Fire
in the
Minds
of
Men

James H. Billington

Fire
in the
Minds
of
Men

Origins of the Revolutionary Faith

with a new introduction by the author

TRANSACTION PUBLISHERS
NEW BRUNSWICK (U.S.A.) AND LONDON (U.K.)

Seventh printing 2007

New material this edition copyright © 1999 by Transaction Publishers, New Brunswick, New Jersey. Originally published in 1980 by Basic Books, Inc., Publishers.

Library of Congress Catalog Number: 98-24144
ISBN: 978-0-7658-0471-6
Printed in the United States of America

Library of Congress Cataloging-in-Publication Data

Billington, James H.

Fire in the minds of men : origins of the revolutionary faith / James H. Billington, with a new introduction by the author.

p. cm.

Originally published: New York : Basic Books, 1980.

Includes bibliographical references (p.) and index.

1. Revolutions—History—19th century. 2. Revolutionaries—History—19th century. I. Title.

HM283.854   1998   98-24144
303.6'4'09034—dc21   CIP

CONTENTS

BOOK III

THE RISE OF THE SOCIAL REVOLUTIONARIES:

THE LATE NINETEENTH AND EARLY TWENTIETH CENTURIES

INTRODUCTION TO THE TRANSACTION EDITION

REISSUING in the late 1990s a book written in the late 1970s, it may be useful to summarize and take a fresh look in light of intervening developments at its main theses and underlying assumptions.

The book suggests that the violent revolutions that convulsed the twentieth century grew out of a faith generated in the nineteenth. Politicized intellectuals created all-encompassing, secular ideologies as surrogates for religious belief within the European world during the century-and-a-quarter between the French and the Russian revolutions. Those who generated this faith and called themselves revolutionaries during this period were generally involved in journalism and rarely exercised real power. They believed that the violent overthrow of traditional political and religious authority would produce an altogether new order that would not just assure prosperity and justice but would also transform the human condition.

There was a basic schism within the revolutionary faith between those who believed most in *fraternity* (that the nation was the vehicle of deliverance) and those who believed in *equality* (that a social class was the vehicle of deliverance). Both of these forms of faith differed fundamentally from the more limited, practical, and anti-authoritarian belief in *liberty* that animated the American War of Independence. Although the American Revolution acquired symbolic significance for both national and social revolutionaries, its essentially liberal ideal exercised relatively little substantive influence on the modern revolutionary tradition as it radiated out from Europe to the world.

The revolutionary faith came out of the wilderness and into power in its most violent and messianic form in the wake of World War I. This bloody conflict delegitimized traditional authority and helped the national revolutionary tradition come to power in Mussolini's Italy and Hitler's Germany; the social revolutionary faith, in Lenin's and Stalin's Russia.

These revolutions created dictatorships and modern totalitarianism. The most violent and authoritarian movements in Germany and Russia each intensified one form of the revolutionary faith by adopting significant elements of the other. Nazism was, literally, an abbreviation for national socialism. Communism was defined as "socialism in one country." One fortified fraternity with equality; the other, equality with fraternity. Each exemplified the distinctive characteristic of the revolutionary faith that "the extremes touch each other." Each subordinated liberty to a new and far more totalistic form of authority than had existed previously. The revolutionary faith was sustained in power at great cost to human life and freedom.

I anticipated in my original introduction that there would be hostility to: (1) the suggestion that belief in revolution was a new kind of religion; (2) the emphasis on ideas and leaders rather than on social, psychological, and other material forces; and (3) the inclusion of exotic figures and symbols that distract focus from the customary hagiographic core of this subject. The desire to preserve a romantic and positive picture of the revolutionary tradition has remained strong in the academy even as that view has generally been repudiated by voters in the last generation.

I believe that history in these last two decades provides some measure of vindication for my suggestion then that the end might be approaching for this political religion—which might in the long run "prove to be only a stage in the continuing metamorphosis of older forms of faith." The two most important "revolutionary" upheavals of the last twenty years have been the Muslim extremist uprising that came to power in Iran and the Catholic-based solidarity movement that started the chain of events that overthrew Leninist rule in Eastern Europe. Both were precipitated by movements from below rooted in religion rather than by new movements from above rooted in secular ideology.

I ended my original work by calling attention to the innovative nature of a still often overlooked earlier event in Poland: the overthrow of Wladislaw Gomulka in 1970. It was the first forcible change of political power brought about by a worker-led uprising in Eastern European since the Russian revolution of 1917. The Solidarity movement that subsequently arose among the same workers posed the kind of challenge to which Leninist control structures proved altogether unable to respond. In 1987, when the prospect for significantly changing any Communist regime still looked bleak, I wrote about Solidarity that it represented "the awesome intrusion into ordinary life of the voice that proclaims both a higher moral standard and a new set of historical possibility." I suggested that "it is not hard to imagine . . . that in the 21st century . . . even in the Soviet Union, historians will look back on Solidarity as an anticipation, if not a prototype, of movements . . . developed to transform their own society in ways radically different from the violent secular revolutionary movements of the past."[1] Not simply in Catholic Poland, but in Protestant East Germany and ultimately Orthodox Russia, the pattern that emerged was non-violent, social rather than political, and tinged with religion. These changes were produced more by "spontaneity" than by the elite "consciousness" that Lenin had prescribed for his revolutionary party, by a desire for evolution rather than revolution, liberty rather than fraternity or equality.

Revolutionary ideology has been thoroughly discredited in the old Soviet empire, where it was most fully put into practice. It has yet to burn itself out altogether on the periphery of European civilization in the Third World. In China, the controlling Leninist hierarchy persists in the revolutionary faith, but massive exposure to the open international economy and improvisational political developments at the grassroots level seemed to be eroding the ideology into a hollow shell.

India, the other great world civilization in Asia, avoided the totalitarian temptation. Its amalgam of Indian nationalism and secular socialism was never revolutionary—and was always leavened by democratic institutions inherited from England, by the Gandhian tradition of non-violence, and by an economy based in many respects on small property holdings and free market relations.

Only in the two smaller Asian nations that had physically fought with the United States—Vietnam and North Korea—did revolutionary ideology maintain much of its force. If the faith in Vietnam seemed to be subject to many of the same erosive effects that it faced in China, the faith was being intensified in North Korea into a virtual state religion including elements taken from pagan sun-god worship and oaths like those that had justified Japanese *kamikaze* missions in World War II.[2]
The desire not only to gain freedom but to recover moral responsibility gave birth to the most important, unexpected, and transformative event of recent times: the sudden collapse of Communism and the Soviet Empire in a few dramatic hours of August 1991. I had the rare privilege of being present in Moscow at that time. In my account, I pointed out how totally different this event was from preceding "revolutions."[3] The movement was entirely spontaneous, radically evolutionary, consistently non-violent, and tinged with religious ideas and symbols. The internal moral revolt against the reigning ideology infected the proponents of the attempted Communist putsch almost as much as it did its opponents.

The contagious series of events that overthrew Communism was dependent on the new electronic technologies as much as the revolutions of 1848 had been on the first advent of the telegraph. The defenders who formed a human wall around Yeltsin's government were responding not to any manifesto or even any clear call to come to his White House. They were responding to an image only recently permitted on Moscow television of the human circle that had formed against previous repressive efforts to maintain Communism in Lithuania. Yeltsin climbed on a tank to make his gesture of public defiance, not by prior plan, but responding instinctively once again to the unforgettable televised image of the young man causing a tank to stop in Tiananmen Square. The age of the fax, e-mail, and the portable phone has created forms of communication no longer subject to central control by repeating the old Bolshevik tactic of simply capturing the post office, the telegraph office, and the train station. The final paroxysm of revolutionary violence by the extremists in Moscow in October 1993 took the form of an attempt to seize the television center.

What seemed genuinely new as the second Christian millennium neared its end was the seeming consensus that whatever was wrong with an aging democratic experiment in America, a shaky one in Russia, highly secularized ones in Western Europe, dangerously fanatical, and often demagogic ones in the third world—the remedy should not be to legitimize total violence and totalitarian controls in the name of any ideology.

I concluded the epilogue of my original narration of the revolutionary faith by noting that Castro's Cuba seemed to be the major remaining locus of legitimacy for politicized intellectuals still clinging to the revolutionary faith. As I write this introduction in January 1998, the 72–year-old Fidel Castro, the century's longest reigning revolutionary dictator, has fanned the embers by ritually reburying the remains of the archetypal romantic revolutionary, Che Guevara, while at the same time attempting to refortify his own fading legitimacy by receiving the staunchly anti-Communist Pope John Paul II.

What I have called in this book "the evolutionary alternative" seemed at last to have triumphed. I identified this alternative with Lafayette, a moderate liberal lost in an age dominated by extremists. It has been my privilege, as Librarian of Congress, to succeed in gaining from Lafayette's last lineal descendant, the generous and courtly Count René de Chambrun, permission to microfilm the hitherto largely inaccessible Lafayette collection so carefully preserved at his ancestral estate of La Grange East of Paris. Fuller study of this remarkable figure and of others caught between the extremes of revolutionary reaction are beginning to be made; and more attention is now being paid retrospectively to the universal appeal of the ideals of liberty, rule of law, and constitutional government. People in many nations seem to be seeking to solve problems more pragmatically at the local level and with religious faith shoring up conscience and accountability.

But the 1990s also brought an exaggerated belief that liberal democracy and market economies will solve most human problems and even bring about "the end of history." Alas, the overcrowding of the earth and depletion of its resources, the widespread delegitimation of authority, and the recurrent tendency of human beings to fight with each other in the absence of shared external enemies—all suggest that conflicts and dangers may be ahead that will be at least as great as those wrought by the age of revolution.

This book essentially deals with the nineteenth century. I had originally intended to write a second volume to be called *Revolutionaries in Power* that would have covered the twentieth century. However, the history of the twentieth century has now been well chronicled and its horrors richly exposed. I have had the experience at the Library of Congress first of arranging for a major exhibit of 500 secret documents from the Soviet archives in 1992[4] and then of acquiring for the Library of Congress the ranging photostatic record of documents from the Soviet era accumulated by General Dmitry Volkogonov, former political head of the Soviet Armed Forces, who spent the courageous final fifteen years of his life documenting some of the atrocities and deceptions committed by the Soviet system against its own and other people.

Both Stalin's and Hitler's terrifying reigns were supported by many otherwise educated people. Thus, the mere spread of education throughout the world is hardly a guarantee against the emergence of new forms of violence and repression. Intellectual ingenuity has so far outstripped moral and spiritual development in our time that it is hard to see how the human race will be able to control the awesome powers of destruction that modern science and technology have put in our hands.

I personally believe that the answer to false and illusory beliefs is not an indefinite suspension of all belief, but a providential, Christian belief in responsibility to God and to one's fellow man. But theology and history both teach us that many who profess noble beliefs do evil things; and that many with illusory or no beliefs do good. I am inclined to believe that every system of belief which attracts a large human following must contain at least some aspiration for good within it. In the case of the revolutionary faith, I identified that positive strain at the end of my book with Rosa Luxemburg and her consistent belief in, and practice of, a non-duplicitous movement for social justice transcending traditional national, ethnic, and gender boundaries. The revolutionary fire, Marxist underpinnings, and messianic utopianism of Rosa Luxemburg died long ago. But the substance of such an ideal—in a more moderate but no less passionate form—may continue to influence those who seek to reform or transform the liberal democracies of our time.

JAMES H. BILLINGTON

Notes

1. James H. Billington, "Introduction," *Solidarity and Poland: Impacts East and West*, Steve W. Reiquan, ed., Washington, D.C., 1988, 1–4.
2. This subject is discussed in *North Korea: A Country Study*, Andrea Savada, ed., Washington, DC: Library of Congress, 1994, 41–44, 183–85, and is currently being studied in more detail by Thomas Belke, who is writing a book *Juche! The State Religion of North Korea*.
3. James H. Billington, *Russia Transformed: Breakthrough to Hope, Moscow, August 1991*, New York, 1992.
4. *Revelations from the Russian Archives: Documents in English Translation*, Diane P. Koenker and Ronald D. Bachman, eds., Washington, DC: Library of Congress, 1997.

ACKNOWLEDGMENTS

IT IS BOTH a duty and a pleasure to record my special debt to two institutions that sustained me during the lengthy preparation of this work. The Center of International Studies of Princeton University and its two directors, Klaus Knorr and Cyril Black, gave initial support and encouragement. The full-time administrative demands of the Woodrow Wilson International Center for Scholars, which I have directed since the fall of 1973, have in a sense delayed the completion of this work. But in a deeper sense the Wilson Center has greatly enriched this off-hours labor by providing continuing contact with a diversified, international group of scholars—and by challenging me to do what I was urging on others: the completion of scholarly work on something that matters.

I have benefited during the preparation of this work from various forms of support provided by Princeton University (including a McCosh Faculty Fellowship), the International Research and Exchanges Board, the Rockefeller Foundation (including the Villa Serbelloni), the Aspen Institute for Humanistic Studies, and the Maison des Sciences de l'Homme and Ecole Pratique des Hautes Etudes. I owe a special debt to the two principal libraries I have used, the Firestone Library in Princeton during the early stages of work, and the Library of Congress in recent years. Their supportive staffs—and those of the other libraries mentioned in the list at the beginning of my documentation at the end of this book—have my sincerest thanks. This work was also aided in some ways by my concurrent labors as a writer for *Life* in the late sixties and as a member and as chairman of the Board of Foreign Scholarships (Fulbright program) in the first half of the seventies.

Among the many who have aided me in the preparation of this book, I would like to pay special tribute to Zdenek David, curator of Slavic books at Princeton and then librarian of the Wilson Center; Mernie Weathers, an incomparable executive assistant at the Center; and Midge Decter, an extraordinary editor. I also thank those who gave me specially helpful references, comments, or criticisms in the early stages of this work: Isaiah Berlin, John Talbott, Jerry Seigel, Fred Starr, Robert Tucker, Jacques Godechot, Timur Timofeev, Armando Saitta, Sidney Hook, Rondo Cameron, Leo Valiani, Albert Soboul, Eóin MacWhite, Alan Spitzer, Orest Pelech, Peter Thon, Arthur Lehning, and especially Robert Palmer, Andrzej Walicki, and Joseph Strayer. None of them is, of course, to be implicated in any way with my methods or interpretations.

I have benefited both at Princeton University and at the Wilson Center from the industry of a succession of helpful research assistants, of whom special mention should be made of Joe Coble, Tom Robertson, Neil Hahl, Chris Bown, Wayne Lord, and George Sevich. I am also indebted to typists at both institutions, with special thanks to Virginia Kianka, Mary Leksa, and Virginia Benson.

In the often lonely business of producing a book like this, one is immeasurably aided by the immediate family. I feel grateful not just to my beloved wife, Marjorie, but to our children, Susan, Anne, Jim, and Tom, who have put up with this work on all of our vacations and much of our spare time with good humor for more than a decade. To them, I express my deepest thanks—as I do to friends who have provided all our family with continuing encouragement. In this latter category, I express special warmth and gratitude to the Cadles: to Inge and Caron and to Don, to whom this book is dedicated.

FIRE IN
THE MINDS
OF MEN

INTRODUCTION

THIS BOOK seeks to trace the origins of a faith—perhaps *the* faith of our time. Modern revolutionaries are believers, no less committed and intense than were the Christians or Muslims of an earlier era. What is new is the belief that a perfect secular order will emerge from the forcible overthrow of traditional authority. This inherently implausible idea gave dynamism to Europe in the nineteenth century, and has become the most successful ideological export of the West to the world in the twentieth.

This is a story not of revolu*tions,* but of revolutio*naries*: the innovative creators of a new tradition. The historical frame is the century and a quarter that extends from the waning of the French Revolution in the late eighteenth century to the beginnings of the Russian Revolution in the early twentieth. The theater was Europe of the industrial era; the main stage, journalistic offices within great European cities. The dialogue of imaginative symbols and theoretical disputes produced much of the language of modern politics.

At center stage stood the characteristic, nineteenth-century European revolutionary: a thinker lifted up by ideas, not a worker or peasant bent down by toil. He was part of a small elite whose story must be told "from above," much as it may displease those who believe that history in general (and revolutionary history in particular) is basically made by socio-economic pressures "from below." This "elite" focus does not imply indifference to the mass, human suffering which underlay the era of this narrative. It reflects only the special need to concentrate here on the spiritual thirst of those who think rather than on the material hunger of those who work. For it was passionate intellectuals who created and developed the revolutionary faith. This work seeks to explore concretely the tradition of revolutionaries, not to explain abstractly the process of revolution. My approach has been inductive rather than deductive, explorative rather than definitive: an attempt to open up rather than "cover" the subject.

My general conclusions can be stated simply at the outset—and, for the sake of argument, more bluntly than they may appear in the text that follows.

The revolutionary faith was shaped not so much by the critical rationalism of the French Enlightenment (as is generally believed) as by the *occultism* and *proto-romanticism* of Germany. This faith was incubated in France during the revolutionary era within a small subculture of literary intellectuals who were immersed in journalism, fascinated by secret societies, and subsequently infatuated with "ideologies" as a secular surrogate for religious belief.

The professional revolutionaries who first appeared during the French Revolution sought, above all, radical simplicity. Their deepest conflicts revolved around the simple words of their key slogan: *liberty, equality, fraternity*. Liberty had been the battle cry of earlier revolutions (in sixteenth-century Holland, seventeenth-century England, eighteenth-century America) which produced complex political structures to limit tyranny (separating powers, constituting rights, legitimizing federation). The French Revolution also initially invoked similar ideas, but the new and more collectivist ideals of fraternity and equality soon arose to rival the older concept of liberty. The words *nationalism* and *communism* were first invented in the 1790s to define the simpler, more sublime, seemingly less selfish ideals of fraternity and equality, respectively. The basic struggle that subsequently emerged among committed revolutionaries was between advocates of national revolution for a new type of fraternity and those of social revolution for a new type of equality.

The French national example and republican ideal dominated the revolutionary imagination throughout the first half of the nineteenth century. Exiled Francophile intellectuals from Poland and Italy largely fashioned the dominant concept of revolutionary nationalism—inventing most modern ideas on guerrilla violence and wars of national liberation, expressing their essentially emotional ideal best in mythic histories, vernacular poetry, and operatic melodrama.

Rival social revolutionaries began to challenge the romantic nationalists after the revolutions of 1830; and this socialist tradition increasingly predominated after the forming of the First International in 1864 and the movement of the revolutionary cause from French to German and Russian leadership. Social revolutionaries expressed their essentially rationalistic ideal best in prose pamphlets and prosaic organizations. Their hidden model was the impersonal and dynamic machine of factory industry rather than the personalized but static lodge of the Masonic aristocracy.

No less fateful than the schism between national and social revolutionaries was the conflict among social revolutionaries that began in the 1840s between Marx and Proudhon. The former's focus on destroying the capitalist economic system clashed with the latter's war on the centralized, bureaucratic state. This conflict continued between the heirs of Marx (principally in Germany and Russia) and of Proudhon (among Latin and Slavic anarchists, populists, and syndicalists).

The word *intelligentsia* and the thirst for ideology migrated east from Poland to Russia (and from a national to a social revolutionary cause) through the Russian student radicals of the 1860s, who developed a new ascetic type of terrorism. Lenin drew both on this Russian tradition of violence and on German concepts of organization to create the Bolshevism that eventually brought the revolutionary tradition out of the wilderness and into power.

The revolutionary faith developed in nineteenth-century Europe only within those societies that had not previously (1) legitimized ideological dissent by breaking with medieval forms of religious authority, and (2) modified monarchical power by accepting some form of organized political opposition. In northern Europe and North America, where these conditions were met by Protestant and parliamentary traditions, the revolutionary faith attracted almost no indigenous adherents. Thus, the revolutionary tradition can be seen as a form of political-ideological opposition that arose first against authoritarian Catholicism (in France, Italy, and Poland) and then against other religiously based autocracies (in Lutheran Prussia, Orthodox Russia). The most dedicated and professional social revolutionaries—from Maréchal through Blanqui, Marx, and Bakunin to Lenin—came from such societies and tended to become that rarest of all forms of true believer: a militant atheist. They and other pioneering revolutionaries were largely middle-class, male intellectuals with relatively few familial attachments. Revolutionary movements tended to become more internationalist and visionary whenever women played a leading role; more parochial and pragmatic whenever workers were in command.

Before attempting to chronicle the drama, the dogmas, and the disputes of this new, secular religion-in-the-making, it is important to linger on the mystery and the majesty of faith itself.

The heart of revolutionary faith, like any faith, is fire: ordinary material transformed into extraordinary form, quantities of warmth suddenly changing the quality of substance. If we do not know what fire is, we know what it does. It burns. It destroys life; but it also supports it as a source of heat, light, and—above all—fascination. Man, who works with fire as *homo faber*, also seems foredoomed in his freedom to play with it as *homo ludens*.

Our particular chapter in history unfolds at a time of physical transformation in Europe that was almost as momentous as the first discovery of fire must have been in the mists of antiquity. The industrial revolution was permitting men to leash fire to machines—and to unleash fire power on each other—with a force undreamed of in earlier ages. In the midst of those fires appeared the more elusive flame that Dostoevsky described in the most searching work of fiction ever written about the revolutionary movement: *The Possessed*.

He depicted a stagnant (tranquil?) provincial town that was suddenly inspired (infected?) by new ideas. Shortly after a turbulent literary evening, a mysterious fire broke out; and a local official shouted out into the nocturnal confusion: "The fire is in the minds of men, not in the roofs of buildings." Dostoevsky was writing under the impact of two great fires that disturbed him deeply and heralded the transfer of revolutionary leadership from France to Russia. These fires had broken out in imperial St. Petersburg in the spring of 1861 (where the emancipation of the serfs seemed to have inflamed rather than calmed passions), and in imperial Paris ten years later (where the flaming defeat of the Paris Commune ended forever the era of romantic illusions).

The flame of faith had begun its migrations a century earlier, when some European aristocrats transferred their lighted candles from Christian altars to Masonic lodges. The flame of occult alchemists, which had promised to turn dross into gold, reappeared at the center of new "circles" seeking to recreate a golden age: Bavarian Illuminists conspiring against the Jesuits, French Philadelphians against Napoleon, Italian charcoal burners against the Hapsburgs.

When the most important anti-Napoleonic conspiracy was ridiculed for attempting "to use as a lever something which is only a match," its leader replied that

> With a match one has no need of a lever; one does not lift up the world, one burns it.[1]

The leader in spreading the conspiracy to Italy soon noted that "the Italian flame" had spread "the fire of freedom to the most frozen land of Petersburg." [2] There the first Russian revolution occurred in December 1825. Its slogan, "From the spark comes the flame!" was originated by the first man to predict an egalitarian social revolution in the eighteenth century (Sylvain Maréchal) and revived by the first man to realize such a revolution in the twentieth (Lenin, who used it as the epigram for his journal, *The Spark*).

A recurrent mythic model for revolutionaries—early romantics, the young Marx, the Russians of Lenin's time—was Prometheus, who stole fire from the gods for the use of mankind. The Promethean faith of revolutionaries resembled in many respects the general modern belief that science would lead men out of darkness into light. But there was also the more pointed, millennial assumption that, on the new day that was dawning, the sun would never set. Early during the French upheaval was born a "solar myth of the revolution," suggesting that the sun was rising on a new era in which darkness would vanish forever. This image became implanted "at a level of consciousness that simultaneously interpreted something real and produced a new reality." [3]

The new reality they sought was radically secular and stridently simple. The ideal was not the balanced complexity of the new American federation, but the occult simplicity of its great seal: an all-seeing eye atop a pyramid over the words *Novus Ordo Seclorum*. In search of primal, natural truths, revolutionaries looked back to pre-Christian antiquity—adopting pagan names like "Anaxagoras" Chaumette and "Anacharsis" Cloots, idealizing above all the semimythic Pythagoras as the model intellect-turned-revolutionary and the Pythagorean belief in prime numbers, geometric forms, and the higher harmonies of music. Many of the same Strasbourg musicians who first played *La Marseillaise* in 1792 had introduced Mozart's *Magic Flute* to French audiences in the same city only a few months earlier; and Mozart's illuminist message seemed to explain the fuller meaning of the *jour de gloire* that Rouget de Lisle's anthem had proclaimed:

> The rays of the sun have vanquished the night,
> The powers of darkness have yielded to light.[4]

The rising sun brought heat as well as light, for the fire was generally lit not at high noon on a tabula rasa by some philosopher-king, but rather by some unknown guest arriving at midnight amidst the excesses of Don Giovanni's banquet. "Communism," the label Lenin finally adopted, was invented not by the great Rousseau, but by a *Rousseau du ruisseau* (Rousseau of the gutter): the indulgent fetishist and nocturnal streetwalker in prerevolutionary Paris, Restif de la Bretonne. Thus the revolutionary label that now controls the destiny of more than one billion people in the contemporary world sprang from the erotic imagination of an eccentric writer. Like other key words of the revolutionary tradition it first appeared as the rough ideograph of a language in the making: a road sign pointing to the future.

This study attempts to identify some of these signs along the path from Restif to Lenin. It follows sparks across national borders, carried by small groups and idiosyncratic individuals who created an incendiary legacy of ideas. We will say relatively little about either the familiar, formal organizational antecedents of contemporary Communism (the three Internationals, the Russian Social Democratic party) or the actual revolutionary conflagrations of the period. We shall exclude altogether the contemporary era in which the stage has moved from Europe to the world, and revolutionaries from the anticipation to the exercise of power.

We shall deal repeatedly with the linguistic creativity of revolutionaries, who used old words (*democracy, nation, revolution,* and *liberal*) in new ways and invented altogether new words like *socialist* and *communist*. Their appealing new vocabulary was taken over for nonrevolutionary usage—as in the adoption of *republican* and *democrat* for competing political parties in postrevolutionary America, or in the conservative coöptation of *nation, liberal,* and even *radical* in late nineteenth century Europe. Revolutionaries also originated other key phrases used by nonrevolutionary social theorists in our own century: *cybernetics, intelligentsia*. Even speculation about "the year 2000" began not with the futurology of the 1960s, but with a dramatic work written in the 1780s by the same figure who invented the word communist.[5]

The origins of revolutionary words and symbols is of more than antiquarian interest; for, in the contemporary world where constitutions and free elections are vanishing almost as rapidly as monarchs, revolutionary rhetoric provides the formal legitimation of most political authority.

The historian's path back to origins leads, however, into often murky labyrinths; and requires a willingness to follow seminal figures in leaps of fantasy to remote times and on long marches into distant spaces.[6] Revolutionaries (no less than prophets of the Judaeo-Christian-Moslem lineage) seek to find their "holy other" in historical time. They tend to become more extreme in the present as they idealize an ever more distant past. Those who glorified pre-Christian druids tended to outstrip in fanaticism those who looked only to the early Christians.[7]

Revolutionaries have also pursued a geographical quest for some ideal place where the "holy other" could be wholly present. Activists have often sought out a small, clearly encompassed area within which perfection could become material. The earliest utopias of the imagination and the starting places for many key nineteenth-century revolutionaries were often islands. In their search for sacred space, the original revolutionaries made judgments through an apotheosis of location: left vs. right or mountain vs. plain in the French National Assembly, an inner circle of the dedicated within a broader circumference of the affiliated in their revolutionary organizations. What Cloots called the "world-map of revolution" was explored and charted by a new breed of politicized artists and writers. Flags and songs provided a semaphore of salvation. The bourgeois Third Estate sartorially celebrated its liberation from the aristocratic Second Estate by lowering its knee britches and becoming sans-culottes—only to don the tight new uniforms prescribed by the revolutionary citizen-state.

The revolutionary faith was built more by ideological innovators than by political leaders. He who held actual power during the original French Revolution was generally "a provisional being . . . a creature of exceptional circumstance . . . not a professional of the Revolution." [8] Professionalism began later with a different kind of man: an intellectual who lacked political experience, but saw in revolution an object of faith and a source of vocation, a channel for sublimated emotion and sublime ambition. If traditional religion is to be described as "the opium of the people," the new revolutionary faith might well be called the amphetamine of the intellectuals.

But such characterizations are neither fair to the believer nor helpful to the historian. The wellsprings of this faith are deep, and have sustained men and women on the way to the scaffold of an executioner as well as to the platform of power. The youthful intellectuals who were the prophets and priests of this new secular religion were largely crying in the wilderness throughout the nineteenth century, struggling against overwhelming odds for revolutions that they saw coming mainly with the eyes of faith. It was not self-indulgent pity that caused one of the most militant and original early revolutionaries to compare his wandering life of exile to an eternal purgatory of "suffering without end and without hope":

> I no longer have a friend . . . no relatives, no old colleagues . . . no one writes me or thinks about me any more. . . . I have become a foreigner in my own country, and I am a foreigner among foreigners. The earth itself refuses to adopt me.[9]

Revolutionaries were generally sustained in such loneliness and despair—and protected from ridicule and indifference—by secularized nineteenth-century versions of the old Judaeo-Christian belief in deliverance-through-history. At a deep and often subconscious level, the revolutionary faith was shaped by the Christian faith it attempted to replace. Most revolutionaries viewed history prophetically as a kind of unfolding morality play. The present was hell, and revolution a collective purgatory leading to a future earthly paradise. The French Revolution was the Incarnation of hope, but was betrayed by Judases within the revolutionary camp and crucified by the Pilates in power.

The future revolution would be a kind of Second Coming in which the Just would be vindicated. History itself would provide the final judgment; and a new community beyond all kingdoms would come on earth as it never could in heaven.

A classical, contemporary statement of this belief lies in the founding manifesto of Fidel Castro's revolutionary movement, *History Will Absolve Me*. He represented his own original revolutionary assault on the Moncado barracks as a kind of Incarnation. The subsequent torture and martyrdom of his virile fellow revolutionaries was the Passion and Crucifixion; and Castro's trial by Batista was Christ before Pilate. The Cuban people were promised corporate Resurrection, and their revolutionary apostles Pentecostal power. The coming revolution would fulfill all the Law (the five "revolutionary laws" of the Moncado raiders) and the Prophets (José Martí).[10]

Such total belief in secular salvation is uniquely modern: the sublime creation of the age of political religion ushered in by the American and French Revolutions.[11] Previous political upheavals—even when called revolutions—generally sought a new leader rather than a new order. The norm was revolt rather than revolution—either the "primitive rebellion" of outlawed "social bandits" [12] or the "pursuit of the millennium" by religious prophets seeking to move beyond nature into a state of grace.[13] Never before was the word *revolution* related to the creation of a totally new and entirely man-made order. With the militant, secular French Revolution "a new era opens, that of beginnings without return." [14]

Particularly after the revolution turned to terror in 1793 and to retreat in 1794, many realized that the revolutionary process would not automatically bring deliverance and social harmony. A new species of man, the professional revolutionary, emerged during the "Thermidorean reaction" to keep the dream alive. He argued that the French Revolution was incomplete, and that history required a second, final revolution and a new type of man dedicated to serving it. The full-time revolutionary profession began not with the ruling politicians but with the intellectual activists in Babeuf's "Conspiracy of the Equals," who had little in common with earlier revolutionaries "except in the imagination of the police." [15]

Yet the tradition that developed from the "people of Babeuf" cannot be divorced altogether from "the imagination of the police." For revolutionary and counter-revolutionary forces often lived in a kind of symbiotic relationship. The same writer who first prophesied a new revolutionary society for France in the late 1760s [16] also coined in the early 1780s the prophetic phrase *les extrèmes se touchent*.[17] We shall repeatedly have occasion to note the interaction and often unconscious borrowing between the extremes of Right and Left.

A work of history is, of course, a product of its own time as well as a description of another. This study originated in graduate university teaching during the 1960s, when some Western intellectuals began to think of themselves as revolutionaries. Their voices were often shrill and rarely heeded. Most people in the West remained attached to either their material possessions or their spiritual heritage. Yet within over-developed universities even more than underdeveloped economies there was often a kind of fascination—compounded sometimes with fear and/or secret delight—at the perceived reappearance of a political species long thought to be nearing extinction.

Yet the perspective of history seemed strangely missing among revolutionaries, antirevolutionaries, and voyeurs alike. Activists seemed largely uninterested in the substantial academic literature that had already accumulated by the mid-sixties; and new writing often seemed unusually narrow or polemically preoccupied with immediate issues. There seemed as well to be deeper ideological, cultural, and even professional reasons for continued historical ignorance of the revolutionary tradition.

Ideologically, historical understanding has been muddied in the postwar era by the rhetoric of superpower politics. The American and the Soviet states are each the product of a revolution: the first to proclaim, respectively, a new political and a new social order.[18]

The American Revolution of 1776 was a classic contest for political liberty secured by constitutional complexity. But American sympathy for the simpler cause of nationalism elsewhere (including within the Soviet empire) has often blunted the ability of American leaders to distinguish between revolutions seeking limited liberties and those seeking the more unlimited gratifications of nationalistic fraternity.

The Russian Revolution of 1917 was the classic revolution for social equality. But the Soviet leaders adopted as well the language of liberal and national revolutionaries—and debased the entire revolutionary vocabulary by using it to rationalize imperial despotism. Rejecting Marxism as the progenitor of Stalinism, the liberal West proved, in its technocratic era, almost equally hostile to the anti-authoritarian, Proudhonist alternative to Marxism within the social revolutionary tradition.

Culturally, historical understanding was complicated in America by the voracious overuse of the word revolutionary in a generally non-revolutionary society. Not only was the word abused by advertisers to announce the most trivial innovations in taste and technology, but also by social commentators anxious to contend that a "revolution" was occurring in the politically conservative America of the early 1970s. The revolutionaries were variously identified as drifting flower children,[19] as the technological innovators they rejected,[20] and as humanistic capitalists who presumably had little in common with either.[21] It was only marginally more absurd for a bizarre drifter named Rasputin to characterize his free-form sexual-religious commune of affluent youth as "revolutionary"—and to invent the verb "to revolute":

> . . . let the people do what they want . . . keep them revoluting. Revolution, constantly changing, going on to the next thing. . . .[22]

All of this preceded the cacophonous deluge of Bicentennial messages about the enduring importance of the American Revolution variously interpreted. The day after the two-hundredth anniversary of the signing of the Declaration of Independence, the leading newspaper in the American capital featured a proclamation of "the new American Revolution." But its "new American Maoism" for a "post-Copernican Age" seemed little more than a final sprinkling of intellectual confetti left over from the Age of Aquarius.[23]

Such confusion flows in part from the general modern tendency to attach "a magical, binding and unique meaning to the word 'revolution,'"[24] in an age when "the word 'revolution' is always construed in a positive light."[25] Yet even if the word has been "emptied of all meaning by constant overuse," it does not necessarily follow that it will "soon cease to be current."[26]

Professionally, American academic historians may themselves have contributed—ironically and inadvertently—to the erosion of historical memory about the revolutionary tradition. By devoting inordinate energy to demonstrating either their political "relevance" (the sixties) or their methodological "rigor" (the seventies), many have neglected the enduring obligation of open-minded immersion in the legacy of the past. Cliometricians and cliopetitioners alike may have been too confident that they possessed in the present either a method or a message for the future—and, as a result, were too willing to see the past as an instrument to be used rather than a record to be explored.

As a university-based historian during the early years of this study, my "method" was to ignore professorial debates and to spend my time with old books and new students. The experience gave me an unanticipated sense of "relevance." I was repeatedly struck in the depths of libraries with precedent for almost everything that was daily being hailed as a novelty from the rooftops outside.

I came to know figures like Thomas (Ismail) Urbain, a Black Muslim of the 1830s unknown to those of today. He adopted Islam and Algerian nationalism a century before the same pattern was followed by other black revolutionaries from the same West Indies. Flora Tristan, the Franco-Peruvian founder of the first international proletarian organization, anticipated today's radical feminism, by invading the all-male House of Lords in London of the late 1830s and removing her disguise as a male Turk to dramatize her cause. The struggle between the old and the new left recapitulated much of the Marx-Proudhon conflict. Even the marginalia of leftism such as ideological sky-jackers had precedents in the revolutionary high-jacking of Mediterranean ships by Carlo Pisacane in the 1850s.

The concept of a revolution along generational lines was already fully developed in *Gerontocracy* of 1828 by the future Swiss revolutionary leader, James Fazy. Germany had produced even earlier the prototypical "modern" student counter-culture: rakish dress, long hair, narcotic highs, and sexual lows. Out of this subculture came violent calls for a "propaganda of the deed" long before contemporary terrorists. The anti-traditional musical theater of the early nineteenth century inspired real revolution in a way that rock festivals of the recent past only avowed to do.

But these were minor discoveries of antecedents along the path directed toward constructing an account of origins that might add some insight from fresh historical research to the substantial work that already exists on the modern revolutionary tradition.[27] This study will, it is hoped, broaden the base of enquiry even as it arouses controversy by considering Bonneville and Nodier as well as Babeuf among the founding fathers; Dézamy and Barmby as well as Marx among the communist pioneers; media of communication as well as means of organization; and Radchenko as well as Lenin among the authors of Bolshevism.

This study necessarily deals with only a small part of a rich story. It will not provide the traditional staples of either comprehensive political history or rounded individual biographies. In addition, readers should be specifically forewarned that I am not following any of three familiar approaches to the revolutionary tradition: the hagiographic, the sociological, or the psychological.

Hagiography is the retroactive justification of a revolution in power: the portrayal of precursors in the past for purposes of indoctrination in the present. In this approach, saints and sinners, heroes and heretics are created and catalogued to support the current political judgments of the recognized revolutionary succession. From such an intensely partisan tradition, of course, has come the bulk of historical writing on revolutionaries. The critical historian can find here not only invaluable source material, but also insights from Marxist historical analysis, particularly in the period prior to Stalin when relatively free speculation was still permitted in the Soviet Union.

A massive new Soviet history, *The International Workers' Movement*, will provide an authoritative codification of post-Stalinist orthodoxy. The first two volumes cover the same period as this book, predictably stressing the actions of workers and the doctrines of Marx. But the new periodization, the international perspective, and the assignment of specific sections to different authors—all give this work an interest largely absent from earlier versions of the hagiographic genre.[28] A very different line of saints and devils is traced in the philosophically rich history of Marxism by the brilliant, exiled Polish revisionist and critic, Leszek Kolakowski.[29]

The sociological approach predominates among social historians in the West [30] as well as nonhagiographic Marxists.[31] That the revolutionary tradition was intimately related to forces of industrial development, class conflict, and social change in the modern world is incontestable. But it does not follow—as many sociological historians either assert or imply—that the revolutionary tradition is simply produced or "caused" by these processes. Such an explanation may be argued as a hypothesis or asserted as an act of faith. But it can hardly be called a scientific fact—and it may actually serve to rationalize restriction on the range of enquiry, which the open experimental method should always seek to expand.

Microhistorians of the sociological school have been increasingly critical of those broad histories of the revolutionary era that focus on the diffusion of French power to local elites.[32] There clearly is a need to understand better the widely different regional and social experiences of a complex continent—and for that matter the human variety contained within the French term "Jacobin."

Since our subject is not the politics of the revolutionary era, but the genesis and spread of the revolutionary tradition, it is necessarily the story of a few ideas and of key people. So many of them have been neglected or forgotten that it seems task enough to enlarge the inventory and provide a historical framework for tracing the development of this small, but immeasurably important subculture of nineteenth-century Europe.

The effort here will be to maintain a kind of agnosticism on first causes while bringing into view some relatively neglected data and advancing some new hypotheses. In those areas where intellectual history can approach scientific precision, however, this work will attempt to trace the origins of key words, symbols, ideas, and organizational forms.

The psychological method is currently much in favor as a means of explaining data about men and ideas. Since revolutionaries are intense people at war with accepted social norms, they have become favorite subjects for this kind of analysis—particularly in America.[33] The suspicion remains, however, that Freudian, even more than Marxist, analysis may itself be a somewhat dated technique—at times more appropriate for the period of the historian than for the historical period.

Aside from the recognized difficulties of retroactive psychoanalysis, the fact is that most of the important early revolutionaries seem surprisingly free of unusual personal characteristics. One of the best studies of the emotional side of the original French revolutionaries points out that "the future revolutionaries were almost all docile pupils of Jesuits and Oratorians."[34] Like most other French children of their time, they were fond of their mothers, of their native regions, and of mildly sentimental, apolitical literature.

Revolutionaries in the subsequent, romantic era were rarely as idiosyncratic and antisocial as artists and poets, and less committed to violence than is generally realized. The schools of thought that played the most important roles in developing a revolutionary tradition all saw themselves providing the rationality that would end violence. Politicized Illuminists promised inner moral renewal; messianic Saint-Simonians, an organic order to end revolutionary unrest; Young Hegelians, the peaceful completion of Prussian reforms.

The fascinating fact is that most revolutionaries sought the simple, almost banal aims of modern secular man generally. What was unique was their intensity and commitment to realizing them. This faith and dedication made the revolutionary trailblazers bigger than life—and deeply controversial. Their progress represented, for some, humanity emerging on wings from its cocoon; for others, a malignancy attacking civilization itself.

Most Communists and many Third World leaders still profess to believe in salvation-through-revolution; others fear that this belief still retains the power to immobilize intellectuals in the West who lack "the experience of living in a society where that myth has been politi-

cally elevated to the status of official doctrine." [35] Others see this secular faith fading away as a "post-industrial society" moves "beyond
ideology" into a "technetronic" era.[36] Others may suggest that belief
in revolution was only a political flash fire in the age of energy—now
burning itself out on the periphery as the metropole enters the twilight
of entropy.[37]

The present author is inclined to believe that the end may be approaching of the political religion which saw in revolution the sunrise
of a perfect society. I am further disposed to wonder if this secular
creed, which arose in Judaeo-Christian culture, might not ultimately
prove to be only a stage in the continuing metamorphosis of older
forms of faith [38] and to speculate that the belief in secular revolution,
which has legitimized so much authoritarianism in the twentieth century, might dialectically prefigure some rediscovery of religious evolution to revalidate democracy in the twenty-first.

But the story of revolutionaries in the nineteenth century is worth
telling for its own sake—quite apart from any concerns of today or
speculations about tomorrow. This heroic and innovative record of revolutionaries without power is an awesome chapter in the history of
human aspiration. This study will attempt to let the dead speak for
themselves without overlooking the continuing concerns of the living.
It is a work of humanistic history: the record of what one man who is
not a revolutionary found interesting and important about a number of
his fellow humans who were.

BOOK

I

FOUNDATIONS OF THE REVOLUTIONARY FAITH: THE LATE EIGHTEENTH AND EARLY NINETEENTH CENTURIES

THE CITY is the crucible of modern revolution. The revolutionary tradition, seen from below, is a narrative of urban unrest successively dominated by Paris and St. Petersburg.

Paris overthrew the mightiest monarchy in Christendom in 1789–92, triggered new waves of revolution in 1830 and 1848, and forged a new model for social revolution in the Paris Commune of 1871. By then, there had arisen in St. Petersburg a new type of revolutionary who was to convulse the largest land empire in the world with terror in the late nineteenth century and insurrection in the early twentieth. Three Russian revolutions—in 1905, March 1917, and November 1917—brought the revolutionary tradition out of the wilderness and into power.

Other cities also played decisive roles: Strasbourg, where German ideas entered France and the national revolutionary ideal burst into song in the 1790s; Lyon, where class warfare first fueled the rival social revolutionary tradition in the 1830s; and Berlin, where Marx was first radicalized and where a Marxist revolution failed in 1918–19—dooming the communist cause to confinement in Russia for the next thirty years. The site of legitimacy was not revolutionary St. Petersburg, which took the new name "Leningrad" from the victorious leader; it was the medieval Kremlin within conservative Moscow.

Seen from above the revolutionary tradition is a story of elite, intellectual leaders: a thin line of apostolic succession from Buonarroti to Lenin. The former was the leading survivor and historian of the first organization for secular, social revolution: the Babeuf conspiracy of 1796–97. Like St. Peter among the Romans, Filippo Buonarroti was the rock on which subsequent revolutionaries built. By the time of his death in 1837, social revolutionary leadership had passed to his admirer, Louis Auguste Blanqui, who retained special authority throughout the Paris-dominated era.

Leadership moved from Paris to St. Petersburg through Blanqui's Russian collaborator, Peter Tkachev; his compatriots assassinated the Russian tsar in St. Petersburg in 1881, the year Blanqui died in Paris. When Lenin's older brother was hanged six years later for plotting to kill the next tsar, young Lenin became the vehicle for vengeance and vindication.

Lenin's path from an underground cell to the podium of power began at a particular place in St. Petersburg: the student-run dining hall and library of the St. Petersburg Technological Institute. The revolutionary seed first took root in the early 1890s in this spot, where the young Lenin had his first contact both with the main Marxist classics and with real industrial workers. Within this small area of freedom students not only dreamed of a technologically abundant alternative to tsarism, but also used their technical talents to form the first Russian organization of revolutionary Marxists.

The road that was to lead from the Technological Institute to the Finland Station originated, however, earlier and elsewhere. The first green zone that fertilized the revolutionary seed by turning intellectuals into revolutionaries was the Palais-Royal in the late 1780s. This privileged Parisian sanctuary of the reformist House of Orléans incubated those who wrested power from the ruling royal palace of Versailles in 1789 and from the Tuileries in 1792, long before the Leninists occupied the Winter Palace in 1917. Thus our story begins with the "anti-Versailles" in the heart of Paris, the scene of the first modern revolution. It leads us to Buonarroti, the anti-Napoleon who conceived of the first modern revolutionary organization.

CHAPTER 1

Incarnation

THE MODERN revolutionary tradition begins with both word and deed: prophecy and incarnation. First came the slow growth of the *idea* of secular revolution in early modern Europe. Then came the *fact* of a totally new kind of upheaval within the largest city of the mightiest power in Europe.

The Idea of Revolution

Long before the Second Coming of 1917—and even before the Incarnation of 1789—men brooded about the nature and meaning of the word *revolution*. The term derives from the Latin substantive *revolutio*, which was unknown in classical Latin but was used in the early Middle Ages by St. Augustine and other Christian writers.[1] Translated into Italian as *rivoluzione* in the early Renaissance and then into French and English as *revolution*, the term initially meant the return of a moving object to its place of origin—particularly the movement of celestial bodies around the earth. Copernicans used it increasingly in the sixteenth and seventeenth centuries to describe their unsettling new concept of the earth revolving—axially and orbitally—around the sun. The French savant Jacques Amyot suggested that in sixteenth-century France an understanding of these awesome movements in nature was also necessary for a successful politician:

> Il y a une certaine révolution et préfixion de temps oultre lequel l'homme sage ne se doibt plus entremettre des affaires de la chose politique.[2]

But "revolutionary" change was still generally seen as a return to an earlier, temporarily violated norm: a re-volution back to a more natural order.[3] Even the extremists of the seventeenth and eighteenth centuries who helped prepare revolutions tended to think of restoring preexisting rights and traditions. Judaeo-Christian ideas inspired what many consider the first modern revolution: the Puritan rebellion in seventeenth-century England; and nonconformist religious ideas played a major role in preparing the American revolution.[4] Fanatical religious ideologies dominated the sixteenth-century civil wars that raged within the two great continental powers, the Hapsburg Empire and the French Kingdom. Both sides in both of these conflicts have recently been hailed as revolutionary pioneers. The Dutch revolt against authoritarian Spain has been called the first modern revolution and "the earliest modern expression of democratic ideas." [5] Similar claims have also been made for an earlier revolt in which the roles were reversed, when urban Spaniards rebelled against the predominantly Dutch entourage of Charles V.[6] A leading Calvinist in sixteenth-century France was "one of the first modern revolutionaries," [7] as was his bête noire, the Catholic League, which installed "the first revolutionary reign of terror that Paris was to experience." [8] These Parisian Catholics were probably the most authentic anticipation of the modern revolutionaries. They introduced the term "Committee of Public Safety," the use of barricades, and a program that was "truly revolutionary in the sense that it embodied conscious social antagonisms." [9]

But such revolutionary means still served reactionary ends. Innovative political practices continued to require aggressively Christian ideologies. The grounds for a new approach were prepared by the exhaustion with religious conflict and by the enthusiasm over the scientific method that produced a "crisis of the European consciousness" at the end of the seventeenth century.[10] In the ensuing Enlightenment of the eighteenth century, a critical spirit began to regard Greco-Roman antiquity as a kind of secular alternative to Christianity.[11]

Much of the growing volume of secular political writing in the age of the Enlightenment dealt with the problem of revolution. A pioneering Italian work of 1629 on the causes and prevention of revolution found kingdoms particularly vulnerable to revolution because of their monarchs' misconduct.[12] An anti-Spanish treatise, *The Revolutions in Naples*, appeared in 1647 on the eve of an uprising in Naples led by the fisherman Masaniello against the Hapsburgs.[13] This event stimulated the already well-developed Italian discussion of political revolution.[14] Polemic writers in England during the Puritan Revolution drew in turn on Italian writings. One English work on the Neapolitan uprising coined the classic revolutionary metaphor of a "fire" coming from a small "spark." [15]

The poet Robert Heath appears to have been the first to link political revolution with social change,[16] speaking of a "strange Vertigo or Delirium o' the Brain" drawing England into a revolution that went beyond politics:

> Nor doth the State alone on fortune's Wheeles
> Run round; Alas, our Rock Religion reeles.

He then suggests that the hope of heaven on earth might replace that of heaven above:

> Amidst these turnings, 'tis some comfort yet,
> Heaven doth not fly from us, though we from it.

And finally comes the full new fantasy:

> Nothing but fine Utopian Worlds i' the Moon
> Must be new form'd by Revolution.[17]

Interest in the upheaval which restored moderate monarchy to England in 1688 led to a proliferation of anonymous historical studies in which the term "glorious revolution" was introduced to the continent.[18] In the New World as in the Old, revolution became for the first time a positive political ideal.

The most dynamic of the "enlightened despots," Frederick the Great, saw revolutions as part of the destiny of nations, particularly new ones. In 1751 he wrote that

> . . . fragility and instability are inseparable from the works of men; the revolutions that monarchies and republics experience have their causes in the immutable laws of Nature.[19]

Frederick generally used the word "revolution" in the old sense of revolving back to where nations had been before. But he also began the trend among German thinkers of applying the word to spiritual as well as political change. He said of the Lutheran Reformation:

> A revolution so great and so singular, which changed almost the entire System of Europe, deserves to be examined with Philosophical eyes.[20]

Later Germans, such as Hegel and Marx were, of course, to use just such "philosophical eyes" to see in the liberating reforms of both Luther and Frederick antecedents of the modern, ideologically based revolutionary tradition.

Frederick the Great's interest in revolution as a spiritual and political event subtly influenced many Germans of his time. He created in Prussia a sense of new Promethean possibilities. His impatience with tradition in affairs of state was echoed in the republic of letters by the rebellious poets of the *Sturm und Drang*. Radical Bavarian Illuminists urged in the early 1780s that his secularizing reforms be carried even further through an "imminent revolution of the human mind." [21] Their opponents, in turn, already saw in such a program in 1786 the threat of an "imminent universal revolution." [22]

Thus Germany—not France—gave birth to the sweeping, modern idea of revolution as a secular upheaval more universal in reach and more transforming in scope than any purely political change. This concept was transported to Paris by Count Mirabeau, a former French ambassador in Berlin; it helped him to become the leading figure in the early events of the French Revolution in 1789. His study of Frederick the Great in 1788 had proclaimed Prussia the likely site of a coming revolution, and the German Illuminists its probable leaders.[23] Mirabeau's speeches and writings the following year transferred these expectations of a deep transformation from Germany to France. He became both the leader in turning the Third Estate of the Estates-General into a new National Assembly and "the first to succeed in launching a journal without the authorization of the government." [24] His reputation as the outstanding orator of the Assembly is closely related to his pioneering role in convincing the French that their revolution, though political in form, was redemptive in content. Mirabeau popularized the Illuminist term "revolution of the mind," introduced the phrase "great revolution," [25] and apparently invented the words "revolutionary," [26] "counter-revolution," and "counter-revolutionary." [27] Mirabeau pioneered in applying the evocative language of traditional religion to the new political institutions of revolutionary France. As early as May 10, 1789, he wrote to the constituents who had elected him to the Third Estate that the purpose of the Estates-General was not to reform but "to regenerate" the nation.[28] He subsequently called the National Assembly "the inviolable priesthood of national policy," the Declaration of the Rights of Man "a political gospel," and the Constitution of 1791 a new religion "for which the people are ready to die." [29]

The introduction of the hitherto little-used word *revolution* into the German language sealed the new and quasi-religious usage of the word. Writers and lexicographers initially either bragged or complained, according to their politics, that "we Germans wish so hard to keep [revolution] distant that we do not have even one word for it in our vocabulary"; and the French word was introduced into German precisely "to convey in its nature an impossible movement with speed and quickness"—to inspire awe and suggest a novelty beyond the traditional word for political upheaval, *Umwälzung*.[30]

We shall return to this faith in revolution as something totally new, secular, and regenerative—and to the occult, Germanic sources of this idea. But first, we must briefly consider the events of the French Revolution themselves. For the convulsions that began in Paris in 1789 represented an unprecedented succession of novelties that made Mirabeau's new conception of revolution believable. With mounting intensity and without any clear plan or continuous leadership, France proceeded to create a new political lexicon centered on the word "democracy" [31] and on a new understanding of revolution as a superhuman source of fresh dynamism for human history.[32]

The Fact of Revolution

In the summer of 1789, absolute monarchy and aristocratic authority were overthrown forever in the most powerful kingdom in Christendom. This was the essential French Revolution: the hard fact that gave birth to the modern belief that secular revolution is historically possible. This unplanned political transformation occurred within a period of exactly five months—between May 5, when King Louis XVI opened in Versailles the first Estates-General to meet in 175 years, and October 5, when the king was brought back to Paris as a virtual prisoner of the mob.

The decisive event of these five months was the Third Estate (which represented everyone except the clergy and nobility and was dominated by articulate middle-class lawyers) declaring itself to be the National Assembly. Members of the other two estates went over to join the Third Estate; it resolved in the "tennis-court oath" of June 20 to remain in being "until the constitution of the realm is set up and consolidated on firm foundations." Following the violence in Paris that led to the storming of the Bastille on July 14, a "great fear" spread through the countryside. Fires destroyed many records and symbols of the manorial system. In the course of August the Assembly abolished serfdom and aristocratic privilege and proclaimed the "natural and imprescribable" right of every citizen to liberty, equality, property, and security.

News of a political act—the king's dismissal of his reformist Finance Minister Necker—had fired the original unrest in Paris. Nine days after the Bastille fell the Paris mob hung Necker's successor, and political authority was restored by the Marquis de Lafayette. He arrived on a white horse—literally as well as symbolically—and took military command of Paris on July 15, lending legitimacy to upheaval, and serving with Mirabeau as a founding father of the revolutionary tradition.

Wounded at age nineteen while fighting for American independence in the Battle of Brandywine, Lafayette had returned to France hoping that the American Revolution "might serve as a lesson to the oppressors and an example to the oppressed" in the Old World.[33] He presented a key to the Bastille to Washington, used American rhetoric to help draft the *Declaration of the Rights of Man and Citizen*,[34] and lent dignity as head of the new national guard to the fateful march on Versailles on October 5.

Yet this seeming guarantor of continuing order amidst revolutionary change was soon denounced not just by the Right, but by the Left as well. Burke's conservative attack on the French Revolution listed "Fayettism" first among the "rabble of systems." [35] On the revolutionary side, "Gracchus" Babeuf, just a year after the fall of the Bastille, excoriated Lafayette as a conceited and antidemocratic brake on the revolutionary process.[36] Later revolutionaries, as we shall see, repeatedly raged against him.

Mirabeau, also a marquis but less elegant than Lafayette, was more central to the early revolutionary events. Rejected by his fellow aristocrats for election to the Estates-General, the pock-marked Mirabeau accepted election by the Third Estate; he infused it with *la passion politique*.

The constitutional monarchy favored by Lafayette and Mirabeau could not survive the attempt of the king to flee Paris in the summer of 1791 and the outbreak of foreign war in the spring of 1792. Revolutionary France formally proclaimed a republic in August 1792; massacred 1,100 alleged domestic foes in Paris in September, and publicly guillotined King Louis XVI in January 1793. External and internal violence increasingly polarized politics and split the National Assembly into the original "right" and "left." [37] The subsequent equation of the left with virtue dramatized revolutionary defiance of Christian tradition, which had always represented those on the right hand of God as saved and those on the left as damned.[38]

During this time the armed masses in Paris tended increasingly to reject the politics of the Assembly, arguing that

> Le *Côté Droit* est toujours gauche
> Et *le gauche* n'est jamais droit.[39]

The crowd that had invaded the Tuileries Palace to imprison the king on August 10, 1792, broke into the Assembly on May 31, 1793, and in the summer mobilized in the *levée en masse* to resist counter-revolutionary foes in the countryside and on the borders.

The subsequent history of the armed revolution reveals a seemingly irresistible drive toward a strong, central executive. Robespierre's twelve-man Committee of Public Safety (1793–94) gave way to a five-man Directorate (1795–99), to a three-man Consulate, to the designation of Napoleon as First Consul in 1799, and finally to Napoleon's coronation as emperor in 1804.

After 1792 a growing split developed between the stated ideals of the revolutionary republic and their practical implementation. Marxists have represented this conflict as the inevitable clash of the "proletarian" quest for a social revolution and the "bourgeois" desire to consolidate newly acquired property rights and political power. But social consciousness at the time was focused on the shared hatred of foreigners and aristocrats; and in pre-industrial Paris the distinction between the working and middle classes was not yet clear. The more significant split was between the political consciousness of the articulate lawyers and leaders of revolutionary France and the mundane, apolitical demands of the urban masses for food, security, and something to believe in.

The leaders repeatedly failed to satisfy the Parisian populace. Lafayette, who in April 1792 had favored war in order to rally France behind the constitutional monarchy, was soon drowned out by the more bellicose and radical Brissot. The Brissotists, or Girondists, were in turn swept aside by the more extreme Jacobins in the late spring of 1793. The relatively moderate Jacobinism of Danton was then supplanted by Robespierre; his reign of terror claimed some forty thousand domestic victims in 1793–94. Yet none of these figures was able to bring stability.

Robespierre, the most radical political leader of the revolutionary era, was also the first to turn decisively against the Paris mob. He broke up its sectional assemblies in the fall of 1793 and executed the extreme *enragés* or Hébertists in the spring of 1794—shortly before he too was guillotined in July. The retrenchment that followed, the so-called Thermidorean reaction, checked a seemingly inexorable drift to the left. The new republican Constitution of 1795 was far less radical than that written in 1793 (but never put in effect). Two years later the attempt of the Babeuf conspiracy to organize a new revolutionary uprising was crushed by the five-man Directory with no difficulty. Though Napoleon rose to power through the revolutionary army and used revolutionary ideas to expand French power, he (like the constitutional monarchs who were restored to power after him) was generally seen not as an heir to the revolution but as its repudiator.

The revolutionary tradition reached maturity when fighting broke out again on the streets of Paris against the restored Bourbons in July 1830. Lafayette, by then an old man, emerged to legitimize a return to constitutional monarchy, and helped establish in power Louis Philippe of the House of Orléans. The linkage was deeply appropriate. For the original revolution of 1789 that had been led by Lafayette can in a sense be said to have begun in the Parisian pleasure dome of Louis Philippe's father, Philip of Orléans: the Palais-Royal. There in the shadow of the Tuileries Palace, Philip had decided to accept the revolution and rename himself *Egalité* rather than remain loyal to his cousin, King Louis XVI. It was this Philip who renamed the great public gardens of the Palais-Royal—in which the mob that stormed the Bastille first formed—"the garden of equality." And it is in this revolutionary garden of Eden, this unlikely Bethlehem, that the story of the revolutionary faith properly begins.

CHAPTER 2

A Locus of Legitimacy

AS PARIS overthrew the old regime, its citizens felt an almost desperate need for some new source of authority. The story of this need is usually told in terms of political or social forces, but it can also be told in terms of an ideological and geographical search for legitimacy.

If one were to use a single word to describe what the original French revolutionaries were really seeking, it might well be a key term later used by the Russians: *oprostit'sia*, to simplify. The desire for radical simplification (even of oneself as the reflexive verb suggests in Russian) impelled intellectuals following Rousseau to reject personal pretention as well as social convention. A similar striving toward simplicity compelled politicians leading up to Robespierre to rely increasingly on liquidation as well as inspiration. At the root of everything lay the passionate desire of thinking people to find a simple, unifying norm for society like the law of gravity that Newton had found for nature.

In their drive toward revolutionary simplicity Frenchmen melded many estates into one state; discarded innumerable titles for the uniform "citizen," "brother," and "*tu*"; supplanted elaborate rococo art with a severe neo-classicism; discarded complex Catholic traditions in the name of Dame Nature or a Supreme Being; and replaced reasoned argument with incantational slogan. The early revolutionary call for "one king, one law, one weight, one measure" prefigured later French evangelism in spreading the use of the metric and decimal systems.[1] Throughout the inventive revolutionary era, new symbols and societies seemed to be searching for *le point parfait*: "the perfect point" within a "circle of friends." These were the strangely appropriate names of two leading Masonic lodges that flourished in Paris during the Reign of Terror.[2]

But where was the "perfect point" on which to base a new secular faith? For many, the progressive simplification of the political process provided a kind of answer by reducing the locus of popular sovereignty from a National Assembly to an executive of twelve, five, three, and finally one man. Precisely under Napoleon, however, the professional revolutionary tradition began. The appearance of conspiracies within Napoleon's armies at the height of his power revealed an unsatisfied revolutionary thirst for something more than pure power.

Violence was part of what revolutionaries sought—and was in many ways their ultimate form of radical simplification. A thousand hopes and hatreds could be compressed into a single act of blood ritual, transforming *philosophes* into *révolutionnaires*. As the darkest mystery of the revolutionary faith, violence was at first mainly discussed by reactionary opponents, who saw the revolutionaries preempting the promise of ancient religions to provide *salut par le sang*.[3] Revolutionary violence has been best described metaphorically as a volcanic eruption or the birth pain of a new order. Because revolutionaries always believe their violence will end all violence, it might also be described as the sonic boom at which controls must be reversed, the vortex of a whirlpool in which a helplessly descending object may suddenly be hurled up to freedom.

The mark of blood distinguishes real revolution from mythic melodrama about the storming of a Bastille or a Winter Palace. The drama resembles rather that of a medieval passion play—in which, however, the act of crucifixion rather than the fact of resurrection provides *le point parfait* for a new beginning. Belief in a purely secular salvation leads the modern revolutionary to seek deliverance through human destruction rather than divine redemption. We shall trace the course of revolutionary violence from a romantic, Italo-Polish phase in the early nineteenth century to an ascetic Russian form in the late nineteenth and early twentieth centuries.

Yet the same lava that was to destroy a decadent Pompeii was also to fertilize a new Eden. The original search for revolutionary legitimacy involved not just the razing of a Bastille and beheading of a king, but also the quest for sacred space in which perfection might appear and oracles might speak. The story can be traced through both places and people. It begins in the cafés of the Palais-Royal and leads on to the neglected figure of Nicholas Bonneville.

The Cafés of the Palais-Royal

Nowhere—the literal meaning of Utopia—first became somewhere in the Palais-Royal. In the cafés that ringed the gardens of this great royal enclosure in central Paris, the "heavenly city of the eighteenth-century philosophers" found earthly roots; high ideals were translated into coarse conversation; salon sophistication became bourgeois bravado; reform moved through revolt to revolution.

The Palais-Royal had political origins as the creation of Cardinal Armand de Richelieu, the father of *raison d'état* in modern France. The palace was transformed into an enclosed complex of galleries, exhibition halls, and entertainment centers in the early 1780s—and was opened to the public by the reform-minded Philip of Orléans. His avarice rapidly converted it into a profitable center of pleasure where "all desires can be gratified as soon as conceived."[4] In the late spring of 1787, Philip built *Le Cirque*—a large oval enclosure more than one hundred meters long in the middle of the garden—for large meetings and sporting events.

The cafés in the arcades and the "circus" in the center of the Palais-Royal incubated an intellectual opposition that went beyond the mild, Whiggish reformism of the London coffeehouses that the House of Orléans had originally sought to imitate. The Palais-Royal became "a sort of Hyde Park of the French Capital," "the place where public opinion is formed," "the agora of the city in ferment," "the forum of the French Revolution." [5]

If the French Revolution can be said to have begun in any single spot at any single moment, it may have been in the gardens of the Palais-Royal at about 3:30 in the afternoon of Sunday, July 12, 1789, when Camille Desmoulins climbed up on a table and cried *Aux armes!* to the milling crowd. He was suggesting a collective Parisian response to the news that had just come from Versailles about the king's dismissal of Necker. Within half an hour of his speech, the crowd began coursing out onto the streets carrying busts of Necker and the Duke of Orléans.[6]

The moment was dramatic—in the most intense and literal sense of the word. The Palais-Royal had attracted an expectant audience. A minor operatic composer had set the stage, helping Desmoulins to mount what he called *la table magique* taken from the Café Foy. A green ribbon attached to Desmoulins's hat (by some accounts a green leaf plucked from a tree) provided the new costume: a badge of nature and of hope to brandish against the unnatural emblems of a hopeless aristocracy. The urban hero was (like Saint-Just and Babeuf to come) an intellectual journalist from rural Picardy. In response to his harangue, the supporting cast of hundreds spilled out into the streets. Their immediate purpose was the demonically appropriate one of forcing all the theaters in Paris to cancel their evening performances—as if to remove from the city any drama that might rival their own. Having shut the theaters, they converged on the greatest open square in Europe, the Place Louis XV, which they helped transform into a theater of revolution.

Under the equestrian statue of the king's father, the crowd brandished the busts of the king's dismissed minister and of his suspect cousin. The first act of the revolution/drama began at 8 P.M. in the square when stray fire from royal troops created the first martyrs of the revolution and the mob responded by sacking nearby armories. The drama was to return repeatedly to this great, open-air theater for its climactic scenes: the execution of the king in January 1793 (with the setting renamed Place de la Révolution), and the Easter liturgy celebrated by Tsar Alexander for the entire Russian army after the final defeat of Napoleon in 1815 (renamed again as Place de la Concorde).

In July 1789, however, the great square was only a point of transit for the Paris mob as it drove on to express in the center of Paris the destruction that had previously begun in the periphery with the razing of forty royal customhouses. The ultimate destination of the crowd that first acquired an identity on July 12 was, of course, the sparsely populated prison and armory known as the Bastille; but their original assembly point had been the Palais-Royal. Located about halfway between the Place Louis XV and the Place de la Bastille, the Palais continued to play a central role in the choreography of conflict during the early years of the revolution.

The habitués of the Palais were, in a way, the original "people" of revolutionary rhetoric; and the mob that assembled there periodically, the model for revolutionary mobilization. By early August, police were coming from other sections of the city to deal with the disorders reigning in the Palais-Royal and the dangers that could result from them.[7] If the Palais-Royal was not yet unified behind the republicanism of Desmoulins, it echoed the Anglophilia of the Duke of Orléans in hailing the events in France as "cette glorieuse Révolution." [8] Petitions against a royal veto were carried to the assembly in Versailles from the "citizens assembled in the Palais-Royal," [9] who constituted themselves as a kind of informal voice of revolutionary authority in the city. Songs in praise of the soldiers said to have refused orders to fire on the people were improvised "in the name of the citizens of the Palais-Royal." [10] "Lacking a King, Paris found a chief in the Palais-Royal." [11]

The locus of legitimacy was the critical issue, and the ultimate protagonists were the king's court at Versailles on the one hand and the headless "forum of the people" in the Palais-Royal at Paris on the other. Standing between them, however, in the summer of 1789 were the newly constituted National Assembly, still under the king's shadow at Versailles, and the formal government of Paris, still at the Hotel de Ville, on the Rue de Rivoli, halfway between the Palais-Royal and the Bastille. On August 30 a crowd of fifteen hundred set off from the Palais-Royal to the Hotel de Ville for the first of two unsuccessful petitions to gain official backing for a march on Versailles.[12] Finally, on Sunday, October 4, 1789, a large group formed in the Palais-Royal; it was joined by other Parisians to march on Versailles the following day, and brought both the king and the National Assembly back to Paris.

Paris itself thereafter became the battlefield. The king resided in the Tuileries Palace; popular authority, in the Palais-Royal just across the Rue Saint-Honoré. The National Assembly was relocated close to both in the drafty building of the former royal riding academy overlooking the Tuileries gardens.

The terminology used to characterize factions within the assembly revealed a thirst for the spatial sanctification of immaterial ideals. Legitimacy was identified with a physical location: "left" or "right," "mountain" or "plain." The middle position in the assembly between the two extremes became known as "the swamp" (le marais): the morass occupied by those unfit for either land or sea. One of the earliest historians of the revolution characterized le marais in polarized terms that anticipated later revolutionaries' denunciation of the "center" as "unprincipled," "opportunistic," and lacking the conviction of either right or left:

> Between these two extremes, men of secret votes and silent cowardice stagnate, always devoted to the strongest party and serving the powers that be. The place occupied by these eunuchs in the Convention was called the *Swamp*; it is called the *Center* in modern assemblies.[13]

Then, with the division of Paris into forty-eight sections on June 22, 1790, the Hotel de Ville was effectively superseded by a new form of popular government: the Commune of the Paris sections; and the Section of the Palais-Royal (later called the Section de la Montagne) became the largest sectional government in the center of the city.[14] News of divisions and debates in the National Assembly often came first from participants relating their accounts at the nearby cafés in the Palais-Royal. Rumors were manufactured there that the king was planning to flee France by assuming masked disguises or by digging a secret canal to Saint Cloud.[15]

The Palais-Royal played a central role in revolutionary Paris for three reasons. It offered, first of all, a privileged sanctuary for intellectuals where they could turn from speculation to organization. Second, its owner and patron, the Duke of Orléans, represented the point through which new ideas broke into the power elite of the old regime. Finally, the Palais provided a living link with the underworld of Paris and with the new social forces that had to be mobilized for any revolutionary victory.

Royal ownership assured immunity from arrest within the Palais-Royal; and from 1788 to 1792 a host of new organizations were formed and key meetings held there. Amidst the ferment of 1789 literary and artistic talent was rallied to the revolution by pioneering, if often short-lived, clubs: the Lycée de Paris, Lycée des Arts, Musée Français, Athénaum, and Club de 1789.[16] The revolutionary theater found a home there first in the Théâtre des Variétés, which had opened in 1785, and then in the new Théâtre de la République to which many outstanding actors of the national theater, including the legendary Talma, moved in 1792.

The mob that burst forth from the Palais-Royal in July 1789, carried a bust of Philip of Orléans along with one of Necker, and the mob that went to Versailles in October also acclaimed the king's cousin. As the owner of the Palais-Royal, Philip was seen as a patron of the revolutionary cause within the royal elite. His journey to London later in 1789 was seen by some as part of an Anglophile's maneuvering to move France closer to constitutional monarchy. Philip had written his own *Regulation of Life for the Palais-Royal* in February 1789; among other things it called for formal Wednesday evening soirées of twenty-five thinkers.[17]

His personal sponsorship of the Musée Français in his apartment and of various publications as well as open-air dramas in the gardens of the Palais led many conservatives to assume that the revolutionary tumult was in some sense the result of an Orléanist conspiracy.

Shortly after the proclamation of a republic on September 15, 1792, Philip of Orléans presented himself to the new communal government of Paris with a request to be renamed *Egalité*, and to have the garden of the Palais called the "garden of equality." [18] He paid tribute to his experience as a Freemason for providing him with a "sort of image of equality," but gave thanks that he had now "left behind the phantom for the reality." [19]

The rebaptized head of the House of Orléans was then elected a member of the Convention—over Robespierre's opposition. Two months later a decree of the Convention challenged the sincerity of Philip's conversion, suggesting that he "speculated on the revolution as on his jockies" and had simply acted in a way "most convenient to his interests." [20] Jean Paul Marat cast further doubt on Philip's "civic dedication" (*civisme*). When a revolutionary leader was assassinated in the Palais-Royal on January 20, suspicion of Philip deepened, and the Convention unleashed a kind of storm-trooper organization, the so-called defenders of the republic, for raids on the Orléanist redoubt.[21] When Philip's son, the future King Louis Philippe, defected to the counter-revolutionary camp together with General Charles François Dumouriez in the early spring, Philippe-Egalité was arrested—and eventually guillotined on November 6, 1793.

The Palais-Royal was the center in Paris not just of high politics and high ideals, but also of low pleasure. Along with the "political effervescence" fostered by "agitators whose mysterious existence seems more appropriate for a novel than for reality" appeared raucous publications that mixed politics and pornography, such as *The National Bordello under the sponsorship of the Queen, for the use of Provincial confederates.*[22] Philippe-Egalité once again showed the way. His long-time mistress, Mme. de Genlis (later Citoyenne Brûlart), was a kind of princess among the prostitutes of the Palais as well as a "governess of the princes." The new personal secretary he brought to the Palais in 1788, Choderlos de Laclos, was the author of *Les Liaisons Dangereuses* and a pioneer of the liberated pornography that flourished during the revolutionary era.[23] Laclos's friend, the Marquis de Sade, opened a bookstore in the Palais during the turmoil to sell his dark masterpieces; every form of sexual gratification that he described was available in the cafés and apartments of the Palais complex. The gardens were the gathering place for prostitutes, and respectable women did not appear in the Palais-Royal after 11:00 A.M.[24] Even before the revolution, the Palais-Royal had generated a counter-morality of its own. A defiant prostitute who refused to give herself to the Comte d'Artois became a folk heroine, and a café, *La Vénus*, was named in her honor.[25] The promenade of boutiques and galleries in the center of the Palais where contacts and assignations were usually made (the so-called Gallerie de Bois or Camp des Tartares) had as its central sculpture "la belle Zulima," [26] a wax statue of a naked woman done in realistic flesh color.

Cafés were the heart and soul of the Palais-Royal. About two dozen ringed the Palais-Royal and beckoned strollers from the gardens into the arcaded pleasure spots which were—literally as well as figuratively—the underground of Paris. Like the Cirque in the middle of the gardens (five-eighths of which was dug out below ground level), the cafés were mostly underground. Some of the most important names— Café du Caveau, Café des Aveugles, and Café du Sauvage—suggest the fetid air, mysterious darkness, and indulgent abandon that characterized these subterranean retreats. The Café des Aveugles offered twenty separate "caves" for the sexual and narcotic delectations of its customers, who usually descended there after lighter, alcoholic preliminaries at the Café Italien directly above.[27] For those who remained in, or returned to, the Café Italien (also known as the Corazza) passions turned political, and politics became international because of its large Italian clientele.

The verb "to politic" (*politiquer*) may even have originated in the café language of the Palais.[28] A special kind of politics emerged in this ambience. Playful irreverance and utopian speculation were preferred to pedestrian practicality. It was not the politics of those responsible for exercising power in the National Assembly or within the Paris Sections. It was a politics of desire fashioned over drinks that induced blissful oblivion, such as the *non-lo-sapraye* (fractured Italian for "You will never know it"), and after sweets designed for gluttons (such as the ice-cream confections of the Café Tortoni).[29]

The cafés of the Palais-Royal were also filled with votive objects of the emerging new faith in the applied sciences. In the Café Mécanique, "the ancestor of our automatic bars," [30] drinks appeared from trap doors, which were part of an elaborate set of levers and other devices illustrating various principles of Newtonian physics. Illusion became reality in the Café des Milles Colonnes, where mirrors magnified a few columns into a thousand. The stove that warmed the Café Italien was shaped like the pioneering balloon flown by Joseph Montgolfier, who himself frequented the café.[31]

This complex of cafés made the Palais-Royal seem, to the most acute observer of Paris on the eve of revolution,

> the capital of Paris, a sumptuous little city within a large one; the temple of voluptuousness.[32]

The sanctuary within this temple was the Café Foy, before which Desmoulins issued his famous call to arms on July 12, 1789. The Foy was the only café that had both the privilege of serving tables within the garden and control of a passageway out of it onto the Rue de Richelieu. Thus, it became the "portico of the Revolution," [33] the precise point at which Desmoulins's followers first moved from talk to action on the streets:

> During these months of excitement, the Café Foy was to the Palais-Royal, what the Palais-Royal was to Paris: a little capital of agitation within the kingdom of agitation.[34]

The Foy earned a mantle of martyrdom when it was shut down briefly by the king later in 1789, and the cafés of the Palais-Royal continued to politicize the populace of Paris in emotionally satisfying ways that neither the National Assembly nor the sectional governments could altogether duplicate. As one relatively neutral observer wrote in 1791:

> When a posterity more reflective and enlightened than the present generation studies the history of the French Revolution dispassionately, it will not be able to believe that cafés became the supreme tribunals within a city at the center of a free state. The Café de Foy and the Café du Caveau . . . are today two republics in which the most pronounced intolerance takes the name of patriotism.[35]

In this period "cafés grew and formed clubs; their tables became tribunals; their habitués, orators; their noises, motions."[36]

As the quarreling among revolutionaries became more intense, each faction tended to have its own café within the Palais—serving as both outpost and headquarters. The Café du Caveau was a gathering place for the Girondists who prepared the demonstrations of August 10, 1792, that overthrew the monarchy and established the First Republic. The Café Italien was an assembly point for the more radical Jacobins who eventually occupied the National Assembly and established the revolutionary dictatorship in the early summer of 1793.[37]

But the Jacobins operated mainly outside the Palais, deriving the name for their nationwide organization from the Jacobin monastery where the Parisian leaders first met. The Jacobin politicians were deeply suspicious of the Palais-Royal because of its obvious lack of discipline and at the same time out of contrary fear that it might ultimately fall subject to the discipline of a potential claimant to the throne: Philip of Orléans. They feared not only the royalists, who also controlled cafés within the Palais, but also the foreign friends of the Revolution who enjoyed the hospitality of the Palais-Royal. Thus, during the nationalistic mobilization of 1793, when all Paris became a theater of political conflict, the Jacobin dictatorship of Robespierre curtailed the freedom of the Palais-Royal. The café headquarters for the Jacobins and Babeuvists were some distance away on the left bank. Thus, long before the Cirque was burned down in 1798, and the cafés cleaned out by Napoleon in 1802, the Palais-Royal lost its centrality.

But why was the Palais-Royal able to mobilize mass emotions so successfully during the early years before full state power and military emergency could be invoked against it? The truth seems to be that the cafés provided not just a protected place for political meetings, but also the intoxicating ambiance of an earthly utopia. Distinctions of rank were obliterated, and men were free to exercise sexual as well as political freedom. In the course of a single visit, one might sip such libations of liberation as a new tricolored liquor, savor foreign foods in perfumed *boîtes*, see the *laterna magica* trace the history of the world in the apartment of Philippe-Egalité, visit a quasi-pornographic wax museum in the arcades, attend a melodrama which included music and acrobatics in the Cirque, and then go underground for entertainment that ranged from ventriloquism by a dwarf to sex with the seven-foot two-inch Prussian prostitute, Mlle. Lapierre.[38]

In such an atmosphere, illusion and fantasy mixed with material gratification and made the ideal of total secular happiness seem credible
as well as desirable. Hedonistic awakening was combined with political and intellectual discussion in an atmosphere of social equality and
directness of communication that had been unknown among the aristocratic conventions of the old regime. All races were represented
among the servants, entertainers, and shopkeepers of the Palais. Two
blacks (known as Aladin and Scipio) were revered rather in the manner
of court "fools" during the Renaissance, and were even called upon to
resolve conflicts.[39] The form of communication was egalitarian. The
often scatological language of the cafés was incorporated into plays
produced by the Duke of Orléans in his "garden of equality." His so-
called *genre Poissard* introduced irreverent forms of speech that soon
found their way into revolutionary journalism.

The Palais-Royal was an intensely verbal place, infecting Paris and all
of France with its revolutionary rhetoric and iconoclastic speech. As
one pamphlet noted already in 1790:

> The Palais-Royal is a theater, which imprints a great movement on the
> capital and on all the provinces of the French kingdom![40]

The anonymous writer was describing an incident in which Mirabeau
had been challenged by a mob in the Palais; and the implication was
that legitimacy lay no longer with the orator of the Assembly, who hides
"under the mask of national interest," but with the spontaneous people
in the Palais.[41] The Palais had become not just "the temple of patriotism
and wisdom," but also the point of combustion for *la révolution sentimentale:* that "immense and quasi-universal explosion of sensibility"
that began with Rousseau and helped transform a political crisis into
an emotion-charged upheaval. "From May to October 1789, there is no
scene . . . which did not end in tears and embraces." And many of those
scenes began in the Palais-Royal:

> . . . a sacred temple where the sublime sounds resound in celebration of
> this revolution that is so happy for the French nation and of such good
> augury for the entire universe.[42]

Within the café a small group of trusted friends often met at a table
and gradually formed a basic new unit for revolutionary activity: the
"circle." Mercier noted that even before the outbreak of revolution in
1789

> . . . the taste for circles, unknown to our fathers and copied from the En-
> glish, has begun to become naturalized.[43]

Unlike the English, the French in the Palais-Royal became "grave and
serious once gathered in a circle." [44] A small group could move beyond
the surface conviviality of the café to deeper dedication in a circle:
unified by the pursuit of truth, a sharing of inner thoughts, and the
"strength of a uniform equality." [45]

The most important such body to appear in the Palais-Royal during the turbulent and creative early years of the revolution was the Social Circle (*Cercle Social*), which was in some ways the prototype for the revolutionary organizations of the future. Its founder, Nicholas Bonneville, was as important and innovative in his day as he has been neglected since. It is to this remarkable figure that attention must now be turned.

Nicholas Bonneville and Oracular Journalism

Editorial offices no less than cafés were breeding grounds of the new revolutionary faith. Indeed, at almost every crucial point of the French Revolution, journalists stood at center stage—or perhaps left-center, with active political leaders slightly to their right.

The Abbé Sieyès, a denizen of the Palais-Royal [46] and a leading voice of the Third Estate in 1789, suggested that the Fourth Estate of journalism may have been even more important than the Third:

> The printing press has changed the fate of Europe; it will change the fate of the world. . . .
> The press is for the immense spaces of today what the voice of the orator was on the public square in Athens and Rome.[47]

The Fourth Estate in many ways replaced the First, the Church. In revolutionary France journalism rapidly arrogated to itself the Church's former role as the propagator of values, models, and symbols for society at large. Indeed, the emergence of dedicated, ideological revolutionaries in a traditional society (in Russia of the 1860s no less than in France of the 1790s) depended heavily on literate priests and seminarians becoming revolutionary journalists. Like church-state relations in an earlier era, the relations between the journalists and the politicians of revolution involved both deep interdependence and periodic conflict.

The new breed of intellectual journalist during the French Revolution created both the basic sense of legitimacy and the forms of expression for the modern revolutionary tradition. Journalism was the only income-producing profession practiced by Marx, Lenin, and many other leading revolutionaries during their long years of powerlessness and exile.

The story of the link between journalism and revolution—one to which we shall repeatedly return—began with the sudden imposition at the onset of the revolution of two new conditions on journalists: the granting of unprecedented civil liberties and the assignment of broad new tasks of civic mobilization.

The idea that events in France were part of a process greater than the sum of its parts was popularized by the new journals which sprang up in 1789 like *Révolutions de France et de Brabant* and *Révolutions de Paris*. When the latter ceased publication in February 1794, it proclaimed that the people were now in power and that *la révolution est faite.*[48] But by then the Reign of Terror was at its height, and a new species of journalist-agitator had educated the masses to believe that the revolution was not at all completed: they were men like the Swiss-Sardinian doctor Jean Paul Marat and the Norman libertine Jacques-René Hébert, who had begun his journalistic career while serving as a ticket seller at the Théâtre des Variétés in the Palais-Royal.

Marat broke the unspoken taboo against using the press to call openly for violence against fellow Frenchmen.[49] He institutionalized the perpetual denunciation of traitors—often writing from hiding or exile in his *L'Ami du Peuple*. He in many ways anticipated and validated the main ideas of the Jacobin dictatorship—attacking both the Girondists and the Palais-Royal. When murdered in his bath on the eve of Bastille Day, 1793, he became a martyr of the uncompleted revolution and was transfigured immediately into an icon by David's famous painting. Five other journals appeared to perpetuate Marat's title; two others called themselves *Véritables Amis du Peuple*.[50]

The more earthy Hébert provided the people not with a friend, but with a spokesman: the coarse but candid "Father Duchêne," a figure of folklore well-known in the vaudevilles of Paris and in the cafés of the Palais-Royal. Hébert delivered his own editorials in the rough language of this mythical personality, who became a kind of Everyman for the Parisian mob and lent his name to Hébert's newspaper, *Père Duchêne*; he inspired even more imitators than Marat.[51] Hébert popularized the revolutionary technique of anathematizing people not as individuals but rather for the sins they allegedly personified: *Brissotisme, Buzotisme,* and so forth.[52]

Père Duchêne reached beyond the realm of commentary and even of agitation to exercise for brief moments direct revolutionary leadership. Hébert had found the secret of arousing the animal instincts of the mob through the power of the printed page. The appeal of *Père Duchêne*[53] was so great that he reappeared in every revolution of nineteenth-century France along with *Mère Duchêne, Les Fils du Père Duchêne,* and so forth.

This rough-hewn personification of the revolution was more than merely the hero of a popular morality play or the mouthpiece for the left wing of the revolution. He represented a ritual desecration of authority, something that was as important to the cultural revolution as was the legal change in authority to the political revolution. The celebrated profanity in Hébert's journal not only appealed to the masses, but also encouraged them to overthrow the secret tyranny of language exercised by aristocratic French and its elaborate conventions of classical restraint. The forbidden words of Hébert both heralded and legitimized formerly forbidden acts carried out during the Reign of Terror. Many early, aristocratic supporters of the revolution had their tongues silenced by Hébert before their heads were removed by Hébert's readers.

Along with the seizure of power, there came a "seizure of speech," a *prise de parole*. Indeed, the four-letter outbursts of the youthful demonstrators in the late 1960s echoed the political shock tactics of Hébert, who

... never began a number of the *Père Duchêne* without putting in a *foutre* or *bougre*. This gross vulgarity signified nothing but signaled . . . a total revolutionary situation [by using language] . . . to impose something beyond language which is both history and the part one is to play in it.[54]

In a highly verbal culture linguistic shock was essential to the sustaining of the revolutionary spirit. The intimidating effect of aristocratic or academic speech had to be shattered by

... the seizure of the forbidden word, that which the established order proscribes because it destroys its legitimacy. The word which is both hidden and forbidden; the word which has been buried under accumulated generations of alluvial respectability.[55]

Hébert cut through these layers with a vulgarity that fed the rage of the Parisian populace when food supplies ran low late in the winter of 1793–94. In demanding social controls and economic redistribution, the journalist exceeded the limits that politicians could tolerate. Martyred by Robespierre, Hébert was rediscovered in the 1840s as a forgotten hero of the revolution and a fresh model for militant revolutionary journalists frustrated by bourgeois culture and anxious for social rather than political change.

But among all the pioneers of revolutionary journalism, Nicholas Bonneville was perhaps the most original. He was the first to issue the famous cry of *La Marseillaise: "Aux armes, citoyens!"* even before it was used to summon the mob to the Bastille.[56] From May to July 1789, Bonneville's new journal *Le Tribun du Peuple* directed attention beyond the revolution then taking place to "the revolution that is being prepared." [57] He looked for deliverance not to any political republic, but to "the republic of letters": [58] a rallying of intellectuals to lead mankind.

Bonneville saw his new journal as a "circle of light," whose writers were to transform the world by constituting themselves as "simultaneously a centre of light and a body of resistance." [59] They were to be "legislators of the universe," [60] preparing a "vast plan of universal regeneration," [61] and opposing "those pusillanimous beings whom the indifferent crowd call moderate people." [62] The supreme authority was not to be any elected official, but a "tribune": a modern version of the idealized tribal commander of the uncorrupted early Romans. The revolution to come must be led by a "tribune of the people," a reincarnation of the special leaders first chosen by the plebeian legions in 494 B.C. to defend them against the Roman patricians.

On the eve of the first anniversary of the seizure of the Bastille, Bonneville became the first to use the most basic weapon in the revolutionary seizure of speech. He substituted the familiar, plebeian form of address, *tu*, for the formal, aristocratic *vous* in addressing the king of France.[63]

Though Bonneville was elected secretary of the assembly of representatives of the Paris Commune that met in June 1790, it was basically through his new journal that he worked to exercise his "tribunat dans la République des lettres." [64] In the seventeenth and last issue of his *Tribun*, he proclaimed his intention to provide the revolution with "a mouth of iron . . . a kind of tribune that will always be open." [65] He published a *Bulletin de la Bouche de Fer* in the summer,[66] and in October put out the first issue of *La Bouche de Fer*, which he saw as a kind of public oracle:

> C'est la force magique
> Et sa Bouche de fer sauve la République.[67]

The first issue called *La Bouche* "a different, superior power," a "fourth power" [68]—a power outside and above the three branches of government that the American Revolution had taught European reformers to admire. This "superior power" had a right and obligation to conduct censorship and denunciation in defense of the revolution. Its mission was "universal surveillance" on behalf of that "multitude of good citizens who are not yet enlightened enough to know what they desire." [69]

Reporters for Bonneville's journal were "tribunes of the people," countering the despotic tendencies not only of monarchs, but also of patrician assemblies. These tribunes were not just to represent their region, but were also to know and report "the heart of their people." [70]

All nations and languages were to send messages to Bonneville's letter box, which was shaped like an iron mouth. This "mouth" was to swallow and digest the words it was fed and then to announce its counsel to "friends of truth" everywhere. Just as "mouths of gold" spoke of war, so the "mouth of iron" announced the coming of universal peace.[71] Indeed, its distribution on the streets was to be announced by trumpeters.[72] Although Bonneville's journal ceased publication on July 28, 1791, the echoes of its trumpets did not die out.

In the early years of the revolution, Bonneville and other literary journalists in effect invented a new, post-aristocratic form of French that was rich in neologisms and hailed as *la langue universelle de la République*.[73] This language was forced on the dialect-rich provinces as a means of destroying local loyalties in a time of national danger. After 1792 the documents of the central government were no longer even translated into provincial dialects; in some ways a "body of language" replaced the body of the king as the symbol of French unity.[74]

This new language was derived from the living speech of the revolution itself. Revolutionary French destroyed many oral traditions of the provinces and countryside in the course of radiating its own song and speech out from Paris. In the hands of Bonneville's associates, men like Anacharsis Cloots, the "orator of the human race," the spoken language tended to recapture its primitive function of communal incantation. Bonneville's closest friend, Claude Fauchet, was a curate who helped storm the Bastille and then stormed the pulpit with a new genre of revolutionary sermon. In the very citadel of Catholic France, Notre Dame Cathedral, Fauchet used words that anticipated Lincoln to call for a new kind of government:

pour le peuple, par le peuple, au peuple.[75]

Many revolutionary leaders had been trained in rhetoric by the Jesuits and in oratory as prosecuting lawyers or preaching curates. Philosophers in the prerevolutionary period had increasingly sought "less to prove than to move, less to demonstrate than to touch."[76] As a young advocate, Robespierre had dreamed of stimulating

> . . . within hearts this sweet shudder by which sensitive souls respond to the voice of the defender of humanity.[77]

"Vous frémissez, messieurs!" Danton said to the National Assembly as it prepared to found the first French Republic in 1792. This "voluptuous shudder" seemed to be a "symbol of the contagion of the word." [78] It reflected as well the decisive transformation made by Danton himself ("the Mirabeau of the populace") in revolutionary rhetoric: the discarding of classical metaphors and aristocratic forms for earthy speech directed at the masses.[79] Oratory in this new idiom fed the fever of 1792–94 and dominated the new civic rituals.

Revolutionary journalists often seemed to echo, if not actually to reproduce, the spoken word. Spontaneous speech was thought to approximate the language of nature itself. There was a revulsion that was almost physical against any writing not directly inspired by revolutionary ideas. Saint-Just denounced "the demon of writing," which led to the "tyranny of bureaus." [80] Cloots warned against "men of letters who were not men of ideas." [81] Bonneville cried out almost audibly against "the mania of decrees":

> Point de décrétomanie ou nous perdons les moeurs et la liberté! [82]

Bonneville insisted that the authority of revolutionary intellectuals should supplant once and for all that of authoritarian politicians. He had been one of the first to revile Necker before the revolution; to denounce Lafayette as a potential "Caesar," and to warn against Jacobin ambitions with the slogan *point de société dominatrice*.[83]

The appearance of revolutionary intellectuals in the modern world is inseparable from their reverence for *le peuple-Dieu*. For Bonneville the only antidote to the aristocratic indulgence of "talking societies" was immersion in the language of "the people." Bonneville had in mind, of course, not the words actually spoken by ordinary people but what he thought of as the hidden language of their true desires, the expression of the goodness they preserve when living naturally as "brothers and friends." [84] Well before the revolution, Bonneville had urged the aristocratic Condorcet to speak more simply. If writers do not inspire the people, who "always have a rapturous feeling for nature," the fault lies with the aristocratic *philosophe*'s own loss of touch with the "language of fire," the "universal language: sighs and tears." [85]

In his proto-romantic search for pure origins and radical simplicity, Bonneville suggested that both speech and worship began when man first placed fire in water and heard the whistling sound *is-is*. He contended that the Cathedral of Notre Dame had been superimposed on an earlier, more universal cult of Notre-Isis.[86]

The legitimizing myths of the revolution became inextricably connected with key words drawn from the language of "sighs and tears" and used for incantation more than explanation. The rational discourse of the philosophes was engulfed by a torrent of terminology created by intellectuals for plebeians, repeated in staccato shouts, and italicized or capitalized on fly-sheets and wall posters. Literate reformers of an earlier generation bitterly denounced the new "disposition to dominate conversation" with *idées forces*, to profit from "the power of badly defined words," and to camouflage denunciations by using "on dit que . . ." rather than "a precise and human nominative." [87] But they recognized that the new journalists had found the secret of arousing the masses:

> The people, burdened with their daily work, have neither the ability, time, nor desire to read. This enormous mass of people could never have been led into the terrible movement of these past three years by metaphysical, philosophical, or eloquent works. Other levels were needed. . . . not books, but words: liberty, tyranny, despotism. . . .[88]

In revolutionary Paris at the height of the terror in 1794, words had become weapons. Robespierre silenced Hébert in March, and justified further censorship by a special study of language in May, which described words as "the bonds of society and guardians of all our knowledge."[89]

From the still undisciplined Palais-Royal, however, came a call for the direct translation of words into deeds, in a pamphlet appropriately entitled *L'Explosion* by Jean-François Varlet, a protégé of Hébert and Bonneville, warning that "despotism has passed from kings to committees." [90]

If words ruled the world, ultimate power could be thought to inhere in the compilation of the ultimate dictionary. Efforts to do so were in fact made by two literary friends of Bonneville, and of each other, Restif de la Bretonne and Louis-Sébastien Mercier. Each of them wrote detailed descriptions both of ordinary Parisian life and of the Palais-Royal at the beginning of the upheaval.[91] The "universal" language each sought to create was the language of aspiration in the city both loved, and of imagination in the section they knew best.

Restif attempted to compile a *Glossographe* for a new universal language that would free French from being merely "a dialect of Latin." [92] Mercier devoted most of his energies in the revolutionary era to a magnum opus that appeared only in 1801: *Neology or Vocabulary of Words That Are New or to Be Renewed*. Mercier compared his own accomplishment to Bonaparte's conquest of territory for the republic, describing himself as *le premier livrier de la France*—a position apparently comparable in the republic of letters to Napoleon's first consulship in the republic of politics.[93] After falling out with Napoleon, Mercier continued to work on his partially suppressed and never completed *Universal Dictionary of Language*.[94]

Like Restif and Bonneville, Mercier died forgotten and has continued to be largely neglected by historians of the revolution. But unlike the other two, his importance for the subsequent development of the revolutionary tradition does not require special attention; Mercier is properly remembered primarily for anticipating the French Revolution. His remarkable utopian work of 1768–81, *The Year 2440*, predicted the destruction of the Bastille [95] and a future republican form of government for France. The republic was to be based not on institutional mechanisms, but on a democratized language that would have "reinstated equal dignity for words as well as men. No single word will be vile," [96] and people throughout the world will be nourished by words from journals "twice as long as English gazettes." [97] When the revolutionary conflagration finally came, Mercier traced its origins to Rousseau,[98] and saw it spreading through words that "crackled" in contemporary usage. The introduction to the German edition of his *Year 2440* found his picture "full of fire," [99] and Mercier used the same metaphor four years later to suggest prophetically the link between ideas and revolution:

> . . . the flame of philosophy . . . has been lit and dominates Europe: the wind of despotism in curbing the flame can only stir it up and billow it into larger and brighter bursts.[100]

The ultimate keeper of this flame was the most secret inner group within the Palais-Royal: Bonneville's "Social Circle." This organization combined the Masonic ideal of a purified inner *circle* with the Rousseauian ideal of a *social*, and not merely a political, contract. There may have been some continuity with a prerevolutionary Club of the Social Contract or Social Club under Philip of Orléans, to which Bonneville had belonged.[101] He appears first to have conceived of this new organization in October or November of 1789, and first to have formed it in the summer of 1790 out of the Thursday editorial meetings of his *Tribune of the People*—initially as an organ of surveillance and censorship for *La Bouche de Fer*.[102]

Bonneville distinguished his new organization from all other revolutionary clubs. "The Social Circle, which seeks *neither masters nor disciples*, is not at all a club," he insisted in the first issue of *La Bouche*.[103] Members had secret cards and assumed names. They comprised an inner group within a broader "patriotic circle of the friends of truth," [104] and *La Bouche* was their "hierophantic" interpreter of truth to those outside.

Bonneville sought to organize in the Cirque of the Palais-Royal a "Universal Confederation of the Friends of Truth," and attracted some six thousand members to its opening session in October 1790.[105] Bonneville appears to have viewed it as a kind of rival ideological parliament to the National Assembly, organized by "old friends united in principle and in heart long before the birth of the National Assembly." [106]

The constitution of the confederation, published in November 1790, described it as the servant of the Social Circle "and of all the circles of free brothers (*francs-frères*) affiliated with it." [107] "Circles of free brothers" may have existed in Utrecht, Geneva, Genoa, and Philadelphia —all had correspondence centers for the Social Circle.[108] Another main outlet appears to have been London, where Bonneville had lived and written just prior to the revolution and where a printing press and formal branch of the Social Circle were founded under "one of our English franc-brothers"—John Oswald.[109]

Oswald was an uprooted Scottish soldier-of-fortune who had fought in both America and India, worked as a jeweler and veterinarian, and become proficient in an astonishing range of languages including Arabic, Greek, and Portuguese.[110] One of the first foreigners to hail the French Revolution, Oswald became, in effect, Bonneville's London correspondent. He translated from and contributed to Bonneville's publications, and transmitted them to "franc-Scottish" and "franc-Irish" as well as to "Anglo-franc" brothers.

Bonneville's English friends denounced the English constitution, long admired by French reformers, as a parliamentary despotism. It represents poor people in the way "wolves represent sheep." [111] Oswald personally joined the military struggle of the French Republic against the British-led coalition. In Paris in 1793, just before going off along with his two sons to die in battle in the Vendée, he published *The Government of the People; or a Sketch of a Constitution for the Universal Common-wealth. By John Oswald Anglo-franc, Commandant of the First Battalion of Pikes, in service of the Republic of France.*[112] "A Constitution for the Universal Common-wealth" was the only one worthy of the "Universal Confederation of the Friends of Truth."

In his major work for the Universal Confederation of the Friends of Truth, Bonneville saw social justice radiating out from "the center of the social circle," and truth generating the "electricity" of virtuous conduct.[113] He provides one of the first rationalizations for the rule of an intellectual elite: "In intellectual organization, truth is the center to which all should gravitate." [114] The very dedication to Truth, however, may require the tactical concealment of some truths

> . . . not out of gratuitous cruelty, but in order to secure little by little, universally, the innumerable steps that must be taken on our ladder.[115]

"All the parties" should respect *La Bouche de Fer*, since it "serves none of them," [116] but only Truth.

Bonneville's Friends of Truth envisaged the universal rule of "the republic of letters," not the parochial control of any political republic. Authority was to come not from below by assembling the *états généraux*, but from above by the *confédération des écrivains généraux.*[117]

Bonneville's group was a self-conscious, self-proclaimed intellectual elite. They were *les intelligences supérieures* capable of finding *une lumière vive . . . dans les sphères très-élevées de la maçonnerie.*[118] The hope of humanity lay, therefore, in purifying the intellectual elite, not in imposing any checks upon its power. The main reason for fear was external: the persistence of irrational *violence par les imaginations mal reglées.*[119]

Bonneville's concept of rule by "superior intelligences" represents the first revolutionary equation of abstract intelligence with concrete people claiming political authority. Thus, Bonneville launched the idea of an inner intellectual "circle" as the controlling unit of a secret international movement. He seems even to have anticipated the future east-ward migration of this idea through the German *Kreis* and the Polish *koła* to the Russian *kružhok,* when he wrote even before the revolution:

> In France, in Italy, in Germany, and above all in Russia, they are cher-ishing the hope of one day being admitted into the miraculous secrets by the beneficent superiors who watch over all the members of the society.[120]

Bonneville anticipated both the idea of an elite intelligentsia and the special receptivity of Russians to this concept. It seems appropriate that the key founder (Count Dmitriev-Mamonov) of the pioneering group (the Order of Russian Knights) within the first Russian revolu-tionary movement (the Decembrists of the 1820s) had not only read Bonneville, but insisted:

> For the basic design of a plan I know of no more suitable book than *La bouche de fer de Bonneville.*[121]

In a chapter of his work for the Friends of Truth entitled "On the Theory of Insurrections," Bonneville described how "a beloved magis-trate" would appear before his people in the new order to conduct a naturalistic version of Holy Communion:

> Friends, this is *the body* of the sun which ripens the harvest. This is the body OF THE BREAD *which the rich owe to the poor!* [122]

He addressed his readers not as Freemasons (*franc-maçons*) but as *Francs-cosmopolites*—an altogether new breed combining the natural order of the early Franks and the "universal fraternity" of the modern Enlightenment. After a Hymn to Truth invoking the need "to conquer the light," [123] Bonneville intoned:

> CERCLE du PEUPLE FRANC, pour forth with a sure hand thy luminous rays into the dark climates.[124]

A remarkable appendix spoke of "magic circles" and reduced major political systems to graphic circular representations of how the parts relate to the center of power. The impression created by his *cercles con-stitutionels* was that both the original constitution of England under Alfred and the constitution of revolutionary France represented simple, symmetrical systems compared with the constitution of England during or since the Puritan Revolution.[125] Yet even the purest of political cir-cles seemed implicitly inferior to the social circlé, which would realize "the perfectibility of all governments" [126] by creating an egalitarian so-ciety: the perfect circle in which all points are equidistant from the center, Truth.

The Universal Confederation of the Friends of Truth represented one of the first efforts of a small circle of intellectuals systematically to propagate radical social ideas to a mass audience. The Confederation advocated a *grande communion sociale* that would provide social bene-fits, universal, progressive taxation, and the extension of civic equality to women and blacks.

"Of the Paris political clubs the *Cercle Social* was the first to advocate feminism." [127] It called for circles of women to accompany those of "free brothers," [128] and formed on February 15, 1791, in the Cirque of the Palais-Royal a feminine Society of the Friends of Truth with the Dutch Etta Palm (née D'Aelders) as president.[129]

The Social Circle was also relatively sympathetic to the cause of the blacks. Among the many engravings and medallions that Bonneville's artistic brother François designed for the Social Circle, two of the best depicted in classical style a black man and a black woman bearing respectively the legends:

> I am thy equal. Color is nothing, the heart is all, is it not, my brother?

> In freedom as thou art: The French Republic in accord with nature has willed it: am I not thy sister? [130]

From the beginning Bonneville's stress on social equality rather than political discipline and the determination to be "universal" and hospitable to foreigners rendered his organization suspect to the Jacobins. They accused Bonneville of building an explosive "new volcano" in the underground cafés whose crater was "the mouth of hell." (*La bouche d'enfer* was a play on words with the title of Bonneville's journal.)[131]

In February 1791, Bonneville answered the Jacobin accusation that his program was "incendiary" by agreeing that he was in truth attempting to generate "the warmth of universal fraternity." [132] His combustible material was often foreign. Thomas Paine moved in 1791 from his London association with Mirabeau's former secretary to take up residence with Bonneville and his wife and to become their closest friend. Fresh from completing his famous defense of the French Revolution, *The Rights of Man*, Paine together with another American in Paris, Joel Barlow, helped impart a sense of apostolic linkage between republican America and revolutionary France.[133]

Bonneville argued against Marat's call for a revolutionary dictatorship after the king tried to flee abroad in 1791:

> No more king! No dictator! Assemble the people and face the sun. Proclaim that the law alone will be sovereign.[134]

Their belief in a totally legal order led Bonneville and Paine to oppose the two key political decisions of the First French Republic: the execution of the king and the establishment of Robespierre's dictatorship. The Jacobins rejected Paine's argument that revolutionaries should rise above the death penalty, and Marat denounced Bonneville as a "base flatterer" in the pay of Lafayette.[135]

The murder of Marat intensified the fear of foreign subversion—and the suspicion that the cosmopolitan Palais-Royal was its breeding ground. Bonneville's principal collaborators on *Chronique du Mois* (the journal he founded after the *Bouche de Fer*)—Brissot and Condorcet —were killed, and Paine and Bonneville's other foreign friends were imprisoned. The weapon that Charlotte Corday had used to kill Marat had been purchased in the Palais-Royal.[136] Suspicion focused on foreigners: the Belgian Proli (who had edited since 1791 the journal *Le Cosmopolite* in sumptuous offices above the Café Corazza); the Spaniard Guzman (whose gambling center was thought to smuggle money); the English, Irish, and Americans in a nearby hotel, who were thought to be Orléanists; and Dutch, Germans, and Italians involved in the short-lived foreign legions.[137]

Bonneville himself escaped arrest, and continued to publish works identified as coming from "the press," the "press and library," or "the directors" of "the Social Circle" even though the organization itself ostensibly ceased functioning in 1791. In fact the press had always been the heart and soul of the Social Circle. So long as it continued to operate, the concept of an international, egalitarian transformation of society continued to grow and deepen. While on a revolutionary mission for the new republic in September 1792, Bonneville sent back an independent report addressed to "Free Citizens, directors of the press of the Social Circle, Paris." [138] Thereafter Varlet, the leading opponent on the left to Robespierre's dictatorship, wrote pamphlets for the press of the Social Circle. As president of the Central Revolutionary Committee of the Paris sections, he preached "permanent insurrection" as the logical means of supporting "direct" democracy.[139]

Varlet later joined Babeuf's proto-Communist Conspiracy of Equals, and continued—along with Sylvain Maréchal, author of the conspiracy's Manifesto—to publish with Bonneville's press. The novel of Restif that first introduced the word communist to a general audience and many of the plays of Bonneville's friend Mercier also appeared under Bonneville's imprimatur. Even Babeuf, who was connected at an early date with Bonneville's confederation, built his conspiracy of 1796 around an oracular journal that used the original title Bonneville had introduced six years earlier: *The Tribune of the People*.

But the republic was at war in 1792, and so it was inevitable that the locus of legitimacy was to shift away from the Palais-Royal. A nation at arms in the name of "the people" could no longer tolerate elite prophets of cosmopolitan confederations and universal Truth.

Para-military "defenders of the republic" began systematic forays early in 1793 into the Palais-Royal to apprehend alleged foreign and aristocratic sympathizers. By midyear France was in the middle of a civil as well as a foreign war. Paris was suffering a shortage of bread and fuel on the one hand and an excess of inflammatory patriotic journals on the other. The center of power had moved from the Girondist assembly to the Jacobin dictatorship. The locus of legitimacy was moving from closed to open space, from the editorial office to the public festival, from the Café de Vénus to the Champs de Mars, the great military parade ground of Paris on the left bank of the Seine.

The Fields of Festival

There was almost certainly no serious conspiracy within the Palais-Royal. Philip of Orléans was too weak to constitute a political threat, and no café-based organization had the structure of support to rival either the national network of Jacobin clubs or the sectional governments within Paris.

Yet what Nicholas Bonneville created within the permissive ambiance of the Palais-Royal was nothing less than the prototype of a modern revolutionary organization. It had global political pretensions ("a universal confederation") based on ideological convictions ("friends of truth") under the discipline of a secret inner group (the Social Circle) who pretended to translate Rousseau's general will into revolutionary strategy through an oracular journal ("the mouth of iron").

Physically, Bonneville's organization may be thought of as a series of concentric circles. The outer circumference was the high colonnaded quadrangle of the Palais-Royal; the second circle, the enclosed Cirque where the Universal Confederation of the Friends of Truth met in 1790–91; and the inner circle was where Bonneville's own group met in a café even further underground than the subterranean Cirque.

Bonneville sought legitimacy, not power, and he is thus overlooked by modern historians for whom struggle among political factions is somehow more real than the contention of political symbols. Yet the quest for legitimacy is no less important to trace than is the politics of power if we are to penetrate the minds of revolutionaries and not merely describe the externals of the revolutionary process. Bonneville made the most thorough effort to replace the circle of the court at Versailles with a new circle of authority in Paris. But "the people" still needed something to rally around, a common point of reference if not of reverence, new rituals to replace the rituals of Versailles and Notre Dame.

The search for authority in a landscape newly stripped of familiar landmarks led many to look beyond language for direct certainty. Disoriented men and women unconsciously discarded the familiar "reference" symbols used in conventional communication and reached out for "condensation" symbols that might directly represent truth itself.[140] If the inner circle was a condensed symbol of perfection and equality (opposing the linear, hierarchical symbols of the old regime), the circle required a center: some common point of reference to unify and equalize all the points on the circumference.

The unifying point of authority within Bonneville's circle was the press. It was the totem within the Social Circle, the larynx behind the mouth of iron. The press became and has remained the core of revolutionary counter-authority to modern political tyranny. The smell of printer's ink is the incense of modern revolutionary organization.

But for all its importance, the printing press could not provide the unifying authority for society, or even a condensation symbol for the revolutionary faith. In the first place, the printing press was a complex machine rather than a simple expression of nature. Revolutionary authority juxtaposed the simple and natural to the complex and traditional. If the circle was the microcosm of a purified nature, any central symbol within it would have to be a distillation of Nature. In the second place, the function of the printing press was to produce written reference symbols, not direct condensations or representations of things. Revolutionary Paris was not prepared to follow any linear parade of words or train of thought. Such products of aristocratic complication would lead to dispute and division rather than to unity of feeling and purpose.

Insofar as words played a unifying role in the early years of the revolution, it was through the slogans of orators like Mirabeau and Danton rather than through the structure of arguments. A painting of the murdered Marat and an etched image of Père Duchêne were better known than was any article of Marat or Hébert. Slogans and images changed with the passions that inspired them; they were fleeting points of reference for a fickle populace.

· But there were also solid symbols that commanded broad allegiance; they provided rallying points for popular rituals of unity during the early years of the French Revolution. First, of course, was the Bastille itself. This architectural embodiment of unyielding authority provided a condensation symbol for the old regime and in late June and early July, a target for the hitherto diffuse unrest of Paris. France first found its revolutionary identity not only by storming the Bastille but also by razing it utterly, creating in the heart of Paris a field of nature where the towers of tradition once stood. From the stones of the leveled fortress eighty-three small models of the Bastille were built and sent to every department of France "to perpetuate there the horror of despotism." [141] The site of the Bastille itself became a cleared space: a *tabula rasa*. Many proposals were made to fill it with symbols of a new order, but the first to be realized was the enormous, sphinx-like statue of Nature erected there for the Feast of Unity and Indivisibility in 1793 on the first anniversary of the overthrow of the monarchy. Designed by the brother-in-law of David, the statue was to be the rallying point for a predawn gathering to sing a "Hymn to Nature" by Gossec, to hear the poet Herault de Sechelles read an invocation to nature, and then to join in a ritual that was nothing less than a secular fusion of baptism and communion rites beneath a "fountain of regeneration representing Nature":

> From her fertile breasts (which she will press with her hands) will spurt an abundance of pure and healthful water. From it shall drink, each in his turn, the eighty-six commissioners sent from the primary assemblies . . . a single cup shall serve for all.[142]

The equivalent of the consecration of the host came from the act of the president of the Convention in filling the first cup and pouring it on the ground as he walked in a circle around the statue of Nature, "watering the soil of liberty" and tracing the circle within which believers must come to share the common cup.[143]

Dame Nature was a rival authority not just to the king, but to the church. On the eve of the first anniversary of the seizure of the Bastille the Cathedral of Notre Dame celebrated not a Christian mass, but a musical "hiérodrame" of the revolution called *La Prise de la Bastille*.[144] By the time of the Feast of Unity and Indivisibility three years later, the high altar in Notre Dame had been replaced by a "mountain" of earth from which an actress dressed in white intoned Gossec's "Hymn to Liberty" like a Druid priestess. She invoked a kind of secular counter-trinity: Mother (nature), Daughter (liberty), and Holy Spirit (popular sovereignty):

> Descend, o Liberty,
> daughter of Nature. . . .[145]

From its negative focus on sending miniature Bastilles to every department of France, the revolutionary imagination soon progressed to positive symbols like planting a tree of liberty. A tree had the incalculable advantage of being an organic product of nature: a symbol of regeneration rooted in the earth but reaching up to heaven. Popular festivals soon took place in local communities around the ritual of planting such a tree. There was a natural equality in the circle of those who gathered for this open-air, communal event, and there was continuity with the apolitical tradition of planting and decorating a maypole. But the tree of liberty was a living totem: an acceptable new form of verticality amidst the leveling impulses of the revolutionary era. The tree was preferably a young oak, which symbolized strength and youth and did not cast shadows. Communal activities were to be conducted openly in the sunshine nearby in defiance of secretive tyrants, who, in the words of one orator, never felt

> . . . obligated to expose all their acts of governing to the light of day. They abandoned the trees for the interior of their houses where they forged the chains that subjugated posterity.[146]

Trees of liberty were often fertilized with the ashes of patriots killed in battle, and were used to replace crosses in public places; they were venerated for their mute pedagogy as "silent teachers of the community." [147] In the feast commemorating the execution of King Louis XVI, the planting of a tree of liberty was the central, obligatory ritual.[148]

The tree of liberty was now said to be fertilized by the blood of kings—blood that came from the third and most famous focus of revolutionary ritual: the guillotine. The guillotine was first employed in Paris on April 25, 1792, to execute an assassin who had been apprehended three months earlier in the Palais-Royal. Viewed from the open air around liberty trees, the subterranean recesses of the Palais seemed particularly suspect. Already in 1790, the police had referred to "this shadowy cloaca," and the extraordinary device that was unveiled to avenge the murder there was a mechanical device for decapitation championed by an "enlightened" member of the National Assembly, Dr. Guillotin, in order to democratize and humanize capital punishment. The execution did not take place until the new machine had been tested on both animals and human corpses; and it occurred publicly with electric effect—inspiring both revulsion and fascination.

If the rituals around trees of liberty were essentially dances, those around the guillotine were dramas of the highest order. The guillotine was a hypnotic attraction in the great squares of Paris; it became the leading actor in these open-air theaters. After its debut in the Place des Grèves, the guillotine moved in August 1792 into the Place du Carousel, directly in front of the royal palace. In April 1793, it was left out on permanent public display, and transferred in May to the most prominent public place in Paris, the Place Louis XV, where it remained until the end of the Reign of Terror. Each gesture of each prominent figure on the way to the scaffold was invested with meaning, and legends were spun out of the alleged final words of many who perished on this sacrificial altar.

The guillotine turned the revolution into a drama that all could understand. It was the Enlightenment on display, punishing all equally without causing unnecessary suffering. *La sainte guillotine* was the awesome heroine of a morality play; the ending was known, but there was the perpetual possibility of minor variation in individual performances. This mass for the masses offered the certainty of blood sacrifice and the promise of collective redemption. By the end of the Terror, children were being given toy guillotines and sparrows for practice executions.[149]

This collective ritual in the public places of Paris made anything taking place on an indoor stage seem pale by comparison. The event was free and (to cite the slogan that the theaters had adopted from the Bonneville-Fauchet circle) *par et pour le peuple*. Talma and his colleagues at the pro-revolutionary Théâtre de la République in the Palais-Royal were frequent spectators at the greater drama taking place outdoors. Evreinov, the man who directed the greatest open-air revolutionary pageant of the twentieth century—the recreation by the city of St. Petersburg of the Bolshevik seizure of power—has perhaps best characterized the revolutionary play that unfolded in Paris:

> In eighteenth century France, the competition between life in actuality and life on the stage had reached the point where no one could say which was more theatrical. In both there were pompous, overstudied phrases, a mannered refinement of bows, smiles and gestures; in both, showy costumes . . . courtyards . . . powder, rouge, beauty spots, monocles and very little of one's "natural" face. . . .
> And then a reaction began. . . . The first to "come to his senses" on life's stage was Jean-Jacques Rousseau; the first on the theatrical stage was Talma. Both of them, lackeys in their youth, wanted to return the conceited lords of life back to naturalness.

More than a political revolution was needed to expose "the theatrical pomposity of the hierarchical system of its life."

> The first revolution changed only the *mise-en-scène* and changed the roles. . . . Having established a purely theatrical equality, the first thing to be concerned with was costume: the painter David sketched the costume of the "free citizen," the actor Talma tried it on in the theatre, and the people approved it and adopted it. The wigs were burned, the back of the

neck was cut short, and people began to greet one another with a spasmodic nod of the head, imitating those who were guillotined.[150]

The revolution's "passion for theatricality" extended even to the bodies of the decapitated victims, as "people played with them, sang to them, danced, laughed, and greatly amused themselves with the awkward appearance of these actors who so poorly played their 'funny' roles."

> In a word, the Great Revolution was as much theatrical as political. Only those succeeded who had an artistic temperament and sense of timing. Incorrigible actors, utterly unhappy to be without a director, the people soon discovered one in the person of Napoleon: an actor who dared to teach the great Talma himself.[151]

But the search for legitimacy involved more than the dance around the liberty tree and the drama of the guillotine. It involved a festive attempt to realize utopia, not in the enclosed Palais-Royal but in the open air: to transform old Paris into a new Jerusalem; to move from the guillotine's kingdom of fear to a republic of rejoicing in which Dame Nature was Queen. One revolutionary proposing changes in Parisian street names asked:

> Is it not natural that from the Place of the Revolution one should follow the Street of the Constitution to that of Happiness? [152]

The very geography of Paris was invested with moral meaning, and the only question for the believing revolutionary was where in Paris is that Place of Happiness and how does one get there.

Revolutionary Paris declared, in practice, that happiness lay in an open field to be reached by festive procession. The destination for the first and the last of the great revolutionary festivals was the largest open space in central Paris, its ultimate amphitheater for the drama of revolutionary redemption: the Champs de Mars.

Some one hundred thousand Parisians dug up this large military review ground and created a natural earthen arena for the Feast of Federation on July 14, 1790, the first Bastille Day. More than three hundred thousand Frenchmen from all over the country marched in procession through driving rain to hear a vast chorus commend the unified French nation to the Sun: "pure fire, eternal eye, soul and source of all the world." [153] The Champs de Mars became the "metaphysical center of Paris"; [154] and the revolutionary choreographers decided that henceforth

> National feasts can have no enclosure except the vault of the sky, because the sovereign, that is to say the people, can never be shut into a circumscribed place.[155]

The constitution was delivered to the people from that open sky to an open field by balloon on September 10, 1791. As the venerated dead were being moved from open Christian graveyards into closed pagan pantheons, living revolutionaries moved from Christian cathedrals into pagan parks—driven by a kind of cosmic claustrophobia.[156]

A procession from the ruins of the Bastille was combined with the popular assembly in the Champs de Mars on the second Bastille Day in 1791. By the time of the Feast of Indivisibility in August 1793, the procession was in fact organized into a kind of five-act drama of revolutionary redemption. Stops along the way resembled stations of the cross. The predawn gathering watched the sun rise over the statue of Nature at the Place de la Bastille. The group picked up strength as it surged through Paris, which was "drowned in a sea of flowers." [157] The cortege flowed into the Tuileries (le Jardin National), where the twenty-four hundred delegates of the forty-eight sections of Paris were joined by the entire National Convention and fifty members of the Jacobin Club (*la société mère*), who melded into the procession to the Champs de Mars. So many flowers, fruits, and even vegetables were carried that the festival has been called a "vegetable metamorphosis of Paris." [158] A float at the center of the procession was drawn by eight bulls with gilded horns carrying a printing press and a plow—each under a tree of liberty. The Champs de Mars was newly planted with trees, and the spectators from previous festivals now became participants on the giant "mountain" raised up as an altar to Nature with one hundred thousand people on it singing antiphonal responses to cues from trumpets and cannon.

Paralleling the development in festivals from assembly to procession was the shift in the locus of legitimacy from space to time: from nature to history. With the formal adoption of a new revolutionary calendar by the Convention in the fall of 1793, utopia became temporal. Nowhere became sometime—and time was just beginning a new march that would be "novel, majestic and simple like equality." [159] Nature itself sanctified the founding of the new era on the day of the sun's autumnal equinox: September 22, 1792. At the very moment when "equality was marked in the skies between days and nights" and "the sun passed from one hemisphere to another," authority on earth "passed from monarchical to republican government." [160]

The new calendar reflected "the rationality and simplicity of nature," and provided an "eloquent nomenclature" of neologisms suggesting "a vague 'rural and agricultural' ideology." [161] The calendar was divided into the four seasons with new names of months designed to suggest the mood of each: mournful *ôse* endings for winter months (Pluviôse, Ventôse), spring names in *al* suggesting new growth (Germinal, Floréal). The week—based on the religious idea of seven days of creation—was eliminated altogether. Sundays and saints' days were replaced by feasts consecrating natural (largely agricultural) objects: trees, fruits, domestic animals. The latter, wrote one of the authors of the calendar, should be "far more precious in the sight of Reason than beatified skeletons dragged from the catacombs of Rome." [162]

He rejoiced that *cultivation* had replaced *cult* in France, invoking nature in both its senses—as higher law and as simple countryside—as the supreme authority of the new order. In announcing the need to complete the "physical" revolution with a revolution in the moral order, Robespierre had proclaimed "the universal religion of Nature." [163] Varlet labeled 1793 "the first year of truth" and addressed a new Declaration of the Rights of Man "in the social state" to the "people of nature." [164] A new version of *La Marseillaise* began

> Voici le jour où la Nature
> Reprend ses droits sur l'univers. . . .[165]

The last great festival on the Champs de Mars (the Feast of the Supreme Being on June 8, 1794) was the largest (five hundred thousand participants), the simplest, and the most profoundly pastoral. Animals of warfare were excluded, with only peaceful cows and doves permitted in the cortege. The couplet for sunrise urged participants to begin the day "in the fields" *tête-à-tête avec une fleur*; and the "vegetable exuberance" under sunlit skies caused many to believe in a kind of greening over of the guillotine.[166] "The instrument of death had disappeared under the trappings and flowers." [167] The revolutionary calendar seemed to be heralding a new "life of fêtes." [168] But within a few weeks, Robespierre himself had been guillotined, utopian expectation had receded, and the Champs de Mars had become once again a place for military drill. The only innovative festival to be held there in the later revolutionary period was a national industrial exposition for workers in 1798, the first exhibit of this kind in modern France.[169] The Champs de Mars had become a field for displaying iron, and the great iron totem, the Eiffel Tower, eventually rose to dominate the very fields on which the festivals of Nature had once unfolded.

One speaker later looked back on the great festivals as representing "in the navigation of life what islands are in the midst of the sea: places for refreshment and rest." [170] It was a more powerful image than the former participant may have intended, for many of the most dedicated revolutionaries felt the need to retreat at some point in the turmoil to real or imagined islands.

The first major festival after the fall of Robespierre was his apotheosis on October 11, 1794, when a special island was created for his remains in a pond in the Tuileries. The service was a kind of rural repudiation of indoor entombment in the Pantheon, a tradition that prevailed from the reburial of Voltaire in 1791 to that of Marat as recently as September 21, 1794. Behind musicians in rustic dress, botanists followed in Robespierre's cortege bearing the inscription: "The study of Nature consoled him for the injustice of men." [171]

The event was a throwback to the past—an imitation of Rousseau's burial on an island within a lake at Ermenonville—and, at the same time, a symbolic anticipation of things to come. Just as Rousseau had sought political "relevance" by writing a constitutional proposal for the island of Corsica, so later revolutionary pioneers tended to find either hope or solace in the miniaturized isolation of a "natural" island—from the pioneering popularizer of communism in the 1840s, Goodwyn Barmby, who successively sought out the islands of Sark, Man, and Wight for his first "Communistery," to the leader of the rival tradition of revolutionary nationalism, Giuseppi Garibaldi, who repeatedly returned like Antaeus to renew his strength on the small island of Caprera.

Those who were to lead the Babeuf conspiracy under the Directorate all retreated for a time under Robespierre to islands of one kind or another. Buonarroti, one of the conspirators of whom we shall hear a good deal later, tried to put egalitarian ideals in practice first in Corsica and then on a small island off Sardinia. Babeuf retreated even within Paris to the relative tranquility of the Ile de la Cité to define his agrarian ideal in the relative obscurity of the food administration. Restif repeatedly returned to the even quieter Ile Saint-Louis, on which he wrote endearing graffiti and to which he addressed his own epitaph.[172]

More's original *Utopia* had been located on an island;[173] and the first modern communist utopia, Morelly's *Code of Nature*, arose out of his earlier utopian fantasy about "floating islands" and provided the inspiration for Buonarroti's own island experiment.[174] Morelly's radically utopian ideas about material equality and the redistribution of property helped draw Babeuf and Buonarroti together into the Conspiracy of Equals. They turned for ultimate ideological guidance to a popularizer of Morelly and a choreographer of revolutionary festivals: Sylvain Maréchal.

Maréchal was impelled to revolutionary utopianism—which came to include extreme atheism and anarchism—both by Rousseau and by the German preromantic poets. He used the pastoral forms of the latter to write in 1779 a long elegy, *The Tomb of J.-J. Rousseau*, returning regularly to his island burial place and publishing a second edition at Ermenonville itself upon the outbreak of the revolution. Calling himself the Shepherd Sylvain, he drew a picture of pastoral perfection in *The Golden Age* in 1782 and already in 1785 used the term "community of goods" to describe his egalitarian ideal.[175]

In the early years of the revolution he wrote *Dame Nature at the Bar of the National Assembly* and a *Code of Nature* of his own.[176] In 1793 he published at Bonneville's press a blueprint for a new golden age which called for reorganizing society into small "families" modeled on the communal peasant units of the Auvergne and Franche Comté.[177] Well before his *Manifesto of Equals*, Maréchal warned that "the revolution is not completed," and that there will be "a new and more equal distribution of goods." [178]

Under the Directorate, Maréchal retreated from the Champs de Mars to the private islands of his imagination. He and his friends returned to underground cafés—but no longer to the arcaded splendor of the Palais-Royal, which had been largely transformed into fashionable restaurants for the *jeunesse dorée* (whence lobster thermidore and "Tortoni" ice cream).[179] The hard core of committed revolutionaries now met in the more plebeian cafés: the Café Manoury on the left bank and the Café des Bains-Chinois on Montmartre, where Maréchal composed songs for his red-haired mistress:

> Tu nous créas pour être égaux.
> Nature, ô bienfaisante mère.[180]

> Thou created us to be equal
> O beneficent mother nature.

The repeated return of the revolutionaries to the cafés suggests that Dame Nature was not just a chaste classical statue representing rational order and pastoral simplicity. She was also a seductive sorceress offering the emotional gratification of both mother and mistress. Dame Nature was a Goddess with two faces: a Janus who looked back to the "rationalism" of the eighteenth century and forward to the "romanticism" of the early nineteenth. The modern revolutionary, born at the juncture of these two eras, worshipped both images. He drew intellectually on the belief that Nature represents some higher order of perfection, and emotionally on the belief that Nature provides earthier forms of satisfaction. We shall turn to the former, philosophical concept of Nature when we examine the surprising sources of revolutionary ideas about organization. Here we must linger for a moment on the psycho-sexual element in the revolutionary understanding of nature.

One must note in passing the importance of Laclos and De Sade in the ambiance of the Palais-Royal, the fact that many innovative revolutionary thinkers from Mirabeau to Maréchal were major collectors and authors of literary pornography, and the not-untypical *ménage à trois* of Bonneville's wife with Bonneville and Paine (the former naming his second son after the latter and permitting his wife to move back to America permanently as Paine's companion).

Paine's closest American friend in Paris, Joel Barlow, imagined that there were "natural" sexual origins for festive revolutionary symbols. He traced trees of liberty to the phallic symbol of the Egyptian cult of Osiris—carried thence to Greece and Rome, where "Bacchus was known by the epithet Liber, so that the Phallus became the emblem of Libertas." [181] Barlow derived the "Phrygian" red cap of liberty from a Roman symbol for the head of the phallus,[182] and he decried with solemnity the substitution of a maypole and the celebration of May 1 for the older and richer phallic festival of the Liber Deus on the vernal equinox:

> Men have forgot the original object of the institution, the phallus has lost its testicles, and has been for many centuries reduced to a simple pole.[183]

Restif, who introduced the word "communist," first burst on the European literary scene with a vivid depiction of a foot fetish in his novel of 1769, *Le Pied de Fanchette, ou l'orphéline française*; he proceeded to produce a virtual encyclopedia of sexual fact and fantasy climaxing in his defense of prostitutes, *Le Pornographe*, of 1779 and his endless accounts of Paris by night.[184] The very act of writing his communist work, *Monsieur Nicolas*, has been described as "a shockingly direct sublimation of Restif's erotic drives." [185] As Restif himself explained:

> Failing the physical satisfaction so ardently desired, my imagination gorged itself on ideas. . . .[186]

But revolutionary communism was not the main destination of the awakened romantic imagination, which gorged itself rather on the rival tradition of revolutionary nationalism, which swept through France in 1793 and overwhelmed all ideological competition.

To understand this powerful, visceral force, we must turn to new media of expression, new psycho-sexual drives, new physical locations. One must look to the second city of the French Revolution, Strasbourg; to the dark genius who came to rule it, Saint-Just; and to the seemingly improbable fact of German influences on French nationalism. One must consider as well that most immaterial yet emotional form of cultural expression: music.

CHAPTER 3

The Objects of Belief

WHILE SEEKING to legitimize their revolution by sanctifying a place, a process, or even a picture, Frenchmen still sought to define their beliefs in words. There was a trend toward radical simplification, however, as they increasingly tended to substitute labels for arguments. In attempting to state simply the purpose of secular society under popular sovereignty, they found three basic answers. Each was expressed by one of the words of the most important slogan of the era: liberty, fraternity, and equality.

Each of these three ideals had ancient origins, but each acquired a new mystical aura during this period. At the beginning of the revolution they had blended into a trinitarian unity. But there were deep, inherent differences between the three concepts, and much of the subsequent history of the revolutionary tradition involved recurring and widening conflict between these rival ideals.

First came the *political* ideal of securing freedom through a constitutional *republic*. This was the original revolutionary cause of *liberty* —defined in terms of constitutional rights and popular legislatures. Property no less than people was to be freed from traditional bondage to nonproductive authority—an idea that made the republican ideal attractive to entrepreneurs of all sorts.

Second came the *emotional* ideal of experiencing brotherhood in a new kind of *nation*. This was the romantic vision of *fraternity*: the discovery amidst a struggle against others that one's immediate neighbors are one's brothers—linguistically, culturally, geographically—fellow sons of a common fatherland.

Finally came the *intellectual* ideal of creating a nonhierarchical socioeconomic *community*. This was the rationalistic concept of *equality*: the collective sharing of goods within a community free of all social and economic distinctions.

In general terms, the first ideal may be identified with the Enlightenment reformism of the eighteenth century; the second with the romantic nationalism of the nineteenth; the third with the authoritarian communism of the twentieth. The post-1789 history of the revolutionary tradition was to show the gradual, near-universal spread of the first ideal—followed by growing conflict between the other two. Though political "liberation" spread from France in the eighteenth century through Europe in the nineteenth to the wide world in the twentieth, the split between the rival ideals of national and social revolution grew and deepened.

In considering these ideals, then, we shall concentrate attention not so much on the first ideal, which arose in the relatively familiar debates culminating in the creation of the First French Republic in 1792. We shall focus more on the less understood rival ideals of national and social revolution which arose to serve the more elusive goals of brotherhood and equality. Fraternal nationalism dominated the period of war and terror from 1792 through 1794; egalitarian communism appeared during the subsequent period of seeming stagnation under the Directory.

Liberty: The Republican Ideal

The replacement of a monarchy by a republic was the major accomplishment of the initial period of the revolution. In the course of 1793, the republican ideal was sealed in blood by the execution of the king, in ink by the drafting of a radical constitution, and in time by the adoption of a revolutionary calendar.

La république represented the Enlightenment ideal of a rational political order; it replaced old privileged distinctions with the single category of "citizen," the rule of kings with the rule of law: *royaume* by *loyaume*.[1] Humanity was thereby freed from the arbitrary authority of the past in favor of rational perfectibility in the future—through laws established by popular assemblies and through virtue inculcated in secular schools.

"Republican" and "republicanism" had been transformed from terms of opprobrium to labels of pride by the American Revolution—particularly during the six months of intense debate prior to the Declaration of Independence on July 4, 1776.[2] Thomas Paine's *Common Sense*, published in January 1776, played a decisive role through its secular, millenarian insistence that "we have it in our power to begin the world over again" by establishing a new constitutional union.[3]

Yet "republican" was not a major rallying cry in America during the debates leading up to the Constitution of 1787, and the American experience with republican rule did not prove very appealing to Euro-

peans in the 1780s.[4] In the debates over the first revolutionary constitution for France during the summer of 1789, the Abbé Sieyès's call
for direct popular rule by a single legislative chamber prevailed over
the rival idea of an American-style balanced government with a bicameral legislature and an executive (that is, a royal) veto.[5]

The movement toward republican government in France and the discussion of its proper constitution did, however, generate genuine excitement—not least in Paine's own defense of the French Revolution against
Burke in 1791:

> What were formerly called revolutions were little more than a change of
> persons or an alteration of local circumstances . . . what we now see in
> the world . . . is a renovation of the natural order of things, a system of
> principles as universal as truth. . . .[6]

When the First Republic was formally established, Paine moved to Paris,
accepted French citizenship, founded the first "republican" society in
Paris, edited a short-lived journal, *The Republican,* and attracted the ire
even of Jacobins by his quasi-devotional use of the word "republican." [7]

Paine was only one of many foreigners to find a new identity as a
citizen of the revolutionary republic; Babeuf only one of many Frenchmen to refer to "republican" as "this sublime word." [8] The continuing
debate about a constitution (even after the adoption of one in 1791)
lent an added aura to that word as well. In the first issue of a new
revolutionary journal in 1792, Bonneville insisted that

> . . . this *health-giving* word, this *sacred* word CONSTITUTION! . . .
> must exercise a prodigious influence on the destinies of the human race.[9]

Fascination grew in late 1792 and early 1793 as the Convention prepared the more radical republican Constitution of 1793. Though never
put into effect, its text was carried like a holy object from the Bastille
to the Champs de Mars in the great feast of August 10, 1793; [10] it remained a venerated model for many political revolutionaries well into
the nineteenth century.[11]

One of the few demonstrable results of the two greatest upheavals
within France in that century—the Revolution of 1848 and the Paris
Commune of 1871—was the reestablishment of constitutional, republican governments: the Second and Third Republics respectively. The
major (though more short-lived) expression abroad of the revolutionary
French ideal was the founding of satellite republics: Batavian, Cisalpine,
Helvetian, and so forth. As we shall see, the Europeanwide revolutionary tradition began as a series of republican, constitutional conspiracies against an imperial Napoleon and the monarchical restoration
that followed him.

But, in 1793 revolutionary France was ready to reject many republicans including Paine and other foreigners gathered in Paris around
journals like *Le Cosmopolite* and talking ecumenically about "the great
human republic." [12] By then, Frenchmen were inventing modern nationalism—and the worship of its exclusive and elusive ideal, *la grande
nation.*

Fraternity: The Rise of Nationalism

The second new ideal to emerge in the French Revolution was that of *la nation*: a new fraternity in which lesser loyalties as well as petty enmities were swept aside by the exultation of being born again as *enfants de la patrie*: children of a common fatherland. The nation was a militant ideal that was largely discovered on the *jour de gloire* of battle and best expressed in the *levée en masse* of 1793: the prototype of modern mass conscription on a "national" scale.

The American Revolution had originated the concept of independence as a political rather than a philosophical ideal—creating in effect a new nation through a revolution. But the United States did not call itself a "nation" in the Declaration of Independence, or constitute itself as a nation in the modern sense. There was no new language to be asserted, no mythologized antiquity to be created, no continuing foreign threat bordering on the new territorial entity. The official designation "United States" was the only formal name of a major country prior to the creation of the Soviet Union that contained no ethnic or national designation. In America, a "sense of nationhood was the child, not the parent of the Revolution." [13]

In the French Revolution, on the contrary, the concept of a "nation" was central even though no new country was created. The word *nation* soon predominated over the older and more paternalistic term *patrie*.[14] Flags, feasts, and songs were all said to be "national," and Bonneville, while organizing the Paris militia in the summer of 1789, warned against *ennemis de la nation*.[15] Citizens of the old regime were forced to communicate in the French language, which until then had not been the basic tongue of many living under the French crown.

The word *nation* had been used in Roman times to describe a native community smaller than a people but larger than a family—and in the late Middle Ages to describe regional student groups within universities and differing groups within church councils. Prerevolutionary France used the term for a representative group of aristocrats. In choosing the name *assemblée nationale* (instead of *représentants du peuple français*), the revolutionary Third Estate sought to give itself, in effect, aristocratic status.[16]

The term *nation* was not widely understood at first. Peasants forced a well-dressed man to cry "Vive la nation!" early in the revolution, then begged him: "Explain to us just what is the Nation." [17] But the label was soon understood to define a new type of popular sovereignty that was territorially and linguistically unified and often more absolute than monarchical authority. God Himself was reborn in early revolutionary tracts as the "Savior of the Nations," [18] "the august and sublime national Areopagus"; [19] and prayers were addressed to "the body of the Nation." [20]

The concept of *la nation* gave tangible definition as well as higher legitimacy to the revolution.[21] The revolution acquired spatial dimensions and was henceforth embodied not in complex republican institutions but in simple concentric circles. The borders of France were an outer, ideological mote; Paris the inner citadel; the National Assembly the "perfect point" of authority within Paris itself. The revolutionary nation was proclaimed "indivisible," and its borders expandable. The archenemy of the French Revolution, the Abbé Barruel, introduced the term "nationalism" to denigrate the new form of parochial, secular selfishness that he felt was replacing universal Christian love as the human ideal.[22]

Militant nationalism reached the European masses largely through Napoleon: "the first ruler to base a political regime exclusively upon the nation . . . the most powerful purely national symbol that any nation has had." [23] Some were positively inspired by his example of nationalism (the Poles and Italians); others were negatively stimulated to form national movements against him (the Spaniards and Prussians). By the end of his career Napoleon's *grande armée* had in effect supplanted the revolutionary *grande nation*. That army was two-thirds foreign by the time of its decisive defeat in the "Battle of the Nations" in 1813 by a coalition of the nationalisms he had awakened throughout Europe.

Nationalism remained the major revolutionary ideal until the final quarter of the nineteenth century. Its mysterious power and continuing mutations make essential a closer look at its origins. The birth of this new ideal was both sublime and bloody, involving the heights of music and the depth of terror. The birth of a nation takes us beyond the Paris of Robespierre to the Strasbourg of Saint-Just.

The Song from Strasbourg

Strasbourg, the largest city of the lower Rhine, was France's major link with Europe—with a Catholicism that was more than Gallican (the bishop retained political allegiance to the Holy Roman Emperor); with a religion that was more than Catholic (a third of Strasbourg was Protestant); and with a culture that was more than French (most of the city spoke German). Strasbourg had been France's most important continental conquest during the century and a half prior to the revolution. When the upheaval came, this exposed outpost felt particularly vulnerable. The bishop's patrimony was confiscated, the German-speaking university was shut, and the great pentagonal fortress built by Vauban was reinforced by an elite "army of the Rhine."

Strasbourg did not just accept, but amplified and transformed, the rising new French nationalism—internalizing German ideas even as it combated the external threat of German arms. Unlike Paris, Strasbourg was not distracted by competing factions and multiple political institutions. Its quasi-medieval municipal structure gave Strasbourg relative unity within itself and solidarity with the surrounding Alsatian countryside. Even its café culture was an establishment activity devoid of Parisian license and radiating *Gemütlichkeit*.[24] The twice-elected Protestant mayor of revolutionary Strasbourg, Frédéric Dietrich, unified the city with a family having both French and German branches (Didier and Dietrich), a multilingual Swiss wife, and a bilingual salon where old antagonisms tended to melt away.

In the early beleagured months of 1792, a national consciousness was intensified by the growing sense that an enemy was near and war was likely. The normal population of fifty thousand had been swollen by friends of the revolution fleeing from Austria and Prussia, and by volunteers from all over France coming to reinforce the garrison city on the Rhine. The news that both Germanic monarchs had declared war on revolutionary France reached Strasbourg before Paris; and, on the night of April 24, 1792, Dietrich commissioned a young engineering captain from his salon, Claude-Joseph Rouget de Lisle, to write a song that would arouse the polyglot army to resist the anticipated Hapsburg attack. In the feverish inspiration of one night, he wrote a song that rallied a people as had no other song since Luther's *Ein feste Burg*.[25] Originally called *Chant de guerre de l'armée du Rhin*, its surprisingly bloodthirsty lines were sung with special zest by newly arrived volunteers from afar. The contingent from Marseilles gave the song from Strasbourg its permanent name: *La Marseillaise*.

The origin of *La Marseillaise* in Strasbourg was not accidental, for this was the city in which the rich musical culture of Germany flowed into France. It had both French and German cathedral choirs, French and German opera houses, and the finest orchestras in prerevolutionary France outside of Paris and Versailles. Strasbourg manufactured instruments as well as melodies. The great piano manufacturer Ignace Pleyel became Kapelmeister in the Strasbourg Cathedral in 1789. Drawing on both Catholic pageantry and Protestant hymnography, Strasbourg produced an original revolutionary repertoire, introducing elaborate musical compositions into open-air revolutionary festivals via the Pleyel-Rouget de Lisle *Hymn of Liberty*.[26] First performed on September 25, 1791, it used the entire audience as a chorus for the first time, a technique that was only later transported to Paris. The austere words of Rouget renouncing "the vain delirium of profane gaiety" and "soft voluptuousness" suggested the revolutionary puritanism that lay ahead.[27] *La Marseillaise* was from the beginning a kind of corporate production. When Rouget first presented the rough melody to the mayor in his salon, Dietrich, who was a tenor, became the first to sing it, and his violinist wife, the first to orchestrate it. *La Marseillaise* electrified the nation going to war. The two leading composers of the Opéra Comique, Dalayrac and Gossec, composed *Offering to Liberty, Religious scene on the Marseillaise*.[28] This "religious scene" was taken out of the theaters into army camps. Choruses of women knelt before statues of liberty singing the verse, "*Amour sacre de la patrie . . .*" as a hushed prayer, then rising to sing the final verse with a percussion accompaniment that "would make the pavement leave the street for the frontier."[29] The leading composer of the era, André Gretry, congratulated Rouget for creating "*musique à coups de canon*,"[30] and in his *Guillaume Tell*,[31] perhaps the most popular new opera of the revolutionary era, began the popular practice of inserting the anthem directly into operatic scores.

The tide of passion aroused by music soon engulfed its early patrons. In 1792, Dietrich was swept out of office as a moderate accused of affinities with Lafayette. Musical militance intensified at the Strasbourg celebration of the first anniversary of the founding of the republic on August 10, 1793, when Pleyel and Rouget de Lisle staged their remarkable *The Allegorical Alarm Bell*.

Described as "a battle in music," the pageant took place in the newly transformed cathedral underneath seven bells suspended from the cupola. The bells (like the enormous chorus and cast) had been gathered in from all over Alsace; they were to be melted down for cannon immediately after the production. The first part was purely orchestral ("the arousal of the people"). When alarm bells rang, the second movement ("the battle") began. Only when all combat was finished did human voices burst forth for the first time—in a triumphant chorus ending with *la victoire est à nous*.[32]

So great was the Strasbourgeois belief in the unifying power of music that its craftsmen invented a new system for printing the notes of the new national music. So great was the fear of evocative melody that the priests, who later restored Catholic authority to the cathedral, decreed that only bleak plainsong and organ drone would henceforth be permitted in ordinary worship.[33]

Music reached a special crescendo in Strasbourg precisely during the Terror. It seems appropriate that the first guillotine was made by a piano maker in Strasbourg named Schmidt and was first brought to Paris to be used on a living person on April 25, 1792, at almost exactly the moment that Rouget de Lisle was finishing *La Marseillaise*.[34]

Strasbourg brought France the excitement not just of the German musical tradition, but also of the German theater. The antitraditional, anti-Hapsburg dramas of Friedrich Schiller were usually introduced into France by performances in Strasbourg, and the principal translations of Schiller into French were made by Nicholas Bonneville when he was studying in Strasbourg during the 1780s. The early German romantics inspired the altogether new type of play that Bonneville wrote in 1789 to commemorate the fall of the Bastille. It was a *Tragédie Nationale* designed for the *peuples-germains . . . peuples-frères* worthy of entering a new *société fraternelle*.[35] Bonneville appealed to Camille Desmoulins to institutionalize this "national" genre as a kind of rebuke to "the lackeys of the Court" who favored light entertainment devoid of moral purpose.[36]

Strasbourg became the major continental correspondence center for Bonneville's Social Circle, and the place for translating and publishing its works for distribution in the German world.[37] Charles Nodier, a later pioneer in secret revolutionary organization and the inventor of the antitraditional, partly musical genre of melodrama, discovered German literature through Bonneville's translations, and dedicated his *Essays of a Young Bard* to Bonneville. Inspired by Schiller/Bonneville and by "romanticism" (a word first used in Bonneville's circle),[38] Nodier passed on his implausible plots and iconoclastic heroes to his famous literary protégé, Victor Hugo.

The principal teacher of Nodier in Strasbourg was Eulogius Schneider, the most original, imaginative—and violent—of the many Germans who emigrated to revolutionary Strasbourg. Schneider, a former Capuchin monk, became an Illuminist in Neuwied and a popular professor at Bonn until he was dismissed for heresy in June 1791.[39] He led the radical republican overthrow of Mayor Dietrich, composed the first German translation of *La Marseillaise,* edited two extremist journals, founded a special unit for popular revolutionary indoctrination throughout Alsace called *la Propagande,* and served as chief prosecutor of the revolutionary tribunal in Strasbourg.[40]

Nodier later recalled with aesthetic fascination an execution where Schneider's "propagandists" wearing red hats and tricolor sashes and with large hunting knives, lectured the spectators. After genuflecting before the scaffold, the principal orator

> . . . delivered a panegyric to the guillotine in the name of liberty . . . I felt a cold sweat appear on my forehead and wash down over my eyelids.[41]

The Reign of Terror came early to Strasbourg, during the long seige that began in August 1793. Schneider took over the German theater in Strasbourg as his headquarters and popularized the word "denunciation" in the revolutionary vocabulary.[42] The mayor of Strasbourg insisted that the word "inn" be substituted for the feudal term "hotel" throughout the city,[43] and the Germans writing in Schneider's journal brought a new flood of rustic metaphors into French revolutionary nationalism. The Prussian Anacharsis Cloots in his Patriotic Crusade spoke of the French nation's historic right to control the Rhine:

> The mouths of the Rhine, the ancient frontier of Gaul will sing the hymn of liberty in the shadow of our victorious banner . . . let us rush en masse to the banks of the great river, and never again will a German crowd in on the soil of the newborn France.[44]

Cloots had seen the first festival on the Champs de Mars as a return of the French people to being "all Germans and all brothers." Another German witness compared it to the ancient barbarian ritual in which "the Franks, a free union of Germans, gathered yearly in order to declare to the king the sovereign will of the people." [45]

The ancient German tribes became a mythic prototype for the sovereign "people" within a revolutionary "nation." Bonneville's alternative to the indulgence and selfishness of modern civilization was a virile, pre-Christian communalism of "the free man" (*homme franc*) such as Tacitus had described among the early Germans. Bonneville praised Frankish tribalism in his *Manifesto of the Friends of Truth* in 1789; [46] later he praised the barbarians over their "civilized" oppressors in his "Prophecy of an Old Druid against the Romans." [47] Bonneville saw the nation learning from "the university of nature," with a modern "Druid" like himself helping it rediscover the lost language of truth:

La nature est un livre immense à dévorer,
La langue en est perdue, il faut la recouvrer.[48]

Nature is an immense book to be devoured,
Its language is lost and must be recovered.

That language was largely German—not just the "sighs and tears" of the early romantics so well known to Bonneville, but also the compound words with abstract appositions, like *Peuple-Dieu*, which he imported wholesale into the French language. There were many other contributors to this process in addition to Bonneville, Cloots, and their friends: J.-G. Saiffert, the doctor of Philip of Orléans who led the short-lived German legion in Paris and was called "the vandal"; [49] A. G. F. Rebmann, the leading publisher of German journals in Paris; [50] and the Frey brothers, German-speaking Jews from Strasbourg, one of whom wrote a defense of terror by a minority: *Philosophie Sociale*.[51]

In trying to weed out "the verbiage of the defunct French Academy" [52] and "create a language, make a religion" [53] for *la nation*, Bonneville drew heavily on Germanisms and followed the Strasbourg custom of publishing tracts bilingually.[54] "People" (like "Nation" and other symbolic substantives) acquired a capital letter in the Germanic fashion in new French phrases like *Peuple-Roi*, *Peuple-Dieu*, and *Peuple-Sauveur*. Cloots's pledge of allegiance to *la nation* required capital letters throughout:

> My profession of faith is as reassuring for the patriot as it is terrible for the treasonous: I BELIEVE IN THE INFALLIBILITY OF THE PEOPLE.[55]

Partly created by German influences in France, *nationalism* was first so named by a French exile in Germany, the Abbé Barruel. Herder, the original romantic lover of organic variety, had in fact previously used the words *Nationalismus* and *Nationalism* in a cultural sense as early as 1774.[56] Herder's image of a rustic, virtuous, and musical German nationality was admired by radical French thinkers as they sought to define their own "national" identity. Long before Madame de Staël's *Germany* of 1810, Schneider's pupil, Charles Nodier, spoke rapturously of

> . . . that marvellous Germany, the last country of poesy and belief in the West, the future cradle of a strong society to come—if there is any society left to be created in Europe.[57]

For the romantic political imagination, the locus of legitimacy no longer lay in a city, but in a nation; that "nation" sometimes seemed to speak with a rustic German accent.

The Saint from Picardy

By the early fall of 1793, Strasbourg was dispirited by terror from within and the threat of German occupation from without. The Alsatian city was the exposed outpost of the revolutionary nation—the point toward which advancing Prussian and Austrian troops appeared to be converging—at a time when Lyon, the second city of France, had already fallen to counter-revolutionaries and a peasant revolt raged in the Vendée. On October 17, Paris sent a special proconsul of *la nation* to rally people and collect provisions for the army of the Rhine. In a little over two months in Strasbourg, he curbed the excesses of the extremists, energized the indifferent masses, and headed the soldiers, who turned back the invaders in a stunning series of victories. The man who led this salvation of the revolutionary nation was the quintessential youthful revolutionary, Louis-Antoine de Saint-Just.

Saint-Just gave living legitimacy to the revolutionary ideal. He was by far the youngest member of the twelve-man Committee of Public Safety which exercised executive authority in Paris. But because the committee met largely in secret in the Tuileries Palace and did not communicate in regular ways with the people, its authority depended heavily on the deeds and examples of those it sent out in the name of the nation.[58] Unlike other members of the committee, Saint-Just had no prior, practical experience as a lawyer, engineer, priest, journalist, or even actor. Too young to be anything but a child of the revolution, he became in 1793–94 its embodiment.

Legitimacy no longer lay in a place, a symbol, or a song; it lay in a revolutionary apostolate of twelve. The center of ascetic coolness within this heated group was the young man from Picardy whose very name summoned up images of sanctity. The locus of legitimacy was narrowing to a point: "that ideal location where the creative and divine forces have their greatest and most potent concentration."[59] The secular, revolutionary drama was converging, like Dante's *Divine Comedy*, toward "the point in which all time is present."[60] And that point was not simply Saint-Just himself, but the nerve center within his head. His friend Camille Desmoulins wrote that Saint-Just

> . . . regards his head as the keystone of the republic and carries it on his shoulders with respect like a holy sacrament.[61]

Another fascinated contemporary felt sure that some "secret" was hidden behind the "shade of general anxiety, the somber accent of preoccupation and defiance, an extreme coolness in tone and manners" of his large head. Saint-Just's leadership role cannot be explained as resulting from the characteristics now often ascribed to revolutionary leaders. He was not "charismatic"—lacking Robespierre's flair for the inspirational and the theatrical. Nor was he particularly "violent"—he purged Schneider and ended public executions in Strasbourg. He developed neither the bloodthirsty rhetoric of a Marat nor the theory of violence of an Oswald. Saint-Just was not a moralist, and he was not essentially interested in power in the purely political sense. He ceded formal positions of authority to others and never partook in the practical play of peacetime political deliberation.

Saint-Just has been described as "an idea energized by passion";[62] he might also be characterized as passion disciplined by an idea. His passion was the raw, sensual energy of an emancipated romantic sensibility. As a sixteen-year-old provincial youth, he began writing a book about a nearby medieval castle and seduced the daughter of a local aristocrat in one of its rooms. Forced to run away to Paris, he haunted the Palais-Royal on the eve of the revolution, and composed in a "spirit of vertigo" a vast pornographic poem designed to show "the general analogy of customary behavior with madness." [63] His tableaux, which included a transformed representation of the Palais-Royal, made no clear distinction between heaven and hell, good and bad, humans and animals.[64] With the outbreak of the revolution, he wrote a play in which illusion and confusion once again gave way to desire. The main character seeks to experience anything and everything in order to be

> ... original, original ...
> Je veux vivre à mon sens désormais
> Narguer, flatter, parler, me taire, rire
> Aimer, haïr! [65]

> ... original, original ...
> I want to live henceforth in my own way
> To defy, flatter, speak, be silent, laugh
> To love, to hate!

But the passions are rarely satisfied in Saint-Just's early writings; they are indeed increasingly sublimated into a vague longing for some new kind of earthly greatness:

> L'amour n'est rien qu'un frivole besoin
> Et d'un grand coeur il doit être loin.[66]

> Love is nothing but a frivolous need
> To be kept far away from a great heart.

The challenge to a "great heart" in 1789–90 was to beat with the revolution; his passions soon became absorbed in the two sides of it —the organizational and the ideological—that political leaders tended to neglect.

Organizationally, he formed a national guard in the small town of Blérancourt and led the guardsmen in such rituals as the public burning of counter-revolutionary books. Ideologically, he turned to writing (on three tables in the open air) his *Spirit of the Revolution* and his uncompleted and unpublished *Nature*.[67] Saint-Just in effect withdrew from the pettiness and divisions of the old dying order to develop the central beliefs of the new one.

He was suspicious of mass movements, and considered the storming of the Bastille simply "the drunkenness of slaves" and the great festivals the staging grounds for demagogues.[68] Nor was he interested in the rights of man or the formulas of constitutions. These were the work of "petty thieves in the holy sanctuary." [69] He went beyond Rousseau's social contract (*contrat social*) in his call for a new social order (*état social*) "founded solidly only on nature." [70]

With no vision of the future, almost no knowledge of the past, and surprisingly little concern with the present, Saint-Just became the first ascetic of the revolution, cutting himself off from people in order to serve "the people" totally:

> I shall speak of all peoples, of all religions, of all laws as if I myself did not adhere to any . . . *I detach myself from everything in order to attach myself to everything.*[71]

Rousseau had pointed the way from total loneliness to totalistic attachments. His removal from the society of his day was the indispensable psychological prerequisite to his revolutionary conception of nature as

> . . . a totality saturated with moral content . . . at one and the same time "paradise lost" and the permanent possibility of beginning everything anew.[72]

Saint-Just, however, provides the first suggestion of the total removal from normal attachments later called for in the *Revolutionary Catechism* of Nechaev, who enjoined revolutionaries to cut "every tie with the civil order, with the educated world, and with all laws." [73]

Arguing that "all is relative in the world" and "truth alone is absolute," Saint-Just saw the only hope for ending "the circle of corruption" in a return to "original virtue"—a secularized inversion of original sin.[74] "Original virtue" implied renewed communion with the primitive simplicity of nature.

Elected as a representative to the Convention in September 1792, Saint-Just returned to Paris just after the founding of the Republic and proclaimed the Convention to be "the point toward which everything is compressed." [75] The legislator converging on such a sacred spot is not to be a sophist dealing with words, but an "oracle" or a *pontifex* in the original Roman sense of a human bridge between higher truth and a confused humanity.[76] Assigning himself this larger-than-human role at the center of power, Saint-Just quietly became in October secretary to the main office of the Convention and the most powerful advocate of regicide on the floor of the Assembly. His argument for killing the king was totally impersonal and dispassionate. The monarch was not considered a human being at all, but a universal abstraction, "the King of Kingdoms." He was the counterpoint to the new point of sovereign power in the Convention; and Saint-Just impelled that body forward to the revolutionary point of no return, arguing against "a compassion which involuntarily corrupts one's energy." [77]

His radical simplification provided at last a compelling metaphor for the French nation to replace that of the king's body just as it was being severed. He revived the old image of the human body itself, which personalized the agony and affections of the nation in a way that the mechanistic metaphors of the eighteenth century never could. "The enemies of the republic are in its intestines." Its leaders are largely "worms." The best hope lies in a "great heart" and "great nerves" as well as in "the audacity of magnanimous virtue." [78] Saint-Just expressed model revolutionary contempt for individual good deeds in a "sick" society:

> The particular good one does is a palliative. One must wait for a general sickness great enough for general opinion to feel the need for measures

capable of doing good. *That which produces the general good is always terrible.*[79]

His image of the nation as a single body made any loss of territory as painful as an amputation. In the early spring of 1793 he saw the nation threatened with death "if division is attached to territory,"[80] and set off on the first of three special missions to rally the resistance in exposed provinces. Working on the Constitutional Committee of the Convention, he failed in his campaign to create an eighty-four member executive formed from a nerve center in each department; but he succeeded in inserting into the Constitution of 1793 an unprecedented constitutional provision against ever making peace with a foreign power occupying any French territory.[81]

In his great speech on October 10, 1793, calling for a revolutionary dictatorship, Saint-Just denounced all traditional government as "a world of paper":

> The prolixity of governmental correspondence and orders is a mark of inertia; it is impossible to govern without laconicism. . . .
> The bureaus have replaced the monarchy; the demon of writing makes war upon us and we cannot govern.[82]

With the Committee of Public Safety now "placed in the center," the cause of all misfortune in the nation had been determined to be "the vicissitude of passions."[83] The only passion that could give constancy to the nation prior to the inculcation of virtue was terror, which he saw as a means not of punishing crime, but of fanning popular energy and audacity.

Although Saint-Just's argument for terror was reluctant and his use of it in Alsace limited, his legitimation of it encouraged the fresh wave of pedagogic violence that began with the public execution of Marie Antoinette on October 16. Saint-Just left for Strasbourg the next day; on the day following a new play opened in Paris that introduced the metaphor of a volcano into the previously tranquil image of an island utopia. Despite the urgent need for explosives at the front, the Committee of Public Safety authorized the delivery of twenty pounds of saltpeter and powder to the Theater of the Republic to produce the onstage volcanic eruption that pitched rocks and smoldering charcoal into the audience at the end of Sylvain Maréchal's *Last Judgment of Kings*.[84]

This was precisely the image that Saint-Just had used long before the revolution in connection with his first discussion of "terror";[85] and Maréchal's enormously successful play in a way substituted a new "natural" image as a focus of awe and terror in place of the guillotine, which Saint-Just had avoided using for public executions in Strasbourg. There was a suggestion of orgasm in the Saint-Just–Maréchal image of eruption—just as there was a suggestion of nudity in Maréchal's subsequent opera depicting a priest shedding his robes "to renounce my imposture . . . in the eyes of nature."[86]

Saint-Just, too, turned to the emotive power of music. On the way to Strasbourg, he sang Italian songs,[87] and left behind in Paris a lost opera which he had worked on with an Italian composer for an opening just a few nights after Maréchal's *Last Judgment*. His *Sélico ou les nègres* was apparently built around the intense friendship of two brothers involved in slaying a tyrant; this sense of masculine comradeship-in-arms enabled Saint-Just to identify the nation with brotherhood in an almost physiological way.[88]

Brought up entirely by his mother and sisters, Saint-Just discovered *la fraternité* along with *la nation*. On his first mission of mobilization to the provinces in the spring of 1793, he wrote that the nation "is not at all the sun, it is the community of affections." [89] His posthumously published vision of an ideal society promotes his concept of brothers-in-arms into quasi-erotic attachment. He proposes that every twenty-one-year-old declare his friendships publicly in the temple and repeat the ritual at the end of every winter. If a man leaves a friend, he is required to explain the motives behind it before the people; and "is banished if he refuses . . . [or] says he has no friends, or renounces his beliefs in friendship." Friends are to fight in battle together; are held responsible for each other's crimes; and "those who remain united all their life are to be buried in the same tomb." [90]

Saint-Just's worshipful companion on the mission to Strasbourg, Le Bas, felt the same kind of fraternal loyalty that Saint-Just in turn showed to Robespierre. Saint-Just never distanced himself from Robespierre at the end, as he might easily have done. He never married, and his engagement to Le Bas's sister seems to have been mainly a token of friendship for his companion in Alsace.

Militant fraternity in the service of the nation allowed no room for sorority—or indeed for fraternization with women. Saint-Just and Le Bas destroyed Schneider in Strasbourg for indulging not just in distractive sex and excessive violence, but also for taking a German wife, Sarah Stamm, at the height of the battles with foreign invaders in December. Schneider had threatened both the ethnic and the sexual homogeniety of the French legions; his wife was executed along with him in April, 1794.[91] A foreign threat was once again coupled with feminine temptation in the case of Etta Palm d'Aelders, the radical feminist within Bonneville's Confederation, who was denounced for foreign links.[92] In late 1793, the nation was applying standards of loyalty that were more exclusive, Spartan, and homophile than anyone educated in the cosmopolitanism of the Enlightenment could have imagined.

At the popular level, too, a sudden surge of feminine participation in revolutionary activity was permanently repressed during the nationalist mobilization of late 1793. An "Amazon corps" of four thousand young women had appeared briefly in Bordeaux and a feminine "Friends of Liberty and Equality" in Lyon.[93] Within Paris, women "took the most violent initiative and surpassed by a good deal the fury of men" [94] in the debates of May 31, 1793, which moved power out of the Assembly and into the streets. All of this feminine activity vanished along with the Revolutionary Republican Society, a Parisian society of female sans-culottes, which became "the first target of the Jacobin assault upon the popular movement"[95] in the fall of 1793. Its demand for women to wear the red cap of male revolutionaries outraged the central revolutionary leaders. On October 31, the Convention outlawed all female clubs and societies.

The antifeminine sentiment that swept through Paris was almost certainly related to the parallel process of mobilizing men for military service. The unprecedented *levée en masse* involved tearing thousands of young men away from their mothers and linking them together by the masculine mystique of militant nationalism. Female and foreign identities were already blended together. The word for "Austrian" was spelled in the feminine form even when French grammar called for a masculine ending.[96] Whether or not the red hat was a phallic symbol as Joel Barlow contended, the wearing of it by women in Paris clearly seemed to threaten the male leadership. Fabre d'Eglantine, one of the principal choreographers of the revolutionary festivals, invoked a kind of domino theory of prospective feminine annexations of male weaponry/sexuality. After the *bonnet rouge*, women would take the gun belt and then the gun itself, he warned.[97] The official report to the Convention on the role of women urged against any participation in politics by a sex that is congenitally "exposed to error and seduction":

> . . . women, by their constitution, are open to an exaltation which could be ominous in public life. The interests of the state would soon be sacrificed to all the kinds of disruption and disorder that hysteria can produce.[98]

The hysteria was largely in the minds of the men who voted—with only one dissenting vote in the entire Convention—to outlaw all women's associations. In this atmosphere, Marie Antoinette, who had been relatively neglected as a target of abuse in the early years of the revolution,[99] became a target for a savage hatred that bordered at times on sadism. Her execution on October 16 began a series of public guillotinings of the great symbolic women of the era in a short space of time. Charlotte Corday, the killer of Marat, Olympe de Gouges, author of a *Declaration of the Rights of Women*, and finally the Girondist leader Madame Roland on November 8—all provided spectacular executions for the Parisian masses. The popular imagination, which had already substituted inexpensive etchings for aristocratic engravings,[100] received its gynephobic icon in the form of David's pencil sketch of an ugly, but still arrogant, Marie Antoinette on the way to her humiliating end. The contrast is striking in both medium and message with the idealized neo-classical male nude warriors that were to dominate David's vast oil canvases in glorification of *la grande nation*. Subconscious fear of revenge might well explain the strange apprehension that later haunted both Robespierre and Saint-Just of being assassinated by women.[101]

As the very embodiment of militant, male *fraternité*, Saint-Just wrote to Robespierre from Alsace that there were "too many laws—too few examples."[102] In the last months of his life, Saint-Just observed the "strictest austerity of habit," avoided all contact with women,[103] and led the struggle against indifference and factionalism.[104] Late in April of 1794, he journeyed to the front with Le Bas one final time to share in the great victory at Fleurus late in June. When the vanquished Austrians before Charleroi brought him an envelope with terms of surrender on June 25 and began speaking to him of honorable arrangements, Saint-Just interrupted them to say that he would not open it, and demanded unconditional surrender:

> We cannot either honor or dishonor you here, just as it is not in your power to either dishonor or to honor the French nation. There is nothing in common between you and me.[105]

Ironically, the victory that assured the survival of the nation removed the need for terror and for the emergency that had justified the first governmental body ever to describe itself officially as "revolutionary." Robespierre and Saint-Just were both executed and the Committee of Public Safety dissolved a month after the victory.

As befits the chiaroscuro politics of apocalypse, there was one final fabulous feast of fraternity just before the fall of Robespierre. If the Feast of Federation in 1790 had represented "the first day of the sublime dream of fraternity," [106] Robespierre's spectacular Feast of the Supreme Being on June 8, 1794, suggested the beginning of its unending summer. The winter, the foreign armies, and the guillotine all seemed to have passed; and the last stage in revolutionary simplification had occurred with Robespierre's election as president of the Convention and proclamation of a new religion of maximum simplicity: "the Cult of the Supreme Being."

Designed to be the first in a series of regular national festivals, the Feast of the Supreme Being turned the volcano into a peaceful mountain of floral beauty and choral unison on the Field of Mars. Women were admitted and given a separate but equal place in the hitherto homophilic rituals. Even the ascetic Saint-Just saw in the proceedings the beginnings of a pedagogic program that might truly inculcate virtue in a corrupt world. Here at last was Sparta plus song. Paris had been transformed not into a city based on some preexisting conception, but into "an eternal model of assembly, simplicity and joy."[107] In hailing the Supreme Being, Robespierre proclaimed that its "true priest" was "nature":

> . . . its temple, the universe; its cult, virtue; its festivals the joy of a great people . . . renewing the sweet bonds of universal fraternity.[108]

The euphoria was short-lived, though much of the new secular simplicity survived together with many of the national festivals in the Cult of Theophilanthropy under the Directory. The "fraternal meals" of the last weeks of Robespierre's rule [109] and the "fraternal embrace" which ended the festival were followed by a final, fratricidal burst of terror and factionalism which brought down the emergency government.

Saint-Just illustrated within the leadership the mass phenomenon within the populace of dedicated young soldiers harnessing their passion to a national cause. He was a prototype for the ascetic revolutionary of the future. Through him the locus of legitimacy moved away from physical place and political formula to living example. That example was made awesome by the icy calm, the *sang-froid*,[110] he maintained throughout the quarreling and violence of his last days. Saint-Just had the serenity of one who had surrendered himself long before death to a transcendent ideal, to "the spirit of the revolution," and realized the goal of human "regeneration."

The passion of Saint-Just was cold rather than hot. It imploded into intelligence rather than exploding into indulgence. That intelligence charted a course of constancy and toughness in the turbulent final weeks of rule by the Committee of Public Safety. He resisted both Robespierre's apparent moves to make peace with foreign enemies and his tendency to personalize his struggles with moderates. At the same time, Saint-Just seems to have been far bolder than Robespierre in attempting to appeal over the heads of the Convention to the revolutionary army in a final effort to forestall the conservative drift.

Whatever his exact role, Saint-Just retained till the end a cool contempt for the "dust" of ordinary life, the "softness" and idleness of those who gave themselves over to the process of corruption rather than to that of regeneration.[111] The "spirit of the revolution" was resisted not just by "the force of things"—about which he often impatiently complained; there was also the lack of force among revolutionaries themselves—the backsliding from *l'esprit de la révolution* into *le bon esprit* of aristocratic salons:

> . . . *l'esprit* is a sophist which leads all virtues to the scaffold. . . .[112]

Within the proud head of Saint-Just as he went to *la sainte guillotine* may have lain that most sublime of all contradictions in revolutionary thought: the need for a tyranny of virtue to prevent the recurrence of tyranny surrounded by vice. His apparent attempt to by-pass the Convention with the army, his revelation that Augustus Caesar was his greatest hero of antiquity, his mysterious references to Oliver Cromwell, and Robespierre's final likening of him to Charles IX, author of the St. Bartholomew's Day massacre [113]—all indicate that this just saint who sought no personal power may have felt impelled to justify absolute power.

The national ideal of fraternity reached its apogee in the execution of Saint-Just following the Roman suicide of his younger revolutionary "brother," Le Bas. The rival ideal of communitarian equality appeared during the Thermidorean reaction that followed. Its leader, Babeuf, was, like Saint-Just, a native of Picardy with a similar nostalgia for agrarian simplicity and antique virtue in a corrupted world.[114] Its supreme cultural expression was not Robespierre's singing festival of fraternity, but Sylvain Maréchal's prosaic *Manifesto of Equals*. If Maréchal took his image of revolution-as-volcano from Saint-Just, he derived the more important idea of a revolutionary Second Coming from Robespierre. Maréchal's concept of the political upheaval of

1789–94 as the harbinger of a second, social revolution arises directly from Robespierre's valedictory at the Feast of the Supreme Being:

> A new world has appeared beyond the limits of the world. Everything has changed in the physical order; everything must change in the moral and political order. Half of the world revolution is already done, the other half must be completed. . . .[115]

Equality: The Vision of Community

The third new ideal to arise out of the French Revolution was that of *communauté*: a new type of social and economic community based on equality. Though this ideal was the least articulated at the time (and the least important politically throughout the nineteenth century), it has important roots in the revolutionary era. The revolutionary egalitarianism of Babeuf, Maréchal, and Restif de la Bretonne is the progenitor of modern Communism—and of revolutionary socialism, the rival ideal of revolutionary nationalism.

The new egalitarian communalism was rooted in Rousseau's call for a social contract that would repudiate inequality among men and legitimize authority by permitting the "general will" to unify the community on a new basis. Rousseau's contract was generally interpreted in purely political terms during the French Revolution, but the germs of a socioeconomic interpretation also emerged from two sources: the rhetoric of the American Revolution and the reality of the French countryside.

The American Declaration of Independence offered as its first philosophical justification of separation from England the ideological assertion "that all men are created equal." By pronouncing this to be "self-evident," the Declaration also initiated the tendency of revolutionary publicists to proclaim the obviousness of truths that had never before even been thought about by more than a handful. The more secular French Declaration of Rights in 1789 proclaimed men to be equal only "in respect of their rights"; but later revolutionaries thought also of the "pursuit of happiness" proclaimed by the Americans—and the radical Constitution of 1793 affirmed (as the Americans never did) that "common happiness" (*le bonheur commun*) was the aim of society and "oppression against the body of society" (*corps social*) a justification for insurrection.[116]

The proto-communist idea that "common happiness" might be realized at the expense of private property ownership began to appear relatively early in the cosmopolitan Parisian circles that ultimately proved anathema to the nationalistic Jacobin leaders. A petition on "the agrarian laws" by an Anglo-Irishman James Rutledge, who called himself a "citizen of the universe," urged in 1790 the establishment of a

social order (*état social*) with "no ownership of property." [117] This idea
of a *lex agraria*, a modified land distribution in the manner of Tiberius
and Caius Gracchus during the Roman Republic, was systematically
propagated at the same time by Bonneville's principal collaborator in
the Social Circle, the Abbé Fauchet.[118] The idea became a special favorite of the provincial clergy who identified with their rural parishes.
The Abbé Cournand went even further, declaring that "in the state of
nature, the domain of man is the entire earth" and arguing that all landowners should have plots equal in size, non-hereditary, and non-trans-
ferrable.[119] Other "red curates" found an almost religious exaltation in
identifying with the masses and articulating a social ideal that went beyond Parisian politics to suggest secular salvation. Thus, Pierre Dolivier
was almost saintly in self-denigration as he petitioned for acceptance
into the Bonneville-Fauchet Universal Confederation. I am, he said, the
lowliest of men:

> . . . simple and even too simple, without knee britches and without a
> hearth (*sans culottes et sans feu*), but not without passion for the work of
> bringing into being the kingdom of universal justice.[120]

This universal ideal found local roots in the grievances of the French
countryside. These were brought to Paris in May 1790 by François-
Noël Babeuf, a young prisoner from Picardy who had led a local tax
revolt against the continued levying of indirect taxes by the National
Assembly. Babeuf had been brought up in the country, trained as a commissioner of land deeds, and studied land utilization but with relatively little interest in politics. In Paris, he discovered the concept of
the agrarian law by establishing links first with Rutledge and then with
the Universal Confederation,[121] which gave an ideological cast to his
earlier primitive ideas about a "collective lease" (*ferme collective*) and
the redistribution to the poor of confiscated church lands.[122] His opposition to the moderate political revolution was dramatically signaled by
an attack on Lafayette in the summer of 1790. This *Letter of a Deputy
from Picardy* was distributed in the Palais-Royal,[123] where Babeuf drew
up plans to publicize a radical feminist *Confédération des Dames*, perhaps in connection with the Universal Confederation.[124]

He identified the communal government in Paris with local rural authority in common opposition to the parasitic national government.
Elected as administrator of the department of the Somme in September,
1792, he returned to Paris to adopt in the spring of 1793 the name
"Gracchus" in his quest for "real economic equality" (*égalité de fait*)
and some new kind of "general happiness unknown throughout the
ages." [125] It is to that revolutionary search that we must now turn.

The Conspiracy of Babeuf

The origins of the social revolutionary tradition—no less than those
of the national revolutionary—lie in the military mobilization of 1793.
Social revolutionaries like Babeuf—unlike the nationalist majority typified by another native of Picardy, Saint-Just—had a special affinity for

the international military units that formed briefly in 1793. Babeuf had known Rutledge even before the revolution, and late in 1789 he signed on as a regular correspondent from provincial Roye for the international *Courrier de l'Europe* published in London.[126] Arriving in Paris in February, 1793, Babeuf joined the agitational "legion of people's liberators," serving as secretary to the Franco-Haitian Claude Fournier, who had led the storming of the Bastille from the Palais-Royal and kept the name "the American."[127] He then briefly became secretary to a Dutch officer in charge of the Batavian legion[128] before retreating to the food administration of the Paris Commune.

When Fournier was not chosen to lead the revolutionary assault against the conservative uprising in the Vendée, Babeuf appears to have despaired of finding a meaningful role in the exciting events of 1793. During a period when nationalist armies were singing *La Marseillaise* rather than reading proto-socialist tracts, Babeuf wrote to his protector Sylvain Maréchal that he envied Rousseau's capacity to sustain himself by writing music:

> I have no such talent, and am therefore more unhappy. But I shall learn to compose with typography.[129]

He became a master composer in his chosen medium. In and out of prison during the Reign of Terror, Babeuf repeatedly turned to typography and journalism. His perennial protector Maréchal directed him first to Bonneville's press of the Social Circle in April and then to his own *Révolutions de Paris* in December of 1793.[130] After the overthrow of Robespierre, newspapers became "more of an arm of struggle than a source of information";[131] and Babeuf founded in September, 1794, his own arm, *Journal of the Freedom of the Press*, hailing journalism as the means of keeping alive the revolutionary spirit and struggling to implement the Constitution of 1793. His ideas soon went beyond radical republicanism and the denunciation of Robespierre's tyranny. He began to discover posthumously in Robespierre "the genius in whom resided true ideas of regeneration";[132] and, in 1795, he founded his *Tribune of the People*: the first journal in history to be the legal arm of an extralegal revolutionary conspiracy.

Babeuf's *Tribune* was an organ of strategy, not just an outlet for rhetoric. Its criticism of other revolutionary journals and its effort to define a coherent line make it a distant ancestor of Lenin's *Iskra* and *Pravda*; and its prospectus defined a social goal as well as a moral mission. At the head of each issue stood the italicized phrase, "The aim of society is the happiness of the community."[133] Babeuf rejected the "right of property" guaranteed in the Declaration of Rights of Man in favor of the "state of community",[134] arguing that society should provide "common happiness" through "perfect equality."[135]

Alongside the journalistic proclamation of a new social ideal came a new type of revolutionary organization. The national network of Jacobin clubs, which had been largely destroyed by the overthrow of Robespierre, was no longer taken as the model. In a long manifesto of November 1794, "On the need and means of organizing a true popular society," he likened the relationship between earlier "clubists" and the masses to that of "the Christian sermonizer vis-à-vis the benevolent congregation." He called for a militant society to end all subservience to the "aristocracy of riches" and to begin "the reign of republican virtues." [136]

Arrested in March 1795, Babeuf used his six-month imprisonment in Arras to perfect his ideas of a true "popular society." All were to be equal and dedicated to developing collectively commerce, agriculture, and (in a striking addition for this period) industry. Such a society was to come about through a new geographical base and a new militant organization. In an important letter of July 28, Babeuf provided perhaps the first outline of a program for completing the revolution, and anticipated the later idea of a secure base area for militant revolutionaries.[137] He speaks variously of "our Vendée," [138] the "Sacred Mountain," or "the plebeian Vendée." [139]

"Advancing by degree, consolidating to the extent that we gain territory, we should be able to organize." [140] "Enemies of the human race" fear the militance of "numerous phalanxes" [141] by revolutionaries who will give up their traditional occupations to advance the struggle.

Babeuf fled backward in time and forward in revolutionary consciousness when he moved from the ideal of a Roman legion to that of a Greek phalanx as the model for the revolutionary struggle. His effort to form a "phalanx of sans-culottes" in the spring of 1793 failed, but the image reappeared in Saint-Just's call for new forms of socio-military support for the revolutionary government in October. Anacharsis Cloots, the deracinated "orator of the human race," saw the revolutionary army of France not as a national body at all, but as the new Greeks fighting for all civilization as

. . . phalanxes of interpreters, of translators of the universal law.[142]

Babeuf used the term *phalange* for the formations needed to realize the social as well as the military discipline of his new *communauté*; and the term was to have a venerable history in subsequent revolutionary usage.[143]

The original phalanx in search of a new society arose directly out of revolutionary journalism. Late in 1795, the Club of the Pantheon began meeting by torchlight in the crypt of the Convent of Sainte Géneviève ("the Cave of Brigands") to discuss the program of Babeuf's *Tribune*. Babeuf, who had returned to Paris in September 1795, assumed leadership of the club, which claimed two thousand members. Accused of fomenting civil war, Babeuf invented the classical revolutionary riposte that such a war already existed: the war of the rich against the poor.[144] He accepted with pride the accusations of his foes that his friends were "anarchists . . . men who want to be always making revolution." [145]

In November, Babeuf published the first in the new genre of social revolutionary manifestos which would culminate in Marx's *Communist Manifesto* of 1848. Babeuf's *Plebeian Manifesto* was both a philosophical inventory (a *manifest* of what was needed to bring about "equality in fact" and "the common good") and a call for a popular uprising (a *manifestation*, "greater, more solemn, more general than has ever been done before").[146]

When a police raid led by the young Napoleon Bonaparte shut down the Club of the Pantheon on February 28, 1796, Babeuf and his associates turned their attention inward on their "Conspiracy of the Equals." Seeking now to revive rather than revile the dictatorial methods of Robespierre, they constituted themselves on March 30 as the Secret Directory of Public Safety.

Decisions of the directory were reached collectively and announced anonymously.[147] In place of individual signatures on leaflets and letters, there was the designation "public safety" or the words of the revolutionary trinity in triangular form—with "common happiness" substituted for "fraternity." [148] Each member of the central insurrectionary committee was to be concurrently active in other areas from which he could report back to the inner circle. The secret center was to communicate outward through a network of twelve trusted "instructors," with each responsible for mobilizing a broader insurrectionary force in one of the twelve *arrondissements* of Paris. The secret directory met almost every evening. It published in printings of at least two thousand not only the theoretical *Tribun du Peuple*, but also a fly sheet, *L'Eclaireur du Peuple* for the ordinary worker.[149] Methods of mobilization included the active enlistment of affiliates by small groups of activists or *groupistes*, who gathered around newly and prominently displayed revolutionary posters. The number of those loosely recruited grew to seventeen thousand,[150] and the conspiracy increasingly focused on the army as the crucial recruiting ground for insurrection. The decision to put a military committee of the conspiracy directly in touch with the secret directory enabled an informer to discover the inner circle and expose it to police arrest.[151]

The conspirators were guardians not only of the revolutionary hope for social equality, but also of the vision of Saint-Just that true revolution would take men beyond politics. All government—and not just some governments—would somehow be destroyed by a true revolution. "To politic" (*politiquer*) was a verb invoked with contempt by Babeuf, whose *Plebeian Manifesto* ended with a call for "total upheaval" (*bouleversement total*). "May everything return to chaos, and out of chaos may there emerge a new and regenerated world." [152] The conspiracy envisaged the establishment of a "great national community" in which all goods were owned in common and shared equally. This "community" was eventually to supplant—by either attractive example or coercive force—all other systems of political and economic authority.

Imperceptibly within Babeuf's conspiracy arose the myth of the unfinished revolution: the idea that the political upheaval in France was only the forerunner of a second, more portentous social revolution. Babeuf's journal called in 1795 for the reality rather than the appearance of revolution:

Ce n'est plus *dans les esprits* qui'il faut
faire la révolution . . . c'est dans les choses. . . .[153]

A few months later in 1796 Babeuf explained that "the epoch of these great revolutions" had created a situation

> . . . where a general upheaval in the system of property ownership is inevitable; where a revolt of the poor against the rich is a necessity that nothing can prevent.[154]

Already in his *Plebeian Manifesto*, Babeuf had begun to develop a sense of messianic mission, invoking the names of Moses, Joshua, and Jesus, as well as Rousseau, Robespierre, and Saint-Just. He had claimed Christ as a "co-athlete" and had written in prison *A New History of the Life of Jesus Christ*.[155] Most of the conspirators shared this belief in Christ as a *sans-culotte* at heart if not a prophet of revolution. The strength of the red curates within the social revolutionary camp intensified the need to keep Christian ideas from weakening revolutionary dedication. Anacharsis Cloots helped break up Bonneville's Social Circle by attacking the Abbé Fauchet for extolling the levelers of the Puritan Revolution. Cloots juxtaposed the certainty of Nature ("always living, always young, always the same") to the ambiguities and contradictions of the Gospels.[156] The antique ideal that the Babeuvists adopted as an alternative to Christianity was that of the Spartans—militant, ascetic, rooted in the land, and deeply hostile to the artificially cerebral and crassly commercial life of the new "Athens": bourgeois Paris under the Directorate.[157]

But the only sure antidote to the vestigial appeal of Christian ideas lay in atheism, which was the special contribution to the Babeuf conspiracy of Sylvain Maréchal, the man who called himself l'HSD, *l'homme sans dieu*, and produced for the revolutionary movement a totally secular version of the messianic idea of a Second Coming. Maréchal had repeatedly declared that "the revolution will not be complete until men share the fruits of the earth as they share the rays of the sun." [158] His neglected *Corrective to the Revolution*, written at the height of revolutionary exaltation in 1793, insisted that

> The Revolution is not complete. . . . The revolution is still only in words and all in theory. It does not yet exist in fact.[159]

Maréchal said the revolution was not yet real, because men were not happier; they would never find happiness without higher principles; and they could never discover such principles under conditions of social inequality:

> Tant qu'il y aura des valets et des maîtres, des pauvres et des riches. . . .
> La Révolution n'est point faite.[160]

In another study of 1795, Maréchal added an element of urgency, suggesting that the preceding, purely political revolution may have made life even worse. "Merchants have become aristocrats, a thousand times more dreadful than the feudal nobility." [161]

It was only a short step to the prophecy of the *Manifesto of Equals* which Maréchal wrote for Babeuf's group:

> The French Revolution is but the precursor of another revolution, far greater, far more solemn, which will be the last.[162]

Babeuf was arrested and the conspiracy destroyed on May 10, 1796. In his court defense and final letters, he appeared surer of his role than of his ideas—dealing with the government often as if he were another government. He viewed himself as the precursor of something new, and bade farewell in a moving last letter to his family as he prepared for a "perfectly virtuous sleep." [163]

The conspiracy sounded a reprise on many themes of the revolutionary faith. The solar myth of the revolution blended with the café breeding ground of activism in the *Chant des Egaux* sung at the Café des Bains-Chinois:

> Sortez de la nuit profonde.
> . . . Le Soleil luit pour tout le monde! [164]

This song was itself the revolutionary counter to the *Reveil du peuple*, introduced after Thermidore as the reactionaries' rival to *La Marseillaise*.

Just as the greatest Christian theologians had defined God as "the coincidence of opposites," so Babeuf took the new faith in revolution to the level of sublime paradox. The justification for launching a new revolution was to "terminate the revolution"; [165] the means of ending "the spirit of domination" was to obey an elite hierarchy; and the way to avoid the tyranny of "factions" was to accept a single leader. The miraculous move to true popular sovereignty was to take place on a springtime "Day of the People" in which some seventeen thousand direct supporters [166] were to rise up in Paris at signals from bells and trumpets. This apocalyptical political act would bring an end to politics.[167] Born out of the vision of island utopias, this realization of instant equality planned to banish opponents immediately to preselected islands in the Atlantic and Mediterranean.[168]

Few accepted Babeuf's egalitarian ideal; but many were haunted by his example. There were, moreover, some grounds for fearing that the conspiracy had foreign links. Representatives of the radical Batavian Republic (the revolutionary regime proclaimed amidst continuing chaos in the Netherlands in 1795—and the first anywhere to adopt officially the revolutionary slogan liberty, equality, fraternity) had some contacts with the French conspirators. Babeuf had once served in the Batavian Legion, and a major uprising by cannoneers of the national guard occurred in Amsterdam on the same day that Babeuf was arrested in Paris.[169] There were echoes of the Babeuf conspiracy in the two countries that in many ways dominated the revolutionary tradition during the early nineteenth century: Italy and Poland.

Babeuf's Italian collaborators sought early in 1796 to persuade the ruling Directory in Paris to support an uprising of "popular movements" in Italy that would lead to a "general revolution" and a unitary state

aligned with France. Guglielmo Cerise, Babeuf's former secretary, and
Buonarroti, his future historian, sought to organize and promote a revolution in Piedmont that would confront the French authorities with
a fait accompli—and push the Directorate closer to the Babeuvist position. Buonarroti argued eloquently against French military rule in Italy,
urging instead "the prompt formation of popular authorities" by the
local populace.[170] But his revolutionary vision was derided by French
military leaders,[171] who launched under Napoleon a conventional military invasion in April. The entry of French troops into Italian villages
was celebrated, however, not with local uprisings, but with Catholic
masses—prompting a friend of Buonarroti's to complain bitterly:

> One does not found a democracy with a magnificat. Instead of illuminat-
> ing churches, it would be better to light up (that is, to burn) feudal
> castles.[172]

Frustrated in Piedmont, Babeuvist activists moved on to Milan, where
they briefly helped organize a local militia and introduced the Italian
tricolor prior to the arrival of Napoleon. The Babeuvists helped form
the hierarchical revolutionary organization the Society of Lights (or
Black League), founded by Cerise and others in Bologna late in 1798.
Though this organization failed to realize what Godechot has called
the best opportunity to unify Italy prior to 1860, it did leave a legacy
of experience with secret, nationwide revolutionary organization which
was later to benefit the Carbonari.[173]

The echo of Babeuvism from occupied Poland was more distant and
muffled. A conspiratorial peasant organization of 1796–97 led by a veteran of both the American and French wars of revolution proclaimed
the slogan "Equality or Death," and may have been influenced by the
Babeuf conspiracy.[174]

Within France, there were flickers of revival among the surviving
Babeuvists—notably in July 1799, when they gathered to form a Society
of the Friends of Equality and Freedom. Such activity was snuffed out
with the arrival of Napoleon later that year.[175]

Yet the hope did not die that the revolution was not yet complete
and might still produce a new morality, if not a new type of man.
The coming revolution was to be Babeuf's *bouleversement total*. Such
expectations were intensified by conservative critics like Burke's German translator (and the future secretary of Metternich), who popularized the phrase "total revolution." [176]

What was the nature of the revolution yet to come? There was a
difference—and at times open conflict—between the Saint-Just–Robespierre ideal of a moral revolution within a nation and the Babeuvist
belief in a "universal" social revolution. But there were human links
between the two ideas through the two most important surviving members of the conspiracy: Buonarroti and Maréchal. For both of them social
and moral revolution were one and the same thing. Their shadowy
careers point, as we shall see, to some surprising philosophical and
organizational roots common to both ideals.

The Communism of Restif

The revolutionary concept of *communauté* may have come less from the high culture of the Enlightenment than from the low culture of popular journalism. Babeuf had been influenced by *The Year 2440*, the prophetic utopian work of one great chronicler of Parisian life, Sebastien Mercier.[177] The word "communism" was introduced to the world by Mercier's friend and fellow journalistic chronicler of Paris, Restif de la Bretonne: the "Rousseau of the gutter," the "*Jean-Jacques des Halles.*" [178]

Restif's verbal invention came out of a life that was—literally—fantastic. His literary production filled nearly 250 volumes with cosmic, social, and sexual fantasies that no one has yet fully catalogued. His writings anticipated everything from interplanetary travel to atomic energy, and encompassed almost every imaginable sexual fetish and perversion.[179]

Inexhaustible, erotic energy made him as compulsive as he was creative. He was possessed with the mystique of the new journalistic medium—inventing hundreds of new words and a bewildering variety of typographical formats. His attachment to printing was almost physiological. He worked for many years as a type-setter and often composed his works directly on his home type-setting equipment without a manuscript.[180] Every aspect of the formal production of a literary work contributed to his total message. His choice of typography, use of italics, overuse of capitalization (often in the middle of words), misuse of accents, and endless invention of pseudonyms and neologisms [181] —reflected an almost religious fascination with the production of the printed word.

Legitimacy for the partisans of egalitarian community flowed from the printing press. Restif's only political activity during the revolutionary era was his attempt beginning in 1789 to organize a productive association for printers and typographers.[182] His works provided an unparalleled descriptive panorama of lower-class life. Distinctions between fact, fiction, and fantasy were swept away by his gushing stream of consciousness. Restif remained the purest form of self-centered intellectual from his youthful days in rural Burgundy to his later years as a nocturnal street-walker in Paris. Wherever he was, Restif lived only in his own self-created world of words, his maze of monologue.

In 1785, Restif published a review of a book describing a communal experiment in Marseilles. He cited a letter of 1782 from the book's author, who described himself as an *auteur communiste*—the first known appearance in print of this word.[183] The author, the educational theorist Joseph-Alexandre-Victor Hupay de Fuvea, later submitted a vast, utopian educational plan to his friend in Aix, Mirabeau, when he set off for the Estates-General in 1789. He lived on to write a *Republican Koran* during the revolution,[184] and to propose that all citizens wear green uniforms with pink trimming as they marched to work daily in

a *grande promenade de la communauté*.[185] But his most remarkable
work was *The Project for a Philosophical Community* of 1779, which
may be considered the first full blueprint for a secular, communist
society in the modern world.[186]

Hupay made a "moral and literary announcement" in 1778 that he
was taking up a subscription to set up his ideal "plan for social and
political life" near Marseilles.[187] His plan was a potpourri of utopian
ideas: the communal ideal of the Moravian Brethren combined with
the legislative ideas of Mably; the social theories of "the new world
and the new Eloise" (that is, the unspoiled Indians and the natural
man of Rousseau's *Nouvelle-Héloïse*).[188] All would speak French, "the
language of reason and truth," and children would be educated communally up to the age of five to insure freedom from past prejudices.[189]
Rigid "tables of exercises and studies" were prescribed for subsequent
education, and a *Plan Géométral* drawn up for the community featuring two large statues: "the divine PLATO, Prince of Legislators, Inventor of the Communal Life (*Communauté de vie*)" and "J.J. ROUS-
SEAU, Citizen of Geneva, Investigator of the principles of Human Education." [190] A privileged exit from this "house of meeting" of the
community was shown leading to a special place for "communities
formed by Children married within the Philosophical Community." [191]
This was presumably a kind of philosophical master race living in
"equality and union" and "the most perfect sociability." [192]

> . . . a Spartan people, the true nursery of a better race of men than
> ours.[193]

But where was the new Spartan race to come from? Was there anyone
who might really aspire to set up the "community of moral-economic
rule" based on an egalitarian "community of goods"? [194] There is no
record of any serious attempt being made in the vicinity of Marseilles;
but there is in the text ample and altogether prophetic indication that
he thought it might most easily be realized in Russia.

Hupay—like many *philosophes*—was inspired by the ambitious reform plans of Catherine the Great, the prototypical "enlightened despot."
Her pretentious early writings led him to believe it might be possible
"to put into practice the beautiful laws of the Republic of Plato," to
create "an entire city of philosophers" which would "be called Platonopolis." [195] Such an ideal community would be easier to establish in
Russia than in the West precisely because it was an authoritarian society with coercive power "where each lord could more easily become
the father and benefactor of his serfs." [196]

Hupay, however, was an unnoticed minor figure. His letter to Restif
in 1782 had been prompted by reading the latter's seminal *Le Paysan
perverti, ou les dangers de la ville*. In the fourth volume of this work,
Restif announced his intention to provide a "new Emile" that would
enrich the pedagogic ideas of Rousseau's original *Emile* with a social
program inspired by Rousseau's *Discourse on Inequality*. This section
of Restif's work concluded with a model statute for a *bourg commun*

in which private property was limited to immediate needs for clothing and furniture.[197] For Restif, the noble peasant had been "perverted" by advancing civilization. He could be restored to wholeness only by the establishment of a new "philosophical community" based on "the sentiments of the best authors and the principles . . . of the New World." [198]

In 1781, Restif wrote a literary fantasy describing an egalitarian society, where there was only one law.

> All must be common among equals. Each must work for the common good. All must take an identical part in work.[199]

This was in many ways the most sophisticated of all the utopian islands to appear in prerevolutionary literature. It depicted not only the innate goodness of the inhabitants of the Island of Christina, but also the compatibility of their unspoiled egalitarianism with advanced ideas brought back to the island from "Megapatagonia" (an idealized version of France). Thus the "French Daedelus" sought not just to fly away from a decadent France to an island paradise, but rather to rescue an egalitarian society from "the people of the night," ruling over it by providing an eighteen-article "Codex of the Megapatagonians" which decreed the common ownership of all property and the uniform work obligations that the oppressed islanders secretly wanted.[200]

An even more ambitious work in the following year introduced the term "community of goods" and suggested the "manner of establishing equality" in "all nations of Europe." [201] Thus, Restif was able to refer his correspondent, the self-proclaimed "communist author," to works of his own that had already taken his communist ideas beyond the outline in *Le Paysan perverti*.

Communism may in part be one of the new ideas blown back across the Atlantic by the original revolutionary "wind from America." [202] Both Hupay's "project" and Restif's *Le Paysan* were conceived in 1776. In his commentary on Hupay's letter, Restif argued that "the people of brothers of Philadelphia" have opened the possibility for "that union and that community of moral and economic rule . . . that excludes all vain and external distinction." Restif spoke of the coming of a supranational community that would end "the puerile rivalry which confounds states and drags all of them together into ruin and crime." [203]

Even more crucial to the communism of Restif was its close identification with the peasantry; the peasants had been perverted by the cities, but retained the moral force to build communism. On the eve of the revolution, Restif wrote a pamphlet urging that peasants be admitted as a fourth estate to the Estates-General; [204] and on the first anniversary of the fall of the Bastille, Restif wrote another pamphlet warning rural Frenchmen coming to Paris for the Feast of Federation against the evils of the city.[205]

Although Restif prided himself on belonging to no club or party, his writings of the early revolutionary period seem to envisage a further uprising (*soulèvement général*) to support his broad plan for social justice:

Mettez toute la nation en communautés . . . faites une insurrection générale, partagez.[206]

From his appeal for agrarian communalism submitted to the Estates-General in 1789, he turned in late 1792 and early 1793 to the Convention with an appeal for what he now called his *plan de communauté générale*.[207]

In February 1793, Restif used the term *communism* as his own for the first time to describe the fundamental change in ownership that would obviate the need for any further redistribution of goods and property.[208] His detailed exposition of communism (and regular use of the word) began the following year with a "Regulation . . . for the establishment of a general Community of the Human Race" in his *Monsieur Nicolas or the human heart unveiled*.[209] In this work, Restif insisted that the absolute elimination of private property would end human need but not individual initiative. He saw communism as a more effective cause for rallying the French army than the "uncompleted republic" of the Directory. The republicanism of the post-revolutionary United States was also attacked for providing only "nominal" equality.[210] In a communist society, all citizens would accept the obligation to work—and to declare publicly their annual production goals at the beginning of each year. Neither possessions nor professions could be passed on from father to son.[211]

Communism was the best of eight possible forms of government[212] and would give birth to a new political system: "the only one worthy of reasonable men."[213] Only a communist order could bring to an end seduction by money and the attendant corruption and vice.[214] Restif's proposed regulations for the human race proposed communal ownership, communal eating, and a new *monnaie communismale* to replace traditional forms of exchange.[215]

As the revolution progressed, Restif intensified his commitment to his communist ideal, which he traced back to his *Andrographe* of 1782. But it was a lonely vision; and Restif had to print many of his own books in his basement in such small editions that many have been lost. He printed *Monsieur Nicolas* in an edition of two hundred on paper of such low quality that the book remained largely unknown for nearly a century.[216] His *Posthumous Letters*, also written in 1796, could not be published until 1802; then they were immediately confiscated by the Napoleonic censorship. He compared the ideal communist society of the future with other societies by describing a series of interplanetary visits. Appropriately, in view of his erotic interests and preoccupations, Venus was the site for his communist society of the future. The manuscript of his final communist fantasy, *The Cage and the Birds*, has been altogether lost. All we know is the one line Restif devoted to "the birds" in his *Posthumous Letters*:

Mais le Communisme les retenait dans l'égalité.[217]

Others besides Restif disprove the suggestion that there was no "communism" in the French Revolution and that the revolutionaries all accepted the sanctity of private property.[218] Jean-Claude Chappuis, who lived in the same building as Restif during the late 1790s, attacked the Declaration of the Rights of Man for its defense of property rights, anticipating Proudhon by nearly a half a century in labeling property as "theft." [219] Another proposal of 1795 argued for *la communauté des biens-fonds, communauté d'industrie* and urged the formation of small territorial communes.[220]

Restif's three-volume *Philosophie de Monsieur Nicolas* of 1796 called for a *communauté universelle,* and talked about "the Communists" as if they were active and numerous in the real world.[221] The question of whether Restif was alluding to, or in some way connected with, Babeuf's concurrent conspiracy takes us deeper into the occult labyrinths of Paris where modern revolutionary organization began. But it is worth glancing first across the continent to the open spaces of St. Petersburg, where real Communists eventually were to come to power. The first of many Russians to comment substantively on Restif was the founder of a distinctively Russian tradition of revolutionary intelligentsia: Alexander Radishchev. Writing in his famous *Journey from Petersburg to Moscow* in the first year of the French Revolution, Radishchev blasted the libertarian excess and sexual permissiveness of Restif's communism [222]—providing a hint of the more ascetic and puritanical version that was to come.

The Bonneville Connection

The possibility of links between Restif's verbal communism and Babeuf's active conspiracy has never been seriously considered—partly because historians of the revolution have been slow to acknowledge the importance of Restif, but perhaps even more because the paths of investigation lead into dark corridors of the human imagination that Western positivists no less than Eastern Marxists prefer to ignore. But before plunging in to explore in all seriousness the occult origins of revolutionary organization, it might be well to summarize such evidence as exists for the possibility of actual links between those seminal figures whom we have found to share so many ideological affinities.

While no public suggestion of a link between Babeuf and Restif was raised at the former's public trial, the authorities, as they prepared their case, apparently believed that such a link existed.[223] Historians now can hardly hope to find more conclusive evidence than the prosecutors were able to amass at the time before deciding not to press the connection in court. But Babeuf repeatedly used the word *communauté* (and inventions like *communautistes*) in the revolutionary manner of Restif; [224] and Restif tantalizingly ends *Monsieur Nicolas,* the magnum opus in which he first set forth his full-blown communist ideal,[225] with a reference to Babeuf followed by three dots. He may have been suggesting that the imperatives he provided were flowing into the Babeuvist movement that was just beginning.

A more serious link almost certainly lies in Maréchal, the journalistic protector and sponsor of Babeuf's early career who knew Restif well before the revolution and before meeting Babeuf. Maréchal's still obscure role in the conspiracy—like Restif, he escaped prosecution altogether despite his direct involvement—leads back in turn to the links that Babeuf, Restif, and Maréchal all had with Bonneville's Social Circle.

Bonneville was perhaps Restif's closest friend, seeing him "almost daily" in the mid and late 1790s.[226] Bonneville's most extreme revolutionary associate, Jean-François Varlet, lived in the same building as Restif at the time he was beginning his collaboration with Babeuf.[227] Bonneville secretly printed Restif's basic communist treatise, *Monsieur Nicolas*, in his own home along with the follow-up treatise, *Le Philosophie de Monsieur Nicolas*, and Varlet's *Explosion*.[228]

Babeuf had close knowledge of (if not direct contact with) the Social Circle in 1790, placing the *Bouche de Fer* at the head of his own list of journals;[229] and in December 1790, signing his name "*Babeuf de la société de la confédération universelles des amis de la vérité.*"[230] He may have had continuing contact with the Confederation in Picardy, where there was special provincial enthusiasm for the Confederation.[231] He could have had personal contact with Bonneville in Paris in December 1790, or again in April 1793, when Maréchal suggested that Babeuf take a job as typographer for the press of the Social Circle.

At that exact time, Maréchal was engaged in an intensive program of publication at Bonneville's press; and both of his major works of 1793, *Correctif à la révolution* and *Almanach des républicains*, bore the mysterious new designation "*à Paris chez les Directeurs de l'Imprimerie du Cercle Social.*" It would appear that Maréchal himself was one of the "directors" of this press; and that this press, which continued to publish works by Maréchal and other Babeuvists, linked in some way Bonneville's circle with Babeuf's conspiracy.[232]

Important further evidence for suggesting such a link can be found in the neglected pamphlet of Varlet, which appeared in 1792 as the first document to bear the imprimatur of "the directors of the press of the Social Circle." His *Project for a Special and Imperative Mandate to Those Mandated by the People to the National Convention* purported to be "printed at the expense of *sans-culotes* [sic]" and seemed to call for little less than a social revolution. It was a warning of the dangers of "legislative tyranny" in any central assembly within the new republic where "careerists" may claim to "represent" the people while failing to satisfy their concrete social and economic needs. In order not to betray what Varlet was the first to call "the second revolution," he bluntly instructed "those mandated by the People":

> You will cement the social pact. . . . You will lay the foundation that has so far been neglected of social happiness.[233]

Thus Maréchal appears to have derived his concept of a needed second, social revolution from his fellow "director" of Bonneville's press. Maréchal's subsequent participation in the Babeuf conspiracy was kept secret until revealed in Buonarroti's *History* in 1828, which explained that materials on Maréchal's "definitive legislation of equality" were hidden in a place inaccessible to the police. Any such materials have remained hidden from scholars as well, so the precise nature of Babeuf's links with Maréchal and the surviving "directors" of the Social Circle cannot be determined.

There is strong reason to believe, however, that Babeuf borrowed heavily from the Bonneville he had admired in 1789–90 in shaping his own conspiracy in 1795–96.[234] Babeuf took both the title and function of his key journal from Bonneville's earlier *Tribune of the People*. He adopted this new name at precisely the point when his journalism assumed the oracular and mobilizing functions Bonneville's journal had claimed for itself during the Parisian insurrection of 1789. Posters to be distributed by the Babeuvists alluded to the precedents of 1789 (rather than 1792) not only to attract a broader base of support but also to suggest an uprising beyond politics of the kind first envisaged in Paris by Bonneville. Babeuf revived Bonneville's favorite fantasy of using trumpets in the streets to make announcements, his stress on social goals and *bonheur commun,* and his assignment of leadership roles to women.[235] Babeuf may also have adopted from Bonneville the more general idea of a network of reporters-supporters and of a secret inner circle directing a broader public confederation.

Bonneville's Social Circle had a far more extensive program than is generally realized during the two years prior to Robespierre's dictatorship in the summer of 1793.[236] The Social Circle was, moreover, more radical in social policy then than were the rival Jacobins—setting up an agitational organization for wage earners and artisans in 1791, the *Point central des arts et métiers,*[237] writing pioneering treatises on insurrection,[238] and calling for

> equality above all, equality between men, equality between the departments, between Paris and the rest of France.[239]

These militant egalitarian ideals attracted new interest after the fall of the Jacobin dictatorship and the parallel deepening of the economic crisis in Paris. Although the nature and the extent of Bonneville's activity after Thermidore is still obscure, he became even more closely linked with Restif and Mercier—and remained active and influential until 1800, when Napoleon shut the last journal of the Social Circle, *Le Bien-Informé* after Bonneville compared Napoleon to Cromwell.[240]

Whatever the precise links of Babeuf to Bonneville, of both with Maréchal, and of all with Buonarroti, a common force shaped them all: romantic occultism. It is to this unfamiliar, but unavoidable world that one now turns in an effort to map the mysterious and to approximate answers to the question of origins.

CHAPTER 4

The Occult Origins

of Organization

AFTER the fall of Robespierre, and especially after the trial of Babeuf, the French Revolution in some sense ended. Those who sought to keep alive the high hopes of the early revolutionary era no longer focused their faith on the ongoing process of innovation in society as a whole, but instead retreated to the secure nucleus of a secret society where intense conviction need not be compromised by the diffuse demands of practical politics.

Their myth of the unfinished revolution lent to such secret societies the special aura of an elect anticipating the Second Coming. The mantle of revolutionary legitimacy passed from the rulers of France to small conspiratorial groups throughout Europe. These groups echoed the secrecy and utopianism of Bonneville's circle and Babeuf's conspiracy more than the open political activity of the Jacobin clubs and the parliamentary assemblies.

Moreover, because of the increasing effectiveness of the political police, secret societies tended to move even further underground. Thus under Napoleon, conspiratorial societies with hierarchical discipline became the dominant form of revolutionary organization, and in the 1820s under the conservative restoration they produced a wave of revolutions throughout Europe.

Historians have never been able to unravel the tangled threads of this tapestry—and in recent times have largely given up trying. The most important recent study confines itself to tracing the history of what people *thought* about the secret societies rather than what the societies in fact were.[1] But the problem will not go away simply because we lack documentation on the numbers and the nature—and at times even the very existence—of these organizations.

The plain fact is that by the mid-1810s there were not just one or two but scores of secret revolutionary organizations throughout Europe—extending even into Latin America and the Middle East. These groups, although largely unconnected, internationalized the modern revolutionary tradition and provided the original forum for the general debate in the modern world about the purposes of political power in a post-traditional society. And it was they who in the process of modernization pioneered a phenomenon by now familiar: impatient youth forming their own organizations to combat monarchical-religious authority.

The story of the secret societies can never be fully reconstructed, but it has been badly neglected—even avoided, one suspects—because the evidence that is available repeatedly leads us into territory equally uncongenial to modern historians in the East and in the West.

In what follows I shall attempt to show that the modern revolutionary tradition as it came to be internationalized under Napoleon and the Restoration grew out of occult Freemasonry; that early organizational ideas originated more from Pythagorean mysticism than from practical experience; and that the real innovators were not so much political activists as literary intellectuals, on whom German romantic thought in general—and Bavarian Illuminism in particular—exerted great influence.

Buonarroti: The First Apostle

The continuous history of international revolutionary organization begins with a lonely individual in exile, Filippo Giuseppe Maria Lodovico Buonarroti. Largely unknown until in 1828 at the age of sixty-seven he published his *History of the Babeuf Conspiracy*, thereafter he was the patriarch to a new generation of revolutionaries until his death in 1837. He is largely remembered today as a kind of Plato to Babeuf's Socrates—recording the teachings and martyrdom of the master for posterity. But he was also the first apostle [2] of a new religion: the first truly to become a full-time revolutionary in the modern sense of having total dedication to the creation by force of a new secular order.

Buonarroti, the oldest of five sons of a noble Florentine family, was a direct descendant of Michelangelo. He showed an early aptitude for French and for music: the two languages used by Italians to express hopes higher than those they found in their own vernacular. French was the language of philosophy and progress for the aristocratic Enlightenment in Tuscany as elsewhere, and music, of course, was the language of longing.

These languages of rational reform and of lyric hope were important to the young Buonarroti. His family was largely impoverished; by the time he was elected to the noble order of Saint Stephen in 1778, the handsome, seventeen-year-old Florentine had acquired a sense of self-importance he had no way of sustaining. A poor aristocrat in an economically stagnant city, he sought satisfaction in the life of the mind. Thus he became the prototypical radical intellectual: gifted, self-indulgent, and restless—with a penchant for politics.

Buonarroti was directed by his father to the study of law at Pisa,[3] and his earliest thoughts about radical social change may have occurred during his first voyage out of Tuscany to Marseilles in the summer of 1780. He was shocked by his discovery of urban poverty[4]— and perhaps also stimulated by the cosmopolitan atmosphere of the French Mediterranean port. Returning to study at Pisa, he fell under the spell of the Italian followers of Rousseau and Morelly who dominated the faculty.[5]

By late 1786, Buonarroti had chosen the public career characteristic of almost all revolutionaries: journalism. He founded a short-lived weekly journal in Florence which sought simultaneously to combat religious superstition in Tuscany and to awaken political consciousness. Published in French, the language of the Enlightenment, his *Journal Politique* was conceived "dans le goût des Gazettes Angloises," and appeared at the beginning of 1787 as

> . . . a collection of the deeds transpiring in the four corners of the World, and above all in Europe, seeking to inspire interest and to make one take note of the march of Nations to their greatness or decadence.[6]

By seeking "to talk politics (*politiquer*) with those who shall wish to listen to us,"[7] Italy would find the path to greatness. Buonarroti's journal praised both the new American constitution for its guarantees of religious and journalistic liberty, and the religious battles of the Jansenists and the Dutch republicans against the forces of tradition.[8] During the first days of the French Revolution, Buonarroti enthusiastically propagated the new ideas as an editor and bookseller in Leghorn, and he was exiled to Corsica early in 1790.

In the decade that followed, he refined into modern form the two central myths of the revolutionary tradition: belief in an uncompleted revolution and faith in a perfect alternative rooted in nature. The first myth he established through cultivating the memory of Babeuf and by pioneering a new approach to revolutionary organization. And he refined the myth of nature by carrying it beyond sentimentality into revolutionary practicality. This latter contribution, unrecognized even among Buonarrotian scholars, began with his stay in Corsica from 1790 to 1792. In these years, the very ones when Babeuf was first formulating his radical "agrarian law" in Picardy, Buonarroti discovered an idealized state of nature in rural Corsica (with occasional visits to Sardinia and other neighboring islands).[9] His *Patriotic Journal of Corsica* in 1790 [10] defended the French Revolution in Rousseauian terms, arguing that "general happiness" can be found only "in the state of nature" where alone we realize "the faculty of acting according to the determination of our will." [11]

His baptism by fire occurred during the Corsican years when he joined the campaign of revolutionary France against Sardinia in 1792. He became a propagandist-legislator for the only successful part of the expedition: the occupation of the small Island of San Pietro. Describing his function in that idyllic spot as "teaching the sweet doctrine of nature," [12] he drafted for it a model republican constitution, which he called *The Code of Nature*.

Faced with the general failure of the Sardinian expedition, Buonarroti left for Paris late in 1792. He had been one of the foreigners designated as citizens of the First French Republic. On April 29, 1793, Buonarroti argued successfully before the Convention in Paris for the incorporation of his island utopia into the French Republic under the new name of *Isola della Libertà*, the Island of Liberty.[13] Buonarroti's first arrival in Paris began a life-long infatuation. The revolutionary city seemed to him magically able to lift people out of their private pettiness into shared enthusiasm:

> I admired that metamorphosis by which long dominant personal interests were fused into a common interest that became the passion of all.[14]

He saw the main thing to fear as betrayal from within. In the only treatise that Buonarroti wrote during his first stay in Paris, *The Corsican Conspiracy Entirely Unmasked,* he warned the French people against creeping counter-revolution by "rich egoists" who were in fact "enemies of equality." [15] "Great treasons" arise from those who lacked "holy enthusiasm" for creating a new type of community. This pamphlet of 1794 was a savage denunciation of the alleged betrayal of the Corsican revolution by its supposed leader and hero General Paoli. Having led the original rebellion against Genoese tyranny, Paoli had returned to Corsica after a long exile and allied himself with the English in opposing the French-supported republicans. Paoli symbolized the revolutionary-turned-opportunist. Buonarroti denounced him as a type, and called for a new sort of man to complete the revolution. To prevent future Paoli's in France, he suggested—in a passage prophetic of future revolutionary history—that there was a "great need for a great purge." [16]

As the Reign of Terror descended on Paris, Buonarroti moved back onto the front lines of revolutionary advance into Italy. He joined Robespierre's younger brother Augustine and the young Napoleon Bonaparte with the French armies on the Italian Riviera early in 1794. On April 9, Buonarroti took charge of revolutionary rule in the Ligurian city of Oneglia. He began the "organization of the peace" by setting up a centralized system of "revolutionary agents" designed to mobilize the population against "agents of tyranny" still serving the Italian aristocracy and priesthood.[17]

Buonarroti's proclamation of May 9 to the people of Oneglia may be considered the first statement of his apocalyptical egalitarianism. He insisted that all men are created "equal, free, and to be happy" and that any distinction whatsoever is an open violation of the law of nature.[18] In Oneglia, the young aristocrat felt an exhilarating identity with the simple people. He incessantly used the term *sans culottes*, and affected penury by insisting when he was arrested that he possessed only one suit of clothes:

> I have never attached myself to any powerful person. I have always lived modestly, sometimes in poverty. . . . No one would dare say that I have ever loved money . . .[19]

Until the end of his days, he kept with him as a kind of talisman the certificate indicating that he had been admitted to *La Società Popolare* "after having undergone a purifying scrutiny." [20]

After helping to set up a new system of public instruction and a local Festival of the Supreme Being and of Nature, Buonarroti was arrested on March 5, 1795. In the Paris courtroom he defended his use of terror in Oneglia against "the enemies and émigrés that infested us," but stressed the pedagogic nature of his rule:

> . . . my manner of terrifying consisted in preaching our principles and interests to the inhabitants; in placing in their hands proclamations and books in their language in a familiar and intelligible style . . .[21]

In his successful defense he insisted that he "never belonged to any party." [22] He anticipated the authentic revolutionary posture of purporting to serve a universal cause beyond the petty, quarreling factions of the moment.

By 1796, Buonarroti had moved away entirely from his sentimental understanding of nature to a revolutionary concept of law and obligation.

> The law of nature differs essentially from what is called the state of nature. The first is the result of experience and reflection; the second, of first impressions and ignorance.[23]

He henceforth sought "to lead men back to nature" [24] not by following the mossy path "of the native living alone in the forests," [25] but by creating an egalitarian community in Paris itself. After his acquittal in 1795, Buonarroti joined the Babeuf conspiracy in an effort to realize "this sweet community." [26] He was rearrested with Babeuf and the other conspirators in 1797, imprisoned in Cherbourg, then sent to the Island of Re under close scrutiny before being permitted by Napoleon to move to Geneva in July 1806.[27]

Buonarroti remained in Geneva for the next seventeen years except for fourteen months he spent in Grenoble during 1813–14. He became the first in a long line of revolutionaries—culminating in Lenin—to use Switzerland, "the land of Jean-Jacques" as he called it,[28] as a secure mounting base for revolutionary activity.

The precise history of Buonarroti's activities during this period will probably never be known. He conceived of two successive secret organizations to command the international revolutionary movement: the

Sublime Perfect Masters and *Monde*. Neither organization appears to have had much substance, but Buonarroti's unremitting efforts inspired and at times guided the resistance to Napoleon. Some of his fellow Babeuvists were active in the intrigues of the Philadelphians, which culminated in the first serious republican attempt to overthrow Napoleon, led by General Claude-François Malet in 1808, and Buonarroti had direct contacts with the second, more formidable conspiracy of Malet in 1812.[29] Buonarroti's role was even greater in the revolutionary conspiracies that proliferated during the Restoration following the final defeat of Bonaparte.

Though Buonarroti never succeeded in formally enlisting many followers, his ideas influenced many young soldiers and students who had been politically awakened by the Napoleonic wars. Indeed, Buonarroti brought a certain Napoleonic quality to his own plans for revolution. Like Bonaparte, he had begun his political career as an obscure Franco-Italian on the Island of Corsica; and had been an early agent of French revolutionary expansion into Italy. At the end, on St. Helena, Napoleon paid grudging tribute to his revolutionary nemesis:

> He could have been very useful to me in organizing the Kingdom of Italy. He could have been a very good professor. He was a man of extraordinary talent: a descendant of Michelangelo, an Italian poet like Ariosto, writing French better than I, designing like David, playing the piano like Paesiello.[30]

Buonarroti did not, however, return the compliment. He wrote Babeuf's son that Bonaparte "delivered the *coup de grâce* to the revolution." [31] As he and his contemporaries struggled to keep revolutionary dedication alive under Napoleon, Buonarroti became ever more deeply imbued with romantic occultism. This very tendency to the occult owed, paradoxically, a good deal to Napoleon. Since Napoleon claimed to embody the Enlightenment, his revolutionary opposition cultivated anti-Enlightenment ideas. Since Napoleon posed as the bearer of universal rationalism—openly imposing the Code Napoléon, the metric system, and French administrative methods wherever he went—his opponents secretly fled to exotic fraternal organizations to nurse their protest. Since, moreover, Napoleon's opposition included extreme monarchists as well as extreme republicans, concepts of the Right often filtered into the programs of the Left.

The Masonic lodges of Geneva provided the ambiance in which Buonarroti formulated in 1811 his first full blueprint for a new society of revolutionary republicans: the Sublime Perfect Masters.[32] Both the society's name and the three levels of membership proposed for it had been adopted from Masonry. Indeed, Buonarroti sought to work through existing Masonic lodges: to recruit through them, influence them, use them as a cover, and (if necessary) even undermine them.

His final aim was the original Babeuvist one of putting into effect on a continental scale the revolutionary republican Constitution of 1793.[33] His colorful blueprint for doing so—rich in Masonic symbolism—provided the prototype for modern revolutionary organization. The society was secret and hierarchical. Only those in the inner circle were told that the organization sought radical social change as well as a republican constitution. Elaborate precautions of secrecy were increasingly taken. Printed forms signifying the grade of membership were to be burned—or if necessary swallowed—in case of detainment or danger.

Buonarroti's organization called for a morality of its own; a kind of moral Manicheanism within the revolutionary elect. They were the agents of good against evil, freedom against tyranny, equality versus egoism. His inner circle, the "great firmament" of Nature, was a political authority clearly superior to Napoleon, let alone other petty princelings.

The Milieu of Freemasonry

Although Buonarroti's revolutionary organization went far beyond any Masonic models, it was clearly influenced by his five-year immersion in Masonic meetings in Geneva. So great, indeed, was the general impact of Freemasonry in the revolutionary era that some understanding of the Masonic milieu seems the essential starting point for any serious inquiry into the occult roots of the revolutionary tradition.

Masonry imparted to the revolutionary tradition at birth the essential metaphor that revolutionaries used to understand their own mission down to the mid-nineteenth century: that of an architect building a new and better structure for human society. Masons believed they were recreating in their fraternal societies the "natural" condition of cooperation that prevailed among those earlier, artisan masons who shaped stones for a common building.

The progression of each "brother" from the stage of apprentice through journeyman to master required philosophical and philanthropic accomplishment rather than social status. "Free" masonry was, thus, a moral meritocracy—implicitly subversive within any static society based on a traditional hierarchy. Men of intelligence and ambition in the eighteenth century often experienced within Masonic lodges a kind of brotherhood among equals not to be found in the aristocratic society outside.

The rituals leading to each new level of membership were not, as is sometimes suggested, childish initiations. They were awesome rites of passage into new types of association, promising access to higher truths of Nature once the blindfold was removed in the inner room of the lodge. Each novice sought to become a "free" and "perfected" Mason capable of reading the plans of the "Divine Architect" for "rebuilding the temple of Solomon," and reshaping the secular order with moral force.

Masonry ritualized fraternity and provided upward mobility more easily than outside society. The Masonic title of "brother" fulfilled on the continent some of the function of blending bourgeoisie and aristocracy that was assumed in England by the envied term "gentleman." [34] In the Masonic milieu, normally conservative people could seriously entertain the possibility of Utopia [35]—or at least of a social alternative to the ancien régime. Philip of Orléans was the titular head of French Masonry (the Grand Orient); and most of the pro-revolutionary denizens of the cafés of the Palais-Royal were his Masonic "brothers."

In the early days of the revolution, Masonry provided much of the key symbolism and ritual—beginning with the Masonic welcome under a "vault of swords" of the king at the Hotel de Ville three days after the fall of the Bastille.[36] To be sure, most French Masons prior to the revolution had been "not revolutionaries, not even reformers, nor even discontent"; [37] and, even during the revolution, Masonry as such remained politically polymorphous: "Each social element and each political tendency could 'go masonic' as it wished." [38] But Masonry provided a rich and relatively nontraditional foraging ground for new national symbols (coins, songs, banners, seals), new forms of address (*tu, frère, vivat!*), and new models for civic organizations, particularly outside Paris.[39]

Most important for our story, Masonry was deliberately used by revolutionaries in the early nineteenth century as a model and a recruiting ground for their first conspiratorial experiments in political organization. Buonarroti was entirely typical in adopting the names of two Masonic lodges, "perfect equality" and "perfect union," for his first two revolutionary clusters in Geneva. These lodges had originated in the 1760s in opposition to absolute monarchy and aristocratic privilege respectively.[40] Buonarroti drew up his first blueprint for "the sublime perfect masters" during his active membership of 1806–13 in a lodge of "perfect equality" in Geneva,[41] and defined "perfect equality" as its goal. The lodges of "perfect union" left their impact on the revolutionary organization Union founded in 1813–14 in Grenoble during Buonarroti's visit there by his future collaborator Joseph Rey.

The Illuminist Model

If Freemasonry provided a general milieu and symbolic vocabulary for revolutionary organization, it was Illuminism that provided its basic structural model. The organizational plan that Buonarroti distilled from two decades of revolutionary experience in Geneva (and basically remained faithful to for the rest of his life) was simply lifted from the Bavarian Order of Illuminists. This radical and secular occultist movement was organized on three levels in a secret hierarchy: church, synod, and areopagite. Buonarroti's revolutionary version of this structure defined the "church" as the local cell headed by a "sage," who was alone linked with the regional "synod." The members of each synod ("the sublime elect") were headed by a "territorial deacon," who supervised the activities of all "churches" in the region. The highest "areopagite" grade (also called "the Great Firmament") sent out its own "mobile deacons" to control the synods and supervise propaganda and agitation.[42]

It may be well to trace in some detail the nature and impact of this baffling movement, because its influence was far from negligible and has been as neglected in recent times as it was exaggerated in an earlier era.

The Order of Illuminists was founded on May 1, 1776, by a professor of canon law at the University of Ingolstadt in Bavaria, Adam Weishaupt, and four associates. The order was secret and hierarchical, modeled on the Jesuits (whose long domination of Bavarian education ended with their abolition by the Papacy in 1773) and dedicated to Weishaupt's Rousseauian vision of leading all humanity to a new moral perfection freed from all established religious and political authority.

Weishaupt did not so much invite intellectuals to join his new pedagogic elite as taunt them to do so. He radiated contempt for men of the Enlightenment who "go into ecstacies over antiquity, but are themselves unable to do anything," [43] and insisted that "what is missing is the force to put into practice what has long been affirmed by our minds." [44]

That force was to come from an altogether new type of secret society, which would have "much more the characteristics of a militia in action than an order with initiations." [45] The purpose of ascending the Illuminist hierarchy was not so much to attain wisdom as to be remade into a totally loyal servant of a universal mission. "We cannot use people as they are, but begin by making them over." [46] Weishaupt's elaborate process of recruitment involved creating in the novices a psychological dependence on the process that was transforming them. "Insinuators" (those who brought in new members) were to proceed "little by little following detours":

> . . . giving birth first to imprecise and vague desires, then, when the candidate himself experiences them, show him the object that he will then seize upon with his own two hands.[47]

The "object" was the card pledging the new member's desire for admission to the next higher level of the order. At this point of eagerness, the "insinuator" became the "superior," and made it difficult for the newcomer to enter into the next circle. The "postulant" might indeed have to face intense scrutiny during a two-year "novitiate" and a thirty-page questionnaire asking him about everything from his taste in clothes to his position of sleeping in bed. This nerve-wracking process sought to mobilize a new elite whose purpose was

> . . . neither to conquer territories nor to impose authority, nor to gather riches . . . [but] the more difficult conquest of individuals. Their indifference, passive or obedient submission is not enough. Their total confidence without reservation, their enthusiasm, must be gained.[48]

The revolutionaries' primitive vision of the world as a dualistic struggle between the forces of darkness and of light may originate in the neo-Manichaean view of Weishaupt's followers that their elect group of "illuminated ones" was engaged in struggle with "the sons of darkness," their categorical name for all outside the order. The name for the order was initially uncertain (Perfectibilists was used and Bees considered); [49] but the name Illuminist was apparently chosen from the image of a sun radiating illumination to outer circles. At the very center within the inner circle of Areopagites burned a candle symbolizing the solar source of all illumination. The Zoroastrian-Manichaean cult of fire was central to the otherwise eclectic symbolism of the Illuminists; their calendar was based on Persian rather than classical or Christian models. [50]

Pseudonyms and symbols, which had precise esoteric significance in Masonic lodges, became deliberate instruments of camouflage for the Illuminists. Ingolstadt was both Eleusis and Ephesus; Munich was Athens; Vienna, Rome. Weishaupt's own Illuminist name of Spartacus, the leader of a slave revolt in ancient Rome, provided a hint of revolutionary commitment; but his original key collaborators took the names of the Greek Ajax and the Egyptian Danaus respectively, and other names ranged from Tamerlane to Confucius. [51]

The Illuminists attempted to use the ferment and confusion in Freemasonry for their own ends. Weishaupt joined a Masonic lodge in Munich in 1777; and attempted to recruit "commandos" (groups of followers) from within the lodges of the Bavarian capital. Late in 1780, Weishaupt's campaign spread to all of Germany and to the pseudo-knightly higher orders of Masonry with the entrance into Weishaupt's inner circle of Baron Adolph Knigge. He was a native of Hanover and a leader of occultism in Frankfurt, which soon replaced Munich as the leading "colony" of the movement. For five intensive years (until Knigge left the order in July 1785), the Illuminists recruited largely among those who had belonged to the most popular of the German higher Masonic orders, the Strict Observance. The Illuminist technique was, first of all, to discredit the more conservative rival order by fair means (helping the conference of occult orders at Wilhelmsbad in 1782 to determine that the Strict Observance Lodges were not in fact descended from the Knights-Templars) and foul (arguing that the Strict Observance Lodges were secretly controlled by "unknown superiors" who were in fact Jesuits in disguise). [52]

The Illuminists coöpted the organizational structure of their conservative Masonic rival; in the process, they acquired some of the mysterious allure that they had not possessed as an arid cult of rationalistic intellectuals. Illuminism also became much more political.

Weishaupt appears to have initially seen Masonry as a kind of intermediate training ground for Illuminists—after they had entered the order but before they joined the secret inner circles. [53] Then, under Knigge's guidance, he developed a system of three successive "classes" that incorporated all existing "grades" of Masonry as preliminary to a higher class of Illuminist grades. The first two classes (the preparatory and the middle) incorporated the three traditional grades and the higher symbolic grades of Masonry respectively.

The third or "administrative" class was the most original—and indicated by its very name the political implications of Weishaupt's plan for the moral renovation of humanity. Its first two grades, those of "small secrets" and "great secrets" respectively, led up to the third and highest grade: the Areopagites, where all the ultimately irrelevant symbols were discarded for the pure reign of natural liberty and equality. Within this final grade—totally secret from all others—the "ennobling of motives" [54] was complete, the social contract was restored, and a new "inner politics" would provide both the nucleus and the model for a transformed world. These divisions within the Illuminist hierarchy were popularly described in ecclesiastical terms. The first two classes encompassing all past Masonic stages were the "Church"; the first two grades of the administrative class, the "Synod"; and the final, Areopagite stage represented man freed from all authority to live in egalitarian harmony.

This promise of total liberation terrified the German-speaking world, and the order was subjected to ridicule, persecution, and formal dissolution during 1785–87. Weishaupt was banished to Gotha and kept under surveillance. But the diaspora of an order that had reached a membership of perhaps two thousand five hundred [55] at its height in the early 1780s led to a posthumous impact that was far greater throughout Europe than anything the order had been able to accomplish during its brief life as a movement of German intellectuals. In France, the publication by the Bavarian police of Weishaupt's correspondence and other documents in 1787 created more fascination than fear. The *Essay on the Sect of Illuminists*, published the following year by the brother of a former functionary of the Prussian court, intrigued rather than horrified. Even the erotic imagination of the Palais-Royal could not have improved on the description of an alleged Illuminist initiation: Marks were made with blood on the prostrate nude body of the candidate. His testicles were bound by a pink and poppy-colored cordon; and he renounced all other human allegiances before five white-hooded phantoms with bloody banners after a "colossal figure" appeared through a fire. Finally, the bands and marks were removed, and he was accepted into the higher order by drinking blood before seven black candles.[56]

The decisive book in popularizing the Illuminist ideal was Count Mirabeau's *The Prussian Monarchy under Frederick the Great*, which also appeared in 1788. Written in large part by a former Illuminist, Jakob Mauvillon, Mirabeau's work distinguished rationalistic Illuminists from "mystical" occultists, hailing the former as leaders of a movement the "great aim" of which was "the improvement of the present system of governments and legislations." [57] Mirabeau took much of his new, totalistic concept of "the revolution" directly from Illuminist models; he almost certainly transmitted something of this ideal to his influential protégés, Camille Desmoulins and Etienne Dumont (the friend and protector of Thomas Paine in London), who served successively as his personal secretary.

Nicholas Bonneville was, however, the decisive channel of Illuminist influence. He was converted to Illuminist ideas during the first of two visits to Paris (in June 1787) by Weishaupt's leading associate in the final political stage of Illuminism, Christian Bode. A friend of Lessing who had come to win Frenchmen away from their own drift into conservative occultism, Bode apparently converted the German-speaking Bonneville (then working as a lawyer for the Parlement) to a faith that combined Illuminist symbols and radical ideas of popular sovereignty.[58] Bonneville immediately began his unsuccessful attempt to convert Condorcet to the more active faith, hailing the imminent coming of "the People-King," the liberating "flame of the world" foreseen by the "sage" Rousseau.[59]

Bonneville saw popular liberation as a kind of blindfolded mass entry into an Illuminist sanctuary:

> Take away from the people the bandage that covers their eyes. . . . Place the hand of the People on the veil . . . it will soon be torn aside.[60]

Accused by contemporaries of making "the title of Citizen a grade of Illuminism," [61] Bonneville argued in Illuminist terms that "the integral man is God," and that from the center of the social circle there will

> . . . emanate a *circle of light* which will uncover for us that which is hidden in the symbolic chaos of masonic innovations.[62]

In his massive study of 1788, *The Jesuits Driven from Free Masonry*, Bonneville developed the basic idea of Weishaupt and Bode that Masonry had been infiltrated by Jesuits, who had to be driven out by some new order opposed to tyrants and priests. Bonneville's version of the Illuminist ideal interested figures as widely removed as Saint-Just and Desmoulins in Picardy and Dietrich and Schneider in Strasbourg.[63] The substantial German influx into Paris itself included former Illuminists like the Saxon physician of Philip of Orléans, Jean-Geoffrey Saiffert, the Frey brothers, and the journalist Rebmann.[64] Occult—possibly Illuminist—influence is detectable in Babeuf's first clear statement of his communist objectives early in 1795—inviting a friend to "enter into the sacred mysteries of agrarianism" and accepting fidelity from a *chevalier de l'ordre des égaux*.[65] Babeuf's subsequent first outline for his conspiracy spoke of a "circle of adherents" "advancing by degree" from *les pays limotrophes* to transform the world.[66] Babeuf's secret, hierarchical organization resembled that of the Illuminists and of Bonneville. The strange absence of references by Babeuf and the others to the man who formulated their ultimate objectives, Sylvain Maréchal, could be explained by the existence of an Illuminist-type secrecy about the workings of the inner group.[67] The conspirators may have viewed Maréchal as the "flame" at the center of the "circle." As such, he would have had to be protected by the outer circle against disclosure to profane outsiders. His mysterious designation of Paris as "Atheopolis" and himself as *l'HSD* (*l'homme sans dieu*) represented precisely the ideal of Weishaupt's inner Areopagites: man made perfect as a god-without-God.

As for Buonarroti (who codified the legend of Babeuf and first revealed Maréchal's role), he had been fascinated with Illuminism even before the revolution. Already in 1787, he drew ideas from Mirabeau and noted the struggle of Illuminism with Catholicism in Bavaria.[68] A hint that Buonarroti may even have been committed to Illuminism is provided in

a forgotten journal of 1789 by a group of young Italians who had been
influenced by Illuminism while studying in Bavaria. Excited by the
political news from France, these students drew up plans in Innsbruck
("Samos") to set up a journal capable of promoting the total transformation of humanity set forth in the Illuminist ideal. Late in 1789, they
published in Sondrio, on the Italian side of the Alps, a journal that may
well have been the first ideological revolutionary organ of modern
times: *Political Appendix to all the gazettes and other news sheets*. . . .

The journal purported to move beyond politics, by providing a kind of
pedagogic guide for the revolutionary reading of all other publications.
The editors insisted: .

> The Appendix is not a gazette, but rather a reasoned course of Legisla-
> tion, of Government, of Political Economy, applied to the present revolu-
> tions of Europe.[69]

Its ideal was "happy equality"[70] as "preached by the citizen of Geneva"[71] and embodied in a "social constitution."[72] This ideal clearly
went beyond the purely *political* reading of Rousseau favored among
French politicians of the revolutionary era. The more radical social
ideal had released on Europe "the energy of the winds, which are
bursting forth violently against oppression."[73]

The first issue praised the Weishaupt-Mirabeau concept of a "revolution of the mind" as the proper objective of the "century of the illuminated."[74] It identified this type of revolution with the Bavarian Illuminists ("the company which Count Mirabeau has compared to the Priests
of Eleusis"),[75] and distinguished their ideal from spiritualist distortions. The editor followed the Illuminist practice of adopting a pretentious pseudonym, "Lazzaro Jona" (suggesting perhaps Lazarus, Jonah,
and the return of truth from death), and hailed as a friend "Abraham
Levi Salomon," the "recorder" (*estensore*) of the *Patriotic Journal of
Corsica*.[76] A footnote identified this figure as "the cavalier Buonarroti,"
a "man of spirit."[77] Since Buonarroti is the only contemporary Italian
mentioned by name in the journal, Buonarroti would seem to have had
some special connection with the *Appendix* as well as with the *Patriotic
Journal*, "the first revolutionary journal in Italian,"[78] which he
launched soon after being banished to Corsica in October 1789. Certainly there is stylistic and substantive continuity between Buonarroti's
Journal Politique of 1787 and the short-lived *Appendix* and *Patriotic
Journal*. The second and final number of the *Appendix* spoke of a forthcoming special issue that would provide "a political course on the Revolution in France and the affairs of the other powers."[79] But this issue
never appeared, and Buonarroti soon immersed himself in revolutionary
activity within France.

Gioacchino Prati, a young student from Trentino who later became
one of Buonarroti's closest collaborators, traced the Illuminist connection when he contended that Buonarroti's first revolutionary organization, the Sublime Perfect Masters, "was instituted during the first
French Revolution" and was "composed of four concentric circles"—
each with its own secret profession of faith.[80] The outer circle was

designed to attract "the large mass of Liberals, who, like the Radicals, strive for universal suffrage and popular institutions." Inside was a secret, second circle composed of "staunch democrats." The final, inner circle was unknown to the others and pledged to absolute egalitarianism.

Whether or not Buonarroti was in effect propagating an Illuminist program during his revolutionary activity of the 1790s, he had clearly internalized a number of Illuminist ideas well before the massive borrowing in his revolutionary blueprint of 1810–11. He had adopted the Illuminist pretension of recovering a natural religion known only to "Illuminated" sects in the past. He saw himself as "reintegrating" "in its ancient forms the religion of nature, reason" [81] by reviving the legacy of a bizarre genealogy: "the Persians of Cyrus, the initiators of Egyptian priests, the holy Hermandad of Spain, the apostolate of Jesus, the Anabaptists, and above all the Jesuit order." [82] He followed Weishaupt and Bonneville in attaching special importance to the Jesuits, whom he sought both to imitate and to liquidate. His secret ideal was from the beginning, according to Prati, the egalitarian Illuminist one of breaking down all "marks of private property."

> Let the Republic be the sole proprietor; like a mother, it will afford to each of its members equal education, food and labour.
>
> This is the only regeneration aimed at by philosophers. This is the only rebuilding of Jerusalem. . . .[83]

Such borrowings from Illuminism seem substantial enough to challenge the long-accepted judgment of the leading student of the subject that, after 1790, Illuminism "having disappeared from history . . . lived on only in legend." [84] There seems good reason to believe that Illuminist influence was not so much a "legend" as an imperfectly perceived reality.[85] The same historian's perplexed observation that "the police legend" about Illuminists began to "develop with more amplitude and originality" in the Napoleonic era [86] points to a surprising source of Illuminist influence. Illuminist ideas influenced revolutionaries not just through left-wing proponents, but also through right-wing opponents. As the fears of the Right became the fascination of the Left, Illuminism gained a paradoxical posthumous influence far greater than it had exercised as a living movement.

The Pythagorean Passion

As we have seen, a vast array of labels and images was taken from classical antiquity to legitimize the new revolutionary faith. Two relatively neglected names were central to the development of an ideal identity among revolutionary intellectuals: the image of the revolutionary as a modern Pythagoras and of his social ideal as Philadelphia. These two labels illustrated the proto-romantic reaching for a distant Greek ideal as a lofty alternative to the Roman images of power and conquest that had dominated France as it moved like ancient Rome from republic to empire under Napoleon. Pythagoras and Philadelphia represented a kind of distillation of the high fraternal ideals common both to the occult brotherhoods of Masonry and Illuminism and to the idealistic youthful mobilization to defend the revolution in 1792–94. The two labels recur like leitmotifs amidst the cacophony of shifting ideals and groups during the recession of revolutionary hopes at the end of the eighteenth century and the beginning of the nineteenth.

Precisely during this dark period the modern revolutionary tradition was born—echoing the romantic Napoleonic belief that all things were possible, but looking for a lost Hellenic ideal rather than to the recovered Roman empire of the new Caesar.

Pythagoras, the semi-legendary Greek philosopher, provided a model for the intellectual-turned-revolutionary. He became a kind of patron saint for romantic revolutionaries, who needed new symbols of secular sanctity.

According to tradition, the great geometrician of antiquity was driven from Samos, Greece, in the sixth century B.C. to Crotona in Southern Italy, where he allegedly founded a religious-philosophical brotherhood to transform society. Radical intellectual reformers throughout antiquity periodically revived and embellished this tradition. Neo-Pythagoreans flourished in Alexandria in the second century B.C.; and a later group of Pythagoreans produced Apollonius of Tyana in the first century A.D., a wonder-working sage who was in his time a major rival to Christ. Though organized movements faded away, Pythagorean ideas recurred in medieval Christianity, which for a time represented Pythagoras as a hidden Jewish link between Moses and Plato.

An undercurrent of fascination with Pythagorean thought in the High Renaissance and Enlightenment came to the surface during the French Revolution. Weishaupt's final blueprint for politicized Illuminism, written during the first year of the French Revolution, was entitled *Pythagoras*; and, as extremists sought some simple yet solid principles on which to rebuild society, they increasingly turned for guidance to Pythagorean beliefs in prime numbers and geometric forms. Early, romantic revolutionaries sought occult shortcuts to the inner truths of nature, and repeatedly attached importance to the central prime numbers of Pythagorean mysticism: 1, 3, 7, and above all 5. Pamphleteers of the Right suggested that prime numbers provided a secret organizational code for revolutionaries; one particularly ingenious effort of 1797 derived the entire structure of revolutionary history from the number 17. Bonneville had begun the fad on the Left, suggesting even before the revolution that the number 17 held the key to understanding the Jesuits' secret take-over of Masonry.[87]

However bizarre it may appear to later revolutionaries and historians alike, this Pythagorean passion seriously influenced the organizational activities of the first revolutionaries. We have seen how the Illuminists made the first halting efforts systematically to use the forms of occult Masonry for ulterior conspiracy—pointing the way for Bonneville, Buonarroti, and the early professional revolutionaries. But the wild profusion of exotic symbols and higher orders also fed a much broader and more open impulse: the search for simple forms of nature to serve as a touchstone for truth amidst the crumbling authority of tradition. The increasingly manic search for simple, geometric harmonies within Masonry in the 1770s and 1780s reveals the radical thirst for revolutionary simplification at its purest.

This quest for legitimizing simplicity spilled out of closed lodges into open assemblies in 1780. Occultists became politicians, and made special use of the two most important Pythagorean geometric symbols— the circle and the triangle—in dramatizing their challenge to established power. These two forms became symbols of divinity in medieval Christianity.[88] They increasingly dominated the hieroglyphics of the higher Masonic orders [89]—and the imagination of prerevolutionary utopian architects who often sought to build only with "geometric figures from the triangle to the circle." [90] Since many early leaders of the revolution saw themselves as mason-architects, they felt some affinity with this ongoing campaign to combat the aristocratic rococo style with the "rule of geometry." Reassured by Newton's law of gravity about the circular harmony of the universe, they felt that man's mastery of mathematical laws made him "possessor of the secret of the solar universe" destined to organize human society rationally.[91] At the same time, the proto-romantic philosophy of German occultism inspired many to see man not as a cog but as a dynamic "living point destined to become a circle" [92] with a "field of vision comparable to a circle whose circumference grows without end." [93]

But before borders could expand, monuments had to be built in the center. The architectural plans for Paris during the early months of the revolution reveal a special fascination with the three-dimensional forms of the triangle and circle: the pyramid and the sphere. Two of the most important monuments proposed in 1791—to the glory of the French nation on the Bastille and to the memory of Mirabeau—were independently designed as giant pyramids.[94] The pyramid form became even more popular after Napoleon's return from Egypt, though it was soon superseded in public places by the more elongated obelisk. Even before the revolution, utopian architects had felt drawn to "the sublime magnificence of the sphere." The pure form reappeared in the sketch for a Newton Memorial (a sphere with nothing inside except a small grave lit from a single beam of sunlight), a necropolis for the revolution (an empty globe in the middle of a cemetery), and a proposed Temple of Equality (a huge sphere on columns containing a smaller sphere inside).[95]

The Circle

The later Pythagoreans had been the first school of classical antiquity systematically to contend that the earth and universe were spherical in shape and finite in form. Numbers and music expressed the hidden harmonies of an ultimately spherical natural perfection. The central reality of human life was the transmigration of human souls from one body to another—all moving in cycles like the universe itself. Eighteenth-century Pythagoreans were specially excited by the Illuminist idea of progressive human purification from the lower cycles of animal nature to the heavenly spheres of pure intelligence. The Illuminists' hierarchy of circles—moving inward from "church" to "synod" to the Areopagite center—suggested the concentric circles in the universe itself. The flame at the center of the final, inner circle was assumed to be an image of the inner fire of the universe around which the earth and all planets revolved.

Occultists may not have always believed in such images literally, but they did usually feel that some secret inner circle held out the promise of both personal redemption and cosmic understanding. Added to this traditional belief in an esoteric higher wisdom was the new promise of German romanticism for liberation. The concept of a charmed inner circle gave a spatial dimension to the romantic longing for liberty. The life of "the circle" was one of liberation—freeing oneself even from bodily limitations for life in the heavenly spheres, freeing society from the constraints of inherited tradition.

Weishaupt appears to have been the first to use the term "circle" to designate a new type of political organization making both individual moral demands and universal ideological claims. Weishaupt described his recruitment of Illuminists from within Masonic lodges in Munich as "the progress of the ⊙" in the political area. He introduced italicized variants of the Latin word (*circul, circl*) into his German writings to explain the politicization of the movement, which he propagated by means of "circulars" and "circulation." [96]

The idea of circles was central to the caricature of Illuminism by Marquis de Luchet no less than to Bonneville's imitation of it. In two key chapters of his exposé, Luchet described the "circle" as the key nine-man cell of conspiracy: the "administrative committee" for an altogether new type of human society in which "each member of a circle belongs equally to all the others" and "has broken all the links which attach him to society." [97] The conservative Rosicrucians who dominated the Prussian court after the accession of Frederick William II in 1786, created their own rival conception of a nine-man *Zirkel*. Propagators of the Illuminist ideal variously tried to attack the Rosicrucian "circles of corruption" [98] and/or to incorporate them into their own plans for occult "circulation." [99]

We have already seen how Bonneville envisaged a global transformation on the Illuminist model through "magic circles" radiating the ideas of his central "social circle" out to the entire CERCLE DU PEUPLE FRANC. With the recession of revolutionary expectations in the late 1790s, Bonneville (and his associates like Thomas Paine and Sylvain Maréchal) clung—like Weishaupt in exile before them—to the image of oneself as Pythagoras: an exiled but "relevant" intellectual building a new brotherhood of deliverance for the future.

Bonneville even before the revolution had traced the Illuminist ideal to Pythagoras, who "brought from the orient his system of true Masonic instruction to illuminate the occident." [100] After the demise of his effort to "square the social circle" [101] via his organizations of the early 1790s, Bonneville wrote verses on "the numbers of Pythagoras," [102] proclaiming that "man is God" and will "become angelic" by widening the circle of universal brotherhood:

> O Cercle Social!
> Espoir toujours plus doux, d'un pacte général;
> Des peuples opprimés ta ligue fraternelle
> Jura la délivrance, entière, universelle.

> O Social Circle!
> Ever sweet hope of a general pact;
> Thy brotherhood of oppressed peoples
> Has sworn eternal, universal deliverance.

As romantic hyperbole mounted, Bonneville immolated himself figuratively on the altar of primitive Germanic purity and the solar myth of revolution. The idealized "people" had become

> Libre et pur comme l'air, et dans ma république,
> Tout est fraternité, parenté germanique. . . .

> Soleil d'un autre monde, et dans ta Majesté
> D'un nouvel Univers sois la Divinité . . .
> Je brûle. . . .[103]

> Free and pure as air, and in my republic,
> All is brotherhood, German parenthood. . . .

> Sun of another world, in thy Majesty
> Become the divinity of another Universe . . .
> I am burning. . . .

Thomas Paine, who lived in a *ménage à trois* with Bonneville and his wife from 1797 to 1802, believed that the Druids and Pythagoreans had combined to provide an occult ideological alternative to Christianity. *An Essay on the Origin of Free Masonry*, written after his return to America (with Bonneville's wife) and immediately translated into French by Bonneville, insisted that the natural sun worship of the Druids had not been destroyed but merely diverted into Masonry.

At its apogee of influence in 1792, the Social Circle began to publish new crypto-revolutionary works by the high priest of mysticism from Lyon, Louis-Claude de Saint-Martin. This long-time foe of the Enlightenment had suddenly discovered in the mysterious chaos of revolution the possibility of building a new Jerusalem by means of Pythagorean forms and numbers. "A radiant sun has detached itself from the firmament and come to rest over Paris, from whence it spreads universal light." The "new man" can perceive that light by contemplating concentric circles that converge on a point within the flame of a lighted candle, thereby "reintegrating" himself with the primal elements of air, earth, and water. As man moves toward pure spirit, revolutionary democracy will become "deocracy." [104]

The image of Pythagoras as the heroic model for all revolutionaries was most fully developed in the great valedictory work of Sylvain Maréchal: his monumental, six-volume *Voyages of Pythagoras* in 1799.[105]

Maréchal's Pythagoras urged armed uprising ("not with words [but with] bow and arrow"),[106] invoking a metaphor that was to become a classic of revolutionary rhetoric:

> It is necessary to seize the suitable moment . . . with the smallest spark a great fire can be ignited . . .[107]

The ideal of the heirs of Pythagoras is:

> Own everything in common, nothing for yourself . . . the equality of nature . . . the republic of equals.[108]

The final volume of *Voyages*, listing 3506 alleged "laws of Pythagoras," under "Revolutions" advises that

> . . . the history of an entire people often lies entirely in the life of a handful of men.[109]

That "handful of men," who enabled the revolutionary tradition to survive Napoleonic oppression, were very different from the dramatis personae of most history books. They were not—as we have seen—political–military leaders, but journalist–intellectuals; they were influenced not so much by the rationalism of the French Enlightenment as by the occultism of the early German romanticism. Maréchal's work was widely distributed in the German-speaking world; [110] but, prophetically for the future, it was most appreciated in the distant Russian Empire in the atmosphere of vague religiosity and unfocused reformism under Tsar Alexander I. Beginning in 1804, Maréchal's *Voyages* began to appear in official government journals in a Russian translation at the rate of one volume a year. Another Russian journal concurrently published 150 "rules of Pythagoras," taken from Maréchal's sixth volume.[111] Maréchal's Russian promoter was a protégé of the imprisoned occultist, Nicholas Novikov, whose pseudonym was "lover of truth" and whose secret gatherings in the late eighteenth century had begun the *kruzhkovshchina* (mania for circles) of the modern Russian radical tradition.[112]

The dream of a revolutionary Pythagorean organization animated the first flush of youthful political activity in the Russian Empire after the defeat of Napoleon. A student group in Vilnius held nocturnal meetings in spots of natural beauty, listening to the occult wisdom of an "arch-illuminated" visitor from an inner circle; and the tradition of "free Pythagoreans" spread throughout the Polish-influenced regions of the empire.[113] In the Western Ukraine, three young Russians formed a "society of Pythagoras" in May, 1818, and drew up "rules of the Pythagorean sect." [114] They proposed the classical three concentric circles of membership, the third representing Plato's Republic. From this group eventually came the Society of the United Slavs, which sought to realize this Hellenic ideal throughout the Slavic world, and russified the three grades of membership into "brothers, men and boyars." [115]

Early Russian radicals often argued in terms of rival laws of Pythagoras—some stressing the "two laws of Pythagoras" forbidding private property and requiring shared ownership; others stressing the "rule" that weapons and friendship could conquer all; others insisting on the primacy of moral perfection over legal reform: "Do not create laws for the people; create people for the laws." [116]

One of the earliest circles to feed into the Decembrist revolt of 1825 was the still-mysterious Green Lamp. One of its leaders wrote for the society a utopian picture of St. Petersburg three hundred years in the future, where Tsarism and Orthodoxy have, in effect, been overthrown by Pythagorean forms. There is a circular temple with a plain, white marble altar and an open arch. Music is the only art medium permitted. A phoenix with an olive branch has replaced the decapitated two-headed eagle (the two heads of the imperial seal, allegedly representing despotism and superstition).[117] Alexander Pushkin, the greatest of Russian poets, referred to the Green Lamp as a circle in which "beloved equality sat in Phrygian cap by a round table." [118] Though not so deeply involved in occultist revolutionary circles as his Polish counterpart, Adam Mickiewicz, Pushkin shared his fascination with the dedication and sacrifice that seemed to be found only within a magic circle of youthful revolutionaries. The "circle" was, in short, the supreme symbol of what a Russian Masonic song of the period called

> Those truths of holy law
> Given you by Geometry.[119]

The Triangle

Seeking some secure way to enlist those outside their inner circles, revolutionaries found inspiration in another key Pythagorean symbol: the triangle. If the circle suggested the objective—the egalitarian perfection of nature—the triangle suggested the way to get there.

The triangle, a key symbol for all Masons, had particular meaning for Pythagoreans as the simplest means of enclosing a surface with straight lines. The triangle expressed harmonic relationships (such as that of the Pythagorean theorem) and became a key symbol in revolutionary iconography. The revolutionary trilogy (Liberty, Equality, Fraternity) and the tricolor (red, white, and blue) each adorned one side of the omnipresent triangle on seals and stamps.

Pythagorean occultism gave added importance to the symbol. Franz von Baader's influential *On the Pythagorean Square in Nature* of 1798 suggested that the three elements of nature—fire, water, and earth— had to be energized by an "all-animating principle" or "point of sunrise," represented as a dot in the center of an equilateral triangle $\triangle$.[120] Any letter, symbol, or maxim that a revolutionary group wished to venerate specially was given this central place of occult authority within the inevitable triangular seal.[121]

Maréchal introduced the occult idea of triangular harmonies into his "CHARTER OF THE HUMAN RACE" in 1793, announcing the three-fold duties of man to be a father, son, and husband as "traced by Nature on man": "a triangle beyond which he dare not pass with impunity." [122] This seemingly traditional ideal is revalidated for the liberated "man without God" by seeing him as a kind of secular trinity: three persons in his own substance. Maréchal often placed his own atheistic sobriquet HSD inside a triangle.

In building their nuclear organizations, early revolutionaries showed a mania for triangular forms. The original Illuminist idea of a nine-man inner circle was soon discarded as too susceptible to police penetration, and subsequent plans for reorganization broke the circles down into three-man "triangles." [123] One man from an inner group was to recruit two from an outer group for apprenticeship; and an almost indefinite chain of interconnected organizations could then be formed. Any one member need know only two others—from one other group either below or above—outside his three-man cell.

This process of triangulation may not have been implemented by the Illuminists—or even conceived by them. The alleged Illuminist plans were published by the Bavarian government as part of an exposé, and may have been edited to appear more incriminating.[124] But whether the Right invented this tactic of the Left or merely publicized it, it was soon adopted in revolutionary circles. This intimate and relatively secure triangular form of organization has recurred in modern times: in Vietnam, Algeria, and even the Soviet Union.[125] Shortly after his arrival in Geneva in 1806, Buonarroti and his friends took the lead. His program of 1808–9 for the Sublime Perfect Masters was saturated with triangular symbols. The sign of the grade was ⊙; [126] and the altar in the sanctuary to which a new member was brought was only one point in a triangle of shrines. The other two points represented the ocean (of new life, the element of water) and the volcano (or revolution, the element of earth).[127] To the east, behind the altar-ocean-volcano triangle, three candles burned in a candelabrum in the form of an equilateral triangle beneath a semicircle signifying the equator (which in turn signified the circling of the entire globe and the perfection of eternity).[128]

The three men who faced this symbolic picture of the universe may have provided the model for Buonarroti's triumvirate form of organization. At the center of this human triangle facing the symbolic triangles was the North Star, leader of the other two Grand Stars. The Polar Star was clearly the one to steer by, and it became a favorite label for revolutionary journals.

Under the assumed name of Camille, Buonarroti joined the mildly pro-republican Masonic lodge of Sincere Friends in Geneva in order to recruit revolutionaries. However, he was under surveillance, and the lodge was infiltrated by police and shut in 1811. He then tried to continue its meetings secretly, apparently reorganizing it with expanded participation of the military under the new name Triangle.[129] Nothing more is known of this organization, but the choice of name and the circumstances of police repression may indicate the beginning of triangular organization.

Such a system of interlocking secret cells was apparently used in the first major plot to kill a king in post-Napoleonic Europe: the Spanish Triangle Conspiracy of 1816.[130] Like Buonarroti's associates, restless young Spaniards were in transition from conspiring against Napoleon toward a broader concept of combating monarchs of all kinds. The Sublime Perfect Masters must have been sympathetic, even if they were not connected, with the Spaniards' attempt to kill the restored Ferdinand VII, who had rejected the liberal Constitution of 1812 and reinstituted the Inquisition.

This triangular method of organization remained a basic means of enforcing conspiratorial security throughout the 1830s; and was translated back into Germany in the statutes of 1836 for the first revolutionary organization of German émigrés in Paris: the League of Outlaws. From its local "tents" to its central "campfire," this progenitor of the original League of Communists kept various levels of organization ignorant of one another. One man in each large group formed the connecting triangle with one other secret representative from a group at his own level and one connecting representative to both of them from a higher level.[131]

The Philadelphian Fantasy

The new secular revolutionary, then, found a model in Pythagoras (the action-oriented intellectual), a starting place in the circle (the microcosm of perfection), and a building tool in the triangle (the basic unit of organization). But what was he building? What was the macrocosm that the next and final revolution would reveal?

The answer was, quite simply, a universal community of brotherly love, which revolutionaries designated by its Greek name, Philadelphia. The Circle of Philadelphians, conceived in 1797 and constructed some years later, was the first important revolutionary organization to arise in France after the suppression of the Babeuf conspiracy. It epitomized the occult conspiracies of the Napoleonic era and anticipated the larger revolutionary movements of the 1810s and 1820s.

The name Philadelphia provided both the sanction of revelation and the promise of revolution. Two lost cities of antiquity had been called Philadelphia: one in the Holy Land near present-day Amman, the other in Asia Minor and mentioned in the Book of Revelation. But the word also suggested William Penn's idealized "green countrie towne" in Pennsylvania, whence came the revolution that established the United States of America in 1776. In the years leading up to the French Revolution, the word acquired further evocative associations from both the deepening occultism of the Old World and the continuing ferment of the New.

The word Philadelphia entered French Masonry during a rising tide of occult influx from Germany with the founding of a Primitive Rite of Philadelphians in Narbonne in 1780.[132] The Germanic order of Strict Observance, with its chivalric imagery and hermetic teachings, had swept into France through Strasbourg on to Bordeaux in the late 1770s; and the German-sponsored Rectified Scottish Rite established itself in Lyon as the leading occult order in France,[133] causing contemporaries to describe the Lyonnais as "our Germans," whom "obscurity does not bother." [134]

The attempt of the Narbonne group to proclaim a primitive rite was pressed farthest in Paris in the remarkable, proto-romantic lodge of the Nine Sisters. German influences again predominated through the founder of the lodge, a Swiss Protestant pastor, Court de Gébelin. From his first arrival in Paris from Berne in 1763 until his death in a mesmerist bath in 1784, Court preceded Herder in glorifying the German language and seeking the secrets of nature in the sounds of primitive speech.[135] In 1773 he published the first of nine volumes of a megalomanic inventory of sounds, signs, and symbols: *Monde primitif analysé et comparé avec le monde moderne.* By the third volume, he moved from lamenting man's lost happiness to insisting that unity "among nations" could be rediscovered through a primordial language in which vowels were sensations; consonants, ideas; and all writing, hieroglyphic.[136] On July 5, 1776, he founded the radical, occultist Nine Sisters, which became a kind of "UNESCO of the Eighteenth Century," attracting 180 members including 40 foreigners within two years.[137] Reading Court's *Monde primitif* became part of its ritual; and by the eighth volume Court advocated "a single political order . . . a single grammar of physics and morality . . . an eternal and immutable religion which creates perfection in man." He rejected "words" for "things"—by implication radical social reform.[138]

The occultism of the Old World blended with the revolutionism of the New through two of Court's closest associates in Paris: Benjamin Franklin and M. L. E. Moreau de Saint-Mery. Franklin, who arrived in Paris from the real Philadelphia just before Christmas in the revolutionary year 1776, was initiated by Court into the Nine Sisters, became its Venerable Master,[139] and collaborated with Court on the lodge's fifteen-volume collection of political miscellany. The Nine Sisters subsequently printed the constitutions of all thirteen American states and became, in effect, "the first school of constitutionalism that ever existed in Europe." [140]

Moreau de Saint-Mery, who was secretary of the educational arm of the Nine Sisters, conveyed back across the Atlantic to Cap-Français in Haiti a magical faith in the transforming power of science which rivaled the faith in voodoo of the oppressed natives. In 1784, Moreau and his brother-in-law founded the Circle of Philadelphians, praising the city of Franklin ("destined to become the metropole of a great Empire") and disassociating their circle from all traditional literary societies or academies. They used the language of occult Masonry in referring to the "last degree of perfection," and the restoration of an "ancient knighthood (*chevalerie*)" "to unveil the truth." [141] The Philadelphians claimed a radical secular identity as an "ideal little society, an image of the great future society" with "perfect equality . . . no rank, no precedence," and a commitment to the civic education and advancement of the native Creoles.[142]

In the occult circles of this lush colony it was easy to contend somewhat patronizingly that "France needs a revolution. But . . . it must be enveloped in mystery." [143] The Philadelphians became revolutionary leaders in Cap-Français during 1789–91 before the blacks rose up in July 1791, and other white colonists turned against them. They later reminisced that

> We took the intoxicating cup of novelty without realizing that it contained poison that would tear up our own intestines.[144]

Brissot, who was close to the Creole Miranda in Paris and others linked with the Philadelphians in Haiti, was accused of "trying to make Paris a new Philadelphia"; [145] the hotel near the Palais-Royal, where Parisian leaders met with English, Irish, and American friends of the French Revolution, was nicknamed *Hotel de Philadelphie*; and the magic word was used to suggest subversive internationalism in Germany and Poland as well.[146]

Cloots, Court's closest collaborator, had foreseen already in 1781 that the Nine Sisters would create "citizens of the world" by "forming an immense circle whose center is in Paris, but whose rays penetrate everywhere." [147] In his final work in 1793, he foresaw a future in which France will have become

> . . . a fraternal city, the city of *Philadelphia*, whose circumference necessarily embraces the entire universe, the whole human family (*famille antropique*). National and sovereign unity will be expressed by a single word: *Philadelphia*.

Philadelphia thus became the name of a truly universal republic centered on Paris. Just as the National Assembly had become "the resumé of the world-map (*mappemonde*) of the philanthropists," so "the commune of Paris will be the meeting place and central funnel of the universal community."

> Europe and Africa and Asia and America will give themselves over to the vast and happy city of PHILADELPHIA.[148]

Court's romantic ideal of recovering the *monde primitif* found its final revolutionary expression in Maréchal's *Voyages of Pythagoras*. Already in 1779, Maréchal had idealized Rousseau's island burial place as *l'Habitat de Philadelphie*.[149] Now, twenty years later, this protégé of Court invoked the term *monde* without an article to describe not just a microcosm of pastoral perfection but a special fraternity to perpetuate the legacy of Pythagoras and revolutionize the world. At the end of his travels, Maréchal's dying Pythagoras summons his followers:

> Let us agree among ourselves to call *monde*, that is to say, a masterpiece of harmony and perfection, what other men designate as the universe, heaven, the globe.
> May our school, our adoptive family, be for us a *little world* (*monde*) as harmonious as the great one! [150]

Maréchal may have been the source of the term *monde*, which Buonarroti finally settled upon for his inner organization.[151] But the Philadelphians were the first to realize Maréchal's vision; and their history is best told through the bizarre figure of their founder, Charles Nodier: the last of the literary, Germanophile occultists to play a pioneering role in revolutionary organization.

Nodier's Pentagon

Yet another geometric model for revolutionary organization was suggested by the occult symbol for the universal love of humanity: the pentagon. This five-sided object provided the image of five-man cells for the first organization of opposition to arise within Napoleon's army —which is what the Philadelphians were.

Their plan of organization was conceived in 1797 by Nodier, exiled from Paris of the Directory to his native Besançon, which he renamed "Philadelphia." His organizational plan developed to the point of mania the Pythagorean fascination with the number 5. Five is the mean number between 1 and 9, and the mystic figure that emerged when these and intervening odd numbers were added together and divided by the number of digits.[152] The number acquired revolutionary significance in the new calendar, which had five special days (the *sansculottides*) each year set apart from any of the twelve months for special celebrations, and especially under the new five-man Directory, which replaced the "apostolic" twelve-man Committee of Public Safety as the ruling executive arm of the revolution.

In Nodier's original blueprint, the Philadelphians appear as both the guardians of festive purity for the *sansculottides* and as a potential counter-Directory. The pentagon was their sign of friendship and recognition; a five-pointed star with the number five engraved on it was their seal. Initiations took place at five o'clock on the fifth day of the month, when members were to face the setting sun—wherever they happened to be—for five minutes to renew their vows to the brotherhood. Power to revise the statutes was confided in "the five oldest brothers." [153]

The five-man cell appeared concurrently for a brief period in Ireland,[154] Italy,[155] and Poland,[156] and became the dominant revolutionary unit in France beginning with the formation of a directoral committee and a web of five-man brigades by the student organization of 1819, the Friends of Truth.[157] The five-man, quasi-military unit dominated the conspiratorial organizations of Blanqui and the first group ever to call itself "Communist," the *Travailleurs-Egalitaires* of 1840 in Paris.[158]

The five-man unit acquired added mystique in the East. The Russian Decembrists were to call for five-man ruling committees in both the executive and legislative branches of a post-revolutionary government,[159] and added martyrological meaning to the number when their five leaders were executed early in 1826. The concept of a nationwide network of five-man cells controlled by a central "five" would be revived in the Land and Liberty organization of the early 1860s [160] and dramatized a decade later in Dostoevsky's *The Possessed*. The idea was to spread back to the western and southern Slavs through a series of organizations which saw the four ordinary members of each cell as the "fingers" of a single hand, with a single leader ("the thumb") as the sole connecting link with the next, higher level.[161] This image would appear in the name of the South Slav revolutionary "Black Hand," whose assassination of the Hapsburg Archduke in 1914 was to bring on World War I, which would in turn give birth to the October Revolution in Russia.

The original Philadelphians achieved no such prominence, and Nodier's vision of an army secretly transformed from within into a revolutionary brotherhood of fives never developed. But an organization did gradually emerge and involve itself in anti-Napoleonic plots through the exotic figure of Charles Nodier. His career ranged from Parisian cafés to revolutionary armies to the popular stage—then on to journalism in Ljubljana and a visit to Russia at the very time that the first revolutionary societies were forming there.[162] Whether or not he had any influence in the East, he anticipated the Eastern-type alienated revolutionary intellectual.

Nodier's vivid imagination was shaped by the revolution from the time, in 1790, when as a ten-year-old boy he led a delegation of "enfants de la patrie" in greeting the delegates returning to his native Besançon from the Festival of Federation in Paris. On that occasion young Charles held a banner showing an eagle with a tricolor in its beak,[163] standing at the head of 200 little girls dressed in white. Like Robespierre, he was much influenced by a Masonic father, who was the principal orator of the Besançon lodge "Perfect Union." [164] He went with his father to Paris; and, at age twelve on New Year's Day in 1793, read a poem calling for "the punishment of traitors by the republican dagger." [165] He wrote parodies of the Lord's Prayer ("Our father who art in Hell. . . .") and of the Creed:

> I believe in Sieyès, the father almighty, and in Robespierre, his beloved son, who suffered on the 9 Thermidore, was guillotined, dead and buried. . . .[166]

He fell under the spell of German romantic literature and of Eulogius Schneider, his tutor in Strasbourg, where he was arrested by Saint-Just in 1794.[167] Returning to Paris as the revolution turned to the right, he took refuge in writing fantasies, often under the influence of opium, in erotic engagements with young men, and in the contemplation of suicide.[168] His attention returned to the revolution when he attended the trial of the Babeuvist group which began in February 1797. The dramatist in him particularly warmed to the handsome figure of Buonarroti, calm under questioning and with his faithful wife at his side.[169]

With the border between fact and fantasy thoroughly blurred in his mind, the eighteen-year-old Nodier returned in 1797 to his native Besançon and drew up his Rules of the Philadelphes. He almost certainly began there his collaboration with the other leader of the Philadelphes, Jacques Rigomer-Bazin, a radical journalist from Le Mans who had participated in the Babeuf conspiracy and was exiled to the Jura at about the same time as Nodier.[170]

Nodier's discussion group at the Café Marrulier in Besançon and his later society of white-robed *Méditateurs*, who met in an abandoned monastery near Passy, were occult literary groups under the dominant influence of Bonneville and German romanticism.[171] Influenced by Bonneville's translations of Schiller, Nodier, and Bazin invented the new dramatic genre—melodrama—and slowly brought into being the occult organizational blueprint of the Philadelphians. Nodier was arrested in 1799; Bazin placed under surveillance after the first assassination attempt against Napoleon on Christmas eve of 1800; and Nodier rearrested in 1803 when an English newspaper revealed him as the author of the anti-Napoleonic poem *La Napoléone*.

Their first real organization appears to have been the Conspiracy of the Alliance, formed in opposition to the crowning of Napoleon as emperor by the Pope in Notre Dame Cathedral on December 2, 1804. The group contemplated kidnapping Napoleon as he passed through the Jura on his way to Milan to receive the crown of Italy in March 1805.[172]

Some form of Nodier's original Philadelphian blueprint—at least its basic core of five inner fives—came into being in or around Besançon under the empire. The key ingredient was the participation of two military leaders from the Jura: General Malet and Colonel Oudet. Malet became the leading anti-Napoleonic activist inside the French military until his execution after the uprising of 1812. Oudet was the romantic hero of the first of these abortive uprisings before dying under mysterious circumstances just after the Battle of Wagram in 1809.

Oudet was the charismatic leader for whom Nodier's miscellaneous band of self-indulgent but imaginative intellectuals desperately longed.[173] He appealed to them as a handsome young man of action. Conservative by temperament and scarred by youthful duels, Oudet fascinated Nodier and Bazin as a real-life version of the heroes they had created in their melodramas. Nodier likened Oudet to the hero of Schiller's *Conspiracy of Fiesco*;[174] and he saw Oudet as a kind of anti-Napoleon—a figure like Napoleon bigger than life and driven by the nobility of struggle more than by clarity of convictions. Oudet was apparently converted to revolutionary conspiracy in 1801–02, while serving as military commandant on the islands of Ré and Oléron where Buonarroti and others were imprisoned. Whether or not he was won over by his captives,[175] he made common cause with General Malet, deriving inspiration for revolutionary republican activity against Napoleon from the earlier counter-revolutionary uprising in the Vendée. They "professed admiration to the point of enthusiasm for the Vendéens," contrasting their grass-roots fidelity to the cowardly flight of the aristocratic émigrés. Malet seemed almost to envy the "Happy Bourbons," whose dynasty was virtually relegitimized by "the devotion of the Vendée." [176] Nodier noted an affinity of spirit between the extremes of Left and Right:

> During the Revolution, Jacobinism and the Vendée provided all the moral elevation that there was in France.[177]

"Moral elevation" was more important than a precise political goal for the romantic imagination. Most distasteful was the *juste milieu*: venal, compromise politics based on petty interests rather than noble goals.

A single, melodramatic hero leading a simple organization—this was the Philadelphian fantasy: the radical, sublime simplification that would lead to revolution. Nodier's task was to find the lost language for the coming kingdom of brotherly love: a form of speech worthy of Oudet, the leader who left him speechless.[178] Thus, at the very time the first Philadelphian conspiracy was taking shape in 1808, Nodier was propagating the "primitive idioms" of natural man in his *Dictionary of Onomatopea* and his *Theory of Primitive Languages*; and extracting 283 thoughts from Maréchal's *Voyages of Pythagoras* for his *Apotheosis of Pythagoras, Warnings of Pythagoras*, in a limited edition with pseudoantique inscriptions.[179] The city of publication, his native Besançon, was no longer referred to as Philadelphia, but as Crotona, the city where Pythagoras's active brotherhood had been founded.

Malet planned in 1808 to overthrow Napoleon while he was occupied in Spain and to set up a temporary dictatorship in the name of the French Senate that would prepare a republican constitution for France. The plot was uncovered and five hundred arrested. But, in 1809, Malet returned to Nodier's original idea for the Philadelphians of a fusion between Jacobin and royalist foes of Napoleon into a conspiracy that was "properly speaking neither royalist nor republican." [180] Malet was planning in 1809 to announce the overthrow of Napoleon in Notre Dame Cathedral in order to reassure the Right.[181] He included two aristocratic royalists in the government he proposed to form after the coup he planned for October 1812 when Napoleon was in Russia. He appealed to royalists with his message to the army:

> Show France and Europe that you are no longer soldiers of Bonaparte, just as you are not soldiers of Robespierre.[182]

Malet's insurrection at dawn on October 23 very nearly succeeded. He seized the bank, treasury, and other key municipal buildings in Paris and gained the allegiance of two battalions after announcing that Napoleon had died in Russia. But he never disarmed the police; his followers fell into disarray; and some fifteen hundred were arrested. Before Malet was executed, he made a courtroom response worthy of Nodier's melodramas to the prosecutor's question of who his collaborators had been: "You yourself, sir, and all of France if I had succeeded." [183]

By that time, Nodier was in exile in distant Ljubljana, suspected of counter-revolutionary activity but undaunted in his romantic fantasies. The newly found Slavs now represented primitive, natural purity, the Sparta of his dreams, the "last and touching shelter of the ancient ways." [184] The ideological intensity of his original Philadelphian ideal had not survived beyond 1809 when Oudet was killed and Bazin was imprisoned, where he remained for the rest of the Napoleonic era. Henceforth anti-Napoleonic activity among Frenchmen was concentrated in military cabals pointing toward opportunistic insurrection.

Buonarroti's Monde

The grandiose ideal of an occult revolutionary brotherhood was taken up with even greater intensity by the Italian version of the Philadelphians, the Adelphians.[185] Formed no later than 1807 among exiles in Paris under Buonarroti's friend, Luigi Angeloni, the Adelphians seem to have considered themselves even more consciously than the Philadelphians an inner controlling organization within a broader revolutionary movement. The Italians, too, used pseudonyms (including Weishaupt's "Spartacus") and code words ("secret" for "revolution," "money" for "arms") [186] while legitimizing violence through occult symbols. Inner circles were now said to represent the letter O—suggesting the martyred Oudet, the verb to kill (*occide*), and the Olympians of imagined antiquity.[187] There was even an Italian version of the melodramas of Nodier and Rigomer; because the revolutionary imagination of the Italians in France was shaped by the heroic plays and Masonic fantasies of Francesco Salfi's romantic revolt against the "languid imagination" of his complacent countrymen.[188]

Buonarroti reestablished his links with broader revolutionary movements through Angeloni and the Adelphians, whose statutes of 1811 coincided with and strongly resembled his own first blueprint for the Sublime Perfect Masters.[189] On July 22, 1812, he issued "from below the Equator" the first "decree of the Great Firmament" incorporating both Adelphians and Philadelphians into a new order. A counsel of three members was to propose each new member.[190] Though there is no evidence of any direct response to this call, Buonarroti's entourage was at least loosely linked with Malet's final conspiracy.

During the Restoration, he refined his concept, insisting that "instruction on the falsehood of Christian revelation" be given before conferring the title *Tieboar* ("Tyrannum interfice, Bona omnia antiqua recupera"),[191] writing a Latin *Profession de foi* for both the outer, five-man circles ("the Synod of ⊙") and the inner, three-man circle ("the Church of ⊙").[192] He expanded his contacts with the French, but placed his hopes increasingly on Italy and used the German Illuminist term *Weise* for the central figure in the inner circle of Sublime Perfect Masters.[193] As the tide of revolution seemed to rise again, Buonarroti dipped once more into the world of the occult for his second and last blueprint for a world revolutionary organization: *Monde* or "world."

He saw this revolutionary microcosm, *Monde*, as liberating and unifying the macrocosm, realizing (in the words of the password of the final grade) *felicitas-consensus* for all the world. Buonarroti assumed the new pseudonym of Polycarp,[194] naming himself for the early Christian evangelist who had bridged the gap between the first apostles and the institutional church. He meant to represent a similar historic link between the apostles of the revolutionary era and the institutionalized movements of the Restoration. He sought to establish connections with other movements through "mobile deacons" and to strengthen authority by invoking occult titles like "archont" for Angeloni.[195] The documents also speak of *frères intimes*, who were to watch for spies and test the loyalty of new members, and of a new set of four grades: adolescent, man, theologian, and philosopher.[196]

His occult structures were all thinly staffed, and often represented more a figment of imagination than a fact of organization. But they captured the imagination even as the police captured them—the awakening romantic imagination of the young in restless search of "the miracle that will release each of them from mediocrity." [197] The Philadelphians in France, the Adelphians in Italy, and Buonarroti's "world" in Geneva—all saw themselves as the "party of the vanquished" [198] dedicated to a vague republican-constitutional ideal into which everyone poured his private hopes for an alternative to Napoleon. The radical republican Constitution of 1793 was generally accepted as the ideal precisely because it had *not* been put into practice. The new generation, having had its hopes raised in the 1790s and dashed in the early 1800s, was clearer about what it opposed (Napoleon) than what it wanted. As Nodier recalled:

> The republic was for my generation a verbal talisman (*un mot talismanique*) of unbelievable power . . . the name of a government that could be anything one wanted except that which actually exists.[199]

Political romanticism believed in youth against age—and in heaven on earth:

> Not in Utopia, subterranean fields,
> Or some secreted island, Heaven knows where!
> But in the very world, which is the world
> Of all of us,—the place where, in the end,
> We find our happiness, or not at all! [200]

This thought sounds so familiar to the modern secular mind that it is more likely to be thought banal than revolutionary. Yet it represented in its time an extraordinary, almost unprecedented form of faith—a faith made all the more intense (like that of Marx later) by its repudiation of the inherited images of (and the very word) utopia.

> Romanticism is neither of the Right nor of the Left. . . . The characteristic of romantic politics is that it is a politics of the miraculous.[201]

Extreme solutions appealed to romantic young believers in this "politics of the miraculous." "*On n'arrive point au sublime par degrés*" (One does not reach the sublime by gradual steps), wrote Mme. de Staël, a spiritual leader of the more moderate opposition to Napoleon and a popularizer of German romanticism.[202]

The man who validated in real life the "politics of the miraculous" was Napoleon himself. He had returned from the land of the pyramids to deliver France from mediocrity and all of Europe from encrusted habit, inspiring French Masonic lodges to sing:

> Poursuis, Napoléon, fais encore un miracle,
> Etonne l'Univers par un nouveau spectacle,
> . . . les Français ne reverraient-ils pas Corneille et Racine reparaître?
> Tu peux ce que tu veux; commande, ils vont renaître.[203]

> Pursue them, Napóleon, make another miracle,
> Dazzle the Universe with a new spectacle.
> Could not the French see Corneille and Racine reappear?
> You can do what you will; command, they'll be here.

The new generation of revolutionaries looked to the sun of the Enlightenment from under the shadow of Napoleon. They internalized his Prometheanism even as they opposed his imperialism. The first attempt at a secular socialist cosmology (that of Fourier) and the first authentically revolutionary ideologies (those of Hegel and Saint-Simon) were conceived during the reign of Napoleon and under his impact. Buonarroti was a kind of mirror image of the emperor, bringing a certain Napoleonic quality to his own plans for revolution.[204]

The mundane question of how Buonarroti made a living during his lonely years as a revolutionary exile leads one into the most sublime of all regions to Pythagoreans: music. Napoleon was not the only person to admire the musical talent of Buonarroti, who supported himself throughout his long career by giving piano and singing lessons—often retiring from all human company for long solo sessions. A French visitor to Geneva in 1811 described how Buonarroti's "superb and inspired head" rose above the piano:

> He was dreaming, improvising, then reining himself in to produce fireworks on his instrument with long, agile and powerful fingers, bursting into songs without words that seemed to be the explosion of mysterious thoughts. . . .[205]

"Songs without words" were for the Pythagoreans the ultimate form of conversation of the cosmos with itself. The "music of the spheres" was the highest form of discourse, expressing "the harmony of creation, or rather of the world as it should be." [206] The occultist Antoine Fabre d'Olivet, who composed all manner of fantastic works in the revolutionary era climaxing in his *Golden Verses of Pythagoras*,[207] left behind a posthumous work that proclaimed music as "the science of harmonic relationships of the universe." [208] The very word *music* was said to have blended primitive Egyptian and Celtic roots into a Greek name [209] "when Pythagoras appeared in Greece, rich with all the illumination of Africa and Asia, about nine centuries after Orpheus," and left behind a sect "which even today is not entirely extinct." [210]

Fascination with music as the lost language of liberation led Buonarroti's friend, Luigi Angeloni, to publish in Paris a dissertation on the medieval origins of musical notation even as he was organizing his Adelphian revolutionaries.[211] For the romantic mind, music was the realm of freedom: the most spiritual of the arts, releasing emotion yet creating order in the dimension of time. Music freed man from spatial and material limitations for a new sense of boundless expectation. Music was the expression of modern, "Faustian" man, for whom infinite striving had replaced the finite mastery of classical forms,[212] the language of hope which was specially "open to the future." [213]

The music in the life of Buonarroti and Angeloni, the melody in the melodramas of Nodier, Bazin, and Salfi—all were expressions of aspiration rather than inspiration, of emotion rather than intellect. The text for Buonarroti's "songs without words" was to be provided by the leader of the last important revolutionary organization he directly founded: the Flemish Society of Brotherhood, of Jacob Kats in the 1830s.[214] Kats, who lived on to influence the German émigrés in Brussels who gathered around Karl Marx to create the Communist League, chose Pythagoras as his revolutionary pseudonym and projected the Pythagorean ideal in his revolutionary mystery drama *The Earthly Paradise*. He flooded music into the play—and later into the Flemish lower classes broadly, creating the first theater for popular Flemish music in Brussels during the Revolution of 1848.[215]

This was, as we shall see, the wave of the future. For music became the handmaiden of ethnic rather than class consciousness, of fraternity rather than equality. The medium of music found its message in the romantic era on the operatic stage in the service of national rather than social revolution. But the belief in the liberating power of music derived from the occult fascination of the Pythagorean pioneers of the revolutionary tradition with discovering the lost harmony of nature. They sought a language that went beyond words to sounds—a legitimacy that moved beyond space to time.

The Interaction of Extremes

Well before the revolution, Mercier, the friend of Bonneville, Restif, and Nodier, had introduced the phrase *les extrèmes se touchent* as a chapter heading in his *Tableaux de Paris*. He was anticipating a fateful fact about the early revolutionaries and a reappearing reality of revolutionary dynamics: the affinity and unconscious borrowings between the extremes of Right and Left.

The interaction of extremes affected the revolutionary tradition in two ways: dialectically and symbiotically. Dialectically, the radical, secular Illuminists on the Left developed their sense both of universal, pedagogic mission and of secret, hierarchical method from the conservative Christian Jesuit order on the Right. The Illuminist strain represented the hard, ideological core of the revolutionary faith as it developed from Bonneville through Babeuf to Buonarroti.

Symbiotically, the broader spectrum of opportunistic revolutionary leaders and functionaries drew in the early days of the French Revolution on an equally broad range of reactionary, pseudo-chivalric higher orders of Masonry. The symbiosis became even more intimate during the Napoleonic era when monarchists and republicans borrowed repeatedly from one another while collaborating in common opposition to Bonaparte.

The dialectic of Left-Right interaction began as we have seen—like so much else in the "French" Revolution—in Germany well before 1789. Adam Weishaupt had derived his concept of hierarchical organization in pursuit of a global mission directly from the Jesuits,[216] and Knigge had described the Illuminist program as one using Jesuit methods to combat Jesuit objectives, a "counter-conspiracy of progressive, enlightened forces." [217] Subsequent Illuminist propaganda contended that there was a secret Jesuit conspiracy, and that the nominally abolished order had established underground links between Bavarian Jesuits and Berlin Rosicrucians.[218] As the conspiracy mania grew, Weishaupt himself was accused of being a secret Jesuit.[219] The Illuminists became more revolutionary in the course of the 1780s precisely in the process of winning converts from conservative Masonic lodges of Strict Observance.

The anti-Illuminist campaign of German conservatives in the 1790s was in many ways simply an echo of the anti-Jesuit campaign that the radical Illuminists themselves had launched in the 1780s. Revolutionaries began to take Illuminist ideas seriously (long after Illuminism as a movement was dead) because of the panic that the Illuminist label seemed to produce among conservatives. Buonarroti appears to have first discovered the Illuminists through an antagonistic exposé by the archconservative Elector of Bavaria.[220] The "great fear" of an "aristocratic conspiracy" in the summer of 1789 in France helped create the conspiracy it assumed; and conservative fears during 1790 of an "infernal cabal" of revolutionaries may have helped shape Buonarroti's first plans for forming such a cabal.[221]

The Illuminist myth both "crystallized the antirevolutionary forces of central Europe" [222] and—paradoxically—revived hopes among some revolutionaries. How the fears of the Right dialectically became the fascination of the Left is illustrated by the case of Hungary. Ignatius Martinovics, a Catholic priest and physics professor, was hired by the Hapsburg police to report on the alleged Illuminist danger in Budapest. He became absorbed in his subject, however, and soon drew up plans to provide Hungarian radicals with an Illuminist-type, hierarchical organization. Martinovics wrote separate catechisms in May 1794 for both the open Association of Reformers and a secret, inner Association of Liberty and Equality.[223] The first organization was to accomplish a political revolution for national independence; the second, a social revolt on behalf of the serfs. Martinovics, the self-proclaimed Democritus of the Mountain, was soon arrested along with many of the two hundred to three hundred conspirators. (Despite a final reversion to collaboration with the police, Martinovics was beheaded in May 1795.) [224]

The dialectical interaction of Right and Left was also a factor in the prerevolutionary popularization of the ideas of Rousseau and Court de Gébelin within France. Of course, the literary cult of Rousseau in the

1780s led in some cases directly to the political cult of 1790–94. But Court de Gébelin's own Rousseauist work, *Duties of the Prince and of the Citizen,*[225] was probably less influential among radicals than the dialectical impact of reactionary attacks such as that of the Abbé Le Gros, *Analysis of the Works of Rousseau and Court de Gébelin.* Le Gros unintentionally revived interest in the occult thought of the deceased Court by suggesting already in 1786 that Court was merely codifying the subversive ideas of Rousseau in a desire "to effect in the Universe the greatest of *revolutions.*" [226]

The interborrowing between monarchists and republicans in common opposition to Napoleon began with the very first acts of resistance to his dictatorship in 1800. The "infernal machine" (a cart loaded with gunpowder) detonated in the rue Nicaise in Paris by royalists appears to have imitated an earlier machine designed by Jacobins.[227] The intellectual discussion group that took shape at the same time on the rue des Marins brought together elements of the two extremes and gave birth to the Philadelphians, who also mixed royalists and republicans. The Philadelphians followed the Babeuvists in idealizing from the Left the grass-roots heroism of the Vendée on the Right.

Extremists tended to share a common opposition to moderation that was more intense than their opposition to one another. This attitude was a legacy of the revolutionary era and its basic drive toward radical simplification. Moderate positions tended to complicate political calculation—and they inspired a special contempt among activists on both sides. Robespierre coined the scornful term *modérantisme,* which "is to moderation what impotence is to chastity." [228] Either Left or Right, "mountain" or "plain" was preferable to "the swamp" or moderate Center in the National Assembly.

The interborrowing between extremes was particularly striking in backward agrarian regions on the European periphery: the Iberian and Italian peninsulas and Russia. These centers of resistance to Napoleonic authority were among the first to produce revolutionary movements after his demise. Tsar Alexander I mixed both revolutionary and reactionary impulses within himself. Both Metternich and his leading foe on the Left (the Italian Carbonari) believed that the tsar supported the Italian revolutionaries.[229] In Poland, where a national Masonic network converted itself into a new revolutionary organization (the Polish National Society of Freemasons) in 1819–21, a key revolutionary leader was concurrently head of the secret police.[230] The Polonophile Society of the United Slavs, the most revolutionary Russian group of the period, promised the ideal of pan-slav solidarity, which eventually became the reactionary alternative to revolutionary ideology in Russia.

British leadership in the anti-Napoleonic struggle encouraged the blending of Right and Left throughout southern Europe—from Greece through southern Italy and Sicily to Spain and Portugal. The British *medium* for mobilizing elites politically was often the conservative Scottish orders of Masonry; [231] but the main English *message* (constitutional limitation on royal power) was a revolutionary concept in these lands of absolutism. As early as June 1803, British intelligence advised

... that the Republicans and the Royalists were very numerous and if they
could be brought to trust each other . . . a revolution might be operated.[232]

Although such trust was never achieved, Right-Left collaboration became commonplace in the national resistance movements to Napoleon.
In Portugal, for instance, republican Philadelphians collaborated with
the conservative English commander, the Duke of Wellington.[233]

Spain provided perhaps the most striking illustration. The central
point of mobilization for the army-based revolutionary societies was established in 1809 in the former headquarters of the Inquisition. Members of these societies were haunted by continuing uncertainty as to
whether their allegiance was to a king more conservative than Napoleon or to a revolution more radical than that of the French. Right-
Left confusion extended to the hardy Basques, who lent important leadership to the protracted Spanish resistance against Napoleon. They
became (and have remained) inventive practitioners of the irregular warfare that wore down the French conventional forces. The most important guerrilla leader, Francisco Espoz y Mina of Navarre, who later led
the revolutionary army that battled the right-wing Carlists, nevertheless
went through an extreme monarchist phase of his own in 1814, when he
formally executed by a firing squad a copy of the Constitution of 1812.
Another key guerrilla leader, Jerónimo Merino of Burgos moved in the
opposite direction to become a leader of the same Carlists. Yet another
guerrilla, Merino's lieutenant Eugenio Aviraneta of Irún, ended up as
the leading apostle of continuing revolutionary conspiracy in the Hispanic world. He founded a five-man central revolutionary cell in Northern Spain (*El Aventino*), sought international support for establishing a
republic in Zaragoza in the early 1820s, and remained active in republican conspiracies down to the middle of the century, including making
trips as far afield as Mexico and the Philippines.[234]

Symbiosis between the extremes of Right and Left is evident in the
career of the man who became the leading counter-revolutionary of the
era: Joseph de Maistre. As a young and ambitious magistrate, de Maistre became a Mason in 1773 and called for an American Revolution
even before the Americans did in his politically charged eulogy of 1775
to the King of Sardinia:

> Liberty, insulted in Europe, has taken flight to another hemisphere. It
> coasts over the Canadian ices, arms the peaceful Pennsylvanian, and from
> the heart of Philadelphia cries out to the British. . . .[235]

De Maistre later confessed that only a radical conversion by the
Jesuits kept him "from becoming an orator in the Constituent Assembly." [236] De Maistre took his own positive ideal from the negative portrayal of conservative Catholicism in Germany by the revolutionary
Mirabeau.[237]

De Maistre's counter-revolutionary manifesto of 1796, *Considerations
on France*, betrayed a hypnotic fascination with the revolution more
extreme than that shown by earlier antirevolutionaries. De Maistre
outdid the revolutionaries themselves in insisting on the absolute nov-

elty of the revolution. It was a direct, mysterious act of providence, a "miracle" of evil calling for a counter-miracle: the establishment of papal theocracy.[238]

Far from being a simple throwback to medieval Catholicism, de Maistre's call had a modern ring which derived from his long exposure to German romantic thought while in exile.[239] His long residence in St. Petersburg led him to predict that upheavals in that country would henceforth be led not by peasant Jacqueries like that of Pugachev against Catherine the Great, but by "Pugachevs from the universities." [240]

De Maistre called from the Right for violent measures to restore authoritarian rule by the pope. Maréchal argued from the Left for a similar militant dictatorship in a memorandum to Napoleon of 1798. He pointed out, like de Maistre, the virtues of war and the dangers of degeneracy in any peace negotiated before the process of "regeneration" was underway.[241] He called in vain on Napoleon to lead the failing revolution in terms similar to those used by de Maistre imploring the pope to lead the counter-revolution. Napoleon was urged to become a

... dictator not just of the French republic, but of all the other powers of Europe ... *the Founder of a universal and federative Republic.*[242]

Maréchal echoed Buonarroti's fear of a compromise peace brokered by England such as Napoleon's fellow-Corsican Paoli had accepted.[243] The model for liberation was Napoleon's Italian campaign: "You revolutionize Italy first, and then preach prudence and calm." [244] De Maistre, who became Sardinian ambassador to St. Petersburg, turned to Russia as the elemental, uncommitted power that might somehow save Europe. Maréchal seems to have entertained, if he did not espouse, this thought at the end of his remarkable *History of Russia* of 1802. Ostensibly the work seeks to discredit all autocratic government, representing Russian history as an unmitigated series of crimes and attacking those like Voltaire who purported to find hope there. Insisting that "truth is always brutal," [245] Maréchal seemed at times to be attacking Napoleon as well. But, in a darkly brilliant supplement to this otherwise dull work, the veteran revolutionary presented a blueprint for the suppression of revolutionary movements: *The Good and Last Advice of Catherine II to Paul I.*

Maréchal likened it to a new version of Machiavelli's *Prince*; and it is indeed a political classic, which deepens the mystery of Maréchal's late years and his seeming immunity from arrest even during periods of extreme reaction. The work reveals either the extraordinary penetration by the extreme Left into the thinking of the extreme Right—or possibly even some final movement of Maréchal from one extreme to the other.

Maréchal's Catherine instructs her son on how to prevent the "distant political revolution which will befall us if its giant steps are allowed to continue as they have for seven years." [246] "Learn from me," she advises, "the science of conjuring with popular storms. Prevent them by waging war far away: all shall then be permissible for you as long as your arms shall be victorious." [247] The danger of the future lies in the growth of a free press, for "one cannot do what one wills with a reasoning people"; [248] and in the restless new intellectuals who may "form a state within the state."

> If the feeble and unfortunate Louis XVI . . . had not committed the signal imprudence of a call to savants and publicists for advice on the deplorable state of his finances, the unfortunate prince would still be reigning.[249]

A modern prince must get their advice but not permit them to publish for a broader audience. The public must not be courted with favors but dazzled with "the magic of the throne" and kept "breathless" with activity: wars, parades, and festivals.

> Do not leave the people time to think. . . . The common lot of men love movement. . . . Stagnant waters become spoiled and produce disease.[250]

Princely rule is threatened either by "armed confederations" like Poland or "unarmed confederations that are called *clubs* in England, and under the name of societies and patriotic circles have brought a deluge of crimes and calamities to France." [251] The true monarch must maintain "sang-froid in great political crises" and indifference to the fate of individuals, for he is "a being below God only, but above all men." [252]

> At the height where we are placed, my son, we need have regard only for the ensemble; and here again we model ourselves on nature, which seems to abandon to themselves those beings that it no longer needs.[253]

Maréchal seems to see his own egalitarian position as the most dangerous challenge to the old order. Catherine denounces "these vile magistrates of the people" who "write ostentatiously the word *equality* at the head of their decrees." [254] She advises her son that there is nothing to be done with the "handful of parvenus" who would lead France into that "den of thieves" known as democracy except to outshine them in wisdom and purity.

This political polarization into revolutionary and reactionary positions —each understanding the other better than any position in between— became characteristic of the Restoration. Paul Didier, leader of the first and most seminal revolutionary conspiracy of that era, had been an arch-royalist during the revolutionary and Napoleonic periods. He argued in his *Spirit and Vow of the French* (1799) and his *Return to Religion* (1802) for a unitary, total faith as the essential bond for society.[255] He preferred, therefore, to move all the way over to the revolutionary camp rather than support the compromise formula of a constitutional monarchy after 1815. The unsuccessful conspiracy that he mounted just north of Grenoble was denounced by perplexed royalists as the act of one "who has now betrayed successively all the governments in France for 20 years." [256] Didier's defense was that

> I do not wish to defy either laws or men; I am only defying irreligion.[257]

The romantic temperament called for heroism in the name of faith and tended to rule out middle positions. The term "ultra," used in France to describe the extreme, theocratic Right, was invoked in Italy for revolutionaries of the far Left. Moderate defenders of the compromise settlement of 1815 in France were saddled with the less complimentary label of "doctrinaire."

Perhaps the two most influential new reactionaries of the era were both refugees from the revolutionary occultist infatuations of an earlier period. Karl Eckhartshausen, the leading propagator of the antirevolutionary mysticism of the "Holy Alliance," was a Bavarian who had briefly joined and subsequently studied at length the Illuminist Order.[258] Joseph de Maistre, the most influential among the ultramontanist breed of reactionary, had been a leader of radical occult Masonry in prerevolutionary France.

The most important two figures in systematizing the police repression of revolutionary forces in France were both former revolutionary extremists. Joseph Fouché, who organized Napoleon's political police, had made his reputation as the organizer of the Feast of Equality in 1794 in Lyon after leading there perhaps the bloodiest single episode against counter-revolutionaries in the entire Reign of Terror.[259] Simon Duplay, who compiled the "green book" of all known political conspiracies since 1792 for Napoleon, had lost a leg fighting for the revolution at Valmy and subsequently served as Robespierre's secretary.

In one of the last letters which de Maistre received just before his death in 1821, Lamennais (who was moving in the opposite direction from ultramontanism to an ultrademocratic faith in the masses) wrote prophetically:

> There will be no more middle way between faith and nothingness. . . . Everything is extreme today; there is no longer any dwelling place in between.[260]

BOOK

II

THE DOMINANCE OF
THE NATIONAL
REVOLUTIONARIES:
THE
MID-NINETEENTH
CENTURY

IN THE POST-NAPOLEONIC ERA, the revolutionary tradition broke out from the cocoon of conspiracy and into flight on the wings of nationalism. Though they generally rejected the universalist rhetoric of the French revolutionary era, the new nationalists were following the French example of a militant, musical mobilization of the masses against foreign foes during 1792–94. Italy and Poland, which had responded the most enthusiastically of all foreign peoples to the French Revolution, remained the leaders of European nationalism and the most inventive theorists of revolutionary violence.

The national revolutionary cause was identified almost everywhere with liberal constitutionalism up until the Revolution of 1830. Thereafter, however, the nationalist ideal of *fraternité* was increasingly dissociated by revolutionaries from the *liberté* of the liberals—particularly in central and eastern Europe. And in western Europe, constitutional liberalism lost some of its earlier links with revolutionary nationalism —becoming an experimental, evolutionary alternative to the revolutionary path which increasingly emphasized ideology and violence. In the 1840s a new generation of revolutionaries turned to socialist rather than nationalist ideals—reviving the banner of *égalité* as a rival to the *fraternité* of national revolutionaries. The long struggle thus began between the two main branches of the revolutionary faith. Paris remained the Mecca of the faith; but the dominance of nationalism waned after the defeat of the revolutions of 1848; and the last Parisian revolution—the Commune of 1871—became a legend and model for the social revolutionaries of the future.

This entire, Francocentric period of revolutionary ferment was suffused with a florid romanticism that sought to mobilize the imagination with naturalistic imagery. In an age of accelerating industrialization and urbanization, there seemed a compensatory need to identify revolutionary organization with pastoral simplicity. Dame Nature was no longer mathematical but organic. Her servant was no longer an aristocratic mason building a temple in stone but a democratic "charcoal burner" returning to a primeval forest.[1] Beyond the forgotten folklore and neglected vernacular that nationalist revolutionaries everywhere sought to recover lay an imaginary golden age.[2] In the Latin American revolutions this idealized state of nature was associated with the period prior to foreign dominance: a return to an Aztec idyll after "a sleep of three centuries" in the Mexican Revolution of 1808–10;[3] to pastoral, sixteenth-century Araucania in the subsequent Chilean (and to some extent the Argentine and the Peruvian) Revolution.[4] In the Latin part of North America, too, the earliest uprising of French Canadians against Anglo-Saxon dominance in 1837 was led by a "secret association of brother huntsmen."[5]

Social revolutionaries no less than the dominant national revolutionaries sought to begin building a new world by recovering vanished perfection and familial feelings in rural settings. Buonarroti's Parisian rival to the nationalistic Carbonari, his True Italians, called themselves Families—as did Blanqui's pioneering social revolutionary organization of 1834, the Society of the Families. Blanqui replaced his Families with an organization with even more pretensions of recreating the harmonies of nature: a Society of the Seasons organized into a hierarchy of weeks, months, and seasons. The pioneering communist society in Lyon in 1836 was the Society of Flowers, which assigned each artisan member the name of a flower or plant and met early in the mornings in a beautiful forest setting overlooking the river Saône.[6] The pioneering German social revolutionary group that met in Paris at the same time, the League of Outlaws, adopted the pose of rural bandits and organized into huts, mountains, and national huts, then into tents, campfires, and campfire points.[7] Independently in Switzerland, French-speaking social revolutionaries called themselves the Society of the Swan,[8] closely followed by a German-speaking group which organized itself into leaves, buds, blossoms, and fruits—with a seed at the center.[9] And in England, the trail-blazing socialist ideas of Robert Owen were popularized by a revolutionary theory of history allegedly derived from studying beehives. Humanity was simply to follow the bees through five successive revolutions: noble savagery, pastoral occupations, farming, and industry on to the final creation of a community of goods by the wise bee.[10]

The main product of the romantic return to nature was not, however, ideal socialist alternatives but real nationalist movements. The image of a nation as a vitalistic, natural organism legitimized the revolutionary nationalism that dominated the Francocentric period. Since this supra-personal national ideal continues to baffle modern man as consistently as it arouses him, it may merit unconventional scrutiny: of its songs and signs, of its "people" and their violence. This "springtime of nations" was seeded by the Italian charcoal burners (*Carbonari*), and the full harvest has not yet been reaped.

CHAPTER 5

The Conspiratorial
Constitutionalists
(1815–25)

IN MARCH 1814, as the armies of the European monarchies entered Paris, all hopes for revolution seemed to have ended. Babeuf's son committed suicide; and Simon Duplay committed to the flames his "green book," which alone might have provided a definitive history of early revolutionary conspiracy. But no sooner had he destroyed this massive inventory of those who had "troubled the tranquility of France" since 1792 than he was forced to begin another. Working for the restored Bourbons from 1815 until his death in 1827, he compiled some fifteen thousand dossiers on real-life organizations far more fanciful than Nodier's Philadelphians or Buonarroti's Sublime Perfect Masters. In his view, the seminal revolutionary organization was Didier's; and the key role in developing a revolutionary movement throughout France was played by the Masonic Association of Misraim, allegedly the original Egyptian Rite with 90 degrees of membership.[1]

The resurgence of revolutionary activity during the restoration reached far beyond occult conspiracies within France. Indeed, the decade 1815–25 saw a new generation of liberal, constitutional revolutionaries for the first time mobilize mass followings behind national rather than universal goals. The conspiracies that challenged the conservative "world restored" at the Congress of Vienna [2] represented in effect the first political youth movement of modern times. As an all-European species of the early nineteenth century, the liberal revolutionaries anticipated an important extra-European phenomenon of the early twentieth: the secret conspiracy of young officers and intellectuals seeking expanded access to political power in a stagnant, traditional society.

Indispensable to a politicized youth movement is the raising of hopes by a tradition-shattering political leader. Like Frederick the Great for the original *Sturm und Drang* generation of the 1770s in Prussia or the Kennedys for the youth movement of the 1960s in America, Napoleon Bonaparte was the inescapable model for a restless generation that had never known any other leader. Napoleon was less a father figure than a kind of idealized older brother beckoning the young into battle against patriarchal authority. At the same time, Napoleon was bigger than life, having risen "above the earthly thought of founding a dynasty," accepting instead

> . . . the providential mission . . . to destroy the isolation of peoples, spread civilization afar, shatter the diadems.[3]

He had, in short, attempted what others had only dreamed of: the political transformation of the world.

Napoleon's messianic reappearance from Elba for the "hundred days" prior to his final defeat at Waterloo had restored the image of Napoleon as revolutionary rather than tyrant. He had adopted the constitutional banners of civil liberties and a federal distribution of power. He had at last brought to his side the Marquis de Lafayette, the symbol of successful constitutional revolution in both America and France.

Whether young Europeans fought for or against him, Napoleon left them with a thirst for heroism and even martyrdom. He widened horizons, raised appetites, and infected young Europe with political passions. The three nations that dominated the revolutionary tradition of the early nineteenth century—France, Italy, and Poland—were precisely those in which the cult of Napoleon was most developed.

The new revolutionaries awakened during the Napoleonic era did not yet seek sweeping social change; but they clearly wanted something more than mere political independence and constitutional reform. Mickiewicz spoke implausibly of combining Christ and Napoleon; Piasecki alluded vaguely to "the creation of a new people." [4]

But to ask what it was they really wanted is to pose the most unanswerable—if most important—question about the revolutionary vocation. Mapping utopia may be more conducive to reverie than to revolution. Any precise list of demands may lead to ennervating discussion and division among the revolutionaries—and provides the opportunity for selective coöptation by the existing powers.

Thus, the success of early conspirators in arousing large sections of Europe against existing authority did not come from any finished vision of the society they sought. Nor can their dynamism be explained simply as the by-product of the perpetually rising bourgeoisie. The main force of the industrial revolution had not yet reached the continent; and the revolutionary movement was strongest—in Iberia, Italy, Greece, and Russia—where the bourgeoisie was weakest and the leadership primarily aristocratic.

The revolutionary movement's principal stated objective—limiting monarchy by a formal "constitution"—was perhaps its least understood aspect. The French ambassador to Naples asked a peasant in the Apulia early in 1818: "Just what is this constitution you are demanding?" and received the answer:

> I don't know anything about it, but they had better give us one.[5]

The romantic world view of the young revolutionaries was shaped not just by the spell of Napoleon but also by the experience of camaraderie within their own small groups. These exclusively masculine fraternities sublimated eros into aspiration—providing dislocated young men in a turbulent era with a simple community of faith that suggested some earlier, less complicated time. The fraternal *groupuscule* was the model; the "politics of the miraculous" was the motor; a revolutionary Second Coming was the destination.

The most important movement of the era was the Italian Carbonari: the first to mobilize the masses for a national cause through a secret organization. Attracting in a short space of time an unprecedented membership of at least three hundred thousand,[6] they presented a danger to the conservative restoration that reached far beyond Italy. They posed a direct challenge to both the stability and the legitimacy of Hapsburg rule, the linchpin of the post-Napoleonic order. The Carbonari threatened the twin pillars of the Metternichean order, traditional borders and monarchical authority, precisely where their hold was weakest: in the divided Italian peninsula.

The Forest Fraternity

When Buonarroti's key collaborator spoke of the revolutionary movement during the restoration as "this party of the Jura,"[7] he provided insight into the genealogy as well as the geography of the revolutionary tradition. The original Philadelphians of the 1790s had come from the wooded and relatively unspoiled Jura region between Besançon and Geneva; Buonarroti and his friends operated there until he moved to Brussels in 1824;[8] and the romantic idea of recovering a lost golden age continued to flourish there down to the formation of Bakunin's final alliance of romantic revolutionaries, the *Fédération Jurasienne* of the early 1870s. Dostoevsky sent his antirevolutionary caricature of Bakunin, Nicholas Stavrogin of *The Possessed*, off to commit suicide in the Jura, but nevertheless pays grudging tribute to the revolutionary dream, "the Geneva idea":

The golden age is the most implausible of all dreams. But for it men have given up their life and strength; for the sake of it prophets have died and been slain; without it the people will not live and cannot die.[9]

From the Jura at the beginning of the nineteenth century came the first purveyors of the dream to arouse the masses: the society of Good Cousins, Charcoal Burners.[10] This rural mutation of Masonry from Besançon was transplanted by the Napoleonic armies to southern Italy, where it was politicized and popularized throughout the Kingdom of Naples during the rule of Napoleon's maverick brother-in-law, Joachim Murat (1808–15). A leading role was played by a veteran of the Besançon group, Jean-Pierre Briot, whose fascination with a new type of forest fraternity was apparently fueled by the experience of escaping from Austrian imprisonment into the Black Forest and by his own political experience as revolutionary commissioner for the Island of Elba in 1801–02, before moving to Naples and founding the first Carbonari group in 1807.[11]

This new ritual order drew on the same type of extended family structures and protective loyalties that was later to produce the Mafia.[12] It attracted lesser aristocrats and untitled professional people who had not become as extensively involved in traditional Masonic lodges as their counterparts in northern Italy.[13] The Carbonari increasingly drew a hitherto quiescent populace into civic activity, and posed an immediate threat to the traditionalist Bourbon King Ferdinand I, when he was restored to the Neapolitan throne in 1815.

Carbonari ritual in the South was far more effective in mobilizing the masses than traditional Masonic ritual in the North. Naturalistic and familiar symbols replaced the occult and mathematical language of Masonry. The charcoal burners were an artisan brotherhood in the woods, not an esoteric order in a temple; they met in a bourgeois shop (the literal meaning of *vendita*, the term used for their local cells) rather than an aristocratic lodge; and they bade their members follow a patron saint (Theobald, who allegedly renounced civilization for the simple life of the charcoal burner) rather than to seek out the esoteric secrets of Solomon, Pythagoras, and the like. Most important, the Carbonari used popular religious symbols in this intensely Catholic region.

Membership was attained by initiation into a kind of higher Christian fraternity. The postulant for the second grade of membership received a crown of thorns analogous to that of Christ's own passion. Later, as the society became more explicitly political, initiation came to include the path of Calvary past Caiaphas, Herod, and Pilate. The implication was that Christ had pointed out the path of resistance to civil power, church, and king alike. The final, fourth degree of initiation involved a binding to the cross and receipt of the stigmata before being rescued and accepted as a grand-master, grand-elect pledged to fighting tyranny.[14]

The path of the Carbonari from philanthropy to political ambition has never been clearly mapped. But here again it appears that the fantasies of reactionaries played a role in determining the identities of revolutionaries. The Carbonari account of the group's origin appears to have been adopted from the account given in Abbé Barruel's counter-revolutionary exposé, according to which Scottish fugitives had been seeking liberty in the forests as charcoal burners. King Francis I of France was allegedly aided by them when he got lost on a hunting mission, was then initiated into their rites, and became their protector.[15]

By 1812, the Carbonari had assumed their characteristic structure of secret local cells ruled by a higher one: the *Alta Vendita*. The Carbonari became, in effect, a pyramidal counter-government in the Kingdom of Naples, with a self-appointed mandate to assemble a legislative body from other tribes (the ethnic-territorial subdivisions of the Carbonari). Carbonari organizations soon spread into the papal states and other Italian provinces, melding a new constitutional ideal with the age-old dream of a united Italy.

The Carbonari combined all three beliefs that we have seen to be crucial to the revolutionary tradition: belief in an uncompleted revolution, in the authority of Nature against tradition, and in secret, hierarchical organization.

Belief in an uncompleted revolution was particularly widespread in Italy, which had provided some of the most dramatic echoes and notable foreign supporters for the original French Revolution and the Napoleonic reforms. The Italian middle class was angered at the return of a conservative monarchy without even the partial guarantee of constitutional liberties offered by the French Charter of 1815.

The society viewed itself as heir to a rich line of sects and societies that had kept alive "the unaffected language of nature," and could guide man "to the contemplation of never varying nature, to the love of man collectively." [16] Although "the tender name of brother has been renounced" by a humanity that has fallen prey to violence and intrigue,[17] one could at least become a "good cousin" through the Carbonari.

The space surrounding the meeting place was the forest in which goodness had been preserved by the charcoal burners. Each apprentice wore a small fragment of wood—hoping that it would be transformed into the higher form of charcoal and he into a charcoal burner. The Grand Master used an axe as his gavel on a wooden block, the symbolic trunk of a tree to which all branches of the society were organically related. These branches all shared common roots in the earth, and were part of a great common tree, whose leaves reminded the secret fraternity

> . . . that as our first parents, after having lost their innocence, covered their shame with leaves, [so] the Good Cousins ought to conceal the faults of their fellow men, and particularly those of the Society.[18]

Secrecy became almost a way of life for the Carbonari, with their meetings concealed from public view, secret handclasps, passwords, and pass-signs. Hierarchical discipline was also important. The Grand Master exercised absolute power over the agenda. No good cousin could speak at a meeting without permission from the head of the line in which he was seated; and penalties were prescribed for failings either in personal morality or in Carbonari ritual.

The wooden ladder—symbol of man's climb to perfection—was always present on the table of the lodge master; and a principal sign of both the apprentices and the masters was known as the "ladder." [19] Their ritual of recognition—the vertical extension of both arms downwards with clenched fists—may be a distant ancestor of the future revolutionary salute: the raised, single-armed clenched fist. Bundles (*fasci*) of sticks also lay on the table of the master—a symbol that harked back to ancient Rome and would be revived in the Rome of Mussolini. For the Carbonari the bundles signified "the members of our respectable order, united in peace." [20]

In order for each piece of wood to be transformed symbolically into the purer, more useful form of charcoal, each meeting was conceived of as a ritual purification by fire in the furnaces of a secret grotto within a forest.[21] Those who progressed on to the level of the great elect faced the most awesome of these ordeals by fire. The Grand Master entered through the secret single door from the West.

Two guards called "flames" are placed at either side of the door, with two sabres like flames of fire.[22]

The members sat in triangular lines in a triangular room under three over-hanging candles symbolizing the three sources of enlightenment in the great firmament (sun, moon, and northern star). The meeting was opened with seven solemn strokes of the axe by the Grand Master upon the ceremonial tree trunk to the East, now decorated not just with symbolic fire but with "numerous yellow flames." [23]

Those deemed unworthy of admission could be excluded if "black balled" with charcoal in a black book. There was quite literally a burning obligation to meet the society's demands for both secrecy to outsiders and full disclosure to fellow members. The names of repeatedly errant members were burned from the membership rolls at public meetings.[24]

The Carbonari provided an ideal meeting ground for those who were politicized by the revolutionary era and shared its vague resolve to "rid the forest of its wolves." [25] By 1817, the society was printing pamphlets that suggested withholding tax payments until the king granted a written constitution.[26] Political involvements increased until the Carbonari led the successful Neapolitan uprising in July 1820. Then, when Austrian troops came in to put it down, the Carbonari led a similar revolution in Piedmont to the north.[27]

These spectacular if short-lived Italian upheavals were the decisive events of the Restoration era for the revolutionary tradition. They were the central link in a chain of constitutional revolutions that had begun five years earlier far to the west with colonial rebellions against Spain and ended five years later with the defeat in the east of the Russian Decembrists. The Italian upheaval was inspired by the successful revolution in Spain in January 1820; [28] and the Italians in turn helped inspire the Russians.

International Echoes

The first—and the only successful—echo of the Carbonari began with a secret conclave of revolutionaries held in the fall of 1820, at the very time when counter-revolutionary powers were meeting at the Troppau Congress. A group of East Europeans gathered in Izmail at the mouth of the Danube heard plans for a forthcoming upheaval in Greece outlined by an organization remarkably similar to the Carbonari: the *Philiki Hetairia* or Brotherly Association. Formed by Greeks in nearby Odessa in 1814,[29] it resembled the Italian organization in its initiation rites and oaths, its mixture of Masonic and Christian symbols. There were four levels in its hierarchy, supplemented later by three specially recruited higher levels under a seven-man directorate. This complex, secret structure grew rapidly, largely within the Greek merchant community of the Mediterranean. Its affiliates spread from Gibraltar to the Russian Black Sea ports. It provided a rallying cause and a refuge for disgruntled Balkan veterans of a decade of intermittent struggle against the Turks.

The Hetairia had four advantages over the Carbonari: an important sponsor within the continental power structure (General Alexander Ypsilanti, aide-de-camp to Tsar Alexander I); a non-European foe (the Moslem Turks); a more explicitly political focus (its basic higher and lower orders being those of citizen and administrator respectively); and, above all, a song. For the Greek national movement had been called into being by a militant, anti-Turkish hymn, the *Thourios,* which electrified the Greek people with a rapidity "perhaps unique in history" even before its author-poet, Rhigas Velestinlis, was arrested with his flute and two wood instruments and turned over by the Hapsburgs to the Ottomans for execution in 1798. If the rudimentary organization of "good cousins" that he had founded in Vienna with branches in Belgrade and Bucharest was in some respects a forerunner of the Hetairia, his anthem anticipated the evocative role we shall find music repeatedly playing in nineteenth-century national revolutions.[30]

Since the song of Rhigas appealed to all Balkan peoples, and the Hetairia of Ypsilanti (whom Rhigas had once served as secretary) was strong throughout the Balkans, hopes rose for a widespread insurrection to be supported by Russian arms against the Turks. But the assassination in 1817 of the militant Karageorge, the former elected head of constitutional Serbia, deprived the Hetairia of its most powerful ally. The failure of an uprising in Moldavia and Wallachia early in 1821 dampened visions of a Danubian or trans-Balkan liberation.[31]

Nevertheless, the uprising that began in Greece in March 1821, revived hope for revolution elsewhere, stimulating the romantic imagination with the ideal of liberating shrines of classical antiquity and appealing even to conservatives as a crusade of Christian solidarity. Greek independence was finally achieved only after the great powers installed a conservative monarch; and the entire Greek struggle became in many ways a safety valve for the revolutionary impulses of the age. Even conservative monarchs subscribed to the "revolutionary" cause of fighting the Turkish Sultan.

But radical romantics also imagined themselves renewing links with the cradle of democracy, and the Greek national revolution assumed an enduring historical importance for the revolutionary tradition. It raised the prestige of constitutional revolution throughout Europe at the very time when that cause seemed most humiliated. It gave an imaginative boost to the cause of national—as distinct from social—revolution; and it mobilized politically the influential romantic writers.[32] Shelley wrote his last drama *Hellas* in its praise; and its literary sympathizers helped popularize the new designation "liberal" for those who sought to limit kings and clergy with constitutions and civil liberties. Lord Byron helped found the new quarterly *Liberal* and published his *Verse and Prose from the South* in 1822, and secured his position as romantic hero of the age by dying as a revolutionary volunteer in Greece two years later.

The liberal ideal did indeed come from the South. If after Italy Greece became the chosen cause of European revolutionaries in the 1820s, in the preceding decade it was in Spain that "liberal" first became inscribed on the banner of national revolution.[33] The birth of the term "liberal" in Spain—used in opposition to the term "servile"—marks the conscious appearance of Manichaean combat terminology among revolutionaries.[34] The establishment of constitutional rule the following years involved in the revolutionaries' eyes, more than a mere victory of "democrats" over "aristocrats" (the sharpest polemic dualism of the French revolutionary era). The new "liberal" revolution marked the birth of a new type of "liberal" man, freed at last from a heritage of servility.

Lord Castlereagh introduced the word in the House of Commons early in 1816, by denouncing the Spanish "Liberales" as "a perfectly Jacobinical party." [35] By then, the new ideal had already spread to France during the one hundred days of renewed hopes that followed Napoleon's dramatic return from Elba in March 1815. Joseph Rey of Grenoble, where Napoleon received one of his most tumultuous welcomes, told the emperor in April that the age of "liberal ideas" and "liberal constitutions" had dawned; [36] and that Napoleon should head the new movement as "the favorite foster child of the most liberal of revolutions." [37]

After Napoleon's defeat at Waterloo and final exile, many older figures, like Lafayette and Cousin, who had rallied to him during his "liberal" period, were impressed with the constitutional charter under which the restored Louis XVIII promised to rule. Lafayette confided to Jefferson his intention "to unite ourselves with the constitutional throne of the Bourbons while struggling to make it as national and liberal as possible." [38]

But to the younger generation, the "national and liberal" banner was sullied almost from the beginning. Napoleon had raised great expectations in his last one hundred days. Many young soldiers and students who had never known any other model could not accept a Bourbon restoration: "They swore that France would rise again from its days of mourning." [39]

In February 1816, Rey formed in his native Grenoble the first French secret society of the restoration period: the *Union libérale*.[40] It appears to have had both international inspiration and ambitions, disguising its statutes as an extract from the *Boston Gazette* of 1796.[41] It recruited French political exiles in Germany, Switzerland, and Belgium,[42] and followed the tradition of Buonarroti in superimposing a third grade on two lower, Masonic-type grades of membership. Rey was inspired by his close contacts with Germany and later became an active agent in Switzerland for Buonarroti's plans for an international revolutionary organization.[43]

Union soon established links with the respectable revolutionaries who provided the backbone of what was soon to be called the French Carbonari: Lafayette, Voyer d'Argenson, Dupont de l'Eure, and Victor Cousin. At the same time the swelling postwar student population in Paris began independently to use Masonic lodges for republican agitation. An organization, formed soon after September 1818 under the Illuminist name Friends of Truth, became a center for student radicals and gained more than one thousand members.[44]

The proliferation of organizations and demonstrations in France during 1819–20 reveals no single directing force or program. Yet the student circles of the restoration shared with the police spies who pursued them the implausible assumption that the agitation of a few would somehow produce a convulsion among the many. The students felt—all appearances to the contrary notwithstanding—that innovation through sudden political change was the destiny of modern France. Accordingly, their task was simply to throw out the foreign-imposed rule of the Bourbons. The antimonarchical party known as the Independents was thus infiltrated by students who substituted the subversive Spanish label "liberal" and introduced the even more terrifying Italian term Carbonari for their organization.

Using Masonic organizations for revolutionary mobilization through the Friends of Truth, the students converted the journal *The French Aristarchus* into a legal outlet for revolutionary ideas in 1819. The same group attempted to organize a revolutionary "directorial committee" and a classical conspiratorial web of five-man cells ("brigades").[45] Little direction was given, and these brigades often resorted to uncoordinated violence; but they represented the first large-scale deployment in France outside of military organizations of this cellular type.

The French students of 1820 introduced the typical modern justification of revolutionary violence as a necessary defensive measure against the forcible undermining of their constitutional rights:

All the efforts made by a people to reconquer the constitution which violence or intrigues have torn away from it are legitimate.[46]

The innumerable mini-revolts of the French Carbonari [47] were born of the belief that making manifest what was secret would somehow trigger revolutionary change. There was an exaggerated faith in the power of a demonstration (*manifestation*) or proclamation (*manifeste*). This faith related directly to the belief that some new spiritual power was being generated within the secret society.

The young revolutionaries sometimes compared their power to that of magnetism and electricity—those newly discovered forces in nature that seemed to reveal new powers beyond those described by Newtonian mechanics.[48] Prati made a pilgrimage to visit Mesmer before joining Buonarroti in a revolutionary career,[49] and Buonarroti had an equally typical interest in Swedenborg.[50] Revolution was related directly to spiritualism by Barbès, one of the key figures in the secret revolutionary societies of the 1830s.[51] Robert Owen, who influenced both Rey and Buonarroti, eventually became a full-time spiritualist.[52]

In this atmosphere, revolutionaries turned to Buonarroti as "an occult power whose shadowy tentacles extended over . . . Europe." [53] Buonarroti sought to use the Carbonari organizations as he had Masonic ones earlier, and he probably collaborated with the French republican delegation that went to Naples in the mid-1820s to establish connections with the Carbonari.[54] His principal friends and protectors in Geneva, the Fazy brothers, were a key link between the Italian and French movements.[55] James Fazy was specially fascinated by the revolutionary potential of youth, and soon wrote perhaps the first programmatic declaration of generational war in modern times. His *Gerontocracy* of 1828 saw revolutionary struggle as a necessary response to a political system that denied participation to anyone under forty; and to an ideology that frustrated the enthusiasm of youth for applied science as a means of unleashing human productivity.[56]

Buonarroti himself crossed into Savoy from his frequent meeting place with revolutionaries just across the Swiss border at Nyon, initiating Frenchmen into the first grade of Carbonari membership.[57] His close associate Prati established a Carbonari *vente* in Lausanne [58] and became a point of contact between the directorate of the French Carbonari and the *Alta Vendita* in Naples. Prati had become a member of the Swiss Bible society and wrote a tract praising Swiss reformers which was published in a variety of languages (including Romansh) in the Swiss town of Chur [59]—a frequent point of reunion with German-speaking revolutionaries. Within Italy, Carbonari organizers also sometimes traveled as agents of the Bible society [60]—lending some credence to the widespread fear that this new, missionary-oriented organization was potentially subversive if not covertly revolutionary.[61]

After the arrests in Piedmont of the Carbonari, revolutionaries there apparently sought links with the Buonarrotian Grand Firmament.[62] Prati discussed with Joseph Rey, then in exile in Bern, a possible "European Union" to be based on Rey's *Union* in Grenoble. Prati attempted to coordinate an anti-Hapsburg attack in the Tyrol with Hapsburg troop movements against Naples, and to recruit soldiers "to act in conjunction with General Berton," the principal provincial insurrectionist in France.[63]

Buonarroti's associates formed a triumvirate in eastern Switzerland in April 1820 to recruit twelve men from different countries to act as leaders of the coming republican revolution and to organize a web of supporting secret societies among soldiers, craftsmen, and students. The specific inclusion of students was probably the work of the most remarkable member of the triumvirate, Karl Follen of Giessen: "the first student leader of modern times . . . the prototype for all the student leaders of the next century and a half." [64] Follen, an extremist leader within the new German student societies (*Burschenschaften*), soon joined other youthful émigrés in Swiss exile to form a revolutionary League of Youth (*Bund der Jungend*) which also sought to establish links with the Carbonari.

The *Burschenschaften* were assertively masculine and Francophobe societies that had arisen during the national struggle against Napoleon. They emphasized vigorous gymnastics; and in 1818, on the first anniversary of their outdoor festival at Wartburg, some one thousand five hundred students in long hair and open-necked, unbleached linen shirts proclaimed a "universal students' union"—"the first overt, self-conscious assertion of the intellectual elite as a political force in modern history." [65]

As a leader of the Union's left wing, which admired the French Revolution as much as German antiquity, Follen had already in 1814 formed a German reading society which later became a German culture and friendship society, but was best known by its intervening designation—the blacks—after the color of its members' favorite velvet attire. Seeking a republican constitution for a united Germany based on the 1793 model from revolutionary France,[66] Follen soon became obsessed with the question of how to move from endless discussion to concrete action. "Life without science," he concluded was better than "science without life." [67] In a series of Sunday afternoon meetings with trusted friends, he formed an activist revolutionary band, "the unconditionals," who toyed with the idea of selective political assassination. They argued that perjury and murder "against the great robbers and murderers of popular freedom" might be a duty. Members were "unconditionally" bound to follow the dictates of the group, and "if matters come to the worst, all who are wavering in their opinions must be sacrificed." [68] Moving from Giessen after its student association was shut in 1818, Follen became a lecturer and counselor to student radicals in the permissive atmosphere of Jena. One student put his ideas into practice on March 23, 1819, by fatally stabbing Kotzebue, a prominent playwright thought to be an agent of the Holy Alliance.

This assassination, which forced Follen to leave Germany, had an electric effect on wavering revolutionaries. Prati—who was soon to join Follen as a triumvir of Buonarroti's Great Firmament—later recalled his feelings on first hearing about the event in a Swiss inn:

> It seemed as if this was a signal for a general combat . . . from that moment all my mind became as it were inflamed for political strife; from that moment I plunged headlong in a continual series of conspiracies and revolutionary commotions.[69]

Reflecting on this turning point in later years after he had ceased to be an active revolutionary, Prati noted the inspirational effect of ideologically motivated violence:

> . . . such is the power of political fanaticism, and party spirit, that a murder committed with cold deliberation upon a gentleman of great literary renown . . . instead of eliciting any signs of compassion for the victim among the most moral and inoffensive nation of the world, elicited the most enthusiastic sympathy for the assassin.[70]

Along with Prati and Buonarroti, Follen drew up plans in 1821 in Chur for a secret revolutionary organization which was largely German in composition, but more universal in its aims than earlier Carbonari-type groups. This League of Youth was alleged to be the activist arm of an ultrasecret League of Men who were supposedly already scattered throughout society and ready to constitute after the revolution a new republican government. Preparations for the revolution were assigned to the youth organization, which began recruitment in Germany during the summer of 1821 through a Jena student who had gone to Italy to participate in the Carbonari revolt earlier that year.[71] The idea of a *Männerbund-Jünglingsbund* has no precise antecedent in Germany and may have been an effort to realize the first two grades of Buonarroti's *Monde*: men and adolescents.[72]

The German republican movement was, however, swept away in a flood tide of repression. The leading ministers of the German-speaking world meeting at Carlsbad throughout August 1819 abolished the *Burschenschaften* and introduced uniform censorship and political supervision of the universities. Most members of the League of Youth were arrested; and, by the end of 1824, Follen was forced to leave Switzerland. He dreamed of founding a German state in America as a secure base for mounting further revolutionary agitation in Germany and throughout Europe, but he soon settled down to become a Unitarian minister and the first professor of German literature at Harvard University.

The wave of insurrections against monarchs was broken in 1823, when a French royalist army invaded Spain and rescued the king with relative ease from the constitutional obligations he had assumed in 1820. French and other foreign republicans formed a Legion of European Liberty to fight for the Spanish liberals, but this proved as futile as efforts of the International Brigade on behalf of the Spanish Republic in the 1930s. In both cases, the trend of the times was towards the Right. Fears were felt as far away as the United States—by President Monroe in the 1820s even more acutely than by President Roosevelt in the 1930s. In December 1823, Monroe propounded his doctrine condemning intervention in the New World, fearing that the Holy Alliance might seek to reassert its sway in newly independent Hispanic America.

Within Europe, the victorious conservative tide produced a fresh crop of fanciful theories about "the Hydra of Revolution." [73] Writers denounced not only republicanism but Masonry and Pythagorean symbols. The new rector of the University of Kazan, Michael Magnitsky, went so far as to insist that the Pythagorean theorem no longer be taught in schools except as a theological proof of the Trinity. The sides of the right angle were the Father and Son; and the hypotenuse, whose square so harmoniously equalled that of the other two, represented the love of God coming down to man via the Holy Ghost.[74] An anonymous study of 1823 suggested that aristocratic patrons of revolution should first renounce their own titles (Lafayette should call himself neither Marquis nor General, but farmer; Voyer D'Argenson, "iron-master" rather than Viscount, and so forth), and presented a prototypically conservative view of the subversive effect of an expanding educational system:

> . . . the man, who can read and write, fancies himself on an equality with his superiors, and, instead of earning his bread by honest labour, he meditates on state matters, and becomes a politician, and in his heart a traitor.[75]

The reaction seemed to climax in 1824 with the accession to the French throne amidst medieval pageantry of the ultraconservative Charles X. Masonry and the Carbonari were outlawed by kings and condemned by the pope. Organized discussions of any kind became suspect, and civil liberties waned throughout the continent.

Russian Reprise

The last echo of the constitutional rebellions came in distant Russia with the Decembrist revolt late in 1825, in which major themes of the earlier rebellions in western and southern Europe were played back in reprise.

An ill-coordinated coalition of several secret organizations sought to force Russia to accept some form of constitutional limitation on tsarist power after the death of Alexander I. Its leaders were young officers and even younger students who brought unusually high hopes out of the Napoleonic period. Russia had first shared with Napoleon the dream of dividing up the civilized world and then had taken the lead in defeating him. Those young officers who had entered Paris triumphantly at the beginning of Holy Week 1814 and celebrated en masse the Easter liturgy in the square where Louis XVI had been guillotined (now renamed Place de la Concorde) could not easily readjust to the petty perspectives of provincial Russian life. The Turgenev brothers, the first to form plans for a secret society, testified to the impact of the wartime experience on their political consciousness:

> The circumstances of the last war reinforced a soldier's material strength with moral strength, the strength of opinion. They had fought for the fatherland, for freedom, for independence. Then suddenly it was proposed to turn these giants back into gingerbread soldiers! And by whom? Political pygmies.[76]

The Turgenevs followed the familiar revolutionary pattern of deriving their organizational ideas not directly from an earlier revolutionary group, but rather from conservative attacks on a previous secret society (the German *Tugendbund*).[77]

More like the quasi-religious Italian Carbonari than the secular French movement, young Russians dreamed of bringing spiritual rebirth to Europe by consummating Alexander I's marriage of "religion and liberty." They sought to use Masonic lodges, beginning with the Lodge Astrea—named for the Goddess of Justice, who had been the last to leave the Elysian fields before the end of the Golden Age.

Just as the Carbonari at first enjoyed the patronage of Murat, so the Russian Decembrists received initial encouragement from Alexander himself. He actually joined the Lodge Astrea and vaguely implied that the parliament which the Poles maintained within his expanded empire might provide a model for the rest.

The characteristic move towards increased secretiveness and radicalism began with the transformation in 1818 of the Society for the Salvation of the Fatherland into the Union of Welfare, which then developed a proto-governmental structure. A secret meeting in Moscow early in 1821 set up a "constituent Duma" and regional councils of the Union. The split between constitutional monarchists and radical republicans—characteristic of the Italian, French, and Spanish movements alike—was reproduced in Russia in the conflict between the federal ideas of the Northern Society and the Jacobin version of a unitary republic in the Southern Society. As elsewhere, there were partisans of regicide: a small group of youth who dreamed as early as 1816–17 of a twelve-man brotherhood that would kill the Imperial family at night on the road to Tsarskoe Selo.[78]

The Decembrist movement was both the last chapter in a century-long struggle of Russian aristocratic reformers and the starting point of the modern Russian revolutionary tradition. If the revolt was also part of the European-wide chain reaction of constitutional risings against traditional monarchies, the leaders already displayed many of the distinctive characteristics of later Russian revolutionaries—stoic, humorless asceticism combined with a cult of brotherhood and Schilleresque theatricality.[79]

In December 1825, the more revolutionary faction of the movement, the so-called Southern Society, mounted a doomed uprising in the Chernigov Regiment. The leading theorist of this group, Paul Pestel, was one of the most inventive revolutionary thinkers of his time anywhere in Europe. He was one of the few to argue for an authoritarian, centralized revolutionary state that would consciously create a single nationality and press for egalitarian social reforms.[80] He followed the Buonarrotian pattern of making extensive use of Masonic lodges and symbols,[81] and anticipated Buonarroti in calling for an immediate provisional government after a revolution.[82]

As the son of a former governor of Siberia and a veteran of the Napoleonic wars, Pestel had traveled widely. His pan-European, even worldwide perspectives bordered on megalomania, but also reflected the reality of Russian power. After 1815, the incorporation into Russia of western regions—the Baltic provinces and Poland—added non-Russians into the agitation for political reform.[83]

Meanwhile in St. Petersburg, conservative ministers and bureaucrats (often German) had been appalled by the new wave of German student unrest in 1816–18 and developed a kind of domino theory of revolution spreading east from Germany through Poland to Russia. Then came word of conspiracy even further east, with returning veterans setting up small secret societies even in places like Orenburg and Astrakhan. The virus seemed to spread even to the Arctic north, when the secretary to the governor of Olonetsk set up a secret society called the French Parliament in Petrozavodsk.[84] The barrage of revolutionary reports from afar created a giddy sense among youthful Russians of "another mail delivery, another revolution." [85]

To Pestel, the experience of the early 1820s in Spain, Portugal, and Naples demonstrated the treachery of kings and the hopelessness of constitutional monarchy. Even in France and England constitutions were only masks for monarchical despotism. Revolution inside Russia might lead to international war. After Napoleon's experience, no one would dare invade Russia, so revolution there "will spread safely and immediately to other countries whose people are even more bent on revolution." [86]

The all-European nature of the revolutionary contagion is illustrated by the affinity that the Decembrists felt for the revolutionary constitutionalists at the opposite extremity of the continent: in Spain. The Spaniards' original "little war" (*guerrilla*) of popular resistance to Napoleon in 1808–09 had anticipated and influenced the Russians' "partisan war" against him in 1812–13. Young Russian officers had shared with distant Spaniards a sense of common victory and—uniquely in Europe—of contact with the inarticulate masses who made the new guerrilla tactics possible. The Decembrists took as their principal model for a constitution that of the Spanish liberal monarchy of 1812; and for their eventual uprising, the bloodless Spanish Revolution of 1820.[87]

The Decembrists may also have been more closely related to other European revolutionary movements than has yet been realized. The original Union of Salvation was formed in 1816 among Russian officers traveling back and forth to France at precisely the time Rey founded his model *Union*. Once again, the Russians developed similar plans for working through Masonic lodges with a secret, three-stage hierarchy.[88] F. N. Glinka, the principal founder of the Union of Salvation, appears to have been influenced by a twice-translated French work describing "the institute of Pythagoras." [89] The charter of the successor organization, the Union of Welfare, borrowed directly from the French *Union*;[90] its stated aim of establishing "the common good" with "social ownership" suggested the Babeuvist tradition; and its unexplained title, "the green book," repeated that of Duplay's dictionary of conspiracies. An inner group of an Illuminist-Buonarrotian type may have been contemplated. Allusions to an unnamed head and special watchman among the five members of the root council suggest the ultra-secret new fourth grade of observers that Buonarroti was then introducing into his organizational plans.[91]

The conspirator whom Buonarroti sent from Geneva to Italy in 1822 to organize revolutionaries internationally later wrote that "skilled and numerous emissaries were sent at that time to Germany, Poland, and even to Russia." [92] As early as 1819, a sympathetic French observer told of an ultra-secret revolutionary group in Italy, the consistory.

> . . . it is principally in Russia that the conspirators place their hope . . . precisely because there is something vague and undetermined in its aim, which encourages all expectations. One must also add that the men of the consistory are solicitously entertained by the Russians—accredited or not— who pass through Italy.[93]

Whatever the specific connections, the general fascination of young Russians with western revolutionary movements—and above all the Carbonari—is undeniable. Russians had many contacts with Italian revolutionaries, and tried to establish links early in 1819.[94] The Grand Duke Michael toured Italy in the same year together with his (and the tsar's) tutor, Laharpe, who had become a leader of the Swiss Carbonari in close contact with the Italian movement.[95] In May, a leading Russian periodical published an article in praise of the Sect of Pythagorians, beginning its catechism with questions allegedly asked by Pythagoras himself: "What is universal? *Order*. What is friendship? *Equality*." [96] Their credo went, if anything, beyond Buonarroti:

> Not having any private property, not knowing false pride and vain praise, far from petty things that often divide, they competed with one another only in doing good. . . . They learned to use things in common and forget about ownership.[97]

A brief uprising in the tsar's favored Semenovsky Regiment in 1820 led, however, to repression in Russia and thus in turn to increasing Polish dominance of revolutionary activity in eastern Europe. The Poles had deeper links with the Italian movement through both a common background of collaboration with Napoleon and a common Catholic culture.

The special commission that investigated the Decembrists during the first half of 1826, after their doomed uprising, suggested that their regional organization was modelled on the five regional *ventes* of the French Carbonari.[98] Moreover, the Italians were so well informed of the plans of the Russian movement and so optimistic about its potential that they continued to expect a second and conclusive uprising by the Decembrists in the spring of 1826: the original secret date chosen before the abortive rising of December.[99]

But the Decembrists did not rise again. Five leaders were hung and the others sent off to Siberia. Epithets and mud were hurled at them en route by a populace that (like that of Spain two years earlier) showed that it did not share the elitist interest in revolution.

Mediterranean Diaspora

A decade of international constitutional agitation against the conservative restoration had come to an end. The revolutionary picture in 1826 was one of total disorder. Left behind were only an aura of romantic heroism and a few martyrs. But the period had been one of critical revolutionary experiment and political tutelage—not least for one of the youngest of the French Carbonari, Auguste Blanqui. Even as a twenty-year-old boy, late in 1825, Blanqui had drawn inspiration from the Decembrists: "five martyrs of liberty . . . illustrious victims that European democracy has inscribed on its martyrology" for having opened "to Russia the era of progress and liberty." [100] He was to keep alive the conspiratorial spirit throughout the nineteenth century, and to help transmit it back to a more receptive Russia in the 1870s.

Within Russia itself, a revolutionary tradition distinctive in many ways began atop Sparrow (now Lenin) Hills overlooking Moscow when the youthful Herzen and Ogarev swore together their "Hannibalic oath" to "sacrifice our entire lives" to the struggle that the Decembrists had begun.[101] Many ideas of the Russian revolutionary tradition were to come from Herzen,[102] and some of its organizational ideas from Ogarev.[103] Russia, as we have seen, was the last to turn to revolution in the crisis of authority that followed the Napoleonic wars. A century later, after the next great continental war, Russia was to be the first.

But for all its international echoes and prophetic anticipations, the post-restoration decade of revolutionary activity belonged largely to the Italians. The Carbonari had been the first secret organization to lead a large-scale revolution in modern Europe. Despite its failure and disintegration, the Carbonari awakened enthusiasm for a united Italy; and provided a model for others. Its surviving members retreated into a sub-culture of localized groups—sometimes taking the names of their local *vendita*, sometimes inventing new ones, sometimes dissolving into other groups.

The Carbonari diaspora produced a bewildering variety of atomized protest groups. Classic revolutionary cells appeared with such colorful names as "five in a family" and "the seven sleepers." The hasty military training grafted onto the Carbonari during the uprisings of 1820 left a legacy of militance, intensified by the execution of some eight hundred Carbonari leaders after the uprising was put down. Veterans of the struggle formed new militant groups like the Sons of Mars of 1820 and the American Hunters (*cacciatori Americani*), who met for drills in the pine woods near Ravenna. There were the black bellies (*pancie nere*) of Rome, the shirtless ones (*scamiciati*) and vampires (*vampiri*) of Naples, the imitators of Sand (the young assassin) in Sicily. Reactionary groups, such as the piercers (*bucatori*) of Tuscany, may have forged a link with "social bandits" keeping alive folk traditions of local resistance to central authority.[104] Extremist groups sometimes appear to have had broader connections throughout Italy, such as the destroyers (*sterma-*

tori); and beyond, such as the devils of London and Greeks of silence.

The era of the Carbonari left behind a legacy of conspiracy and frustration that was to lead Italians and Poles to develop new theories of revolutionary violence to which we shall return. It also provided a precedent and legend for the Mediterranean area that broke the hold of authoritarian fatalism and influenced a host of subsequent uprisings from the good cousins of the forest of Oran in Algeria in 1848 [105] to the Young Turks a half century later.[106]

CHAPTER 6

National vs. Social Revolution (1830–48)

THE PERIOD between 1830 and 1848 witnessed the most fundamental internal conflict within the modern revolutionary tradition, that between national revolution and social revolution. It was then that men began to confront a question that still arises: Should the coming revolution create a new nation of cultural brotherhood that obliterates the lines between classes? Or a new classless society that breaks down national borders? Should revolutionaries rely on the emotional appeal of nationalism or the intellectual appeal of social equality?

This enduring question was posed implicitly in the mid-1790s. As early optimism faded, French revolutionaries began to ask if the fulfillment of their stalled revolution lay in *fraternité* or *égalité*: the building of a *grande nation* as Napoleon urged or of a new social *communauté* as called for by Babeuf. The more popular idea was—and has generally remained—that of a nation, and of what the Spaniards were the first to call "national revolution." [1]

After the revolutions of 1830, romantic nationalism lost its automatic linkage with constitutional liberalism. As nationalism developed a new revolutionary intensity of its own, it began to confront a Babeuvist revival from which the rival tradition of social revolution emerged.

The Revolution of 1830 in France raised more hopes than it could satisfy by merely removing the last Bourbon king of France. A new generation was excited by the "three glorious days" of July when men were once again willing to stand and fall on one or the other side of the barricades. The poet Alfred de Vigny wrote almost breathlessly upon the outbreak of insurrection in Paris in July 1830:

> Since this morning they are fighting. The workers have all the bravery of Vendéens; the soldiers, the courage of an imperial guard; Frenchmen every-

where. Ardor and intelligence on the one side, honor on the other. . . . Poor people, great people, warriors all.[2]

This romantic love of heroism—whether Vendéen or revolutionary—made it difficult to reconcile oneself to the *juste milieu* of Louis Philippe. France seemed to have been reborn out of sheer enthusiasm; a month later a new nation was in fact born out of spontaneous upheaval in Belgium; and this in turn inspired a heroic national revolution in Poland. The picture of nations rising in arms against foreign rule provided new hope for national and social revolutionaries alike. But nationalists were far more numerous, and Italians led the way. Having provided the previous model through the Carbonari, Italy now devised the prototype of a national revolutionary organization in Giuseppe Mazzini's Young Italy.

The rival call for social rather than national revolution was sounded at the same time as Mazzini's appeals. In 1831, just as Young Italy was formed among émigrés in Marseilles, French artisans farther up the Rhone at Lyon turned a riot into an insurrection, inspiring a new language of class warfare. French poets in 1831 spoke of a "universal uprising" and of a revolutionary volcano unleashing a "lava of new Spartacuses" to level out inequality and insure that "there will be no more bastard children on our native soil." [3]

In the same Lyon, Mazzini used the same metaphor while recruiting for an armed invasion of Savoy that he hoped would set off a chain reaction of nationalist revolutions. "If we act resolutely, if we show one spark of real fire, Italy is a volcano." [4] Shortly after the invasion attempt aborted and his legion dissolved early in 1834, a second and more massive social upheaval convulsed Lyon, inspiring some to speak of "the great final revolt of the proletariat." [5]

If dramatic new models for social revolution came from Lyon, the leadership still came from Paris. Here the awakened romantic imagination was forced to confront the prosaic reality of Louis Philippe's bourgeois monarchy. With growing desperation, Parisians turned in the 1830s to Mazzini's aging Italian rival, Buonarroti, who had returned at last to Paris in 1830 for the final seven years of his life. He and a younger Frenchman of Italian ancestry, Auguste Blanqui, created there in the 1830s the modern belief in a coming social revolution. In contrast, Mazzini set up a series of revolutionary nationalist organizations—Young Italy and Young Europe—precisely to oppose the "Parisian principle": the dependence of an entire continent on one French city.

The conflict between national and social revolutionaries was, in essence, between romanticism and rationalism: the nationalists' emotional love of the unique and organic against the socialists' intellectual focus on general laws and mechanistic analysis. The nationalists saw revolution as a "resurgence" (the Italian *risorgimento*) or even "resurrection" (the Polish *zmartwychwstanie*) of an individual nation. Social revolutionaries saw it as an extension of the scientific universalism of the Enlightenment. If revolutionary nationalists were often poets like Petöfi in Hungary and Mickiewicz in Poland celebrating the uniqueness of their vernacular idiom, social revolutionaries like Blanqui tended to view themselves as educational theorists teaching universal principles.[6] If national revolutionaries tended to exalt the vitalism of youth and the "springtime" of their nation, social revolutionaries tended to cluster around autumnal symbols of mature wisdom: the sexagenarian Buonarroti in the 1830s, Blanqui prematurely aged from prison in the late 1840s, and Marx already remote and venerable in the British Museum after 1850.

The inability of either tradition to understand the other is illustrated by the astonishingly inaccurate appraisal of nationalism in Marx's *Communist Manifesto*, written on the very eve of the widespread nationalist upheavals of 1848.

> The workingmen have no country. . . . National differences and antagonisms between peoples are daily more and more vanishing. . . .[7]

Nationalism rather than socialism remained the dominant revolutionary ideal even after the failures of 1848–50. The First International, which called itself explicitly a "Working Men's Association," sought out Mazzini before it turned to Marx for leadership at its founding in 1864.

The Dominant Nationalists

Revolutionary nationalism attracted a variety of social groups whose pattern of life had been disrupted by the early stages of the Industrial Revolution. The new radical nationalists came neither from the factory-centered proletariat (which hardly even existed on the continent in 1830) nor for the most part from the commercial or industrial bourgeoisie. Three general characteristics seem to have been shared by most of those who identified revolution with nationalism during this period—whether they were East European aristocrats, Franco-Italian junior officers, German students, or educated artisans.

Politically, national revolutionaries sought for themselves—and demanded for others—a greater share of political power than monarchs were willing to give. The drive for power appropriated the new idea of popular sovereignty and pushed into the background the earlier Enlightenment concern about constitutional forms and rational balance.

Socially, the new nationalists were almost all displaced people. Whatever their class status, they had generally lost the sense of structured expectations that traditional societies had hitherto provided. Whereas the revolutions of 1820 had occurred in traditional societies (Spain, southern Italy, Greece, and Russia), the revolutions of 1830 affected regions where the workings of a market economy were relatively advanced: Belgium, Rhineland Germany, northern Italy, Paris, and Poland.

Defeated or frustrated revolutionary exiles congregated after 1830 in victorious Paris and Brussels, or in the even more economically sophisticated urban centers of London and Geneva. There, a combination of unnatural exile and urban anomie often created a compensatory longing for the family-type structures and rural images which became characteristic of revolutionary nationalists. The perception of creeping mechanization and uniformity created a sometimes manic desire to assert the peculiarity and humanity—even the divinity—of one's own tradition. Revolutionaries no less than reactionaries of the romantic era began to look back longingly to the Middle Ages at precisely the time when they first confronted the modern, industrial era.

Occupationally, the national revolutionaries tended to work in the communications media. Whatever their class origin, the new revolutionaries came together not just in Masonic-type meetings and military conspiracies, but in editorial offices and theaters. With an almost missionary spirit they invented, debated, and transmitted ideas and identities for hitherto inert sections of the European population. Their greatest spiritual adventure seemed to lie in defining the mission for one or another of the many "peoples" who had been suppressed in the eighteenth century by the artificial conventions of aristocracies and the subtle tyranny of French culture.

Social revolutionaries were, of course, also affected by political ambition, exile, and the new means of communication. But, during this relatively early stage of industrialization, class identities were not so clearly perceived as national ones. Thus the nationalists were more successful in attracting a mass following. In the wake of 1830, they renewed their efforts to arouse the peoples of Europe against the monarchical power of what the Polish poet Mickiewicz called the "Satanic Trinity" of Russia, Prussia, and Austria.

The Mazzinian International

The man who did the most to incite the peoples of Europe against their kings was the Genoese Giuseppe Mazzini. A veteran of the Carbonari who had been imprisoned during the Revolution of 1830, Mazzini saw his life's mission as an "apostolate" that would provide martyrs as well as teachings for a new type of national society. In exile in 1831, he founded the model society for modern revolutionary nationalism: Young Italy. He collaborated for a time with Buonarroti's new Society of True Italians, but soon rejected the latter's continued dependence on French leadership, as well as its hierarchical "spirit of caste," and challenged the idea that a small group of deracinated conspirators could be trusted even provisionally with dictatorial power by a people with the cultural wealth of Italy.[8] He insisted that a truly Italian movement could never tolerate either terror or one-man rule, both of which he saw emerging from Buonarroti's approach. (Buonarroti in turn denounced Mazzini's links with rich Lombards, arguing against any attempt to invade Piedmont without the aid of France.) [9]

Mazzini renounced his own profession as a lawyer, and often criticized the French emphasis on legal rights rather than moral duties. Jansenist teachers had filled him with a moralistic religiosity; and romantic literature had infected him with a compulsion to produce inspirational writing. More than one hundred large volumes of his collected works still do not exhaust his prose production. He particularly excelled in the most personal of all genres: letters to friends; and his web of association and influence was Europe-wide.

Philosophically, Mazzini provided a universal and not merely a parochial Italian rationale for a nationalistic movement. He spoke of one master (God), one law (progress), and one earthly interpreter (the people). No "people" is complete until it becomes a nation. "The individual is too weak and humanity too vast." [10] True nations are not in conflict, but are only the proper organic units—geographically, linguistically, culturally—of a harmonious international order.

Symbolically, the Italian cause assumed the role that the struggle for Greek independence had played in the preceding period. It fired the romantic imagination throughout Europe with the image of a seat of idealized antiquity bathed in sunlight and beauty, longing for heroic rebirth, bidding everyone unite against a common oppressor: the Hapsburgs, who had replaced the Turks.

Politically, the Italian national movement seemed to hold out the most realistic prospects for success. German nationalists were hemmed in by the Prussian and Austrian monarchies; the Poles had been crushed by the Russians; and other movements were only beginning. The Italians, on the other hand, had international advantages as well as a powerful indigenous revolutionary tradition. Italy was remote from the center of the Hapsburg empire and accessible to potential foreign sources of support: France, Switzerland, and even seaborne England. Mazzini was able to mobilize on French and Swiss soil an international legion of French, Germans, Swiss, and Poles under a Polish commander to join with Italians in an aborted attempt of January 1834 to invade Savoy and trigger revolution in Italy.[11]

Organizationally, the Italian movement formally became the center of a European movement on April 15, 1834, when Mazzini attempted to keep the international character of the legion alive by founding Young Europe in Bern, Switzerland. Organized under a committee of seven Italians, five Germans, and five Poles, Young Europe soon added a Young Swiss affiliate and smaller groups for France, Spain, Hungary, and Scandinavia.

Mazzini's alternative to the Buonarrotian centralism of a "universal monarchy controlled from Paris" [12] was a federation of nationalist movements. By the summer of 1835, there were 86 clubs of Young Italy (74 inside Italy with 693 members), 62 Swiss clubs with 480 members, 50 Polish clubs, and 14 each for Young Germany and Young France.[13] Penetrated by spies and torn by disputes between the Italians and the Germans, the organization was expelled from Switzerland in August

1836; and after Mazzini moved to London in January 1837, it virtually ceased to exist. But the example of trans-national collaboration in the cause of nationalism had been established and securely identified with Italy. Mazzini's nationalist International was the first of many attempts throughout the nineteenth century to draw revolutionary nationalists together in a common struggle against traditional monarchies. The international importance of the Italian cause extended even beyond Europe in the late thirties and early forties. Giuseppe Garibaldi, who had been converted by Mazzini and condemned with him for attempted insurrection within the Piedmontese armed forces in 1833, took the cause of national revolution in its purest Italian form to Latin America. He joined the struggle to defend the new nation of Uruguay from the incursions of its giant neighbors, Brazil and Argentina.

With a ship named the *Mazzini* and an Italian Legion mobilized under his command to "serve the cause of nations," Garibaldi went to battle under a black flag with a volcano at the center (symbolizing respectively the mourning of Italy and its coming revolution). His legion acquired its "red shirt" uniform by expropriating smocks in Montevideo which were intended for export to the slaughterhouses of Argentina.[14] These, the original "bloody shirts," were henceforth to camouflage the blood of men rather than cattle. This characteristic Italian revolutionary uniform was later brought back from the New World to the Old when Garibaldi returned with his legion to Italy on a ship named *Speranza*.

On the open deck of this ship of "hope," Garibaldi and his followers gathered nightly on the high Atlantic in a circle for patriotic singing. Such rituals—suggestive alike of Christian vespers and pagan incantation—were characteristic expressions of communal revolutionary expectation in the romantic era. When the *Speranza* finally landed in Spain early in 1848, Garibaldi learned that revolution had already broken out in Italy. It was as if life itself had echoed their chorus, just as hope was heading home.

Garibaldi rushed onstage in Nice like a heroic tenor, and aroused his audience with dramatic appearances all over Italy. His subsequent rallying of besieged republican Rome against assaults from all sides, the tragic death of his beautiful Brazilian wife and companion-in-arms, Anita, and his final departure for the United States in June 1850, on the *Waterloo*—all have some of the quality of Italian opera spilling over onto the stage of history. It seems appropriate that Garibaldi in exile prepared for his glorious revolutionary return to the Italian scene in a house that he shared on Staten Island with the greatest operatic tenor of his day, Lopenzo Salvi.[15]

Indeed, it is well worth pondering the actual, if surprising, way in which opera itself, this most Italian of art forms, interacted with—and even helped to shape—revolutionary nationalism in Europe generally and Italy in particular. For the telling though elusive interaction between theater and life that was evident during the French Revolution became even more striking in the case of opera and revolution in the nineteenth century.

The Operatic Stimulus

The connection between revolution and the musical theater was recognized by one revolutionary at his trial in the summer of 1832:

> People have left the churches for the theaters . . . opera is a spectacle
> to *awaken and excite* the senses . . . a vast reservoir of powerful sensual
> excitements.[16]

Opera so far had been written only for the few and rich, but in the future, it must "awaken and excite" the masses for social transformations—taking advantage of the large audiences to spread ideas through agitators known as *chefs d'attaque* [17] at a time when political assemblies were prohibited.

The "leaders of the attack" on the existing order in the early nineteenth century were the national revolutionaries; [18] and the emotional power of romantic nationalism was heightened by its intimate ties with opera.

Of course, nationalism cast its spell through many art forms. From David to Delacroix, there were pictorial icons. The revolutionary call was sounded in the dramas of Schiller and Hugo—and answered by the vernacular poets who became revolutionary leaders in 1848: Lamartine in France, Petöfi in Hungary, Mickiewicz in Poland, Herwegh in Germany. But revolutionary nationalism was a visceral ideal that reached beyond pictures and poems to the most immaterial—and emotionally evocative—medium of the romantic era: music. Mazzini, while he was forming Young Europe, hailed the revolutionary potential of music as a form of human communication

> which begins where poetry ends . . . the algebra of the spirit . . . the
> perfume of the whole universe . . . which the materialism of our age has
> hidden, not exiled from the world.[19]

Deepest of all was the connection with operatic melodrama. By linking music with vernacular language and local folklore, opera became the vehicle for national consciousness—unifying fragmented, often illiterate audiences. The dream of attaining total human happiness through the creation of a new nation required extraordinary leaps of faith. Belief in a national revolution was somehow easier for those who were already immersed in the unreal world of opera where social, spiritual, and even sexual satisfactions were simultaneously obtained through the magic of music.[20]

There were three stages in linking the operatic stage to the national revolutionary cause. First, in the 1760s, had come the birth of the *opéra comique*, which lifted out of low bourgeois culture its combination of "little songs" (called *vaudevilles*) and spoken dialogue to express everyday sentiment and to evoke direct emotional reactions from the audience. Gone was the aristocratic ideal of disciplining rather than arousing the passions—and the subordination of melody to a rhetorical text.

Second had come the rapid development in the early days of the

French Revolution of a propagandistic, revolutionary message for the *opéra comique*. Revolutionary operas required ever more crude plots, spectacular settings, and larger orchestras attuned to outdoor acoustics and bombastic military music. Brasses replaced strings as "Apollo put down his lyre, donned a red cap, and picked up a trumpet." [21] Actors playing kings were often physically abused, while republican heroes and choruses were required to repeat revolutionary choruses or insert popular songs into the action.

Guillaume Tell—a landmark opera by two leading figures of the *opéra comique*, librettist Michel Sedaine and composer André Gretry —converted the tale of a fourteenth-century Swiss foe of the Hapsburgs into a roiling revolutionary exhortation. Maréchal also glorified William Tell [22] and collaborated with Gretry on ideological operas during the Reign of Terror. In *The Feast of Reason*, a *sans-culotte* is crowned with a cap of liberty, while a priest hails the liberating effects of publicly shedding his robes. Another Maréchal-Gretry opera, *Denis the Tyrant*, celebrated the need "to inculcate in children . . . the sacredness of equality." [23] The invocation to struggle against tyranny may have been even more intense in a lost opera of the same period by Saint-Just, *Selico ou les Nègres*. [24]

The third and final stage in the linkage between opera and national revolution came during the Napoleonic wars. "Revolutionary pride was transferred to the French armies, which were seen as liberators of the oppressed countries." A new genre of "rescue operas" glorified "the liberation of foreign peoples or individuals suffering under absolutism." [25] The most famous of these was the 1798 work of a police chief in revolutionary France: *Leonora or Wedded Love: A Spanish Historical Play in Two Acts*, which provided the basis for Beethoven's only opera, *Fidelio*, the greatest of all operas of heroic deliverance. The opera was, in effect, banned during the first decade of its existence, with the première delayed by Austrian censors and then by the French entry into Vienna in 1805. Only in the revised version of 1814, amidst the buoyant hopes that followed the defeat of Napoleon, did *Fidelio* emblazon itself on the European imagination. The setting for the final scene in which the prisoners reappear was moved from the dungeon to the open air— just as the thirst for liberation was about to spill out from the operatic theater into real life national revolution.

Music helped keep alive a feeling of unity in divided and humiliated Poland.[26] In 1811, the director of the Polish National Opera Theater, Karol Kurpiński, introduced in Warsaw his new opera *Kalmora*, written on an altogether novel theme for the operatic stage anywhere: the American Revolution. Kalmora, an American girl, is unable to marry a British soldier until after the revolutionaries have defeated the British and convinced him of the superiority of a republic to a monarchy.[27] In 1816, after the Napoleonic wars, Kurpiński tried to identify opera with national struggle in his *Cracovians and Mountaineers*. Consciously reviving the title of an earlier work written just before the first partition of Poland, Kurpiński turned folk dances—the polonaise and mazurka—into symbols of suppressed nationhood.

Kurpiński sought in vain to persuade his most gifted pupil, Frederick Chopin, to develop an operatic tradition for Poland.[28] But Chopin's piano music transposed the same polonaise and mazurka into symbols not just of Polish pride, but of unrealized nationhood everywhere. Schumann described Chopin's mazurkas as "cannons buried in flowers,"[29] and Chopin's benefit concert tours throughout Europe between the revolutions of 1830 and 1848 were themselves dramatic events, mobilizing the emotions for national revolution. Franz Liszt's virtuoso concerts of the same era played a similar role. He dedicated his *Lyon* to Lamennais and called on music to recapture the "political, philosophical and religious power" it had allegedly exercised "in pagan times." He transformed a tune from the Hungarian gypsy violin into the Rákóczi March, and played it as "the Hungarian *Marseillaise*."[30] Berlioz inserted into his *Damnation of Faust* an orchestral form of this march with bass drums suggesting cannons of liberation, which was hailed as a revolutionary symbol at its debuts of 1846 in both Budapest and Paris. The French romantic wrote a host of idiosyncratic works in praise of national revolution.[31]

With their deep musical traditions and leadership in the drama since Schiller, the Germans developed a particularly important national school of opera. In 1817, Carl Maria von Weber first described

> the type of opera all Germans want: a self-contained work of art in which all artistic elements cooperate, disappear and reemerge to create a new world.[32]

Five years later in *Der Freischutz*, he put this new concept into practice. Focusing on a tale from Germanic folklore, he enlarged the orchestra and scrambled the placement of instruments, producing a new dependence on the conductor and preparing the way for the conductor-composer who was to realize his dream of a uniquely German *Gesamt-kunstwerk*: Richard Wagner.

The mature Wagner weaved pagan myth and a seductive new musical idiom into a unique vehicle of modern German nationalism. But his original, youthful turn to revolutionary politics prior to 1848 illustrates the more general romantic forms he later denigrated. His first and most explicitly political opera, *Cola Rienzi, the last of the tribunes*, was completed in Paris in 1840 to celebrate the fourteenth-century Roman revolutionary.[33] The twenty-year-old Frederick Engels wrote a play in praise of the same Rienzi in the same year.[34]

The first organized conspiracy of the Left against Napoleon was an assassination planned to take place during the climactic chorus of an operatic première on October 10, 1800. Less than two months later, the first conspiracy of the Right killed or wounded eighty in its unsuccessful attempt to kill Napoleon on the way to the opera.[35] On both occasions, Napoleon demonstrated his *sang-froid* by continuing on to the opera and watching the performance as if nothing had happened—becoming thereby a kind of operatic hero in his own right.

The stability of the post-Napoleonic restoration was shaken by the assassination of the Duc de Berry in the opera house in Paris on February 12, 1820. And an operatic performance on January 12, 1821 at the Teatro d'Angennes in Turin helped precipitate the revolution that broke out in Piedmont.[36] This forgotten event at the heart of the region that eventually led the struggle for unification of Italy was the beginning of the open, direct link between romantic opera and national revolution. The opera itself was a seemingly apolitical work by one of the most politically conservative composers of the age: *La Gazza Ladra* (The Thievish Magpie) by Gioacchino Rossini. Determined to outdo the Germans in an opera written for Austrian-controlled Milan, Rossini augmented both the size and the volume of his orchestra and began the process of conjuring up new sounds in the score to support new ideas in the libretto. The conflict between a classicist and a romantic over a falsely accused servant girl was given a revolutionary reading by the Italians, who had already felt their emotions aroused by *Moses in Egypt*, Rossini's earlier opera about the chosen people seeking liberation from bondage. The potentially revolutionary message was emphasized more clearly in the Parisian triumph of the new French version of the opera in 1827. Thus, Rossini, who had been Metternich's guest at the Congress of Verona and chief composer to the ultraconservative King Charles X of France, found his audiences identifying his real-life patrons with his operatic villains. He unwittingly abetted the gathering revolutionary ferment with his *William Tell*, which opened in Paris in 1829 and provided a musical model for national liberation struggles.

The excitement of the famous overture, the overall length (nearly six hours), and the emphasis on large choral ensembles—all lent a portentous air to the work. The *William Tell* overture was to be played at the last meeting of the radical circle to which the youthful Dostoevsky belonged in 1849. Orsini's spectacular attempt to assassinate Napoleon III a decade later occurred outside the Paris opera while the orchestra was playing that same prelude to liberation. Two decades later, a French revolutionary on trial in Switzerland explained that his model was Tell, whose "arrow whistles the music of Rossini."[37] The tenor who sang the lead in the original production was permanently radicalized by the experience—leading the singing of *La Marseillaise* atop the barricades during the Revolution of 1830 with sword in hand and cherishing thereafter the vision of a world where "an upheaval would be nothing more than a concert."[38]

The revolutions in France and Belgium in 1830 were highly theatrical: the sudden exits and entrances of kings, the processions and pageantry of volunteer armies, and the festive spirit of Paris and Brussels.

Revolution seemed to be moving from the stage to the street—or perhaps the street was merely reclaiming what it had previously given to the stage. The extravagant melodramas of Nodier's protégé, Victor Hugo, had in many ways anticipated the revolution. The première of *Hernani* on February 25, 1830, was in effect the opening political demonstration of the year. The tale of an outlaw struggling for love and liberation against fate, hate, and the Hapsburg establishment aroused the student audience. The red vest defiantly sported by Hugo's supporters anticipated the revolutionary red flag which was soon to be raised in the open-air theater of Paris; and the anti-traditional beat of Hugo's poetry fed naturally into innumerable operatic amplifications of his plays.[39]

In Brussels, the theatrical catalyst was yet another anti-Hapsburg opera: *The Mute Girl of Portici* by Daniel-François Auber. In this tale of a seventeenth-century Neapolitan insurrection, choral scenes of beggars and shopkeepers swirled around the arresting figure (taken over from popular pantomime) of a dumb heroine. The melodrama had been proscribed in Brussels after the July Revolution in Paris; but the defiant Belgians demanded that it be restored to the repertoire soon after they were asked to honor the birthday of the Dutch king on August 24. After lengthy discussion of cuts, a performance was reluctantly approved for August 25—along with secret orders for stand-by troops.

During the performance, the police chief of Brussels sent a boy out to conduct reconnaissance among the mob that had gathered outside. The informer returned to report rumors that the chief was to be assassinated in his box.[40] At the end of the fourth act, many people left the theater as if in search of their own ending for the revolutionary melodrama. By the time the opera ended with a pyrotechnic onstage eruption of Mount Vesuvius (making spectacular use of new sound and color effects), the lava of revolution was already coursing through the streets of Brussels. Wealthy members of the audience were unable to get out of the theater and into their carriages. Soldiers and police were unable to keep up with (let alone contain) the movements of the mob in search of symbols of authority to burn and destroy.

Thus, an operatic performance triggered the revolution that led to Belgian independence in 1830. Later popular uprisings in Belgium were formed in the knowledge of this bizarre fact. Risings in 1834 were built around demands for another revival of the Auber opera, while later perturbations in Ghent were triggered by a gala performance of *William Tell* at which the student audience confronted the Duke and Duchess of Brabant.[41]

The program to prevent the spread of revolution into Germany in 1830 involved prohibiting performances of *The Mute Girl* and *William Tell* in cities close to the French or Belgian borders.[42] But the fears of those in power became the fascination of those who were not. Continent-wide efforts to restrict the rights of assembly for political purposes after 1830 increased the covert political content of theatrical performances. A recurring theme of the new grand opera which spread out from Paris after 1830 was national uprisings: Druids versus Romans in Bellini's *Norma* (Milan, 1831), conspirators assassinating a king in Auber's *Gustav III* (Paris, 1833), persecuted Protestants against aristocratic royalists in both Bellini's *Puritans* (Paris, 1835) and Meyerbeer's *Huguenots* (Paris, 1836); Jew versus Christians in Meyerbeer's *The Jewess* (Paris, 1835) and versus Babylonians in Verdi's *Nabucco*.

The première of this latter work in Milan on March 9, 1842, brought Giuseppe Verdi into the center of the real-life drama of Italian unification. Verdi, whose very name was to become an acronym for Italian nationalism (Vittorio Emmanuele Re d'Italia), struck a deep vein of

anti-Austrian sentiment with this operatic tale of bondage to King Nebuchadnezzar. The uproar at the end of the first act surprised and frightened the composer, who was seated in the orchestra. The prolonged
standing ovation he received at the final curtain—from the orchestra
as well as the audience—removed all doubt that he had suddenly become a culture hero for the risorgimento. The chorus of captive Jews
from the third act *Va pensiero* (Fly, my thoughts, on golden wings to
the fatherland) had to be resung on the spot at the première. Massed
mourners at Verdi's public funeral in Milan were spontaneously to sing
it again nearly sixty years later. It was to become a kind of informal
national anthem, with its lush lingering melody calling for the deliverance of "my beautiful but lost fatherland."

Nabucco was followed in 1843 by a second patriotic opera, *The Lombards at the First Crusade*, with another chorus of liberation ("Today
the Holy Land shall be ours!"), which also had to be resung at the
première.[43] Verdi turned next to an operatic version of *Hernani*. Melodramatic operas of struggle cascaded from Verdi's pen in the remaining
years leading up to the Revolution of 1848: *Joan of Arc* (1845), *Attila*
(1846), *The Robbers* (1847), and finally, *The Battle of Legnano*, first
produced amidst great excitement in January 1849 in Rome just 12 days
before the establishment of the short-lived Roman Republic.[44] Verdi
subsequently returned to Victor Hugo for his *Rigoletto* of 1851 (based
on *Le Roi S'Amuse*); and escalated to virtual onstage revolution in his
Sicilian Vespers (Paris, 1855). The political censorship required a change
in title for the first Italian performance the following year; and popular revolt against the doge of Venice dominated *Simone Boccanegra*,
which opened in Venice in 1857. Verdi's rewriting of Auber's regicidal
Gustav III as *The Masked Ball* was heavily censored and first produced
in Rome (after the setting was moved from Europe to distant Boston)
in 1859 on the eve of the decisive war of liberation against Austria.

At that crucial point in Italian history, even Verdi's apolitical operas
seemed to be mobilized. Cavour entered the key battle against the
Hapsburgs in April 1859, humming the famed tenor air from *Il Trova-
tore*: "Di Quella Pira."[45] The essential message that national revolutionaries found in Verdi was that of the Roman envoy speaking to the
conquering Hun in the first act of *Attila*: "Take the universe, but leave
me Italy."[46]

There were operatic echoes among social as well as national revolutionaries. Buonarroti gave singing lessons throughout his career, and
his collaborator in both musical and revolutionary activity, Luigi Angeloni, turned from his doctoral dissertation on the origins of musical
notation to writing about opera.[47] Buonarroti's Flemish protégé, Jacob
Kats, wrote the struggle song from Meyerbeer's *Robert le Diable* into
his revolutionary drama *The Earthly Paradise*[48] and created the first
Flemish theater for popular music and drama in Brussels.[49] That supreme symbol of international social revolution, Michael Bakunin, bade
his friends farewell with the chorus of assassins from the *Huguenots*,[50]
and drew on the text of the fourth movement of Beethoven's Ninth
Symphony (Schiller's *Ode to Joy*) to call his followers "beautiful daugh-

ters of the divine spark." On Palm Sunday, 1849, in Dresden, he rushed forward after hearing Wagner conduct to announce that that movement would be exempted from destruction in the forthcoming revolutionary upheaval.[51] Whether or not Bakunin provided part of the model for Wagner's Siegfried, the bear-like Russian suggested to many that a general "downfall of the gods" was imminent in life as well as operatic fancy.

Songs and Flags

Musical militance burst out of the opera houses after 1830 in a flood of song and verse. This "trumpet blast that suddenly rouses a vast camp of nations in arms"[52] led to a profusion of national anthems and banners in imitation of *La Marseillaise* and the tricolor of the original French Revolution.

Louis Philippe adopted and ostentatiously led the singing of *La Marseillaise* as a means of securing his precarious hold on power.[53] The tenor Nourrit and the composer Berlioz led the singing of it on the Paris barricades with a sword and pistol respectively as a baton.[54] Rouget de Lisle, the all-but-forgotten author of the great anthem, hailed Berlioz as "the Vulcan of revolution,"[55] and was freed from prison by donations from the radical songwriter Jean-Pierre Béranger, who described his protest singing as a *"tambour social à ouvrir la marche et marquer le pas."*[56]

The new Marseillaise of 1830 was the "Parisienne," which Lafayette sang onstage with Nourrit at the end of the public theatrical performance that followed his introduction of the new king to the Paris masses at the Hotel de Ville.[57] Its composer, Casimir Delavigne, had contributed a melodrama, *The Sicilian Vespers*, to the unrest of 1819–20; and he soon added to this stirring march for victorious Paris, words to a martial air of Kurpiński for the martyred Poles, the "Varsovienne," which became in many ways the Marseillaise for all defeated nationalities. The Belgian Revolution of 1830 produced the "Brabançonne," which became the national anthem; and the Franco-German crisis of 1839–40 produced a proliferation of nationalistic airs, such as "Watch on the Rhine" and "Deutschland, Deutschland über alles," adapted to Haydn's music and destined to become the future German national anthem.[58]

The national song, of course, had its accompanying flag. In some cases, the song was about the flag (the Romanian "Tricolor," "The Star Spangled Banner").[59] In some, it was simply identified with a banner: *La Marseillaise* with the tricolor, which became the official flag of France after 1830.

To the fourteen-year-old Eugene Pottier, the future author of the "Internationale," the tricolor was "the signal of happiness" when first raised over Paris in July 1830.[60] Each nation suddenly seemed to feel the need for some such signal. A true nation was now thought to require a tricolor—freed of all crosses, crowns, and heraldic reminders of traditional authority and civic inequality. The first creative act of the Belgian revolutionaries after leaving the opera house in Brussels was the crude fashioning of a new banner out of curtains ripped down from the gutted office of the hated editor of *Le National*.[61] The three vertical stripes of the black, yellow, and red of Brabant were identified with the "Brabançonne" and immediately raised over the Hotel de Ville in Brussels.[62]

Like the Belgian, the Italian tricolor (green, white, red) had made its debut in the revolutionary era. The revolutionary legion in Italian Lombardy blazoned on their tricolor "equality or death" and "victory or death." [63] The Hungarian national movement began to gather in the 1840s around its own tricolor of red, white, and green.[64] Romanian nationalists threw up a vertical tricolor of blue, yellow, and red, which became the flag and inspired the anthem "Tricolor" when Romania joined the unrest of 1848.

The black, red, and gold banner was a central symbol of the Hambacher Fest of May 1832. Local colors were swept away by youthful enthusiasm for three-colored cockades and sashes bearing the legend "Germany's Resurrection." [65]

Following the impulse for radical simplification, some demonstrators called for "only one color." [66] However, the idea of one unifying color was most fully developed by social revolutionaries in their search for a banner to rival the tricolors of national revolutionaries. "Our flag can no longer be contained by the sky of France," the visionary prophets of universal social change, the Saint-Simonians, had sung.[67] Their mission was to "unfold in the breeze the battle standard of the workers . . . serve the universe as a torch." [68]

Workers themselves began to provide a real-life banner for this Saint-Simonian fantasy. Having gained few tangible benefits from the revolutions of 1830, they brought out colors of their own in urban demonstrations. In Reims, the black flag (which was later to become the banner of anarchism) made its modern French debut, when on January 15, 1831, unemployed dirt carriers bore a flag of mourning through the streets with the slogan, "Work or Death!" [69]

The future banner of international revolution, the red flag, made its modern debut in Paris during riots and demonstrations after the funeral of a popular general, Maximilien Lamarque, on June 5, 1832.[70] In a nocturnal scene worthy of his own melodramas, Victor Hugo unfurled the red flag that night on the barricades in the Rue de la Chanverie and lit a torch beside it, which, in his words, added "to the scarlet of the flag I don't know what kind of sinister purple." [71] The demonstration of June 5 has been called "the first disturbance that was simultaneously both republican and social." [72] It was organized by republican agitators in the wake of the trial of "the fifteen"—Blanqui and his associates. The red flag, which had been used as a sign of martial law and a signal of alarm during the original French Revolution, was thus revived by a new set of republicans amidst the cholera epidemic of 1832.

Lafayette, who had sanctified Louis Philippe's authority during the

Revolution of 1830 by publicly handing him the tricolor, fled La-marque's funeral in a state of shock upon finding the rival red flag on the coffin of his old comrade-in-arms.[73]

Those who put down the demonstrations of June 1832 saw them-selves defending the tricolor "against the white flag in the Vendée, the red flag in Paris, or the colors of the foreigner on our borders." [74] Not until the Revolution of 1848 did the red flag supplant the black flag as a symbol of proletarian protest and a rival to the tricolor for any signifi-cant body of Frenchmen.[75] And even then, social revolutionaries usu-ally confined themselves merely to moving the red stripe into the center of a revised tricolor.[76] The tricolor remained "the rainbow of the free" even for social revolutions: [77] a banner freed from the "barbarous escutcheons" of "nations which typify brute force with their three-headed eagles and vultures," with colors as pure as "the people" themselves.[78]

The Myth of "the People"

Romantic nationalism was everywhere hailed as the cause of "the people"—a term so vague yet appealing that it seemed to require a spe-cial language of sounds and symbols to express its meaning. Songs and flags helped enlist the emotions and politicize the illiterate. If system-atic ideology was not part of revolutionary nationalism, this concept of "the people" was central to it.

As a counter to rationalism, evocation of "the people" goes back at least to Rousseau's quarrel with the elitist *philosophes* of Paris. Bonne-ville in 1787 had warned the aristocratic Condorcet of the coming of the *Peuple-Roi*,[79] and had written songs about the *peuple-frère*,[80] while Cloots had proclaimed "THE INFALLIBILITY OF THE PEOPLE." [81]

By the 1830s, romantic revolutionaries were speaking almost rou-tinely of *le peuple, das Volk, il popolo, narod,* or *lud* as a kind of regen-erative life force in human history. The new monarchs who came to power after the Revolutions of 1830, Louis Philippe and Leopold I, sought the sanction of "the people" as king "of the French" and "of the Bel-gians," rather than of France or Belgium. Even the reactionary Tsar Nicholas I, three years after crushing the Polish uprising of 1830–31, proclaimed that his own authority was based on "nationality" (as well as autocracy and Orthodoxy)—and his word *narodnost'* also meaning "spirit of the people" was copied from the Polish *narodowość.*

"The people" was a different concept for revolutionary nationalists than for evolutionary liberals (who thought of specific propertied groups to whom the franchise and civic liberties might be extended), or for social revolutionaries (who thought of an industrial proletariat that might provide fresh fuel for revolution). For romantic nationalists, "the people" was simply the source of legitimacy for the exercise of sov-ereign power in the modern nation-state. Its sanction was gained not by the prosaic counting of parliamentary or class divisions, but by the poetic invocation of a forgotten inner unity.

Revolutionary nationalism was fortified in the 1830–48 period by a romantic view of history that contrasted the creativity of the people not only with the kings and bishops who dominated France prior to 1789, but also with the bankers and politicians who rose to dominance after 1830. High priest of this new religion of "the people" was Jules Michelet. Dazzled by the spontaneous mass action of the 1830 revolution in Paris, he published an *Introduction to Universal History* in 1831 as a prelude to his massive epic, *The History of France*, on which he spent most of his next forty years.

To Michelet, France was "not only a nation, but a great political principle," [82] vague enough to include both of "our two great redemptions, by the Holy Maid of Orleans and by the Revolution." [83] The revolution had opened up a "second period" of God's presence on earth. "His incarnation of '89" [84] in France would lead to the resurrection of all peoples. The liberation of the masses during the July days was a foretaste of that "eternal July" yet to come. The spontaneous development of popular unity and popular institutions from July 1789 to July 1790 made the popular festival of federal unity on the first anniversary of the fall of the Bastille more important than the original event itself.

From being "friends of the people" (the leading republican society of 1830–32), radicals soon sought to become the servants thereof. "In the presence of the sovereignty of the people, you must all bow your foreheads into the dust," Voyer D'Argenson told the Chamber of Deputies during a dispute over symbols of authority with the Guardian of Seals in 1834.[85] In the same year, one of the leading former advocates of a Catholic revival under papal leadership, Lamennais, celebrated what was to be his final break with Rome. He retreated to Brittany, shed his clerical collar, and published his passionate and apocalyptical testament to the simple people of Europe as the suffering servant of God: *Words of a Believer*. This immensely influential tract directly inspired Mazzini's *Faith and the Future* of 1835, which he considered his best work.[86] Lamennais's *Book of the People* (1837) went still further in glorifying "the people" as "the poor, the weak, the oppressed." [87] He excited imitators into writing a *Marseillaise of the People, Reign of the People*, and *Gospel of the People*.[88] It seemed not too much to contend that—in the words of a song of the period—"the people . . . is God." [89]

For Michelet the people was both *plebs* and *populos*, both the humble toilers and the spiritual unity of the nation.[90] In his view England was a great empire, but a weak people. Only a people can become a nation; indeed "a nation is a people that has become a person." [91] The English were a kind of antipeople, dedicated to power and prosperity without love and friendship; they were scavengers who have "profited from the entr'acte between the two religions (Catholic and Revolutionary)." [92]

Beyond France, Michelet looked for vindication to Poland and invited as lecturer to the Collège de France perhaps the greatest of all poetic prophets of revolutionary nationalism: Adam Mickiewicz. The crushing of the Polish Revolution was for the poet a crucifixion of the "Christ among nations." In his last lecture at the Collège in 1842, he contended that a messianic mission had been imparted to three peoples: the ancient Israelites, the French, and now the Slavs.

Mickiewicz regarded Poland's temporary destruction twice in one lifetime as a sacrificial offering for the sins of others, necessary to save the peoples of the world. By submitting itself to partition during the French Revolution, Poland had saved revolutionary France from concerted action by the monarchs of Europe. Likewise the Polish rising of 1830, inspired by a sense of fraternity with events in France and Belgium, prevented—even in defeat—Nicholas I from restoring the power of his wife's uncle, King William of the Netherlands.

Intoxicated with the outbreak of a third wave of revolution in 1848, Mickiewicz tried to organize a Polish legion to lead the final liberation of Poland and all mankind. Like Lamartine in France and Petőfi in Hungary, he was a great vernacular poet destined to mount the barricades amidst a popular upsurge. The transfer of the revolutionary cause from Franco-Italian conspirators to an international fraternity of romantic nationalists is illustrated by Mickiewicz's plural version of the old Babeuvist title, *Tribun des Peuples* of 1849.[93]

Already in the 1830s the Poles had assumed a certain leadership in internationalizing revolutionary nationalism. Arriving in Paris in great numbers after the failure of the Polish Revolution in 1831 they organized innumerable protest meetings and petitions against repression by the German as well as the Russian government.[94] Mickiewicz and others expected a German revolution throughout 1832–33 that might lead to guerrilla uprisings and the liberation of Poland.[95] On November 3, 1832, many Poles addressed a proclamation of solidarity to the Jews as another persecuted nation in exile.[96] Mickiewicz died in Istanbul in November 1855, in the arms of a Jewish friend who had his own proto-Zionist dream of liberating Jerusalem.

By the end of 1832, the Polish radicals in Paris had formed a group of 1,500–2,000 (later known as the Democratic Society[97]) to organize popular revolution, not only in Poland but also in the surrounding regions where national aspirations were being repressed by the Hapsburgs and Romanovs. Young Poland became one of the largest sections of Mazzini's Young Europe. When restrictions in Paris became tighter after 1834, the Poles blazed the trail of further revolutionary migration to Brussels and then London (the trail followed by Marx). Of the 4,380 political refugees known to have been in England in 1853, 2,500 were Polish.[98]

The dominant figure in the Polish emigration was Mickiewicz's former history professor, Joachim Lelewel. Head of the Revolutionary Patriotic Society during the insurrection of November 1830 in Warsaw, Lelewel had spoken on July 27, 1831, at the first in a long series of gatherings in Paris to commemorate the Polish uprising.[99] For Lelewel as for Michelet the revolutionary potential of the oppressed people lay not in their material desperation but in the spiritual richness of their communal feelings. "The classes which we call inferior and which follow instinct more closely," said Michelet, "are for that very reason eminently capable of action, ever ready to act." [100] Lelewel gradually came to believe in the capacity of the Slavic peasant masses to accomplish what the Russian empire would not, and the Polish aristocracy could not, do: free the captive Slavic nations. His *History of Poland* was translated from

French into Polish and on into Russian, Czech, and German; and his ideal was widely disseminated from his first clandestine liberation organization of 1831 in Paris, the Vengeance of the People, to his fateful meeting in Brussels in 1844 with Michael Bakunin, who developed further Lelewel's vision of revolutionary potential among the unspoiled Slavic peoples.[101]

There was a certain amount of pure rural nostalgia in the Michelet-Lelewel concept of the people. Both men felt redeemed by their own historical contact with the ordinary people of the past; both compared their profession as historians to the hard but wholesome work of the ordinary laborer; both urged that the wealthy and wise should seek out "mixed marriages" with poor and simple people to unify the nation.[102] Michelet glorified the fishermen of Normandy for forming a "moral union" that looked beyond mere economic interest and helped lead men from "the natural association of family . . . to the grand association, that of our native country." [103] Lelewel saw the communal agrarian institutions of the early Slavs serving the same function.

The revolt of 1846 in Cracow inspired the Polish Democratic Society to plan rapidly (if vainly) for a general *levée en masse* of the entire Polish peasantry. The Polish uprising inspired even the British working class,[104] and provided the first hint of the national uprisings that were to become epidemic in 1848.

The Slavs' answer to the national congresses of 1848, held in Frankfurt by the Germans and in Budapest by the Hungarians, was the pan-Slav congress of Prague convened in the Bohemian National Museum by the romantic Czech historian František Palacký. Like so many revolutionary nationalist gatherings of that era, the Prague congress provided the precedent and the symbols for the conservative chauvinism of a future generation of imperial politicians.[105] At the same time, however, the activities of Bakunin, the dominant Russian representative, revealed that the revolutionary belief in the liberating power of "the people" was moving farther to the left as it moved farther to the east. Having already set forth in a French journal in January 1845 a fluent statement of faith in the revolutionary potential of the Russian peasantry,[106] in December 1848 Bakunin published an "Appeal to the Slavs," urging alliance with revolutionary Hungary and Germany in a "general federation of European republics." [107]

Revolutionary populism—no less than reactionary imperial panslavism—developed from the intellectuals' fantasy of an unspoiled people who longed to be liberated and who offered in turn moral liberation in their midst. In the wake of 1848 populism developed slowly out of the writings of Alexander Herzen and Bakunin, the two leading Russian participants in the events of that year in western Europe.

But it was Michelet who fortified radical nationalism with the kind of antireligious humanism that Russian revolutionaries were to find congenial.[108] His *The People* of 1846 was a revolutionary enconium to plebeian France. When the French Revolution of 1848 failed, Michelet looked east again to Poland for a popular revolution in his *Poland and Russia* of 1851. In reply, Herzen wrote his famous "Open Letter to

Michelet," insisting that the Russian people with their communal land-holding and adjudication truly carried the germ of revolutionary regeneration for Europe.[109] Michelet looked more sympathetically at Russia in his *Democratic Legends of the North* of 1854, but attached even greater hopes to the Danubian Revolution in Hungary and Romania.[110]

Romania became in 1859 the first new nation to emerge from a revolutionary struggle in Europe since Belgium in 1830. Its revolutionary movement represented the convergence of Italian, Polish, and French influences. There was, first of all, the same echo of Mazzini that had also been heard in the 1840s in such far corners of Europe as Ireland and Norway. "Young Dacia" and "Young Romania" [111] appeared in the Danubian region where the three multinational empires—Ottoman, Austrian, and Russian—converged. The lonely bearers of Latin culture in eastern Europe were to develop a new historical consciousness of themselves as heirs to the ancient Roman province of Dacia. The historian Nicolae Bălcescu went to study with Michelet in Paris,[112] and organized the most important of many national revolutionary organizations: *Fratia* (Brotherhood).[113] He edited a nameless weekly and organized secret ten-man cells under a three-man directorate. The militant structure required total obedience to the deacon or priest who catechized the individual member. A militant strategy for national revolt was suggested in Bălcescu's massive historical study of 1844: *Armed Power and Military Art from the Setting up of the Wallachian Principality to our Times.* "Justice and Brotherhood" was their motto and their image of what a national struggle against a foreign power could achieve. In 1846, translations from Michelet's *The People* and the outbreak of the Polish upheaval in Cracow began to bring the Mazzinian ideal into revolutionary reality within Romania. Bălcescu went over to the slogan "fatherland, brotherhood, and liberty," and gave first priority to achieving "unity of ideas and feelings which in time, shall bring about political unification." [114]

During the unsuccessful national revolution of 1848–49, Bălcescu published a new journal *The Sovereign People*, fleeing thereafter to Paris and London, where he represented Romania on Mazzini's European Democratic Central Committee.[115] The tricolor banner which had been proclaimed for revolutionary Romania in June 1848 (red, yellow, and blue with the slogan "Justice—Fraternity") became the flag of a new nation when the two principal provinces, Moldavia and Wallachia formally united to form independent Romania in January 1859.

The idea of "the people" penetrated into the vast Russian empire in a way that illustrates the ambiguity of this romantic concept. Nicholas I invoked the term *narodnost'* more in its narrow meaning of "nationality" than in its broad sense of "spirit of the people." In combating the Ottoman Empire, which he did in the years from the war of 1828–29 to the Crimean War of 1853, Nicholas I found an oppressed "people" to liberate: the Orthodox Slavs under the Moslem Turks.

The *narodnost'* of radical populists, on the other hand, was the unspoiled "spirit of the people"; and their "people" was the Russian peasantry itself. Russian populists sought to rediscover a sense of community from them while liberating them from both feudal oppression and bourgeois exploitation.[116] Finally, for many nationalities within the Russian Empire, "the people" was an oppressed minority seeking both national and social liberation through the words of national poets that appeared in the 1840s from Taras Shevchenko in the Ukraine to Johan Runeberg in Finland.

But the vagueness of belief in "the people" and the danger of conflict between one people and another did not diminish the idealism and high expectations of national revolutionaries. Despite the failures of 1848–49, romantic nationalism remained the dominant revolutionary faith throughout the 1850s. Michelet remained the prophet, Poland the hope, and Mazzini the heart and soul.

As with Michelet and Lelewel, "the people" was for Mazzini a spiritual force—not something to be divided up into interests or classes. In his first journal for the working class, *Apostolate of the People* (the weekly of his Workingmen's Association which he founded in 1840), Mazzini published the first four parts of his most famous work, *The Duties of Man*. The stress on moral obligation was also evident in the slogan he placed over the masthead of a later journal for Italian workers: "Morality, Fatherland, Labor." [117]

He dreamed throughout the 1840s that a "council of mankind" might issue a declaration of principles to supersede French-type declarations of rights.[118] This stress on ethical rather than material imperatives is apparent in his last attempt at a nationalist International: the International Association of 1855–59. Mazzini organized this effort in London, where he had returned after serving in the ruling triumvirate of the short-lived Roman Republic in 1849. He sought to fortify his old faith in a "third Rome" of "the people" replacing the earlier Romes of emperors and popes. He now argued that a broader "alliance of the peoples" was about to be formed by the three great "peoples" of Europe (the Slavs, Germans, and "Gallo-Romans") to renew the common struggle.[119]

But the 1860s destroyed the dream forever. Italy was unified not by the passion of Mazzini but by the realpolitik of Cavour, "the prose translation of his poem." [120] Poland rose and was crushed again in 1863; and Germany chose *Einheit* rather than *Freiheit* as it achieved unity under Bismarck's rule of "blood and iron."

All this was accompanied by war and bloodshed never envisaged by romantic nationalists, who had dreamed of a conflict-free family of nations. The vernacular poets and national historians who were the "ideologists" of nationalism always assumed that the only national war would be that of peoples against kings.

The faith in national revolution remained dominant throughout the 1850s. But the rise of the rival tradition of social revolution had already been foreshadowed in the appearance of deep and conscious class conflict during the revolutions of 1848. Paralleling the emergence of the red flag as a rival to the tricolor was the increasing substitution of *ouvriers* for *peuple* in Paris during May and June of 1848.[121] If the new class terminology was most evident in the petitions and songs that directly reached the masses, the new ideas of social revolution were developed by a small, apostolic succession of elite intellectuals who took their torch from the hands of the aged Buonarroti.

Revolutionary Violence: The Italo-Polish Contribution

Before going on to the social revolutionary tradition, it is necessary to consider the introduction of violence into revolutionary practice by national revolutionaries. There were anticipations of a distinctively new approach to violence in both the American [122] and the French [123] revolutions. In a broad sense as we have seen, the national revolutionary tradition arose in a period of almost continuous war from the massive monarchical assault on France in 1792 to the final defeat of Napoleon by a coalition of national resistance movements. The French provided the precedent; the English, distant support; and the Germans, ideas. But the dedicated cadres who combined practice with theory came largely from Italy and Poland.

The Italo-Polish period of revolutionary violence lasted until the successful unification of Italy and the defeat of the last Polish rebellion in the early 1860s. Thereafter, a very different tradition of revolutionary violence emerged—primarily in Russia and among social revolutionaries. The two types naturally overlapped and, in the early twentieth century, converged in the Balkan no-man's-land of European politics. The shooting of the Hapsburg Archduke Franz Ferdinand at Sarajevo in July 1914 led to World War I and to the new age of total war and totalitarian peace. That fateful assassination was to be the work of a movement inspired by both Italian and Russian revolutionaries.

The difference was that Italo-Polish violence, parochial in aim, was heroic in style. Russian violence, universal in aim, was rationalistic and ascetic in style. The Russian story is well known. The tale of Italo-Polish revolutionary violence has, however, been generally overlooked. Almost all modern ideas on guerrilla tactics or wars of "national liberation" have antecedents if not origins in forgotten writings by national revolutionaries from these two nations. The originality of Italy and Poland derived paradoxically from their fanatical dedication to replicating and perpetuating the revolutionary example of France.

It was in 1794, as the Terror reached its peak in Paris, that the modern theory of revolutionary violence began to emerge in places distant from that capital. In that year, the young Buonarroti established within his revolutionary rule in Oneglia a special school to teach "the theory of revolution." At the same time, in Warsaw, there was a large-scale uprising against the final partition of Poland which included scythe-bearing partisans. Survivors of the insurrection formed a legion of liberation in Italy which grew within a year to ten thousand, and began the long linkage between the two national revolutionary traditions. Fighting with the French in Italy, the Poles dreamed of an eventual return "from Italy to Poland"; and their song later became the Polish national anthem.[124]

The wounded leader of the defeated Polish uprising, Tadeusz Kościuszko, saw the liberation of Poland opening the "epoch of general pacification" to end all human conflict.[125] In exile, he developed the characteristic belief that revolutionary violence would end all other violence. In 1800, he published *Can the Poles recover their independence by armed action?* [126] and answered affirmatively that "a people which aspires to independence must absolutely have faith in its own arms." [127] The combination of militance and self-reliance forced upon the Poles by history guarantees, in effect, that a new quality of man and nation will emerge.

Kościuszko had drawn on eight years of experience in the American Revolution and on the indigenous Polish tradition of Cossack-influenced resistance to earlier Swedish and Russian incursions.[128] He focused on the key unanswered question arising from the Polish experience of 1794: How can a popular army combat superior conventional military forces? The Poles had simultaneously confronted the armies of the three most powerful conservative powers in Europe: Russia, Prussia, and Austria. He was impressed that, despite the impossibility of victory, sustained mass resistance had taken place. Morale had been a factor, but even in purely military terms, a small insurrectionary army could neutralize a much larger conventional force by simply refusing to fight in traditional terms.

Kościuszko may have been the first to use the term "little war"; [129] but his substantial contributions to the American army lay in the relatively conventional areas of designing fortifications for West Point and writing the first military manual for the horse artillery.[130] In Europe, he universalized the struggle for nationhood by denouncing Napoleon as the foe of "every great nationality and still more the spirit of independence." [131] But memory of the resistance movement he had led continued to dominate the Polish imagination; and, four years after his death in 1817, the Polish Patriotic Society was formed with the secret name League of Scythebearers.[132]

The most important writings on revolutionary violence in the 1820s were by the Italians in the aftermath of their unsuccessful uprisings. At the forefront were the members of the *Apofasimèni* or desperate soldiers, formed by veterans of the Spanish, Italian, and Greek upheavals. They perpetuated the Carbonari's secret, hierarchical organization, substituting the military term tent (*tende*) for shop in describing the local unit.[133] The initiation ceremonies placed an almost masochistic emphasis on violence. After a centurion had washed away the servile past of each new member with two ritual drops of water and baptized him as "the terror of tyrants," [134] the neophyte asked—on his knees with his left hand on his heart and right hand on a dagger—for punishment if he should ever betray any of his vows:

> I wish that my eyes be pulled from head, my tongue ripped from my mouth, my body cut and torn little by little; that my bowels be pulled out; that corrosive poison may eat at me with pain—with spasms of the chest, lungs and stomach bringing even sharper pain. . . .[135]

And after this process, the traitor to the *Apofasimèni* was to be quartered, and his remains put on display with the label: "Here was justly punished the infamous————." [136]

The first theoretical reflections on revolutionary violence among Italians occurred as the nonviolent agitation of the Carbonari escalated into unsuccessful military confrontation with Hapsburg power in 1820–21. Buonarroti's associates took the lead. Prati suggested in 1821 organizing a guerrilla-type war using Genoa as a base or "point of action for the Liberals of Italy." [137] The Spanish Constitution of 1812 like the Spanish resistance movement was seen as the model for national resistance to a foreign oppressor.[138]

As the Italian movement was collapsing, Luigi Angeloni wrote a series of letters on the problem of violence which were later published in London as *On Force in Political Affairs*. Proclaiming that "all is force in the universe," he cited Hobbes's gloomy view of human nature (a rare authority for revolutionaries),[139] and found hope only in the struggle that lay ahead between "artificial" and "natural" force.[140] The former, expressed politically through hereditary privilege, must eventually succumb to the latter, which is based on popular sovereignty rooted in majority rule.

Italians after the failures of 1820–21 (like Poles after their setbacks in 1830–31) tended to substitute the distant example of the American Revolution, however little understood, for the tarnished model of France. Angeloni cited the American Revolution as the purest example of "natural force," and the Monroe Doctrine as an indication that this natural force may be turning from a "minor force" into the "major" force in the world.[141]

Angeloni's work impressed his old colleague Buonarroti as he was preparing to publish his *History* of the all-but-forgotten Babeuf conspiracy; and also interested other Italians exiled with Buonarroti in Belgium.[142] Both Angeloni and Buonarroti influenced in turn the most extensive and original treatise yet to appear on irregular revolutionary warfare: the two-volume *On the War of National Insurrection by Bands applied to Italy* by Count Carlo Bianco di Saint-Jorioz.[143]

Bianco had been active in the revolutionary struggle in Piedmont during 1820, and had journeyed to Paris in an unsuccessful effort to coordinate the Italian struggle with other European movements. Returning empty-handed, he was captured and narrowly escaped a death sentence in Turin in 1821. He then led the "Italian lancers" in Spain, stayed on to fight the royalist French troops there in 1822–23, fought briefly for Greek independence, and played a leading role in the *Apofasimèni* before beginning a life of permanent exile in Gibraltar, Malta, Corsica, Algeria, London, and Brussels.[144] Thus, his treatise of 1830 was the summary and synthesis of a decade of active experience —and at the same time an anticipation of the final flurry of violent revolutionary activity that he was about to undertake in Lyon in February 1831, and in Mazzini's efforts to invade and inspire revolution in Savoy in 1831 and 1834.[145]

Bianco's treatise urged Italy to reject timid political philosophers "more foreign than Italian," in favor of a "strong, robust and ardent" political-military mobilization for "national insurrection," such as took place in the United States after "their stupendous swift revolution." [146] He called for a nationwide network of guerrilla bands that would avoid direct combat but raid armories, seek camouflage, and deny the occupying Hapsburgs any local sustenance.[147] Gradually, areas were to be liberated, "bands" coalesced into "flying columns" and then into regular military formations with colors, uniforms, and Roman titles (decurion, centurion, consul, tribune).[148] The insurrection was to produce a model for political organization through its military command structure (four provinces, twenty congregations or cantons, and two hundred smaller units).[149]

The secret of success for a war of peoples rather than kings lay in the political and moral mobilization of the entire country. Arguing implicitly against the dominance of Parisian thinking in the revolutionary tradition, Bianco contended that the possession of a major—or even a capital —city is not important in the early stages of a national insurrection. The real national war against the invader in Spain and Russia began *after* Madrid and Moscow had fallen.[150] Capture of the capital—like the use of identifying uniforms and banners—would come later rather than early. It was important not to be corrupted by the big cities in the formative stages of a revolutionary movement. Rome itself was a "cloaca" of dishonesty; and large cities generally promoted "a luxuriating and effeminate life." [151]

The insurrectionary movement was thus seen as a kind of rural-based moral revival of the nation. Bianco's seven types of military movement prescribed a kind of corporate calisthenics for a people already sinking into *la dolce vita*. There was a sense of athletic adventure in Bianco's preference for light weapons, which put a premium on individual skill and intimate familiarity between man and implement: pikes and pitchforks, the Spanish knife and the Italian *pugnole*.[152]

Violence for Bianco (like "artificial force" for Angeloni) was characteristic only of reactionary states. Bianco (like most later apostles of revolutionary violence) saw himself as a reluctant fighter for national liberation opposing the mercenaries of a degenerate empire. The latter alone fought *per violenza*.[153] Mazzini tried to put his insurrectional theory into practice,[154] but came to depend on émigré exhortation more than insurrectionary action after the failures of the early thirties. Garibaldi would revive the notion of a partisan fighting group in the mid-forties; and the revolutionary failures of 1848–49 in Italy would inspire a return to violence in the fifties—especially in the remarkable uprising led by Carlo Pisacane in 1857, from a ship he had kidnapped on the high seas.

Prior to this, Pisacane had written a long study of the Italian Revolution of 1848–49. A military officer by profession, he laid particular stress on the need for ideological motivation in revolutionary warfare. The word *concetto* (concept) was distinguished from "sterile doctrines" and became almost synonymous with "revolutionary movement." [155] He called for "the revolution of ideas which must always precede the material revolution"; for an insurrectionary movement to spread "from one extreme of Italy to the other with the rapidity of thought"; [156] and for a new type of militant distinguished from the old type of soldier: *militi tutti, soldato nessuno.*[157] Nationalism was "enough for the insurrection, but not enough for victory"; so one must switch slogans "from 'war to the foreigner' to 'war on the ruler.' " [158] He envisaged a blend of Spanish and Russian anti-Napoleonic guerrilla tactics with the new class warfare of the workers of Lyon.[159] Moral factors could defeat material force; and "poetry" would prevail over "grammar" as the revolution spread from the countryside to the cities for final victory.[160]

The Poles became even more innovative than the Italians in the use of revolutionary violence. They built on the almost mystical significance that Kościuszko had attached to the link between peasant and scythe in the insurrection of 1794,[161] and speculated subsequently about using everything from fence posts and table knives to boiling water as weapons for insurgence against traditional armies.[162] They hoped, after their failed uprising of 1830–31, that a chain reaction of revolutions elsewhere would reverse the Russian suppression of Polish liberties. But neither the French unrest of 1832 nor that of Germany in 1833, nor the second Italian campaign against Savoy in 1834 succeeded. One of the relatively moderate leaders of the Polish military uprising of 1830–31 had written a lengthy and radical call to arms, *On Partisan Warfare*, in Paris in 1835; [163] and in the same year, a significant minority of the large Polish émigré population split off from the Democratic Society to form the Polish People organization, which advanced even more comprehensive theories justifying revolutionary violence.

Within the Democratic Society, the most influential proponent of violence, Ludwik Mierosławski, was born appropriately enough on a military wagon in 1814. He had led uprisings in Sicily and Baden as well as Poland, and by the 1830s was arguing that "in a state of revolution, the whole country is transformed into a single communal property in the hands of the revolutionary government." [164] He advocated "salutary" terrorism and mobilization of the peasantry for acts of violence, but still thought in terms of regular warfare against the occupying powers— concentrating against Russia. His ideas found reinforcement in another Polish treatise drawn up in the same year in Paris: *Partisan Warfare as the type most convenient for resurgent nations.*[165]

The Poles lent some of their militance to other national revolutions in 1848. Józef Bem, author of the first modern treatise on rocketry, became commander in chief of the military forces of the Hungarian national army.[166] But he saw the Hungarian Revolution crushed by the bulwark of reactionary antinationalism, by troops from the same Russia that had besieged him in Gdańsk in 1817 and destroyed the Polish insurrection in 1830–31 in which he had fought.

The failure of the 1846 uprising in Poland and of the final uprising of 1863 brought to an end the Polish-Italian period of heroic insurrectionist teachings. Left behind to posterity, however, was the largely overlooked legacy of the most original and prophetic of the Italo-Polish theorists of revolutionary violence, Henryk Kamieński. He so intensified the myth of "the people" as to insist that national revolution was inseparable from social revolution "because he who wishes to achieve his goal must will the means." [167] The means of realizing true national independence and dignity was his strikingly modern concept of a "people's war." This concept was first set forth as the title of the third part of a tract published in Brussels in 1844, partially exemplified in the Cracow uprising that he helped lead in 1846, and finally perfected in his *People's War*, published posthumously in 1866 after his long imprisonment and exile.

A "people's war" differed from a partisan war which was seen by Kamieński as only a tactical form of struggling for "auxiliary goals." A people's war was the totally just struggle of a totally oppressed people like the Poles, involving a total mobilization "in which the number of those fighting equals the numbers of inhabitants of the country." [168] The gentry who had long led Polish liberation movements must either renounce all social privilege and join the struggle or face punishment including death. Factors of morale were more important than weapons; and because the idea of a "people's war" was totally new, its leaders must be created in the struggle preferably among the peasants at the grass-roots level. They must be "apostles" of an egalitarian social transformation as well as tactically skilled military leaders.

The image of the revolutionary spark was given a slightly more modern ring by the widely travelled Kamieński (who lived in Paris and Brussels after 1830, Russia in exile, and France and Algeria in emigration after 1846). Social revolution, he insisted, was "the electric spark over the whole of Poland, set in motion by a magical power" [169] that would arouse the masses to defeat any traditional means of force (and would free national movements in the future from their traditional dependence on external aid or émigré leadership). With great detail—and a constant emphasis on political and moral as well as military factors —Kamieński developed two separate outlines for a four-stage concept of people's war. Initial scattered uprisings would build confidence and organization while avoiding pitched battles with regular units. Then mobile detachments would begin action, gradually merging into larger units. His tactics always included flexible responses to the forms that opposition might take, so that the occupying power (and the vacillating gentry) could never establish any enduring security. There is hardly a concept of modern, ideologically disciplined guerrilla warfare (including trans-national solidarity even with the impoverished Russians) that was not included in Kamieński's treatise, which in its final form was intended for the leaders of the 1863 uprising—but never reached them.

The only important new theoretical writing of the immediate pre-1863 period was Mierosławski's *Instructions to Insurgents* of 1862, which encouraged the Poles to think in more traditional anti-Russian terms despite such novel ideas as the use of armored cars.[170] Mierosławski was a more traditional nationalist, who had fought with Garibaldi and shared the Italians' great hopes for Napoleon III.

Italo-Polish teachings about violence always bore the influence of the French period of revolutionary history. The model was that of the revolutionary *levée en masse* of 1793 out of which a new nation had been born. The Italian and Polish interest in military action was a direct outcome of the military training and aroused expectations of the revolutionary and Napoleonic eras. Italy in the south and Poland in the east of Europe had provided the earliest, most consistent support of both revolutionary and Napoleonic France. These nations continued to nurture romantic hopes of material or spiritual aid from France.

Uprisings had been looked upon as necessary responses to what Angeloni in the aftermath of 1820 called "artificial force" and Cabet in the aftermath of 1830 called the "system of violence" [171] of the Holy Alliance. The Italo-Polish dream of national insurrection was generally based on the expectation that revolutionary France would lead the way. A sense that Napoleon had left that path was what had led in 1800 to the first revolutionary conspiracy to attack him by a Corsican and an Italian.[172] Continued bitterness by Italians at the French rejection of their own revolutionary heritage had led to periodic violence in Paris, culminating in the most grisly assassination attempt of the early nineteenth century by a Corsican Italian veteran of Napoleon's Russian campaign, Giuseppi Fieschi. In July 1835 (on the fifth anniversary of the Revolution of 1830), his improved version of the anti-Napoleonic "infernal machine" fired twenty-five guns simultaneously at King Louis Philippe, killing eighteen innocent bystanders and wounding scores more while missing its target altogether.[173]

Hope waned during the Second Empire of Napoleon III for another revolution in France; and the inevitable violent Italian expression of unrequited revolutionary love came, as we shall see, with Orsini's attempt to assassinate the French ruler in 1858. Finally, when unification came in 1859–61 through war and diplomacy rather than heroic revolution, the dream of such revolution died in Italy. Polish revolutionary hopes were definitively crushed by the massive Russian repression of the last in a long line of Polish insurrections in 1863. The Italo-Polish era of heroic violence had ended; and the new and very different Russian tradition was about to begin.

The Rival Social Revolutionaries

The rival tradition of social revolution, as we have said, was less successful than that of national revolution throughout the 1830–48 period. Social revolutionary leaders were usually lonely émigré intellectuals divorced from the masses. Even among urban workers there was little organized class warfare, let alone proletarian consciousness, outside of Paris and Lyon.

Yet a sense of impending social revolution haunted much of Europe in the 1830s. The conservative de Tocqueville, in the preface to his

Democracy in America of 1835, used the term "social revolution," and spoke of it as "irresistible . . . an accomplished fact, or on the eve of its accomplishment."

There were two main stages in the birth of a social revolutionary tradition, that is, in the transition from the republican conspiracies of the early twenties to the Marxist Communism of the late forties. First came the perfection of the idea of revolutionary dictatorship by Buonarroti in his last decade from 1828 to 1837. During this period, the revived Babeuvist ideal of equality was linked with the proletarian class struggle by some of Buonarroti's followers—and by his successor as chief organizer and symbol of revolutionary conspiracy—Auguste Blanqui.

The second phase, lasting from the late 1830s to 1848, was dominated by émigrés, who both internationalized the impulse towards social revolution and linked it with the working class. This progression of the social revolutionaries from conspiracy to ideology took place in Paris, London, Brussels, and Geneva. In these cities, relatively free expression was possible, and the critical intellect was forced to confront the reality of a new industrial order.

Buonarroti's Legacy

The starting point for a distinct and continuous social revolutionary tradition was the publication in 1828—at the nadir of revolutionary hopes—of Buonarroti's massive memorial to Babeuf: *The Conspiracy for Equality.* It provided at last both an ancestry and a model for egalitarian revolution by publicizing the all-but-forgotten Babeuvists.[174] The book was studied by both émigrés and local Belgians, who were encouraged by Buonarroti to see in a social revolutionary organization the "Archimedean lever" to overturn the world.[175]

The failure of all revolutions since 1789 had, in Buonarroti's view, been caused by a lack of strong leaders prepared in advance to give power to "a revolutionary government of sages." [176] He harkened back to Babeuf's idea of delegating authority immediately to "general commissioners" (*commissaires généraux*) trained in revolutionary "seminaries" and insisted on the need for a "provisional authority charged with completing the revolution and governing until popular institutions come into active being." [177]

Buonarroti urged that the revolutionary regime *not* submit itself to popular elections while initial revolutionary changes were being effected; but fulfill three functions instead: (1) "direct all the force of the nation against internal and external enemies," (2) "create and establish the institutions through which the people will be imperceptibly led really to exercise sovereignty," and (3) "prepare the popular Constitution which should complete and close the revolution." [178]

The ultimate aim of the revolution was the Rousseauian one of returning man to his "natural" state of liberty in which the "general will" prevails. Thus revolutionary power must be entrusted immediately to a "strong, constant, enlightened immovable will," and "the same will must direct the enfranchisement and prepare liberty." [179] "Experience has shown" that the privileged are "very poor directors of popular revolutions" and "the people are incapable either of regeneration by themselves or of designating the people who should direct the regeneration." [180]

Buonarroti provided a mandate for the continued existence of an elite
revolutionary dictatorship, and an implied license for the secret police
surveillance of the future. In his retrospective version of the Babeuf
conspiracy, a final decision had been made by "the secret directory" that

> . . . once the revolution is completed, it would not cease its works and would
> watch over the conduct of the new assembly.[181]

Buonarroti was almost certainly influenced by the more authoritarian
turn of mind among Italian émigrés after the failure of the liberal revolutions of the early 1820s. The theorist of violence Carlo Bianco, who
saw much of Buonarroti during this period, argued that the collapse
of the constitutional regimes in the early 1820s was facilitated by the
very liberties they granted. He insisted that revolutionaries should
establish a strong provisional authority and that no one should "determine in advance the duration." In language strongly suggestive of
Sorel's later paean to Mussolini, Bianco expressed a preference for an
individual dictator: "a *condottiero* with a heart that is hard and inaccessible to any shriek for mercy." [182]

Buonarroti's *History* was a model for modern revolutionary polemics
in its Manichean simplification of a complex story into a clear, cosmic
struggle of evil against good: "egoism" vs. "equality." He immediately
relegated to the camp of egoism almost all who had hitherto written
about the revolution. He then pointed out that "among the parties . . .
there is one on which the wise man should rivet his gaze"; [183] and this
party is presented as a kind of ultimate Masonic order, "the sincere
friends of equality." [184]

Buonarroti had gone to Brussels in 1824 because the Belgian half of
the newly created kingdom of the Netherlands was almost the only
French-speaking area in Europe still tolerant of exiled political extremists. Many aging French revolutionaries had taken up permanent residence there; it was largely among older revolutionary veterans that
Buonarroti gathered the inner circle for his *Monde* organization.

When Charles X abdicated after a struggle with the deputies that
spilled into the streets, the constitutional monarch Louis Philippe succeeded him with the support of that patron and symbol of moderate
revolution, the Marquis de Lafayette. However shocking it was to established kings to see a monarch enthroned by a mob, the spectable was
equally disquieting to extremists on the Left like Lafayette's former
aide-de-camp and associate in the French Carbonari, Voyer D'Argenson.
Likewise, the decision of Jean-Baptiste Teste, a former refugee in Belgium, to become a minister of the new king repelled his brother, the
publisher, Charles Teste. Thus D'Argenson and Teste formed together
with Buonarroti in his last years a kind of revolutionary triumvirate [185]
—the highest Illuminist "triangle," perhaps, or the final inner circle of

his *Monde.* In their eyes, the failure to institute a republic—let alone an egalitarian community—foredoomed the new French regime to failure long before its subservience to bourgeois capitalism made it a commonplace object of criticism and satire.

When revolt broke out in Brussels late in August 1830, French republicans were encouraged to believe that the revolutionary wave had not yet crested. Frenchmen moved into Belgium to defend the revolt; and Charles Rogier, who had many French revolutionary connections, led troops in from Liège to become the president of a provisional government. Buonarroti remained in Paris, but his friends participated in the agitation which led to the formation of a provisional revolutionary government on September 25. Buonarroti and Teste exercised direct, and at times controlling, influence on Rogier; on the more radical Louis De Potter, who briefly headed the provisional government; and on Felix Bayet, who was Buonarroti's secret agent in Brussels.[186] Buonarroti urged the Belgians to provide the "great example" that France had failed to give revolutionary Europe:[187] to form "fronts" for the revolutionary leadership by creating popular societies and journals that would propagate the virtues of a radical republican regime,[188] and to "delay elections . . . *Be dictators if necessary for the well-being of the country.*"[189] Bayet became secretary of a forty-man central meeting pledged to complete the revolution, and worked with De Potter, who attempted to form a Committee of Public Safety.[190]

After several months of internal chaos and external diplomacy, Belgium became independent, but under a conservative constitutional monarchy with the entrepreneurial bourgeoisie as the ruling force. The new king, Leopold I, was a German who had married into the British royal family, just as—at the opposite end of society from him—many workers came from Germany to work in the expanding English-type industries of the bourgeois monarchy. The Buonarrotian legacy of radical republican journals and secret societies affected Belgium throughout the thirties.[191] And Brussels became the residence of Karl Marx during 1845–47, when he was formulating the ideas for his *Communist Manifesto,* and the site of many of the meetings that led to the formation of the Communist League.[192]

In Paris after the revolutions in France and Belgium, Buonarroti's entourage decried not only the failure of the new regimes to proclaim republics, but also their failure to commit themselves to immediate, egalitarian reforms. The Babeuf-Maréchal idea that an élite vanguard must realize the unfinished revolution was revived with a vengeance. De Potter's pamphlet of December 1831, *On the revolution yet to be made,* predicted that "the first really social and popular revolution will fill up in reality and for all time the abyss of revolutions."[193] Teste insisted that "the extraordinary authority of strong, wise and devoted men" should exercise full interim power after any future revolution on behalf of "the most advanced, magnetic, energetic and prudent party in the society."[194]

Buonarroti himself now turned to Italy, where revolution still seemed possible. In 1832, he formed a Society of True Italians with a central

committee (*giunta*) and local "families" designed to inculcate "the social virtue of a free people" [195] while providing shock troops for the
revolutionary high command. The following year, this group allied with
the Reformed Carbonari (radical republican veterans of the original
French Carbonari) into the Universal Democratic Carbonari: the last
effort to realize Buonarroti's dream of an international revolutionary organization. It had loose links with Belgian, Swiss, and German (and
possibly Spanish and Portuguese) movements as well as with France and
Italy.[196] The goal was to realize equality "not in name, but in fact." [197]

The revolutionary conspiracy adopted names for lodges such as Jean-
Jacques and Saint-Just, the Babeuvist term *phalanx* in place of the Carbonari *vente*, and pseudonyms, codes, and security procedures that grew
ever more complex with the mounting police repression. The plan for a
reorganized Carbonari organization involved two grades, the forest and
the mountain—the former recalling the original Carbonari, the latter
the radical Mountain, now being glorified by a growing cult of Robespierre among Buonarroti's associates. But by the mid-thirties both his
foreign links and his "universal" organization had evaporated. Living
in virtual exile in the Parisian home of Voyer D'Argenson until his
death on September 16, 1837, Buonarroti ended up—literally—with
the anagrams rather than the reality of a revolutionary organization.[198]

Buonarroti had survived long enough to become a living legend, and
to attract the admiration of the very young, who were disillusioned
with Louis Philippe in the way Buonarroti had been with the Directory.
Many radical leaders of socialism in the 1840s—Cabet, Blanc, and
Buchez—apparently had contacts with the venerable "Jean-Jacques"
in the mid 1830s.[199]

Buonarroti also influenced the new generation of revolutionary artists
—particularly the revolutionary painter, Philippe-Auguste Jeanron: the
first to represent the proletariat in revolutionary scenes with a realistic
style.[200] Destined to illustrate Blanc's *History of Ten Years* and to direct the Louvre during the revolutionary years 1848–50, in the 1830s
Jeanron attacked not only the official art of the institute ("the Bastille
of artists"), but also the neo-classical imitators of David ("the old regime
in art"). Jeanron produced in the mid 1830s a haunting portrait of
Buonarroti,[201] who in turn inspired Jeanron's proclamation of 1834 that
"After the beneficent storm, EQUALITY SHALL APPEAR UPON THE
EARTH." [202]

Buonarroti had also had a final brush of sorts with the ghost and
legend of Napoleon. The most interesting new associate of Buonarroti's
last years, Jean-Jacques Delorme, was the link with surviving Bonapartists. As a young provincial from Loir-et-cher, Delorme had felt the grass-
roots appeal of the Napoleonic legend, and had been in sympathetic
touch in the late 1820s with circles that "would prefer a Napoleon to a
Bourbon if there were no other choice." [203] His vivid account of his
links with Buonarroti at the same time provides a unique source for
understanding the final revolutionary perspectives of the revolutionary
patriarch.

Delorme journeyed to Paris for a Carbonari-type initiation sealed by

Buonarroti's kiss of brotherhood in the presence of thirty members. He then returned in the early thirties for a largely unsuccessful effort to organize provincial "democratic committees." The triumvirate of Buonarroti, Teste, and Voyer D'Argenson advised him to see in adversity a test of revolutionary commitment: "Let us console ourselves by cultivating virtue," counseled Buonarroti.[204] Concentrate organizational work on youth, where "it is only a matter of preserving it from corruption." [205] Above all, maintain purity of conviction among the cadres even at the cost of diminished overall numbers.

Questioning the hostility to compromise of his revolutionary mentors, Delorme was told by Voyer D'Argenson (after a ceremonial banquet on Montmartre late in 1833) that "profound convictions are intolerant" and that revolutionaries must maintain *la sévérité de l'esprit exclusif.*[206] Anticipating the later Leninist conception of "principled" opposition, Buonarroti insisted on separating revolutionary from personal quarrels. The resulting sense of selfless dedication to an issue served in turn to intensify contempt for rivals in the political arena. "Pure love of equality," Buonarroti wrote in 1834, is "the thread" of Ariadne which will show "the way out of the labyrinth." "Sincere vows" to equality must precede any political activity. Otherwise revolutionary activists will become "enemies of the people and of humanity" and "all political changes will be deceptions and all revolutions incomplete and vicious." [207] Even royalists and Bonapartists now "call themselves republicans to deceive the weak," wrote Buonarroti,[208] as he adopted his final pseudonym of "Maximilien" to dramatize his admiration for Robespierre. Buonarroti also warned against the temptation to drift off into scholarly discussions. Revolutionaries have "no greater enemies than would-be scholars (*les prétendus savants*): such people, petrified with vanity, are the aristocracy incarnate." [209]

Buonarroti's most important new body of followers in the 1830s had been the Polish revolutionary organization founded on the Island of Jersey on October 30, 1835: the Polish People (*Lud Polski*). This group called for the abolition of private property, subdivided itself into communes, published innumerable manifestoes and denunciations of moderate reformists. They thought of themselves as "disciples of Buonarroti," and were "the first . . . publicly to accept his teaching as their own." [210] They took as their slogan Voyer d'Argenson's phrase *l'égalité des conditions sociales,* and urged an interim "dictatorship of the people" to reeducate people after a revolution through

> terrorism, the use of the sword to bring principle into effect, intolerance of all that either now or at any time harms this principle or can endanger our aims.[211]

The movement towards social revolutionary ideas in the 1830s can be vividly illustrated through the brief career of Simon Konarski, who, independently of the Buonarrotians, carried the Polish revolutionary mentality farthest to the east and deepest into the masses.[212] A brilliant student from an impoverished aristocratic family of Polish Calvinists, Konarski had fought as a youth in the Polish Revolution of 1830–31. In the best heroic tradition of his nation, Konarski did not stop when defeat was inevitable, but continued fighting in Lithuania and the eastern marches until mid 1831. After a brief internment, he emigrated to France and Belgium, where he became a protégé of Lelewel and a member of Young Poland. Thus he at first became the quintessential national revolutionary—rushing to Switzerland to participate in the ill-fated Mazzinian invasion of Savoy, keeping with him always both the pistol with which he fought and the flute on which he played patriotic songs.

But the national cause alone could not fully satisfy his revolutionary longings; and in the fall of 1834—a full year before the formation of the Polish People organization—he moved on to his own form of social revolution. In his biweekly Parisian journal, *Midnight,* he called not only for an overthrow of Tsarism, but for expropriating landowners, emancipating peasants with land grants, and equalizing social classes. He also followed the new Buonarrotian pattern of planning for a provisional revolutionary government in his "The Transitional State and the Final Organization of Society."

In 1835, he returned incognito to Poland and established a revolutionary Society of the Polish People (*Stowarzyszenie Ludu Polskiego*) in Cracow, then moved east to organize revolutionary cells in Lithuania, White Russia, and the Ukraine. Across the vast area which stretched from the Baltic to the Black Sea, Konarski spun a conspiratorial web which was estimated to have included about three thousand participants—and which soon became perhaps the first purely revolutionary organization to form a special, separate circle for women.

Arrested at Vilnius late in May 1838, Konarski proved unbreakable under torture, converted his Russian guards, and would have probably escaped had he not insisted that all other prisoners also be released. In a farewell verse to his fiancée from jail just before he was executed by a firing squad on February 25, 1839, Konarski wrote: "I do not wish to go to heaven, while my people are in bondage."

The revolutionary par excellence thus confronted without flinching a hopelessness that extended from this world to the next. He had created—among other things—the first student revolutionary movement ever to take root inside Russia. So great was the fear of his circle of student followers that Kiev University was shut altogether for a year. Imperial Russia in 1839—as Custine's famous book of that year, *Russia,* eloquently pointed out [213]—proved the very heart of European repression. It was of course to be in this same Russia that actual social revolution, dimly foreshadowed in the Konarski movement, eventually took place.

Blanqui

If Buonarroti had become the venerable old man of social revolution in France of the 1830s, the cause was actually more deeply identified with the youthful Auguste Blanqui. Blanqui thought of a revolutionary movement as a force for educating the masses rather than purifying the members; he was better equipped to make revolutionary use of the new possibilities for political agitation under the new constitutional monarchy. Keeping alive the Buonarrotian tradition of secret hierarchical organization, he still gave more concrete social content to the egalitarian ideal.

Blanqui was descended from a north Italian family (Bianchi-Blanchi-Blanqui), and had joined the French version of the Carbonari during its period of decline.[214] His interest in economic questions was aroused by his older brother, the economist Adolphe Blanqui, and also perhaps by the pioneering ideologue-economist Jean-Baptiste Say, whose socialist utopia of 1799, *Olbie*, had envisaged the banishment of all tyrants, parasites, and priests.[215]

Wounded three times in the election demonstrations of 1827, Blanqui set off on foot with a pack for the then almost mandatory "rendez-vous of love" with Greece.[216]

His romantic wanderings, however, took him only as far as conservative Italy and Spain, where he intensified his hatred of both monarchs and priests. He returned to Paris just in time for the July revolution, which permanently affected his imagination:

> No one could forget the marvelous suddenness with which the scene changed in the streets of Paris, as in a *coup de théâtre;* how ordinary clothes replaced formal dress in the blinking of an eye as if a fairy's wand had made the one disappear and the other surge forth. . . .[217]

After the "three glorious days," the only remaining revolutionary task was "gathering in the booty." The failure of national revolutionary leadership to do this gave Blanqui his sense of permanent mission: to provide leadership for a popular social revolution. He was determined to prevent the "unworthy usurpation" of revolutions by political opportunists, the victory of *les hommes du comptoir* over *les hommes des ateliers.*[218]

Blanqui felt from the beginning a profound impatience with excessive verbalizing. He became active in the radical republican Friends of the People formed during the Revolution of 1830 "to conserve for the people the rights they have just conquered." He agitated for universal suffrage and full implementation of the radical Jacobin constitution of 1793.[219]

At his trial on January 15, 1832 (he was acquitted), Blanqui began the modern revolutionary tradition of using the courtroom as a podium for a revolutionary *profession de foi*. To the question "What is your estate?" (*état*) he answered simply "proletariat." When the president of the court insisted "that is not an estate," Blanqui replied:

> How can it not be? It is the estate of 30 million Frenchmen who live by their labor and are deprived of political rights.[220]

Increasing agitation by the Friends of the People for social as well as civic equality began after Blanqui's acquittal in the summer of 1832. Against a background of proletarian upheaval in Lyon and unrest elsewhere, Blanqui developed not only a theory of social revolution based on class conflict, but also the rationale for leadership by an intellectual elite. Blanqui insisted that mental intelligence and physical labor were interdependent needs for a successful revolution:

> Labor is the people; intelligence is the men of devotion who lead them. How could the brutal violence of privilege prevail against this invincible coalition. . . ?

Here in essence was a call for a revolutionary *intelligentsia*: "intelligence" not just as a mental force but as a group of people pledged to social justice.[221]

By 1834, most radical republicans had transferred their activities to the Society of the Rights of Man. This organization was a nationwide, open association under a central committee, with sections of ten to twenty members elected by majority vote. This society gathered in local memberships from a wide variety of groups agitating for civil liberties and republicanism; its variegated local affiliates assumed names as respectable as Washington and Stoicism and as disturbing as Revolutionary Power, Death to Tyrants, and Buonarroti.[222] It was the first national society to extend its educational activities to the working class.

It was largely against the growing strength of this amorphous organization that Louis Philippe early in 1834 directed new laws restricting the rights of association and the press. This action strengthened the hand of revolutionary republicans and helped precipitate new disturbances. Polarization into extremes continued with a new wave of arrests. The following year a former Corsican bandit together with two members of the Society of the Rights of Man made a bloody but unsuccessful attempt with their "infernal machine" to assassinate Louis Philippe and his sons.

The repressions that followed forced republicans to move again from open to secret societies; and the prisons of Louis Philippe became the centers of recruitment for a new wave of revolutionary organization led by Blanqui.

Blanqui led two successive conspiratorial organizations, the Society of the Families and the Society of the Seasons, where in many ways the modern social revolutionary tradition was born. The name "family" was probably taken from Buonarroti's Italian secret society;[223] and its five-member structure came from the French student circles of the early twenties where Blanqui served his revolutionary apprenticeship. Founded in the summer of 1834, the families gained twelve hundred adherents—many of them workers from the militant "revolutionary legions" which had sworn to keep alive the insurrectionary traditions of 1834.[224] The secret hierarchical organization often expanded to include as many as twelve members in a nuclear family cell. There were five or six families to a section; and two or three sections to a quarter, whose leaders were linked with the secret, central committee through a revolutionary agent. Special authority to screen members was invested in a three-man jury; and the catechism for new members reiterated the Buonarrotian message that egoism was "the dominant vice of society" as it now existed and "equality" the "principle basis of society" as it should be. "New aristocrats" ruled by force and money; but the revolutionaries had new allies in the "proletariat," whose lot was now "similar to that of serfs and negroes." The last of fifteen questions and answers for the would-be member of a family was:

> Is it necessary to make a political or social revolution?—*It is necessary to make a social revolution.*[225]

The Society of the Families was crushed through police penetration in 1836. When Blanqui was released from prison in 1837, he reorganized it as the Society of the Seasons with a more proletarian composition and an even more florid form of organization evoking the idea of revolutionaries as mysterious agents of a higher natural order. The basic cell was a week composed of six men with a chief called Sunday. At the next level, four weeks comprised a twenty-nine-man month with a chief called July; three months constituted a season with a chief called Spring. Four seasons made a year with a chief who was the supreme agent of the revolution for the given area. At the head of the Seasons, which at its peak included about nine hundred members, was a triumvirate of leaders: Blanqui, Armand Barbès, and Martin Bernard.[226]

This triumvirate sought to lead not just the revolutionary struggle, but an interim revolutionary government as well.[227] In an insurrection begun on Sunday, May 12, 1839, the Seasons anticipated the Bolshevik idea of striking directly for the centers of power: transport and communication. On a prepared plan they seized the Hotel de Ville and Palais de Justice; but the absence of widespread popular support (the "silence of the streets") made the triumph short-lived. With its leaders condemned to imprisonment in Mont-Saint-Michel, the tradition of revolutionary conspiracy largely ended in Paris.

However, this secret tradition continued to flourish in outlying regions. In the same 1839, much of Ireland lay in terror before the Irish Sons of Freedom and Sons of the Shamrock or Ribbon Society. This secret revolutionary organization had attempted to impose professional discipline on an old and hallowed Irish tradition of agrarian violence by establishing regional brotherhoods in which a master had power over three members, who in turn each commanded twelve brothers.[228] Secret passwords, recognition signals, and ribbons were changed with each season; and carefully targeted beatings ("slatings") were undertaken by leaders such as one Edward Kennedy, who later became the principal informer at their trial in Dublin.[229] There was a central committee in Dublin [230] which apparently entertained some hopes of forming alliances with Scots and even Englishmen.[231]

Ribbonism was feared not only as a kind of counter-government in Ireland but also as an instrument of class warfare within the British Kingdom. In sentencing the principal leader in 1840, the judge spoke of "the protection of the working classes against being duped into the commission of crimes which they never contemplated." [232]

Unlike Blanqui's Society of the Seasons, the Ribbon Society did not attempt a political coup. It was succeeded in the 1840s by Young Ireland, which, as we have seen, was directly linked with Mazzini and that other revolutionary tradition, romantic nationalism; and then, in the 1850s, by the Irish Republican Brotherhood (called Fenians after the pre-Christian warriors), which was largely modeled on the rival Carbonari model of republican conspiracy.[233] Thus, within its own uninterrupted revolutionary tradition, Ireland experienced a typical alternation between national and social revolution, between the Mazzinian and Buonarrotian models for political warfare against the established order.

German Émigrés

One decade after Buonarroti's death in 1837 and eight years after Blanqui's eclipse, the social revolutionary tradition gave birth to the Communist League. A small group of young German émigrés created this short-lived but historic organization. They took over the struggle within the German emigration "between national republicans and communist republicans," [234] and produced a leader for the latter camp in Karl Marx. He fortified the entire European social revolutionary camp with an ideological armory and strategic perspective it had never possessed before.

The scene for this German drama was the liberal metropolitan centers of the non-German world: Paris and London—and, to a lesser extent, Brussels and Geneva. There the possibilities for free expression and assembly were greatest, and the plight of the growing industrial proletariat most inescapable. These cosmopolitan, multi-lingual centers of bourgeois capitalism provided favorable breeding grounds for the tough-minded secularism that eventually prevailed in Marx's *Manifesto*. The first stage, however, in establishing links between émigré intellectuals and indigenous workers was the new surge of romantic religiosity which swept through the intellectuals themselves in the late 1830s and 1840s.

Infatuation with religious ideas helped reassure social revolutionaries that a total transformation of society was still possible even at a time of repression and of disillusionment with the experiments of the early Fourierists and Saint-Simonians. At the same time, religious images enabled revolutionaries to communicate anew with the still-pious masses. This was important in building a base for the top-heavy revolutionary organizations. It was also important psychologically in providing human links for deracinated intellectuals within the impersonal city. Small-group solidarity—face-to-face human relations—was a deep need for sensitive and isolated leaders. The small revolutionary band as a surrogate family with quasi-religious rituals had often answered this need, particularly in Italy.

Some of the new political exiles were, however, attached to ideas, divorced from local allegiances, and seized by a revolutionary vision that was—to use a favorite word of the decade—universal. In the early 1840s, the totally uprooted Franco-Peruvian author of *Peregrinations of a Pariah*, Flora Tristan, drew up in London the first plan for an all-European proletarian alliance, the *Union ouvrière*.[235] In the early

1850s, continental émigrés in London calling themselves "the outlaws" (*proscrits*) formed an alliance of revolutionary nationalists for a "universal republic." These were the first in a series of attempts by political exiles at ecumenical organization that led eventually to the First International.[236]

A certain thirst for conflagration began to infect the intellectuals. Flora Tristan, for instance, called for a purely "intellectual union" of workers, but wanted it animated by "fire in the heart" so that it could constitute "a firebrand in the system." To the suggestion that one must ignite such firebrands, she replied: "Not before one is sure that the fire would be inextinguishable." [237] The more universal the dream of brotherhood the greater the personal need often was for a protective "family" or—to cite another image of Flora Tristan's—a "nest."

It was principally among the Germans that the progression from national to "universal" social perspectives had taken place. Disillusioned with the reactionary turn of their new national leader, Frederick William IV of Prussia, Germans were in any case inclined to a broader perspective by their traditions of theological and philosophical speculation—and also by the absence of a nationalistic émigré subculture such as the Poles and Italians enjoyed in Paris and London.

To be sure, the revolutionary movement among German émigrés, as elsewhere, was initially nationalist, with the formation in 1832 of a German People's Union in Paris and of a Young Germany affiliated with Mazzini's Young Europe the following year in Geneva. Many were veterans of the ill-fated German revolutions of 1830; others had joined émigré Polish nationalists in the Hambacher Fest of 1832 before settling together with the Poles in the safer surroundings of Paris or Geneva. In Switzerland, where the majority of early German émigrés tended to go for linguistic reasons, the religiosity of Lamennais and Mazzini tended to dominate.

Those who went to Paris were, however, mostly secular intellectuals from the Rhineland attracted by the example of successful revolution in France, and quick to imitate the new organizations that were springing up "like mushrooms after rain" in Paris. After the repressive measures of 1834, German radicals in Paris followed their French counterparts in moving towards more extreme organizations, founding in July 1834 the League of the Outlaws (*Bund der Geächteten*). Its leader, Theodore Schuster, was less explicitly revolutionary than his French counterpart, Blanqui, but apparently borrowed directly from Buonarroti's final fantasy of a Universal Democratic Carbonari.[238] Schuster's hierarchical structure had regional tents or foundaries ascending up through provincial camps to a central focus or burning point.[239]

Schuster's *Confession of Faith of an Outlaw*, written in 1834,[240] was perhaps the first example of a portrayal of the coming revolution as a necessary creation of the outcasts of society. He suggested that rejected exiles and outlaws would provide the elemental power of the revolution. Bakunin picked up this idea in the early 1840s,[241] and later popularized it among Russian revolutionary populists.

Schuster, however, anticipated more the Marxist conception of a proletarian revolution than the romantic idea of a bandit uprising. In his journal, *The Outlaws*, which appeared until the society was abolished in 1836, Schuster spoke not only of Buonarrotian social equality, but also of inevitable class struggle. He advocated productive cooperatives as a means of protecting the poor and enhancing their solidarity.[242] Schuster and his associates took a skeptical view of the republican and civil libertarian ideals of the French. The fact that they tended to be working class in origin and at the same time of a relatively high educational level predisposed the Germans to a more concrete, economic approach to the problems of their time. Seeing such problems as common to both France and Germany, they argued that the deepest divisions in Europe were now between social classes.[243] Schuster advocated government intervention to prevent the rule of capitalists over workers through a "cooperative republic." [244]

The Outlaws were the first international organization of social revolutionaries. With about one hundred members in Paris and at least seventy to eighty members in the area of Frankfurt am Main,[245] they soon outgrew their conspiratorial cocoon. Schuster led one group back into the national revolutionary camp via a new League of Germans; [246] but the larger successor organization was the League of the Just, which drew up its statutes in Paris as the Outlaws were disintegrating in late 1837 and early 1838.

The new organization was less hierarchical in structure and more directly responsive to working-class interests than the Outlaws. Though its federative organization and social demands resembled those of Blanqui's Society of the Seasons, there was a new strain of internal democracy. Officers were now elected locally rather than appointed from the center, and orders that violated personal conscience could be ignored.[247] Ten members formed a commune, ten communes a county. Delegates from each county made up a hall (*halle*), which was to elect both an executive committee in charge of political direction and a committee of assistance in charge of material support and adjudication within the one thousand-man society.

No longer content with the abstract political rights of the French republican tradition, the German League of the Just followed the Society of the Seasons in insisting on "the right to existence" and to education as well as the right to vote. They fortified the Buonarrotian call for provisional revolutionary dictatorship with a medical metaphor:

> The state of society having become gangrenous, the people will need—in order to pass into a healthy state—a revolutionary power for some time.[248]

Here was the hint of forthcoming amputations by self-appointed surgeons for the sick society. The organic image of society implicitly challenged the open, contractual concept of politics common to revolutionary republicans. A split soon developed between advocates of political agitation and partisans of a social revolution to create a "community of goods." The former group (called cabinet-makers or carpenters because of the guild affiliation of some leaders) opposed the more revolu-

tionary faction (called tailors or shoemakers). This split between political reformists and social revolutionaries paralleled the schism in
France between radical republicans who sought gains for workers
through the political system, and social revolutionaries like Blanqui
who wished to overthrow it altogether.

One key member of the more extreme tailor faction within both the
Outlaws and the Just was Johann Hoeckerig, who was a protégé and visitor of Buonarroti in his last days. Hoeckerig had founded a short-
lived Franco-German radical journal in 1836 and subsequently introduced a number of Germans into Masonic and revolutionary activity in
Paris—moving even beyond Buonarroti, who had believed in a Grand
Architect though not a Creator God, to pure atheism.[249]

But most of the revolutionary minority among the approximately
eighty-eight thousand Germans in Paris in the 1830s retained a special
quality of religiosity. German workers and craftsmen were closer to a
communal religious life than the cosmopolitan, Francophile intellectuals; and the Germans proved receptive to Lamennais's suggestion that
the alternative to bourgeois exploitation would be some new kind of
social Christianity.[250] Just as uprooted Catholic intellectuals from Italy
and Poland drew hope for national revolution from Lamennais's *Words
of a Believer,* so uprooted Protestant workers from Germany saw the
outlines of a coming social revolution in Lamennais's picture of "the
people" as the suffering servant of God with a messianic destiny.

Karl Schapper, leader of the Paris section of the League of the Just,
had moved from an early allegiance to Mazzini to egalitarian socialism.[251] Addressing his followers as "Brothers in Christ," he described
the coming social revolution as "the great resurrection day of the people" that will sweep away not just the "aristocracy of money," but also
the "aristocracy of the mind." Revolutionaries should beware, however,
of intellectuals, who

> . . . think little of the people and believe that heads filled with book learning
> make them better than other people [and entitled] to make laws and
> govern. . . .[252]

Schapper's anti-intellectual religiosity was intensified and popularized
by the tailor Wilhelm Weitling, who wrote the principal manifesto for
the League: *Humanity as it is and as it ought to be.* Under the influence
of Lamennais's *Book of the People,* which he translated,[253] Weitling
proclaimed himself to be a "social Luther." His clandestinely printed
Humanity conveyed in tones of earthy simplicity the thirst for religious community within the uprooted, newly industrialized working
class. His diagnosis was primitive, and his prescription utopian. But
simplicity and directness reached the new mass audience. Its two thousand copies were widely distributed and discussed, and *Humanity* became the model for subsequent manifestoes of social revolution.

Inequality, Weitling argued, was increasing rather than vanishing in
the face of industrialization. All exploitation and corruption could be
traced to one disease carrier: money. All the goods made by honest

workers as well as their wives, their families, and their very souls have been put up for sale: subjected to the rule of money.

Against the artificial world of this false medium Weitling juxtaposed a utopian alternative to be based on a fusion of the "law of nature" with the "law of charity"—a mélange of Buonarroti and Lamennais, of radical secular enlightenment with visionary Christian sentiment. All individual property ownership and right of inheritance were to be abolished. The value of all products was henceforth to be calculated in terms not of money, but of hours of work. Conflict was to be resolved and rights guaranteed not by republican political forms, but by two totally new social authorities: the "order of families" and the "order of production."

The order of families most likely drew its name and federative structure from Blanqui's Society of the Families. The pyramid ascended from local assemblies elected by universal suffrage up to a supreme Senate which was to appoint an executive director to determine social priorities for each million inhabitants. The natural unstructured social unit, the family—rather than any artificial economic identity—was the basis for all higher social authority.

The order of production divided society into four separate estates: the rural, the worker, the intellectual, and the industrial. The first three were decentralized. But the industrial estate—dealing with public utilities and heavy manufacturing—required a centralized "industrial army," in which everyone between the ages of fifteen and eighteen would be required to serve. The only permissible commercial exchange was that earned by supplementary volunteer labor (during so-called "commercial hours") in special factories in which alone "objects of luxury or fantasy" could be produced.[254]

Weitling initially had no idea of bringing such an order about by violence. Despite many connections with the Society of the Seasons, the League of the Just did little to aid its insurrection of May 1839 in Paris. When, however, many members were arrested in the general repression and the survivors forced to emigrate a second time, the Germans began to explore more revolutionary paths.

The largest element of this new emigration moved to London, and helped form in February 1840 an Educational Society for German Workingmen.[255] Three transplanted leaders of the Paris League of the Just (Schapper, Bauer, and Moll) took the lead in organizing this larger new society, while simultaneously keeping alive something of their smaller old organization.[256]

The Chartist Catalyst

The quasi-Christian influence of Weitling was weaker in London than in Switzerland, where Weitling had initially emigrated. The booming commercial life, the glaring inequalities, and the cosmopolitan atmosphere of the English capital encouraged the Germans to pay increasing attention to social issues and secular criticism. But most importantly, London was the home of the large and internationally minded Chartist

movement, which was widely regarded as the most promising democratic movement of the 1840s.

Chartism has been seen in retrospect as a reformist rather than revolutionary movement: open agitation for rights rather than clandestine
organization for upheaval. The English Reform Bill of 1832 focused
attention on political rather than social change. The Victorian establishment—so the accepted wisdom runs—provided just enough light
at the top of the chimney to persuade the dispossessed to continue
climbing up through the soot rather than to contemplate tearing down
the house.

But Chartism had a European-wide impact on revolutionaries. This
large-scale movement was launched in the 1830s in order to oppose
the authority of a propertied parliament with the more revolutionary
idea of full popular sovereignty: annual elections based on universal
suffrage. The radical proposal of a "people's charter" in 1838 led in the
following summer to a direct challenge to Parliament by a "national
convention" summoned to present a petition with one and one-quarter
million signatures to the House of Commons.

As the subsequent petitions of 1842 and 1848 were also to be, this
was rejected. Much of the Chartist program was to be incrementally
adopted in later reform bills. But the radical wing of the Chartist movement dramatized the continuing possibility of violent direct action by
the working class; and their increasingly desperate search for allies
brought them into collaboration with the German émigrés who left
France after the parallel failure of the Blanquist insurrection in 1839.

Radical Chartists were the first in the modern world both to suggest
(in 1832) [257] and to attempt (in 1842) a nationwide general strike as a
means to power for the working class. The London Working Men's Association, formed by radical Chartists in June 1836, internationalized
their quest for revolutionary action a few months later by issuing a
"Manifesto of Solidarity to the Working Classes of Belgium" in support
of the arrested Buonarrotian Jacob Kats.[258] This pamphlet was distributed in Germany by the League of the Just and used as a means of
raising money. German links with the Chartists became even closer
in 1837 when the latter's more radical members, George Julian Harney
and Bronterre O'Brien, broke away to form the more militant Democratic Association. These two played key roles in pioneering the international social revolutionary tradition.

As early as 1833 O'Brien argued that the working class must have
"complete dominion over the fruits of their own industry."

> An entire change in society—a change amounting to a complete subversion
> of the existing "order of the world"—is contemplated by the working
> classes. They aspire to be at the top instead of at the bottom of society—or
> rather that there should be no bottom or top at all.[259]

A displaced Irishman impressed by his stay in Paris, O'Brien looked to
cosmopolitan London and to foreign support for help in countering the
dominant trend in Chartism towards moderate reformism.[260] Harney's
role as secretary to the Democratic Association was even more impor-

tant. The newspaper he took over in 1843, *Northern Star*, was to become a model for social revolutionaries: *North Star*, the antislavery weekly founded in 1847 by the pioneering American black journalist Frederick Douglass; *Poliarnaia Zvezda*, the first illegal émigré Russian revolutionary publication, which Alexander Herzen brought out in 1855; and *Nordstern*, the first journalistic organ of an all-German workers' party, which took that name in Hamburg in 1862—all used variants of Harney's title.[261]

Weitling arrived in London in the summer of 1844 with an aura of martyrdom following two years of imprisonment for revolutionary activity in Switzerland. The Chartists arranged in his honor the first truly international meeting of social revolutionaries in London on September 22, 1844: the anniversary of the founding of the first French Republic. Hailed as "a martyr in the cause of Communism,"[262] Weitling proposed a toast "to that social organization which leads through republic to the community."[263] A British speaker followed him with a speech that looked even more explicitly beyond politics to a communist society. He argued that the French revolutionaries had "tried convention, directory, consulate and empire, and had found mere political changes insufficient."

> Thus had Babeuf and Buonarroti arisen to declare that without reform and common labor and enjoyment, the end of the revolution was not gained.[264]

He proposed a massive "communist" publication program in French, German, and Italian so that "the world would be revolutionalized."[265]

Those who hoped for international social revolution tended to disregard not just the national question but political issues altogether. The League of the Just proclaimed to the rebellious Silesian weavers in October 1844 that the coming emancipation of the proletariat made the form of government almost irrelevant:

> It is all the same to us whether the state is monarchist, constitutional or republican, so long as it is founded only upon justice.[266]

Excited by the international proletarian cause, the German Educational Society in London began adding foreign members. From a scant thirty members in 1844, they grew by June 1846 to two hundred fifty members, including forty Scandinavians, thirty Germans, twenty Hungarians, and other representatives from Latin and Slavic lands as well as from the Low Countries.[267] The Germans regularized cooperation with French and Polish political exiles through an informal, international society of 1844, the Democratic Friends of All Nations. Its name and organizational ideas were taken from Harney's Democratic Association. On September 22, 1845, German relations with the Chartists were formalized at another meeting to commemorate the founding of the first French Republic. This truly international Festival of Nations led to the founding of the International Democratic Association under Harney, who insisted at the banquet that the word "foreigner" be expunged from the dictionary. In March 1846, Harney founded yet another, even broader, international group, the Fraternal Democrats, with Poland, Germany, France, England, Hungary, Switzerland, and Scandinavia all represented in the secretariat.

Harney issued a manifesto to the workers of America and Britain during the war crisis of 1846 between the two countries, urging that the proletariat not be diverted from social issues into national wars. The League of the Just adopted in the course of 1846 the Fraternal Democrats' slogan "All men are brothers," and made London formally the headquarters of the League.[268]

A similar call for transnational unity in the "abolition of property" had been issued in Switzerland late in 1844 in the pamphlet *What do the Communists Want?* by the leading survivor of Weitling's original communist organization:

> If we speak of the liberation of humanity, we mean that the liberty which we hope for is not German or French or North American freedom, but the real freedom of man.[269]

The message of social revolution was also being spread to the New World. In November 1845 secret members of the League of the Just helped an industrial congress in New York focus on the disparity between the egalitarian language of the Declaration of Independence and the inequalities of the industrial order. Calling themselves "the German Commune of Young America," they led the German community in New York to form a special Social Reform Association within the National Reform Association in America.[270] Their German-language journal, which first appeared in New York in January 1846 under the Babeuvist title, *Tribune of the People,* addressed itself to "the poor, the supplicants, the oppressed." [271] Both the journal and the association attracted attention among German immigrants in major American cities from Boston to Milwaukee to St. Louis.

On July 4, 1846, the German movement in England prevailed on Harney's "Fraternal Democrats" to appeal to the "Workers of America" on the seventieth anniversary of the Declaration of Independence

> . . . to crown the perfection of your institutions with the abolition of the slavery of whites as well as blacks—of the salary as well as the whip; to expel from your legislative assemblies landed proprietors, userers, lawyers, mercenaries and other charlatans and idlers.[272]

Lasting leadership for the social revolutionaries was to come, however, neither from émigré German workers nor from English democrats. The figures who fused proletarian communism with democratic internationalism were two German intellectuals in Brussels: Karl Marx, the learned son of a distinguished jurist from Trier, and Frederick Engels, the widely read and traveled offspring of a wealthy industrialist from Wuppertal. They increasingly came to dominate the social revolutionary camp after beginning their lifelong collaboration in the late summer of 1844. They unified the proletarian cause with secular ideology in a way that was both authoritative and authoritarian.

Their first task was to establish their authority in the crucible of radical journalism by attacking precisely those who were then recognized as the leaders of each of the two forces they sought to bring together. Systematically and simultaneously they attacked both the workers then recognized as the leading spokesmen for the proletariat (Weitling and Proudhon) and at the same time the intellectuals then recognized as the most revolutionary (the left Hegelians). In so doing they gave focus to the social revolutionary ideal and created modern communism. The story of the birth of communism deals with cerebral forces in an era when the romantic force of revolutionary nationalism had weakened. That story will require detailed treatment later in this narrative, not so much because of communism's importance in the nineteenth century, but because of its legacy to the twentieth.

CHAPTER 7

The Evolutionary

Alternative

NATIONAL REVOLUTIONARIES had offered the romantic imagination a new sense of fraternity. Social revolutionaries had provided the early industrial era with a new call for equality. But there were still those concerned primarily with liberty: the third part of the revolutionary Trinity.

The ideal of freedom—expressed in civil liberties, written constitutions, and republican forms of government—continued to have its votaries despite the revolutionary failures of 1815–25. After constitutional regimes came into being in France and Belgian in 1830, political liberals continued to proliferate—and to be widely regarded as revolutionaries.

But old-fashioned constitutionalism had lost its luster for many younger revolutionaries. It seemed too narrowly political, too much concerned with the form rather than the texture of a new society. One can illustrate both the general decline and the peripheral success of liberal-constitutional revolutionaries after 1830 by considering, respectively, the last days of the Marquis de Lafayette and the early career of his Swiss admirer, James Fazy.

Lafayette and the Lost Liberals

As the revolutionary tide ebbed after 1830 and revolutionaries of a new generation were expressing their disillusionment, they began to denounce the patriarchal sponsor of the July monarchy, the Marquis de Lafayette.

The flood of popular songs, lithography, and pamphlets released by the revolution sharpened the taste for a total alternative in society. Moderation provided food for caricature; and, in his last years, the aging Lafayette could not escape. He, who had typified the moderate, constitutional ideal among revolutionaries—a dashing freedom fighter in America, the first ambassador to the United States, and perhaps the most lionized foreign visitor to early America on his triumphal return in 1824–25—was to prove as much a political failure in France as he had been a success in America. His tolerant deism, his belief in natural rights and constitutional propriety, which had earned him so much admiration in America, were to win more enemies than friends in France. He was repeatedly caught between the scissor blades of Right and Left as they cut through him to steely confrontation with each other. Both constitutional monarchies that he backed, that of 1791 and 1830, were undercut from both Right and Left almost as soon as they were promulgated.

Lafayette had attached himself to Washington upon his arrival in America as a boy of nineteen in 1777. But in France he neither found such a leader nor became one himself. His hopes for Louis XVI proved misplaced; and by the end of 1830 his faith in Louis Philippe had faded. Disdain for Napoleon born of a sense of rivalry cut Lafayette off from influence on that era. He had joined Napoleon only for the final, ill-fated Hundred Days, and for an unsuccessful effort (as vice-president of Napoleon's chamber of deputies) to establish Napoleon's son as ruler of France under a regency.

If one accepts the brilliant characterization of his grand nephew and posthumous editor, Charles Rémusat, Lafayette cannot simply be dismissed as a "statue looking for its pedestal"[1] in Lafitte's term, or, in Mirabeau's, as a statesman who *"avait bien sauté pour reculer."* [2] Nor was Lafayette simply an ineffectual moderate, like so many Girondists and Orléanists, addicted to timid compromise or self-interested opportunism. Despite superficial similarities and occasional alliances, Lafayette disliked and fought most such moderates.

"Il n'y a pas de milieu," Rémusat insisted despairingly to Lafayette during the initial revolutionary chaos of 1830.[3] But Lafayette rejected the extreme alternatives of either a republic under himself or a monarchy under the Bourbons. He proposed instead a constitutional monarchy under the new house of Orléans. The opposite of liberal was "doctrinaire," [4] and its political style was moderate, but not unprincipled.

"Moderation," he wrote in the last year of his life, "has never been for me the middle point between any two opinions whatsoever." [5] It was rather a positive commitment "to the cause of liberty" guaranteed by a rule of law and representative institutions; and an equally firm opposition to "the adversaries of the cause under whatever form: despotic, aristocratic, anarchic." In his political testament, Lafayette equated moderation with the militant defense of:

The sacred cause of liberty from the heresies that denature it, the excesses that retard it, the crimes that profane it, and the apologies that would still defeat it—if it had not found refuge in the pure memories and sublime sentiments which characterize the great work of the people.[6]

This "great work of the people" was to have been the establishment of political freedom and civil liberty through the original French Revolution of 1789–91. Despite secure social roots in the aristocracy and ample personal wealth, Lafayette believed that there were revolutions yet to be made. But they were to be limited, constitutional revolutions designed to initiate popular sovereignty and release individual initiative.

When reaction closed in on France with a vengeance in 1824, Lafayette refurbished his image as elder of the revolution with a long and wildly successful trip to the United States. He returned in 1825 to be greeted by insecure student agitators seeking him out for long discussions.

It is hard to determine exactly how intimate and extensive his collaboration actually was with the many revolutionary groups with which he had contact throughout the 1820s. Police investigations were reluctant to probe too deeply when the trail pointed towards such a powerful and respected figure.[7] His hold on the imagination of the young represented in many ways a transfer of messianic expectations following the death of Napoleon in 1821. He presented himself as both the successor to and the antithesis of "the false liberation of Napoleon." By contrast, he seemed to be blending positive sentiments into a program of liberal rationality. His aristocratic remoteness from direct participation in conspiracy made him even more invulnerable as a hero when the conspiracies failed.

In any case, more important than the details of *how* Lafayette collaborated with the new generation of European revolutionaries is the question of *why*. The answer tells us much about the enduring power of the revolutionary ideal. In 1787, prior to the revolution in France, he had argued before the assembly of notables for both toleration of Protestants and a national assembly. He had thus favored legitimizing both the ideological and political opposition, a step that might have helped France to follow the English and Swiss path for preventing the development of a revolutionary tradition. And he argued with no less passion for full popular sovereignty in his last major speech before the Chamber of Deputies just before his death in 1834.

Like his friend Thomas Jefferson, Lafayette continued to believe in renewal through perpetual reëxamination and periodic revolution. But whereas Jeffersonians envisaged such revolutions as taking place within the system, the young French radicals who looked to Lafayette during the restoration were not so sure. Lafayette always viewed himself as working through the system even when cooperating with clandestine revolutionary groups. Like many an aging reformer in later times, he thought he could elevate and educate the young extremists—and perhaps also recover something of his own youth amidst an army of adonis-liberators. Because of his own sincerity and disinterestedness, Lafayette was seduced by these qualities in others. How could he resist a new generation "so irreproachable and interesting which crowded around him and whose disinterestedness, devotion and ardor demanded that he put himself out for them?" [8] He was unable to see that the young conspirators of the restoration sought not so much liberty in his eighteenth-century understanding as the new romantic goals of equality and fraternity. To him, they were the new version of his old regiment. His feeling of duty to the young may also have been compounded by feelings of guilt toward his own son. Like many indulgent liberal fathers of revolutionary children in our own time, Lafayette had neglected his son George and his education because of preoccupation with high politics and public affairs. The boy in turn had become an introverted and narrow revolutionary, idolizing the views of his father but rejecting his incongruously aristocratic style of life and discourse. Within the house of Lafayette there grew up "a disinterested, modest, and exacting fanatic such as one must find in new religions [with] a holy abhorance for men of wit and a marked preference for common men." [9] The constant accusation of hypocrisy that such a young man presented to Lafayette may well have had its effect. In any event, Lafayette's decision to become a father figure to younger revolutionaries may have been in part a belated effort to be a father to his son. He did succeed in winning back his son to a more moderate subsequent political career. But the views of the old lover of liberty never converged with those of the new believers in equality.

Lafayette escaped from the young demonstrator at General Lamarque's funeral in 1832 who had said: "If we were to kill General Lafayette, could not such a good death provide a call to arms?" [10] But, in the following year, he was killed off as a revolutionary symbol with the publication of *Political Life of Lafayette*, written by Buonarroti and his young confrères, which excoriated the Marquis as an anachronism, artificially preserved "like a mummy in its bindings." [11] He was an example of what to avoid—a false friend being more dangerous than a declared enemy.[12]

As he had in so many other respects, Bonneville had, already in the early 1790s, anticipated these new attacks on Lafayette by characterizing him as a "*temporisateur*; a double personality," who, being "nothing in either one party or the other, will be doubly nothing." [13] But to unmask a figure of Lafayette's venerability and stature after 1830 was no easy task. An extraordinary target required innovative ammunition, and the Buonarrotian salvo was in many ways a model for future ritual denunciations by revolutionaries. The tract is not a debate about general ideas, but an illustrative unmasking of a particular individual— all, however, in the name of principle. The "objective" political significance of Lafayette's failings are analyzed with an air of clinical detachment. His "subjective" statements and seeming accomplishments are simply neglected.

Lafayette was said to espouse "egoism" rather than "equality" because of his infatuation with the American rather than the French Revolution. America did not have a real revolution because of "the egoistic character of its leaders" who did not include "a single proletarian" [14] and inherited from England a baleful legacy of legalism and localism.

Federalism defeated unity and created a chaos of ever more inextricable laws. It is the feudal regime reclothed with democratic forms.[15]

The same egoism which caused Americans to turn their backs on revolutionary France in 1793 led Lafayette to the "omission of the word equality"[16] from all his public speeches. Clearly the "hero of two worlds" was no hero to the new social revolutionaries.[17]

Perhaps no role is more difficult to play in modern times than that of the moderate revolutionary: the man who honestly shares both the radical hope for a new start and the conservative concern for older values and continuity. Not unlike a Martin Luther King in a later era, Lafayette stood at the center of events and became the focal point "of all the hatreds and all the prejudices"[18] of a bitter time. If Lafayette never quite drew the lightning of assassination, he faced a thousand jibes from Right and Left and a long period of posthumous obloquy. Just before his death, he spoke wearily in a letter to an old Italian revolutionary of the oscillation between apathy and despotism, which feed on one another to hold back political maturity and social progress. He saw a time coming when

> . . . the great struggle will begin of the two principles, the awakening of the oppressed against the oppressors; and there will be a European conflagration that could have been avoided by a modest adherence to the program of the Hôtel de Ville. . . .[19]

However distasteful this position may have become for old aristocrats, new revolutionaries, and Orléanist opportunists alike, Lafayette remained the outstanding symbol in Europe of moderate hopes for the general revolutionary ideal. Though he lamented the misfortune that resulted from the unsuccessful spread of the revolution to other countries in 1830,[20] he accepted membership in the Polish national guard in 1831 and worked unceasingly on behalf of the fading Polish cause.[21] He concluded that, if royal absolutism was the old foe, popular apathy was in many ways the new one. The corrosive force of indifference had driven sensitive figures like Lamennais into the arms first of reaction and then of revolution. The despair which Lafayette felt over political apathy in France was shared even by his more successful Swiss protégé, James Fazy, during his period of deepest discouragement:

> C'est trop d'avoir à lutter à la fois contre l'indifférence de ses amis et la malveillance de ses adversaires.[22]

But Lafayette never gave up hope. He continued to believe that liberal and national institutions would inevitably be established in "the two peninsulas" (Italy and Spain) as well as in Germany and Poland.[23]

His ideal was always liberty, rather than equality and fraternity. He linked the old virtues of enlightened rationality with the new techniques of constitutional guarantee and parliamentary debate. With his death in 1834, the revolutionary tradition lost its major surviving link with the aristocratic Enlightenment. As the Masonic enconium at his funeral put it:

> the death of Napoleon was the extinction of a volcano;
> the death of Lafayette was the setting of the sun.[24]

But it was the volcano, not the sun, that had dominated the political life of France during the revolutionary era. Lafayette's great moments —the Declaration of the Rights of Man in 1789 and the "three glorious days" of 1830—were overshadowed by the more fateful convulsions of 1792 and 1848 respectively. Each of these eminently political revolutions eventually brought to power a Napoleon. In a world of polarized politics, centralized power, and demagogic leadership, there was little room for a Lafayette.

Fazy and the Swiss Success

The one successful revolution in Europe between 1830 and 1848 occurred in Switzerland. In the space of a few years, the Swiss moved from semi-feudal division under Hapsburg dominance into a federal republic with a bicameral legislature closely approximating the United States. The most important revolutionary leader was James Fazy, whose career provides a rare example of an American-type revolution prevailing in continental Europe. He helped guide Switzerland—despite its geographic and linguistic links with three cultures that pioneered continental revolutionary agitation—France, Italy, and Germany—into the essentially Anglo-American mold of "bourgeois" liberalism.

James Fazy was born into a Huguenot family who had emigrated to Geneva and involved themselves with moderate success in commercial and manufacturing activities. One ancestor was a clock-maker to Catherine the Great and another a cousin of Rousseau. The ideas of the latter exerted a strong influence on Fazy through his mother, and his father was a leading Genevan supporter of the original French Revolution.[25]

Born in 1794, Fazy was subjected to pietistic influences at the school of the Moravian Brethren in Neuwied, then thrust into the heady life of a Parisian university student in the early years of the restoration. He founded a short-lived radical journal, *La France chrétienne* in 1817, and helped organize the French Carbonari together with his brother Jean-Louis and Antoine Cerclet, who (like Fazy's mother) had been born in Russia, and who later became a Saint-Simonian and editor of *Le National*.[26] Fazy's own interest in political journalism led him to write a criticism of the Bank of France, followed by a revolutionary fable and play.[27] His first book-length work, a series of "philosophical and political conversations of 1821," proclaimed "Jesus Christ the first prophet of liberty and equality," and hailed the French Revolution as guaranteeing the spread of "liberalism" even to Asia and Africa.[28]

Early in 1826, he returned to Geneva and founded the *Journal de Genève* in an effort to oppose the political indifference of the restoration era in his native city; but in August, he returned to Paris, where he worked on the *Mercure de France au XIX siècle* and signed protest ordinances against the repressive laws of Charles X on behalf of the journal *La Révolution*.[29]

Fazy's imagination was fired by long conversations about the American experience with Lafayette; and he later recalled a particularly exciting description of America that the Marquis provided him during a long ride from La Grange to Paris.

> . . . if a stenographer had been there to record all that the general said, the book which De Tocqueville later published would have been unnecessary.[30]

In Paris in 1828, he produced a neglected masterpiece, *Gerontocracy*, the first work systematically to identify the revolutionary struggle as one of youth vs. age. He was on the barricades in July 1830, and in the forefront of the radical republican opposition to Louis Philippe immediately thereafter. After harassment by the censorship and payment of a 6,000-franc fine, he returned to Geneva, announcing in 1831 his belief that only something like the "federal system of the USA" would "fulfill the constitutional needs of Switzerland." [31] Having sheltered Buonarroti in the early 1820s,[32] his household became the gathering place of ·Mazzini and other nationalist revolutionaries in the early 1830s.[33] In 1833, he established the first daily paper ever published in Geneva, *L'Europe Centrale*, as a kind of journalistic counterpart to Mazzini's Young Europe. From radical journalism, he turned to radical politics in the late 1830s, producing in 1837 the first draft of an American-type, federal constitution similar to that finally adopted by Switzerland a decade later.

From 1835 to 1841, he devoted much of his energy to a lengthy *History of Geneva*, which exalted the role of ordinary citizens in both developing the city and resisting authoritarianism (Calvinist as well as Catholic). He broke sharply with Buonarroti's Swiss followers when they tried to transform Young Europe into an organ of social rather than political revolution.[34] Despite close friendship with the pioneers of communism in Nyon, Lausanne and Geneva, Fazy opposed from the beginning the restrictions on political freedom and economic growth that he found inherent in their programs. Socialists as well as communists were producing mummies rather than citizens, he believed, by shriveling and binding the dynamic political and economic processes that freedom releases. A report to Metternich in 1847 noted that Fazy's program for Geneva called for both freedoms (of religion and association) and responsibilities (observing laws, promoting education):

> Within these freedoms and limits, James Fazy believes that the life of the Republic will develop entirely on its own into a harmonious liberty

with bodily and spiritual prosperity. He will hear nothing of socialism or communism.[35]

Fazy linked his republican ideal to "bourgeois" commerce, insisting that the increased circulation of money in a free society would itself solve many social problems and end traditional forms of bondage.

Armed in 1841 with yet another new magazine, *La Revue de Genève,* Fazy published a plan for the municipal organization of Geneva and with his brother gathered 950 signatures for a popular petition demanding an elective council. Skillfully allying his own radical minority with liberal deputies on the one side and revolutionary émigrés on the other, he succeeded in getting the council of state to convene a constituent assembly elected by all citizens in November 1841,[36] and successfully resisted in the course of the 1840s the resurgent power of the Catholic Sonderbund within Switzerland. He became on October 6, 1846, head of a ten-man provisional revolutionary government which proved to be one of the most orderly and moderate in modern history. His government reformed the city in concrete ways—breaking the old economic monopolies, democratizing the churches, converting forts into housing and old people's homes, and so forth. Fazy also carried out a second constitutional reform of the city in 1847, which in turn influenced the structure of the federal republic that was established in all of Switzerland the following year.

Fazy was a deputy to the constitutional Diet and a contributor to the federal constitution adopted by Switzerland in 1848. He helped persuade the king of Prussia to renounce his rights to Neuchâtel, and remained head of the government of Geneva until 1864. He was a leader in both the local and national political activity of the Radical Party, in a host of journalistic and economic activities, and in education. He championed the academic study of political economy in Switzerland, and founded the *Institut national genevois* in 1852. He spent his last years lecturing, writing, and sponsoring apolitical civic projects in Geneva.

Fazy had his failures and his enemies. His overall city plan for Geneva was never successfully carried out; and his own precarious financial situation led him into economic speculations that compromised his integrity.[37] His political activity won him enemies in Geneva—and many more among conservative, German-speaking Swiss.[38] Nevertheless, his overall record is one of the most impressive of revolutionary politicians in the nineteenth century. Even conservatives did not interfere with the constitutional reforms that he had so solidly established; and the critical chronicler of his record is probably not exaggerating in saying that "Fazy brought forth a democracy and a new city." [39]

Like so many revolutionaries in England and America, Fazy was absorbed into the political system. In the process, he helped to change it—but was also changed by it. In nineteenth-century Switzerland, as in seventeenth-century England and eighteenth-century America, revolutions enjoyed qualified success; and divisive recrimination soon ended.

In part, one may credit underlying economic changes in all three countries with having kept political changes from being as socially revolutionary as they had initially promised to become. Yet it is not enough simply to speak of rising bourgeois capitalism domesticating political slogans; of yesterday's revolutionary activist becoming tomorrow's conservative raconteur. For the young man who in 1828 wrote the original indictment of rule by old men had emphatically not by the time of his death a half-century later become simply the "debris left over from a time rich in storms" [40]—as he had accused the original French revolutionaries of becoming during the restoration. There is an inner consistency in his life's work—in both the ideas he expressed and the tradition he represented. Ideologically, he articulated as well as anyone what could be described as the progressive, evolutionary alternative to both revolution and reaction. More generally, the Swiss tradition provided a receptivity to incremental change that seems to have represented an effective—and perhaps instructive—immunity to the formation of a revolutionary tradition.

In examining Fazy's ideas, one finds from the beginning the belief in a humanized, personalized democracy—compounded of both the universal ideals of the French Revolution and the intimate, communal experience of his native Switzerland. His roots in a Swiss manufacturing family enabled him to come to grips in a way few radical social theorists in continental Europe were able to do with both the irreversible necessity and the liberating potential of industrial development. Like Saint-Simon, he believed in "the necessity of an industrial revolution as the means of avoiding a new political revolution." [41] But unlike the Saint-Simonians, Fazy did not believe that the industrial age required a new authoritarian ideology and elite. To Fazy, the real conflict was between those societies that were closed and "absolutist" on the one hand and those that were open and "examining" on the other. He feared equally the old ecclesiastical authoritarians and the new political ideologists with their *doctrines alarmantes du sans-culottisme apostolique.*

Restoration France was falsely preoccupied with protecting old wealth rather than creating new riches. Taken up with the short-term political maneuvering of "all these more or less detestable or ridiculous parties," [42] France had allowed itself to become the arena for the debilitating quarrels of old men. The "debris of the emigration" [43] was squabbling with the burnt-out revolutionary "generation of '89," which "began by interdicting its fathers, and ended up disinheriting its children." [44]

Youth must be given power because it was "the virile part of the nation" [45] that did most of the work and uniquely understood "the real needs of the body social." [46] Youth sought concrete socio-economic goals rather than abstract political ideals; and it must be allowed to advance civilization cautiously and experimentally—freed from the ritualized slogans and controversies of the revolutionary era.

This faith in youth was neither a passing fancy nor an abstract idea for Fazy. Much later, as president of the Canton of Geneva, Fazy organized banquets for the schoolchildren of Geneva at which both the parents and politicians paid homage to the children and orphans of the city. Alexander Herzen describes one such banquet during the revolutionary year 1849:

> Fazy delivered a thoroughly radical speech, congratulated the prize-winners and proposed a toast "To the future citizens!" to loud music and firing of cannon. After this the children went after him, two by two, to the field. . . .[47]

With mounting bewilderment, Herzen recalls the spectacle of the parents and other adults forming an avenue and saluting with their weapons Fazy's parade of children:

> . . . they presented arms . . . Yes! presented arms before their sons and the orphans. . . . The children were the honoured guests of the town, its "future citizens." All this was strange to such of us as had been present at Russian school anniversaries and similar ceremonies.[48]

Fazy's bête noire was Spain, whose "absolutist" form of government produced "general apathy" in the populace and a static economy. He sought to build on the good manners and family feeling of small-scale Swiss and German communal life, but to add the benefits of industrial growth. His ideal societies were the open and enterprising countries of England and America. This affection of his suggests a certain deep affinity between the nation he inhabited and those he admired. Fazy, like most political radicals in England and America, remained active to the end and was not forced into emigration. These three nations —unlike those torn between revolution and reaction—provided a continuing opportunity for the innovative radical to make an enduring contribution to his nation's development. Thus, the difference between Fazy and most of his fellow Carbonari, who subsequently either burned out or sold out, lies less in personalities than in political systems.

Fazy perfected the technique of effecting change through peaceful constitutional and electoral agitation. By conceding regularly to his conservative opponents on matters of nomenclature and terminology, he was generally able to prevail on essential matters of democratic rights and guarantees. As he noted after his successful struggle for the adoption of a constitution for Geneva:

> . . . the greatest adversaries of the revolution themselves contributed to the most radical reform—satisfied to triumph over us on some points of detail to which we seemed to cling, and which in fact were of little concern to us.[49]

Fazy used extra-legal means, but in a limited way in order to broaden political participation rather than narrowing it through manipulation or conspiracies. Thus, in November 1841, when the Council of State was blocking the constitutional reform that was called for by Fazy's popular petition, he proposed to go directly to St. Peter's Cathedral and summon the populace to authorize directly a democratically elected body to revise the constitution. Faced with a much more substantial conservative counter-attack in 1846 against the constitution that was adopted in 1842, Fazy did not hesitate to throw up barricades and proclaim a revolutionary government. Herzen described the annexation of power as "an eighteenth Brumaire—for the benefit of democracy and the people." Fazy appeared before the council to announce personally its dissolution. The members nearly arrested him, then asked in whose name he spoke.

> "In the name of the people of Geneva, who are sick of your bad government and are with me," and thereupon Fazy pulled back the curtain on the council-room door. A crowd of armed men filled the hall, ready at Fazy's first word to lower their weapons and fire. The old "patricians" and peaceful Calvinists were taken aback.
> "Go away while there is time!" said Fazy, and they meekly trudged home; and Fazy sat down at a table and wrote a decree. . . .[50]

This is a no doubt exaggerated, but essentially accurate, account of a rare nineteenth-century victory for "the audacity which Saint-Just considered essential in a revolutionary." [51] Even here, the revolutionary act of seizing power was immediately subordinated to a constitutional program; and the ten-man provisional government immediately sought to democratize the city within even as they prepared to defend it from external threats.

Most significant of all was the importance that Fazy attached to individual rights as an aim of the revolution, always to be protected even against revolutionary leaders themselves. His preference for a bicameral legislature, for the maintenance of local as well as central powers, and for checks and balances between the three branches of government —all were rooted in his admiration for the American system. But they also grew out of the suspicions that independent Swiss burghers felt for a long line of authoritarian intruders from the Holy Roman emperors to Napoleon. He sought to retain the political integrity of the cantons to maximize local participation in government and to guard against the "unitary tendencies" [52] on which tyranny builds. His defense of individual rights of press, association, and religion was "more Anglo-Saxon than French in inspiration," the work of a man who had "nothing Jacobin, statist and authoritarian" in his make-up.[53] He defended the diffusion of power by giving a libertarian twist to the doctrine of absolute popular sovereignty traditionally used by Jacobin centralizers.

> The sovereignty of the people is an absolute sovereignty, the whole of which can never be entrusted to anyone . . . The people never delegate more than parts of their sovereignty.[54]

Fazy denounced communism not with conservative outrage, but with liberal disdain. It was an impractical, foreign derangement that could never be "representative of the people," Fazy contended early in 1842. "Foreign governments alone seem to be aware of the presence of communists in our cantons and of their works, which no one among ourselves has seen." [55] Practical Swiss enterprise rejects the alien concept of

> ... the centralization of ownership ... by which German workers admitted into our cantons are preparing a happy future in which they will no longer need to rob, since people possessing anything will already have been forced to give it up.[56]

Swiss family loyalties were likewise contrasted with the communist principle of "the centralization of the family" into "a single great family of humanity." [57]

The Swiss disdain for communism was born both of confidence in their own constitutional revolution and of fear that concrete gains might be sacrificed for abstract goals. Already in March 1842, a Genevan journal noted proudly that Swiss workers in Lausanne had withdrawn from the meetings of German communists

> ... when they discovered that mutual instruction was only a pretext used to conceal some other objective. Communism runs aground on the good sense of the Swiss people.[58]

Fazy also became apprehensive about the authoritarian and centralizing dangers of revolutionary nationalism. Having welcomed Garibaldi to Geneva in 1867 as the personification of "the new generation," Fazy soon turned against him.[59] Increasingly thereafter, he criticized the overconcentration of power in the modern state. He called for the federation of France, Spain, and Italy as a means of extending the Swiss formula to Europe and beginning a continental federation.[60] He also struck a Millsean note of alarm about the gathering threats to liberty from the new tyranny of majorities within democracies. He wrote a "Declaration of Individual Rights," and his last work, *On the Collective Intelligence of Societies*, of 1873 insisted that individual rights must be guaranteed against collective authorities of all kinds.[61]

Individual freedom with continuous openness to *l'esprit examinateur* provided the only chance for progress and the best hope of happiness for Fazy as for the leading liberal progressives of the Anglo-American world in the nineteenth century.

Societies without Revolutionaries

The experience of this particular small country raises a larger general question: Why did the parliamentary regimes and relatively open societies of the United States, England, and Switzerland never transform their own successful revolutions into broader revolutionary movements? Why did these lands, which provided so much early inspiration and continuing asylum for foreign revolutionaries, produce almost no professional revolutionary traditions of their own?

The Anglo-American world was, of course, geographically and linguistically separate from the continent—and had a special, common tradition of evolutionary legal and political development. Yet at the same time without these two nations a modern revolutionary tradition is unthinkable. The Puritan Revolution in seventeenth-century England has been called the first "ecumenical" revolution in terms of projecting a universal vision of man and society.[62] England began the Industrial Revolution a century later, and by the early nineteenth century possessed the world's first industrial proletariat and a rich bouquet of agitational and journalistic activity. Yet England did not produce a revolutionary tradition—let alone a revolution—of its own in the nineteenth century.

Nor did the United States, which had started in 1776 the chain of modern political revolutions. Despite the revolutionary language of the Declaration of Independence and the continuing rhetoric of American politics (with parties using the revolutionary names "Democratic" and "Republican"), the United States contributed little of its own to the modern revolutionary tradition. Like England, America absorbed the defeated. Its underpopulated expanses accommodated the utopian experiments of Owen, Fourier, and Cabet—and later the desperate doings of Irish republicans and east European anarchists. But America provided Europe with no important revolutionary leadership, ideology, or organization. The feedback from the New World to the Old was probably greater from South America than from North America in the nineteenth century. The United States appeared in the international revolutionary movement mainly as the site for the final journalistic flurries of the Communist League and the final organizational collapse of the First International. Even this latter event in Philadelphia in 1876 went largely unnoticed amidst the centennial celebrations of the original American Revolution.

But why did Switzerland, located in the heart of Europe and closely in touch with revolutionary movements throughout the continent, fail to bring forth a revolutionary tradition from its more recent revolution? Switzerland had given Europe the ideal of William Tell and the ideas of Rousseau. It provided shelter for active revolutionaries from Buonarroti in Geneva through Bakunin at Vevey to Lenin in Zurich.[63] It attracted such a large proportion of Slavic revolutionary leaders that the anti-revolutionary Dostoevsky characterized the entire concept of revolution as the "Geneva idea."[64]

The fact of a successful past revolution and a measure of popular representation does not altogether explain why Switzerland, England, and America proved so immune to the formation of indigenous new revolutionary organizations or ideologies. The central example of France proves that a relatively successful revolution and a measure of suffrage were not necessarily an antidote to the development of a professional revolutionary tradition. France, the site of victorious "bourgeois" revolutions in both 1789 and 1830, became the principal breeding grounds for fresh revolutionary ideas and organizations.

What then is the crucial difference between England, America, and Switzerland, where revolutionary traditions did not develop, and France, Italy, and Poland (as well as other Slavic, Germanic, and Latin lands), where they did?

The key difference appears to lie in two common features of the way in which change and opposition developed in England, America, and Switzerland. These were nations that, first of all, had previously experienced and *legitimized ideological opposition* to medieval Catholicism. They were, in short, nations in which Protestantism was, if not the dominant creed as in America, at least a venerable and coequal one as in Switzerland. Secondly, each of these nations in different ways had found ways to *institutionalize political opposition* through an effective system of parties. Whether under a monarch and a centralized parliamentary government as in England or under a federal republic with separation of power as in America and Switzerland, these nations all gave political scope to serious, institutionalized opposition. That opposition, moreover, assumed the disciplined form of a limited number of political parties—usually two major ones.

This is not to say that Protestant rule was not itself intolerant (or indeed bloody, as defeated Irish and Swiss Catholics could attest). Nor was the toleration of political opposition achieved without violence and civil strife at one time or another in all three countries. The institutionalization of ideological and political opposition was in some sense interrelated with—and expressive of—a peculiar type of dynamic and exploitative economic development taking place in all three countries. Only those still clinging to the scientistic simplicities of nineteenth-century thought would say categorically that capitalism was the cause and constitutionalism the effect. Karl Marx and Max Weber suggested exactly opposite conclusions about whether Protestantism caused or was caused by capitalism. A similar stand-off could be extracted from the literature about the relationship between the rise of the industrial bourgeoisie and of liberal democracy.

But there was also an interrelationship—in which cause and effect are again difficult to disentangle—between the presence of Protestant and parliamentary traditions and the absence of revolutionary traditions in the nineteenth century. Thomas Macaulay, the great troubador of Protestant, parliamentary England, spoke of himself as a man who "disliked revolutions and for the same reason . . . disliked counterrevolutions." The passage was cited on the title page of a major treatise by a Hungarian liberal,[65] and could well stand as a preface to the history of parliamentary progressivism. Later generations have rebelled at Macaulay's self-congratulatory "whig interpretation of history."[66] But his conviction that Protestantism and Parliament were the essential antidotes to stagnation and upheaval was widely shared by rising continental politicians in the nineteenth century. Just as Macaulay spread his ideas not only in Parliament, but through his monumental and readable *History of England,* so on the continent the liberative powers of Protestantism and parliamentarianism were celebrated by a host of politicized popular historians of civilization beginning with Guizot and Sismondi.

Much experience in nineteenth-century Europe supports the argument that Protestantism and parliamentarianism provided a kind of alternative equivalent to revolution. The countries perhaps most immune in all Europe to native revolutionary movements were the totally Protestant nations of Scandinavia, which even developed an elastic, simultaneous tolerance for welfare socialism and monarchy. The low countries also provide a validating case. Although Holland had experienced an ideological revolution against Spain in the late sixteenth century, a political one in the late eighteenth, and a revolution for independence in 1830, the low countries were tranquil, thereafter, accommodating into the twentieth century both a monarch and a high degree of social controls. All of this was accomplished incrementally with tolerance for legal opposition and vocal dissent.

Why then was France so different? Like England, America, and Switzerland, France had made constitutional gains through revolution: in the charter of 1815 and the constitutional monarchy of 1830. Yet new revolutionary movements appeared after each of these "victories," and France became the principal center of revolutionary extremism until after the Paris Commune in 1871. Jansenists and *philosophes* had provided France with its own forms of ideological dissent from medieval Catholicism; and the July monarchy had legitimized a measure of political opposition. But France remained polarized into extreme positions.

The attempt to legitimize both ideological and political opposition by Lamennais and the school of Catholic social reform represented perhaps the most powerful effort of the 1830s to provide a coherent middle way. Yet Lamennais, though widely read in the 1830s, failed almost totally in his effort to bring the equivalent of Protestantism and of political democracy into Catholic France.

Lamennais argued for a kind of socialist version of the Reformation within the Catholic Church. He welcomed the revolutions of 1830 precisely because they legitimized political opposition in France and Belgium and therefore freed Catholicism from its links with traditional monarchs. He had some immediate influence among moderates in Belgium,[67] but little in France prior to receiving posthumous praise from both Christian Democrats and Christian Socialists in the twentieth century. For Lamennais was antirevolutionary as well as antiauthoritarian. Although he was never a Protestant and never sat in a parliament, he believed in the need for both a religious opposition within Christianity and a political opposition within the social order.

Without both ideological and political opposition to the status quo, Lamennais feared Europe would either break up through continued civil war between revolutionaries and reactionaries or disintegrate from a loss of all enthusiasm. Like the Protestant revivalists in England, who are often accused of substituting religious for revolutionary fervor among the working classes, Lamennais was a passionate enthusiast. He wrote his first and famous *Essay on Indifference* in 1817 specifically to combat the debilitating trend toward apathy and decay.[68] If he alternated between his early Catholic conservatism and his later courtship of revolutionary socialism, he consistently and above all wanted Europe to share his enthusiasm; to help create a new ideological-political opposition to revitalize an aging civilization. Lamennais's appeal for Christian democracy and social justice was widely heard throughout Catholic

Europe; but only his early conservative and ultramontanist ideas had a continuing resonance in nineteenth-century France.

Unlike America (or Switzerland), where controversy after the original revolution was rapidly ritualized into party politics, French politics remained polarized. Revolutionaries were constantly confronting counter-revolutionaries outside parliamentary bodies, which were often seen as bickering arenas for petty sectarians. Moderate ruling factions rarely felt secure enough to risk letting opposition parties coalesce—or even to tolerate elections that might risk major changes in the exercise of power.

Why was the impact of the two great revolutions of the late eighteenth century so dramatically different on the subsequent political history of America and France respectively? There are of course obvious differences between the tabula rasa of the New World and the clutter of feudal custom and aristocratic privilege in the ancien régime; between the reluctant acceptance by England of a revolution partly rooted in historic rights and the revanchist refusal of traditionalist France to accept structures created by the French Revolution. It may also be argued that the American Revolution was essentially republican, whereas the French was democratic—and thus inherently more extreme.

The successful Swiss Revolution followed the American rather than the French pattern of accepting a federalist solution for state organization. The moderate Girondist formula in Switzerland was rejected by centralizing Jacobins and Bonapartists alike in France. The Swiss Revolution, like the American, distributed power more successfully outside the center than the French. The Swiss and Americans defused the myth of a total revolution to come—both by mythologizing a moderate constitution and by legitimizing political and ideological opposition in the post-revolutionary society.

America and Switzerland—and to some extent England, the low countries, and Scandinavia—rejected the basic impulse of the ideological revolutionary tradition towards radical simplification. Both the American and the Swiss revolutions were consolidated by building more rather than less complex political systems. They were federal rather than centralized; more people participated in the process; and power tended to be diffused. From the time of the Jacobin attack on the Girondists to Buonarroti's attack on the American system, the French revolutionary tradition clearly saw the complexity of federalism as a threat to the simplicity of the revolutionary dream.

America essentially *realized in practice* the reformist ideas of the Enlightenment through a process of evolution.[69] Continental Europe remained throughout the nineteenth century more authoritarian politically than the British Empire had been under George III in the eighteenth century. Thus, Europeans continued to *develop in theory* the more revolutionary, Illuminist concept of realizing total enlightenment through a coming upheaval. The intellectuals who had looked before the French Revolution to "enlightened despots" to transform society now looked to a new source of deliverance: *ideology*. This modern surrogate of religion was born—both as a phrase and as a force—in the political-intellectual opposition to Napoleon. It reached maturity in the mid-nineteenth century, validating and legitimizing the social revolutionary tradition as a rival to revolutionary nationalism. Above all, ideology helped revolutionaries keep alive the simple certainties of their faith against the seduction of Anglo-American empiricism and liberalism. It is to the birth of revolutionary ideology, the ultimate foe of the evolutionary alternative, that attention must now be turned.

CHAPTER 8

Prophecy:

The Emergence

of an Intelligentsia

THE RISE of revolutionary movements in the first half of the nineteenth century was directly related to the development of a new class of intellectuals in continental Europe. This new class created original systems of thought which may be called *ideologies,* and eventually developed a new sense of identity (and a term to describe themselves) as an "intelligentsia."

To be sure, intellectuals were joined at every point by other social and ethnic forces protesting against the conditions of early industrialization and against political reaction. But the ferment that led to revolution in 1848—whatever the final causes—was clearly dominated by intellectuals. They bore the contagion from their studies into the streets, from banquets to barricades, and across national borders. They popularized, legitimized, and internationalized the revolutionary impulse.

A thousand studies remain to be made about the sociology and psychology of this new social force.[1] But the first task for a history of revolutionary movements is to isolate those systems of thought that were most decisive in developing revolutionary commitment among intellectuals in the early nineteenth century; to trace the genesis of those new spiritual creations known as ideologies.

Ideologies have been defined as "the integrated assertions, theories and aims that constitute a socio-political program." They "conceptualize the historical process and orient human beings for shaping it" by creating "a program of collective action" from a "coherent system of symbols." [2] They are in many ways a modern form of religion—all-inclusive in scope, universal in application, historical in focus. To determine which of these systems in the romantic period was most revolutionary, one may begin with Lenin's distinction between the ideologies of revolutionaries and revolutionary ideology. Any inventory of the former in nineteenth-century Europe would have to include republicanism, nationalism, Fourierism, Owenism, Christian messianism, anarchism, populism, and even spiritualism. But few of these were inherently revolutionary ideologies with universal applicability and a clear concept of how present conflict would lead to future happiness. None of these "ism's" offered a clear, secular conception of how history worked and how it could provide both intellectual security and strategic guidance for revolutionaries.

Two of the new systems—those of Saint-Simon and Hegel—offered just such a view of history, and these two systems provided the principal sources of modern revolutionary ideology. Although the ideologies developed only after their deaths, Saint-Simon and Hegel generated the original ideas that spread across national and cultural boundaries to attain nearly universal appeal in an age of nationalism.

There are some parallels between the radically different thought-worlds of the French aristocrat and the German professor. Each sought to update the Enlightenment faith in the underlying laws of nature with a new belief in the dynamic laws of history. Each attracted ambitious young intellectuals with the ideal of a new activist elite. The following of each increased after the master's death (Saint-Simon in 1825, Hegel in 1832), for their respective impact was one of ideas rather than personalities.

Each of these ideas gave rise to a school of thought that took a path ironically different from the one envisaged by the master. Both Saint-Simon and Hegel had developed new views of the world precisely to end revolutionary disruption; yet their followers were at the forefront of renewed revolutionary agitation. Although the influence of both Saint-Simon and Hegel was protean and diverse, it was most decisive on revolutionaries. The impact of both men converged on Karl Marx.

If both Saint-Simon and Hegel were deeply conditioned by the events of the French Revolution, each first articulated his major ideas in the shadow of Napoleon. Each was in some ways an imperialist of the mind, seeking to fulfill in the realm of ideas the universal dominion that Napoleon seemed to have established in the material world.

At the age of forty-two Saint-Simon turned from a life of financial speculation and aristocratic adventure to one of intellectual speculation and adventure. He did so in direct response to the assumed needs of Napoleon, who had just proclaimed himself emperor. Saint-Simon's first serious composition was a proposed curriculum for the new system of thirty lyceums that Napoleon had projected as the basis for civic education [3] and his first major published work an anonymous proposal of 1802–03, addressed directly to Napoleon, for a plan for perpetual peace during the hiatus in warfare that followed the treaty of Amiens.[4]

Hegel's first major writing was done in these same years, following his academic appointment at Jena in 1801. His great ideological treatise, *The Phenomenology of Mind* (or *Spirit*), was written as a kind of intellectual counterpoint to the Napoleonic military conquest of Germany. It was completed with cannon sounding in the background from the battle at Jena, where Napoleon crushed Prussia.

Hegel's philosophy in some ways constituted a revenge of German thought against victorious French power. Saint-Simon's writings on the other hand represented a subtler drama: the first "ideologists" revenging themselves against a political system that had rejected them.

The Saint-Simonians

Largely neglected recent research indicates that revolutionary Babeuvists and Philadelphians may have exercised a direct influence on Henri de Saint-Simon during the first decade of the nineteenth century. Long studied largely as an influence on later revolutionaries, Saint-Simon should also be seen as a figure who was himself perhaps in turn directly influenced by the first conspirators of the Napoleonic era.

The crucial link in the apostolic succession from the Babeuf Conspiracy to the birth of ideology under Saint-Simon is provided by a minor revolutionary playwright and editor, Jacques Rigomer-Bazin, with whom Saint-Simon lived in Paris at several important points during this decade. Bazin may have been linked with Bonneville's Social Circle and was almost certainly connected to the Babeuf Conspiracy while still working as a revolutionary journalist in provincial Le Mans.[5] After moving to Paris, he became close to Maréchal and other survivors of the conspiracy through a circle of radical intellectuals which began to meet regularly at the Café Manège in 1799. The Paris police arrested Bazin in May 1804, and confiscated his *Sketch for a new plan of social organization*, which apparently called for an authoritarian elite of thirty savants to help the poor and create social equality.[6]

Bazin was living with Saint-Simon at the time of his arrest; and the latter clearly borrowed extensively from Bazin in his writings of this period. His *Letter of an Inhabitant of Geneva* (1802–3) called for twenty-one men of genius to open a subscription before the tomb of Newton and begin the scientific reorganization of society. His next work of 1804 adopted the very title of Bazin's confiscated work, adding to Bazin's previous call for a scientific elite an idea shortly to be developed more fully by Bazin: the artist should be the moralist of the new scientific era; and a new type of writer, the *littérateur*, its propagandist.[7]

Bazin played just such a role when he reappeared after his release from prison in 1807 as editor of a new journal *Lettres philosophiques*, which attacked the Catholics and strongly defended Maréchal on behalf of "the party which persists in providing instruction in the progress of philosophy." [8] The journal ostensibly sought to "open a public correspondence among philosophers"; [9] but it appears in fact to have been a medium for communication (and perhaps even coded messages) among revolutionary Philadelphians. Bazin was one of their leaders. He signed a major article, "Dialogue on Philosophy," with the name *Philadelphe;* and the list of 250 subscribers included most leading revolutionaries of the era in an aggregate sum consonant with the society's organization into five-man cells. The supposition seems reasonable that *Lettres* was simply an open organ for a secret conspiracy.[10]

In the last issue of his journal, Bazin issued the classic cry of the alienated intellectual; restless with abstract pursuits, anxious for political relevance, and possessed with his own missionary importance, he announced that he was giving up philosophy altogether for

> . . . un plan d'une plus grande étendue; j'ouvre un plus vaste champ à la critique . . . sur tous les points de la République des Lettres.[11]

Bazin's new journal that was to realize this mission never appeared; he was arrested in the wake of the first conspiracy of Malet in 1808. Released from prison in 1809, Bazin lived secretly and illegally once again with Saint-Simon, who helped him escape into exile.[12] Though their paths did not apparently cross again,[13] Bazin clearly provided in this formative period both a personal and an ideological inspiration for Saint-Simon's vision of an elite of intellectuals transforming not just politics, but all of human society and culture.

To trace the birth of revolutionary ideology one must distinguish between two successive phases of the Saint-Simonian movement: the scientistic and the romantic. The first, scientistic period occupied the last twenty-five years of Saint-Simon's life, which was the first quarter of the nineteenth century. It represented in essence a reaffirmation of the eighteenth-century belief in rational, secular progress. The second, romantic phase unfolded during the decade after the master's death in 1825. Following the invocation in his final work, *The New Christianity,* Saint-Simon's disciples created a fantastic new secular religion with global perspectives that foreshadowed many aspects of twentieth-century thought.

A Science of Man

The scientistic phase of Saint-Simonian thinking grew directly out of the activities of the first people to call themselves "ideologists." Destutt de Tracy, who first popularized the term "ideology" in 1796–97,[14] suggested in the first part of his *Elements of Ideology* in 1801 that traditional metaphysics must be superseded by "ideology," a new method of observing facts, inferring consequences, and accepting nothing not suggested directly by sensation. Building on the tradition of Locke, and of Condillac's *Treatise on Sensation* of 1775, de Tracy maintained that all thinking and feeling were physical sensations in the strictest sense of the word. "Ideology is a part of zoology," he wrote with a certain polemic zest.[15] Happiness is merely the free play of the organs. As his closest collaborator put it: "The brain digests impressions and secretes thought." [16]

Henri de Saint-Simon extended this radical empiricism into the altogether new field of social relations. Having spent eleven months in prison during the Reign of Terror, expecting death at any moment, Saint-Simon had a deep fear of revolution. He dreamed of founding a new science of man as a means both to overcome disorder and to remove the overgrowth of false political rhetoric which concealed the real, material questions of society.[17] Thus, ironically, this aristocrat of the ancien régime seeking to provide (in the words of one of his titles) *the means for bringing an end to the revolution*,[18] ended up popularizing the most revolutionary of all modern ideas: there can be a science of human relations.

Saint-Simon's ideas fell on receptive ears because the original "ideologists" around de Tracy [19] popularized not just a method of analysis but also a vision of society. Among de Tracy's friends within the Second Section of the newly created Institute (devoted to moral and political science), there had grown up in the 1790s the heady belief that the development and application of a new science of humanity could be the supreme creation of the revolutionary era. The journal that popularized this belief in the practical power of science was the influential *Décade philosophique, littéraire et politique* founded in 1794, the year of the Thermidorean reaction. After five years of a tempestuous revolution, this journal and the newly created Second Section of the Institute had sought to focus attention on peaceful, pedagogic changes for the "philosophical decade" ahead.

The controlling group, which de Tracy and Cabanis called *idéologiste*, argued that the key to diagnosing and curing the ills of humanity lay in an objective understanding of the physiological realities that lay behind all thinking and feeling. They were encouraged by the rise of Napoleon; for he had assembled a kind of institute in exile during his campaign in Egypt, surrounding himself with scientists and asking de Tracy and others to join him there. On his return to France, Napoleon accepted membership in the First Section of the Institute, which dealt with the natural sciences. He visited Helvetius's widow, a kind of salon mother to the ideologists. De Tracy's group was led to believe that a "revolutionary academy" might replace popular sovereignty. The first outline of his *Elements of Ideology* in 1801 was designed for use in the new republican schools they expected from Napoleon.[20]

Once securely in power, however, Napoleon became suspicious of the *idéologistes*, denouncing them as *idéologues*.[21] He dissolved the Second Section of the Institute in 1803, forcing these original ideologists into a kind of party of opposition to the emperor. When the daughter of de Tracy married the son of Lafayette, the philosophical and political opposition were joined.

The struggle between Napoleon and the *idéologistes* deeply disturbed both sides—perhaps because each secretly admired the other. Napoleon was a compulsive writer and a would-be intellectual who never had the time to develop these inclinations in himself. The *idéologistes* had a clear thirst for the power that Napoleon seemed to have denied them. Many of them had caught a glimpse in the revolutionary era of an exhilarating, active life in which they might simultaneously debate ideas and shape events. As imperial restriction descended on their academies and journals, the ideologists felt empty and deprived; and their distress was no less keen for being spiritual rather than material.

Saint-Simon provided a broad battle plan for the intellectual opposition. The combat leaders were to be the new politicized journalists whom he called *littérateurs* in his *Sketch* of 1804 and *publicistes* subsequently. Scientific indoctrination and intellectual unity were to be provided in a new "positive encyclopedia" on which he worked from 1809 to 1813.[22] His *Essay on the Science of Man* in 1813 suggested that every field of knowledge moved successively from a conjectural to a "positive" stage, and that the sciences reached this stage in a definite order.[23] Physiology had now moved into a positive stage, just as astrology and alchemy had previously given way to astronomy and chemistry. Now the science of man must move towards the positive stage and completely reorganize all human institutions.

In a sense, Saint-Simon was only reviving the Enlightenment vision of humanity advancing through three successive stages to a scientific ordering of life (in Turgot's *Discourse on Universal History* of 1760); and of universal progress towards rational order (in Condorcet's *Sketch for a Historical Picture of the Progress of the Human Mind*, written in hiding shortly before his death in 1794).

But just as the revolutionary regime condemned Condorcet, so Napoleon shut the Second Section of the Institute. Saint-Simon was forced to publish his early proposals anonymously and usually outside the borders of the Napoleonic Empire. Thus, Napoleon, who had helped inspire the quest for a science of man, also began the process of driving it into social revolutionary paths.[24] Believing that the scientific method should be applied to the body of society as well as to the individual body, Saint-Simon proceeded to analyze society in terms of its physiological components: classes. He never conceived of economic classes in the Marxian sense, but his functional class analysis prepared the way for Marx.

The key problem at each stage in Saint-Simon's successive efforts at social analysis was to determine which social force was capable of applying science to society. During the Napoleonic period he divided society into property owners, workers, and savants, placing all his hope in the latter group's disinterested approach to human affairs. He thought that property owners could be persuaded to see that the savants were natural leaders able to steer humanity away from a revolutionary disruption of the social order.

During the restoration Saint-Simon divided society into two fundamental groups: industrials and idlers. Disillusioned with savants, the men of learning who lacked drive, he turned to *industriels*, the "industrious" (not simply the industrialists), to take leadership away from unproductive priests and politicians. He idealized the *industriels* out of respect not for their ownership of property but for their powers of production. Work was liberative; the beaver and not the lion should be the king of beasts. In his *Letters to the Industriels* and other articles [25] during this period, he envisaged an end to revolution through a new religion with a single commandment: "All men must work." There were idlers (*oisifs*) and industrious ones (*industriels*) within all social groups. The new elite was thus to be drawn from whoever was industrious in agriculture, commerce, manufacturing, and banking regardless of social origins. Saint-Simon was the prophet of meritocracy, seeking to reorder society in the image of the new chessboard he had designed for revolutionary France, with a hierarchy in which the king was replaced by a figure called Talent.

Having failed, however, to win over the industrialists, Saint-Simon turned to one last force for revolutionary support in his last years, 1824–25: "the most numerous and poorest class." He addressed to the self-proclaimed spiritual leaders of the "holy alliance" his final plea for a "New Christianity" of morality without metaphysics, technology without theology. This alone could keep the urban poor from returning to the false god of revolution. "Listen to the voice of God speaking through my mouth," he proclaimed with characteristic lack of modesty in the final words of his last work addressed to the political heads of Europe:

> Turn to true Christianity again, . . . Fulfill all the duties it imposes on the powerful. Remember that it commands them to devote all their strength to the swiftest possible amelioration of the lot of the poor.[26]

Saint-Simon promised to elaborate fully the nature of the "New Christianity." But he died in 1825 and never had a chance to go beyond suggesting that it would resemble heretical Christian sects of the past and would reorganize society to benefit the poor.

Saint-Simon was a truly seminal intellectual force: a father of socialism as well as sociology, and a John the Baptist of revolutionary ideology, crying out in the wilderness of the Napoleonic and restoration eras for a new historicism and moral relativism.

Saint-Simon was one of the first to popularize the distinctive nineteenth-century belief that truth is not absolute but historical, and is realized not in individual thought but in social action. He was one of the first continental thinkers to contend that the Industrial Revolution was more important than the political revolution in France. The key factors in history for him were tools and technological revolutions. Archimedes was greater than Alexander; Newton than Napoleon. The real forces for change in modern society, the *industriels*, far from being aided by the political changes in France, were now burdened with a second group of nonproductive *oisifs*: new politicians alongside old priests.

The bourgeoisie was for Saint-Simon hardly less parasitical than the idle aristocrats of the ancien régime. He rejected liberalism (which soon won over some of his closest friends such as Augustin Thierry) as a negative and critical movement, incapable of reunifying mankind, incompatible with the new positive age of science. He accorded economics primacy over politics, physiology over metaphysics. Government was a social function appropriate to the metaphysical stage of history and was now to be replaced by a rational social organization suitable for the exploitation of nature. The rule of man over man was always oppressive; the rule of men over things, liberative. Even in his most political proposal, his *Reorganization of European Society* in 1814, he urged a clean break with past political systems in favor of a new Economic Parliament of Europe and a trans-national authority to unify Europe through vast public works such as a Danube-Rhine and Rhine-Baltic Canal.

Political authority was to be replaced by *social* authority in his technocratic utopia. It was to be administered by three chambers: Inventions run by engineers, Review run by scientists, and Execution run by industrialists. A supreme college was to draw up physical and moral laws; and two even higher academies, Reasoning and Sentiment, were to be filled by a new breed of propagandistic writer and artist.

Saint-Simon's final call for a new religion represented the culmination of the *idéologiste* attempt to supplant all religion by absorbing it into a progressive scheme of secular evolution. In his commentary of 1802 François Dupuis's *The Origin of All the Cults of Universal Religion* [27] de Tracy suggested that past religions were not simply senseless superstition, but rather a kind of scientific baby talk: the generalized expression in imprecise language of the scientific thought of the age. Religious ritual was, moreover, socially necessary to dramatize scientific principles for still-ignorant people. Saint-Simon viewed his *New Christianity* as just such a necessity for the masses. His death left it unclear whether this faith was designed to provide the moral basis for the new social order or merely an interim faith until the masses were educated to accept a totally scientistic system.

Saint-Simon more than any other figure of his generation excited young Europeans about the liberative possibilities of industry and about reaching salvation through knowledge and mastery, not belief and mystery. After the failure of their conspiracies in the early 1820s, radical youth found both consolation and a new direction in Saint-Simonian ideology. They reassembled in small discussion groups, forming "a congress of philosophers charged with discussing everything that had been left out of the one at Vienna." [28] They were exhilarated both by the new sense of history filtering in from German philosophy and by the study of economics filtering in from England. These interests led to a new appreciation of Saint-Simon. Some directly transferred from Carbonari conspiracies to Saint-Simonian circles, leading one of the best memoirists of the period to characterize Saint-Simonianism as simply "religious carbonarism." [29]

The enormous posthumous influence of Saint-Simon stretched from Russia and Poland to Latin America—eventually reaching the Near and even Far East.[30] His teachings helped form a radical intellectual elite both in Germany (which he considered "infinitely superior in its character, science and philosophy")[31] and in Russia (which he praised as "not yet withered up by scepticism").[32] He influenced the lonely pioneer of Scandinavian socialist thought, young Swedish printer Per Götrek, who translated and popularized Saint-Simonian tracts before turning to Cabet and the *Communist Manifesto*.[33] Saint-Simon produced a permanent impact on bankers and on railroad and canal builders,[34] imparting the vision to look beyond immediate obstacles and traditional inhibitions.

But the greatest Saint-Simonian influence lay within France, first of all on the positivist tradition developed by his friend and sometime pupil Auguste Comte.[35] Comte perpetuated the search for a science of society through a three-staged theory of progress, which he derived from Saint-Simon in 1822. Comte's idea that mankind moved from a "theological" through a "metaphysical" to a "positive" era encouraged a certain indifference to democratic politics (a phenomenon of the passing second stage).

Though essentially apolitical, positivism had authoritarian implications—relying on intellectual authority rather than on the random play of vulgar pressures. The link between enlightenment and despotism in the eighteenth century was not entirely accidental. Saint-Simon had consistently appealed to monarchical authority from his first petitions to Napoleon until his last appeal for a "New Christianity" to the leaders of the Holy Alliance. Saint-Simonians on several occasions sought out Metternich, who expressed admiration for their doctrine and met at length with Michael Chevalier in 1835.[36] Auguste Comte was later to appeal for the adoption of his "System of Positive Politics" to the two most authoritarian potentates in Europe: the Russian tsar and the Turkish sultan.[37] Comte's positivism was perhaps most influential in the courts of antidemocratic regimes in Latin America and the Near East.

More important than Saint-Simon's influence on sociology was his impact on socialism. His followers in the 1830s first gave widespread use not only to the word "socialism," but also—in the course of 1831 alone—to "socialize," "socialization," and socializing the instruments of labor.[38] These usages were at times only an extension of older Saint-Simonian terms like organization and association, but they carried new suggestions of social control and of challenge to liberal individualism.

The first historian of socialism, Louis Reybaud, prophesied in 1836, just after the seeming disappearance of the Saint-Simonians, that they

. . . will be to the social future what a trial balloon is to aeronautical experience. The trial balloon swells up before the eyes of an astonished crowd, rises, grows smaller and smaller, is lost in space. After a short and brilliant role it is no more; but . . . has gained in the process an acquaintance with the atmospheric zones and caprices of the wind which await him. . . .[39]

The technological metaphor seems appropriate, for Saint-Simonian socialism was the creation of students from the Ecole Polytechnique. This "school of many crafts" had trained the engineers and technicians for the revolutionary and Napoleonic armies and was a model of the new antitraditional institution open to talent and dedicated to practical accomplishment.

Social revolutionary Saint-Simonianism was begun by two young students from the Ecole Polytechnique: Olinde Rodrigues, the son of a Jewish banker from Bordeaux, and his young mathematics student, who had fought for Napoleon in the Hundred Days and spent 1821–23 in St. Petersburg, Barthélemy Prosper Enfantin.[40] These two polytechnicians joined with former French Carbonari like Bazard and Buchez to edit *Le Producteur*, in 1825–26, and then in 1828 drew up a systematic *Exposition* of Saint-Simon's doctrine. These Saint-Simonians introduced the phrase "the exploitation of man by man" and the concept of class conflict arising out of "the relationship of the workers with the owners of the instruments of labor." [41]

But it was not until renewed revolutionary hopes in 1830 gave way once more to disillusionment that the Saint-Simonian cult truly flowered. The liberal daily *The Globe*, edited by Pierre Leroux, converted to the new belief in 1831, and a weekly *Organisateur* and the first of a nationwide system of temples of humanity were founded. With these developments, Saint-Simonianism became a mass phenomenon. Gaining at its height perhaps forty thousand French adherents or sympathizers, Saint-Simonianism developed links with prominent intellectual leaders throughout Europe in the 1830s—ranging from Heine to Goethe in Germany, from the liberal Mill to the conservative Carlyle in England.[42] Franz Liszt was an active member, playing the piano at some of the sect's gatherings.

The Saint-Simonians briefly tried to open a new Saint-Simonian college on Christmas Day, 1829, before turning to their temples of humanity in 1831. They were harassed in Paris by governmental restrictions and rumors of scandalous sexual license. When Leroux left *The Globe* later in 1831, and the journal collapsed in the following year, there was a need for a new source of revelation and place of worship.

The Saint-Simonians found both the source and the place by withdrawing in the summer of 1832 into a celibate, communal retreat on Enfantin's family estate at Ménilmontant in the outskirts of Paris. There at 10 P.M. on Bastille Day, the long-haired "father" Enfantin gathered seven of his favorite "children" for their first of four long sessions, revealing his *New Book*: a series of mystical aphorisms suggesting how science was to be applied to society. Rich in Pythagorean number mysticism, Enfantin's revelation concentrated on triadic formulas for the new "organic era." There was the coming harmony of sentiment, industry, and intellect; of the spiritual, material, and rational; and of the worker (a plane), the theorist (a line), and the apostle (a three-dimensional solid).[43]

The commune under Enfantin was short-lived, memorable largely for such customs as the wearing of vests buttoned in the back to enforce dependence on one's fellow man. Their subsequent search for a female Messiah in Egypt was even more bizarre. Yet such efforts represented only the excesses of a general European infatuation with new ideologies, offering hope after the failure of revolutions in the early 1820s and in 1830 to produce a new social order.

Saint-Simonianism contained the implied promise that those involved in its discussions were to be the elite of the new age. Indeed, they can perhaps be considered the first modern "intelligentsia" in the sense defined by Karl Mannheim: a new, classless element free of either the Church control of the past or the regional and class biases of the future; and able to impart a "dynamic and elastic" quality to thought while forcing ideas into the political arena. This "free intelligentsia" was destined, in Mannheim's hopeful view,[44] to produce a society free of prejudice and directed towards rational social goals. The Saint-Simonians for the most part viewed themselves as doing precisely that.

Romantic Globalism

The Saint-Simonians of the 1830s developed plans that exceeded even those of the master, who had dreamed of himself as a new Charlemagne and of him and Mme. de Staël giving birth to a new Messiah. His romantic followers fantasized projects for the rejuvenation of Oceania, India, and China,[45] and launched substantial movements in eastern Europe, the Near East, and Latin America. Saint-Simonian ideas provided new hope for Spaniards exiled in Gibraltar as well as Argentineans exiled in Uruguay.[46] Chevalier, the head of the Saint-Simonian religion in Paris, scouted out terrain in Russia and North Africa, North and South America. He wrote a detailed plan for the minute republic of Andorra,[47] advocating a kind of omnibus pilgrimage to all the cities frequented by Moses, Jesus, and Mohammed.[48]

But the enduring historical importance of the Saint-Simonians lies not so much in their impact on specific groups as in their general effect in quickening expectations throughout the European world. More than any other system of thought, Saint-Simonianism inspired restless revolutionaries with fresh hope in the early 1830s, a time when disillusionment was growing not just with revolution but with the Enlightenment belief in natural laws. As the French Revolution of 1830 trailed off into petty political bickering under a constitutional monarchy, Enfantin and Bazard's *Judgment of the doctrine of Saint-Simon on the most recent events* proclaimed that "in the presence of the impotence and incoherence of the parties, only the Saint-Simonians possess a logical solution to the difficulties." [49]

Saint-Simonianism promised a universal social transformation. The old political revolutions had grown out of French civilization, based on the archetype of 1789–93. But the new type of society vaguely envisaged by the Saint-Simonians might come from almost anywhere. Thus, the Saint-Simonians influenced the new revolutionary nationalism of Mazzini and Young Europe.[50] Mazzini's distant South American echo, "Young Argentina," was independently shaped by Saint-Simonianism, which was the "definitive" influence on "the birth of an Argentine mentality." [51]

At the opposite end of European civilization—both geographically and spiritually—the vision of a new religious community advanced by the conservative Polish Order of the Resurrection was also largely Saint-Simonian in inspiration.[52] Its leader, Bogdan Jański, in turn, tried to convert the liberal John Stuart Mill.[53]

Saint-Simonianism reached beyond Europe most dramatically through the French intrusion into the Near East. Napoleon's Egyptian campaign in the 1790s had introduced the printing press and new ideas into the old civilizations of the Afro-Asian world. In like manner, the Saint-Simonian hegira to the East after their failures in France led to the founding of the first polytechnical school outside Europe (in Egypt in 1834),[54] and to the first export of revolutionary ideology beyond the traditional confines of European civilization. Canning had described the British naval support of revolutions in the Americas in the 1820s as "calling the new world into being to redress the balance of the old." The Saint-Simonian move into the East in the 1830s attempted in a smaller way to call upon the ancient world to redress the failure of social revolution in contemporary Europe. Though there was little response, the stirrings of the Saint-Simonians in the East were prophetic of things to come.

The Saint-Simonians' eastward voyage in 1833 after their failure in France broke the usual nineteenth-century pattern. Revolutionaries in search of a new start had previously gone west to America. Saint-Simon himself had first been stimulated to global perspectives by his experiences as an eighteen-year-old participant in the American Revolution in 1778 and as a would-be builder of a canal to join the oceans through Mexico. Michael Chevalier returned to the master's original source of inspiration to make a new appraisal in 1832–35 of the prospects for Saint-Simonianism in America, Mexico, and Cuba.[55]

Chevalier, however, moved east to those original cradles of civilization that had not yet distorted the revolutionary faith. His *Mediterranean System* in *The Globe* [56] saw peaceful industrial progress reaching out from the Mediterranean via a web of railroads into Asia and Africa as well as Europe. The "sea among the lands" which had cradled wars in the past would now become "the nuptial bed of East and West," [57] the forum for a "universal association" of all peoples. Along with the railroads, two critical canals were needed to increase the worldwide interdependence. The same *Globe* in the same month set forth the first call for a canal through Panama to connect the Atlantic and Pacific following an earlier Saint-Simonian call for a canal to link Europe and Asia through Suez. They also called for a high dam on the Nile.

Chevalier suggested that the fundamental conflict in the world was between East and West. But unlike Kipling and the heroic pessimists of a later age, the Saint-Simonians felt that the twain did in fact meet in Egypt. This land of Napoleonic legend seemed under Mohammed Ali to be entering culturally into the French orbit. Its mighty pyramids and obelisks stood astride the little isthmus of desert at Suez which alone separated the abundant waters of the European and Asian worlds. "The field of battle is worthy of the pyramids which dominate it," [58] wrote "Father" Enfantin:

> One must fertilize the Egypt of Mohammed. We shall not decipher the hieroglyphs of its past grandeur, but we shall engrave on its soil the signs of its future prosperity.[59]

They envisaged a marriage between "the imagination and poetry" of the Orient and "the organization and positive science" of the West.[60]

The Saint-Simonians who went east in 1833 in search of a "feminine messiah" soon focused their hopes on Egypt and on "piercing" a canal through the thin "membrane" of virgin desert, which alone blocked the consummation of East-West commerce. The "universal association" of all peoples through the canal was conceived in the same sexual terms as the cultural intercourse to be consummated in the "nuptial bed" of the Mediterranean.[61]

Nothing less than their own virility seemed to be at stake. Upon his release from prison, Enfantin communicated the order to go east on August 8, 1833, in rhapsodic, erotic verse:

> Suez
> Est le centre de notre vie de travail
> Là nous ferons l'acte
> Que le monde attend
> Pour confesser que nous sommes
> Mâles.[62]

Physical labor wedded a masculine humanity with a feminine earth: *le peuple* with *le monde*.[63] Universal significance was thus attributed to the simple act of intellectuals doing a little work. "The people," who of course had been performing such labor all along, were patronizingly described as the dependent children in the Saint-Simonian "family."

> The people is our family, let us engender them by work, let us embrace, caress the earth . . . let us await the milk of the Woman, but let us men prepare the bread! [64]

God himself was feminine as well as masculine,[65] drawing people in to reunion with nature (and a share of divinity) by a kind of universal libido:

> Cette électricité vagabonde qui circulait du monde à l'assemblée et de l'assemblée au monde et qui traversait les corps sans se fixer. . . .[66]

The Saint-Simonians viewed the *couple-prêtre* of man and woman as the new social microcosm, replacing the atomized individual, and they extended sexual imagery to the macrocosm, the entire world. There was an almost phallic rivalry over who should be the first to awaken the passive femininity of the East. The Saint-Simonians believed that she would be wakened from her slumber and ravished by "Russian cannon" unless their own peaceful technology penetrated the Orient first.[67]

Behind such erotic fantasy lay authentic insight: a prophetic anticipation of the modern belief that total material gratification is not only individually desirable, but universally inevitable. The future will provide the benefits, as it were, of both *l'école polytechnique* and *l'amour polymorphique*. Each will complete his experiences in the life of others, then flow into the lives of all and ultimately perpetuate life itself into eternity—so argued Enfantin in his last work, *La Vie éternelle*.[68] He lifted the older Saint-Simonian idea of transmigration (*palin-genesis*) of souls [69] to its highest level, prophesying both the technological transformation of the earth and the biological creation of a new, androgynous humanity.

The mystical excesses and eastern adventures of Saint-Simonianism deserve attention not solely as data for psycho-sexual investigation. For their eastern expedition may be the first major, organized effort of western, urban intellectuals to apply a secular ideology for radical social change to an idealized, underdeveloped area. Egypt appealed to the Saint-Simonians' Napoleonic delusions. They appear to have believed that they might ultimately return to France from Egypt triumphant and vindicated as Bonaparte had to save an earlier revolution from disintegration. But in place of Napoleon's military victories in the East, the Saint-Simonians saw themselves winning technological triumphs as a prelude to their return. They would lead France not to a short-lived imperial glory, but to an unending age of industrial prosperity.

The First Black Muslim: Urbain

This first call to look East for the light of revolution that had faded in the West found a response in the New World from a gifted member of the group most oppressed in the Americas: the black slaves. Thomas Urbain, one of eight mulatto children born by the black second wife of a French planter and slave trader is perhaps the most interesting and neglected of the original Saint-Simonians. His vision of using the Saint-Simonian religion to liberate black people was, in a way, the last desperate effort of West Indian blacks to find in French culture the liberation promised by the revolt of Toussaint L'Ouverture. At the same time, the journey of Urbain back to an Africa from which he never returned represents the first in a long line of returns to Africa from the New World (and mostly from the West Indies) by black revolutionaries: Padmore, Blyden, Dubois, Fanon, Malcolm X, and Carmichael. But for Urbain, the island remained a kind of paradise lost in his later memories of "the sweetness of creole and family life" and of the young black girl "who initiated me into the first raptures of love in a large woods." [70] When he went to France with his father to study medicine, he adopted as a surname the Christian name of his father, Urbain, and was called Thomas by his schoolmates.[71] Isolated and uncertain of his identity, he was converted to the new religious Saint-Simonianism before he was twenty, went through the monastic phase at Ménilmontant, wandered by foot across Corsica with other Saint-Simonians, and finally headed east with the Companions of the Woman, landing near Constantinople in April 1833.[72]

When he eventually arrived in Egypt, he instinctively "felt himself to be an oriental," [73] and he became a teacher of languages in Damietta and a convert to Islam.

The plague of 1835, which turned some Saint-Simonians like the feminist Suzanne Voilquin to hashish, led Urbain away from drink and the "explosion of sensuality" into a new life as a Muslim. He was impressed by their tolerant attitude toward race and the solidity of Muslim family life [74]—and perhaps also disillusioned by reports from other Saint-Simonians that even isolated groups like the Malabar Christians of India had not preserved the hoped-for island of purity in man-woman relations within Christendom.[75] He found at last a name of his own, that of the prophet Ismaïl, who had also been the son of a slave abandoned by his father, but had allegedly "discovered a source of water near Mecca." [76]

In Algeria, newly colonized by the French, Urbain found his "oasis" in the shadow of Enfantin, "the gigantic palm tree in my desert," [77] who arrived in 1839 with a scientific commission. Urbain, who had moved there in 1837, began a long career as official military interpreter to a series of high French officials beginning with the Duke of Orléans [78] and ending with Napoleon III. Urbain believed that he had been chosen to mediate between East and West; and that the link that he personally represented between the French and the Arabs stood at the pivotal point of a coming reconciliation. "The day is coming," he proclaimed to the Arabs

> . . . when you will place yourself in the midst of the nations to demand an accounting from them of the riches you have deposited in their midst. The Orient and the Occident belong to God and he is pushing the one toward the other.[79]

Urbain immersed himself in linguistic and ethnographic studies of his adopted land. Enfantin's image of reconciling the East and the West seemed in a way to be taking place in Algeria through Urbain, who was half black, half white, "embracing Islam without renouncing Christianity," [80] writing poetry in both French and Arabic.

In 1839 Urbain added a vision of reconciliation between the races to the Saint-Simonian repertoire of conflicts to be resolved in the coming "universal association" of peoples. *The Letters on the black race and the white race*, which he exchanged with the Jewish Saint-Simonian Gustave d'Eichtal, suggest racial reconciliation through the creation of a new mulatto race. Eichtal was clearly fascinated by his personal relationship with Urbain, which had led to collaboration on *The Two Worlds* in 1836–39, a work apparently lost.[81] Eichtal saw his link with Urbain as that of "the black and the Jew: the two outcasts, the two prophets!" and saw the liberation of the two peoples as deeply interrelated.[82] The conversion of blacks like Urbain to Islam was an important first step as it made them "members of the great family of Abraham" and offered via the Koran "the initiation of the black to the book." [83] Eichtal transferred the characteristic romantic glorification of the unspoiled "people" directly to the blacks: "La race noire c'est le monde *sauvage* de Rousseau. . . ." [84] The blending of the races in the Hispanic world (which has gone on from the time of the Moors to present-day Cuba) was seen as a model of the future in the third and last of the *Letters*.[85] The coming mulatto humanity was to be the product of the direct erotic fusion of divided races and sexes.

Urbain seemed to accept Eichtal's view that the new chosen people should begin forging their "alliance of zoology with history" [86] in Algeria. Efforts to establish a new Franco-Arabian college and the pro-Arab *Colonization of Algeria*, which Enfantin published in 1843 on the basis of notes by Urbain, represented the last common effort of the Saint-Simonians to find a place on earth for the immediate transformation of the human condition. The master's final hopes for a "new Christianity" became transferred into the pupils' interest in what might be called a "new Islam." Eichtal developed this idea in *The present and future of Islam in Central Africa*.[87] The very title of the new French-language journal founded in 1844 summarized the new geopolitical vision of these Saint-Simonians: *Algeria: courier of Africa, the Orient and the Mediterranean*.[88]

Urbain was in Paris during the Revolution of 1848. Caught up in "the revolutionary fever," he served with Eichtal in a unit of the National Guard commanded by Rodrigues.[89] The leading Saint-Simonian contribution to revolutionary events in Algeria was the brilliant defense of the leading indigenous revolutionary organization, the Children of Carthage, by the original leader of the Saint-Simonian pilgrimage to the East: Emile Barrault.[90] He lectured the defendants even as he pleaded their case, pointing out the dangers of *fantasmagorie révolutionnaire* in an atmosphere of conspiracy: "*Si la démocratie conspire, elle abdique.*" [91] Most of the European community in Algeria were persuaded by his argument that the revolutionaries were largely a harmless anachronism. They received a light sentence, and the prestige of the Saint-Simonian group was enhanced in Algeria. However, their activities in the antirevolutionary, post-romantic 1850s largely involved either technocratic development or cultural bridge-building—with Urbain the leading advocate of the latter.

After a long career of trying to unify the two worlds (increasingly under the pseudonym *Voisin*, "neighbor"), Urbain issued a ringing, revolutionary defense of the native culture against forced Europeanization in his work of 1860, *Algeria for the Algerians*.[92] This title was the prototype for innumerable anticolonial appeals of later eras. But for Urbain it was personally inspired by the lingering fatal illness of his Mauresque wife, which for him symbolized the suffering of the Arab peoples. Napoleon III was impressed by this and other of Urbain's works. He came to know Urbain as his official interpreter while touring Algiers, and gave the aging Arabophile the impression of adopting his ideas by declaring in 1862:

> How can one count upon the pacification of a country when almost the entire population is incessantly disturbed. . . . It would be necessary to relocate the entire Arab population in the desert and inflict upon it the fate of the Indians of North America . . .[93]

It was a classic statement of the impossibility of sustaining colonial dominance over a hostile culture. The tragedy is not only that Napoleon III did not honor the implied promise of national self-determination, but also that men like Urbain believed that he would do so.[94] It was the last in a long line of Napoleonic illusions which began with Saint-Simon's own proposals to the first Bonaparte and ended with the docile service of surviving Saint-Simonians as bankers and railroad builders for Napoleon III. Even after Napoleon's fall in 1870, Urbain continued to believe that some kind of reconciliation between East and West was in fact taking place within French North Africa.

When another black came from the West Indies a century after Urbain to adopt the Algerian cause as his own, he preached not the reconciling philosophy of Urbain and the early Saint-Simonians, but heroic, therapeutic violence. The time seemed to have come for the "nations of the world" to "account for the riches" taken from the poorer nations as Urbain had predicted. But Frantz Fanon's accounting was not to be made in Urbain's warm confidence that both "the Orient and the Occident belong to God"; but rather in the cold belief that a diabolistic Occident must be defeated by a massive uprising of les damnés de la terre.

Yet these words from Fanon's most famous title came not from a native song, but from the French revolutionary poet, Eugène de Potter, whose hymn to the fallen communards of Paris became the Internationale. It was not just from native traditions or from visionary prophets like Urbain that the "wretched of the earth" were to take their ideas of liberation in the twentieth century. It was also from a new generation of European political revolutionaries tutored less in the romantic Saint-Simonianism of Urbain, than in the grim political prison of Devil's Island on the tropical island Urbain had left behind.

The Hegelians

The "Young" or "Left" Hegelians transformed the vague historicism of Saint-Simonians and others into hard revolutionary conviction. Their influence (like that of the Saint-Simonians) began only after the death of the master. About a decade after the appearance of a Saint-Simonian movement, left Hegelianism appeared in the late 1830s as the generational badge of younger radicals east of the Rhine. Alexander Herzen, a founder of the Russian revolutionary tradition, was typical in moving from an early infatuation with Saint-Simon, whose works he had "carried around like a Koran," to Hegel, in whom he found "the algebra of revolution."[95] The metaphors were well chosen. Saint-Simon provided a vision of material paradise: Hegel, a method for attaining it.

An impatient new generation tended to blend Saint-Simonianism into

Hegelianism during the politically frustrating 1830s. Some older Saint-Simonians turned to the study of Hegel; [96] and young Slavs like Herzen were exhilarated by the more radical Young Hegelians. Herzen wrote from exile in Vladimir in July 1839 that he was contemplating a dissertation on "How is our century a link between the past and the future?" when he came upon the radical treatise of a Polish Hegelian who answered his question with a "philosophy of action." [97]

Nothing better illustrates the transnational appeal of revolutionary Hegelianism. A Russian exile east of Moscow was rejoicing over the work of a Polish thinker writing in German on the basis of a French translation of the works of the dead Hegel. Revolutionary Hegelianism was, however, no less extreme for being derivative. Herzen wrote that Saint-Simon's sentimental "New Christianity" was henceforth forever superseded "by the absolute knowledge revealed by Hegel."

> The future society is to be the work not of the heart, but of the concrete.
> Hegel is the new Christ bringing the word of truth to men . . .[98]

The conversion to Saint-Simonianism of young Germans like Gall and Gans in the Paris of the early thirties preceded, and in a way prepared for, Karl Marx's education in Hegelianism. For Gans was Marx's high-school teacher at Trier; and either he or Marx's future father-in-law may have exposed Marx to the ideas of Saint-Simon there before his infatuation with Hegelian thought at Berlin University.[99] The entire phenomenon of left Hegelianism has indeed been described as "nothing more than a Hegelianized Saint-Simonianism or a Saint-Simonianized Hegelianism." [100]

Prussian Pedagogy

To understand the Young Hegelians, one must move from the adventuresome vistas of the Saint-Simonians to a quieter world of abstract intellectualism: from energetic engineers at the Ecole Polytechnique to brooding philosophers of the University of Berlin. If Saint-Simonianism was the religion of the *polytechniciens* in post-revolutionary France, so Hegelianism was the religion of university students in post-reform Prussia.

The new university at Berlin was the intellectual heart of the Prussian revival after Prussia's humiliation by Napoleon. Hegel was central to its intellectual life not only as professor of philosophy from 1818 until his death in 1831, but for many years thereafter. Founded in 1809, the University of Berlin was in many ways the first modern university —urban, research-oriented, state-supported, free from traditional religious controls.[101] Berlin stood at the apex of the entire state educational system of reform Prussia. Deliberately located in the capital rather than in the traditional sleepy provincial town, the University of Berlin breathed an atmosphere of political expectation and intellectual innovation among both its uncharacteristically young professors (mostly in their thirties) and its gifted students. Berlin was built on a solid German tradition that had already extended and modernized the university ideal—notably at Halle in the late seventeenth century and Göttingen in the mid-eighteenth. But both of these had been lost to the Prussian state in the Treaty of Tilsit in 1807. Thus the hopes of all Prussia were focused on the new university at Berlin, the first to be built around the library and laboratory rather than the catechistic class-room. The university offered entering students the challenge of research rather than learning by rote, the promise of discovering new truths rather than propagating old ones. Education at Berlin was built around sharing the explorations of a professor rather than covering a pre-scribed curriculum. Interest focused on research institutes—twelve were added during the first ten years of the university's existence—rather than on the theological faculty, hitherto the dominant area. Even here, innovation was evident in the intra-confessional, state-appointed theological faculty dominated by the unorthodox Friedrich Schleiermacher.

Berlin University marked a new chapter not only in the development of scholarship, but also in the relationship of education to society. For it was a creation of the state, pledged to train a new Prussian elite. Schleiermacher's most famous work was *Patriotic Sermons*; and the best-known work of Fichte, the first rector and professor of philosophy at the university, was *Speeches to the German Nation* of 1807.

By the time Hegel succeeded to Fichte's chair in 1819, the first flush of optimism in Prussia had faded. Restrictions had been placed on students, and conservative Austria rather than reform Prussia domi-nated the politics of the German-speaking world. But Hegel had a life-long interest in politics evidenced by his substitution of English polit-ical newspapers for morning prayers as a young student of theology. He described newspaper reading as "a sort of realistic morning prayer. One orients one's attitude to the world by God or by that which the world itself is." [102]

Hegel's "world" was largely political. Deeply affected by the aroused hopes of the French Revolution, he focused his philosophy on the goal of universal political liberation:

> No other philosophy has been so much and so intimately a philosophy of the Revolution.[103]

Marxist intellectuals continue to insist on the revolutionary impact of Hegel: as the first major thinker to dwell on both the Industrial and the French Revolutions,[104] as a key influence on Lenin as well as on Marx.[105]

Hegel was particularly impressed with Napoleon, the subconscious model for his ideal of a "world-historical figure." He wrote of Napoleon in Jena in 1806:

> I saw Napoleon, the soul of the world, riding through the town on a reconnaissance. It is indeed a wonderful sight to see, concentrated in a point, sitting on a horse, an individual who overruns the world and masters it.[106]

Here was the ultimate simplification, a *point parfait* for the imperial intellect. Hegel's complex thought was brought into focus by power "concentrated in a point," which made new beginnings possible. When political reaction followed Napoleonic innovations and Prussian reform, Hegel sought to convert philosophy into a political weapon. He succeeded in politicizing philosophy; his lectures satisfied the striving toward power and "relevance" that was inherent in the University of Berlin—and in much of modern intellectual life.

Hegel expressed, first of all, the supreme self-confidence of the thinking man in the value of his thought. Everything became relative to historical context because his own capacity for seeing the whole picture was assumed to be absolute.[107] Accepting the romantic belief that truth was revealed in the peculiarities of history rather than in a static natural order, Hegel nevertheless simultaneously pressed the Enlightenment idea that all was rational. His method applied reason to precisely those phenomena that most interested the romantic mind: art, philosophy, and religion.

He had begun as a student of theology, in search of a theodicy, a justification of the ways of God to man; he ended up instead creating a new God: the "World Spirit." Just as Hegel saw his chair of philosophy giving overall coherence to the intellectual variety of the new university, so the World Spirit provided a unifying rationale to the historical process. Just as Berlin University was the dynamo for regenerating German society, so Hegel's philosophy was its source of dynamism.

Hegel found in the ancient Greeks' insistence on man as a social animal an antidote for lonely romantic brooding. Eternal contemplation of the self was, he discovered, the old idea of hell: the literal meaning of *hypochondria*. The world of the spirit (or mind, the German *Geist* meaning both) provided a way out, because the mind finds satisfaction in its own activity. Charting the life of the spirit—the "phenomenology of mind" as he called it—appeared as a kind of compensation for defeat in battle. Hegel's "science of consciousness" was seen as the controlling force of the universe. His subsequent work suggested that the individual's plight in overcoming "alienation" was related to that of history itself, which alternates between separation and reconciliation. Thesis generated antithesis and was resolved in a higher synthesis following the pattern of thought itself. Like history thought moved upward through such tensions toward the pure life of the spirit—the old Greek ideal of contemplating contemplation.

Young intellectuals in nineteenth-century Europe were fascinated by the suggestion that their own intellectual life and personal alienation put them in special communion with the World Spirit. Reconciling reason and revelation presented no conflict for the self-proclaimed Thomas Aquinas of Protestantism. Hegel viewed all religious creeds historically, as the rational expression of what was implicit in religious feeling at a given moment. One believed in a particular formulation primarily because one believed in the wisdom of the process of which it was a part. Just as political organizations were necessary to give

objective expression to the need for sociability, so churches were needed
to objectify the subjective feelings of awe that all men felt. Ultimate
truth lay only in the process itself—moving through, yet beyond, all
partial, historical forms of expression. History was a process whereby
the absolute mind moves to absolute freedom. The only real freedom
for any individual man lay in knowing its inner laws and ever-changing
necessities.

Thus, Hegel gave a compelling urgency to knowledge about how history worked. All truth was realized in history, and any part of reality
was intelligible only in historical context. Hegel's fragmentary attempts
to decode the historical process inspired a bewildering variety of movements. His argument that certain great men were chosen agents ("world
historical figures") stimulated Carlyle and other theorists of "great men"
in history. His belief in a special role for the German world and the
Prussian state inspired the chauvinistic "neo-Hegelians" of the late nineteenth century. His own political predisposition for evolutionary constitutionalism influenced the so-called *Rechtsstaat* or "rule of law"
liberals. His belief that the mission of the mind was to seek a comprehensive understanding of human phenomena inspired much of the
apolitical, "Germanic" scholarship in the humanities and social sciences
throughout the nineteenth century.

But the most important aspect of Hegel's immense influence was
that which he exercised on the so-called Young or Left Hegelians. This
new generation of radicals drew from his legacy a belief in the dialectical inevitability and revolutionary direction of history.

Of course, like the other Hegelianisms, revolutionary Hegelianism was
based only on a partial reading of Hegel's world picture. Hegel no more
than Saint-Simon intended to start a new revolution; he meant only to
resolve the conflicts of the old. But the sedentary Berlin professor with
his snuff box and *haute bourgeois* style of life hatched the most revolutionary idea of all: the dialectical method.

By suggesting that history like thought proceeds progressively through
contradiction and conflict, Hegel justified a new type of militance based
on what might be called the power of negative thinking. Originally, of
course, the dialectic was for Hegel a positive, reconciling concept. The
general direction was onward and upward. Each new synthesis tended
to lift up (*aufheben*) the level of civilization. But, since history progressed through contradiction, Hegel's method suggested that each new
affirmation necessarily gave rise to negation. This tension, in turn, gave
birth to the "negation of negation," a new synthesis.

Since the essential content of history was thought, the key elements
in its dynamic development were ideas. To understand which were the
critical ones in a given era required a new type of speculative thinking
that transcended the one-sidedness of either unhistorical reasoning
(which he called *raisonnement*) or unreasoning imagination (which he
called *Vorstellung* or "representation," the favorite word of his rival
Schopenhauer). Rather one had to seek through reflection on reality to
gain a "grasp" or "concept" (*Begriff*) of the unfolding truth of history.
By gaining this grasp of the *Zeitgeist* ("spirit of the time") the specu-

lative intellectual acquired a sense of relevance which he otherwise tended to lack in a frenetic world.

Hegel saw history taking man from the realm of necessity to that of freedom through the progressive development of Western civilization —from the advent of monotheism when freedom was posited for the one (God) through the Reformation when it was proposed for all by Luther. Hegel felt that, in the present age, the idea of freedom was at last taking political form through the new type of state that had been proposed by Frederick the Great and partly realized in the Prussian reforms. In a sense, then, the Hegelian vision was simply a sublime justification for Hegel's own vocation as a kind of pedagog-in-chief for reform Prussia. History was transforming abstract ideas into concrete form, and Prussia was the cutting edge. Who could be more important to history than the key figure in the key institution of the key state?

The sense of destiny and self-importance that Hegel imparted to the study of philosophy at Berlin lingered on after his death. But to a new generation of students who flocked to the Prussian capital from central and eastern Europe it was difficult to sustain Hegel's optimism about the state as the chosen instrument of the historical process. After Tsar Nicholas I of Russia crushed the Polish rebellion in 1831 and pronounced his absolutist doctrine of "Orthodoxy, Autocracy, and Nationality" in 1833, he leaned increasingly for support on his conservative relatives in the ruling house of Prussia. When a new king of Prussia, Frederick William IV, disappointed the hopes that attended his coronation in 1840 and proved even more reactionary than his predecessor, a new group of Young Hegelians began to give a revolutionary reading to their master's message.

It had been a decade since Hegel died; and the new generation had never known the exhilaration of hopeful participation in active reform. They had, however, imbibed the visionary hopes of the Hegelian perspective and the exuberant, arrogant intellectualism of Berlin. Each of the two major strands from which Bolshevism was eventually woven —the Russian revolutionary intelligentsia and German Marxism—had its origins in the Young Hegelian movement. The pioneers in both camps were intellectuals of the 1840s—men who were seeking not so much to redress concrete wrongs as to realize an abstract ideal: the Hegelian transition "from necessity to freedom." Before turning to the German Marxist, and the Russian revolutionaries, one must trace the first Slavic awakening which took place under the spell of Hegel and the leadership of the Poles.

Slavic Awakening

A new generation of Poles, humiliated by the disappearance of their nation, found a certain attraction in the new German intellectual atmosphere. Writing largely in the relative freedom of Prussian-occupied Poznań, these Poles turned Hegelianism into a weapon of revolution and invented a new verbal talisman for the Slavs: *intelligentsia*.

The founder of revolutionary Hegelianism, August Cieszkowski, came to Berlin in 1832 just after Hegel's death. During a trip to Paris in 1836–38, he fell under Saint-Simonian and Fourierist influence and published upon his return to Berlin in 1838 his seminal *Prolegomena to a Historiosophy*. Despite his pretentious title and awkward German prose, Cieszkowski brought a simple message that radicalized the master in the guise of providing a final "knowledge of history" (the literal meaning of historiosophy).

History, he contended, moved dialectically through three successive ages: emotion, thought, and action. The first age was that of antiquity, the second stretched from the birth of Christ to the death of Hegel, and the third was the present age which was destined to translate philosophy into action.

Cieszkowski introduced the Greek term *praxis* for the "practical activity" that he felt would be characteristic of the new age. The quest for a "philosophy of action" became central to the most revolutionary thinkers of the group: first radical fellow Poles,[108] then the seminal Russian revolutionary Nicholas Ogarev in 1841,[109] and finally Karl Marx.

In his *Philosophical Manuscripts* of 1844 Marx sought to harness thought to action: both by plunging directly into revolutionary activity and by discarding speculative thought for "the study of social praxis."[110] This activist study of society in its concrete historical context was little more than a German adoption of the "social physiology" of the Saint-Simonians; but it was also a means of overcoming one's sense of separation from other men by discovering a new world in which "total man and total society tend to recover one another."[111] Thus, however much the Young Hegelians may have been providing answers to the real needs of society, they were also answering their own psychological need for a purpose in life: some way of reconciling themselves to living with their fellow man, and even with themselves.

The more lonely and intense the intellectual, the more universal his ideal tended to become. Thus the Poles who had lost their national identity in 1831 and imbibed Hegelianism from nearby Prussia produced a small but highly creative group of ideologists who rejected the dominant ethos of Polish nationalism for the more universal vision of social revolution.

A Polish Saint-Simonian, Bogdan Jański, had been the first to use the term "social revolution" in the 1830s,[112] before going on to found a conservative new religious "order of the Resurrection." Cieszkowski, too, moved from ideology to cosmology in order to sustain an image of worldwide social transformation. To counter Mickiewicz's idea of nation-as-messiah, he suggested that the Lord's Prayer contained a prophecy of a coming social utopia. In his enormous, unfinished work of the 1840s, *Our Father*, he argued that the Kingdom was literally about to come "on earth as it is in heaven." A reintegrated "organic humanity" was to usher in a new age of "the Holy Spirit" in which all national identities would disappear before the Central Government of Mankind, the Universal International Tribunal, and the Universal Council of the Peoples.[113]

In 1843, B. F. Trentowski invented the word "cybernetics" to describe the new form of rational social technology which he believed would transform the human condition. In his neglected work, *The Relationship of Philosophy to Cybernetics; or the art of ruling nations,* he also invented the word "intelligentsia." In a passage challenging the leadership of the nationalist poet Adam Mickiewicz, Trentowski called him out of touch with "the new generation and the new spirit,"

> . . . trembling from fear lest the sceptre with which he rules the Polish intelligentsia be taken from him.[114]

Trentowski had been educated in Germany; and he published his treatise in Poznań, where the Prussian censorship was somewhat more liberal than in the Austrian- or Russian-occupied parts of Poland. The following year, in the same city, the term "progressive intelligentsia" was introduced in a periodical edited by Karol Libelt, a Polish Hegelian who had been educated in Berlin and politicized in Paris.[115] In his *Love of the Fatherland* written in the same 1844, Libelt described this intelligentsia as

> . . . all those who having carefully and broadly obtained an education in higher schools and institutes, stand at the head of the nation as scholars, officials, teachers, clergymen, industrialists—in sum all those who lead it because of their higher enlightenment.[116]

Here, clearly, was an alternate leadership for Poland to the military rule of the occupying powers. The idea blended in with the new theory simultaneously put forward by Cieszkowski that the hereditary aristocracy should be replaced by a new aristocracy of merit.[117] Subsequent usages of the term by the Polish press in Poznań introduced the idea that the "intelligentsia" was separate from the masses.[118]

Libelt and Cieszkowski still looked largely to the old aristocracy to produce the new elite. But Libelt's call upon the youth of Poland to "sacrifice your reality to an ideal," to "fall in love with enlightenment while renouncing the pleasures of the body" was a harking forward to the future. In Russia of the 1860s, intelligentsia first acquired its full-blown modern suggestion of an intellectual elite cut off from traditional allegiances and dedicated to radical social change.[119] Libelt invoked the text of Schiller's poem "Resignation," a poem that had become simultaneously "especially popular in Russia,"[120] suggesting the needed spirit of sacrifice to the founders of its revolutionary intelligentsia, Herzen and Ogarev. The poem offered the choice between satisfaction in the present and hope for the future. There was no question that Slavic revolutionaries had chosen, already in the forties, to live by hope.

Hegelian philosophy gave them hope—even when they rejected it. Belinsky, the founder of Russian radical journalism, wrote in 1838 that Hegel's teachings enabled him "to get along with practical people"[121] by convincing him that they were objectively worthy of study. The Hegelian perspective elevated him beyond what his correspondent Bakunin called "my personal me."[122] Belinsky subsequently rejected the "reconciliation with reality" that Hegel had provided, proclaiming that

... the fate of the subject, the individual, the personality is more important
than the fate of the whole world and . . . the Hegelian *Allgemeinheit*.[123]

But this was "the cry of revolt of a sick man whom the Hegelian medicine has not cured." [124] Indeed, the "medicine" had induced an addiction for an all-encompassing ideology; and the young *révoltés* of Berlin
were producing one in their "philosophy of action." [125]

Ogarev, studying in Germany, pointed the way with his declaration
that "not all that is real is rational, but all that is rational should
become real. The philosophy of action is at present the best trend . . .
a theory according to which irrational reality changes into a rational
one. Praxis is history." Revolutionary action is the cure for alienation,
the appropriate response to the present age, and a means of transforming Hegelian abstractions into "something personal." [126]

Ogarev's friends, the "romantic exiles" Herzen and Bakunin, made
particularly anguished efforts to blend the personal into the universal
and to answer Cieszkowski's call for a new philosophy of action.[127] The
Russians felt the double disability of being provincial aristocrats as well
as alienated intellectuals. They suffered an acute sense of being like
the "superfluous men" of Russian literature, with even less opportunity
than Prussians for meaningful activity in society. But, in a Prussia
more interested in economic growth (through the *Zollverein*, the new
customs union of 1834) than in political or educational development,
many Germans also felt frustrated. Neglected young intellectuals tended
to reaffirm their own worth by exaggerating the worthlessness of the
ruling forces.

None of the leading Young Hegelians had seriously suffered at the
hands of the European authorities; and most of them (including Marx)
appear never to have even been inside a factory. Theirs was a mental
and spiritual revolt—born of new vision rather than old grievances.
They spoke from exile—Russians in Berlin or Paris, Prussians in Geneva or Brussels, Poles everywhere. They spoke with many tongues—
but always in the language of prophecy. Just as Christian prophets had
identified oppressive rulers with the Antichrist in order to heighten expectations of deliverance by the True Christ, so the Young Hegelian
prophets now proclaimed the evil of rulers in order to intensify the
thirst for revolution.

That thirst was stimulated by the order of Frederick William IV of
Prussia to "root out the dragon seed of Hegelianism" [128] in Berlin
by awarding Hegel's former chair in philosophy to his rival: the romantic idealist Frederick Schelling. For the radical pilgrims to Hegel's
shrine, installing Schelling in Berlin was not unlike enthroning the
Antichrist in Jerusalem. His inaugural lecture on "The Philosophy of
Revelation" in November 1841 attracted a glittering audience, [129] including Engels and Bakunin, both of whom excoriated this seeming retreat from Hegelian logic to romantic fancy.

Frustrated in all their youthful hopes, the radical Hegelians began to
long for a revolutionary apocalypse. Bruno Bauer saw in the new philosophy of action "The Trumpet Call of the Last Judgment" to cite the

title of his article of November 1841; [130] and the call for violence was not long in coming. Bakunin proclaimed late in 1842 that "the joy of destruction is a creative joy"; [131] and his friend Proudhon, then under Hegel's influence, began his major work of the mid-1840s with the motto: *Destruam ut aedificabo*: "I destroy in order to build." [132]

But all radical Hegelians—not excepting that bitter foe of Bakunin and Proudhon, Karl Marx—believed that the revolution was to bring freedom through the destruction of the state, rather than through its fulfillment, as Hegel had envisaged. This second generation of Hegelians saw the end of all repressive rule coming. Some like Bakunin argued for a social revolution to overthrow "God and the state." [133] Others like Max Stirner argued for "the ego and its own" [134] to reject all externally imposed authority. Marx argued that social revolution would emerge dialectically from a feudal through a bourgeois to a proletarian order. But Bakunin's anarchism, Stirner's solipsism, and Marx's communism were all sustained by the Young Hegelian conviction that an end to all authority was at hand; and that the "spirit of the times" required a revolutionary rejection of the present power structure.

Revolutionary Hegelianism reached a kind of climax in the life of Edward Dembowski, the aristocratic journalist who was shot at age twenty-three after leading perhaps the most extreme revolutionary regime to appear in nineteenth-century Europe. Dembowski had been a leading agitator in Poznań and the quintessential example of the phenomenon Libelt had been the first to name: the progressive intelligentsia. As a youth of twenty he was struck by the doctrine of creative destruction set forth in Bakunin's article of 1842. The following year, Dembowski published in Libelt's journal the first of several articles in which abstract philosophy was used to justify concrete revolutionary activity. His "Few Thoughts on Eclecticism" argued against using Hegelianism to reconcile contradictions. Such an "eclectic" perspective merely played into the hands of the established rulers. Atheism was essential since "the Left Hegelian school" was at "the absolute pole from religious radicalism." Only pure negation and destruction could lead to concrete, creative action that would affect the "sensual substance" of real life. [135]

His last major article, "Thoughts on the Future of Philosophy" in 1845, argued for a Polish national philosophy of revolution to synthesize German thought and French deeds. [136] He traced the history of parallel sets of German thinkers and French actors: Kant-Robespierre, Fichte-Babeuf, Schelling–Saint-Simon, Hegel-Fourier, and Feuerbach-Proudhon. The last pair exhausted the possibilities of philosophy and social criticism respectively by attaining atheistic materialism on the one hand and a total rejection of political authority on the other. [137] Nothing remained to be done except to translate these ideas into a creative, necessarily bloody revolution on the unspoiled soil of Poland. When peasant insurrection in Galicia triggered widespread unrest throughout occupied Poland, Dembowski found his chance to put this "national philosophy" into practice. The twenty-three-year-old philosopher led the revolutionary government that took power in the Free City of Cracow. The ancient capital had acquired new importance as the only unoccupied part of Poland and a small region where peasants had been emancipated in the Slavic East.

On Washington's birthday of 1846 a national government of Poland was proclaimed there, and two days later Dembowski became de facto leader of the "Republic of Cracow." Its brief ten days of existence shook Europe with a bold proclamation of universal suffrage, national workshops, and the abolition of the system of landlord ownership so that "everybody could make use of land property according to his merits and abilities." [138] Seizing the difficult task of quieting and satisfying the still unruly peasantry, Dembowski set forth from the city to meet the advancing Austrian troops—hoping that they might stay out of the city and neutralize the advancing Russians. But Dembowski was shot by the Austrians, who annexed the last vestige of free Poland after the Russians occupied Cracow on March 3.

The despairing Poles began to turn from soaring philosophy to grim practicalities. Dembowski's elder cousin, Henryk Kamieński pointed the way with two major works published 1843–45: *The Philosophy of the Material Economy of Human Society* and *On the Living Truths of the Polish People*.[139] The first discussed the earthy mechanics of socio-economic change; the second, the tactical uses of revolutionary violence. The latter work called for agrarian revolution via a guerrilla uprising and a careful campaign of revolutionary terrorism. In the exploration of this subject—as in so much else—Poland of the 1840s anticipated Russia of the 1860s. In between came the uprisings in the West: the "revolution of the intellectuals" in 1848, in which neither occupied Poland nor somnolent Russia played any major part.

The Clash of "Isms" in 1848

Early in 1848, a wave of revolutions struck Europe. It reached further and lasted longer than that of 1830. But it failed everywhere—and brought to an end that "exciting sense of almost limitless possibilities" [140] that had previously prevailed among revolutionaries. After 1848, calculation generally replaced exaltation; the prosaic reality of state-building and industrial development supplanted the romantic vision of a new nation or social community. Henceforth, revolutions were basically caused by defeat in foreign wars rather than by internal social upheaval.

Taken as a whole, the revolutions of 1848 seem more fluid than solid: more a flooding of foundations everywhere than a hard seizure of power or definition of program anywhere. There was a contagion of the spirit amidst a confusion of authority.

A new generation of articulate, ambitious thinkers sparked the uprisings. Artisans threatened by social change and other uprooted elements in the great cities of continental Europe provided the combustible material. Traditional structures were weakened by economic depression below and political ineptness above. The resulting swirl of political experiment and poetic enthusiasm has perhaps been best characterized as "the revolution of the intellectuals." [141]

This revolution may have a relevance for the ideologically insecure Western world of the late twentieth century which it did not have for the more confident Europe of the late nineteenth century. As the last great upheaval of an essentially pre-industrial Europe, 1848 drew on many of the same basic elements as the first internal upheaval of the essentially post-industrial West in the late 1960s. Both movements became almost instantly transnational—and cut deepest into society when they succeeded in arousing newly arrived and unassimilated elements within the cities. The Irish in London, the Saxons in Berlin, and the provincials in Paris [142] played roles in the agitation of the late 1840s not altogether unlike that of the blacks in American cities in the late 1960s.

Of course, the revolutions of 1848 were far more extensive than the student-led riots of 1968—and the bonds between intellectual and urban upheaval far stronger. The two waves of unrest also had profoundly different causes. But both had the effect of encouraging conservative trends in the years that followed. The two upheavals shared, moreover, a profound difference from almost all the more ritualized and organized forms of upheaval that appeared during the intervening 120 years of industrial organization and geopolitical conflict among mechanized states. Indeed, 1848 and 1968 form a kind of frame for the geopolitical conflict of the industrial age.

For all their differences, the unrest of 1848 and 1968 each began by bringing down the dominant symbol of political power in the Western World: the last king of France and an "imperial" president of the United States. In each case internal unrest bore an intimate historic link to a remote foreign war. The unrest of the 1840s did not really end until the aroused popular passions of the greatest industrial states of the nineteenth century, Great Britain and France, were channeled off into the first major armed conflicts of the industrial era: the Crimean War of 1853–56. The unrest of the 1960s did not really begin until popular sentiment in the greatest industrial state of the twentieth century, the United States, rose against the war in Vietnam.

There is a similarity between these two wars—as between the revolutions to which Crimea and Vietnam are related. These two destructive wars mark the birth and perhaps the death of the ritual of mass violence organized at home but exercised abroad by liberal industrial states. Both wars were strictly localized in distant places through a gradual process of escalation. The doses were calculated by antiseptic accountants and sugar-coated by ambitious politicians who dramatized the threat of a hostile authoritarian regime taking over—through the domino effect—an unstable area (Russia in the Balkans, China in Southeast Asia). Both wars were entered into by idealistic, innovative reformers (Palmerston and Kennedy/Johnson) and were briefly glamorized by creating heroic fighting models (the Light Brigade, the Green Berets). Success or failure depended in each case on the relevance of new technology and the role of new means of communication. In the Crimea, the London *Times* and the new mass press stimulated the enthusiasm for war and the thirst for victory. In Vietnam, the *New York Times* and the new mass medium, television, helped take America out of the war.

The modern ritual of national warfare through applied industrial power came into being to a considerable extent to channel if not resolve the largely formless but exalted aspirations of the 1848–50 period in industrial England and industrializing France. The ritual may well have exhausted itself in Vietnam in the 1960s, when some of these same aspirations reappeared in post-industrial America in a second, even more formless "revolution of the intellectuals." The ferment of 1968 may have revived at the twilight of the industrial era some of the forms and ideas present at the dawn in 1848.

A central role in this original revolution of the intellectuals in 1848 was played by new ideas (the "isms") and new means of communication (mass journalism). Out of the three basic ideals of the French Revolution—*la république, la nation, la communauté*—came the three new systems of ideas that vied for men's allegiance in continental Europe during the early nineteenth century: *liberalism, nationalism,* and *socialism.* After the reincarnation of revolution in France in 1830, these isms were linked with renewed hopes for revolutionary fulfillment on the part of political, national, and social revolutionaries alike. The revolutions that spread from France in Europe in 1848 can be discussed in terms of the interaction and conflict of these three isms.

We have seen how the cafés of the Palais-Royal provided in 1788–89 the legitimation of a royal patron for free political discussion with a broad public, and mobilized that public for revolutionary action. In like manner, the national banquet campaign for electoral reform of 1847–48 provided the legitimation of a parliamentary activity for an even greater extension of political discussion that led to a new revolution.[143] But, whereas the Paris mob on July 12, 1789, had assembled in one point (the Palais-Royal), were aroused by one grievance (the dismissal of Necker), and finally converged on one target (the Bastille), the new mob of February 22, 1848, assembled diffusely on the streets in support of a banquet campaign that had covered all of France; their grievances were economic; and their processions protested the cancellation of the climactic great banquet in Paris. The crowd that coursed through Paris for two days until King Louis Philippe abdicated lacked the cohesion of the earlier mob that had set out from his father's elegant enclave of cafés sixty years earlier. The Parisians of 1848 were seeking food not drink, an ideological not a geographical locus of legitimacy.

The basic conflict between moderate political and radical social aspirations was apparent from the beginning. Though superficially a classical political revolution like that of 1830, the scenes on the barricaded streets were dramatically different. The people were hungrier, the weather colder. The romantic tenor Nourrit had held center stage in celebrating the "three glorious days" of July 1830. But, in the freezing February of 1848, the revolution found its artistic hero and spokesman in a vaudeville actor, Frederick Lemaitre, playing in a social drama of the street: *The Ragpicker.*

Lemaitre also played in traditional revolutionary melodramas, such as *Toussaint L'Ouverture* written by the poet who became foreign minister of the new provisional government in 1848, Lamartine. But Lemaitre increasingly turned to vaudeville, which had been dramatically linked with revolution ever since the manager of the Vaudeville Theater, Etienne Arago, had shut his theater and bid the audience join the insurgent mob in 1830, proclaiming "there shall be no laughter at the Vaudeville while Paris is in tears!" [144] In preparing for the role, Lemaitre studied directly with a famous Parisian ragpicker who was viewed as a social critic.[145] Lemaitre played the role daily—contrary to Paris custom—after its opening in 1847; [146] and *The Ragpicker* proved in 1848 a *pièce d'occasion* for revolution as had *Hernani* and *The Mute Girl of Portici* in 1830.

A free performance of the play given on noon of February 24 for the people of Paris produced such an "indescribable effect" that "contemporaries are unanimous in attributing to the play an influence on the February Revolution." [147] In the play, Lemaitre had to pick a crown out of a wastebasket, and when he did so the audience burst into singing *La Marseillaise* in communal celebration of the transfer of power from the last French monarch to the people. Cannon sounded, the audience cried *Vive la république!*, and the performance blended into a popular demonstration which Lemaitre called "a truly sublime spectacle." The author of the play, newly returned from banishment, wrote that "a life of exile is a small price to pay for a day like that." [148]

By June, the provisional revolutionary government would be firing on many of those who had felt the sublimity of which Lemaitre spoke. The working people of Paris had begun to echo the ragpicker's complaints about having to "find his bread in the manure pile," [149] and had enrolled 30,000 subscribers for a proposed banquet of the people (costing only 25 centimes rather than the 10 francs of bourgeois electoral banquets).[150] But this popular feast was cancelled, and the bloody "June days" soon followed, pitting liberalism against socialism in the streets of Paris. In the meantime, however, revolution had spread throughout Europe largely under the banner of the third and most appealing ism of the age: nationalism.

Nationalism was, as we have seen, the dominant revolutionary ideology between 1830 and 1848. On the eve of 1848, with the campaign of the Cyril and Methodius Society in the Ukraine and of nationalists under Kossuth in the Hungarian Diet, youthful representatives of the largest sub-nationalities in each of the great multi-national empires, Austria and Russia, led the way. Then early in January 1848, a separatist uprising occurred in Palermo, Sicily; and conservative statesmen became convinced that "the Polish madness" of revolutionary nationalism evinced in Cracow in 1846 was spreading.

When the bourgeois monarchy of Louis Philippe collapsed in Paris late in February, French approval seemed assured for national revolt elsewhere. A French *chansonnier* who had previously seen the French banquet campaign as the beginning of a new "universal feast" of all nations,[151] now rhapsodized that

> Paris est sorti du tombeau . . .
> Radieux comme un Christ nouveau.[152]

Even before the new French government had acquired political form, it justified itself "by natural right and by national right," appealing to the nations rather than the sovereigns of Europe.[153]

As if in response, a flash flood of national revolutions swept from Copenhagen and Amsterdam to Venice and Sardinia. Germany was the whirlpool at the center in its "March days." Metternich, symbol par excellence of antinationalism, resigned and fled. Within a week, Berlin followed Vienna in revolt; the king of Prussia adopted the tricolor of revolutionary Germany; and all authority seemed on the verge of collapse. In this atmosphere, nationalist revolutionaries turned to the constitutional political forms that had provided the banners for revolt at the beginning of the Metternichean era. Thus, the German-speaking world brought to center stage the second revolutionary doctrine of the romantic era: liberalism.

Liberalism dominated European thinking from the assembling late in March of a committee of fifty German leaders in a "pre-parliament" calling for the election of a constituent assembly for a united Germany. In April, a constituent assembly was elected in France in the first nationwide voting by universal male suffrage, and when the provisional government resigned its authority in May, a moderate republican assembly in effect became the government of France. Republics and constitutions were proclaimed in a variety of Italian regions; and a Slavic congress assembled in Prague in imitation of the German assembly that met in Frankfurt on May 18.

The 830-man Frankfurt assembly provided the most sustained and serious effort to realize a new constitutional order on the continent. It sought to extend the French idea of a Declaration of the Rights of Man into a broader Declaration of the Rights of People. But in seeking to represent "the people" directly, the educated parliamentarians of Frankfurt cut themselves off from the existing bases of real power. In a German world that was still politically divided and economically backward, local and princely authorities gradually reclaimed real power from above. Meanwhile, from below, the specter of social revolution in the summer of 1848 increasingly frightened the middle-class liberals of Frankfurt. Yesterday's liberals became today's conservatives, and moderate liberal rule lost its revolutionary luster in Germany as elsewhere.

Socialism along with communism and other slogans of social revolution came to dominate the European imagination, particularly after open class warfare bloodied the streets of Paris in June 1848.

Proletarian unrest following the depression of 1847 had helped precipitate the original February Revolution. The Commission for the Workers, which the provisional government set up in the Luxembourg Palace, soon became the driving force in a gathering social revolution. This Luxembourg Commission of three hundred to four hundred workers provided the forum for working-class demands, some of which (promulgation of the right to work and creation of national workshops) the assembly formally approved.

Foreign apostles of socialist solutions—Robert Owen, Goodwyn Barmby, and Karl Marx—rushed to Paris. "The King of Trade has been conquered by the Man of Work," [154] Barmby proclaimed in March, praising the socialist president of the commission, Louis Blanc, and its vice-president, "Albert the Artisan." [155] On April 22, he wrote to England that "by the time this reaches you Paris will have peacefully socialized its banks, railroads and factories." [156]

By the time that message reached England, however, the conservative swing against proletarian Paris had begun. The Left was badly defeated in the elections to the assembly late in April; well-known revolutionary leaders like Blanqui were arrested in May; and in June some ten thousand workers were killed or wounded and about eleven thousand deported by the forces of the "liberal" assembly.

The "June days" emboldened forces of reaction throughout Europe. Four days after repression in Paris, the Frankfurt assembly turned to the conservative Austrian archduke as "regent of Germany." Shortly thereafter, the assembly called on Prussian troops to rescue it from revolutionary siege of the Frankfurt church in which it met. With the crushing of a revolt in Baden in September and of a proletarian uprising in Berlin in October, the assembly prepared the way for the full-scale return to monarchical conservatism in the German-speaking world, which began with the counter-revolution in the spring of 1849 in Vienna, where the German revolution had started just a year before.

The counter-revolutionary resurgence throughout Europe in 1849–50 benefited not just from the inexperience of intellectuals as political leaders. Equally important were the underlying conflicts that came to the surface between the differing revolutionary ideologies themselves.

Liberalism in Germany had been the main source of revolutionary hope outside France; Marx himself had urged the abolition of a distinct Communist League in the spring of 1848 in order to unify all revolutionary forces behind a consolidated "bourgeois democratic" revolution. But German liberals were unnerved by the rise of a workers' movement, and the specter of communism that this movement raised helped turn older liberals into new conservatives. Even more fundamental was the inner conflict between the once compatible, but now rival, revolutionary goals of national unification and constitutional republicanism. The former proved far more appealing to the masses in times of upheaval. Germans could be aroused by hatred of Russia, and Italians by hatred of Austria. Both Germans and Italians proved willing—at times even eager—to drop liberal republican ideals and accept a king. As long as it was a king of their own who could give them identity, they seemed ready to choose the national ideal of unity over the liberal ideal of freedom: *Einheit* over *Freiheit*.

The failure of 1848 in Germany also illustrated the conflict within liberalism between the desire for a strong rule of law and for increased freedom of the individual. The defeated German liberals of Frankfurt were only a little less authoritarian than the victorious German nationalists. The liberals believed in a strong executive and a weak legislature; [157] and their concept of a "constitutional union" helped divorce the phrase "constitutional" from its previous associations with romantic revolutionary deliverance. *Konstitutionelle* suggested the *juste milieu* of law and order; and this concept of a "constitutional constitution" was in direct contrast to that of a revolutionary constitution. The former bespoke moderation, the latter had promised liberation. Constitutional liberalism ceased to be a revolutionary ideal in Germany not just because of hostile pressures exerted by conservatives, but also because of the definitions that liberals made of their own calling.

Calls for political change became less revolutionary; and calls for social revolution went largely unheard. Even within the dominant revolutionary ism of nationalism, the upheavals of 1848–50 revealed deep conflicts that were never envisaged in the Mazzinian dream of a happy fraternity of federated peoples. German power was asserted at the expense of Danish and Czech identity. Hungary, which produced the most flamboyant and successful of the purely national revolutions, was crushed from above by the rival, reactionary nationalism of Russia and undercut from below by the secessionist nationalism of the Croatians, Serbs, Slovaks, and Romanians.

Reactionary monarchs triumphed everywhere east of the Rhine; and, by 1851, the only hope for revolutionaries seemed to lie in France and England. England had preserved a measure of civil liberties and welcomed political refugees from the continent. France had overthrown its last king and established a republic based on universal suffrage. But England had defused the radical side of its liberal tradition by an ingenious combination of preventive police repression and selective legislative co-optation of the Chartist reform program.

The Chartist demonstration in London of April 1848 involved elements of the largest urban working class and the best-educated lower middle class in Europe. But the proponents of "physical force" had already lost out within the movement. With the failure of the rain-soaked gathering to produce anything more than an ineffectual petition for further democratic rights, England saw 1848 pass without an uprising, let alone a revolution. Liberalism was separated further from revolutionary militance; and the great exhibition of material goods in the Crystal Palace in 1851 turned English eyes away from ideas altogether to the promise of prosperity and evolutionary progress.

France dealt blows of another sort in 1851 to surviving hopes for revolutionary republicanism. On December 2, the anniversary of Napoleon I's greatest military victory at Austerlitz, Napoleon III dissolved the legislative assembly and assumed dictatorial power. Despite stiff resistance to the coup in the countryside, he was able to turn the Second Republic into the Second Empire and establish for a decade a kind of police state sanctioned by plebiscite which reflected a widespread desire for order and stability.[158]

Four days after his coup, Napoleon III returned the Pantheon to the archbishop of Paris, who renamed it (for the third time) the Church of Saint Geneviève—thus dooming to oblivion a unique artistic effort to express the general faith underlying all the ism's. For more than three years, a dedicated team of revolutionary painters under Paul Chenavard had been working on a vast set of designs to redecorate the Pantheon.[159] It was perhaps the most ideologically ambitious artistic project of the 1848–51 era—and a worthy reprise of those first efforts after the death of Mirabeau in 1791 to turn the church into a secular shrine for great men which might inspire revolutionaries to "make the world into a Pantheon." [160]

Chenavard's career reads like a recapitulation of revolutionary romanticism. He had been a member of the claque at the opening of Hugo's *Hernani* on the eve of the Revolution of 1830, an iconographer of Mirabeau and the original National Assembly in the aftermath, the man whom Delacroix asked to see when dying, and—throughout—a faithful son of Lyon both in his passion for the working man and in his Germanic and mystical approach to social questions. At the end of the frieze he designed for the Pantheon to show the progress of humanity stood Saint-Simon and Fourier, whose followers were Chenavard's closest friends in the 1840s.[161] He was commissioned to redecorate the Pantheon in April 1848 by the brother of the socialist leader Louis Blanc (Charles Blanc, the revolutionary Director of Beaux-Arts) and by the radical political leader Alexander Ledru-Rollin, the new Minister of the Interior.

The central element in Chenavard's revolutionary iconography was a vast mural in heroic classical style representing real and mythical figures in a circular panorama of progressive "palingenesis" (continuous rebirth) leading towards universal brotherhood among androgynous supermen. Right-Left interaction is evident in this uncompleted monument of revolutionary faith. The title of his great mosaic under the central dome of the Pantheon, *La Palingénésie Sociale*, was taken directly from a book published in 1827 by his conservative Catholic friend and fellow Lyonnais, Pierre-Simon Ballanche. Ballanche's vision of history as a series of "social rebirths" represented the romantic "politics of the miraculous" at its most fantastic. Although he was politically reactionary and ultimately pessimistic about progress (predicting a return of humanity to animality after its ascent to godhood), Ballanche had inspired many of the most widely optimistic imaginations in the revolutionary camp: the Saint-Simonians in their messianic phase in 1832, and the aged Charles Nodier, who published a futuristic fantasy *Palingénésie humaine* in the same year.[162]

The paintings, sketches, and plans of Chenavard and his associates were relegated to the archives of provincial museums under the Second Empire. Napoleon III, who had swamped Ledru-Rollin at the polls long before claiming to be emperor, felt no obligation to carry out the defeated republican's artistic plans. Like the other experimental political leaders who built new industrial states in the third quarter of the nineteenth century (Bismarck in Prussia, Cavour in Italy), Napoleon adopted bits and pieces of all the older romantic ideals. But the controlling ism's in France were no longer revolutionary ideologies of any kind—whether liberalism, nationalism, or socialism—but rather a new set of apolitical and anti-romantic attitudes which went under the names of realism, materialism, and positivism.

The revolutionary failure of 1848, followed by the Napoleonic coup in Paris, represented an historic turning point: a loss in the locus of legitimacy. From political exile in distant Kazakhstan, one of the ever-prophetic Poles, Zygmunt Sierakowski, wrote that

> Before December 2, I wanted to go to Paris. Today I see only two places in the world for me: New York or Petersburg. . . . If I had the choice, I should perhaps choose Petersburg.[163]

If individual revolutionaries often fled to America, the revolutionary tradition itself migrated rather to Russia. Sierakowski's subsequent impact probably lay less in his public leadership of the Polish uprising in 1863 than in his more silent influence on Chernyshevsky and the rising Russian tradition. The center of revolutionary gravity was moving from national to social revolution, from Paris to Petersburg.

CHAPTER 9

The Early Church
(the 1840s)

Credo: Communism

MORE THAN any other movement within the revolutionary tradition, communism was born with its name. When the word first appeared publicly in 1840, it spread throughout the continent with a speed altogether unprecedented in the history of such verbal epidemics. Unlike earlier revolutionary labels, communism was a new word, associated from the beginning with a new concept.[1]

Rapid dissemination of the term throughout Europe was made possible by accelerated means of communication (mail service regularized by means of the steamboat and steam engine, and the first telegraphy). Those who spread the word were a small group of young journalists whose sole occupation was verbal craftsmanship. Unlike the operatic voices of romantic nationalism, social revolutionaries communicated most naturally in printed prose—the social novel, the critical review, the polemic pamphlet. Out of a veritable ocean of such prose, the word communism emerged as a telegraphic label for an essentially verbal vision. The idea, first popularized in the pages of a novel (Cabet's *Voyage to Icaria*), was refined and finally made manifest by Marx on the eve of revolution in 1848.

The new term brought into focus both the fears of the older generation and the hopes of the new. The word commun*ism* spread before there were any commun*ists*. Indeed, the term was most prominently and insistently used by conservative opponents—demonstrating once again the symbiosis between the fears of one extreme and the hopes of the other. To place the impact of the new label in proper context it is necessary to consider more broadly the history of verbal innovation within the revolutionary tradition.

The Talismanic Word

With almost rhythmic regularity, each decade had produced its own new labels for rallying the revolutionary Left. In the 1790s, friends of the French Revolution invoked the venerable word *democracy* with awesome new effect. *Nation* and *republic* were other old words used in new, revolutionary ways. *Constitution* became important during the subsequent decade of opposition to Napoleonic tyranny. All of these terms lingered on in the revolutionary lexicon—and returned to recapture their original evocative power at later times in distant places.

In the decades that followed the defeat of Napoleon, however, there came a change in the nature of the central, mythic terms favored by revolutionaries. Altogether new words with more sweeping meanings began to replace older words which had more limited associations. These new labels were derived from French words ending in *isme*, and offered the vague but appealing prospect of providing new legitimacy for a European civilization no longer so sure of its churches and kings.

The first new ism, which was invented and widely disseminated at the dawn of the century, was *romanticism*. From its appearance in 1804, the word transcended mere literary usage and implied the active commitment of the human will to a new world view.[2] The proclamation of an ism suggested a new idea requiring active adherents—abstract beliefs in need of concrete commitment. Political content was added by the proclamation of the new and equally self-conscious ism of the next decade, *liberalism*.

But the terms romanticism and liberalism were not as revolutionary as the content of their adherents' manifestoes. Indeed, the jarring novelty of the broad movements we understand by those designations today was somewhat softened for contemporaries by the fact that the accompanying adjectives already had well-established, nonrevolutionary usages. There was no pretense that a romantic or a liberal person embodied in any basic sense some new doctrine requiring the special designation of a neologism such as romanticist or liberalist. The first new isms to create their own new *ists* were socialism and communism. These verbal talismans appeared with timetable punctuality at the beginning of the 1830s and 1840s respectively. But, unlike the liberalism of the 1820s, socialism and communism produced self-proclaimed socialists and communists. The old adjectives social and communal were clearly inadequate to describe the new commitment—in ways that earlier labels like democratic, republican, national, constitutional, and liberal were never felt to be.

The creation and propagation of sweeping new labels such as these was a hallmark of the social revolutionary tradition during the period between the revolutions of 1830 and 1848. Before telling their story, it is worth asking why the far more numerous and successful national revolutionaries of the same period produced no comparable verbal innovations. *Nationalisme*, a word coined in Barruel's widely read treatise of 1797, was rarely used by subsequent national revolutionaries, and does not appear in any major European lexicon until the *Larousse* of 1874.[3]

National revolutionaries, of course, used songs and symbols as much as words. They generally rebelled against any abstract social ideal, proclaimed an almost organic attachment to their own land and culture, and rejected slogans reflecting the rationalistic universalism of uprooted intellectuals. National revolutionaries were also more reluctant than social revolutionaries to adopt terms introduced with scorn and hatred by their opponents. Even Mazzini initially avoided and rarely used the term *nationalism*.[4] Romantic nationalists essentially preached an emotional gospel of love, drawing men of like heritage together into a new type of brotherhood. Social revolutionaries, in contrast, preached the rational restructuring of society. They were a small intellectual elite in search of a mass audience to rival that of the nationalists. Above all, they needed visibility, which could be attained even through negative publicity. This, and a slogan that inspired outrage in the nonrevolutionary, mass press, could be profoundly useful in attracting fresh attention to their ideal of radical social change.

The term *socialist* had a substantial prehistory of random usage as a term of abuse in the eighteenth century. In Italy, Rousseau was denounced as a socialist in 1765,[5] then as an antisocialist in 1803.[6] In France, a radical veteran of Babeuf's Conspiracy used the term socialist in 1797 as an insulting designation for a royalist chief of police.[7]

The word was apparently first used in its modern sense within Robert Owen's original circle of followers. Writing to Owen in November 1822, Edward Cowper urged the participation in a new utopian community of an unspecified person "well adapted to become what my friend Jo Applegath calls a socialist." [8] In 1827, Owen became the first to use it in print. "The chief question between the modern (or Mill and Malthus) political economists and the communionists or socialists," he wrote in *Cooperative Magazine*, is whether "capital should be owned individually or commonly." [9]

It was just after the Revolution of 1830 that *socialism* came into widespread positive usage for the first time, and it rapidly became one of the "sacramental words of the epoch." [10] The word was widely invoked in France during the 1830s just as *liberalism* was falling into disrepute through identification with the bourgeois monarchy.[11] It spread rapidly along with related words (socialize, socialization) and other, more ephemeral terms (societism, associationism) in 1831–33. Whether welcomed or cursed, socialism was generally seen as the necessary counter both to *individualism* and to a narrow preoccupation with purely political processes.[12] The first large public gathering to use the term extensively was a congress of scientists and philosophers at Nantes in April 1833, where "socialists" were contrasted with "political maniacs" (*politicomanes*), "who busy themselves with questions of the constitution rather than turning their eye to the social question." [13]

Another new ism that arose to challenge the alleged hollowness of political liberalism was *radicalism*. Already in the 1820s French thinkers had begun to take over the term radical from English utilitarian reformers.[14] Their idea that change should go to the very root (*radix*) of society had been intensified by the raising of expectations during the Revolution of 1830.[15] Radical was used increasingly in the late thirties —particularly after *republican* became an illegal term.[16] But soon radical, like liberal, began to suggest opposition to revolution. Théophile Thoré, a young revolutionary on trial in 1841, cited the case of a professed radical who announced at a banquet in Rouen early in 1839:

> We are revolutionaries. Yes, friends of the completed revolution in order to prevent new revolutions.[17]

The new word to which the youthful Thoré and his generation turned to vindicate the ideal of social revolution was *communism*.

In March 1840, a conservative German newspaper wrote:

> The Communists have in view nothing less than a levelling of society— substituting for the presently-existing order of things the absurd, immoral and impossible utopia of a community of goods.[18]

This, the earliest documented use of the term, already illustrates the repulsion mixed with fascination that the new concept inspired in European officialdom. Usage spread rapidly throughout Europe.[19] Another conservative German newspaper paid tribute three years later to the "immense power" and polemic passion that the word had come to generate:

> When hostile papers find themselves unable to touch a liberal newspaper, they reproach it for Communist tendencies. . . . One regards a Communist as a criminal against the property of another.[20]

In the 1840s, communism was more a presence in the minds of the propertied classes than an ideal—let alone a reality—for the proletariat. Its beginnings as a movement can clearly be traced to France in the late 1830s. The first formal usage of the term communist in Germany of 1840 alludes to preexistent French reality, and Cabet claimed in 1841 that communism began with discussions in French prisons after the arrests of 1834.[21] Although no written example has been found, the term almost certainly came into being during the late 1830s as one of several new French words derived from the revived Babeuvist term *communauté*. Thus any account of the birth of communism must begin with France.

French Founders

Communism as a new type of class-conscious, revolutionary movement originated in Lyon and Paris in the second half of the 1830s. With the suppression of the workers' movement in Lyon after the insurrection of 1834, a small number of proletarian leaders went underground in search of more extreme remedies. The secret "Society of Flowers" of 1836–38 has been called "the first Communist society"; [22] and it is clear that by 1838 in Lyon "exclusively working class societies had appeared." [23] Likewise in Paris, after the failure of the Blanquist insurrection in May 1839, a small and exclusively working-class organization was founded, the Society of Workers. It sought to sustain the hierarchical revolutionary organization of the Blanquist Society of Seasons, but dramatized its proletarian preoccupations by changing the units "week, month, and season" into "craft, shop, and factory." [24]

Communism as a political ideal and verbal talisman originated, however, not among workers but among intellectuals who provided leadership through smaller groups that arose within or out of these larger organizations. In Lyon, Joseph Benoît and two of the other original "flowers" formed late in 1838 a Committee of Equals to provide an egalitarian program for proletarian activity. Basically forming a society for peaceful propaganda, its members flirted with revolutionary activism, particularly after the visit to Lyon in April 1839 of Blanqui's flamboyant comrade-in-arms, Barbès.[25] Unlike almost all other revolutionaries in the first half of the nineteenth century, Benoît had considerable firsthand experience doing physical labor. Nevertheless, his own *Confessions of a Proletarian* indicated that the dominant formative influences on him were those that characteristically affected bourgeois revolutionary intellectuals: schooling in exile in Geneva, participation in a colorful range of occult circles, infatuation with Rousseau, and, finally, the discovery of Buonarroti's book on Babeuf while imprisoned in 1834.[26]

The decisive new ideological influence on Benoît and his restive colleagues in Lyon was Albert Laponneraye. His remarkable journal, *L'Intelligence*, was later designated "the first Communist organ in France," and Cabet called it at the time "the standard-bearer of the egalitarian party, the communist party." [27] Laponneraye's journal was popular not only in Lyon, but also in Geneva and Lausanne among former followers of Buonarroti, who were simultaneously forming the first movement to call itself communist in Switzerland.[28] *L'Intelligence* began appearing in September 1837, and acquired the aura of martyrdom when Laponneraye's principal collaborator, Richard Lahautière, was tried the following summer for an anti-Catholic article that added the word *Intelligence* to Liberty, Equality, Fraternity.[29] In his courtroom defense, he called for inscribing on "the proletarian banner these four organic words: charity, equality, fraternity, intelligence." [30] Freedom had vanished from the list—as it had in Blanqui's earlier proclamation of "Unity, Equality, Fraternity," [31] and would again in the first Communist Banquet on July 1, 1840, shortly after *L'Intelligence* had been forcibly shut.

"A new era has just begun for the world," the published account of this banquet for some one thousand artisans in the Belleville section of Paris proclaimed in bold italics.[32] A series of speakers proceeded to invoke the word communist for the first time in public, rejoicing that henceforth ordinary politicians (*routiniers politiques*) would never be able to "contain its explosive impact." [33] The words unity and equality recurred throughout the toasts. Their unity was to be "perfect," "indissoluble," and "unalterable"; [34] their equality, "real, perfect, and social." [35] Community, common happiness, and probity were substituted for liberty in the revolutionary trilogy.[36] The only toast that even used the word spoke of "a general and all-inclusive liberty . . . which cannot walk without leaning on its sister and companion equality." [37]

Liberty was thus crippled from the beginning by communists. Their preference for unity and equality was made clear by the senior co-sponsor and principal speaker at the banquet, the former priest Jean-Jacques Pillot. He called on all present to "lay down upon the altar of equality all sentiment contrary to the great unity." [38] He and the co-sponsor of the banquet, Théodore Dézamy, were *communistes immé-diats* [39]—and may be considered along with Laponneraye the true founders of modern communism.

Unlike Benoît and his colleagues from Lyon, these three Parisian jour-nalists were young intellectuals, divorced from personal contact with the working class. They were infatuated with the power of *Intelligence*, the very title of Laponneraye's journal; and it is hard to escape the suspicion that in some sense it was their own power they were seeking through intelligence. In the upwardly mobile atmosphere of the July monarchy, such youthful and bourgeois intellectuals represented the cutting edge of the "revolution of rising expectations." The story of their pilgrimage to the new communist ideal begins—chronologically and ideologically—with Laponneraye.

Laponneraye's *Intelligence* was the first journal successfully to trans-pose the revolutionary visions of middle-class intellectuals into an appealing revolutionary message for the working class. Laponneraye developed two of the three new ideas that the first communists intro-duced into French social thought: a class-oriented view of the French Revolution and a totalistic conception of popular education. He pro-vided a new view of the one historical event that had meaning for even the most illiterate worker, that is, the French Revolution.[40] He helped create a mythic view which has dominated subsequent communist his-toriography: the simultaneous glorification of both the political leader-ship of Robespierre and the socio-economic aspirations of the Parisian proletariat. These two elements had in fact often been in conflict, but they were unified retroactively in order to validate Laponneraye's own desire to provide elite leadership for proletarian power.

The deification of Robespierre was a final legacy of the old Buonar-roti to the new communists. In the last article Buonarroti wrote, "Ob-servations on Robespierre," he had reversed Babeuf's negative view of the dictator, and glorified him as the true successor to "Moses, Pythag-oras, Lycurgus, Jesus and Mohammed." Robespierre alone had fought "gangrene" in society and laid "the base to the majestic edifice of equal-ity and the popular republic." [41]

Laponneraye's popularly written works on French history presented the "incorruptible" Robespierre as a model for contemporary revolu-tionaries in his dedication to public over private interest.[42] Laponne-raye glorified the political style of the Committee of Public Safety and engrossed himself in the first systematic edition of Robespierre's works, which appeared in three volumes in 1840.[43]

But he went further, suggesting that the mission of the contemporary revolutionary was to combine Robespierre with Babeuf: authoritarian means with egalitarian ends. Babeuf's "agrarian law" was to be superseded by a more thorough "repartition, pro-rated according to need," designed to create a totalistic "community of rights, labors and duties." [44]

The second element in the birth of the communist ideal was a new concept of intellectuals and education. Laponneraye argued in his *Democratic Catechism* for "communal and unitary" indoctrination based on an alliance between "intelligence and labor." For him education was a means not just of spreading knowledge, but also of building a new type of human being "in the midst of a society that has turned gangrenous with egoism and corruption." [45] This new type of education sought "the annihilation of egoism" within man and the destruction within society of "this moral anarchy in which intelligences are drowned." [46]

This reference to "intelligences" as an animate plural marks the beginning of the fateful translation of the old idea of abstract intelligence into the modern ideal of an active intelligentsia. Revolutionary vindication is guaranteed by the gathering force of intelligence—a category always implicitly understood to begin with the writer and his readers.

Such intelligence must penetrate and unite with the masses in order to free them from bourgeois corruption, which takes the political form of "liberalism, the off-spring of Girondist federalism." [47] What is needed is "a radical revolution in ways of life." [48] For this revolution, the proletariat will play the role that the Third Estate assumed in 1789—by becoming conscious that it is nothing, and must become everything.[49]

This educational ideal was developed in an even more extreme manner by the second major figure in the birth of communism: Théodore Dézamy. In an essay of 1839 for a contest of the French Academy on the failure to translate Enlightenment into practical morality, the eighteen-year-old Dézamy called for a totally new type of mass education: "communal, egalitarian, harmonious . . . industrial and agricultural." [50] Elite education of all kinds must be abolished. The more education penetrated the masses "the more intelligence will come together." Strong central authority ("a good social mechanism") was required to unify theory and practice, combine mental and physical development, and fill everyone with new "habits of equality and fraternity." [51]

Dézamy argued that the social theorist-turned-revolutionary was the ideal "intelligence" for the new age—replacing the former hidden model of many social reformers: the medical doctor.

> There is no mirage more perfidious than to exalt medicine (or law or literature) over social science. . . . I would compare the doctor to a tailor who puts new cloth on an old suit, and in closing a small hole opens up a larger one.[52]

Such writings announce the third and most important new element in the birth of communism: the metaphysical. Dézamy, a poor young student from Dijon, became in Paris during the early 1840s perhaps the first truly ideological social revolutionary in modern history. He imbued a tempestuous outpouring of pamphlets with an intensified belief in universalism and atheism, the antitheses of the dominant nationalism and religiosity of the age. He developed (before Marx and independently of the Germans) an inner certainty that he was building both the final science and the perfect society.

Armed with such conviction, Dézamy developed a polemic style that was qualitatively different from previous petty wrangling over the details of utopias or the motives of personalities. He stressed the need to discipline intellect for the task of revolution. Leaders of the coming revolution would be neither "believers" (*croyants*) in any religion nor the "wise men" (*savants*) to whom even Buonarroti had looked, but a new type of engaged intellectual: the "knowing ones" (*sachants*) for whom "the aim of philosophy . . . is to conduct men to happiness . . . by science." [53]

The first task of the *sachant* was to rescue the "primordial truths, general principles" of communism from the sentimental distortions of it by the two most famous people identified with the label at the beginning of the 1840s: the venerable Lamennais and the literary prophet of communism (whom Dézamy had once served as personal secretary), Etienne Cabet.

Dézamy had initially joined these two in a united front of social revolutionary opposition to the rise of officially sponsored nationalism that followed the Blanquist insurrection of May 1839, the subsequent war scare with Germany, and the move from restrained occupation to full conquest of Algeria. Dézamy collaborated with Cabet in an antinationalist compendium of 1840, *French Patriots, Read and Blush with Shame*; [54] and Lamennais denounced the government's stationing of military forces in forts around Paris as "new Bastilles." [55] Lamennais became the first in a long line of idealistic radicals to be denounced by governing authorities as "communist" [56]—but was soon denounced in even stronger terms by Dézamy for not being communist enough. Dézamy's excoriating pamphlet of 1841, *Mr. Lamennais refuted by himself*, sought to expunge religiosity from the communist label.[57] His pamphlet of the following year, *Slanders and Politics of Mr. Cabet*, criticized the vacillation (*girouettisme*) of his former mentor, and argued—for the first time—that ideological, and not merely political, discipline was necessary for communism.[58]

At issue once again was form as well as content, roles as well as rules. Cabet had established himself as *the* oracular interpreter of the new communist label. He had to be discredited if he were to be supplanted. He had attained his status through the highly traditional means of creating a literary utopia on an imaginary island (in *Voyage to Icaria* of 1839–40) and presenting a secularized version of a religious credo (in *Communist Credo* of 1841). Dézamy's alternative was his *Code de la Communauté* of 1842. Unlike Cabet's evocative, moralistic *Credo*, Dézamy used the radical Enlightenment model of a rational "code" in the manner of Morelly's and Buonarroti's *Code of Nature*. Unlike Cabet's fanciful *Icaria* Dézamy's prosaic picture concentrated on the material means of attaining the communist end. He began with a quote from Hobbes ("In the community morality comes from things and not from men") and ended with a fold-out chart of a "communal palace" where the communized men of the future would live. In between lay an extended discussion of the rationality and inevitability of social revolution against the compromises of reformist politics on the one hand and the diversion of national revolution on the other.

Dézamy insisted that a communist revolution must immediately confiscate all property and money rather than rely on Cabet's pacifistic education and taxation measures. "With half measures you will not succeed in satisfying anyone." [59] Swift and total change would be less bloody than a slow process, since communism releases the natural goodness of man and "has no plan, no need of employing violence and constraint." [60]

In contrasting his "unitary communism" with Cabet's "Icarian Communism," Dézamy revealed once again the recurring impulse of the revolutionary mentality for radical simplification. In the society of the future there would be one global *congrès humanitaire*,[61] a single language (preferably a neutral, dead language like Latin),[62] and a single form of service as "industrial athletes," [63] who would transform all tasks of construction into communal youth festivals. *"Travailleurs, unissons-nous!"* [64] Dézamy called out in anticipation of the Marxist "Workers of the world, unite!" As an apostle of unity and simplicity, Dézamy denounced the "politics of diversion" which seeks "to detach and distract the workers from egalitarian and communist theories." [65]

The logic of radical simplicity led Dézamy to insist that just as communism was "unitary," its victory would be universal. "Finished Communism" would exist only in a "universal country" [66] that will supersede not just nationalism (which "imprisons equality in the narrow circle of an egoistic nationality") [67] but also any other divisive allegiances such as *famillisme*.[68] There would be no "new holy alliance against the first government embracing Communism," [69] because its ideological appeal would spread rapidly and create "the universal community." [70] Conflict among "unitary Communists" was logically impossible:

> No, no, there can be no splits among Communists; our struggles among ourselves can only be struggles of harmony, or reasoning. . . .[71]

"Communitarian principles" contained "the solution to all problems." [72] The original French Revolution failed because it did not realize that such principles were "the most powerful and most sublime arm for cutting down the enemies that had to be vanquished." Communism was

> . . . the sole, the unique means of destroying, of guillotining in a stroke, not men, not your brothers, but on the contrary all the vices.[73]

Dézamy thus anticipated both the Maoist concept that only "nonantagonistic contradictions" are possible among communists and the high Stalinist idea that killing dissenters is always portrayed as the ritual expulsion of some impersonal form of vice.

An alarmed French police investigator described Dézamy's *Code* as a blueprint for *"la communauté rigoureuse, mathématique et immédiate."* [74] His arrest and trial in 1844 attracted and inspired the most radical foreign intellectuals then in Paris: Arnold Ruge, Moses Hess, and Karl Marx among the Germans and Nicholas Speshnev among the Russians.[75]

In addition to their examples as martyrs, the French founders left behind a legacy of unalterable opposition to supernatural religion. Dézamy's last three major works argued in the course of 1845–46 for a materialist and atheist worldview to supplant Catholicism for "the organization of universal well-being." [76] Already in his prize essay of 1839, Dézamy had spoken of "this sublime devotion which constitutes socialism" [77] and bid the "unhappy proletarians"

> . . . reenter into the gyre of the egalitarian church, *outside of which there can be no salvation.*[78]

For Dézamy—as for his admirer Karl Marx—the atheism of his mature years was not "just an historical or biographical accident," but "an essential premise of his whole theory." [79] The former priest Pillot went even further with his insistence that "Equals know neither God nor the devil." [80]

British Influence

Communism was transnational as well as antinationalist. If the French pioneers soon had German followers, they themselves had drawn more than is generally realized on English sources. England had become important in the repressive atmosphere of the late 1830s as a secure place for revolutionary émigrés to meet each other and publish freely. The Chartist movement in its early, semi-insurrectional stage provided an inspirational example for the awakening political imagination on the continent. By far the most important British catalyst on the early communists, however, was Robert Owen, who decisively influenced two very different founding fathers of modern communism: Etienne Cabet and Goodwyn Barmby.

Cabet spent most of the 1830s in exile in England, where he first published clandestinely in 1839, his enormously influential *Voyage to Icaria*. The novelistic form of his *Voyage* was largely taken from English models,[81] and the content was deeply influenced by the secular sobriety of Owen, who provided Cabet with a rationalistic alternative to the romantic socialism of Fourier, which had hitherto dominated the French imagination.

Owen imparted a new, secular confidence that human nature could be transformed through a cooperative environment. He also preached a lofty contempt for democratic reformism, calling instead for a social transformation outside politics and beyond political borders. His Association of All Classes of All Nations, founded in 1835, was "the first organized socialist movement in England" [82] and a beacon for foreign refugees like Cabet. Owen presented a rationalistic alternative to the romantic moralism of the "prophets of Paris" and appealed to those who, like Cabet, had difficulty relating to the parliamentary perspectives of Whig reformers and Chartist radicals. Owen was a successful manufacturer who had founded concrete, cooperative enterprises on an allegedly scientific basis in both Britain and America. Bitterly attacked by the visionary Fourierists, Owen attracted some support from the more scientistic Saint-Simonians, whose journal published in 1826 the first French discussion of Owen's "System of Mutual Cooperation and Community of Goods." [83]

French Fourierists, in search of a more rational basis for unity, allied with Owenites in 1834–35. One Fourierist complained in May 1834 that the dream of *"un grand parti socialiste"* was still far away.[84] In lodging the complaint, he defined the new ideal, which was brought into being by Owen's principal apostle in France, the youthful editor Jules Gay. A disillusioned Fourierist, Gay journeyed to London in 1835 seeking in Owenism a more scientific and revolutionary doctrine. He persuaded Owen to visit Paris in 1837 with the objective of setting up a *Maison Harmonienne* to unify Saint-Simonianism, Fourierism, and Owenism. Owen also met with Buonarroti shortly before his death, and was feted by the Masonic editor who headed the Universal Statistical Society. The sole organizational result was the establishment of a small French affiliate of Owen's Association of All Classes of All Nations.[85]

Owen had earlier introduced and popularized terms like *communionist* and *communional*.[86] His remarkable book of "Social Hymns" to be sung in the "Halls of Science" of new cooperative communities invoked the word repeatedly and lyrically:

> Community doth all possess
> That can to man be given:
> Community is happiness
> Community is heaven.[87]

Increasing public attacks on Owen's atheism only intensified the master's anticlericalism. In 1839, he changed the name of his association to Universal Community Society of Rational Religionists. At the same time, his teaching of scientific egalitarian community as the true goal of humanity provided new inspiration—through Gay—for those Frenchmen in the 1839–40 period—Dézamy and his associates—who introduced the term communist.[88] Moreover, as far afield as Russia, the *Pocket Dictionary* of the radical Petrashevsky circle used Owenism as its "Aesopian" entry for communism in 1846. Cabet himself, moreover, was so deeply influenced by Owen that the Icarian Communism he brought back from England to France has been described by the leading authority as "merely Owenism Frenchified." [89] Cabet returned to London in 1847 to seek Owen's direct sanction for his project to organize communist emigration to America. Owen in turn went to revolutionary Paris in March 1848; and his pamphlets there calling for a total social reorganization were denounced by the indigenous French Left as "Communist." [90] Owen's final call for a new community "of all classes, all parties and all religions" [91] was echoed in Gay's short-lived journal of 1849, *Le Communiste*.

Cabet may also have derived his belief in the need for a revolutionary dictatorship from another British (or more properly, Irish) thinker, Bronterre O'Brien.[92] But Owen's emphasis on peaceful education kept Cabet from developing O'Brien's linkage of social revolution with Robespierrist dictatorship into the full-blown authoritarianism of Dézamy and the younger generation in France. Meanwhile, another Englishman, Goodwin Barmby gave a more exotic, religious twist to the pacific Owenite ideal and in the 1840s became perhaps the most prolific—and surely the most forgotten—propagandist for communism anywhere.

Christian Fantasies: Barmby

John Goodwyn (usually called Goodwin) Barmby first popularized the term communism in England, linking it with inventive fantasies that were bizarre even for this period of florid social theory.

Armed with a letter of introduction from Robert Owen, he journeyed as a twenty-year-old youth to Paris in 1840, seeking to escape from the "melee of competition" and the limitations of narrow nationalism [93] by establishing "regular communication between the socialists of Great Britain and France." [94] Calling himself "the friend of Socialism in France, in England, and the world," he promised to gather material for a definitive history of socialism and of "all the systems of community" ever devised.[95]

He used the word "community" to suggest rational Owenite organization as an antidote to Fourierist romanticism. "A Community is preferable to a Phalanstère," he had proclaimed prior to his departure from England; [96] but upon arrival in Paris, Barmby was soon caught up in a whirl of Fourierist activities including socialist discussion groups, Fourierist concerts, and lectures on phrenology and "societarian science" in "community coffee houses." [97]

On June 20, Barmby presented "the prospectus and papers of a proposed 'International Association for the promotion of mutual intercourse among all Nations' for which society a provisional committee was lately formed, under the presidentship of an ardent friend of human progressism, in Paris." [98] The Association was designed for people from all countries and limited "neither to sect or party." [99] Although nothing more is known about it, this lost document may well have been the first outline of an international communist organization. It appears likely that its French president was Jules Gay.[100] Barmby was pleased to report back to the Owenites in England that the communist banquet organized by Dézamy and Pillot at Belleville on July 1 served "the community and not the *Phalanstère*." [101]

Though Barmby later claimed to have invented the word communist,[102] his totemistic fascination with the word appears to have begun only after he realized that "the public journals are all on fire at the Communist dinner at Belleville." [103] Barmby was determined not to let the fire go out, and he began tracing "the movements of the communists" in Paris for his English Owenite readers.[104] The French government immediately prohibited any further communist banquets in Paris. But smaller banquets were held in Rouen and Lyon; and Barmby announced late in August that a second communist banquet was to be held at the Institute of Childhood directed by Jules Gay's wife: a *grand Fête* in "about a month" to be built around the secular marriage ceremonies of leading communists. Such hopes came to naught with the government crackdown in the face of widespread strikes late in the summer and the attempted assassination of the king early in the autumn.

On his return to England, Barmby went wild with the new-found label. He founded a Communist Propaganda Society (soon renamed the Universal Communitarian Society)[105] and a journal, *The Promethean or Communitarian Apostle* (soon renamed *The Communist Chronicle*). He described communism as the "societarian science" and the final religion of humanity. His *Credo* proclaimed:

> . . . I believe . . . that the divine is communism, that the demoniac is individualism. . . .[106]

He wrote communist hymns and prayers,[107] called for the building of Communitariums,[108] under a supreme Communarchy headed by an elected Communarch and Communarchess.[109] He called himself "Pontifarch of the Communist Church,"[110] proclaimed the "religion of COMMUNISM,"[111] called for the rejection of Christ's claim to messiahship, and defined communism as a new fusion of Judaism with "Christianism."[112]

In March 1842, Barmby set forth the first communist theory of history: a scheme based on four ages of humanity (an early pastoral stage, "paradization," which leads through feudalization and civilization to "communization"). There were to be four successive stages of communization (from a club or lodge through common production unit and communal city to a total communist society).[113] He instituted a new calendar and proclaimed a new vegetarian diet. From his central communitarium at Harnwell he called for a restoration of the church lands confiscated by Henry VIII—not to the monasteries of the past, but to his "communisteries" of the future.[114]

Barmby soon attracted the backing and counsel of a radical Chartist journalist, Thomas Frost, who transferred Barmby's publications to the veteran printer of the Left, Henry Hetherington. Barmby took advantage of Weitling's arrival in London to increase the size of his "communion" from 70 to 130. He wrote *Book of Platonopolis*, combining traditional utopian motifs (Platonopolis was the name given by Hupay to his original "philosophical community" of 1779) with scientific projections for the future (including some yet to be realized such as a steam-driven automobile). He drew up a list of forty-four Societarian Wants for humanity and a plan of action that rapidly became almost global. He went on a proselyting lecture tour of the north, visited and placed special hopes on Ireland, spoke of five territorial groups for missionary work, and began working through "living correspondents" in Paris, Lyon, Lausanne, Cologne, New York, and Cincinnati.[115] He attached special importance to the plans of his correspondent John Wattles, who founded a communist church near Cincinnati and offered to supply grain to European communists. He sought links with radical sectarians planning to set up an egalitarian commune in Venezuela. But, since they saw themselves only as a political-economic society, they could be considered only "approximate Communists" and a "congregation," not a true "communion" of total spiritual commitment.[116]

Barmby saw communism rendering politics as such obsolete, and he appears to have been the first to use a phrase incorrectly attributed to others:

> In the future, government politics will be succeeded by industrial administration.[117]

In his manic desire to realize heaven on at least a little part of earth, Barmby was driven to the outer islands of the British archipelago. On the Isle of Wight in 1844, he began devising plans for a model "communitarium" on the Island of Sark. From there, he dreamed of establishing "a community of printing and agriculture" throughout the Channel Islands. Nothing came of it, and the more practical Frost rebelled and founded a *Communist Journal* to rival Barmby's *Communist Chronicle*. Barmby in turn began the long history of communist excommunications. Viewing Frost's adoption of the word "Communist" as "an infringement of his copyright" Barmby formally forbade its further use in a document that was "sealed with a seal of portentous size, engraved with masonic symbols in green wax, green being the sacred color of the Communist Church."[118]

Isolated in his own fantasies, Barmby retreated to yet another island, the Isle of Man, to publish his *Apostle* in 1848. No one there or anywhere else appears, however, to have submitted to the bizarre initiation ritual that he prescribed to separate the "approximate" communists from the real ones. His four-staged suggested baptismal rite was to begin with a cold bath (the Frigidary), followed by a hot one (the Calidary), a warm one (the Tepidary), and then vigorous exercise (the Frictionary). All of this was then followed by anointment with oil and perfume: a secular chrism designed to prepare the candidate for "the divine communiverse."[119]

From dreams of an international movement (where progress was recorded nation by nation in his column "Communist Intelligence"), Barmby moved on to become the first to speak of "*National* Communism."[120] After a brief visit to Paris during the Revolution of 1848, he became a Unitarian minister, a friend of Mazzini, and a defender of national rather than social revolution.

His colorful mélange of secular utopianism and Christian ritual is illustrated by the subtitle of his journal of the forties: "The Apostle of the Communist Church and the Communitive Life: Communion with

God, Communion of the Saints, Communion of Suffrages, Communion of Works and Communion of Goods." Within his short-lived "Communist Church," Barmby saw the struggle for Communism in apocalyptical terms:

> In the holy Communist Church, the devil will be converted into God. . . . And to this conversion of Satan doth God call peoples . . . in that Communion of suffrages, of works, and of goods both spiritual and material . . . for these latter days.[121]

Thus, this pioneering communist proclaimed the death of the devil as decisively as later Communists were to announce the death of God.

The rush to heaven on earth was, predictably, led by the Poles. In a book called *Future of the Workers* a Pole named Jean Czynski, the most revolutionary of the Fourierists, was the first to suggest systematically that socialism was to be realized by workers rather than intellectuals. Barmby translated the book into English.[122] Cabet was even more dependent on another Polish émigré, the remarkable self-educated peasant, Ludwik Królikowski. He was Cabet's close collaborator, and the first to popularize a Christianized version of the new communist ideal in his extraordinary journal *Poland for Christ*.[123]

In 1840 the first French journal conceived and edited by workers, *L'Atelier*, proclaimed to "revolutionary workers," that "My kingdom is not now of this world"[124] and carried an engraving of "Christ preaching fraternity to the world."[125] Christ stood atop the globe trampling the serpent of egoism beneath his feet and brandishing a ribbon saying "fraternity" between angels in phrygian caps labelled "equality" and "liberty"[126]—the iconography of the Holy Trinity blended with the trinitarian slogan of revolution.

Other French revolutionary journals of the 1840s spoke of protest banquets as "holy tables" and "holy communisions."[127] The infusion of Christian ideas represented for many "not the degradation of Christian faith, but the regaining of religious enthusiasm."[128]

In Germany, this tendency to identify communism with religion was widespread and more distinctively Christian. The only books cited by Weitling in his manifesto for the League of the Just, *Humanity as it is and as it should be*, were the Bible and Lamennais's *Words of a Believer*. Propagandists were aided by the tendency to identify communism with communion,[129] and by the rhyming of *Jesu Christ* with *Kommunist* in German.[130] An 1842 pamphlet in Paris by one of Weitling's followers called for a new "community of brotherly love" and mutual assistance to bring "pure Christianity" into being among the workers.[131] Another follower penned a utopian dream of the new communist order in the same year, bearing a title that harkened back to the Book of Revelation, but was to be revived by Hitler: *The Thousand-Year Kingdom (Reich)*.[132] Religious fervor helped Weitling's Swiss Communist movement attain by 1843 some 750 German members in thirteen separate associations plus 400 French-speaking members.[133]

Barmby purported to find Weitling's communism "not a faith but a universal science," [134] and urged Weitling to go to Ireland to spread the new revolutionary doctrine. [135] The arrest and trial of Weitling in 1843 and his subsequent expulsion from Switzerland embittered the original communists and inclined many towards an increasingly tough-minded and secular point of view. But religious themes remained powerful in the German movement, [136] and played a more important role in the revolutionary ferment of 1848–51 in Germany than is generally realized. [137]

Indeed, communism probably would not have attracted such instant attention without this initial admixture of Christian ideas. This infusion (1) made credible the inherently implausible idea that a totally different social order was possible "on earth as it is in heaven"; (2) convinced many that this new "Communist" order would fuse Babeuvist *communauté* with Christian communion; and thus, (3) helped for the first time make a transnational social ideal compelling to significant numbers of pious working people.

This debt to religious ideas usually remains unacknowledged or obscured by revolutionary and communist historians—if not condemned out of hand as a retrograde flight from reality. But this turn to religion would seem to represent a "progressive" stage in the development of revolutionary movements—moving beyond the utopian experiments and speculations of Fourierist and Saint-Simonian intellectuals. Religious ideas activated the moral and social consciousness of a hitherto largely passive working class and helped secular intellectuals "in the passage from utopia to reality." [138] For simple workers, it was easier to rally to a communism allegedly founded by "the sublime egalitarian" whose first communion was "the image of future banquets" for a communist society. [139]

The hope for an international communist organization of a quasi-religious nature was advanced by Barmby for a brief time in the immediate aftermath of Weitling's arrival in London in 1844. This "grand event" should "lay the basis by which the Communist Church in England and the Communist Church in Germany can act in concert together." Barmby publicly corresponded with "the Primarchs of the Communist Church of Ireland" about the possibility of a joint missionary trip there with Weitling.

But already by 1845, the tide was turning to precisely the irreligious communism that Barmby feared. [140] Schapper, the most religious leader of the League of the Just, insisted against Weitling in that year that "nothing transcendent" be mixed in with their political discussions; [141] and an Italian in Paris noted at the same time the rise of "the speculative and practical atheism of the Communists." [142] The formation of the League of Communists in December 1847 represented the merger of the two key communist groups opposed to the religiosity of Weitling and Barmby: the London League of the Just and the Communist Correspondence Committee of Brussels. The revolutionary atheism that Karl Marx derived from Ludwig Feuerbach was the new unifying force.

Flight to America?

If the denial of God's heaven was essential to European revolutionary doctrine, so too was the rejection of the belief in a heaven on earth in America. Throughout the nineteenth century, Europeans had escaped defeated revolutions in the Old World by fleeing to the land of successful revolution in the New. Some came in person like Kościuszko; others by proxy like Bonneville, who sent his wife and son when he himself was imprisoned by Napoleon. The revolutionaries provided sinew for the new state. If Kościuszko helped design the battlements and early military manuals for West Point, Bonneville's son became one of its legendary early graduates—the first in a long list of former European revolutionaries to be military leaders in both the Mexican and Civil wars. Bonneville's wife, Margaret, became the companion of Thomas Paine in his last years. His son Benjamin was the aide to Lafayette on his visit to America in 1825–26 and an explorer of the Far West celebrated in Washington Irving's book of 1837: *The Adventures of Captain Bonneville*. Thus, Bonneville's own revolutionary career, which drew its original romantic inspiration from Schiller's plays as well as early revolutionary events in Paris, trailed off into literary romance as well as military history in America.

Flight to America was, thus, a tradition among European revolutionaries. When a number of European communists were to challenge Cabet over this issue in the late 1840s, some of the luster was to be removed from this option.

After the arrest of Weitling and the widespread trials and investigations of 1843, Cabet, as the best-known propagandist of the communist ideal, had faced the problem of giving leadership to the inchoate movement. His attempts to rally broad support against the communist trials of the mid-1840s in France led him to seek some form of transnational organization. He solicited the collaboration of both French and Germans in London for establishing a communal center of five to twenty members to coordinate international propaganda for communism.[143] However, he soon conceived a plan for establishing a much larger settlement in America. He turned his energy to enlisting twenty to thirty thousand "communists" for a massive emigration to America. He envisaged this voyage to a New World "Icaria" not just as an escape, but as an attempt "to create a new direction" for the European movement as well.[144]

In so doing, Cabet was only expanding on the tradition established by followers of Fourier and Owen, whose major communal experiments had also been founded in America. Indeed, he planned to visit Owen, "the venerable patriarch of English Communism," in England during 1847 to secure a kind of blessing for his project.

Cabet's project was, however, criticized by the Germans in London, who insisted that communism be set up in Europe instead.[145] The Londoners were echoing the harsh denunciation by Marx the year before of Hermann Kriege, the leading German revolutionary editor in America, for suggesting that the proletariat could gain a fresh start by settling the empty spaces in America. Marx's position had been supported by all of the Communist Correspondence Committee in Brussels except Weitling, who had already left to join Kriege in America.[146]

In arguing for revolution in Europe rather than flight to America, the German communists in London echoed in amplified form a Buonarrotian position of the 1830s that had gone almost unnoticed outside narrow conspiratorial circles. The Buonarrotians in Paris had opposed the flight of Saint-Simonians to the East as escapism; and, almost alone among active European revolutionaries of the 1830s, they remained hostile to the American experiment. This attitude was expressed by unprecedented attacks on the two most admired European participants in the American Revolution who had subsequently become semilegendary figures: Kościuszko and Lafayette.[147]

In any case, it was the fact that nineteenth-century America absorbed rather than rearmed the many revolutionaries who came to her shores. (The numbers increased sharply after the revolutions of 1848 failed in Europe.) Cabet's Icarian communists settled first in Texas, then in Nauvoo, Illinois; soon quarreled among themselves; then melted into the larger society, as had earlier secular utopians in the New World. Cabet died in St. Louis in 1856, rejected by his few remaining followers.

The only serious movement of social revolutionaries to reach America was the First International, which, however, did not arrive until 1872 after it had already fallen apart and needed a decent place of burial. And when the First International formally collapsed in Philadelphia in 1876, hardly anyone in America even noticed. Erstwhile revolutionaries had become new Americans; and popular attention was fixed on the centennial celebrations in the same city—the city of America's own, quite different revolution.

The continuing struggle "between the proletariat and their oppressors" was to be fought—as the Buonarrotians had foreseen—primarily in Europe. Indeed, the only revolutionary movement to be based in America in the last half of the nineteenth century was the narrowly national Irish Republican Brotherhood.[148]

There is irony in all this, because the original American Revolution had given birth to the radically new idea that a purely political party—without religious or dynastic sanctions—could be the legitimate object of supreme, if not total, human dedication. In the aftermath of independence, Americans had developed intense political passions and "party spirit" as they sought substance for the political life required by their new Constitution.[149] In the course of the nineteenth century, however, America increasingly defined parties more in terms of shared material interests than of shared spiritual ideas, and measured "party spirit" by precisely the kind of reformist electoral activity that by the 1840s the rising generation of European social revolutionaries had come to hate. It is not, therefore, surprising that the political event that most preoccupied even former revolutionaries in America in 1876 was not the last congress of the First International but the purely American and nonideological controversy between Republicans and Democrats over the disputed Hayes-Tilden election. Nor is it surprising that European social revolutionaries in the post-Jacksonian 1840s had not looked to American models in their efforts finally to form a party. In the repressive atmosphere on the eve of 1848, it was difficult for Europeans to share the distinctively American political faith of John Adams that "the blessings of society depend entirely on the constitutions of government." [150] The first attempt by communists to form a party and develop "party spirit" grew not out of the old hopes of the New World, but out of new hopes in the Old World.

The new party for which Marx wrote his manifesto late in 1847 was a largely imaginative anticipation of the more substantial "party of a new type," complete with sacrificial "party spirit" (*partiinost'*), which Lenin created in 1903. Communists of the 1840s had even less impact on the revolution which followed in 1848 than did Lenin's Bolsheviks on the Revolution of 1905. There is, nevertheless, a special importance to studying this first appearance of a communist party in human history. It is an event that should play for later communists something of the role that the Incarnation—or perhaps Pentecost—plays for Christians.

Ecclesia: A New Party

French social thinkers had long dreamt of a political party of an altogether different type from the quarreling factions of the restoration. They wanted a party faithful to "the movement" that had produced the original revolution: [151] an association that had both higher principles and deeper roots than the bourgeois politicians of the July monarchy. The rallying cries of the pre-1830 revolutionaries—constitution, republic, liberalism—were increasingly rejected; but the new generation in the late 1830s and early 1840s was not yet quite ready to accept a direct call for social revolution. Instead, they turned back to the old term of the 1790s: democracy—often fortifying it with the adjectives true or revolutionary. Democracy was associated with the unfulfilled hopes—social as well as political—of the French revolutionary tradition.[152] The term had also acquired romantic new identification with "the people" in Lamennais's sense of the unenfranchised and unfed masses.

Victor Considérant transformed Fourierism into a new socialist political movement by changing the title of his journal from *Phalange* to *Peaceful Democracy*. He spoke of the need for a "social party" to fulfill the needs of a "modern democracy." [153] It was in rivalry to Considérant's *Manifesto of Peaceful Democracy* that Karl Marx wrote his *Communist Manifesto* late in 1847. Marx was seeking to create just such an ideological "social party"—but it was to be revolutionary rather than peaceful, communist rather than socialist. Like Considérant, however,

Marx believed his new party would also be in some sense democratic. It was the international organization of Fraternal Democrats in Brussels that first drew Marx into the discussions about communism with Weitling and others, and it was in the buildings of the Fraternal Democrats in London that the Communist League continued to meet until the police repression in the summer of 1848.[154]

Renewed Democracy

The idea that communism was the fulfillment of democracy excited a new generation of French revolutionary publicists in the early forties. The more authoritarian the early communist writers became in their revolutionary plans, the more insistent they were on the "democratic" nature of these plans. Pierre Leroux led the way, proclaiming that total democracy was the only possible sanction for modern authority and insisting that democracy was not only a "sacred word," [155] but a "religion" [156] capable of providing "a peaceful solution of the problem of the proletariat." [157] He led George Sand and Louis Blanc into popular journalism through his *Revue Indépendante* during 1841–48.

The new radical journalists, however, were having difficulty translating this sacred symbol—democracy—into political reality. Théophile Thoré was thrown into prison in 1840 for telling *The Truth about the Democratic Party*, which was that it must serve "the interest of the most numerous and deserving classes, of the working people." [158] Convinced that many "Communists are in the great democratic current," [159] Thoré persevered in trying to connect the two movements in Leroux's journal [160]—prompting a rebuke from the possessive Cabet, *The Democrat turned Communist in spite of himself.*[161]

Out of the more radical new communist journals which had sprung up in 1841, that is, *L'Humanitaire* and *La Fraternité*, first came the unequivocal suggestion that the "democratic party" must in the modern era be a "communist party." Most of these original communists were little more than twenty years old. They felt that the promise of 1830 had been betrayed, and that even their older mentors, Cabet and Leroux, might be in danger of "decapitating the future." [162] It seems appropriate that the first use of the term *Communist Party* appears to have been by the journal of the young Dézamy announcing the death of Buonarroti's last old comrade-in-arms, Voyer D'Argenson in August 1842.[163]

A Franco-German Alliance

As for the Young Hegelians in Germany, it was not until they began to look toward their counterparts in France that they became truly revolutionary.[164] The original link between the Young Hegelians and the new generation of French social revolutionaries had been Moses Hess, the Paris correspondent of *Die Rheinische Zeitung*. He had suggested that the German drive for philosophical freedom could be realized only through the social equality that the French had called for,[165] and he had intended in the 1830s to write a biography of Babeuf.[166] Influenced also by the Saint-Simonians, he urged in his *European Triarchy* of 1840 a progressive alliance of Prussia with England and France.[167] He was then drawn by Cieszkowski to the Young Hegelians.[168] A new series of articles in 1841, beginning with "Socialism and Communism" and "The Philosophy of Action," launched the long effort to provide a philosophical basis for communism.[169] As a Jew—and later a founding father of Zionism—Hess lent to his belief in communism a messianic fervor looking forward not just to a change of government but to a kind of political "end of days."

Some creative fusion of the two main Western sources of revolutionary inspiration, the French and the German traditions, was a possibility particularly thirsted for by the Russians. Belinsky in 1840 hailed Heinrich Heine, the radical German poet living in Paris, as "a German Frenchman—precisely what Germany now needs most of all." [170] Bakunin's summons to violent upheaval was published under a French pseudonym in the *German Yearbook* of 1842. Another Russian, Bakunin's future friend and sometime collaborator, Alexander Herzen, hailed that article as evidence of the emerging alliance between French politics and German philosophy, "the beginning of a great phase of activization [*Betätigung*]" of the European revolutionary movement.[171]

The editor of the *German Yearbook*, Arnold Ruge, expressed the hope that Bakunin's article would make "some sluggards get up from their beds of laurels" and begin working for "a great practical future." [172] Ruge played a central role as the oldest of the "young" Hegelians, bringing with him an aura of martyrdom from having spent most of the 1820s in prison. His *Halle Yearbook of German Science and Art* in 1840 provided the first authoritative vehicle for declaring the victory of the revolutionary "philosophy of action" over the contemplativeness of previous German philosophy.[173] His rapid succession of journalistic experiments became the medium for this "philosophy of action," just as treatises and lectures had been the medium for the earlier "contemplative" philosophy. His *Halle Yearbook* became the *German Yearbook*, which in turn gave birth among his followers late in 1841 to *Die Rheinische Zeitung*: a deliberate challenge in the newspaper world to the conservative *Kölnische Zeitung*. In 1843, Ruge began to give the Hegelian "party" a revolutionary political line by seeking to "cleanse" Hegelianism of Hegel's own moderate liberalism and by urging Germany to "transform liberalism into democracy." [174]

Thus he introduced the Germans to the French communists' polemic technique of juxtaposing true democracy and false liberalism. He was soon forced to begin a hegira of Hegelians to Paris. He had fled from Prussia in 1841, only to be banished from Saxony (and to see *Rheinische Zeitung* shut) early in 1843. Next he moved to Zurich and then (after considering Strasbourg and Brussels) to Paris, where together with Karl Marx he founded in 1844 the short-lived *Deutsche-Französische Jahrbücher*. Excited as were most Germans by the Parisian atmosphere, Ruge argued that the Young Hegelians would in the new age of *praxis* provide political organization and critical education for the coming social revolution.

Enter Karl Marx

The man who came closest to fulfilling this task was Ruge's young journalistic protégé, Karl Marx. The decisive works in which it was performed were Marx's lengthy critique of Hegel's *The Philosophy of Right*, written in the summer of 1843, and his introduction of the following year to the same work. In criticizing Hegel's last and most political work, Marx applied for the first time his so-called transformative method —reversing the role of matter and spirit—to politics. In the introduction, he used "proletariat" and "communist" for the first time as labels of liberation.[175]

Hegel had contended that beyond subjective "civil society" lay a higher and more universal social objective: the state. The identification of the state as "the march of God through history" may represent the overenthusiasm of the auditor whose notes on Hegel's lecture were posthumously turned into *The Philosophy of Right*. Hegel was, in any case, speaking of an ideal, rather than an existing German state. Nevertheless, Hegel did see a universally liberating mission for the state and for its dedicated "universal class" (*der allgemeine Stand*): the disinterested bureaucracy.

Marx turned this analysis on its head by beginning with states as they actually existed in 1843. Hegel had seen civil society as the imperfect anticipation of an ideal state. Marx described the state as a degraded expression of the controlling material interests in "civil society"—the term *bürgerliche Gesellschaft* now acquiring some of the overtones of "bourgeois" as well as "civil" society. The state bureaucracy was the agent of venal interests rather than of any universal mission.

The concept of a "universal class" was revived a year later in Marx's introduction to Hegel's work, and applied to the "proletariat"—a term that Marx used for the first time in this purely philosophical, Hegelian sense. The "abolition of private property," which the proletariat was to accomplish, was not initially related to any analysis of either capitalism as a whole or the proletariat in particular.

The liberating mission of the proletariat was, however, closely related to the establishment of "true" democracy by universal suffrage. Venal civil society controlled the state through the institution of property, and even advanced forms of representative governments maintained a property requirement for the vote. Universal suffrage would accompany and insure the advent of universal property. The abolition (*Aufhebung*, also meaning uplifting and transforming) of property would also involve the abolition of the state. As with proletariat, Marx first used "communistic" in this philosophical-political context. The abolition of the old political system through universal suffrage would, Marx insisted, "bring out the true communistic aspect of men."

Thus, Marx related the achievement of communism to the cause of universal suffrage. At the same time, the universality which Hegel expected to realize in the ideal state must now be realized instead by abolishing the existing state. Like other radical Hegelians, Marx dreamed of a politics to end all politics. The Hegelian concept of a "universal class" leading humanity to an earthly millennium through a clash of opposites was retained:

> Just as philosophy finds its material weapons in the proletariat, so the proletariat finds its intellectual weapons in philosophy. . . . Philosophy is the head of this emancipation and the proletariat is its heart. Philosophy can only be realized by the abolition (*Aufhebung*) of the proletariat, and the proletariat can only be abolished by the realization of philosophy.[176]

The young Marx was seeking cosmic compensation for political frustration. The Prussian government had failed to realize the exaggerated Hegelian hopes of its becoming "the incarnation of objective morality." [177] Therefore all government—indeed the very business of government—had to be superseded. This eschatological vision was given social content largely by Moses Hess. Through Hess's elaboration of Proudhon, Marx first came to see private property as the root cause for the degradation of man and the ineffectiveness of political reform in bourgeois society.[178]

It was also Hess who first introduced Marx in 1843 to his lifelong collaborator, Frederick Engels, who called Hess "the first Communist in the party" and "the first to reach Communism by the philosophical path." [179] Together with Engels, Hess evolved just such a philosophical concept of a communist party. Developing Hess's idea of a "European triarchy" in a series of articles during 1843, Engels insisted that a German communist movement would arise not out of the "comparatively small" working class, but "among the educated classes." [180]

Hess and Engels began denationalizing the revolutionary ideal by adding French and English perspectives to those of the Berlin Hegelians. Hess tried to provide a transnational outlook by publishing in 1844 in the Paris journal *Vorwärts* the first of a series of communist catechisms.[181]

The special contribution of the young Marx in 1844–45 was to identify this still-idealistic conception of a communist party with both the pretensions of science and the destiny of the proletariat. The idea of a "scientific" socialism based on historical materialism and a rigid theory of class was "uniquely and exclusively" [182] the work of Marx—so Engels later insisted.

The first stage was Marx's break with Ruge over the meaning of an unsuccessful weavers' revolt in Silesia in 1844. Ruge, the *doyen* of radical Hegelian journalists, argued for better political organization and education of the workers. Marx urged, instead, deeper study of the causes of poverty and greater faith in the universal mission of the German proletariat. Members of the proletariat were to become the theoreticians of the world proletarian movement just as the English were to be its economic and the French its political leaders.[183]

In his *The Holy Family* of the same year, Marx broke altogether with the Hegelians—and by implication with his own previous intellectualism. He held up as the model instead the recently suppressed German workers' movement led by Weitling in Switzerland. Two years later, Marx denounced Weitling's Christianized communism (and, more broadly, sentimental idealism) in his *German Ideology*. Marx used "ideology" as a term of abuse for the self-deceptions of German intellectuals. But he himself was, at the same time, creating an ideology in the modern sense: a secular system of ideas based on a theory of history that ultimately promised answers for all human problems.

The "Communist Party" for which Marx soon wrote his manifesto was "ideological" in this latter sense. Marx's polemics against his seeming allies on the Left during the formative period of this "party" reflected his personal desire to annex a pedagogic position with the rising proletariat analogous to that which Hegel had held over the rising Prussian elite for an earlier generation at the University of Berlin. Before turning to the Communist League, which became Marx's "party" in 1847–48, it is important to trace Marx's own quest for a political party to believe in. This search paralleled his philosophical quest and antedated his discovery of either communism or the proletariat.

In his doctoral dissertation of 1841, Marx had placed faith in "the liberal party as a party of a concept . . . [which] realizes real progress." [184] Though soon disillusioned with liberals, he did not immediately embrace those who called themselves socialists and communists. These seemed to him to be more interested in economic theories than in actively advancing "a concept." [185] Marx defended himself late in 1842 against the accusation of being a "communist," [186] and insisted in the following year that communism was only "a dogmatic abstraction . . . a particularly one-sided application of the socialist principle." [187]

Marx's move to Paris in 1843 immersed him in French revolutionary history, and his friendship with Engels introduced him to the study of English economics. Spurned by real-life radicals in Paris (with whom he, Hess, and Ruge attempted to collaborate in the new *German-French Yearbook*),[188] Marx "discovered" the distant German proletariat as the force for revolutionary deliverance. The thought gradually ripened that the longed-for movement of theory into action might in fact be taking place through the "constitution of the proletariat into a class" about which Flora Tristan had spoken in forming her international proletarian society in 1843: the *union ouvrière*.

Politically, the task of the proletariat was the conquest of democracy, which had been compromised by liberalism. Ideologically, the mission was to realize the "human emancipation" that lay beyond the purely political gains of past revolutions: [189] to bring into being what Marx described in his *Philosophical Manuscripts* of 1844 as "realized humanism" or "naturalism." By the time of his expulsion from Paris early in 1845, Marx described both his and humanity's goal as "Communism."

> This Communism is like realized naturalism which equals humanism which equals naturalism. . . .[190]

A Finished Ideology

The crucial new element that Marx brought to communism was dialectical materialism. Here at last was a finished revolutionary ideology with a dynamic historical outlook. It was perfected in the three years he spent in Brussels—1845–48—which were the happiest of his life. Marx forged there the long-sought revolutionary link between France and Germany. But it was not the alliance of active forces envisaged by Hess and Ruge so much as a merger of elements from the two universal ideologies of the preceding era: Saint-Simonianism and Hegelianism.

Philosophically, Marx drew most basically on three new attitudes characteristic of radical Hegelians in the early 1840s: negativism, materialism, and atheism. One has to use Hegel's own dialectical method to explain how such revolutionary ideas could be derived from a politically moderate, philosophically idealist, sincerely Lutheran, and patriotic Prussian professor like Hegel. It seems, indeed, an "ironic" development of "antitheses," through which the "cunning of reason" expressed the "spirit of the times."

Having placed exaggerated initial hopes in the Prussian state, restless Young Hegelians rationalized their disillusionment in the early 1840s by cultivating the sublime idea of its total destruction. Since history proceeds through contradictions (the dialectical "negation of negation"), and since the state had become a negative force, their historical duty was to "negate" the state.

Radical Hegelians also moved from idealism to philosophical materialism in the mid-1840s. Ludwig Feuerbach championed the thought that Hegel's "spirit of the times" was nothing more than a conglomeration of material forces. "Man is what he eats," he argued in a characteristically inelegant pun (*isst*, "eats," *ist*, "is"). Feuerbach later went so far as to explain the failure of the Revolution of 1848 by the dulling effects of a potato diet on the lower classes.[191]

In August 1844, Marx confessed to a "love of Feuerbach[192]—a sentiment he rarely expressed—for pointing the philosophical way to socialism. Feuerbach had substituted materialism for idealism while retaining a monistic, deterministic view of history. Materialism in the 1840s attracted some of those preoccupied with industrialization in northern Europe. By reasserting the monism and determinism of Hegel, Feuerbach reassured radicals that the tension between moral ideals and material reality was only at the level of appearances.

Marx introduced the dynamic idea of dialectical progression into this materialistic monism. Like other earlier metaphysical determinisms (Islam, Calvinism), dialectical materialism provided, paradoxically, an effective call to action. His *Theses on Feuerbach*, written shortly after his move to Brussels, was for Engels "the first document in which is deposited the germ of the new world outlook."[193] It contained his famous dictum:

> Philosophers have only interpreted the world in various ways. The time has come to change it.[194]

A third area of borrowing from the radical Hegelians was Marx's atheism. Whereas Hegel had identified God with the totality of history, his followers took God totally out of it. In a sense, Hegel had prepared the way by placing philosophy above religion, and by subordinating all Gods to his own concept of an all-controlling "world spirit." Contemporaries viewed this as tantamount to atheism; and "the vehemence of attacks from religious quarters on Hegel can perhaps be compared to the reaction in England to Darwin." [195]

Struggle with religion, the original cause to which the young, prepolitical Hegelians had rallied in 1837–38,[196] reached a high level of sophistication in Feuerbach's *Essence of Christianity* of 1841. He distinguished the "true or anthropological essence of religion" (man's need for higher moral purpose) from its "false or theological essence" (belief in God). Marx broke only with Feuerbach's effort to create a new secular religion. However religious in nature, Marx's ideology could never be religious in name. The insistence that it was "scientific" helped protect it against the ebb and flow of enthusiasm that plagued rival revolutionary doctrines. Lenin later rejected "God-building" tendencies within his movement, and subsequent Marxist-Leninists have consistently rejected religious allegiances of any kind within their ranks.

Feuerbach prepared the way for revolutionary atheism by inventing the Hegelian belief that God created man out of his spiritual need to overcome divine alienation. Feuerbach suggested that, on the contrary, man had created God out of *his* material need to overcome human alienation. To Marx, this suggested that alienation was to be solved not by spiritual, but by material forces. Both the source and the cure lay in political economy; its driving force was not ideas but social classes. The class of the future—the class to end all classes—was the proletariat, which had arisen inevitably out of the conflict of the bourgeois with the feudal order. All alienation would be overcome—and all need ended for the Gods that mask repression—when the proletariat overcame its alienation from the means of production that it did not own.

Thus the social revolution so widely discussed in the 1840s—the forcible confiscation of the means of production—became in Marx's analysis the inevitable, necessary, and culminating act of history. Marx became the first to argue consistently that the social revolution was to be made not only *for,* but *by* the proletariat. The intellectual seeking "relevance" could find it only through the working class.

Marx grafted certain key Saint-Simonian beliefs onto his Hegelian view of history: the liberating potential of the Industrial Revolution, the need for a "scientific" analysis of society by classes, the historical destiny of "the poorest and most numbrous class." The German writers from whom he and his friends had learned about French revolutionary thought—Hess in the late 1830s, Stein in the early 1840s—had both attached special importance to Saint-Simonianism. Also, Marx's native town of Trier had been a center of the new Saint-Simonian teaching.[197]

The small group of German émigrés to whom Marx sought to impart his ideology represented an authentic revolutionary intelligentsia—more coherent than the Saint-Simonians of a decade earlier, and more explicitly revolutionary. The dialectical method offered insurance against disillusionment; materialism provided relevance in a time of growing socio-economic stress; and, most important of all, Marx was an indefatigable ideological leader.

Karl Marx remained basically a Hegelian intellectual—always relating individual parts of his analysis to a broader context, writing with voracious interest yet emotional sobriety about an astonishing variety of subjects. The admixture of Saint-Simonian ideas and other Anglo-French social theories helped Marx bring Hegel back "from the blue skies to the kitchen." [198]

Establishing the Movement

But where were the troops for Marx's ideological army? Was there any body attached to his head?

Weitling, the wandering tailor from Magdeburg and Paris, had formed among Germans in Switzerland the first workers' group to call itself communist. Relocated in London, he began in February 1845 a year-long, intermittent discussion with Schapper's more moderate German émigré-faction. Weitling argued that the time was ripe for revolution, which could be made in alliance with criminals and youth on the one hand and with kings and princes on the other.[199] Schapper's group argued for reliance on the communist education of the working classes and rejected Weitling's willingness to tolerate violence and "the communism of Princes" (*Fürstenkommunismus*).[200] But Weitling argued that "simple propaganda helps nothing," [201] and would not be effective unless it promised people a social revolution in their own lifetime.

Schapper, on the other hand, said that communism must strengthen the ability "to develop oneself freely," [202] and "a real system will be developed by our new German philosophers." [203]

The way was clear for Marx and Engels to steer a new path between Weitling's militance and Schapper's moralism. Across the channel in Brussels, they seem to have derived some inspiration from former friends and followers of Buonarroti. They planned to publish a German translation of *History of the Babeuf Conspiracy* which Buonarroti had published there and adopted the Buonarrotian juxtaposition of "egoists" and "Communists." [204] On their first visit to London from July 12 to August 20, 1845, they took the elitist high ground—avoiding the quarreling German workers and discussing international collaboration with radical democratic intellectuals in the Weber Street pub.[205] Engels stayed on alone for the Chartist Festival of Nations in September. Excited that "a Chartist meeting became a Communist festival," he wrote that "Democracy in our days is Communism." [206] Against this background of association with bourgeois democrats rather than German workers, Engels used for the first time the term "proletarian party." [207]

Marx worked first through his Communist Correspondence Committee in Brussels, an organization of about fifteen German writers and type-setters closely linked with Belgian radical intellectuals. Particularly close to Marx were Victor Tedesco, a lawyer from Luxembourg who spoke

Marx's middle German dialect and frequently travelled with Marx, and Philippe-Charles Gigot, whose house was used for meetings and as a mailing address.[208]

The first foreign allies of the committee were the Chartist internationalists, Julian Harney and Ernest Jones, who formed an affiliated London Correspondence Committee in March 1846, despite their suspicions about "the literary characters in Brussels." [209] Three months later, Marx established his first organizational link with the London German community. Marx had been unable to gain followers among Germans in Switzerland where Weitling's influence was still strong, and, despite energetic proselytizing by Engels, had won over only one small element of the Parisian German colony (the furniture carpenters). After driving Weitling to America and Proudhon into animosity in the summer of 1846, Marx and Engels turned for allies to Karl Schapper's group in London, the League of the Just.

Since 1840, this group (though smaller than the Parisian branch of the league) had placed itself at the head of two German worker education associations with some five hundred members including French, Scandinavian, and Dutch émigrés. The London league established formal contact with Marx's committee in Brussels on June 6, 1846, through a long letter from Schapper, Joseph Moll, and seven other "of the most diligent local Communists." [210] They described a vigorous collective life: three meetings a week for their two hundred fifty members (nearly half of them non-German), biweekly gatherings with Harney's group (called Fraternal Democrats), and an educational program including song and dance instruction and a small library in many languages.[211] Though he preferred Marx's concept of a "thorough [tüchtig] revolution" based on an "intellectual [geistige] revolution" to Weitling's unscientific "inanity," Schapper confessed to having once feared that Marx might fan "the scarcely suppressed hate between intellectuals and workers" and install some new "aristocracy of the learned [Gelehrten-Aristokratie] to rule the people from your new throne." [212]

In October 1846, Engels defined "the aim of the Communists" as support of the proletariat against the bourgeoisie through a "violent democratic revolution" that would end private property and establish a "community of goods" (Gutergemeinschaft).[213] Police repression of the Paris branch of the league forced the London league to assume international leadership in this effort. In November 1846, its members called for a "powerful party" to be formed in London around a "simple communist creed, which could serve everyone as a rule of conduct." A congress of the league was called for May 1, 1847, to prepare for an international congress the following year of "the supporters of the new thought (neue Lehre) from all regions of the world." [214]

This call singled out three pressing problems for the forthcoming congress to resolve: (1) alliances with bourgeois-radical groups, (2) attitude towards religion, and (3) the unification of all "social and communist parties." [215] In January 1847, Moll journeyed from London to cement links with Marx in Brussels and with Engels in Paris. These two provided the London group in the course of the next year with comprehensive answers to all three of its questions.

On the question of unification, Marx suggested that unity be based on a revolutionary ideology—universally valid but centrally defined. He inveighed against both the "economists," who accepted passively the logic of capitalist economic development, and the "socialists," who contented themselves with private experiments.[216] Only a clear recognition of the basic antagonism between the bourgeoisie and proletariat would prepare the latter for the "struggle of class against class, which carried to its highest expression is a total revolution." [217]

Marx used the early part of 1847 to write his *Poverty of Philosophy* against Proudhon. This was a dramatic assertion of his own authority against a better-known rival, who had defied him both organizationally and ideologically, and also a text for discussion of the "new doctrine." Later in 1847 Marx arrived in London secure in his vision of revolutionary eschatology. Having exposed the "poverty" of his principal continental rival, he now brought the riches of philosophy to the German colony in London, which was built around "education" associations and was awed by the German intellectual tradition. Armed with his ideology, Marx and Engels now proceeded to offer solutions to the two other tactical problems facing the League of the Just: the attitudes towards religion and towards bourgeois radicalism.

The question of religion was in many ways the most difficult. The proletariat in London had never accepted the philosophic atheism of Berlin and Paris intellectuals like Marx and Dézamy. At the London congress of the League of the Just from June 2 to June 9, the old "utopian" idea of directly establishing a quasi-apostolic "community of goods" among workers was still favored—along with the catechism form for expounding "Communist articles of faith." Engels was apparently the principal author of the creed of the London congress which concluded:

> All religions up to now have been the expression of the historical developmental stages of individual peoples or masses of peoples. Communism, however, is the developmental stage which makes all existing religions superfluous and abolishes them.[218]

Engels verb for "abolition," the Hegelian *aufheben*, suggested uplift to a higher level of synthesis. The tone was condescending and intellectual. But there was not yet any statement of a clear, alternative worldview.

At a second congress, from November 29 to December 8 of that same year, the league defined its purpose as the abolition of property and of the bourgeois class as such. Historical materialism was accepted as the basis for a party statement, which Marx was asked to write.

The *Communist Manifesto* resolved a year of ideological infighting within the League of the Just. The decision to change the name to Communist League (and the first use of the slogan "Workers of the world, unite!") had emerged from the June congress where Marx's influence was still small. Subsequent discussion and propagation of the new Marxist perspective within individual branches of the league appear to have tipped the balance. In late October or early November, Engels composed for the Paris branch "Principles of Communism" designed to combat "The Communist Confession of Faith" drafted by the London branch the previous month. Objecting to the catechistic form,[219] Marx went to London himself to try to seal the debate at the second congress of the league.

The quasi-religious perspective of figures like Schapper sharpened the debates which lasted for ten days. But Marx prevailed, and the first paragraph of the new program bluntly announced that "the aim of the League is the downfall of the bourgeoisie, the rule of the proletariat. . . . and the foundation of a new form of society devoid of classes and private property." [220]

At the same time, Marx also shaped the approach of the new league to the third and last of its unresolved problems: the attitude towards bourgeois-radical political parties. Like other communists of the forties, Marx had opposed the secretive, conspiratorial past of the revolutionists and defined communism as the fulfillment of political democracy. The arguments for an alliance between democrats and communists were particularly forceful in London, where the Chartists' struggle for civil rights seemed to aid their own educational and organizational work.

The tactical alliance between proletarian and bourgeois revolutionaries was put into practice in London through Engels's links with the English Chartists. Concurrently, Marx's Communist Correspondence Committee in Brussels participated in the activities of the Belgian Fraternal Democrats, and acquired a new designation as the German democratic communists in Brussels.[221] Many of its members joined local Belgians in founding the Democratic Association of Brussels in 1847 with Marx as one of the vice-presidents. Marx's trip to London, which enabled him to participate in the second congress of the Communist League, was made possible by an invitation from the London Fraternal Democrats to its Belgian affiliate.[222] The importance of a united front with bourgeois democratic forces was thus naturally stressed by Marx. After returning to Brussels from London, he became president of the Brussels Democratic Association.[223]

The tactic of cooperation with other democratic parties was spelled out in the fourth and final section of Marx's *Manifesto*. Only communists could represent the true class interests of the proletariat, but they needed to ally themselves with radical democratic parties in advanced countries—and with agrarian revolutionaries in backward lands like Poland. Communists needed to support "every revolutionary movement against the existing social and political order of things," but at the same time "bring to the front, as the leading question in each, the property question." Marx saw all this being done openly—and in some sense with the "agreement of the democratic parties of all countries." [224]

Thus Marx provided guidance on all three of the problems from the original 1846 agenda of the League of the Just. He offered ideological unity, rejected religious idealism, and suggested tactical cooperation with bourgeois revolutionaries. He illustrated his belief in "the union and agreement" of all "democratic parties" early in the Revolution of 1848 by dissolving the new Central Committee of the Communist League founded in Paris under his presidency. He argued that the establishment of full civil liberties in revolutionary Paris rendered such an association superfluous.

Disillusionment with the democratic label was soon to develop; but many believed in 1848 that communism was democracy in the social sphere. Like "democracy" in 1789–94, "communism" in 1848 became a major scare word—used "to frighten political rabbits," and, as such, appealing to "all frank democrats aware of the logic of their principle." [225]

Communism vs. Socialism

In the course of the 1840s, the word communism acquired a meaning distinct from socialism. There was, to be sure, much confusion and overlapping. Some, like Marx, used the terms interchangeably at times.[226] Nevertheless, the aggressive propagation of the newer word by young French journalists in the early forties and the halo of martyrdom attached to the "communist trials" lent a special aura to the new term.

Communism was generally distinguished from socialism in any or all of four ways.

First, communism suggested more far-reaching social control than socialism—control over consumption as well as production. At its first congress in June 1847, the Communist League advocated not just socializing the means of production, but also creating a far-reaching "community of goods" for "the distribution of all products according to general agreement." [227] Communism was a new form of life shared in common, not merely a new form of social control.[228]

Second, communism was increasingly associated with a scientific and materialistic worldview in contrast to moralistic and idealistic socialism. With an intensity that grew from Cabet to Dézamy to Marx, communists saw the future order emerging out of the objective necessity of scientific truth rather than from any subjective appeal to moral ideals. Attachment to the communal ideal required detachment from everything else: a distaste bordering on revulsion for romantic sentimentality (the degenerate form of moral idealism), and a militant opposition to belief in God (the ultimate source of moral idealism).[229]

Third, communism was widely associated with political violence in a way that socialism seldom was. This identification was present from the very beginning. In 1840, when one of the original communists attempted to assassinate the king, the trial linked *communistes immédiats* to violent means.[230] Lamennais argued in 1841 that communists unlike socialists had to realize "rigorous and absolute equality" and would therefore be forced "under one form or another" into

... the use of force, despotism and dictatorship in order to establish and maintain it.[231]

George Sand noted that socialists, unlike communists, do not "concern themselves enough perhaps with the present-day struggle." [232] Cabet, in tracing the history of communism in 1842, admitted that its origins lay less in his own nonviolent utopianism than in the Babeuvist tradition of "immediate and violent" revolution.[233]

The communists' belief in the inevitability of an egalitarian order legitimized, if it did not lead to, violence.[234] Communists argued that bourgeois society was already doing violence to humanity. Precisely because the communists saw themselves building the final, violence-free community, they felt justified in undertaking a final, revolutionary act of violence. In his original statement of the "purposes of the Communists" in October 1846, Engels declared that they would "refuse to recognize any other means" to establish communal ownership by the proletariat "except violent, democratic revolution." [235]

Victor Considérant, author of the socialist manifesto that rivalled Marx's, insisted that "communism is before all else a *negative* idea. . . . Not knowing how to unravel the Gordian knot, it cuts it." [236]

Russian socialists tended to agree. Herzen in 1844 defined communism as "primarily negative, a storm-cloud charged with thunderbolts, which like the judgment of God will destroy our absurd social system unless men repent"; [237] and, a few years later as "the socialism of revenge . . . close to the soul of the French people, which has so profound a sense of the injustice of the social order and so little respect for human personality." [238] Within Russia, the *Pocket Dictionary* of the Fourierist Petrashevsky circle listed communism in April 1846 at the end of a series of opposition groups descended from "the party of Milton" in the English civil war reaching even beyond the "radicals." [239] The suggestion was made that the future society be divided between "Fourierists" and "communists," [240] who were said to differ by locating the source of evil, in competition and in private property, respectively.[241] But the heart of the difference—in Petrashevsky's own words —lay in the fact that "Fourierism leads gradually and naturally up to that which communism wants to institute forcibly and in an instant." [242]

The fourth way in which communism generally differed from socialism by the late 1840s was in its reliance on the power and authority of the working class. Even Herzen, despite his fear of communism, called it in 1844 "closer to the masses." [243]

From Homelessness to Universality

The small band of intellectuals that moved the social revolutionary camp toward communism had one common characteristic: homelessness. They generally owned "neither castles nor cottages," [244] and, in the words of a French student of the rise of communism, comprised a "species of proletarian that is described by the term *Heimathlosen*, that is to say, people without hearth or home." [245] Physical homelessness was often deepened into spiritual alienation by three characteristics shared by most of the original communists: youth, unrewarded intellectual precocity, and the loneliness of exile.

The most extreme communists were extremely young. The original communist banquet of 1840 had been organized largely by radicals in their late teens as a counter-banquet to the more genteel evenings of older electoral reformers. The systematic atheism with which Dézamy rejected Cabet (and Marx, Weitling) expressed the rebellion of the very young against men sometimes old enough to be their fathers.

The ideological passion of Dézamy and Marx was also the channel of expression for intellectual talent and personal ambition that could find no adequate rewards in existing society. These men turned against the patriarchs of communism in the French and German worlds seeking to free the new ideal from the "utopian" mode of social experiment characteristic of an earlier generation.

But where could the young who rejected paternal and divine authority find a home of their own? Ultimately not in space, but in time; not in the places of geography, but in the flow of history. Historical ideology offered cosmic compensation for the lack of a particular dwelling place. The social revolutionary became a pilgrim without a holy land, but with a wholly certain view of history.

This vision flourished in lonely exile. The path to communism began with Buonarroti, an Italian exiled from Corsica to France to Switzerland to Belgium. Communist organization began among Germans exiled into non-German-speaking regions: in French-speaking Switzerland, France, Belgium, and finally England. Communism never took root inside Germany even during the turmoil of 1848–49, nor among the large, German-speaking regions of Switzerland and the United States. Revolutionary communism also proved stronger among Frenchmen exiled after 1848 to Jersey and London than it ever had been in Paris.

The social revolutionaries who formed the Communist League in London were young, uprooted, and largely denationalized intellectuals. The core was *Heimathlosen* Germans surrounded by a miscellany of Flemish-speaking Belgians, Anglicized Irishmen, multi-lingual Swiss and Scandinavians.

The twenty-nine-year-old Marx could become a senior statesman in such a group. He was the prototypical displaced intellectual: a Berlin Hegelian who had discovered French social thought in Paris and then digested English economics during a second exile in Belgium. The "Communist Party" for which he purported to be speaking in his *Manifesto* existed only in his prophetic imagination. This "party" was a kind of *pied-à-terre* for a few intellectuals cut off from the main currents of European politics on the eve of revolution.

Marx provided no real navigational course for the storms that broke out early in 1848 within a few weeks of publication of the *Manifesto*. But he did find a homing point for the compass: the coming classless society. The inexorable movement towards this end overrode and superseded all personal or parochial considerations. Man's proper home in the interim lay not in any castle on the sand, but in the stream of history itself.

Faith in a coming "universal" liberation [246] reinforced Marx's faith in historical materialism. In all the roles he subsequently filled—as an active counsellor to revolutionaries, as a journalistic commentator on current events, and as a scholar working on his never-finished *Capital* —Marx radiated the exhilarating belief that local conflicts necessarily feed into a process leading to universal revolution. His hopes focused on western Europe, where bourgeois society and its redemptive proletariat were most advanced; and he generally saw progressive significance in the spread of European institutions: German above all—but French, English, and even Russian when at the expense of Asian backwardness.[247] Even amidst the pressing happenings in Cologne during 1848–49, Marx's articles in *Neue Rheinische Zeitung* repeatedly found revolutionary relevance in remote events. On the Taiping rebellion, he suggested in 1853 that

> . . . the Chinese revolution will throw the spark into the overloaded mine of the present industrial system and cause the explosion of the long-prepared general crisis, which, spreading abroad, will be closely followed by political revolutions on the Continent.[248]

A few years later, a Spanish upheaval prompted him to conclude that "the revolution is imminent and will take at once a socialist character." [249] On the eve of his death, assassinations in Russia inspired the thought that Russian events might serve as a "signal to the revolutionary development of the West" [250] and thus to universal liberation.

Marx's genius offered rootless revolutionaries anywhere a new kind of shelter—in nothing particular, but something universal. That something combined Hegelian historicism and Saint-Simonian scientism: inevitability and perfectibility. Whereas other socialists and communists offered revolutionary ideas, Marx provided a revolutionary ideology. By developing it at a relatively young age, Marx was able to stake a claim as strategist-in-chief of proletarian revolution that he was able to sustain for another forty years. His younger collaborator, Engels, continued that role for eleven more years after Marx died in 1883, beginning an apostolic succession with an increasingly disputed lineage.

Marx's special position was based largely on two factors that he emphasized for revolutionary thinking during the turmoil of 1848–50: the destiny of the proletariat and the necessity of dictatorship. The first of these elements was introduced by Marx on the eve of the Revolution of 1848, the second in its aftermath. Marx invested both concepts with the kind of universal significance that assured their continued appeal long after the memory faded of revolutionary events in which Marx played only an insignificant part.

"The Proletariat"

Once again a word was crucial. Much of the sudden rise to prominence of the numerically insignificant communists can be traced to their ability to dramatize their own connection with something they were the first systematically to label "the proletariat."

There was, of course, something very tangible behind the label. The spread of industrial machinery and the factory system throughout western Europe had created by the 1840s a growing body of manual laborers working for uncertain wages in new urban environments. The conditions in mine and mill were often brutal; and the new industrial laborer had none of the pride of product and self-respect of traditional artisans. He tended to become a subordinate statistic in the ledgers of investment and accounting, and shared similar experiences and grievances with workers in other countries.

Nevertheless, there was little internal communication—let alone shared identity—among these workers. They tended to quarrel more among themselves than with anyone else—and to exacerbate rather than supplant all the older ethnic, religious, and national conflicts of humanity. The number of factory workers was still insignificant outside of England, and their sense of collective importance was even smaller.

Marx's distinctive accomplishment was to establish the idea widely that history was producing a single force of deliverance known as "the proletariat" with a single head ("organ of consciousness"), the communist party. It is as important to trace the revolutionary intellectuals' myth of "the proletariat" as it is to analyze the actual conditions and concerns of working people in the industrial era.[251]

The term proletariat came into modern use in the seventeenth century as a general, contemptuous term for the lower classes.[252] More positive connotations appeared in the eighteenth century through Rousseau and some Babeuvists.[253] The word was identified with class conflict in Sismondi's influential *New Principles of Political Economy* of 1819. Sismondi's "social economics" challenged the classical economists' indifference to the social consequences of the free play of market forces, which had led not to increased happiness for the people, but rather to the impoverishment of "the proletariat." He argued that, whereas the Roman proletariat lived at the expense of the people, the modern bourgeoisie was living at the expense of the proletariat.

After the Revolution of 1830, some argued "the need of special representation for the proletarians" in the assembly;[254] but an increasing number followed Blanqui in identifying "the proletariat" with social struggle outside all existing political arenas.[255] Lamennais wrote that the common objective of both socialists and communists was "to abolish the proletariat and to liberate the proletarian."[256]

The reality of class conflict was affirmed in a host of new publications of the early 1840s,[257] and the need for active class struggle was intensified by the younger communists' battle against Cabet's pacifistic communism. A defender of Babeuf launched an early attack on Cabet in August 1840, announcing, "Je ne suis pas littérateur, mais un prolétaire. . . ."[258]

Per Götrek, a Swedish printer who had personally known Cabet,[259] brought some of the large Workers' Education Circle in Stockholm into the discussions of the London League with his pamphlet of 1847 stressing the link between the proletariat and communism: *On the Proletariat and its Liberation by the Path of True Communism.*[260] Victor Tedesco wrote *Catechism of the Proletarian,*[261] which spoke of class conflict between "the rich and the proletarian." [262] The European worker's condition was like that of the black slave in America: "The negro is the slave of man. The proletarian is the slave of capital." [263]

Marx's conception of the proletariat may well have been influenced by Götrek and Tedesco, who later worked respectively on the first Swedish and French translations of the *Communist Manifesto.*[264] Tedesco's influence was greater, since he was personally close both to Marx and to Wilhelm Wolff, the organizer of the German Workers' League, which was founded in Brussels in 1847.[265] Wolff accompanied Engels to the first meeting of the Communist League in London in June 1847; and Tedesco accompanied Marx to the second meeting in December. Brussels radical circles had, if anything, even more class consciousness than those in Paris.[266] Marx was also influenced by Lorenz von Stein's *Socialism and Communism in Contemporary France,* which had first popularized the communist ideal in Germany, by explaining that

> Communism, as the expression of proletarian class consciousness, may sharpen the opposition and the hatred between the two large classes of society. . . . Communism is a natural and inevitable phenomenon in any nation which has developed from a market society into an industrial society and which has given rise to a proletariat. There is no power in the world that can prevent the growth of Communism.[267]

Marx's theory of history and of dynamic class conflict was first set forth fully yet concisely in the *Communist Manifesto,* in January 1848. "The history of all hitherto existing society is the history of class struggles," [268] proclaimed the opening sentence of the first of its four sections, "bourgeois and proletarians." This arresting beginning suggested not only a simple program—class struggle against the bourgeoisie—but at the same time a messianic calling for the party that could deliver humanity from its bondage. "The proletariat alone is a really revolutionary class," [269] the chosen instrument of a class war to end class war.

Only in part two, "proletarians and communists," was the new type of party mentioned. It derives all its sanction (though not necessarily any of its members) from the proletariat. The new party was in no way separate from the proletariat or opposed to "other working class parties," but was the only group to represent "the proletariat as a whole." [270] As such, the communist party has an obligation when participating in any national movement to "bring to the front the common interests of the entire proletariat, independent of all nationality." [271]

After only a few pages of discussion, all mention of a communist *party* ended. Engels, at the time of writing the *Manifesto,* had written that "communism is no doctrine, but a movement." [272] Although the *Manifesto* suggests a number of egalitarian measures to be undertaken after the seizure of power, these are to be undertaken not by a party, but by "the proletariat" itself, creating "a vast association of the whole nation" in which "public power will lose its political character." All class antagonisms would vanish as men entered a new type of "association in which the free development of each is the condition for the free development of all." [273]

The third section of the *Manifesto* was a criticism of rival socialist theories, an excellent example of the denunciatory literature endemic among revolutionaries in the 1840s. At the same time it was a virtuoso exercise in class analysis—relegating each school to its own form of historical oblivion by showing its "feudal," "bourgeois," or "petit bourgeois" nature. Names were for the most part avoided; and positive recognition was extended—albeit somewhat patronizingly—only to three "utopian" socialists: Saint-Simon, Fourier, and Owen. Their plans for the future allegedly awoke the critical imagination and corresponded to "the first instinctive yearnings" of the proletariat "for a general reconstruction of society." [274]

The final short section of the *Manifesto* prescribed a variety of tactical alliances for "the communists." Marx insisted in the manner characteristic of earlier revolutionaries that the violence of revolution would in reality only bring to a rational (and thus final) conclusion the violence and disruption already begun unconsciously and prolonged irresponsibly by the bourgeoisie. It was *they* who had disrupted the family, taken away private property from most of humanity, and replaced home education by social education. The communists sought only to champion a movement which, by completing these processes in a society free of class antagonisms, would bring all this disruption to an end.

Dictatorship

Despite the ringing rhetoric of its final "WORKERS OF THE WORLD, UNITE!", the *Manifesto* was largely unnoticed until well after the revolutions of 1848–49. As a document of its own time, it was inaccurate in its two major predictions for the immediate future: that national antagonisms were vanishing before a new transnational proletariat; and that the coming wave of revolution would focus on Germany and move from a bourgeois to a proletarian revolution.

The Communist League, for which the *Manifesto* was written, also played only a minor role in the revolutionary events. After the return of its leaders to Germany in the spring of 1848, the membership of the London League was a scant eighty-four; [275] and the membership elsewhere was scattered and divided.

Marx was mainly preoccupied with editing *Neue Rheinische Zeitung* from May 1848 until its demise the following May. He provided not so much practical revolutionary guidance as an Olympian overview of political and economic developments that often seemed far removed from his readers.[276] "The music in them," one worker wrote, "is pitched too high for us; we cannot whistle it." [277] Bitterness grew with the repression in Germany and with the failure of the proletarian-bourgeois democratic alliance to stem the tide. A letter of April 22, 1849, denounced Marx as "a learned Sun-God . . . not touched by that which moves the hearts of human beings." For him human suffering allegedly had "only a scientific, a doctrinaire interest." [278]

Radicalized by his own arrest and trial in Cologne and then by the suppression of his journal, Marx returned to London in the autumn of 1849 and reversed the opposition he had expressed in the spring towards reconstituting the Communist League. He helped reorganize it, and issued a first address to it in March 1850.[279] But dissension soon tore it apart, and Marx's activities were increasingly concentrated on the refinement of his theory of revolution in two great works on recent events: *Class Struggle in France* (1850) and *Eighteenth Brumaire of Louis Bonaparte* (1852). These, together with the *Communist Manifesto* and the first sketch in 1849 of his theory of socio-economic development (later expanded in *Critique of Political Economy* and *Capital*), represented the heart of his vision and revolutionary legacy.

His writings in London, beginning with his *Manifesto* for the reconstituted Communist League, stressed the transnational nature of the coming social revolution. His tone became almost eschatological in the continuation of *Neue Rheinische Zeitung*, which was written in London, printed in Hamburg, and distributed in America as well as Europe. He expected it soon to become a weekly and then a daily; [280] but only six numbers appeared between March and its demise in November 1850.

His international perspective offered not only cosmic consolation, but also fresh hopes for revolution. The workers had been crushed in Paris only because "everywhere in the continent" the leadership of the bourgeoisie had "entered into open alliance with feudal monarchy against the people," while the working class formed no such international alliance. But the French repression also revealed the "secret" that any government now was forced "to maintain external peace in order to conduct a civil war internally."

> Peoples just beginning their struggle for national independence were delivered over to the power of Russia, Austria, and Prussia. But at the same time the fate of these national revolutions was made dependent on the fate of the workers' revolution. Their seeming self-sufficiency and independence from the great social upheaval had vanished.[281]

Pointedly singling out the three most nationalistic revolutionary movements in Europe, he added:

> Neither Hungarian, nor Pole, nor Italian will be free as long as the worker remains a slave.[282]

The victory of the counter-revolution had created—by its own international character—conditions for the universal victory of revolution. His interpretation—in form if not in content—was strikingly like that of religious messianists who occasionally joined the revolutionaries of 1848, arguing that the triumph of the Antichrist announced the imminent Second Coming of Christ. Marx, too, saw Armageddon coming:

> Every new workers' revolution in France inevitably involves a new *world war*. A new French revolution will be obliged now to leave the national

arena and *conquer the European arena* in which alone the social revolution of the XIX century can be realized.[283]

"The problem of the worker can nowhere be resolved within national borders." [284]

> Class war within French society will be transformed into world war between nations. The revolution will begin only when world war places the proletariat at the head of the nation controlling the world market, at the head of England.[285]

He hoped that conflict would develop between the temporarily triumphant bourgeoisies of France and England. This in turn would unify the French and English proletariat—and represent the "organic beginning" of the final revolution.

> The present generation is reminiscent of those Jews whom Moses led through the desert. It must not only conquer a new world, but also leave the scene in order to give way to a people ripe for the new world.[286]

By the end of 1849 it had become clear that the German and French revolutions had failed to produce a new order (and the Chartist movement had failed to produce even a serious uprising). But the cause of social revolution had at least acquired a banner of its own to match the myriad colors of the national revolutionaries. In Paris in 1848 the red flag had replaced the black flag as the favored banner of the proletariat. "Only when steeped in the *blood* of the June insurgents," Marx wrote in 1850, "did the tricolor become transformed into the flag of the European Revolution—the *red flag*." [287] At an international gathering of November 10, 1850, Marx's friend the Chartist Julian Harney became the first man publicly to repudiate his own national banner in favor of the red flag of revolution.[288]

But the workers did not follow this banner. The revolution had collapsed everywhere except among the orators in London, where a revolution had never taken place at all. It was a time of crisis for a committed ideological revolutionary. Marx had believed in a universal revolution, which was fading into universal failure. History manifestly refused to follow his manifesto. As a participant, Marx proved largely unable to communicate with workers, let alone lead them.

The standard response to such disappointment was emigration to America for a new start. The flight of German revolutionaries to the New World after 1848 represented one of the most massive movements of its kind in the century.[289] Marx and Engels themselves briefly planned to emigrate to America in August 1850.[290] But they rejected this alternative along with the second one of substituting reformist for revolutionary goals within Europe.

Marx followed instead a third course characteristic of a small number of Germans remaining in exile within Europe: the intensification of messianic commitment. Almost uniquely among the revolutionary extremists, however, Marx avoided acts of adventurism or fantasies of fresh conspiracy. Indeed, he fortified his commitment not by undertaking any new activity in the 1850s, but rather by refining his revolutionary theory. Incarcerating himself in the British Museum, he widened his strategic perspectives with journalism and wrote his massive theoretical works: *Critique of Political Economy, Grundrisse,* and *Das Kapital.*

The main immediate conclusion that Marx derived from the setbacks of 1848–49 was that there was need for a revolutionary dictatorship to act on behalf of the proletariat. In propounding this doctrine, he drew close to Blanqui, whose ideas would also provide fortification for Lenin at a later time.

In April of 1850, Marx and Engels joined Harney and others in London to draw up plans for the Universal League of Revolutionary Communists—a short-lived last effort to transform the revived Communist League into a guiding force for secret revolutionary organizations throughout Europe. The statutes of this organization contained the first clear formulation of the concept of an interim "dictatorship of the proletariat":

> The aim of the association is the overthrow of all the privileged classes, the subjection of these classes to the dictatorship of the proletariat by sustaining the revolution in permanence until the realization of Communism, which has to be the final form of the organization of human society.[291]

Marx first related the term "dictatorship of the proletariat" to his theory of history and class struggle in March 1852. The Buonarrotian idea of a transitional elite dictatorship was thus transformed into its "Marxist" form of class dictatorship as the necessary preliminary to a classless society.[292]

After 1848 many revolutionary leaders had discussed the need for some kind of dictatorship to defend revolutionary democracy from counter-revolution. The term "dictator" still had some of its ancient Roman connotations of temporary martial law in behalf of a republic [293]—although Marx had also used it as a term of abuse.[294] The term did not yet have its modern despotic ring. German communists had also used the term approvingly, beginning with Weitling in 1845:

> Should we call communism to the fore through revolutionary means, then we must have a dictator who governs over everything.[295]

In Cologne during the 1848 revolution, Marx rebuked the assembly for failing to exercise dictatorship "in the face of the daily growing threat of counter-revolution." [296]

> Every provisional state set up after a revolution requires a dictatorship, and an energetic dictatorship at that.[297]

A decade earlier, after the failure of the insurrection of 1839 and Blanqui's imprisonment in Mont-Saint-Michel, Blanquists had fled to London. Blanquist émigrés now turned again to the question of "what the people should demand the day after a revolution." [298] In 1848, as in 1839, they had seen insurrection crushed and the master imprisoned (in remote Belle-Ile in the Bay of Biscay).

Marx had already known (and may have been influenced by) Blanquists in Belgium, particularly Jacques Imbert who had served with Marx as co-vice-president of the Brussels Democratic Association.[299] A large-scale publication effort was planned, though never realized, by the Blanquists in London; and consideration was given to founding together with the London communists a new organization on the model of the Central Republican Society, which Blanqui, Dézamy, and others had set up between the February Revolution and the June repression of 1848. Blanqui had argued then for (1) placing military and political power immediately and directly in the hands of the working class, and (2) postponing elections so that the interim organizations of the revolutionary proletariat would have time to reeducate the masses in terms of their true interests rather than outmoded political categories.[300]

In the context of forming a united revolutionary front with the Blanquists, Marx introduced the term "dictatorship of the working class" in place of his previous term "rule [*Herrschaft*] of the proletariat" in January 1850.[301] Although Marx cited it as a "brave slogan of the revolutionary struggle" which had anonymously appeared in Paris in 1848,[302] it seems probable that he had simply taken it from the Blanquists. He had been brought into close touch with the newly arrived followers of Blanqui at a dinner in London given by Harney and other radical Chartists late in 1849. The French Blanquists joined Engels, Marx, and Harney to provide leadership for the Universal League of Revolutionary Communists. The statutes (written in French by the most "Blanquist" of the Germans, August Willich, who was then specially close to Marx) proclaimed the aim of overthrowing the privileged classes and submitting them to

. . . the dictatorship of the proletariat by maintaining the revolution in permanence until the realization of communism.[303]

The final section of Marx's *Class Warfare in France*, written at this very time, equates the "revolutionary proletariat" with "the party of Blanqui." [304] All was not lost because

The *proletariat* is more and more uniting around *revolutionary socialism*, around *communism*, which the bourgeoisie itself has baptised with the name *Blanqui*.[305]

Marx's language becomes almost totally derivative in the use of characteristic Blanquist terms of abuse ("juggler") and expressions of physical aversion for utopian "reveries" that distract from making revolution. The victory in the Paris election of March 1850 by Paul Louis Deflotte, "a friend of Blanqui's . . . the June insurgent, the representative of the revolutionary proletariat," is cited by Marx as proletarian revenge for the massacres of June 1848. "Behind the ballot papers lay the paving stones." [306] He then uses—for the first time—the phrase "dictatorship of the proletariat," linking it immediately with his other new term "permanent revolution." [307]

The suggestion of Blanquist influence on Marx is anathema to later Marxists, who seem committed both to exaggerating Marx's originality and to caricaturing "Blanquism." Even when not subject to Soviet discipline, Marxists insist that Marx did not take the term from Blanqui and used the term to contrast his "class dictatorship" with Blanqui's elitist conception.[308] Far from establishing a lack of Blanqui's influence, however, such usage only indicates a deeper linkage. For Marx tended to denounce the ism behind an individual in the act of borrowing his idea—just as he reviled the persona of a rival leader he was seeking to displace. Adopting an idea from Blanqui created a compensatory need to denounce "Blanquism."

Blanqui's influence on Marx during this period is further illustrated by Marx's taking over of another term that was to become important in revolutionary history: permanent revolution. Marx had rejected such a concept when it was suggested by working-class leaders in Cologne during 1848–49; [309] but he embraced "revolution in permanence" as the "war cry" of the reorganized Communist League in March 1850.[310] Marx saw permanent revolution as a necessary condition of any future "dictatorship of the proletariat" if it was to be different in kind from the "dictatorship of the bourgeoisie."

The circulars sent from the London Central Committee to the German members of the Communist League in March indicated that the classical Illuminist-Buonarrotian-Blanquist type of conspiracy had taken root among Germans. Emissaries from London were instructed to recruit people to the league from within existing revolutionary organizations. There should be two classes of membership; an outer circle of local and provincial groups that knew nothing about the inner circle; it alone was to be told of "the communist consequences of the present movement." The secret, hierarchical movement was to be entirely manipulated by the London Central Committee, which would sanction selective terror against "hated individuals or public buildings associated with hated memories." [311] The leadership suggested that the Communist League should prepare Germans to fight even more against petty bourgeois democrats than against reactionaries in the next phase of revolutionary warfare.

Following the defeat of the workers' insurrection in Paris in July 1850, Marx decided that further revolution was unlikely; and by August, he fell out with Willich, who fought a duel with one of Marx's followers early in September. In the course of rewriting the statutes of the Communist League, Marx denounced Willich and his followers on September 15 for relying on "the will of revolutionaries as the sole motor of revolution" [312] and flooding the movement with petty bourgeois elements so that "the word 'proletariat' is now used as an empty word, as is the word 'people' by the democrats." [313] But Marx's plans for reorganizing the league did not force a split with the "Blanquist" Willich. Marx took the unusual steps of sanctioning two separate groups in London, while transferring the league's headquarters to Cologne.

Though smaller than ever in numbers, the German-based league gained a measure of new life late in 1850 through its links with a much larger if nonrevolutionary national organization of workers: Stephen Born's brotherhood (Verbrüderung). Marx was largely excluded from the league, but continued to be represented by many younger revolutionaries.[314]

Nor were links with the French Blanquists affected by Marx's estrangement from the Willich group in London. Marx and Engels translated into both German and English Blanqui's denunciation of moderate socialists sent by him from prison to a Banquet of Equals held in London on February 24, 1851. Blanqui said, among other things, that in the future,

> All governments will be traitorous which, having been lifted up on the shoulders of the proletariat, do not proceed immediately with (1) general disarmament of bourgeois troops and (2) the armament and organization into national militia of all the workers.[315]

The Communist League came to its end in May 1851. The movement which had begun with a German tailor (Weitling) bearing communist proposals to the League of the Just twelve years earlier ended when another German tailor (Peter Nothjung of the Cologne Central Committee) was arrested in a Leipzig railroad station on May 10 carrying most of the important documents of the league.[316]

Engels's *Revolution and Counter-Revolution in Germany* of 1851–52 blamed the failure of the German revolution on the timidity of the bourgeois liberals who led it. But some share of the blame might also be allotted to the extremism of the communist program, which frightened workers as well as bourgeois liberals and gave a pretext for repression to reactionaries.[317] The displaced journeymen who provided the rank and file for the German upheavals felt threatened by intellectuals who sought to manipulate them with unfamiliar terminology. As was to be the case later—in Italy on the eve of Mussolini and Germany on the eve of Hitler—extremism on the Left played a role in preparing the way for reaction on the Right.

Marx's own postmortem was concentrated on France. He had translated Blanqui's blunt aphorism "Who has iron has bread" for the Banquet of Equals in February 1851.[318] But by the end of the year he realized that the established authorities had all the iron and could dispense the bread to the weary masses. Blanqui remained in prison; and the last great popular uprising of the era (of one hundred thousand rebels against Napoleon III's proclamation of dictatorship) in December 1851, was crushed with five hundred killed and twenty thousand convicted.[319] There was no major upheaval in France and no further mention of the "dictatorship of the proletariat" anywhere until the Paris Commune twenty years later.[320]

Marx sent his famous "Eighteenth Brumaire of Louis Bonaparte" to his close friend Joseph Weydemeyer in 1852 for publication in his short-lived new weekly journal, *Die Revolution.*" [321] "Blanqui and his comrades" were designated by Marx as "the real leaders of the proletarian party, the revolutionary communists." [322] (The last three words were excised in later editions after Marx began to view Blanqui as a rival rather than an ally. There is no indication of the deletion in the supposedly complete and academic Soviet edition.[323]) Weydemeyer had just written a militant article, "Dictatorship of the Proletariat," [324] in New York, and Marx's letter of March 5, 1852, to his old friend contained the fullest definition Marx ever gave of the concept:

> ... the class struggle necessarily leads to the dictatorship of the proletariat which itself constitutes only the transition to the abolition of all classes and to a classless society.[325]

Marx emerged from the crisis convinced of the need for dictatorial leadership in any future revolution. The Blanquist belief in an unending revolutionary struggle provided hope in the face of the European reaction. Trotsky was to revive the concept of "permanent revolution" in a similar period of depression after the Russian Revolution of 1905.[326] But most expressions of hope tended to come from the New World rather than the Old. Willich, Weydemeyer, and Weitling (for the second time) had emigrated; other pioneering social revolutionaries like Cabet and Harney soon followed; and Marx himself became a writer for the *New York Tribune*. Militantly atheist "Communist Clubs" were formed among German émigrés in New York, Chicago, and Cincinnati during 1857–58.[327] But for the most part, the early dream of social revolution in Europe was simply grafted onto the national dream of an expanding America, while in Europe many of Marx's German associates became absorbed in the nationalist mystique of the German drive for unity; his old friend Moses Hess became a visionary Jewish nationalist.[328]

Marx, however, continued to believe in the inevitability of a social revolution global in scope and permanent in nature. Looking back in 1860 on his experiences with the Communist League, Marx would not seem overly distressed that a "party in the altogether ephemeral sense of the word has not existed for eight years." For in his more lofty meaning of the word—"By party, I understand party in the great historical sense"—such a party was only beginning to exist:

> The League, like the Society of Seasons in Paris, like hundreds of other societies, was only an episode in the history of the party, which is everywhere spontaneously growing on the soil of contemporary society.[329]

Thus, the confused and quarrelsome history of the Communist League was only an episode in the creation of a greater party to come, a "party in the great historical sense." It seems appropriate that the only other "episode" Marx mentioned was Blanqui's Society of the Seasons. In arguing for a centralized revolutionary dictatorship in the name of a semimythologized, monolithic proletariat, Marx had moved close to the positions of Blanqui. This evolution in turn heightened the conflict which had already opened up among social revolutionaries between Marx and the passionately anti-ideological, anticentralizing Pierre-Joseph Proudhon.

CHAPTER 10

Schism:

Marx vs. Proudhon

THE DEEPEST and most fundamental conflict among social revolutionaries is that which recurs between intellectuals who propose to speak for working people and workers who attempt to use the language of intellectuals. Marx, the intellectual par excellence, had his two earliest and bitterest quarrels with the two physical toilers who most effectively articulated the revolutionary cause of the working class in the 1840s: Wilhelm Weitling and Pierre-Joseph Proudhon.

Weitling was in effect excommunicated by Marx during a personal confrontation at the latter's home in Brussels on March 30, 1846. A neutral witness recalls how Weitling attempted to discuss revolutionary strategy "within the bounds of common-place liberal talk." Suddenly, Marx broke the polite euphoria:

> Tell us, Weitling, you who have made such a noise in Germany with your preaching: on what grounds do you justify your activity and what do you intend to base it on in the future?

It is the classic voice of the intellectual, certain that he understands the interests of the working class as a whole, indifferent to the short-sighted opinions of individual workers, contemptuous of leaders like Weitling who arouse the masses "without any firm well-thought-out reasons for their activity." Weitling responded by touching Marx's rawest nerve: his lack of human links with the working class.

> Weitling consoled himself for the evening's attacks by remembering the hundreds of letters and declarations of gratitude that he had received from all parts of his native land and by the thought that his modest spadework was perhaps of greater weight for the common cause than criticism and armchair analysis of doctrines far from the world of the suffering and afflicted people.

On hearing these last words Marx finally lost control of himself and thumped so hard with his fist on the table that the lamp on it rung and shook. He jumped up saying: "Ignorance never yet helped anybody!" [1]

Marx responded by asserting his intellectual superiority and pedagogic mission; and the thumping of his fist did not stop until Weitling had been driven to America and friends like Moses Hess driven to tell Weitling that he would "have nothing more to do with your party." [2] Marx followed this attack with a circular against Hermann Kriege, who had moved from collaboration with Marx in Belgium to editorship of an American journal with the Babeuvist title, *Tribune of the People* (*Volkstribun*). Marx excoriated Kriege's mindless sentimentality (pointing out that Kriege used the word "love" thirty-five times) and his belief that the social problem could be solved in land-rich America by "turning all men into owners of private property." [3]

Many years later, in the longest and last of his many major works denouncing rival radicals, Marx made it clear that the pamphlet against Kriege had in effect been part of a conscious ideological purge:

We published at the same time a series of pamphlets, partly printed, partly lithographed, in which we subjected to a merciless criticism [the reigning ideas] of the League. We established in its place the scientific understanding of the economic structure of bourgeois society as the only tenable theoretical foundation. We also explained in popular form that our task was not the fulfillment of some utopian system but the conscious participation in the historical process of social revolution that was taking place before our eyes. [4]

The field was clearer to impose his program on German émigrés after Weitling went to America early in 1847 to aid Kriege and rescue his followers from their nationalistic deviation of the previous year: supporting the war against Mexico. But Kriege's *Tribune of the People* soon died, and Marx vaulted past the distant Weitling into international leadership of the communist movement.

Marx's conflict with Weitling revealed a characteristic blend of contempt for the man and respect for his role. Marx saw nothing personal in his attacks on Weitling. Indeed, Marx paid tribute to Weitling's previous function of launching a revolutionary social critique of the existing order. But Weitling by the mid-forties represented to Marx that most obstructive of anachronisms: a historical leader whose time had past. Weitling was unable to fulfill the historical position of egalitarian, proletarian leadership which he himself had created. In order to fill this position himself, Marx moved beyond the German-speaking world to mount a similar, simultaneous attack on Proudhon: the leading proletarian revolutionary within the French citadel of the revolutionary faith. The clash that developed between Marx and Proudhon proved the most important among social revolutionaries in their time—and may remain the most relevant for our own.

For two decades after their first falling out in 1845, Marx and Proudhon fought in bitter rivalry for leadership of the new proletarian movement. They drew increasing numbers of followers into a widening range of disputes. In the 1860s (after the death of Proudhon), Marx's daughters inveighed against Proudhonism even while dancing at the festivals of the First International.[5] In the 1960s (after the "death of ideology"), the heirs of Proudhon, in effect, answered back to the Marxists with the festivals of the "new left."

The Marx-Proudhon conflict can be analyzed on two quite different levels: as a personal-political clash between rival nineteenth-century revolutionaries, and as a broader ideological conflict of divergent but enduring radical ideals.

The Clash of Men

The personal conflict between Marx and Proudhon was most intense during its first phase just prior to the Revolution of 1848. But it was to continue until Proudhon's death in 1865; and an insulting obituary by Marx helped ensure that the clash would continue between rival groups. The battle between Marxists and Proudhonists was central to the discordant history of the First International from 1864 to 1876— and to the tensions that continued thereafter between Latin and Slavic revolutionaries on the one hand and German Social Democrats on the other.

It was not so much a battle of ideas as a clash of the moralistic and the authoritarian temperaments over the question, should revolutionaries have an ideology? Marx answered Yes—and became the enshrined authority for the more than a billion people who had come to live under communist rule by the mid-twentieth century. Proudhon's negative answer made him the ancestor (often unacknowledged) of anarchistic alternatives, which rarely succeeded but never quite disappeared.

In 1844, during the critical turning point in his life, the twenty-five-year-old Karl Marx first came to know the thirty-five-year-old Proudhon. The quarrels that soon developed between them aggravated almost every exposed nerve of the young Marx at a precarious time of transition from his youth as a philosopher to his maturity as a revolutionary. Proudon seemed to challenge not just Marx's ideas, but his very identity.

In the months just before his expulsion from Paris in February 1845, Marx was blending his personal struggle with philosophical alienation into a world historical theory in which proletarian revolution would overcome all human alienation. He was expecting his first child, but had not yet formed his firm collaboration with Engels or fully elaborated his new views. His break with the philosophical idealism of his former Hegelian friends was completed. But he had not yet established any concrete links with either the proletariat or the revolution—the objects of his faith. Youthful Germanic hopes for a "holy alliance" with the French revolutionary tradition, which had brought Hess, Marx, and the others to Paris, had been rudely dispelled. The *Deutsch-Französische Jahrbücher* of 1844 had failed to attract a single French contributor. Marx, like other recent radical arrivals from Germany, had been ignored and occasionally ridiculed by leading French revolutionaries.

Thus Marx felt a deep need for a French connection as he entered into extended discussions with Proudhon soon after the latter arrived in Paris from Lyon on September 25, 1844. Proudhon was the most arresting and famous radical personality in France: authentically plebeian and fearlessly polemic. Proudhon represented a link both with the revolutionary France that the Germans admired and with the proletariat that Marx personally professed to serve. As early as 1842, Marx had praised Proudhon above other French socialists as a "penetrating" figure. Early in 1844 Marx had sought to praise the working-class communism of Weitling by calling him "even better than Proudhon." [6]

Marx particularly admired the power and simplicity of Proudhon's *What is Property?* of 1841. Proudhon answered bluntly: "Property is theft," and went on to suggest that the "proletor" would expropriate the proprietor and establish property rights equal for all. Marx admired Proudhon's forceful clarity in insisting on a social revolution along class lines. Throughout 1844 Marx contrasted the Frenchman favorably with the abstract Germans. He called *What is Property?* a "scientific manifesto of the French proletariat" [7] which

> has the same importance for modern economics that Sieyès' *What is the Third Estate?* has for modern politics.[8]

This was high praise, even when softened by a patronizing tone. Proudhon had begun to explore precisely those problems that were most central to Marx's own new outlook: the economic basis and class nature of revolutionary conflict. Proudhon had contended that even if the proprietor paid his workers the full day's wage they had commanded before moving into a factory, he would still not be paying them for the "collective force" that produced new wealth out of "the union and harmony of the workers, the convergence and simultaneity of their efforts." [9] Marx praised this analysis in *The Holy Family*; and what Proudhon called the "error in counting" (the disparity between the sum of the workers' wages and the value of the goods produced) may have been the starting point for the Marxist theory of surplus value. Marx seemed to draw from Proudhon in the first instance the idea that the basic form of capitalist exploitation was the appropriation of work not paid for by the owner: the "surplus value" accumulated after paying the worker the lowest wage that the market would permit.[10] But whereas Proudhon invoked Ricardo's theory that labor was the source of all value as a moral imperative for achieving equality in the future, Marx alluded to it as a scientific tool for analyzing exploitation in the present.[11] In his *Philosophical Manuscripts* of 1844, Marx had begun to see future liberation in the overcoming of the "alienation" of the worker ("living labor") from the means of production which were owned by the capitalist ("dead labor"). Two essays of 1844 began to suggest that the proletariat might be the historical force for overcoming this alienation and liberating all of humanity from this exploitation.[12] By the time of the *Communist Manifesto*, Marx had thoroughly distilled the view that "the bourgeoisie . . . produces . . . its own gravediggers" and that its overthrow by the proletariat was to come about through historical inevitability and not Proudhonian exhortation.

Proudhon made little mention of Marx in his early writings. But Marx later claimed to have given him a philosophical education; and there may be traces of a brief infatuation with the new Marxist perspective in Proudhon's rather uncharacteristic expression from a letter late in 1844:

> One must abandon the subjective point of departure so far adopted by philosophers and legislators and seek outside of the vague conception of the just and good the laws which can serve to determine it . . . objectively in the study of the social relations created by economic facts.[13]

The fatal break between the two men came in 1846 after Marx had gathered together his thoughts and a nucleus of German followers in Belgium. It was a two-staged split affecting first the organization and then the ideology of the revolutionary movement—with a deep personal and cultural animus underlying both.

The organizational break came as a result of a letter from Marx of May 5, 1846, asking Proudhon to become the French correspondent of a new international revolutionary organization. The letter spoke of committees of correspondence, but cautioned of a need for extreme secrecy and contained a peculiar postscript added by the Belgian Philippe Gigot, whom Marx had designated as his cosigner of letters from the Brussels center. Gigot denounced as a "charlatan" and "parasite" the German radical Karl Grün, who had arrived in Paris just as Marx was leaving.

Karl Grün was resented by Marx as someone who, in effect, had taken his place. For Grün was the latest self-appointed ambassador of German philosophy to Parisian revolutionaries, the author of a new book defining the nature and meaning of current revolutionary ferment,[14] and a rival courtier for the favor of Proudhon. "Proudhon is the only Frenchman completely free of prejudices that I have ever known," Grün had written.[15] Proudhon reciprocated the admiration, and addressed a sharp response directly to Marx, whom he apparently assumed to be the true author of the entire letter.

Proudhon went far beyond the questions raised in the letter to suggest deep doubts about Marx himself. Proudhon expressed willingness to work together to discover the laws of society, but feared that Marx had not yet risen above the German penchant for "a priori dogmatism":

> Let us not fall into the contradiction of your compatriot Luther who having overthrown catholic theology, immediately turned to his own excommunications and anathemas, to found a protestant theology.[16]

Thus, Proudhon feared the authoritarianism in Marx even when he himself was being offered a major share of the authority.

> Because we are at the head of a movement, let us not make ourselves the chiefs of a new intolerance, let us not pose as the apostles of a new religion, even if it should be the religion of logic and reason.[17]

Such sentiments were clearly threatening to the much younger Marx, who felt immune from religion, and newly inspired by economic dogma. But Proudhon went still further to challenge Marx's new-found faith in sudden—even violent—social change. Proudhon characterized this as a "shove" (*secousse*) rather than a true revolution:

> I prefer to have proprietorship (*propriété*) burned over a slow flame rather than to give it new force by making a Saint-Bartholomew of property owners . . . our proletarians have such a great thirst for science that one who gave them nothing to drink except blood would not be welcome among them.[18]

Proudhon characterized Marx's faith in violent revolution somewhat patronizingly as a phase that he, Proudhon, had also gone through in his younger years. He defended Grün in human terms as a father faced with abject poverty who had continued the education in German thought that Marx had helped begin. In a somewhat provocative conclusion, Proudhon asserted his own authority as the more experienced, older figure, and suggested that Marx and his associates help promote the German translation of Proudhon's forthcoming book that Grün was preparing.[19]

The work to which Proudhon referred was his massive *System of Economic Contradictions or Philosophy of Poverty* of October 1846. In direct response, Marx wrote *The Poverty of Philosophy*, which he finished in June 1847: [20] the only book-length treatise against a single man and the only work in French that Marx ever wrote.[21] It was given a key role in spreading the "new teaching" that Marx succeeded in making the ideological underpinning of the Communist League by the end of 1847. His personal conflict with Proudhon thus became part of an organizational struggle for the allegiance of social revolutionaries. The Marx-Engels collaboration was sealed and their earliest organizational efforts conducted against this background of polemics with Proudhon.

At critical stages of Marx's subsequent revolutionary career, moreover, Marx would again be confronted by rival prophecies from the abrasive Frenchman. Marx's interpretation of 1848, for instance, seemed challenged by Proudhon's *General Idea of the Revolution* of 1851, which denounced the perversion of the revolutionary ideal into "materialist centralization." [22] Proudhon's *La Révolution démontrée par le coup d'état du 2 décembre* of July 1852 was a deliberate counter-interpretation to Marx's famous "Eighteenth Brumaire of Louis Bonaparte," filled with maddeningly paradoxical judgments which even included an appeal to Napoleon III to become the champion of social reform.[23] Marx contemplated (and may have written) a critique of Proudhon's *General Idea*; [24] and Engels composed an attack on Proudhon at the time, which was long unpublished.[25] Marxists have repeatedly echoed the master in accusing Proudhon of courting, if not in effect urging, collaboration with Napoleon III.[26]

Later, when Marx finally saw ideology and organization coming together into the First International in 1864, Proudhon produced a final series of writings that both conflicted in theory with Marx's *Critique of Political Economy* and helped prevent in practice French workers from collaborating harmoniously with Germans. Proudhon substituted talk of justice for economic analysis; direct moral appeals to "the working classes" for the ideological politics of "the proletariat."

Proudhon's death on January 19, 1865, was all but celebrated by Marx in an obituary for the January edition of the German journal *Sozial-demokrat*, which has been subsequently used as a ritual preface or appendix to Marxist editions of *The Poverty of Philosophy*. Marx repeated his earlier negative judgment in a letter to a leading German Social Democrat:

> He wants to soar as the man of science above the bourgeois and the proletarians; he is merely the petty bourgeois, continually tossed back and forth between capital and labor, political economy and communism.[27]

Followers of Proudhon

The ghost of Proudhon lived on to haunt Marx for at least the remainder of the nineteenth century. Proudhonist opposition to centralism and ideological dogma dominated both the First International and the Paris Commune of 1871—the two most important phenomena in the development of the social revolutionary tradition in the West during the remaining years of Marx's life.

The organizational-political aspect of the Marx-Proudhon conflict began while Proudhon was still alive—with the first attempts to organize international proletarian cooperation after the disastrous failures of 1848–51. Proudhon emerged from these years with much the greater reputation—earned as an active journalist in Paris who had consistently called for radical, immediate social change and as one of the very few newly elected members of the assembly who used his position to protest publicly the June massacres of 1848.

As far afield as quiescent Denmark, there was an immediate response to Proudhon's vision of a new internationalism based on mutual aid and small-scale cooperatives rather than on national units and parliamentary politics. A remarkable young medical student, Frederik Dreier, in his *Future of the Peoples of the World* in 1848 set forth the vision of an international of small-scale cooperatives speaking a new common language. He founded a small artisan organization largely inspired by the ideas of Proudhon.[28] Thus, the first approximation of the cooperative movement in northern Europe, which later became a major contribution of Scandinavia to modern socialism, was Proudhonist in inspiration. But Dreier died in 1853 at the age of twenty-five, and the movement never had the chance to develop.

Another immediate, if even more distant echo of Proudhon came from

America. A tall, handsome graduate of West Point and Harvard Divinity School, William Greene of Massachusetts, published in 1850 a Proudhonist book, *Mutual Banking*, and proceeded to set up a system of land banks to promote mutualism in the New World. In 1853, he moved to Paris, where he met Proudhon and remained until the Civil War. After a brief tour of duty in the Union Army, he became a labor organizer, dividing his time between America and France, where he joined the French section of the First International.[29]

The beginnings of an international working-class movement can be traced to April 1856, when a predominately Proudhonist delegation of French workers arrived in London with an "Address from the workers of France to their brothers, the workers of England." It proposed a League of Workers of All Nations to supplant capitalism everywhere with Proudhonist producer and consumer cooperatives.[30] Then, in 1862, Napoleon III conceded to his restless working class the right to elect a delegation to the London International Exhibit of 1862. This was the first independent political activity of French workers since the Napoleonic coup; and the 750 delegates spread international political awareness among the French proletariat. The most influential proletarian leader was a pure Proudhonist, Henri-Louis Tolain, who independently arranged for a second working-class delegation to London in 1863. Its meetings proved more militant, featuring speeches in support of the Polish Revolution and establishing links with the newly founded London Trades Council.[31] A call was issued for an international gathering the following year—which proved to be the founding meeting of the First International.

Marx prevailed over the Mazzinians within the central committee in the drafting of the general rules and the inaugural address for the new organization late in 1864. Marx's fear of the Proudhonists was evidenced in his successful insistence on substituting a London meeting of the central committee (General Council) for its first congress, which had been scheduled for Belgium in September 1865. But conflict with the Proudhonists flared into the open at the conference and continued to dominate the first four congresses which were held on an annual basis in Switzerland or Belgium (Geneva, Lausanne, Brussels, Basel). The underlying issue was almost always the same: the insistence of the Proudhonists on a working-class movement based on trade unions and cooperatives that would avoid becoming involved in political or ideological questions. The French initially tried to limit membership in the International to manual workers, for they had a deep distrust of the rhetoricians and savants who had so long misled the Parisian workers with political slogans.

Proudhon had written an influential pamphlet in April 1863 urging true democrats to boycott the polls ("the political church of the bourgeoisie") in the elections scheduled for May.[32] The same antipolitical tone pervaded both the *Manifesto of the 60* of February 1864, whose signatories included only workers, and Proudhon's own posthumously published *On the Political Capacity of the Working Classes*.[33] At the congresses of the International in the late sixties, the French consistently opposed general resolutions on remote and largely symbolic international issues (Poland) or measures of reform that depended on enforcement by the power of the state (child labor laws).[34] To Marx, however, such issues were not ends in themselves, but useful "guerrilla fights" [35] for mobilizing proletarian consciousness and solidarity in the struggle against capitalism. Though not present at any of the early congresses, Marx exercised increasing control through his position on the General Council and his energetic talent as drafter and tactician. The Brussels Congress of 1868, which attracted a record one hundred delegates, committed the International to the policy of nationalizing the means of production—largely by wooing some of the swollen Belgian delegation away from the Proudhonist French position. César de Paepe, leader of the Belgian section which hosted and dominated the congress, described his movement into alliance with the Marxist position as being "de-Proudhonized." [36] The congress at Basel in the following year confirmed the decline of Proudhonist influence by endorsing the common ownership of land, which the Proudhonists considered equivalent to "collective tyranny." [37]

The relatively nonviolent Proudhonists were, in effect, supplanted within the International by the more militant and revolutionary form of anarchism represented by Bakunin, who for the first time attended a congress at the International in 1869. But during the Franco-Prussian War and the subsequent civil war fought within France against the Paris Commune, it was the Proudhonists (including Proudhon's friend and portraitist, Courbet) who completely dominated the Paris federation of the International. They provided seventeen of the ninety-two elected representatives of the Commune.

After the war and revolution of 1870–71, the nonviolent antistatism of Proudhon reasserted its appeal to a new and chastened generation of social revolutionaries. Proudhonism gained a new following in agrarian southern and eastern Europe. Seminal propagandists of populism like Nicholas Mikhailovsky in Russia and Svetozar Markovič in Serbia translated Proudhon's works; [38] and Proudhon's ideas inspired Pi y Margal, leader of the antinationalist Federal Party in Spain, and others from Portugal to Mexico.[39]

In western Europe, Proudhonism remained a dominant current throughout the 1870s and 1880s. Prior to the great industrial expansion of the 1890s and the concurrent growth of the Second International, the "petty bourgeois" Proudhonist ideal of gaining immediate recompense in goods or property had continuing appeal. In a time of political repression, many preferred to develop working-class institutions apart from bourgeois politics altogether. Outside of Germany, Marxism responded effectively to Proudhonism and its ideological allies only after forming the first Marxist journal in France (Jules Guesde's *Egalité* of 1877), and the first Marxist circle among the Slavs (Plekhanov's "Liberation of Labor" in 1882).

The last European Congress of the First International (Geneva, 1873) and the first Congress of the Second (Paris 1889) were each preceded and challenged by a rival international congress sympathetic to Proudhonist ideas in the same city: the Geneva founding congress of the anti-authoritarian international in 1873 and the Paris international Congress of Possibilists in 1889. The first was a militant gathering that far outshone the pallid Marxist congress a week later; the latter congress of 1889 was, however, as the name Possibilists suggests, only an attenuated version of the Proudhonist message: a reformist search for the possible. The main group of Possibilists was overshadowed by the larger and more cosmopolitan gathering of Marxists, whose rival centennial commemoration of the French Revolution led to the founding of the Second International.

A splinter group of the Possibilists, however, led by the militant Jean Allemane, who was like Proudhon a printer, kept alive the quasi-anarchistic Proudhonist legacy as well as the emphasis on direct action by workers themselves: "No white hands; only hands with callouses!" [40] More militant than the Possibilists, but deeply opposed to the dogmatism and centralism of the Marxists, the Allemanists helped transmit the heritage of Proudhon to the new revolutionary syndicalists as they formed in the early 1890s. The basic unit for this movement was the local version of a trade union, the Bourse de Travail, which was deeply Proudhonist in its working-class composition and emphasis on local authority and direct action. If the future belonged to the better organized Marxists, who soon gained control of the Second International, the rival Proudhonists seemed still to dominate the militant workers' movement in France and most of the Latin world. As a leading German Social Democrat of the period explained:

> Every time that the workers' movement finds itself thrown back on itself, far from bourgeois temptations, far also from the advice of its own chiefs— those who proclaim themselves their chiefs—it naturally recovers Proudhonism, this Monroe Doctrine of the Proletariat. [41]

Although anarcho-syndicalism continued to flourish in the Latin world at least through the Spanish Civil War, Proudhonism is generally seen as a transitory phenomenon of the period that preceded large-scale industrial and imperial expansion in the 1890s. The First International and the successor congresses of the 1870s and 1880s involved only a small fraction of the European working class. Relatively skilled workers from larger cities containing a variety of industries were in the forefront. There was little involvement of the unskilled masses from the new metallurgical and mining industries or from the newer factory cities built around one controlling industry. [42] If the old artisan class was in decline, the new factory proletariat had not yet fully emerged. As late as 1896, 534,000 of 575,000 industrial establishments in France had less than ten workers. [43] The expansion of heavy industry, larger factories, and unskilled labor prepared the way for new mass movements more receptive to chauvinist appeals from the Right and Marxist direction on the Left. There seemed new relevance to Marx's critique of Proudhon as "petty bourgeois"; but in a time of little-understood change, Proudhon's "petty bourgeois" ideal of preserving a measure of private property and local autonomy had continuing appeal.

Enduring Issues

Beyond the personal passion of Marx and Proudhon and the political polemics of their followers lay a deeper conflict about ideas that is of continuing importance to those in search of radical social change.

At first glance, the intensity of the Marx-Proudhon struggle seems surprising. Conservatives, liberals, and earlier romantic socialists all saw many similarities between the two. Taken together, Marx and Proudhon represented the point of transition—indeed, of no return—from the sentimental theorizing of the pre-1848 period to the no-nonsense toughness of modern mass revolutionary movements.

Both had a confident vision of history that attached central importance to fulfilling the aborted hopes of the French revolutions of 1789 and 1848. This faith actually grew stronger in the wake of 1848, since both men absorbed themselves in fortifying their basic faith with long theoretical writings during the disillusioning aftermath of the defeated revolution. Both believed that social revolution could resolve the social and economic contradictions in the real world. They were the first important continental revolutionaries to study English classical economics at great length (even before 1848), and to view the working class as the chosen instrument of the ultimate liberation of all mankind.

Both believed that all preceding socialisms were utopian and, in Proudhon's phrase, *rêveries fantastiques:* private experiments rather than suitable vehicles for the total transformation of society. Both rejected the traditional institutions of bourgeois liberalism more systematically than their predecessors, and were deeply opposed to nationalism and the ideal of national liberation (though each reflected some national prejudices from his own background). Both were creatures of the new *feuilleton* style of writing in the early 1840s and of the concurrent moves from philosophy to polemics, history to politics, academic dialogue to radical action groups.

Yet the differences between Marx and Proudhon—and between their conscious followers and unconscious heirs—were profound. Conflict raged in at least six areas: philosophical, historical, moral, political, economic, and religious. Each of these domains became a battlefield for the continuing struggle between "authoritarian" communists and "petty bourgeois" mutualists in the nineteenth century. Some or all of them have recurred in the continuing twentieth-century debate between collectivist and libertarian impulses on the Left.

(a) *Philosophically,* there was a difference from the first time the two men met in 1844. The young Marx was an authentic product of the intellectual self-confidence of the University of Berlin: believing that all questions were answerable, and all problems soluble in an absolute system of truth that he was in the act of discovering. Proudhon, ten years older and far better known, was a self-taught plebeian deeply suspicious of intellectual abstraction. "You will never imagine," he wrote on reading some economists, "the terrible effect which a learned theory produces when used in a destructive way." [44] He rejected the very image of a Pythagorean harmony in nature which had been so fundamental to earlier revolutionaries:

> I do not find anywhere, neither can I understand, that melody of the great All, which Pythagoras thought he heard.[45]

Like Marx, Proudhon made his living writing; but there was a profound stylistic difference between the rough, paradoxical (Marx called it "muscular") prose of the provincial Frenchman writing in the prisons of Paris and the logical, acerbic polemics of the Rhineland German writing in the British Museum.

(b)   Their *different views of history* were evidenced in the contrasting uses they made of Hegel's thought. Broadly stated, Marx turned Hegel upside down, making his theory materialistic rather than idealistic; but he maintained the basic Hegelian view that reality was monistic and that history was moving necessarily and dialectically toward the realization of an ideal future order. In contrast, Proudhon left Hegel right side up, maintaining the Hegelian image of history as a process of ideas unfolding through contradictions. But he denied the objective, monistic view of reality, substituting the dualism between "ought" and "is" of the subjective moralist. He further denied that there was any necessary "synthesis" to the contradictions of social life. Proudhon's definition of revolution was the "defatalization" of history rather than the final resolution of its problems.[46]

Proudhon's first major work, *The System of Economic Contradictions,* insisted that the intellect could discover necessary contradictions in society—but no certain syntheses. To Marx, this was "the poverty of philosophy": a confession of philosophical bankruptcy that would disarm revolutionaries by taking away any rational hope for the course of history. Proudhon's imperfect understanding of Hegel was easily demonstrated by the young Marx, who explained that Proudhon "glorifies contradiction because contradiction is the basis of his existence." [47]

(c)   Proudhon's view of history was rooted in a *moral philosophy* closer to the stern moralism of Kant than to the impersonal historicism of Hegel. Marx called him "the French Kant"; and Kant helped lead Proudhon to speak not of a progressive dialectic which resolves everything, but of antinomies that can never be resolved.[48] Proudhon found in the Kantian discovery of insoluble philosophical antinomies a source not of despair, as Marx contended, but of guidance for understanding the comparable antinomies in social life. The economic analysis of his *System of Contradictions* found paradox built into the very development of an economy: the need for more poverty to create greater wealth; the pursuit of happiness leading to greater unhappiness, and so forth.

But Proudhon insisted that the agony of contradiction would not lead to despair or resignation as long as man did not look on the situation with complacency or cynicism. The real answer for society was not the mythic conclusion of some future, final synthesis; but the realistic possibility that at every stage the contradictions which are part and parcel of life itself could be held in equilibrium. Proudhon spoke of a dynamic ever-changing equilibrium: an "equilibration" between forces that would never either vanish or lose their venality. The balancing of such rival forces, though always tense and precarious, was the highest good that man can hope for on earth.

In society, contradictions are brought into equilibrium by Justice, which was for Proudhon a moral absolute. Justice was a higher principle that somehow struggled to control the historical process. Good and evil were not relativized and subordinated to historical necessity as in Hegel, but kept as transcendent values in themselves. He insisted on rejecting any scheme in which the distinction between good and evil was not fundamental. Marx noted that Proudhon had reduced Hegel's dialectic to "the dogmatic distinction between good and bad." [49]

History for Proudhon was a kind of development of the idea of Justice, which he described variously as "the great ideal," "a mystery," and "the very essence of humanity." [50] This justice was the unending defense of human dignity realized through the moral struggle of the individual conscience. Evil lay not in social relationships, but in the human will; and therefore the proletarian cause would not in itself save humanity as Marx contended.[51] Proudhon called Marx utopian for believing that society could be improved "without stirring up renewed consciousness of justice." [52] Marx for his part considered Proudhon utopian for making mankind dependent on the moral idealism of the individual, and the workings of an unhistorical, metaphysical conception of justice.

(d) *Politically*, Proudhon's attitude differed sharply from that of Marx—although both believed that the coming revolution would ultimately bring an end to any oppressive rule of man over man. Marx's economic determinism argued that the revolution would be accomplished by the proletarian conquest of political power; and that this process would require a new type of political party and an interim "dictatorship of the proletariat." Proudhon, believing in moral determinism, argued that the revolution could be realized only through concrete social and economic change; and that this process required a rejection of all political activity in favor of immediate social changes producing tangible economic benefits.

During the Revolution of 1848 Proudhon eschewed political debates, insisting that a parliamentary division is "1000 times more idiotic" than the ceremony of annointment with holy oil.[53] He concentrated instead on mounting a direct attack on what he called "industrial feudalism": the abuse of property ownership to accumulate unearned profits and enserf workers with "the leprosy of interest." He proposed a system of people's banks to grant virtually free credit. This would stimulate economic activity without increasing the power of the government or of large, impersonal business enterprises.

Marx rightly pointed out that this was a *petit bourgeois* conception; for Proudhon sought not to end the ownership of property, but only to end ownership without labor—profit without work. He sought to realize equality by "an identity of the labor and capitalist" that would not deny the acquisitive instinct in man, but rather would make capital immediately available to all, and thus would achieve an equilibrium between liberty and order.[54]

(e)   *Economically*, the essence of their argument was that Marx believed property should be abolished, while Proudhon believed it should be distributed. In the Hegelian language of their polemics, Marx defined communism—whose essence was the liquidation of private property—as the final synthesis of history. Proudhon saw communism only as an "antithesis" of capitalism—and thus necessarily as one-sided and false as the "thesis" of capitalism itself.[55]

Proudhon's new *révolution sociale* was to be made not by the violent seizure of political power at the center, but rather by the nonviolent development of a new system of equal contracts at the local level. Direct agreement of man to man was to undermine and replace that artificial contract between citizen and government, between worker and capitalist. Free credit was to stimulate the *moral* goal of a fairer distribution rather than the *economic* goal of greater production.

Proudhon in the 1850s and 1860s moved beyond the simple anarchism of his early works [56] and related his vision of the coming social revolution to two new concepts: *mutualism* and *federalism*. The word mutualism he took from long prior usage among the artisans of Lyon. It was, thus, one of the few isms with an authentic origin among workers rather than intellectuals. On June 28, 1828, workers in Lyon organized a society of *Devoir Mutuel* or *Mutuellisme*, with a program of education and mutual aid designed above all to further the self-sufficiency and self-respect of the silk weavers in the city. The date came to be annually celebrated as "year _____ of the regeneration"; [57] and in the subsequent uprising of November 1831, a more militant *Association des Mutuellistes* also briefly played a role. The workers of Lyon generally preferred to call themselves *mutuellistes* rather than *prolétaires* during the turbulent years leading up to the Revolution of 1848; and the term connoted workers organizing themselves in militant pursuit of their own immediate needs and material interests.

This mutualist tradition of Lyon was never dominated either by intellectuals or by republican politicians. The proud, provincial bastion of Lyon was suspicious of either intellectual or political centralization, which inevitably meant Parisian dominance. The strong artisan traditions of the silk industry made Lyonnais workers additionally hostile to the centralization and monopolization of economic power.

Proudhon's native Besançon was far closer geographically and spiritually to Lyon than to Paris. Proudhon spent much of the crucial period from 1843–47, when he was writing his most important works, in Lyon. He took the Lyonnais label and applied it to his own ideal of a new type of free contractual relationship among individual artisans in a common enterprise.[58] Proudhon's mutualism represented a social revolutionary ideal much in the air in the mid-nineteenth century but largely forgotten in the twentieth because it was opposed to communism. In like manner, Proudhon's political ideal of federalism was widely admired in the mid-nineteenth century,[59] but has been obscured since by the dominant, rival concept of nationalism.

Federalism was "mutualism transported to the political sphere," the political principle which could alone check the "materialist centralization" of the modern national state.[60] Federalism was Proudhon's reluctant concession to the need for political organization: the only hope he saw for avoiding nationalistic wars and for preserving the equilibrium between order and freedom. So deep was Proudhon's commitment to the federal principle that he opposed most of the fashionable international revolutionary causes of the 1860s: the unification of Italy, the independence of Poland, the Union side in the American Civil War. He contended in each case that misguided politicians were simply creating larger and more impersonal concentrations of power with the aid of deceptive political slogans.[61] Of Mazzini, Proudhon asked:

> Does he know what he has done for the Italian pleb in making him a fanatic for unity? He has established the reign of the bourgeoisie over him.[62]

Proudhon had a consistent—many have called it reactionary—preference for smaller and more personalized social units. His passionate defense of the traditional rural family (and attendant hatred of the "pornocracy" of Paris) was part of a relentless localism that tended to prefer Burgundy to France, Franche Comté to Burgundy, and the individual family and village to Franche Comté.[63]

Marx attacked this attitude as "Proudhonized Stirnerism: everything to be dissolved into little groups or communes . . . while history comes to a stop."[64] Marx's global perspective favored "the establishment of large-scale economies and polities and the assimilation of smaller cultures and languages."[65] Marx and Engels had a special contempt for "small relics of people . . . got up in popular dress," and a certain infatuation with "the right of the great European nations to separate and independent existence."[66] Thus, he generally favored the struggles of larger, more advanced nations to become states (Italy, Hungary), supported smaller struggles that might aid larger ones (Ireland-England), and praised "national classes" whose interests spearheaded the struggle of a nation with a special historical destiny (the bourgeoisie in Germany 1848–49). Against the Proudhonist argument that the Polish cause was a "Bonapartist invention" to divert working people from real social issues, Marx insisted in the First International that the Poles deserved continuing international support both because Poland was a great "historical" nation and because its nationhood was prerequisite to a German revolution.

In his hostility to all forms of centralized power, Proudhon attacked Rousseau with particular venom for having made political tyranny "respectable by making it proceed from the people."[67] Proudhon saw more deeply than most other radicals into the dangers of war that were inherent in the very creation of the modern industrial state. War was being made likely not just by the monopoly of physical power and ideological authority invested in the state—but also because standards of behavior had ceased being moral and were becoming aesthetic. Abstract slogans and remote border conflicts had become matters of psychic significance to the uprooted masses who were increasingly seeking artistic genius in their leaders.[68]

Marx occasionally advocated war (usually against Russia), but viewed it as a means of hastening social revolution and thus as a passing phenomenon. Proudhon feared that war had an enduring psychological appeal and suggested its inevitability in a world of sovereign nations: "War is the most ancient of religions and it will be the last." [69] In his view *political* conflicts tended necessarily to become wars. Since conflict could not be eliminated from human life, the ending of war required the elimination of politics. By concentrating on social rather than political causes, France now had the opportunity to redirect the attention of humanity into an area in which "the jurisdiction of war is incompetent" and thus "create a new spiritual order." [70] The "creative valor of war" would not be denied or suppressed but rather "transposed" into creative labor in which the "warrior virtues" of individual pride and team effort were equally engaged.[71]

The creator of this new order—which Proudhon called in his late works a "third world," a "new democracy"—was to be the "working classes" of France. In his final, posthumously published On the Political Capacity of the Working Classes, Proudhon urged the development of a new ethos of "democratic simplicity" within the working classes: the nonviolent building of an egalitarian social order by mutualism at the local level and boycotts against the bourgeois order at the national level.

(f) *Religion* was a final area of difference between Proudhon and Marx; they had radically differing attitudes towards the Judaeo-Christian heritage. Marx was a confident philosophical atheist. Though well versed in scripture as a youth, he showed almost no interest in it as an adult. His hero was Prometheus, who took fire away from the gods; and his perspective was patronizing if not contemptuous towards both his Jewish heritage and the Christian tradition of Germany into which he had been baptized. Religion he viewed as the opium of the people [72] and the confusion of the intellectuals.

Proudhon, on the other hand, was deeply and permanently disturbed by Christian teachings. He was not at all a believer in any conventional sense. But his writings were saturated with religious symbols and scriptural passages. He described the dominant influences on his life as the Bible first, then Adam Smith and Hegel. The last two he shared with Marx; but the first was distinctive to Proudhon. In many ways he was probably a more thorough reader of the religious than of the economic or the philosophical text, since he read both Latin and Hebrew but never mastered the English of Smith or the German of Hegel.

He had become acquainted with the Bible as a young typesetter for religious texts in his local community,[73] and made an early contrast between the biblical idea of justice and compassion and the society of comfort, callousness, and complacency all around him. He developed a special revulsion for "neo-Christian" sentimentality—"those fools who admire Christianity because it has produced bells and cathedrals"—and a lifelong hatred for "religion offering itself as a safeguard to the middle class." [74]

For Marx, this use of religion by the ruling class was natural and inevitable; a superstructure of religious rationalization that was bound to perish with the revolutionary destruction of the substructure of bourgeois social forms. But Proudhon was deeply disturbed by any identification of Christianity with the bourgeois order of Louis Philippe or Napoleon III. He became a passionate spokesman for the current in French social thought that sought to separate Christ from the Church: to equate social radicalism with true Christianity. Proudhon hated the Saint-Simonian conception of a "New Christianity," the belief that the people need a new religion to reconcile them to a new scientific elite. Proudhon did not seek any new religion, but rather the final victory of Justice on earth, which he increasingly came to identify with the realization of Christ's teachings. Christ to Proudhon was the starting point of Revolution and the supreme teacher of Justice—and thus the man who validated both of Proudhon's key concepts.[75] He believed with Tolstoy that "only that revolution which is impossible to stop is a fruitful revolution"; [76] and that Christ had started it.[77]

Although best known for his influence on French socialists and foreign anarchists, Proudhon also influenced many unorthodox religious prophets of radical but nonviolent social change. Tolstoy took the title for his greatest novel, *War and Peace,* and some of his subsequent anarchist ideas from Proudhon.[78] Martin Buber saw Proudhon's mutualism as part of the moral inspiration for the Israeli kibbutzim, which constituted in turn a rival approach to social ownership to that of Soviet collectivization.[79] Radical "personalists" and worker-priests in France after World War II also found inspiration in Proudhon. His substantial foreign following was greatest in those countries that combined powerful religious traditions with reactionary and authoritarian social structures.

Although Proudhon's influence has been most fully traced in the Latin world, it was probably most important in Russia. The unique traditions of Russian populism were deeply influenced by Proudhon from the beginning through his formative personal impact on Herzen and Bakunin, the two principal pioneering authors of its ideology. Russian populism developed in the years just after Proudhon's death in 1865 into a near perfect embodiment of Proudhonist ideas. The glorification of a nonviolent social revolution through the commune and artel was antipolitical mutualism at its best. The anti-ideological, quasi-Christian, and anti-authoritarian populist ideology also shared Proudhon's fear of the cities, of central government, and of the entire lexicon of liberal constitutionalism. Like the Proudhonist socialists in late nineteenth-century France, the Russian populists divided into a moderate "possibilist" wing (the "legal populists") and a more violent "anarcho-syndicalist" wing [80] (the terrorists in the People's Will organization and later in the Socialist Revolutionary party).

The Russians' passion for ultimate answers led them to develop Proudhon's antisystematic moralism into a heroic philosophy of action.

Closest to an ideological expression of this attitude, which underlay most of Russian populism, was Nicholas Mikhailovsky's "subjective method." It insisted that "man with his flesh and blood, his thoughts and feelings" must be both the means and the end of the revolutionary struggle. *Lichnost'*, the fullness of personality in every man and woman, could never "be forgotten for an abstract category"; and the heroic, often anarchistic belief that they were waging a "struggle for individuality" kept the Russian populists' belief in "the people" from becoming a mask for collectivism.[81] An aristocratic convert to revolutionary populism in the late 1860s, Peter Kropotkin, provided an eloquent new voice for Proudhonianism. After living among the watchmakers of the Jura, observing their disciplined mutualism, and talking at length with the predominately Proudhonist exiles from the Paris Commune, Kropotkin returned to St. Petersburg to help set up the first group to organize and politically educate urban workers in Russia, the so-called Chaikovsky circle, where much of the broader agitation of the 1870s originated. Kropotkin amplified Proudhon's ideals by substituting the moral imperative of "mutual aid" for "scientific" theories of conflict; and he drew up in late 1873 a kind of populist manifesto that repudiated all forms of constitutionalism in favor of a federation of independent local communities controlled by the workers and peasants themselves.[82]

Concurrently in the West, Bakunin was developing from the Proudhonist tradition an even more militant form of revolutionary anarchism. Bakunin's resultant struggle with Marx was, as we shall see, in many ways a continuation of the earlier Proudhon-Marx conflict. But Russia in the twentieth century (like Germany in the late nineteenth) was to follow Marx rather than Proudhon. For Marx had analyzed the Industrial Revolution more fully, and accepted the medium of political struggle more naturally. Although few workers ever read his writings, in the late nineteenth century Marx's claim to scientific authority exercised increasing appeal to the first generation ever to experience near universal primary education in secular state schools. Marx's unfinished masterpiece of the post-1848 period *Capital* was impenetrable for the average worker. He nevertheless felt

> . . . a superstitious respect for that which he does not understand. There were two conditions: that it explain both the suffering he endures and the end it proposes. Proudhon never knew how to satisfy either condition.[83]

Yet despite Proudhon's inherent flaws and the seeming triumph of Marxism in the twentieth century, the ghost of Proudhon has not been entirely laid to rest. For the "new left" of the 1960s bore many striking resemblances to the old Proudhonism. There was, first of all, the intense moralism and quasi-anarchic rejection of almost all established authority. There was the accompanying Proudhonian desire to put power directly in the hands of "the people," primarily by the nonviolent strengthening of local communal structures. At the same time there was a deep antagonism to dogma and "idea-mania" [84] as well as an indifference to history,[85] and suspicion of science. They followed Proudhon in protesting against remote central power, and arguing for immediate concrete benefits against the distant, symbolic goals promoted by governments.[86] They even revived (albeit unconsciously) the mystical term "third world." The "third world" of the new left was the nonwhite, extra-European world oppressed by both capitalism and communism. But this new "third world"—like the old—was believed to be the bearer of a new social order because of its very lack of participation in the existing processes of power. Marxist hagiographers in the U.S.S.R., meanwhile, detected the hand of "neo-Proudhonism" behind a bewildering variety of anti-authoritarian impulses; and denounced at great length the "return to Proudhonism." [87]

The original Marx-Proudhon controversy took place in the bleak period of European socialism: the third quarter of the nineteenth century. Early utopian experiments had failed; the revolutions of 1848–50 had been crushed; and the mass movements of the late nineteenth century had not yet been coalesced. The industrial bourgeoisie and the great state-builders—Cavour and Napoleon III, Bismarck and Disraeli—seemed everywhere triumphant. Yet both Marx and Proudhon continued to believe that bourgeois society was doomed; and both reaffirmed in the darkest period of all—the 1850s and 1860s—their belief in a coming social revolution.

Marx based his revolutionary faith on an all-encompassing system of truth; Proudhon offered in the last analysis only an impassioned belief in Justice. Perhaps there is an analogy with thirteenth-century Europe, when the outward prosperity of medieval civilization was at its height, but when two new mendicant orders appeared to preach prophetically of its inner weakness: the Dominicans and the Franciscans. Marx was the modern Dominican, the system-building Thomas Aquinas of the revolutionary church; Proudhon was its St. Francis. The former spoke primarily to the intellect, the latter mainly to the emotions. The Franciscans were always further from power and closer to heresy; but it was the Dominicans who lit the fires of the Inquisition and of Savonarola.

CHAPTER 11

The Magic Medium: Journalism

"THE PRESS is a drum which leads to the frontier," wrote Armand Marrast, editor of the newspaper *National* during the upheavals of 1848 in Paris.[1] The frontiers were physical as well as spiritual, for just as journalism moved men to revolution, so journalists often manned the movements that resulted. Marrast, who as a young man had helped write the libretto for Rossini's *William Tell*, had moved on to the drumbeat of journalism and became the mayor of revolutionary Paris.

The last king of France was deposed literally as well as figuratively by journalists. Emile Girardin, the founder of the first cheap mass paper in Paris, *La Presse*, went to Louis Philippe and told him to get off of his throne late in the morning of February 24, 1848.[2] At that very moment, the new provisional government was being formed in the office of another newspaper (Flocon's radical *La Réforme*) after consultation with the editorial staff of a third (Marrast's *Le National*).[3]

Sweeping freedom for the press was among the provisional government's first decrees. The profusion of revolutionary printing could not be contained in regular journals. It soon spilled out into posters, fly leafs, and placards, which Barmby likened to "pulses of intellectual movement which we count by the minute"—a counter-volley against "the murderous musketry of a dead and driving despotism." This unprecedented outpouring represented "handwriting on the wall to the Belshazzars of the earth!"[4] at a time when "printers must become princes."[5]

Whether it was cause or effect, barometer or spark plug, the press played a role that was as central in the revolution of young intellectuals in 1848 as had been the Masonic-type conspiracy in the revolutions of young officers during 1815–25. A decade of florid journalistic criticism set the stage for 1848. But the link between journalism and the modern revolutionary tradition goes back much further and may even validate the hypothesis that "every revolutionary change in the means of communication is followed by a change in the entire structure of society." [6]

The extraordinary importance of journalism to the French Revolution has already been stressed. Whether at the mass level of mobilizing men and popularizing ideas à la Marat or Hébert or at the elite level of inventing new words and forms à la Bonneville or Restif, journalists provided the drumfire driving Frenchmen on to new concepts as well as to new conquests.

The impact of the "fourth estate" during 1789–94 is all the more remarkable for having occurred in a largely pre-industrial era. Industrialization vastly increased both the number and importance of journalists; and a large number of revolutionaries developed an almost physiological attachment to printing along with a personal dependence on journalistic writing.

The hum of printing machines and the smell of printers' ink were close to the revolutionary movement at every critical moment during its progression from conspiracy to ideology. Restif is the prototype—inventing the word communist and fantasizing about "the year 2000" during the French Revolution in private communion with his own home printing press—designing his own type face and typography, rejoicing in the physical act of printing and in the company of fellow printers. In like manner, Joseph Applegath, the first man to use the word socialist in its modern sense, was an engineer and "creator of the printing presses from which the modern machines were derived." [7] Typographic technicians from the Ecole Polytechnique played a major role in the Saint-Simonian movement. Henry Hetherington, the pioneer of the cheap, unstamped radical press and a key early organizer of English Chartism, had been the apprentice of Luke Hansard, the famed parliamentary printer. His life was spent quite literally around printing presses; and court orders to suppress his activities were often accompanied by the physical destruction of press and type with blacksmiths' hammers.[8] The spread of Owenite doctrines to the working class was largely the work of Hetherington and other printers such as George Mudie from Scotland.[9] Hetherington was also instrumental in launching the journalistic activities of Barmby, who in turn repopularized the word communist.[10] Schapper, the founder of the League of the Just, had been a student of forestry and was interested in the production of paper and print as well as of radical ideas. Proudhon learned to read while working as a printer's apprentice. Apprenticeship in the printshop induced a visceral sense of identification with the working classes in the songs of Béranger [11] as well as in the pamphlets of Proudhon.

Compositors played a key role in the formation of revolutionary circles among German émigrés in the late 1830s. The German community in Paris had become increasingly revolutionary long before Marx joined their ranks in 1843. A Paris police report traced the leading role of the society of "German demagogues" and its subordinate "action society"— both founded in 1838. Two of the three leaders of the former group were identified as printers (a Rauchfuss from Prussia via Swiss secret societies, and the "clever and influential demagogue," Trappe of Dresden). The individual leader of the "action society" was a "worker printer" from Hanover named Rust, who under a variety of pseudonyms had fled from Göttingen in 1830 to Belgium, Switzerland, and the international revolutionary campaign against Savoy before coming to Paris in 1837.[12]

From this pioneering group Weitling and Becker drew the talent and precedent for the original communist publication campaign of the early forties in Switzerland.[13] Particularly after hopes of revolution were dashed by the failure of the insurrection of 1839 in Paris, the German "action society" turned its activities in Belgium and Luxembourg entirely to printing and propaganda.[14]

Journalism was the most important single professional activity for revolutionary Saint-Simonians and Hegelians. Hegel as a young theology student had directly substituted the reading of English newspapers for morning prayers—a distant anticipation of the modern educated man substituting the Sunday newspaper for Sunday church. The Saint-Simonians regarded the press as the medium for propagating the theology of their new religion of humanity (just as the theater was to provide its new liturgy).[15]

The profession of revolutionary journalism blended most closely with new means of communication in Brussels of the 1840s. Marx's years of crucial ideological development climaxing in the *Communist Manifesto* were spent in Brussels, precisely when he was perfecting his mature profession as à journalist.

Brussels had become a center both of legal revolutionary journalism and of rapid industrial development after the successful Belgian Revolution of 1830. Buonarroti published his history of the Babeuf Conspiracy in Brussels, reminding his associates there that Babeuf had founded *Journal de la Liberté de la Presse* before his *Tribun du Peuple*. Buonarroti's Belgian followers like Jacob Kats, Louis de Potter, and Felix Delhasse directed their activist impulses largely into journalism,[16] and intoxication with the new medium increased as Brussels became the hub of rail and telegraphic links between France, England, and North Germany. The remarkable Belgian social theorist Napoleon Barthel argued that these new media of communication hailed the advent of a "scientific religion of humanity," which he called "normalism." Versed in the occult study of phrenology and magnetism, Barthel moved from a *Philosophic Manifesto* of 1839 on to his strange outpouring of the revolutionary year 1848: *On physical telegraphy in general, and in particular on the electromagnetic telegraphic system of Napoleon Barthel.*[17]

The marriage of the printing press to telegraphy and a mass audience in the late forties fascinated the restless and uprooted émigrés like Marx. The very titles of journals to which the German radicals contributed suggested the mobilization of words to technology: the liberal Leipzig, *Locomotive*, the socialist *Westphälische Dampfboot* (Steamboat), and Gutzkow's Hamburg daily *Telegraph für Deutschland*. Marx had been active on the *Dampfboot*,[18] and placed articles in the *Tele-*

graph in collaboration with Engels, whose polemic journalistic career had begun in 1841 on yet another journal named *Telegraph*.[19]

The lifelong collaboration of Marx and Engels thus began in journalistic activity in Brussels: their founding of the Communist Correspondence Committee in 1846, and of *Deutsche Brüsseler Zeitung* the following year. Their first organizational use of the label communist was for the Correspondence Committee, which apparently sought to infiltrate the correspondence networks and wire agencies centered in Brussels in order to place material in a wide spectrum of European journals.

This Correspondence Committee apparently had links with a leftist news agency, the Brussels Correspondence Bureau, which Marx's close collaborator, Sebastian Seiler, had helped found in 1844.[20] A radical Swiss journalist and former collaborator with Marx on the *Rheinische Zeitung*, Seiler employed Marx's brother-in-law Edgar von Westphalen in his bureau. Brussels was the ideal base of operations. Relatively free from censorship, it was the point of convergence for the three great wire services that were revolutionizing journalism: Reuters of Britain, Havas of France, and Wolff of Germany. Their lines were to meet in Brussels; and Marx and Seiler were waiting.

Not only the early hopes, but also the seminal quarrels of the revolutionary movement developed in the shadow of the printing press. Schapper was Marx's proofreader on *Neue Rheinische Zeitung;* Stephen Born was his typesetter on *Deutsche Brüsseler Zeitung*. Marx rejected the "true socialism" of the Young Hegelians and the quasi-religious communism of Weitling by attacking their respective journals: the *Westphälische Dampfboot* and *Volkstribun*.[21]

Thus, émigré journalism preceded and helped shape Marx's ideas on revolutionary organization. A similar sequence was to recur with Lenin, whose organizational ideas were largely worked out in the activities of his journal *Iskra* in 1900–02, before a distinct Bolshevik party emerged in 1903. Both German Communism and Russian Bolshevism were founded by émigrés largely immersed in journalism, meeting in the same two cities of Brussels and London a half century apart.

To understand the origins of the ideological journalism that played such a central role in the German and Russian movements, one must begin with the prior history of revolutionary journalism in France. In this as in so many other areas, Germany and Russia in the second half of the nineteenth century were keeping alive hopes that had been previously raised and then frustrated in France.

The French Awakening

The rise of revolutionary hopes in France was closely linked with changes in communications. Precisely in this field the new technology of the English Industrial Revolution first joined the new ideas of the French political revolution in the early nineteenth century. The results were as explosive for European politics as was the simultaneous first fusion of nitrogen and glycerin into the new raw material dynamite.

The almost simultaneous discovery of practical methods for machine producing paper and for accelerating printing with steam power produced by the 1820s the first major changes in printing in two centuries.[22] The resulting advent of modern mass journalism produced changes in thought no less far reaching than those produced earlier by the introduction of a phonetic alphabet and of a printing press (the "chirographic" and the "typographic" revolutions).[23] The role that Luther, the Gutenberg press, and the vernacular Bible had played in the sixteenth century was, in many ways, played by Walters of the *Times* and Girardin of *La Presse* at the beginning of the nineteenth.

It seems appropriate that the word *magazine*—used already in the eighteenth century for thick weekly and monthly journals of criticism —was used to describe concentrations both of explosive powder and of polemic print.[24] The unstamped working-class press of the 1830s was, in the words of one French observer, "simply a machine of war"; [25] and the flowering of a cheap daily press after the repeal of the tax deepened the passion for conflict. There may have been a special critical bias to the printed culture of France, for it took shape more under the influence of Rabelais and Montaigne than of a vernacular Bible. As a French journalist-revolutionary in the 1840s put it:

> Study of the French press reveals a characteristic of its own that is eminently distinctive: by the very fact that it exists, it is revolutionary . . . the great successes, those which are revived from century to century, belong only to the revolutionary writers.[26]

The powerful role of the press during the French Revolution made subsequent rulers of France fear another Marat or Hébert. Restrictions on the press grew, and were systematically imposed by Napoleon. "If I loosen my bridle on the press, I shall not stay in power for three months," he explained.[27] Of the seventy-odd journals with political content published in the Paris region in 1800, only four remained in existence (all under restrictions) by 1811.[28] Napoleon viewed the English press as one of his major foes, and made intensive efforts to counter it, to influence it, and even to buy it off.[29] His own semi-official *Moniteur* did little to arouse public support. Indeed, "Napoleon may have made more enemies with this unfortunate journal than with his cannon." [30] During his brief restoration after Elba in 1815, Napoleon raised expectations of a free press—as did the Charter of 1815 after Napoleon's final deposition.

A brief flicker of the old flame of revolutionary journalism appeared in *Nain tricolore* of Robert Babeuf, the oldest of the conspirator's three sons.[31] (The other two died in 1814 as faithful soldiers of Napoleon: Caius as a soldier in the *grande armée*, Camille as a suicide from the Vendôme tower at the sight of the allies' entry into Paris.) But Robert followed his father's path into the battlefield of journalism. As a bookseller, printer, and sometimes pamphleteer in Paris, Lyon, and Switzerland, he kept the old revolutionary tradition alive throughout the Napoleonic period. After he was tried and sentenced to Mont-Saint-Michel for publishing a new journal in 1816, he wrote in prison an eight-volume *Martyrology of the French Revolution or Monumental Collection dedicated to the memory of the victims by their families.* When released in 1818, he was placed under police surveillance for twenty years, and moved away from revolutionary circles. But in the late twenties, he renewed association with Buonarroti, his "tender friend" [32] and his father's biographer, thus providing a thin thread of continuity between the revolutionary journalists in the 1790s and those in the 1830s.

During the restoration, Napoleon's *Journal de l'Empire* reassumed its earlier title *Journal des Débats*; and energy was transferred from the battlefield of empire to that of journalism by the "youth of 1815":

> . . . with the collapse of the imperial system, when their arms fell with exhaustion, their intellects rose up to satisfy their need for activity. Works of the spirit succeeded fatigues of the body.[33]

Journals sprang up for all factions within the assembly—extending to the far fringes of Right and Left. The reactionary royalist "ultras" who boycotted the new assembly found journalistic voices as did radical republicans too inflammatory for the assembly and thinly disguised partisans of a Napoleonic restoration. Whatever their position, journals were partisan political organs with no separation of news and editorial functions. Only a few centrists around Guizot had anything approaching a commitment to freedom of expression and ideological diversity for its own sake; and such moderates were ridiculed as "doctrinaires."

French journalistic polemic found particularly rich echoes among the Poles, who fortified old phrases through ritual repetition and added a halo of martyred heroism.[34] Restrictions and censorship began in central Europe with the Carlsbad Decrees of 1819, which were followed in France by the institution of a preliminary censorship in 1820. A continuing alteration of fortune on a generally descending curve of freedom ended in efforts by Charles X to suspend freedom of the press altogether on the eve of the Revolution of 1830.

The revolutionaries of 1830 in both France and Belgium looked forward to

> . . . the day when every citizen shall be able to have a press in his home, just as he has the right to have pen and paper.[35]

Among the many new journals, some began to argue for social as well as political change. Broad new vistas were suggested by the very titles of the two most important journals: *The Future* and *The Globe.*

The first issue of *The Future* on October 16, 1830, marked the emergence of the Abbé Lamennais in full-time journalism. Until he was condemned by the pope and his journal shut two years later, Lamennais rocked the Catholic world by urging an alliance of the church with revolutionary change rather than established authority. "The appearance of this journal was so to speak an event not just in France, but in the entire Catholic church," one of his followers reminisced.[36]

More important was Pierre Leroux's *Globe*, with which modern ideological journalism basically begins. *The Globe* had previously been the special organ of romanticism with a staff

> . . . young and free of all attachment to the past . . . a new generation . . . smitten with liberty, eager for glory, above all young. With the naive faith of youth, generous illusions, limitless hope, they flattered themselves that they could avoid the pitfalls of their fathers and seize the conquests of the revolution while repudiating its crimes.[37]

In October 1830, after a number of his liberal collaborators on the *Journal* had accepted positions in the government of Louis Philippe, Leroux transformed *The Globe* into a conscious Saint-Simonian organ, which became central to the "evolution of French romanticism toward socialism." [38] Dedication to social change was stressed in the solemn pronouncement: "The publication of the *Globe* is not a speculation: it is the work of an apostolate." [39] The journal announced that it would be distributed free to the new Saint-Simonian churches springing up throughout France, and it was disseminated in theaters, gardens, and so forth. *The Globe* vaulted from printings of two thousand five hundred in September 1831 to four thousand two hundred in January 1832.[40] Its provincial correspondents were to recruit adherents as well as to produce an inward flow of news and an outward distribution of propaganda.[41]

Leroux soon broke with the Saint-Simonians, but only to propagate even more aggressively their basic idea of using the media of communications for social propaganda. He became a kind of lexicographer-in-chief of the revolutionary Left—through his *Revue Encyclopédique* (from 1831), *Nouvelle Encyclopédie* (from 1834), his *Revue Indépendante* (which he co-edited with George Sand in 1841 and effectively turned over to Louis Blanc in 1842), and his *Revue Sociale* (from 1843). He was the first to popularize the word socialism, largely as a term of abuse for the Saint-Simonians ("who would transform humanity into a machine"), and the term individualism (an even worse English heresy "which, in the name of liberty, turns men into rapacious wolves").[42] He gave a new religious intensity to the word humanity [43] and coined the word solidarity [44] for the social doctrine that he hoped would unify it. He himself fell victim to the dynamic of denunciation by labels. Having denounced the Saint-Simonians for building a "new papacy" with their *mot talismanique* of socialism in the 1830s, he was accused of the same tendency in the 1840s by the rising critical star Sainte-Beuve, who said of his *Revue Indépendante* that "the end is communism and Leroux is its pope." [45]

Leroux had an almost totemistic fascination with the new medium. His attachment to the printing press might almost be called Oedipal. The first article he ever wrote appeared in 1822 under the name of his mother, who had died the previous year; and the article set forth a visionary plan for a new typography—the *pianotype*—that would operate like a piano and make the very act of setting type an aesthetic experience.[46] (Another printer attempted a little later to set up a similar piano typesetter in Lyon.) Utopian expectations of the press anticipated great expectations that developed for society itself.

Across the Atlantic, Josiah Warren of Cincinnati concurrently sought to propagate a revolutionary message in America through a totally new typographical format involving a high-speed press, type moulds and facings, stereotype plates and cylindrical printers. A veteran of Owen's New Harmony, Warren was perhaps the first to popularize the word socialist in the New World. He eventually defined his unique blend of pacifistic anarchism as universology—arguing that political forms of rule were now irrelevant, that "public influence is the real government of the world," and that printing should henceforth be the main arm of "this governing power." [47]

Whereas Warren was opposed to "the forming of societies or any other artificial combination," [48] Leroux sought some new principle of human association. In the same 1833, when Warren wrote *The Peaceful Revolutionist,* Leroux's brother Jules addressed an appeal "to typographical workers" on the "necessity of founding an association aimed at making workers owners of the instruments of labor." [49] Pierre Leroux's last major journal was the product of a printing association he established in a small town in the *Massif Central,* purporting to provide a "temple" for humanity and a "peaceful solution of the problem of the proletariat." [50]

Louis Philippe's ministers saw a free press as the "universal dissolvant" [51] and staged more than four hundred press trials during 1831–32.[52] The example of England was seen as a further danger; for the philosophical radicals used the press to create pressure for the broadening of suffrage in the Reform Bill of 1832.[53] An official French enquiry on the press in 1833 noted with alarm the power of the new medium:

A book is cold and slow like a protracted monologue before an absent spectator. In a journal on the contrary the consequence follows the action. This idea which you hurl onto paper will make a tour of all of France tomorrow . . . It forms secret links between the journalist and unknown friends that it has never seen and never will, but for whom its thinking is vital food . . .[54]

Fearing that this "food" was creating its own appetite, the French government enacted restrictive press laws in September 1835.

The real challenge to the radical press came, however, less from government restrictions than from bourgeois distractions. In 1836, Paris revolutionized journalism by creating two newspapers that were sold at half the previous price and were designed less to instruct than to divert. Emile Girardin's *La Presse* and Dutacq's *Le Siècle* appeared almost simultaneously in July and ushered modern mass journalism onto the stage of history. The daily press was now pledged "to study well the general taste and constantly to satisfy its changing requirements (*ses mobiles exigences*)." [55] Girardin sought to provide "publicity of facts and not polemic of ideas." [56] He and Dutacq developed the already established tradition of sensationalist *canards*—journalistic fictions that had begun in 1784 with the "discovery" in Chile of a monstrous harpie fifteen feet high and twenty-two feet long, and been encouraged by Louis XVIII.[57] Also important were the *romans-feuilletons*, which reached the public through the new medium, beginning with Alexander Dumas's smashingly successful *The Three Musketeers* in *Le Siècle*.

The new mass dailies moved "beyond ideology," substituting entertainment for politics, creating literary heroes in the absence of real political ones. In the decade following 1836, the readership of dailies in Paris increased from 70,000 to 200,000.[58] Journalism became a substitute for both politics and education in a society where access to the assembly and to the universities increased hardly at all during the same period. As one Frenchman noted in 1838: "In a country where there is more liberty than education, the press attempts to determine (and not just repeat) what everyone thinks." [59] He saw the mass press building a "new democracy" by providing a tribunal for the people that was "higher than the tribunal of judges, the throne of kings, and, I shall say, even the altar of the living God." [60]

The Power of Pictures

Pictures became a favorite weapon of the new radical journalism for the first time in November 1830, when the lithographed cartoons of the twenty-two-year-old Honoré Daumier began to appear in the new weekly *La Caricature*. The word caricature came from the Italian *caricare*: to load a weapon, and there was more than a little explosive power in the new pictorial press. Men in the mass could often be reached through pictures more easily than through words: through the common denominator of emotion rather than the uncommon quality of reason.

The turn to visual effects, to "journalism made flesh," [61] helped move journalism even more deeply into social criticism. The French Revolution had been enshrined in the imagination essentially as a series of tableaux: the tennis court oath, the storming of the Bastille, and the endless processions to the guillotine or the battlefield. Napoleon had combined royal theatricality with revolutionary iconography. From David to Delacroix, French painters sought to give pictorial form to revolutionary longings. Visual symbols on coins and calendars, statues and posters provided both semaphore and sacrament for the revolutionary faith.

Louis Philippe tried unsuccessfully to codify the visual paraphernalia of the revolutionary tradition in public building and civic symbols. But the unforgettable images from his time were not monuments built for him but cartoons drawn against him. Daumier, who had, ironically, formerly been an apprentice in the Museum of the Monuments of France, brought a sculptor's vitality to his monuments of political satire against the *roi-mitoyen*. He was not deterred either by six months in prison, after portraying the king as Gargantua in 1832, or by legal restrictions against caricaturing royalty in 1835. Daumier merely moved into the richer field of social satire against the bourgeoisie in general. In his own daily *Le Charivari* as well as in *La Caricature* and another new journal *Le Corsaire*, he stimulated class consciousness probably more than any socialist pamphleteer with his picture of the bourgeoisie as a "legislative paunch" of bloated self-interest.

No words could dispel his pictures once they were planted in the popular imagination. Lamennais observed that "wit itself and talent are on the side of the republic." [62] Crayoned lithography provided the first means of inexpensively reproducing a drawing "unchanged, actually as the artist made it," [63] and it required no access to the subject being represented. The department of the Seine in Daumier's time supported 24 lithographic houses with 180 presses and 500 workmen.

Daumier's lithography provided an indelible negative picture of bourgeois society for modern journalism. Many of his prototypes were subsequently codified almost mechanically into the cartoon culture of the U.S.S.R.

The development of pictorial journalism through line engraving to off-set photography, however, involved technologies that were more expensive than revolutionaries could afford. A new age of pictorial distraction began with the first appearance of *Punch* in 1841, followed within two years by *Illustrated London News*, *L'Illustration* in Paris, and *Illustrierte Zeitung* in Leipzig. [64] Mass pictorial journalism thus moved beyond ideology to entertainment and thence—in part out of sheer boredom—to chauvinistic enthusiasm. The rapturous sonnet of dedication in the first issue of *The Illustrated London News* seemed prophetic of imperial wars to come:

> To the Great Public—that gigantic soul
> Which lends the nation's body life and light
> And makes the blood within its vein grow bright
> With gushing blood. . . .
>
> . . . The page of simple news
> Is here adorned and filled with pictured life
> Colored with a thousand tints—the rainbow strife
> Of all the world's emotions. [65]

Converging technological developments—the coming of regular steamboat service throughout Europe in the 1830s and the beginning of new railway lines—prepared the way for mass journalism to spread its own pictures of "the rainbow strife of all the world's emotions." If it had taken George IV nearly two months to learn of Napoleon's death in 1821, by 1840 news traveled from London to Paris (by carrier pigeon) in seven hours. [66] The age of the foreign correspondent and news agency began in 1835, when Charles Havas, an arms maker who seemed to sense the explosive power of the press, formed *L'Agence Havas* in Paris. Electric telegraphy first became a regular part of a news service on the *Morning Chronicle* of London in 1845.[67] A telegraphic correspondence bureau was established by Bernard Wolff in Berlin in 1849; and linkage was made by these two telegraphic networks with the last—and ultimately most important—service when Reuters of England extended lines through Brussels to Aachen in 1850 and completed the Dover–Calais cable in 1851. By the end of the decade the three services were exchanging news, and in another decade they began to work out a division of world-wide coverage.[68]

However, the creation of a world-wide news network led not to peace, but to a restless search for fresh foreign adventure. The new telegraphic technology brought in excitement from abroad even as it increased police control at home. The network of telegraphic communications that had developed in England of the 1840s helped to assure the effective and uniform suppression of the Chartist movement,[69] just as the railroad facilitated Napoleon's repression of Parisian unrest across the channel.

Revolutionary journalism had sought to engage the ears as well as the eyes—through such journals as *La Ruche Populaire,* founded in 1839 by the Saint-Simonian folk-singer, Jules Vinçard. The Germans in particular developed a style that might almost be called incantational. Already in 1818–19 the Weimar paper *Patriot* (the organ of the most revolutionary "Unconditionals" within the Burschenschaften) set forth their aims in a *Grosses Lied*—"Ein Reich . . . ein Gott, ein Volk, Ein Wille . . ." [70]—in a way that seemed an eerie anticipation of Nazi incantations at Nuremberg in 1934. Karl Follen's brother, Adolf Ludwig Follen, argued that "newspapers are the wind by which the weather cocks turn." [71] He sought to stimulate a mass popular revolution in Germany by journalistic propaganda that relied heavily on songs of heroism and sacrifice. His agitational songbook, *Free Voices of Fresh Youth,* helped inspire Karl Sand to commit political assassination in 1819 by invoking a host of historical models from William Tell to the contemporary insurrectionist Andreas Hofer.[72]

The German communist press in Switzerland in the early 1840s added a quasi-religious element reminiscent at times of the Reformation pattern of hymn singing and family devotional readings. Songs and responsive readings were printed in a variety of forms to be read aloud— at communal workers' meetings rather than silently and individually by the bourgeois fireside. There was even a "Communist Lord's Prayer":

> Also sei's! In deinem heil'gen Namen
> Werfen wir den alten Trödel um:
> Keine Herrn und keine Diener! Amen!
> Abgeschaft das Geld und Eigentum! [73]

> So be it! In thy holy name
> We'll overturn the old rubbish;
> No masters and no servants! Amen!
> Money and property shall be abolished!

Ideological Journalism in Germany and Russia

This mobilization of the emotions through the press helped create an almost religious conception of journalism within a new generation of German and Russian exiles. Made desperate by the failure of 1848, they developed the new idea that a journalist was not merely an "apostle," but a prophet and priest as well. They shared the belief expressed by a dying Communist a century later that their very souls "would permanently corrode" if they did not perform their sacred duties on a daily basis:

> I held on to my profession in the manner of religion. Editing my daily article was the daily sacrament.[74]

Such ideological dedication among communist journalists of the mid-twentieth century was in some ways only the delayed result of the communications revolution a century earlier: the discovery of the word communism in the journalism of the 1840s and the linkage of ideological journalism to revolutionary organization in the 1850s.

Victorian London was the holy city for the new faith in the power of the press. Mill had written that "the subversion of established institutions is merely one consequence of the previous subversion of established opinions." [75] Julian Harney, when founding both the radical wing of the Chartist movement and the Democratic Association in 1837, had stressed the dependence of both upon journalistic support: "A new age will commence" only with "the liberation of the press." [76] The pioneering communist Théophile Thoré defended himself at his trial in 1840 as a kind of Socrates, who had substituted printer's ink for philosopher's hemlock:

> Thanks to printing and to the press, we have today means of intellectual propaganda that the ancients did not imagine. Without going out to converse in the shops and preach on the squares, we can send the radiations of our thought directly in the hearts of men of good will.[77]

Barmby saw the media replacing Christ as well as Socrates:

> Since the discovery of the printing press . . . the mission of the editor has by degrees superseded that of the parson-priest, the desk has become more useful than the pulpit, the leading Saturday article more saving than the drawling Sunday sermon.[78]

Belief in the priestly function of radical journalism led to feelings of saintly succession among journals. The Hungarian revolutionary tradition built on the charismatic power of Louis Kossuth's daily *Pesti Hírlap* (*Journal of Pest*), which vaulted in the first six months of 1841 from sixty to five thousand subscribers.[79] The Russian revolutionary tradition built similarly on the appeal of the radical journalist of the 1840s, Vissarion Belinsky. His example of passionate protest through "thick journals" legitimized the revolutionary impulse and compensated for the lack of political opposition. An apostolic line of succession followed Belinsky's death in 1848: Chernyshevsky and Dobroliubov of *The Contemporary* in the late 1850s and early 1860s, Pisarev of *The Russian Word* in the mid-sixties, and Mikhailovsky on Belinsky's former journal, *Annals of the Fatherland*, in the late 1860s and 1870s.[80]

It might be said that true ideological journalism had in many ways begun with the Young Hegelians of the early 1840s. As a member of this coterie, Marx helped explore plans for journals that never came into being (*Zeitschrift für Theaterkritik* and *Archiv des Atheismus*),[81] then collaborated on some that did (*Deutsche Jahrbücher* and *Rheinische Zeitung*); and he first became a polemic leader in 1842 at the age of twenty-four when he was made chief editor of the *Rheinische Zeitung*. His journal set itself up as the rival to the hitherto dominant *Augsburger Allgemeine Zeitung*. In the German world a political press was coming into being even before there was a legal political association. Marx explained the advantages of such inverted development in the New Year's issue of his journal for 1843. German newspapers could play an exalted pedagogic function on the awakening political imagination, he said, and not merely deal with complex interest groups like the English and the French, who had to respond to "existing, already formed power." The infant German press was not bound passively to "express the thoughts, the interests of the people. You first create them or rather impute them to the people. You create party spirit." [82]

Thus in Marx's view journalism had the responsibility of creating "party spirit," the direct ancestor of Lenin's *partiinost'*. For both men this desire to create party spirit preceded the firm idea of a political party.

It was as the editor of *Rheinische Zeitung* that Marx was first introduced to economic questions when he was forced to develop opinions about productivity in the Mosel and about the general problems of free trade and tariffs.[83] Much of his subsequent education in political economy was conducted in the form of seminars with editorial colleagues.[84]

The revolutionary fire burned brightest in the journals of the émigrés in cities like Paris, Brussels, and London (to which Marx fled successively), and in Switzerland and America. In such places, the journal became the rallying point and organizational center for a desperate and alienated constituency. The Thuringian preacher's son Julius Fröbel moved to Switzerland in 1835 and established a new publishing house, which he characterized as the "armory of the party of the future"; [85] this "armory" helped Weitling forge the ideological weapons of the first communist organizations.

The revolutionaries who had left Europe in large numbers after 1848–50 and embarked on a new life in America rarely fed back any significant arms or ideas to their former comrades in the Old World.[86] Marx, of course, had in a way also fled to America—in the sense of using Charles Dana's New York *Tribune* as his new journalistic outlet. In his journalism in the 1850s, he enlarged the global perspective he had already introduced on the *Neue Rheinische Zeitung* in Cologne during the turmoil of 1848. The Cologne Workers' Union had been the only one in Germany with its own official journal; [87] thus Marx was free of the responsibility of dealing with local affairs in his periodical, and he ranged widely over remote areas of time and space in search of instructive material for revolutionaries. The latest student of the period argues that one must speak of a "party of the *Neue Rheinische Zeitung*" during this period rather than of a "Party of the League of Communists." [88] In London Marx plunged deeper into journalism, enriching his reports with material from the British Museum and from the daily press, which was fed by Reuters' News Agency. His journalistic analyses helped account for his failure to finish his magnum opus, *Das Kapital*.

Marx's major disputes with Weitling and Proudhon before the Revolution of 1848, and with Stephan Born during it, were in many ways those of intellectual against artisan in the presence of the printing press. Marx invoked the political symbols and strategic perspectives of the new journalism. His opponents were preoccupied with the concrete concerns of local workers—sometimes only of the typographers. Marx's quarrel with Proudhon was, in this respect, an amplified repetition of the antagonism between the intellectual journalists who were the original French "communists" and the proletarian *L'Atelier* in the early 1840s.

Those with firsthand experience of physical labor like Born and Proudhon played a greater role in the events of 1848 than did their cerebral protagonists like Marx. Typographers who were particularly active included Claude Anthime Corbon, vice-president of the constituent assembly; and George Duchêne, delegate of the typographers to the Commission of Labor in 1848 and founder of Proudhon's journal *Le Représentant du Peuple*. This journal and its successors *Le Peuple* and *La Voix du Peuple* exercised great authority in revolutionary Paris; and the Leipzig journal *Brotherhood*, edited by two working typographers from the "Gutenberg League," spawned a network of journals throughout Germany, and inspired pioneering working-class journals elsewhere: *The Herald* in Prague, *The Workers' Journal* in Budapest.[89]

In the 1840s, the life of the editorial and typographical staff of a radical journal became a kind of model for the new society. Here truly was a sense of community, built around a journal designed for ordinary men in contemporary language. Physical and mental work existed in balance and harmony. The tension between man and the machine was not yet present, because the modern linotype had not yet entered the craftsman's print shop. Its product was for the profit of mankind rather than of some absentee owner.

Corberon, who with Buchez founded *L'Atelier*, the first French journal produced exclusively by and for workers, saw in the very act of composing type a liberation of labor from routine. He was the master of several crafts including wood sculpture, and he saw the production of a journal as a kind of Masonic initiation into a new type of fraternity.[90] Born, who was both compositor and writer for Marx's journal in Brussels, had a similar vision of the collective work of producing journals as a model for future socialist enterprise. The strike of printers and compositors he led in Berlin in April 1848 was the best organized and sustained direct action taken by German workers on their own behalf during the early revolutionary days. The national German movement of workers to improve their lot in the summer of 1848 by workers congresses and strikes grew in good measure out of the national assembly of printers in Mainz in June. Born remained at the heart of it, as president of the Central Committee of Workers, as the moving spirit of its official "social political" organ *Das Volk*, and as Berlin correspondent of Marx's *Neue Rheinische Zeitung*.[91]

Printer-artisans also played a key role in French events of 1848. Duchêne and other typographers had been leaders in the banquet campaigns of the 1840s; and the typographers' union, which had numbered 3,000 already at the beginning of the decade,[92] provided an image of solidarity against both the higher bourgeoisie and the new, more impersonal techniques of printing.

Here was an informal alternative both to the depersonalized new economic system of the bourgeoisie and to the political and legal mechanisms they offered the working class. In England, Belgium, and Switzerland as well as in France typographers began to form societies and organize banquets in the 1849–51 period, echoing the slogan: "Toward the institution of a universal, typographical free-masonry!"[93]

The simple artisan ideal of human friendship unpolluted by machines and undiluted by bureaucracies was of course to be overwhelmed by the massive industrial growth of the late nineteenth century. But the belief lived on that a printed journal could be the authentic voice of a popular revolution—and its typographical-editorial workshop a kind of model for a new communal life-style.

Proudhon perpetuated this idea even after the National Guard burst into his office to break his printing press and scatter the type. In the repression that followed, Proudhon's collaborator Duchêne was subjected to so many trials and fines that he finally turned to the prosecutor and wearily said, "L'addition, s'il vous plaît."[94]

Though the "bill" came to 50,000 francs and ten years in prison, Proudhon was soon free again to revive *Le Peuple* as *La Voix du Peuple* on October 1, 1849, with Alexander Herzen as collaborator and financial supporter.[95] The Russian émigré and his friends saved Proudhon from the clutches of Emile Girardin, who had recognized Proudhon's talent and sought to coöpt him through financial subsidy.[96] After Proudhon's *Voix* and *Le Peuple de 1850* were shut down, Girardin finally succeeded in taking over much of the personnel and lexicon of revolutionary journalism for his new journal of 1851, *Le Bien-Etre Universel*.[97] It was hard to promise anything more than "universal well-being," and the enormous printing of 100,000 copies impressed Napoleon III, who in turn took over Girardin's twin techniques of coöptation and distraction.

Proudhon's journals established him as the leading spokesman for a revolutionary social alternative to centralized bourgeois rule in France. And Herzen, baptized in revolutionary journalism on Proudhon's publications of the revolutionary era, transferred this tradition to Russia, founding in 1857 in London the first illegal revolutionary periodical in Russian history: *Kolokol* (*The Bell*).

Herzen's publication electrified a Russia exasperated by defeat in the Crimean War and filled with expectations of a fresh start under the new tsar, Alexander II. Herzen also benefited from the fact that the journalistic media had become in the German and Slavic worlds during the 1840s a form of liberation from the confines of the university with its abstract speculation and lengthy lectures divorced from everyday reality. When Belinsky ("the furious Vissarion") transformed Pushkin's old journal, *The Annals of the Fatherland*, into an organ of active social criticism, "the world of politics in miniature" [98] in 1842, worried police officials referred to the journal as a "party." [99] The socialist novels of George Sand were translated along with French radical criticism; and a secret police report identified the "party of Belinsky" with "pantheism, communism, socialism . . . robespierrism." [100]

Belinsky died just before the outbreak of revolution in 1848; and Russia did not participate in the revolution but rather plunged into a severe period of reaction. Herzen filled the vacuum by propagating the idea that the revolutionary initiative had passed from West to East, above all to Russia with its peasant communalism and hostility to bourgeois institutions. Herzen transposed into the Russian peasant commune the enthusiasm that his French friends Michelet and Proudhon had felt for the communalism of the fishermen of Britanny and the craftsmen of Jura respectively. The distinctive belief of Russian revolutionary populism that the commune provided the germ of a new social order was set forth by Herzen in a letter he wrote to Michelet in the dark days of 1850 from the French Riviera.[101]

Writings of or about Michelet and Proudhon (as well as Mazzini, Victor Hugo, and others) were included in the almanac *Polar Star*, which first appeared in the summer of 1855, marking the beginning of an uncensored Russian press. Operating first with lithographs, then with type face largely transported by hand from Paris, Herzen and Ogarev placed pictures of the five martyred Decembrists on the cover and included works of Belinsky within.[102]

A supporting network of secret correspondents within Russia provided part of the nucleus of future revolutionary movements.[103] *Polar Star*, together with *The Bell*, the supplement that appeared more frequently and soon supplanted it, began a large publication campaign in London that led to the creation of revolutionary populism. Soon appearing in printings of 2,500–3,000, *The Bell* coined its two great slogans: "to the people" and "land and liberty." Illegal student publications began appearing in the fall of 1858 in response to, and often in deliberate imitation of, Herzen's *Bell*—as typical titles suggest: *The Living Voice, My Own Ring, The Last Sound,* and *The Echo*.[104]

The birth of a new extremism inside Russia is partly traceable to the discovery of Herzen's *Bell* by a young aristocratic student in Moscow, Peter Zaichnevsky. His imagination was fired by discovering the word socialist "almost on every page" of Herzen; and he turned all his energies "to seeking every possible chance to get hold of books which spoke of this [word]." [105] He secretly took the lithograph used to reproduce university lectures, and in 1859 began to make copies of Western revolutionary writings. He was preparing to publish his translation of Proudhon's *What Is Property?* when arrested in 1861. Alarmed officials conducted an inquiry into the press; it revealed that only 96 of 150 private presses in Moscow had obtained official authorization. [106]

Surveillance began, and repression received new impetus, when Zaichnevsky gathered together a student group known as "the Society of Communists" and formed "the first free Russian Press" later in the year. Moving for safety from Moscow to Riazan, this society—the first ritually to invoke the terms socialist and communist on Russian soil—began the long Russian tradition of revolutionary audacity by daringly distributing its pamphlets into the chapel of the Winter Palace during services on Easter Monday of 1862. [107] In May, it issued the incendiary manifesto *Young Russia*.

This remarkable call to revolutionary terrorism suggested that journalists might be leaders of the "revolutionary party" in its struggle for power with the "imperial party." Zaichnevsky rebuked Herzen for lapsing into reformism and liberalism, for failing to realize that "it is time to begin beating on the alarm bell (*nabat*) and summon the people to revolt, not to mouth liberal slogans (*liberal'nichat'*)." [108] Zaichnevsky thus provided the rival name—*Nabat*—for the major journal of Russian conspiratorial Jacobinism which was later published abroad by his friend and sometime collaborator Peter Tkachev. [109]

A different group, but one that came from the same new subculture of revolutionary journalism, took Herzen's slogan "land and liberty" as the name for a secret revolutionary organization inside Russia in 1862. The organization was inspired by an illegal journal of 1861, which had daringly printed four issues on the press of the General Staff in St. Petersburg. Land and Liberty took shape later in 1861 around the editorial staff of the St. Petersburg journal *The Contemporary*; [110] and established contact with *The Bell*, which published in London its proclamation of 1862, *To the Young Generation*, and subsequent special publications for soldiers, Poles, and sectarians. In the fall of 1862, Land and Liberty sent abroad its leading typographer, who set up a new press in Bern and discussed plans to unite with—or perhaps absorb and supplant—Herzen's publication effort in London. [111] Then, in 1862, Land and Liberty began printing major proclamations inside Russia in another illegal publication: *Freedom*.

Martyred heroism accrued to the movement with the arrest and trial of two of its leading writers, Michael Mikhailov, the youthful poet believed to have written *To the Young Generation*, and Nicholas Chernyshevsky, the radical literary critic who proceeded to write in prison *What Is To Be Done?*, a novelistic exhortation to self-sacrifice and communal living. Lenin was only continuing a long tradition of veneration mixed with imitation of Chernyshevsky when he took the title for his own blueprint for a new type of party, *What Is To Be Done?* from the pioneer of Russian revolutionary journalism. [112] At the same time, Lenin took the title for his pioneering journal *Iskra* (*The Spark*) from the journal of that name founded by another writer associated with Land and Liberty, V. S. Kurochkin. A poet, caricaturist, and translator of Béranger's revolutionary songs, Kurochkin together with a cartoonist founded his *Iskra* in 1859, and proceeded to satirize the bourgeoisie in the spirit of Daumier. There was another *Iskra,* too, among the illegal student publications; and in 1862, another of Lenin's journalistic titles, *Pravda,* was anticipated in the journal of a White Russian follower of Chernyshevsky: *Muzhitskaia Pravda* (Peasant Truth).[113]

Land and Liberty anticipated Lenin not just in words, but in the basic technique of using journalistic activity to organize as well as educate a revolutionary movement. The centrality of journalism to the Russian revolutionary tradition was firmly established in the five years that followed the first sound of Herzen's *Bell.* But Land and Liberty was crushed and revolutionary journalism swamped in 1863 by the reactionary nationalism that swept through Russia as a result of the uprising in Poland. It is to the waning of revolutionary nationalism in most of the European world in the third quarter of the nineteenth century and to the rise of the counter-revolutionary mass press that attention must now be turned.

CHAPTER 12

The Waning of

Revolutionary Nationalism

FRANCE had dominated the revolutionary era from 1789 to 1850; and its main legacy to the world lay in the creation of national revolutionary movements. These grew partly in imitation of the revolutionary nation-in-arms of 1793, partly in reaction to subsequent Napoleonic conquest. The other nations that helped inspire this "springtime of nations" were the Americans, whose revolution had preceded the French, and the Poles and Italians, who most faithfully echoed French ideals.

The ideal of national revolution had been inspired originally by the American Declaration of Independence. The Italians added the idea of recapturing past glory and discovering new manhood through a national struggle. The revolutions of 1830 and 1848 had both been dominated more by national than by social revolutionaries, by what the Russian minister Nesselrode called the "Polish disease" (national self-determination) spreading throughout Europe.

The dominant ideology of revolutionary nationalism faded after the failure of revolution in 1848. The second half of the nineteenth century witnessed a dramatic metamorphosis of nationalism, through both death and transfiguration.

Death came with the decisive divorce of nationalism from the revolutionary ideal in the heart of Europe. The final unification of Italy and Germany in the 1860s was accomplished by the industrial-military-diplomatic strength of an established state rather than by romantic revolt in the name of a new national ethos. Piedmont and Prussia in effect conquered Italy and Germany, while the Polish uprising of 1863 was crushed by Russian power after providing a last hurrah for romantic, revolutionary nationalism.

Revolutionary nationalism was then transfigured into reactionary im-

perialism during the final quarter of the nineteenth century. Nationalism, the old cause of idealistic revolution against authority, reappeared
as a means of diverting domestic discontent within industrial Europe
into emotional support for expanding European state power.

This new nationalism of the European imperial era—and the revolutionary reaction to it—are part of another story: the global drama of
the twentieth century. Here one must deal only with the death of the
old revolutionary nationalism in the fateful period that ended with the
Franco-Prussian War of 1870–71. A new journalism and a new Napoleon
were factors: and the last of the French revolutions—the Paris Commune
of 1871—was a watershed.

The Last Heroes

Despite failure in 1848, hopes remained strong for more national revolutions throughout the 1850s. Revolutionaries everywhere took heart at
the defeat in the Crimean War of Russia, the pillar of European reaction, which had extinguished the revolutionary nationhood of Poland in
1831 and of Hungary in 1849. National revolutionaries were further
emboldened by Napoleon III's encouragement to movements of self-
determination against the conservative, antinationalist empires of both
the Romanovs and the Hapsburgs.

The Polish cause retained its European-wide appeal despite the death
of its symbolic leaders: Chopin during the revolutionary ferment of
1848–49, Mickiewicz in the midst of the Crimean War in 1855. The
latter was in the process of raising national legions not just for the
Poles, but also for other oppressed nationalities, including the Jews.
He died in Constantinople in the arms of his Jewish friend Armand
Lévy, who in turn raised a companion Jewish legion, "the first Jewish
military unit of modern times." [1] Its dream was to liberate Jerusalem,
its flag was to be "the scroll of the Law." [2] Lévy subsequently became
the leading French propagandist for the Romanian nationalist movement. [3] The emergence of a new Romanian nation from the conference
at Paris in 1859 provided a thread of hope for belief that the tide of
revolutionary nationalism might still be rising.

German nationalists, frustrated in the Old World, flooded into the New
World after 1849, bringing extreme ideas about a new nationalist international. A German Revolutionary League was founded in Philadelphia
with the support of the original radical Hegelian, Arnold Ruge, and an
even more radical apostle of tyrannicide, Karl Heinzen. Their plan, drawn
up by a former member of the revolutionary government in Baden, advocated a messianic world federalism to be led by the United States.
Cuba and Santo Domingo were to be annexed first, then Mexico and
Latin America. Following this, the "infederation" [4] of Europe was to be-

gin with England. The defeated Hungarian revolutionary Kossuth on his triumphal tour of America in 1851 aroused sentiment everywhere; and in the following year a revolutionary People's League for the Old and New World was briefly organized in Wheeling, West Virginia.

But the revolutionary impulse could not be revived from America; and the frustrated nationalism of the new German arrivals found its only outlet in the rising nationalism of America itself. In 1853, two German revolutionary immigrants published *The New Rome*, which anticipated in a remarkable manner the geopolitics of a century later. It predicted that Europe was now eclipsed by greater powers on either side: reactionary Russia and revolutionary America; and that the decisive struggle between them would be fought largely in the air. "Europe will be first Cossack, but then Yankee." [5]

The center of revolutionary hopes within Europe was London, to which Kossuth soon returned. Mazzini and other national revolutionaries formed there in 1850 a European Democratic Central Committee. Its publication was in French; but it had national subcommittees of Italians, Poles, Germans, Austrians, Hungarians, and Dutch.[6] After the Napoleonic coup of 1851, revolutionary exiles with messianic expectations poured into London at an even greater rate.[7]

Social revolutionaries formed the *Commune révolutionnaire*, an international fraternity of revolutionary socialists established in 1852 under French leadership in London with a branch on the Island of Jersey. Its introductory brochure was drawn up for delivery to France on the anniversary of the founding of the First French Republic. Subsequent pamphlets and its regular propaganda organ, Victor Hugo's *L'Homme*, were smuggled into France in such ingenious hiding places as a bust of Queen Victoria.[8]

For this self-proclaimed heir to the revolutionary commune of 1792 in Paris, the vistas were universal. The *Commune* called for a "universal democratic and social republic" and a "holy alliance of the peoples." [9] It joined with the left wing of the Chartist movement to form early in 1855 an international committee, which in turn joined German communists and Polish socialists in a more inclusive International Association on August 10, 1856.[10]

This association was the last of the old-fashioned international revolutionary organizations rather than a prototype of the First International.[11] It was essentially an organization for dinners and discussions by émigré intellectuals. They busied themselves with a revolutionary social calendar, which commemorated almost every prominent arrival and anniversary. But they also began to question the belief in national revolution and in political reforms without social change.

The failings of nationalism were also those of liberalism; so concluded the ill-fated Russian Petrashevsky circle late in 1849:

> The movement of nationalities is a product of liberalism because socialism is a cosmopolitan doctrine standing above nationality. . . . The movement of nationalities is antithetical to the success of socialism, distracting the vital forces of society away from subjects capable of increasing social well-being and forcing the resort to war—with arms.[12]

Suspicion of nationalism grew in eastern Europe after the revolution-ary events of 1848–49. Nationalism had bred repression of one people by another—Russian against Hungarian, and Hungarian against other Slavs. In western Europe, Cabet and others attacked the symbol of lib-eral national revolution—Mazzini—in a brochure of 1852, *French So-cialists to Mr. Mazzini*.[13] He was denounced at greater length in a man-ifesto of December 1858, *To the Republicans, Democrats and Socialists of Europe*, which accused Mazzini of becoming a wealthy apologist for "law and order":

> . . . the Italian patriot, the representative of the republican bourgeoisie, who has inscribed on his banner "law and order." [14]

Having told the proletariat to "put off social problems," he should now at least tell "his friends to put aside their plutocratic tendencies." [15]

After further rebuking all "plutocratic republicans" of Europe, the manifesto called for a rejection of nationality:

> The States of Europe reunited in one sole democratic and social republic in which all the citizens must be producers before becoming consumers. . . . a union between the Proletarians, Democrats, Socialists of Europe is at the present moment an absolute necessity. . . . "union" is the order of today, "action" will be that of tomorrow.[16]

The incorrigibly nationalistic Poles soon left the organization alto-gether. New egalitarian rules introduced in January 1859 (dealing with complete equality of the sexes and a quasi-anarchist definition of the revolution as "absolute negation of all privileges, absolute negation of all authority") [17] hastened the Poles' departure—and the organization's collapse. Its last known publication on June 13, 1859, urged that no sides whatsoever be taken in purely political conflicts between na-tions, such as the Franco-Austrian War in Italy. One must avoid "mu-tual laceration within the masses" in a time when

> . . . the "Marseillaise" puts forth its full-sounding tune in order to celebrate the adventures of crowned heads . . . whose power takes root in the enmity of nationalities.[18]

The International Association established affiliates in American cities (sometimes called *Kommunistenklub*) and attached importance to Ca-bet's communist communities in America. The association pleaded with the latter not to spoil their noble experiment with petty bickering and thus enable the exploiters of Europe to say: "How can you hope to make society communitarian if a few communists cannot even live in harmony?" [19]

But Cabet's fading utopia was a weak reed on which to lean; and few in Europe noticed the appearance in New York in 1859 of Joseph Dé-jacques's remarkable new antinationalist journal, *Le Libertaire*, which criticized Garibaldi for wearing a red shirt without advocating revolu-tion.[20]

Social revolutionaries found secure ground in Europe only in London with the first meeting of French and English workers' delegations in

1862 and the establishment of the First International two years later. The founding meeting of this International Workingmen's Association on September 28, 1864, brought working-class organizations together with émigré intellectuals in Saint Martin's Hall where, nine years earlier, many of the same participants had founded [21] the International Association.

Ernest Jones, the aristocratic godson of the Duke of Cumberland, had opened that earlier meeting in the same Saint Martin's Hall on February 27, 1855, with a withering attack on the concept of nationality. Jones had succeeded Harney as the chief revolutionary internationalist among the Chartists, and he led Chartism's last effort at political organization (the so-called "parliament of labor" at Manchester in March 1854) and its last major journal (the *People's Paper*). In 1864, he addressed himself ecumenically to all "men of Europe":

> Kings have invented the idea of hostile nationalities so as to split the unity of peoples. . . . For us, nation is *nothing*, man is *all*. For us, the oppressed nationalities form but one: the universal poor of every land.[22]

Jones, the greatest nineteenth-century English poet of the class struggle, portrayed a simple struggle of good with evil:

> . . . all men are brethren—but some are Abels and some are Cains, and this is a gathering of the Abels of the world against the crowned and mighty Cains who have murdered them.[23]

The history of the First International was one of continuous controversy among social revolutionaries over how "the Abels of the world" should combat the Cains, who controlled the land and did not act as their brothers' keepers.

Once the cause of national revolution began to wane, social revolutionaries quarrelled among themselves with new intensity; but just before founding the First International in 1864, Mazzini and his friends made one last attempt to revive the dream of a European-wide alliance of nationalist revolutionaries. The Italians provided the spark for this last flicker of romantic, revolutionary nationalism. While other émigrés were talking to each other in London, Mazzini and his followers made sensational, secret incursions into Italy; these fascinated readers of inexpensive new mass journals in Europe throughout the 1850s.

A climax came when a group led by Felice Orsini threw three bombs at Napoleon III on January 14, 1858, missing the target but killing 8 people and wounding 148. The handsome Orsini had twice before been condemned as a political prisoner, and he enjoyed enormous popularity in England, where he had conducted a lecture tour and sold within a year some 35,000 copies of his 1856 book, *Austrian Dungeons in Italy*.[24] The London trial of Orsini's French friend, who had helped prepare the grenades, "turned into a trial of Napoleon III" [25] and resulted in the defendant's acquittal as well as increased publicity for the revolutionary nationalist cause. Orsini himself was tried and executed in Paris; but his final plea to Napoleon III to take up the cause of Italian national liberation was, in effect, heeded in 1859, when Napoleon joined Piedmont in war against Austria.

There was a sense of *déjà vu* in all of this. The original professional revolutionaries at the beginning of the nineteenth century had dreamed of executing an earlier Napoleon—and viewed his attitude toward Italy as a test of his claim to be defender of the revolution. Even the name of the first revolutionary organization reappeared. The major society through which the new Italian revolutionaries recruited allies in London, Brussels, and Geneva was called the Philadelphians. Like the earlier society of the same name, it was an outgrowth of Masonry, which provided international connections and an outer shell of secrecy for recruitment. Some prominent socialists like Louis Blanc drifted into the camp of the national revolutionaries in London through the Masonic Lodge of United Philadelphians.[26] Most leaders of the International Association refused to sign the association's official condemnation of the Mazzinian program in December 1858; and many began collaborating with Mazzini even before the association collapsed in 1859.

The Italian national rising against the Hapsburgs momentarily revived the romantic belief in liberation through national revolution—even though the Italian success was more the work of Piedmontese statesmen like Cavour and of new bourgeois organizations like the National Society than of Mazzinian revolutionaries.[27] Seeing Italy unified with the aid of Napoleon III, Hungarian and Polish revolutionary organizations in London began exploring new possibilities for conspiracy and possible collaboration with the new Bonaparte. Common interests among democratic nationalists seemed suggested by the appearance in London of vernacular revolutionary journals in German and Russian, that is, Hinkel's *Hermann* and Herzen's *Bell*. Even hitherto nonrevolutionary nationalists like the Czechs began advocating through émigré spokesmen like Josef Frič a broad coalition of anti-Hapsburg national revolutionaries. Frič and Hinkel clashed bitterly, however, in 1859 with Marx and Engels, who preferred German hegemony over the Czechs, and Magyar rule over the other Hapsburg Slavs.[28]

The arrival of Bakunin in London in 1861 after a long imprisonment helped revive the romantic dream of a revolutionary Slavic federation. When revolt broke out in Poland in 1863 and a national government was set up, contacts and consultations were established with Czech and Croatian revolutionaries as well as with Hungarians and Italians.[29] A kind of anti-Hapsburg alliance of revolutionary nationalists came into being—and was formalized in a convention signed with Garibaldi in June 1864. Italian and Polish revolutionary forces pledged to continue the anti-Hapsburg struggle until all Slavs subject to Vienna achieved full autonomy.[30] But the document was signed just as the Polish rebellion was being crushed and Victor Emmanuel was drawing back from further struggle with the Hapsburgs. As Germany, Italy, and even Hungary proceeded to achieve new national stature, the Slavs remained the main bearers of the old ideal of liberation through national revolution.

In January 1864, Bakunin arrived in Florence and embarked on a feverish decade of revolutionary activity in which old and new, fact and fantasy, were difficult to disentangle. To some extent, this was only a replay of the revolutionary past: a visit to Garibaldi on the Isle of Caprera, another attempt to create revolutionary organization through Masonic lodges, and his joining at Garibaldi's suggestion of the new lodge, *Il Progresso Social.* He wrote a lost *Catechism of Free Masonry,* and an organizational outline: *Aims of the Society and the Revolutionary Catechism.*[31] Bakunin also wrote blueprints for a series of phantom international revolutionary brotherhoods: an International Secret Society for the Emancipation of Humanity in 1864, an International Fraternity or International Alliance of Social Democracy in 1868, and a final Socialist Revolutionary Alliance in 1872. Behind it all was the vision of a lost natural society—with each cell a family and all members brothers.

But there was also real novelty in Bakunin's focus on a social revolution that opposed any form of national authority. In these last years he had become an authentic revolutionary anarchist. He organized the first Italian organization explicitly to oppose the socialist to the nationalist ideal: the Alliance of 1864, which directly challenged Mazzinian deference to familiar political and religious modes of thought. After moving to Switzerland in 1867, Bakunin also tried to recruit a social revolutionary following from within the liberal republican League of Peace and Freedom. He then led his Genevan recruits into his International Alliance—and also into the First International, where there began his long struggle with Marx and the Marxists. Bakunin's Alliance virtually created the Italian and Spanish branches of the First International; and his ideas found much greater resonance than those of Marx among the Swiss and Slavs.[32] Bakunin also attracted a following from the working class—first in Spain, where revolution had overthrown Queen Isabella in 1868 and aroused new social expectations; then in Italy, where Bakunin's following increased after the death of Mazzini in 1872.[33] Hope of affiliation with Bakunin's Alliance attracted to Geneva in March 1869 the young Serge Nechaev, who stayed on to write his *Catechism of a Revolutionary.*

Although Bakunin linked revolution to anarchism in his final years, his strategic perspective remained in some respects national. He argued that the Russians, Italians, and Spaniards were revolutionary by nature;[34] and that world reaction was concentrated in the one nation in which he and other Young Hegelians had once placed their highest hopes: Germany. In search of a locus of evil to provide chiaroscuro contrast with the lands of liberation, Bakunin imparted to the Germans as a nationality the same demonic genius that Marx attributed to the bourgeoisie as a class. Germany became a kind of antinationality, which had deformed Bakunin's native Russia into a "knouto-Germanic empire."[35] The peoples of eastern and southern Europe, by contrast, were invested with precisely the qualities that the Germans had renounced, those of spontaneous, anti-authoritarian brotherhood.

Bakunin revived Weitling's belief in outlaws and brigands as potential revolutionary recruits, and sought to link conspiratorial action directly to the masses:

> A few hundred young men of good will are certainly not enough to create a revolutionary power without the people . . . but they will be enough to re-organize the revolutionary power of the people.[36]

If Bakunin in the 1860s was a throwback to the romantic para-military conspirators of the 1810s and 1820s, his great revolutionary contemporary and sometime collaborator, Giuseppe Garibaldi, echoed the romantic nationalism of the 1830s and the 1840s. He became the last authentic hero of the fading nationalist revolutionary cause in the late 1860s and the 1870s.

Garibaldi belonged, like Mazzini, to the London Philadelphians.[37] He had grown to bigger-than-life dimensions as a symbol of national liberation by carrying his struggle during 1836–48 to Latin America, the original seedbed of revolutionary struggle against the Holy Alliance. As early as 1843 he had formed an Italian legion in Uruguay; it had taken as its uniform red shirts that were originally designed for workers in the slaughterhouses of Buenos Aires.[38] This red-shirt uniform became associated with human slaughter and the bloody shirt of revolutionary martyrdom after the crushing of the Roman Republic. Garibaldi, who had inspired the besieged defenders, saw his Brazilian wife and revolutionary companion die on the retreat from Rome in 1849.

The trappings of romantic melodrama surrounded the Italian revolutionaries in the final stages of their long struggle for national unity. Alexander Dumas sailed his yacht *Emma* into the Bay of Naples and put fourteen tailors to work on the deck manufacturing red shirts for Garibaldi's insurgents.[39] Some of them wore black with a flaming Vesuvius on the front—calling up an image of revolution long associated with the Neapolitan struggle against the Hapsburgs.

Garibaldi reentered the scene to lead the anti-Austrian liberation struggle in uneasy alliance with Cavour. When Cavour enraged him by ceding his birthplace (Nice) to France, Garibaldi set off from Genoa on May 6, 1860, with his famed thousand men for the final liberation of Sicily and Naples. There the revolutionary impulse had first appeared in the beginning of the century, and there the struggle with the Hapsburgs had an age-old appeal.

The way had been prepared for Garibaldi's astonishing success in conquering the South and uniting it with northern Italy by the remarkable uprising of 1857 led by the Neapolitan nobleman Carlo Pisacane, the first ideological hijacker of the modern era. Pisacane was a professional military officer who had fought in Algeria and with Garibaldi in defense of the Roman Republic of 1849. On June 25, 1857, by prearrangement with other impatient revolutionaries in Mazzini's entourage, Pisacane forcibly took over the postal steamer *Cagliari* as it left Genoa, converted it into a romantic flagship of revolutionary deliverance, and headed south. He released some four hundred prisoners on the Isle of Ponza (mistakenly believing them all to be political prisoners), continued to Capri, and (after the failure of a hoped-for revolution in the Naples area) went on to Calabria.[40] After some success in gaining popular support there, he saw his forces dispersed, and shot himself.

Pisacane mixed elements of transnational social revolution into his call for a national rising in Italy. He enlisted the English machinists aboard the *Cagliari* and alluded to imminent French support. Indeed, "great fear" of social revolution swept through Italy—and was to haunt Garibaldi even in victory.[41] (The romantic idea that a nation could be inspired to revolution by a ship of liberation lived on only among the isolated, unreconstructed Irish, who founded their greatest revolutionary organization, the Fenian brotherhood, on St. Patrick's day 1858. In an improbable series of episodes based in America during the next quarter century, the Fenians chartered the sailing ship *Catalpa* to rescue political prisoners from western Australia, and then commissioned the first American submarine, the *Fenian Ram*, to provide an underwater link between America and Ireland that could escape English dominance of the surface of the ocean.[42])

Like Mazzini, Garibaldi had hesitated to mix the national cause with the semi-anarchistic social radicalism of Pisacane. But when his own campaign proved victorious in the same southern regions three years later, Garibaldi felt some of the same bewilderment in victory that Pisacane had felt in defeat. Liberation brought a decline in revolutionary élan, and a disillusioned Garibaldi soon returned to Caprera. The effect of his victory everywhere in Europe, however, had been too electric to permit his early retirement. Early in October 1860, a month before he escorted King Victor Emmanuel into newly liberated Naples, Garibaldi called for an international legion of French, Polish, Swiss, and German volunteers.[43] They were to aid in the completion of Italian national liberation; but Garibaldi later suggested that these formations might also aid in the liberation of their own homelands. The first head of his international legion was a Pole; and many in the Polish uprising against Russia in 1863 wore red shirts and sang Italian songs.[44] On behalf of these Poles, the last serious efforts were made to give reality to this old ideal of an international revolutionary army. Consultations were held in Dresden and Turin; and a Polish-Italian pledge of simultaneous anti-Hapsburg uprisings in Galicia and Venice was agreed upon with Garibaldi in a three-day international gathering in June at his island retreat.

The London-based Philadelphians gathered together many former members of the recently deceased International Association to support Garibaldi's campaign.[45] Like this Masonic group, the names of the other allies in this loosely structured revolutionary campaign read like a summary of romantic conspiracy during the preceding half century: the spark of a Polish uprising, the fantasies of London-based émigrés (including Russian ideas of imminent uprisings among religious dissenters, peasants, and soldiers), the rumors of possible Napoleonic deliverance, and the inevitable Verdi melody—a kind of *Internationale* for revolutionary nationalism—the *Hymn to the Nations* of 1862.[46]

Recruitment for the international legion was most effectively publicized by Johann-Philipp Becker in Hamburg; he participated in both the Italian and Polish uprisings, and campaigned in support of Garibaldi through his journal in Hamburg, *Northern Star*.[47] In July 1863, Becker journeyed to the Jura region—the birthplace of both the first

Carbonari and the first Philadelphians—to prepare for an international congress which invited in Garibaldi's name the leaders of national democratic movements from throughout Europe. Convened at Brussels on September 26–28 with Pierre Coullery of the Jura [48] as chairman and Becker as vice-chairman, the congress adopted a resolution to form the *Association Fédérative Universelle de la Démocratie*, a society similar in name to the Democratic Association founded in Brussels sixteen years earlier. This Brussels association of 1847 had been supplanted by the London Communist League. In like manner, the new Garibaldian Democratic Association would be superseded one year later by a second London-based international organization dedicated to social revolution and dominated by Karl Marx: the International Workingmen's Association, subsequently known as the First International.

In London of 1864, the dominant passion among political exiles was not the founding of the International, but the organization of a tumultuously successful visit by Garibaldi. The Philadelphians helped organize it, and nationalist refugees from the recently crushed Polish uprising helped fan enthusiasm to a fever pitch. The spectacle of Garibaldi's arrival sent fresh blood coursing through even the most hardened revolutionary arteries. Goodwyn Barmby burst forth from his rural Unitarian parsonage in Wakefield, Yorkshire, to hail the arrival of this hero from "full, deep-bosomed Italy." Garibaldi, he announced, was the liberator of everything from trees and birds to lonely nuns in their convents.[49]

Herzen, disillusioned by the failure of revolution in Poland and rejected by younger Russian radicals, threw a dinner party for this one shining symbol of victorious revolution; the dinner ended with *Baba à la polonaise* and *Plombière de glace à la Garibaldi*.[50] Even French exiles, who rarely looked to foreigners for revolutionary guidance, hailed Garibaldi as a harbinger, if not a model, of their own liberation.[51]

For a brief initial period, the First International included in its general council a substantial number of Philadelphians and Italian nationalists. With their removal from the general council in the autumn of 1865 and the concurrent collapse of Mazzini's efforts to establish a new international of nationalist revolutionaries (variously referred to as a Universal Republican Alliance and an International Republican Committee), a half century of romantic revolutionary conspiracy came to an end.

If that period of revolutionary activity had been dominated by national revolutionaries, the next half-century was to be dominated by the more prosaic social revolutionaries of the first two proletarian internationals. The revolutionary appeal of nationalism had been undercut by the triumph of a conservative governmental nationalism under bourgeois auspices—in the newly unified Germany of Bismarck and Italy of Cavour; in post-Civil War America; in the proclamation of dominion status for Canada in 1867; and even in two events in eastern Europe during the same 1867: the adoption of a dual-nationality, Austro-Hungarian Empire by the Hapsburgs and the nationalistic enthusiasm aroused in Romanov Russia at the Moscow Pan-Slav Congress.

Romantic nationalism had been built on the twin pillars of an assertive vernacular culture and a heroic revolutionary movement for political self-determination. Important late-blooming examples appeared on the fringes of imperial Europe in the late nineteenth century among the oppressed Irish of the British Empire in the West and the oppressed Jews of the Romanov Empire in the East. But the Dublin stage and Irish Republican Army, like the Yiddish theater and Zionist and Bundist movements, were brilliant exceptions to the rule. The prevailing nationalist trends in the late nineteenth century were those of industrial development and territorial expansion by national states, which made varying degrees of concession to the parliamentary political forms of English or French liberalism. The dominant radical opposition was now to seek social more than political change, whether people thought of themselves as social revolutionaries or social democrats.

The romantic nationalist dream did not die dramatically, but like Garibaldi himself merely faded away. Almost totally a man of action, unable to understand the political and economic complexities of the new industrial world, Garibaldi fought for the French in 1870–71 and served brief, bewildered careers in both the Italian and the French parliaments before retiring to his island in the Mediterranean near Corsica, whence had come much of the inspiration for his ideal of an unspoiled natural order. After he died in 1882, his simple dream of popular revolution without any clear political program or social content lived on mainly in the adulation with which the nonrevolutionary Anglo-American world regarded this "hero of two worlds." Through posthumous glorification by the great Cambridge Victorian George Trevelyan and the great Princeton Wilsonian Walter Phelps Hall, he became a legend. The future of the revolutionary movement, however, belonged not to this consummate man of action, but to the supreme man of theory, Karl Marx, who was to die only one year after Garibaldi.

But Marx's heirs might never have come to power among the northeastern Slavs had not the heirs of Garibaldi established an earlier hold over the southwestern Slavs. The assassination of Archduke Franz Ferdinand by the conspiratorial nationalist Young Bosnia organization in July 1914 led directly to World War I, which made possible the Russian Revolution. Young Bosnia inherited the Mazzinian tradition of Young Italy. Its idealistic, nationalistic aims, quasi-Masonic forms,[52] and ethos of youthful sacrificial dedication—all represented a reprise in the 1910s on the preceding revolutionary movements of neighboring Italy. One of the two Young Bosnians tried for the assassination inscribed in his diary just after the fateful event the words of Mazzini:

> There is no more sacred thing in the world than the duty of a conspirator, who becomes an avenger of humanity and the apostle of permanent natural laws.[53]

Garibaldi remained the symbol of the struggle for national "resurgence" throughout the Balkans—from the mountains of Albania, where he was known as "a descendant of Skanderbeg" (the great national hero) to Russophile Bulgaria, where radical youth often wore a shirt called a *garibaldeika*.[54] Added intensity was provided by the Russian revolutionary movement, which radiated outward its own revolutionary pan-Slavic nationalism and dated back to the 1870s, when Bakunin and Garibaldi had rallied to the support of the Bosnian uprising against Turkey in 1874–75, a year before the tsarist government intervened militarily.[55] In the last years of his life, Bakunin was to make a final effort to recruit insurrectionary support for the South Slavs, thus transferring his hopes of a revolution back to Slavic lands. From the peasants of Bosnia, he was to turn in 1875–76 to the populists of St. Petersburg. And just after his death in 1877 Russian revolutionaries would begin the great chain of eastern European political assassinations that led to Sarajevo.

Mass Journalism

Thus it was in the 1860s and 1870s that the old hopes for revolutionary nationalism and the old modes of conspiracy moved from the industrializing center to the rural periphery of Europe. Coupled with this was another insidious and powerful development that undermined any possibility for keeping alive the dream of revolution in the minds of the masses: a new type of journalism. The revolutionary journalism of an intellectual avant-garde, which, as we have already seen, was absolutely central to the 1830–48 period, subsequently became swamped in the competition for popular attention by a new mass press—a press that was either nonrevolutionary or antirevolutionary.

The ideological journalism of the revolutionary tradition came to suffer rivalry from two different sources: (1) the prosaic, largely apolitical journals of workers themselves, and (2) the chauvinist press with its dazzling sensationalism which transformed nationalism from a revolutionary to a reactionary cause.

Proletarian Preoccupation

Journalism produced by working people has almost always been non-ideological, and only rarely revolutionary. This type of journalism began in England and America, where working-class readers were from the beginning preoccupied with immediate issues and material interests. Such perspectives encouraged reformist attitudes that Leninists would later call "trade-unionist," "tail endist," and *ouvrieriste*.

In America, embryonic unions created the first journals edited by and for workers. The pioneers were first the skilled artisans working with intellectuals in the Working Men's Movement in Philadelphia [56] and then the literate German immigrants who came to comprise one-third of the population of American cities.[57] Their journals all tended to be absorbed into the reformist politics of the New World. Even the later generation of transplanted communists, like Marx's friend Joseph Weydemeyer, began to redirect their journalistic energies into the political mainstream—as is symbolized by Weydemeyer's movement in the early 1850s from a journal called *Revolution* to one called *Reform*.[58] Karl Marx himself became a regular contributor in mid-1852 to the bourgeois, reformist newspaper of an ex-Fourierist, Charles Dana's *New York Tribune*.[59]

In England initially, the working class proved more threatening to European authority. Beginning in 1830, scores of untaxed periodicals with an increasingly proletarian editorship and readership began to appear illegally.[60] They helped prepare the mass base for both the Chartist movement and organized trade unionism—with Irish immigrants playing the radicalizing role that German immigrants had in America.[61]

In France, a working-class press first came into being in the immediate aftermath of 1830 (*Le Journal des Ouvriers, Le Peuple, journal des ouvriers rédigé par eux-mêmes,* and *L'Artisan,* with Lyon adding *L'Echo de Fabrique* and the anti-Parisian, anti-intellectual *La Tribune-Prolétaire* in 1831).[62] At the end of the decade an even larger and more aggressively *ouvrieriste* press appeared with the indefatigable former Saint-Simonians in the lead: [63] Jules Vinçard's *La Ruche Populaire,* a "journal of workers edited and published by themselves" in 1839, Philippe Buchez's *L'Atelier,* an even more important journal which was founded by and intended exclusively for salaried, physical laborers.[64]

The point about these working-class journals was that they showed little interest in the theories of revolutionary intellectuals *about* the working class. *Atelier,* for instance, rejected the ideological pretensions of the original French communists in making the attainment of material happiness "a complete social doctrine . . . an entire system of philosophy," [65] and the rhetoric of Leroux in speaking of humanity "as if it were a real person." [66] The working-class press was particularly suspicious of socialist ideologists; and, in the period of expanded opportunity between the fall of Louis Philippe in 1848 and Napoleon III's coup in 1851, Proudhon's influence was great and workers' journals tended to be "more revolutionary than socialist." [67] But the prestige of revolutionary manifestoes was already shattered by the repression of June 1848; [68] and Napoleonic restriction and coöptation blunted the revolutionary inclinations of surviving proletarian journals.

Once again the center of working-class journalism returned to the freer atmosphere of England. The great exhibit of 1851 in the Crystal Palace and the reformist role of the Liberal party seduced many former radicals with the promise of incremental material improvements and upward mobility within the system. When, in 1855, the "tax on knowledge" was at last completely abolished and stamping by the government was no longer in force, the main beneficiary of the new freedom of the press turned out to be the new sensationalist mass journalism. Once the goal of freedom had been attained, the very Chartist journalism that had been agitating for that freedom ironically collapsed.[69] London did not cease to provide haven and ideas, but by 1860, revolutionary leadership—and the Chartist tradition of revolutionary journalism —had passed to other nations.

The International Workingmen's Association of 1864 grew out of a tradition of French workers' delegations visiting London—which itself grew out of Chartist attempts to develop Anglo-French collaboration in the 1850s.[70] The mature Marx, however, saw relatively little revolutionary possibility in either the French or the English working-class sponsors of the First International. He increasingly placed his hopes on the rising German Social Democratic movement, the only place where proletarian journals did not seem to imply renunciation of revolution.

Chauvinistic Distraction

The rise of a new working class created deep fears in the 1850s and the 1860s. With the memory of 1848 still vivid, European statesmen not only provided social benefits to the populace in order to defuse social protest, but also entered the journalistic lists themselves to help shape public opinion. Conservatives like Bismarck and Disraeli no less than an erstwhile friend of revolutionaries like Napoleon III developed journalistic outlets and "socialistic" programs. Even in Russia, the Ministry of the Interior was involved in founding the first working-class journal in that country in 1875.[71] Thus began the long government tradition of attempting to infiltrate or direct the organization of the working class in the large industrial complexes of late nineteenth-century Russia.

The real weapon against workers from 1848 to 1914 was, however, the new patriotic press. It hypnotized the masses everywhere—hitching the old romantic nationalism to the new wagon of industrial state power. England led the way in the 1850s, with a patriotic press that first put pressure on a weak Liberal government to intervene in the Crimean War of 1854–56, and then championed the purge of all corruption and inefficiency that impeded victory. This war, the bloodiest in Europe during the century between Waterloo and Sarajevo, drowned out whatever was left of the Chartist passion for social reform within England. Radical journalists in England contributed to the hysteria by baptizing it a "people's war" and "war of the nations" against reactionary Russia.[72] Marx, who was a leading Russophobe among revolutionary journalists of this period,[73] had high hopes that the war might call into being a revolution as "the sixth power of Europe." [74] *The Times* introduced telegraphic dispatches from special war correspondents and war photographers to make this distant war seem more immediate and vivid than the more urgent domestic problems. *The Times* encouraged its readers, moreover, to kibbitz on the management of the war; and ended up depicting it as a kind of crusade for civilization, which provided both the heroism of the Light Brigade [75] and the healing mission of Florence Nightingale.

William Russell, a brilliant Irish correspondent of *The Times*, helped mobilize popular opinion for the war over the heads of vacillating politicians, and helped summon up instant outrage about its conduct that

brought down once unassailable military leaders. After victory he became "a sort of king without a crown." [76] In 1855 *The Times* had a
daily print order of 61,000, more than ten times that of its rivals; [77]
and a new weekly began publication in November 1855 with the flat
statement that "this country is governed by *The Times*." [78]

During the Crimean War, *The Times* found an imitator in England's
French ally, *Le Figaro*, which from its inception in 1854 also appealed
to mass patriotism from beneath a format of conservative respectability. The full-blooded patriotic exhibitionism that soon developed in the
London *Daily Telegraph* was also characteristic of the journalistic experiments of Girardin and others late in the reign of Napoleon III.

The French coined the word chauvinism for this attitude, drawing
the name from the popular culture of the music halls. An old vaudeville, *La Cocarde Tricolore,* had ridiculed an uncritical follower of Napoleon I, Nicholas Chauvin, for repeatedly singing:

> Je suis français
> Je suis Chauvin

If French journalists discovered chauvinism on the eve of the Franco-
Prussian War, their British counterparts created a similar ism of their
own to describe a parallel burst of popular patriotism during the Balkan War of 1878. Drawing from an expletive used in pubs ("jingo"
meaning gosh), the British press began to speak of *jingoism*. The *Daily
News* of March 13 described excessive patriotism as the creation of "the
new tribe of music hall Patriots who sing the Jingo song." [79] But the
press itself provided the orchestration.

As the "music hall patriots" urged Britain to fight Russia again, the
Russians began to produce their own jingo press. Indeed, the creation
of a new, antirevolutionary mass journalism in Russia provided a striking illustration of reactionaries pre-empting the techniques and cancel-
ing out the appeal of a pre-existent revolutionary journalism.

The story begins with Michael Katkov, who had been a radical in the
late 1850s and was the first to use the word *nihilist* in print inside
Russia. Late in 1862, Katkov purchased *Moscow News,* a journal that
had previously been a semi-official state organ and had only recently
become a daily newspaper. He assumed the editorship on New Year's
Day 1863, and within ten days the Polish uprising began. Katkov responded with what Herzen described as his "cruel crusade against Poland." [80] Playing on antiforeign feelings within Moscow, St. Petersburg's ancient rival, Katkov proved that a privately owned press outside
the capital could be even more reactionary than official governmental
ones in St. Petersburg. He defined his *Moscow News* as "the organ of
a party which may be called Russian, ultra-Russian, exclusively Russian"; [81] and its circulation soared to an unprecedented twelve thousand.[82] Using his previous experience in the radical ambiance of the
"thick journals," Katkov gave an ideological cast to repression, arguing
that he favored "not the crushing of Polish nationality (*narodnost'*),
but the summoning of it to a new political life with Russia." [83] Making
ample use of feuilleton inserts and of anti-intellectual letters to the

editor, Katkov's journal helped impel the imperial government to overcome initial indecision and launch a campaign of repression. Katkov then introduced illustrations into the land of icons—representing the new military governor-general, Muravev, as a popular hero and the distant Herzen as a devil infecting Russia with foreign discord. This journalistic campaign of patriotic mobilization helped shrink the readership of Herzen's *Bell* in the course of 1863 from more than 2,500 to less than 500.[84] The campaign, moreover, emboldened Katkov to press early in 1866 a campaign against the revolutionary virus at home. He insisted that "the true root of the upheaval lies not in Paris, Warsaw, or Vilnius, but in Petersburg." [85] The enemy became not outright revolutionaries, but liberals in high places "who do not protest against the powerful influences that give aid to the evil." [86]

The leadership of former revolutionary sympathizers in developing a new antirevolutionary journalism increased in the late 1860s through the serialized writings of two veterans of the radical Petrashevsky circle of the 1840s: Feodor Dostoevsky and Nicholas Danilevsky. Dostoevsky's *The Possessed*, published in Katkov's journal, caricatured Nechaev's revolutionary conspiracy with unprecedented metaphysical depth and satiric power. Danilevsky provided a seemingly scientific rationale for expansionist pan-Slavism in his *Russia and Europe*, which described a coming struggle for survival between the "Romano-German" and "Slavic" worlds. Danilevsky's work was published in a new reactionary monthly of 1869; its name, *The Dawn* (*Zaria*), was coöpted from the revolutionaries' lexicon. Contributors included Herzen's former collaborator, Vasily Kelsiev, as well as the leading "antinihilist" novelist of the sixties, A. F. Pisemsky.[87] Dostoevsky's novel began appearing in 1871 (just as Danilevsky's articles were being republished as a book) in Katkov's *Russian Herald*. So important was this new journal felt to be in the ideological war against the revolutionaries that when Katkov died in 1887, a special session of the Council of Ministers was called to consider the "crisis." The journal was moved from Moscow to St. Petersburg to encourage even closer links with official policy.[88]

Reactionary pan-Slavism was rarely promoted directly by government officials and never became an official ideology in tsarist Russia.[89] Rather it was the creation of the new right-wing mass journalists who were often former radical intellectuals redirecting revolutionary impulses into foreign areas. Katkov, who previously encouraged rebellious students at Moscow University, remained a periodic agitator for radical legal reform. A former friend and patron of Belinsky on *Annals of the Fatherland*, A. A. Kraevsky, launched in 1863 a new reactionary journal, *The Voice* (*Golos*), and sponsored its growth from 4,000 readers to more than 22,000 at the time of the pan-Slav enthusiasm of 1877.[90] In that year, A. S. Suvorin took over the St. Petersburg daily *New Times* (*Novoe Vremia*), and transformed it into an even more influential pan-Slav newspaper. He added a second edition and a new motif of anti-Semitism, which became in the 1880s a principal theme of the new reactionary journalism concurrently developing in Russia's German-speaking neighbors to the West.[91] Yet even this gazette continued to use revolutionary rhetoric about "new times." Suvorin himself in his youth had written a story called *Garibaldi* that was read aloud for inspirational purposes at the soirées of radical intellectuals.[92]

The new industrialism helped enable the chauvinistic mass press to replace the ideological journalism of the early nineteenth century. The crucial change in the source of financial support from subscribers to advertisers did more than inhibit direct criticism of capitalistic institutions. It freed journalists from the pressure to deal with the immediate and local interests of their readers. Journalists in the late nineteenth century were encouraged by their editors to create remote identities and symbolic issues for their anonymous urban audience. News stories had to be ever more dramatic in order to compete with the growing volume of gaudy advertising. The situation grew worse at the turn of the century with the arrival of pictorial and headline journalism. The regular use of photographs, sensational headings, and special editions accelerated the drift towards the excitement of passions through anti-revolutionary nationalism. The "thick journals" of an earlier age seemed slow-moving and dull. The disenfranchised readers had lost control. The path was straight from Girardin's pioneering decision to rely on advertisers for basic support to the mass chauvinism that helped launch World War I.

Napoleon III and "Imperialism"

The drama of deradicalizing the masses through a new type of journalism unfolded most vividly in the France of Napoleon III. In ways that contemporaries never understood—and historians have only begun to investigate—Napoleon turned revolutionary nationalism abroad into a means of political repression at home, and transformed revolutionary Saint-Simonian social ideas at home into a means of economic expansion abroad.

One cannot speak of the third Napoleon without speaking of the first; for the new Napoleon rode to power in large measure on the reputation of the old. Napoleon III was elected president of the Second French Republic by an overwhelming vote in December 1848, and was awarded dictatorial powers three years later by an even more staggering vote. The Napoleonic legend had continued to cast its spell over many revolutionary intellectuals.

The original French Revolution brought Napoleon I to power, and the original professional revolutionaries of the early nineteenth century came together largely to overthrow him. Revolutionary thinking about power was, thus, influenced from the beginning by this supreme man of power. He set the agenda for a generation by shattering all the old political legitimacies: by politicizing the Enlightenment ideal of universal rationality (the metric system, the Code Napoléon); and by imposing it all on a backward world. Above all, he fed the romantic imagination with an aesthetic fascination with power—and with the possibilities of changing the map and the life of Europe.

Whether they came from the armies that fought with Napoleon (French Philadelphians, Polish Philomats, and most Italian Carbonari) or against him (Russian Decembrists, Spanish *comuneros*, German *Tugendbund*), the early revolutionaries were youthful soldiers who spoke French and thought in the grand Napoleonic manner. There was, then, a hidden model or "superego" for the original revolutionaries. Bonaparte was Prometheus unbound, a parvenu in power; and the young revolutionary was almost always both a restless Promethean and an outsider in search of power.

The most important revolutionary ideologies of the restoration era —Saint-Simonianism and Hegelianism—were born under the Napoleonic star. They continued to attract intellectuals who sought to provide purpose for (and thus gain access to) power. This politicization of the intellect intensified under Napoleon. Saint-Simon first began writing specifically in order to perfect and complete the Napoleonic reforms. His long and unsuccessful campaign to reach Napoleon directly gave him a permanent predilection for seeking out a power capable of putting his ideas into force. Hegel was enraptured by the Napoleonic conquest of Germany, and saw the hand of providence in the completion of his *Phenomenology* at the time of the Battle of Jena. His final political vision appears to have been a synthesis of Prussian reform with Napoleonic universality.

The rational reintegration of society preached by Hegel and Saint-Simon was inconceivable without the strange combination that Napoleon introduced into the world: a despot ruling in the name of liberation. However un-Napoleonic may have been the final hopes that Saint-Simon placed in the working class and Hegel in the Prussian state, the impulse to look for some universal secular transformation of society came as much from the concrete fact of Napoleon as from the abstract rhetoric of the revolution.

The Napoleonic legacy thus helped create the original revolutionary ideologies; and the Napoleonic legend helped in more subtle ways to revive and intensify the revolutionary impulse in the 1840s.[93] The boredom with the politics and style of Louis Philippe would not have been so acute in a land that did not have a Napoleon to remember. The insecure Louis Philippe, in search of some genealogy of legitimacy, cultivated an identification with Napoleon. He returned the ashes of Napoleon to Paris for reburial in the Invalides, and erected his statue in the Place Vendôme.

There had long been a body of Frenchmen who considered themselves reform Napoleonists as distinct from militaristic Bonapartists. In the 1840s their ranks were swelled by others whose political hopes focused on Napoleon's nephew, the future Napoleon III, who had been active in the Italian revolutionary movement and had vainly tried twice to have himself proclaimed emperor in the late 1830s. This new Napoleon wrote in 1839 the influential *Des Idées Napoléoniennes,* which called for a new supra-political authority avoiding all doctrine and seeking only concrete benefits for the masses.[94]

This influential work, which sold 500,000 copies in five years,[95] reflected the ideas of the Saint-Simonians whom Napoleon had befriended during his English exile of the late 1830s. He followed them in preferring administrative solutions over ideological or political ones and in his early interest in a possible canal through Nicaragua to further the "mystic marriage of East and West." [96]

The young Saint-Simon had progressed from early dreams of becoming a new Charlemagne to his final appeal for justice to "the poorest and most numerous class." Napoleon III in like fashion turned from writing a life of Charlemagne in the early forties to a new vision of increasing production and ending unemployment in his work of 1844: *Extinction of Pauperism.*[97]

Napoleon III did not share Napoleon I's fatal opposition to ideology. Unlike the first Napoleon, who came back from Egypt and Italy as a man of war, the third Napoleon returned to France from London as a man of ideas. He adopted as his own the Proudhonist proposal for workers' associations and benefits, and transformed the Saint-Simonianism of his youth into an authoritarian industrialism and an anticlerical positivism that greatly strengthened the French state [98] (and, incidentally, helped to gain for many surviving Saint-Simonians lucrative positions in banking, industry, and government service). In this respect Bismarck was his imitator, transforming Hegelianism, the ideological system hitherto prevalent among German revolutionaries, into a new and conservative German nationalism. The roots of this neo-Hegelianism lay in the tract of 1857 calling for the building of a monument to Hegel, but warning that none would be adequate "until the German nation would build its state into the living temple of purest realism." [99] When Bismarck became premier of Prussia five years later he capitalized on the passion of Hegelian intellectuals for political relevance by enlisting many of them in the tasks of German state-building. Many came to believe that Hegel's vision of a rational, ordered society giving birth to a neo-Hellenic flowering of high culture might soon become reality in the new Germany Bismarck was building.

The principal "Napoleonic idea" was the coöptation of French revolutionary rhetoric by the patriotic press, which Napoleon III controlled brilliantly. The problem of the press was inescapable for anyone trying to restore order to France. Triumphant in elections, Napoleon faced the challenge of a free press:

> . . . the great question of the century . . . the greatest difficulty for constitutional order, the greatest danger for weak governments, the decisive proof of strong ones.[100]

Initially, Napoleon III reacted negatively to the challenge. But his harsh press laws of 1852 were gradually relaxed. He provided a general amnesty for the press in 1859, and soon entered the lists of chauvinistic journalism with his own anticlerical, quasi-socialist *L'Opinion Nationale*.

Napoleon created the "national opinion" that he purported to describe. So thoroughgoing was his control of the press that one critic complained before the legislature in 1862: "There is one journalist in France . . . the Emperor." [101] In addition to controlling the news agency Havas and flooding the market with sloganized pamphlets (*L'Empire c'est la paix, Le salut c'est la dynastie*), Napoleon bought off opposition newspapers, streamlined the official *Le Moniteur*, and added a readable evening edition in 1864. This *Petit Moniteur* was published in editions of 200,000 and sold at a depressed price of six centimes— thereby undercutting all other competitors, who had to pay a minimum tax of five centimes on each issue. The satirist Maurice Joly, in his *Politics of Machiavelli in the Nineteenth Century* of 1864, described the technique as "neutralizing the press by the press itself." [102]

Napoleon was a master of coöptation and public relations. He often offered prominent radical personalities jobs while stealing their slogans. He sponsored banquets and even associations for workers, and sought to channel their growing search for solidarity. Housing projects, mutual aid societies, and other meliorative programs were introduced and lauded with publicity on his imperial tours. Unlike Fazy in Switzerland, who introduced worker benefits out of long conviction and after careful study, Napoleon simply adopted what his monitoring of public opinion convinced him was expedient.

Historians have reached radically different verdicts on the motives and even on the results of the emperor's program.[103] Essentially, he seems to have prepared the way for the characteristic political formula of the Third Republic: the combination of revolutionary rhetoric and practical reliance on a permanent centralized administration left over from the first Napoleon.

Napoleon continued his support of the Italian nationalist movement abroad, and espoused other, more remote national revolutionary causes. However, the suspicion soon grew that he was attempting to reroute abroad the popular impulses towards social revolution that had appeared at home in 1848 and 1851. "Emperor of the French" rather than of France, he increasingly seemed to use overseas adventure for domestic prestige: war in the Crimea in 1854–56, conquest of South Vietnam in 1862, and the disastrous attempt to conquer Mexico in 1866–67. All of this called forth a new word of rebuke from his erstwhile journalistic friends: *imperialism*. This, the last of the great isms to find a name, was used to describe the rapid expansion of European power overseas in the last two decades of the nineteenth century; but the term began with journalistic questioning of Napoleon III in the final "liberal" period of his reign.[104]

Napoleon's scourge during these final years was the last great polemic innovator of revolutionary journalism in the Francocentric era: Henri de Rochefort. His remarkable career illustrated both the vulnerability of Napoleon as a leader and the ultimate victory of his chauvinist ideal.

Rochefort came out of the same low culture that had created the terms chauvinism and jingoism; he was a vaudeville writer and a pupil of both Blanqui and the chansonnier Béranger. He served his journalistic apprenticeship on *Figaro* before launching in the late 1860s his radical *La Lanterne* and *La Marseillaise* and contributing to Victor Hugo's new *Le Rappel* of 1869. Rochefort's was the direct voice of proletarian ribaldry: a Daumier in prose with just a suggestion of Rabelais, promising to "register the misery of the laborers" alongside "the toilets of the Tuileries." [105] The very title of his first journal dispensed with the romantic past and invoked the plebeian image of a gaslight atop an iron support on a Parisian street corner. "The Lantern," Rochefort bluntly explained, "can serve simultaneously to illuminate honest men and to hang malefactors." [106] His principal target was Napoleon, whom he assaulted with an unprecedented barrage of animal metaphors.[107] His journal soared to an unprecedented printing of 500,000,[108] and its easily concealed, pocket-sized format gave it European-wide distribution. When forced to flee to Brussels, Rochefort resumed publication of *The Lantern* with a model declaration of revolutionary independence from coöptation by Napoleon:

> The role of the government is in effect to amnesty me as soon as possible; but my role is not to let them . . . It is original, it is even burlesque. . . .[109]

Although Napoleon succeeded in having the weekly shut later in 1869, Rochefort simply transferred his energies to a daily, *La Marseillaise,* which one of his collaborators called "a torpedo launched at high speed against the metal plates of the imperial navy," and a future leader of the Paris Commune called a "machine of war against the Empire." [110] If France was still the "light of the world" [111] for foreign revolutionaries, his journal was the main beacon.

Rochefort and his associates "proposed to rally the entire European socialist party to establish through the journal permanent relations between all the groups." [112] Such plans were fanciful, but his format was widely imitated. Students in distant St. Petersburg (including Marx's principal Russian correspondent, Nicholas Danielson) tried to set up a journal with the same title and format.

Within France, Rochefort's appeal was so great that it had to be combatted not just with repression, but also with rival attractions. Girardin moved into the vacuum, and, as we have seen, he became in the late years of Napoleon's reign a leading troubador of nationalism and foreign war. Taking over the moribund *La Liberté* in the late 1860s, he lifted its circulation from 500 to 60,000 through a journalistic revolution that was "perhaps as significant as that of 1836 of which it was in any case the natural consequence and prolongation." [113] The new mass audience that he thus created found its excitement no longer in *The Three Musketeers* and the gossip columns of *La Presse,* but in images of actual combat in the real world—telegraphic dispatches of distant military adventures, bulletins of a rising and falling stockmarket, and athletic contests that *La Liberté* was the first to cover regularly in its new section, *le monde sportique.*

Rochefort himself was eventually seduced by the new chauvinism—despite having served ten years in New Caledonia for supporting the Paris Commune and having founded a new journal of revolutionary opposition to moderate republicans (appropriately named *The Intransigent*) on Bastille Day 1880. He swung to the Right late in the decade to support General Boulanger, moved further to the Right a decade later during the Dreyfus case, and left *The Intransigent* altogether in 1907 to spend the last six years of his life writing, for the conservative, nationalist *La Patrie*.

One need not fill out in full the story of the chauvinistic press and how it grew in the late nineteenth century. Many of the innovations used to sensationalize news originated in America: photographic political illustrations (in the *New York Daily Telegraph* of 1873), linotype (in the German-American press of Baltimore in 1885), and a host of devices used by William Randolph Hearst after his acquisition of the *New York Journal* in 1895. Seeking to outshine Pulitzer's *New York World*, Hearst used aggressive patriotism as the cement for a journalistic empire.[114] He all but created the Spanish-American War of 1898. He sent the illustrator Frederick Remington to Cuba on the eve of war to provide pictorial evidence of Spanish transgressions. Remington wired back to Hearst, "Everything is quiet. There is no trouble here. There will be no war. Wish to return." Hearst replied with the famous: "Please remain. You furnish the pictures and I'll furnish the war." [115]

A typical journalistic move from the revolutionary Left to the chauvinistic Right—the motion so common in superpatriotic journalism—was that made by the most politically influential left-wing French journalist of the late nineteenth century: Georges Clemenceau. His transformation into the ultra-militant leader of France in World War I illustrated how mass politics had replaced not only the conservative statecraft of the restored European monarchies after Waterloo but also the French-led tradition of revolutionary opposition. The decisive watershed year for many (including the young communard Clemenceau) was 1871, which sealed the victory of reactionary chauvinism over revolutionary nationalism. The German victory over France in the Franco-Prussian war led to the crowning of a new German emperor in Versailles. The concurrent "liberation" of Rome and its designation as the Italian capital added new imperial associations to the achievement of Italian unity.

Germany and Italy—the foci of hopes throughout the early nineteenth century for an extension of revolution beyond France—thus achieved final union in 1871 not through a revolution of their peoples, but through the military and diplomatic power of their leading sub-states: Prussia and Piedmont. Bismarck's Germany realized *Einheit* (unity) at the expense of *Freiheit* (freedom), under an emperor rather than a constitution. Italy under Cavour was subordinated not to Mazzini's "Rome of the people," but to the Rome of a new king. The Vatican council of 1871 proclaimed its faith not in Lamennais's vision of popular liberation from below, but in the infallibility of papal authority above.

The most dramatic and fateful event of the watershed year, 1871, was, however, the rise and fall of the Paris Commune. It triggered the swing to the Right throughout Europe—and opened up new horizons for the revolutionary Left.

The Paris Commune

The Paris Commune of 1871 was the largest urban insurrection of the nineteenth century—and precipitated the bloodiest repression. It was a watershed in revolutionary history: the last of the Paris-based revolutions, bringing to an end the French domination of the revolutionary tradition.

The Paris uprising was the first example of mass defiance of the new military-industrial state in modern Europe. The Commune created—however briefly—an alternative, revolutionary approach to the organization of authority in modern society. Successful subsequent revolutionaries in Europe followed the communard example of making revolution only in the wake of war. Whereas the revolutions of 1789, 1830, and 1848 had occurred in times of peace, those that rocked Russia in 1905 and 1917, and brought other communist regimes into power in China, Yugoslavia, and Vietnam in the 1940s, were the direct outgrowth of foreign wars.

The Commune left a legacy of legends as well as lessons. It provided the Russian Revolution with holy relics (Lenin was buried with a communard flag, and the spaceship Voskhod was equipped forty years later with a ribbon from a banner of the Commune); and with holy images (the classic icon of class conflict in Eisenstein's *October*—bourgeois ladies jabbing fallen workers with pointed parasols—was taken from a mural in the Paris museum of the Commune).

Myths of the Commune abounded among anarchists as well as Social Democrats in the period prior to World War I; [116] among Chinese cultural revolutionaries of the 1960s [117] no less than Russian political revolutionaries fifty years earlier; [118] among the New Left as well as the Old in the Western world.

Insofar as all later revolutionaries were to find unity among themselves, it was in the singing of the great hymn that emerged from the martyrdom of 1871: the *Internationale*.

The simple fact of the Commune was that a revolutionary alliance ruled Paris for seventy-two days in the spring of 1871. It began as a patriotic protest against capitulation to the Prussian siege of Paris by a provisional French government formed after the defeat and flight of Napoleon III in September 1870. But the Commune soon became a vehicle for proletarian protest against the modern centralized state. An internal social revolution became a means of restoring pride to the nation after the state had suffered defeat in a foreign war. There were echoes as far afield as the Muslim quarter of Algiers [119] and provincial Russia. The leader of a student circle moved between Vilnius and St. Petersburg, signing his name "Communist" and proclaimed on April 14, 1871; "The World Revolution has already begun." He named his short-lived journal *The Gallows*, and trailed into anonymity with an appeal to his countrymen on May 4 to "respond where you are to dying Paris . . . to arms! to arms!" [120]

For the historian of revolution, the Commune may be seen as the most extreme moment of a revolutionary cycle in France which began when Napoleon tried to liberalize his empire in 1869–70—and ended only with the formal constitution of the Third Republic in 1875.[121] The movement was, moreover, narrowly Parisian. Although there was sporadic insurgency in support of the Commune in other French cities, only in Paris was a new communal government elected and able to exercise authority.

For the historian of the revolutionary tradition, the Commune represents a crucial turning point from the previous dominance of national political revolution to the coming emphasis on transnational social revolution. To be sure, the Commune originated in the intensification of nationalistic militance during the war with Prussia that began in the summer of 1870. The Parisian Central Committee of the swollen National Guard opposed the armistice of January 1871 and spoke of the resistance possibilities of a new *levée en masse*. Nationalistic Paris turned revolutionary when the new central government of Thiers tried unsuccessfully to seize the guns of the Paris National Guard on March 18, 1871. Thiers fled to Versailles, and the patriotic leaders of France elected an eighty-one-member Commune as a rival government—or, as some would say, a rival to government.

This new participatory form of revolutionary administration resisted till near the end Jacobin and Blanquist demands for strong executive leadership, and militantly combatted the authority of the republican National Assembly at Versailles. The Commune attempted to move beyond traditional politics, reviving dreams of a fundamental transformation of the human condition on a large scale for the first time since 1792–94.

Aspiration was no less intense for being unfocused. At first during January and February, hopes seemed to move from national to social revolution, as "vigilance committees" allied themselves into a "revolutionary Socialist Party." [122] As the Commune developed, social revolutionaries avoided formal parties, but generally divided themselves into anticentralizing Proudhonists and elitist, statist Blanquists.

About half of the ruling body were manual workers; and another, partially overlapping, half had been involved in working-class political agitation of the 1860s. There was an authentic proletarian quality to the Commune's efforts to establish cooperative industrial organization and professionally oriented secular education.

The verbal talisman of this unexpected social revolution was the word "Commune" itself. To most, it suggested "a demand for decentralization of authority—a federal state where small self-governing groups or units would become the dominant feature." [123] The expulsion of the national government from Paris on March 18 was described as a *révolution communaliste*.[124] It represented essentially a search for communal authority and communal benefits. Marx and the First International were only distant commentators despite the efforts of the Versailles government to equate communalism with communism.[125]

A strangely festive air prevailed in revolutionary Paris under the *souveraineté sauvage* [126] of the masses, from the parades that proclaimed the Commune on March 28 to the rapturous destruction of a totem of the Napoleonic cult, the Vendôme tower, on May 16 just hours before the Commune was crushed. March 28 was proclaimed "the festive wedding day of the Idea and the Revolution" [127] amid general expectations of realizing "something more than a nominal republic," "the thing instead of the name." [128]

In what Lenin called this "festival of the oppressed," even funerals became processions of civic dedication. These and other ceremonies were often punctuated by the sounds of the new weapons firing on Paris. As one revolutionary poet wrote:

> The clash of cymbals can be heard in the dreadful silence between rounds of firing; and merry dance airs mingle with the rattle of American machine-guns.[129]

The new guns, of course, prevailed; and the "merry dance airs" gave way to a dance of death. In the "bloody week" that followed the final entry of the Versailles troops into Paris on May 21, 1871, some 20,000 communards were killed. Another 13,000 were subsequently sent to prison or exile. Physical horror was accompanied by an attempt—largely unprecedented in prior repressions of revolutionary movements—to treat revolutionaries as pathological criminals.[130]

The defeat of France by Prussia and then of the Paris Commune by the Versailles-based government seemed to represent the consistent crushing of ideas by power. France had still been seen as the homeland of revolutionary brotherhood; and surviving nationalist revolutionaries throughout Europe had rallied to the French cause. The last commander-in-chief of the Paris Commune itself was the Pole Jarosław Dąbrowski, who died heroically on the barricades.[131] Garibaldi and his Polish counterpart Józef Hauke-Bosak (leader of the Polish national insurrection of 1863) joined hands to assume military command of the unsuccessful defense of Dijon against the Prussians; and this last great hero of Polish nationalism died his martyr's death there.[132]

Defeat of the Paris Commune and the subsequent disintegration of the First International brought to an end the French era of modern revolutionary history. For nearly a century since the Great Revolution of 1789, Paris had been the principal center of expectation and the scene of revolution. The rallying cries of the 1830s and 1840s—socialism and communism—were first sounded in Paris, where the genie of popular political journalism was also first released. In Paris, the fantasies of intellectuals provided spiritual ideals for a materialistic age—and prophetic prefigurations of almost every later revolutionary movement. All the congresses of the First International had been held in French-speaking areas on the immediate periphery of France—as if the leaders of European revolution sought to be as close as possible to a promised land only temporarily denied them.

That hope died when the conservative Third Republic rose on the grave of the Commune—and proved to be the most enduring form of government in modern French history. Thus, ironically, the French period of revolutionary history was ended by the very republican system of government that the original French revolutionaries had fought to establish. Versailles, where the forces assembled to destroy the Commune, worked its belated revenge against revolutionary Paris. The Tuileries Palace, which the original republicans of 1792 had stormed to establish the First Republic, was burned by the communards as the revolution staged its own final immolation scene. The Third Republic enlisted the economic power of the industrial bourgeoisie and the military might of the new centralized state. It wedded yesterday's revolutionary slogans (republican government, secular education) to today's vested interests.

Both the founding of the Third Republic in 1871 and its final dissolution in 1940 occurred in the wake of military defeat by Germany. In the history of revolutionary movements no less than that of national armies, the period of French dominance was to be succeeded by one of German dominance.

The French Republic was as much a conservative, unitary state as Bismarck's empire; and France soon followed Germany in transforming the revolutionary nationalism born in the late eighteenth century into the reactionary imperialism of the late nineteenth.

With nationalism crushed and republicanism discredited in France, social revolution alone remained intact as a revolutionary ideal. Within the Commune there had been two conflicting types of social revolutionary: decentralizing Proudhonists (emphasizing direct rule by and benefits for the workers) and authoritarian Blanquists and Jacobins (who in the dying days of the Commune established a dictatorial Committee of Public Safety). But there was no real leadership for either party. Proudhon had been dead for six years; and Blanqui was arrested and immobilized before the Commune was formed. Perhaps the closest any individual came to becoming a unifying leader was the moderate Jacobin Charles Delescuzes; and he gained special status only by dying on the last barricades.

The thoroughness of the repression within France placed the burden of continuing the social revolutionary tradition on leaders from other lands. Two in particular, Bakunin and Marx, sought to define the lessons of the Commune and carry on its tradition. The conflict between them became in the embittered aftermath of the Commune as central as was the struggle between Marx and Proudhon a quarter century earlier.

Marx vs. Bakunin

The fight between Marx and Bakunin was in many ways only a deepening of the Marx-Proudhon conflict. Once again, it was a civil war among social revolutionaries who shared more assumptions than either cared to admit.

Both Marx and Bakunin had been radical Hegelians at the University of Berlin. Both developed almost simultaneously an early, lifelong commitment to the coming revolution to end all social inequality. Both were convinced internationalists who rejected any purely national revolution. Both sought to base their struggle on oppressed social classes, rejecting the elite conspiratorial traditions of the past. Neither participated in the Commune, but each argued that its heroic tragedy vindicated his own revolutionary ideas.

Their conflict had in a sense already begun in 1843, when Bakunin insisted that the communist movement, then only in its infancy, was a deeply authoritarian foe of revolutionary liberation.[133] Man's desire for local and national identity could be crushed, he argued, because communism was the expression of

> a herd of animals organized by compulsion and force and concerned only with material interests, ignoring the spiritual side of life.[134]

In the 1850s, when Marx was writing in the British Museum, Bakunin languished in tsarist prisons. In the 1860s, when Marx was establishing a central authority among northern European revolutionaries in London, Bakunin threw himself into a series of movements in southern Europe that intensified his anti-authoritarianism and anticipated the anticentralism of the Commune.

By 1866, Bakunin had concluded that local, autonomous communes were the only legitimate form of political authority. Two years later, he spoke of replacing the modern state altogether with a "federation of the barricades." His concept foreshadowed the Soviets that would later emerge in Russia: a ruling council of "one or two deputies for each barricade . . . always responsible and always revocable." [135]

Bakunin rejected emphatically the Buonarrotian tradition of hierarchical organization pointing towards a provisional revolutionary dictatorship. He also sharply criticized the German socialists for their dangerous insistence that "the political revolution must precede the social revolution." [136] Against the German Social Democrats' stated goal of "a free people's state," Bakunin insisted that "the words *free* and *people's* are annulled and rendered meaningless by the word State." [137]

He set forth a plan for a European-wide revolutionary movement against state power in all its forms on the eve of the Franco-Prussian War. The originality of Bakunin's program lay in his call for a worker-peasant alliance. He insisted that revolutions narrowly based in cities tended simply to seize the existing power of the central state and then superimpose their authority on the countryside. Elitist, urban-based revolutionaries like Marx tended to radiate intellectual contempt for the peasantry by denigrating their religious faith and their individualistic methods. Bakunin himself was just as hostile to these peasant attitudes, but he nevertheless argued that a display of hostility would only perpetuate the separation of the peasantry from its natural revolutionary ally: the proletariat.

> There is no point in extolling or denigrating the peasants. *It is a question of establishing a program of action which will overcome the individualism and conservatism of the peasants.*[138]

Such a program lay in unification for "the extirpation of the principle of authority in all its possible manifestations."[139] Without such a common objective, ordinary people in the cities and the countryside might be distracted by demagogues into a meaningless civil war under rival banners of political oppression—peasants rallying to monarchy, workers dying for a republic. The lower classes had to be liberated from attachment to either banner and unified by a Proudhonist-type social revolution that would "foster the self-organization of the masses into autonomous bodies federated from the bottom upward."[140]

Bakunin sought to begin this international anarcho-socialist revolution in the cities of southern France. He placed special hopes on Lyon, where his disciples staged a demonstration in March 1870. If Paris were to succeed first, he insisted, it must renounce immediately all claim to govern and organize France.[141] In the spring of 1870, he envisaged revolution spreading from France to the neighboring urban centers of Italy and Spain, and on through the dissident Slavs in the Hapsburg Empire to his native Russia.[142]

In September 1870, immediately after the decisive Prussian defeat of the French army and the demise of Napoleon III, Bakunin arrived in Lyon to lead a brief communal uprising; it was soon echoed in Marseilles. His appeal of September 25, *The Revolutionary Federation of Communes*, identified Bismarck's Prussia as the main foe of social revolution. Even before the final defeat of the French armies, he spoke of the need to "put down the Prussians within in order to move with confidence and security against the Prussians from without."[143] He incited immediate communal revolution, because the centralized French state was destined henceforth to be "little more than a vice-royalty of Germany";[144] and he called for "a war to the death" between "popular revolution" and "the military, bureaucratic and monarchical despotism" of Germany.[145]

The second wave of revolution struck France when the Paris Commune arose in the spring of 1871. Bakunin played no direct role; but in exile in Switzerland, he feverishly wrote his longest work, part of which was published in July 1871: *The Knouto-Germanic Empire, or the Social Revolution.*

The genius of the Paris Commune was, in Bakunin's view, to present an authentic social revolutionary alternative to "God and the State"— the twin sources of all oppression.[146]

For Bakunin, the villains within the revolutionary camp were the

Jacobin leaders, who eventually imposed "dictatorial and governmental conceptions" on the Commune, and Mazzini, who had misled the Italian revolution with "obsolescent religious idealism" into "the political lust for state grandeur." [147] Insisting that social revolution must be "diametrically opposed" to political revolution,[148] Bakunin made his last substantial group of conversions to the revolutionary cause at Mazzini's expense between the summer of 1871 and the summer of 1872, when an Italian Federation of the International was founded by his new followers in Rimini.

Other future anarchists like Johann Most in Austria would independently echo Bakunin's view of the Commune as the harbinger of the most fundamental of all social revolutions.[149] And among the Slavic and Latin peoples, where the state was particularly authoritarian (and where industrial development was not far advanced), the Bakuninist vision dominated the revolutionary imagination.

Bakunin's principal rival was, of course, Karl Marx, who embodied precisely the authoritarian German instincts and political preoccupations that Bakunin detested.

Characteristically, Marx's great essay on the Commune, "Civil War in France," was written in the form of an address of the General Council to the membership of the International Workingmen's Association. Lacking much of a following among the rank and file of the International (outside of its relatively small number of English- and German-speaking affiliates), Marx consistently sought to work through the executive structure of the London-based General Council of the International rather than through its autonomous federations and general congresses. Marx's essay was written as the final executions in Paris were taking place. In it, Marx not only rediscovered the revolutionary passion of 1848, but also anticipated the new polemic style of 1917 and beyond.

There was, first of all, a reaffirmation of the necessary link between revolution and violence: "Paris armed was the Revolution armed . . . a slaveholders' rebellion." [150] He then proceeded to explain the success of the repression largely by depicting Alphonse Thiers as a villain without parallel even in Marx's rich repertoire of polemic vitriol. This "parliamentary Tom Thumb, permitted to play the part of a Tamerlane" [151] was portrayed as "a virtuoso in perjury and treason," with "vanity in the place of a heart"—"a monstrous gnome" [152] who

has charmed the French bourgeoisie for almost half a century, because he is the most consummate intellectual expression of their own class corruption.[153]

Marx extended the usual revolutionary argument about violence as a necessary posture of defense into the contention that Thiers was "the real murderer" of the Archbishop of Paris, whom the communards had killed along with sixty-four other hostages.[154]

The Commune encouraged Marx to believe that new political forms could advance social revolution—just as it encouraged Bakunin to argue that political forms had held the Commune back from social revolution. Marx traced its origins to political forces. For him the Commune was not—as it was for Bakunin—a kind of metaphysical opposite to the

Germanic principle of authority; for Marx the Commune was a dialectical development that arose out of French politics as "the direct antithesis to the Empire." [155] The Commune emerged logically from the Empire, in Marx's view. Napoleon's industrialization created a revolutionary proletariat; Napoleon's imperialism armed it and created the wars among nations that the mobilized working class was now converting into wars between classes. Lenin's argument of the World War I period in *Imperialism, The Highest Stage of Capitalism*, was anticipated in Marx's contention that imperialism under Napoleon III has already become

> the ultimate form of the State power . . . [of] full-grown bourgeois society . . . for the enslavement of labour by capital. . . .[156]

Marx's vision of the Commune as an instrument of political deliverance from imperial war was likewise later transposed into Lenin's vision of the Soviets as a political mechanism for establishing proletarian power during World War I. Even Lenin's confidence in the power of the urban revolution to penetrate the countryside may have been anticipated in Marx's ill-founded belief in "the appeal of the Commune to the living interests and urgent wants of the peasantry." [157] When Lenin reached for a slogan for the confiscation of private property in 1917, he borrowed one that Marx had attributed to the less confiscatory communards: "the expropriation of the expropriators." [158]

In 1871 as in 1848, Marx turned for support to the most remorseless of revolutionaries: the followers of Blanqui. These "Blanquists," whom Marx ridiculed in tranquil times as "alchemists of revolution," provided Marx in times of trouble with an antidote to despair—and to disintegration within the revolutionary camp.

New followers had gathered around the legendary Blanqui after his release from prison in 1865; and he published for them a manual for insurrection in 1869: *Instructions for an Armed Seizure*.[159] Though Blanqui was again in prison by the time of the Commune, his followers gained prestige by their leadership within it. After the defeat of the Commune, leading Blanquists under Edouard Vaillant were coöpted as heroes into the General Council of the International. Marx cooperated with them in transforming this London-based executive body into a kind of embryonic embodiment of the concept that Marx had derived from the Blanquists in 1848: a "dictatorship of the proletariat." He diverted the broader congress of the International scheduled for 1871 into a conference in London that he controlled in alliance with the Blanquists.[160]

The common enemy of Blanqui and Marx in 1848 had been Proudhon, and their shared foe in 1871 was Proudhon's anarchistic heir, Bakunin. Marx deliberately excluded Bakunin from the invitation list to the special conference of the International in London in September 1871. This Blanquist-Marxist gathering then proceeded to transform the hitherto relatively loose International into a disciplined political organization, centrally led by the General Council and explicitly committed to conquering political power.

The Bakuninists replied at a rival congress in Sonvilier two months later that hierarchical and political means could never be used to gain social revolutionary ends. The "Sonvilier circular" proclaimed that it was impossible "for a free and egalitarian society to come out of an authoritarian organization," [161] and insisted that revolutionary organizations had to be miniature examples of the new society rather than branches of a political party.

In the first half of 1872, the conflict gave birth to a new vocabulary. In March, Marx revived the word *anarchist* as a pejorative term for the Sonvilier group; and he sent his son-in-law Paul Lafargue to Spain to attempt to destroy Bakunin's political foothold there. The Bakuninists replied by introducing in June—for the first time in history—the term *Marxist* to characterize the new efforts to establish authoritarian control over the International. They denounced Lafargue as an agent of "the Marxist conspiracy" and an "apostle of the Marxist law" (enforcing whatever Marx wanted).[162] Bakunin fortified his own polemic language with another new term: *authoritarian communist*.[163]

Marx and Bakunin each accused the other of organizing a conspiracy. Each drew a measure of support from a surviving faction of communards. A curious anticipation of future revolutionary history lay in the names used to designate the more and less authoritarian communard factions: *majoritaires* and *minoritaires*. These terms, majoritarian and minoritarian, were to recur in the Russian *bol'shevik* and *menshevik*.[164] In both cases, the aggressive adoption of the majority label by the authoritarian party transformed a tactical majority within a small gathering into the pretense of representing the majority of a larger total body.

Lenin's Bolsheviks were as much a minority in the Russian Social Democratic movement as were the Blanquist majoritarians within the Paris Commune. But the label was deftly annexed by the former on the basis of a majority in key meetings of the 1903 party conference and by the latter on the basis of a brief majority within the leadership during the last days of the Commune. Another verbal anticipation of later Russian revolutionary history came with Bakunin's invention of the term *socialist revolutionary* in juxtaposition to Social Democrat.[165] Likewise, the international organization that Bakunin had founded in the summer of 1868 as the International Alliance of Social Democracy was recreated early in September 1872 as the Socialist Revolutionary Alliance.[166] Bakunin thus originated the label that was eventually adopted by the largest revolutionary party in late imperial Russia. Like the Bakuninists, the later Socialist Revolutionaries attached a key role to the peasantry that was never admitted by the urbanized Social Democrats.

The Marx-Bakunin conflict came to a head when Marx himself went for the first time personally to a congress of the International—at the Hague in September 1872. He succeeded in having Bakunin expelled, and tried with the aid of the Blanquists to require all member organizations to advocate the conquest of political power as the necessary prerequisite to proletarian revolution. However, most national sections of the International rallied instead to the Bakuninist banner at a series of congresses held in defiance of Marx later in 1872. The International held a sixth congress in Geneva in September 1873, and a final one in Philadelphia three years later. But, in effect, it ceased to function after 1872. Following the Hague Congress, Marx moved its General Council to New York to prevent Bakuninist control. But Bakunin's followers steadily extended their influence in Europe—taking the allegiance of many local membership bodies out from under the limited central authority that Marx had established.

The International was, of course, destroyed not so much by internal conflict as by the repressive conservative tide that swept through Europe after the Paris Commune. Bakunin's Revolutionary Alliance, which was conceived well before Bakunin joined the International in 1868, survived through the Jura Federation. Marx's fierce *ad hominem* attacks on Bakunin and his drive for a central authoritarian structure over the International never gained widespread support.

Slavic and Latin groups within the International particularly sympathized with the Bakuninist view that Marx "like the cuckoo, came to hatch his egg in a nest that was not his own." [167] Many continued to believe that revolutionary leadership would still come from France— and then spread to those "peoples and *fragments of peoples* who have the revolutionary flame." [168] Many shared Bakunin's view that Marx had repudiated revolution as a search for liberty and had institutionalized the same "pan-Germanic" authoritarianism within the proletarian camp that Bismarck had introduced into bourgeois political life. Shortly after the epithet Marxism came the taunt Bismarxism.[169]

The conflict between Marx and Bakunin in the early 1870s further atomized an already decimated Left; and, in effect, destroyed the social revolutionary tradition in western Europe for a generation. With Bakunin soon to die and Marx aging and somewhat isolated, the international revolutionary tradition in the early seventies lost its active leadership as well as its first international organization. The Marx-Bakunin fight left a legacy of bitterness and of unresolved issues that were to recur in subsequent generations. The First International left behind a number of national organizations as well as a new tradition of transnational proletarian authority that was to inspire numerous other congresses in the seventies and eighties until—on the centenary of the first French Revolution—a Second International was to be founded in 1889.

Meanwhile, in the course of the seventies, a new generation of revolutionaries grew up without the sense of geographical focus that Paris had previously provided. Revolutionaries now tended either (1) to organize the working class within the new bourgeois state in the hope of taking it over (the Social Democratic position of most "Marxists") or (2) to combat the state as such, using new violent tactics (Slavic populism and Latin anarcho-syndicalism being dual heirs to the "Bakuninist" tradition).

The new concept which rationalized—if it did not help inspire—the turn to violence among both these groups in the 1870s and the 1880s was the Bakuninist idea of "propaganda by the deed." This doctrine—if it may be called that—was first articulated in late August 1870 as the basis for the revolutionary uprisings Bakunin was about to incite:

> Let us leave now to others the matter of theoretically developing the principles of the social revolution, and let us content ourselves with broadly applying them, with *incarcerating them in deeds* . . . henceforth we must propagate our principles no longer by words, but *by deeds*.[170]

Beyond "propaganda by the deed" lay a new interest in the broader subject of revolutionary violence—reflected by desperate anarchism and syndicalism in the West and by an altogether new type of ascetic violence in the East. For all Europeans who attempted to sustain the revolutionary vision in the later nineteenth century, the memory of the Commune remained sacred, and its glorification provided compensation for the hostile atmosphere of the antirevolutionary industrial state.

The Lost Romance

The romantic, heroic mentality died with the Paris Commune. Both revolutionary nationalism and French leadership were undercut, and the intangible, indispensable element of romance faded forever from the world of banners and barricades. The communards had gutted the Tuileries Palace and toppled the Vendôme tower—symbols respectively of monarchical and Napoleonic authority. But the Third Republic created no monument capable of symbolizing legitimacy or even eliciting emotional support. In the late nineteenth century, the Parisian skyline was dominated by two new cultural symbols that sought to move beyond the political past—but only provoked further polarization. Sacre Coeur, the new Cathedral of the Sacred Heart, lifted its great white cupola over the former communard headquarters on Montmartre—the fruit of a nationwide Catholic subscription campaign to expiate the sins of the Commune. On the opposite, left side of the Seine soon arose the 984-foot Eiffel Tower, the iron symbol of the new industrial city over the Champs de Mars on which the original romantic, revolutionary festivals had been enacted.

The conservatism of the Sacre Coeur combined with the industrialism of the Eiffel Tower to produce a new kind of state power capable of annexing and transforming the forms of romantic nationalism. Heroic violence of the Italo-Polish variety gave way to the modernized, mechanized violence of the new mass conscript armies of the late nineteenth century. The musical melodrama that had accompanied and ennobled revolutionary nationalism was replaced on the forefront of musical experiment by a new type of opera that heralded the rise of the Germano-Russian stage of revolutionary development.

Modernization of Violence

The grisly repression of the Commune revived an apocalyptical element that had all but vanished from revolutionary thinking after 1848. Dostoevsky likened the fires in the Tuileries to those of the Last Judgment. Lenin later spoke of "the struggle for heaven," and Pottier of *la lutte finale*.

This "final struggle" of proletariat with bourgeoisie was not, of course, to begin in earnest for another quarter of a century, when once again the military defeat of a European power prepared the way for internal uprising. Humiliation by Japan in 1904–05 would lead Russia into its era of revolutions; and Lenin—the man who eventually led the revolutionaries to power—would turn for guidance to the period of the Commune. Indeed his first move as an exile in Switzerland on hearing that urban fighting had broken out in Russia in 1905 would be to begin reading and translating the military memoirs of a leader of the communards' military resistance: Gustave-Paul Cluseret.

Selections from Cluseret's three-volume work were translated by Lenin's wife, and published with a preface by Lenin in March 1905.[171] Cluseret's hatred of sentimentality and his emphasis on careful planning under a "general staff of revolutionaries" appealed to the post-romantic mentality; and his careful emphasis on seizing the key points of existing governmental power provided a rough advanced blueprint for the Bolshevik seizure of power in St. Petersburg in 1917.

Cluseret modernized revolutionary violence. He infused revolutionary thinking with the knowledge of modern, mass warfare he had gained through firsthand participation in the two bloodiest wars of the century between 1815 and 1914: the Crimean War and the American Civil War. A graduate of St. Cyr and a winner of the Legion of Honor for his repression of revolutionaries in 1848, Cluseret had drifted into the revolutionary camp via military service with Garibaldi's red shirts and the Irish underground in America. Arriving in war-torn France as the emissary of Bakunin in Lyon, he rapidly rose to become commander-in-chief of the last phase of the military resistance in the Paris Commune. His knowledge of modern warfare was enriched by his friend and adviser, the hard-line American Union General, Sheridan, who had been with Moltke and the new Prussian military machine during its lightning victories over Napoleon III.

Cluseret's retrospective writings on the Commune advocated a new kind of total war in which "no quarter is to be expected since none is to be given," [172] and provided blunt tactical suggestions for a fresh, unromantic approach to street fighting: attack by night, neutralize fire power by concealment, occupy corner houses, and so forth. Military and civic education had to be closely integrated [173] in a new type of revolutionary militia that would destroy property rather than people and constantly cut bourgeois lines of communication and supply by means of flying columns. Even the Germans could not have sustained a long war against this kind of opposition; [174] and no modern state would be able to resist an armed and disciplined revolution that was determined to replace "the basis of society" rather than to "replace only people" as conspirators had been doing since the last real revolution in 1792.

Cluseret's advocacy of violent means for visionary ends was based on the belief that a social rather than national revolution was approaching:

> The work of the second and supreme Revolution will be to replace anew the social axis of capital in order to hand it over to labor.[175]

Such a specter on the Left was used by the Right to justify threats of counter-violence that helped keep France polarized—and often paralyzed —during the troubled life of the Third Republic.

Cluseret's new stress on social rather than national goals, discipline rather than romance, was most fully accepted farther to the east; and, when urban social revolutionaries finally did gain power, it was in St. Petersburg in 1917 under the leadership of Cluseret's Russian admirer. Lenin's revolutionary career fused the two major new forces that had arisen to dominate the imagination of the Left after the defeat of the Paris Commune: German social democracy and Russian populism. These movements grew out of the rival traditions of Marx on the one hand and of Proudhon and Bakunin on the other. They reflected as well a new and more professional attitude towards the problems of organization and violence respectively within the new industrial state. The rise of social democracy and populism within the Prussian and Russian empires respectively signaled the waning of French influence and the onset of the Germano-Russian period of revolutionary history.

The Mutation of Opera

Turning from the mundane of violence and organization to the sublime, the decline of both romanticism and revolutionary nationalism in the 1860s and 1870s can be traced through the transformation of opera. This musical medium was, as we have seen, a touchstone of revolutionary passion; and its mutations in this period reflect the transfer of the ideological center of gravity in Europe from the Franco-Italian to the Germano-Russian world.

As we have said, realism and materialism prevailed in France after the defeat of the Paris Commune. George Sand, the great romantic novelist, complained in her old age to Gustave Flaubert, the new realist, that she suffered from *idiotisme auditif* in the new era. She was no longer able to dream of romantic transformations of reality, to be both man and woman, to "make words and music at the same time."[176]

Like everything else, music was put at the service of the state. Opera, yesterday's medium of revolution, became today's handmaiden of reaction. *The Mute Girl of Portici*, which had precipitated insurrection forty years earlier, was used in 1870 to mobilize France for its reckless war with Prussia. At a performance just after Napoleon III's ill-fated declaration of war, the cast of the Paris opera lingered onstage to sing *La Marseillaise*. The excited audience urged them to add the warlike song from the Franco-Prussian crisis of 1840: "Nous l'avons eu, votre Rhin allemand." When the cast protested that they did not know the words, the weathervane journalist Girardin shouted down from the loges: "It will take longer to learn it than to take it!" [177]

Verdi, the patriarch of earlier revolutionary nationalism, retreated from politics altogether during the crisis of 1870–71. With the unification of Italy safely behind, he concentrated his attention of getting scenery and costumes safely out of Paris for the première in Cairo of his new opera, *Aida*, heralding the opening of the Suez Canal. This old Saint-Simonian dream of a canal connecting East and West through Egypt had become a reality in 1869; but it heralded the arrival not so much of the "new Christianity" as of the new imperialism. After the opening of *Aida* in December 1871, Verdi withdrew altogether into the majestic, apolitical worlds of religion (*Messa de Requiem*) and Shakespeare (*Otello* and *Falstaff*). And *Aida*, which might have been seen as a drama of national liberation a decade before, was instead treated as sheer spectacle—particularly as it was mounted on the largest opera stage in the world at the new Paris opera after 1875.[178]

Meanwhile, at the new theater of the Bouffes-Parisienne, traditional opera was supplanted altogether by the operettas of Offenbach, which became the rage of the gaslight era in Paris. Light music for the masses —like the new mass journalism—provided diversion for reactionary imperialists rather than inspiration for revolutionary nationalists.

Offenbach's musical model caught on in one empire after another. It arrived in Britain at the very time of the taking over of the Suez Canal and the preparation of the title Empress of India for Queen Victoria. In 1875, Gilbert and Sullivan wrote the first of their immensely successful patter operas, *Trial by Jury*, as the opening number for an evening of Offenbach. Concurrently, in yet another antirevolutionary empire, Hapsburg Vienna was enchanted by one musical confection after another that cascaded from Johann Strauss II, in the wake of his first successful operetta, *The Thousand and One Nights* of 1871.

Offenbach's show-stopping suggestive dance routine, the cancan, was a popular feature of his operettas; it was to become a symbol of imperial decadence and inanity to the more somber revolutionaries who now loomed beyond the Rhine.[179] In Germany and Russia a new kind of grand opera arose in marked opposition to the romantic, Franco-Italian musical tradition. The parallel emergence of the very different figures of Richard Wagner and Modest Mussorgsky heralded a rejection of the romantic lyricism and uncomplicated optimism of the Latin school. Ideologically, their operas expressed a new nationalism completely divorced from any revolutionary message.

If there was a decisive moment of this transition from the Franco-Italian to the Germano-Russian dominance of nationalistic opera, it might well have been the winter of 1862–63 in St. Petersburg, when a new kind of opera was born in the Russian north. Alexander II had commissioned Giuseppe Verdi to write the only opera he composed during his service in the new Italian parliament from 1861 to 1865. The world première of this opera, *La Forza del Destino*, in St. Petersburg in November 1862 was followed in February 1863 by the arrival of Verdi's

German rival, Richard Wagner, as guest conductor in St. Petersburg. Wagner's "music of the future" excited the awakening Russian sensibility, and inspired immediate imitation in Serov's opera *Judith* of 1863. Wagner contrasted the warmth of the Russian reaction and the coolness of the French reception of his "music of the future" by suggesting that "the Russians now live in the future." [180]

Most Russians feared the seductive appeal of Wagner even as they hailed his rejection of Franco-Italian models. A gifted group of young Russian composers withdrew altogether from the St. Petersburg Conservatory to form a new Free Music School dedicated to discovering an authentically Russian musical style, free from all foreign influence. The genius of the group, Mussorgsky, produced in the late 1860s and 1870s a Russian national opera to rival the concurrent German achievement of Wagner. Taken together, their accomplishments mark the end of the link between nationalism and revolution which had been a hallmark of romantic Franco-Italian opera.

In a purely artistic sense, both Wagner and Mussorgsky were far more antitraditional (and in this general sense revolutionary) than Verdi and other giants of the Franco-Italian opera. Each of them sought to transcend the romantic idiom—and indeed Western musical tradition altogether. Each sought to derive a new musical language directly from "the people" and new subject matter from the collective subconscious of vernacular folklore. The radical differences between the two giants tell us more than a little about the very different inner aspirations of post-romantic nationalism in Germany and Russia respectively. Wagner and Mussorgsky played important roles in the development of national consciousness in each country. Indeed, their music provides a kind of prophetic foreboding of the two most fateful revolutionary upheavals of twentieth-century Europe: the national socialism of Hitler's Germany and the socialist nationalism of Stalin's Russia.

Wagner delivered—quite literally—the deathblow to the lyric theme of romantic love which had been central to the operas of romantic nationalism. Subconscious longing replaced lyric melody in *Tristan and Isolde*, which was first produced in 1865. The first four notes opened up the abyss of chromatic modern music; and the lovers were transformed into foredoomed nocturnal figures overwhelmed by a music of the subconscious, which achieved harmony only after a final orchestral orgasm left both lovers dead upon the stage.

After taking lyricism away from the theme of love, Wagner proceeded to an affirmation of German nationalism in his next great opera, *Die Meistersinger*. First performed in 1868 after the Prussian defeat of Hapsburg Austria, the composer found himself enamored of Bismarck's successes and under the secure patronage of the even more conservative King Ludwig of Bavaria. "My real self," he wrote joyously, "is roaming the streets of Nuremberg"; and a triumphant sense of German superiority burst forth at crucial moments in his tale of the prize contest in medieval Nuremberg. A heroic crescendo verging on a military march rose up when Hans Sachs, the symbol of German cul-

ture and virtue, punctuated his monologue on the vanity of the world
with

> Wie friedsam treuer Sitten,
> getrost in That und Werk,
> liegt nicht in Deutschland's Mitten
> mein liebes Nürenberg!
>
> How peaceful and faithful
> Secure in its deeds and ways
> Lies in the midst of Germany
> My beloved Nuremberg!

Meistersinger projected not a revolutionary but a conservative nationalism. The old Sachs enabled the young Walter to win the prize;
and Sachs ended with a warning against "foreign thoughts and foreign
ways":

> ehrt eure deutschen Meister,
> dann bannt ihr gute Geister!
> Und gebt ihr ihrem Wirken Gunst,
> zerging' in Dunst
> das heil'ge röm'sche Reich,
> uns bleibe gleich
> die heil'ge deutsche Kunst!
>
> Honor your German masters
> If you would prevent disasters!
> Take them into your heart;
> Let the Holy Roman Empire
> fall into dust.
> We'll have instead
> Our holy German art!

Wagner provided a "holy German art" through his monumental *Ring
of the Nibelungen*, which was completed by 1874 and given its first
complete performance in 1876 at the theater-shrine newly completed
for him at Bayreuth.

To the new, imperial generation of German nationalists in the late
nineteenth century, the Rhine was to become not just the artery of the
fastest growing industrial complex in the world, but also the mysterious
source of a golden ring capable of bringing mastery over the world and
the downfall of the gods. Whether or not one accepts the Freudian
critique of Wagner as promising phallic deliverance through Siegfried's
sword and Parsifal's spear, there is clearly a mobilization of sublimi-
nal emotions in Wagner's music. The young Adolph Hitler was an avid
Wagnerite, returning time and again to the opera house in Linz to see
the entrance of the knight in shining armor in *Lohengrin*, proclaiming
Meistersinger as his favorite opera, and staging his own theatrical triumph in Nuremberg in the monumental rally of 1934.

Very different were both the music and the message of Mussorgsky's
"popular music dramas" in Russia—but equally destructive of the romantic lyricism and revolutionary nationalism of the Franco-Italian
school. In his search for a unique national idiom, Mussorgsky sought
to discover his new musical language in the unspoiled sounds of or-

dinary people, attempting at one point to extract music directly from
the sounds of the babbling masses at the Nizhni-Novgorod fair.

In his desire to make music express a truth that was both realistic
and moral, Mussorgsky turned for inspiration first to the prose texts of
Nicholas Gogol, then to Russian history and the greatest dramatic text
of Russia's greatest poet: Pushkin's *Boris Godunov*. He spent 1868–74
—the exact period when Wagner was completing his *Ring*—writing
Boris, his only completed opera. This greatest of all Russian national
operas dealt with a period of internal upheaval and uncertain modernization very much like that of Alexander II's Russia: the "time of
troubles" at the beginning of the seventeenth century. Calling it a
"popular (*narodny*) music drama," Mussorgsky built up to the final scene
in the Kromi forest which he called a "picture of the people" [181] and
which the critic Stasov soon dubbed the "revolutionary scene."

This tumultuous scene directly followed the death of the guilt-ridden
Tsar Boris and presented a succession of would-be leaders for the Russian people of the early seventeenth century who were strikingly suggestive of similar forces contending for the allegiance of the Russian
people in the turmoil of the 1870s. The scene also represented a kind
of revolutionary variant on the preceding scene in which Boris died
amidst the decorum of a Boyar Duma. Whereas all was hierarchy and
orderly procession within the tsar's palace, all was chaos and dis-
orderly flight in the forest. The rousing anti-authoritarian chorus *Slava
Boiarinu, Slava Borisovu* was sung during the famous "movement to the
people" by radical students who went to the countryside in search of
revolutionary allies in the summer of 1874 just a few months after the
première of the opera.

Authority was desecrated beginning with the mock coronation scene
of the boyar Khrushchev (sic) and continuing with the humiliation of
the hero of popular Russian folklore (the holy fool) and the symbol of
arrogant, foreign ways (the Jesuits). Finally Mussorgsky's "people"
found their voice in the soprano's cry of *smert', smert'* (death, death)
at the orgiastic climax of a regicidal chorus. It was all remarkably
prophetic of the role that women were to play in the revolutionary
movement that eventually assassinated Alexander II. The masses in
Mussorgsky's opera—like the Russian masses after the death of Alexander II—rushed to embrace a new tsar rather than to form a new revolutionary order.

But the last word for Mussorgsky was pronounced by the holy fool
left alone on the stage alongside an alarm bell and a flickering flame,
no longer able either to prophesy or to pray, but only to lament. The
people were no longer the idealized *narod* of populist revolutionaries,
but a hungry *liud*, without food or hope. Bleak realism had triumphed
over revolutionary romanticism; and the same bleakness was to dominate Mussorgsky's subsequent effort to write a national trilogy of Wag-
nerian scale in his uncompleted final opera, *Khovanshchina*.

At the height of revolutionary unrest in 1877 he considered briefly the
eighteenth-century peasant rebel Pugachev as a possible operatic subject; but returned at the end to the seventeenth-century Old Believers

who had supported the Khovanskies in resisting the westernizing innovations of Peter the Great. Mussorgsky's *Khovanshchina* ended like Wagner's *Ring* with the main characters consumed on stage by a giant fire. But there was a deep difference between the two immolation scenes. Mussorgsky ended with the bass voice of an Old Believer priest bidding everyone mount the pyre in bleak tones of resignation. Wagner ended with a kind of transfiguration as Brünnhilde ecstatically climbed into the fire joyfully to greet her husband. Mussorgsky suggested that the Russian people both yearned for political change and were unlikely to find deliverance along that path. So stirring to the imagination was the "revolutionary scene" of *Boris*, however, that when Lenin was forced to go into hiding briefly outside St. Petersburg amidst the revolutionary crisis of 1917, he reputedly answered the enquiry of where he was going by the simple reply, "to Kromi."

Thus opera by the end of the nineteenth century had become ritualized entertainment for the reactionary, rather than inspirational excitement for the revolutionary. Social revolution in the age of industrialism and imperialism had become a grim and prosaic matter.

The would-be makers of the social revolution did, however, find a new song to replace *La Marseillaise*, which had lost some of its revolutionary luster when its final codification as the national anthem of the Third Republic was supervised by none other than the republic's chauvinistic scourge, General Boulanger.[182] The rival anthem for social revolutionaries was to come into use at the opening of the fourteenth congress of the French Workers Party on July 20, 1896. Meeting at a time of gathering national rivalry and with an unusually large number of German and other foreign delegates present, the congress was disrupted by a chauvinistic group shouting "Down with Prussia," waving the tricolor, and singing *La Marseillaise*.[183] The French socialists responded by singing Pottier's "Internationale" in the musical version composed in 1888 by a Belgian for a workers' chorus in Lille.[184] Thus, an all-but-forgotten poem from the time of the Paris Commune and a scarcely noticed musical arrangement suddenly became the song of revolutionaries looking beyond national identities to transnational, working-class solidarity. Beginning with the congress of the Second International at Paris in September of 1900, it became the practice of international gatherings of socialists to end their meetings with the singing of this hymn,[185] which has generally remained the anthem of those who believe in revolution through class rather than national identity.

The Francocentric age of revolutionary nationalism had begun in Strasbourg in April 1792, when *La Marseillaise* first rallied a revolutionary nation to resist invading German monarchs. The age ended in the same Strasbourg in August 1870, when new German invaders subjected its civilian population to four nights of devestating, continuous bombardment. This unprecedented atrocity announced "a new military age" [186] in which mechanized violence would lead to social revolution. Alsace, which had ignited France with song in 1792, smoldered in resentment as a German province after 1871—and became a *casus belli* in 1914.

Nationalism had been taken over and deradicalized by the great state builders of the post-1848 era: Napoleon III, Cavour, Bismarck. Romantic nationalism remained the dominant ideology of the less-developed and politically disenfranchised fringes of Europe (Ireland, the Balkans); and, by the turn of the century, had gained new vitality in the non-European world seeking to resist European imperial domination. But the most important new developments in the European revolutionary movement between 1848 and 1914 lay within the rival tradition of social revolution. It is to the growing pains of this very different, transnational tradition largely within Germany and Russia that attention must now be turned.

BOOK

III

THE RISE OF THE SOCIAL REVOLUTIONARIES: THE LATE NINETEENTH AND EARLY TWENTIETH CENTURIES

CHAPTER 13

The Machine:

German Social Democracy

EUROPE after the Franco-Prussian War and the Paris Commune entered a new age of social and political conservatism. But it was profoundly different from the royal restoration at the beginning of the century. A new industrial order had created a new interdependence through the railroad, the steamboat, and the telegraph. Individual countries had transformed nationalism and republicanism from revolutionary slogans into forms of social discipline. The new national state possessed the military and police power to suppress revolutionaries; and the state was gaining the productive powers and political skills to provide consoling social benefits to the masses.

After two decades of intermittent warfare among European states, European leaders now turned their militant energies outward for three decades of imperial expansion against the non-European world. Imperialism proved to be a more effective rallying cry than revolution with the European masses; and, for at least two decades after the Paris Commune, the revolutionary tide seemed to be waning—if not disappearing.

The symbol and source of dynamism in the new industrial state was the machine. It was the throbbing heart of the new manufacturing metropole—a magnet pulling people in from the countryside like loose metal filings. The machine mobilized the masses for productivity, made them factors in its factories. It was the magician of modernity, transforming raw material from within the earth into finished power over it. The machine also became Moloch in motion, spreading the sovereignty of steel throughout the world by steamboat and locomotive. Better machine locomotion permitted Prussia to unify Germany and defeat France.[1] European armies began thereafter to mechanize mass murder by adopting that terrible technological by-product of the American Civil War: the machine gun.[2] Both the firearms of the new German army and the engines of the new British navy were propelled by a new kind of force. Power in both cases was directed through a central shaft; and, by swirling the tube, the power was vastly increased for expelling a shell or propelling a ship.

Rifling the bore of a gun was nothing less than "the first missile revolution";[3] and the turbine engine was "one of the most important inventions in the entire history of power."[4] Whether driven by steam or water, it enabled man to generate electricity. Countries like Italy which lacked coal were at last able to produce power for industrial production. Then, in 1885, one year after the appearance of the first usable steam turbine, an internal combustion engine was applied successfully to ground transportation by Daimler and Benz in Germany. New mobility was provided by internal combustion and the use of oil for industrial energy. No longer did man simply draw flame from coal in one place to produce steam power from water in another. Power was now directly generated by exploding volatile new fuels—oil and gas—directly inside the machine. The machine thus came to contain violence within itself. It was soon mass-produced by other machines as the American system of interchangeable parts combined with German skill in precise microscopic measurement.

The new mechanized world rendered obsolete the romantic ideal of a natural order and the poetic, melodramatic style of earlier leaders. The subconscious model for revolutionary organization subtly changed from that of a *structure* to that of a *machine*. Gone now was the older architectural image of masons building a new "temple" for humanity through the personal exertion of their mental and moral faculties. In its place there slowly appeared the concept of a modern political machine driven by thermodynamic force and impersonal calculation. There was an accompanying change in revolutionary personnel. Professional people, often with aristocratic backgrounds, who viewed themselves as creative builders of an ideal order, now gave way increasingly to a new type of intellectual-organizer preoccupied with shaping an effective organization for, if not from, the working class.

The change from moral to functional purposes did not represent the triumph of "technology" or "organization" as such within the revolutionary tradition. Rather it represented the victory of one aspect of technology (the dynamic, standardized, and environmentally independent *machine*) over another (the relatively static, unique, and environmentally dependent *structure*).[5]

Power was now thermodynamic not charismatic: hot, hard, and movable, rather than cool, elegant, and static. The romantic belief in the power of heroic individual will faded after the death of the last Napoleon. Increasingly, relentlessly, the late nineteenth century identified power with the essential elements of the heat engine itself: mechanical organization and violence. The machine itself was a model of organized violence; and revolutionaries were learning its lessons as they turned to the problems of organization and to the possibilities of violence for mobilizing the masses.

The frontiers of discovery for the revolutionary tradition in the age of the machine were in central and eastern Europe. The old centers of gravity—France, Italy, Poland—faded in importance, as the new type of organization appeared in Germany and new uses of violence were developed in Russia.

Thus we return again to fire; it was the blast furnaces and fire-driven machines of the Ruhr, the Saar, and Silesia that during the second half of the nineteenth century transformed a localized, semirural German people into the most industrialized and urbanized major nation in Europe. The fire-driven machinery which stood behind the rapid industrialization of Germany was a product in effect of a "second industrial revolution." Whereas the first Industrial Revolution a century earlier in England emerged through the trial and error of artisan-craftsmen, the new German accomplishment emerged rather from the laboratory of the scientist-engineer.[6] The ability of the new German state systematically to apply the discoveries of scientific research to factory production enabled it to outstrip France as the greatest power in continental Europe in ways that were even more decisive than the military victory of 1870–71.

Social Democracy represented a systematic attempt by the Germans to convert their short-lived revolutionary conflagration of 1848–50 into the more disciplined, slow-burning fire of a modern political machine. The German Social Democratic party sought to organize workers as rationally within society as the new engineers had organized machines inside the factory.

Germany also supplanted France as the focus of revolutionary hopes; and the poignant irony of this dramatic change can be illustrated by recounting the history of one French family: the Carnots. Germany in the late eighteenth and early nineteenth centuries produced nothing to equal the technological genius of this gifted family of scientist-engineers; yet a newly united Germany in the late nineteenth century succeeded far more than a newly polarized France in applying their ideas to society.

Lazare Carnot had been the leading military engineer and "organizer of victory" for the original French Revolution against the counter-revolutionary intervention of German princes in 1793–94. His son Sadi, reflecting sadly on the subsequent English victory over Napoleon and the exile of his father to Germany, concluded that the steam engine was the source of England's triumph. He thereupon probed its secrets and unlocked the theory of thermodynamics which made high pressure, fire-driven engines possible. His *Reflections on the Motive Power of Fire*, written in 1824 when he was twenty-eight, has been called "the most original work of genius in the whole history of the physical sciences and technology";[7] but it was to be his only book, for he died of cholera in 1832.

It was the Germans who developed most successfully both Lazare Carnot's concept of a military machine and Sadi's theory of the heat engine. The former came with the victories of the Prussian army in the war of 1870–71. The latter followed in the next fifteen years as N. A. Otto developed the four-stroke engine; Rudolph Diesel began work on the engine bearing his name; and Gottlieb Daimler and Karl Benz, working independently of each other, developed the first modern automobile engine.

By the time Sadi Carnot's *Reflections* was reissued in 1878 by his brother Hippolyte, Germany had supplanted both England and France as the most dynamic industrial power in Europe. When Hippolyte's son, another Sadi Carnot, became president of France in 1886, it appeared that his engineering experience and personal stature might recapture for the Third Republic a position of industrial as well as political leadership in Europe. He repelled the neo-Napoleonic challenge from the Right by General Boulanger, but was assassinated from the Left by an Italian anarchist at a banquet in Lyon in 1894.

German Social Democracy provided a form of social discipline against precisely that sort of random violence. It arose from the massive introduction of the technology of the Carnots into the very different political culture of imperial Germany. The German Social Democratic party became the first organized political body in modern times to gain an authentic mass following among the working class. But the Social Democratic party has a cloudy historical image. Marxist-Leninist historians must necessarily accord some recognition to the first mass organization formally to adopt Marxism as a doctrine, the largest political party in imperial Germany, and the principal vehicle for mediating Marxist teachings to the broader world in the period before World War I. On the other hand, these historians find it necessary to remain faithful to Lenin's harsh judgments during the last decade of his life of the German Social Democrats. It remains perplexing even to the non-Leninist Left that the German Social Democrats failed (1) to take—or even to share—power in imperial Germany and (2) to prevent—or even to resist energetically—the German entrance into World War I.

The German Social Democrats occupied a position within German politics that was as ambiguous as their role in world history. They were neither a revolutionary conspiracy nor a political party operating through an accepted system. They were, instead, a kind of "non-participating opposition" [8] within the most powerful state in Europe. Even more than the Second International, which they often dominated but did little to preserve after 1914, the Social Democrats represented a bridge between the Francocentric revolutionary conspiracies of the European era and the mass movements and global politics of the twentieth century.

Social Democracy provided a new type of revolutionary leader. He did not attain power. He remained in the wilderness—but as an organizer rather than a prophet. The German party represented the point of transition in the history of revolutionary movements between revolutionaries without power in the nineteenth century and power without revolutionaries in the twentieth.

The "Communist party" about which Marx spoke in the 1840s had been more an object of faith than a matter of fact, and he extolled it subsequently not for anything it did, but for its spiritual essence as the first "party in the great historical sense." There seemed to have been three key characteristics for such a party: (1) unity through ideological discipline, (2) total dedication to the proletariat as a class, and (3) freedom from restricting parochial perspectives. Marx and Engels discovered no such party anywhere during the revolutionary recession of the 1850s, and never saw more than a potential embodiment in the International Workingmen's Association during its brief history from 1864 to 1872. Despite Marx's efforts to control and discipline it, this amorphous body never became a "party" in this or any other sense.

Thus, the party that formed in Germany under the label Social Democratic was probably the most important political expression of Marxism during Marx's lifetime—even if it was largely unconnected with the International and not yet sufficiently disciplined ideologically to be a "party" in Marx's "great historical sense." Its name expressed its aim of social rather than national revolution—and its identity as something more than liberalism and less than communism.

Revolutionaries have repeatedly sought to give new vitality to an old label by attaching fresh adjectives to the word democracy. The first youthful communists in the early 1840s described themselves as "true" and "fraternal" democrats. Aging Stalinists a century later attempted to refurbish the tarnished communist cause by referring to "people's" democracy,[9] democracy "of a new type,"[10] or "national" democracy.[11] "Social" democracy was the new label of hope for chastened revolutionaries in Germany after 1848, fortifying democracy, the political term for rule of the people, with an adjective suggesting economic justice as well.[12] The term was first invoked by an organized group during the aftermath of the 1849 uprising in Baden.[13] Social democracy became the primary label for the fresh spread of the social revolutionary ideal east of the Rhine in the late nineteenth century, and was gradually linked with Marxism.

Lassallean Origins

The flamboyant founder of German Social Democracy, Ferdinand Lassalle, seemed an unlikely type to usher in the new age of machine organization. He had dreamt as a youth of leading the German people in battle; and he assumed at various points in his brief adult career the posture of a poet or philosopher, and the personal demeanor of a brooding lover and demagogic orator. His debonair appearance and admiration for Garibaldi made him an uncongenial personality for Marx, who once called him (to the embarrassment of Marxist hagiographers) a "union of Jew and German on a negro foundation." [14]

Lassalle had worked with Marx on the *Neue Rheinische Zeitung* in Cologne during 1848–49, and had developed ideas on revolutionary organization different from those of the Communist League. Lassalle's concept of a party was derived not so much from the ideas of Marx's manifesto as from the practices of his newspaper, from what his best biographer calls "the party of the *Neue Rheinische Zeitung*." [15]

Lassalle argued that the Communist League failed because it had been held together only by very general ideas which were "indigestible without education" and unsuitable for practical application. The needed mechanism for day-to-day tactical deliberations took place during the editorial discussions of the *Neue Rheinische Zeitung*, where Marx exercised discipline, while benefiting from criticism. The result was not the individual dictatorship inherent in the structure of the Communist League, but a collective "dictatorship of insight" (*Diktatur der Einsicht*) [16] by a small group struggling through mutual criticism towards an objective understanding of historical necessity.

Lassalle viewed the failure of Marx's journal to reach a broader audience during 1848–49 largely as an organizational shortcoming. The Cologne group had simply found no structured way of relating the communist high command to the proletarian army. Lassalle spelled out his organizational remedy after the collapse of the journal and the subsequent flight of Marx from Germany in May 1849.

Two new structures were prescribed; and each was designed simultaneously to aid the political education of the masses and to provide popular advice and approval for the leadership. First came the periodic "mass meeting" (*Volksversammlung*) where a carefully prepared program was presented, and a mass mandate produced for a broad line of strategy to be pursued over a long period of time. Second came a permanent cluster of smaller, popular organizations (of which Lassalle's People's Club in Düsseldorf was a kind of model). They developed limited mandates for specific actions of a tactical and local nature.[17]

During the 1850s, workers' associations were outlawed, and Lassalle spent most of his energies writing on legal, economic, and even literary matters. But he continued to correspond with Marx and to procure journalistic commissions for him—regarding Marx as an absentee leader who shared his view that the Rhineland would eventually become the base for revolutionizing Prussia. Political agitation revived in Germany at the end of the decade, stimulated by the Italian victory over the conservative Hapsburg Empire in 1859. The ensuing unification of Italy revived political agitation for German unification. Lassalle was immediately plunged into the practical problems of the Prussian political awakening, and he found himself in increasing conflict with the more theoretical and global perspectives of Marx in London. They differed, first of all, over who was the greatest enemy of the proletariat in the war of 1859—Engels indicating Napoleon III (who aided Italy); and

Lassalle, the Hapsburgs. Marx wrote Engels that Lassalle's intractability on this issue meant that "we must now absolutely insist on party discipline." [18] But they never found a basis for dialogue let alone discipline. When the new Prussian king declared a political amnesty early in 1861, Lassalle proposed reviving the *Neue Rheinische Zeitung* and bringing Marx back to Germany to assume leadership of "the party." But neither Marx's visit to Berlin nor Lassalle's return trip to London in 1862 succeeded in working out a formula for collaboration. Nor did Lassalle gain Marx's approval of his program calling for universal suffrage and state aid to producer cooperatives during the national electoral campaign of May 1862. Marx criticized Lassalle for his lack of international perspective and his naïveté about universal suffrage, which Napoleon III had manipulated into sanctioning a dictatorship. But Lassalle pressed on, and led the gathering of fourteen representatives at Leipzig in May 1863 in forming the All German Workers' Association, "the first independent national labor organization" in German history.[19]

Lassalle turned to the proletariat not out of affection but out of conviction that the German middle class was incapable of championing popular rule. German liberals had formed a new Progressive party in 1861, but Lassalle believed them to be paralyzed by "fear of the people":

> Our liberal bourgeoisie cannot smash the military state, cannot win political freedom.[20]

Universal suffrage and direct elections were prerequisites to democracy, which liberals no longer sought in their hearts. Producer cooperatives were needed to lift the workers above subsistence and give them a taste of the "social democracy" to come.

Arguing that "the working class must constitute itself as an independent political party," [21] Lassalle increased the size of his organization from about four hundred to nearly one thousand by early 1864.[22] Lassalle rejected Marx's counsel of making common cause with the numerically stronger liberals, and he gave the German working class an orientation towards self-conscious separation from the rest of society which never basically changed. Intellectuals who applied for membership in a local branch of Lassalle's new organization had to be cleared by party headquarters. The adjective *geschlossene*, which many Lassalleans attached to the word working class, meant closed as well as united.[23]

The Social Democratic party emerged from these small beginnings, rallying the primarily Protestant ranks of the working class. In the process of achieving "self-isolation" and "negative integration" [24] into the imperial German state, the Social Democrats unconsciously internalized to some extent not just the military discipline of the state it opposed, but also its growing bureaucratic mentality. The German version of the recurring phenomenon of interborrowing between the extremes of Right and Left began in the early 1860s, which were the formative years of both the new reactionary German state and the new working-class movement. For, whether or not German Social Democracy was "crippled from birth," it was clearly haunted from the cradle by the looming presence of Otto von Bismarck. His long dominance of German political life began when he was summoned to become minister-president of Prussia during the constitutional crisis of September 1862. Viewing the working-class movement as a tactical ally in his struggle with the liberals, Bismarck sought out Lassalle to discuss the latter's proposal for universal suffrage as a possible means of strengthening the monarchy. Bismarck also commissioned a conservative journalist to examine the questions of workers' benefits raised in Lassalle's program—old age insurance and state regulation of factory conditions—and to draw up proposed social legislation for the workers (it was vetoed by the liberals).[25]

Lassalle, from his side, saw opportunities for the German working class in Bismarck's struggle with the liberal propertied classes. The working class could tactically use the power of Bismarck's state to dispossess the liberals and set up producer cooperatives. The latter would provide the economic base (and universal suffrage the political vehicle) for an eventual takeover of the central state by the organized party of the working class. Marx, who objected at this time to Lassalle's concept of interim cooperation with the Prussian state, was himself later to be accused of "Bismarxism." [26] Thus the early history of German Social Democracy is closely linked to the efforts of the Iron Chancellor alternately to manipulate, to coöpt, or to suppress his steadily growing opposition on the Left.

Lassalle did not live to see the process unfold. He died in a duel over an aristocratic woman's honor in August 1864, just a few weeks before the founding of the First International. He died like a romantic figure of a bygone era—but had spoken in some ways like a prophet of the distant future. His demagogic addresses to mass audiences ("the all-destroying power of human speech") [27] and his admiration for Bismarck ("a man" as distinct from the "old women" liberal politicians) [28] prefigured in a way the later German fascination with the radio voice and aggressive masculinity of National Socialism.

Efforts at organization in the Lassallean tradition were built around a journal: first the Hamburg *Nordstern,* then the Berlin *Sozial-Demokrat,* founded in December 1864. Its editor, Johann Baptist von Schweitzer, succeeded Lassalle as head of the All German Workers' Association and soon described the new journal as the "Organ of the Social Democratic Party." [29] Schweitzer popularized Lassalle's argument with Marx through a serialized novel, which showed liberals deceiving the workers by inciting them to overthrow feudal governments and then taking over political power and exploiting the workers even more ruthlessly.[30] Marx reacted to Schweitzer even more angrily than to Lassalle, breaking relations altogether early in 1865 for three years. Marx gave the proletarian Social Democratic organization the disparaging label of sect while the nonrevolutionary, bourgeois Volkspartei was called a party, since it supported Marx's call for resisting Prussian control of a unified Germany.[31]

But the middle-class liberals whom Marx first saw as allies were immobilized by Bismarck's spectacular military victory over the Hapsburgs in 1866. For fresh hope Marx turned to a second working-class party less attached to Bismarck's Prussia than the Lassalle-Schweitzer organization: an amalgam of workers and intellectuals that formed the Social Democratic Workingmen's party at Eisenach in 1869.

The leading "Eisenachers," Wilhelm Liebknecht and Johann Philipp Becker, were Marx's closest German friends, and like him were cosmopolitan, multi-lingual intellectuals forced into exile after the failure of revolution in 1848–50. They had both been far more active militants than Marx, having fought in the armed uprising of 1849 in Baden. Becker remained in Switzerland throughout the 1860s and became the guiding force behind *Vorbote*, an official journal of the First International which began to appear in January 1866.[32] Liebknecht, Marx's closest German protégé in London in the 1850s, became his most effective supporter within Germany after returning in 1862. He collaborated closely with the woodworker and orator August Bebel. They were both elected to the North German Diet in 1867, reaffirming the need for a tactical alliance with what remained of the liberal opposition to Bismarck.

Liebknecht and Bebel acquired an aura of heroism by resisting the Franco-Prussian war, converting into propaganda platforms first their seats in the Reichstag and then their positions as defendants in the Leipzig trial of 1872. The Eisenachers alone were formally linked to the First International; and they developed a number of procedures that were to become standard in mass revolutionary organization: a ritual of formal expulsion and (after their congress of 1873) an insistence that party members cannot concurrently hold positions in another political organization.[33]

Thus, despite their inferiority in numbers to the Lassalleans, the Eisenachers brought disproportionate strength to the merger between the two groups organized at Gotha in 1875. The seeming victory of the Lassalleans at that time, signified by the acceptance in the program of unification of the Prussian state as the framework for socialist development and of producer cooperatives as the means for distributing wealth to the workers, drove Marx to strong denunciation. He wrote his last great theoretical tract on the link between communism and revolution: his *Critique of the Gotha Program*. He decried the "vulgar socialism" involved in seeking distributive justice through any existing state mechanism. For the second (and last) time in his writings, he articulated the need for a "dictatorship of the proletariat." The existing bourgeois state, he reminded his German readers, must be destroyed altogether by revolution, and the means of production seized by the proletariat. Only after this event—when a new interim form of class dictatorship has been established—could social justice be achieved and oppressive political power begin to "wither away."

Dictatorship would wither away because it would lack any roots in class oppression. As an expression of the universal class in possession of the means of production, a dictatorship of the proletariat would be short-lived: a transitional phase of communist society (which later Marxist theorists would call "socialism"). Marx deferred all hope for distributive justice to the second, "higher phase" of the coming communist society. Then alone would society be ruled by the law: "From each according to his ability, to each according to his needs." [34]

Marx from afar could not provide leadership for German Social Democracy. But Marxism as an ideology did begin to make a decisive impact after Engels's *Anti-Dühring* began to appear throughout 1877–78 in *Vorwärts*, the official journal of the new united party. Like other leading Marxist texts, this affirmation of doctrine took the form of a blistering attack on a rival. Eugen Dühring was a prolific and iconoclastic teacher at Berlin University, who argued in essence that Marx's preoccupation with economic laws was blunting the healthy passion for political revolution in Germany. In counterattacking with gusto this idol of radical Berlin, Engels wrote the first popular exposition of Marxism as a coherent revolutionary doctrine; it has remained the most widely reprinted work by Marx and Engels after the *Communist Manifesto*.[35] Engels's work was initially denounced, in part out of political sympathy for Dühring who had been dismissed from the university. But the work deeply impressed the new emerging leaders of Social Democracy: young Karl Kautsky and Eduard Bernstein as well as Liebknecht and Bebel. Growing popular acceptance of the Engels tract was a major milestone on the path towards the formal adoption of Marxism as the official ideology of the German Social Democratic party.

The polemic posture of *Anti-Dühring* transformed Marx's image in Germany—even for those who could not understand his ideas. For the first time Marx appeared clearly to be defending the working class and its economic concerns against the abstractions of a professor. Engels helped free Marx from the charge of excessive intellectualism by leveling the same charge against Dühring. Marx's followers soon broadened the attack against "the socialism of professors" (*Kathedersozialismus*) generally. Marx annexed the rival's role, however, even while denouncing his person. He gained the position of pedagogue-in-chief to the revolutionary movement, transferring the locus of quasi-ecclesiastical authority for the working classes from political teaching pronounced in Berlin University to economic science derived from the British Museum. His largely unread *Capital* became a greater source of authority than the complete works of Dühring. The discovery of Marxism occurred just on the eve of the twelve-year period of antisocialist restrictions that began in 1878. Marxist reassurances that revolution was ultimately determined by economic laws and not political activists fortified the Social Democrats against the discouragement that might otherwise have descended on a movement that was now suddenly forbidden to hold any meetings or to continue any publications outside the Reichstag.

The Social Democrats had steadily increased their strength from two Reichstag seats in the elections of 1871 to nine in 1874 and twelve in 1877. An alarmed Bismarck used the pretext of two inept assassination attempts against the emperor to pass in 1878 antisocialist restrictions that remained in effect until the chancellor left office in 1890. During this period, Bismarck revived his earlier interest in social legislation for the workers—providing insurance and retirement benefits in an effort to undercut the Social Democratic hold over the proletariat. The reorganized German political police in Berlin received during the period of restrictions some 18,000 reports from agents assigned to cover the revolutionary agitation in which the Social Democrats were presumed to be leaders.[36]

This persecution, albeit limited, helped purge the party of any Lassallean illusions about working through the state. Organizational work continued among the proletariat under Bebel's leadership. Earlier attempts to use intellectual journals as the basis for organization gave way to a growing network of social and fraternal bodies for working people that closely paralleled those which the churches had traditionally provided. Women's, youth, and sporting organizations appeared under Social Democratic auspices—and served as vehicles for both recruitment into the party and outward dissemination of its propaganda.

At their Copenhagen Congress in 1883, the Social Democrats professed to entertain "no illusions" of obtaining progress through parliaments. Writing to Bebel the following year, Engels hailed "the party" as a kind of army: as the "general staff" and the first mass Marxist organization on a national basis.[37] The party continued to grow: from 300,000 votes netting twelve Reichstag seats in 1881 to twenty-four seats in 1884 and thirty-five in 1890, when the party polled nearly one and a half million votes—about one-fifth of the total.[38] The following year, at Erfurt, during the first congress held after the fall of Bismarck and the repeal of the antisocialist laws, the party formally declared itself to be Marxist with the blessing of the aged Engels and of his young protégé in London, Karl Kautsky.

Kautskian Orthodoxy

It is hard to understand in retrospect how Karl Kautsky could have exercised the preeminent authority that he established at the Erfurt Congress and maintained for a quarter of a century. He never held a formal political position in either the party or the parliament, and his turgid prose was unintelligible to many ordinary workers. His tendency to find guidance in Marx for almost everything was so single-minded that a colleague once said: "Kautsky would always feel he had to demonstrate that Marx even wet his diapers in an orthodox way." [39]

His long apprenticeship with Engels in London and his role as literary caretaker of Marx's and Engels's papers suggested that he was a kind of apostolic successor to the founders. His new journal, *Die Neue*

Zeit, was founded with the blessing of Liebknecht and Bebel in 1883 in Stuttgart. It combined the old concept of revolutionary guidance from a central journal with the new function of defining Marxist positions on philosophical and cultural as well as political questions. Kautsky brought to his task a truly international background: a Czech father, a German mother, with both Italian and Slavic ancestors, a Viennese education, long residence in England. He fortified his party with the Marxist assurance that proletarian revolution was inevitable and could "neither be hastened nor delayed." [40] The Social Democrats were "a revolutionary party, but not a party which makes revolution." [41] In a letter to Marx's biographer in 1893, Kautsky suggested that Marx's "Dictatorship of the Proletariat" could be realized by an English-type parliament with a Social Democratic majority. [42]

He pioneered the tradition of defining a Marxist party line in a center between Right and Left deviations. [43] His influence grew internationally, as the German party inspired imitators elsewhere and increasingly dominated the Second International during the decade after its founding in 1889.

Kautsky's pedagogic role was imitated by the founding fathers of the Social Democratic movements which soon arose in the two conservative multinational empires of eastern Europe: Victor Adler in Hapsburg Austria and George Plekhanov in Romanov Russia. [44]

Adler like Kautsky had a partially Czech background, a Viennese education, and a close personal relationship with Engels. A medical doctor and an urbane intellectual, he led the Austrian party after its non-ideological founding in 1874 until the time in 1889 when he succeeded in inviting Kautsky to draft a purely Marxist program committing the party to the seizure of political power. The Austrian party in turn influenced the working-class movements of other leading nationalities of the Hapsburg Empire: notably the Hungarians and the Czechs. The tendency of Social Democratic groups to relate in a federative rather than a subordinate manner to the Austrian party led in 1895 to the first use of the term "national socialism." [45]

Plekhanov published in Geneva in 1882 the first Russian translation of the *Communist Manifesto*. The following year he formed the first Russian Marxist group, the "Liberation of Labor," and published *Socialism and the Political Struggle*, the first of the ideological treatises that made him rival Kautsky as the leading theoretician of international Marxism. The development of Social Democracy within Russia was to occur later; but during the decade from 1885 to 1894, Social Democratic parties on the German model were also founded in Belgium, Hungary, Bulgaria, Poland, Romania, and Holland. In the midst of this period, the Second International was founded in Paris on the centenary of the storming of the Bastille. Adler and Plekhanov were leading speakers; Marx's surviving relatives were present; and the German Social Democratic delegation of eighty-one was the second largest among the nearly four hundred representatives of twenty national delegations.

Only gradually did the Second International fall under the dominance of the German Social Democrats, and it never quite became what Lieb-knecht had urged at the first congress: "a single united organiza-tion." [46] The International was founded in France on a French anniver-sary with the French delegation in a clear majority (221). Only at the fourth congress (London, 1896) were anarchists, syndicalists, and other anticentralizers decisively rebuffed by the creation of a central organization and the requirement that members accept the need for political action (implicitly on the German Social Democratic model). At the next conference (Paris, 1900), the German organizational model was drawn upon further with the establishment of a permanent, paid secretariat: the International Socialist Bureau in Brussels. This central body lacked the strong personal leadership that Marx had provided through the General Council of the First International and the fifty to seventy members of the council of the bureau held only four meetings a year; but the pretension of paragovernmental authority was unmistak-able. The executive committee of the bureau prepared for and executed commands from the congresses, which were henceforth formally named International Socialist Congresses; their designated purpose was "to be-come the Parliament of the Proletariat," whose resolutions would "guide the proletariat in the struggle for deliverance." [47]

Effective leadership in the Second International was exercised more by the German Social Democratic party than by the council of the bu-reau or by the Brussels secretariat. Party caucuses produced a generally unified German position in advance of the congresses of the Interna-tional. The Paris Congress of 1900 and the Amsterdam Congress of 1904 were each preceded by a German party Congress (at Hanover in 1899 and Dresden in 1903).

The Amsterdam Congress of the International in August 1904 repre-sented "the highest point in the influence of the International" [48] and perhaps the high point as well of German control. Kautsky's formula-tions calling for a recommitment to class struggle and to the revolu-tionary use of parliamentary power were forced through the congress by a disciplined German delegation backed by the prestige of electoral success in winning eighty-one seats and three million votes in 1903. The next congress, in 1907, was the first ever held in Germany; and the German Social Democrats had the largest group (289) within the largest total delegation (886) ever to appear at a congress of the Inter-national. German cultural trappings dominated the proceedings from the opening singing of a Lutheran hymn in which the word for their party replaced the word for God: *Ein feste Burg ist unser Bund*.[49]

The German party had massively expanded its organization after 1903, forming small town and rural cells, children and youth groups, cultural evenings for worker-poets, and finally in 1906 a central party school. There was also a steady increase in journalistic activity as the number of conservative and liberal papers declined in relation to those of the Social Democrats.[50]

Essentially, the Germans had prevailed over the French, Marx over Proudhon, objective and scientific over subjective and utopian socialism. This was the battle that Liebknecht and Bebel had fought against Proudhonist ideas within Germany in the 1870s; and that Jules Guesde concurrently waged less successfully in France. Guesde established in 1877 the first Marxist weekly, *Egalité,* and defined in 1879–80 the first Marxist program for France. The same basic conflict spread to Russia, beginning with Plekhanov's call of 1883 to substitute a Social Democratic program for the antipolitical Proudhonist tradition of Russian populism.[51]

Engels's final blessing on the German model was contained in his last major work before his death: a new preface in 1895 to Marx's *Class Struggles in France.* Engels modified if he did not "revise" the semi-Blanquist tone of Marx's classic, suggesting elections rather than insurrections as the path to power. Steady gains in general elections gave the German Social Democrats "a special position . . . a special task" as "the decisive 'shock force' of the international proletarian army." [52]

Kautsky became the custodian and perpetuator of Engels's evolutionist and determinist optimism in interpreting the Marxist heritage.[53] The German model of Social Democracy seemed to be on the road to vindication in the period leading up to World War I. Organizational activity grew rapidly in a sub-culture that included cooperative stores, chess clubs, and even burial societies. The number of leaflets increased in the space of one year (1911–12) from 33.5 million to 114 million[54] after the elections of 1912, and leadership in effect passed to the parliamentary group of the party that was composed largely of authentic workers.

The German working class was more numerous, better educated, and superior in professional status to that of France or Russia. It created not just an effective political machine, but also the appealing image of "a global counter-society ready to substitute itself for the established society." It kept hope alive at two levels with "its double ambition to be something right away and to be everything when the moment comes." [55]

But the moment never came. Indeed, the German tide may have crested as early as the Stuttgart Congress in 1907. Internal organizational activity subsequently acquired a life and logic of its own. Preambles to executive reports at party gatherings came to resemble state pronouncements; financial statements acquired the solemnity of governmental budgets; and annual congresses required weeks of preparation and grew to four days in length.[56] The revolutionary impulse simply drowned in an ocean of bureaucracy.

The Social Democrats also absorbed some of the nationalistic ethos of imperial Germany. They had helped secure in 1907 international proletarian opposition to national wars (either "by parliamentary or by social action"). But they began to reflect a characteristically German dislike of England and Russia, and a tendency to absorb the Polish movement rather than to foster its independence. They accepted the nationalistic belief of ordinary Germans that they were defending civilization against Russia in August 1914, and reluctantly but unanimously voted for the credits that helped launch the war and doom the Second International.[57']

The Struggle with Revisionism

The concept of a Marxist party as an instrument for the ideological discipline of mass political action was a distinctive legacy of German Social Democracy to the Russian revolutionary movement. The latter was deeply and permanently influenced by the way the German party at the turn of the century overcame the growing demand within it to substitute reform for revolution. A pragmatic, piecemeal strategy seemed to be only an extension of the basic decision to concentrate Social Democratic efforts on gains in the parliament. There was added appeal in the seeming trend towards reformism within France and England. This German "struggle against revisionism" dominated the revolutionary imagination in central and eastern Europe during the period between the tiny first congress of the Russian Social Democratic party in 1898 and the large second congress in which the party as a whole and the Leninist Bolshevik wing were both born.

Kautsky popularized the theoretical term *revisionism* to denounce those who "revised" Marx's teachings into evolutionary reformism. Kautsky successfully isolated, labeled, and denounced as an ism something that had hitherto existed only as tendency.[58]

In a bold departure from revolutionary orthodoxy during an electoral banquet of 1896, a leading French socialist, Alexandre Millerand had argued that capitalism could now be effectively supplanted by partial nationalization and municipalization of the means of production. Such a strategy necessarily involved political collaboration with radicals and liberals in the assembly against monopoly control of the economy.[59] Banquets, which had led men to the barricades fifty years earlier, now led them to the ballot box. Electoral gains in May 1898, combined with the threat from the Right during the Dreyfus Affair to cause a prime minister to invite Millerand in 1899 to become minister of trade and industry in his new government.

This unprecedented spectacle of a revolutionary socialist in a bourgeois government split French social revolutionaries into two altogether new parties. On the one hand, the charismatic figure of Jean Jaurès rallied former "possibilists" and other reformists into a new French Socialist party pledged to "revolutionary evolution" (the progenitor of modern, democratic socialism in France). On the other hand, the Blanquist Edouard Vaillant and the Marxist Jules Guesde formed the rival Socialist party of France (the ancestor of the modern French Communist party). It accepted the warning of Marx's son-in-law Paul

Lafargue in 1899 against the "parliamentary gangrene" of "pact-making" opportunism—agreeing to participate in elections but refusing any ministerial role that might "lull the combative ardor of the party." [60] Meanwhile the French trade union movement coalesced independently into the General Confederation of Labor (CGT), which perpetuated the antipolitical Proudhonist tradition and proved more influential among the masses than either of the socialist parties.

The moderate reformist impulse was strengthened throughout the labor movement by the formation in 1902–03 of an International Secretariat of National Trade Union Centers.[61] The eleven countries represented were largely the Protestant countries of northwestern Europe where revolutionary traditions were almost nonexistent; and the controlling force in both the permanent secretariat and the biennial international conferences tended to be the moderate wing of the German Social Democratic movement. Independent international influence was exercised by the even-less revolutionary trade union movement of Great Britain. This growing movement swamped the weak Marxist Social Democratic Federation in England, which had briefly sought to provide revolutionary leadership for the labor unrest of the late 1880s. British unions were enticed by incrementalism, and unlike their German counterparts were creators (not creations) of a political party. The British elected labor delegates to parliament first as a bloc within the Liberal party in 1886 and 1892, and then formed the Independent Labor party in 1893. The success of the British unions in enacting progressive legislation encouraged others to consider the advantages of a unionism that was

> wage conscious rather than class conscious, interested primarily in collective bargaining, and non-socialist, if not anti-socialist.[62]

Optimism within the working class about evolutionary social progress was paralleled by growing socialist conviction among upper-class intellectuals. The Fabian Society founded in 1883 played a catalytic role, preaching the "inevitability of gradualness" in the movement towards a socialist society. Taking their name from the Roman warrior Fabius, who learned to wait patiently before striking a fatal blow against Hannibal, the Fabians were less doctrinaire in their reliance on the masses than the Social Democrats. They feared that "the revolt of the empty stomach ends at the baker's shop." [63] They rejected not just revolutionary tactics, but also the concept of class struggle, arguing in effect that

> the conflict between bourgeois and proletarian might produce industrial unrest; it would not produce socialism.[64]

The Fabians saw themselves "permeating" all elements of English society with the rationality of socialism. They generally stood apart from either the Marxist disputes of the Social Democratic Federation or the political activities of the Labor party.

Fabian ideas deeply influenced Eduard Bernstein, the leading German Social Democratic exile in London in the 1890s. Through him, the nonideological reformism of late Victorian England was transformed into the Marxist heresy of revisionism. German Social Democracy became less democratic in the process of rejecting Bernstein—and, perhaps more suitable thereby for later adoption in authoritarian lands further east.

Bernstein was one of fifteen children of a poor Jewish plumber in Berlin. A brilliant student and writer, he had since 1881 edited the official party newspaper *Der Sozialdemokrat,* and was close to Engels during his long exile in London. Beginning with articles in 1896 and ending in the publication of his *Evolutionary Socialism* in 1899, Bernstein argued forcefully that Marx's teachings required systematic revision in the light of economic developments since his death. He argued that a capitalist collapse was not inevitable, and a catastrophic revolution increasingly improbable. Wealth was in some ways being spread (rather than concentrated in ever fewer hands) under the capitalist system, and class distinctions blurred (rather than ever more sharply polarized). He argued that the Social Democratic party could substantially increase its influence if it

> could find the courage to free itself from outmoded phraseology and strive to appear as what in fact it now is, a Democratic Socialist party of reform.[65]

Bernstein returned to Germany in 1901 after twenty years of enforced exile and was elected to the Reichstag the following year. He gained considerable support within the trade union movement and in south Germany, where Social Democrats were already active in local government. He proposed that the German Social Democrats follow, in effect, the Millerand precedent by insisting on the vice-presidency of the Reichstag and thus participating in the formal exercise of government power. But this suggestion and the evolutionary reformism behind it were decisively rejected at the Dresden conference of the party in 1903, and at the Amsterdam Congress of the Second International the following year.

Bernstein had brought to Germany the view widely expounded throughout the European Left that capitalist society might "grow into socialism without a violent revolution." Yet the argument seemed more appropriate to England than to Germany, where the executive was not finally responsible to the Reichstag. Behind the imperial executive in Germany, moreover, stood the antidemocratic and antisocialist force of military and Junker power. Finally, and not least important, was the long attachment of Social Democrats to the consoling myth of a coming revolution which had sustained them during the long period of the antisocialist laws. They could not bring themselves to abandon the idea in theory—even if they did in practice. Thus, revisionism was stamped out as a threat to the revolutionary faith. As Liebknecht put it to Bernstein at the onset of the controversy:

> Islam was invincible as long as it believed in itself. . . . But the moment it began to compromise . . . it ceased to be a conquering force. . . . Socialism can neither conquer nor save the world if it ceases to believe in itself.[66]

Kautsky remained the prophet of this New Islam. He guarded the faith intact and kept the believers united with his interpretation of the Koran of Social Democracy, *Capital*. But unlike Mohammed, he was not to be "the seal of the prophets." For it was in Russia, not Germany that revolution first broke out in the twentieth century (1905), and that social revolutionaries eventually came to power (1917). The Marxist mantle of doctrinal infallibility passed thereafter to the leader of that revolution, V. I. Lenin, who anathemized Kautsky in much the same way that Kautsky had condemned Bernstein twenty years earlier in his *The Proletarian Revolution and the Renegade Kautsky*, written late in 1918 on the eve of the First Congress of the Third International.

Before turning from Germany to Russia, one must ask the nagging questions always posed about the German Social Democrats. Why did they not attain—or more aggressively seek—power? Why did they become so preoccupied with parliamentary elections? How could they end up supporting the patriotic rush to war in 1914—providing in effect proletarian cannon fodder for the bourgeois state they were theoretically pledged to overthrow?

Much of the Social Democrats' "failure" can be attributed to adverse outside forces. They had the misfortune to be a revolutionary movement in a nonrevolutionary age. The enormous concentration of physical power in the new industrial state of the late nineteenth century rendered spontaneous, internally generated revolution all but impossible. Even in combustible Paris by 1870–71, a foreign power had to smash the existing state machine before a revolution could occur.

But part of the explanation for the Social Democratic "failure" lies in the nature of the movement itself. As we have seen, it conceived of power in an altogether different way from the revolutionary movements of an earlier era, the difference described earlier as the shift from a Masonic to a machine model of revolutionary organization.

The Masonic models of the Francocentric era had conceived of power in architectural terms as the enclosure of space by a structure: [67] locating legitimacy within an inner lodge or circle; revalidating politics through the structure of a constituted assembly rather than the body of an anointed monarch; liberating others by enclosure within a *grande nation*; ultimately seeking to "make the world a pantheon." [68] But the new German state even more than the Third Republic in France had simply coöpted for conservative ends these images of the national revolutionary era. The "springtime of nations" had given way to the long hot summer of industrial unrest and imperial expansion. The new machine model of the German Social Democrats expressed the replacement of national by social revolutionary ideals.

The Germans drew from the machine the image of power as the dynamic development of material force in time, rather than the progressive conquest of segments of space through moral heroism. The Social Democratic party was not the expression of some philosophical-moral ideal. It was a material, political instrument of the working class. This class had no single geographical location, no center of sanctification in a lodge or circle. It was a widely scattered, prosaic group of human appendages to the machines of a powerful, newly unified state. German Social Democracy, therefore, saw its avenue to power in a political strategy that developed over time rather than in para-military efforts to "liberate" oppressed areas. The object of revolutionary strategy was to gain control over the means of production which were widely dispersed, not to seize directly the concentrated political power of the state.

The success of the Social Democratic party as a political machine gave it a vested interest in the very national state within which its power was increasing. Having lost the sense that earlier revolutionaries had of a separate identity, a fraternal conspiracy anchored in its own sacred space, the new mass organization was unable to preserve its distinctiveness from the established political system.

Most important of all, the Social Democrats—like most other political organizations in the long period of peace and progress prior to World War I—lacked that sense of prophetic foreboding that alone could have prepared them for what was to come. Germany was particularly removed from violence during this period; it was perhaps the most internally tranquil country in Europe for the quarter of a century prior to 1914.[69]

Possibly only those who lived more intimately with violence could sense the coming of total global war. Violence in Germany on the eve of World War I still lay sheathed within the machines of a disciplined state. Further to the east, violence was less easily confined and controlled. The first major war of the twentieth century, the Russo-Japanese conflict of 1904–05, led directly to revolution in Russia in 1905. And when violent war came again in 1914, Russian Social Democrats proved more prepared than their German counterparts to move boldly.

The Germans, having lost the older dependence on moral heroism, were thus unable to muster the courage to resist the rush to war in 1914. In Russia, however, where violence was central to the revolutionary tradition, a revolutionary Social Democratic opposition to the war developed on a semiprophetic basis. Vladimir Lenin foresaw the flame of a coming revolution when others saw only the smoke of war. Lenin worked towards the Bolshevik victory of 1917 through the Russian version of a German Social Democratic party. But he built on a unique—and uniquely violent—Russian revolutionary tradition, to which detailed attention must now be turned.

CHAPTER 14

The Bomb:

Russian Violence

THE REVOLUTIONARY FLAME had been slow to ignite in Russia. The spark blown in from abroad by Decembrist officers died in the snows of Siberia. The flames lit later by student revolutionaries under Alexander II were also extinguished. But that fire continued to smolder underground, and burst out into three revolutionary conflagrations in the early twentieth century.

During the second half of the nineteenth century, Russia and socialism replaced Poland and nationalism as the main revolutionary force in eastern Europe. Then, in 1917, the social revolutionary tradition was to come to power in Russia, producing the first decisive break in the ideological unity of European civilization since the Protestant Reformation.

How and why did Russia move from the conservative somnolence of the late years of Nicholas I in the early 1850s to the revolutionary turbulence that greeted Nicholas II forty years later? How was revolutionary socialism able to prevail in a land hitherto renowned for reactionary nationalism? No question is more important in the history of the revolutionary tradition than the origins and nature of the peculiarly Russian revolutionary tradition.

The tradition stands—like Russia itself—as the bridge between Europe and Asia. The Russian revolutionaries of the late nineteenth century represented both a reprise on the Europeans of the early nineteenth century and an anticipation of the extra-European revolutionaries of the twentieth. The proper monument to the Russian revolutionary tradition should not be one of those healthy, heroic workers celebrated in Stalinist sculpture, but rather some simple, sickly student with the two heads of Janus: one looking back to European inspiration, the other forward to a global transformation.

The importance of Russia to the world lies not just in the material victory of the Bolshevik Revolution but also in the prior spiritual conquest within Russia of a highly cerebral and uniquely intense variant of the European revolutionary tradition. Indeed, the transformation of the old Russian Empire into the new Union of Soviet Socialist Republics resembled in some respects the transformation of the Roman Empire from paganism into Christianity under Constantine the Great in the fourth century A.D. The imperatives for the change arose not just from the practical problems of an aging empire, but also, more deeply, from its loss of ideological legitimacy. The origins of the turn to a new belief by an old empire must, in both cases, be sought in the long years of preaching, martyrdom, and quiet conversion to the new faith within the realm of the old. Just as the Constantinian Revolution originated in the underground history of a previously illicit faith, so the Bolshevik Revolution "began" with the development within Russia of the most totalistic branch of the European revolutionary faith.

There was a dark side to this distinctiveness. For the Russians may be said to have unlocked the secrets of violence—just as the Germans uncovered those of organization. If the machine symbolized the German revolutionary movement, the bomb symbolized the Russian. The explosive implement was no less a product of the new industrial technology than was the implosive machine, but the bomb was more radically democratic (anyone could make and have access to one) and more directly terrifying.[1]

The Russian fascination with explosives dates back to the early Muscovite tsars,[2] but was intensified by the western economic expansion of the late nineteenth century. In search of minerals and fuels to feed its expanding industrial production, western Europe explored Russia and other outlying regions with the aid of new blasting materials. The Swedish inventor of dynamite, Alfred Nobel, conducted much of his early work in St. Petersburg and established by the turn of the century the largest oil fields in the world at Baku.[3]

From Nobel's first underwater detonation of dynamite in 1862 through the perfecting of nitroglycerine compounds in the early 1870s, Europe was presented with powerful new explosives equally suitable for blasting minerals or killing people. The explosives exercised a certain scientific fascination for the new radical student generation, since chemistry seemed to be one of the least romantic and most materially useful forms of science. Chernyshevsky justified the new revolutionary asceticism with a chemical metaphor. The warmth people need came not from sentimentality, but from a cold match striking the hard surface of social reality and lighting thereby a fire. Revolutionary students developed an almost sacramental reverence for chemical mixtures. Dmitry Mendeleev, who wrote his *Principles of Chemistry* and codified the periodic table in St. Petersburg during the late sixties, remained a youthful role model for young revolutionaries down to Lenin's older brother in the mid-1880s.[4] Art no less than science required chemical anointment; and the leader of the new Russian national school of music was a chemist, Alexander Borodin, who regularly prepared a special compound of chemicals into which the compositions of his colleagues were immersed for preservation.

The supreme revolutionary organization of the era, the People's Will, ended the reign of Alexander II with a rain of bombs. It is a haunting fact that the People's Will revealed neither its name nor its program until November 1879—*after* the first bomb had exploded in a first attempt to assassinate Alexander II.[5] The regicidal explosion was thus the organization's first public statement; and when one of its leaders was arrested, extraordinary attention was devoted to analyzing the seventeen kilograms of dynamite discovered upon him. The experts gloomily concluded that the explosive was an original, high quality compound made inside Russia and easily replicated.[6]

In its final plans for the successful assassination of the tsar on March 1, 1881, the People's Will attached special importance to the bomb even while recognizing that shooting might be cheaper and surer:

> It would not have created such an impression. It would have been seen as an ordinary murder, and thus would not have expressed a new stage in the revolutionary movement.[7]

The Russian tradition did indeed express a "new stage in the revolutionary movement." The assembling of bombs became a communally unifying force no less important than the printing of leaflets in the revolutionary cell. The dynamite workshop (*masterskaia*) which the People's Will first formed in the late seventies reappeared in the student group of Lenin's older brother in the late eighties—and then again in the "technical bureau" of Lenin's own Bolshevik party and other such groups proliferating throughout Russia at the turn of the century.[8]

The Russian tradition first acquired distinctive shape in the 1860s amidst the raised expectations of Alexander II's reform period. As we know, Herzen, the leader of the first Russian revolutionary organization, Land and Liberty, had for nearly a decade been close to such national revolutionaries as Lelewel, Worcell, Mazzini, and Fazy in Geneva. During the period of Alexander's reign, Herzen had even entertained the classical Italo-Polish hope of realizing a constitutional monarchy through "reform from above."

Yet hardly had Herzen begun to organize from London a conspiracy to achieve this than his leadership was rejected by Chernyshevsky and the "new men" of the 1860s within Russia. By 1863, the Italo-Polish tradition had been in effect supplanted in Russia by the more violent ideology of a new generation. The intensity of its quarrel with the older generation (like that of Bazarov with his elders in Turgenev's *Fathers and Sons* of 1862) heralded something profoundly new.

The new Russian tradition which emerged in the 1860s can be analyzed in terms of five evocative words central to it: *nihilism, intelli-*

gentsia, populism, terrorism, and *anarchism.* Each word had been used before elsewhere, but acquired through Russian usage both a new meaning and a new world-wide currency. Taken together the five terms suggest uncompromising, total opposition to the status quo. They may be said to have replaced in practice (even as they pretended to serve in theory) the revolutionary idea of the earlier, Francocentric period: *liberty, equality,* and *fraternity.*

The Slogans of the Sixties

Nihilism

Youth movements begin with a "revolution of rising expectation" during an age of political reform. The original revolutionary student movement had arisen in Germany a half century earlier out of hopes raised by the reforms in Prussia. American student revolts a century later were to grow out of the renewed sense of political possibility generated by the Kennedy era and the civil-rights movement. In like manner, exaggerated youthful expectations of change under Alexander II led— perhaps inevitably—to disillusionment deepening into despair once his reforms came to be seen as partial and incomplete.

The sense of being a unique generation usually feeds not only on exaggerated expectations of reform, but also on identification with a political leader who seems to represent a charismatic agent of change. Perhaps the first self-conscious student generation in revolt were the *Sturm und Drang* poets and pamphleteers of the 1770s in Germany. Their glorification of the will in opposition to convention was in many ways subtly shaped by the model of Frederick the Great, who defied both Prussian tradition and the European balance of power. The original revolutionaries of the early nineteenth century were young officers and students whose imagination had been aroused by Napoleon; and he continued to inspire romantic rebels throughout the century.

Mazzini's Young Italy and Young Europe introduced in the early 1830s the romantic notion that youth as such should rebel against what Fazy called "gerontocracy." Once again, hopes were raised (by the Revolution of 1830) only to be dashed by the failure of revolution to spread, and by the subsequent return in Belgium and France of "revolutionary" new monarchs to conservative ways. The vitalistic idea that the young generation itself should complete an artificially arrested reform program kept revolutionary enthusiasm alive among Poles and Italians during the "springtime of nations" leading up to 1848.

But the assertion of generational identity among young Russians in the 1860s had a new ideological quality.[9] They had no desire to complete the program of concrete reforms begun by Alexander II. They rejected the entire traditional society—and indeed all else save their own newly discovered evangelical faith in scientific method. Total negation was born in part out of disgust with the incompetence of old Russia that had led to humiliating defeat during the Crimean War, and in part out of long-repressed resentment against the pretension and antirationalism of Romanov Russia. The uniqueness of Russia had been asserted with extravagant pride in the doctrine of official nationality in 1833 and identified with social conservatism as Russia crushed revolutions in Poland of 1831 and in Hungary of 1849. After defeat in the Crimea, young people wanted to end this attitude of acceptance, and the term *nihilist* was invented and popularized in Turgenev's *Fathers and Sons* of 1862 to characterize the new negativism that proclaimed "two plus two is four and all else is nonsense." [10]

This extreme rejection of existing tradition was confined almost exclusively to the student population. As in Prussia of the 1810s, a government bent on reform after defeat in war suddenly opened up educational opportunities and sought to organize the expanding student population into traditional regional groupings. The Russian *zemlia-chestva* was a literal translation of the earlier German *Landsmann-schaften* (and a direct borrowing from the *Korporationen* organizations at Dorpat, the German-speaking university within the Russian Empire). But just as the German students formed their own anti-aristocratic and antitraditional *Burschenschaften*, so the Russian students in the late 1850s developed their own more democratic groupings which met to define and defend student rights: the *skhodki*, named after the label used for traditional peasant assemblies.[11] The sense of unlimited possibility generated in these gatherings contrasted sharply with the squalid conditions in which the students were forced to live. The Russian student population nearly doubled in the six years that followed the sanctioning of unlimited university enrollment in 1855, and many of the student complaints about Russian society as a whole were in some cases projections of their own grievances against the cramped conditions of Russian student life.

Much of the subsequent behavior of radical Russian students followed the earlier pattern of German students during the revolutions of 1848–49: the printing of journals, the founding of "free academies," the attempts to recruit army support (successfully in Baden in the summer of 1849), and the heroic efforts to rescue their ideological heroes from prison (such as the escape of Johann Kinkel from the Spandau prison engineered by the twenty-year-old Karl Schurz).[12] The term nihilist had been popularized in Karl Gutzkow's tale of 1853, *Die Nihilisten*, to characterize the materialism of the German students in the disillusioned aftermath of 1848.

Young Russians eagerly absorbed the materialism of German writers of the 1850s like Büchner and Molleschott, often fortifying their new convictions with theological intensity derived from seminary backgrounds. Unlike the Germans, however, the Russians had not failed in revolution. Nihilism was for them an expression not of disillusionment, but of rising political consciousness. Defeated German revolutionaries either fled abroad or settled down. But frustrated radicals in Russia never had a chance to rise in 1848. Further frustrated by the repression of Nicholas I's last years, they felt a new sense of possibility with the advent of a new tsar in 1855. Thus, young Russia developed a subculture of intense expectation that never tired of attempts to free political prisoners. Unlike Germans who went to America, Russians sent to Siberia never lost faith in a coming revolution.

The totalistic quality of the Russian revolutionary tradition owed much to the authoritarian nature of the tsarist system. Never had the interdependence between the extremes of Right and Left been more evident than in late imperial Russia, where the liberal reformism of Alexander II's early years was undermined by both terror on the Left and counter-terror from the Right. Revolutionary populism vied with and intermixed with reactionary pan-Slavism in the 1870s; the assassinations on the Left that climaxed in the killing of Alexander II were followed by pogroms of the Right under Alexander III. Revolutionaries and police not only studied but interpenetrated one another's activities so deeply that it was sometimes impossible to disentangle an individual's real allegiance.

The deepest roots of revolutionary totalism in Russia, however, perhaps lay in the student subculture and its rituals of togetherness. The decisive element was not just the political activation of nonaristocratic students,[13] but also the development within the elite educational institutions of a "two-track pattern of educational promotion, with one path leading to political revolt." [14]

This path first appeared within the Aleksandrovsky Lyceum in the 1840s, then within the university in the late 1850s and the early 1860s, and finally within the technical schools (the Medical-Surgical Academy and the Technological Institute) as they assumed more importance in the late 1860s and the early 1870s. These highly selective institutions of the Russian government provided automatic advancement into the imperial state; but in the 1860s they also became "a crucible for the tempering of radical revolt among students for whom social origins had lost real meaning." [15] In the impersonal capital of St. Petersburg, a city built for parades rather than people, the university population had more than doubled from 1855 to 1859.[16] This swollen student population was cut off from its parochial and patriarchal past and infected simultaneously with the political ambition of imperial St. Petersburg and the intellectual vistas of a European university. The students thus combined "elitist attitudes and egalitarian habits." [17] They developed an intense communal life built around libraries, mutual aid funds, lithographed publications, and even (with the active help in 1860 of the university law faculty) student courts.

The student subculture developed from the formal life of the university. Illicit books and subjects provided a counter-curriculum more appealing than the "irrelevant" subjects presented in university lectures. The students began to entertain fantasies about remaking the broader society in their own image; and student discussion groups increasingly provided a "protective environment" [18] for outright revolutionary recruitment. Student life in its early, apolitical phase already contained the germs of a social alternative to the tsarist order. The *skhodki* provided a kind of legislature; the commune (*obshchina*) a kind of judiciary; the cooperative (*artel*) a productive enterprise based on distributive economic justice. Their discussion groups for themselves and their literacy schools for others made up a total educational system. All that was missing was a strong executive to challenge the tsarist government; and this came in the late 1860s in the person of Serge Nechaev, the first revolutionary nihilist of the modern world.

The students' path from positions of privilege and promise into revolutionary opposition began with demonstrations on purely student issues, which spread to provincial university centers like Kazan and Kharkov by the late 1850s. In Kiev in the fall of 1859, an idealistic surgeon launched the Sunday School movement, using the one nonworking day of the week to provide free tutorials for peasants living in the city. This pioneering effort at popular education acquired a political coloration when one of the tutors, P. V. Pavlov, a young Kievan opposed to serfdom, became professor of Russian history at St. Petersburg University in 1861. He glorified past westernization (the age of Boris Godunov and the quasi-parliamentary zemsky sobors) in his lectures, and participated in the impressive network of 28 Sunday schools in the capital, which involved, some 450 volunteers teaching basic literacy to some 5,000 indigent students.[19]

Far from pacifying the students, the emancipation of the serfs in February 1861 only intensified their unrest. A demonstration of 350 St. Petersburg students in March was followed by a second one of 400 in April. A fumbling effort to try one student for embezzlement in the spring led to further organized protests. By the time the long-sought abolition of student uniforms was conceded in the summer of 1861, the move was resented as an official plot to remove a common bond of solidarity.[20]

Student unrest became a student movement with the sudden appearance in St. Petersburg early in September 1861 of the revolutionary proclamation "To the Young Generation," written by Nicholas Shelgunov (a veteran of the Crimean War radicalized by subsequent travel abroad) and revised by Michael Mikhailov, a young poet who lived in a *ménage à trois* with Shelgunov and his wife. Mikhailov smuggled six hundred copies from Herzen's press in London back to Russia in a false-bottomed trunk, and distributed this call to the "young generation" to reject not only the institutions of old conservative Russia but the reform proposals of the new liberals as well, and to "move boldly forward to revolution."[21] The purpose of the proposed revolution was the establishment of popular sovereignty, and the means could be violent:

> If to achieve our ends, by dividing the land among the people we have to kill a hundred thousand of the gentry, even that will not deter us. . . .[22]

Mikhailov's arrest early in September and his subsequent trial represented the first official persecution of a spokesman for radical youth.

His personal heroism in insisting on sole responsibility for the pamphlet helped rally students not just to his case, but to his cause. In contrast to some later student movements that would present amnesty for themselves high among their demands, the revolutionary student movement in Russia put personal demands last in order to vindicate their principles.

Fear of the growing student unrest led the university authorities in St. Petersburg at the beginning of the new term on September 22 to shut the unused lecture rooms that the students ordinarily used for their meetings. This led to a forced entry into the closed Hall of Acts by some five hundred students on the twenty-third, followed the next day by a march of one thousand through the streets to the home of the curator of the university. Such unprecedented acts caused further arrests, and a similar demonstration in October in Moscow—the first of its kind there—led to 340 arrests and 37 detentions. On December 20, the University of St. Petersburg was formally closed. Students meanwhile began to feel exhilarated with the experience of building a kind of counter-university. The sign "University of St. Petersburg" was tacked on the Peter and Paul Fortress, where Mikhailov was being held incommunicado. Young demonstrators confined in Kronstadt set up their own "republic" in prison. University students established their own "free university" to continue the process of public enlightenment with the aid of some of the younger professors who resigned from the university to protest its forced closing.

The free university along with the Sunday School movement were broken up in March 1862 with the sudden nocturnal arrest of Pavlov, the professor who had been central to both. But most of St. Petersburg University did not open until August of 1863. During that final eighteen months when there was in effect neither university nor counter-university, the student movement reached a frenzied climax that did much to set the future course of the Russian revolutionary tradition.

First of all, Herzen and Ogarev tried rather clumsily during this period to introduce a classical Western style revolutionary organization into the amorphous Russian movement. But their Land and Liberty hardly even touched, let alone controlled, unrest inside Russia.

The arrest of Nicholas Chernyshevsky, in the summer of 1862, his long imprisonment in the Peter and Paul Fortress before trial, and his final exile to Siberia in May 1864 provided the young generation with a hero and martyr. The famous work that he published during this period of imprisonment, *What Is To Be Done? or Tales of the New People*, provided a kind of model for the new believers in a rational socialist order. Chernyshevsky's ideal was a student commune ruled by utilitarian puritanism, seeking to become both a productive cooperative enterprise and a center of enlightenment for the masses. His valedictory answer to the question *What Is To Be Done?* emphasized the need for communal structures and social rather than political goals. The book gave guidance to the student quest for a new way of life and society which in turn produced on Russian soil a new type of professional revolutionary. Fanatical, ascetic belief in science was the key. Scientism was for Chernyshevsky and his younger friend, Dobroliubov, largely a case of the "exchange of catechisms" by former seminarians replacing one absolute belief with another "without any internal struggle." [23]

The student subculture came to be identified with violence among the people when a sudden series of fires swept through St. Petersburg in the spring of 1862. In inflammable, wooden Russia, fear of fire was endemic; and rumors of Bohemian arsonists reached "down to the last hut, to the homeless peasant." [24] And generalized fears were specifically attached to the new student revolutionaries when the pamphlet *Young Russia* appeared in May 1862, precisely at the time of the major fire. This document was the work of two Moscow students, Peter Zaichnevsky and Pericles Argiropulo, and it marked the beginning of a Russian revolutionary tradition demonstrably different from anything in the West.

The two students had once had loose links with Herzen's Land and Liberty, and Zaichnevsky had studied the Polish Revolution of 1830–31, admired Mazzini, and made his debut as a revolutionary orator in February 1861 at a Catholic requiem in Moscow for students slain in Warsaw.

But *Young Russia* differed from any manifestoes of the Mazzinian persuasion (1) in its almost sacramental exaltation of the violent act and (2) in its identification of violence with social rather than national revolution. There was the uncanny prophecy:

> The day will soon come when we will unfurl the great banner of the future, the red banner. And with a mighty cry of "Long Live the Russian Social and Democratic Republic" we will move against the Winter Palace to wipe out all who dwell there.[25]

Violent class war would occur between the imperial party and the "party of the people" in Russia, "which destiny has ordained shall be the first country to realize the great cause of Socialism." If there is resistance

> we will cry "To your axes" and then we will strike the imperial party without sparing our blows just as they do not spare theirs against us.[26]

Land and movable wealth were to be redistributed and "social" factories established. A revolutionary elite would have to "take dictatorship into its own hands and stop at nothing," and only then give power to a national assembly elected by universal suffrage. Otherwise elections could lead to the end of revolution as in France of 1848.

Their program of "putting oneself at the head of every movement" [27] was initially condemned as an elitist Western import by Herzen and Bakunin from London—and even initially by Chernyshevsky from St. Petersburg. In truth, however, *Young Russia* represented a comprehensive revolutionary program authentically rooted in Russian reality.[28] In the first place, the manifesto grew out of the new, scientistic nihilism. Zaichnevsky had come from his small provincial estate in Orel to Moscow University to study mathematics. He turned to politics not out of personal privation, but out of ideological determination to "defend the rationality of socialism." [29] He made use of the lithograph process, which reproduced university lectures, to circulate long passages from two influential sources of the new nihilism: Feuerbach's atheistic *Essence of Christianity* and Büchner's materialistic *Force and Matter*. At the time of his arrest the police also found an unfinished manuscript translation of the original plebeian manifesto: *What Is Property?* by Proudhon, whose rough-hewn egalitarianism made him perhaps the most influential single Western revolutionary within Russia at that time.[30]

At the beginning of 1861 Zaichnevsky had broken off from one discussion group, the Library of Kazan students, to form a small but intense group of five to seven members which apparently used the name The Society of Communists and became thereby the first "Communist" group on Russian soil.[31]

Zaichnevsky was among the first student agitators to cultivate mass support for social revolution. His group worked intensively through the Moscow Sunday School movement,[32] and then turned to more active revolutionary agitation in the countryside. Zaichnevsky set out on horseback from Moscow on May 21, 1861, to spread socialist ideas and develop revolutionary strategy among the peasants of his native Orel.[33] A split soon developed with Argiropulo, who argued that "to preach does not mean to fight." [34] Zaichnevsky contended in effect that preaching must—if it was serious—escalate into confrontation and even conflict.

Public confrontation with deceptive officials and timid reformers would help strip away the respectability of official Russia, just as the rhythmic student chant of *chelovek-cherviak* (man is a worm) was breaking up any remaining aura of sanctity about obligatory theology lectures.[35] Preaching socialism, in Zaichnevsky's view, was not merely an educational act, but also a dramatic one. Even if the witness should end up sending the agitator to the gallows, the image of the truly dedicated revolutionary would haunt his persecutor just as the Christian martyrs had haunted the declining Roman nobility.

Arrested on the personal order of Tsar Alexander II, Zaichnevsky nonetheless succeeded in completing *Young Russia*. He stunned Russian society with its opening lines:

> Russia is entering the revolutionary stage of its existence. . . . Under this regime a small number of people who own capital control the fate of the rest . . . everything is false, everything is stupid, from religion . . . to the family. . . . a revolution, a bloody and pitiless revolution . . . must change everything down to the very roots . . . we know that rivers of blood will flow and that perhaps even innocent victims will perish. . . .[36]

The same student life of Moscow that had nurtured Zaichnevsky brought about within a few years the fulfillment of his prophecy. Moscow was traditionally less sympathetic to Western, liberal ideas than

St. Petersburg, and more intimately in touch with the dissenting religious traditions of old Russia. Moscow had been the center of much of the reactionary nationalist revival that had accompanied the crushing of the Polish rebellion in 1863. The Moscow Slavic Congress of 1867 became the launching site for a new reactionary pan-Slav ideology—with the city providing lavish subsidies and its newspapers enthusiastic support. In contrast to the more moderate, transnational Congress of Slavs in Prague in 1848, the Moscow Congress became a vehicle for Russian chauvinism.[37]

Once again, the mutually re-enforcing nature of the extremes became evident. Moscow, the new center of reaction, was also the new breeding ground for revolution. About ten Moscow students, mostly from the Volga region, had in the course of 1864 formed a secret revolutionary group called simply The Organization; and within it there emerged an even smaller and more secret group known as Hell, which purported to be linked with a European Revolutionary Committee.[38] Central to these groups was a certain longing to sacrifice—if not suffer—together. They emulated the ascetic life-style (sleeping on floors and communal sharing) advocated in *What Is To Be Done?* by Chernyshevsky.

Chernyshevsky himself became the ultimate model for the new generation—both in his rejection of Herzen and the older radical nobility [39] and in his acceptance of a martyrdom reminiscent of early Christianity.[40] The new thirst to translate words into deeds was first expressed in a series of pacts and plots among young Muscovites to free Chernyshevsky. The most exotic of the new communes, the Smorgon Academy of 1867–69 (named for a wooden region in the Urals where gypsy bears were trained), planned to blow up a train to free Chernyshevsky and to smuggle him abroad to found a revolutionary paper. But they settled for sending one of their own members to Geneva in 1867 to reprint *What Is To Be Done?*

This group also idolized the figure of Dmitry Karakozov, the young Moscow student and member of Hell, who was executed for his unsuccessful attempt to assassinate Tsar Alexander on April 4, 1866. However clumsy his attempt, it did in some ways open a new era of "propaganda by deed"—of terror and counter-terror, which was finally to lead to the killing of the tsar fifteen years later.

Hell preached a new and sublimely suicidal theory of assassination. Members made vows of celibacy, secrecy, and complete separation from all family and friends from the past. The goal was the assassination of the tsar—preferably on Easter Sunday. It was hoped that this would begin a broader campaign by other "sections" of a "European Revolutionary Committee" to exterminate monarchs everywhere. The assassin on the eve of his sacred act was deliberately to conceal his true identity not just with a false name, but by assuming a false personality—ostentatiously adopting a drunken and talkative manner totally at variance with his real revolutionary dedication. Immediately prior to the deed, he was to disfigure his face beyond recognition; immediately after, he was to take poison—leaving behind only a manifesto from "the organization," which would be assured thereby an impact that peaceful propaganda could never have. The manifesto from the mythical European revolutionary committee that Karakozov left behind so traumatized the government that after his secret trial and public execution, it arrested anyone who even visited his grave.[41]

This atmosphere of fearful expectation set the stage for the arrival in Moscow of Nechaev, the dark genius of the Russian tradition. Unlike almost all other revolutionaries of the 1860s, Nechaev came from a working-class family. His father had been a textile worker and his mother a seamstress in the bleak city of Ivanovo-Voznesensk, the center of the early Russian textile industry.[42] When he was nine years old, a year after the death of his mother, Nechaev began working as a messenger in one of the factories of this "Russian Manchester" on the upper Volga.

For him, the escape to student life in Moscow was a special kind of liberation. He avidly absorbed the mythology of the revolutionary student circles of the late 1860s, which tended to fuse and confuse into a single heroic tradition the ascetic scientism of Chernyshevsky, the call to violence of Zaichnevsky, and the attempted tsaricide of Karakozov.[43] He simultaneously reviled the inadequacies of all past revolutionaries and used his own lower-class background as a kind of certificate of special merit. He alone had suffered in the past—and would call for the deliberate acceptance of suffering and sacrifice in the "common cause." A Romanian student leader in Moscow, Zemfiry Ralli, had pioneered the professionalization of revolutionary organization by trying to model a secret society directly on Buonarroti's Conspiracy.[44] Ralli then went abroad to become Bakunin's principal editor; and Nechaev soon followed him to Geneva, gaining accreditation from Bakunin's mythical "World Revolutionary Union." While abroad, Nechaev drew up and published his famed *Catechism of a Revolutionary*: a bleak guide for the creation of a totally revolutionary personality and for the calculated manipulation of others for the revolutionary cause.[45]

This was not the first *Revolutionary Catechism*;[46] and was in many respects a continuation of Bakunin's efforts to adopt Masonic rituals for a revolutionary manual. But the document also represented a final revolutionary answer to Chernyshevsky's question: What is to be done? To the ascetic rationalism of Chernyshevsky, Nechaev added the distilled hatred of the most brilliant survivor of the extreme revolutionary circles of the 1860s: Peter Tkachev.

Tkachev was part of the harassed St. Petersburg wing of all the major Moscow-based extremist groups of the 1860s from Young Russia to the Smorgon Academy. He spent much of the decade in prison, which solidified his intense identification with Chernyshevsky.[47] He was one of the first Russians to embrace economic materialism[48]—and may have led Nechaev into taking approving notice of Marx.[49] Tkachev mastered the "aesopian" art of conveying revolutionary messages through legal journalism; and in 1868, he published an article that profoundly influenced Nechaev: "Men of the Future and Heroes of Bourgeois Mediocrity."

Tkachev suggested that the "new men" of Chernyshevsky were acquiring a focus that would enable them (by implication) to destroy the hated "bourgeois mediocrity" (*meshchanstvo*). All that was ultimately needed was that "all their efforts and aspirations converge towards one point: the advent of the triumph of their idea." [50] They had to be people who gave themselves "wholly and with total self-denial" to this "idea," which was, of course, social revolution in Russia.

Nechaev provided such single-minded decisiveness. This was the one attribute praised even by his detractors, and it was precisely the one needed to lead quarreling intellectuals. Nechaev appointed himself, in effect, to be chief executive officer of the student movement, which had hitherto performed only legislative and judicial, economic and educational functions. Nechaev apparently viewed himself as a rival executive authority to the tsar. He adopted a series of nicknames suggesting authority: the king, the baron, *Liders* (from the English leader), *Barsov* (from the Russian lord), and *Nachalov* (from the Russian chief), the eagle, and *Volkov* (from the Russian for wolf). He began using the imperial we, and may have been in touch with an extremist group that planned to blow up the tsar's train near Elizavetgrad in the late summer of 1869.[51]

Nechaev attempted to instill into the student movement a new model of revolutionary dedication forged in the crucible of the 1860s. He invoked coarse peasant language—and concentrated his recruiting within the Agricultural Institute in Moscow, where such an idiom had an intimidating effect. He seemed to feel a special affinity for Balkan revolutionaries, with their tradition of blood feuds and vengeance. From his early friendship with the Romanian Ralli in Moscow through his visit to the Bulgarian leader Khristo Botev en route back to Russia in 1869 to his admiration for the Serbian assassins of King Michael Obrenovich and his own assumption of a Serbian identity, Nechaev prefigured the close link that was to develop between Balkan and Russian revolutionaries of the new type.[52]

For Nechaev "the revolutionary is a doomed man" who "has severed every tie with the civil order, with the educated world . . . if he continues to inhabit it, it is only to destroy it more effectively." [53] The catechism told the new type of revolutionary how to utilize different categories of the society he was bent on destroying. The important and intelligent were to be killed; the important and unintelligent were to be left alone, since their stupidity would drive the uncommitted to revolt. A third category, "animals and high-ranking personalities, neither intelligent nor competent," were to be blackmailed if their "dirty secrets" could be unearthed. Revolutionaries should pretend to follow a fourth category of "ambitious politicians and liberals of various sorts," while forcing them on to more radical steps that make it impossible for them to turn back. Fifth were doctrinaire or rhetorical revolutionaries, who had to be forced to move beyond mere talk and theory into active demonstrations. This would serve the dual purpose of killing off the weak and tempering those who survived into hard-core activists in the future. In a final category were women, who would be either the best revolutionaries of all or else figures to be treated like the third and fourth categories of men.[54]

The *Catechism* distinguished the coming "comradeship" *tovarish-chestvo* from Western organizations with their "respect for property, traditions . . . 'civilization' and 'morality' " and even from the "brother-hoods" of Bakunin.[55] Nechaev had returned from Geneva with a membership card in the "general committee" of Bakunin's mythical new "World Revolutionary Union," and he proceeded to found both a journal and an organization under the name *Narodnaia Rasprava* (The People's Summary Justice). Its official seal spoke of "the Russian Section of the World Revolutionary Union," and displayed an axe surrounded by the words "Committee of the People's Summary Justice of February 19, 1870."

This was the designated date for a revolutionary uprising: the ninth anniversary of the peasant emancipation and the bicentenary of the peasant uprising of Stenka Razin. Nechaev journeyed to Vladimir and Ivanovo in search of peasant recruits for his revolutionary elite, which was organized into a small number of five-man cells. As the connecting link and driving force, Nechaev led the central group on November 21 into the collective murder of a student participant who like Nechaev had worked in a factory in Ivanovo and bore the Everyman name of Ivan Ivanovich Ivanov. The slain Ivanov, an illegitimate child and former prison guard, may have drawn the assignment to kill the tsar within the core group of *Narodnaia Rasprava*, perhaps with explosives being prepared in a bookstore on the outskirts of St. Petersburg. He may have then had to be executed because of doubts about his reliability.[56] Or his death could have been a calculated crime designed to tighten the loyalty and cohesion of those implicated in it. In either event, tsaricide appears to have been part of the plan to trigger the social revolution on February 19, which also included recruitment among the workmen of the Tula munitions factories.

Nechaev, who fled abroad in mid-December after Ivanov's corpse was discovered, became the object of a massive manhunt in London, Paris, and Switzerland. He was, in effect, tried three times for the murder: first, through the fictionalized version in Dostoevsky's *The Possessed*, which began to appear serially in Katkov's *Russian Herald* in 1871; second, in his own formal trial after his arrest in Switzerland on August 14, 1872, and extradition to the Russian government; and finally by the tsar himself. Upon hearing of Nechaev's defiant calls for revolutionary revenge at his mock execution ceremony, Alexander II changed his sentence from twenty years hard labor to *"forever in prison,"* [57] personally underlining these words.

Yet even in total isolation within the Peter and Paul Fortress, Nechaev exercised a certain hypnotic impact on his captors. He eventually taught some of them to write in code; and, as other political prisoners began to fill up the fortress in the later 1870s, Nechaev instructed some of them in "disinformation": the spreading of false manifestoes to confuse the populace and terrorize officialdom. Once it was discovered in the late 1870s that Nechaev was still in St. Petersburg rather than Siberia, plans to free him began to replace the earlier project of freeing Chernyshevsky. After the execution of the tsar on March 1, 1881, sixty-nine soldiers were arrested on suspicion of collaborating in planning his escape, and the prisoner was put into deeper isolation within the prison. He died mysteriously on November 21, 1882, choosing perhaps the anniversary of the murder of Ivanov for his own suicide.[58]

Intelligentsia

With no acknowledgement of earlier Polish usage, the word *intelligentsia* was introduced into the Russian language in 1861 in an article describing south Russian students in the Hapsburg Empire.[59] It soon became the "verbal talisman" of the new Russian student generation as a whole—laden with far more universal meaning than it had ever had for the Poles.

Moderate liberals, romantic Slavophiles, and rationalistic Westernizers no less than revolutionaries all seized on the term. The intelligentsia was alleged by all of them to hold the secret of a national awakening through mental mobilization against the bureaucratic inertia of old Russia. Westernizers built on a long tradition of reverential usage of the French word *intelligence* by radical pioneers like Chaadaev and Herzen.[60] Slavophiles like Ivan Aksakov propagated the image of a Russian intelligentsia as a classless moral force seeking to be closer to the suffering common people than the intellectuals of aristocratic Poland.[61] Even conservative officials began speaking about "the development of a people's intelligentsia" [62] (*narodnaia intelligentsiia* meaning both a national and a people's intelligentsia).

Ideological expectations soon outstripped practical possibilities. By the late 1860s, the revolutionaries had taken over exclusive claim to the new label, and to the strong sense of collective righteousness that hung about it. Nicholas Shelgunov, the first radical to popularize the term, had envisaged in his *Proclamation to the Young Generation* of 1861 a relatively apolitical, new elite, "the intelligentsia of the country," [63] emerging from the enlarged student population. Within a decade, Shelgunov had introduced the word *intelligent* (with a hard *g*) as the singular of intelligentsia and a badge of belonging. He also made the moral distinction between a true and false *intelligent*.[64]

Pisarev and Mikhailovsky, who became in succession the two most influential radical journalists in Russia after the arrest of Chernyshevsky in 1862, saw the intelligentsia as "the moving force of history," [65] and history itself moving in accordance with progressive laws set down by Saint-Simon's protégé, Auguste Comte.[66] Bakunin and Lavrov, the two principal theorists and leaders of the revolutionary emigrant community, were moved more by the Hegelian brand of ideology—evident in Lavrov's appeal (in his influential *Historical Letters* of 1868–69) for the "critically thinking personality" to become "a conscious, knowing agent of progress." [67] Implicit in all the dated quarrels of the late 1860s and the early 1870s over "formulas of progress" and three-staged theories of history was a shared thirst for ideology as such: for some scientific, secular set of beliefs about history and social change that purported to universal validity.[68] In order to sustain the radical traditions of the earlier sixties during the repressive atmosphere that followed the assassination attempt of 1866 one needed the reassurance of history. Thus, the nihilist became the intelligent. He had moved from iconoclasm to ideology.

In addition to its concern for introducing science into society, the intelligentsia developed a passionate commitment to social justice. The radical intellectual was not generally thought to be fully *intelligentny* unless he believed in what Mikhailovsky called the "two-sided truth." Mikhailovsky insisted that there was deep meaning in the fact that the Russian word for truth, *pravda*, meant both objective, scientific truth (*pravda-istina*) and justice (*pravda-spravedlivost'*).[69] The intelligent had to be committed to both.

Though the first body of people to conceive of themselves as an intelligentsia viewed themselves as evolutionary friends of science and rejected Nechaevism as a pathological aberration, the convergence that soon developed between the intelligentsia and the revolutionary cause was already foreseen by Peter Tkachev, the human bridge between these two traditions in the late 1860s. As "the only person who defined the intelligentsia in specific terms in the 1860s," [70] Tkachev saw it as an insecure new social group created by the great reforms, yet left with "no other means of existence except intellectual labor." [71] Though economically and culturally dependent on the ruling classes, this growing category of intellectual workers was socially and psychologically closer to the proletariat. Rendered almost as insecure as the worker by his vulnerability to the market, the intellectual retained nonetheless the ability to identify his unhappiness with that of all society and to conceive of a full-blown revolutionary alternative. Tkachev believed that most intellectual workers would become supine servants of the state, willing to settle for "complete freedom in the sphere of his specialty, but nothing more." [72] But he also saw the possibility of a saving revolutionary remnant producing what he characterized in a letter to Engels of 1874 as a "socialist *intelligentskaia* revolutionary party." [73]

Tkachev sought to find the basis for such a party through close association with Blanqui from the time he went into exile in 1873 until he delivered the eulogy at Blanqui's burial in 1881.[74] Tkachev and Nechaev had little practical success, but affected a kind of *coup d'imagination* with their ascetic version of Blanqui's idea that an amoral elite must both make the revolution and rule after it. Violence was not just tolerated but exalted by making "the success of the revolution" the sole admissible passion. As one of Nechaev's followers put it: "Absolute honor does not exist; there is only party honor." [75] Even before any party had formed, the need had been defined for the kind of sacrificial party spirit that Lenin was later to call *partiinost'*.[76] But the new self-

conscious intellectuals needed to link their sense of dedication to the
social reality of backward peasants and workers. The force for this
union—such as it was—was Russian populism.

The Banners of the Seventies

Populism

Populism was never a fixed doctrine but rather a vague social ideal
common to many agrarian societies undergoing rapid but uneven modernization. The two major movements to call themselves populist in
the late nineteenth century occurred on the rural periphery of European
civilization: in Russia and America. Common to both (and to later
populist movements) was a thirst for social regeneration that idealized
the older agrarian-based human relationships yet ironically prepared
the way for the further consolidation of centralized economic and
political power.

Populism became a mode—and not just a mood—of thought when an
educated elite defended the ways of a backward region or economic
sector confronted by the advance of capitalism and a market economy.
It was cultivated by those whose education had alienated them from
native roots and values yet who sought symbolic and psychic compensation in the idea that "the people" would produce "some sort of integrated society" [77] that would avoid the depersonalized elitism of capitalism. Thus populism tended to revive romantic faith either in a
threatened culture (the earlier Russia Slavophiles) or region (the later
American populists).

As Russia moved towards massive Europeanization, its intellectual
elite suddenly discovered the *narod*, making the Russian peasant the
repository of all their hopes and personal needs for a more humane
social order.

Russian populism began with the compulsive ethnographic search
within the university subculture of the 1860s for an alternate way of
life among the Russian peasantry. At exactly the moment when students were leaving the universities for revolutionary activity in 1862–63,
young artists broke away from the established St. Petersburg conserva-
tories of painting and music to form the new more plebeian groups
known as the "wanderers" and "mighty handful" respectively. The best
products of this new orientation—the paintings of Repin and the music
of Mussorgsky—sought to depict the life and truth of the simple people; and the late sixties and the seventies were filled with a veritable
explosion of fact and fantasy about peasant life in Russia. Students of
Russian popular life like Afanas'ev and Khudiakov were active in the
revolutionary ferment. Radical students consistently rallied—even in
their most nihilistic period—to lecturers delving into ethnographic his-

tory of old Russia like Pavlov of the Sunday School movement, and Kostomarov, whose lecture in the spring of 1861 brought on a key student disorder. The seminal radical thinker in Kazan, Afanasy Shchapov, turned to social issues through his study of materials on the Old Believers and the Russian North which were transported from the Solovetsk Monastery in the White Sea to Kazan during the Crimean War. The first populist-like circle in Moscow (the *vertepniki* or den of thieves) took shape in the last months of the Crimean War under the leadership of a former Old Believer, who became a leading collector of old Russian songs as well as a propagandist for democratic and atheistic ideas.[78] The author of an unprecedented series of books on beggars, taverns, and holy fools in old Russia, Ivan Pryzhov, became an active member in Nechaev's five-man revolutionary cell.[79]

The isolation of student life and the abstraction of scientific study thus created among students a deep need for some psychic link with "the people"; and by the late sixties, the quest moved from ethnography to real life. Bakunin helped the move out to the masses with his renewed calls for active links with the insurrectionary impulse purportedly latent in the peasantry. But the dominant new trend of the late 1860s and the early 1870s rejected both Bakunin's romantic vision of gangs (*shaiki*) in the manner of Stenka Razin and Nechaev's network of ascetic revolutionary fives.

The new, nonviolent populism began with a second wave of student unrest in 1868–69 that led to the closing of the Medical-Surgical Academy in St. Petersburg in March 1869. A group of some fifteen students, most of whom were medical students like Mark Natanson, came together in a two-story wooden house in St. Petersburg to form a dedicated and disciplined commune. Nicholas Chaikovsky, from whom the circle took its name, referred to it as an order.

The Chaikovsky circle was collectively dedicated to opposing the elitism and violence of Nechaev. Yet the moralism of the group was so intense that it gave birth to a set of rituals that in their own way heightened revolutionary fanaticism. Meetings involved a strange mélange of therapy and strategy. A great premium was attached to "objective" analysis of both personal morality and social questions. The later, Leninist practice of obligatory group- and self-criticism may have had its roots in the *Chaikovtsy's* practice of "the criticism of each by all." They believed that "the objective analysis of the characteristics and peculiarities of a given individual at a general meeting of everyone" would provide "the exact method for the regulation of relations between individuals and society." [80] The influence of this circle radiated out to a new student generation through a series of manifestoes and a growing, nationwide web of Circles of Self-Education and Practical Activity.

Populism was an essentially Proudhonist-type movement that was antidoctrinaire and egalitarian with a passion for older communal institutions, decentralized federal structures, and mutual aid societies that dealt directly with pressing social needs and bypassed the political arena altogether. As with earlier utopian socialist movements in the West, the populist socialism of the Chaikovsky circle was weakened by the flight of Chaikovsky himself to the New World.[81] Even more than their Western counterparts, however, the populist pioneers in Russia derived profound personal satisfaction from their self-appointed roles as "critically thinking" agents of the historical process.

Seeking a link with "the people" the intellectual elite turned first to the urban workers, whose plight had been "discovered" through V. V. Bervi's *Position of the Working Class in Russia* in 1869.[82] Within the Chaikovsky circle, Prince Peter Kropotkin, newly returned from an ethnographic expedition to Siberia, professed to see in the new working class "the purest revolutionary element." [83] He proposed ending the "privileged labor" of intellectuals and managers by closing all institutions of higher learning and opening up "schools of trade mastery" for the direct benefit of the workers.[84] By 1873–74 the workers had become the focus of activity for the Chaikovsky circle and the main hope of Kropotkin for combatting the amoral statists (*gosudarstvenniki*) both within and without the revolutionary camp. The anarchist Kropotkin saw a new revolutionary type, "the people's agitator" (*narodny agitator*), emerging from the working class independent of both intelligentsia and "any leadership from émigré parties." [85] He distinguished between those who were only temporarily and insecurely employed in factories (*fabrichnye*) and those with permanent employment (*zavodskie*). The former, he insisted, were bound to be revolutionary; the latter, reformist.[86]

But the quest for the masses inevitably led back to the countryside, where more than four fifths of the Russian population still lived. In the "mad summer" of 1874 more than two thousand students left universities and cities to live among "the people." So intense was the intellectuals' desire to establish identity with the peasantry that Jewish students accepted baptism—not out of conversion to Christianity but out of a desire to share this part of the peasant experience. As so often in revolutionary history nature seemed to be imitating art. Some students went out "to the people" singing the chorus of rebellion from the insurrectionary final scene of Mussorgsky's *Boris Godunov,* which had its premier early in 1874. Some went to live among the Volga boatmen, as if responding to the dramatization of their plight in Repin's famous painting of 1870–73, "Haulers on the Volga" by learning "to hate with their hate." [87]

The repression of the movement to the people and new restrictions on the émigré student colony (particularly the large one in Zürich) brought back to St. Petersburg and Moscow an angry and disillusioned student population. At the same time, the revolutionaries' belief in their ability to outmaneuver tsarist authorities was fanned to new heights by the spectacular escape of Prince Peter Kropotkin from prison in the summer of 1875. A precision-drilled team of outside revolutionaries rescued this famous convert to revolution from the high nobility by a combination of such theatrical devices as signals by balloon and a gypsy violin, and by a message smuggled in a watch by a French-speaking female visitor.[88]

Kropotkin and others who followed him abroad immediately began sending back new revolutionary propaganda. Amidst gathering expectation, some four hundred young radicals persuaded a priest in the Kazan Cathedral in St. Petersburg to celebrate a liturgy in honor of Chernyshevsky on December 6, 1876; [89] then met outside for the first open revolutionary demonstration in Russian history. Participants included not only the aging veteran Zaichnevsky of Young Russia, but the youthful George Plekhanov, who in the following decade was to found the first Russian Marxist organization.

Unfurling a red banner and proclaiming, "Long live the Socialist Revolution, long live Land and Liberty," the demonstrators gave the loose "revolutionary populist group of the north" a new identity as Land and Liberty (*Zemlia i Volia*). By memorializing Chernyshevsky and revising the name of their original revolutionary organization of the 1860s, the Russians dramatized once more their growing sense of tradition. They emulated the established practice of heroic courtroom martyrology throughout the long series of political trials beginning with the "trial of fifty" demonstrators in January 1877, and reaching a climax in the "trial of the 193," which ended just a year later. The latter, the largest political trial ever held in tsarist Russia, was a tumultuous affair extensively covered by the press.[90]

Meanwhile, Russia went to war against Turkey; and militarization at home helped move the Russian tradition onto a path previously taken by only a few: terrorism.

Terrorism

The terrorist turn was inspired by the increased activity of extremist groups in south Russia, particularly in Odessa and Kiev. Odessa was under military administration, and revolutionary leaders there drew on sectarian religious ideas as well as on a quasi-criminal subculture to spawn new forms of extremism. Odessa produced "the first revolutionary organization made up of wage earners," the South Russian Union of Workers in 1874. [91] Kiev simultaneously generated a series of insurrectionary movements (*buntari*) including the largest peasant-based revolutionary organization of the mid-1870s, the Fighting Brotherhood.

Right-Left confusion was evidenced again by the movement that developed in Chigirin near Kiev involving nearly one thousand peasants in a fantastic secret society allegedly led by the tsar himself to liberate the peasants from the nobility. The purported new government was to be a Council (*Soviet*) of Commissars, and the new militia (*druzhiniki*) was to destroy the nobility with pikes and axes.[92]

At the same time Land and Liberty was moving towards greater violence. The controlling "basic circle" created a group pledged solely to "disorganization." This included all violent activities: the forced freeing of prisoners, the killing of police spies, and the "systematic destruction of the most harmful or prominent members of the government." [93]

Terrorism began to dominate the Russian revolutionary movement in the fall of 1877 largely because of two Ukrainian members of Land and Liberty: the dashing and charismatic Valerian Osinsky ("the warrior") and the ascetic wealthy patron of the movement, Dmitry Lizogub ("the saint").[94] They suggested that a direct, disciplined political struggle against the autocracy should take priority over everything else in Russia; and that the sterile debate between propagandists (Lavrovists) and insurrectionists (Bakuninists) should be put aside in favor of a common political campaign. There was an unacknowledged disparity between violent means and moderate ends. Osinsky argued that "urban terrorists" should "terrorize the government" into providing the same constitutional liberties that he had previously sought as a liberal in Rostov on the Don.[95]

Russia was electrified by the first such effort: the nearly successful attempt on January 24, 1878, to murder the St. Petersburg Chief of Police, Fedor Trepov, by a former friend of Nechaev, populist propagandist in Kiev, and typesetter for Land and Liberty, Vera Zasulich. A skillful defense and fascinated newspaper coverage turned her trial into a political investigation of the intended victim rather than a criminal trial of the would-be assassin. Despite her obvious guilt, she was acquitted in March, borne out of the courtroom on the shoulders of 1,500 to 2,000 rejoicing students,[96] and spirited abroad to become a heroine of the revolutionary emigration.

Osinsky and his Kievan colleagues echoed Zasulich with several assassination attempts accompanied by public declarations of the reasons. Beginning in March 1878, they used a red oval seal containing an axe, knife, and pistol and the label "executive committee of the Russian social-revolutionary party." [97] There was as yet no such organization; but the term "executive committee" became central to the People's Will organization that formed the following year.

In May 1878 one of Osinsky's protégés killed the police chief of Kiev; in August an affiliated group attempted to assassinate the tsar in Nikolaev; and in April 1879 a terrorist near the Winter Palace fired five shots at the tsar announcing at his trial, "We revolutionary socialists have declared war on the government." [98] Osinsky and his comrades were executed shortly thereafter; and the imperial government declared a state of siege, dividing Russia into six military districts. In response, the People's Will organization was formally constituted in the summer of 1879 to fight autocracy "with the means of William Tell," using a highly centralized para-military organization that soon involved between four and five thousand.[99]

The structure represented an almost complete return to the Buonarrotian tradition of secret, hierarchical conspiracy. Each member pledged to the high cause "every possession. . . . all personal sympathies and antipathies, all strength and life itself." Each member accepted "absolute subordination to the majority" at every level of the organization and the absolute authority of the higher over the lower level. Beyond two lower levels of "agents" stood the third, inner group, the famed "executive committee" which used the designation "agent third degree" in dealing with all others in the organization.[100] They sought both to disguise the identity of the controlling group and to inspire the vague fear that other inner circles might exist even beyond their own.

The People's Will generally called itself an "organization" till early 1880, and thereafter a "party." [101] From the beginning it rejected the possibility of functioning as an open organization, and insisted that members could be brought in only by coöptation after a period of apprenticeship as a "candidate." Local "struggle groups" were to be under total discipline of the central organization. In the fall of 1879, nationwide local organizations began to proliferate. A dramatic explosion on November 19 derailed a train that was supposed to contain the tsar; and on February 5 a massive explosion in the Winter Palace killed eleven and injured fifty-six. "Political crime," wrote a despairing reactionary journalist, "has become a veritable national tradition." [102]

The People's Will came to conceive of itself as a kind of alternative government with its own central "administration" (five members and three "candidate" members) within the executive committee. The organization derived its authority from two founding "congresses" at Lipetsk and Voronezh in the summer of 1879; developed local organizations throughout Russia (often existing as separate student, peasant, and worker groups); provided for a kind of legislature (*obshchee sobranie*); mobilized "struggle groups" as a kind of Cossack striking force (even referred to by the Cossack term *atamanstvo*); and described its program of carefully targeted terror as the "ministry of justice of the revolution." [103] They revived the old term "partisan war" to describe their campaign against the tsarist government; [104] but the striking new features of their campaign were (1) their massive (and surprisingly successful) efforts to win over large numbers of active sympathizers and passive supporters within the ruling class, and (2) their almost mystical dedication to their chosen instrument of "people's justice": the bomb.

They gained a protective outer circle of supporters by their selfless dedication and asceticism, which attracted liberal and radical intellectuals to write under pseudonyms for their journal. They also won over protectors and "concealers" (*ukrivateli*) within the official government establishment, which enabled their nationwide network of communication to function.[105]

Dedication to the bomb was institutionalized in the summer of 1879 with the organization of three "dynamite centers" in St. Petersburg to assemble bombs for the final struggle with the autocracy.[106] These centers began to acquire some of the ritual centrality to the life of the new organization that had hitherto been provided by the printing press. While presses remained important to the People's Will, its distinctive new institution was the terrorist cell located near a railroad depot, police station, or official residence. Women were included, giving the cell the external appearance of a peaceful family group. But in some windowless inner room or deep-burrowed tunnel the real business of the "struggle group" took place: the assembly and deployment of bombs.

Andrei Zheliabov, who became the leader of the final terrorist campaign that led to the assassination of Alexander II on March 1, 1881, had been fascinated as a youth by the use of dynamite to kill fish in the Black Sea. He remained in many ways more fascinated with Nobel's explosive toy than with the tactic of terrorism. Born to a peasant family, he had refused to join Osinsky's first wave of southern terrorism in 1877–78 because of its aristocratic leadership. Thus, when he entered the lists in 1879, his peasant background gave a freshly authentic populist quality to terrorism.

Nicholas Kibalchich, the ingenious designer of the nitroglycerin assassination packages of the People's Will, believed that he was provisioning a new type of revolutionary movement that would come from within the new industrial cities and bring about the "complete merging of the political and social revolution." [107] If there was a totalism about his conception, there was also a professionalism about his craftsmanship. His bombs were carefully designed to have a destructive radius of only about a meter, requiring closeness to the victim and minimizing any possibility of escape for the assassin.

When Alexander II and his assassin both lay fatally wounded by the second bomb thrown at his carriage in St. Petersburg on March 1, the third reserve "thrower" rushed forward to aid the fallen monarch with his bomb under his arm as if offering a pillow to the dying tsar.[108] Zheliabov likened the terrorists' spirit to that of the nonviolent early Christians. Their moral fervor inspired the novelist Tolstoy and the theologian Solovev to send impassioned appeals for clemency for the assassins. The letter of explanation by the Executive Committee of the People's Will was addressed to the new tsar nine days after the murder of his father and stressed their agonizing reluctance to use violence and their hope for a peaceful transfer of power to the people.

Kibalchich confirmed the picture of the noble and reluctant terrorist —going to the gallows unafraid, dedicating even his last hours before execution to the service of humanity by feverishly trying to design a rocket-propelled flying machine.[109] The ascetic terrorist sacrificing himself for a new era of freedom and science remained a model for Russian students even amidst unprecedented repression in the 1880s.

Almost alone among Russian revolutionaries, George Plekhanov at a meeting of émigrés in Paris denounced the People's Will for having succeeded only in putting an "Alexander with three stripes in the place of an Alexander with two." [110] Plekhanov's small splinter group, Black Redistribution, had split off from the People's Will at its founding congress in June 1879, insisting on stressing economic over political goals. He opposed the "firework displays" of political assassination just as he had previously rejected the "childish hopes" of the Bakuninists for popular insurrection.[111] He was to establish the rival Marxist tradition, slowly and painfully, in the emigration during the 1880s and 1890s; but even he recognized that "to speak up then against the terrorist struggle of the intelligentsia was completely useless: the intelligentsia believed in terror as in God." [112]

What was the origin of such a belief? Whence came the "God" to whom Russian Marxists themselves would eventually pay homage?

Contrary to popular belief, terrorism did not come from the Reign of Terror in the original French Revolution. To be sure, the Committee of Public Safety formally endorsed "terror as the order of the day," and tolerated a Draconian program particularly in endangered border areas such as Alsace under Saint-Just and Eulogius Schneider. But the committee viewed these as extraordinary, wartime measures and anathematized *terrorisme* just as Babeuf later denounced *furorisme*.[113]

Marx briefly embraced "revolutionary terrorism" as a slogan and an expedient after the seeming defeat of other revolutionary methods late in 1848. He saw it developing in response to "the cannibalism of the counter-revolution," and revealed the dark secret of its appeal. Terrorism was the ultimate method of revolutionary *simplification*, the antidote to both complexity and confusion, the "only one means"

> *to shorten, to simplify, to concentrate* the murderous death throes of the old society and the bloody birth pangs of the new. . . .[114]

It was only in Russia of the late 1860s and the 1870s that this violent, heroic form of simplification became the chosen label and preferred course of revolutionary action against established authority. The Russians added to the basic ingredients of political terrorism ("a source of violence, a victim and a target" [115]) the concept of terrorism as a "ministry of justice of the revolution." [116] In the most important single treatise on the subject, Nicholas Morozov of the People's Will Executive Committee described terrorism as "the most just of all forms of revolution," [117] since it struck only those who were guilty of crimes against the people. Active terrorism, moreover, provided a kind of baptism in blood for the bloodless intellectual. The children of privilege were rendered fit for the people's "struggle of equals" by accepting both the risk of death and the obligation of murder. A commitment to violence, in Morozov's view, set the revolutionary off from the talkative liberals who were "purely platonic" in both "love of the revolution and hatred of the government." [118] The terroristic act provided the "moment of fever break" (*tochka pereloma*) [119] for the apprentice revolutionary seeking to overcome the inertia of the wellborn and the inhibitions of the intellectual.

The Lasting Legacy

Blanquism: The Legacy Within

The terrorist tradition that the turbulent age of Alexander II left behind to Russia was both anarchistic and authoritarian. It was anarchistic in its determination to "disorganize" and destroy all existing state power. It was authoritarian in its reliance on a disciplined, hierarchical organization to accomplish the task. Thus, the People's Will left a deeply divided legacy. Although the story is complex, authoritarian strains generally predominated within Russia, anarchist ones in the echoes abroad.

It is deeply ironic that Blanquist ideas should have dominated the internal Russian legacy of the People's Will. For Blanqui himself remained almost unknown inside Russia throughout his long life; and the Russian advocates of Blanquism, Nechaev and Tkachev, died not long after Blanqui himself in the early 1880s. But precisely because Blanquist ideas became important only during the dramatic, last years of the People's Will, they had the appeal of novelty and the aura of martyrdom. The combination created a fatal fascination. During the repressive reign of Alexander III (1881–94) an appealing glow hung over this dictatorial tradition far more than over the more democratic ideals of populism. The clearest sign of continued veneration for the terrorists' "propaganda of the deed" lay in the disparaging name that radicals of all varieties attached to this period: the age of small deeds (*malye dela*). The longing for great deeds—suicidal assassinations, dramatic escapes, heroic coups—exercised disproportionate appeal within the new student generation of the 1880s to which both Lenin and his elder brother belonged. Thus Blanquism—like Hegelianism and Saint-Simonianism, the original revolutionary ideologies of the European intellectual elite during the period of small deeds that followed the revolutions of 1830—appealed to a rising generation of intellectuals only after the death of the master. And once again in a place unforeseen by the man who gave his name to the ism.

The Blanquist turn within the People's Will organization can be identified with the journey abroad late in 1880 of Morozov and of an even more interesting theorist of terrorism, a wealthy Bessarabian landowner and intellectual, Gerasim Romanenko. The two returned to Russia in 1881 to play an important role in the Executive Committee of the People's Will during its final year of full operation. Whether or not they had been sent abroad as foreign representatives of the People's Will [120] or merely rose to prominence during the period when the organization was preoccupied with the assassination of the tsar, these two men clearly played a key role in the final turn to Blanquist ideas within the People's Will.

Morozov had been in touch with Tkachev and other Blanquists in Paris in 1880; and Tkachev had written Morozov on November 1, 1880, that "your program perfectly coincides with mine." [121] Romanenko, who stayed on in the West a half year longer than Morozov, had links with both Tkachev and his Polish patron Turski.[122] In Geneva he published a remarkable call for a "terroristic revolution" as the most efficient, just, and bloodless form of social warfare under modern conditions. It appeared under the title *Terrorism and Routine*.[123] Romanenko argued that only intellectuals could lead a modern revolution. They were "the most conscious revolutionary group" that alone could break the fatal hold of "routine" and of "philistinism" in everyday life. The "conscious" elite was, moreover, needed to provide leadership for the "spontaneous" and undisciplined masses.

The basic Leninist juxtaposition of a "conscious" vanguard with the "spontaneous" masses along with Lenin's exalted idea of a "party" as an "organ of consciousness" thus have clear origins in the final Blanquist teachings of the People's Will.[124]

From his return to Russia in the summer of 1881 until his arrest in Moscow on November 8, Romanenko was active on the Executive Committee of the People's Will. During this period of extreme government repression, the "party"—as the People's Will now called itself—replied by increasing its Blanquist emphasis on violence. A letter of the Executive Committee to comrades abroad spoke of an "exclusively military uprising with the aim of a seizure." [125]

Blanquists perpetually fantasized that the capture of power was within their grasp, and always insisted on power as the prerequisite for social revolution. So it is not entirely surprising that Romanenko in prison should have attempted to persuade the tsar himself to launch the social revolution. He wrote a remarkable letter to Alexander III, using both sides of forty-six pages, seeking to convert him to socialism. It was delivered by the minister of the interior to the tsar at his Gatchina estate [126] just when other messengers were telling him that a fresh infusion of youth was reviving the decimated People's Will.

On the first anniversary of the assassination, a "central university circle" in St. Petersburg had circulated a hectographed periodical, *Struggle*, calling for "the youthful intelligentsia" (*intelligentnoe iunoshestvo*) to pick up the revolutionary torch.[127] This group was in touch with both the remnant of the Executive Committee and some peripheral survivors of the People's Will; [128] it, too, was crushed not long after the arrest in February 1883 of the last survivor of the original Executive Committee of the People's Will, Vera Figner. She hurled out a final gesture of Blanquist bravado that became part of the folklore of the new student generation. She insisted that as a sign of good faith to the young the government should release not an ordinary terrorist but the aged Nechaev himself.[129]

One of the most dynamic of the new radical students, Lev Shternberg, wrote a new defense of terrorism in 1884, after being sent away from St. Petersburg to Odessa. He insisted that terrorism was the least bloody form of revolution in a country so dependent on an intelligentsia for leadership.[130] He attempted to create a new Executive Committee in Ekaterinoslav in September 1885. After his arrest the following year, he became famous among political prisoners for his constantly repeated slogan—impeccable in its superficial piety, yet unmistakable in its revolutionary allusion to the People's Will: "The God of Israel still Lives!" [131]

The revolutionary God did indeed refuse to die. Late in 1883, a young poet-philosopher in St. Petersburg University organized a Union of Youth that attempted (1) to establish links with the scattered workers' sections of the People's Will, with Polish revolutionaries, and with émigré Russians in Paris; and (2) to unify them all through an underground journal, *The Revolutionary*, and through a new tactic of decentralized "factory-agrarian terror" designed to rebuild organizational strength at the local level.[132] After arrests destroyed the Union in St.

Petersburg late in 1884, survivors in Kazan attempted to provide fall-back support and continuity.[133] It was from this Volga region in the deep interior of Russia that new strength soon appeared in the form of Alexander Ulyanov, Lenin's older brother.

Ulyanov, a brilliant and idealistic young student from Simbirsk, helped form in 1886 in St. Petersburg a new Terrorist Fraction of the People's Will, which echoed all the classic features of Russian revolutionary movements led by young intellectuals—and amplified the new dedication to elite terrorism.

The group first took shape as a central union of regional student groups (*soiuz zemliachestv*) at St. Petersburg University. Sasha Ulyanov, a young student of the natural sciences, served in all thirteen of the groups that came from the Volga region.[134] He was also secretary of a scientific-literary society and an eager student with a characteristically evangelical dedication to the natural sciences, arising early in the morning during the summer months to get the maximum benefit for his experiments of the long days of natural sunlight.[135]

All the understanding this young provincial scientist had of broad social and political questions was derived from the traditions of the radical intelligentsia. His entire extracurricular life in St. Petersburg was devoted to the ritual veneration of people or events hallowed in the radical pantheon. The closing in 1884 of the revolutionaries' favorite legal journal, *The Annals of the Fatherland*, rendered young Ulyanov almost incapable of taking his first examinations at the university. He attended the lectures of Vasily Semevsky on the plight of the Russian peasantry as a ritual demonstration of solidarity with a teacher who had been denied a doctorate for being oversympathetic to peasants. Ulyanov helped organize the first public demonstration in St. Petersburg since 1876: a peaceful procession of four hundred students to the graveyard of revolutionaries, the Volkovo cemetery, on February 19, 1886, the twenty-fifth anniversary of the emancipation of the serfs. In November, he was thrilled to be part of the student delegation that participated in a daylong, one thousand-man demonstration at Volkovo to commemorate the twenty-fifth anniversary of the death of Chernyshevsky's closest journalistic collaborator, Nicholas Dobroliubov.[136]

Thus, young Ulyanov was a pure acolyte of the radical, scientistic intelligentsia when he turned to help organize the Terrorist Fraction of the People's Will, the first political group anywhere to call its members "terrorists." They argued that constitutional rights were indispensable in forming a workers' party in Russia; and that a renewed terrorist threat was the surest way of impelling the government to make concessions. The first assault of the People's Will had induced vacillation; a second effort would induce concessions. A renewed and "decisive terrorist struggle" was further needed because of the special obligation in Russia to "wage war on two fronts with capitalism and with the government" and to "lift up the militant temper of advanced society."[137]

In one of the debates leading up to the decision of Ulyanov's Terrorist Fraction to attempt an assassination of Alexander III on the sixth anniversary of his father's death, a dissenter urged that they pay attention to changing reality: "Statistics are more frightening than bombs." [138] But for all his scientism, Ulyanov was committed to bombs. Indeed, Ulyanov explained to the group the functioning of the missile projectile they planned to use. *Propagande par le fait* meant for him the propagation not of scientific facts, but of terrorist feats. His statement of the fraction's program was read by the intended victim, Alexander III, while Ulyanov was in prison awaiting execution. The tsar covered the manuscript with apoplectic notations, but consoled himself at the end with Ulyanov's remark that "under the existing political regime in Russia almost any part of this activity is impossible." "This is comforting," the tsar wrote.[139]

But the tsar did not find much comfort; the omnipresent uniforms guarding him henceforth continued to be challenged—as in primitive societies—by the power of the mask.[140] The mask gave an ordinary man a new identity; an anonymity that bred fear and uncertainty; a public "image" that was grotesque, yet awesome and bigger than life. Unlike the uniforms of power that—however oppressive—at least defined clear roles, the new revolutionary mask destroyed all links with the familiar and the predictable, all loyalty and accountability to normal human society.

The mask was part of the equipment of the professional revolutionary in Russia already in the 1860s. Hell had preached the need to disfigure one's own face before assassinating an opponent. The Den of Thieves and Bear Academy had cultivated a wild appearance to enhance their shock effect on society. One of the eerie echoes of the People's Will, a terrorist group of 1886 called "the lancers," masked even their bombs by disguising them as dictionaries.[141]

When young Ulyanov appeared with his Terrorist Fraction, the men in uniform assumed that the regional student organization to which he had previously belonged, the men of the Kuban and Don, masked a revolutionary group dedicated to peasant rebellion and frontier violence.[142] After Ulyanov and his fraction were crushed in 1887, a mask could not be worn in the great urban centers of St. Petersburg and Moscow, where police controls made terrorist organization almost impossible. But the mask spread back to the expanses of the Russian South whence it had first come a decade earlier—from Lizogub and Osinsky in the Ukraine and Zheliabov on the shores of the Black Sea. Beyond the efforts of Romanenko and Shternberg and others to perpetuate in the South the terrorist tradition of the People's Will, there emerged new projects and groups of which the most impressive was the Conspirators. Its program echoed Ulyanov's Terrorist Fraction, but was dedicated more to organizing urban terrorist cells than to performing terrorist deeds.

The organization was centered in Kiev with branches in Kharkov and Kazan from 1884 to 1892, when its headquarters moved to Moscow. Though it never mounted the active campaign it was ostensibly preparing, its organization served as a training ground in sustaining the conspiratorial sense of solidarity that was becoming institutionalized in the Russian tradition. At the time of its demise in 1903, this group fed members into Lenin's *Iskra* as well as into other revolutionary organizations in the South.[143] By then, the mask had returned north to reestablish links with the radical student subculture in St. Petersburg through Ulyanov's younger brother, Lenin. His Bolshevik party was deeply rooted in distinctively Russian revolutionary tradition; and represented, as we shall see, not so much a "party of a new type" as the final formation of the party his brother had dreamed of. Behind the new mask of Marxism was the old figure of a revolutionary intellectual establishing political authority through the incantation of scientism and populism and the tactics of terrorism.

Anarchism: The Echo Beyond

The ideal of a constitutional political revolution had spread at the beginning of the nineteenth century from the center (France) to the southern and eastern periphery of Europe. In the late nineteenth century—as if in revenge—the ideal of a total social revolution beyond politics spread back from the periphery into the center. Masonic officers had borne the revolutionary message out to Russia at the beginning of the century, speaking aristocratic French and calling themselves liberal or republican. Impersonal wire services now carried the new message back to the center at the end of the century in the earthy vernacular of mass journalism under headlines about TERRORISM, NIHILISM—and above all, ANARCHISM.

The term *anarchism* became popular in the West at precisely the time when Russian revolutionaries were tending to abandon it in favor of *terrorism*. The most widely read émigré writers about the Russian revolutionary movement (Kropotkin and Kravchinsky) had left Russia when terroristic tactics were still identified with the "disorganization" of state power and before the People's Will formed as a kind of revolutionary counter-state. They thus identified terroristic tactics with anarchistic ideals; and in the West this identification was to remain dominant. Western press coverage within Russia also tended to accept at face value the heroic anti-authoritarian rhetoric of the revolutionaries. Thus anarchism tinged with idealism and sanctified by martyrdom became a new verbal talisman for many otherwise dispirited revolutionaries.

Many in the West were infected by "moral contagion from acts which strike the imagination."[144] Soon after the first shots were fired at Alexander II in May 1878, five attempts—an unprecedented number—were made to assassinate crowned heads of Europe. The leading new convert to anarchist-terrorism in the West, Johann Most, praised the "Russian method" and hailed the slaying of Alexander II with an editorial in London.[145] Two years later he supported from afar a conspiracy to throw a bomb at the kaiser; and he was arrested in England for supporting the assassinations by Irish revolutionaries of the British chief secretary and the undersecretary for Ireland. The mania was spreading, and the horror of anarchism expressed in the press made it a label of fascination and even of pride to some intellectuals in hitherto nonrevolutionary countries like Holland, England, and the United States. Johann Most took the label with him to America in 1883. The anarchist ideal was propagated in both England and America by an increasing number of exiles from the Romanov Empire: Russians and Ukrainians fleeing political persecution in the 1870s followed by Jewish exiles fleeing religious persecution in the 1880s.

The term anarchist struck special fear in the hearts of those who were building the new industrial states of the late nineteenth century, for anarchists identified the centralized state itself as the enemy. For the same reason anarchism provided a banner of new hope to a generation in France that had become disillusioned with politics: first by a decade of republican repression after the Commune and then by the decision of the rival Blanquists to support the right-wing challenge to the Third Republic of General Boulanger "in the hope that it was the prelude to a great revolutionary crisis." [146] Thus began the fateful tendency of putschist revolutionaries on the Left to see in a right-wing challenge to liberal republican authority a tactically useful stage in preparing for their own social revolution. This thinking proved successful for Lenin, who was to view Kornilov's rising against Kerensky's government in September 1917 as a "gun rest" for his own revolutionary rifle. The same thinking by German Communists in 1933 was to have disastrous consequences, when Hitler was seen as a transitory Kornilov tactically useful for destroying the Weimar Republic.

The richly reported struggle of Russian revolutionaries was increasingly identified in the West with the label anarchist. The activist intellectuals of the 1870s called themselves the "true," the "new," and the "young" intelligentsia,[147] and brought with them in their westward diaspora the image of pure truth opposing unbridled power. Anarchistic opposition to all power was often imparted in the West by the remarkable women who played a leading role in the Russian movement—and often enjoyed second careers as wives or leaders of Western radical movements.[148] But the distinctively anarchist ideal was most effectively popularized in (and beyond) western Europe by three prominent members of the Russian higher nobility: Michael Bakunin, Prince Peter Kropotkin, and Count Leo Tolstoy.

Bakunin glamorized violent insurrection with the anarchist label, particularly in Latin Europe, during the late 1860s and the early 1870s. Kropotkin extended and intensified Bakunin's anarchist vision while toning down his incendiary excesses after arriving in France in 1876, the year of Bakunin's death. Even more than Bakunin, Kropotkin exerted his greatest influence in western Europe rather than in his native land.[149]

The third great aristocratic anarchist, Tolstoy, provided massive authority for the new ideal by renouncing his brilliant literary career in the late 1870s and retreating to the barefoot simplicities of his country estate—rejecting the authority of church, state, and any science or art devoid of moral purpose. Tolstoy became a pole of magnetic attraction for the diverse discontents of the late imperial period: the "moral tsar" of Russia and anarchist counselor to the world until his death in 1910. Prose novels had been vehicles for social revolutionary ideals since the time of George Sand and Cabet's *Voyage to Icaria*. Now the latest social revolutionary ideal, anarchism, claimed the allegiance of the world's greatest living novelist for the final thirty-five years of his life.

In glorifying an ancient label of abuse, the Russians followed in the footsteps of Proudhon along a trail already blazed in Latin Europe by followers of both Proudhon and Bakunin. Anarchism had previously been rejected by revolutionaries, who viewed the label as a conservative defamation if not a provocation.[150] Babeuf noted the "scandalous affection" of established authority for the threats of anarchists.[151] Anarchism became a positive revolutionary label with a continuous history only in 1840, when Proudhon invoked the term as a badge of pride and a verbal shock weapon.[152]

Left Hegelianism had given anarchism a new appeal through Bakunin and others in the 1840s. Having previously accepted Hegel's exaggerated expectation that politics would transform the human condition, Hegelians now exaggerated the benefits to be accrued from dispensing with politics altogether. This dialectical leap of a truly Hegelian kind was particularly congenial to Slavs dwelling under autocracy; and the anarchist ideal as the "antithesis" of autocracy proved equally appealing in conservative, Catholic Spain and Italy.

Anarchism became a major force through the brotherhoods and alliances that Bakunin organized within and beyond the First International, constituting a kind of Left opposition to authoritarianism and Marxism and convening a host of international meetings in sites ranging from Geneva (1873) to Paris (1889) during the interregnum between the collapse of the First International and the birth of the Second.[153]

The Spanish and Italian movements were at the forefront. The Italian Federation of the First International survived the international parent organization and became the largest and most militant anarchist organization of the 1870s and the 1880s. It attracted more than 30,000 members by the mid-seventies to ten regional federations, extending throughout Italy into Sardinia.[154]

Though he shared the stage with Bakunin and Tolstoy in spreading the anarchist ideal, Peter Kropotkin was by far its most influential proponent among western revolutionaries. Beginning his long stay in western Europe in 1876, he filled the void left by the demise of the distinctively Bakuninist International the following year. He dominated the last three annual anarchist congresses held in the Jura (1878, 1879, 1880). He began to attract a new international following for his teaching that "insurrectionary deeds . . . the violent expropriation of property and the disorganization of the state" could progressively destroy the national state and establish federated communal organizations throughout Europe. He left the term populism behind in Russia and rejected Bakunin's term collectivism for anarchist-communist or simply anarchist.[155] His knowledge of European languages and his experience with both scientific expeditions and revolutionary adventures within Russia enabled him to speak with authority in the West. He channeled his major energies into the international anarchist movement rather than the Russian revolutionary cause. His steady stream of publications attracted a growing following, and his arrest in 1882 gave him the mantle of martyrdom.

The philosophical perspective of Kropotkin's anarchism fell somewhere in between the violent atheism of Bakunin and the nonviolent religiosity of Tolstoy.[156] Kropotkin's Swiss journal, *Le Révolté,* proclaimed in 1879 "permanent revolt by word of mouth, in writing, by the dagger, the rifle, dynamite." [157] Yet he subsequently also said: "A structure based on centuries of history cannot be destroyed with a few kilos of explosives." [158] His emphasis on mutual aid and small-scale cooperatives suggested a peaceful, Proudhonist return to a manageable human scale and to distributive justice more than a violent, romantic war against state authority.[159]

Kropotkin's vision dominated the anarchist movement from the time the anarchist congress convened its forty-five delegates in London on Bastille Day in 1881. No genuinely international congress of anarchists was to meet again until a week-long gathering of eighty delegates in Amsterdam in the summer of 1907. Throughout the intervening period, however, the specter of a Black International haunted Europe. Kropotkin's prolific writings lent respectability to the proposition that "outside of anarchy there is no such thing as revolution." [160] Agreeing with Tolstoy that "the only revolution is the one that never stops," he saw man's struggle for freedom as the rational, progressive liberation from all restrictive authority.

Anarchists pressed this uncompromising antipolitical faith with far greater success in the 1890s than has generally been remembered. They gained some measure of allegiance from more than one hundred thousand Frenchmen,[161] most of whom followed the peaceful ideal of Kropotkin rather than the call of "Dame Dynamite." Anarchists dominated in many ways the early congresses of the Second International until they were expelled at the insistence of the statist German Social Democrats at the London Congress in 1896. Anarchists opposed not only the manifestly political and increasingly bureaucratic Social Democrats; they also began to challenge the more closely related syndicalists for daring to create political structures of their own.[162]

At Amsterdam in 1907, they demonstrated that even the limited solidarity of a congress could not be sustained. Anarchism fragmented anew, and prior to World War I worked more as a catalyst within other revolutionary movements than as a unitary force. As a delegate to one of their innumerable and disputatious gatherings put it: "We are united because we are divided." [163]

Yet anarchism did produce a unitary, transnational impact that makes it important for the history of the revolutionary tradition. For it became a scare word of unprecedented power in the Western world and it kept alive a quasi-religious, totalistic belief in revolution during an era of positivism, skepticism, and evolutionary progressivism. Anarchism as a label became a focus for the suppressed fears of the era; and nowhere more than in America. The arrest in 1920 of two poor Italian anarchists, Sacco and Vanzetti, and the long agony leading to their execution in the electric chair in 1927 ritualized the rejection of the revolutionary ideals that had arisen in America at the beginning of the twentieth century. "Anarchy" and "anarchism," Katherine Anne Porter was to reminisce years later, inspired "terror, anger and hatred," [164] which enabled a counter-revolutionary chorus to drown out the "duet of two great voices telling a tragic story": [165] Kropotkin and Emma Goldman.

A kind of anarchist revolution did occur in the New World, in the very year when Sacco and Vanzetti were arrested in Massachusetts. The location was the most implausible outpost of human habitation, the Patagonian Peninsula, where Latin America narrows into an arrow pointing towards Antarctica. There, in 1920, Antonio Soto, an émigré Spanish classmate at the Military Academy in Toledo of the future Fascist dictator of Spain, Francisco Franco, led oppressed Chilean and Argentine peons in a brief and tragic revolution. Soto had been impelled to flee military service by a reading of Tolstoy and had worked as a stagehand in an Argentine theater before moving south to lead his short-lived revolution in the name of Proudhon, Bakunin, and Kropotkin. His red and black flag was burned, some fifteen hundred people (mostly poor sheep farmers) shot, and the polyglot anarchist uprising suppressed by the Argentine army.[166]

The Russian dream faded out on this remote frontier of European civilization at almost exactly the time in 1920 it effectively died in Russia itself. When the new Soviet government was finally to defeat the White opposition in the Russian Civil War, it would turn for a "major surgical operation" on the substantial and varied anarchist forces that had hitherto fought with it.[167] The great Ukrainian anarchist leader Nestor Makhno would flee abroad; and the man who had inspired him, the aged Peter Kropotkin, would die early in 1921 in Moscow deeply disillusioned with the new Soviet dictatorship for having reestablished the "Jacobin endeavor of Babeuf." [168] With the leading anarchists dead or gone, the anarchist spirit as well was to be crushed the following month, when the anti-authoritarian revolt of the Kronstadt sailors was cruelly repressed and its leaders shot by Soviet authorities.

CHAPTER 15

Revolutionary Syndicalism

THE LATIN and English-speaking worlds also saw an upswing in violent revolutionary activity during the later nineteenth and early twentieth centuries. They produced no political mechanism so impressive as the German Social Democratic party, no revolutionary intellectuals so intense as the Russians. Yet out of increased working-class violence they produced a new tradition that can be described as revolutionary syndicalism: a linking of trade union organization (*syndicats*) with mass action aimed at the creation of a new social order.

Revolutionary syndicalism followed Proudhon and Bakunin in rejecting the political arena and all forms of centralized power. In France the movement was strongest, and the line of descent from Proudhon the most direct. But revolutionary syndicalists emphasized violence more than Proudhon had—and in a manner different from Bakunin's concept of a primitive military insurrection. They were, of course, forced to work against the tightened police controls and repressive regulations instituted in the wake of the Paris Commune, and they turned to the potential of factory-based organizations for waging a new type of war from below—and from within—the new urbanized, industrial state.

It seems ironic that labor violence and revolutionary syndicalism flourished within precisely those societies where private property, parliamentary rule, and Victorian propriety seemed most securely established: republican France, newly independent Italy, and (to a lesser extent) the low countries, England, and the United States. The syndicalist tradition was least important within the conservative monarchies of Austria, Russia, and Prussia.

Revolutionary syndicalism arose in the relatively liberal nations partly because of their tolerance of new forms of working-class association. To some extent the workers simply rejected the values and institutions of the bourgeoisie in the lands where the middle class had gained the greatest power. But revolutionary syndicalism also expressed a deeper malaise about liberal values—and perhaps even about Western political culture generally: the desire to assert oneself violently within—if not against—the new industrial ethos and its "progressive" pretensions. The violent impulse was expressed in the new gunboat imperialism abroad, and in the agitation of anarchists, separatists, suffragettes, at home in Europe; it contributed to "the strange death of liberal England" —and perhaps of the Western "liberal" consensus more generally.[1] Restless ennui led much of the European intellectual *avant-garde* to acquire a certain taste for violence during the long, lingering autumn of relative peace and progress prior to 1914. Edwardian excess challenged Victorian values at the beginning of the new century; and a large number of leading intellectuals actually welcomed war when it finally came in 1914.[2]

Working-class violence thus emerged as only a part of the general problem of violence in the industrialized Western nations. During the 1871–1914 period the modern European state achieved an almost absolute monopoly on the exercise of violence within its own borders. Such a concentration of power was always implicit in the concept of a secular state that was totally sovereign and territorially defined. Liberal industrial states felt a special moral tension between their monopoly of physical power and their stated pluralism of values and institutions. The tension, like the power, was new; political leaders tended simply to project both the power and the problem out into the world rather than to deal with it at home. There was, thus, a psychological need for the "new imperialism," whatever its economic and ideological motivations. But imperialism served only to channel—and never to harness—the new forms of violence available to the state. It was a dangerous game, for the imperatives were territorial, not categorical. The players soon ran out of space that could be easily taken away from inhabitants and divided among conquerors. The contest returned in 1914 to the disputed no man's lands between the European powers themselves—the Balkans, the Baltic marches, the Franco-German border. Violence, which had been latent, became blatant; and machine-gun fire, artillery shrapnel, and poison gas tore apart the fabric of European society during the 1914–18 war.

Well before Oswald Spengler published *The Decline of the West* in 1919, Europeans had begun to think of themselves as beleaguered Romans awaiting their fall. In *Chitral, Beau Geste,* and other such late nineteenth-century tales Europe had rediscovered the Renaissance theme of lonely men with superior values overwhelmed by barbarians from beyond—"a theme that had been of scarcely any significance at all in Western literature from the Renaissance onward."[3] The founder of the Salvation Army suggested that "the heart of darkness" lay not in Africa, but "in darkest England."[4] His "way out" of the urban blight was to provide direct material charity for the neediest while infusing them with spiritual rather than material militance. The greatest playwright of late Victorian England, George Bernard Shaw, pointed to the rival revolutionary road, leading his Major Barbara away from her army of salvation to his camp of socialism.[5] Fresh recruits were provided not so much by Shaw's evolutionary, nonviolent Fabian society as by the new wave of organized class agitation typified by the great strike of London dockworkers in 1889.

By then full-blown revolutionary syndicalist movements had emerged in France, Italy, and Spain; this revolutionary current had reached the western and eastern frontiers of European civilization via the Industrial Workers of the World (IWW) in America and the socialist revolutionaries in Russia. One must explore this powerful new movement in its native Western habitat—considering its impact on the early career of Mussolini on the Right before returning to the revolutionary upsurge in Russia and the emergence of Lenin on the Left.

The "General Strike"

Modern trade unions were not initially—and have never been primarily—revolutionary. Nor was violence central to the trade unions that gradually developed among skilled workers on a craft basis. These unions concentrated on immediate material issues capable of at least partial gratification, and rarely embraced an ideological or strategic perspective. Demonstrations and strikes seldom had political objectives, and such "associational" or "modern" violence as occurred was less destructive than the last outbreaks of the earlier "communal" or "reactionary" forms of violence.[6]

The economic depression of the mid-1870s gave rise to a more militant type of trade union organization, which developed in Britain and then in France once unions became fully legal in 1876 and 1884 respectively.[7] This "new unionism" of unskilled and semi-skilled workers in large industrial factories, mines, and transportation gained notoriety as well as self-confidence in the successful London Dock Strike of 1889. The subsequent rapid growth of large-scale industrial unions throughout Europe and America was closely related to the increasing use of strike tactics for revolutionary purposes. The new militants used strikes both to challenge the "labor aristocracy" within older unions and to raise the revolutionary consciousness of the masses.

The great hope was to build towards a "general strike"—a collective act of resistance by a united working class that might lead to the overthrow of both the economic and political dominance of the bourgeoisie. Like most other major ideas of the modern revolutionary tradition, the concept has its origins in the time of the original French Revolution. It was Sylvain Maréchal who had in 1788 made the first suggestion of unified proletarian protest against the economic and political organization of modern society. Maréchal spoke of "the imperative of the collective stoppage of productive forces" by "the most numerous class."[8] C. F. Volney independently suggested a few years later an international, antimilitarist form of work stoppage. Comparable ideas of massive resistance from below were variously advocated by Lequinio, the Breton "citizen of the globe," by Marat (in his "Supplication of the 8 million unfortunate ones"), and by Pierre-Gaspard Chaumette, the leader of the insurrectional commune that established the republic in August 1792. Chaumette had argued in June 1791 that violence would not be needed against a tyrant:

> Just do not support him and he will crumble of his own weight and be destroyed like a great colossus with the pedestal removed.[9]

The idea of a general strike first arose within the working class itself in England, where the Industrial Revolution was most advanced. In 1792 an educated Scottish shoemaker, Thomas Hardy, began a London Corresponding society, which soon founded branches in manufacturing centers in the Midlands and in Scotland; it might be called the "first independent political working class movement in history." [10] By 1795, when many of its leaders were imprisoned, the society had 80,000 members. And in October 1795, it was able to rally 150,000 workers to demonstrate against Pitt and his war on revolutionary France; subsequently the tradition spread through the United Irishmen, which drew up plans for a mass invasion to liberate Ireland with the aid of French revolutionary forces.

Some of the working class turned directly against the machines of the new factory system during the late years of the Napoleonic wars. The Luddite movement, with its widespread smashing of new textile machines, spread rapidly from its origins in Nottingham late in 1811. Its repression triggered further, more organized violence from technologically displaced artisans. As early as 1817 there had been talk in Great Britain of a general strike. The term was first popularized in the 1830s by an Irish printer in Manchester,[11] and made the subject of a remarkable theoretical treatise by a nonconformist minister who had become the proprietor of a London coffee house.[12] The first attempt at such a strike in an industrial nation occurred in 1842 in Britain; it was led by one who as a boy had seen the "Peterloo massacre" of peacefully demonstrating workers in 1819 and had then traded his father's hand loom for a power loom and destitution in a factory.[13]

A more sustained general strike occurred in Barcelona in the summer of 1855. Here as elsewhere the working class was turning from communal to associational violence; and a secret new labor organization, *Unión de Clases*, led the strike, calling for "association or death" and for a popular militia.[14] This *huelga general* provided a model for what was to become a vigorous Spanish tradition of revolutionary syndicalism. Antipolitical, anticentralizing labor unrest would continue to excite the Spaniards—and particularly the Catalonians—from the time of their first enthusiastic reception of Bakuninist ideas in the fifty-thousand-man anarchist movement of the early 1870s to the formation in Barcelona in 1936 of that seeming contradiction in terms: an anarchist government.[15]

Proudhon taught Latin Europe in his last years that the general strike should be the central weapon of a major political movement, leading to what he eventually called "the new democracy." Electoral polls should be boycotted in favor of developing a new ethos of self-help on concrete matters, "democratic simplicity" in ordinary living, and preparation for a radical transformation of society by a massive boycotting of all bourgeois institutional structures. The inventive Girardin, then close to Proudhon, had suggested on December 3, 1851, the day after the coup d'état of Napoleon III, that the only effective answer would be not armed resistance but a "universal strike." [16] Under Proudhon's tutelage, the French suggested to the early councils of the First International that such a strike might serve reformist and pacifist ends. The Belgians suggested at the Basel Congress that local workers' councils and a national Chamber of Labor might "take the place of the present government." [17] A Polish exile linked the strike idea with more militant tactics in a pamphlet written for French workers in 1869, *La Grève*; [18] and there were efforts to launch a general strike of workers against the Franco-Prussian War.[19]

This conception was echoed in 1871 by the anti-parliamentary and anti-Marxist Sonvillier Circular of the Jura Federation, which expressed opposition to "political socialism" and to all forms of state power. It saw the emerging new trade union organization (*syndicat*) as far more than "a transitory phenomenon bound up with the duration of capitalist society." It was the missing "cultural ideal" for socialism, and provided

> . . . the germ of the socialist economy of the future, the elementary school of socialism. . . .[20]

The general strike helped give corporate identity to the rising French trade union movement. Even more important, it sustained among the workers a sense that there still was a uniquely French revolutionary tradition. It helped check the drift which followed the defeat of the Paris Commune towards either the English-style reformism of Paul Brousse and the "possibilists" [21] or the doctrinaire Marxism of Jules Guesde's "revolutionary collectivism." [22]

What gave the militant unions new revolutionary potential was the geographic solidarity they managed to achieve—to begin with, among the textile workers of Catalonia in the 1870s. Rather than organizing unions according to craft or trade, the northern Spaniards organized all trades and crafts into local area units. These provided territorial power bases that served "an educational role in the present" as they prepared to assume an "executive role in a revolutionary society to come." [23] Similar bases of geographic strength began to appear in Italy (*camere del lavoro*) and particularly in France (*bourses du travail*), which soon became the center of the syndicalist movement.

French unionists were impressed with the American sympathy strikes for the anarchists executed after the Haymarket riot of 1886. In 1887, the first *bourse du travail* was formed in Paris. The Bordeaux Congress of French trade unions in 1888 endorsed the tactic of the general strike and equated it with social revolution. The revolutionary general strike became a rallying point in the formal consolidation of the French General Confederation of Labor (C.G.T.) during the late 1890s. At the

Marseilles Congress in 1892, Aristide Briand suggested that a "universal strike," represented "legal force" rather than "violent force." [24] As strike activity intensified, the idea grew that a general strike might develop spontaneously out of some incident and escalate into revolution. A railroad delegate to the C.G.T. Congress of 1896 insisted: *"The general strike will be the revolution, peaceful or not."* [25]

If there was a central leader of anything so deeply anti-centralistic as French revolutionary syndicalism, it was Fernand Pelloutier. This passionate young journalist dominated the revolutionary imagination of the French working class from the time he became secretary of the new Fédération des Bourses du Travail in 1895, until he died in his study at age thirty-three in 1901.

Of all the long list of middle-class intellectuals to claim revolutionary leadership in the nineteenth century, Pelloutier probably made the deepest effort to study and understand the actual conditions of the working classes [26] and came closest to bridging the gap between workers and intellectuals. His *Revolution by the General Strike* [27] of 1892 called for direct action to bring these two elements together for the common creation of a new ethos and a new society.

The Bourses du Travail provided a new form of worker self-government that had immediate pedagogic and potential political functions, like the territorially consolidated union organizations in Catalonia. Pelloutier sought to expand it from a mere provider of aid and information into a kind of local, territorially based counter-government by and for the workers. Perhaps as few as 1.25 percent of the French workers were directly involved in the Bourses; [28] but they nevertheless dominated the proletarian imagination in France by keeping alive the vision of an alternate social order. With Pelloutier's death in 1901, revolutionary syndicalism lost its most dynamic leader; but its ideas gained broader influence as the Federation was absorbed into the C.G.T.

The use of strike tactics enormously expanded at the turn of the century throughout industrial Europe. Belgium offered a dramatic example—responsive as it was to all three of the great European labor movements: the German drive towards party organization, the British preoccupation with practical reforms, and the French thirst for direct, heroic action. Focusing on political objectives, the Belgians produced three great strikes—each more universal and disciplined than the last —in successive decades (1893, 1902, and 1912–13). Their example inspired imitation in neighboring Holland,[29] where the Protestant pastor, Domela Nieuwenhuis, repeatedly called on the Second International to accept the ideal of a trans-national general strike as the proletarian preventive for war.

The Second International generally stressed political organization on the Social Democratic model rather than syndicalist strikes. But the latter inspired special fear, because direct action posed a direct threat to the privileged classes who felt they "must find a means of defense or be conquered and crushed." [30]

Sweden, another hitherto tranquil northern nation, produced a successful general strike in 1902, which prepared the way for universal suffrage five years later. If the Swedes subsequently followed the English rather than the French in using trade unionism largely for incremental economic benefits, the month-long Swedish strike in 1909 was nonetheless "the most complete, non-revolutionary general strike, for distinctly economic purposes, in the history of the labor movement up to the outbreak of the Great War of 1914." [31]

Revolutionary syndicalism was, however, largely a product of Latin Europe. A week-long general strike of 150,000 workers in Barcelona in 1902 was followed by an even more ambitious strike in Italy in 1904, the new syndicalists in Spain and Italy increasingly drawing strength and inspiration from France.

France became the center of revolutionary syndicalism in the early twentieth century,[32] producing more strikers than either England or Germany,[33] an unparalleled record of successes in major strikes,[34] and a series of new techniques for direct action including the serial strike (*la grève tournante*, which stopped production by staggered pauses without leaving work), sabotage,[35] and the labeling and boycotting of products.

The leading theorist of French syndicalism after the passing of Pelloutier was another middle-class journalist and long-time official of the C.G.T., Emile Pouget. In such works as *The ABC of revolution* and *How we shall make the revolution,* he set forth a blueprint for paralyzing the modern state without using weapons. He argued that the state could not police the far-flung lines of communication and transportation on which it depended; and that the moral force of a *prise de possession* by the workers would cause the army masses either to join their striking brethren—or, if forced to fire by their superiors, to rebel against their own officers. Pouget followed Proudhon in rejecting all parliamentary strategies and intellectual dogmas—especially socialism which always seeks "to move towards the revolution along statist paths." [36] He went beyond Proudhon, however, in arguing for the liberation of women; and in providing an explicit picture of the post-revolutionary society, according to which a "Federal Congress" was to confirm the spontaneous decentralization of all authority that the revolutionary process would accomplish. Freedom from prejudice was to be assured by a new educational system that would exclude all study of the past and include only physical education and the exact sciences. The new society was to be based not on another Declaration of the Rights of Man, but on "absolute respect for the rights of the child." [37]

Revolutionary syndicalism purported to ignore the political arena altogether. But news of the successful, nationwide general strike during the Russian Revolution of 1905 and the transfer at about that same time of the main location of the labor wars from northern France to the Paris region suggested to some that Paris might once again prove to be the site of revolution.[38]

Though deeply Proudhonist and nonideological, French syndicalism produced a sublime theorist in Georges Sorel. He sought to inspire workers with his call to heroism and his myth of a general strike that would transcend the *gymnastique révolutionnaire* of the C.G.T.[39]

Sorel was the son of a bourgeois monarchist from Normandy and the cousin of a great historian of the French Revolution, Albert Sorel. Until the age of forty-five, he was a little-known civil engineer, inspecting roads and bridges and developing a deep contempt for the political life of the Third Republic. His first two books appeared in 1889, hailing the heroic poetry and tribal ethics of the Old Testament as an antidote to the crude utilitarianism of the day and saluting the death of Socrates as a proper reward for his corrosive and antisocial rationalism.[40]

In 1892, he retired on a government pension to begin a new career as a social critic and uncrowned philosopher-in-chief of syndicalism. Though far more deeply influenced by Proudhon,[41] he embraced Marxism as a necessary cure for the corrosive scepticism of the age and a doctrine that promised to find in the proletariat "something worthy of survival" in a corrupt age.[42] His hatred of bourgeois society was far more intense than Marx's, and tinged with aesthetic contempt. Sorel saw only a decadent world of self-serving interest groups, self-indulgent intellectuals, and venal leaders rationalizing their lack of all conviction into pacifistic principles. The English were scorned for treating wars like athletic contests; the French, for succumbing to an arid rationalism easily coöpted by the Third Republic. He rejected the Enlightenment heritage traditionally honored by French revolutionaries, and the "illusions of progress" that had led the French to worship the state, and workers to engage in demeaning political activity.[43]

Sorel found an alternative in the proletarian *bourse du travail,* which was "a thing of conscience, rather than an instrument of government." [44] The trade unions which formed around each bourse and immersed workers directly in strike activity provided a heroic alternative to bourgeois politics. The proletariat as a class provided the only hope for regeneration in a society where the upper classes were decadent, the middle classes philistine, and the lower classes a perpetual prey for the rhetoric of either ambitious Jacobins or reactionary Catholics.

The proletariat to fulfill its mission must build on revolutionary pessimism rather than evolutionary optimism: on the heroic, emotional conviction that something *must* be, rather than the petty, intellectual argument that something *will* be. Beliefs in harmonious development and social peace were those of a decaying bourgeoisie, hoping to drag others down to its level. To avoid such degradation, the proletariat must base itself squarely on a myth: on "armed pessimism," which was capable of inspiring "heroic acts" like those of the early Christians and the first Calvinists. Believing the world totally damned, they armed themselves with a "will to deliverance" that "changed everything from top to bottom" before the critical spirit and pallid optimism of the Enlightenment transformed Calvinism into "simply a lax Christianity."[45]

Commitment of a religious kind was a "necessary imposture" in human affairs.[46] The redeeming myth for the proletariat in a post-religious age was the "great proletarian general strike." This was neither an economic strike (simply for material benefits) nor a political strike (subordinate to political ambitions). Sorel describes the Proletarian General Strike unapologetically as a "myth." [47] Myth for Sorel was "a power that stirs the soul . . . a vision of life," [48] which the proletariat could keep alive only by rejecting every temptation "to imitate the middle class." [49] Class war was the most essential and forgotten concept in Marx,[50] the proper form of heroic combat for modern man, and the indispensable source of *élan vital* for a revolutionary proletariat. Precisely because the *bourses du travail* and *syndicats* were *not* political bodies, they were capable of leading the revolution. The workers must, however, unite in believing that a coming Proletarian General Strike would totally supplant the existing political order. The danger was that this messianic event might be perverted into a "political general strike" controlled by politicians seeking to take over (or even to join) bourgeois institutions of government.[51]

Violence was the indispensable ingredient: the chivalric *rite de passage* for the proletariat on the path to power, the "clear and brutal expression of the class war," [52] which would clarify issues by polarizing society. Capitalism "at present stupified by humanitarianism" would regain "the warlike qualities it once possessed," [53] and the proletariat would close ranks with the enthusiasm of medieval warrior-crusaders. Thus, through Sorel, ideas from the old Left unintentionally became weapons for the new Right. After the bloodshed of World War I, the sublime violence that Sorel had prescribed for the syndicalists would become part of the rationale for Fascism.

The leading French politician of the era, Georges Clemenceau provided a classic illustration of the internationalist Left turning into the nationalist Right. He had used his newspaper of 1880, *La Justice*, to build a reputation as a crusading foe of corruption and a defender of the little man (a technique also used by Hearst in domestic counterpoint to his call for crusades abroad). Clemenceau had also served periodically as the leader of the extreme Left within the Chamber of Deputies. But it was radical journalism that had remained the favorite medium of the former communard: his new journal of 1897, *L'Aurore*, had printed Emile Zola's famous exposé of the right-wing machinations behind the Dreyfus affair.

Yet when Clemenceau himself acceded to power as minister of the interior in 1906, he advocated using military force to suppress domestic disorder. After he became premier later in the year, he dwelt even more systematically on the need for national strength. By the time he launched his new journal of 1913, *L'Homme Libre*, he had become a militant patriot pure and simple. He called for rearmament against the German threat, total mobilization once the war began, and a fanatical "will to victory" that vaulted him into the premiership at the age of seventy-six for the final push to victory. Clemenceau gave his chosen commander for the last battles, Ferdinand Foch, the Napoleonic title Marshal of France, and insisted on imposing humiliating peace terms on the vanquished Germans at Versailles. He sent Foch to join another former revolutionary who had turned to counter-revolutionary nationalism, Józef Piłsudski, in the last and best-armed effort to crush the Bolshevik Revolution in Russia.

The most striking case of mutation from the old Left to the new

Right occurred in Italy, which fashioned out of post-war chaos and syndicalist unrest the first Fascist regime in modern history. Its author —and the founding father of the modern radical Right—was a former left-wing socialist and lifelong admirer of Lenin: Benito Mussolini.

The Fascist Mutation

Italy played a special role in the age of labor wars throughout Europe. There were venerable traditions of violence; and anarchists, who had issued the first call for a revolutionary "propaganda of the deed" in 1876 in Italy,[54] helped more than in most countries to organize the general strike of 1904. It was the largest up to that time;[55] more than one million workers participated. Since parliamentary procedures and political parties did not evoke deep allegiance in Italy, the syndicalist call for direct action outside the political arena had a particular appeal. The Italian general strike of 1911 against the invasion of Tripoli put into practice the original syndicalist idea of the 1890s: a strike within to oppose war without. The last congress of the Second International (Basel, 1913) recorded many pledges of transnational proletarian action against any coming war. The Italians provided the most serious practical response by staging in June 1914 the last great general strike before the conflict.[56] Though confined to one tumultuous week, the Italian strike helped keep Italy—alone of the major European powers— from entering the war immediately after it broke out in July 1914.

The agitation for Italian intervention began precisely among the revolutionary syndicalists, who feared that revolutionary France might be crushed and reactionary Austria emboldened to invade Italy. The syndicalist passion for heroic myth and direct action fatefully linked the old Left with the new Right. In agitating for Italian intervention, syndicalists helped form "bands [fasci] for revolutionary action." They represented war and revolution as parts of one ennobling process that would free Italy from both monarchical rule and parliamentary procedure. Italian syndicalists echoed Sorel's parallel efforts in France during the immediate prewar years to combine nationalist and syndicalist forces in opposition to bourgeois democracy.[57]

Mussolini was literally baptized into the revolutionary tradition. His father, a radical blacksmith, gave him the name of the Mexican national revolutionary, Benito Juarez. The young Mussolini became a revolutionary socialist, and as a professing Marxist spent some of his youth in refuge in Switzerland. In 1908 at the age of twenty-five, he became editor of a journal of the Socialist party, La Lotta di Classe (The Class Struggle). In 1911 he was jailed for five months for agitating against the Italian conquest of Libya; and in December of the following year he became editor of the official journal of the Socialist party, *Avanti!* (Forward), which he with the collaboration of the Russian anarchist Angelica Balabanov made a militant revolutionary outlet with syndicalist leanings.

His journalistic activity as head of an official party organ bore striking resemblance to that of Lenin just a decade earlier. Like Lenin, Mussolini assumed personal responsibility for using his editorial position to determine a general political line. Just as Lenin had attacked "parliamentary cretinism" (in *Iskra* and *Vpered*, also meaning "Forward"), so Mussolini ridiculed in *Avanti!* the parliamentary illusions of less militant socialists. Mussolini also started a smaller theoretical review, *Utopia*,[58] to provide guidance for the creation of a "socialist culture" —again recalling Lenin's founding of an ideological journal (originally *Zaria*, later *Bol'shevik*, now *Kommunist*) to complement the daily tactical guidance of a party newspaper (*Iskra*, later *Pravda*).

Mussolini, of course, diverged sharply from Lenin by embracing a radical interventionalist posture in World War I. He was expelled from the Italian socialist party in October 1914 and founded in the following month his most famous journal, *Il Popolo d'Italia*, in which he forged his own militant synthesis of syndicalism and nationalism. He argued that war on the allied side would serve both to defeat the reactionary German Empire and to mobilize the masses for direct action against the effete liberal rule of the bourgeoisie. Anyone afraid "to go out and fight in the trenches will not be found in the streets on the day of the battle." The time had come to "shout loudly" something "I would never have pronounced in normal times," that "fearful and fascinating word: War!"[59] His characterization of the war as the "miracle" which would end the old order and create conditions for the new foreshadowed the coming totalitarianism, but also echoed the original romanticism of the revolutionary and Napoleonic eras with its "politics of the miraculous."

The weak liberal democracy that emerged in Italy after the war faced revolutionary challenges from both the syndicalist occupation of plants and the new revolutionary party that Mussolini created by transforming syndicalist *fasci di azione rivoluzionaria* into new *fasci Italiani di combattimento*. The central symbols invoked by Mussolini were almost all taken from the romantic nationalistic tradition of the *Risorgimento*. Mussolini's *Il Popolo d'Italia* played on memories of Mazzini's *L'Italia del Popolo*;[60] his rhetoric revived Mazzinian hopes for a "third Rome" —not of emperors or popes, but of "the people"; and his hymn of self-praise, "Youth" (*Giovinezza*), was a reprise on Mazzini's image of Young Italy. Using the classical *mise en scène* of the national revolutionary tradition, Mussolini and his followers staged in the opera house of La Scala in Milan, the "first planned violence of post-war Italy,"[61] a disruptive nationalist demonstration of January 1919. Even the black shirts of Mussolini's followers combined the anarcho-syndicalist color with the classical Garibaldian costume. Mussolini's fusion of violence and myth earned the admiration of Sorel, who described him as "not an ordinary socialist . . . a *condottiere*."[62]

Mussolini's Fascism was thus both a revival of revolutionary nationalism [63] and an adaptation of revolutionary syndicalism. The break with his former belief in socialism was dramatized in April 1919, when he helped burn the headquarters of *Avanti!*, the socialist newspaper he had once edited. In July, the Fascists offered to help the government suppress a planned general strike.[64]

During the second half of 1919 and in 1920, Italy produced the most nearly successful syndicalist revolution in European history. Beginning with the metal workers of Turin and spreading rapidly throughout much of the industrialized north, factory councils were established as a rudimentary form of decentralized worker self-management. This campaign was less violent and political than the maximalist position within the socialist party yet more completely opposed to the bourgeois state than the parliamentary wing of the party. When employers refused to deal with the councils, there occurred in September 1920 a spectacular and largely peaceful "occupation of the factories" by 400,000 workers with millions more following along throughout Italy.

Despite the appearance of red flags and "red guard" organizations in many factories, the recent Russian Revolution did not exercise a major impact on the Italian events. The Turin intellectuals, Antonio Gramsci and Palmiro Togliatti, who were later to become founders and leaders of the Italian communist party, neither initiated nor controlled the short-lived worker take over of the instruments of production of 1920.[65] Their enthusiasm over its raw vitality and their frustration over the missed opportunity for a full annexation of power led them to force a split in the Italian socialist party at Leghorn in January 1921, and to create their own, more disciplined and political communist party of Italy.

Out of Gramsci's intellectual visions and pedagogic efforts to provide leadership for the proletariat during the "failed revolution" of 1920 came the word and ideal of *hegemony*. It revived the essentially syndicalist ideal of the total cultural reintegration of an autonomous proletariat rather than a mere political dictatorship as the aim of revolution. The enthusiasm of the young Gramsci over the heroic potential of the proletariat for building "the future city" or "the new order" [66] recalled Sorel—even if it derived from the rejection by students within Turin University of the dull positivism of Italian intellectual life. But the struggle for proletarian hegemony required the leadership of intellectuals; cultural organizations and the means of communication were more important than parliaments and elections in preparing the way. Intellectuals, in Gramsci's view, were at least potentially free from the enervating decadence of bourgeois politics. Italy had so far produced only a "passive revolution"—one in which the state had created a political dictatorship of bourgeois liberals, without gaining the assent, let alone the involvement, of civil society. Thus the existing Italian state was held together by force rather than hegemony. The proletariat had the opportunity with the aid and tutelage of progressive intellectuals to revive the vitality of civil society by creating the hegemony on which a real revolutionary transformation of society could be based.[67]

But political power was to be seized in Italy and a new cultural hegemony imposed not by Gramsci and the Communists, but by the rival revolutionary party which was also formed in 1921, the Fascist party of Italy. Its first secretary was a former syndicalist organizer, Michele Bianchi. He bore the original Italian version of the name of Auguste Blanqui, whose famous phrase "who has steel has bread" had been placed at the beginning of the first issue of Mussolini's *Popolo d'Italia*.[68]

The victory in Italy of the Fascists' national revolution rather than of the Communists' social revolution owes more than a little to the tactics of the losers. Gramsci's first known political article had defended Mussolini's interventionism in World War I, based on the argument that war might destroy the bourgeois state and bring revolution nearer.[69] His crucial decisions in late 1920 and early 1921 brought Mussolini to power—and illustrated once again the frequent interdependence of the extremes of Right and Left.

Gramsci, Togliatti, and the others made the fateful decision during the post-war crisis to join the extremist advocate of close Moscow ties, Amadeo Bordiga, in splitting the Italian Socialist party and leaving the Left hopelessly divided on the eve of Mussolini's drive for power. Gramsci's subsequent suffering in Fascist prisons, the Italian Communists' rapid repudiation of Bordiga as a Left deviationist, and Togliatti's deathbed criticisms of high Stalinism (exemplified by the tyrant of Hungary, Matthias Rákosi, who had been a key Soviet agent at the Leghorn conference)—all do not obscure the tragedy inherent in the original formation of a separate Italian Communist party. That party was formed in deliberate response to the externally imposed "21 conditions" of the new Leninist International. Gramsci and the others tragically assumed that by concentrating their fire against a weak liberal democratic state and reformist socialists, they would hasten their own revolutionary conquest of power—rather than that of the little understood forces on the Right. The appeal of national over social revolution prevailed once again; and the chauvinist Right came to power in 1922.

The same fateful misperceptions were to plague the German Communists a decade later. They were to see the weak Weimar Republic and the rival Social Democrats on the Left as more serious opponents than the Nazis on the Right. Hitler like Mussolini would be thought to be only a transitory phenomenon who would prepare the way (as Kornilov had done in Russia during 1917) for the serious revolution on the Left, which allegedly alone had the mass base to last.

The failure to distinguish clearly between rival revolutionary parties was more justifiable in the Italian than in the German case. Mussolini, Bianchi, and others had, after all, been pure political products of the revolutionary tradition; and they extensively adopted syndicalist techniques in organizing their movement into a controlling national party. Fascist economic unions were used to mobilize the masses; and after the march on Rome in 1922, the Fascist corporative state was organized along vertical lines by industries in a manner previously favored by syndicalist strike organizations. The irony is intense and twofold. Syndicalist ideas were used to help pave the way for the very centralization of political power that the syndicalist tradition had come into being to prevent. More importantly, social revolutionary ideals and expectations were extensively drawn upon (especially in the early period by the so-called *fascismo della prima ora*) to legitimize a revival under right-wing auspices of the rival national revolutionary tradition.

The syndicalist tradition also played a role in preparing the way for other Fascist regimes that subsequently emerged in Spain and Portugal. Throughout Latin Europe, syndicalists had legitimized violent direct action against liberal democratic institutions and had frightened conservative Catholics into the arms of a new form of pseudo-revolutionary nationalism. The final validating illustration was provided by another right-wing dictator who succeeded in overthrowing a fledgling democracy in the 1920s: Józef Piłsudski. Poland like Italy had been a bastion of the original national revolutionary tradition of the Francocentric era, and of its expressive romantic violence. These two national traditions had inspired Europe with much of its revolutionary dynamism prior to the period of Germano-Russian dominance in the last third of the nineteenth century. Like Mussolini, Piłsudski was a left-wing socialist journalist brought up in the period of disillusionment and confusion at the turn of the century. Like Mussolini, Piłsudski rode to power largely by adapting his training on the Left to the needs of the Right—and by consciously playing on memories of a once-revolutionary nationalism. Like Mussolini, Piłsudski created what Spengler would call a pseudomorphosis (a falsified transformation) of the revolutionary heritage.

Piłsudski had been implicated through his brother in St. Petersburg in the same plot to assassinate the tsar in 1887 for which Lenin's older brother was executed. Sentenced to a five-year exile in Siberia for procuring chemicals to aid the plotters, Piłsudski returned to Poland to join the Polish socialist party (formed in Paris in 1892) and to found in 1894 an illegal underground journal, *Robotnik* (The Worker). As with Krupskaia on Lenin's *Iskra*, Piłsudski's wife was his key collaborator, and they were arrested together in 1900 in their secret editorial offices in Łodz. Piłsudski admired Lenin's militance, but saw possibilities for a revolutionary national resurgence of his country amidst the violence of World War I. Proclaimed chief of state with dictatorial powers when Poland at last achieved independence in 1918, Piłsudski immediately plunged into combat with Lenin's rival regime to the east. Like Mussolini's struggle with the pro-Bolshevik Italian socialists, Piłsudski's conflict with Lenin was in many ways an intramural conflict between the national and social revolutionary traditions. Piłsudski fought other Poles (such as Lenin's chief of secret policy, Felix Dzerzhinsky, whose parallel career in revolutionary journalism began at about the same time and place as that of Piłsudski).[70] Piłsudski's program for a federation of independent national states centered on Poland; in opposing the imperial power of both Russia and Germany it was in many ways a throwback to the romantic Mazzinian nationalism of Young Poland in the early nineteenth century.[71] But his slow consolidation of dictatorial power betrayed the democratic substance of those earlier visions of national revolution as the path to human liberation.

If syndicalism in Europe thus found itself absorbed into a new kind of radical nationalism of the Right, in the United States in the same period it found its purest expression as a doctrine of ecumenical social revolution.

The Western Frontier

Like a prairie fire that burns brightest on the periphery, revolutionary violence became most intense in the outlying regions of Europe in the late nineteenth century. The Balkans, Ireland, and even Australia became major centers of violent unrest. The eastern frontier produced the Russian Revolution; but forgotten fires also burned on the western frontier. In the very year that the Russians produced the first successful nationwide general strike (1905) the Americans founded the first and only international organization pledged to revolution by means of the general strike: the Industrial Workers of the World (IWW).

As it entered the industrial age full blast in the 1870s, America had plunged into "the bloodiest and most violent labor history of any industrial nation in the world." [72] Industrial violence in America was focused on gut economic issues rather than ideological ones.[73] The heart of unrest was the great metropolis of the American interior: Chicago. The new city of stone and steel that arose from the ashes of the great fire of 1871 produced in 1875 the first Education and Defense Society, where workers met regularly and drilled with firearms. Six years later, Chicago hosted the first gathering of Americans advocating social revolution by means of armed resistance to authority.[74] The first May Day for workers was proposed in Chicago in 1886; and the first broadly based industrial strike was launched there in 1894: the Pullman strike. Chicago was also the scene of the Haymarket riot of 1886, which created the first modern revolutionary scare in America, and of the founding of the IWW in 1905.

This American version of revolutionary syndicalism was a continent-wide movement that involved the oldest cities of the East, the newest mines of the West, some factories in the Midwest, and the railway network that connected them all. For the first time since the American Revolution a significant number of Americans—most of them working people—called for the overthrow of their rulers.

This revolutionary movement of the American industrial era unfolded in two successive, if overlapping stages. Each represented in some ways a delayed (if unconscious) repetition of earlier efforts by European revolutionaries. First came a period of heroic, anti-authoritarian protests led by immigrant workers in northeastern America and reminiscent of the romantic Italo-Polish tradition of revolutionary violence. Then followed the revolutionary syndicalist organization (the IWW) led by western miners and reminiscent of earlier efforts by the French.

Ethnic Unrest

The vital new ingredient in America that linked violence with revolutionary ideas was the flood of immigration that began in the mid-nineteenth century. As the country acquired new manpower from Europe to build railroads, tunnel mines, and fill factories, it also acquired a fresh infusion of ideas. In the early period these ideas came mainly from revolutionary nationalists of Catholic origin, who often became social revolutionaries in predominantly Protestant America.

Ireland played a particularly important role, providing 44 percent of the 3.5 million immigrants who came to America from 1840–54.[75] The Irish brought with them a rich revolutionary tradition of secret organization and defiance of authority. Irish immigrants (led by the younger brother of a leading Irish revolutionary of 1848) led the rebellion of gold miners in the Eureka Stockade on the Australian frontier in 1854; [76] and the Irish dominated the more sustained unrest among Pennsylvania coal miners in the 1860s and the 1870s.

After the suppression of the Ribbonmen in the late 1830s and the famine years of the mid-forties, revolutionaries in Ireland became more extreme and resourceful. Some new secret societies revived the old agrarian tradition of dressing in women's clothes (the "Lady Rocks" and "Lady Clares"); [77] and the Irish countryside began to talk about an altogether new secret society under a legendary Molly Maguire.[78]

The Molly Maguires acquired an importance in the New World that they never had in Ireland. They became the defenders and organizers of the Irish immigrants who flooded into the newly opened coal fields of Pennsylvania. Anthracite mining was new to the Irish, who as Catholics were suspect and subjected to frequent unemployment, particularly in the recession following the Civil War. They looked for protection to the Molly Maguires, who organized largely in taverns as a secret, militant arm of the Ancient Order of Hibernians. They captured the imagination of America with their work stoppages climaxing in the Long Strike of 1875 against the Reading Railroad.

A former radical Chartist, Allan Pinkerton, championed the counterattack by the railroad owners, infiltrating the Mollies, and using "flying squadrons" to break the strike and arrest its leaders. A sensational series of trials led to the hanging of twenty leaders in 1877, including the eight members of the inner, secret center. Legends arose on the Left—and fortified a new literature of reassurance on the Right: the detective story. Just as Pinkerton provided a model of detective work in the service of the status quo, so Arthur Conan Doyle, after creating Sherlock Holmes, immortalized Pinkerton's tale of triumph over the Irish miners in The Valley of Fear of 1915.

The Molly Maguires were by no means the only Irish revolutionary

movement to develop in America. The most important of all Irish secret
societies was founded in America on St. Patrick's Day in 1858: the Irish
Republican Brotherhood, sometimes called simply "the organization,"
but usually known as the Fenians (from the name of legendary Irish
warriors of antiquity).[79] Some members returned to fight in Ireland,
others participated in three spectacular if unsuccessful Fenian attempts
to attack the British in Canada: from New York in 1866, Vermont in
1870, and across to Manitoba in 1871.[80]

Their seaborne exploits rivaled those of Pisacane and Garibaldi. They
took over a ship which they renamed *Erin's Hope* and sailed from New
York to Ireland with weapons in 1864; they chartered a vessel and sailed
to Australia in 1876 to rescue Irish prisoners;[81] and they terrified the
British five years later by commissioning *The Fenian Ram*, the first
modern submarine built in America, for secret missions to Ireland.[82]

As the Fenians went underwater, a rival group went underground: the
Clan-na-Gael or United Brotherhood, whose alternate name, The Triangle, recalled the mysticism of older occult organizations.[83] They entertained plans for everything from sinking ships and blowing up the
House of Commons to assassinating Queen Victoria.[84]

The revolutionary impulse in America of the late nineteenth century
became linked with anarchism and assassination through the new wave
of unskilled immigrant workers, often from southern and eastern Europe, who were largely excluded from the dominant union, the American
Federation of Labor, which was founded in 1886.[85] Three presidents
were shot to death in the forty-year period after the outbreak of the Civil
War. Lincoln was killed a year before and Garfield four months after
the first and last assassination attempts respectively on the life of Tsar
Alexander II. But the American assassins were lonely, idiosyncratic figures—closer to the emotionalism of the Italo-Polish tradition than to
the ascetic, ideological tradition of Russia. Indeed, the two most important political assassinations to come out of American anarchism at the
beginning of the century were committed by Italian and Polish immigrants respectively.

Gaetano Bresci, a frail immigrant from Florence, had organized a
group of anarchists in Paterson, New Jersey, known as *L'Era Nuova*
(The New Era). Alone and unknown, he bought a cheap revolver, and
practiced using it quietly in a woods near Weehauken while his wife
and daughter picked spring wild flowers. He returned quietly to Italy
under the guise of seeing his aged mother; instead, he murdered
Umberto, king of Italy, on July 29, 1900, as he left an athletic festival
near Milan.[86] A year later, in another place of pleasure (the Temple of
Music at the Pan-American exhibition in Buffalo), President McKinley
was shot by a shy immigrant from Poland, Leon Czolgosz.

Behind and beyond these isolated acts lay an element of Russian inspiration, enriched with a strain of prophetic Judaism from the ghettos
of eastern Europe. Czolgosz confessed to having been inspired by hearing a speech by the mother figure of anarchist activism in America,
Emma Goldman.[87] Bresci's survivors in the New Era group joined in
the anarchist agitation (culminating in the antiwar and antidraft move-

ments during World War I), led by Goldman and her close friend and fellow Russian, Alexander Berkman.[88]

The Russian-Jewish immigration gave American anarchism of the gilded age its most inventive leaders. Their port of entry, New York, began to assume the supportive role for other revolutionary movements that it had previously played only for the Irish. Revolutionary anarchism spread from a movement previously formed in London: the Federation of Jewish Anarchists, which had brought together Yiddish-speaking artisan-emigrants from Russia in the 1880s and 1890s to hear Kropotkin and other Russians.

Their leader had been a remarkable German gentile, Rudolph Rocker, who had learned Yiddish only after joining the group, and later became the conscience as well as the historian of international anarchism.[89] The son of a musical typesetter and a skilled bookbinder, Rocker lived on to see his library and archives burned by the Nazis [90] and his hopes of seeing anarchism realized undercut by Communists in Barcelona and then dashed by Franco during the Spanish Civil War.[91] In his old age, he immigrated to America and saw in its libertarian tradition the best hope for his fading dreams.[92]

But the dream of an anarchist America never faded for Emma Goldman.[93] She, like Berkman, had transplanted to America Russian revolutionary hopes along with the Judaic idea of a promised land.[94] Their rich, lifelong collaboration began in August 1889 at a chance meeting in a café on the Lower East Side frequented by radicals.[95] Three years later, Berkman daringly tried to extend anarchist terror to economic as well as political oppressors. On July 23, 1892, he tried to kill the steel tycoon Henry Clay Frick, who had recently ordered reprisals against strikers in Homestead, Pennsylvania. Goldman had imitated Sonia in *Crime and Punishment*, becoming a streetwalker in order to raise money for a suit of clothes that would make Berkman presentable enough to get into Frick's office.[96] She passionately defended Berkman after his arrest, and continued to advocate forceful resistance to authority in her journal, *Mother Earth*, from 1906–17.

Johann Most, the leading violent anarchist in America, probably wished Goldman had gone elsewhere for her revolution when she lashed at him with a horsewhip at a public meeting for criticizing Berkman. Most (like Rocker) was a bookbinder whose youthful imagination had been captured by the spontaneous anti-authoritarianism of the Paris Commune. His bearlike appearance and inspiring oratorical powers reminded many of Bakunin. He served briefly as a Social Democrat in the Prussian Reichstag, which he denounced as a "Theater of Marionettes." He then moved to Austria, from whence he was subsequently banished "forever." [97] In London he was deeply influenced by blow-by-blow accounts of the terrorists' struggle within imperial Russia. Then, he set off to America, and in 1883, drew up a charter for an international congress of revolutionary "communist anarchists." [98]

In Pittsburgh, Most called for revolutionary anarchism to use a violent "propaganda of the deed" to raise the proletariat's consciousness of the gap between rulers and ruled.[99] Anarchists began to assume just such a leading role in Chicago in 1886 after a decade of mounting industrial unrest. To protest the killing of six striking workers at the McCormick harvester plant, anarchists organized a meeting on Haymarket Square on May 4. Despite its peaceful, oratorical nature, the police forcibly intervened, and in the ensuing meleé seven were killed by a bomb. Outraged public opinion led to the hasty conviction of the anarchist leaders and the hanging of four, though the actual felon was never discovered.

Most was implicated and imprisoned. The court entered into evidence his treatise written just before Haymarket: *Science of Revolutionary War —Manual for Instruction in the Use and Preparation of Nitro-Glycerine, Dynamite, Gun-Cotton, Fulminating Mercury, Bombs, Fuses, Poisons, and so forth.*[100]

Most's guide for "arming the people" benefited from his experience at an explosives factory in Jersey City. With a certain zest he contemplated using "hand grenades and blasting cartridges . . . the proletariat's substitute for artillery." [101] Larger bombs were even more promising:

> That which reduces what had been solid rocks into splinters may not have a bad effect in a court or monopolist's ballroom.[102]

Most nonetheless disapproved of the Haymarket bombing and refused to defend Berkman. Nor did the Chicago anarchists approve of Most and his journal—having founded a rival organ, *Anarchist,* on the eve of Haymarket.[103] To most anarchists, however, Most remained an "example of a man who refused to be bowed by imprisonment, ridicule, calumny." [104] Henry James used him as the model for the mysterious Hoffendahl in *Princess Casamassima* of 1886.

Most helped the European revolutionary tradition find roots within the new industrial working class in America. Because he wrote and spoke powerfully in German as well as English, he reached the largest and best-established of all minority groups in urban America: the Germans. He revived the little-known arguments for violence of a German foe of Marx, Karl Heinzen,[105] reprinting his defense of tyrannicide on the very day that McKinley was shot.[106] Only one copy was sold (to the arresting officer),[107] but the final line provided an incriminating text: "Let us save humanity with blood and iron, poison and dynamite!" [108] Most was once again jailed for a year.

Well before he died in 1906, Most was forgotten and attention was turned away from these American echoes of European revolutionary romanticism. A more organized threat to the status quo had appeared in the form of a revolutionary trade unionism that in some respects surpassed the French syndicalist tradition, the IWW, born in the year of the first Russian Revolution.

A Syndicalist "International"

Perhaps one million people held IWW cards at some time during 1905–15,[109] most of them new immigrants. Both their leader, William D. Haywood, and their "most dynamic figure," Frank Little, were part Indian, and both were blind in one eye. The early life of the large-framed Haywood reads like a melodrama of the old West. Born in Utah the son of a pony-express rider, "Big Bill" went to work as a boy in lawless mining towns and was married at an early age to "Nevada Jane" Minor.[110] When she was thrown from a horse and permanently incapacitated, Haywood took to drink, to poetry reading, and to leading a "war in the Rockies" against mine owners; he centered on the gold-rush town of Cripple Creek, Colorado. In the first great strike (in Cripple Creek in 1894), local authorities remained neutral. As a result, victory was won by Haywood's new organization, the Western Federation of Miners, which had been founded by metal workers in Montana the year before. The second Cripple Creek strike lasted for nearly two years and finished in bloody disaster for the union in 1904. By then, the overall number of strikes in America had increased from 1,000–1,300 in the early 1890s to nearly 4,000; and Haywood had turned his attention to a broader arena.

At the founding convention of the IWW in a sweltering room in North Chicago in the summer of 1905 he presided over 203 delegates. Here at last was a thoroughly indigenous American revolutionary organization hailed as the "Continental Congress of the Working Class," [111] and endowed with a characteristically American nickname, "the Wobblies." The initial gathering officially represented only 52,000 workers; but its perspective was as sweeping as its symbol: a globe (sometimes a sun) bearing the letters IWW.[112] The IWW gained a following in the United Kingdom (particularly in Glasgow and among Celtic minorities), which grew after Haywood's visit of 1910–11 to Europe; there were also echoes of the IWW in Mexico, Chile, and Scandinavia, and a substantial branch in Australia.[113]

The IWW most resembled the branch of revolutionary syndicalism with which it probably had least contact: the Spanish. The objective of forming "one big union" divided into industrial departments and comprising in effect a kind of shadow government resembled the Hispanic ideal of a consolidated *sindicato único*. The regional concept of organizing all workers west of the Mississippi (natural for an organization three fourths of whose founding members were from the Western Federation of Mines) was reminiscent of the recurrent ideal of basing a new syndicalist order territorially on Catalonia.[114]

The IWW was, however, most directly influenced by the French. The founding congress of the IWW endorsed the ideal of a "Social General Strike"; and Haywood's *The General Strike* hailed the Paris Commune as "the greatest general strike known in modern history." [115] Ben Williams, the polemic typesetter for the IWW publication *Solidarity*, drew on his extensive knowledge of French to translate syndicalist ideas of direct action and particularly organized industrial sabotage. "We need not 'advocate' it, we need only to explain it. The organized workers will do the acting." [116]

The IWW organized two particularly dramatic and protracted strikes, involving about 25,000 textile workers each in 1912 in Lawrence, Massachusetts, and in 1913, in Paterson, New Jersey. These strikes represented authentic folk events for working-class America successfully transferring the musical, visual, and dramatic images of heroism hitherto associated with romantic nationalism over to the previously prosaic cause of proletarian internationalism.

The ten-week strike that began in Lawrence in January 1912 was highlighted by the evacuation of the hungry children of strikers, which created nationwide sympathy after their arrival in Grand Central Station. Lawrence itself provided a kind of continuing, open-air ethnic festival. Only 8 percent of the strikers were native-born Americans; [117] much of the oratory was in Italian and other foreign languages. The arrested strike leader and editor of *Il proletario*, Arturo Giovannitti, wrote poems in both English and Italian as well as a long and powerful introduction to an English translation of Pouget's *Sabotage* from his prison cell in Lawrence.[118]

A confusion of tongues found unity in song. It was "as if the great American melting pot had suddenly boiled over" to produce "a revolution with a singing voice." Even such a sedate commentator as Ray Stannard Baker was impressed:

> It is the first strike I ever saw which sang. I shall not soon forget the curious lift, the strange sudden fire of the mingled nationalities at the strike meetings when they broke into the universal language of song.[119]

The "strange sudden fire" became a holy torch when the general strike moved from the cotton plants of Lawrence to the silk mills of Paterson. Flags as well as songs were central to this great strike in the spring of 1913.

The striking workers in Paterson actually manufactured American flags when they were on the job; and on Flag Day, March 17, they unfurled a massive stars and stripes of their own under a sign proclaiming:

> We wove the flag; we dyed the flag;
> We live under the flag; but we won't scab under the flag.[120]

Even more remarkable than the rituals of the strike was its symbolic reenactment at a Pageant of the Paterson Strike before a packed Madison Square Garden on June 7, 1913. Financed by the wealthy Mabel Dodge and produced by journalists and artists who congregated in her Fifth Avenue home, the pageant involved more than one thousand of the actual strikers. They were trained as performers and brought through New York in a parade towards the tower of the Garden, which shone with a ten-foot high IWW sign in red lights. Inside, they reenacted the major experiences of the strike in a stunning display of living, multimedia theater. At one point the funeral of a slain Paterson striker was reenacted. As the procession of one thousand workers moved down the aisle with a casket to the widow, some felt the athletic arena transformed into a kind of temple for the consecration of revolution. As Mabel Dodge later recalled

> I have never felt such a high pulsing vibration in any gathering before or since.[121]

These "high pulsing vibrations" did not altogether die out despite the financial losses of the pageant, the failure of the Paterson strike, and the rapid decline of the IWW from its peak membership of some one hundred thousand in 1912 to virtual collapse following its opposition to the American war effort after 1917. The man who had largely conceived and written the pageant in New York, John Reed, went on to glorify the Mexican Revolution in his *Insurgent Mexico* of 1914, and then to write the most influential single account of the Bolshevik Revolution of 1917: *Ten Days That Shook the World.*

A romantic poet from Oregon, correspondent for the radical *Masses,* and sometime lover of Mabel Dodge, Reed was an enthusiast in search of a cause. He was a typical American sports enthusiast, whom his friend and classmate Walter Lippmann called "the most inspired song and cheer leader" at Harvard.[122]

Yet, this well-bred radical intellectual also felt the characteristic populist passion to rejoin the common people. A young girl who went to prison in the Paterson strike told Reed that "we were frightened when we went in, but we were singing when we went out." [123] Anxious to share in this form of regeneration, Reed went to Paterson, and was briefly imprisoned in a four-by-seven-foot prison cell with eight other pickets. He became emotionally involved with the strike, mobilized his friends for the pageant, and then set off on a journalistic argosy in search of a hero. He went first to Pancho Villa in Mexico, then to both the western and eastern fronts in World War I, and finally to the feet of Lenin and Trotsky as they drove for power in October 1917. Reed's classic account received the imprimatur of both Lenin and his wife Krupskaia. The cheerleader found a game worthy of his enthusiasm. The real-life, "unrolling pageant of the Russian masses" [124] replaced pageants in Madison Square Garden.

Despite a bloody, heroic history of labor wars, the United States did not winnow any enduring revolutionary tradition from the experience of the early twentieth century. The two main reasons for this fateful failure of the Left were nationalist pressure from without and corrosive disunity from within.

As had also been evident in the case of Italy, whoever controlled the banner of nationalism tended to determine the nature of the syndicalist legacy everywhere after World War I. In the United States, labor unrest was doomed by its opposition to the nationalist fervor that swept through America during and after the war. The social revolutionary intensity and the internationalism of the IWW (and the anti-war, anti-allied sentiments of many Germans and Irish in the labor movement) provoked a patriotic backlash. The decade from the American entry into war in 1917 until the execution of Sacco and Vanzetti in 1927 may be regarded as a period in which a new nationalism rose in America and largely crushed its perennial rival, the social revolutionaries.

But disunity on the Left had undermined revolutionary syndicalism in America long before persecution and prosecution from the Right crippled it irrevocably during the Red Scare of 1918–20. Neither intellectuals who might have provided the leaders nor working people who might have comprised the troops accepted, for the most part, labor militance. Revolutionary intellectuals dissipated their modest numbers in theoretical debates and in political squabbles within the fragmented socialist parties: Eugene Debs's reformist Socialist Party of America and Daniel De Leon's smaller, Marxist Socialist Labor party. Lenin once called the Curaçao-born, European-educated De Leon "the greatest of modern socialists—the only one who has added anything to socialist thought since Marx." [125] But De Leon was as politically inept as he was intellectually brilliant.

Even at their peak, the IWW and its militant allies never represented more than a fraction of the American working-class movement. Samuel Gompers's American Federation of Labor (AFL) grew from two to four million members between 1914 and 1920; and continued to dominate organized labor in America. The most serious effort to revolutionize it from within came from William Z. Foster, one of twenty-three children born to slum-dwelling Irish immigrants. He was a former IWW member who studied in France syndicalist methods of working for revolutionary ends within larger, conservative unions. His first effort at "boring from within," the Syndicalist League of North America, never gained more than two thousand members during its brief existence from 1911–14. Foster turned next to a new type of "amalgamated" union, which, like the syndicalist federations in Europe, brought both the craft and industrial unions of a given industry into one amalgamated body for united strike efforts. He formed such bodies first in the Chicago stockyards, then in the great steel complexes of Chicago and Pittsburgh. In the fall of 1919, a great nationwide steel strike was launched under the group which Foster had organized with AFL consent the year before, the National Committee for Organizing Iron and Steel Workers.

Foster planned to "catch the workers' imagination and sweep them into the union *en masse*" by launching "a hurricane drive simultaneously in all the major steel centers." [126] He sought something less than Sorel's general strike leading directly to revolution, but something more than mere economic gains within the existing system. The strike lingered on into the winter and was supported as far afield as Seattle, Washington, where workers took over the shipyards and launched a city-wide general strike.[127] The steel strike was broken slowly but decisively by the application of corporate and police power in the same state of Pennsylvania where the Molly Maguires had first introduced America to labor violence a half century before. After the abolition of the National Committee in the summer of 1920 and a final wave of labor violence during the depression of 1921–22, the age of militant syndicalism in America came to an end.

Foster subsequently became a Communist and an unwavering advocate of the Moscow line. So did his successor as head of the American Communist Party, another Irish veteran of the labor wars, Eugene Dennis. But their party was never to become more than what Marx would have called a "sect." [128] Reed, Haywood, and most other IWW veterans who immigrated to the new Soviet state were soon disillusioned.[129]

Like syndicalism in general, the IWW in particular was deeply anti-authoritarian. Its combination of violent strike action and demands for worker control "had not been the exclusive property of the IWW, but the main theme of a dozen years of fierce class conflict in America." [130] If the IWW never had a chance, it always had a song—thousands of them. More successfully than any other social revolutionaries, the IWW broke the monopoly that national revolutionaries had held on the use of music for mobilizing the masses; and their best-remembered hero was appropriately a wandering song writer from the American frontier, the Swedish immigrant Joe Hill. His execution by a firing squad in Utah in 1915 transformed him into an "Arthurian figure of the proletariat, who will return from the grave to help workingmen everywhere," [131] inspiring them to sing in the meantime: "I dreamt I saw Joe Hill last night, alive as you and me. . . ."

CHAPTER 16

The Path to Power: Lenin

LENIN brought the revolutionary tradition out of the wilderness and into power. In so doing, he produced the first major break in the basic unity of European civilization since Luther.

The Bolshevik Revolution—the first ever made in the name of a doctrine of impersonal, materialistic determinism—was profoundly shaped by the charismatic leadership of this single man. Returning from long exile in April 1917 in a sealed train through war-ravaged Europe, Lenin led his native Russia in the overthrow of its new provisional democracy. He boldly seized power in St. Petersburg in November; renamed his Bolshevik wing of the Social Democratic party communist in the following March; held on to power throughout a long Civil War and against foreign intervention; and formed the Third, or Communist, International in January 1919, in repudiation of the democratic socialism of the Second International.

Once state power was consolidated throughout the world's largest land empire, the revolutionary tradition faced entirely new opportunities—and problems. What had been proclaimed as a social revolution with full respect for national self-determination became a form of bureaucratic state socialism confined to one country and largely imposed by Great Russia on its old imperial clients. Lenin, however, lived to see—and to be implicated in—very few of the grim realities of a revolution in power. He ruled in health over a country at peace for only about a year: between the end of civil conflict early in 1921 and his first stroke in 1922. The new state had barely defined itself politically as a "Union of Soviet Socialist Republics," when Lenin died in January 1924, long before the massive social transformations of agricultural collectivization and forced industrialization.

Lenin's main contribution to history, therefore, lay not so much in his improvisations as a statesman as in his accomplishments as a revolutionary. He broadened the appeal of Marxism as a revolutionary doctrine from its original focus on urban workers in liberal Western societies to a global ideology suitable for the intellectual elites and peasant masses of the authoritarian, extra-European world.

The German Legacy

By Russifying a German doctrine, Lenin was in a sense fusing the two sides of his own heritage. His father was a partly Tatar Russian and his mother a German, and Lenin seemed to combine the familiarity with violence and the ruggedness of a Volga Russian with the organizational discipline of a German.

The German part of his inheritance was less important, but has been perhaps too much neglected in recent years. German models and assistance were as important to the Russian social revolutionaries of this era as French models and aid had been to the Polish national revolutionaries who dominated the preceding era of eastern European revolutionary history. Lenin's political vehicle to power was a Russian variant of the German Social Democratic party. His active leadership began with the founding of his journal, *Iskra* (the Spark), in Germany in 1900; and his final move to power began when the Germans allowed him transit from German-speaking Zürich through to St. Petersburg in April 1917. The German ties with Bolshevism were subtle and opportunistic on both sides, and were by no means those of a simple paid client. But there was a base of common interest not just between Social Democrats in the two countries but also between the German government and the Russian revolutionary movement. They shared a common opposition to tsarist power from the time that the anti-German Franco-Russian alliance was first concluded in 1894; and the opposition deepened with the growing dependence of Russian capitalism on France.

On the eve of World War I Russia owed France the largest debt between nations in history.[1] The new Soviet government became initially dependent on Germany in its hopes first for a supporting revolution from below, then, after the Rappallo agreement in 1922, for economic and military aid from above.

The German connection dates from the very beginnings of Russian Marxism, which remained until the early twentieth century, a kind of Germanophile minority movement within the Russian revolutionary tradition.[2] The time of testing for Russian Marxists came with pioneering efforts in the 1890s to lay concrete foundations within the Russian working class for the abstract Western doctrine of proletarian revolution. Lenin's genius lay in his application of the Russian tradition of an intellectual vanguard organization to the new reality of restless agitation and rising aspirations among the industrial working class.

The pace of Russian industrialization began to accelerate rapidly in the late 1880s. After the nationwide famine and cholera epidemic of 1891, the influx of destitute peasants into the cities increased dramatically. Waves of new workers came from primitive and rural backgrounds into large new factories and urban complexes creating fresh opportunities for revolutionary mobilization. But the traditional problem remained: a gap between intellectual leaders and ordinary people.

The first to bridge the gap was one of the few early Russian Marxists to come from the lower class: Pavel Axelrod. Originally a Jewish Bakuninist, he was dazzled in the mid-1870s during two trips to Berlin by the combination of discipline and worker participation in the German Social Democratic party. He saw in their cultural activities and workers' holidays a "prototype of life in the future socialist society." [3] Axelrod joined Plekhanov's anti-anarchist, anti-terrorist Black Repartition group, when it rebelled against the conspiratorial politics of the People's Will, emigrated to Geneva in 1880, and in 1883 formed the first Russian Marxist organization, the Liberation of Labor.

Its first program (1884) did not frontally reject the terrorism of the Russian tradition, but criticized its reliance on political conspiracy. German Social Democratic influence was evident in the call for a broad spectrum of class-based workers' activities and for the Lassallean idea of government aid to producer cooperatives. A second program (1887) introduced the Marxist concept of a proletarian dictatorship by referring to the "seizure of political power by the working class" as the "inevitable precondition" of radical social change.[4]

Though Marxist in *content*, this small émigré movement took the traditional *form* of a Russian revolutionary circle: a small band of exiled intellectuals seeking unity and hope in a new Western ideology promising universal liberation. The only significant group inside Russia to establish links with them in the 1880s was the short-lived (1883–86) Party of Russian Social-Democrats, which was in fact led by a Bulgarian student at the Technological Institute in St. Petersburg. The first significant Russian-led group was the Social Democratic Society, organized by a Russian student at the Institute in 1889 and posing as its objective the training of "future Russian Bebels." [5]

The German virus reached Russia largely through the mass-based Social Democratic movements which developed within the western parts of the Russian Empire. By the early 1890s the avenue of contagion led from Germany through Warsaw into western Russia and on to St. Petersburg itself, the historic "window to the West" of the Eurasian Empire. The railroad gauge broadened as the tracks moved east; so also did the vistas for revolutionary activity.

Among the first bearers of infection were the energetic Jewish workers confined by law to the pale of settlement in western Russia. Their international connections and German-like Yiddish language assured easy and early exposure to German ideas. Like the German workers, the Jews had a relatively high level of culture which made their civil and political deprivations particularly galling. The situation worsened drastically for Jews in the 1880s, when anti-Semitic pogroms were introduced as a lightning rod for popular discontent in western Russia and the Ukraine. With their very identity thus threatened, some Jews turned to their own, intense form of nationalism, Zionism, which eventually

helped found the state of Israel. Other Jews found a prophetic alternative in the General Union of Jewish Workers in Russia and Poland,
better known as the Bund, which was created in 1897, the year of the
first Zionist Congress in Basel, and was at the turn of the century the
largest and best organized Social Democratic organization in the Russian Empire.[6] If Zionism was in many respects a uniquely intense
variant of the national revolutionary tradition, the new Social Democratic organizations exemplified the rival tradition of social revolution.

As if in reaction to the multi-nationalism of the Russian Empire,
the first Social Democratic party within its borders, the Social Democratic party of Poland and Lithuania, created in 1893, proved to be
the most profoundly anti-nationalist of any social revolutionary party.
Out of the common national humiliation of Poles and Jews, the new
party was prodded by the Polish-Jewish Rosa Luxemburg into rejecting
all narrow nationalist movements in the name of international proletarian revolution. The Polish party was formed in deliberate opposition to the new Polish populist party (The Polish Socialist party or
PPS), which had accepted a separate national identity for Poland at its
founding in 1892. The Social Democrats insisted that the Polish proletariat should fight only for the common social struggle against the
tsarist system—never, even as a tactical matter, for any national cause.

By the late 1880s, Polish no less than Jewish workers were generating forms of grass-roots proletarian activity[7] that had heretofore been
largely unknown to the Russian revolutionary movement with its historic reliance on elite intellectual leadership. One Polish activist of this
period, Waclaw Machajski, developed during his Siberian exile in the
1890s an extreme indictment of the parasitic intellectual leadership
within the Social Democratic movement.[8] His call for a "workers' conspiracy" to create a truly classless movement[9] went unanswered; but
Makhaevshchina was to become a powerful current of thought on the
Russian Left. It built on the established anti-intellectual traditions of
Proudhon, Bakunin, and the Russian anarchists and helped revive the
populist passions that would lead to the formation of the revolutionary
rival to the Social Democrats, the larger but more amorphous Socialist
Revolutionaries or SR's.

Intensified anti-intellectualism resulted from the larger scale of contact that intellectuals were at last having with workers, who were often
illiterate and deeply hostile to theoretical ideas of any kind. In the
deep interior of Russia this conflict was particularly severe—as in the
case of the founder of the first Marxist groups on the upper Volga,
Nicholas Fedoseev.

Fedoseev built on the radical organizations that developed in the early
1880s as provincial imitations of the intellectual circles of St. Petersburg. He led a group of young intellectuals in Vladimir to oppose terrorism and to work for a closer link between peasants and workers—
thereby overcoming two perceived weaknesses in the People's Will organization.[10] But he had no better answer than anyone else to the
problem of the gap between intellectuals and the lower classes—even
after his conversion to Marxism. By 1888, he had established in Kazan

the first full-fledged Marxist circle in the Volga region, with the expressed purpose of creating authentic working-class political leaders like Bebel, not theoreticians like Kautsky.[11]

Despite energetic organizational efforts and a program of illegal publications stretching from Vladimir to Kazan, Fedoseev never realized his dream. He was arrested in the summer of 1894 and sent on a long and arduous journey through the Russian North to Verkholensk in distant Siberia. There he sought to retain his sanity by writing a major Marxist treatise on the economic causes for ending serfdom in Russia. But he was denounced as a bourgeois intellectual, and the isolation and humiliation visited upon him by fellow prisoners left him despondent and isolated. In the summer of 1898 he ventured forth into the taiga and shot himself.[12]

The anti-intellectualism that appears to have hounded Fedoseev to his death in Siberia also animated working-class agitation at the other end of the Russian Empire in Vilnius. The large Jewish proletariat there took the lead in juxtaposing concrete action among workers to the abstract argumentation of intellectuals. One Jewish worker, Arkady Kremer, recommended "agitation" as a corrective to the previous emphasis on "propaganda" conducted by intellectuals. He was himself then challenged by an even more anti-intellectual Jewish worker, Abraham Gordon, who accused Kremer of viewing workers as "cannon fodder of the revolution," seeking to manipulate them while retarding their true political education.[13]

The call for direct proletarian action was brought from western Russia to St. Petersburg in 1893 by Yury Martov, a Russified Jewish intellectual who had been exiled to Vilnius after participating in the workers' demonstration at the funeral of Shelgunov in 1891. He returned to St. Petersburg in 1893, armed with Kremer's *On Agitation* as a guide book for mass action.

The drive towards agitation was an eastern echo of the western syndicalist passion for direct action. But it was something much deeper as well. The revolutionary tradition was striving for roots in the soil, liberation from its century-long dependence on "verbal talismans." There was a thirst if not for blood, then at least for some kind of blood ritual: a longing to be reborn and not merely republished.

Thus Martov went even further than Fedoseev, who had rejected the label Marxist, rejecting as well the terms socialism and social democracy. He sought to break the inherited habits of thought as well as the assumptions of leadership by Russian intellectuals. He wanted workers to unify around an accumulation of specific struggles rather than the refinement of general concepts, and he was the most important figure in drawing the twenty-odd Marxist groups that sprang up within the capital into the Union of Struggle for the Emancipation of the Working Class, which took shape late in November 1895: "the first Russian Social Democratic organization that made mass agitation the pivot of its activity."[14] The Union's Vilnius program of accelerated agitation on behalf of the specific needs of workers sought to raise their level of political consciousness, not just their economic well-being.

The organization championed strikes and published some seventy agitational leaflets before its disintegration in 1897.

Lenin's first organizational affiliation had been as an eighteen-year-old youth from the fall of 1888 to May 1889 with the pioneering circle in Kazan led by Fedoseev. But Lenin entered the stage of history as the coleader with Martov of the Union of Struggle and its most effective pamphleteer.

Superficially, Lenin was simply another provincial intellectual radicalized by early experiences. Shortly after his arrival in St. Petersburg on August 31, 1893, he gained acceptance in Marxist discussion groups largely as the younger brother of a martyred revolutionary. Expelled from Kazan University for participating in a student demonstration, he had found a new Western "bible" in Samara (Marx's *Das Kapital*). In St. Petersburg, his Marxist education continued within the circle of a young electrical engineer, R. E. Klasson, who had founded in 1890 the first serious Marxist discussion group in St. Petersburg before setting off to study German Social Democracy first hand from 1891–93. Lenin's future wife, Nadezhda Krupskaia, had belonged to Klasson's circle, which had sought to bridge the gap between thinker and worker by leaning initially more on Lassalle, who had pioneered mass mobilization, than on the more theoretical Marx.[15]

Lenin's first long work, *What the "Friends of the People" are and how they fight the Social Democrats* (hectographed in 1894), echoed Engels's final view that famine and plague were accelerating the pace of capitalist development in Russia; and that Russia could progress to revolution only through a period of capitalist development. Lenin visited Germany in the summer of 1895. Arrested early in December 1895 for his role in organizing the Union of Struggle, Lenin spent a year in a St. Petersburg prison, followed by three years in a Siberian exile that was far more pleasant than that of his earliest Marxist mentor, Fedoseev. Granted solitude, the companionship of his wife, and access to a large library, Lenin wrote his most technical economic work, *The Development of Capitalism in Russia,* which was published legally in 1899. It was a final assault on the populist illusion that Russia could somehow avoid the capitalist stage of economic development. Then in 1900 began his long exile in the West, where he founded the journal *Iskra* in 1900 and the Bolshevik party in 1903.

Prior to this "Iskra period" (1900–3), Lenin gave few indications of his future divergence from the still-dominant German model of Social Democracy, especially in its theoretical translation by Plekhanov.[16] If Plekhanov provided philosophical arguments for Marxism out of his extensive contacts with German Social Democrats abroad,[17] Peter Struve joined Lenin on the economic front in attacking populism after he was "carried away by German Social-Democracy and its successes" on a trip to Germany.[18] His *Critical Notes on the Problem of Economic Development of Russia* sold out an entire edition of one thousand two hundred within two weeks of its publication in 1894,[19] boldly contending that Russia's woes came not from the fact that capitalism was developing on Russian soil, but from the weakness of that development.

Though Lenin and Struve met and quarreled briefly late in 1894, such conflicts did not then occupy either of them long. They and all others calling themselves Marxists felt too dependent on each other and on the Germans after the repression that followed the industrial unrest of late 1895 and 1896 inside Russia. Struve went abroad for consultations with German Social Democrats in Berlin and with Plekhanov's Liberation of Labor group and the Jewish Social Democrats in London. He returned in the autumn of 1896 to become the editor of a formerly populist journal, *Novoe Slovo*; and he provided the imprisoned Lenin with books and printed articles smuggled from Lenin's cell before the latter's exile to Siberia.[20]

Though decimated by the repression in St. Petersburg, Social Democracy left behind Unions of Struggle and Workers' Committees throughout much of the Russian Empire. The "fetishization of organization" [21] acquired from the Germans increased the desire for nationwide consolidation in Russia. Representatives of the newly formed Jewish Social Democratic Bund met clandestinely in Minsk with representatives of six other small groups on March 1–3, 1898, for the first and founding congress of the Russian Social Democratic Workers' party. Its manifesto, written by Struve, declared the struggle for the "total conquest of political liberty" to be "the most immediate task of the party." [22] A Central Committee and party organ (*Rabochaia Gazeta* of Kiev) were chosen; Lenin was designated director of pamphlet publication; and Plekhanov's group was charged with foreign liaison. The Central Committees of both the Jewish Bund and the Russian party were, however, arrested almost immediately; and the printing press of the Kiev journal was confiscated. Only with the formation of the rival, neo-populist Socialist Revolutionary party (1901) and the refounding of a Social Democratic party (1902–3) was Russia to acquire enduring nationwide revolutionary organizations. Until unrest swelled into revolution in 1905, the various Marxist groups of the Russian Empire still tended to look to the German party for leadership. Indeed, German authority in some respects increased as the growing flood of Russian revolutionary emigration [23] turned increasingly to Berlin. To understand the Leninism that took shape on the eve of the Russian Revolution of 1905, one must turn from the German seed to the Russian soil in which it grew, and consider both the new type of *apparatchik* which first emerged in these formative years and the recurrence in Russia of the classic theme of Right-Left interaction.

Russian Roots

In a new introduction to Marx's *Class Struggles in France*, published early in 1895 just before his death, Engels hailed the German Social Democrats as the "party of overthrow" which had emerged unbroken from underground existence and was destined to become the new state religion of the very empire that had persecuted them.[24] If one simply substitutes the Russian for the German Empire, Engels can be credited with a prediction of things to come. At the very time in the 1890s when the German Social Democrats were becoming too involved in the existing system to remain a "party of overthrow," the Russians were becoming too estranged from their system to settle for anything less.

The remarkable revival of the Russian revolutionary tradition after the 1880s grew in part out of the deep interior of Russia itself, where Lenin had spent the first twenty-three years of his life. Like Stenka Razin, leader of the greatest of all Russian peasant upheavals, Lenin was born in Simbirsk (now Ulyanovsk) and spent all of his formative years in the Volga region on the border between Europe and Asia. There the authority of distant, Westward-looking St. Petersburg was never entirely legitimized—and the dangers of frontier violence never entirely absent. Of his many revolutionary pseudonyms, he eventually settled on the one derived from the coldest and easternmost of the great Siberian rivers, the Lena.

If Lenin drew strength like Antaeus from his Siberian exile in the late 1890s, he drew his organizational ideas from the ascetic, self-sacrificial traditions of the Russian revolutionary tradition. His dedication to this tradition enabled him to remain largely unaffected by Western exile after 1900, and to change the state religion of the Russian Empire from Orthodox Christianity to his kind of Orthodox Marxism within six months of his return in April 1917. One must turn, therefore, to the peculiarities of a Russian tradition which Marx underestimated to understand the revolution which deified him.

Lenin was baptized into the revolutionary faith by the hanging of his older brother, Alexander, in May 1887, for participating in a plot to assassinate the tsar.[25] His path to the revolutionary profession was otherwise altogether typical of established Russian tradition. He was a middle-class intellectual, the radical son of a liberal father. After being expelled from Kazan University for participating in a student demonstration, he gained both the time and the motivation to study the works of earlier Russian revolutionaries, particularly Chernyshevsky.[26] He was first exposed to Marxism in Fedoseev's circle through reading the authoritative *Das Kapital* rather than the exhortative *Communist Manifesto*. During the four years he spent in Samara on the upper Volga from October 1889 to August 1893, Lenin had considerable contact with a powerful survivor of the Russian Blanquist tradition, who later wrote that "the idea of the dictatorship of the proletariat had already occurred to him." [27]

After moving to St. Petersburg to study law in 1893, Lenin plunged into the ideological struggle against the populist belief that mass support for any revolution must come from the peasantry. Mikhailovsky, whom Lenin had met in Samara in 1892, became a special polemic target in Lenin's *What the "Friends of the People" are and how they fight the Social Democrats* in 1894.

This work already revealed two enduring and interrelated characteristics of Lenin as a revolutionary: his focus on power and his contempt for the intelligentsia. Lenin sought not so much to refute the populists' misunderstanding of Marxism or their errors of analysis (the main complaints of simultaneous antipopulist tracts by Plekhanov and Struve respectively), but rather to wrest away from the populists the appealing title of "friend of the people."

Mikhailovsky stood in a kind of apostolic succession to Herzen and Chernyshevsky as the journalistic spokesman of the revolutionary intelligentsia, and Lenin sought in effect to substitute himself for Mikhailovsky as heir to that sacred tradition. One of his most important and original slogans was first formulated in another work of the same year, this time addressed not to his populist foes but to an insufficiently militant Marxist ally. Rebuking Struve for using "the language of an objectivist and not a Marxist (materialist)," Lenin insisted: "Materialism contains within it, so to speak, a *party spirit (partiinost')*" that requires addressing all social questions from the perspective of class warfare and rejecting the narrow "spirit of the circles" (*kruzhkovshchina*) in which intellectuals simply talk to each other.[28]

Lenin threw himself into the polemic campaigns of the Union of Struggle, which had at least succeeded in linking the intellectual elite with genuine working-class organizations. More than 70 percent of the more than one hundred fifty identified members of the union were workers,[29] yet the organizational structure of the union followed the established conspiratorial traditions of Russian revolutionaries rather than anything even faintly resembling German Social Democracy.[30] A "directing center" of five intellectuals headed by Lenin stood at the center of the organizing group of seventeen. Three regional groups in St. Petersburg were each headed by one of the five directors.[31] The two key directors (Lenin and Martov) were exempted from local affiliations to provide strategic direction and ensure maximum security. There were no workers in the central directorate; and proletarian participation was apparently confined to the special category of "worker-organizers" who provided the link between the Social Democratic circles of different plants within each of the three districts.

Martov (leader of the fraction called "the young") appears to have done more than the "elder" Lenin to lead the St. Petersburg union away from the traditional tutorial relationship to the lower classes. His concept of agitation combined the syndicalist idea of direct action on immediate issues with the Marxist conviction that each individual action should deepen proletarian confidence that "the struggle will not stop until the complete emancipation of the workers from the oppression of capital is achieved."[32]

Lenin participated in the union for only a few weeks before he was arrested, but he continued to communicate with the organization fairly freely during his year in prison prior to exile. The question of the extent of Lenin's influence on the group has unnecessarily preoccupied historians, who have not yet perhaps devoted enough attention to the

possible influence of the group on Lenin. For Lenin's associates during
this period remained close to him throughout the decade from his first
arrival in St. Petersburg until the formal birth of the Bolshevik party in
1903. Most of them played important roles during Lenin's short-lived
rule over the new Soviet state. Whatever the exact nature of Lenin's
leadership over them, he also clearly needed them to build a political
organization. Thus, Lenin's key associates of this formative decade can
be described as the first Leninist *apparat*: the "men of the apparatus"
(*apparatchiki*) who preceded—and in many ways created—the Leninist
"party of a new type."

Lenin's key associates were almost all middle-class intellectuals drawn
to revolutionary activity not so much out of deep conviction as out
of the inertial habit of the St. Petersburg student subculture. Unlike the earlier student radicals who were consumed by ideas, these
young Marxists were basically technicians in pursuit of careers. They
were trained in engineering tasks for jobs in the rapidly growing industrial sector of the Russian Empire; they sought to apply the professional standards acquired in their technical training to revolutionary
activity as well. They came together in a single place in St. Petersburg
that may have been as important in incubating revolution there as the
Palais-Royal had once been in Paris. Just as the royal house of Orléans
had unintentionally provided sanctuary for proto-revolutionary intellectuals in the late 1780s, so the imperially favored Technological Institute offered a century later a sheltered hothouse in cold St. Petersburg
for new revolutionary growth.

The Technological Institute

The St. Petersburg Practical Technological Institute of Emperor Nicholas I had produced its share of revolutionary heroes in the 1870s and
experienced its share of restrictions in the 1880s, including the reintro-
duction of the hated student uniform. What enabled the institute to provide the strategic command post for the next stage of revolutionary unrest was the creation in one corner of its massive pentagonal courtyard
of a separate three-story building, which was completely controlled by students and eventually became in effect a liberated zone for revolutionaries.

Originally built in 1879–80 as an apolitical student dining facility,
the building became the center for a growing range of student-run
activities, particularly after the formation in 1884 of the "society of
technologists," which initially focused on the problem of finding jobs.
This inner building became both a gathering place and a citadel for
the new generation of students who were helping Russia enter the
industrial era. The institute was the largest technical school in Russia, bringing more than five hundred students together in one concentrated location (unlike the dispersed buildings of the university), and
subjecting them to a harsh common regimen of laboratories and workshops that "reminded one considerably more of a factory or plant than
of anything taking place in a university." [33]

Some of the pioneering Jewish Social Democrats arrived at the institute from Vilnius in 1885, and further contacts with revolutionary centers were facilitated by the founding of an affiliated institute at Kharkov the following year. A Polish student apparently first introduced Marxist ideas to the institute; the student dining facility provided a secure meeting place; and the well-stocked library in the same student-run building soon included at least four copies of *Das Kapital*, which was otherwise almost unobtainable in St. Petersburg. By the early 1890s, each higher educational institution in the capital had acquired (in the words of Lenin's future wife, Nadezhda Krupskaia) "its own physiognomy." The Forestry Institute was a center of populism, the University of "legal Marxism," and the Technological Institute of revolutionary Social Democracy.[34]

The first group to combine the study of Marxism with the organization of workers was led by a railroad engineer at the institute, Mikhail Brusnev. The key figure in this circle was a young Siberian student at the institute, Leonid Krasin. His account of these years sounds at first like a repetition of earlier circles of the Russian revolutionary intelligentsia. The students discovered the progressive use of scientific discoveries for revolutionary ends (from the Greek fire to Kibalchich's bomb); identified with the traditions of the intelligentsia (demonstrating at the funeral of Nicholas Shelgunov in 1891); and appointed themselves leaders over the workers, among whom allegedly, "the intellectual is needed for systematic activity and propaganda."[35]

Yet that link with the working class represents one of those powerful turning points in human history. Brusnev's new circle of 1891 suddenly plunged the intellectual avant-garde into the real world of the Russian working classes. Brusnev himself was the nonintellectual son of a Don Cossack with broad connections in the working class. He and Osip Tsivinsky, another Pole with practical experience among the proletariat, worked with Krasin, who became the leader of a new group of Social Democratic textile workers.

The great divide between intellectuals and workers was bridged in rituals that had some of the qualities of baptism into a new life. Krasin had to don older clothes, take a new name ("Nikitich"), and move across the city from the world in which electricity had been introduced to a world still largely in darkness. He learned workers' slang and incorporated some of it into a proclamation for a strike in the St. Petersburg port district in 1890; but his language was denounced as too *bashkovity* (eggheaded) by workers who resented following a leader too young to grow a full moustache.[36]

Brusnev's followers used familial forms and designations like "father" for the leading worker-organizer and "uncle" for Brusnev's leading collaborator.[37] And there were more than a few wives. Krupskaia was only one of four female teachers who participated in the new evening "Sunday School" for workers organized by the Brusnev circle and ended up marrying one of the male revolutionaries.[38]

But the only way of ultimately bridging the gap between intellectuals and workers was by forcing both to become something neither of them had been before: full-time, professional organizers. Thus, in 1890 was born in effect the first systematic cadre training program of the modern revolutionary tradition: the so-called Circle of Organizers (*kruzhok organizatorov*). The tradition of the People's Will was modified by the technical and managerial training of the Technological Institute itself in a move towards the professionalization that was essential to combat more sophisticated police methods.

The Circle of Organizers met secretly during the worship hours on Sunday and on workday evenings; and the inner party apparatus of the future can be viewed as its direct lineal descendant. The circle essentially organized the Shelgunov demonstration in March and the first May Day demonstration in 1891; Krasin organized on its behalf in the same year the first Social Democratic women's organization in Russia.[39] There were concerted efforts to recruit seminarians in the Theological Academy of the Alexander Nevsky Lavra and to start a parallel organizing effort in the Taganka section of Moscow; but police repression decimated the organization, expelling one hundred students including Krasin from St. Petersburg after the Shelgunov demonstration, and arresting Brusnev himself the following year. Their departure served only to scatter new ideas of Social Democratic organization into the various regions of Russia where the expelled and arrested organizers were sent. Krasin had a chance to play the role of spreading the gospel of Social Democratic revolutionary organization in Nizhni-Novogord, Irkutsk, the Crimea, Kharkov, and finally in Baku, where he was given a key engineering job in an electrical company by the exiled originator of the Social Democratic agitation in the Technological Institute, R. E. Klasson.[40]

Klasson and Krasin were part of a kind of electricians' mafia, which enjoyed a certain immunity from prosecution because of the desperate need in a rapidly industrializing economy for native technology. Gleb Krzhizhanovsky of Samara, another product of the St. Petersburg Technological Institute, became a legend in the revolutionary underground for his skillful use of electrical technology for revolutionary purposes, and was repeatedly aided in exile by classmates from the institute.[41]

The most famous alumna of Klasson's original Marxist discussion group in the St. Petersburg Technological Institute of 1890 was Krupskaia. She joined the Brusnev circle in 1891, met Lenin several months after his arrival in St. Petersburg in 1893, was arrested and exiled in 1896 not long after Lenin, and married him in Siberia in 1898.

But the man who more than any other individual realized Krasin's dream of professionalizing Social Democratic cadres within St. Petersburg during the 1890s was a taciturn Ukrainian named Stepan Radchenko. From the time he joined the Brusnev circle in 1891, he became in effect its leader. He may well have been the most important single figure in holding the Social Democratic movement together for the rest of the 1890s. He is surely the most neglected of all the founding fathers of Bolshevism.

The First Apparatchik: Radchenko

Radchenko's importance lay not in ideas—he never wrote a single published article—but in his role as a technician among technicians. He was perhaps the first truly professional *apparatchik*, a man not of grand plans, but of a hundred carefully executed details: the relatively noble progenitor of an altogether frightening species.

Nothing is known about his activities from the time in 1887 he arrived in St. Petersburg from Kiev to study at the Technological Institute until his first appearance in a Marxist circle in 1890. He clearly played an important role in deepening the links between intellectual circles and workers' organizations, and his conspiratorial genius enabled him to be the sole member of the circle to elude arrest during the police crackdown in the summer of 1892. Radchenko became the first of the "eternal students" who were to become so characteristic of later, Stalinist youth festivals—staying on at the Technological Institute even after completing his courses in 1892 to continue the work of Brusnev.[42] He brought Krzhizhanovsky into the revived circle in 1892 and Lenin the following year (along with both his and Lenin's future wives). Just as Radchenko had accompanied Lenin at key moments in the 1893–95 period in St. Petersburg, so his wife Ludmilla Baranskaia subsequently accompanied Krupskaia in exile. Both before and after Lenin's Siberian exile, Radchenko's apartment was the site of more key meetings than anywhere else. Radchenko was part of the five-man inner directorate of the Union of Struggle in St. Petersburg in 1895–96; the sole delegate from St. Petersburg to the founding congress of the Russian Social Democratic Labor party at Minsk in 1898; a principal contact with Lenin when he returned from Siberia in February 1900; and the main representative in St. Petersburg of *Iskra* later in the year.

The crucial, simple fact about this ubiquitous yet strangely silent figure was that he was the man who could get things done. In a world of expansive talkers, he was the one who could act quickly and effectively. He was the indispensable man who could, at short notice, find the place for a secure meeting,[43] print a leaflet, forge a passport, find and deliver money, deliver and pick up mail, and provide supplies ranging from secret ink to statistical information. Radchenko's original circle in the early 1890s was called "the technologists." [44] He soon professionalized Krasin's circle of organizers, creating a "technical bureau" at its core, which became in many ways the only body to have a continuing existence amidst the fluid Social Democratic groups that proliferated in St. Petersburg during the early 1890s.

Radchenko's style was radically different from either the courtroom histrionics of the revolutionary populists of the 1870s or the icy bravado of a Nechaev in prison disputing with his guards and fantasizing princely titles for himself. Radchenko avoided both the limelight and the prison cell, remaining perpetually, professionally, in the shadows. Though twice arrested, he was not held for long prior to 1902. The police could never find incriminating materials on his person. His grateful fellow revolutionaries—not he himself—assigned him titles of revolutionary nobility; and they were titles appropriate to the new military-industrial society in which their movement was now operating: *inzhener, general,* and *direktor.*[45] These pseudonyms—engineer, general, and director—were continuously used by a revolutionary generation reluctant to confer title of any kind on anyone.

Radchenko's pivotal role in early Social Democracy was, however, not just the result of faceless technical competence. He was looked to as the man who could communicate effectively between a hard core of revolutionaries and a softer outer penumbra of sympathizers. He was thus not a sectarian conspirator, but a true *apparatchik* who expressed loyalty to the inner cause precisely by extending his contact outward for purposes of recruitment, intelligence, and manipulation. In the words of a key contemporary and coworker, Radchenko was a leader in "diplomatic relations with the legal Marxists and with other Social Democratic groups in the capital: and with different organizations of intellectuals, circles of writers, students, and cultural activists." [46] He was also a communications link between the earliest Marxists on the upper Volga (the followers of Fedoseev) and the émigrés in Switzerland.[47]

Two factors in his youthful background helped Radchenko become apparatchik-in-chief of the St. Petersburg intellectuals. He had been immersed in the professional revolutionary traditions of the Ukraine and, at the same time, in the practical experience of dealing with working people.

Radchenko was the second oldest of eleven children born to a merchant father of Cossack descent near Chernigov, where he acquired a sense of regional pride in the native sons of that region (Lizogub, Zheliabov, and Kibalchich) who had first infused revolutionaries in St. Petersburg with a commitment to terrorism. He always referred to the student dining hall of the Technological Institute, where he recruited intellectuals for revolutionary activity, as the "Zaporozhian Sech'," the legendary site of Cossack freedom and self-determination on the lower Dnepr. He leaned heavily in all his activities on a kind of Ukrainian network. He retained close links with Kiev, which created the largest Union of Struggle outside St. Petersburg and provided half of the six organizations that met with Radchenko to form the Russian Social Democratic Labor party in 1898. Radchenko appears to have depended on his brothers, his Ukrainian schoolmates, and his Ukrainian assistant, A. Malchenko, for the anonymous and variegated forms of assistance he perpetually needed. When pressed to break his silence and explain where he procured supplies for his fellow revolutionaries, he answered, "through Polish technologists," [48] and his familiarity with the Polish language and Polish revolutionaries in the western Ukraine probably were sources of aid and support.

In January 1894, after Martov received a doctor's permission to return to St. Petersburg, he counselled his revolutionary friends to cease thinking of themselves as displaced Jews and Poles, to stop fantasizing about "broad plans," and "to go humbly as 'students' to Radchenko and his 'elders' into the already existing Petersburg organization in the same way that I went as a student to the Marxists in Vilnius." [49] Rad-chenko's group absorbed and propagated Martov's theory of direct agitation among workers, which had arisen from his contacts with Polish workers in prison and Jewish organizational work in Vilnius.[50] Martov viewed Radchenko's pioneering work in reaching the working classes as an antidote to what he then characterized as the "Blanquism" of most St. Petersburg-based revolutionaries.[51]

Radchenko appears to have moved easily and invisibly among workers in St. Petersburg.[52] He introduced Lenin into his Sunday circle of workers when Lenin came to St. Petersburg briefly in the fall of 1891 to ascertain conditions for entering the university. Radchenko at that time led both Lenin and the workers in the discussion of Marxism.[53] He became "the guide of other revolutionaries into the working milieu"; [54] and Lenin, like everyone else, regarded him as "our most skilled conspirator." [55] Radchenko arranged to finance and print most of the early Marxist attacks on the populists, including Lenin's *What the "Friends of the People" Are* of 1894; and it was in his flat that Lenin and other St. Petersburg Social Democrats proclaimed themselves a Union of Struggle for the Liberation of the Working Class.[56] Radchenko's importance increased after Lenin and other leaders were arrested in December 1895; and he played a leading role in the gathering of July 18, 1896, in a forest outside St. Petersburg where the Union of Struggle organized itself for a further round of strikes.[57] Arrested in August, he was released in November to assume uncontested command of the organization. He was its (and St. Petersburg's) sole delegate to the founding conference of the Russian Social Democratic party at Minsk in 1898, and was probably responsible for inserting the word "labor" into the official name of the party.[58]

Radchenko played a decisive role in beating down the proposal of St. Petersburg workers to create a separate treasury for purely economic needs and struggles.[59] He thus anticipated Lenin's opposition to "economism" divorced from the political struggle. Indeed, he may even have originated this "Leninist" attitude. Recent Soviet archival research indicates that Radchenko opposed Lenin's first advocacy of agitation among workers in the fall of 1894 as a repudiation of revolutionary militancy in favor of "the fight 'for a five-copeck piece,' 'for boiling water' and for other economic demands." [60]

Thus from the time he was released from prison late in November 1896 until he was rearrested in 1902 and exiled for the remaining nine years of his life, Radchenko was the most important single leader among St. Petersburg Social Democrats. During this period, a remarkably common set of assumptions developed among professional Social Democratic organizers. With the exception of a few aristocratic intellectuals like Struve, who always believed in freedom more than in equality, most Social Democrats accepted conspiratorial means to accomplish social revolution. They believed that both general Marxist propaganda and specific proletarian agitation were needed to produce a popular "party" that would be more than an intellectual "sect." [61] Even Martov, the future Menshevik and leader of the "young" rivals to the Radchenko-

Lenin "elders," preached the need for "a conspiratorial organization" to be "embedded in a wide social democratic party." [62]

Russian revolutionary Social Democrats were deeply disturbed by the sudden appearance of "economism," the Russian form of the reformist German "revisionism." After a severe crackdown on the Union of Struggle in December 1895, strikers in 1896–97 had turned away from militant Social Democratic objectives towards the pursuit of purely economic goals. Almost immediately after the founding of the new Russian Social Democratic Labor party, both its designated official party organization in the emigration (The Union of Russian Social Democrats Abroad) and its official journal within the Russian Empire (*Rabochee Delo*, "the workers' cause") accepted the new emphasis on attainable economic goals rather than unrealistic political revolutionary plans.

In 1899, there was a new and more violent turn to labor unrest (centered among metallurgical workers in St. Petersburg and the Ukraine) and a marked revival of student unrest. Lenin and the other exiled agitators of an earlier era sent from Siberia a "protest of the seventeen" against the drift of Social Democracy away from revolution. In that final year of exile, Lenin devised the basic implements for building a new revolutionary party to check the drift to reformism and mobilize the new unrest.

He began with that basic building block of modern revolutionary organizers: a three-man, central cell. In correspondence with Martov and Potresov, Lenin spoke of them as the "troika" or "triple alliance" who would accomplish the "conquest of the party" upon their release.[63] Their main weapon was to be the favored device of totalistic revolutionaries since Bonneville's *Tribun du Peuple* and *Bouche de Fer*: an ideological-political journal. Its title *Iskra* (The Spark) and its epigraph, "from the spark comes the flame," revived a classic metaphor; and Lenin extended it by calling his journal "an enormous bellows that would blow every spark . . . into a general blaze." [64]

Lenin went abroad with Potresov, allied himself with Plekhanov and other anti-economist émigrés, and began publishing *Iskra* in December 1900 in Germany with Krupskaia as co-editor. In "Where to begin?," published in the fourth issue in May 1901, Lenin summoned up the Bonneville-Babeuf image of a newspaper as a "tribune" designed to "awaken in all strata of the people . . . a passion for political arraignments." [65]

The central newspaper became for Lenin "not only a collective propagandist and collective agitator, but also a collective organizer." "Technical work itself" for the new journal would create "the net of local agents for a unified party . . . accustomed to execute regularly detailed functions on a nationwide scale." [66]

The very process of distributing the journal involved creating the nucleus of a new party: "a network of agents that would automatically form itself in the process of establishing and distributing a common newspaper . . . doing precisely such regular work as would guarantee the greatest probability of success in the case of an uprising." [67]

Thus, Lenin blended—as none since the Saint-Simonians had—the concept of a central journal of ideological indoctrination with a system of nationwide organization dedicated to social revolution. Lenin added the element of conspiratorial organization that originated with Babeuf and reached a new intensity in the Russian revolutionary tradition. The production of *Iskra* became intertwined with the perfecting of cyphers, pseudonyms, and false addresses; while the press was also used for such tasks as printing false passports (Bulgarian and German being easier than Russian to forge).[68] The flow of information out of Russia and the distribution of the journal in from the editorial center in Munich involved a clandestine transportation system which operated through a host of illegal centers and, by 1903, involved some one thousand *Iskrovtsy*.[69]

A number of Lenin's former comrades helped form local *Iskra* cells in the regions where they were sent after Siberian exile: Krasin in the Caucasus, Malchenko in Nizhni-Novgorod, and Martov, the third of Lenin's "triumvirs," in and around Poltava.[70] Radchenko's wife also set off for Poltava in the summer of 1900, launching a remarkable family effort to weave a net of supporters throughout Russia. Lenin had almost certainly relied on the Radchenkos for local arrangements earlier in 1900, when he stopped off in Pskov en route from Siberia to Western exile.[71] Radchenko's wife (known as "Pasha" and *direktorsha*—the "directress") helped organize successively the two most important Ukrainian centers for *Iskra* and the southern transportation route for smuggling the journal from abroad.[72] Radchenko's younger brother Ivan (known as "Arkady" and "Kas'ian") set up a secret press in Kishinev which began reprinting *Iskra* on Russian soil.[73] Stepan himself became the principal agent in St. Petersburg, and Lenin asked him in April to set up a kind of bibliographical review board for *Iskra* of works published inside Russia.

Lenin first asked him to enlist for the *Iskra* net the young intellectuals who had formed the revolutionary extremist group *Sotsialist*, and then dispatched an emissary to work through Radchenko in setting up a regular organization in St. Petersburg that would link *Iskra* with the remains of the Union of Struggle.[74] In the late summer of 1901, the "director" was renamed "general" in a kind of battlefield promotion for Radchenko by the revolutionary underground.[75] Up until his arrest and the effective end of his career on December 4, 1901, he played a key role in the "socialist postal service" used to distribute the journal—the trunks with concealed compartments, the dummy addresses (*iavki*), the writing of messages in invisible ink between the lines of innocuous publications (so-called *lastochki* or "swallows").[76] When his arrest was followed by that of his wife, his brother Ivan took over leadership of the St. Petersburg bureau of *Iskra* and played a leading role in the Organizational Committee formed inside Russia to prepare for a congress of the Social Democratic party. He represented *Iskra* at the preparatory conference in Pskov before he, too, was arrested late in 1902.

Though they were unsuccessful in forming stable, central leadership within Russia, the *Iskra* groups did succeed in spreading propaganda and new agitational techniques into many local settings. The characteristic structure was a small inner cell of organizers (often with a name like Spartacus), which would publish fly sheets weekly and distribute them widely (sometimes in colored paper in children's schools or thrown randomly into theaters when the lights went down). The organizers would also arrange small meetings of twenty-five to thirty committed Social Democrats to discuss contemporary problems (*letuchki* or flying meetings) and larger gatherings of thirty to one hundred fifty that included nonparty sympathizers (*massovki* or mass meetings).[77]

The Organizational Committee for *Iskra* inside Russia first began the widespread usage of the word *partiiny* (party-spirited)—often reinforced with the prefix *obshche*, indicating a common, overall, or higher party spirit.[78] Lenin was responding to Marx's earlier call for a "party in the great historical sense": a revolutionary body capable of conquering power.

Partiinost' in this sense was the direct opposite of that amateurism in technique and provincialism of perspective described by the term *kustarnichestvo*, a word Lenin began using regularly to denounce the sloppiness in method and absorption in local concerns that *Iskra* organizers found dominant within the masses themselves. Just as economism might blunt the revolutionary aims of a "party in the great historical sense," so *kustarnichestvo* might blunt its centralized discipline. The word had been used traditionally to describe the primitive methods of home industries in Russia. Lenin clearly preferred methods of revolutionary organization appropriate to the modern industrial era of large-scale factories. He needed his "directors" no less than did the bourgeois owners of factories; his "generals" no less than the tsarist protectors of privilege.

In December 1901 (the very month that "the general," Stepan Radchenko, was arrested), Lenin first used the pseudonym "N. Lenin" under which he was to become commander-in-chief of the revolutionary army.[79] His articles in *Iskra* can be thought of as revolutionary communiques—usually focused on a single theme which was often reducible to a single slogan, invariably enlisting emotion as well as intellect in the pursuit of some immediate goal.[80] Lenin saw all his *Iskra* associates as engaged in a kind of basic training for a future revolution, "doing precisely such regular work as would guarantee the greatest probability of success in the case of an uprising." [81]

Like any other modern army, Lenin's Bolshevik party depended on the invisible work of trained technicians: *apparatchiki* like the Radchenkos. Their professional anonymity has made it almost impossible to reconstruct the full story of what they did to create a Social Democratic party; but it is possible to identify another place in St. Petersburg that played at the turn of the century almost as important a role as the Technological Institute. The German model of Social Democracy was in some ways transmitted and transformed into a dynamic new Russian revolutionary organization through the new Siemens-Halske factory in St. Petersburg. Radchenko went to work there after his expulsion from the Technological Institute in 1893; and his technical duties enabled him to have constant access to the means of transportation and communication for the *Iskra* net.[82] Krzhizhanovsky likewise used his training as an electrical engineer to set up the most important single center of *Iskra* activity in the interior (in Samara); [83] and he was later strategically placed for Bolshevik organizational work by Leonid Krasin, who had worked for Siemens in Germany and returned to resume Bolshevik activity in Russia as an official Siemens representative: first as head of the Moscow branch and supervisor of its electrification program and thence to St. Petersburg as head of all Siemens operations in Russia.[84] Thus, some of the dynamism of the Russian proletarian party came from the German capitalist firm that had invented the dynamo.

Krasin inherited Stepan Radchenko's revolutionary nickname, "director"; [85] and he—like the other original technologist-apparatchiks—would play an important role in the management of the new Soviet state.[86] But the man who turned all their tactical technology into revolutionary strategy was, of course, Lenin himself.

The Master Builder

The most distinctive feature of Lenin was his single-minded focus on political power.[87] He was, as we have seen, a professional revolutionary before he became a Marxist; and he related his new doctrine more insistently to the struggle for power than had Marx himself. It is almost impossible to conceive of Lenin in exile following the example set by Marx of writing miscellaneous paid articles for the "bourgeois" press and devoting years of his life to a purely theoretical magnum opus like *Capital*. He was never as much at home in the British Museum as was Marx, the doctor of philosophy from Berlin in its golden age. Lenin studied fitfully and wrote rapidly. His prematurely abbreviated university career immersed him not in classical philosophy, but in the most political subject it was possible to study in Kazan and St. Petersburg: the law.

Lenin had adopted Marxism as a necessary alternative to the populist path for destroying autocracy. He adopted Marxism not as an open body of criticism for understanding society, but as a finished blueprint for changing it. In contrast to many other Marxist intellectuals in Russia, Lenin adhered almost uncritically to the main schema of Marxism until the final push to power in 1917, modifying the doctrine only slightly during and after the Revolution of 1905.

During his period of exile prior to that revolution, as we have seen, Lenin created a "party of a new type" to lead the struggle. In so doing, he followed more the Marx who periodically identified with Blanqui than the Marx and Engels who later accommodated themselves to German Social Democracy. In *Iskra*, journal though it was, Lenin was not defining a doctrine so much as driving towards a destination. In his first sketch of a battle plan, "A Letter to a Comrade on our Organizational Tasks," he described himself as leading an orchestra. The conductor needs to know "precisely who is playing which violin and where . . . who is playing wrongly . . . and who should be transferred how and where in order to correct the dissonance." [88] His self-image in *What Is To Be Done?* is that of a master builder who "lays down a thread . . . visible to everyone" so that individual bricklayers will have a line to follow—each laying separate bricks yet realizing that there is a "final goal of the common work." [89] Lenin was not so much defining a general line as threading a specific path. As he attempted to orchestrate the sounds coming from Russia, he heard two major forms of dissonance. His special genius lay in demonstrating that discord from both "right" and "left" had the same basic source: "spontaneity."

The necessary counterforce to such discord was "consciousness," the source of discipline within an otherwise amorphous movement. But consciousness must be a source of discipline, not dissipation. Therefore, Lenin's tract began with an assault on "freedom of criticism" as a dangerous slogan that would inevitably dilute revolutionary militance into democratic reformism.[90] Freedom of criticism gave rise to "opportunism," "economism," and "trade unionism" by blunting the basic Marxist belief in the class struggle as the moving force of history. Unaided by the higher "consciousness" of a revolutionary ideology, the working class everywhere risked being limited to its "spontaneous" impulse to satisfy immediate wants. They became vulnerable thereby to the bribery of the bourgeoisie, which was made ideologically respectable by the ideology of "economism."

But the terrorists on the Left also indulged in the sin of spontaneity. As the bourgeois intellectuals, they could not transcend their class origins. The working class as a result became infected with "the spontaneity of the hottest indignation of the intellectuals" that produced random violence without cumulative effect.[91]

Thus Lenin introduced the chiaroscuro technique of modern communist polemics: the brightening of a changing line by the darkening of rivals on either side into "left" and "right" deviations: terrorism and economism, "adventurism" and "tail-endism," left and right "liquidators" after the failure of revolution in 1905, and finally in the postrevolutionary era, the "infantile disorder" of "leftism" and the "bootlicking" "capitulationism" of "the renegade Kautsky." [92] Stalin ritualized this process into a formula of rule by alternating purges of "left" and "right" (beginning with Trotsky and Bukharin respectively).[93]

For Lenin, however, Marxism was the ideological cement needed for a harassed revolutionary movement—not pliable putty for a purveyor of power. Rather than more "theories of revolutionaries," the Russian movement required a "revolutionary theory" and a "conscious" vanguard able to interpret and implement it. Thus Lenin issued his call for a secret, hierarchical organization of full-time professional revolutionaries to build a new type of party.

Lenin's innovation in Russian revolutionary tradition lay in his insistence that this was a Marxist party whose interests were entirely those of the proletarian class. The relationship of his vanguard party to the working class was rather like that of a central nervous system to the body. It was indispensable to the body, but equally inseparable from it. Individual cells within this nervous system were thus inseparably bound *both* to the system of which they were a subordinate part and to the particular part of the body in which it functioned. Thus, "the centralization of the secret functions of the *organization* does not at all mean the centralization of all the functions of the movement." [94] Leninists were obliged to participate in all forms of activity that were genuine expressions of proletarian class interest ("the movement") but to owe their basic allegiance at all times to the party: the organ of "consciousness" that alone gave the movement direction. From the beginning, therefore, there was a kind of provisional quality to the allegiance of any Leninist to anything outside his own elite organization. Lenin left no doubt of his determination to enforce that discipline, placing on his title page as if in answer to the question of the title itself: *What Is To Be Done?* the citation from a letter of Lassalle to Marx during the period when both were close to Blanqui:

> . . . Party struggle lends a party strength and vitality, the greatest proof of the weakness of a party is its diffuseness and the blunting of strongly defined boundaries, a party strengthens itself by purging itself. . . .[95]

Lenin waged his struggle at the Second Congress of the Russian Social Democratic Labor party held in Brussels and London from July 17 through August 10, 1903. He emerged at the end with both the name and the nucleus for his "party of a new type," Bolshevism. His faction took its name, "the majority," from the position it gained by following what was to become a classic "Bolshevik" technique: sheer persistence in pressing positions and never leaving meetings. Lenin was in a clear minority in the crucial voting on the definition of a party member, when the congress formally rejected Lenin's insistence on a definition that emphasized central discipline and a full-time commitment.[96] But Lenin persevered; and the majority support for Martov's more democratic formulation eroded when representatives of the Jewish Bund and the "economists" left the congress in protest over other issues. Lenin used his temporary majority to elect his followers to the board of *Iskra*, officially designated as the central organ of the party, and to the Central Committee. Although by the end of the year Lenin was to lose this majority on *Iskra* (and later on the Central Committee), Bolshevism was born; and the larger, but more democratically disputatious group within the Social Democratic party was permanently adorned with the label of Menshevik, or "minority." [97]

Through a long series of tactical struggles with the Mensheviks involving many shifting alliances, Lenin consistently refused to compromise his concept of democratic centralism for the sake of some democratic consensus. He condemned the "toy forms" of democracy used by liberal politicians. He feared that any general campaign for voting rights in the Russian Empire would simply lead to another "imperial plebiscite" expressing the attachment of the backward peasant masses to the tsar, just as the French masses had voted for Napoleon III.[98] Lenin preferred to call for a "constituent assembly," which was born in the French Revolution as an expression of revolutionary enthusiasm, rather than to call directly for a popular legislature which might deflect such enthusiasm into reformist channels.[99]

Widely denounced as an "ultra-centralizer" and a "Blanquist," Lenin consistently acted as if his Bolshevik faction was in fact the organ of consciousness of the proletariat. After forming his new type of party, his major accomplishment was retooling its Marxist ideology for use in the less-developed world that the partly Asian, largely peasant Russian Empire represented.

The first step was the explicit accommodation of bourgeois intellectuals within the proletarian vanguard. Just as a mysterious transformation of personal identity was thought to have occurred upon entering the inner circle of the original Bavarian Illuminists, so upon entering Lenin's party "any distinction between workers and intellectuals must be completely obliterated." [100] The class function of this party was, in effect, to rebaptize intellectuals like Lenin as full-fledged proletarians. Such a ritual was essential because intellectuals were indispensable to any revolutionary elite.[101] Explicit sanction for bourgeois intellectual leadership was essential in countries totally dependent for leadership on a small educated elite. Immediately after the Party Congress of 1903, Lenin appealed energetically to "revolutionary students" to raise their own "consciousness" by accepting his leadership.[102]

Even more innovative was Lenin's willingness to accommodate the peasantry within his alliance of progressive forces. Using an industrial metaphor, he was later to speak of a metal fusion (*smychka*), or "clamp," joining workers and poor peasants. In his lengthy writings on the "rural poor" in 1902–3, he relied on Kautskian analysis and German illustrations, seeing hope for the peasantry only in their conversion into a rural proletariat of wage workers. But once revolution broke out in 1905, he immediately sensed the inadequacy of the classical Marxist formula of a "dictatorship of the proletariat" as the prescribed form of revolutionary rule. In early March 1905, he sketched the outline for an article suggesting that the proletariat and the poor peasantry together constituted the "real bearers of this revolution." He expressed fear that an isolated uprising by the proletariat might lead only to a "spontaneous dictatorship of the proletariat," [103] which would presumably be drowned in a counter-revolutionary tide as was the insurgent Paris proletariat in June 1848.

At rival party congresses held in April 1905 the Bolsheviks showed more active interest than the Mensheviks in inciting and organizing the peasantry, even while recognizing the rural masses to be "spontaneous and politically unconscious." [104] Then in the summer of 1905, Lenin's *Two Tactics* set forth a Marxist redefinition of the provisional government in a post-revolutionary society as a "revolutionary-democratic dictatorship of the proletariat and the peasantry." [105]

Lenin returned to Russia from his Swiss exile in November 1905 during the unrest of the general strike into what he then called "the revolutionary whirlwind." Two months of ill-fated incitement to armed insurrection were followed by two years of organizational consolidation within a Social Democratic party that was nominally united at the Stockholm Congress in April 1906 and formally acknowledged the principle of "democratic centralism." [106] Lenin urged boycotting the elections to the first Duma and taking part in the elections to the second; but as the Dumas were prorogued and reactionary rule descended, he once more retreated to the emigration in November 1907.

His major work in exile (*Materialism and Empiriocriticism* of 1908) seems to any educated Western mind an unusually dated and turgid exercise in polemic overkill against long-since-forgotten philosophers of science. Yet this work was important to Lenin in defending the claim of Marxism to represent scientific truth. His insistence on the scientific nature of his own Marxism intensified its appeal to the westernized elites of the less-developed lands. For them, Western science represented less an introduction to the experimental method of the laboratory than the acceptance of ultimate truths capable of shattering the shackles of traditional religion. Lenin's party of a new type provided, thus, a vehicle not just for the ambitions of intellectuals—but also for their quasi-religious visions of apocalyptical social transformation and their quasi-familial need for rituals of belonging and reassurance.

His combination of political intensity and scientistic pretensions produced an important modification in the Marxist attitude towards religion. On the one hand, his attitude prior to the outbreak of revolution in 1905 was politically pragmatic and far more flexible than the Mensheviks and other Marxists. *Iskra* made extensive use of the established channels for smuggling religious books into Russia; [107] and in *What Is To Be Done?* Lenin saw many of the persecuted sectarian religions in Russia providing "a means and occasion for political agitation, for drawing the masses into political struggle." [108] At the Congress of 1903, one of Lenin's closest associates urged an alliance with these "popular democratic elements" in the struggle against "bourgeois democracy." He argued that Social Democrats could help raise the "political consciousness of the millions who comprise the people's democracy," [109] and launched a journal *Rassvet* (The Dawn) and a campaign with Lenin's approval to work with religious dissenters "in order to draw them to Social Democracy." [110]

Once the Revolution of 1905 was underway, however, Lenin turned from being merely anticlerical to being militantly antireligious. At the very height of revolutionary expectations late in the year, Lenin broke decisively with what had been the standard position of European Social Democrats since the Gotha program—religion was a private matter. He insisted that while religious beliefs might be private in relation to the *state*, "under no circumstances can we consider religion to be a private matter with regard to our own *party*." [111] No past religion nor any future religion, even of the proletariat itself,[112] was acceptable. The "science" of

Marxism was both necessary and sufficient for salvation, with Lenin an infallible and solely secular pope.

Lenin's doctrine had a special appeal to intellectuals from oppressed nationalities within and beyond the Russian Empire. Basically, he foresaw an end to all national identity in the coming universal social revolution, and already at the 1903 Congress had expressed the centralizer's hatred and suspicion of the federal principle which dated back to the Jacobins' critique of the Girondists. But in his first writing on the national question in 1903 he recognized that the "autonomy" of oppressed nationalities might be necessary under Russian conditions,[113] and hailed the entry of "inflammable material into world politics" [114] when the revolution in Russia was followed by an upheaval of 1906 in Persia and by the Young Turk revolt of 1908 in the Ottoman Empire. Lenin was open to the thought that "the European worker has Asian comrades," and violently opposed the support of any national cause in World War I. He opposed the war effort with a small but energetic group of left-wing Social Democrats in Switzerland during 1914–16, and went beyond the others in favoring the defeat of his own country.[115]

His crowning work of this period codified for the less developed nations an easily understandable demonology.[116] Imperialism was the "highest" or final stage of capitalism, and war was its inevitable by-product. War was not the conscious policy of anyone, but the form of convulsive collapse that capitalism assumed in its last stage, when the large capitalist states were consuming the smaller ones as well as their own and the external proletariat. The task of the proletariat was to turn the imperialist war among nations into a civil war among classes.

Lenin's theory of imperialism escalated the class struggle to the level of a global apocalypse. In this last stage, the European bourgeoisie had lost all its progressive features of an earlier era. It was now dominated by parasitic bankers who performed no entrepreneurial function and, in effect, started war "by clipping coupons." In the less developed Asian lands, Lenin believed the bourgeoisie might still have revolutionary potential, however; and one of the first proclamations of the new Bolshevik regime was its "Declaration of the Rights of Toiling and Exploited People."

Like the nine-headed beast in the Book of Revelation, the "ravening beasts" of finance capitalism were for Lenin a sign that the end of history was near. The millennium, of course, was the coming classless society. And just as the antichrist preceded the true Christ in Christian eschatology, so the imperialist war had concentrated power and mobilized the masses in ways that would make a proletarian take-over easier.

The chance for power came late in World War I, when the Russian Empire was staggered by the loss of five million killed and fifteen million removed from the economy. As winter set in in 1916 with a dwindling grain supply and 800 percent inflation, Russia was rocked by three successive shock waves. First came the revolt "from above" of moderate liberals, the so-called "progressive bloc" in the Duma. They killed Rasputin, the symbol of imperial decadence, in January 1917, and sought to set up a regency under the Grand Duke Michael that would provide responsible, constitutional government with civil rights and local autonomy. Second came insurgency "from below" on March 8, 1917, when demonstrations led to fighting in St. Petersburg with one thousand casualties and to the replacement of tsardom by a Provisional Government pledged to convene a Constituent Assembly. At the same time the executive committee of the St. Petersburg Soviets set up an independent workers' authority which grew steadily alongside the power of the provisional democratic government and created counterparts in other cities during the brief period between the end of tsardom in March 1917 and the success of Bolshevism in November.

The third shock wave was the Bolsheviks' *coup d'état* in November 1917, engineered and led by Lenin after his return from Switzerland to St. Petersburg in April. Lenin brought with him the aura of an authentic alternative to the suffering and quarreling of war-torn Russia; and he proved himself in the dazzling six months leading up to his own revolution, a master tactician bordering on genius.

His first and most essential step was to identify himself in a time of total confusion with the most utopian of all revolutionary positions: the anarchist vision of an imminent end to all authority. Lenin recognized that in a time when traditional ties have been severed, the most extreme position may suddenly become the most practical one for mobilizing the masses. Thus, just after the fall of the tsar and before returning to Russia, Lenin asked for Bakunin's writings on the Paris Commune. He proceeded to write his great and influential treatise of the revolutionary year, *State and Revolution*. It was a work of anarchist fantasy—to be sure, a fantasy once shared with Bakunin briefly by Marx during their period of common excitement over the creative potential of the new forms of worker self-governance thrown up by the Paris Commune.

With the passion of an anarchist, Lenin rejected the parliamentary bodies of the bourgeoisie, who were seen as putting brakes on the revolutionary process. Lenin saw this as one of those periods when history was moving like a racing locomotive rather than a "slow freighter." [117] At such a time, there was a need for the "arming of the whole people" and the spontaneous political formation of "the people constituted in communes." At such a moment the "conscious" vanguard party must put itself in tune with the "spontaneous" popular movement, which sought to smash the oppressive structures of the past and to create "democracy without parliamentarism." [118] Reaffirming all the while his "scientific" Marxist authority, Lenin suggested that the total smashing of the bourgeois state was imminent. The "dictatorship of the proletariat and poor peasantry" that was to follow the revolution would "wither away" in the very near future. Since all coercion had its roots in class oppression, all instruments of coercion would simply vanish in the classless society. In Lenin's astonishingly utopian image, any conflict or excess after a successful proletarian revolution would require "no special machine, no special apparatus of suppression."

> This will be done by the armed people themselves as simply and as readily as any crowd of civilized people even in modern society interferes to put a stop to a scuffle or to prevent a woman from being assaulted.[119]

Having maintained Marxist orthodoxy during his long years of emigration, Lenin suddenly appropriated not just this dream of the anarchists, but the most visionary ideas of almost all his other revolutionary competitors as well. He took over the Mensheviks' long-standing insistence on the Soviets as a major instrument for proletarian political expression and promoted it as the only instrument of political legitimacy (his slogan "All power to the Soviets!"). He annexed the Socialist Revolutionaries' long-standing call for the direct peasant expropriation of the land (adding "bread and land" to his already established call for "peace" to make a trinity of popular demands). And he took over the hitherto rejected view of Trotsky and Parvus that revolution in Russia could directly "grow over" in an "uninterrupted" procession from a bourgeois-democratic to a proletarian phase.[120]

Lenin also suddenly embraced a gifted group of brilliant, deracinated intellectuals that he had previously held at arm's length. They provided the indispensable oratorical and organizational talent for mobilizing the masses. His companion on the sealed train that brought him back to Russia was a gifted Polish-Jewish revolutionary who had been active on the left wing of the German movement: Karl Sobelsohn, who had taken his revolutionary name "Radek" from the hero of a novel modeled on Machajski,[121] and he became a principal emissary of Lenin to the outside world during the early days of the new regime. Upon arrival, Lenin recruited a like-minded anti-intellectual group of intellectuals in St. Petersburg headed by Trotsky and known as the inter-regional group (*mezhraionka*).[122] These magicians of the word were essential for the mobilization of the mind that rapidly took place. Two of the newly baptized Bolsheviks—Lunacharsky and Trotsky—dazzled the working classes of St. Petersburg with their oratory conducting a kind of nightly revolutionary variety show at the Cirque Moderne, which became a popular rallying and reunion center rather like the Cirque of the Palais-Royal in Paris in the early days of the original French Revolution.

As other organized bodies disintegrated, the smallness of Lenin's following seemed less of a drawback, and the tightness of his organization more of an advantage. But the final source of strength was the quality of total self-discipline that he bore within himself. To be sure, the Bolshevik party grew ten times from its low point of 25,000 at the time of the March Revolution to the take-over of St. Petersburg six months later. But it was the disciplined generalship of Lenin that enabled this still relatively small political group to lead a revolution and totally dominate the new regime.

If there was one external element that was decisive in enabling the Bolsheviks to overthrow Kerensky's Provisional Government late in

1917, it was clearly the decision of the conservative military leader, General Kornilov, to march on Petrograd and fatally cripple the Provisional Government from the Right. This action from one extreme weakened the centrist government of Kerensky and enabled the other extreme to assume increasing leadership in the capital. This dramatic dependence of the Left on the Right at the threshold of power points to a deeper element in the rise of Leninism and in the history of the modern revolutionary tradition generally. It is to this dark subject that attention must next be turned.

The Symbiosis of Extremes

The revolutionary tradition returned in early twentieth-century Russia to its original pattern of early nineteenth-century France. As under Napoleon I, so under Nicholas II, revolutionary leaders were elite conspirators hounded into secretive methods by political police. In both eras, revolutionaries sought to terminate autocracy with assassination and to challenge imperial domination with democratic ideology.

Most important of all the similarities between the age of the first French emperor and the age of the last Russian emperor was the interaction of the extremes. In Russia even more than in France, the Left and the Right deeply influenced each other. The symbiosis of extremes became a fateful and enduring feature of the Russian revolutionary tradition.

In the first decade of the nineteenth century, extreme republicans and royalist "ultras" had been thrown together in conspiracy against Napoleon. The head of the reactionary political police that combatted the revolutionaries for Napoleon had previously been a fanatical revolutionary commissioner and apostle of *la révolution intégrale*.[123] The seminal figure within the Babeuf Conspiracy, Sylvain Maréchal, appears to have survived through some kind of special indulgence from, if not relationship with, the police.

But the perhaps inevitable symbiosis between revolutionary conspirators and the police who pursue them was to reach an ever greater pitch of intimacy and intensity in the Russian setting. Because the police presence was so all-pervasive in late-imperial Russia, it influenced both the Russian revolutionary movement and the political structure that the movement produced after gaining power.

The growth of a secret political police arm of the Right in Russia was, from the beginning, linked with the development of revolutionary organization on the Left. The "Third Section" of the Imperial Russian Chancery had been created in direct reaction to the Decembrist uprising of 1825. Though *de jure* a part of the tsar's chancery, it remained a small organization, dependent in practice on a highly visible blue-uniformed gendarmery. It had ceased to be effective long before it was abolished in 1880, for it was able to deal only with individuals, not organizations. The revolutionary movement had entered the stage of professional organization in Russia, and the police were to respond in kind.

The modern Russian secret police originated with the formation of a special "division for the defense of order (*po okhrane poriadka*) and security" in the St. Petersburg police after the first attempt on the life of the tsar in 1866. Amidst the renewal of assassinations, a new Department of State Police was created in 1880 with special sections for the defense of order in Moscow and Warsaw.[124] The new secret organization enjoyed nothing like the privileged position outside the bureaucracy of the tsar's recently abolished Third Section. It began only as a small ad hoc group of special security sections (*okhrannye otdeleniia*) of the police, under an assistant minister of the interior. But—particularly after the establishment of a secure headquarters on the fifth floor of the police headquarters in St. Petersburg in 1898—the Okhrana (Watchguard), as it was incorrectly but persistently called, became a vast police empire. Seven new sections were set up in the provinces in 1902; and authority was invested in new security regions (*okhrannye okrugi*), which numbered between seventeen and twenty-six by 1914 with twenty-six special sections and perhaps as many as seventy-seven district offices.[125]

The reorganization in 1883 of the Department of State Police into the Department of Police with the function of political security produced an organizational structure to match the professionalism of the revolutionaries. The police relied on emergency powers created by the Law of August 1881, which permitted virtual military dictatorship in any area where "conditions of alarm" had been created among the populace. This "extraordinary power of defense" (*chrezvychainaia okhrana*)[126] could be introduced only with the approval of the tsar, but was in fact often invoked for the remaining years of the Russian Empire. The secret police of the Soviet era also began its even more extensive secret police operations as an "extraordinary commission" (*chrezvychainaia komissiia–Cheka*) under supposedly temporary and emergency conditions.

Alexander III's antirevolutionary campaign was initially led by an emergency organization formed directly within the imperial court: the Sacred Brotherhood (*sviashchennaia druzhina*). It published a journal of provocation in Geneva called *Pravda* (Truth) in an effort to discredit the revolutionaries by its extremism. The Brotherhood planned to assassinate prominent revolutionaries abroad even while negotiating with others for their agreement not to disrupt the new tsar's coronation. But this organization was dissolved in November 1882 when the emergency had passed; and its files were turned over to a new foreign section (*zagranichnaia agentura*) of the Police Department, which became in effect the overseas branch of the Okhrana.

The resultant growth of overseas police activities centered on the Paris embassy inclined the Russian Empire toward growing dependence .

on France, where the traditions of *agents provocateurs* and paid informers had reached a new sophistication under Napoleon III,[127] and where
the Paris Commune had left conservatives in a state of perpetual counterrevolutionary vigilance. The system of prisoner identification and
police filing on which the success of the Okhrana was based (the Ber-
tillon system) was imported wholesale from France.[128]

The Paris-based antirevolutionary campaign provided a testing ground
for the Okhrana's strategy of parallel reliance on external informers
and internal penetration of revolutionary groups. A leader of the foreign agentura, Peter Rachkovsky, broke up the last émigré press of the
People's Will in Geneva in 1886. His subsequent discovery of revolutionaries with bombs in Paris in 1890 was publicized in such a way as
to discredit the revolutionary movement before liberal opinion and to
help ease the way for further Russo-French police cooperation in the
years leading up to the historic alliance between the two governments
in 1894.[129]

Inside Russia, the techniques of penetration and provocation developed rapidly within the secret police. Many of the police leaders were
Baltic German disciplinarians like V. K. Plehve, who became director
of the Police Department in 1881, deputy minister of the interior from
1884 to 1892, and minister of the interior and chief of gendarmes
from 1902 until he was blown up by a terrorist bomb in July 1904.

Southern Russia, from whence terrorist violence first came to St. Petersburg in the 1870s, became the main staging ground for governmental
counter-violence in the 1880s. Kiev was referred to as *skorpion* (the
scorpion) in the usually anodyne coding system of the Okhrana.[130] General Strelnikov, who initiated mass searches, arrests, and pogroms in
Kiev, was assassinated in March 1882 by Stepan Khalturin, who had previously tried to blow up the Winter Palace and became the last successful assassin-martyr of the People's Will.

In response, the police developed a new professionalism exemplified
by Lt. Col. Gregory Sudeikin of the St. Petersburg Okhrana. He began
recruiting political prisoners to be double agents, as in the case of
Serge Degaev, who became a police agent inside the surviving leadership of the People's Will. Though Degaev later changed his mind and
assassinated Sudeikin as a kind of propitiatory act,[131] the damage
had been done. The precedent had been established for the confusion
of identities between the rival clandestine empires of Right and Left
within the Russian Empire. Sudeikin argued with seeming sincerity that
only collaboration between the Okhrana and the People's Will could
institute the reforms that Alexander II had promoted through liberal
institutions. This argument that reform in Russia could occur only
through, and not in opposition to, the police had apparently persuaded
Degaev to collaborate with the Okhrana.

The continued sparring between the police and revolutionaries took
place in a twilight world of tacit understandings, personal alliances,
and even mutual admiration. Close combat sometimes led to secret
embrace. Names that were introduced on the Right (*Pravda* for a
newspaper, *druzhiniki* for "volunteer" vigilantes) later reappeared in

the vocabulary of the Left. Pasternak revived the name of Strelnikov, the original apostle of violence on the Right, as the name for his personification of the revolutionary Left in *Doctor Zhivago*. The "extraordinary" measures of the late tsarist police prepared the way for the "extraordinary commission" of the early Soviet era.

By the time the Okhrana acquired its own special headquarters on the fifth floor of the police building at 16 Fontanka Quai in St. Petersburg in 1898, Russia had a professional counterrevolutionary organization with careful files based both on agents' reports and the systematic reading of mail in its "black cabinet." A typical file entry on a revolutionary recorded all his known human relationships on radial lines leading out to different circles: red for terrorist links, green for political friends, yellow for relatives, and brown for people known to deal with his revolutionary contacts.[132] Another set of cards used different colors to distinguish among revolutionary (and potentially revolutionary) affiliations: red for S.R.'s, blue for S.D.'s, yellow for student organizations, white for professional associations, green for anarchists. There were between two and three million of these cards on file by 1911. The number of documents received by the police passed 100,000 in 1900 and continued to increase.[133] Reports of external spies (*filery* from *fileurs*) were collated with those of internal spies (*sotrudniki*); and preparations were laid for mass arrests at the times of greatest revolutionary activity (and thus of maximum visibility).[134]

The counterrevolutionary police in many ways became a mirror image of the revolutionaries. They adopted *klichki* (pseudonyms) of their own including the distinction between "elders" and "the young" which the revolutionaries of the 1890s used; they enlisted their own *mamochki* and *nianki* (mothers and aunts, like those of the revolutionaries to host and keep watch respectively over the "safe houses" where secret meetings were held and messages exchanged); and they classified their agents according to the type of revolutionary each was dealing with: terrorist agents, propagandist agents, and typographist agents. A special importance was attached to the last in recognition of the central role that secret presses played as a rallying point for underground revolutionaries:

> . . . to uncover a secret printing press—that was the dream of every "blue uniform" from the youngest recruit to the greyest general . . . "liquidation with typography"—this was the present that opened the way to celebration, promotion, decoration— [135]

The counterrevolutionary empire of the Okhrana metastasized throughout Russia like an uncontrollable malignancy. In distant Vladivostok, a Kievan student who had been repelled by the revolutionary demonstrations during Lent assumed a leading role in the two leading journals so that the Okhrana could control them.[136] In Finland, at the other extremity of the empire, Leonid Men'shchikov moved in rapidly with a staff of two hundred to promote and enforce the Russification of that proud and independent people.[137]

The peculiar unevenness of Russian political development aided the counterrevolutionary Okhrana just as it did the revolutionary parties.

The lack of broad participation in the political process deprived regular governmental procedures of any broad sense of legitimacy to resist attacks from either Right or Left. At the same time, the relatively vigorous development of legal procedures made it difficult to gain convictions in court. Thus the Okhrana was under mounting pressure to use clandestine methods and, if possible, to gain confessions from the accused to assure conviction. In this way the Okhrana became ever more deeply intermeshed with the life of the Left in order to establish the intimacy needed to induce information and seduce confession.

But seduction worked both ways. It proved difficult to involve oneself with the Left without entering into its ideals and aspirations. There developed, therefore, in the late-imperial period, a twilight world of uncertain allegiances and identities. However much the Okhrana and the revolutionaries opposed one another in principle, they shared in practice a common subculture of intrigue, anonymity, and excitement. They were the dynamic forces in a static society; and it was easier to change sides than to leave this alluring world altogether. Without the collaboration of Okhrana officials like Michael Bakai from Warsaw and later Leonid Men'shchikov, Vladimir Burtsev could never have formed in Paris his remarkable revolutionary police and detective bureau to combat the Okhrana abroad by adopting its own tactics of surveillance and penetration.[138]

The most important forms of Right-Left symbiosis were those of the two most famous Okhrana leaders to penetrate the revolutionary movement: Serge Zubatov and Yevno Azev. These were the central figures in the efforts of the Okhrana to undermine what they perceived as the two most serious threats to the regime: Social Democratic programs to organize the working class and the Socialist Revolutionary revival of political terrorism. If these two famous provocateurs from the Right did not succeed in destroying either movement on the Left, they did in many ways lock the extremes into new kinds of interdependence.

Zubatov had been involved with revolutionaries as a student, and began working for the Okhrana after his arrest in the mid-1880s. Working as a police *sotrudnik*, he helped liquidate the last press of the People's Will in Tula in 1887, recruiting in turn Men'shchikov from among those arrested.[139] As Social Democratic agitation among urban workers increased during the 1890s, many tsarist officials concluded that passive waiting for a second round of violence was an inadequate response. Zubatov felt that the monarchy itself should take the lead in organizing the workers. He prepared a memorandum in 1898 on the workers' question, and in 1901 journeyed to Kharkov to study worker organizations. In May, he organized for the Moscow Okhrana a new working-class organization to rival that of the Social Democrats: the Moscow Mutual Aid Society of Workers in Mechanical Trades. Ex-Social Democrats were its leaders, and lectures on working-class institutions in the neo-medieval Historical Museum on Red Square its first important activity.[140]

Zubatov's campaign to win the workers away from the politically subversive intelligentsia was extended to the Jewish community in

Minsk, Vilnius, and Odessa, where Jewish Independent Labor parties were established with varying degrees of success as a rival to the Social Democratic Bund. If Zubatov's protégés staged a pro-tsarist demonstration on February 19, 1902, to commemorate the emancipation of the serfs and defuse revolutionary mass movements, they also summoned in November the first legal grievance meeting of Russian workers in St. Petersburg in the Vyborg tractor plant. More Social Democrats became involved—especially those with authentic proletarian roots like I. Babushkin, a veteran of the Union of Struggle in St. Petersburg. Even Lenin, who vehemently denounced the movement, was willing to use it for his own purposes of gathering information and disseminating propaganda.[141] Thus Zubatov's expressly pro-monarchist organizations unwittingly provided vehicles for fresh revolutionary agitation and recruitment—rather as the Masonic lodges had for earlier revolutionaries. Indeed, Zubatov was dismissed shortly after the general strike in Odessa in July 1903 because of official fears that his organizations were doing more to advance the revolutionary cause than to impede it.

The real benefit to the Left of this initiative on the Right came in the Revolution of 1905. The revolution was, in the first place, launched by the dramatic massacre on "Bloody Sunday" (January 9, 1905) of demonstrators led by an organization spun off from the Zubatov movement. Father Gapon, the priest and former sheep tender who headed the demonstration, had previously known Zubatov and later entered into formal relations with the Okhrana. The Assembly of Factory and Mill Workers which he founded early in 1904 was built up with the knowledge and support of the police in Petersburg; but by March 1904 it had developed its own program for social and political reform which was kept secret from the authorities.[142] Thus Gapon's organization was able to take the lead in the demonstration of January when 150,000 of the city's 175,000 industrial workers mounted a nonviolent strike and drew up a petition to Nicholas II for modest economic concessions as well as an end to "government by bureaucracy." [143]

Mounted troops fired at the several processions moving from outlying industrial regions in to the center of St. Petersburg. When the main procession led by Gapon arrived singing hymns in the open square before the Winter Palace, hoping to deliver their petition to the tsar, they were fired on and brutally dispersed. Gapon, who was in full ecclesiastical regalia, was protected by the Socialist Revolutionary P. Rutenberg, who threw him to the ground and aided his escape—only to help hang him in March 1906, after he returned to Russia and appeared to be establishing links with the police.[144]

"Bloody Sunday" precipitated nearly two months of sympathy strikes in some 122 cities and numerous mines and railway lines throughout the empire.[145] Another wave of strikes rose after May Day, which fell on a Sunday, and militancy was intensified by the rising counterrevolutionary violence of the chauvinistic "Black Hundreds." The defeat of the Russian fleet by the Japanese in the Tsushima Straits on May 14 and the mutiny of the Battleship Potemkin on the Black Sea a month later shattered the illusions of Russian imperial power. The ensuing unrest was more violent and more concentrated in the heart of Great Russia than before. Spin-off elements from the Zubatov movement again appear to have played a more substantial role than is generally recognized in the two most important revolutionary innovations that followed: the first "Soviet of Workers" and the great general strike of October 1905.

Ivanovo-Voznesensk, the textile center where Nechaev had been raised two hundred miles northeast of Moscow, launched on May 12 the longest strike of the year involving some fifty thousand workers.[146] The first Soviet or "workers' council" arose when the 151-man strike committee (which included 25 women) assumed para-political functions following the flight from the city of frightened government officials and factory owners. The Soviet formed its own militia, assumed powers of local price regulation, and convened a daily open meeting on a small grassy peninsula on the Talka River which was referred to as "the cape of Good Hope." [147] This "free university on the Talka" was disrupted by Cossack troops and the Black Hundreds, but continued until July 19.

In adopting the name "Soviet" and in such incidental demands as a request for a national holiday on February 19, the textile workers in Ivanovo-Voznesensk may well have been influenced by precedents among the Moscow textile workers whom Zubatov had largely organized. Zubatov's leading organizer in Moscow had declared himself already in 1902 to be president of the "Soviet of Workers of the City of Moscow"; [148] and the plans for Zubatov's organizations elsewhere had included elections to other "Soviets of Workers." [149] The example of Ivanovo soon inspired the Moscow workers to establish their own Soviet, but economic demands in the petitions drawn up by veterans of Zubatov's organization continued to dominate the agenda in Moscow until the great general strike of October.[150]

Some Moscow veterans of the moderate Zubatov petition campaign of early 1905 were radicalized and joined with the Bolsheviks,[151] who attached significance to the revival in Ivanovo of the slogan "workers of the world, unite," and ended their own tribute with the words, "Long live socialism!" [152] Meanwhile, the most formidable of all Soviet organizations was formed in that bastion of radical politics, the Technological Institute in St. Petersburg, where Menshevik influence was strongest among Social Democrats and where Trotsky arrived with a galvanizing theoretical presence in mid-October just as the great general strike was beginning.[153]

The Great October Strike presented the world with its first clear demonstration of the revolutionary potential of a nation-wide strike in a modern industrial state. It began almost accidentally with a walkout of printers in Moscow and St. Petersburg. As the strike was taken up by railway workers, the government lost those sinews of transportation and communication it needed to control a continent-wide empire. Strike activity spread to the armed forces, the national minorities; and it was beginning to arouse the peasantry when the frightened autoc-

racy issued its manifesto of October 17, promising civil liberties and
a consultative national assembly, the Duma.

But public disorder did not subside. After the leaders of the St. Petersburg Soviet were arrested on December 3, its Moscow counterpart
started a new general strike four days later—with Lenin's belated and
misplaced encouragement. The strike soon became an armed uprising
in Moscow, "the only case during the revolution in which tsarism faced
a substantial opponent on the field of battle." [154] Its bloody suppression
and the collapse of the strike on December 19 ended the "days of freedom," and pacification of the unrest in the countryside continued during
1906.

The uneasy establishment of the Duma system under a reluctant tsar
gave way to pure reaction when the opposition-dominated Second
Duma was shut in June 1907 and the electoral laws revised.

The succession of war and revolution in 1904–06 markedly increased
the level of violence within the Russian Empire. In outlying regions
like the mountainous Caucasus, there were 1,150 acts of terrorism
between 1905 and 1908.[155] Traditions of local brigandage merged with
Russian revolutionary traditions, and non-Russian insurgents often
identified with the Social Democratic party rather than with the more
rural and Russian-dominated Socialist Revolutionaries. Among those
serving a revolutionary apprenticeship in the Georgian underground
was the young Joseph Stalin, who served as a mysterious liaison officer between the Caucasian bureau of the Bolshevik wing of the party
and its fighting squads. Here, as elsewhere, his ability to survive in-
ternecine feuds and repeatedly to elude the police or escape from
prison strongly suggests that Stalin himself probably collaborated to
some degree with the Okhrana in his early years.[156]

The only collective Okhrana arrest of Bolsheviks before 1914 was
that of the Bolshevik members of the Second Duma,[157] which drove
Lenin's party underground—and into closer contact with underground
agents of the Okhrana. Two of Lenin's closest friends and protégés
during the period of exile that ensued were *sotrudniki* of the Okhrana: David Zhitomirsky and Roman Malinovsky. The former was close
to Lenin in Paris after 1908, the latter in Cracow after 1912. Despite
warnings from Burtsev to Lenin of his connections with the Okhrana,
Zhitomirsky continued to enjoy Lenin's companionship and apparent
confidence as late as 1915.[158] Malinovsky remained so close to Lenin
that, even when his complicity with the Okhrana was revealed after
the revolution, he returned to the U.S.S.R. in the apparent confidence
that he would be welcome.[159] Lenin refused to acknowledge Malinovsky or save him from summary execution. While there is no reason to
believe that Lenin himself had links with the Okhrana,[160] there is also
no doubt that he directly benefited from the Okhrana's campaign to
prevent unification of the Social Democratic party. The Okhrana's arrest of the leading Bolshevik champion of reunification with the Mensheviks, Alexis Rykov, was useful to Lenin in preparing the way for
Malinovsky's elevation in 1912 to the Bolshevik Central Committee as
Lenin's key ally in resisting unification.[161] Miron Chernomazov, who

succeeded Stalin in 1913 as editor of the Bolsheviks' journal, *Pravda*, was yet another agent of the Okhrana.[162]

But the larger Socialist Revolutionary party posed a different problem. As the direct heir to the populist revolutionary tradition, the S.R.'s had to be combatted frontally. Their hard core "fighting organization" had embarked on a campaign of assassinations which represented an immediate threat to the government. The Okhrana gave the organization the mock-imperial code name "Boris,"[163] and began a direct—and successful—frontal war on the new organization.

Its founder was a gifted Jewish pharmacist from Kiev, Gregory Gershuni, who sought to subordinate terrorist attacks to a disciplined overall strategy of the S.R. party.[164] As before, terrorism was the work of the youth movement. The campaign had been launched by a student attempt to kill the minister of education in February 1901 and led to the first organized movement of revolutionary youth in Rostov in 1902.[165] But the material concerns of the workers became more important than the students' familiar calls for "ideological unification" in the revolutionary struggle.[166]

The Okhrana's greatest coup was the placing of a former revolutionary, Yevno Azev, to succeed Gershuni as head of the Fighting Section of the S.R. party in 1903. Though working for the Okhrana, Azev made no effort to prevent the assassination of his nominal chief, minister of the interior Plehve, in 1904. He became a member of the S.R. Central Committee the following year, and helped the Okhrana make its two largest mass arrests of the revolutionary era: of almost all delegates to the first S.R. party congress at Imatra in January 1906 and of the Fighting Section of the party in March in St. Petersburg.[167]

Azev was finally exposed by Burtsev and formally denounced late in 1908 and early in 1909. He could never have sustained his imposture for so long without a measure of sincerity in his profession of revolutionary commitment; Azev had, indeed, been Burtsev's only public supporter during the latter's terrorist period in the 1890s.[168] Many continued to believe that the assertion of Azev's police ties was itself a provocation.

The destruction of the terrorist wing of the S.R. party did not bring an end to revolutionary violence, because terrorism had moved beyond the control of the S.R. party even before the Revolution of 1905. The incendiary agent of antidiscipline was the destructive anarchism of the *bezmotivniki*, the "without motive" group within the largely Jewish Black Flag movement in Bialystok and of the smaller group called "Intransigents" in Odessa. Inspiration from abroad came in the anarchist publication *Bread and Freedom*, which began to appear in 1903 with Bakunin's dictum on the masthead: "The Passion for Destruction Is Also a Creative Passion."[169] The terrorist revival among the intellectuals spread to the countryside during the Revolution of 1905. Wires were slashed and crops burned, and the S.R.'s were unable to channel violence into their desired end of an "organized expropriation of the land."[170] While the S.R.'s substituted "fighting squads" for their "fighting organization," the far more violent Maximalists split off to

form their own terrorist squads. The Maximalists killed thirty-two and
wounded the son and daughter of Prime Minister Stolypin in August
1906. Rebuked by an outraged public and even by the S.R. Central
Committee, the assassins replied that "the real cause of the public's
profound grief is that Stolypin himself . . . is still alive." [171] Though
the pace of terror subsided after 1906 thanks to the "Stolypin necktie"
(the hangman's noose) and "Stolypin trains" (bearing convicted revolutionaries to Siberia), Stolypin himself was assassinated in the Kiev
opera house in 1911. Appropriately, the assassin had been a police
agent among the revolutionary anarchists in Kiev. Though he appears
to have acted "without instructions from any revolutionary organization or the police," [172] the impulse to assassinate had been inculcated
by experience with both.

Identification with the dedication and heroism of the terrorist tradition was a major factor in assuring the S.R. party a certain continued
preeminence as *the* revolutionary party of Russia. Even after the Bol-
shevik-led October Revolution in 1917, the S.R.'s outpolled them by
nearly two to one in the elections of November 25 for the Constituent
Assembly: the only free, multi-party election by universal suffrage ever
held in Russia.[173]

The revival of terrorism in early twentieth-century Russia paralyzed
the will even of those who opposed it. More powerful than the reality of
terrorism was the fear of it. There was fear of the unknown: the mysterious bomb always about to explode in Bely's hallucinatory novel of 1911,
Petersburg.[174] There was fear of some preternatural link between terror
and biblical apocalypse in the novel of 1909, *The Pale Horse*, by Boris
Savinkov, the S.R. leader in the assassinations of Plehve in 1904 and of
the Grand Duke Sergius the following year. Even the original theorist of
Russian terrorism, Nicholas Morozov, began blending revolutionary ideas
with apocalyptical speculation in his *Revelation in Thunder and Storm:
The Birth of Apocalypse* of 1907.[175] The final image was that of Christ-as-
revolutionary, leading armed "apostles" into windswept St. Petersburg in
Alexander Blok's great poem of January 1918: "The Twelve."

Labor violence grew steadily after the massacre of workers in the
Lena gold fields in 1911, but was soon diverted into the organized
violence of World War I. That war was the one indispensable prerequisite for revolution in Russia, and it began with an event that blended
perfectly the Italo-Polish and the Russian traditions of violence. The
assassination of the Archduke Franz Ferdinand at Sarajevo on July 1914
was a classical anti-Hapsburg gesture of the kind that the Serbs had
taken over from the neighboring Italians. At the same time it was a
political assassination more reminiscent of their supporters in Russia.
Popular enthusiasm in Russia for going to war was produced in large
measure by crypto-revolutionary sympathy for the South Slavs. The
disastrous war ended for Russia in a revolution and civil war in which
the final, rival purveyors of violence were both Polish revolutionaries:
Piłsudski and Dzerzhinsky.

Józef Piłsudski led the final battle against the Soviet state in 1920–21.
He was the leader of newly independent Poland and the final expres-

sion of the national revolutionary tradition. A veteran of the conspiracy that claimed the life of Lenin's brother in the 1880s and of "fighting squads" that conducted spectacular raids against banks and arsenals in Russia and Poland during the Revolution of 1905, Piłsudski now returned with an army as the avenging embodiment of a Poland finally freed from Russian domination.

Piłsudski was an apocalyptical hero for the new Right in Russia, which had lived in symbiotic intimacy with the old Left in the prerevolutionary emigration. The novelist Dmitry Merezhkovsky wrote a book in 1921 hailing Piłsudski as the man of God sent to deliver Russia from the Bolshevik Antichrist.[176] In the emigration again after 1917 (as after 1905), Merezhkovsky revived many of the occult ideas from which the revolutionary tradition had originally sprung—such as the Illuminist concept of radiating world-wide influence through concentric three-man circles.[177] Merezhkovsky drifted uneasily on to Mussolini and later to Hitler in search of some kind of new force to free the world from bureaucratic atheism and permit a "religious revolution" to unfold. Thus, the romantic revolutionary mentality of Merezhkovsky and some of his S.R. friends like Savinkov helped fortify Piłsudski's passionate belief that only a nationalist theocracy of the Right could prevent a universal atheist autocracy on the Left.

The leading defender of the new atheistic autocracy in Russia was another Pole, Felix Dzerzhinsky. He was the ultimate social revolutionary just as Piłsudski was the distillation of revolutionary nationalism. Whereas Piłsudski was a product of the nationalist Polish Socialist party in the 1890s, Dzerzhinsky had been an early adherent in the mid-1890s of the first Marxist party in the Russian Empire: the Social Democratic party of Poland and Lithuania. Dzerzhinsky founded his Extraordinary Commission (Cheka) for the defense of the revolution just a few weeks after the seizure of power and rapidly turned it into the most awesome political police empire the world had ever seen. He soon formed a Trust to penetrate émigré organizations abroad, and succeeded in luring back to Russia figures like Savinkov, who publicly renounced his anti-Soviet views before mysteriously dying in a Soviet prison.[178] Dzerzhinsky began to attach "special sections" to Soviet missions abroad—almost as if his organization were a continuation of rather than a reaction to the Okhrana.

Dzerzhinsky had in fact been educated in tsarist prisons and Siberian exile, where he spent about half of his adult life prior to 1917. A wellborn and devout Catholic who used to force his brothers and sisters to pray regularly, he exchanged his Christian catechism for a Marxist one during his first year at the University of Vilnius and left to become an agitator among workers in nearby Kovno. He learned almost everything he knew from the tsarist police who pursued him and incarcerated him six times. Among the revolutionary extremists with whom he was imprisoned, the old Russian tradition of self-immolation had been revived in the late imperial period.[179] Dzerzhinsky described socialism as a "torch" rather than a doctrine;[180] and himself as a fighter who must be either "entirely in the fire" or "carried to the cemetery." [181]

When he was finally borne to his resting place in the Kremlin wall near Lenin, he was hailed by Stalin as having "burned himself out for the proletariat." [182] Radek spoke of him as the great "disinfector" of the revolution; [183] and each periodic, ritual purge on which the police empire came to depend was known as a "cleansing" (*chistka*).

All of these metaphors suggest that Dzerzhinsky represented a kind of purified essence of the revolutionary faith. Whereas Lenin had described his profession as "journalist," Dzerzhinsky answered a similar questionnaire with "revolutionary—that's all." [184]

Here at last was the radical simplification that revolutionaries had so long sought: faith tested by flame. Dzerzhinsky represented the dedication that power could not corrupt. He was simplicity incarnate, the self-effacing defender of the revolution, working sixteen hours a day in a simple building that once housed an insurance company. Far more than Robespierre, Dzerzhinsky deserved the title "incorruptible."

Two weeks after Lenin's death, he became chairman of the Supreme Council of the National Economy as well as head of police. The fatal blending of these two functions had begun; and his police empire was turned after his death two years later into Stalin's personal instrument of political and economic terror. The weapon Dzerzhinsky had created to defend a simple faith was used against those who continued to make things complicated. Soviet intelligence destroyed the Russian intelligentsia. If the sword was wielded by Stalin, Dzerzhinsky had forged it. Dzerzhinsky, in his last years, was, perhaps appropriately, Stalin's most important ally in leadership battles with Trotsky and other rivals for the mantle of Lenin.

The reign of the secret police under Stalin far surpassed anything remotely imagined by the Okhrana.[185] Though Stalin's successors dismantled most of the concentration camps, the "extraordinary" power of the police remained. A biographical film glorified Dzerzhinsky in the early Brezhnev era under a title *Veliky Podvig* (the "great deed") traditionally used to describe the heroic and saving work of saints. Nearly a quarter of a century after the gigantic likenesses of Stalin had fallen from public places throughout the Soviet Empire, Dzerzhinsky's massive, forty-foot statue still loomed in front of the secret police headquarters he first established in the Lubianka near the Kremlin.

For all their use of provocateurs, the tsarist Okhrana never engaged in the counterassassinations abroad that the Soviet secret police were to attempt. Indeed, the growing concern for due process at trials and relatively humane treatment in prison and exile made the Okhrana's campaign against the revolutionaries far less severe and effective than that of its Soviet successors. There were only four mass arrests by the Okhrana in the early twentieth century,[186] and Lenin like many others enjoyed relatively good conditions for reading and writing during his far-from-arduous exile in Siberia.

If the new Soviet rulers were schooled in cruelty and technique by their tsarist predecessors, they clearly went beyond a mere recreation on the Left of what they had experienced from the Right. They made their revolution in October 1917 not against tsarism, but against the democratic Provisional Government that had replaced it. The Leninist regime preached in its passionate early days a violently antinationalist repudiation of the war effort to which the Provisional Government of Kerensky had recommitted Russia. The Bolsheviks brought with them a new sense of ideological legitimacy and mission that freed them from the moral inhibitions of the Old Order. Their revolution in power went beyond the symbiosis of the old extremes to build a brave new world that proclaimed totalitarian peace as the only sure alternative to total war.

There were three fundamental "problems of Leninism" that his myriad followers have been left to deal with. These questions go beyond the basic, general problems of Marxism: whether or not there is only one answer to all questions, and whether or not secular society is perfectible.

Leninism poses the added problems of (1) an ethical double standard: contrary yet equally binding moral obligations to participate fully in mass movements yet to render absolute allegiance to an inner elite; (2) an antidemocratic bias which may have been caused by the conditions of pre-revolutionary Russia, but continues to be defended as universally valid; and finally, (3) the absence of any but the most naive plans for just administration after a successful revolution. As a leading Western biographer of Lenin's performance after taking power has observed: "What commenced to wither away was the idea of withering away." [187]

But it would be misleading as well as unfair to end a discussion of Lenin with the impression that the apparatus of the party and the internalizing of Russian autocratic methods were the essence of his legacy. The heart of Leninism was the figure of Lenin himself: a self-disciplined, essentially puritanical figure in whom the revolutionary passion for simplification found its human embodiment. He saw himself as the simple servant of a revolution greater than himself—speaking directly to the proletariat the concise slogans and pronouncements that sealed the success of the Bolshevik Revolution. The fundamental revolutionary longing to *oprostit'sia*, to simplify things, found verbal incarnation in Lenin's call in April 1917 for "bread, peace, and land" and in his proclamation in November that everything now belonged to everybody.

CHAPTER 17

The Role of Women

LENIN'S Revolution in November 1917 was mounted against a rival revolutionary regime that had briefly and provisionally brought democracy to Russia in the revolution of March 1917. Lenin's social revolution was doomed to confinement in one country after the final defeat of the attempt at revolution in Germany in January 1919.

Women were central to both the original victory in St. Petersburg and the final defeat in Berlin. Women had only slowly gained prominence within the revolutionary tradition; but they had assumed special importance within the German and especially the Russian movement. The March Revolution in St. Petersburg was triggered by a mass demonstration for International Women's Day. The January upheaval in Berlin was ended by the murder of the only revolutionary personality of the era to rival Lenin in stature: Rosa Luxemburg.

As in Brussels in August 1830, so in St. Petersburg in March 1917 a festive popular event had unintended broader consequences. Just as an operatic performance had triggered a national revolution in 1830, so an essentially apolitical women's demonstration started the chain of events that led to social revolution in 1917. There is a kind of inner logic in both cases. Romantic operatic melodrama was, as we have seen, a symbol of and stimulus to the visceral cause of national revolution. The women's cause, on the other hand, was equally linked to the more rationalistic, rival tradition of social revolution.

For a final reprise on the story of revolutionaries without power, it might thus be appropriate to turn to the role of women, a largely powerless social group in nineteenth-century Europe. Their slow emergence to prominence in the broader revolutionary movement reflects the gradual rise of social over national revolution, the replacement of the Franco-Italian-Polish leadership by the German and Russian movements. Women brought special strengths to these latter movements in non-Catholic Europe—enabling each to become a total subculture capable of surviving repression, coöptation, and isolation by authoritarian governments and hostile societies. Women became particularly involved in revolutionary events during the aftermath of World War I, producing in Rosa Luxemburg perhaps the most authentically prophetic revolutionary of the early twentieth century.

This discussion of the involvement of women in the revolutionary traditions can only scratch the surface of a complex problem. Necessarily excluded from our consistent focus on ideological innovators and leaders are the great bulk of rank-and-file revolutionaries who happened to be female, and of feminists who were more or less revolutionary. At almost any given point throughout the period under consideration, some women simply shared and echoed the political and economic demands being advanced by men. Others sought to change only the social role of women, who were still confined to fixed and subordinate roles in the patriarchal European family system. The former group more or less passively accepted the agenda set by male revolutionaries; the latter group only occasionally and episodically identified with the largely male revolutionary movement.

Our discussion will focus on a third category: innovative feminine revolutionaries, prophetic women who were both original and important within the revolutionary movement. Such women often brought to the broader movement a special aura of moral superiority, born in part out of their very exclusion from power. Their criticism of European society tended to be especially far-reaching, to point towards a social revolution beyond local perspectives. On occasion, they went even beyond the social dimension altogether to suggest new sexual, cultural, and psychological dimensions for revolutionary thought. Because these are subjects of renewed interest at present and of uncertain significance for the future, this final retrospective look at revolutionary origins will focus on women.

The French

As with so much else, the history of women revolutionaries begins in the turmoil of the French Revolution. Thinkers in the Enlightenment had concentrated largely on the limited question of how education would improve the lot of women.[1] The otherwise proto-revolutionary Rousseau was the first in a long line of convinced antifeminists within the French Left. Women played few leading roles in the American Revolution or in the initial stages of the French. A small group of revolutionary feminists soon appeared in France, however. Olympe de Gouges, "the high priestess of feminism,"[2] drafted (and tried to obtain Marie Antoinette's sponsorship of) a *Declaration of the Rights of Women* to supplement the *Declaration of the Rights of Man*. Mary Wollstone-craft rebuked Burke for rejecting the French Revolution, wrote a *Vin-dication of the Rights of Women*, and journeyed excitedly to republican Paris in 1792. As the wife of the libertarian anarchist William Godwin and mother of the wife of the romantic atheist poet Shelley, she was a kind of matriarch of the female revolutionary tradition despite her lack of influence in her native England or in Scandinavia, to which she repaired after leaving revolutionary France.[3]

Bonneville's Social Circle was almost alone in seeking radical equal-ity for women, largely through its remarkable feminist spokesperson, the Dutch Baroness Etta Palm d'Aelders.[4] The only thinker to link a radical social vision with revolutionary ideas about the role of women (and speculation about the polymorphous possibilities of sexual ex-perience) was, as we have seen, a man: the inventor of the word Com-munism, Restif de la Bretonne.

The dominant spirit of the French revolutionary era was that of *Les Révolutions de Paris*, advising women to stay home and "knit trousers for our brave sans-cullotes." [5] "Politically, women at the close of the Revolution were worse off than at the beginning"; [6] and, in the settle-ment of 1815, women gained no new rights except of inheritance and divorce—with the latter soon revoked by Louis XVIII.

The temper and legacy of the Napoleonic era was aggressively mas-culine. There had been a kind of struggle within France between the feminine world of the salons and the masculine world of the *grande armée*. Napoleon's most tenacious internal foes had been women: first the *idéologues* gathered around the last of the salon mother figures, Mme. Helvétius; and then the liberal romantics gathered around Mme. de Staël.[7]

The revolutionaries of the Restoration era in continental Europe were exclusively masculine: small bands of junior officers from the Napo-leonic wars and male students who banded together in Masonic-type fra-ternal organizations. Buonarroti, the pioneer of social revolution, broke with this exclusively male recruitment pattern of the early national revolutionaries. In exile in Switzerland during the early Restoration, he sought to work through acquaintances who had taken temporary teaching jobs in girls' schools to recruit women for his trans-national revolutionary organization. He "always found among women greater disinterestedness, devotion and constancy than among men." [8] His principal aid claimed to have "created among young ladies a real army of republican blue stockings" [9] in Switzerland. But Buonarroti's inner revolutionary organization seems never to have admitted women—ap-parently because of two problems that he identified: the congenital insolence of men (who treat them as "pieces of domestic furniture") and the inability of women to get along with each other under stress.[10] Prati added his own more venal complaint that women in radical meetings were so unattractive as to cause "the most ardent lover of womankind to make an eternal vow of celibacy." [11]

In England feminism proved a reformist rather than a revolutionary cause. The movement for women's suffrage had begun as early as 1818–19. The original version of the People's Charter called for universal *adult* suffrage, which was only later revised to *manhood* suffrage.[12] English feminism, like American, moved in the bourgeois mainstream in pursuit of the vote and rarely attached itself to socialism as an ideology or to the proletariat as a class.[13]

In France, however, a truly revolutionary feminism became a major force between the revolutions of 1830 and 1848. The realm of politics and power was still a man's world, but the advent of women into journalism brought more ranging moral concerns about society as a whole and a new strain of pacifistic internationalism. Women helped extend horizons beyond the often narrow political perspectives of earlier all-male conspiracies to broader visions of a transformed humanity.

The ever-ingenious Saint-Simonians led the way by proclaiming that the coming social revolution would be led by a feminine messiah. Disillusioned with the purely political Revolution of 1830 and with their own failure to establish a new society in Paris under "Father Enfantin" in 1832 ("the year of the father"), a large group of Saint-Simonians proclaimed 1833 "the year of the mother," named themselves *les compagnons de la Femme*,[14] and set off to the East in search of a female saviour. Their leader, Barrault, proclaimed himself the "Saint Peter of the Feminine Messiah" and saw favorable omens in volcanic eruptions, the appearance of Halley's Comet, and the death of Napoleon II (presumably the last possible male messiah). Barrault addressed an appeal *To Jewish Women,* hailing them for rejecting the idea of a male messiah and producing instead the "bankers of kings" and "the industrial and political link among peoples." Against his belief that the Jews might produce the new feminine messiah, another Saint-Simonian argued that India produced more sensuous goddesses and a more truly "androgynous God" than Jewish "male authoritarianism."[15]

There was a kernel of deep seriousness in all of this. The idea that androgyny (the state of Adam before the fall) was the only truly liberated human condition had, since Boehme, been a central concept within the occult tradition. The romantic preoccupation with overcoming "alienation" led some beyond the social dimension into questions about the basic, biological alienation of one sex from another. Androgyny appeared both as the goal of humanity and the key to immortality in Enfantin's last work, *La Vie Eternelle* of 1861.[16]

Fourier believed that social renovation required the harmonizing of 12 basic passions and 810 "principal characters" created by their interplay. Even many who did not entertain his kind of fantasies were intrigued by his concept of total liberation and of gratifying the passions in gourmet phalansteries. Emancipation of women from their limited, familial roles was a particularly pleasing aspect of his system; and the term "feminism" was apparently introduced by Fourier.[17]

The Saint-Simonians argued that a man and woman together (*le couple prêtre*) should replace the individual as the basic unit of society to insure both equality between the sexes and sociability within society.[18] Building a new type of family was for them a prerequisite for renovating society. With the failure both of the political Revolution of 1830 and of their own mass propaganda campaign of 1831, the radical Saint-Simonians thought that women no less than workers might provide new messages of liberation. Among the feminine converts for creating a new "family" was an orphaned proletarian girl, Suzanne Voilquin, who joined (together with her husband, sister, and brother-in-law) the journal of women workers, *La Femme Libre*. Because the title lent itself to ridicule, she soon changed it to *La Femme de l'Avenir* and then *La Femme Nouvelle, ou Tribune Libre des Femmes*. But these journals failed, as did the journey East in search of a feminine messiah.[19]

This voyage to the East may seem in retrospect either a comic fantasy or a pathetic reprise on Napoleon I's expedition to Egypt. It did, nevertheless, direct Saint-Simonians to the land that eventually built a monument to their belief in reshaping the water routes of the world: the Suez Canal. Moreover, their adventures did lead to a feminine messiah of sorts. For en route to the East, Barrault met and converted to the new Saint-Simonian doctrine a then-obscure twenty-five-year-old second mate on the ship, Giuseppe Garibaldi.[20] He was destined to become not only one of the most successful revolutionaries of the century—but one of the most deeply dependent on a woman.

In 1839, after many more ocean voyages and several years of revolutionary freebooting in Uruguay and Brazil, Garibaldi suddenly lost his Italian comrades in a shipwreck and drifted desolately off the coast of Brazil. According to his own testimony, he resolved to find a woman as his only hope, spied through his ship's telescope a magnificently athletic creole, went ashore to tell her "you must be mine," and brought her back on board.[21] Whatever the exact truth of the story, there is no doubt that Anita, his "Brazilian Amazon," saved him from ruin. Throughout the next decade she was inseparably at his side even during long horseback rides and hard fighting, until she died in 1849 outside Rome amidst the collapse of the revolutionary republic they had briefly established there.

The newly active women of France in the early nineteenth century were neither revolutionaries nor messiahs: no longer *dames* but not yet *citoyennes*. If men had celebrated their revolutionary opposition to the aristocracy sartorially by becoming *sans-culottes*, some women now also began to defy bourgeois convention by assuming male dress.[22] Journals for women slowly moved from fashion and gossip to social satire and reform.

Saint-Simonian feminists disrupted a speech by Robert Owen in Paris in 1837 in a manner foreshadowing later internal protests within the Left against "male chauvinism." The young woman who denounced the absence of women from Owen's podium was challenging the identification of radical social reform with the arid rationalism and exclusively masculine organization of Owen's principal host, César Moreau, founder of the Société de Statistique Universelle and editor of *L'Univers Maçonnique*.[23]

The most important new aspect of social ferment attributable largely to women was a passion for pacifism and nonviolence. Delphine Gay and George Sand collaborated in a campaign for the abolition "of all violent penalties, and the suppression of wars" in the moderate Christian *Journal des Femmes*, which began appearing in 1832. Eugénie Niboyet, the editor of several journals for women and a leading feminist in Paris, founded in Lyon the first pacifist periodical: *La Paix des Deux Mondes*.[24]

The entrance of women into revolutionary activity was directly related to the emergence of a social revolutionary tradition as a rival to nationalism. However colorful the example of Anita Garibaldi, women played almost no role in the Italo-Polish national revolutionary movements. Of the 5,472 Polish émigrés registered in France in 1839, almost all were revolutionary nationalists and less than two hundred were women.[25] The most remarkable new prophet of pacifism and anti-nationalism in the pre-1848 period was another Latin American who came closer than Anita Garibaldi to filling the role of a female messiah: Flora Tristan y Moscozo. The daughter of a Peruvian aristocrat allegedly descended from Montezuma and the future grandmother of Gauguin, Tristan was the first to conceive of a truly denationalized class solidarity among the proletariat.[26]

At the conclusion of the physical and spiritual wanderings amply recited in her *Peregrinations of a Pariah*, Tristan joined together in the 1840s the causes of women and workers, the two "pariahs" of the modern world.[27] After leaving her husband, who had nearly murdered her, and reverting to her maiden name, Tristan went to London. Horrified by its poverty and inhumanity, she called it "the monster city" (*La Ville Monstre*).[28] She went everywhere, from the House of Lords (whose all-male premises she entered disguised as a Turk)[29] to the famous lunatic asylum of Bedlam, on a visit to which she appears to have acquired her sense of a messianic calling.[30]

Tristan toured France seeking adherents for her projected *Union Ouvrière*, gained the collaboration of George Sand, and corresponded with German journalists about her idea of a "universal union" of workers.[31] She associated the term *proletariat* not only with the economic category of propertyless workers, but also with the moral mission of saving humanity from all its divisions—including those between the sexes. The hero of her truly fantastic socialist novel, *Méphis or the Proletarian*, was a rich banker who simultaneously comes under the spell of a feminine messiah and declares himself a proletarian.[32]

Tristan remained florid in fantasy till her death early in 1844. She contended that Christ's second coming would be far more cheerful than his first, since he would no longer be single but accompanied by a *femme-guide*.[33] She also argued that the three persons of the Trinity should in the coming socialist age be represented as Father, Mother, and Embryo.[34]

Her last book was written together with the occultist Abbé Constant, as she immersed herself in a bizarre subculture of mystical feminists under the influence of his *The Assumption of the Woman*.[35] The most fantastic were the "fusionists," who proclaimed the Feast of the Assumption in the year 1838 as the "first day of the year Evadah," in which a new androgynous species (recombining Eve with Adam, as the name indicates) would begin transforming the Earth. Speaking as *le Mapah* (the combination of mama and papa), the prolific author of this fanciful cult persisted in his beliefs, later proclaiming 1845 as "the year one of the paraclete." [36] The Saint-Simonian D'Eichtal argued that the doctrine of the trinity was in reality "une haute formule ZOOLOGIQUE" for harmonizing all earthly conflict. The "male" white race and the "female" black race were to generate "the new mulatto humanity . . . still in the cradle." [37]

Flora Tristan contributed to "the emancipation of women"—the subject of her first book and title of her last one.[38] But her real importance—and that of the new women journalists of the 1840s generally—lay in their infecting the broader socialist movement with distinctive concerns that properly reflect (in part at least) their sex: a commitment to nonviolence, an internationalist opposition to any purely national revolution, and a special sympathy for the forgotten, "invisible" sufferers of the new industrial society: prisoners, mental patients, and victims of religious and racial discrimination.[39] In her last year, she gained ten thousand signatures for her petition to free the blacks.[40] Having once been shot by her imperious and incestuous husband, Tristan felt that women had to play a central role in the coming social struggle to preserve nonviolence as "intellectual power succeeds brute force" [41] in human affairs.

In America, the cause of women's rights was also often linked with that of Negro rights and of nonviolence.[42] Oberlin College, which pioneered the admission of blacks on an equal basis with whites, also became in 1841 the first to graduate women. The two causes were blended together in a remarkable American contemporary and counterpart of Flora Tristan: Frances Wright. She was the rarest of all phenomena: a dedicated revolutionary in a prosperous, post-revolutionary society.

The daughter of a wealthy Scottish merchant, Frances (Fanny) Wright published in London in 1821, *Views of Society and Manners in America*, which inspired revolutionaries throughout Europe during the Restoration era and led to an intimate, lifelong contact with the sixty-seven-year-old Marquis de Lafayette. On their first meeting, he paid tribute to her writings about the American Revolution:

> You have made me live those days over again. . . . We were an army of brothers; we had all things in common, our pleasures, our pains, our money, and our poverty.[43]

Her hopes mingled with his memories. She moved in for long periods into the room underneath his in his estate at La Grange. America was, in Wright's words, "our utopia"; [44] and their shared belief in the perfection of the New World formed the basis of a "friendship of no ordinary character" [45] between them. Repeatedly rumored to be his mistress, she tried in fact to become his adopted daughter. After returning to London, she corresponded with him incessantly (often in cypher) throughout the era of Carbonari intrigues. She accompanied him to America in September 1824, remained with him throughout most of his long, triumphal tour, and returned to France for five years of renewed association in the revolutionary summer of 1830.

A handsome woman nearly six feet tall, Fanny Wright often appeared in white, toga-like attire. She gave her friends names from antiquity (Jeremy Bentham was "Socrates"), and became herself a kind of classical goddess for many young revolutionaries. She acted as companion and consoler to the Irish martyr Wolfe Tone in New York, the Italian General Pepe in London, and an unidentified lover known only in her correspondence by the revolutionary pseudonym of Eugene.[46]

In the second half of the 1820s, Fanny Wright attempted to put into effect a grandiose plan to free the American slaves by integrating blacks into a new type of egalitarian community: new plantations that would be converted into productive Owenite settlements. Working closely with the son of Robert Owen (and attempting to enlist the widow of Shelley), she set up a pilot multi-racial community first in Nashoba, Tennessee, and then in the main Owenite settlement of New Harmony, Indiana. On July 4, 1828, she became the first woman in the New World to deliver the main address in a large public celebration of this national holiday.[47]

She became an ardent Jacksonian and moved to Philadelphia amidst the gathering labor turmoil which saw the establishment of the first labor paper in history, the *Mechanics' Free Press*, in 1828. In New York City she founded a radical propaganda society, the Free Enquirers, that celebrated Thomas Paine's birthday as its major event and established branches in other cities, partly on the Carbonari model.[48] Still preoccupied with the racial question, she set off to Haiti with a group of blacks and a radical French printer and educator, Guillaume Sylvain Casimir Phiquepal D'Arusmont, whom she married in 1831 after becoming pregnant.

In 1830, first elated, then soon disillusioned by the July Revolution in France, she concluded that only in America could the final, universal revolution be realized. She saw it as atheistic, egalitarian, and anarchistic. In the final seventeen years of her life after her return to America in 1835, she bought the Cincinnati home of the anarchist Josiah Warren, and championed "the ridden people of the earth" against "the 'booted and spurred' riders." She became increasingly apocalyptical as the radical tide receded in post-Jacksonian America. On the eve of 1848, she predicted that America was on the verge of a new "fourth age" of humanity. Christianity, "the religion of kings" had given way to feudalism, which was replaced in America first by "the Banking and Funding System" and now by a totally secular religion of the people.[49]

A radical conception of the role of women was central to her revolutionary teaching. She had taken Lafayette in 1824 to hear the pioneer of women's education, Emma Willard, in Troy, New York; and she was so opposed to the use of the male term "brotherhood" that she changed the classic revolutionary slogan of "liberty, equality, fraternity" into "liberty, equality and altruism." [50] But she made enemies by advocating that children be removed from their parents at the age of two and placed in publicly supported schools that would inculcate egalitarian ideas. Her opposition to the institution of the family and to all organized religion put her at odds even with the radical abolitionists; and her desire rapidly to mix the races into a new, uniformly mulatto population activated racist sentiment. She died largely forgotten in 1852. The milestones in women's emancipation in the Anglo-American world had passed her by: the beginning of the women's suffrage movement at the Anti-Slavery Convention in London of June 1840, and the first convention on women's rights summoned by the Society of Friends in western New York in the summer of 1848.[51]

It was in Europe, not America or Great Britain, that feminism became linked with revolution.[52] Fanny Wright had first been attracted to the revolutionary cause by reading a history of the American Revolution written by an Italian, who had projected onto the American experience his own hopes for Italian national liberation.[53] The *grande dame* of radical feminism in New England, Margaret Fuller of Brook Farm, became a true revolutionary only in Italy, where she was swept into the Revolution of 1848 after visiting France and George Sand in 1847.[54]

The European upheaval of 1848–49 produced a host of new feminist journals, many with revolutionary positions. The first women's daily in France, *La Voix des Femmes*, appeared in March 1848 as a "socialist and political journal"; and was followed by *La Femme Libre*, *La République des Femmes* (which published *La Marseillaise des Femmes* in its first issue),[55] and *La Politique des Femmes* (a journal of working-class women which soon changed its name to *L'Opinion des Femmes*). A remarkable group of young women demonstrated under the banner *Vésuviennes* in March, issued a *Manifeste des Vésuviennes* in April, and proceeded to set up an egalitarian female commune in Belleville, where the original Communist Banquet had been held.[56]

But women's liberation was still far away. Ribald journals ridiculed women's demands,[57] and most revolutionaries remained patronizingly indifferent to the "lady Vesuviuses." Delphine Gay complained that the cry "long live the provisional government!" was equated with "long live the provisional ladies!" [58]

Women played a leading role throughout the 1840s in glorifying the art forms of ordinary workers and peasants, proclaiming that, in the present era, "the creative role in poetry belongs to the proletariat, to the people." [59] This literary populism which swept through Europe in the 1840s owes its deepest debt to the most influential woman of her age, one of the few who dared wear men's clothes and adopt a man's name, George Sand. Almost singlehandedly she turned the serialized novel into seductive socialist propaganda. Beginning with her *Spiridon* of 1838, written under the influence of Lamennais, she flooded France with a new kind of fiction, which challenged both the historical novel of Stendahl and the realistic novel of Balzac. She purported to depict man not as he was or is, but "as I wish he were, as I believe he shall be"; [60] and she fired the revolutionary imagination of the 1840s by identifying this ideal with peasant and proletarian in a romantic, almost sensuous manner. But Sand faded away as a revolutionary voice after the failures of 1848. The Second Empire of Napoleon III proved even more aggressively masculine in spirit than the First Empire of Napoleon Bonaparte.

Women played a major role in the Paris Commune. The forces of the Right, which attacked with special vehemence in their propaganda *les pétroleuses*, the "women incendiaries" who allegedly set fire to Paris, arraigned more than one thousand women in the repression that followed.[61] A first sign that Russian women were to take away the leadership role of revolutionary womanhood from the French may be detected in the dominant role assumed by Russian émigrées in the two principal women's organizations in the Commune, the Union of Women and the Montmartre Women's Vigilance Committee.[62]

One final female leader of the French revolutionary tradition arose from the martyrdom of the Paris Commune: Louise Michel. She reasserted with new intensity the characteristic Sand-Tristan themes of internationalism and pacifism. Variously known as *la Vierge rouge, la sainte laïque,* and *la flamme révolutionnaire*,[63] she was as inflammatory in speech as she was demure in appearance. Perennially dressed in black with a high white collar, she defended herself eloquently at the trial of communards, endured prison in New Caledonia, and returned to become the uncompromising apostle of the anarcho-syndicalist dream of *la grande grève*.[64]

Michel was one of those leaders who belonged to no party "but to the Revolution as a whole." [65] By the turn of the century she was perhaps the most passionate and outspoken foe of militarism in Europe. Denied a visa by the United States and expelled from Belgium, the very suggestion that she might venture abroad anywhere unleashed a flood of protests and appeals to the Quai d'Orsay.[66]

She spoke eloquently on questions that revolutionaries usually avoided. After nearly dying early in 1904, she outlined a revolutionary attitude towards death before a large audience in Paris. She lent beauty to revolutionary atheism, describing death as a mere "incorporation into the elements," a radiation outward from the body of aromas and colors, a return to the simplicity that she remembered in New Caledonia after a typhoon. The complexities of human language would simply disappear; and a simple song "composed by a nihilist" would fill the air and enable one to descend into "the hole of shadows . . . beating back with one's arms the walls of an abyss." [67]

As if to parody the purity of such faith, the various revolutionary factions in France quarreled bitterly over the right to dispose of her body when she died in Marseilles on January 9, 1905. Anarchists vied for her remains with Rochefort, the former revolutionary journalist who had supported her financially even after his turn to reactionary nationalism. Her funeral was the largest popular procession in France since the burial of Victor Hugo twenty years earlier.[68] As her body was lowered into the grave, the cry rang out, "Long live the Russian revolution! Long live anarchy!" [69] On the very day of her burial, the Russian Revolution of 1905 had broken out. It was a revolution she had predicted just before her death,[70] and was led by a movement in which women played a more central role than they ever had in France.

The Russians

The example of George Sand helped implant within Russia the revolutionary consciousness that prepared the way for 1905 and 1917. The two greatest writers who participated in the pioneering socialist circles of the 1840s in Russia, Dostoevsky and Saltykov, both considered Sand a leading force in activating their social consciousness and one of the supreme personalities of the century.[71] Had she lived beyond her premature death in 1842, Elena Hahn, a novelist and early advocate of women's rights, might have been the Russian George Sand.[72] Had Konarski's revolutionary network in western Russia not been destroyed in 1839, the organizer of its special women's circles, Ewa Felinska, might have become the Russian Flora Tristan.[73] Had the Russia of Nicholas I not turned repressive in its later years, it might have imbibed the revolutionary feminism of Suzanne Voilquin and other Saint-Simonians who moved from Egypt to Russia in the late 1830s, bringing with them the vague idea that Nefertiti and Cleopatra provided models for the new feminism.[74] Most influential of all in the 1840s was Herzen's novel in imitation of George Sand about an illegitimate Russian girl in which the cause of female liberation was linked to that of liberating the serfs.[75]

Under the more liberal rule of Alexander II, the role of women and the women's question became centrally important to the Russian revolutionary tradition. The young seized on the issue of women's rights in part because of the unusually subordinate position historically assigned to women in Muscovite society. Here also was an issue that directly, emotionally affected university students themselves newly released from the social and doctrinal rigidities of a seminary-based secondary school and anxious to break with the matriarchal dominance and patriarchal discipline of the traditional Russian family. The greatly increased university population of the early 1860s sought a new communal ethic and life-style that would provide both social justice and sexual satisfaction.

Whatever their individual motives, the new generation as a whole adopted women's rights as perhaps its main social cause during the period between the emancipation of the serfs in 1861 and the discovery of the urban proletariat about a decade later. Chernyshevsky provided an ascetic model of the "new woman" as well as the "new man" in his *What is to be done?* [76]

Mikhailov, who had preceded Chernyskevsky as a martyr in the sixties, made his radical reputation as an apostle of women's liberation. Influenced by Saint-Simonians whom he visited in Paris, Mikhailov terrified church officials even in distant Siberia with his proposals to "take away the bridle from women." [77] He exemplified the new ethics by living in a *ménage à trois* with Nicholas Shelgunov and his wife (who bore Mikhailov a child), and by accepting guilt as sole author of the proclamation *To the Younger Generation*—saving the principal author, Shelgunov, from imprisonment.[78]

Nicholas Mikhailovsky, the most influential populist journalist inside Russia throughout the final third of the nineteenth century, also cut his polemic teeth on this issue. From his first three published articles as a boy of seventeen in 1860 to his laudatory preface of 1869 to John Stuart Mill's *Rights of Women*, Mikhailovsky devoted much of his energies to the cause of women.[79] *Woman's Herald*, printed in St. Petersburg during 1860–68, the last and most radical feminist journal of the 1860s, attracted contributions from influential writers like Lavrov and the novelist Gleb Uspensky, who were to dominate the populist era.

Russia in 1869–70 followed England by just a few months in pioneering the admission of women to advanced study in its major universities.[80] Female students proceeded to play a major role in the intensified radical agitation of the early seventies. In Zürich, the major center of Russian study abroad, 103 of the 153 students at the university were women.[81] So central to the budding revolutionary movement were the new women's groups (from the women's club for logical speech to the Fritschi group, named for their baffled Swiss landlady) [82] that the alarmed Russian government in December 1873, ordered all women students to return from Zürich by the end of the year. The male minority demonstrated their solidarity with the women by returning also; and the women reciprocated by participating in both the movement to the people of 1874 and the subsequent turn to terrorism. Almost every dramatic moment of the 1870s produced the heroic example of a young woman. Vera Zasulich, a typesetter in St. Petersburg, opened the campaign of political terror by shooting the police chief of St. Petersburg in January 1878. When she gained acquittal by her courtroom oratory, she provided a successful model for turning the criminal trial of a would-be assassin into the political trial of the intended victim.

The final plans for the successful assassination of Tsar Alexander II on March 1, 1881, were supervised by a frail twenty-six-year-old blonde, Sophia Perovskaya. Another female conspirator, Gesya Helfman, provided the major human interest of the trial (and gained the only reprieve from the gallows) when it became known that she was pregnant.

A male revolutionary observed that "women are more cruel than we men"; [83] and this tended to be true in fantasy as well as in fact. The women's choral cry of "Death! Death!" provided both the orgiastic musical climax and the murderous message of the mob in the final "revolutionary scene" in the Kromi forest of Mussorgsky's *Boris Godunov*.

In the atmosphere of reaction under the new Tsar Alexander III, yet another woman named Faith (Russian *Vera*) kept alive the revolutionary faith. Vera Figner played the leading role within Russia in preserving for much of the decade a vestige of the old People's Will organization, her memoirs providing one of the best human chronicles of the movement.[84] Maria Oshanina, the third woman veteran (along with Perovskaya and Figner) of the executive committee of the People's Will, was a leading Jacobin centralizer and major transmitter of conspiratorial ideas to the new revolutionary movements of the 1890s.[85]

Though often mistresses to the young revolutionaries, women were also often mother figures. Alexandra Weber, for instance, provided maternal care and companionship successively to each of the two rival leaders in the revolutionary emigration of the 1870s: nursing Bakunin in his last years, then serving as the intimate confidante of Lavrov.[86]

Inside Russia, the illegal press of the original Land and Liberty organization, which defied police detection for four years in the early 1860s, was housed in the flat of an elderly woman nicknamed "Mother of God." Revolutionaries recalled entering her premises "with the sense of awe experienced by the faithful crossing the threshold of a temple." [87] Such images were not simply a figure of speech; the revolutionary tradition was influenced here by Russian sectarian religion, often centered on a female leader known as a "Mother of God." Land and Liberty published a special journal for religious dissenters and gave itself the coded designation *Akulina*, from a female saint whose name was used both by a famous sectarian prophetess and by the flagellant sect that went to the extreme of self-castration.[88]

Women tended to be more revolutionary than feminist in Russia. They unhesitatingly used femininity for revolutionary purposes—arranging a fictitious marriage to provide conspiratorial cover, hiding a revolver in a muff, stuffing a detonator in a corset.[89]

The distinctive role of women in the Russian movement was to purify and intensify terror, not to articulate ideas.[90] Thus women took the lead in sustaining the terrorist tradition after the destruction of the People's Will organization (about half of the sentences to life at hard labor in the 1880s were imposed on women)[91] and in reviving that tradition in the early twentieth century. One third of the members of the "fighting organization" of 1902–10, which gave the Socialist Revolutionary party moral and numerical leadership among Russian revolutionaries, were women.[92] These women viewed revived revolutionary violence not so much as a calculated political tactic, but rather as an expression of "the urge for moral wholeness." [93] They often displayed an "almost reverent" attitude towards the terroristic act.[94]

After the Revolution of 1905, women played leading roles in both the Maximalist pursuit of terrorist raids and plans (often altogether outside the discipline of the Socialist Revolutionary party) and in the deepening self-criticism among terrorists in Siberian prison and exile.[95] One key Maximalist, appropriately the great-granddaughter of a Decembrist, described this process of re-examination in Siberia as an intensification of commitment rather than an examination of tactics. Everything the women had done "was again analyzed from the point of view of its purity."[96] This passion for purity fueled a growing desire among women revolutionaries to be the one to throw the bomb,[97] to be sentenced to death,[98] or even to immolate one's self in prison. As if reverting to the self-burning tradition of the Old Believers (where women, too, had played a leading role),[99] women terrorists in the populist-S.R. tradition used this awesome tactic to express the sincerity of their faith: Sofia Ginsburg in 1890, Maria Vetrova in 1897, and Sofia Khrenkova, a village teacher and mother of three, in 1908.[100]

Fire was moving from the minds of men to the bodies of women. Their bodies like their faith were usually pure. Both forms of purity were sealed by the heroic act of martyrdom, which lent to the words of women an authority that they could not otherwise easily command in Russian society.

Terrorist women were generally selective, restrained, and even self-sacrificial in their use of violence. Evstoliia Rogozinnikova, a twenty-one-year-old scholarship student at the St. Petersburg Conservatory of Music, apparently used her beautiful figure—heavily perfumed in an elegant black dress—to gain entry into the main prison administration in St. Petersburg, where she shot the director. She was forcibly prevented from carrying out her original intention of blowing up the entire building by detonating the thirteen pounds of high explosives that she had packed into her bodice and used to enhance her bust.[101] As she was executed three days later in St. Petersburg, new Joans-of-Arc began to appear in the provinces, lending compelling moral authority to the belief in social revolution during this darkest period of reaction. Sincere young girls repeatedly faced old male judges after assaulting their all-male targets. Yet they continued to win the battle for the hearts and minds of men as well as women not just by their courtroom testimony, but by gladly going to die "as one would to a holiday festivity."[102] A peasant girl terrorist was typical as well as prophetic, when she proclaimed in a Kiev courtroom in 1908 just before killing herself that "our death, like a hot flame, will ignite many hearts."[103]

The Germans

Turning from martyrs to leaders, one moves from largely noble Russian women, who were in many ways the purified final embodiment of the Russian intelligentsia,[104] to more hardheaded German women who brought organizational and ideological discipline into the revolutionary camp through the Social Democratic movement.

Marx had paid relatively little attention to the revolutionary role, let alone the feminist cause, of women.[105] He had envisaged the disappearance of the authoritarian family prior to 1848, and rejected the intense antifeminism of Proudhon. But he had a Victorian family life himself; and Engels spoke for both of them in saying that the German communists' effort to emancipate women during the 1848 revolution had produced only a "few blue stockings, some hysteria, a good portion of German family quarrels—but not even one bastard." [106]

Though German women revolutionaries never approached the intensity of the Russians (at least until the female terrorists of the 1960s),[107] they did pioneer in founding unions for women,[108] and the first of a host of Social Democratic women's organizations in the mid-1870s. The cofounder of the German party, August Bebel, produced his theoretical work, *Woman and Socialism*, in 1879, five years before Engels's less influential and more theoretical *Origin of the Family*.[109]

The German movement received an injection of Russian intensity when its leading woman, Clara Zetkin, visited St. Petersburg as revolutionary unrest was mounting in 1878, became fascinated by the Russian example, and married a Russian. After the repeal of Bismarck's antisocialist laws of 1878–90, she founded a special paper for socialist women, *Equality* (*Die Gleichheit*), which became an international journal after she cofounded an International Socialist Women's Congress in 1907. Women were, however, underrepresented in the German party leadership; and at times Zetkin and the Austrian leader Adelheid Popp were the only women leaders to be found in the large German-speaking delegations to the congresses of the Second International. Zetkin's parallel "Women's International" collapsed after a final, desperate Women's Conference against World War I in 1915 at Bern.[110] As a friend of Lenin, a Communist, and the oldest member of the Reichstag, Zetkin presided over the penultimate meeting of the last freely elected German parliament before Hitler.[111]

Meanwhile, Zetkin's movement had found fulfillment in Russia. Within a year of her Socialist Women's Congress, the Russians had assembled one thousand women for the First All Russian Congress of Women in 1908.[112] When Zetkin designated March 8 International Women's Day in 1910, the Russians celebrated it with special intensity. The annual demonstration led to repression in 1914 and prevented the launching of the special journal, *Rabotnitsa* (The Woman Worker) planned by Lenin's wife Krupskaia, his sister Anna Elizarova, and his closest female friend, Inessa Armand. The holiday was next celebrated three years later with the demonstration that led to the overthrow of tsarism on March 8, 1917. After the Provisional Government was in turn overthrown by the Bolsheviks, *Rabotnitsa* was revived, a Second Women's Congress held in 1917, and a special Women's Section (*Zhenotdel*) of the Central Committee established first under Armand then under Kollontai.[113] They fought to realize the equality for women that was formally guaranteed by the Soviet Constitution—extending the concept with particularly radical effect into the traditionalist societies of Central Asia, using the public ritual of "tearing off the veil" from Muslim women [114] who became the "surrogate proletariat" for an enforced social revolution.[115]

Rosa Luxemburg

But by far the greatest of all women revolutionaries of the early twentieth century was Clara Zetkin's friend Rosa Luxemburg. She added to Russian and German involvements the passion of her native Polish revolutionary tradition and the prophetic intensity of her Jewish ancestry. She opposed both elitist Bolshevism and reformist Social Democracy. Luxemburg presented for a brief moment at the end of World War I the vision of a revolution big enough to unite Germans and Russians, to resolve the Polish, Jewish, and women's question all at once. With her death in 1919, the vision faded of a revolution that would be uncompromisingly both international and democratic.

Born to a Jewish merchant family in Russian Poland, Luxemburg was impressed as a fifteen-year-old girl with the working-class agitation in Warsaw that began in the winter of 1885, well before comparable unrest in St. Petersburg. She was briefly connected with the major organizations of revolutionary socialists within Poland, "Proletariat" and "Second Proletariat," before fleeing to Zürich in 1888.[116] In that émigré center of Russian and Polish Marxists, she met her lifelong revolutionary companion and future husband, Leo Jogiches (Tyszka), shortly after he too fled abroad in 1890. He had been a revolutionary leader in Vilnius, where Jewish women had played key roles in beginning Social Democratic organizations within the Russian Empire.[117] He briefly established contact with Plekhanov's Liberation of Labor group, then transferred allegiance along with Luxemburg to the Social Democratic party of the Kingdom of Poland and Lithuania. Beginning in 1893, she participated in every congress of the Second International except the final one in 1913, and was in every sense of the word an international figure.

Luxemburg began her lifelong struggle against national parochialism by rejecting the cause of Polish independence, which had been espoused by the larger Polish Socialist party (PPS) founded in 1892. She argued instead for total Polish involvement in the destruction of tsarism. Her struggle in Poland for a Marxist proletarian party against the populist, peasant-based PPS paralleled the conflict between Marxists and populists in Russia. She internationalized her perspective by expanding her interest to include the struggle of Poles under the Hapsburgs and Hohenzollerns as well as under the Romanovs.[118] Her industry abroad made the Polish party an effective pressure group in the Second International, and she became the driving force behind the theoretical journal of the Polish party.[119] But she settled in Germany after 1898, and transferred her main energy thereafter into the struggle against Bernstein's revisionism within the Social Democratic party. Like Lenin, she combined an uncompromising revolutionary faith with great tactical flexibility based on subtle ideological distinctions. She argued that prior to a revolution socialists could and should serve in parliaments that make laws, but never in an executive branch which enforces them.[120] She relied more than Lenin on institutions spontaneously generated by the proletariat, and made the most sustained effort of any leading Marxist to adapt the new Latin ideal of a general strike into a skeptical German Social Democracy.

She invented the term "mass strike," not as a "crafty device discovered by subtle reasoning," but as a description of what the complacent Germans might learn from the Russian revolutionary experience of 1905.[121] For Luxemburg, the mass strike was a new form of proletarian class struggle that had superseded the bourgeois barricades of 1848–49 and even 1870–71. The mass strike was a spontaneously generated phenomenon that was not called into being, and could not be manipulated on its course by any self-proclaimed elite.[122] The mass strike unified the political (antiabsolutist) and economic (anticapitalist) struggles, and progressed necessarily from the *demonstrative* to the *fighting* stage. After initial demonstrations had overcome inertia and stimulated political consciousness, fighting would begin spontaneously and usually accidentally. Out of the shared experience of combat, new forms of proletarian politics and culture would emerge.

In Luxemburg's view, the Russian Revolution of 1905 failed because the economic struggle, which had led to nationwide political struggle during the October general strike, relapsed back thereafter into parochial economic conflicts. But since this was the first revolution in which the proletariat had assumed the leading role, she urged the German Social Democrats to regard it "as their own" and to learn from it. Above all, the Russian example showed the "bureaucratised" Germans how a less organized movement can leapfrog over a less active one— and how organization can grow out of struggle rather than the other way around.[123]

Her emphasis on the "spontaneous" leadership of the masses in the revolutionary process put her at odds with Lenin. She had been one of the first to criticize Lenin's emphasis on the vanguard role of the party as representing "ultra-centralism," "the sterile spirit of the night watchman," dictatorship *over* the masses rather than *of* the masses.[124] She saw Lenin as guilty of the same "subjectivism" and "Blanquism" that had haunted Russian populism; and she consistently rejected Lenin's willingness to allot a progressive role to national revolutionary movements in the coming social revolution. In her unfinished study of the Bolshevik Revolution (written while in prison in Breslau/Wrocław) Luxemburg insisted that democratic forms be applied immediately under the dictatorship of the proletariat. She censured the reliance on terror and the dissolution of the Constituent Assembly by the Bolsheviks, translating the word democracy into "people's hegemony" (*Volksherrschaft*) in an effort to find a vocabulary adequate for her idea.[125] Her criticism of terror in 1918 was ultimately the same as her original criticism of party elitism in 1903: that it leads to an atrophy of initiative and a growth of the very bureaucratic rule that revolutions should supplant.[126] Parallel criticism of Lenin's elitism was given a special aura of disinterested purity by the most revered revolutionary woman within Russia, Vera Zasulich, who had moved from populism to Marxism.[127]

Despite their deep differences and criticisms of each other, Luxemburg resembled Lenin in leading a Left opposition within a prewar Social Democratic party, in developing a global vision that provided outward courage and inner serenity, in linking capitalism to imperialism and war, and in seeing national war as inevitably leading to social revolution.

During the period of reaction between the ebbing of the revolutionary tide in Russia in 1906 and the outbreak of World War I, both Lenin and Luxemburg sought to fortify the ideological fervor of their respective parties with major new theoretical writings. Luxemburg sought to use not merely journalism, but also the party school at Berlin as a vehicle for attacking the more cautious and doctrinaire wing of the party and for radicalizing future party leaders. This technique was adopted first by the "left Bolsheviks" under Bogdanov at Capri (1909) and Bologna (November 1910 through March 1911) and then by Lenin at Longjumeau outside Paris in the summer of 1911.[128] Luxemburg also preceded Lenin in making a Marxist analysis of imperialism, and she paralleled Lenin in her radical boycott of World War I. Her famed "Junius brochure," written in prison in 1915, rejected the key argument used by the German Social Democrats to rationalize their support of the war effort: that it was a defensive war against the Russian peril.[129] She insisted that no isolated defensive war was possible for major powers in the age of imperialism. The Russian proletariat, she said, was now at the forefront of revolution, and not merely part of the reactionary monolith that it had seemed to Marx at the time of the 1848 revolution and to most German Social Democrats ever since. In the war, Luxemburg saw new possibilities for revolution. When she was released from prison and arrived in Berlin on November 10, 1918, the day before the final armistice, she plunged into a delirium of activity designed to realize a social revolution in Germany.

Her ill-fated attempt at revolution played back in reprise many of the basic themes and symbols of the revolutionary tradition. Even her choice of revolutionary pseudonyms betrayed an unconscious harkening back to origins. From Junius (originally used by the Strasbourgeois Jewish revolutionary Frey in Paris during the great French Revolution), she moved to the Gracchus of Babeuf, on to the Spartacus adopted by the original German progenitor of revolutionism, Adam Weishaupt. Her Spartacus League adopted in December 1918 the label Communist, which Restif had invented and Lenin revived. "I don't have time to think about what will happen to me," she wrote Clara Zetkin, adding in French—as if reverting to the basic language of the tradition itself— *C'est la révolution*.[130] She denounced the liberals as "little Lafayettes" in a final article [131] before moving to direct the revolution through a daily journal bearing the classical label of social revolution: *Red Flag* (*Rote Fahne*). She also planned on a theoretical weekly to bear a title describing its scope, *Die Internationale*.

Hers was a revolution of the young. At the founding conference of her new Kommunistische Partei Deutschlands (Spartakusbund) late in December, her husband was the only delegate (out of 127 from 56 localities) over the age of fifty.[132] Hers was a movement led by journalistic intellectuals. One of its few victories was the occupation of the Wolff telegraphic bureau in Berlin—the heart of the same communications system that had so fascinated Marx when he first came in contact with its extremity in Brussels.

Luxemburg was too penetrating an analyst of society not to realize that there was no hope for immediate revolution; and she argued against the illusions of her principal corevolutionary Karl Liebknecht. Since, however, she was committed to a mass-based general strike and to a revolutionary struggle against the national assembly, she saw no alternative but to join the disorganized struggle that ensued in January. Her Spartacists combatted armed forces that were returning from the front and attempting to establish the authority of the national assembly and of the more conservative Social Democrats. A general strike attracted mass participation, and led to a brief seizure of centers of transportation and communication. But Luxemburg lacked both Lenin's organization and his ability to translate strategic vision into concrete battle plans. The revolutionary Spartacists and their allies were soon shot down and Luxemburg was killed together with Liebknecht on the night of January 15.

Hitler's National Socialism was to be the final gargoyle of masculine revolutionary nationalism. Luxemburg's uncompromising socialist internationalism was its polar opposite: the culmination of the antinationalist, antimilitarist tradition among women revolutionaries. Her implacable opposition to any participation in World War I had been echoed in Russia by the leading radical feminist Alexandra Kollontai, who joined Lenin's Bolshevik party in 1915 largely because of his opposition to the war. Like Luxemburg and Zasulich, Kollontai identified revolution with the spontaneity of working-class initiative rather than the elite Leninist party. She outlived the others and became a member of the Workers' Opposition after serving as the first commissar for public welfare following the Bolshevik Revolution.[133]

That revolution was the first to proclaim equal rights for women. Krupskaia, Zetkin, and others joined Kollontai in claiming universal significance for this aspect of the new order. Increasingly, however, the revolution in power seemed to provide more the obligation to perform old types of work than the opportunity to build a new type of society. Despite formal gains for women in civic and occupational equality, the founding mothers, no less than the founding fathers, saw their hopes disappointed.[134] The Soviet state relied on precisely that combination of terror and bureaucracy that Luxemburg had feared.

Rosa Luxemburg had brought to the revolutionary tradition a special womanly fullness of sensibility largely absent from the Germano-Russian period of revolutionary history. Indeed, she brought back something of the expressive humanism of the earlier Italo-Polish period into the arid puritanism of the Social Democratic tradition, which both Lenin and his barren coworker and wife, Krupskaia, epitomized.

Luxemburg had expressed the special, universal criticism of society that women of unusual ability and sensitivity like Wright and Tristan had voiced before. She breathed inspiration into the grim Social Democratic movement often through a network of other women: Louise Kautsky, with whom she remained an intimate friend even after breaking with Kautsky in 1910; [135] Clara Zetkin, the early foe of revisionism and intimate correspondent of her last years; and Sophie Liebknecht, to whom she addressed inspiring letters from prison in her last years. She was never a feminist, sharing unashamedly in the distinctively feminine experiences of being a companion and cook.[136] But she brought to the revolutionary movement a warmth of engagement without self-indulgence that was generally foreign to male revolutionaries in the nineteenth century—let alone to the dull functionaries of the twentieth.

Rosa Luxemburg stood in a prophetic line of revolutionary women who renounced both home and country in search of the promised land. The list stretches from Etta Palm, a Dutch woman in Paris; through Flora Tristan, a Peruvian in Lyon; to Saint-Simonians in Egypt; to Frances Wright, the Scottish wife of a Frenchman on the American frontier; to Russians in Switzerland, on to this Polish-Jewish leader who sought to replicate the Russian Revolution in Germany.

Rosa Luxemburg was not just a prophet of revolution—of its failure in Germany [137] and its deformation in Russia—but an embodiment of revolutionary simplicity. Beyond all the words written by this most articulate of all revolutionary journalists,[138] lay a simple faith beyond reason—in transnational, proletarian perfectibility; in violent struggle as a creative process and prerequisite to victory; and in those original myths of the revolutionary tradition: in an unfinished revolution and a perfect natural order.

The essential vision that she affirmed in her life and validated by her death is perhaps best contained in her description of the simple perfection she once found on primitive Corsica. Islands had provided the perennial locus of utopia, from the imagination of Thomas More to the reality of Sand on Majorca or Garibaldi on Caprera. Luxemburg described Corsica, where Buonarroti and Urbain had found inspiration, as an ideal alternative "to the Europe of today," a place to satisfy that deep desire of revolutionaries to *oprostit'sia*: to simplify things. Writing from prison to Sophie Liebknecht, Luxemburg recalled recovering "the silence of the beginning of the world" amidst the rustic purity, and finding the archetypical unspoiled "people" in a poor peasant family that passed silently by "precisely in harmony with the landscape." She felt inspired "to fall on my knees as I always feel compelled to do before some spectacle of finished beauty." [139] She proposed to Liebknecht that the two women journey together to Corsica for a kind of pilgrimage of renewal, reviving the original metaphor of the revolution as rising sun:

> We must go there and . . . cover the whole island on foot, sleeping each night in a new lodging place, greeting each morning along the way the rising of the sun.[140]

But Luxemburg went instead from prison to a martyr's death with Liebknecht's husband. She reaffirmed her faith in the ultimate victory of revolution in her last written words, which returned to the older, messianic metaphors of her Judaic heritage:

> The revolution will "raise itself up again, clashing," and . . . proclaim to the sound of trumpets: *I was, I am, I shall be*.[141]

Such a passionate life and dramatic death left behind not just a legend but a kind of haunting presence. When social revolutionaries finally came to power in Germany, not spontaneously after World War I but via the Russian army after World War II, the Stalinist regime in East Germany tried in vain to represent itself as the vindication of her hopes.[142] She had written shortly before her death that true victory lay "not at the beginning but at the end of revolution." [143] The suspicion grew that that victory—and her revolution—was perhaps still to come.

Some have seen posthumous vindication of her vision in the revived invocation of her name during the late 1960s and the early 1970s: by French and Italian student radicals, by female German terrorists, or by admirers of new anti-imperialist movements in the third world and the cultural revolution in Mao's China.[144] But Luxemburg was a Eurocentric believer in the spontaneous leadership of the modern industrial proletariat. She may have found her most authentic reincarnation within the proletariat in her native Poland. Only there had her memory been deeply and continuously honored within a Soviet-dominated Communist party. In December 1970, the Polish working classes spontaneously rose in a mass strike against bureaucratic despotism unguided by any external political or intellectual elites in a move that surprised both East and West. The strike produced in Poland the first forcible change of political leadership by direct proletarian action in Europe since 1917.

The unexpected overthrow of Gomulka seemed a poetic vindication of Rosa Luxemburg. The strike began in Szczecin on the border area between the Polish and German worlds where she had spent much of her life. It brought down a man who had just succeeded in expelling almost the last of Luxemburg's fellow Jews from that region in which they had historically suffered so much. It was almost as if Rosa Luxemburg had returned like the Dybbuk in a Jewish mystery play to take over the body of a Polish worker and avenge the repudiated heritage of Gomulka's Jewish wife.

Could the revolutionary faith remain active at all within the neo-authoritarian, post-revolutionary bureaucracies of Eastern Europe in the late twentieth century? If that faith does survive or revive in those lands where Rosa Luxemburg lived and died, it seems likely to be moved by her ghost stalking the stalags of Stalinism and the dachas of its directors. To them, she can speak of forgotten dreams—reminding them that a Jewish woman once argued that Poles should unite with Russians for their common good; that Germans would benefit from revolution in Russia; and that social revolution would directly abolish both the national identities and the authoritarian controls that repress the creativity of working people themselves.

Epilogue: Beyond Europe

THIS HISTORY has dealt with revolutionaries who functioned inside Europe and without power during the period from the late eighteenth to the early twentieth centuries. There is no room here to discuss the legacy of their ideas to those who have subsequently exercised massive state power in the name of revolution. The very different world since 1917—of total war and totalitarian peace, of Stalin's early identification of revolution with power and of Mao's final search for a revolution beyond power—all of this would require another volume with its own special techniques of analysis and texture of description.

A brief epilogue can perhaps suggest only one key feature in the movement from the nineteenth to the twentieth century: the spread of the revolutionary political faith from Europe to the awakening East. By the early twentieth century, revolutionary nationalism much like that of Europe in the early nineteenth century was spreading through the Afro-Asian world in a kind of global chain reaction against the "new imperialism" of the great European powers.

The primary place of combustion for this nationalist revival was the political no-man's land that stretched out beyond the Danube to the banks of the Tigris and the Nile. This was the East nearest the West, the Middle or Near East, the locus of the Eastern Question. This original cradle of Western civilization became the breeding grounds for the new age of anti-Western revolutions. If the Francocentric era of revolutionary activity had as its main enemy the Hapsburg Empire and the Germano-Russian era focused on the Romanov Empire, the epoch of world revolution began with revolt against the Ottoman Empire.

The upsurge of violent revolutionary nationalism began with an unjustly neglected echo of earlier European movements: the Internal Macedonian Revolutionary Organization. Started as an anti-Ottoman organization in 1893, it began its never-successful efforts to produce a Macedonian nation with the slogan "Better an end with horrors than horrors without end." Excessively romanticized in their own time as heroic mountain rebels fighting the cruel Turks,[1] the IMRO deserves a fresh look by a later generation as perhaps the first modern national liberation movement: using underground broadcasting, urban terror, and a strategy consciously designed to bring international opinion to bear on a local political situation.

The "broadcasting" occurred on Elijah's Day, July 20, 1903, when gramophones hidden behind icons in Macedonian Orthodox churches suddenly burst out with the prepared message: "Brother! The hour has come to begin the struggle. . . . Down with Turkey and with tyranny. Hurrah!" [2]

The urban base for the movement was the cosmopolitan port city of Salonika, where a group of high school students first known as Rabblerousers and then as the Crew studied the Russian revolutionary movement and drew up ambitious terrorist plans of their own. Seeking to combat economic as well as political tyranny—and to attract international attention in the process—this group spent better than two years digging an enormous tunnel under both the Constantinople and Salonika branches of the Ottoman Bank. The plan was to blow up simultaneously both buildings, while unleashing a series of coordinated explosions throughout the city of Salonika. The explosions began on the morning of April 28, 1903, on board a French ship unloading munitions for the Turkish army; and by the end of the day, other explosions had plunged the city into smoky darkness and unleashed a reign of fierce reprisal by Turkish troops.

IMRO thus made a crude and ultimately suicidal attempt at instant revolution. Apart from the hopeless odds against the Turks, the rebels in the cities were not coordinated with the IMRO leaders in the countryside, whose uprising during the summer of 1903 lasted only a little longer and never gave much reality to their self-proclaimed "government of the woods." Nevertheless, its attempts to plan, discipline, and concentrate resources on focused surprise attacks were prophetic of the guerrilla warfare of the future. IMRO took refuge in the technique of sudden attack and then total disappearance back into the countryside, and it became almost impossible to stamp the movement out altogether. "When a Turkish division thinks that it has located a body of troops," a colonel observed, "it suddenly discovers that what it has found is only a group of peasants busy tilling the soil." [3] After the revolution of the Young Turks in 1908, IMRO revived, and continued to rally its countrymen to the perpetually frustrated cause until crushed in 1934 by the very Bulgarian army that had once provided training for many of its original cadres.

IMRO was the least successful of Balkan revolutionary movements in building a nation, but the most successful in terms of longevity in exercising power and waging combat. From within five years of its first organization in 1893, the pyramidal organization, whose basic cell was a group of ten men, exercised effective power over much of Macedonia, denying crops, taxes, and safe residence to the occupying powers. Secret annual congresses determined policy, use was made of "safe" base areas in Bulgaria in the early years and of a complex structure of committee leaders (*comitadji*), military bands (*chetas̄*), and church and educational organizations, which acted as a kind of cultural "front" for clandestine organization.

Terrorism moved into alliance with mass national liberation struggles in the colonized, rural Balkans; and similar movements soon developed in the Asian parts of the Ottoman Empire—and beyond.

The Russian Revolution of 1905 opened a new, global "era of revolutions," producing—literally—an electric effect. The generator of the revolution was in many ways the St. Petersburg Technological Institute, which summoned the first student rally on the day after the first massacre of demonstrators before the Winter Palace (on "bloody Sunday," January 9, 1905); [4] survived a military siege of its student building; [5] and convened the first Soviet of workers in its lecture hall. Krzhizhanovsky, the electrical specialist and Bolshevik activist in St. Petersburg during 1905, saw the electric transmitter as representing "the transition from the anarchy of capitalist production to production by plan." [6] He later helped Lenin redefine communism in terms of the two things that were literally introduced to Russia within the walls of his alma mater, the Technological Institute: "Soviet power plus electrification." [7]

Electric wire service permitted the events of an unfolding revolution to be reported in 1905—for the first time in history—on a day-to-day basis throughout the world. The effect was particularly great outside of Europe, where the new imperialism had infected new regions with Western revolutionary ideas. The proud and ancient civilizations of Asia were particularly sensitive to the expanding power of the European states. The unprecedented news that an Asian nation (Japan) had defeated a European imperial power (Russia) in the war of 1904–5 encouraged new leaders to mobilize the revolutionary potential of the "external proletariat" in the less developed but densely populated East.

Internal revolution in Russia following wartime defeat by an external Asian power produced immediate Eastern echoes: both on minority groups within the Romanov Empire and in the Asian states just across its borders.

Unrest moved first across the turbulent Caucasus to Iran, where in December 1905 a general strike broke out in Teheran even as the general strike was collapsing in Moscow. In Tabriz, by September 1906, the first of several Persian workers' councils (Soviets) fashioned on the Russian revolutionary model was established. Full suppression of the Persian revolutionary movement was assured only with the Anglo-Russian joint intervention of 1911. [8] In that year, the first modern revolution in China overthrew the Manchu dynasty. Its leader Sun-Yat Sen was also influenced by the Russian Revolution of 1905 and the tradition that lay behind it. He had met with Russian revolutionary leaders like Gershuni in Tokyo, where he set up a Russian-type student-based revolutionary movement in 1905 built around a journal similar to Herzen's *Bell*. [9] The Russian example also influenced the turn toward strikes and insurrection of Young India, [10] and the revolution of the Young Turks which overthrew a corrupt sultan in 1908.

The earlier Young Ottoman organization of the 1870s had been influenced by the rise of a Russian revolutionary tradition after defeat by Russia in the Russo-Turkish War. Now a Young Turk movement arose based on a secret cell of officers in Salonika. They sanctioned a mixture of strike tactics and armed resistance similar to that of Armenian secret societies under the apparent influence of the Russian revolutionary movement of 1905-6.[11]

The rising of Asian revolutionaries to oppose European empires repeated in many ways the rise of European revolutionaries against the Hapsburg Empire a century earlier. Mazzini's Young Italy and Young Europe were the direct ancestors of the Young Turks and other young national movements in Asia. As in early nineteenth-century Europe, Asian national revolutionaries of the early twentieth century included vague ideals of social revolution in their dreams of national liberation.

Asian revolutionary nationalism in the early twentieth century frequently followed the patterns of its European prototype. The Chinese revolutionary movement prior to 1911, for instance, was as dependent as the Russian movement had been on the leadership of émigré ideological journalists (Sun-Yat Sen in Hawaii and Japan, much of the future Communist leadership in France).[12] The same émigré guidance was essential for the Vietnamese Revolution, with Ho Chi-Minh living successively in Paris, Moscow, and Canton. Left-Right interaction is also evident in the Soviet training of the son and successor of Chiang Kai-shek, head of the Nationalist regime on Taiwan; and in the strange pattern of transmission of terrorist ideas from Vietnam. Some right-wing French terrorists (the OAS) appear to have learned their techniques while imprisoned by the left-wing terrorists in Vietnam. The French Right in turn imparted a similar schooling back to the Algerian Left (the FLN), whose successful terrorist methods pay tribute again to the symbiosis that occurs when *les extrèmes se touchent.*

If Asian revolutionaries echoed European ideas in the twentieth century, European revolutionaries had occasionally echoed Asians in the nineteenth. The most sophisticated theorist of national insurrection among the ever-prophetic Poles had moved ever farther afield in his search for inspirational models: from the relatively familiar Spanish and Russian resistance to Napoleon, to the Serbian and Albanian resistance to the Turks, the Algerian to the French, the peoples of the Caucasus to Russia, and finally of Afghanistan to England during the war of 1838-42. As Russian troops streamed into that mountain land in the last days of the 1970s, it seemed eerie to read a Polish exile of the 1840s urging close study of the Afghan resistance to an earlier imperial invader "because there it will be possible to uncover the source of the rebuilding of Poland." [13]

As Africa later followed Asia in its awakening, a new theorist of revolutionary violence journeyed—like Ismail Urbain a century before —from the West Indies through France to Algeria. Frantz Fanon re-echoed many of the themes of the original Italo-Polish apostles of heroic violence a century before. "Violence, alone," he insisted, "makes it possible for the masses to understand social truths" and is a "cleansing force" that "frees the native from his inferiority complex and from his despair and inaction." [14] "To shoot down a European is to kill two birds with one stone, to destroy an oppressor and the man he opposes at the same time." [15] But his message was less original than he thought. His style reflected more his Western training as a psychologist than the real thinking of the third world. Only perhaps in Castro's Cuba was there any continued response to Fanon's arousing Africa to revolutionary violence; and that response depended on the power of Cuba's imperial benefactor, the U.S.S.R. Cuban revolutionaries themselves—from Martí's long years as a revolutionary journalist editing *The Golden Age* in New York in the late nineteenth century [16] to Castro's long exile in Mexico and in the maquis—repeated many of the themes of the national revolutionary tradition. When a Cuban national revolution came into conflict with the imperial power of the first nation to be born in revolution, the United States, it attracted considerable sympathy—but more among well-fed young students in the overdeveloped West than among the hungry in the underdeveloped world. Utopia for many intellectuals had simply returned to a tropical island in the New World—which is where the intellectuals of early modern Europe had always imagined it might be.

NOTES

Abbreviations

Because many of the published books used in the references are extremely rare, I have identified the present location of a copy by means of the following abbreviations:

BA   Bibliothèque de l'Arsenal, Paris
BH   Bibliothèque Historique de la Ville de Paris, Paris
BM   British Museum, London
BN   Bibliothèque Nationale, Paris
BO   Bodleian Library, Oxford
CA   Cambridge University Library, Cambridge, England
CO   Columbia University Library, New York City
EU   Emory University Library, Atlanta, Georgia
GL   Goldsmith's Library, University of London
HU   Widener Library, Harvard University
IA   International Institute of Social History, Amsterdam, Holland
IF   Istituto Giangiacomo Feltrinelli, Milan, Italy
LC   Library of Congress
LL   Lenin Library, Moscow, USSR
NP   New York Public Library, New York City
PU   Firestone Library, Princeton University
YU   Sterling Library, Yale University

Explanatory Note

Place of publication will *not* be listed for any French-language work published in Paris, any German-language work published in Berlin, any Russian-language work published in Moscow, any Italian-language work published in Rome, or any Polish-language work published in Warsaw. For English-language works, L = London, NY = New York City.

The full title of journals will be given except in the cases of the frequently cited *Annales Historiques de la Révolution Française*, which will be *Annales Historiques*; and the *Annali del'Istituto Giangiacomo Feltrinelli*, which will be *Annali*. For Marx and Engels's *Gesamtausgabe*, Berlin, 1927 ff., I have used the standard abbreviation, *MEGA*.

The full first name is given of any figure who is substantively important as a person in the development of the revolutionary tradition; only the first initial is given for figures who are cited only as authorities or authors.

Introduction

1. General Claude-François Malet, cited in C. Nodier, *Souvenirs et portraits de la révolution*, 1841, 3d. ed., 308. The rejected metaphor of revolutionary organization as an Archimedian lever capable of lifting the world was also widely used in the early nineteenth century and later adopted by Lenin.

2. Luigi Angeloni, cited in G. Berti, *Rossiia i ital'ianskie gosudarstva v period risordzhimenta*, 1959, 432.

3. J. Starobinski, "Le mythe solaire de la révolution," in "Sur quelques symboles de la révolution française," *La Nouvelle Revue Française*, 1968, Aug, 56–7.

4. "Die Strahlen der Sonne vertreiben die Nacht, Zernichten der Heuchler erschlichene Macht." These last solo words of *Die Zauberflöte* are pronounced before the Temple of the Sun, which—by the end of the revolutionary era—was represented by a circular sun in the midst of a giant triangle (see J. Baltrušaitis, *La Quête d'Isis. Introduction à l'Egyptomanie*, 1967, 57), thus linking the solar myth with the occult geometric symbols that subsequently became central to professional revolutionary organizers.

5. Restif de la Bretonne, *L'Année 2000*, published as a supplement to *Le Thesmographe, ou idées d'un honnête-homme sur un projet de règlement, proposé à toutes les nations de l'Europe, pour opérer une réforme générale des loix: avec des notes historiques*, The Hague, 1789, 515–56. The only important recent study of Restif's revolutionary ideas dates the completion of this work from 1788. It was republished in 1790. See A. Ioannisian, *Kommunisticheskie idei v gody velikoi frantsuzskoi revoliutsii*, 1966, 187, 211.

A second fantasy on the same subject was published by a German communist for use in France at the beginning of the 1840s, *Paris en l'an 2000*, which depicts a historian lecturing in that year in Notre Dame Cathedral to an incredulous audience about the horrors of the by-gone age of war and class conflict. See A. Saitta, *Sinistra Hegeliana e problema italiano negli scritti di A. L. Mazzini*, 1968, 394, 402. A third such utopian fantasy was Edward Bellamy's more widely read *Looking Backward, 2000–1887* of 1888, on which see S. Bowman, *The Year 2000*, NY 1958. See also the Soviet entry into this field: V. Kosolapov, *Mankind and the Year 2000*, Brooklyn Heights, NY, 1976; as well as H. Kahn and A. Wiener, *Year Two Thousand*, NY, 1967. M. Abensour refers to *Paris en l'an 2000* (by an executed veteran of the Paris Commune, Dr. Tony Moilin, a work unavailable in major libraries) in "L'Histoire de l'utopie et le destin de sa critique," *Textures*, 1973, nos. 6–7, 24 n. 2.

6. The tendency to validate revolutionary action by an imagined past is analyzed by the Polish Marxist Kazimierz Kelles-Krauz, in his "The Law of Revolutionary Retrospection as a Consequence of Economic Materialism," *Ateneum*, 1897; discussed in L. Kolakowski, *Main Currents of Marxism*, II, *The Golden Age*, Oxford, 1978, 211–2. But one example of the neglected cosmic dimensions in the thought of a hard-headed, major revolutionary is A. Blanqui, *L'Eternité par les astres. Hypothèse astronomique*, 1872. Blanqui's abundant further speculations in this area are presently being researched from the untouched manuscript material in BN by M. Abensour.

7. See, for instance, the rich analysis of the radicalizing role played by the evocation of Irish paganism among literary supporters of the Irish revolution: W. Thompson, *The Imagination of an Insurrection: Dublin, Easter 1916: A Study of an Ideological Movement*, NY, 1967.

8. R. Cobb, "Quelques aspects de la mentalité révolutionnaire," *Revue d'Histoire Moderne et Contemporaine*, 1959, Apr–Jun, 119.

9. Carlo Bianco, a letter of Mar 8, 1837, cited in L. Carpi, *Il Risorgimento italiano*, Milan, 1886, III, 179.

10. *History Will Absolve Me*, L, 1968, 43–5, 77–8, 101–4. Castro used Dante's *Inferno* to set up his lengthy account of Batista's atrocities (62–3).

11. See R. Palmer, *The Age of the Democratic Revolution*, Princeton, 1959–64, 2 v; J. Godechot, *France and the Atlantic Revolution of the Eighteenth Century, 1770–1799*, NY, 1965; and the latter's fuller exposition and transnational bibliography: *Les Révolutions (1770–1799)*, 1965, 2nd ed.

12. E. Hobsbawn, *Social Bandits and Primitive Rebels*, NY, 1959.

13. N. Cohn, *The Pursuit of the Millennium*, L, 1957, for the medieval period; and, for the most important example from the Reformation, E. Bloch, *Thomas Münzer als Theologe der Revolution*, Munich, 1921; also in French. G. Lewy, *Religion and Revolution*, Oxford, 1974, has valuable bibliography and traces the interaction between the two in a wide variety of times and places. But its suggestions of similarity and continuity between earlier religious movements and modern secular revolutions are not supported by any serious analysis of the latter.

14. M. de Certeau, "La Révolution fondatrice, ou le risque d'exister," *Etudes*, 1968, Jun–Jul, 88.

15. Cobb, "Aspects," 120.

16. Louis-Sébastien Mercier, *L'An deux mille quatre cent quarante. Rêve s'il en fut jamais*, 1768–71, reprinted with a valuable introduction by R. Trousson, 1971. As with his friend Restif, the playwright Mercier was seen as a subversive vulgarizer of Rousseau and was nicknamed *le singe de Jean-Jacques*.

17. Title of a chapter in Mercier, *Tableau de Paris*, 1782, IV.

18. Like almost every generalization about revolution, this is subject to debate—

the Dutch revolt against Spain in the sixteenth century having created a new republic, the Mexican revolutionary constitution of 1917 having proclaimed social as well as political objectives. But neither of these events had the ecumenical impact of the changes in the USA and USSR.

19. "There is a revolution coming. It will not be like revolutions of the past . . . the revolution of the new generation." C. Reich, *The Greening of America*, NY, 1970, 4.

20. J. Revel, *Ni Marx Ni Jésus; de la seconde révolution américaine à la seconde révolution mondiale*, 1970, tr. as *Without Marx or Jesus*, NY, 1971.

21. J. D. Rockefeller, *The Second American Revolution*, NY, 1973; and, independently, J. Beré, "The Second American Revolution," *Vital Speeches*, 1978, Jan 15, 208–11.

22. Cited in J. Johnson, "The Children of God," *Potomac*, 1975, Apr 12, 15.

23. T. Wertime, "The New American Revolution," *The Washington Post*, 1976, Jul 5, A23, hides his essentially Proudhonist call for rural virtues and decentralization in a pretentious muddle of pop-Hegelian prophecies: ". . . the acts of birth of the Great American Mother have been almost continuous. . . . A tiger of change is upon us . . . born in some part of the womb of the American frontier. . . ."

24. R. De Felice, *Interpretations of Fascism*, Cambridge, Mass, 1977, 191.

25. J. Monnerot, *Sociologie de la révolution*, 1969, 7.

26. As suggested by J. Pocock, *Politics, Language and Time*, NY, 1971, 3. J. Ellul also complains at length about confusions in the usage of the term (*Autopsy of Revolution*, NY, 1971, 100 ff., 177 ff., 197 ff.) but then adds to the confusion with a title that suggests revolutions are ending, and an ending suggesting that his own "necessary revolution" may be just beginning.

27. Outstanding as a philosophical-political discussion is H. Arendt, *On Revolution*, NY, 1963; as a general sketch of the intellectual origins of Bolshevism is E. Wilson, *To the Finland Station*, NY, 1940.

28. *Mezhdunarodnoe rabochee dvizhenie*, 1976–78, 3 v. The 21-man editorial commission is under the presidency of the veteran Central Committee ideologist, Boris Ponomarev: the first volume treating "the rise of the proletariat and its formation as a revolutionary class"; the second, 1871–1904; the third, 1905–17.

29. *Main Currents of Marxism. Its Rise, Growth and Dissolution*, Oxford, 1978, 3v. The first volume, *The Founders*, deals with the philosophical origins of Marxism; the second (and in my opinion the best), *The Golden Age*, deals with the varied development of Marxist thought in the period of the Second International (1889–1914); and the third, *The Breakdown*, deals with the Stalin era and beyond. A projected multi-volume history of Marxism by the Italian Communist Party may prove more interesting than most such collective, official publications, since it is scheduled to include contributions by non-Communists and dissident Marxists.

30. For a critical introduction to the immense literature on the nature of revolution, see I. Kramnick, "Reflections on Revolution: Definition and Explanation in Recent Scholarship," *History and Theory*, 1972, no. 1, 26–63; also discussions by two historians of the Puritan Revolution: L. Stone, "Theories of Revolution," *World Politics*, 1966, Jan, 159–76; and P. Zagorin, "Theories of Revolution in Contemporary Historiography," *Political Science Quarterly*, 1973, Mar, 23–52; as well as E. Hermassi, "Toward a Comparative Study of Revolutions," *Comparative Studies in Society and History*, 1976, Apr, 211–35; and M. Hagopian, *The Phenomenon of Revolution*, NY, 1975.

See also P. Calvert, "The Study of Revolution: A Progress Report," *International Journal*, 1973, summer; S. Wolin, "The Politics of the Study of Revolution," *Comparative Politics*, 1973, Apr, 343–58; and a neglected discussion of the revolutionary theories advanced by revolutionaries themselves: R. Larrson, *Theories of Revolution. From Marx to the First Russian Revolution*, Kristianstad, 1970. For a survey of "the changing nature of the 'revolutionary ideal,'" during the last 200 years, see R. Blackey and C. Paynton, *Revolution and the Revolutionary Ideal*, Cambridge, Mass, 1976; also their anthology *Why Revolution?*, Cambridge, Mass, 1971; and Blackey's *Modern Revolutions and Revolutionists. A Bibliography*, Santa Barbara/Oxford, 1976. The methods of Marxism and Western political sociology are combined in a comparative historical analysis of three modern revolutions by T. Skocpol, *States and Social Revolutions. A Comparative Analysis of France, Russia, and China*, Cambridge, 1979, with useful bibliography 295–303, notes 7, 18, 20, 97, and 380–90. Other sociological syntheses not included in Skocpol are A. Decouflé, *Sociologie des révolutions*, 1968; and W. Overholt, "An Organizational Conflict Theory of Revolution," *American Behavioral Scientist*, 1977, Mar–Apr, 493–552. The substantial German literature on the subject is overlooked in Skocpol and almost all of the studies referenced here. See, for instance, H. Wassmund, *Revolutionstheorien*, Munich, 1978; and, for an extra-European perspective, K. Kuman, *Revolution—The*

Theory and Practice of a European Idea, L, 1971. See also J. Goldstone, "Theories of Revolution: The Third Generation," *World Politics*, 1980, Apr, 425-53.

A recent Soviet discussion (M. Barg, "Sravnitel'no-istoricheskoe izuchenie burzhuaznykh revoliutsii XVI–XVIII vv," *Voprosy Istorii*, 1975, no. 9, 69–88) proposes a step-by-step comparison of three major "bourgeois revolutions" (the German peasant wars of the sixteenth century, the Puritan Revolution in the seventeenth century, and the French Revolution in the eighteenth) as an antidote to the alleged chaos of Western historiography. Both his polemic crudeness and his doctrinal hostility to a synchronous approach are in sharp contrast to the most outstanding single Soviet study of the revolutionary process in early modern Europe: B. Porshnev, *Frantsiia, Angliiskaia Revoliutsiia i evropeiskaia politika v seredine XVII veka*, 1970, which treats all of Europe from 1630 to 1655. Other important discussions of the revolutionary process during the period prior to the French Revolution and the development of the revolutionary tradition as traced in this work are J. Elliott, "Revolution and Continuity in Early Modern Europe," *Past and Present*, 1969, Feb, 35–56; and P. Zagorin, "Prolegomena to the Comparative History of Revolution in Early Modern Europe," *Comparative Studies in Society and History*, 1976, Apr, 151–74.

A comprehensive Soviet effort to reconcile Marxist pretensions of developing a scientific theory of revolution with Soviet requirements for defending the evolving policies of a state allegedly ruled by such a science is provided in M. Seleznev, *Sotsial'naia revoliutsiia*, 1971, useful mainly for its accounts of internal Soviet discussions of the 1960s.

31. An important and neglected "sociological model of the revolutionary process" came from the short-lived Czech reform period and includes comparative graphs of the English, French, and Czech revolutions (the latter defined as 1414–50). See J. Krejčí, "Sociologický model revolučního procesu," *Sociologický časopis*, 1968, no. 2, 159–73. A recent attempt to introduce new distinctions into traditional Marxist categories is J. Topolski, "Rewolucje w dziejach nowożytnych i najnowszych (xvii–xx wiek)," *Kwartalnik Historyczny*, LXXXIII, 1976, 251–67. He distinguishes (264–6) between six types of revolution: pre-capitalist, early bourgeois, bourgeois, bourgeois-democratic, early proletarian, and socialist.

32. These complaints are voiced repeatedly by R. Cobb, for instance, in his review of a good recent history confined to one region (S. Schama, *Patriots and Liberators. Revolution in the Netherlands, 1780–1813*, NY/L, 1977) in *Times Literary Supplement*, 1977, Jul 29, 906–7.

33. The systematic attempt in this area by E. Wolfenstein (*The Revolutionary Personality: Lenin, Trotsky, Gandhi*, Princeton, 1967) makes its case more persuasively for Gandhi than for the more traditional revolutionaries. J. Seigel improves on earlier efforts (such as A. Künzli, *Karl Marx. Eine Psychographie*, Vienna, 1966) in extending this method to Marx: "Marx's Early Development: Vocation, Rebellion and Realism," *Journal of Interdisciplinary History*, 1973, Winter, 475–508; and, in the context of his entire career, *Marx's Fate. The Shape of a Life*, Princeton, 1978.

W. Blanchard, *Rousseau and the Spirit of Revolt: A Psychological Study*, Ann Arbor, 1967, is the work of a professional psychologist who speaks of the "moral masochism" of Rousseau. B. Mazlish, one of the better psycho-historians, discusses the secularization of the ascetic ideal in the French Revolution, but concentrates his attention mainly on Lenin and Mao in *The Revolutionary Ascetic: Evolution of a Political Type*, NY, 1975. Sociological and psychological analysis is combined with particular effectiveness for Rousseau and Robespierre in F. Weinstein and G. Platt, *The Wish to Be Free: Society, Psyche and Value Change*, Berkeley/Los Angeles, 1969.

In a class by itself is the psychological portrait of the earliest Russian revolutionaries' combination of asceticism and theatricality by Yu. Lotman, "Dekabrist v povsednevnoi zhizni (Bytovoe povedenie kak istoriko-psikhologicheskaia kategoriia)," in *Literaturnoe nasledie dekabristov*, Leningrad, 1975, 25–74. Despite some terminological opacity, this article provides a tantalizing hint of the analytic insight that the remarkable Soviet school of semioticians could undoubtedly bring to bear on more contemporary subjects if they were not restricted to writing about distant times and places.

34. M. Trahard, *La Sensibilité révolutionnaire (1789–94)*, 1936, 28, also 35–7.

35. P. Berger, "The Socialist Myth," *The Public Interest*, 1976, Summer, 15.

36. D. Bell, *The End of Ideology; or the Exhaustion of Political Ideas in the Fifties*, Glencoe, 1960; Z. Brzezinski, *Between Two Ages: America's Role in the Technetronic Era*, NY, 1970; and Bell, *The Coming of the Post-industrial Society: a Venture in Social Forecasting*, NY, 1974.

37. This line of thought arises from, though is not suggested by, N. Georgescu-Roegen, *The Entropy Law and the Economic Process,* Cambridge, Mass, 1971.

38. See the call for a "second Protestant Reformation" by the former sponsors of the People's Bicentennial Commission of 1976, J. Rifkin and T. Howard, *The Emerging Order: God in the Age of Scarcity,* NY, 1979.

These erstwhile advocates of social revolution suggested that evangelical Christianity might spearhead a revolution yet to come in the same 1979 that saw fundamentalist Islam dominate an unexpected revolution in Iran and a relatively traditionalist Pope draw mass crowds in many countries far in excess of those commanded by any political leaders.

Chapter 1

1. See the exhaustive unpublished doctoral dissertation of F. Seidler, "Die Geschichte des Wortes Revolution. Ein Beitrag zur Revolutionsforschung," Munich, 1955, 14, 20–3 (LC).

2. Cited in Seidler, 167.

3. See V. Snow, "The Concept of Revolution in Seventeenth-Century England," *The Historical Journal,* V, 1962, no. 2, 167–74; Seidler, 108 ff., esp. 114.

4. See M. Walzer, *The Revolution of the Saints: A Study in the Origins of Radical Politics,* Cambridge, Mass, 1965; B. Bailyn, *The Ideological Origins of the American Revolution,* Cambridge, Mass, 1967.

For the particular importance of religious ideas in the American revolutionary ferment, see A. Heimert, *Religion and the American Mind: From the Great Awakening to the Revolution,* Cambridge, Mass, 1966; W. McLoughlin, "The American Revolution as a Religious Revival: 'The Millennium in One Country,' " *New England Quarterly,* XL, 1967, 99–110; and H. Stout, "Religion, Communications and the Ideological Origins of the American Revolution," *William and Mary Quarterly,* 1977, Oct, 519–41. C. Brinton's *Anatomy of Revolution,* NY, 1938, set the pattern for subsequent comparative study by treating the Puritan Revolution as the first modern revolution. A neglected earlier analysis sees the English upheaval as the first "universal" revolution: A. Onu, "Sotsiologicheskaia priroda revoliutsii," in *Sbornik statei posviashchennykh Pavlu Nikolaevichu Miliukovu,* Prague, 1929.

5. G. Griffiths, "Democratic Ideas in the Revolt of the Netherlands," *Archiv für Reformationsgeschichte,* 1959, 50; also his "The Revolutionary Character of the Revolt of the Netherlands," *Comparative Studies in Society and History,* 1960, Jul, 452–72, which finds the main attributes of Brinton's model for revolution present in the Netherlands taken as a whole during this period.

6. J. Maravall, *Las Comunidades de Castilla. Una primera revolución moderna,* Madrid, 1963, sees the urban Spanish rebellion of 1521 against the Hapsburgs as "one of the first explosions" of both national and social revolution (65).

7. D. Kelley thus characterizes the remarkable hero of his *François Hotman, A Revolutionary Ordeal,* Princeton, 1973.

8. H. Koenigsberger, in *New Cambridge Modern History,* Cambridge, 1971, III, 302; also his "Early Modern Revolutions," *Journal of Modern History,* 1974, Mar, 99–110.

9. J. Salmon, "The Paris Sixteen, 1584–94; The Social Analysis of a Revolutionary Movement," *The Journal of Modern History,* 1972, Dec, 540.

For a new version of the repeated attempt since Engels to represent the deeply religious peasants' uprisings in Germany during the Reformation as a pioneering modern revolution, see P. Blickle, *Die Revolution von 1525,* Munich/Vienna, 1975.

10. P. Hazard, *La Crise de la conscience européenne, 1680–1715,* 1967, is the classic account of these intellectual changes.

11. P. Gay, *The Enlightenment: An Interpretation. The Rise of Modern Paganism,* NY, 1966, especially Book One, "The Appeal to Antiquity."

12. Ottavio Sammarco, *A Treatise concerning Revolutions in Kingdoms,* L, 1731, esp. 51–2. The original Italian edition was in Turin, 1629. For the background to the Masaniello uprising, see R. Villari, *La rivolta antispagnola a Napoli: Le Origini (1585–1647),* Bari, 1967.

13. *Le Rivoluzioni di Napoli. Descritte dal signor Alessandro Giraffi,* Venice, 1647, and many subsequent editions.

14. The Masaniello uprising also inspired nineteenth-century revolutionaries through influential operatic and literary recreations. See M. Lasky, "The Novelty of Revolution," *Encounter,* 1971, Nov, 37–9, esp. n. 24.

15. James Howell, *Parthenopoeia, or the History of the Most Noble and Renowned*

Kingdom of Naples, 1654, discussed in Lasky, "The Birth of a Metaphor: On the Origins of Utopia and Revolution," *Encounter,* 1970, Mar, 32. For more detail, see Lasky, *Utopia and Revolution,* Chicago, 1976; for a magisterial survey of 2,500 years of utopian thought combined with concern that "the creative utopian spirit" may be "drowned by the roar of self-proclaimed ideal societies in operation" or blocked out by television's "clatter of special effects" and by the "applied utopistics" of "the pseudoscience of prediction," see F. and F. Manuel, *Utopian Thought in the Western World,* Cambridge, Mass, 1979, and the review by R. Nisbet, *The New Republic,* 1979, Nov 10, 30–4.

16. According to Lasky, "Birth," *Encounter,* 1970, Feb, 35. Lasky's discussion supplements materials cited here with copious English illustrations and Spanish discussions from the later sixteenth century about the possibilities of revolution in England.

17. Ibid., 36.

18. A group of Parisian publications ranging from *Révolutions d'Angleterre* (1670) to *Histoire de la révolution d'Irlande* (1692), along with seven English pamphlets with "revolution" in the title between 1689 and 1693, are all in BO. K. Griewank (*Der neuzeitliche Revolutionsbegriff. Entstehung und Entwicklung,* Weimar, 1955, 182–9) itemizes *Histoires des révolutions* for almost every country past and present in the late seventeenth and early eighteenth centuries; and there were many others such as R. Vertot's *Histoire des révolutions arrivées dans le gouvernement de la République romaine,* 1719, 3v, which was translated into Polish (J. Sapieha, Warsaw, 1736) and republished in many editions.

The word occurred as the title of a play (Catharine Cockburn, *The Revolution in Sweden,* L, 1706), the pseudonym of a pamphleteer (William Revolution, *The Real Crisis or, the necessity of giving immediate and powerful succour to the Emperor against France and her present allies,* L, 1735), and an adjective describing a new kind of politics: *Revolution politicks: being a compleat collection of all the reports, lyes and stories which were the fore-runners of the great revolution in 1688,* L, 1733. (On this, see H. Horwitz, *Revolution Politicks: The Career of Daniel Finch, Second Earl of Nottingham, 1647–1730,* Cambridge, 1968.)

The English settlement was referred to as "our late Happy Revolution" as well as "glorious": *The Revolution and Anti-Revolution Principles Stated and Compar'd, the Constitution Explained and Vindicated, and the Justice and Necessity of Excluding the Pretender maintain'd,* etc., L, 1724, 2d ed., 5 (LC).

A vast world atlas of 1763, which charted all political changes of mankind from Noah to Louis XV (excluding "révolutions intérieures" within states), was entitled *Les Révolutions de l'univers,* 1763 (CA).

The Jesuit Pierre-Joseph Dorléans was the first to deal with the history of revolutions as his sole subject in his *Histoire des révolutions d'Angleterre depuis le commencement de la monarchie,* 1693, 3 v, which described 1688 as "la révolution qui met encore l'Europe en feu." See K.-H. Bender, *Die Entstehung des politischen Revolutionsbegriffes in Frankreich zwischen Mittelalter und Aufklärung,* Munich, 1977, 40 n. 1, 132. For a bibliography and chronological list of histories of revolution in the seventeenth and eighteenth centuries, see 184–201.

19. Frederick the Great, *Oeuvres,* II, 325, cited in Seidler, 91 n. b.

20. *Oeuvres,* II, 235, in Seidler, 236 n. a.

21. A. Weishaupt, *Nachtrag von Weitern Originalschriften,* Munich, 1787, 80.

22. F. von Baader on Aug 14, 1786, cited in H. Grassl, *Aufbruch zur Romantik; Bayerns Beitrag zur deutschen Geistesgeschichte 1765–1785,* Munich, 1968, 431.

23. Mirabeau, *De la Monarchie prussienne, sous Frédéric le Grand,* L, 1788, V, 406 ff.; discussion in Griewank, 231.

24. According to J. Godechot, ed., *La Pensée révolutionnaire 1780–1799,* 1964, 25.

25. Griewank, 230–2; see also Seidler, 183.

26. According to the unpublished dissertation of T. Ranft, "Der Einfluss der französischen Revolution auf dem Wortschatz der französischen Sprache," Giessen, 1905, 123; and Seidler, 185 n. 1. Mirabeau first used "revolutionary" on Apr 19, 1789, and the word was in general use by the fall.

27. F. Brunot, *Histoire de la langue française des origines à nos jours,* 1967, IX, 618 n. 7, 8. The former note raises the possibility that the word may have been originated by A. Rivarol, who himself later became a counter-revolutionary.

28. Godechot, *Pensée,* 127.

29. Cited in J. Thompson, *The French Revolution,* Oxford, 1966, 27; Brunot, IX, 623–4 respectively.

30. Cited from J. von Campe, *Über die Reinigung und Bereicherung der Deutschen Sprache,* 1794, in Seidler, 205. See also the entire section, "Verdeutschungen des Wortes Revolution," 204 ff.

In 1783, a learned Prussian courtier suggested that the German world was subject only to *révolutions passagères, particulières et intestines,* and would be a bulwark in Europe against any *révolution totale.* The Germans would naturally oppose *toute révolution trop grande et dangereuse à la sûreté et à la liberté générale.* Ewald Friedrich von Hertzberg, *Dissertation sur les révolutions des états et particulièrement sur celles de l'Allemagne,* Berlin, 1787, 122–26, cited Bender, 142.

31. R. Palmer, "Notes on the Use of the Word 'Democracy,' 1789–99," *Political Science Quarterly,* 1953, Jun, 203–26. For quantification of the use of terms: M. Tournier, et al., "Le Vocabulaire de Révolution," *Annales Historiques,* 1969, Jan–Mar, 109–24, and materials referenced 111–2.

G. von Proschwitz ("Le vocabulaire politique au XVIII⁰ siècle avant et après la Révolution. Scission ou continuité?" *Le Français Moderne,* 1966, Apr, 87–102) argues for continuity, but proves only that the basic terms of nonrevolutionary parliamentary politics (majority, constitutional, opposition, etc.) had been adopted from England well before the revolution. Polemic political usage of the term dates at least from the Dutch Revolution. A pamphlet of 1583 opened with the assertion that "there live no happier people than the Swiss, because *Democratia*—that is, an honest, well-appointed bourgeois (*borgerlijcke*) government—is established there." Text in Griffiths, "Democratic Ideas," 62–3.

The term was widely and diversely used at the time of the American Revolution (see R. Shoemaker, " 'Democracy' and 'Republic' as Understood in Late Eighteenth Century America," *American Speech,* 1960, May, 83). James Wilson, an author of the American Constitution, saw it vindicating "the democratic principle." (Cited in ibid., 89). But most identified democracy with chaos in any but small states. They argued rather for republicanism, agreeing with Madison that "democracies have ever been spectacles of turbulence and contention . . . and have in general been as short in their lives as they have been violent in their deaths." *The Federalist,* no. 10; also citations in Shoemaker, 88.

32. An understanding championed by both counter-revolutionaries like Joseph de Maistre and revolutionary enthusiasts like Georg Forster. See K. Julku, "La conception de la révolution chez Georg Forster," *Annales Historiques,* 1968, Apr–Jun, 227–51. Julku may overstate the case in suggesting (251) that, by comparison, eighteenth-century usage of the word seems almost "pastoral." Even in the seventeenth century, a dynamic, political understanding of the term "revolution" is detectable. See, in addition to Seidler and Griewank, J. Goulemot, "Le mot Révolution politique (fin XVIII⁰ siècle), *Annales Historiques,* 1967, Oct–Dec, 417–44.

33. Cited in Thompson, *Revolution,* 41–2.

34. L. Gottschalk, *Lafayette in the French Revolution, through the October Days,* Chicago, 1969, 225.

35. "Remarks on the Policy of the Allies with respect to France," *Works,* L, 1803, II, 138.

36. V. Dalin, *Grakkh Babef; nakanune i vo vremia velikoi frantsuzskoi revoliutsii, 1785–1794,* 1963, 265–6.

37. See Brunot, IX, 769–71, for early usages, derived from the location of the different parties within the National Assembly.

38. J. Laponce points out that in all major language-cultures except the Chinese, the notion of left was associated with secular opposition to traditional social and religious custom: "Spatial Archetypes and Political Perceptions," *American Political Science Review,* 1975, Mar, 17; also R. Hertz, "The Pre-Eminence of the Right Hand: A Study in Religious Polarity," in R. Needham, ed., *Right and Left: Essays on Dual Symbolic Classifications,* Chicago, 1973. Prior Pythagorean and Manichean use of the left-right duality are discussed (along with E. Bloch's ingenious ancestry for the modern left in *Avicenna und die Aristotelische Linke*) in V. Fritsch, *Left and Right in Science and Life,* L, 1968, 139.

39. Brunot, IX, 769.

Chapter 2

1. The magisterial work of W. Kula, *Miary i ludzie,* 1970, 429–573, shows that the demand for unified and standard weights and measures was widespread (and altogether baffling to contemporaries) even in the *cahiers de doléance* before the revolution.

2. P. Chevallier, *Histoire de la Franc-Maçonnerie française. I. La Maçonnerie: Ecole de l'Egalité 1725–1799,* 1974, 360–4. *Le Point Parfait* was actually founded during the Terror, becoming "the last to receive its constitutions from the Grand-Orient." 363.

3. Joseph de Maistre, *Oeuvres complètes,* Lyon, 1884, V, 125–6.

4. A. Ducoin, *Etudes révolutionnaires. Philippe D'Orléans-Egalité*, 1845, 22. On the Palais-Royal during the revolution, see S. Lacroix, *Actes de la Commune de Paris pendant la révolution*, 1896, VII, first series, appendix IV, 596, for precise information; R. Heron de Villefosse, *L'Anti-Versailles ou le Palais-Royal de Philippe Egalité*, 1974, 201, for stimulating, but undocumented discussion.

5. C. Rogers, *The Spirit of the Revolution in 1799*, NY, 1949, 108; F. Fosca (pseud. of G. de Traz), *Histoire des Cafés de Paris*, 1934, 74. S. Bradshaw, *Cafe Society. Bohemian Life from Swift to Bob Dylan*, L, 1978, 31.

6. The account here is derived from the detailed information and careful reconstruction of R. Farge, "Un Episode de la journée du 12 juillet 1789. Camille Desmoulins au Jardin du Palais-Royal," *Annales Révolutionnaires*, 1914, VII, 646–74. Supplementary materials and versions (Traz, 75 ff.; Heron de Villefosse, 235–6; J. Morton, *The Bastille Falls*, L, 1936, 12–4) do not materially alter Farge's account. G. Rudé's study of the event from the bottom up refutes the romantic picture of a mass movement, showing that between 800 and 900 probably assaulted the Bastille (even though some 250,000 or more were under arms in Paris), and that few unemployed or even wage earners were involved. See *The Crowd in the French Revolution*, Oxford, 1959, 56 ff., 180–1; *The Crowd in History*, NY, 1964, 99 ff., 126, 250. Neither Farge's argument that the events were not a simple response to Desmoulins's leadership, nor Rudé's demonstration that the crowd was not simply driven by hunger or direct grievance (as they had been in attacking the customhouses) indicates the important mobilizing role played by the clientele of the Palais-Royal. In this respect, as in many others, traditional, semi-legendary accounts, which both of these authors refute in detail, may nevertheless come closer to the truth by providing (as Farge and Rudé never do) an overall accounting for the event.

7. Lacroix, *Actes*, first series, 1894, I, 97–8.

8. Ibid., 114.

9. Ibid., 423–4.

10. Rogers, 207–9.

11. Ducoin, 68.

12. P. Dominique, *Paris enlève le roi*, 1973, 59–60.

13. Ducoin, 196.

14. E. Mellié, *Les Sections de Paris pendant la révolution française*, 1898, 22–5. There were 2,400 active citizens in the Section of the Palais-Royal, as distinct from 1,700 in the Tuileries, 1,200 in the Vendôme, 900 in the Champs-Elysées, etc.

15. Traz, 74–5.

16. Lacroix, *Actes*, first series, 1897, VI, 340–50; second series, I, 232–3. Also *Athenaeum ou idées d'un citoyen sur . . . le Palais Royal*, 1789, a 63-page work (BH).

17. G. Du Boscq de Beaumont and M. Bernos, *La Famille d'Orléans pendant la révolution d'après sa correspondance inédite*, 1913, 3d ed., 214–6. The *Règlement de vie pour le Palais-Royal*, dated Feb 20, 1789, was the guide for "le nouveau genre de vie." More detail on the subject of the House of Orléans during the revolution may well be provided in a work announced for the *Journal of Modern History*, 1979, Dec, but unavailable for this study: G. Kelly, "The Machine of the Duc d'Orléans and the New Politics."

18. *Moniteur*, 1792, Sep 17; Ducoin, *Etudes*, 184.

19. Du Boscq de Beaumont, 272.

20. Ducoin, 225, also 192–3.

21. Ibid., 245, 209; Rose, *Babeuf*, 131.

22. A. Tuetey, *Repertoire général des sources manuscrits de l'histoire de Paris pendant la révolution française*, II, 1892, iii, xiii-iv, xviii; H. Cros, *Claude Fauchet 1744–1793. Les Idées politiques, économiques, et sociales*, 1912, 27–8.

23. Du Boscq de Beaumont, 8–9; Ducoin, 87 ff.; Heron de Villefosse, 224 ff.

24. Ibid., 22 esp. n. 1.

25. Traz, 73.

26. Heron de Villefosse, 215. For the exact layout of the Palais-Royal and discussion of subsequent changes and modifications of this remarkably well-preserved and surprisingly neglected Parisian monument, see J. Hillairet, *Connaissance du vieux Paris*, 1956, 185–200.

27. Traz, 32–7.

28. Ibid., 37.

29. Ibid., 75, 129.

30. Ibid., 47.

31. Ibid., 49, 83.

32. Mercier, *Tableau de Paris*, Amsterdam, 1789, 132; and the entire section on the Palais-Royal, 132–46.

33. The Goncourts, cited in Traz, 79.
34. Ibid.
35. B. de Reigny, *Almanach général de tous les spectacles*, 1791; Traz, 37.
36. The Goncourts, Traz, 79–80.
37. Ibid., 81, 83. For the Palais's importance in the unrest leading to the Republic, see J. Peltier, *The late Picture of Paris; or a faithful narrative of the Revolution of the Tenth of August*, L, 1792, I, 219–20, 231, also 31.
38. Traz, 75; "La Lanterne Magique au Palais-Royal," in Du Boscq, 19–25; also 216; Hillairet, *Connaissance*, 190.
39. Du Boscq, 68.
40. *Grande Aventure arrivée hier au soir au ci-devant vicomte de Mirabeau, au Palais-Royal*, no place or date, but 1790, 21 (BH). Some indication of the new language used in the Palais is in Rogers, 66–70.
41. *Aventure*, 19.
42. Ibid., 18.
   See André Monglond's undeservedly neglected *Le Préromantisme français*, Grenoble, 1930, 2 v, for the "explosion of sensibility . . . no scene . . . which did not end in tears and embraces" (II, 406, 408), and for the general theory that the French revolution developed partly from a prior *révolution sentimentale* (I, 276, and "Les origines sentimentales de la révolution," II, 79 ff.).
   The intensity of the revolutionary cult of sensibility is illustrated by denunciations of "the vice of *insensibilité*" and by the proliferation of neologisms invented to describe those who produce the distortions of *sensiblerie, sensiblomanie*, or *sentimanie* (II, 444–6).
43. Mercier, *Tableau*, X, 133.
44. Ibid.
45. Ibid., 136.
46. P. Bastide, *Sieyès et sa pensée*, 1970, 51–4.
47. Speech to the National Assembly of Jan 20, 1790; extended citation in *Paris révolutionnaire*, 1848, 326.
48. L. Prudhomme, *Histoire des journaux et des journalistes de la révolution française, 1789–1796*, 1846, II, 230–2. The term "journalism" was not yet in use during the revolutionary period (Brunot, IX, 808), and its retroactive use tends slightly to trivialize a profession that was designated with more exalted titles at the time.
49. This I believe to be more accurate than Aulard's suggestion that Marat alone advanced a theory of violence during the period: A. Aulard, "La théorie de la violence et la révolution française," *Études et leçons sur la révolution française*, 1924, ninth series, esp. 12–6. Marat's exhortations did not come as close to providing a "theory" as others like John Oswald.
50. L. Hatin, *Histoire du journal en France 1631–1853*, 1853, 61–2. The title of Hébert's first revolutionary pamphlet, a collaborative effort early in 1790, shows the importance to him of both the favorite entertainment form of the Palais-Royal and its almost indulgent delight in flagellating the aristocracy: *La Laterne magique, ou Fléau des aristocrates*.
51. G. Walter, *Hébert et le Père Duchêne*, 1946, 38 ff.; list of imitators and successors, 357.
52. Walter, 365–6, and his entire invaluable appendix: "lexique de la langue d'Hébert," 359–99.
53. See the introduction by A. Soboul to the reprinted facsimile edition of *Père Duchêne*, 1968.
54. R. Barthes, *Degré zéro de l'écriture*, 1953, 7. For discussion of this tactic in May, 1968, by student revolutionaries in Paris, see M. de Certeau, *La prise de parole*, 1968.
55. A. Decouflé, "La révolution et son double," *Cahiers Internationaux de Sociologie*, 1969, Jan–Jun, 33–4.
56. In a speech to the electors of Paris, Jun 25, 1789, reprinted in *La Chronique du Mois*, 1792, May, 95, 101 (LC). This early period of revolutionary activity is discussed in the unpublished thesis from the Sorbonne of C. Delacroix, *Recherches sur le Cercle Social (1790–1791)*, 1975, kindly made available by A. Soboul. The only significant published study is P. Harivel, *Nicolas de Bonneville, Pré-romantique et révolutionnaire 1760–1828*, 1923, which is purely literary and pays little attention to revolutionary activity. Rudé (*Crowd in Revolution*, 59) identifies Bonneville as "The original promoter of the *milice bourgeoise*." Important material on his later revolutionary activities not used in these other studies is in P. Caron, "La Mission de Loyseau et de Bonneville à Rouen (Septembre 1792)," *La Révolution Française*, 85, 1932, 236–58, 326–44; also biographical information on the Bonneville family,

345–9. The fire in the Palais-Royal of 1798 destroyed Bonneville's papers from this period and makes a reconstruction of his role particularly difficult.

57. "La révolution qui se prépare," *Tribun,* 47.

58. *Tribun,* 104, 114, 148–9 (BN). See also Delacroix, 10.

59. *Le Tribun,* 114.

60. Ibid., 104.

61. Ibid., 44.

62. Ibid., 37 ff.

63. A. Aulard, "Le tutoiement pendant la Révolution," *Etudes et leçons sur la révolution française,* 1914, third series, 28 n. 1. Aulard, following the practice of other great historians of the revolution, dismisses this pioneering usage by Bonneville as purely "poetic" and systematically neglects his importance even while pointing to his innovations.

64. Letter of Bonneville to unidentified "Friends of Liberty" in Jun, 1790; Lacroix, *Actes,* first series, 1898, VII, 572.

65. Delacroix, 10. This work itemizes for the first time the substantial revolutionary activities of Bonneville, who helped provision Paris and Rouen. Even after acting as secretary of the communal assembly of June 1790, he continued to address both the mayor and the heads of Paris districts as a *Représentant de la commune* (Lacroix, *Actes,* first series, 1898, VII, 565–71.)

A valuable doctoral dissertation that came to my attention too late for general use in this work (G. Kates, "The Cercle Social: French Intellectuals in the French Revolution," Chicago, 1978) argues that the Social Circle originated in the struggle of the Commune of Paris against the mayor (16 ff.) and later against the National Assembly (101 ff.). Kates positively identifies 121 members of the Confederation of whom only two were apparently manual workers (51–2).

66. Dalin, *Babef,* 317.

67. Lacroix, *Actes,* VII, 578.

68. Delacroix, 21.

69. Ibid., 36.

70. *La Bouche de Fer,* I, 1790, 54, also 50 ff. The program is set forth in *Du cercle social qui en a conçu le dessin . . . et de tous les cercles de francs-frères qui lui sont affiliés,* 1790, discussed in R. Rose, "Socialism and the French Revolution: the Cercle Social and the Enragés," *Bulletin of the John Rylands Library,* 1958, Sep, 144.

71. Contrast by Fauchet, discussed in A. Mathiez, "Sur le titre du journal 'La Bouche de Fer'," *Annales Révolutionnaires,* XIX, 1917, 690. Delacroix (13) attributes without reference the title to Virgil's *Aeneid;* but it seems rather to derive from *Georgicon,* II, 43–4: mihi si linguae centum sint, oraque centum, Ferrea vox.

72. Ibid., 687,

73. Letter of Dec 1, 1792, from the Director of the Department of Corrèze to the Minister of Justice, cited in M. de Certeau, D. Julia, and J. Revel, "Une Ethnographie de la langue," *Annales,* 1975, Jan–Feb, 27. See also, more fully, the same authors' *Une politique de la langue. La Révolution française et les patois,* 1975; and J.-R. Armogathe, "Néologie et Idéologie dans la langue française au 18e siècle" *Dix-Huitième Siècle,* 1973, no. 5, 27–8.

74. Suggested by Certeau in conversation, Jul 1975, elaborating his discussion in "Ethnographie," 28.

75. Early in 1791, cited in Delacroix, 53, 70.

76. Trahard, *Sensibilité révolutionnaire,* 41, and the entire section "Le recours à l'éloquence."

77. Cited in ibid., 189.

78. Ibid., 185.

79. A. Aulard, *Les Orateurs de la révolution,* 1907, II, 198–9 and ff.

80. Saint-Just, *Oeuvres* (ed. Gratien), 184.

81. Cloots, *La République universelle ou adresse aux tyrannicides par Anacharsis Cloots, orateur du genre humain,* 1793, 82.

82. Bonneville, *Le Nouveau Code Conjugal, établi sur les bases de la Constitution . . . ,* 1792, 25 (LC).

83. *La Bouche de Fer,* 1791, Apr 3, cited in Delacroix, 83.

84. For Bonneville's juxtaposition of *associations parlières* to *sociétés de frères et d'amis,* see *Chronique du Mois,* 1792, Jul, 82.

85. *Lettre de Nicolas de Bonneville, avocat au Parlement de Paris à M. le Marquis de Condorcet,* L, 1787, 41 (BN). "Hymne à la verité," *La Poésie de Nicolas Bonneville,* 1793, 155 (BA); and Bonneville's translation of *Jules de Tarante,* cited in Harivel, 92.

86. Baltrušaitis, *Quête,* 28, 30–1, 65–6; *Poésie de Bonneville,* 123 ff.

87. Citations from the unpublished doctoral dissertation of D. Gordon, *A Philosophe views the French Revolution: the Abbé Morellet (1727–1819)*, Princeton, 1957, 257–60. See also Morellet, "Remarques philosophiques et dramatico-morales sur la particule ON," *Mélanges de littérature et de philosophie*, 1818, IV, 219–30.

Similar arguments were used earlier: (1) by literate loyalists who criticized American revolutionaries for abusing the word liberty "whose very sound carries a fascinating charm" and for unleashing "an Enthusiasm in politics, like that which religious notions inspire, that drives Men on with an unusual Impetuosity, that baffles and confounds all Calculation grounded upon rational principles." (Cited in Stout, "Religion," 534) and also (2) by moderate constitutionalists in the French Revolution, who cautioned already in 1789 about "the power and danger of words" when used by leaders who "would burden us with chains while speaking of liberty" (*Révolutions de Paris*, 1789, Nov 7–14, 3) and later claimed that "the name of liberty killed liberty itself." M. J. Chenier, brother of the poet who was guillotined, cited in Gordon, *Philosophe*, 254). For more material on the opposition of key philosophes to the revolution, see A. Kors, *D'Holbach's Coterie. An Enlightenment in Paris*, Princeton, 1976; also R. Mortier, "Les Héritiers des 'philosophes' devant l'expérience révolutionnaire," and S. Moravia, "La Société d'Auteuil et la révolution," *Dix-Huitième Siècle*, VI, 1974, 45–57, 181–91.

By relating the process of political popularization in America to a prior tradition of religious revivalism, Stout helps explain why the American Revolution was not so terminologically innovative as the French practical, institutional inventiveness. G. Wood ("Rhetoric and Reality in the American Revolution," *William and Mary Quarterly*, 1966, Jan, 26) asserts the general importance of "frenzied rhetoric" during the American upheaval but offers no illustration of any new terms.

88. Morellet, "Apologie de la philosophie contre ceux qui l'accusent des maux de la révolution" (1796), *Mélanges*, IV, 329.

89. Report of Abbé Grégoire, cited in M. Mormile, *La "Néologie" révolutionnaire de Louis-Sebastien Mercier*, Rome, 1973, 199.

90. Varlet, *L'Explosion*, 7 (BM). At the height of its own war against bureaucracy and inherited tradition, the cultural revolution in China urged the rejection even of the original slogan of revolution: "Tear Aside the Bourgeois Mask of 'Liberty, Equality, and Fraternity,'" *Peking Review*, 1966, Jun 10, esp. 13.

91. Mercier, *Tableau*, X, 132–46; Restif, *Le Palais-Royal*, 1790, 3v. The friendship of Mercier and Restif is discussed but not explored by R. Trousson in Mercier, *L'An*, 21–2. Mercier inherited Restif's papers at death: M. Chadourne, *Restif de la Bretonne ou le siècle prophétique*, 1958, 350 n. 2.

92. Mormile, 25–6; also Restif, *Mes inscriptions, journal intime*, 1889, preface.

93. Mormile, 157–8, 164 n. 24. The term is probably derived from Bonneville's *livriste*.

94. Ibid., 201–2. For Mercier's indebtedness to the innovators of revolutionary terminology, especially Mirabeau, Bonneville, and Restif, see ibid., 230–1, 306, 337–8, 347–8.

95. *L'An* (ed. Trousson), 63–4.

96. *L'An* (ed. 1786), III, 160, as cited in Mormile, 170.

97. *L'An* (ed. Trousson), 388. See the imaginary extracts from gazettes in 22 different parts of the world, 388–415.

98. Mercier, *J.-J. Rousseau considéré comme l'un des premiers auteurs de la révolution*, 1791; also Mormile, 155.

99. Cited in Trousson, 68.

100. *Eloges et discours philosophiques*, xv, cited in Trousson, 22. Like so many other philosophes, Mercier was tempted to visit Russia to realize his utopian plans, and tried unsuccessfully to go early in the reign of Catherine the Great. See the unpublished doctoral dissertation of T. Zanadvorova, *Lui-Sebast'ian Mers'e i ego utopichesky roman "2440-i god,"* Leningrad, 1947, 16.

101. Cros, *Fauchet*, 29; and discussion of the Social Circle, in which he was Bonneville's principal collaborator, 25–41.

102. Lacroix, *Actes*, first series, 1898, VII, 577, 567, 564, 585–90.

103. *La Bouche de Fer*, 1790, I, 3.

104. Ibid., second pagination, 1–4, for the "Prospectus pour le Cercle Patriotique"; and 5–12, the "Portrait du Cercle Social."

105. Estimates in Rose, 146, which differ somewhat from those in Lacroix, *Actes*, first series, VII, 597.

106. Ibid., 585.

107. Delacroix, 33–4.

108. Rose, 144.

109. Ioannisian, *Idei*, 43, 39–40.

110. Ibid., 35–8, supplements the still basic account of A. Lichtenberger, "John Oswald, écossais, jacobin et socialiste," *La Révolution Française*, XXXII, 1897, 481–95.

111. John Oswald, *Review of the Constitution of Great Britain*, 3rd augmented edition (Paris, 1792), "and sold at the Cercle Social" cited Ioannisian, *Idei*, 47. An important role in this campaign was also played by the English priest, David Williams, whose *Lessons to a Young Prince by an Old Statesman on the Present Disposition in Europe to General Revolution* (1791) was translated and republished in *La Bouche*, and who influenced Bonneville even before emigrating to France as an honorary "citizen" of the republic. *Idei*, 41–2.

112. A French translation appeared in the same year: ibid., 49–50 and ff.

113. *De l'Esprit des religions. Ouvrage promis et nécessaire à la confédération universelle des amis de la vérité*, 1792, 249, 88 (LC).

114. Ibid., 88.

115. Ibid. (appendices of the second edition), 118.

116. Ibid. (appendices), 132.

117. Cited from an unreferenced work of the Social Circle in *Mercure de France*, 1790, Dec 18, 96.

118. Cited from Fauchet in ibid., 108.

119. Ibid.

120. *Les Jésuites chassés de la franc-maçonnerie et leur poignard brisé par les maçons*, L, 1788, I, 27.

121. Cited in V. Semevsky, *Politicheskie i obshchestvennye idei dekabristov*, St. Petersburg, 1910, 402. See also M. Kalushin, ed., *Pushkin i ego vremia*, Leningrad, 1962, 165–6 n. 3.

122. Bonneville, *Esprit*, 129–30.

123. Ibid. (appendices), 326, 322, 343, 333.

124. Ibid. (appendices), 334. According to the hostile account in the *Mercure de France* (Dec 18, 1790, 98), Bonneville addressed these words to the sun with the invocation: *ECLAIRE, le Monde sera eclairé.*

125. Illustrations and textual keys, ibid., 236–43. Much of this was borrowed from David Williams. See Ioannisian, "Dzhon Osval'd i 'Sotisal'ny Kruzhok,'" *Novaia i Noveishaia Istoriia*, 1962, no. 3, 66–7.

126. *Esprit*, 250.

127. J. Abray, "Feminism in the French Revolution," *American Historical Review*, 1975, Feb, 49, following the judgment of Aulard, cited 50.

128. *Bouche*, I, 3; Etta Palm, *Appel aux françaises sur la régénération des moeurs, et nécessité de l'influence des femmes dans un gouvernement libre*, 1791, 25.

129. In addition to her *Appel aux françaises*, see *Discours de Mme. Palm d'Aelders, hollandaise, lu à la confédération des amis de la vérité*, Caen, n.d.; and, on the Société des Amis de la vérité, A. Mathiez, *La Révolution et les Etrangers*, 1928, 96.

130. E. Hamy, "Note sur diverses gravures de Bonneville représentant des nègres (1794–1803)," *Anthropologie* (1899), X, 42–6. Bonneville's associate, John Oswald, insisted that the "rights of man" be extended not only to women and slaves, but to animals. See his *The Cry of Nature, or an Appeal to Mercy and Justice on behalf of the persecuted animals*, L, 1791 (BN).

131. Alekseev-Popov *Sbornik . . . Volgina*, 329.

132. Lacroix, *Actes*, first series, VII, 601.

133. M. Conway, "Thomas Paine et la révolution des deux mondes," *La Revue Hebdomadaire*, XXVI, 1900, May 26, 478; XXVII, Jun 2, 74–5. Recent work on Paine offers no important new material on his Paris stay, and generally overlooks the study by Conway, which characterizes (XXVII, 75 n. 2) Paine's *Declaration of the Volunteers of Belfast* (1791) as the first public manifesto in support of the French Revolution outside France. Barlow also later wrote a *Letter Addressed to the People of Piedmont*: see J. Woodress, *A Yankee's Odyssey. The Life of Joel Barlow*, Philadelphia/NY, 1958, 134.

134. Cited and discussed in Conway, 479; for Jacobin alarm at the circle, 480–2.

135. Marat, *Izbrannye proizvedeniia*, 1956, III, 126; Dalin, *Babef*, 324.

136. Morton, *Bastille*, 205.

137. Mathiez, *Etrangers*, 37, 105–11. The Swiss, too, had their "bureau of correspondence" close to the Palais-Royal (34). For the furious antiforeign campaign of late 1793, 138 ff.

138. Text in Caron, "Mission," 334–5.

139. Rose, 153–66; Ya. Zakher, "Zhan Varlet vo vremia iakobinskoi diktatury," *Novaia i Noveishaia Istoriia*, 1959, no. 2, 113–26.

140. For the difference between referential symbols, which suggest ideas linguis-

tically, and condensation symbols, which in some way directly express or look like the object described, see E. Sapir, *Language: An Introduction to the Study of Speech*, NY, 1921; and discussion in Laponce, "Archetypes," 11, n. 1.

141. Hillairet, 12.

142. Description of the program drawn up by David in *Chronique de Paris*, 1793, Jul 18; translation in Henderson, 357–8; illustration of the fountain, 356.

143. J. Tiersot, *Les Fêtes et les chants de la révolution française*, 1908, 95 ff.

144. Tiersot, 27–30.

145. Ibid, 107: Descends, ô Liberté, fille de la Nature:
Le peuple a reconquis son pouvoir immortel;
Sur les pompeux debris de l'antique imposture,
Ses mains relèvant ton autel. [Tiersot, 107.]

146. Citizen Guiboust in a speech to the popular society of the Section of the Republic, cited in M. Ozouf, *La Fête révolutionnaire 1789–99*, 1976, 301–2; see also Abbé Grégoire, *Essai historique et patriotique sur les arbres de la liberté*, an II.

147. Ozouf, 313, 315–6, 302.

148. Ibid., 310.

149. J. Crocker, "The Guillotine," *Essays on the Early Period of the French Revolution*, L, 1857, 550, 519–71.

150. N. Evreinov, "Teatralizatsiia zhizni," in *Teatr kak takovoi*, Berlin, 1923, 50–1. For full discussion of Evreinov's theories and their impact on his own reenactment of the storming of the Winter Palace (subsequently largely incorporated into Eisenstein's film *October*), see the forthcoming Princeton doctoral dissertation of P. Thon, to whom I am indebted for this citation.

151. Ibid., 51. For another sustained depiction of the French Revolution as theater ("of demonic picturesqueness . . . Latin perfection of form"), see E. Friedell, *A Cultural History of the Modern Age*, NY, 1954, II, 380–5.

152. Citoyen Grégoire, *Systèmes de dénominations topographiques* (1793), cited in B. Baczko, *Lumières de l'utopie*, 1978, 369.

153. Tiersot, 40.

154. Ozouf, *Fête*, 177.

155. Declaration of Sarrette, cited Ozouf, 152.

156. Ozouf, 157.

157. Michelet, cited in Tiersot, 157.

158. Ozouf, 178; detailed account Tiersot, 156–67; Baczko, *Lumières*, 263–71.

159. Report of the principal author of the calendar, G. Romme, cited in Baczko, "Le temps ouvre un nouveau livre à l'histoire. L'utopie et le calendrier révolutionnaire," *Lumières*, 214. See also A. Galante Garrone, *Gilbert Romme. Storia di un rivoluzionario*, 1959; and, for Romme's little-known influence on his Russian ward, Count Paul Stroganov, Dalin, *Liudi*, 9–21.

160. Romme, cited Baczko, *Lumières*, 215.

161. Ibid., 217, 223, 224.

162. Fabre d'Eglantine, cited in Henderson, 402; also 399–401.

163. Mathiez, "Robespierre et le culte," 224.

164. *Declaration solenelle des droits de l'homme dans l'état social*, 1793 (repr. 1967), 4.

165. Text in Dommanget, "La Fête et le culte de la raison," *Annales Révolutionnaires*, IX, 1917, 355.

166. Ozouf, 136–7; A. Mathiez, *Autour de Robespierre*, 1925, 123–4; also 117–20.

167. C. Nodier, cited in Ozouf, 130.

168. Ibid., 131.

169. The importance of this exhibit is stressed in Walter Benjamin, "Paris, capitale du XIXe siècle," *Oeuvres*, 1971, II, 129.

170. Cited in Ozouf, 205 n. 1.

171. Tiersot, *Fêtes*, 202–4.

172. M. Thiebaut, "Restif à Carnavalet," *La Revue de Paris*, 1935, Jan 15, 439. "Apprends ô ma chère Ile/ Que je puis mourir,/ J'ai fini mon grand ouvrage." Restif's fullest prerevolutionary picture of a communist utopia is that of an imaginary island in *La Découverte australe par un homme-volant, ou le Dédale français; Nouvel très philosophique. Suivie de la lettre d'un singe*, Leipzig, 1781; discussed most fully in Ioannisian, "Utopiia Retifa," 181 ff. J. Pinset, in citing a variant version of Restif's hymn of praise to his beloved island, refers to the island as representing not so much the site of a social utopia as the psychological focus of "the great, egocentric romantic pilgrimage." "Les Origines instinctives de la révolution française," *Revue d'Histoire Economique et Sociale*, 1961, no. 2, 201.

The infatuation with idealized islands as a refuge from artificial social convention is again traceable to Rousseau. See E. Wagner, *L'Ile de Saint-Pierre ou l'île de Rousseau dans le lac de Bienne*, Bern, n.d.; Monglond, *Préromantisme*, II, 44 ff.

Further stimulus was provided by Charles Garnier's series: *Voyages imaginaires, songes, visions, et romans cabalistiques*, Amsterdam/Paris, 1787–95, esp. VIII, 1787: *L'Isle inconnue*.

173. The literature on utopias has become enormous and increasingly repetitious in recent years. More introduced the Greek word for "nowhere," *Utopia*, in his picture of an imaginary voyager discovering an ideal society: *De optimo reipublicae statu, deque nova insula Utopia*, Louvain, 1516; and some subsequent Reformation tracts published in Antwerp were listed as coming from Utopia. M. Kronenberg, "Forged Addresses in Low Country Books in the Period of the Reformation," *The Library*, 1947, Sep–Dec, 81–3. Similar dreams of an ideal order like those of Andreas and Campanella arose in the wake of the religious wars in the early seventeenth century (just as Plato's *Republic* had appeared after the suffering and division of the Peloponnesian Wars); but secular utopianism begins with the awakening of the geographical imagination and of social criticism in the literature of the Enlightenment.

The earliest secular utopias—like many of the most recent—saw men overcoming sexual as well as social divisions. Gabriel Foigny's *Les Aventures de Jacques Sadeur*, 1676, and Varrasse d'Alais, *Histoire des Sévérambes*, 1677, depicted, respectively, a society of hermaphrodites and a communal life with eight hours of pleasure a day (Reybaud, *Etude*, 37–40, 54, 60). But secular literature soon began to invest real places with the utopian qualities of perfection. The tendency to idealize European experiments (the Jesuit state of Patagonia in Paraguay) gave way to more radical praise for the unspoiled Indians themselves, beginning with plays like *Dialogues or Encounters between a Savage and the Baron de la Houta*, 1704. In the course of the eighteenth century, "heroic" utopias inspiring men to action increasingly prevailed over "escapist" utopias lulling men to quiescence. This progression in J. Szacki, *Utopia*, Warsaw, 1968, is similar to the one that C. Rihs traces from "sentimental" to "revolutionary" utopias in *Les Philosophes utopistes; le mythe de la cité communautaire en France au XVIIIe siècle*, 1970; and to the distinction of E. Bloch between "uchronias," which look back to a heroic past, and "utopias," which are future-oriented sources of militant optimism and secular revolution. See Bloch, *Das Prinzip Hoffnung*, 1955, II; and *Geist der Utopie*, Frankfurt/Main, 1964; also P. Furter, "Les fonctions de l'utopie," *L'Imagination créatrice, la violence et le changement social*, Cuernavaca, 1968, 3/11–3/41. B. Baczko, "Lumières et Utopie. Problèmes de Recherches," *Annales*, 1971, Mar–Apr, 355–86, inclines rather to the view that utopian ideas generally lead to reformism rather than revolution. L. Sargent, "Utopia—The Problem of Definition," *Extrapolation*, 1975, May, 137–48, discusses none of the preceding works and deals mainly with narrower literary and structural problems. For an uneven but often stimulating series of short papers and discussions on social ideas in utopias, see *Le discours utopique. Colloque de Cerisy*, 1978.

Utopian thought helped launch the revolutionary search for "symbolic geography" (Certeau, "La révolution fondatrice," 81 ff.): for some tangible, secular locus for an alternative society. The disruptive potential of this mode of speculation was increased when combined with the "polemic, irreligious and socially revolutionary" tendency to juxtapose natural law to Christian tradition. R. Lenoble, *Esquisse d'une histoire de l'idée de nature*, 1969, 365. In addition to this searching study of attempts since classical antiquity "to construct against the myths of one's time a coherent Nature subject to laws" (927), see also the works of G. Atkinson, esp. *Le Sentiment de la nature et le retour à la vie simple (1690–1740)*, Geneva, 1960, and of G. Chinard, esp. *L'Amérique et le rêve exotique dans la littérature française au XVIIe siècle*, 1963, 2v; also L. Crocker, *Nature and Culture: Ethical Thought in the French Enlightenment*, 1963; and P. Van Tieghern, *Le Sentiment de la nature dans le préromantisme européen*, 1960.

174. The still mysterious Morelly's *Code de la nature, ou le véritable esprit de ses loix, de tout tems negligé ou méconnu*, appeared in five editions between 1757 and 1773, following on his *Naufrage des isles flottantes, ou Basiliade*, Messina, 1753, which purported to be translated from an Indian work. See R. Coë, "A la recherche de Morelly," *Revue d'Histoire Littéraire de la France*, 1957, Jul–Sep, 326–8.

Babeuf's program for economic redistribution and welfare was so closely based on Morelly's *Code of Nature* that he has been called "Morelly turned into a man of action." H. Baudrillat, *Dictionnaire d'économie politique*, 1852, I, 427; cited by M. Dommanget, *Babeuf et les problèmes du Babouvisme*, 32. See also R. Coë, "Le théorie morellienne et la pratique babouviste," and the appended discussion between Dautry, Saitta, and Coë, *Annales Historiques*, 1958, Jan–Mar, 38–64; for Morelly's links with an alleged "literary communist" movement of the eighteenth century, Coë, *Morelly: Ein Rationalist auf dem Wege zum Sozialismus*, 1961, 9; and, for Babeuf's direct testimony of derivation, 296.

175. G. Likhotkin, *Sil'ven Mareshal' i "zaveshchanie Ekateriny II,"* Leningrad, 1974, 18–20. *Le Tombeau de J.-J. Rousseau*, 1779; *L'Age d'or, recueil des contes pastoraux par le berger Sylvain*, 1782. The dominant poetic influence was that of the German-speaking Swiss painter-poet S. Gessner.

176. No copy has apparently survived. See O. Karmin, "Sylvain Maréchal et le Manifeste des Egaux," *Revue Historique de la Révolution Française*, 1910, I, 513.

177. *Correctif à la Révolution*, 1793, discussed Ioannisian, *Idei*, 149–59. This work has been called the founding treatise of modern anarchism by one of its leading historians: M. Nettlau, *Der Vorfrühling der Anarchie*, 1924, I.

178. Cited in Karmin, "Maréchal," 511; also Dommanget, *Maréchal*, 455.

179. G. Pariset, *Etudes d'histoire révolutionnaire et contemporaine*, 1929, 129–30.

180. Cited in Thompson, *Babeuf*, 28; also 27–9, and Ioannisian, *Idei*, 223.

181. Barlow, "Genealogy of the Tree of Liberty," unpublished, undated manuscript, Houghton Library, Harvard, bMS Am 1448 (13), 22.
This could be one of the relatively few French revolutionary rituals to be derived directly from American revolutionary precedent, if Arthur Schlesinger is correct in his suggestion that Thomas Paine introduced into France the practice of eulogizing liberty trees: "Liberty Tree: A Genealogy," *New England Quarterly*, Dec 1952, 453. But Schlesinger's learned study explores only the American side. He seems unaware that this practice developed in France well before Paine's arrival, and quaintly patronizing in his suggestion that Barlow was simply writing "for his own amusement" (436 n. 1).

182. See the loose page added to Barlow, "Genealogy," 25, on the liberty cap, which was allegedly adopted by the Romans as the cap that signified the gift of liberty to a slave.

183. Ibid., 23. The erotic aspects of revolutionary symbols will apparently be dealt with in a forthcoming Polish work of M. Janion, who has already written on "the fevers of romanticism": *Goraczka romantyczna*, 1975.

184. *Le Pied* was translated the following year into German and, in 1774, into Russian in St. Petersburg, where Restif's works generally received a warm reception. See G. Buachidze, *Retif de la Bretonn v Rossii*, Tbilisi, 1972, esp. 102–9. For a convenient bibliography in French of Russian work on Restif neglected in Western scholarship, see 328–40. *Le Pornographe ou idées d'un honnête-homme sur un projet de règlement pour les prostituées*, L/The Hague, 1779; see discussion in Poster, *Restif*, 33–50, and material referenced in 97 n. 1 on Restif's own possible foot fetish.

185. Poster, 99.

186. Ibid., and *Monsieur Nicolas*, I, 359. Like almost all Western writers on Restif, Poster seems unaware of the importance of this "communist" work—and relates erotic impulses to literary forms rather than to social or revolutionary substance.

Chapter 3

1. Brunot, IX, 641.

2. W. Adams, "Republicanism in Political Rhetoric before 1776," *Political Science Quarterly*, 1970, Sep, 397–421. For widespread prior identification of republican forms with the negative features of the Commonwealth in England, see P. Maier, "The Beginnings of American Republicanism 1765–1777," in *The Development of a Revolutionary Mentality*, Washington, 1972, 99–117. See also C. Robbins, "European Republicanism in the Century and a Half Before 1776," ibid., 31–5.

3. Cited and discussed in G. Dutcher, "The Rise of Republican Government in the United States," *Political Science Quarterly*, 1940, Jun, 209. He also credits John Adams with simultaneously turning the word into a badge of merit and authoring a model republican constitution for Massachusetts (which, alone of all formed prior to 1787, remains in force). Ibid., 209–11.

4. G. Ghelfi, "European Opinions of American Republicanism during the 'Critical Period,' 1781–1789," unpublished doctoral thesis, Claremont, 1968. American writers of the 1780s who considered their revolution incomplete looked for its fulfillment in a formal constitution rather than in further social change. See D. Higginbotham, "The Relevance of the American Revolution," *Anglican Theological Review*, 1973, Jul, 33–4.

5. Palmer, *Age*, I, 489–502.

6. *The Life and Works of Thomas Paine*, New Rochelle, 1925, VI, 206.

7. *Républicain ou le défenseur du gouvernement représentatif* lasted only four issues. Dalin, *Babef*, 407–8. Paine saw "a new era that is going to wipe despotism from the face of the earth" ushered in as revolutionary republicanism became "universally extended." See his *Lettre de Thomas Paine au peuple françois*, 1792, Sep 25, 3, 7 (EU).

8. Dalin, 405.

9. "Constitution," in *La Chronique du Mois*, 1792, Jan, 3. This journal like *Républicain* was edited by a group that included Bonneville, Paine, Condorcet, and Brissot. Bonneville likens the constitution of the state to the constitutions of nature itself and of the human body—with "the people" its "blood" (4).

10. A. Mathiez, "La Constitution de 1793," *La Revue de Paris*, 1928, Jul 15, esp. 318 ff.

11. Successive periods of this tradition, which became essentially nonrevolutionary, are traced in G. Weill, *Histoire du parti républicain en France de 1814–1870*, 1928, and J. Scott, *Republican Ideas and the Liberal Tradition in France, 1870–1914*, NY, 1951.
The word "republican" was used as early as 1770 in France as a virtual synonym for revolutionary. J. Godechot, "Pour un vocabulaire politique et social de la révolution française," *Actes du 89 congrès national des sociétés savantes. Section d'histoire moderne et contemporaine*, I, 1964, 371–4. The concept of citizen also acquired radical meaning prior to the revolution (A. Dubuc, "Le Journal de Normandie avant et durant les états-généraux," in ibid., 387 n. 7), and came to be resented by some as a new term of privilege during the revolution (Godechot, ibid., 373).

12. *Lettre de Paine*, 3, 7; Palmer, *Age*, II, 113–23.

13. W. Nelson, "The Revolutionary Character of the American Revolution," in C. McFarland, ed., *Readings in Intellectual History. The American Tradition*, NY, 1970, 159. The American concept of independence and nationhood probably exercised its main influence on the Latin American revolutions that began in 1808. See J. Lynch, *The Spanish American Revolutions. 1808–1826*, a valuable synthesis that is weak in discussing ideas. The concept of *independencia* will be treated in a forthcoming study of German Arciniegas; and the historical luster of this term probably accounts for the intensive recent use of its opposite (*dependencia*) by Latin American nationalists to characterize their continued cultural and economic dominance by North America without direct control.
The first Declaration of Independence in Europe after the outbreak of revolution in France (that of the nearby Belgian province of Brabant in October 1789) repeatedly refers to "the nation" and "the body of the nation," and insists that "the will of the nation is always the supreme law." Godechot, *Pensée*, 68, and 67–9. The word "nation" entered the vocabulary of American politics in the ideological modern sense largely after the outbreak of the French Revolution through idiosyncratic ideologists like James Wilson, then associate justice of the Supreme Court who asked rhetorically in *Chisholm vs. Georgia* in 1793: "Do the people of the *United States* form a NATION?" (G. Dennison, "The 'Revolution Principle': Ideology and Constitutionalism in the Thought of James Wilson," *Review of Politics*, 1977, Apr, 187). The first university course taught on the American Revolution (at Harvard in 1839) used a history written in 1809 by an Italian nationalist who had become a French revolutionary activist in order to inculcate a full-blown romantic nationalism for which there were still no American texts. Carlo Botta, *History of the War of the Independence of the United States of America*, Philadelphia, 1821, 2v; discussed by M. Kammen, *A Season of Youth*, NY, 1978, 282–3 n. 83. D. Donald contends that presidents before Lincoln "generally avoided the term" (nation), and that the Civil War led to the widespread adoption of the European term and the end of the tendency to refer "to the United States in the plural." *Liberty and Union*, Boston/Toronto, 1978, 215.

14. J. Godechot, "Nation, patrie, nationalisme et patriotisme en France au XVIIIe siècle," *Annales Historiques*, 1971, Oct–Dec, 494–6.

15. Delacroix, 9.

16. G. Zernatti, "Nation: The History of a Word," *Review of Politics*, 1944, Jul, 352–8, 361–5.

17. Account of Apr, 1790, by Nicholas Karamzin, cited in Brunot, IX, 638.

18. *Le Magnificat du tiers-état*, 1789 (EU).

19. *Symboles des Patriotes françois, ou Credo des anti-aristocrates*, 1790, 7 (EU).

20. *Litanies du tiers-état*, 1790 2d. ed. 10–1 (EU).

21. This line of interpretation is suggested, though not developed, in the stimulating new study by a Breton separatist J. Y. Guiomar, *L'Idéologie national. nation représentation propriété*, 1974, 91–4. J. Gottmann sees a new conception of territorial sovereignty emerging from the French Revolution as the basic characteristic of a nation: *The Significance of Territory*, Charlottesville, 1973, 74–6.

22. *Mémoires pour servir à l'histoire du jacobinisme*, Hamburg, 1798–9, III, 184; cited in Godechot, "Nation," 500.

23. L. Krieger, "Nationalism and the Nation-State System: 1789–1870," in *Chapters in Western Civilization*, NY, 1962, 3d. ed., II, 113.

24. Z.-E. Harsany, *La Vie à Strasbourg sous la révolution*, Strasbourg, 1963, 99, lists 73 cabarets, 86 outdoor rotisseries, and 33 brasseries in Strasbourg in 1789, and describes (89–99) this "golden age of cafés."

25. The basic picture presented here is that established by J. Tiersot, *Histoire de la Marseillaise*, 1915, 27–9, which can be supplemented by A. Dietrich, *La Création de la Marseillaise: Rouget de Lisle et Frédéric de Dietrich*, 1917, and confirmed in P. Martin, "Propos autour d'un tableau historique: Rouget de Lisle chantant la Marseillaise," *Saison d'Alsace*, 1964, Winter, 108–11.
It had long been argued that the melody could not have been invented so rapidly and must have been taken from some forgotten operatic work of the period—variously said to be Dalayrac's *Sargines ou l'élève de l'amour*, Grétry's *La Caravane de Caire*, or a lost work of Méhul, to whom Rouget de Lisle dedicated his published collection of 1796. Tiersot carefully refutes these claims and insists that Rouget was the sole author of both words and music: *Histoire*, 410–22. More recent speculation has focused on possible borrowings by Rouget from an oratorio based on Racine's *Esther*, composed by the music master at the Cathedral of Saint-Omer, where Rouget was stationed previously. See M. Vogelais, *Quellen und Bausteine zu einer Geschichte der Musik und des Theatres in Elsass*, Strasbourg, 1911. A. Gastoué, "L'air de la Marseillaise, naquit-il à Saint-Omer?" *Echanges et Recherches*, Roubaix, 1939, Jan 148–53, answers the question with a decisive no, insisting that the composition was original. At the same time, he indicates that Rouget drew some key phrases from local military terminology ("enfants de la patrie" and "aux armes, citoyens") and from *Sargines* ("entendez-vous le bruit de guerre . . . Marchons, marchons"). See also further references and discussion in J. Mouchon, *La Musique en Alsace*, Strasbourg, 1970, 136.

26. Harsany, 109–10 and ff.; R. Reuss, *La Cathédrale de Strasbourg pendant la Révolution*, 1888. "Ein feste Burg" was itself adapted for the revolution: M.-J. Bopp, "La Poésie politique pendant la révolution," *Deux Siècles d'Alsace française*, Strasbourg/Paris, 1948, 184.

27. Bopp, 195–6.

28. Tiersot, *Histoire*, 68–71. This *Offrande de la liberté. Scène religieuse sur le chant des Marseillaises* was first performed on Sep 30, 1792.

29. Ibid., 71. See also ibid., 63–7; and L. Fiaux, *La Marseillaise: Son Histoire dans l'histoire des français depuis 1792*, 1918, 148, 346–7; also B. Shafer, *Faces of Nationalism: New Realities and Old Myths*, NY, 1972, esp. 136; and, more generally, J. Leith, "Music as an Ideological Weapon in the French Revolution," *The Canadian Historical Association: Historical Papers Presented at the Annual Meeting*, 1966, 126–40.

30. Fiaux, 32.

31. J. Chailley, "La Marseillaise et ses transformations jusqu'à nos jours," *Actes du 89 congrès national des sociétés savantes*, 1964, I, 16.

32. For description of *La Révolution du 10 août ou le tocsin allégorique* and the judgment that it was the most important festival held outside of Paris during 1793, see Tiersot, *Les fêtes*, 117–9.

33. *La Musique en Alsace*, 136.

34. Croker, *Essays*, 549–51, corrects the still widespread belief that the first such machine was made in Paris by either the scientist Guillotin or the surgeon Louis.

35. Bonneville, *L'Année MDCCLXXXIX ou Les Tribuns du Peuple*, nd., v, 80, (BA).

36. See the *Assemblée des représentants de la Commune de Paris. Extrait du procès-verbal*, 17 juin 1790, and the handwritten attached letter of Bonneville to Camille Desmoulins, which are not catalogued but located next to a copy of *L'Année*: Rf 17044 (BA).

37. Document and discussion by Mathiez in *Annales Révolutionnaires*, VI, 1913, 101–2, and VIII, 1916, 437.

38. Harivel contends (*Bonneville*, 141) that Bonneville's friend Letourneur first used "romantic" in its modern sense; but his undated example almost certainly derives from prior German usages discussed by A. Lovejoy, who ascribes the first use to Schlegel but also stresses the importance of Schiller: *Essays in the History of Ideas*, NY, 1955, 183–207.

39. See the neglected doctoral dissertation by E. Nacken, *Eulogius Schneider in Deutschland (1758–1791)*, Bonn, 1931, published only in part as *Studien über Eulogius Schneider in Deutschland*, Bonn, 1931. The basic studies are F. Heitz,

Notes sur la vie et les écrits d'Euloge Schneider, Strasbourg, 1862; L. Erhard, *Euloge Schneider. Sein Leben und seine Schriften*, Strasbourg, 1894; E. Muhlenbeck, *Euloge Schneider*, Strasbourg, 1896; and the series of articles by R. Jaquel in *Annales Historiques*, VIII, 1931, 399–417; IX, 1932, 1–27, 103–15, 336–42; X, 1933, 61–73; XII, 1935, 218–48. Schneider's tutoring of Nodier and others in Strasbourg and the transmission of proto-romantic ideas is discussed in T. Fach, "Die Naturschilderung bei Charles Nodier," *Beiträge zur Geschichte der romanischen Sprachen und Literaturen*, IV, 1912, 5.

40. See F. L'Huillier, "Les grands courants de l'opinion publique," *Deux siècles d'Alsace*, 244–50; Tiersot, *Histoire*, 73; *Annales Historiques*, IX, 1932, 21–7, 103; and Harsany, *Vie*, 257–9.

R. Palmer finds Schneider the only revolutionary to use the counter-revolutionary term "Propaganda," *Twelve Who Ruled: The Committee of Public Safety in the French Revolution*, Princeton, 1941, 187–90. The best source for this insufficiently studied institution would seem to be the history written in prison by Schneider's close associates: *Histoire de la propagande et des miracles qu'elle a faits à Strasbourg . . .* , referred to in R. Jaquel, "Un terroriste alsacien: Le cordonnier Jung," *La Bourgeoisie Alsacienne*, Strasbourg, 1967 (repr. of 1954), 253 n. 86.

41. Nodier, *Souvenirs*, 21; and section on Schneider, 13–33.

42. Harsany, 107; Schneider, "Über die Denunziationen," *Argos*, III, 1793, Sep 26, 297–301.

43. Harsany, 101.

44. "Patriotischer Kreuzzug," *Argos*, 1793, Aug 31, Sep 3, cited in *Deux siècles*, 260.

45. G. Forster, *Ein Lesebuch für unsere Zeit*, Weimar, 1952, 346.

46. Text in Harivel, 153.

47. Bonneville, *L'Hymne des combats*, 1797, 5; also his *Les "Francs-Germains" nos ancêtres*, discussed in Brunot, IX, 633.

48. "La Druide," *La Chronique du Mois*, 1792, May, 7. Fauchet's article "On the University of Nature" (*Bouche de Fer*, 1790, no. 25, 385–97) is discussed by Alekseev-Popov, *Sbornik Volgina*, 305.

49. Mathiez, *Etrangers*, 67. Nodier stresses his role in Paris even more: *Souvenirs de la Révolution et de l'Empire*, 3d ed., 1864, I, 245–6; II, 24 ff.

50. N. von Wrasky, *A.G.F. Rebmann. Leben und Werke eines Publizisten zur Zeit der grossen französischen Revolution*, Heidelberg, 1907.

51. Mathiez, *Etrangers*, 112–7, 142, 153–7. Palmer has correctly noted (*Age*, II, 117) that "the foreign revolutionaries . . . remain one of the mysteries of the French Revolution." No aspect of the mystery has been less explored than the impact within France of the largest neighboring nationality, the German. One of the few studies that even raises the question is S. Stern, *Anacharsis Cloots der Redner des Menschengeschlechts. Ein Beitrag zur Geschichte der Deutschen in der französischen Revolution*, 1914.

52. Cloots, *La République*, 190.

53. Bonneville, *Le Vieux Tribun et sa Bouche de Fer*, 27; cited in Brunot, IX, 633 n. 2.

54. Such as his incendiary "Prise des armes," *La Chronique*, 1972, May, 94–101.

55. *Appel au genre humain, par Anacharsis Cloots, représentant du peuple sauveur*, nd, 20. These capitalized words end the pamphlet.

56. Herder, *Sämtliche Werke*, 1891, V, 510; R. Ergang, *Herder and the Foundations of German Nationalism*, NY, 1931, 110–1. The possibility that Barruel may in fact have taken the term from prior usage by Herder or some other German is given support by Palmer's analysis of Barruel's work as almost exclusively dependent on German sources and authorities: *Age*, II, 251–4.

57. Statement of 1803, cited in Harivel, *Bonneville*, 79. See also 77–118 for German literary influences in France from the beginnings of the 1780s.

58. Palmer, *Twelve*, 3–6; on Saint-Just, 9–10, 73–7; and, on his mission to Strasbourg, 177–201.

59. Laponce, "Archetypes," 12.

60. "il punto, cui tutti li tempi son presenti," *Paradiso*, XVII, 18.

61. Cited in A. Ollivier, *Saint-Just et la force des choses*, 1954, 32. This fundamental work (by a friend of Camus, with an introduction by Malraux) unfortunately lacks precise documentation on many key points. This work can be usefully supplemented by M. Abensour, "La Philosophie politique de Saint-Just," *Annales Historiques*, 1966, Jan–Mar, 1–32, Jun–Sep, 341–58; by the articles and bibliography by J.-P. Gross, *Actes du Colloque Saint-Just*, 1968; and by E. Walter, "Politics of Violence: From Montesquieu to the Terrorists," in K. Wolff and B. Moore, eds., *The Critical Spirit. Essays in Honor of Herbert Marcuse*, Boston, 1967, 121–49.

62. Palmer, *Twelve*, 74.

63. Ollivier, 38–41.

64. Ibid., esp. 57 ff. Ollivier sees this neglected play *Organt* as a key to Saint-Just's development, and points (55) to another subsequent lost work, *Dialogue entre M. D. . . . et l'auteur d' "Organt."*

65. Cited from *Arlequin Diogène,* in ibid., 57.

66. Ibid.

67. Ibid., 71, 117, 94, on *L'Esprit de la révolution,* finished late in 1791; on *De la Nature, de l'état civil, de la cité ou la règle de l'indépendence,* which Abensour dates between Sep 1791 and Sep 1792, see the bilingual edition edited by A. Soboul: Saint-Just, *Frammenti sulle Istituzioni republicane,* Turin, 1952.

68. Ollivier, 69–70.

69. Ibid., 228–9.

70. *Frammenti,* 133.

71. Ibid., 174. Italics added.

72. B. Baczko, *Rousseau solitude et communauté,* Paris/The Hague, 1974, 141–2. The first part of this rich study argues persuasively for the retroactive application of the overused term "alienation" to Rousseau; and the second part, for the centrality of a twofold concept of nature in Rousseau as the denial of what is and the affirmation of what might be. See also E. Reiche, *Rousseau und das Naturrecht,* 1935; and for the impact on Saint-Just, S. Kritschewsky, *J.J. Rousseau und Saint-Just: Ein Beitrag zur Entwicklungsgeschichte der sozialpolitischen Ideen der Montagnards,* Bern, 1895, esp. 30–1.

73. Text in B. Dmytryshyn, *Imperial Russia,* NY, 1967, 241.

74. Ollivier, 75, 78–9.

75. Ibid., 88.

76. Ibid., 88–9.

77. Ibid., 173, 187.

78. Ibid., 168, 252, 110.

79. *Oeuvres de Saint-Just* (ed. J. Gratien), 1946, 296–7. Italics in original.

80. Ollivier, 232.

81. Ibid., 233–9.

82. Ibid., 296; *Oeuvres* (ed. Gratien), 184.

83. Ollivier, 297.

84. D. Hamiche, *Le Théâtre et la révolution,* 1973, 174; text, 269–305. For provincial performances and imitations, see M. Dommanget, *Sylvain Maréchal. L'égalitaire, "l'homme sans Dieu." Sa vie, son oeuvre (1750–1803),* 1950, 258–73, esp. 260–1.

The image of "the word revolution" as a "trumpet of the Last Judgment" resonating "in the four corners of Europe" was used already in May 1791 in the *Révolutions de Paris* for which Maréchal wrote (A. Aulard, *The French Revolution. A Political History,* NY, 1910, I, 257). Independently in 1793 the German radical Georg Forster wrote that "the lava of the revolution is flowing and no longer spares anything." Julku, "Conception," 251.

85. Section from *Organt* describing his "holy shuddering" in contemplating the lava inside Mount Etna "where *Terror* resides" capable of ending "the sleep of tyrants." Ollivier, 52.

86. "Dans le temple de la Raison,/ Aux yeux de la nature,/ Je viens me mettre à l'unison,/ Abjurer l'imposture." *La fête de la raison. Opéra en un acte,* 1794, 20. Copies of this and another little-known Maréchal-Grétry opera, *Denis le Tyran. Opéra en un acte,* 1794, are in IA.

87. Ollivier, 36–7.

88. Knowledge of this work is derived solely from the review of a performance printed in *Gazette Nationale ou le Moniteur Universel,* 1793, Oct 22 (repr. 1847, XVIII, 171), identifying the author only as "citoyen Saint-Just," the composer as "Mengozzi." The latter is undoubtedly Bernardo Mengozzi; and the former, probably the revolutionary leader as A. Soboul contended in bringing this notice to my attention. Another Saint-Just, however, the brother-in-law of Cherubini, later wrote operas of a lighter sort with French collaborators: See A. Pougin, *L'Opéra-comique pendant la révolution de 1788 à 1801,* Geneva, 1973, 247, 207, 213.

89. Ollivier, 233; *Oeuvres* (Gratien), 292.

90. *Oeuvres* (Gratien), 306.

91. Schneider was arrested the day after his marriage, with Le Bas playing an uncharacteristically major role: Harsany, *Vie,* 310 n. 628; Mathiez, *Etrangers,* 174.

92. Mathiez, *Etrangers,* 94–8. She appears to have been victimized by the retroactive application of a previously unknown concept whereby "citizenship" in one country was seen as incompatible with communicating with representatives of another.

93. Clara Zetkin, *Zur Geschichte der proletarischen Frauenbewegung Deutsch-*

lands, 1958, 16–7, on these neglected groups—whose dimensions may be somewhat exaggerated by the revolutionary enthusiasm of the author. For other provincial examples, however, see Abray, "Feminism," 50 n. 40.

94. Jules Michelet, *Les Femmes de la révolution,* 1898, 115.

95. M. George, "The 'World Historical Defeat' of the Républicaines-Révolution-naires," *Science and Society,* 1976–1977, Winter, 412; also 432–7 for the "male chauvinist" denouement.

96. Censer, *Prelude,* 97–8.

97. Abray, 56.

98. Cited from report of A. Amar on behalf of the Committee of General Security in Abray, 57.

99. Censer, 96–7.

100. On the etching (done from life and distributed rapidly) as the popular answer to the aristocratic engraving during the revolutionary period, see H. Mitchell, "Art and the French Revolution: An Exhibition at the Musée Carnavalet," *History Workshop,* 1978, Spring, esp. 127–9.

101. Thompson, *Revolution,* 553.

102. Dec 14, 1793, in *Oeuvres complètes de Saint-Just* (ed. C. Vellay), 1908, II, 161, echoing his complaint that "the laws are revolutionary, those executing them are not." Report to the Convention of Oct 10, 1793, in *Oeuvres* (Gratien), 174.

103. According to E. Hamel, the earliest biographer of Saint-Just and the one most disposed to find female companions for him at every turn, in Ollivier, 505.

104. Report to the Convention on factions, Mar 13, 1794, in Saint-Just, *Discours et Rapports* (ed. A. Soboul), 1957, 171; and the beginning of his famous last defense of Robespierre: "Je ne suis d'aucune faction; je les combattrai toutes." Ollivier, 614.

105. Ibid., 510.

106. Tiersot, *Fêtes,* 41.

107. "Un modèle eternel de rassemblement, de simplicité et d'allégresse," Ozouf, 332.

108. Tiersot, *Fêtes,* 128.

109. Thompson, *Revolution,* 551–2, on the *repas fraternels.*

110. The word is invoked in a description by his colleague in the Committee of Public Safety, Bertrand Barère: Ollivier, 654.

111. Ollivier, 649, 597–8.

112. Ibid., 652–3.

113. Ibid., 651–2, 655. A life of Cromwell was found in his room after his execution, 650 n. 1. These attitudes contrast with earlier criticism of Cromwell and of Christianity for its subordination to Constantine. A. Malraux characterizes Saint-Just as "passionately totalitarian" by the end: Ollivier, 17.

114. See M. Dommanget, "Saint-Just et la question agraire (en rapport avec ses origines paternelles et la terre picarde)," *Annales Historiques,* 1966, Jan–Mar, 33–60.

115. Cited in A. Mathiez, "Robespierre et le culte de l'être suprème," *Annales Révolutionnaires,* 1910, III, 219.

116. Mathiez, "Constitution de 1793," 314–5.

117. The "Questions sur les loix agraires," ostensibly published in London, re-produced in Saitta, *Buonarroti,* I, 285, who attributes the piece to Rutledge, then resident in Paris.

118. Rose, *Babeuf,* 101.

119. L. Bernstein, "Un plan socialiste sous la révolution française," *International Review of Social History,* 1937, II, 209. See Abbé Antoine de Cournand, *De la propriété, ou la cause du pauvre,* 1791 (but written in 1789, according to Ioannisian, *Idei,* 13); also Dalin, *Babef,* 427–35.

120. Cited in Ioannisian, *Idei,* 55. The text of his plea for acceptance into the Friends of Truth (cited 54) is reproduced as an appendix to Delacroix.
A work of Dolivier was found on Babeuf at the time of his arrest: *Essai sur la justice primitive pour servir de principe générataur au seul ordre social,* 1793. See Ioannisian, *Idei,* 58–9.

121. Rose, *Babeuf,* 73, 101–2.

122. Ibid., 39, refutes Dalin's hopeful suggestion that Babeuf's concept of a *ferme collective* already represented the essentials of the Soviet "collective farm" in 1786.
On this complex question, see G. Lefebvre, "Les origines du communisme de Babeuf," *IXe Congrès international des sciences historiques. Rapports,* I, 561–71; discussion in II, 237–43; also Godechot, "Travaux récents," in *Babeuf, Buonarroti,* 12–4; and R. Legrand, "Babeuf en Picardie," 22–34.

123. On the *Lettre d'un deputé de Picardie,* and the abundance of copies dis-covered by police in a raid on the Palais-Royal in August, see Rose, 78, 365 n. 10.

124. Ibid., 78.

125. Ibid., 141.

126. Ibid., 44, 62.

127. Fournier considered himself the first figure to turn *l'esprit publique* into *l'esprit militaire*, by arousing the Palais-Royal on June 30, 1789; and, in his project for a *cercle d'éducation*, proposed the beginnings of a revolutionary military school: *Mémoires secrets de Fournier l'américain*, 1890, 5, 42–4; also A. Espinas, *La Philosophie sociale du XVIII siècle et la révolution*, 1898, 219–23; and Dalin, *Babef*, 508–14. who corrects some dating in Aulard's introduction to Fournier's memoirs.

128. On Babeuf's links with Noë Makketros, Rose, *Babeuf*, 138–9, corrects Dalin.

129. Cited in Dalin, 516.

130. Espinas, 225; Dalin, 516; Rose, 138, 151.

131. Aulard, *Paris pendant la réaction thermidorienne et sous le diréctoire*, 1896, I, art 2 of intr., x. Newly discovered material indicates that Babeuf favored unlimited press freedom: R. Legrand, "Les manuscrits de Babeuf conservés à la Bibliothèque Historique de la Ville de Paris," *Annales Historiques*, 1973, Oct–Dec, esp. 573.

132. Letter to Joseph Bodson, Feb 28, 1796, in M. Dommanget, ed., *Pages choisies de Babeuf*, 1935, 285. See also 165–6.

Recent surveys updating the bibliographical discussions on Babeuf by Dommanget and Rose are Dalin's "L'historiographie de Babeuf," *La Pensée*, 1966, Aug, 68–101; and "The Most Recent Foreign Literature on Babeuf," *Soviet Studies in History*, 1973, spring, 353–70.) Dalin's *Babef* covers only the period prior to the conspiracy. The first volume (of four) covers Babeuf's writings up to 1789 (*Sochineniia*, 1975, I), has also appeared in French, and includes hitherto unpublished work in the USSR.

133. Prospectus in *Pages*, 228; justification of the new title in 169–71.

The recently reproduced (1966) edition shows that the new slogan began to appear regularly with no. 19 of *Journal de la liberté de la presse*; the new name *Le Tribun du peuple ou le défenseur des droits de l'homme* being adopted with a five-page explanatory footnote only with no. 23.

134. Response to Pierre-Antoine Antonelle of 1796, *Pages*, 268–70.

135. *Manifeste des plébéiens* of 1796 from *Tribun du peuplee* in *Pages*, 250–64. These phrases are repeatedly italicized. The undated prospectus of the *Tribun* is in *Pages*, 228–31.

136. Cited from the text in G. Lecocq, *Un Manifeste de Gracchus Babeuf*, 1885, in *Pages*, 172–3. On the eclipse of the Jacobin clubs, see J.-A. Faucher, *Les Clubs politiques en France*, 1965, esp. 23.

137. C. Mazauric (*Babeuf et la conspiration pour l'égalité*, 1962, 116 n. 1) sees this passage standing at the head of a line of thought about base areas for revolutionary warfare which moves through Blanqui and others to Mao.

138. Letter of Jul 28 to Charles Germain, *Pages*, 219–20.

139. *Pages*, 257, 264.

140. Ibid., 219–20.

141. Ibid., 215.

142. Cited in H. Baulig, "Anacharsis Cloots conventionel," *La Révolution Française*, 41, 1901, Dec, 435.

143. Charles Fourier, at the beginning of the nineteenth century, proposed that *phalanges* of about sixteen hundred withdraw from society to form *phalanstères*, the socialist equivalent of *monastères*. (A. Bestor, Jr., "The Evolution of the Socialist Vocabulary," *Journal of the History of Ideas*, 1948, Jun, 270–1.) These phalanxes championed peaceful social idealism from the first effort by a Romanian journalist in Bulgaria (F. Manuel, *The Prophets of Paris*, Cambridge, Mass, 1962, 208–9) to the enclave of New England intellectuals at Brook Farm. The same term was revived by Fascists a century later: From the *Falanga* of Polish Fascists who later became Stalinists (A. Bromke, "From 'Falanga' to 'Pax,'" *Survey*, 1961, Dec, 29–40) to the elite units (*falanges*) of Franco's successful military revolution against the Spanish Republic.

But the main continuing thread of usage—and that most faithful to Babeuf—was that of Filippo Buonarroti, Babeuf's disciple, future biographer, and historic revolutionary in his own right, about whom we shall have a good deal to say later. Buonarroti's followers were to reach as far afield as the Flemish *Phalange flamande Anneessens* of the 1830s. (A. Galante Garrone, "Buonarroti en Belgique et la Propagande Egalitaire," in *Babeuf et les problèmes du Babouvisme*, 1963, esp. 221–5; drawing largely on J. Kuypers, *Les Egalitaires en Belgique, Buonarroti et ses sociétés secrètes, d'après des documents inédits, 1824–1836*, Brussels, 1960.) Auguste Blanqui called for a homogeneous *phalange* of activists capable of providing militant leadership, of acting as the "forceps of revolution," (Marx and Engels, *Sochineniia*, II, 596) while the original German Communist leader Wilhelm Weitling mobilized in the early 1840s a "brotherly phalanx" for equality among émigrés in London.

Bakunin in his correspondence of 1870 with Nechaev, argued that the Russian revolutionary students of the 1860s were "a true youth . . . without status or homes" who could uniquely provide the needed "phalanx" for "the people's revolution." (Letter of Bakunin to Nechaev of Jun 2, 1870, first published by M. Confino in *Cahiers du Monde Russe et Soviétique*, 1966, Oct–Dec, 626.)

The recurrence of this Babeuvian-Buonarrotian term may be merely fortuitous; and revolutionary genealogies are notoriously elusive. But there is within Babeuf's original revolutionary "phalanx"—particularly as idealized retrospectively by Buonarroti—an interesting foreshadowing of the passion for purity—and for purge—of the modern professional revolutionary.

144. Babeuf, *Pages*, 249–50. The figure of 2,000 is given by Buonarroti only. For a concise and critical discussion, see D. Thomson, *The Babeuf Plot*, L, 1947, 21 ff.

145. *Pages*, 265–7.

146. "Manifeste des Plébéiens," in *Pages*, 256, and text 250–64. *Le Manifeste des enragés* of 1793 by the revolutionary priest Jacques Roux was not originally so entitled and lacked the systematic structure of Babeuf's work. See Dommanget, *Jacques Roux. Le curé rouge*, n.d., 53, text 83–91.

147. Mazauric, 138–40. He follows the careful argument of A. Saitta in refuting suggestions of serious dissent within the conspiracy. Saitta shows that at least six of the seven were in essential agreement with Babeuf's program. "Autour de la conjuration de Babeuf, Discussion sur le communisme (1796)," *Annales Historiques*, 1960, no. 4, 426.

148. See P. Bessand-Massenet, *Babeuf et le parti communiste en 1796*, 1926, 28; also Mazauric, 139.

149. The full title was *L'Eclaireur du peuple, ou le défenseur de 24 millions d'opprimés*. See Mazauric, *Babeuf*, 190–1.

150. M. Dommanget, "La Structure et les méthodes de la conjuration des égaux," *Annales Révolutionnaires*, XIV, 1922, 282. Facts about the conspiracy are from 177–96 and 281–97.

151. According to the detailed, though often unreferenced account in K. Bergmann, *Babeuf: Gleich and Ungleich*, Cologne, 1965, 346–51.

152. *Pages*, 264.

153. *Tribun du peuple*, no. 35, 1795, Nov 30, 97. Italicized in the original (and placed in quotation marks).

154. *Pages*, 272.

155. M. Dommanget, "Tempérament et formation de Babeuf," *Babeuf et le babouvisme*, 32–3. Dommanget departs from his usual thoroughness in discussing the implications of a trend of thought which he—like most admirers of the early revolutionaries—apparently finds either distasteful or embarrassing. Invocation of Christ also occurs in the key document first setting forth his Agrarian Law, the letter of Sep 10, 1791 (*Pages*, 122); but Dommanget excludes other works of Babeuf that discuss this theme.

156. G. Avenel, *Anacharsis Cloots. L'Orateur du genre humain*, 1865, I, 233, and 220–69; Fauchet's religious ideas are in his *De la religion nationale*, 1789.

157. The Spartan Jacobins had earlier been contrasted with the Athenian Girondists. See Ozouf, *Fêtes*, 327 ff.; and E. Rawson, *The Spartan Tradition in European Thought*, Oxford, 1969.

158. Cited with multiple references in Dommanget, *Maréchal*, 308.

159. *Correctif à la Révolution*, 1793, 306. The work was published anonymously, but a poem signed S.M. is printed opposite the title page. (BN)

160. Ibid., 307.

161. Cited from Maréchal, *Tableau historique des événements révolutionnaires*, 1795, 160, in Kucherenko, 168.

162. R. Postgate, ed., *Revolution from 1789 to 1906*, NY, 1962, 54; see, however, the more diluted document actually adopted by the secret directory of the conspiracy: 56–7.

163. *Pages*, 311–3.

164. Espinas, 248. This was the chorus.

165. Ibid., 285.

166. For the breakdown in the tabulation by Buonarroti, Rose, 264.

167. Ibid., 244–58; Espinas, 282–4. The latter's description suggests the insurrection as a kind of *fête*.

The basic appeal for leadership from Charles Germain to Babeuf invoked for the first time the metaphor of the revolutionary elite as a motor within a machine:

"Let us rally our forces to a common center. The party which seeks the rule of pure equality would be only a faction unless you declare yourself its leader; you must be its motor. . . ." Espinas, 241 n. 1.

168. Ibid., 361.

169. Palmer, *Age*, II, 180, and 195–7, minimizes the likelihood of links between the Dutch and the Babeuf conspiracy. W. Fishman, *The Insurrectionists*, L, 1970, 42, assumes direct coordination, but misdates the Amsterdam uprising and offers no evidence.

170. J. Godechot, "Le Babouvisme et l'unité italienne (1796–1799)," *Revue des Etudes Italiennes*, 1938, Oct–Dec, 270 and 265 ff. Some supplementary material is in Onnis, *Buonarroti*, 38 ff., who unaccountably makes no apparent use of the Godechot article.

171. Godechot, 268, for the text of a diatribe against Buonarroti from the army to the ministry of foreign affairs on Apr 9, 1796: "he knows nothing about the world and its affairs . . . he is seeking a mission whose vast object is completely undetermined."

172. Ibid., 272. Buonarroti's friend was the "revolutionary commissioner" with the Napoleonic army. Both his position and his complaint resemble those of political commissars with Communist armies in our own times against the narrowly pragmatic perspectives of professional soldiers.

173. Ibid., 273–83.

174. M. Kukiel suggests a possible Babeuvist influence in *Próby powstańcze po trzecim rozbiorze. 1795–1797*, Cracow/Warsaw, 1912, 253. I. Miller stresses indigenous Polish roots: "Vozzvanie Frantsishka Gozhkovskogo," in *Iz istorii sotsial'no-politicheskikh idei. Sbornik statei k semidesiatipiatiletiiu Volgina*, 1955, 365–75.

175. Bergmann, *Babeuf*, 487–9.

176. Friedrich von Gentz, *Über die Moralität in den Staatsrevolutionen*, 1797, cited in Griewank, 248.

177. Rose, 32, 98.

178. G. de Nerval, *Les Illuminés. Récits et Portraits*, 1929, 113. This is one of the most imaginative discussions of Restif's ideas. For a closer analysis of texts from a different point of view, see the equally neglected work of Ioannisian, "Utopiia Retifa de lia Bretonna," *Izvestiia akademii nauk SSSR, otd. obshch. nauk*, 1931, VII seriia, no. 2, 171–200, no. 7, 833–56.

R. Darnton has stressed the general importance of what he calls "grub street" radicals in "The High Enlightenment and the Low-Life of Literature in Pre-Revolutionary France," *Past and Present*, no. 51, 1971, 81–115.

179. This prophetic aspect of Restif is fully discussed (though at times exaggerated) in Chadourne, *Restif*.

180. Ioannisian, *Idei*, 181.

181. Nerval, 111–2.

182. First proposed in *Le Thesmographe*, The Hague, 1789, 2d part, 511–4; discussed Ioannisian, "Utopiia," 180–1; and later in *Idei*, 219–22, with valuable new detail along with the gratuitous ideological homily that Restif's typographical work (which was of a highly skilled, artisanal type) gave him some kind of proto-proletarian perspective.

183. *Les Contemporaines communes, ou avantures des belles marchandes, ouvrières, etc., de l'âge présent*, Leipzig, 1785, 2d ed., XIX, second unnumbered pagination after paragraph no. 69 (BM).

184. See his *Règlement d'éducation nationale*, 1789, iii, vi–xiv (BN). He also sent the plan to Volney, who rejected it. The plan was based on his earlier project (vi–vii) and was reasserted and elaborated in his *Généralif, maison patriarchale et champêtre*, Aix, 1790 (BN). See also his *Alcoran républicain ou institutions fondamentales du gouvernement populaire ou légitime pour l'administration, l'éducation, le mariage et la religion . . . par l'auteur de la communauté philosophe*, 1794. J.-M. Quérard, *La France littéraire*, IV, 167, describes Hupay as "an ardent disciple of Swedenborg," but this is hardly evident from his secular, Rousseauist writings.

185. Material in Ioannisian, *Idei*, 99.

186. *Maison de réunion pour la communauté philosophe dans la terre de l'auteur de ce projet. Plan d'ordre propre aux personnes des deux sexes, de tout âge et de diverses professions, pour leur faire passer dans des communautés semblables la vie la plus agréable, la plus sainte et la plus vertueuse*, Euphrate (Aix) and Utrecht, 1779. Copy in Houghton Library, Harvard. Ioannisian (*Idei*, 97) considered this work to have vanished altogether. P. Jacob (pseud. of Lacroix) reproduces the title more correctly, though less completely, than either Restif or Ioannisian: *Bibliographie et iconographie de tous les ouvrages de Restif de la Bretonne*, 1875, 209–10.

187. *Maison*, 3, 34. It was to be in a pleasant climate far from the "tumult" of the city.

188. Ibid., 3, prospectus opposite title page, and particularly 32 ff., 158–70, on the Moravians, who apparently helped publish the work in Utrecht.

189. Ibid., 11–2, 87–8.

190. Ibid., chart of the Maison, opposite 8, in which these two labels are the only ones in italics.

191. Ibid., opp. 8.

192. Ibid., 6, 26.

193. Ibid., 45.

194. Ibid., 6, 221. This is the earliest use of the phrase *communauté des biens.*

195. Ibid., 144–5.

196. Ibid., 146. For the general fascination of Western intellectuals with the possibilities for realizing radical reform on Russian soil in the eighteenth century, see A. Lortholary, *Le Mirage russe en France au XVIIIe siècle*, 1951.

197. See J. Childs, *Restif de la Bretonne—Témoinage et Jugements. Bibliographie,* n.d.; F. Prigault, "Restif de la Bretonne communiste," *Mercure de France,* 1913, Dec 16, 732–9.

198. *Contemporaines,* XIX, second unnumbered pagination, 3.

199. Cited in Ioannisian, *Idei,* 190, from *La Découverte australe par un homme-volant ou le dédale français. Nouvelle très philosophique,* Leipzig, 1781, 3v.

200. Ioannisian, "Utopiia," 184 ff. Nerval implies (*Illuminés,* 267) that this work—as well as his later ideas of interplanetary travel—may have been inspired by acquaintance with the balloonist Montgolfier.

201. *L'Andrographe ou idées d'un honnête-homme, sur un projet de règlement, proposé à toutes les nations de l'Europe, pour opérer une réforme générale des moeurs, et par elle, le bonheur du genre-humain,* The Hague, 1782, 82.

202. For other aspects, see the compendium by C. Mancéron, *The Wind from America,* NY, 1978; P. Sagnac, "Les origines de la révolution française: l'influence américaine," *Revue des Etudes Napoléoniennes,* 1924, Jan–Feb, 27–45.

203. *Contemporaines,* XIX, second unnumbered pagination, 3.

204. *Le plus fort des pamphlets. L'ordre des paysans aux États-généraux,* Feb 26, 1789, published under the pseudonym Noilliac (BN).

205. *Avis aux confédérés des LXXXIII départemens, sur les avantages et les dangers du séjour à Paris,* 1790 (BN).

206. Citations from *Le Thesmographe* in Ioannisian, *Idei,* 214–5.

207. Ibid., 230.

208. Usage of Feb 26–7, 1793, in *Les Nuits de Paris, ou le spectateur nocturne,* his diary of the revolution, part 8–17, 1794, 460–1, discussed by Ioannisian, "Iz istorii," 116, who does not, however, discuss the origin of the term.

209. *Monsieur Nicolas, ou le coeur humain dévoilé,* 1794–7, in the new ed., 1959, VI, esp. 309, 311. Restif attached great importance to names and chose Nicholas for his communist novel because he believed the name was composed of two Greek words meaning "victory of the people." Buachidze, 159.

Monglond presents *Monsieur Nicholas* as the culmination of the Rousseauist process of externalizing emotions and claiming sincerity through the genre of a confession (*Préromantisme,* II, 322 ff.), and analyses the "nostalgic voluptuousness with which he returns to rural infancy." (II, 326)

210. Ioannisian, "Iz istorii," 120.

211. Ibid., 121.

212. Discussed in Ioannisian, *Idei,* 236 ff.

213. *Monsieur Nicolas,* VI, 257. There is an unreferenced, isolated usage of *communiste* by Mirabeau in 1769 (in the sense of copropriétaire) listed in A. Dauzat, et al., *Nouveau Dictionnaire etymologique et historique,* 1964, 182; and another isolated usage of the revolutionary era listed in Brunot, IX, 1123.

214. *Monsieur Nicolas,* VI, 311.

215. Ibid., 313 ff. See M. Poster, *The Utopian Thought of Restif de la Bretonne,* NY, 1971, for other, related aspects of his thought.

216. Ioannisian, *Idei,* 232.

217. *Les Posthumes,* 1802, IV, 314; Ioannisian, *Idei,* 240–5.

218. L. Gottschalk, "Communism during the French Revolution, 1789–1793," *Political Science Quarterly,* 1925, Sep, 438–50.

219. Ioannisian, *Idei,* 132–6, 117.

220. A. Lichtenberger, "Un projet communiste en 1795," *La Révolution Française,* XXIX, 1895, 490, 492.

221. Ioannisian, *Idei,* 240–1. Speculation ranged widely on where on earth examples could be found. Restif argued that only the American Indians and Moravian Brethren provided worthy illustrations in the New World (where contemporary examples were generally sought); *Idei,* 237; but Restif's friend Gaspar Beaurieu insisted with wild inaccuracy in 1794 (in the new edition of *L'Elève de*

la nature of 1766, cited in *Idei*, 82) that the "inhabitants of Virginia" provided an admirable example of cooperative labor without private ownership of property.

222. A. Radishchev, *Puteshestvie iz Peterburga v Moskvu*, Moscow/Leningrad, 1935, 202–3; discussion in Buachidze, 62–4, where hidden sympathy for Restif is also hypothesized. Radishchev's founding role is proclaimed not just by Soviet critics, but also by N. Berdiaev in his *Origins of Russian Communism*, which identifies Radishchev as the first "repentant nobleman" to heighten moral conscience to revolutionary intensity. Like so many of the French, Radishchev was deeply influenced by German proto-romantic ideas during the prerevolutionary era.

223. Ioannisian, "Utopiia," 854 n. 2. The call, issued in 1931 by Ioannisian, for an archival investigation of this problem has remain unanswered even by Ioannisian himself.

224. Dalin, *Babef*, 589.

225. *Journal intime de Restif de la Bretonne*, 1889, 81, 123, 305, 309; cited Ioannisian, "Iz istorii," 123.

226. Ioannisian, *Idei*, 33–4.

227. Ibid., 117; Rose, "Cercle," 154, 165–6; also Zakher, "Varlet," 113–26.

228. B. Guegan, "Restif de la Bretonne apprenti, prote et imprimeur," *Arts et Métiers graphiques*, 1934, Dec 35; Poster, 144.

229. Dalin, *Babef*, 317.

230. Ibid., 319.

231. Dalin, "Babeuf et le Cercle Social," *Recherches internationales à la lumière du Marxisme*, 1970, no. 62, 65–6.

232. Ibid., 66–7. Babeuf began to work closely with Maréchal early in 1793 and was influenced by reading his works in prison the following year: Ioannisian, *Idei*, 159–60; G. Kucherenko, *Sud'ba "Zaveshchaniia" Zhana Mel'e v XVIII veke*, 1968, 141 ff., 165 ff.

233. Jean Varlet, *Projet d'un mandat spécial et impératif, aux mandataires du peuple à la convention nationale*, 1792, 22, 7, 9, 13, 15. Varlet did not foresee, however, the need for radical egalitarian measures so much as "the gradual disappearance of excessive inequality" once the accountability of central legislatures to grass-roots assemblies was secured: 13 and 11–4.

The nature and extent of the activities of the Social Circle press can probably never be determined because of the fire that destroyed records in the Palais-Royal; but the press survived at least until 1800, through the journal of 1797–1800, *Le Bien-Informé*, edited by Bonneville and Mercier under the imprimatur of *l'imprimerie-librairie du Cercle Social*. This journal (BN) compared Napoleon with Cromwell (see biography of Bonneville in *Biographie universelle*, 1843, V, 38) and represents a continuation of the intimate association that Mercier clearly had with the press (publishing there a host of writings from his *Fictions morales* of 1792 to his *Le Libérateur* of 1797).

234. Ibid., 71–2. Dalin, the only scholar ever even to consider a Bonneville-Babeuf connection, concludes (in an uncharacteristically superficial analysis) that there is "no doubt about the fact that the Social Circle exercised no influence on the formation of the communist revolutionary conception of Babeuf." (*Babef*, 325; repeated verbatim in "Cercle," 73). But Dalin's discussion does not support any such judgment, never dealing with the nature of this conception (or indeed with ideas, organizational forms, or even revolutionary dynamics). He generally ignores the role of Maréchal and Varlet, let alone Restif; shows no curiosity about the survival of the Social Circle Press; and seems ideologically impelled to detach Babeuf at all points from the less socially radical views of Fauchet and Bonneville. If, of course, the influence were organizational and conspiratorial, the *complete* absence of written references to Bonneville (with whom Dalin admits Babeuf was closely familiar: *Babef*, 325) could be a sign of deliberate concealment. Babeuf's papers are notoriously silent on the conspiratorial side.

Babeuf attacked Bonneville as a "false tribune of the people" after Bonneville established his *Old Tribune of the People* in 1796 as a rival to Babeuf's new *Tribune*. Babeuf likened Bonneville to the treacherous tribune Rufus Manlius who "sold himself cravenly to the party of the rich in Rome" in order to destroy the true tribune, Gracchus. Babeuf distinguished the brief period of Bonneville's authentic tribunate in 1789 from his subsequent descent into "ministerial intrigue" and "slavish dependence" on "Mirabeau and other patricians." The excessive anger and Babeuf's erasure of his signature as "Babeuf of the Confederation of the Friends of Truth" may betray the classical technique of excoriating a revolutionary rival in the process of annexing his ideas and role.

235. Espinas, 282–4, also 247 n. 1.

236. Kates, "The Cercle Social," charts for the first time the vast dimensions of the publishing program it sustained after ceasing public activities in the summer

of 1791. See esp. 158–237 for the journals, and 272–85 for the 193 books published. At its height in 1792–3, the publishing empire constituted a radical brain trust subsidized by the Girondist government, harshly critical of Jacobin centralism, regularly publishing an intellectual review (*Chronique du Mois*), an inexpensive journal for urban posting (*Sentinelle*), a daily newspaper (*Bulletin des Amis de la Vérité*), and two journals taken over from others: *La Feuille Villageoise* for the French peasantry and *Le Créole Patriote* for the colonized West Indians. Kates, however, sees the entire group as a simple perpetuation of the Enlightenment; and his study does not seriously investigate either the occult connections or the post-Thermidore legacy of the Circle.

237. Kates, 110–12.

238. See particularly the work of Bonneville's friend and fellow translator, J. Dusaulx, *De l'Insurrection parisienne et de la prise de la Bastille*, 1790; T. Mardar, *Des Insurrections, ouvrage philosophique et politique sur les rapports des insurrections avec la prospérité des empires*, 1793, and the work of J. Oswald discussed later.

239. Cited Kates, 210. The Social Circle equated Robespierre with the royalists because of authoritarian tendencies noticed even before his ascent to power. See J.-B. Louvet, *A Maximilien Robespierre et ses royalistes*, 1792; Kates, 211.

240. Monglond stressed Restif's ties with Mercier and Bonneville (II, 173, 323 n. 2). He also pointed out the inadequacies of the sole monograph ever written on Bonneville (its neglect both of Parisian links with German writers and of Bonneville's role in the revolution). Unfortunately neither Monglond's review ("Nicolas de Bonneville. A propos du livre de M. Philippe Harivel," *Revue d'Histoire Littéraire de la France*, 1926, Jul–Sep, 408–14) nor his *Préromantisme* seriously discuss what the role of Bonneville actually was.

Whatever their personal links, Babeuf clearly echoed Bonneville's symbolic language in defining the destination for his organization. Babeuf focused the impulse for radical simplification onto a single-minded political program by suggesting a more inclusive concept of that "central" or "perfect" point that might provide new legitimacy. His conspiracy was to converge on a *point unique* located in space (the circle of conspirators), time (the coming social transformation), and sentiment (the enduring quest for human satisfaction). The stated purpose of Babeuf's conspiracy was "to mark in advance a single point, towards which you will all strive without division, modifications, restrictions, or nuances; and to be circumscribed within a narrow circle of virtuous men, isolated from all who could oppose divergent and contradictory views—from everything which could not be fused into the one and perfect sentiment of the highest point of goodness." Cited in J. Talmon, *The Origins of Totalitarian Democracy*, NY, 1970, 186.

Chapter 4

1. J. Roberts, *The Mythology of the Secret Societies*, NY, 1972, intelligently discusses (9–16) the reasons for neglect of the subject. His own approach, however, might lead the uninformed reader to believe that the myth itself was the major reality rather than the phenomenon.

2. The invaluable historical account by a Swiss socialist G. Kuhlmann (based on information from A. Becker and sent to Metternich by his chief of intelligence in Mainz in March 1847) called Buonarroti "the first apostle of modern Communism." Barnikol, *Geschichte*, 14.

3. His teacher noted in 1780 Buonarroti's "rare talent" and "romantic" (*romanzesco*) imagination: "Everything exists only for the moment with him. Dissipation rapidly follows study." See M. Morelli, "Note biografiche su Filippo Buonarroti," *Critica Storica*, IV, 1965, 536; and 521–64, for new material on these early years.

4. Ibid., 536.

5. The basic account of the influence of Francophile Italians on Buonarroti by D. Cantimori (*Utopisti e Riformatori italini, 1794–1847*, Florence, 1943, 128–77) should be supplemented by P. Onnis Rosa, *Filippo Buonarroti e altri studi*, 1971, esp. 161 ff.

6. L. Basso, "Il Prospetto a stampa del 'Journal Politique,'" *Critica storica*, VI, 1967, 863.

7. Ibid.

8. L. Modona, "Un Numero del 'Journal Politique,'" *Critica storica*, VI, 1967, 866; and 868 ff.

9. E. Michel, "Le Vicende de Filippo Buonarroti in Corsica (1789–1794)," *Archivio Storico de Corsica*, IX, 1933. The seminal work on this period is still

A. Galante Garrone, *Buonarroti e Babeuf*, Turin, 1948. E. Eisenstein, *The First Professional Revolutionist: Philippo Michele Buonarroti (1761–1837), A Biographical Essay*, Cambridge, Mass, 1959, 161–90, provides a valuable bibliographical essay and a good general narrative. Subsequent scholarship and bibliography are conveniently summarized in *Dizionario biografico degli italiani*, 1972, XX, 148–61.

10. The first 32 issues of this rare journal (Apr 3–Nov 27, 1790) have been reprinted with some biographical information in *Bulletin de la société des sciences historiques et naturelles de la Corse*, Bastia, 1919, 1921, nos. 389–92, 421–4. The pages are numbered consecutively with an index appended 221–68. The serial probably went on at least through no. 36–7. See 219 n.

11. Open letter of Buonarroti in *Giornale*, Jun 12, 1790 (reprinted in *Bulletin*, 112–3), replying to a bishop who had written that supporters of the confiscation of church lands "stink of social heresy" (*"da ogni parte puzzate di eresia sociale . . ."*) and threaten to throw men back to chaos (*"nello stato de natura"*). Ibid., 109, 112.

12. Cited in Onnis, *Buonarroti*, 213.

13. Speech in *Moniteur Universel*, Apr 30, discussed in Onnis, 213.

14. Cited in Onnis, 167.

15. *La conjuration de Corse entièrement dévoilée*, 1794, 3. I attribute his authorship on the basis of the early addition of Buonarroti's name in ink in the anonymously published copy in BM. Not discussed in the standard works of Buonarroti by Saitta and Garrone, this work has his stylistic and terminological characteristics. His opposition to Paoli is discussed by Arnault-Jay-Jouy in *Biographie nouvelle de contemporains*, 1827, 572–3. Among many Italian revolutionaries with whom Buonarroti maintained contact in Oneglia and Paris were Corsicans like Salliceti, who was later a kind of political commissar with Napoleon's army in Italy.

16. *Grand besoin d'une grande purgation*, ibid., 14.

17. Onnis, "Filippo Buonarroti Commissario Revoluzionario a Oneglia nel 1794–95," in *Buonarroti*, 62–5. See also other works referenced in J. Godechot, "Travaux récents," 5–6.

18. Onnis, *Buonarroti*, 68, also 169.

19. Ibid., 138.

20. Ibid., 87–8.

21. Buonarroti's defense speech, reprinted Onnis, 137.

22. Ibid.

23. Saitta, *Buonarroti*, I, 117–8.

24. Ibid., I, 118, citing Buonarroti's principal memorandum on revolutionary organization, reprinted II, 91–116.

25. Ibid., II, 93.

26. Ibid., II, 140, for Buonarroti's discussion of *cette douce communauté* as "not an impossible thing" to realize and a goal that only "levity, depravity or weakness" could cause one to oppose.

27. Details of this long period (relieved only by his affair with Teresa Poggi) in Onnis, 303–11.

28. M. Pianzola, "Filippo Buonarroti in Svizzera," *Movimento Operaio*, 1955, Jan–Feb, 123.

29. The most thorough account of these contacts is now D. Tugan-Baranovsky, "General Male, 'obshchestvo filadel'fov' i Napoleon," *Frantsuzsky ezhegodnik*, 1973, 1975, esp. 184–8.

30. Cited in V. Dalin, "Napoléon et les Babouvistes," *Annales Historiques*, 1970, Jul–Sep, 417–8.

31. Ibid., 413.

32. Growing police fears of Buonarroti and of his Masonic associations in Geneva are documented by M. Pianzola, "La mystérieuse expulsion de Philippe Buonarroti," *Cahiers Internationaux*, 1954, Dec, 61; also "Svizzera," 124.

33. Basic discussion in Saitta, *Buonarroti*, I, 79–119, is supplemented by A. Lehning, "Buonarroti and His International Secret Societies," *International Review of Social History*, I, 1956, 112–40, esp. 119–20; more recent studies referenced in Godechot, "Travaux récents," 1 n. 25–30.

34. See the valuable exploratory article of D. Ligou, "Un source important de l'histoire du XVIIIe siècle. Le fond maçonnique de la Bibliothèque Nationale," *Actes du 89 congrès national des sociétés savantes (Section d'histoire)*, 1965, 38.

35. J. Servier, "Utopie et franc-maçonnerie au XVIII siècle," *Annales Historiques*, 1969, Jul–Sep, 409–13; also other articles in this issue devoted to the question of Masonic links with revolution.

36. On the use of the *voûte d'acier* on Jul 17, see J. Palou, *La Franc-maçonnerie*, 1972, 187.

37. D. Mornet, *Les Origines intellectuelles de la révolution française (1715–1787)*,

1954, 375; discussion 357–87; bibliography, 523–5; and outside of France, Billington, *Icon*, 712–4. A. Mellor, *Les Mythes maçonniques*, (1974) also minimizes Masonic influence, though vaguely acknowledging the influence of the occultist revival on the revolutionary movement.

38. Ligou, "Source," 46, also 49.

39. This subject has never been comprehensively studied. For the best discussions in general terms, see O. Karmin, "L'Influence du symbolisme maçonnique sur le symbolisme révolutionnaire," *Revue Historique de la Révolution Française*, 1910, I, 183–8 (particularly on numismatics); J. Brengues, "La Franc-maçonnerie et la fête révolutionnaire," *Humanisme*, 1974, Jul–Aug, 31–7; Palou, 181–215; R. Cotte, "De la Musique des loges maçonniques à celles des fêtes révolutionnaires," *Les Fêtes de la révolution*, 1977, 565–74; and the more qualified assessment of Ligou, "Structures et symbolisme maçonniques sous la révolution," *Annales Historiques*, 1969, Jul–Sep, 511–23.

For the heavy reliance on Masonic structures in provincial civic rituals, see, for instance, F. Vermale, "La Franc-maçonnerie savoisienne au début de la révolution et les dames de Bellegarde," *Annales Révolutionnaires*, III, 1910, 375–94; and especially the monumental work for la Sarthe which lifts the level of research far above anything done for Paris: A. Bouton, *Les Franc-maçons manceaux et la révolution française, 1741–1815*, Le Mans, 1958. See also his successor volume *Les Luttes ardentes des francs-maçons manceaux pour l'établissement de la république 1815–1914*, Le Mans, 1966.

In the New World, where the links between Masonic and revolutionary organizations were particularly strong, rival revolutionary parties sometimes assumed the names of rival rites. In Mexico, for instance, *escoceses* (pro-English "centralists" from Scottish rite lodges) battled *yorquinos* (federalists from the rite of York introduced by the first U.S. ambassador, Joel Poinsett). See A. Bonner, "Mexican Pamphlets in the Bodleian Library," *The Bodleian Library Record*, 1970, Apr, 207–8.

40. Ligou, "Source," 42–3, 46–7. *La Parfaite Egalité* arose in Franche Comté and generally supported the magistrates of the Parlement in opposition to the "Sincerity" lodges of the royal intendants.

Because of the extreme secrecy of these groups and the preoccupation of the police with Buonarroti himself, we know very little about who else participated, but there were apparently old friends from Oneglia and French exiles such as Jean Marat (a watchmaker and brother of the martyred journalist) with whom Buonarroti lived in Geneva. See Onnis, *Buonarroti*, 225 esp. n. 13.

41. O. Karmin, "Notes sur la loge et le chapitre, La Parfaite Egalité de Genève," *Revue Historique de la Révolution Française*, XII, 1917, Jul–Dec, 314–24.

42. Lehning, "Buonarroti," 116 and 121 ff. This terminology was later transformed into more secular, traditional Masonic form: church became lyceum; synod, academy; sublime elect, perfect Masons; sublime perfect masters, true architects. Saitta, I, 86.

43. Cited in S. Landa, "Konspiracje oświeceniowe i tajne organizacje polityczne," *Przegląd Historyczny*, 1967, no. 2, 247. The closest approximation to a modern, scholarly account of this neglected movement is probably L. Wolfram, *Die Illuminaten in Bayern und ihre Verfolgung*, Erlangen, 1899–1900, two parts.

R. von Dülmen, *Geheimbund der Illuminaten. Darstellung, Analyse, Dokumentation*, Stuttgart, 1975, provides the fullest bibliography of books written on or about the Illuminists during the revolutionary era—88 from 1784 to 1800: 423–9. J. Rogalla von Bieberstein, *Die These von der Verschwörung 1776–1945*, Bern/Frankfurt, 1976, provides the best account of the successive stages in the codification of the theory of an Illuminist conspiracy (95–137), and shows the transfer of this aroused suspicion to the Jews, beginning with the Napoleonic period (161–3). An unpublished doctoral dissertation inaccessible to me is W. Hofter, "Das System des Illuminatenordens und seine soziologische Bedeutung," Heidelberg, 1956.

44. Weishaupt, *Pythagoras oder Betrachtung über die geheime Welt und Regierungskunst*, Frankfurt, 1795 (originally 1790), 385; cited in Le Forestier, *Les Illuminés de Bavière et la Franc-maçonnerie allemande*, 1914, 596.

45. J. B. Baylot, *La Voie substituée. Recherche sur la déviation de la franc-maçonnerie en France et en Europe*, Liège, 1968, 64. The neglected works of Landa and Baylot (using Masonic materials from the Low Countries and the Slavic countries, respectively) are the first studies to enlarge the horizons both materially and conceptually of this problem since Le Forestier.

46. Letter of Weishaupt to K. Zwack (his most important original collaborator), Mar 10, 1778, cited in Landa, 246.

47. Letter of Weishaupt to Zwack (almost certainly misdated as Mar 21, 1772), cited in Baylot, 38.

48. Ibid., 38.

49. Ibid., 37; Wolfram, *Illuminaten*, part 1, 16, 22.

50. Baylot, 39–40, for these and other details on terminology, drawing on new sources.

51. Weishaupt, *Einige Originalschriften des Illuminatenordens*, Munich, 1787, 1–2; Baylot, 40–2.

52. Baylot, 44–8, 56–7; Le Forestier, *L'Occultisme et la franc-maçonnerie écossaise*, 1928, 2d ed., 311; J. Droz, *L'Allemagne et la révolution française*, 1949, 404–9. According to E. Lindner, the Duke of Brunswick himself joined the Order of Illuminists in 1783: *Die königliche Kunst im Bild. Beiträge zur Ikonographie der Freimaurerie*, Graz, 1976, 200.

53. Baylot characterizes Masonry as being placed "en sandwich" between the two stages of Illuminism: Ibid., 43.

54. Weishaupt, *Pythagoras*, 308; cited Le Forestier, *Illuminés*, 596.

55. Estimate of Mathiez in *Annales Révolutionnaires*, VIII, 1916, 433.

56. J. P. L. de la Roche, Marquis de Luchet, *Essai sur la secte des illuminés*, 1789, 2d ed., 73–6. Both first and second editions appeared in 1789, a third edition augmented by Mirabeau in 1792. See Chevallier, *Franc-maçonnerie*, I, 317.

57. *De la monarchie*, V, 99–100; cited by Mathiez, *Annales Révolutionnaires*, VIII, 1916, 434–5; also Chevallier, 320–1, for Mauvillon's role. D. Ligou is skeptical of Mirabeau's association with Masonry ("Mirabeau, a-t-il été Franc-maçon?" in *Les Mirabeaux et leur temps*, 1968, esp. 118–23), but generally ignores the Illuminists and betrays ignorance by referring to Weishaupt as "Weiskaupf."

58. Even less is known about Bode and his mission than about other aspects of Illuminism during the period following its official suppression. His real name was apparently Theodor Heinrich Bode. Princely patronage was important in enabling him (and others) to spread Illuminist ideas beyond Bavaria to Germany as a whole (Grassl, 220–1). His protean activities are most fully discussed in *Fragmente zur Biographie des verstorbenen Geheimen Rats Bode in Weimar*, Rome, 1795. See also Harivel, 23–5; Frost, I, 41–2; and (for Bode's influence on Bonneville) Grassl, 269–71.

Knigge appears to have had a direct influence on revolutionaries in Germany similar to that which Bode's diffusion of Illuminist ideas exercised in France. See the encomia of the German Jacobins on the occasion of Knigge's death in 1796: H. Vögt, *Die deutsche jakobinische Literatur und Publizistik 1789–1800*, 1955, 150–3.

No one has yet sorted out facts from counter-revolutionary propaganda in *Fragmente*. Before his death in 1793, Bode was apparently a composer of military music (E. Lennhoff and O. Posner, *Internationales Freimaurerlexikon*, Zurich/Vienna, 1966, 196–8); and he shared Bonneville's literary interests as a translator of English proto-romantic literature (J. Wihan, *Johann Joachim Christoph Bode als Vermittler englischer Geisteswerke in Deutschland*, Prag, 1906).

59. *Lettre à Condorcet*, 31, 29, 12.

60. Ibid., 37.

61. Critique of *Mercure de France*, 1790, Dec 18, 121 (misreferenced in Harivel, 155).

62. *Les Jésuites*, I, 26; also *De L'Esprit des religions*, 249, 88.

63. *Les Jésuites* appeared almost immediately in Leipzig in a German translation by Bode, who in turn impressed Friedrich Schiller with the image of a Jesuit conspiracy against the Enlightenment (see Schiller's letter of Sep 10, 1787, "Die jetzige Anarchie der Aufklärung wäre hauptsächlich der Jesuiten Werk," Grassl, 290). Thus Bode influenced both the German playwright and his French translator, Bonneville, who immediately published two more works, extending the Illuminist argument to a denunciation of the Scottish Rite Masons as well as of the Jesuits: *La Maçonnerie écossaise comparée avec les trois professions et le secret des Templiers*, and *Les Jésuites retrouvés dans les ténèbres*, discussed in Mathiez, *Annales Révolutionnaires*, VIII, 1916, 435 n. 2. Darnton suggests that Restif as well as Mirabeau and Bonneville may have been a channel for Illuminist ideas entering France: *Mesmer*, 132–3. Rich if unsorted new material suggesting both the Illuminist borrowings and the widespread following of Bonneville are in Baylot, *Voie*, 103–7.

Ollivier (*Saint-Just*, 96–116, 149–50) sees German influence on the lodge of the Amis Réunis to which Saint-Just belonged prior to the revolution, Saint-Just communicating with Bonneville from Picardy in 1791, and an occult group aiding Saint-Just in his election to the assembly the following year. Desmoulins probably imbibed Illuminist ideas while serving as secretary to Mirabeau; and Bonneville addressed a play commemorating the fall of the Bastille with a romantic, Masonic format to Desmoulins: see BA, Rf 17043, 1–4; Rf 17044.

Dietrich translated works of Bonneville's Social Circle into German and had no less active interest in the occult than his rival in revolutionary Strasbourg, Schneider, who had been an active Illuminist. The basic work of Mathiez (*Annales Révolutionnaires*, VI, 1913, 102–3; VIII, 1916, 437) can be supplemented by P. Leuillot, "Bourgeoisie d'Alsace et franc-maçonnerie aux XVIIIe et XIXe siècles," *Bourgeoisie alsacienne*, 343–76.

64. There has been no serious investigation of these figures since Mathiez, *Révolution et les étrangers*, esp. 61, 67, 117–8, 142. Mathiez's suggestion that Rebmann provided a channel for Illuminist ideas is not supported by the work to which he refers: N. von Wrasky, *A. G. F. Rebmann. Leben und Werke eines Publizisten zur Zeit der grossen französischen Revolution*, Heidelberg, 1907, but the many-sided activities of this and other German activists in Paris have never been adequately studied.

65. Dalin, *Babef*, 435, also 15, for Babeuf's letter to Charles Germain; Espinas, 241, for his reply. Rose (*Babeuf*, 189) describes Germain with all the characteristics of an occultist without suggesting such an identity.

66. Dommanget, *Pages choisies*, 219–20.

67. The discussion in Dommanget, *Maréchal*, 297–322, is largely devoted to arguing against the thought that Maréchal might have been spared arrest by connections in high places—and never considers the possibility of Illuminist influences or rules of secrecy. The suggestion that Maréchal might even have collaborated with the police in the denunciation of the conspiracy (made by G. Pariset, *Babouvisme et maçonnerie*, Strasbourg, 1924) is effectively refuted by Baylot (*Voie*, 96 ff.), whose identification of Maréchal's membership in the occult lodge La Céleste Amitié and of Maréchal's contempt for "ordinary masonic lodges" would be thoroughly compatible with an imitation if not a perpetuation of Illuminism.

68. Modena, "Numero," 868–72.

69. *Appendice politica a tutte le gazzette e altri foglietti di novità o sia la spezieria de Sondrio*, II, 1790, 1. Museum of the Risorgimento, Milan.

70. Ibid., 101.

71. Ibid., 4.

72. Ibid., 101.

73. Ibid.

74. Ibid., I, 1789, 78–9.

75. Ibid., 79.

76. Ibid., II, 2, 45; I, 134–5.

77. Ibid., I, 135.

78. According to Onnis, *Buonarroti*, 165. C. Francovich contends (*Albori socialisti nel Risorgimento; contributo allo studio delle società segrete (1776–1835)*, Florence, 1962, 85) that the journal was an imitation of the Masonic *Café politique d'Amsterdam*. The political hero of the young Buonarroti, Leopold of Tuscany, is praised in the *Appendix* (I, 33 ff.) for attempting to enact Rousseau's "social contract" (*patto sociale*); but I can find no reference in the *Appendice* to the supplement entitled "The Century of Joseph II" allegedly written by an Italian thinker, idealizing the enlightened despot who "opened the path to great revolution," according to Francovich, 85.

79. *Appendice*, II, 160 n.

80. Though Prati would have been too young to participate in the original Buonarrotian conspiracies (suggested by Francovich, *Albori*, 87), the implication of Prati's necessarily guarded account of their relationship is that of a longstanding link. Prati called him "my greatest friend . . . the greatest political character I ever met in all my life . . . the most amiable, talented, vigorous, and elevated mind Italy has produced for some centuries . . . a Prometheus-like energy, bidding defiance to the powers of the earth. . . . In better times, and among less enervated nations, Buonarroti would have been to the continent what Lycurgus and Solon had been to Sparta and Athens." *Penny Satirist*, 1838, Apr 21, 2; Apr 28, 1; also 1839, Mar 16, 1. See also P. Pedrotti, *Note Autobiografiche del cospiratore trentino Gioacchino Prati*, Rovereto, 1926; and, for another example, M. Rigatti, *Un illuminista trentino del secolo XVIII, C.A. Pilati*, Florence, 1923.

For the role of foreign intermediaries in bringing Illuminist ideas into Italy, see G. Berti, *I democratici e l'iniziativa meridionale nel risorgimento*, Milan, 1962, esp. 146–7, 156 ff.; and *Aus den Tagebüchern Friedrich Münters. Wander- und Lehrjahre eines dänischen Gelehrten*, Copenhagen/Leipzig, 1937; discussed in A. Faivre, *Eckartshausen et la théosophie chrétienne*, 1969, 83–4, 652–4. Illuminist ideas appear to have influenced pioneering revolutionary propaganda for a united Germany in southern Germany during 1796 (see K. Obser, "Der Marquis von Poterat und die revolutionäre Propaganda am Oberrhein im Jahre 1796," *Zeitschrift für die Geschichte des Oberrheins*, VII, 1892, no. 3, 385–413; Godechot, "Unité," 259); perhaps also the peasant uprising in the Tyrol in 1809 (apparently suggested

by A. Fischer in a manuscript confiscated by the Gestapo during World War II).
H. Koplenig, "Revendications agraires dans l'insurrection tyrolienne de 1809: Egalitairisme paysan ou influence Buonarrotiste?" *Babeuf et les problèmes*, 205–14; also Pedrotti, 27–8), and probably the more aristocratic north German "League of Virtue" (*Tugendbund*) of 1808–9 (Pedrotti, 25 n. 1, 37 n. 1, 69–74, n. 2; also the French police report in the otherwise unreliable work of N. Webster, *Secret Societies and Subversive Movements*, L, 1924, 265, and 258–65, and F. Brokgauz and I. Efron, eds., *Entsiklopedichesky slovar'*, XXXIV, 1902, 31–2).

81. Definition of Knigge in 1782, cited in C. Francovich, "Gli Illuminati di Weishaupt e l'idea egualitaria in alcune societa segrete del Risorgimento," *Movimento Operaio*, 1952, Jul–Aug, 562, also 559, 556.

82. Saitta, II, 105; also discussion I, 114–9. New documents of a slightly later period lead M. Vuilleumier to assume Illuminist origins of the Sublime Perfect Masters in his discussion of more general Masonic links: "Buonarroti et ses sociétés secrètes à Genève," *Annales Historiques*, 1970, Jul–Sep, 475–6, 494–7.

83. Citations from Prati's account (*Penny Satirist*, 1938, Mar 10) reproduced with commentary by Saitta, "Una conferma irrefutabile: il terzo grado Buonarrotiano," *Critica Storica*, VIII, 1969, 709–10. There is no direct testimony beyond Prati's general statements that this social-revolutionary egalitarianism of Buonarroti predated his involvement in the Babeuf conspiracy. Dating of Buonarroti's fragmentary writings is notoriously uncertain; and the clearly Illuminist elements in his formulations could predate or postdate the conspiracy.

84. Le Forestier, *Illuminés*, 715; also valuable discussion in Francovich, "Illuminati," 553–97.

85. A careful recent scholar (Spitzer, *Old Hatreds*, 9–16) finds police records to be relatively reliable as the work of pedestrian officials lacking the time or talent to create legends. Mathiez more than 60 years earlier wrote wisely that "If it is ridiculous to explain the Revolution by an Illuminist plot, it is no less ridiculous to suppose that the friends and ideas of the Illuminists played no role in it." (Review of Le Forestier in *Annales Révolutionnaires*, VIII, 1916, 437). The gaps in Le Forestier are illustrated by his failure even to discuss the Social Circle, ignorance of which is indicated by his designation of "sic" after his sole mention of the term: *Illuminés*, 669.

86. Ibid., 702 and ff.

87. In *Les Jésuites*, Bonneville finds the key dates all composed of digits that total 17: 287 (the alleged founding of the lodge by St. Alban), 926 (the history by Athelstan), 1646 (founding of a lodge by Charles I), and 1692 (founding of a Jesuit college by James II). See Harivel, 23. The last date, of course, totals 18.

88. G. Poulet, *Les Metamorphoses du cercle*, 1961, xxviii–xxix n. 33.

89. See, for instance, in the section on the higher grades, illustrations in Linder, *Kunst*, 84, 119, 123, 161.

90. Abbé Laugier, *Essai sur l'architecture*, 1755, 2d ed., 206; cited in D. Kaufman, "Three Revolutionary Architects: Boullée, Ledoux, and Lequeu," *Transactions of the American Philosophical Society*, 1952, 44.

91. Poulet, 88.

92. Ibid., 141. Poulet relates this image to Fichte's philosophy of opposition between "the I and the non-I" in which the world becomes, in effect, the place for "the imposition of the I on the non-I" and man's drive for expansion of his ego becomes "not simply psychological. It is ontological." In the resulting cosmology of romanticism man is simultaneously "center by the active principle of his thought, circle by its infinite extension." Ibid., 145, 141, 147.

93. Ibid., 185–6.

94. M. Tourneux, *Répertoire général des sources manuscrites de l'histoire de Paris pendant la Révolution française*, V, 1899, 5; and Mirabeau monument model on view in the Carnavalet Museum.

95. Projects respectively of Etienne-Louis Boullée, Claude-Nicolas Ledoux, and Jean-Jacques Lequeu, illustrated and discussed respectively in Kaufman, 461–2, 523, 553. Other citations and titles drawn on here are on 471, 483, 521.
Pierre Patte (not discussed in Kaufman) produced the most extensive prerevolutionary argumentation for the morality of circular shapes as essentially more egalitarian and communal: *Essai sur l'architecture théâtrale* (1782), 40 ff. See also D. Rabreau, "Architecture et fêtes dans la Nouvelle Rome," in *Les Fêtes de la révolution. Colloque de Clermont-Ferrand (juin 1974)*, 1977, esp. 364 ff.

96. Weishaupt, *Einige*, 8, also 7; *Nachtrag*, 136, also 158; and "Circulare an die Logen," in ibid., 133 ff.

97. Luchet, *Essai*, 54, 67, 91; and the chapters "Circles" and "Proofs used to Concentrate an Illuminist member of a Circle."

98. K. Epstein, *The Genesis of German Conservatism*, Princeton, 1966, esp. 107

ff.; on the *Zirkel der Verderbnisse* as distinct from the Illuminist *Circul*, see J. Popp, *Weltanschauung und Hauptwerke des Freiherrn Adolph Knigge*, Leipzig, 1930, 82, 88.

99. Bonneville, *Les Jésuites*, I, 27, illustrates the radical cooptation of Rosicrucianism.

100. *Les Jésuites*, I, 17. Benjamin Franklin had been lionized as "the Pythagoras of the New world" by Maréchal and others after serving as "Venerable" of the occult Masonic lodge of the Nine Sisters in prerevolutionary Paris with Bonneville, Sieyès, Desmoulins, Cloots, Danton as well as Maréchal. (Cited from Maréchal, *Dictionnaire des athées anciens et modernes*, 1800, in A. Aldrich, *Franklin and His French Contemporaries*, NY, 1957, 192; and, for earlier French references to Franklin as Pythagoras: 225, 232.) The most remarkable attempt to use the lodge structure of occult Masonry directly for revolutionary purposes during the early years of the revolution, "The True Light," also invoked the name of Pythagoras: "Masonry in France despite all the brilliant mechanism of its grades is very far from the morality of the School of Pythagoras." Circular letter of Mar 5, 1792, urging democratization of the Grand Orient by "La Vraie Lumière": Chevallier, I, 355.

101. Alekseev-Popov, 303.

102. "Les Nombres de Pythagore," *La Poésie de Nicolas Bonneville*, 1793, 199 ff. (BA).

103. "Cercle Social," Ibid., 143–6.

104. T. Paine, *An Essay on the Origin of Free Masonry*, L, 1818, 5; see also 5–7, 14. It was originally published posthumously, NY, 1810, and translated into French by Bonneville in 1813: Harivel, *Bonneville*, 15.

The materials used and cited here from Saint-Martin are from his fantastic *Le Crocodile, ou la guerre du bien et du mal, arrivée sous le règne de Louis XV, poème épiquo-magique en 102 chants* (originally 1799), 1962, esp. 32, 188; the end of his *Traité de la réintegration*, in R. Amadou, *Trésor martiniste*, 1969, 48–50; and N. Chaquin, "Le Citoyen Louis-Claude de Saint-Martin, théosophe révolutionnaire," *Dix-Huitième Siècle*, VI, 1974, 213, 223. Saint-Martin's key works of 1792 (*Ecce Homo* and *L'Homme nouvel*) were both published by the Social Circle. Chaquin refutes the still widespread misidentification of Saint-Martin with counterrevolutionary theocracy, developing a line of thought suggested by new information assembled in M. Serecka, *Louis-Claude de Saint-Martin. Le Philosophe inconnu. L'Homme et oeuvre*, Wrocław, 1968. See also the semantic analysis of an allegedly "revolutionary ideology" by G. Gayot and M. Pecheux, "Recherches sur le discours illuministe au XVIIIe siècle," *Annales*, May–Aug, esp. 698–701. For bibliography, see Amadou, *Trésor*, 231–37.

105. *Voyages de Pythagore . . . suivis de ses lois politiques et morales*, 1799, 6v.

106. *Voyages*, V, 354.

107. References from the Russian edition of the *Voyages* in Kucherenko, 183 and ff.

108. Ibid., 329, 332, 333.

109. *Voyages*, VI, 33.

110. Maréchal first sent *Voyages* to the same Hamburg publisher who had printed Abbé Barruel's exposé; and, though eventually published in Paris, it was simultaneously distributed in Basel, Breslau (Wrocław), Metz, Strasbourg, and Vienna—all in or near the German-speaking world: Dommanget, *Maréchal*, 349.

111. Yu. Oksman, " 'Pifagorovy zakony' i 'Pravila soedinennykh slavian,' " in N. Druzhinin, ed., *Ocherki po istorii dvizheniia dekabristov*, 1954, 485–7, 490. Another of Oksman's studies (*Vosstanie chernigovskogo pekhotnogo polka*, Leningrad, 1929, xxxv–xxxvi, 2) discussed possible derivation from Maréchal of the "Pythagorean sect" in Russia and its subsequent development, as did his review in *Katorga i Ssylka*, 1928, no. 2, 174–5.

112. On Novikov as *pravda-liubov'* and on the euphoria of Alexander's time, see Billington, *Icon*, 242–59. On Novikov's protégé, D. Dimitrevsky, who launched the six-volume Russian serial translation (Moscow, 1804–10), see Druzhinin, *Ocherki*, 485 ff. See also G. Likhotin, *Sil'ven Mareshal' i 'Zaveshchanie Ekateriny II,'* Leningrad, 1974, who confesses (50) that the theme of Maréchal's influence in Russia "still awaits its researcher."

113. S. Landa, "U istokov 'ody k iunosti,' " *Literatura slavianskikh narodov*, I, 1956, 29–33; and discussion of the parallel transformation of Philomats at Vilnius (to whom Mickiewicz belonged), 9 ff. Landa discusses Russian echoes in "Konspiracje," 243–65.

114. Oksman, in Druzhinin, *Ocherki*, 475, 502 ff. His argument for a continuous tradition is strengthened by evidence and by his reluctance to suggest unsubstantiated links.

115. G. Luciani, *La Société des slaves unis, 1823–1825*, Bordeaux, 1963, 60. This

work supplements the unimaginative M. Nechkina, *Obshchestvo soedinennykh slavian*, 1927.

116. Druzhinin, *Ocherki*, 508, also 502, 509 ff.

117. A. Ulybyshev, *Son* (1819), written in French, translated and published by B. Modzalevsky, "K istorii 'zelenoi lampy,'" in *Dekabristy i ikh vremia*, 1927, I, 53–6; see also 41–2. For a detailed recent study, which differentiates it from other Russian utopias without realizing the Pythagorean sources, see the unpublished doctoral dissertation of D. Neuenschwander, "Themes in Russian Utopian Fiction: a study of the utopian works of M. M. Shcherbatov, A. Ulybyshev, F. V. Bulgarin and V. F. Odoevskij," Syracuse, 1974. See also Lotman, "Dekabrist," *Nasledie*, 56–60.

118. Cited in Nechkina, *Dvizhenie*, I, 246.

119. T. Sokolovskaia, "Masonskie kovry," *More*, VI, 1907, Apr, 424. Russian Masonry developed at least two sets of geometric symbols as equivalents for the letters of the alphabet. See Sokolovskaia, "Masonskaia tainopis'," *Russky Arkhiv*, II, 1906, 399–400.

120. F. von Baader, *Über das pythagoräische Quadrat in der Natur oder die vier Weltgegenden*, Tübingen, 1798, in *Sämtliche Werke*, Aalen, 1963, III, 266–7; also 249. Baader's main influence was on the conservative idea of a "Holy Alliance," a triangle of power in which "three kings from the East" (an Orthodox Russian, Protestant Prussian, and Catholic Austrian) were unified by the Holy Spirit to provide the "point of sunrise" in post-Napoleonic Europe. Baader's *Über das durch die französische Revolution herbeigeführte Bedürfniss einer neuern und innigern Verbindung der Religion mit der Politik*, was circulated to the three monarchs in 1814 and published in Nürnberg, 1815. See H. Schäder, *Die dritte Koalition und die Heilige Allianz*, 1934, 65–70; F. Büchler, *Die geistige Wurzeln der Heiligen Allianz*, Freiburg, 1929, 53–60, for these and other German occult influences.

121. Within Le Mans alone, one finds triangular seals of lodges containing the star of the "triple social knot," the eye of surveillance, the "E" of Eleusis, and the words "Age d'Or" illustrated in A. Bouton, *Les Francs-maçons manceaux et la révolution française, 1741–1815*, Le Mans, 1958, 100, 252, 275, 286.

S. Hutin discusses the revolutionary symbolism of the equilateral triangle as a "luminous delta," each side of which represents past, present or future: *Les Sociétés secrètes*, 1970, 71.

122. Maréchal, *Correctif*, 313, 314. Maréchal also insisted on sanctifying childbirth at republican marriages by singing to the music of *La Marseillaise*: "Aux armes, couple heureux, comblez votre destin!/ Neuf mois, neuf mois;/ Et donnez nous un fier Républicain!" *Recueil d'hymnes républicains et de chansons guerrières et patriotiques*, np, nd, 19 (BH).

123. "I have two directly under me into which I breathe my entire soul, and these two each have two others, and so forth. In this manner I am able, in the simplest way, to set thousands of people into movement and flames. In this manner the Order must be organized and operate politically." Weishaupt, *Originalschriften des Illuminatenordens*, Munich, 1787, II, 32. The chart accompanying his commentary is reproduced with misleading commentary and no references in Webster, *Secret Societies*, 224. On the long history of the triangle as a religious symbol, see G. Stuhlfauth, *Das Dreieck. Die Geschichte eines religiösen Symbols*, Stuttgart, 1937.

124. So suggested by R. Eckart, "Aus den Papieren eines Illuminaten," in *Forschungen zur Kultur-und Litteraturgeschichte Bayerns*, III, 1895, 208. Fascination with multiple, interlocking triangles in occult Masonry led to such bizarre debates as whether the letter "G" inside the central triangle of one symbol (which included six other triple triangles) stood for the Grand Architect of the Universe (God), the higher science of Geometry, the hermaphrodite god of the Gnostics, or the usurpation of Masonry by the General of the Jesuit Order (Bonneville's position). See E. Lesueur, *La Franc-Maçonnerie artésienne au XVIIIe siècle*, 1914, 205.

125. The three-man cell is particularly favored by those revolutionaries who, like the original European ones at the beginning of the nineteenth century, view themselves as vehicles for the education as well as the mobilization of a people. The three-man cell became basic to Vietnamese Communism; and transposed to Algeria in the 1950s, it was graphically illustrated in the movie *Battle of Algiers*. The system of three-man cells unknown to each other recurred among dissident groups in the USSR in the late 1960s: P. Sormani, "Dissidence in Moscow," *Survey*, 1971, Spring, 18–9.

126. Saitta, II, 79–80.

127. Sketched reconstruction of the interior of the sanctuary in Radice, 76.

128. Saitta, II, 61, 78–9.

129. Lehning, 119–20, supplemented by F. Ruchon, *Histoire de la Franc-Maçonnerie à Genève de 1736 à 1900*, Geneva, 1935, 99–120. G. Weill, using a police re-

port of Mar, 1812, identified Buonarroti, Villard, and Terray of Lyon as the original "triangle": *Revue Historique*, LXXVI, 1901, May–Aug, 261.

130. On the still mysterious *Conspiración del triángulo*, see E. Astur, *Riego*, Oviedo, 1933, 102. V. de la Fuente, *Historia de las sociedades secretas antiguas y modernas en España*, Barcelona, 1933, 270–6, esp. 270 for Illuminist influence; also M. LaFuente and J. Valera, *Historia general de España*, Barcelona, 1889, XVIII, 203–4; and F. Suárez, *La Crisis política del antiguo régimen en España (1800–1840)*, Madrid, 1950, 2n ed., 60–1.

131. This principle can be extrapolated from the statutes discovered in the Merseberg archives in East Germany and reprinted in *Bund der Kommunisten*, 1970, I, 975–82, esp. articles 14, 52b, 23, and 33a, for the links between the ascending levels: Zelt/Lager/Kreislager/Brennpunkt.

132. Lantoine, *Histoire*, 220; R. Gould, "Military Masonry," *Ars Quatuor Coronatorum*, XIV, 1901, 45. An earlier, unrelated group of "Philadelphians" had also arisen from among German occultists: followers of Jacob Boehme in London. See N. Thune, *The Behmenists and the Philadelphians*, Uppsala, 1948.

133. The Rectified Scottish Rite was established in France at two conferences (Lyon in 1778 with the aid of a Lutheran clergyman, and Wilhelmsbad in 1782 under the patronage of the Duke of Brunswick) with the mystic Jean-Baptiste Willermoz as leader. See B. Guillemain, "La Franc-maçonnerie comme utopie: J. B. Willermoz," in *Le Discours utopique*, 259–68; A. Joly, *Un Mystique lyonnais et les secrets de la franc-maçonnerie. 1730–1824*, Macon, 1938.

The best general account of the rise of occultism within French Masonry prior to the revolution is in Chevallier, *Histoire*, I, 211–56. The decisive starting point was the foundation in Paris of the Grand Orient in 1773 and the loosening of French dependence on the more casual, philanthropic Masonry which originated in England and had been limited to three grades. The proliferation of higher levels began with the spread of the rival system of "Scottish" Masonry. The influx into France of German occultism—a strikingly neglected subject in the Francocentric historical literature—often took place within the 33 levels of the Scottish Rite.

134. E. Faguet, cited in J. Triomphe, *Joseph de Maistre. Etude sur la vie et sur la doctrine d'un matérialiste mystique*, Geneva, 1968, 494 n. 22. This biography supersedes all other studies of the future ultramontanist reactionary who began as a partisan of Scottish Rite Masonry when it was imported from Germany into France and wrote a history of Masonry for the Duke of Brunswick at the time of the Wilhelmsbad Congress: reprinted in E. Dermanghem, ed., *La Franc-maçonnerie. Mémoire inédit au duc de Brunswick (1782)*, 1925. For the more general diffusion of mystical ideas in Lyon, see J. Buche, *L'Ecole mystique de Lyon. 1776–1847*, 1935.

A favorite label among Lyonnais occultists was "friend of truth"; a more secular group of occultists in Avignon used its Greek form, *Philalèthes*; and these in turn may have given birth to the Philadelphians of Narbonne. See the neglected study of the head of the *Philalèthes*, the Polish Count Grabianka, by J. Ujejski, *Król nowego Izraela*, Warsaw, 1924; and the general, European-wide treatment of the group as a "mystical international," in C. Garrett, *Respectable Folly. Millenarians and the French Revolution in France and England*, Baltimore, 1975.

135. P. Schmidt, *Court de Gébelin à Paris (1763–1784)*, Geneva, 1908, by no means exhausts this subject. Court was a Parisian partisan of the German Reformation, which he considered the first break with tyranny since Nebuchadnezzar, and was the first Frenchman to discuss the proto-romantic artistic ideas of Johann Winckelmann (*Monde primitif analysé et comparé avec le monde moderne*, 1775, III, xviii). Court's fascination with language preceded Herder's similar search for the *Ursprache* of primitive man, which was also influenced by occultism: see R. Unger, *Herder und der Palingenesiegedanke*, Frankfurt, 1922.

136. Court de Gébelin, *Monde*, III, 450, 284–5. There are lengthy extensions of the title for each of the nine volumes that appeared in 1773–84. The second edition of 1787–9 was larger and the one generally studied during the revolution.

137. N. Hans, "Unesco of the Eighteenth Century. La Loge des Neufs Soeurs and Its Venerable Master, Benjamin Franklin," *Proceedings of the American Philosophical Society*, XCVII, 1953, Oct 30, 515–6. Hans estimates a total membership of 400 for the entire period 1776–92. The records of the organization were destroyed by the Gestapo in World War II.

138. *Monde*, VIII, xvii–xx.

139. Schmidt, *Court*, 153.

140. D. Hill, "A Missing Chapter of Franco-American History," *American Historical Review*, XXI, 1916, Jul, 714. See also *Affaires de l'Angleterre et de l'Amérique*, 1776–8, 15 v.

141. B. Maurel, "Une Société de pensée à Saint-Domingue. Le cercle des phila-

delphes de Cap-Français," *Franco-American Review*, 1938, Winter, 143–67. M. Arthaud, *Discours prononcé à l'ouverture de la première séance publique du cercle des philadelphes, tenue au Cap-François le 11 mai 1785*, 1785, 2–3, 9. YU, Franklin collection. See also the biographical sketch of Moreau de Saint-Mery in the introduction to his *Description . . . de la partie française de l'Isle Saint-Domingue*, 1958, vi–xxxvi. Moreau and Arthaud were married to French sisters from Louisiana. I have been unable to locate in any library in the United States, Western Europe, or the West Indies a work referenced in L. Pingaud: A. Salles, *Le Cercle des philadelphes du Cap-Français*, Saint-Domingue, 1784. Another direct channel from the "Nine Sisters" and other occult orders to the Philadelphes was Bacon de la Chevalerie. See Maurel, *Saint-Domingue et la révolution française*, 1943, 27–32.

142. Maurel, "Société," 156; Arthaud, 18–9, 43 ff. Possible Illuminist influence may be detected in their desire to regulate all social conduct by the "general will of the circle" and their use of a hive of swarming bees as a symbol. Maurel, 149. Cap-Français was also the center of Scottish Rite Masonry and provided Paris not only with militant organizers like Fournier l'Américain, but also with the original theorist of revolutionary denunciation and purge, François Boissel, author of the *Catechism of the Human Race* in 1789. Ioannisian, *Idei*, 250–1.

143. Maurel, "Société," 250–1.

144. Maurel, 167; also 163–4, and C. James, *The Black Jacobins*, NY, 1963, 2d ed., 85 ff.

145. E. Philips, "Pennsylvanie, l'âge d'or," *American Historical Review*, 1930, Oct, 13, also 2; and Mathiez, *Etrangers*, 62.

146. Ibid., 37; Stettiner, *Tugendbund*, 5; Landa, "Konspiracje," 250, and "Isto-kov," 26.

147. H. Baulig, "Anacharsis Cloots avant la révolution," *La Révolution Française*, 1901, Aug, 154.

148. Cloots, *La République universelle ou adresse aux tyrannicides*, 1793, 162–3.

149. Maréchal, *Tombeau*, 4.

150. Maréchal, *Voyages*, V, 354. His bibliography begins (367) by stressing that *philosophie et monde* are the two "happy expressions" that Pythagoras left behind to humanity.

151. The term is used in the proclamation dated 1820 by Isambert (*Charbonnerie*, 94; text in Saitta, II, 138), though most authorities follow Saitta in dating the formal designation of the central Buonarrotian organization as *monde* from about 1828. No one has advanced any theory in all the rich literature on these organizations about the derivation of the term—let alone discussed possible borrowings from either Maréchal's *monde* or Court's *monde primitif*.

152. Delatte, *Constitution*, 15–7.

153. Text of his *Règlement de la Société des Philadelphes*, Nov 25, 1797, in Pingaud, *Jeunesse*, 231–4, esp. articles 5, 13–5, 22–3, 25. The five-pointed star was also the symbol of the terroristic Italian "Red Brigades" of the 1970s.

154. The United Irishmen, founded in 1791 to establish links with the French Revolution, combined Catholics and Protestants under a secret, 5-man center, which sought to work through similar subordinate committees. The classic biography of their leader alleges a "close connection between Freemasonry and the United Irishmen," arguing that "a large proportion of Masonic Lodges were practically revolutionary committees." (F. MacDermot, *Theobald Wolfe Tone*, L, 1938, 89.) Frost insists that there was "very little of the Masonic element at any time" in the United Irishmen, but that their reorganization of 1795 created a "system closely resembling that of the Illuminati" (*Societies*, I, 62, 60). A former police official in Ireland argues for far-reaching Illuminist impact (largely on the basis of the neglected pamphlet of R. Clifford, *The Application of Barruel's Memoirs of Jacobinism to the Secret Societies of Ireland and Great Britain*, L/Dublin, 1798) in H. Pollard, *The Secret Societies of Ireland. Their Rise and Progress*, L, 1922. See especially Appendix A, "Illuminism and the United Irishmen," 257–63. None of these studies provides documentation.

After suppression of the United Irishmen in 1797–8 and the act of Union with England in 1801, Irish revolutionaries gradually regrouped into the more narrowly Catholic Ribbon Society, whose hierarchy of 1805 revealed a master and three close followers, each of whom had 12 subordinate brothers (E. Lennhoff, *Histoire des sociétés secrètes au xixe et xxe siècles*, 1934, 139–42). This "apostolic" model of the 12-man unit tended to prevail in Catholic Ireland over the Pythagorean model. Indeed, the United Irishmen also used units of 12 (T. Williams, ed., *Secret Societies in Ireland*, NY/Dublin, 1973, 63).

Irish techniques appear to have influenced other rural, religious communities like Sicily, Iberia, and Latin America, where Irish soldiers sometimes settled (often after serving with British-sponsored anti-Napoleonic armies). This subject has never been adequately explored. See, however, F. Melgar, *O'Donnell*, Madrid, 1946, 7–20; S. Clissold, *Bernardo O'Higgins and the Independence of Chile*, NY/Washington, 1969, 11–6, 63.

155. The Babeuvist "Black League" in Italy during 1798–9 relied on 5-man committees of "the most purified" in each major city but also had an executive committee of 4 and a superior committee of 8, which together comprised an apostolic 12: Godechot, "Unité," 278 ff.

156. See the geometric figure dominating both sides of the leaflet announcing the conspiratorial organization in Poland under Gorzkowski in 1796–7, particularly the figure depicting a square of 25 connected small circles surrounding prime number groupings of similar circles, as reprinted in Miller, "Vozzvanie," opposite 370. See discussion 369–75.

157. B. Pance, "Les Etudiants sous la restauration," in *Paris révolutionnaire*, 1848, esp. 267–8.

158. C. Johnson, *Utopian Communism in France. Cabet and the Icarians, 1839–1851*, Ithaca/L, 1974, 74–5.

159. In the plan of P. Pestel', leader of the more extreme Southern Society and a deep student of Masonic and Pythagorean lore: *Vosstanie dekabristov*, V, 32.

160. Land and Liberty proposed a network controlled by a "5" that included Chernyshevsky. (See Ya. Linkov, *Revoliutsionnaia bor'ba A. I. Gertsena i N. P. Ogareva i tainoe obshchestvo "zemlia i volia" 1860-kh godov*, 1964, 242; E. Vilenskaia, *Revoliutsionnoe podpol'e v Rossii* [60-e XIX v.], 1965, 149; and A. Yarmolinsky, *Road to Revolution*, NY, 1959, 125.)

The idea of 5s was apparently taken from Russian émigrés in London, who had in turn probably borrowed it from Mazzini (F. Venturi, *Roots of Revolution*, NY, 1960, 267, and 760–1 n. 37–9). The only source for this derivation is A. Sleptsov, the main channel for transmitting ideas between London and St. Petersburg (see Sleptsov's memoirs in *N. G. Chernyshevsky, issledovaniia i materialy*, Saratov, 1962, esp. 266–8). Linkov (166–7, 242) follows the usual Soviet practice of minimizing foreign influences.

161. South Slav revolutionaries formed an anti-Turkish organization *Omladina* with a cellular net centered on a 5-man "honorary" presidium (Garibaldi, Mazzini, Cobden, Herzen, and Chernyshevsky), and a Russian revolutionary Ivan Bochkarev forged a link by organizing Serbian students in St. Petersburg, then journeying to Belgrade in 1867 to attend a meeting of *Omladina* (Venturi, 352–3). A later organization bearing the same name (the short-lived Czech *Omladina* of the 1890s) developed the metaphor of the hand. See A. Veselý, *Omladina a pokrokové hnutí*, Prague, 1902, 167–73; G. Simmel, "The Sociology of Secrecy and of Secret Societies," *American Journal of Sociology*, 1906, Jan, 478–9.

162. His visit to Odessa has never been studied beyond the brief discussion in Pingaud, *Jeunesse*, 122 ff. The substantial literature on Nodier (like the sole study of Bonneville by Harivel) concentrates on narrowly literary matters such as his invention of melodrama and his influence on Victor Hugo and the early romantics. See J. Larat, *La Tradition et l'exoticisme dans l'oeuvre de Charles Nodier (1780–1844). Etude sur les origines du romantisme français*, 1923; and A. Olivet, *Charles Nodier, Pilot of Romanticism*, Syracuse, 1964. There are bibliographical studies by Larat (1923), E. Bender (Lafayette, Ind., 1969), and S. Bell (Chapel Hill, 1971). There is disappointingly little on his activity as a journalist in Ljubljana in R. Maixner, *Charles Nodier et l'Illyrie*, 1960. M. Salomon, *Charles Nodier et le groupe romantique*, 1908, is still a stimulating study, as is M. Hamenachem, *Charles Nodier. Essai sur l'imagination mythique*, 1972. See especially "les attraits du cercle," 65–81.

163. Pingaud, *Jeunesse*, 15–9.

164. Hamenachem, *Nodier*, 76 n. 8.

165. Text in *Annales Révolutionnaires*, IX, 1916, 117.

166. Cited in P. Minet, *Souvenirs de la révolution et de l'empire de Charles Nodier*, 1966, Jul 13–4 (ms. of a broadcast, in BA, Fol. z.1478).

167. Salomon, 16–8.

168. Mathiez, "Charles Nodier opiomane et épileptique," *Annales Révolutionnaires*, X, 1918, 403–5; *Biographie des suicides*, 1808; Pingaud, 49.

For his love of the "theater of phantoms" and suggestion that it enact the resurrection of Mirabeau, see P. de la Vassière, "Charles Nodier conspirateur," *Le Correspondant*, 1896, Oct 25, 291–4, based on a letter to his sister, apparently from 1802.

169. P. Shchegolev, "Filipp Buonarroti i ego kniga 'Zagovor ravnykh,'" *Leningradsky Universitet. Uchenye zapiski. seriia istoricheskikh nauk*, LII, 1940, 239–40.

170. Bazin had, like Nodier, first been inspired by participating in the Feast

of Federation in 1790. The only serious discussion of this prolific and neglected figure is in A. Bouton, *Francs-maçons*, 212, 267–74.

171. Vassière, 295; Minet, 14; Viatte, *Sources*, II, 161; and A. Lebois, "Un Breviaire du compagnonnage: *La Fée aux Miettes* de Charles Nodier," *Archives des Lettres Modernes*, 1961, no. 40, 226. Nodier hailed Bonneville variously as his "Columbus," "the most simple and exalted heart that I have known in all my life," and the "Isaiah of masonry." Roberts, *Mythology*, 272 n. 60; Cros, *Fauchet*, 26; also Salomon, 264–5; Hamenachem, 10.

172. Salomon, 60–1.

173. Nodier described the group as "romantics of the epoch, a species of literary pariah with no banner, no chief, no journal"; *Souvenirs et portraits de la révolution*, 1841, 3d ed., 322–5. A plan for an organization of *frères voyageurs* was found on Bazin when he was arrested: Baylot, Voie, 77 n. 9.

174. V. Lombard de Langrès, *Histoire des sociétés secrètes de l'armée et des conspirations militaires qui ont eu pour objet la destruction du gouvernement de Bonaparte*, 1815, 25. This work, sometimes attributed to Nodier or Bazin, is linked with Lombard by Bouton, *Francs-maçons*, 267 n. 9.

Modern conspiracy in some ways derives from fascination with the Genoese republican conspiracy of Fiesco against Charles V. This anti-Hapsburg plot was partly aided by the French in the sixteenth century, and subsequently inspired both a theoretical treatise by the 18-year-old Cardinal de Retz (*Conjuration de Fiesque*, 1632) and the pioneering melodrama of the young Schiller (*Die Verschwörung des Fiesco*, 1782–3). The impulse to struggle is built into the very title of Bazin's *Jacqueline d'Olzebourg. Mélodrama en 3 actes, orné de pantomime, danses et combats*, 1803; and he died in a duel defending his honor after a performance.

175. This possibility is suggested by the discussion in Tugan-Baranovsky, "General Male," 184.

176. Nodier, *Souvenirs*, 309; and the entire section "Malet et Oudet," 303–39.

177. Cited in Pingaud, *Jeunesse*, 204.

178. Nodier praised Oudet for recapturing the lost "link with divinity" of human speech, when "words were no longer imprisoned in the tip of a pen and drowned in an inkwell." *Souvenirs*, 328, 331.

179. *Apothéoses de Pythagore. Imprécations de Pythagore*, Crotona (Besançon), 1808. See Salomon, 64–5 on his *Dictionnaire raisonné des onomatopées françaises*, produced for libraries and lycées in Paris; and 68 for his *Théorie des langues primitives*, which was apparently either not completed or not published. Bazin concurrently published brochures periodically (*Lettres françaises* and *Lettres philosophiques*) which appear to have been more directly propaganda organs of the Philadelphians: Bouton, 272, Baylot, 134.

180. Cited in Pingaud, 242.

181. Tugan-Baranovsky, "General," 182; also Lombard, *Histoire*, 17 ff.; Pingaud, 160–82; Gould, 42–8; Frost, I, 171.

182. D. Tugan-Baranovsky, "Vtoroi zagovor generala Male," *Voprosy Istorii*, 1974, no. 8, 101; also Frost, I, 149 ff.; Lehning, "Buonarroti," 119–22; and works referenced in Saitta, I, 81–2 n. 12. E. Guillon, *Les Complots militaires sous le consulat et l'empire*, 1894, still usefully supplements more recent works in matters of detail: but Guillon like de la Vassière can mislead modern scholars with his extreme contentions that Nodier in effect simply imagined the Philadelphians. O. Pontet, *L'Accacia*, 1905, 190, went so far as to contend that even the existence of Oudet was invented. For a careful account that incorporates recent discoveries and assesses the Philadelphians' influence without exaggerating their organization, see Baylot, "Des Philadelphes de ce que l'on en imagine et de ce qui en procède," *Voie*, 73–92.

183. Cited in L. Villefosse and J. Bouissonouse, *L'Opposition à Napoléon*, 1969, 307; also Tugan-Baranovsky, "Vtoroi," 106.

184. Salomon, 88.

185. Soriga, *Società*, 110. Saitta considers the two organizations identical, I, 81. Tugan-Baranovsky surveys other literature on the two societies ("Vtoroi," 107–8). The neglected Masonic study of F. Radice suggests that Buonarroti may have been a consultant to the Adelphes, who may in turn have had an independent prior existence: "Les Philadelphes et les Adelphes," *Ars Quatuor Coronatorum*, LV, 1944, esp. 71, 89–92.

186. Radice, 69–71; Gould, 44–5; and J. Dautry, "Babuvistskaia traditsiia posle smerti Babefa i do revoliutsii 1830 g.," *Frantsuzsky ezhegodnik*, 1960, 1961, 181.

187. Radice, 76–7; Frost, I, 165 ff.

188. C. Nardi, *La Vita e le opere di Francesco Saverio Salfi (1759–1832)*, Genoa, 1925, 105; also the section on his Masonic writings, 189–98, and on "I melodrammi," 105–20. Though the later term for melodrama was *melologo*, Salfi both

used the general French term and exemplified Nodier's type of emotional combat drama which bore this designation was pioneered by Rousseau's *Pygmalion* of 1762.

189. I accept the date of 1811 suggested by the transcriber of the Adelphian documents in the Public Record Office of London (Radice, 88), and 1812 as the time of amalgamation with the Philadelphians (Radice, 79), despite the possibilities he inconclusively raises of later dating or both. The invaluable Adelphian documents reproduced in *Ars Quatuor Coronatorum*, LV, 1944, 89–117, are—like most material in Masonic publications—mysteriously overlooked and unused by almost all historians of these movements. See also Saitta, II, 61.

190. Archives Nationales, F7 6684, 283. There are two sets of police copies of the decrees and statutes of the Grand Firmament of the Sublime Perfect Masters. The file has been only selectively used and was in disarray when consulted. I assembled and used the most complete of the two sets.

191. Archives Nationales, F7 6684, 286. Undated "Extrait du rituel à l'ouverture de chaque Eglise."

192. Archives Nationales, F7 6684, 284. Undated "Profession de foi du Synode de ☉, ou rassemblement des Sublimes-Elus"; and "Profession de foi de ☉, ou rassemblement des Sublimes Maitres Parfaits." See also D. Tugan-Baranovsky, "Buonarroti i missiia Andriana," *Voprosy Istorii*, 1977, no. 1, esp. 124.

193. Archives Nationales, F7 6684, 299. Undated "Livre des Statuts des Sublimes Maitres Parfaits." In the undated parallel text "Livre des Statuts des Sublimes-Elus," "Les Illuminés" in Germany are one of the five "already formed secret societies" that revolutionaries at this second level are to make use of: 289.

194. Tugan-Baranovsky, "Buonarroti," 127.

195. Ibid., 129.

196. Archives Nationales, F7 6684, 295. Undated "Règlement des Eglises et des Synodes."

197. Characteristic of the "new mentality" created by German romantics in the 1790s in the important study of H. Brunschwig, *Enlightenment and Romanticism in Eighteenth Century Prussia*, Chicago, 1974, 181–2.

Two other works that also suggest a revival of belief in the miraculous in the romantic era and relate this development to revolution are M. Abrams, *Natural Supernaturalism: Tradition and Revolution in Romantic Literature*, NY, 1971 (arguing that faith in apocalypse by revelation was replaced by faith in apocalypse by revolution), and R. Winegarten, *Writers and Revolution: The Fatal Lure of Action*, NY, 1974 (criticizing the "romantic revolutionism" that replaced religion with "fictitious absolutes"). The Polish poet Cyprian Norwid called revolutions "earthly miracles": *Dziela wszystkie*, III, 390.

The word "miracle" recurs repeatedly in firsthand accounts of revolutionary events. "All was miraculous in that meeting . . . more beautiful than all the harmony in the opera," wrote one observer of the National Assembly just after the outbreak of war in April 1792; the key military victory was "the miracle at Valmy"; Fauchet, awaiting death in the Conciergerie, was said by his cellmate to radiate *le goût du merveilleux*: Monglond, *Préromantisme*, II, 409–10, 131, 18.

198. F. Wey, *Vie de Charles Nodier de l'Academie française*, 1844, 12; cited in Fach, "Naturschilderung," 9.

199. *Fragmens sur les institutions républicaines. Ouvrage posthume de Saint-Just précédé d'une notice par Ch. Nodier*, 1831, 10–1 (PU).

200. W. Wordsworth, *The Prelude*, XI, 140–4 (original ed. 1850).

201. Brunschwig, 183.

202. *Corinne, ou l'Italie*, 1820, I, 117 (original ed. 1807).

203. Bouton, *Francs-maçons*, 280.

204. On St. Helena, Napoleon not only paid tribute to Buonarroti but also read Nodier's *Jean Sbogar* (1818), about a Dalmatian bandit whom Nodier placed at the head of his imaginary *frères du bien commun*. Salomon, 89; Hamenachem, 42.

205. Pianzola, "Svizzera," 128.

206. Faivre, *Eckhartshausen*, 544, also 443 ff.

207. *Les Vers dorés de Pythagore*, 1813. Extracts in A. Tanner, ed., *Gnostiques de la révolution. Fabre d'Olivet*, 1946, 103–53. This remarkable figure was descended from a family of persecuted Huguenots and influenced by Court and German occultists. He wrote major *pièces d'occasion* for the Feast of Federation (*Le Quatorze Juillet*, a poetic drama, 1790), the victory at Toulon (*Toulon soumis*, an historic opera, 1794), and the coronation of Napoleon as emperor (*Oratorio*, 1804). Tanner, 279–86.

208. Fabre d'Olivet, *La Musique expliquée comme science et comme art at considérée dans ses rapports analogiques avec les mystères religieux, la mythologie ancienne et l'histoire de la terre*, 1896, 1.

209. Ibid., 46–7.
210. Ibid., 81, 82.
211. L. Angeloni, *Sopra la vita, le opera ed il sapere di Guido d'Arezzo*, Paris, 1811.
212. O. Spengler, *The Decline of the West*, NY, 1939, I, 282; also 183 ff. for his general distinction between "Faustian" and "Apollonian" man.
213. E. Bloch, *Das Prinzip Hoffnung*, as paraphrased in Furter, *L'Imagination*, 1/12; also, on Bloch's view of music as a collective, revolutionary art form, 1/10–1/13.
214. Kuypers, *Les Egalitaires*, 80–1.
215. On Kats's Tooneel der Volksbechaving, see Kuypers, "Les liens d'amitié de Karl Marx en Belgique (1845–48)," *Socialisme*, LVIII, 1963, 412, and works referenced therein.
216. See "Der 'Jesuitismus' als persönliches Ordensprinzip Weishaupts," in Grassl, *Aufbruch*, 184–7.
217. Ibid., 238.
218. This theme from Knigge, *Über Jesuiten, Freymaurer und deutsche Rosenkreuzer*, Leipzig, 1781, is magnified in F. Nicolai, *Beschreibung einer Reise durch Deutschland und die Schweiz im Jahre 1781*, Berlin/Stettin, 1785. The high point of paranoia appears to have been reached in Weishaupt's *Apologie der Illuminaten*, Frankfurt/Leipzig, 1786. For discussion of these and other works, see Grassl, 236–59.
219. E. von Göchhausen, *Enthüllung des Systems der Weltbürgerrepublik*, Leipzig, 1786; Grassl, 266–7.
220. Modena, "Numero," 869–70.
221. Onnis, *Buonarroti*, 208–9.
222. J. Droz, "Le légende du complot illuministe en Allemagne," *Revue Historique*, 1961, Oct–Dec, 316. The best general description of this epidemic of fear is in Roberts, *Mythology*, 118–45. The most learned contemporary attempt to trace a "cosmo-political" conspiracy was by the Scottish chemist J. Robison, "The Illuminati," in *Proofs of a Conspiracy Against all the Religions and Governments of Europe*, L, 1798, 4th ed., 100–271, and the notes added for this edition which summarize the other exposé literature.
The Abbé Barruel popularized the idea of a spreading international plot led by Illuminists through three successive stages: "Condorcet refused to obey God, Brissot refused to obey kings, and Babeuf refused to obey the Republic or any magistrates or governing officers whatever." *Mémoires*, cited in Palmer, *Age*, II, 252. J. Starck and others subsequently corrected Barruel by distinguishing Illuminism more clearly from Masonry.
Fear of Illuminism tended to vary in inverse proportion to proximity; and was perhaps most extreme in distant America, where real Illuminists were absent and revolutionary enthusiasm waning by the late 1790s: see V. Stauffer, *New England and the Bavarian Illuminists*, NY, 1918, esp. 238, 291 ff.; R. Buel, Jr., *Securing the Revolution. Ideology in American Politics, 1789–1815*, Ithaca, 1972, 167 ff.; D. Davis, ed., *The Fear of Conspiracy*, Ithaca, 1971, 35–65. For the subsequent absorption of this issue into American Federalist politics, A. Briceland, "The Philadelphia Aurora, the New England Illuminati, and the Election of 1800," *The Pennsylvania Magazine of History and Biography*, 1976, Jan, 3–36.
223. G. Barany, *Stephen Széchenyi and the Awakening of Hungarian Nationalism, 1791–1841*, Princeton, 1968, 20 ff., on Martinovics. The discussion by M. Kajtai ("German Illuminati in Hungary," in L. Miklos and F. Szenczi, eds., *Studies in Eighteenth Century Literature*, Budapest, 1974, 325–46, esp. 333 ff.) suggests that Hungarian Illuminism was closer to Masonry and more directly an outgrowth of the original German movement than elsewhere. A renegade Illuminist in the Hapsburg capital of Vienna, Leopold Hoffman, first identified revolution with Illuminism. Grassl, 267–9.
224. The account of Benda, "Die ungarischen Jakobiner," in W. Markov, ed., *Maximilien Robespierre, 1750–1794*, 1958, 441–72, is supplemented by E. Wangermann, *From Joseph II to the Jacobin Trials*, L, 1969, who corrects the date of execution, 170 n. 6. See also C. Kecskemeti, "Les Jacobins hongrois (1794–1795)," *Annales Historiques*, 1973, Apr–Jun, esp. 224–6, 232–3.
225. *Devoirs du prince et du citoyen, ouvrage posthume de M. Court de Gébelin, pour servir de suite à la déclaration des droits de l'homme*, 1789. Court is left out altogether (and his associates and fellow admirers of Rousseau, Cloots, and Maréchal overlooked) in G. McNeil, "The Cult of Rousseau and the French Revolution," *Journal of the History of Ideas*, 1945, Apr, 197–212.
The immense subsequent literature on this subject and controversies about it are

soberly summarized in R. Barny, "Jean-Jacques Rousseau dans la révolution," *Dix-Huitième Siècle*, VI, 1974, 59–98, without, however, mentioning this line of influence leading to Maréchal.

226. Abbé Charles François Le Gros, *Analyse des ouvrages de J. J. Rousseau de Genève et de M. Court de Gébelin, auteur de Monde Primitif*, Geneva/Paris, 1786, 24.

227. H. Gaubert, *Conspirateurs au temps de Napoléon I*, 1962, discusses these and subsequent conspiracies.

228. Report to the Convention on the Principles of Revolutionary Government in Godechot, *Pensée*, 193.

229. S. Askenazy, *Łukasiński*, Warsaw, 1929, I, 400; Berti, *Rossiia*, 420–1, who points out that Buonarroti was unique among Italian revolutionaries in not sharing this illusion. P. Robiquet, who sometimes exaggerates Buonarroti's involvements, suggests that Buonarroti himself may have collaborated with the Right at an early point. See "Buonarroti, une émeute cléricale à Bastia en juin 1791," *La Révolution Française*, LIV, 1908, 502–4.

230. On A. Rozniecki, see Askenazy, *Tsarstvo pol'skoe 1850–1830 gg*, 1915, 73–7. Walerian Łukasiński, the main martyr of the society, inspired subsequent generations of Polish and Russian political prisoners who saw or met him during his long incarceration of more than 40 years.

231. Sòriga, *Società*, 80–92, also 115 ff. for the influence of the Philadelphians. Napoleon had organized his own Masonic-type organizations in the army to combat the Scottish influence. See F. Rousseau, "Les Sociétés secrètes en Espagne au XVIIIe siècle et sous Joseph Bonaparte," *Revue des Etudes Historiques*, 1914, Mar–Apr, 184.

232. Lord Pelham to the Earl of Malmesbury, from the latter's diary of Jun 10, 1803, in *Diaries and Correspondence of James Harris, First Earl of Malmesbury*, 1845, 2d ed., IX, 271. This passage is cited without reference in Frost, *Societies*, I, 151–2. Frost's two-volume history is a surprisingly sophisticated and unjustly neglected treatment by a veteran journalist and eyewitness chronicler of the Chartist movement, hampered only by inadequate documentation.

233. F. Rousseau, "Sociétés," 189. See also references in M. Kukiel, "Lelewel, Mickiewicz and the Underground Movements of European Revolution (1816–33)," *Polish Review*, 1960, summer, 62 n. 5.

234. His remarkable career is traced by the great Basque novelist Pio Baroja, *Aviraneta o la vida de un conspirador*, Madrid/Barcelona, 1931, see esp. 15, 29–32, 84; and (for his links with Merino) 41–50, 54. Aviraneta's Mexican years are discussed in *Mis memorias íntimas, 1825–1829*, Mexico, 1906. Of his many writings on guerrilla warfare, see particularly *Las guerrillas españolas o las partidas de brigantes de la guerra de la independencia*, Madrid, 1870.
More generally on the confusion of allegiances, see F. Rousseau, "Les Sociétés secrètes et la révolution espagnole en 1820," *Revue des Etudes Historiques*, 1916, Jan–Feb, 1–33.

235. *Eloge de Victor-Amédée III*, Chambéry, 1775, cited in Triomphe, *Maistre*, 98.

236. De Maistre, *Oeuvres complètes*, Lyon, 1886, XIII, 204.

237. Triomphe, 498.

238. R. de Felice, *Note e Ricerche sugli "illuminati" e il misticismo rivoluzionaria* (1789–1800), 1960, 59.

239. In Lyon before the revolution, in Lausanne, and St. Petersburg as an émigré. See "Joseph de Maistre et l'Allemagne," in Triomphe, 498–576.

240. De Maistre, *Quatres Chapitres inédits sur la Russie*, 1859, 27.

241. *Correctif à la gloire de Bonaparte ou lettre à ce général*, Venice, 1798, 15, also 22–3. It is signed "P. S. M. l'H. S. D." (*l'homme sans Dieu*).

242. Ibid., 8–9, 28.

243. Ibid., 29. Maréchal also shared the general fascination of revolutionaries with the Jesuits, and in his major literary work of the 1890s adopted the slogan of the order, simply substituting "virtue" for "God." *Ad majoram gloriam virtutus*, epigraph to *Le Lucrèce français; fragmens d'un poème*, year VI (BH).

244. *Correctif*, 25–6.

245. *Histoire de la Russie réduite aux seuls faits importans*, L/Paris, 1802, 323 n. 1. italicized and identified as the words "of a famous personage." The second edition in 1807 identified the work as "par l'auteur du Voyage de Pythagore."

246. From the section *Les bons et derniers avis de Catherine II à Paul Ier trouvés parmi les papiers de l'impératrice de Russie, après sa mort*, in *Histoire*, 362–3.
The analysis by Likhotin shows that the testament was accepted as basically authentic by approving conservative scholars in the nineteenth century. A partially fictionalized account of early radical Masons exiled to Smolensk under Catherine portrays them as grateful for the document because it stripped away illusions of

intellectuals about those exercising power. N. Rylenkova, *Na staroi smolenskoi doroge*, Smolensk, 1961, 11–2; Likhotin, 66 n. 21.

247. *Histoire*, 363.
248. Ibid., 364.
249. Ibid., 365.
250. Ibid., 366, 373, 374.
251. Ibid., 377.
252. Ibid., 383, 375.
253. Ibid., 383.
254. Ibid., 381.
255. *L'Esprit et le voeu des français* and *Du retour à la religion*, discussed in A. Ducoin, *Paul Didier. Histoire de la conspiration de 1816*, 1844, 9–13. The former work (whose authorship was not known until his trial) says: "The revolution is a wheel which the genius of evil turns at his pleasure. We are all chained to it, and he whose pride is flattered by arriving at the summit, will soon be cast down by a slight push." Ducoin, 10–1 n. 1.
256. Ibid., 96.
257. Ibid., 164.
The student of police intrigue, L. Grasilier, suggested (*Rétif de la Bretonne inconnu*, 1927) that Restif served as a police informer to successive governments of opposite persuasions—a hypothesis rejected by F. Funck-Brentano (*Rétif de la Bretonne*, 1928, 312). Monglond's summary of the controversy (*Préromantisme*, II, 324 n. 2) concludes that Restif was attached to the "black cabinet" of the French police in April, 1798, as a translator of Spanish.
258. Faivre, *Eckhartshausen*, 75, also 72–84, 619–38, supplementing other material in Billington, *Icon*, 279 ff.
259. Brengues, "Apport," in *Les Fêtes*, 589; H. Buisson, *Fouché, duc d'Otrante*, Bienne, 1968.
260. Text in·De Maistre, *Oeuvres complètes*, XIV, 371–2.

Book Two

1. J. Brengues, *La Franc-maçonnerie du bois*, 1973, stresses the importance of this transformation from dead stone to living wood, which was even then referred to as heralding a "green revolution" (292). A neglected example in another area is the Italian operatic composer during the revolutionary era in Paris, Bernardo Porta, who favored woodwind instruments for romantic, ideological reasons—believing especially that instruments made from the wood of medicinal trees would cure people by their music. T. Fleischman, *Napoléon et la musique*, Brussels/Paris, 1965, 105–6.
2. On the early history of this idea, see W. Veit, *Studien zur Geschichte des Topos der Goldenen Zeit von der Antike bis zum 18. Jahrhundert*, Cologne, 1961. For the romantic transformation of the idea by a prototypical poet at the end of the eighteenth century, see H.-J. Mähl, *Die Idee goldener Zeitalters im Werk der Novalis*, Heidelberg, 1965.
For an important Marxist analysis of how retrospection of a golden age became "genuinely revolutionary," particularly through Rousseau and as the imagined age becomes ostensibly more remote in time, see K. Kelles-Krauz, *Pisma wybrane*, Warsaw, 1962, I, 202–3, also 188–225; and his "La Loi de la rétrospection révolutionnaire," *Annales de Sociologie*, II, 1895, 315–38.
3. "Un sueño de tres siglos," discussed in L. Villoro, *El Proceso ideologico de la revolución de independencia*, Mexico, 1967, 146–53.
4. S. Collier, *Ideas and Politics of Chilean Independence, 1808–1833*, Cambridge, 1967, 212 ff. A play of 1819 written about the leader Bernardo O'Higgins, *The Triumph of the Natural*, portrays the last descendant of the old Araucan Indians boarding a frigate and prophesying that the perfection of nature will be recovered by sailing forward under O'Higgins's command (215 n. 2). Lautaro, the leader of the Araucanian opposition, lent his name to the original Masonic lodge (founded by Miranda in London in 1796) which was expanded into a chain of lodges in Chile, Argentina, and Peru involving O'Higgins and others in the preparation of national revolutions. See the Masonic study by A. Zuñiga, *La logia "Lautaro" y la independencia de America*, Buenos Aires, 1922, 33–43; and the bibliographical discussion and comparison with the Carbonari by J. Eyzaguirre, *La logia Lautarina y otras estudios sobre la independencia*, Buenos Aires/Santiago, 1973, 1–14.
5. On these "frères chasseurs," J. Bernard, *Les Rouges. Libéralisme, nationalisme*

et anticléricalisme au milieu du XIXe siècle, Québec, 1971, 20; and, on the broader movement, O. Tiffany, *The Canadian Rebellion of 1837-8*, Buffalo, 1905 (repr. Toronto, 1972), 61 ff.

6. See the remarkable testament by the *chef d'atelier* from Lyon who led this movement, Joseph Benoît, *Confessions d'un prolétaire*, 1968, 59; also M. Buffenoir, "Le Communisme à Lyon de 1834 à 1848," *Revue d'Histoire de Lyon*, VIII, 1909, 348.

7. Silbernagl, "Die geheimen politischen Verbindungen der Deutschen in der ersten Hälfte des neunzehnten Jahrhunderts," *Historisches Jahrbuch*, XIV, 1893, esp. 803–6. An alternate translation for the successive names of the central headquarters (*Nationalhütte and Brennpunkt*) as "national shelter" and "focal point" loses the naturalistic overtones of the German.

8. On *la société du cygne* in the Vaud, see E. Barnikol, ed., *Geschichte des religiösen und atheistischen Frühsozialismus*, Kiel, 1932, 18.

9. W. Weitling's system of *Blatt, Knospe, Blute, Kern* is set forth in his *Das Evangelium des Armen Sünders*, Bern, 1845, chapter x: "Die Organization der Propaganda."

10. The role of John Minter Morgan's *The Revolt of the Bees* (serialized in *Co-operative Magazine*, 1826) in popularizing Owen is discussed in W. Armytage, *Heavens Below. Utopian Experiments in England 1560–1960*, L, 1961, 131. The first use of the term "Communionist" as a social rather than religious term was in *Co-operative Magazine*, 1827, Nov, 509 (Bestor, "Evolution," 278), and in the later 1830s the radical Owenites called themselves "Communionists" and established *The Working Bee* as their weekly journal.

Already in 1840, the first historian of socialism, L. Reybaud, noted that the impulse behind the utopian experiments of Owen and Fourier were "a return to nature rather than a call to the refinements of civilization" (*Etude*, 25). Fourier went even farther in the direction of pastoral fantasy with his famous "phalanstery," his contrast between false and ugly vs. "natural and attractive" forms of association, and his cosmic vision of natural harmony and erotic links even between astral bodies.

Chapter 5

1. See citation from the text of "Mémoire sur les sociétés secrètes et les conspirations sous la restauration par Simon Duplay," *Revue Internationale des Sociétés Secrètes*, II, 1913, Mar 5, 547–50, also the biographical preface by L. Grasilier, esp. 513–5, 518, and added text, 526–47. See also Spitzer, *Old Hatreds*, 190–3; Baylot, "L'Affaire de Misraïm," *Voie*, 223–31.

2. H. Kissinger, *A World Restored: Metternich, Castlereagh and the Problems of Peace, 1812–22*, Boston, 1957.

3. Trelat, "La Charbonnerie," *Paris révolutionnaire*, 220–1.

4. Cited in Landa, *Dukh*, 274.

5. Cited in Baylot, *Voie*, 168.
For the alleged confusion by ordinary Spaniards of *constitución* with *constipación*, see F. Radice, "An Introduction to the History of the Carbonari," *Ars Quatuor Coronatorum*, LIII, 1942, 105. This history (serialized LI, 37–90; LII, 63–163; LIII, 48–140; LV, 35–66) is a major neglected work in the field, rich in material if uneven in interpretation and written from a Masonic perspective.

Conflicting testimony about the widely believed confusion of *Konstitutsiia* in Russia with the name of Grand Duke Constantine's wife is summarized in Nechkina, *Dvizhenie*, II, 323–4; and J. Michelet, *Légendes démocratiques du nord*, 1968, 164 n. 147. Nechkina insists that this is only a later anecdote read back into the "government version" of the event.

6. This estimate by General Pepe is the lowest of several gathered by Radice, *Ars*, LIII, 92. For other contemporary estimates 2–3 times larger, see Landa, "Konspiracje," 256.

7. Andryane, *Souvenirs*, II, 173.

8. Buonarroti himself frequently visited in the region from Geneva (and from Grenoble, where he resided intermittently 1812–15) and restored his revolutionary "stamina" by "metaphysical revery" during long walks in the countryside which enabled him to read the "hieroglyph" contained in "the mysterious language of universal nature." Andryane, II, 157; Prati, "Autobiography," *The Penny Satirist*, 1837, Jun 17, 3; Aug 26.

Buonarroti later read and may have been influenced by a lost brochure of 1831 by "J.B. (du Jura)," *The Age of Gold unveiled, or a plan of civil, political and religious organization* (Saitta, I, 168 n. 112), and he subsequently imparted this vision to his Belgian followers as evidenced in the play *The Earthly Paradise* (J. Kats, *Het Aerdsch Paradys of den Zegeprael der Broederliefde*, Antwerp, 1836, BM, discussed in Kuypers, *Egalitaires*, 80–1) down to the remarkable 736-page plan for the egalitarian reorganization of Europe by the Flemish brewer, Napoleon de Keyser, *Het Natuer-Regt*, Brussels, 1854, in Kuypers, 131.

9. This dream of Versilov (*A Raw Youth*, 1874) amplifies the first statement of this idea in a suppressed chapter of Dostoevsky's preceding novel (the "confession" of Stavrogin from *The Possessed*, 1870–72).

10. The basic studies of the Jura group are by C. Godard, *Les Bons Cousins charbonniers*, Besançon, 1896; and *Le Catéchisme des Bons Cousins charbonniers*, Besançon, 1903; the most plausible derivation of the Neapolitan from the Besançon "good cousins" is by A. Mathiez, "L'Origine franc-comtoise de la charbonnerie italienne," *Annales Historiques*, V, 1928, Nov-Dec, 551–61. The supposition of a link is convincingly supported by Spitzer (though selectively skeptical of some of the evidence advanced, *Old Hatreds*, 232 n. 60); by F.-A. Isambert, *De la Charbonnerie au Saint-Simonisme. Etude sur la jeunesse de Buchez*, 1966, 99 n. 3; and indirectly by the terminological borrowings cited in Radice, *Ars*, LI, 1940, 60.

11. J. Godechot, etc. *The Napoleonic Era in Europe*, NY, 1971, 155; Brengues, *Franc-maçonnerie du bois*, 190–1. Important supplementary details on Briot (who is, however, incorrectly called Pierre-Joseph) in Baylot, *Voie*, 167–75, and 230–1, where his later involvement in the Misraim movement in France is documented.

12. See Hobsbawm, *Bandits*, chapter III.

13. G. Leti, *Carboneria e massoneria nel risorgimento italiano*, Bologna, 1915, 69 ff. See also J. Rath, "The Carbonari: Their Origins, Initiation Rites, and Aims," *American Historical Review*, 1964, Jan, 353–70; also for the importance of South Italian leadership, Berti, *Democratici*, 148 ff.; and for early Hapsburg apprehensions (and fantasies such as suggestions of linkage to Illuminism), Lennhoff, 17–9.

14. Lennhoff, 25–8; Radice, *Ars*, LIV, 1943, 143–4.

15. See the anonymous *Memoirs of the Secret Societies of the South of Italy, particularly the Carbonari*, L, 1821 (a work rich in documentary material and extracts), esp. 4–8 (BO).

16. From papers of the conspirators of Macerata, 1817, printed in the minutes of the trial in Rome, 1818, in *Memoirs*, 31.

17. Ibid., 26–7.

18. Ibid., 28, also 27–30.

19. M. Saint-Edme, *Constitution et organisation des carbonari*, 1821, 90–1. This work of June 1821 contains the basic statutes, which correspond in respect to the first grade with another set of documents in O. Dito, *Massoneria, carboneria, ed altre società segrete*, Turin, 1905. The validity of the Saint-Edme documents has generally been upheld by recent scholars such as Isambert, who, however, suggests (*Charbonnerie*, 97 n. 1) that the documents are probably of later provenance than the 1807 date suggested by Saint-Edme, whose correct name was Edme Théodore Bourg.

20. *Memoirs*, 29 no. 9.

21. Ibid., 86, describes members as "faggots for our furnaces."

22. Saint-Edme, 94–5.

23. Ibid., 94–6.

24. "Regulation of the vendita," in Saint-Edme, 47.

25. Lennhoff, 18–9.

26. *Memoirs*, 82.

27. In North Italy, much of the preparation for revolution had been done by the Masonic lodges which had been politicized by the influx of young pro-French officers prior to their forced dissolution in 1814 (R. Sòriga, *Il primo Grande Oriente d'Italia*, Pavia, 1917). This process occurred only after 1814 in Spain, but developed very rapidly (de la Fuente, *Sociedades*, I, 209–313). It also affected Portugal, but largely by way of Brazil, where the brief republican uprising of 1817 had a partly Masonic provenance (V. Chacon, *História das Idéias socialistas no Brasil*, Rio de Janeiro, 1965, 13–6). For greater detail on the genesis of the rich secret society tradition in Brazil, see Buarque de Hollanda, *História*, II (*O Brasil Monárquico*, 1), 194–216.

28. G. Spini, *Mito e realtà della Spagna nelle rivoluzioni italiane del 1820–21*, 1950. There was also borrowing from the constitution that the English had helped introduce into Sicily in 1812.

29. G. Arsh, *Eteristskoe dvizhenie v Rossii*, 1970, esp. 167 ff. For discussion of the Greek movement in its European context and interaction with other Balkan movements, see D. Djordjevic, *Révolutions nationales des peuples balkaniques 1804–1914*, Belgrade, 1965, 31–56.

30. A. Dascalakis, *Rhigas Velestinlis. La Révolution française et les préludes de l'indépendance hellénique*, 1937, 90, 78, 71; also 83–94 for the impact of the song,

61–82 for the clear separation of Rhigas's embryonic organization from the later
Hetairia. The national consciousness of the Illyrian movement also received its
earliest stimulation from revolutionary songs written by the Slovenian and Croatian
affiliates of Martinovics's Hungarian revolutionaries. See V. Bogdanov, "Hrvatska
revolucionarna pjesma iz godine 1794 i učešće hrvata i srba u zavjeri Martino-
vićevih jakobinaca," *Starine*, XLVI, 1956; I. Leshchilovskaia, *Illirizm*, 1968, 46–7.

31. N. Botzaris, *Visions balkaniques dans la préparation de la révolution grecque
(1789–1821)*, Geneva, 1962; M. Lascaris, *Le rôle des grecs dans l'insurrection serbe
sous Karageorges*, 1933, 2–21; S. Samoilov, "Narodno-osvoboditel'noe vosstanie 1821
g. v Valakhii," *Voprosy Istorii*, 1955, no. 10, 94–105, and for the interest of the
Southern Section of the Russian Decembrist movement in the Greek revolt of 1821,
see I. Iovva, *Yuzhnye dekabristy i grecheskoe natsional'no-osvoboditel'noe dvizhenie*,
Kishinev, 1963.

32. This remarkable literary infatuation, unequaled perhaps until the Spanish
Civil War evoked a similar response in the 1930s, is discussed in W. St. Clair, *That
Greece Might Still Be Free: The Philhellenes in the War of Independence*, NY, 1972.

33. In 1810, Spaniards began using the term *partido libre* to designate those
favoring a free press and constitutional reforms, substituting the term *partido liberal* with the same meaning in 1813. M. Cruz Seoane, *El primer lenguaje constitu-
cional español*, Madrid, 1968, 158.

34. A "political-literary war between liberals and serviles" was announced in an
article of that title in *El Semanario patriótico*, 1811, Aug 29, discussed in Seoane,
158–9. The contrast was heightened by hyphenating the term "servile" to accentuate
its component parts *ser-vil*, "to be vile" (157). Neutrality was not possible in the
polarized moral climate: "No seas neutral/ O servil o liberal" (166).

For another discussion of the sudden politicization of a term with multiple earlier
Spanish uses, see J. Marichal, "España y las raíces semánticas del liberalismo,"
Cuadernos, 1955, Mar–Apr, esp. 57–60.

35. This is the earliest usage suggested in the most thorough discussion of the
migration of the term from Spain (E. Halévy, *A History of the English People 1815–
1830*, NY, 1923, 81 n. 1). The usages cited therein are not included in the *Oxford
English Dictionary*, 1933, VI, 237–8, which lists a venerable tradition of nonpolitical
meanings: liberal arts (as distinct from mechanical techniques), freedom from
restraint in speech or action, and freedom from philosophical prejudice. The only
instance cited therein of a modern political usage prior to 1812 is in 1801 by Helen
Maria Williams, who uses the term only very generally in the sense of a moderate
foe of despotism. (*Sketches of the State of Manners and Opinions in the French
Republic*, L, 1801, I, 113. See also 63.)

36. *Adresse à l'Empereur par Joseph Rey de Grenoble, président du tribunal civil
de Rumilly*, 2d ed., 1815, Apr 4, 7–8 (BM).

37. Ibid., 9.

38. Unreferenced citation in P. Thureau-Dangin, *Le parti libéral sous la restauration*, 1876, 9 n. 1. The slightly later usages that began with the negative usage of
1817 are documented in G. de Bertier de Sauvigny, "Liberalism, Nationalism, Socialism: The Birth of Three Words," *Review of Politics*, 1970, Apr, 153–4. See also
E. Harpaz, *L'Ecole libérale sous la restauration, Le "Mercure" et la "Minerve"
1817–1820*, Geneva, 1968.

39. Trelat in *Paris révolutionnaire*, 227. See also F. de Corcelle, *Documents pour
servir à l'histoire des conspirations, des partis et des sectes*, 1831, and I. Tchernoff,
Le parti républicain sous la monarchie de juillet, 1901, 34 ff.

40. P. Onnis Rosa, "Propaganda e Rapporti di Società Segrete intorno al 1817
(Rey, Blanc, Buonarroti)," *Rassegna Storica del Risorgimento*, LI, 1964, Oct–Dec,
481.

41. Ibid., 483.

42. These details in Spitzer, *Old Hatreds*, esp. 212–5, apparently relying on the
account by Rey in *La Patriote des Alpes*, 1841, Oct 1.

43. On Rey and *Union*, Isambert, 82, and materials referenced, 82 n. 4; and
Lehning, 125. On what is known of Buonarroti in Grenoble, Pianzola, 127–8. The
term "union" could have been derived either from the "Union of Hearts" Lodge in
Geneva (Pianzola, 124 note 7) or from the "Perfect Union" Lodge of Grenoble
itself, on which see F. Vermale, "Joseph de Maistre, Franc-Maçon," *Annales Révolutionnaires*, II, 1909, esp. 367–8. The society "Les amis de L'Union Parfaite" formed
in Leghorn in 1796 also seems to have adopted Masonic forms for revolutionary
ends under the influence of Italian Illuminists. See Francovich, *Albori*, 89–90. Rey
was a frequent visitor to Germany (G. Weill, "Les Mémoires de Joseph Rey," *Revue
Historique*, 1928, Jan–Apr, esp. 293–6, 302–3), and was almost certainly imitating
the *Tugendbund* (Onnis, "Propaganda," 482).

44. The origins of the group are described vividly in J. Flotard, "Une nuit d'étu-

diant sous la Restauration (du 19 au 20 août 1820)," *Paris révolutionnaire,* 197–215. The overall atmosphere and organization of the student generation are discussed in Isambert, 45–84, who dates (70) the formal existence of this lodge from Jun, 1820.

45. *Paris révolutionnaire,* esp. 267–8. For details on the 5-man sub units, see the hostile, anonymous study *The Carbonari; or, the Spanish War assigned to its Real Cause,* 1823, 8 (BO). Each department, however, was to have a supervisory committee of 9 members, while "the committees of surveillance" that were responsible for security were to be 3-man groups reporting to censors elected for three months (ibid., 8, 18–20).

46. "Des conspirations et des coups d'état," in *L'Aristarque français,* 1820, Mar 14, cited by Isambert, 81, who labels it "one of the most explicit declarations of war on the regime of the Bourbons."

47. Fully itemized and described in Spitzer, *Old Hatreds,* 77–141, 189–209.

48. See the terminal section on magnetism in J. Witt, *Les sociétés secrètes de France et d'Italie,* 1830, 140 ff; also the first chapter on magnetism in A. Viatte, *Victor Hugo et les illuminés,* Montreal, 1942, 13–32; and more generally his *Sources occultes.*

49. Prati, "Autobiography," *Penny Satirist,* 1838, Jan 21, Feb 3. Mesmer counseled against revolution as most spiritualists also did. For the earlier revolutionary interest in Mesmer, see Darnton, *Mesmerism.*

50. Saitta, 1, 115, 170; also Viatte, *Hugo,* 33–53, for the general revival of interest in Swedenborg after 1830.

51. Tchernoff, 39.

52. His biography was written by the leading historian and popularizer of spiritualism, Frank Podmore: *Robert Owen, A Biography,* L, 1906, 2v.

53. Andryane, *Souvenirs,* 134, who also likens Buonarroti's words to "the oracles of the sybils."

54. Argued by Isambert, 95–6.

55. Jean-Louis Fazy was close to both Buonarroti and the Italian movement (Vuilleumier, "Buonarroti," 485–8). His more famous brother James directed the activities of the French Carbonari in the regions near Geneva. See H. Fazy, *James Fazy,* Geneva, 1887, 16–23; also A. Calmette, "Les Carbonari en France sous la restauration," *Revue de la Révolution de 1848,* IX, 1912–13, 412–4, for the infiltration of the Carbonari into France independent of Buonarrotian intermediaries.

56. *De la Gérontocratie ou abus de la sagesse des vieillards dans le gouvernement de la France,* 1828. For discussion of this subject, which concludes that one should not "ask of the notion of age that which the notion of class is alone capable of providing," see L. Maxoyer, "Catégories d'âge et groupes sociaux: Les jeunes générations françaises de 1830," *Annales,* 1938, Sep, 385–423.

57. See confirmation from a low-level participant in such an initiation in Savoy in 1821, and in meetings at the home of the former *conventionnel* and Masonic leader, François Gentil; in M. Vuilleumier, "Deux documents inédits sur le saint-simonisme, l'influence de Lamennais et Buonarroti en Savoie (1821–1831)," *Cahiers d'Histoire,* VII, 1963, no. 2, esp. 220–2. For meetings in Lyon during this period, see Andryane, *Souvenirs,* II, 153–6.

58. "An Autobiography," *Penny Satirist,* 1838, Mar 3, 1.

59. See the *Breve esposizione storica della Riforma avvenuta già trecent' anni nella Svizzera e nei Grigioni. Scritta nell'idioma tedesco . . . da G.G. degli Orelli, volgarizzata dal di lui amico D.G. dei Prati membro della società bibblica,* Chur, 1819. This and other versions are in BM as are his later works in favor of Pestalozzian education. See particularly *On the Principles and Practice of Education,* L, 1829. Orelli was professor of the cantonal school of Chur, which also later provided employment for Carl Follen and asylum for other émigré radicals.

60. Radice, "Philadelphes," 83, for an important illustration in 1820.

61. Such fears were greatest in Russia, where its influence was greatest. See A. Pypin, *Religioznyia dvizheniia pri Aleksandre I,* Petrograd, 1916; also see J. Clarke, "The Russian Bible Society and the Bulgarians," *Harvard Slavic Studies,* III, 1957, 67–103, for its interaction with political events in the Balkans.

62. Prati, *Penny Satirist,* 1838, Mar 10.

63. Ibid., Mar 3, May 4. Spitzer, *Old Hatreds,* 269 n. 175, and referenced letters from Prati and Follen to Joseph Rey in apparently Aesopian language, 268 n. 174.

64. Feuer, *Conflict,* 59.

65. Ibid., 58.

66. Their draft constitution, *Grundzüge für eine künftige deutsche Reichsverfassung,* is discussed in W. Schröder, "Politische Ansichten und Aktionen der 'Unbedingten' in der Burschenschaft," *Wissenschaftliche Zeitschrift der Friedrich-Schiller Universität Jena,* XV, 1966, no. 2, 228–9.

67. Ibid., 227.

68. Ibid., 61. See also on the "blacks" and other elements not discussed in Feuer, G. Spindler, *Karl Follen: a biographical study*, Chicago, 1916, 17–23. For the impact of French revolutionary ideas, ibid., 29–47, esp. 31–2; also R. Pregizer, "Die politischen Ideen des Karl Follen," in *Beiträge zur Parteigeschichte*, Tübingen, IV, 1912, 22 ff.

69. *Penny Satirist*, 1838, Jan 20, 2.

70. Ibid.

71. Adolf Karl Christian von Sprewitz, a young theologian from Rostock whose remarkable career is chronicled in the neglected study of Silbernagl, "Verbindungen," 786 ff. Connections with Italy through Switzerland are discussed in detail with better documentation by M. Barazzoni, "Le società segrete germaniche ed i loro rapporti con i cospiratori lombardi del 1821," *Rassegna Storica del Risorgimento*, XIX, 1932, 89–138.

72. The concise discussion by Lehning, 125–6, based largely on the autobiography of Prati, does not make this connection. Prati refers to the organizations as *Maennerband* and *Ingendband* (*Penny Satirist*, 1838, Feb 10). For details on the *Jünglingsbund* (a term that has a different, earlier usage) see H. Haupt, *Karl Follen und die giessener Schwarzen*, Giessen, 1907. The central role in the League of Youth was played by the third of Buonarroti's triumvirs, Wilhelm Snell, who had planned since 1814 to unite German revolutionaries in a single league with three levels of membership. See Silbernagl, 776, 787 ff.

73. See *The Carbonari; or The Spanish War*, 4: "The Hydra . . . reared its head in Naples and Piedmont . . . took refuge in Spain . . . once more raised its blood-stained crest."

74. N. Bulich, *Ocherki po istorii russkoi literatury i prosveshcheniia s nachala XIX veka*, St. Petersburg, 1905, II, 271. Perhaps there was some kind of subtle revenge on Pythagoras and the Greeks for inspiring so many romantic revolutionaries in the fact that modern, non-Euclidian geometry was discovered by Magnitsky's friend and protégé at Kazan, Nicholas Lobachevsky.

75. *The Carbonari; or, The Spanish War*, 10. The author identified junior officers and nonvocational students as the principal fomentors of revolution.

76. S. Turgenev, letter of Nov 1, 1820, cited in Landa, *Dukh*, 229. For the equally eloquent testimony of N. Turgenev, see Yu. Oksman, *Dekabristy. Otryvki iz istochnikov, 1823–5*, 1926, 76–82, 2.

77. Landa (*Dukh*, 48–58) discusses the influence on their group of H. Schmalz, *Über politische Vereine*, 1815, as well as other more temperate critiques of the *Tugendbund*, including that of the famed historian B. Niebuhr, who apparently originated the expression "state within a state" (51).

78. *Materialy po istorii vosstaniia dekabristov*, 1927, IV, 134–8, 159, 176; X, 283. I. Gorbachevsky, *Zapiski, pis'ma*, 1963, 313 n. 17.

79. Lotman, "Dekabrist," *Nasledie*, 55, 61–2, 65–6, 70–1, and esp. 43–7 for the cult of Schiller.

80. Pestel's sketch for the future organization of society was drawn up between 1820 and 1825 and published posthumously as "The Russian Law" (*Russkaia Pravda*—also carrying the meaning of "Truth"). For the text, P. Shchegolov, *Russkaia Pravda P.I. Pestelia*, St. Petersburg, 1906; for discussion, I. Lubin, *Zur Charakteristik und zur Quellenanalyse von Pestel's Russkaia Pravda*, Hamburg, 1930; and J. Schwarz-Sochor, "P.I. Pestel, The Beginnings of Jacobin Thought in Russia," *International Review of Social History*, III, part 1, 1958, 71–96.

81. N. Druzhinin, "Masonskie znaki P.I. Pestelia," in *Muzei revoliutsii SSSR, vtoroi sbornik statei*, 1929, 12–49; also V. Semevsky, "Dekabristy Masony," *Minuvshie Gody*, 1908, Feb, 1–50, Mar, 127–70.

82. M. Dovnar-Zapolsky, *Tainoe Obshchestvo dekabristov*, 1906, 305.

83. For links with Poland and Lithuania, P. Ol'shansky, *Dekabristy i pol'skoe natsional'no-osvoboditel'noe dvizhenie*, 1959; with the Baltic provinces, Yu. Lotman, *Uusi materjale dekabristide voitlusest balti aadli vastu*, Tartu, 1955.

84. Two particularly influential memoranda prepared for the Russian court were Alexander Sturdza, *Mémoire sur l'état actuel de l'Allemagne*, 1818, mainly on education; and Count Benckendorff's on secret societies, reprinted in M. Kovalevsky, *Khrestomatie po russkoi istorii*, 1923.

The Orenburg society spoke of enlisting the Bashkirs to help liberate Tatars in Central Asia, and then (if successful) to press on to establish a republic in India. V. Petrov, "Tainoe obshshestvo otkrytoe v Astrakhani v 1822 godu," in *Tainye obshchestva v nachale xix stoletiia*, 1926, 19; also 9–31.

The Petrozavodsk society illustrates the harmlessness of many of these ostensibly political organizations. It sought only to encourage the study of foreign things in that northern provincial center; and the assumed name chosen by its leader was

Matvei Fadeevich Don Kichot Lamanchsky, a clear allusion to the eminently non-revolutionary hero of Cervantes novel. See "Frantsuzsky parlament v Petrozavodske," *Katorga i Ssylka*, XIII, 1924, 132–4.

85. *Chto pochta, to revoliutsiia*. N. Turgenev, cited in N. Nechkina, "Dekabristy vo vsemirno-istoricheskom protsesse," *Voprosy Istorii*, 1975, no. 12, 13. This is a belated, but welcome effort by the long-time Soviet student of the movement to relate it to other contemporaneous revolutions. She includes vistas not discussed here (contemporary events in Scandinavia, the accounts of a Russian sailor back from Brazil), but never really considers Russian dependence on anything Western.

86. From the trial of Pestel in *Vosstaniia*, IV, 112, 90–1. Pestel believed the revolution would spread even to "those two opposites England and Turkey" (ibid., 105). He had earlier advocated war against Turkey for Greece in 1821 partly to hasten social change in Russia: Schwarz, 93–4.

87. Gorbachevsky, 26; Nechkina, "Dekabristy," 10–1, 16, and *Dvizhenie*, I, 305–6; and A. Mazour, *The First Russian Revolution, 1825*, Berkeley, 1937, 97 (though his reference to *Vosstaniia*, V, 31, is inaccurate). See also Mazour, 97 n. 35; Billington, *Icon*, 65a–3 n. 67, 68; and the account of the Spanish legion that defected from Napoleon's army in Russia in 1812 and its cordial links with the Russians in E. Marliani, *Espagne et ses révolutions*, 1833, 90–2.

Spanish influence was also important on the Russian poet Denis Davydov, who was the first to develop a theory of "partisan" warfare, and to popularize the term "people's war" (E. Tarle, *Sochineniia*, 1959, VII, 686). Five days before the battle of Borodino, Davydov took 50 hussars and 80 cossacks out of regular units to harass Napoleon with unconventional warfare and to recruit peasants by using a blend of Asian and European methods and choosing leaders from those proven in battle "and not from clerks in central offices" (*Opyt teorii partizanskogo deistviia*, 1819, 76–7, also 42). He stopped speaking French and wearing aristocratic clothes, arguing that "in a people's war one should not only speak the language of the masses (*iazykom cherni*), but also adopt their customs and dress" (*Dnevnik partizanskikh deistvii 1812 goda*, in *Voennye zapiski*, 1940, 208. This work, begun in 1825, too late to influence his Decembrist friends, was finished in 1838 and first published in full only in 1860: ibid., 437–8.)

Perhaps the most brilliant practitioner of guerrilla warfare against Napoleon was the northern Haitian leader Sans Souci, who was feared even by the native leader Jean Christophe, who assassinated him early in 1803 (H. Trouillot, "Le Vodou dans la guerre de l'indépendance," *Revista de Historia de America*, 1972, Jul–Dec, 87–90). Late in 1813, Napoleon himself drew up plans for a national resistance movement to the expected invasion of France for *corps de partisans* fighting with farm implements a total war with *point de règles* and the promise of *patentes de partisan* granting extensive rights to local leaders (Vermale, *Conspirateur*, 84–5.) But all these precedents were virtually unknown. The major influence from the period was the conservative Prussian general Karl von Clausewitz, whose section on the "arming of the people" for a "people's war" provided a systematic treatise on defensive guerrilla warfare: *Vom Krieg*, Bonn, 1952, 697–704, and 618 for the use of the term "partisan." His influence came much later, however, largely on Lenin; and the dominant influences for most of the nineteenth century were Italian and Polish writers to be discussed later.

88. Nechkina, after decrying the lack of study of this founding group and establishing its purely Masonic forms, lamentably fails to consider possible foreign influences on "the first Russian revolutionary organization": *Dvizhenie*, I, 141–7.

89. Druzhinin, *Ocherki*, 477–8, traces the idealization of Pythagoras to Jean-Jacques Barthélemy's "Entretien sur l'Institut de Pythagore," in his long-awaited and much reprinted four-volume *Voyage de jeune Anacharsis en Grèce*, first published in 1789.

90. Demonstrated by A. Pypin (in the notes to *Obshchestvennoe dvizhenie v Rossii pri Aleksandre I*, St. Petersburg, 1900, 547–76) and not effectively undermined by Nechkina (*Dvizhenie*, I, 185 ff.). Oksman, *Dekabristy*, 78, 82, sees the influence of the Tugendbund; Semevsky, *Idei*, 311–3, the Neapolitan Carbonari. Rey's own principal associate, Hugues Blanc, also went to Russia in 1817. See Onnis, "Propaganda," 498. For detail, see M. Wischnitzer, *Die Universität Göttingen und die Entwicklung der liberalen Ideen in Russland in ersten Viertel des 19. Jahrhunderts*, 1965, 139–79; and S. Landa, "O nekotorykh osobennostiakh formirovaniia revoliutsionnoi ideologii v rossii 1816–1821 gg.," in M. Kalushin, ed., *Pushkin i ego vremia*, Leningrad, 1962, 86–98.

Like the French Carbonari, the Russian organization worked through a Masonic lodge of friends of truth, used a root council to control regional branches, which had the characteristic French membership of 10–20. G. Perreux, *Au Temps des sociétés secrètes*, 1931, 65, points out that this number was used "to respect and at the same time get around article 291 of the penal code." Compare Nechkina, *Dvizhenie*, I, 207.

91. On the *bliustitel'*, see Nechkina, *Dvizhenie*, I, 205; on the *gradi di osservazione*, Saitta, I, 104–5. (Note also the Buonarrotian use of the mysterious letters VV, AA, which Saitta reads, 104 n. 68, as *Veri Amici*.) Buonarroti in turn may have derived the idea of an observer from Bonneville's *Social Circle*, which mentions the position OBSERVATEUR du Cercle Social already in the first issue of *La Bouche de Fer*, I, 1790, 229. The pseudonym "Observer" is still used for high-level ideological pronouncements in leading Communist journals.

92. Andryane, cited in Semevsky, 376–7.

93. Letter from Rome of Oct 27, 1819, in Saint-Edme, 211.

94. See the anonymous letter from Rome of Jul 12, 1819, in Saint-Edme, 202; also Semevsky, *Idei*, 365–7. For rich itemization of contacts throughout 1815–20, see M. Koval'skaia, *Dvizhenie karbonariev v Italii 1808–1821*, 1971, 175–202.

95. Lennhoff, 44–5. He underscores Metternich's fear that Russian diplomats in Italy might use the Carbonari against the Hapsburgs. For the impact of the Carbonari on literary figures of the era, see 74 ff., and Landa, "Konspiracje," 256, who stresses Greek as well as Italian examples.

96. The anonymous article, "Sekta pifagoreitsev," *Vestnik Evropy*, 1819, May, no. 9, 36. Oksman attributes these articles to I.I. Davydov: Druzhinin, *Ocherki*, 505.

97. Ibid., 38. The article is, in effect, continued with a second piece, "Dukh sekty sokratovoi," in the same journal, 1819, May, no. 10, 110–20.

98. *Vosstaniia*, IV, 141–2. This remains plausible despite Pestel's denial, 157. Earlier in the interrogation Pestel acknowledged links with Germany and Hungary as well as Italy, 107. Also Oksman, 212.

99. Semevsky, *Idei*, 364–7, 374–5. Semevsky, who pays more attention than later scholars to foreign influence, insisted (377) that "the relations of Russian revolutionaries to secret societies of Western Europe still require many investigations."

100. Cited in M. Dommanget, *Les idées politiques et sociales d'Auguste Blanqui*, 1957, 341.

101. A. Herzen, "Nik i Vorob'evy Gory," *Polnoe sobranie sochinenii i pisem'*, St. Petersburg, 1919, XII, 74. The two subsequently returned alone "once or twice a year" to this "place of pilgrimage."

102. Venturi, *Roots*, chapter 1, esp. 1–2; also M. Malia, *Alexander Herzen and the Birth of Russian Socialism, 1812–1855*, Cambridge, Mass., 1961, esp. the last sentence of section 2, 425.

103. S. Utechin, "Who Taught Lenin?" *Twentieth Century*, 1960, Jul, 8–16; P. Scheibert, *Von Bakunin zu Lenin: Geschichte der russischen revolutionären Ideologien, 1840–1895*, Leiden, 1956, 222–31.

104. All these groups—and many others—are listed in Radice, "History."

105. M. Emerit, "Une société secrète: Les bons cousins de la forêt d'Oran," in *La Révolution de 1848 en Algérie*, 1949, esp. 76–86.

106. The Albanian-born Ibrahim Temo, who founded in 1889 the "secret patriotic society" in Istanbul which led to the Young Turk movement, had been deeply influenced on visits to Brindisi and Naples by the role that the Carbonari had played in Italian history. See E. Ramsaur, *The Young Turks. Prelude to the Revolution of 1908*, Princeton, 1957, 15–6. See also C. Buxton, *Turkey in Revolution*, L, 1909, 44–8, for their Carbonari-like initiation rites.

Chapter 6

1. P. Vilar, "Patrie et nation dans le vocabulaire de la guerre d'indépendance espagnole," *Annales Historiques*, 1971, Oct–Dec, 529; and more fully in Seoane, "El nuevo concepto de nación," in *El primer lenguaje*, 63–81.

The Poles consistently preferred the word "nation" to "patrie," but generally preferred not to use the word "revolution." See J. Borejsza, "Portrait du révolutionnaire polonais," *Acta Poloniae Historia*, XXX, 1974, 135, 125–7.

2. *Journal d'un poète*, 1935, I, 101, cited in Leroy, *Histoire*, 382–3.

3. Barthelémy and Méry, whose *L'Émeute universelle* and *Némesis* (from which these extracts are made) are discussed and cited in F. Rudé, *L'Insurrection lyonnaise de novembre 1831. Le mouvement ouvrier à Lyon de 1827–1832*, 1969, 677–9.

4. Cited and dated Jul, 1933, by S. Barr, *Mazzini: Portrait of an Exile*, NY, 1935, 59.

5. This phrase *la grande révolte finale du prolétariat* anticipates the opening line of the *Internationale* written in 1871, and is cited from the anonymous *Aperçu sur la question du prolétariat*, which appeared in the preface to the novel *La révolte de*

Lyon en 1834 ou la fille du prolétariat, 1835, by Rudé, *Insurrection*, 719, who suggests (716) that the author "L.S." might be the former Saint-Simonian Léon Simon.

6. Blanqui viewed education as "the force that governs the world" and "the only real revolutionary agent." A. Spitzer, *The Revolutionary Theories of Louis Auguste Blanqui*, NY, 1957, 53–4. Spitzer stresses this neglected concern of the famed insurrectionist, esp. 47–64.

7. Text in R. Tucker, ed., *The Marx-Engels Reader*, NY, 1972, 350.

8. On this conflict see Garrone, *Buonarroti*, 342–85; also F. Della Peruta, "Mazzini e la Giovine Europa," *Annali*, V, 1962, 11–147; and E. Hales, *Mazzini and the Secret Societies*, L, 1956, esp. 59, 80.

9. Weill, "Buonarroti," 272–3.

10. *The Duties of Man and Other Essays*, L, 1907, 52.

11. The total numbers (almost certainly less than the 780 men Mazzini claimed) included 200 Poles and 150 Germans and Swiss. Only some 300 got as far as the border of Savoy. See Hales, *Mazzini*, 118–9; Barr, *Mazzini*, 64.

12. Circular of Apr 19, 1834, cited in Della Peruta, 19–20.

13. These figures (in H. Keller, *Das "Junge Europa," 1834–1836*, Zürich/Leipzig, 1938, 53) were probably not the peak. Schieder (*Anfänge*, 120) indicates that Young Germany increased from 172 members in mid 1835 to 268 by early 1836.

14. C. Hibbert, *Garibaldi and His Enemies*, Boston/Toronto, 1965, esp. 21–2.

15. M. Maretzek, *Revelations of an Opera Manager in 19th-Century America*, NY, 1968, 10–1.

16. Duveyrier, whose co-defendants were Rogé of the Opéra Comique, Urbain, and Cayol: *Religion Saint-Simonienne. Procès en la cour d'assises de la Seine les 27 et 28 août 1832*, 1832, 183–4 (Einaudi Foundation, Turin). The Saint-Simonians, whom we shall discuss subsequently, dreamed of including an opera house alongside a palace of industry in their temples of humanity, and made florid operatic experiments on their mission to the East that followed this trial. See P. Gradenwitz, "Félicien David (1810–1870) and French Romantic Orientalism," *The Musical Quarterly*, 1976, Oct, 471–506.

17. Vinçard aîné, *Mémoires épisodiques d'un vieux chansonnier saint-simonien*, 1878, 77, 115–6.

18. National revolutionaries, of course, often derived their practices from universalistic socialists. Garibaldi, for instance, may well have taken his tradition of singing in circles on shipboard (Hibbert, 29–30) from prior experience with this Saint-Simonian practice (Vinçard, 80 n.) during his earlier voyage to the Near East with them.

19. G. Mazzini, "Philosophy of Music" (1833) in *Selected Writings* (ed. N. Gangulee), L, 1945, 250–1. His namesake, Andrea Mazzini, gave a characteristically Italian twist to Left Hegelianism in his "Philosophy of History of Music," in Apr 1840, proclaiming that singing was the language of liberation reconciling "the infinite to the finite." Saitta, *Sinistra*, 21.

20. D. Fernandez suggests that opera was a way of organizing primordial reality especially for Italians in a way that was more comprehensive and less narrowly cerebral and personal than the theater—the latter expressing *moi*, the opera, *ça*: "L'Opéra, révélateur de la société italienne," *Annales du Centre Universitaire Méditerranéen*, XXIV, 1971, 14–5.

Recent writers on opera and revolution have dealt mainly with the self-conscious productions of Weimar Germany: A. Porter (*The New Yorker*, 1973, Jan 6, 59–62) with Brecht/Weill; W. Panofsky (*Protest in der Oper*, Munich, 1966) with the revolutionary restaging of classical operas, including the pre-revolutionary works of Handel: 37–8, 43–4, 83, and discussion, 68–73.

21. P. Lang, "French Opera and the Spirit of the Revolution," in H. Pagliaro, ed., *Irrationalism in the Eighteenth Century*, Cleveland/L, 1972, 108.

Insufficient attention has been paid to the operatic compositions and theories about the musical stage of such proto-revolutionary figures as Rousseau and Beaumarchais. The latter's plays both inspired later operas by others and helped incite the original French Revolution. Napoleon later remarked "If I had been king, a man such as he would have been locked up . . . *The Marriage of Figaro* is already the revolution in action." Cited in F. Grendel, *Beaumarchais*, L, 1977, 220.

On the other hand, too much attention may have been paid to the alleged revolutionary messages in Mozart. R. Koch's argument for Illuminist influence on Mozart's last opera is viewed skeptically by J. Chailley, *The Magic Flute: Masonic Opera*, NY, 1971, 62–5; and C. Rosen points out the purely musical reasons even for passages that sometimes excited revolutionaries (such as the rousing accompaniment to Don Giovanni's "Viva la libertà.") *The Classical Style*, NY, 1971, 94–5.

Starobinski, however, suggests a deeper link between the late Mozart operas and the coming of revolution, arguing that Mozart depicts the role confusions of a dying order ("this vertigo without future or past . . . in which social ranks are lost, and bitterness, pleasure, transvestite illusion, blame and pardon are all confused"). He finds the voluptuous passions of Don Giovanni (for whom "the only religion is liberty" and "limits exist only to be transgressed") prophetic of the early, aristocratic phase of the revolution in which the erotic energy of "the heroic and scandalous figure of Mirabeau" universalized libertarian goals. *The Magic Flute* vindicates the ideal of revolutionary reconciliation and the "solar myth of the revolution" with its final proclamation that "the rays of the sun have dispelled the night." See his "Mozart Nocturne" in "Symboles," 51–5.

22. Maréchal's program for public instruction in the revolution (*Almanach des républicains*, 1793, 1–5) began with a long section on Tell, who was credited with inventing the revolutionary red cap. The earliest American opera of which the music has survived was written in 1796 on Tell. See discussion of Benjamin Carr's *The Archers, or Mountaineers of Switzerland* and other operas on Tell in H. Weinstock, *Rossini*, NY, 1968, 446–7.

23. "Aux yeux de la nature,/ Abjurer l'imposture." *La Fête de la raison. Opéra en un acte*, 1794, 20. *Denis le Tyran. Opéra en un acte*, 1794, 11. The text dates the first performance on Aug 23, 1794 (after the fall of Robespierre). Copies in IA.

In *La Fête*, the priest promises to go to Rome and preach his new faith to "a sans-culotte pope." But the mayor—with the austere caution of those supervising revolutionary reeducation—warns that the priest must first prove himself worthy "par une conduite civique." Ibid., 22.   .

24. Knowledge of this work is derived solely from the review of a performance printed in *Gazette Nationale ou le Moniteur Universel*, Oct 22, 1793. The reprint (1847, XVIII, 171, brought to my attention by A. Soboul) identified the author only as "citoyen Saint-Just," the composer as "Mengozzi."

25. Lang, 111.

26. Z. Lissa, "Muzyka jako czynnik integracji narodowej," *Kwartalnik Historyczny*, LXXVI, 1969, no. 2, 367–73.

27. This text, recently rediscovered in separate parts (the text in Warsaw, the music in Cracow), has been restored by the director of the Warsaw Chamber Opera, S. Sutkowski, to whom I am indebted for this account.

28. H. Opieński, "Les premiers opéras polonais considérés dans leurs rapports avec la musique de Chopin," *Revue de Musicologie*, 1929, May, 92–8.

The Kurpiński opera (*Krakowiacy i Górale*) is sometimes called the *New Cracovians* to distinguish it from the earlier opera. Most reference works mysteriously persist in dating the arrival of a Polish national school of opera only from *Halka* of 1848. The *mazurka* was used as the symbol of Western arrogance in Russian national operas beginning with Glinka's *A Life for the Tsar* (Ivan Susanin) of 1836.

29. R. Schumann, *Gesammelte Schriften über Musik und Musiker*, Leipzig, 1954, I, 279.

30. Cited in A. Laster, "Musique et peuple dans les années 1830," *Romantisme*, 1975, no. 9, 77; E. Haraszti, "Berlioz, Liszt and the Rákóczi March," *Musical Quarterly*, 1940, Apr, 212.

31. Ibid., 216–8 (also 214 for other proto-revolutionary marches of this period); and S. Katonova, *Muzyka rozhdennaia revoliutsiei*, Leningrad, 1968, 16–25, for Berlioz's musical infatuations with various revolutions.

32. Review of Hoffmann's *Undine*, cited in Weber, *Sämtliche Schriften*, Berlin/ Leipzig, 1908, 129.

33. J. Deathridge, *Wagner's "Rienzi,"* Oxford, 1977, 25–8, brings out the influence on Wagner of the Saint-Simonian Heinrich Laube and the idea of art as propaganda for a new "organic" era.

34. "Engels: Volkswut mit Liebe," *Der Spiegel*, 1974, Jul 1, 88–9.

35. Gaubert, *Conspirateurs*, 47, 57; Fleischman, *Napoléon*, 105–15.

36. E. Giglio-Tos, *Albori de Libertà. Gli studenti di Torino nel 1821*, Turin/ Genoa/Milan, 1906, 27 ff.

37. Paul Brousse (then an anarchist, later a moderate "possibilist" leader of French socialism) on trial following the two attempts on the life of the German emperor in 1878, cited in J. Joll, *The Second International, 1889–1914*, NY, 1966, 15 n. 2. On Dostoevsky and the Palm-Durov circle, *Russkaia Starina*, XXX, 1881, 698.

38. Laster, 79–80; and W. Crosten, *French Grand Opera. An art and a business*, NY, 1948, 39; the tenor Adolphe Nourrit viewed Rossini as "a casualty of 1830" when the latter drew back from activism and ceased writing operas (Crosten, 115). Rossini did, however, improvise a funeral composition (that has not survived) for the Carbonari leader, Silvio Pellico, on the latter's death in 1854; Weinstock, *Rossini*, 251, 464.

39. G. Franceschetti, *La fortuna di Hugo nel melodramma italiani dell'ottocento*,

Milan, 1961, 191, shows that Verdi's adaptation of *Hernani* was but one of many, and discusses other, forgotten composers' adaptations with provocative titles such as *Il Bandito* and *Il Proscritto*.

40. Report of the director of police in Brussels to the minister of justice in the Hague, in C. Buffon, *Mémoires et documents inédits sur la révolution belge*, Brussels, 1912, 564–76. More generally, see Crosten, 112; and for the special excitement generated by the duet "Amour sacré de la Patrie," see T. Juste, *La Révolution belge de 1830 d'après des documents inédits*, Brussels, 1872, II, 11–2.

41. F. van Kalken, *Commotions populaires en Belgique (1834–1902)*, Brussels, 1936, 16–7, 23, 40–1.

42. See example in J. Legge, *Rhyme and Revolution in Germany*, L, 1918, 103.

43. T. Ybarra, *Verdi: Miracle Man of Opera*, NY, 1955, 61; modified by F. Walker, *The Man Verdi*, NY, 1962, 150–2. This opera produced a second wave of excitement when first presented at Paris in 1847 under the new title *Jerusalem*.

44. The impact of this opera is particularly stressed in R. Bosworth, "Verdi and the Risorgimento," *Italian Quarterly*, 1971, Spring, 3–16.

45. F. Toye, *Giuseppe Verdi: his life and works*, NY, 1931, 112. For the directly inspirational role of the chorus "Guerra, Guerra" from *Norma* earlier the same year in Milan, see P. Olivier, "Les Grandes Heures de La Scala," *Diapason*, 1978, Jul, 51; and, for the interaction between Juarez's revolutionary victory in battle against the Hapsburgs in Mexico the following year and a performance of the *Huguenots*, see R. Roeder, *Juarez and His Mexico*, NY, 1947, I, 264.

46. Isaiah Berlin argues for an essentially apolitical Verdi throughout in two articles entitled "The Naiveté of Verdi," *Hudson Review*, 1968, spring, 138–47; and *The New Republic*, 1979, Oct 6, 30–4.

47. L. Angeloni, *In lode d'una maravigliosa non meno italica cantate che tragica ed anche comica attrice (Giuditta Pasta), canzone, etc.*, L, 1833; and *Alla valente ed animosa gioventu d'Italia esortazioni patrie, cosi di prosa come di verso*, L, 1837.

48. *Het Aerdsch Paradys*, 49. For an example among the Germans, see the text for an opera by the Young Hegelian Arnold Ruge that was inspired by a visit to the statue of Spartacus placed in the Tuileries after the July Revolution: *Spartacus, Oper in drei Acten in Sämtliche Werke*, Mannheim, 1848, V, 235–84. He explains his intention as the fortification of a radical message with "the magic of music," 234.

49. J. Kuypers, "Les liens d'amitié de Karl Marx en Belgique (1845–48)," *Socialisme*, LVIII, 1963, 412.

50. Yu. Steklov, *Mikhail Aleksandrovich Bakunin. Ego zhizn' i deiatel'nost*, 1926, I, 125.

51. R. Wagner, *My Life*, NY, 1911, II, 466 and ff. E. Istel, *Revolution und Oper*, Regensburg, 1919, stressed the influence of Bakunin on Wagner and contrasts Wagner's and Mozart's festival centers as representative of revolutionary and prerevolutionary art respectively. See "Bayreuth oder Salzburg?" 62.

52. Gottfried Keller (describing the revolutionary poet Georg Herwegh, who collaborated with Liszt in writing revolutionary songs), cited in Legge, *Rhyme*, 203. For the relation of violence to music, see 203–19; also the collection of K. Kuhnke, "Die alten bösen Lieder," *Lieder und Gedichte der Revolution von 1848*, Ahrensburg/Paris, 1970.

53. Account by Etienne Arago in *Paris révolutionnaire*, 408 and n. 1.

54. Katonova, *Muzyka*, 17; J. Halévy, *Derniers souvenirs et portraits*, 1863, 156–7.

55. Katonova, 17.

56. Cited in J. Lucas-Dubreton, *Béranger*, 143; also 107–8. The discussion 109–52 suggests that Béranger may have been the most important single "ideologist" of the pre-1830 period. J. Puech shows how deeply he had made his mark already during the previous revolutionary period, "Les Chansons de Béranger poursuivies en 1821," *La Révolution de 1848*, Jun–Jul–Aug, 313–27.

57. *Life of Lafayette including an account of the memorable revolution of the three days of 1830*, Boston, 1835, 240–6; also M. Leroy, *Histoire des idées sociales en France. De Babeuf à Tocqueville*, 1962, 382; and the rich general discussion 377–428.

58. The young author moved, typically, from membership in an idealistic student society called "universality" (*Allgemeinheit*) through an unhappy visit to Paris to his nationalist composition. See V. Fleury, "L'Auteur du 'Deutschland, Deutschland über alles,' " *La Révolution de 1848*, 1936–37, Dec–Jan–Feb, 193–201. The crisis also produced a "Marseillaise of Peace" to oppose the flood of nationalism. See Jules Gay, *Le Socialisme rationnel et le socialisme authoritaire*, Geneva, 1869, 129–30 n.

59. For the transposition and slowing down of the old Anglo-Irish drinking song "Anachreon in Heaven" and its linkage with the Francis Scott Key poem written during the defense of Fort McHenry in 1812 into the song which formally became

the American national anthem only in 1931, see V. Weybright, *Spangled Banner. The Story of Francis Scott Key*, NY, 1935, 119–68.

The circle of 13 stars on a field of blue officially adopted for the flag of the United States on Jun 14, 1777, was probably derived from Masonic symbolism (the official proclamation of "a new constellation" in the firmament), though this is not suggested in the classic study of G. Preble, *History of the Flag of the United States of America*, Boston, 1880, 2d rev. ed., esp. 259 ff.

In the early nineteenth century, Germans and Poles like Americans used revised versions of the English national anthem: the Germans substituting "People to Arms!" (*Volk in Gewehr!*) and the Americans "Let freedom ring!" for "God save the King!" Pregizer, *Parteigeschichte*, IV, 56, also 86–90; and Askenazy, *Łukasiński*, I, 145.

Conservatives felt obliged to defend themselves with national anthems of their own—the Hapsburgs converting another Haydn melody, the Romanovs adopting a hymn previously used in the mess halls of the Prussian army. See V. Tapié, *The Rise and Fall of the Hapsburg Monarchy*, NY, 1971, 246; and "Kto kompozitor nashego nyneshniago narodnago gimna," *Russkaia muzykal'naia gazeta*, 1903, no. 52, 1313–4. For the penetration of La Marseillaise even to Siberia as a counter-anthem of protest, material should be found in E. Kuklina, "*Marsel'eza" v Sibiri*, Novosibirsk, 1975, a work announced in *Sovetskie Knigi*, 1975, no. 1, chast' 1, 14, but unavailable in any leading libraries.

60. From "Vive la liberté," which like most of Pottier's early songs is based on an air of Béranger. Text in Eugène Pottier, *Oeuvres complètes*, 1966, 33; see also his "Les trois couleurs," 36. The editor of Pottier's works, P. Brochon, has written a number of works about the rise and social importance of the protest song. See particularly *Chanson sociale de Béranger à Brassens*, 1961; also V. Skerlitch, *L'Opinion publique en France d'après la poésie politique et sociale de 1830 à 1848*, Lausanne, 1901.

These materials can be supplemented by articles by Puech (in *La Révolution de 1848*) on songs of the Saint-Simonians (XXX, 1933, Mar–Apr–May, 21–9), about Poland (XXXVI, 1939, Mar–Apr–May, 19–35), and on the revolution of 1848 itself (XXXIII, 1936, Jun–Jul–Aug, 82–97). Music and multi-lingual texts (in French, German, Polish, and English) of the Soviet versions of some of these songs were provided in *Proletarskie pesni SSSR*, 1932.

61. An eyewitness broadsheet describes the sacking of the office of Libry Bagnano and fashioning of the new flag, noting that "as in Paris the sanguary (sic) struggle was not disgraced by pillage." See *Revolution in the Netherlands, Insurrection at Brussels* np, nd (L, 1830, Aug 27). Copy in rare books collection, LC.

62. Ibid.

63. E. Ghisi, *Il tricolore italiano (1796–1870)*, Milan, 1931, exhaustively studies the derivation of the Italian from the French tricolor via Lombardy in the 1790s. See also the account of the introduction of green-white-red tricolor scarves in North Italy in the 1790s in Prati, *Penny Satirist*, 1837, Jul 8.

64. The German and Hungarian were the only non-vertical tricolors. Both became prominent only during the revolutions of 1848. The Hungarian colors were a conscious reversion to those of Maria Theresa; the German colors, a rejection of the vertical blue-red-green adopted by the Burschenschaften. (See P. Wentzcke, *Quellen und Darstellungen zur Geschichte der Burschenschaft und der deutschen Einheitsbewegung*, Heidelberg, 1939, XVI, 217–23 (and 199–259 for the addiction of German student organizations to colors). The Italian colors represented a rejection of the red, white, and black of the Carbonari.

65. V. Valentin, *Das hambacher Nationalfest*, 1932, 32–7.

66. "Die vielen Farben sind Deutschlands Not,/ . . . Nur eine Farb' und ein Vaterland!" ibid., 37.

67. "Notre drapeau n'a plus assez du ciel de France,/ Des minarets d'Egypte il faut qu'il se balance." Les Chants du travailleur. *Recueil de chansons et poésies sociales avec 37 airs notes en musique publié par Vinçard aîné*, 1869, 171.

68. ". . . déroulons à la brise/ L'oriflamme des travailleurs,/ . . . qui marchent en avant vers la terre promise!" ibid. ". . . déployez votre immense drapeau,/ . . . Qu'à l'univers il serve de flambeau," ibid., 67. Other examples of the flag metaphor are ibid., 1–2, 99.

69. M. Dommanget, *Histoire du drapeau rouge des origines à la guerre de 1939*, 1967, 45, 48–9. Asa Briggs has indicated to me that a black flag appeared at the time of the Peterloo massacre in 1819. The black flag appeared in Lyon about a month after Reims (47).

70. Carefully established ibid., 51.

71. Ibid., 55.

72. Tchernoff, 271. Others imply that this was already characteristic of the demonstrations of 1831. See Leroy, *Histoire*, 399.

73. A. Bardoux, *Les dernières Années de Lafayette, 1792–1834*, 1893, 422–3. Seen generally by moderates as a reminder of the Terror, the flag was blamed even by those who used it for the failure of their uprising: Dommanget, 55–6, 59–60.

74. Dommanget, 58.

75. Ibid., 50, 69 ff. Dommanget suggests that the use of the red flag was by no means as widespread in Paris in 1848 as subsequent revolutionary historiography usually contends. Among other studies, F. Wendel, *Die rote Fahne*, Hamburg, 1927, adds details on international usage but without documentation, and J. Slayton, *The Old Red Flag*, Pittsburgh, n.d., 12–3 (PU) traces modern usage to Pulaski's legions during the American Revolution and includes ingenious, fanciful derivations from classical antiquity. A. Schoyen, "From Green Flag to Red" (*The Chartist Challenge*, L, 1958, 171–98) shows that the red flag made partial incursion into the vacuum left during 1848 by the discrediting of the green banner of the Chartists.

An unpublished essay of E. Gombrich (kindly lent me by the author) traces an anticipation of the red-for-tricolor substitution in the replacement of the *bonnet rouge* (the Phrygian cap) for the *cocarde tricolor* during the original French Revolution. The red cap had social rather than political overtones, since it was taken from a Swiss regiment that had rebelled against aristocratic officers in Aug 1790, been subsequently sentenced as galley slaves, then lionized in Paris as popular heroes after amnesty in Nov 1791: *The Dream of Reason. Propaganda Symbolism in the French Revolution*, 13–6. The publication by the Bavarian government of alleged Illuminist documents during the revolution attributed the red cap to the Illuminists: *Die neusten Arbeiten des Spartacus und Philo in dem Illuminaten-Orden*, Munich, 1794, 71.

76. Goodwyn Barmby, the original English popularizer of the word communist, "Letters from Paris," no. 1, *Howitt's Journal*, III, 1848, Mar 25, 207.

77. Ibid., no. 7, 1848, May 6, 301. Barmby contrasts this "heavenly iris that blooms as a sign of hope" with the American flag, which "may have its stars for its states, but it also has its stripes for its slaves."

78. Ibid. Garibaldi already excluded the cross of Savoy from the tricolored banner of his Italian legion in Brazil in 1836: Parris, *Lion of Caprera*, 47. The colors were often thought to symbolize the moral virtues of each people—the green, white, and red of the Italian banner allegedly representing faith, hope, and charity.

79. *Lettre . . . à . . . Condorcet*, 31.

80. *Hymne des combats*, 5 ff.

81. Conclusion of Cloots, *La République universelle*, 20. Capitalization in the original.

82. Michelet, *The People*, L, 1846, 26.

83. Ibid., 161.

84. Ibid., 137.

85. The remark, at a meeting of Jan 6, 1834, precipitated "movement and agitation" in the chamber. M. Voyer D'Argenson, *Discours et opinions*, 1846, II, 414.

86. G. Salvemini, *Mazzini*, L, 1956, 35 n. 1; Hales, *Mazzini*, 139–42, 205–6.

87. *Livre du peuple*, 185, cited Leroy, 445.

88. The former two are hymns by Adolphe Louis Constant, a former priest and later founder of modern French occultism under the name Eliphas Lévi (See P. Chacornac, *Eliphas Lévi. Rénovateur de l'occultisme en France*, 1926, 112); the *Evangile du peuple* of 1840 was by Alphonse Esquiros, who was imprisoned for identifying Christ as a "liberator and revolutionary," but went on to equate democracy with the Kingdom of God in his *Histoire des montagnards*, 1847 2v. See A. Zévaès, "L'Agitation communiste de 1840 à 1848," *La Révolution de 1848*, 1926, Dec, 1036–9.

89. Song of Vinçard, cited in Leroy, 408.

90. P. Viallaneix, *La Voie royale. Essai sur l'idée de peuple dans l'oeuvre de Michelet*, 1959, 292–306. See also 241–8 on the impact of 1830, and 439–71 on the philosophy of nature with which his idea of the people was undergirded.

91. Viallaneix's paraphrase of Michelet's ideal in *Voie*, 538. Compare (Salvemini, *Mazzini*, 51) Mazzini's idea of nations as "the individuals of humanity."

92. Cited in G. Monod, *La Vie et la pensée de Jules Michelet*, 1923, II, 231.

93. See M. Kridl, *Mickiewicz i Lamennais; studyum porównawcze*, Warsaw, 1909; and "Two champions of a New Christianity: Lamennais and Mickiewicz," *Comparative Literature*, 1952, summer, 239–67; J. Bourilly, "Mickiewicz and France," in W. Lednicki, ed., *Adam Mickiewicz in World Literature*, Berkeley/Los Angeles, 1956, 243–76; and L. Mickiewicz, "Michelet et Adam Mickiewicz," *Revue des Deux Mondes*, XX, 1924, 168–87. E. Krakowski, *Adam Mickiewicz, philosophe mystique*.

Les sociétés secrètes et le messianisme européen après la révolution de 1830, 1935, lacks documentation and does not cover as much as its title promises; but it indicates the occult roots of Mickiewicz's prophecy—a theme more fully developed in W. Weintraub, *Literature as Prophecy, Scholarship and Martinist Poetics in Mickiewicz's Parisian Lectures*, Gravenhage, 1959. For the lectures themselves, see *Les Slaves. Cours professé au Collège de France (1840–41)*, 1849, 5v; for the journal see *Trybuna Ludów*, Cracow, 1935. The official newspaper of the present-day Polish Communist party reverts back to the Babeuvist title, *Trybuna Ludu*.

For an overall survey of the often underappreciated impact of the Polish revolutionary tradition on Europe generally, see H. Jabłoński, *Międzynarodowe znaczenie polskich walk narodowyzwoleńczych XVIII i XIX w*, 1966.

94. De la Hodde, *Histoire*, 89–90.

95. Kukiel, "Lelewel, Mickiewicz," 74–6, and references.

96. Raphaël, "Les rapports polono-israëlites et l'insurrection de 1830–31," *La Révolution de 1848*, 1926, Apr–Dec, 788–93.

97. B. Hepner, *Bakounine et le panslavisme révolutionnaire*, 1950, 223–4, and esp. "Le messianisme polonais," 215–35.

98. English police statistics in A. Lehning, "The International Association (1855–1859)," *International Review of Social History*, III, 1938, 201. Borejsza ("Portrait," 136) estimates that 8–9,000 Poles resettled in Western Europe during the "great emigration" after 1831. The literature linking Polish revolutionaries with the revived Carbonari and other groups closer to Buonarroti than to Mazzini is reviewed with convincing skepticism by W. Zajewski, "Prądzyński, Lelewel i mit o Karbonarskim podziemiu," *Kwartalnik Historyczny*, LXXI, 1964, no. 4, 977–85.

99. The "national revolution" in Poland was said to be that of the Lithuanians and Russians as well. See the brochure (including Lelewel's speech, 22–3), *Les Polonais les lithuaniens et les russiens celebrent les premiers anniversaires de leur révolution nationale du 29 novembre et du 25 mars 1831*, 1832. There was also a Lithuanian and White Russian national society founded on Dec 10, 1831, in Paris, just five days before Lelewel's Polish national committee. See A. Barszczewska, "Société lituanienne et des territoires biélorusses et ruthènes à Paris 1831–1836," *Acta Baltico-Slavica*, VI, 1969, 75–102.

100. *The People*, 87.

101. The thesis that the idea of the socialist potential of the peasant commune was borrowed by Bakunin and Herzen from Lelewel (B. Nikolaevsky, "Za vashu i nashu volnost'—stranitsi iz istorii russko-polskikh otnoshenii," *Novy zhurnal*, 1944, no. 7, 252–76) is viewed skeptically by Malia (*Herzen*, 473) and by A. Walicki (in a joint seminar meeting with Nikolaevsky at Harvard University in 1959). Glorification of ancient Slavonic communalism was widespread in the Polish emigration, and could have come from many figures other than Lelewel. See, for instance, P. Brock on the leading figure of the *Lud Polski*, "Zeno Świętosławski, a Polish forerunner of the Russian *Narodniki*," *American Slavic and East European Review*, XIII, 1954, no. 4, 566–87; and, more fully, his *Revolutionary Populism in Poland*, Toronto, 1977, which contends that Poland in effect produced a full-fledged agrarian populist movement between its revolutions of 1830 and 1863, anticipating most of the main features of the better-known Russian movement that followed.

For the mutation of the "conservative utopia" involved in Slavophile idealization of the peasant commune into the revolutionary utopianism of the populists, see A. Walicki, "Slavophilism and Populism: Alexander Herzen's 'Russian Socialism,'" in *The Slavophile Controversy. History of a Conservative Utopia in Nineteenth-Century Russian Thought*, Oxford, 1975, 580–601.

102. M. Serejski, *Joachim Lelewel 1786–1861. Sa vie et son oeuvre*, Wrocław/Warsaw/Cracow, 1961, 56.

103. *The People*, 132, and the section, "Association of the Fishermen of Normandy," 131–7.

104. H. Weisser, "The British Working Class and the Cracow Uprising of 1846," *Polish Review*, 1968, winter, 3–18, esp. 9–10.

105. Whereas Bakunin and an Old Believer bishop from within the Hapsburg Empire had been the only Russians among the 340 delegates at the Prague Slavic Congress of 1848, Russian representatives and pro-Russian declarations completely dominated the Moscow Slavic Congress of 1867. For this transformation of panslavism from a radical cause into reactionary Russian doctrine, see M. Petrovich, *The Emergence of Russian Panslavism, 1865–1870*, NY, 1956.

For neglected conspiratorial activities of this period in Lithuania and White Russia, see D. Fajnhauz, *Ruch konspiracyjny na Litwie i Bialorusi 1846–1848*, Warsaw, 1965. For the Balkans in the 1840s, see Djordjević, *Revolutions*, 66–85.

The revolutionary idea of a Slavic peasant uprising against landowners had conservative origins in the agitation of the 1840s near Lublin by a Catholic priest, Piotr

Ściegienny, using a forged appeal of Pope Gregory XVI to organize a clandestine movement to banish landowners and unite with the oppressed Russian peasantry. See I. Narsky, "Razvitie revoliutsionno-demokraticheskoi filosofskoi mysli v Pol'she 30-40-kh godov XIX veka," *Moskovsky universitet, uchenye zapiski* (fil. fak.), 169, 1954, 87–91. This technique was repeated in the Ukraine thirty years later in the forged appeal of the tsar for insurrection against the upper classes. See Venturi, 582–3.

106. Large segments from the text (from *La Réforme*) are in Venturi, *Roots*, 47–9. Venturi (48) considers this "the first time . . . that the forces and problems of what was later to become Russian populism had been singled out and publicly described."

107. Cited in Venturi, *Roots*, 56. See also Carr, *Bakunin*, 163–89, for discussion of the *Appeal*. The text with other important materials on Bakunin's activities during this period is in J. Pfitzner, *Bakuninstudien*, Prague, 1932, 78–106.

The identification of Slavs with peace and democracy goes back to Herder, and was forcefully developed in the 1820s by the Slovak romantic poet Ján Kollár. See H. Kohn, *Pan-Slavism*, Notre Dame, 1953, 16; T. Masaryk, *Meaning of Czech History*, Chapel Hill, 1974, 55–6.

Although there was no indigenous version of the revolutions of 1848 within the Russian Empire, the Ukrainian Society of Cyril and Methodius contrasted Slavdom with Muscovitism, just as the revolutionary "Catechism of the Russian People" in Paris contrasted a "People's" with a "Tsarist" Russia. See the key document *Zakon bozhii*, reprinted in P. Zaionchkovsky, *Kirillo-mefodievskoe obshchestvo*, 1959, 156–60; and I. Golovin's "Katekhizis russkogo naroda," in "Pervaia revoliutsionnaia broshiura russkoi emigratsii," *Zven'ia*, 1932, I, 195–217.

108. Viallaneix, *Voie*, 471–9, juxtaposes the ultimately nonrevolutionary, Christian understanding of "the people" of Lamennais with the more revolutionary outlook of the mature Michelet.

109. Text of the letter of Sep, 1851, subsequently entitled "The Russian People and Socialism," is in Herzen, *From the other shore and the Russian people and socialism* (intr. I. Berlin), L, 1956, 165–208; discussion in Malia, *Herzen*, 395–409.

110. Phrase used by Michelet in *Légendes*, 239. For his writings on Romania in the 1850s, see 209–59.

111. C. Bodea, *The Romanians' Struggle for Unification—1834–1849*, Bucharest, 1970, 130 ff.

112. Ibid., 117 ff. See also I. Breazu, *Michelet si românii*, Cluj, 1935; and the unpublished Harvard doctoral dissertation of J. Campbell, "French Influence and the Rise of Rumanian Nationalism. The Generation of 1848," 1940.

113. Details from the volume commemorating the hundredth anniversary of his death in 1852: *Nicolae Bălcescu. A Fighter for Freedom*, Bucharest, 1953, which indicates (67–8) that the coded statutes of the Brotherhood have not been preserved.

114. Bodea, 120. For the influence of Mickiewicz on Bălcescu, see A. Zub, "Les Rapports roumano-polonais à la veille de la révolution de 1848," *Revue Roumaine d'Histoire*, 1975, no. 4, 623–4.

115. A. Otetea, ed., *The History of the Romanian People*, Bucharest, 1970, 359, 372. As elsewhere in the romantic era, theatrical performances played an important role in arousing national revolutionaries. Just as the Greeks in Bucharest had been aroused to action in 1819 by a performance of Voltaire's *Brutus*, so Bălcescu was inspired by the youthful demonstration triggered by a performance of Shakespeare's *Julius Caesar* in Bucharest in January 1848. The flash point came when Brutus cried out "Death to tyrants!" See the only partly fictitious account of C. Petrescu, *Un Om între oameni*, Bucharest, 1956.

116. For the development of this idea among the populists, see "The first myth: belief in 'the people,' " in J. Billington, *Mikhailovsky and Russian Populism*, Oxford, 1956, 86–98.

117. L. Ravenna, *Il Giornalismo mazziniano*, Florence, 1967, 72 n. 2, 282.

118. Salvemini, *Mazzini*, 35–8.

119. See Mazzini's response to the invitation of the international committee at the head of the "Rapport annuel du comité international à toutes les nationalités" of Mar, 1856, reprinted in Lehning, "Association," 251.

120. As characterized by Herzen in his letter to Turgenev of Jul 20, 1862, in *My Past and Thoughts*, L, 1927, VI, 20. On his links with Mazzini, see W. Giusti, "A.I. Herzen e i suoi rapporti con Mazzini e l'Italia," in *L'Europa Orientale*, 1935. Giusti's *Mazzini e gli slavi*, Milan, 1940, makes clear the continuing importance of the Polish national cause to Mazzini, but also reveals (237–55) a growing interest in Russia after 1848. The romantic hero of the 1848–9 events in Italy, Giuseppe Garibaldi, also had strong feelings towards the Poles. See A. Lewak, *Corrispondenza polacca de G. Garibaldi*, Cracow, 1932.

121. For qualification of this trend see M. Tournier, "Le Mot 'Peuple' en 1848: désignation social ou instrument politique?" *Romantisme*, 1975, no. 9, 6–20, an anticipation of his forthcoming book *Vocabulaire ouvrier en 1848, Essai de Lexicometrie*.

122. Tactical borrowing from native Americans may have combined with ideological mobilization to give the militia in the American Revolution some of the qualities of a modern "people's liberation" army: J. Shy, "The Military Conflict as a Revolutionary War," in S. Kurtz and J. Hutson, eds., *Essays on the American Revolution*, Chapel Hill, 1973; also F. Pogue, *The Revolutionary Transformation of the Art of War*, Washington, D.C., 1974.

The most remarkable colonial American anticipation of irregular revolutionary warfare is, however, the neglected figure of James Smith of Kentucky, who was captured and adopted by Indians at age 18 in 1755 and applied their methods to frontier fighting after escaping in 1759. His militia in western Pennsylvania, the Blackboys, wore loin clothes, leggings, and painted faces; and in 1767 he raided Fort Bedford, which became "the first British fort in America that was taken by what they called American rebels." *An account of the remarkable occurrences in the life and travels of Col. James Smith*, appendix and notes by W. Darlington, Cincinnati, 1907, 123.

Smith tried unsuccessfully to gain United States government support for irregular warfare in 1777 and again in 1799. He wished to avoid the British mistake of trying to wage conventional warfare in the New World, urging his fellow Americans to emulate the native Americans' closeness to nature, emphasis on proven merit, and ability to tie up superior numbers through camouflage, ambush, and surprise. His original *Remarkable Occurrences* (Lexington, Kentucky, 1799) was expanded and revised shortly before his death as *A treatise on the mode and manner of Indian War. Their tactics, discipline and encampments, the various methods they practice in order to obtain the advantage, by ambush, surprise, surrounding, etc.*, Paris, Kentucky, 1812.

123. The work that came closest to suggesting distinctive new forms of warfare for a revolutionary regime was the almost unnoticed brochure written by Bonneville's friend, the Scottish soldier of fortune John Oswald. He drew on previous experience with the British army in India and America for his *Le tactique du peuple ou nouveau principe pour les évolutions militaires, par lequel le peuple peut facilement apprendre à combattre par lui-même et pour lui-même, sans le secours dangereux des troupes réglées* (BN), dated late 1792 or early 1793 by Ioannisian, *Idei*, 38.

The basic revolutionary drive toward radical simplification is evident in Oswald's announced determination "to discover a principle of movement that is simple, easy and natural," but which is only sketched in the 12-page pamphlet.

124. A. Gieysztor, etc., *History of Poland*, Warsaw, 1968, 407.

125. *Kościuszko au peuple français*, Paris, n.d., 35. The copies in LC and BM are catalogued with the dates 1792 and 1796 respectively. The text makes it appear to be an appeal addressed after the uprising of 1794.

126. *Czy Polacy wybić się mogą na niepodległość?*, first published anonymously in Paris (fictitious place designation of Perekop na Donu), 1800, reissued with intr. by E. Halicz, Warsaw, 1967, and attributed to Kościuszko's secretary, Józef Pawlikowski. M. Kukiel attributes the work to Kościuszko himself: "Les origines de la stratégie et de la tactique des insurrections polonaises au XVIIIe et au XIXe siècle," *Revue internationale d'histoire militaire*, 1952, no. 12, 326–45.

The work, inspired and probably dictated by Kościuszko, had a seminal if delayed impact on the Polish revolutionary tradition. See Kukiel, "Military Aspects of the Polish Insurrection of 1863–64"; *Antemurale*, 1963, VII-VIII, 363–96; and articles in W. Biegański, etc., eds., *Histoire militaire de la Pologne*, Warsaw, 1970, 114–92.

127. *Czy Polacy*, 69, cited in *Histoire militaire*, 132.

128. On the Polish tradition of the *arrière-ban* dating at least from the resistance to the Swedish invasion of 1655, see J. Kowecki, *Pospolite ruszenie w insurekcji 1794*, 1963, and *Histoire militaire*, 133 ff. E. Halicz, *Partisan Warfare in Nineteenth Century Poland. The Development of a Concept*, Odense, 1975, attaches seminal importance to this tract of Kościuszko for Europe more broadly as well as for the Polish tradition.

129. See *Histoire militaire*, 132, 160. This is, of course, the literal meaning of the Spanish *guerrilla*.

130. Ibid., 124–7; also his manual *Manoeuvres of horse artillery adapted to the service of the United States*, NY, 1812; and E. Brink, "Kościuszko—Forefather of American Artillery," *Field Artillery Journal*, XXII, 1932, May–Jun, 303–13.

131. Cited in E. Alexander, "Jefferson and Kościuszko," *Pennsylvania Magazine*

of History and Biography, 1968, Jan, 99. Kościuszko's extraordinary will commissioned Jefferson to use his entire legacy to purchase either freedom or education for Negroes: ibid., 92–3.

132. This organization represented for M. Kukiel the first clear adaptation of Carbonari forms into eastern Europe: "Lelewel, Mickiewicz and the Underground Movements of European Revolution (1816–33)," *Polish Review*, 1960, summer, 63.

133. Radice (*Ars*, LIV, 162) dates the founding from 1821; C. Francovich (*Idee sociali e organizzazione operaia nella prima metà dell'800, 1815–1847*, Milan, 1959, 49) inclines towards 1823. Garrone, 335–6 n. 2, discusses the Greek name and origin of the society, inclining toward a later date of beginnings. The leaders ritually adopted the names of ancient Roman—particularly military—heroes. See A. Ghisalberti, *Cospirazioni del risorgimento*, Palermo, 1938, 39, also 31–58.

134. N. Naldoni, "Sulla setta degli Apofasimèni," *Atti del XXVII congresso per la storia del risorgimento*, Milan, 1948, 467; and 465–72.

135. Ibid., 467.

136. Ibid. Many Italians (including Bianco) fought at some time with the French in Algeria. See E. Michel, *Esuli italiani in Algeria (1815–1861)*, Bologna, 1935.

137. Prati, *Penny Satirist*, 1838, Mar 31.

138. Ibid., Mar 17, 2.

139. *Della forza nelle cose politiche ragionamenti quattro di Luigi Angeloni Frusinate dedicati all'Italica nazione*, L, 1826, Part II, 151 ff., also 166. Angeloni denounces the powers of Europe for reneging on their promise to free and unite Italy (203–4), and finds General Malet, who "served both France and Italy," the only admirable leader of the era (206–7, also 211).

140. Ibid., the third "ragionamente," 1 ff.

141. Ibid., 61–88. Angeloni describes himself as "one of the first promoters (*promovitore*) in France of that true American form of liberty (*quella vera libertà americana*)," 207. Earlier in his first political work of 1814, he had seen both the USA and the Swiss federations as models for Italian unification. *Sopra l'ordinamento che aver dovrebbono i governi d'italia, ragionamento di Luigi Angeloni, Frusinate*, Paris, 1814, 12–3. See also his *Dell'Italia uscente il settembre del 1818, ragionamenti IV di Luigi Angeloni, frusinate, dedicati all'italica nazione*, Paris, 1818, 2v. There is no adequate study of Angeloni, who ended up in a London poorhouse in 1842, and died the following year. (See L. Fasso, *Lettere di esuli*, Lucca, 1915, 126–7.) The best work is still G. Romano-Catania, *Luigi Angeloni e Federico Confalonieri*, Milan, 1898.

142. M. Battistini, *Esuli italiani in Belgio (1815–1861)*, Florence, 1968, 205.

143. *Della Guerra nazionale d'insurrezione per bande, applicata all'Italia. Tratato dedicato ai buoni Italiani da un amico del paese*, Italy, 1830, 2v (two copies of this rare work, apparently published in Malta, are in the Brera, Milan).

144. L. Carpi, *Il Risorgimento italiano*, Milan, 1887, III, 176; Battistini, *Esuli*, 376–8; and Della Peruta's bibliographically rich short biography in *Dizionario biografico degli Italiani*, 1968; X, 226–9. There is no adequate modern study—and no full-length biography at all—of this remarkable figure. For the relationship of his book to the rich history of Italian insurrection, see P. Pieri, "Carlo Bianco conte di Saint Jorioz ed il suo trattata sulla guerra partigiana," *Bollettino Storico-Bibliografico Sub-Alpino*, LV, 1957, 373–424; LVI, 1958, 77–104; bibliography 375–6.

145. V. Parmentola, "Carlo Bianco, Giuseppe Mazzini e la teoria dell'insurrezione," *Bollettino Domus Mazziniana*, V, 1959, no. 2, 5–40; also Garrone, 333–42, on the interconnections amidst the excitement of 1830–1 between Buonarroti and Mazzini. Though the collaboration between national and social revolutionaries did not long survive the disaster in Savoy, Bianco's influence on Mazzini enabled him to exercise an enduring, if largely unacknowledged impact on the revolutionary tradition. See Pieri, 95–104. Allusions are made to a revision of this work *Manuale pratico del rivoluzionario italiano desunto del trattato sulla guerra d'insurrezione per bande*, which was apparently an incompleted manuscript drawn up in connection with preparations for the second Savoy expedition of 1833, though Pieri refers to it as if it were published "(Italia, 1833)," 374–5.

146. *Della Guerra*, I, xii, lxx, 51.

147. Ibid., 170 ff.

148. Ibid., 198 ff.; see also Pieri, 79, and 290–2, for the higher titles and complex staffing under figures like the "great Celiarca" and the "Topographer-General."

149. Pieri, 77.

150. *Della Guerra*, I, 25 ff.

151. Ibid., 19, also 18 ff. and Pieri, 382.

152. For Bianco on weapons and clothes, see *Della Guerra*, I, 176 ff.

153. *Della Guerra*, I, 301.

154. For the nature and impact of the Italian insurrectionist tradition prior to 1848, see Francovich, "L'azione rivoluzionaria," in *Idee*; also S. Mastellone, *Mazzini e la "Giovine Italia,"* Pisa, 1960. Mazzini's own basic theory was contained in his *Della guerra d'insurrezione conveniente all'Italia*, Marseilles, 1833.

155. According to the introduction of F. di Tondo to the new edition of Pisacane, *Guerra combattuta in Italia negli anni 1848–1849*, Turin, nd., 3. The work, originally completed in Lugano on Oct 25, 1850, was first published there in 1851.

156. Ibid., 200–1, 187.

157. Ibid., 190.

158. Ibid., 195, 202.

159. Ibid., 191–3, 206.

160. L. Cassese, *La Spedizione de Sapri*, Bari, 1969, 12–5.

161. Kościuszko wrote in his postmortem of 1800 (*Czy Polacy*, 90, cited in *Histoire militaire*, 132) that "there was no arm capable of resisting the scythe and no army in Europe that one could not have defeated with scythes." On the myth of the scythe see Halicz, 44–5, 175, 183.

162. *Histoire militaire*, 176–7, for many examples and references. The Polish fascination with light, portable weapons may also have owed something to the two pistols (engraved *E pluribus unum*) that Kościuszko had received as a farewell gift from George Washington (ibid., 125).

Kukiel suggests a possible influence of Kościuszko on Bianco ("Military Aspects," 368–9), though his speculation seems questionable in view of his misidentification of Bianco elsewhere ("Problèmes des guerres d'insurrection au XIX siècle," *Antemurale*, 1955, 80). Bianco's work is wrongly attributed to Mazzini in *Histoire militaire*, 181. Halicz shows Bianco to have been influenced by Kościuszko (21), and to have influenced key Poles (77–9) as well as Mazzini (45, 92–3).

163. Wojciech Chrzanowski, *O wojnie partyzanckiej*, 2nd ed., Paris, 1835. He stressed the importance of sudden attack and ambushes (78–9) and escalated (77) the preferred hand firearm from the pistol to the "short carbine." Even an extreme monarchist, Ludwik Bystrzonowski, contributed to the discussion of partisan uprisings. See *Histoire militaire*, 173–4 and n. 16.

164. P. Brock, "The Political Program of the Polish Democratic Society," *Polish Review*, 1969, summer, 1; Kukiel, "Military Aspects," 370–2.

165. Written by a friend of Mazzini, Karol Stolzman, *Partyzantka; czyli, Wojna dla ludów powstających najwłaściwsza*, Paris, 1844. See also H. Kamieński (pseudonym Filaret Prawdowski), *O prawdach żywotnych narodu polskiego*, Brussels, 1844. Lelewel insisted in the same year that "national insurrection" was "the surest means of arriving at national independence." *Histoire de Pologne racontée par un oncle à ses neveux*, Paris/Lille, 1844, I, 328.

166. The remarkable treatise, *Notes sur les fusées incendiaires*, was prepared for the liberal commander-in-chief of Poland (and hero of the Decembrists), Grand Duke Constantine. It was lithographed in 1819, and published in German in Weimar, 1820. Bem also later published a treatise on the military use of "steam machines." See L. Komuda, "Constructor and Hero," *Poland*, 1973, Dec, 31–2.

167. *Katechizm demokratyczny*, Paris, 1845, 49; cited Halicz, 168. His section, "Henryk Kamieński's 'People's War,'" for extended treatment (156–89).

168. *Wojna ludowa przez X. Y. Z.*, Bendlikon, 1866; cited in Halicz, 159. This pioneering treatise with its concept of total self-reliance and mass mobilization for insurrection was translated into French for use in the underground resistance to Nazi occupation as *Insurrection est un Art*, tr. J. Tepicht, 1943. See Walicki, "Problem of Revolution," 36. Kamieński believed in ideological as well as military mobilization, and just before he completed his *People's War* in 1863, he founded and edited a non-periodical journal in Geneva with another name that was to be taken over later by the Russians: *Prawda* (Truth).

169. Cited in Halicz, 160.

170. *Instrukcja powstańcza*, Paris, 1862, discussed Kukiel, "Military aspects," 371–3.

171. Cabet, *Révolution de 1830 et situation présente*, 1832, 176.

172. Gaubert, *Conspirateurs*, esp. 47, 57; N. Forssell, *Fouché the man Napoleon feared*, NY, 1970, 122 ff. The first Jacobin plot was immediately followed by the first (and more destructive) royalist one, exploding the first "infernal machine."

173. R. Burnand, *L'Attentat de Fieschi*, 1930.

174. The English translation by Bronterre O'Brien, *History of Babeuf's Conspiracy for Equality*, L, 1836, was subsequently widely reprinted and excerpted. It allegedly sold about 50,000 copies in a short space of time (B. Barère, *Mémoires*, 1844, IV, 92). The suggestion of Dommanget, *Pages*, 12–3, repeated by Saitta, that there was a first English edition in 1828 is refuted by Garrone, *Buonarroti*, 413 n. 1. The best

edition of the original French work (whose full title is *Conspiration pour l'égalité dite de Babeuf, suivie du procès auquel elle donna lieu, et des pièces justificatives, etc., etc., par Ph. Buonarroti*) is edited with a preface by G. Lefebvre, 1957, 2v.

175. Buonarroti's memorandum commemorating Bastille Day, 1828, written just before publication of his *Conspiracy*. Saitta, II, 92. This metaphor, later invoked by Lenin, was used by Nodier in 1815 (*Histoire*, 28) and by Jean Witt, another historian of secret societies in 1830 (*Sociétés*, 6 n. 1).

176. Saitta, II, 136–9. Buonarroti did not include Russia in his list of failed revolutions, perhaps because the Decembrists had developed a variety of ideas on this subject (See M. Murav'ev, "Ideia vremennogo pravitel'stva u dekabristov i ikh kandidaty," in *Tainye obshchestva*, 68–87). The main group called for a three-month rule by provisional power during which full authority would be transferred to a new national assembly (84); but some Decembrists envisaged the provisional government affecting radical social reforms (70).
There is no certainty that Buonarroti had any contact with Decembrists until the mid-1830s through the brothers N. and A. Turgenev in Paris (see the latter's "Parizh," *Sovremennik*, 1836, no. 1, 275), though Semevsky suggests the possibility of more extensive contacts (*Idei*, 536).

177. Mazauric, *Babeuf*, 173–4. The author reveals the sensitivity common to Leninists who live in Western democracies about the reluctance of "provisional" revolutionary governments ever to "wither away." He rebukes the editor of Babeuf's work, Lefebvre, for "not making enough of a distinction between the organization of the provisional political and social dictatorship . . . and the period beyond for which one foresees, as Buonarroti tells us, the progressive participation of all citizens in the direction of the Communist state," 173 n. 1.

178. Saitta, II, 139.

179. Saitta, I, 125. A good overall discussion of the origin of this idea is in Garrone, "La dittatura rivoluzionaria," in *Buonarroti*, 310–22.

180. Saitta, II, 138.

181. *Conspiration*, I, 114–5.

182. Cited in Garrone, 338. Buonarroti called for "the wisdom to invest a man of the temper of Robespierre with a dictatorship." *Conspiration*, I, 114 n. 1.
For Bianco's writings on the need for a strong provisional government to rule Italy between the disappearance of Hapsburg power and "perfect liberation," see Pieri, 77; and Bianco, *Della Guerra*, I, 256–7, other phrases I, 198 ff., and the section *Del governo provisionale fino alla perfetta liberazione d'Italia*, II, 207–44. He argued that the tragic experience of Spain argued against either dissipating authority in assemblies or prematurely receiving foreign ambassadors. Hence the need for a *Condottiero Supremo* even within the provisional government: *ibid.*, II, 229–31, 239 ff.
Saitta hypothesizes that Buonarroti's *Veri Italiani* were in fact identical with Bianco's *Apofasimèni* (*Buonarroti*, I, 203, supported by E. Ragionieri, *Belfagor*, VI, no. 1, 1951, Jan, 112–3). Bianco includes the *Adelfi*, *Filadelfi* and the Buonarrotian Sublime Perfect Masters in his list of specially revered predecessors: *Della Guerra*, I, 55.

183. *Conspiration*, I, 23.

184. Ibid., 30, 38–9. The party of egoism "sighed after the riches, the superfluities and the fame of Athens," while the party of equality "wanted the frugality, the simplicity and the modesty of beautiful days in Sparta" (25). Repeated warnings against "false friends of equality" imply a need for purification among the elect if the "perfect unanimity" (100) of Babeuf's model conspiracy is to be recreated.

185. For a good characterization of this trio, see Eisenstein, 104–16. Her book is somewhat sparse on their relation with Buonarroti's Belgian friends and activities, and should be supplemented by the subsequent works of Kuypers and Garrone.

186. The centrality of Buonarroti's influence is stressed in Garrone, "Buonarroti en Belgique et la propagande égalitaire," *Babeuf et les problèmes*, 218; key letters of Teste to Rogier in Garrone, *Buonarroti*, 463; Kuypers, *Egalitaires*, 33; Kuypers supersedes Saitta and Garrone by identifying (32) Bayet as the mysterious "good Henry" working for Buonarroti. Lehning reserves judgment in "Buonarroti et la révolution belge de 1830. Un article inconnu," *Annales Historiques*, 1960, Oct–Dec, 531 n. 9.

187. In the rare article that Buonarroti published anonymously in Paris on Nov 3. This is reprinted in ibid., with an introduction by Lehning (530–6) that stresses more than the text seems to merit the subdued nature of the message.

188. Letter of Buonarroti to Teste of Oct 26, in Saitta, II, 115.

189. Cited from *L'Emancipation*, Nov 2, the journal founded by Bayet in Brussels,

in Garrone, *Babeuf,* 219 (who added italics without so indicating); original in Kuypers, 29.

190. Garrone, *Babeuf,* 218.

191. Itemized in Kuypers, 35–66.

192. Garrone in *Babeuf,* 224–5; C. Andler, *Le Manifeste Communiste de Karl Marx et F. Engels. Introduction historique et commentaire,* nd, 35 ff.

193. *De la Révolution à faire d'après l'expérience des révolutions avortées* (also translated into Italian), cited in Saitta, I, 147. He opposed summoning assemblies of any sort, which are of use only "for putting brakes on the chariot of revolution, for deadening the élan of the people" (148).

194. *Projet de constitution républicaine et déclaration des principes fondamentaux de la société,* 1833, in Saitta, I, 151. See also the letter of De Potter to Teste of Mar 10, 1832, in Saitta, II, 155–7. Young Etienne Cabet also called in Sep, 1832, for a *gouvernement provisoire* to enforce security after a revolution and conduct elections after "a delay sufficient . . . so that electors could acquire a fully enlightened opinion on the qualities that it is important to search for in deputies." *Révolution de 1830,* 93–4. But Cabet, unlike the Buonarrotians, tolerated constitutional monarchy, 97–8.

195. From the statutes of the *Famiglia* in Garrone, *Buonarroti,* 351 n. 2.

196. Kuypers, 35 and ff. for detailed study of its operations in Belgium; Garrone, *Buonarroti,* 349 ff. for the complex links between this and other organizations.

197. Kuypers, 44.

198. G. Isambert. "Les Anagrammes de Buonarroti," *La Révolution Française,* XXXVII, 1899, 455–62.

199. M. Rousseau, "Filippo Buonarroti et les artistes français sous la monarchie de juillet," *Revue des Études Italiennes,* 1938, Apr–Sep, 162–3.

200. Ibid., 163–6; see also Egbert, *Radicalism and the Arts,* 191–4.

201. Reproduced in Rousseau, "Buonarroti," opposite 160. See also opposite 163 for the bronze medallion of Buonarroti's profile made by the sculptor (and future mayor of the second *arrondissement* of revolutionary Paris) David D'Angers.

202. From *Espérance,* 1834, cited in Rousseau, "Buonarroti," 165.

203. Cited in R. Bouis, "Filippo Buonarroti nei ricordi di un democratico francese," *Movimento Operaio,* 1955, Nov–Dec, 889. This valuable article (not used by Saitta or Garrone) includes extended excerpts along with full discussion of Delorme's *Mémoires d'un prolétaire,* begun in 1846, apparently largely completed before 1848, but never published in full. See also 907 for later Buonarrotian links with Bonapartist agents.

204. Bouis, 895.

205. Ibid., 896.

206. Ibid., 897–8.

207. Ibid., 901.

208. Ibid., 896.

209. Ibid., 911.

210. Cited from the basic documents (H. Temkinowa, ed., *Lud Polski: Wybór dokumentów,* Warsaw, 1957, 227) in P. Brock, "The Socialists of the Polish 'Great Emigration,' " A. Briggs and J. Saville, eds. *Essays in Labour History,* L, 1960, 146. This article (140–73) contains invaluable documentation to materials in English as well as Polish on revolutionary Western influences on the Polish emigration. Supplementary material is in L. Zieliński, *Emigracja polska w Anglii w latach 1831–1846,* Gdańsk, 1964.

211. Cited in Brock, "The Socialists," 148. See also his "The Political Program of the Polish Democratic Society," *The Polish Review,* 1969, summer, 8; and *Populism,* 99 n. 2.

212. The basic study of S. Kieniewicz, *Konspiracje galicyjskie,* 1950, is conveniently summarized with supplementary bibliography in the same author's article in *Polski Słownik Biograficzny,* 1968, XIII/3, 477–9, from which this account is derived. The name of the journal, *Midnight* (Północ), can also be translated as *North.*

213. Marquis de Custine, *Russia,* L, 1854 (first published Paris, 1839).

214. M. Dommanget, *Auguste Blanqui des origines à la révolution de 1848,* Paris/The Hague, 1969, 11–2, 37–8.

215. Ibid., 32–3.

216. Ibid., 43.

217. Ibid., 63.

218. Ibid. The unpublished memoir of his nephew Lacambre (ibid., 61) juxtaposes Blanqui to "the opportunists."

219. Tchernoff, *Le parti,* 237 and ff.

220. Ibid., 270–1, first published in *Procès des quinze,* 1832, 77–86.

221. Dommanget, *Blanqui des origines*, 138. The passage was apparently written early in 1834 (129–30). Blanqui's "L'intelligence, ce sont des hommes de dévouement . . ." thus defines "intelligence" as people devoted to both thought and revolution. The German pejorative usage of *Intelligenz-Intelligenzen* during the Revolution of 1848–49 is closer in sound to the Russian *intelligent-intelligentsia* (R. Pipes, "'Intelligentsia' from the German 'Intelligenz'? A Note," *Slavic Review*, 1971, Sep, 616–7), but Blanqui's affirmative usage is closer in meaning to the revolutionary Russian usage of the 1860s.

222. Tchernoff, 289–92, and Eisenstein, 121 ff., gather the arguments for believing that Buonarroti tried to work through this organization. See his "Elegy to Equality" specifically addressed to the society in Saitta, II, 157–60.

223. Tchernoff generally seems to underrate Buonarroti and overrate Saint-Simon as influences. Dommanget (*Blanqui. Des Origines*, 151–4) provides the fullest discussion of Buonarroti's elusive, but unmistakable impact on the Blanquists, but does not include the derivation of the "family" idea. S. Bernstein (*Auguste Blanqui and the Art of Insurrection*, L, 1971, 45–6) is more tentative than Dommanget on Buonarrotian influence.

224. These figures, but not these connections and derivations, are made by Tchernoff (374, 380 and ff., also 89–90).

225. Text of the questions and answers in Dommanget, *Blanqui. Des Origines*, 149; see also discussion 147 ff.

226. The latter two each exemplified an element that was to characterize social revolutionary movements in the twentieth century: the racial outcast and the alienated intellectual. Barbès was a flamboyant creole from Guadalupe who turned his military training in France into the service of revolutionary insurrection. Martin Bernard had been successively infatuated with the Greek Revolution, Saint-Simonianism, and Fourierism before becoming a typographer in the direct service of Blanqui's organization.

227. Bernstein, 81–3.

228. Lennhoff, 141 ff. These structural and organizational aspects are neglected in the recent study by J. Lee, "The Ribbonmen," in T. Williams, ed., *Secret Societies in Ireland*, Dublin, 1973, 26–35.

229. See M. Martyn, *Ribbonism in Ireland: An authentic report of the trial of Richard Jones*, Dublin, 1840, 50 ff. PU.

230. Ibid., 16.

231. Ibid., 15–9.

232. Ibid., 139–40.

233. Lennhoff, 146–7.

234. Characterization by the outstanding contemporary source, Karl Ewerbeck, head of the Paris section of the League of the Just and principal German popularizer of Cabet: *L'Allemagne et les allemands*, 1851, 589.

235. J. Puech, *La vie et l'oeuvre de Flora Tristan. 1803–1844 (l'union ouvrière)*, 1943, 423.

236. See their journal, *Proscrit: Journal de la république universelle*, and discussion in A. Zévaès, "Les proscrits français en 1848 et en 1851 à Londres," *La Révolution de 1848*, 1924, Jan–Feb, 358 ff.

237. From the invaluable account based on her speeches at a meeting in the summer of 1843 in A. Ruge, *Zwei Jahre in Paris*, Leipzig, 1846, 94–5.

238. W. Schieder, *Anfänge der deutschen Arbeiterbewegung (Die Auslandsvereine im Jahrzehnt nach der Julirevolution von 1830)*, Stuttgart, 1963, esp. 22–4.

239. Andler, *Manifeste*, 8 ff. Also C. Wittke, *The Utopian Communist, A Biography of Wilhelm Weitling*, Baton Rouge, 1950, 21, on the *Zelte* or *Hütten, Kreislager* and *Brennpunkt*. The statutes of the *Geächteten* are in L. Ilse, *Geschichte der politischen Untersuchungen welche . . . in den Jahren 1819 bis 1827 und 1833 bis 1842 geführt sind*, Frankfurt/Main, 1860, 571–9.

240. *Glaubensbekenntnis eines Geächteten*, Paris, 1834. This rare, 12-page pamphlet is reprinted by W. Kowalski, *Vorgeschichte und Entstehung des Bundes der Gerechten*, 1962, 183 ff. For international links and influences, see Garrone, *Buonarroti*, 427–30; Mikhailov, *Istoriia*, 37–40; and (for the role of a Mason from Heidelberg who apparently knew Buonarroti) W. Koppen, *Jacob Venedey*, Frankfurt/Main, 1922.

241. Steklov, *Bakunin*, I, 144. This pre-Marxist idea of revolution-as-prison-revolt derived from Weitling and was to recur briefly in the post-Marxist 1960s radical vision of a "revolution in the streets" to be led by an outlawed *Lumpenproletariat*, the vision of an Eldridge Cleaver and a Frantz Fanon. See E. Cleaver, "On the Ideology of the Black Panther Party," *The Black Panther*, Jun 6, 1970, 15; derivation from Fanon's *Wretched of the Earth* discussed ibid., 12–4; development in

B. Franklin, "The Lumpenproletariat and the Revolutionary Youth Movement," *Monthly Review*, 1970, Jan, esp. 19–20.

242. See H. Schmidt, "Ein Beitrag zur Geschichte des Bundes der Geächteten," *Die Neue Zeit*, XVI, 1898, I, 150 ff.; and on the *Nationalwerkstätte*, Schieder, 196 ff.

243. Andler 12 ff., Schieder, 223–4.

244. For all his social radicalism, Schuster may have collaborated with any or all of three different governments. See Mikhailov, *Istoriia*, 37–40.

245. Silbernagl, "Verbindungen," 808–9.

246. Ibid., 811 ff.

247. See particularly Articles 11 and 25 of the Statutes of the League (more often then called "League of Justice, *Gerechtigkeit*," than "of the Just, *Gerechten*" as history has labeled it), from the text in H. Förder et al., ed., *Bund der Kommunisten*, 1970, I, 92–8, and comment 993–5.

248. Cited in Andler, 22.

249. Johann Hoeckerig, *Souvenirs d'un révolutionnaire allemand*, 1942 (published in Paris with an intr. by J. Bossu under the false date of 1937, BN).

250. See "Religiöser Radicalismus: der Einfluss Felicité de Lamennais," in Schieder, 227–39. There were no less than three different German translations of *Paroles d'un croyant* in 1834, the very year of its appearance. For the estimate of Germans in Paris see E. Schraepler, "Der Bund der Gerechten; Seine Tätigkeit in London 1840–1847," *Archiv für Sozialgeschichte*, II, 1962, 5.

251. *Bund der Kommunisten*, I, 63. The manuscript of his proposal of 1838 to establish a "Community of Goods" (*Gütergemeinschaft*) is discussed in Schieder, 242 ff., and published for the first time, 319–27, also in *Bund*, I, 98–107. Schapper ended his speeches with "amen" (Schieder, 244). For more details see the unpublished doctoral dissertation by A. Fehling, "Karl Schapper und die Anfänge der Arbeiterbewegung bis zur Revolution von 1848: Ein Beitrag zur Geschichte des Handwerkerkommunismus," Rostock, 1922.

252. *Bund*, I, 99 and ff. on the *Geistesaristokraten*.

253. W. Seidel-Höppner, *Wilhelm Weitling*, 1961, 203 n. 5.

254. *Die Menschheit wie sie ist und wie sie sein sollte*, first edition published anonymously, Paris, 1838, 2d Bern, 1846; text reproduced in edition by E. Fuchs, Munich, 1895, discussed Andler, 24–9. Hungarian and Norwegian translations both appeared in 1840.

255. On the *Deutsche Bildungsverein für Arbeiter*, which continued to exist (though in transmuted form) until 1914, see Lehning, "Association," 194 ff.

256. E. Kandel', *Marks i Engel's—organizatory soiuza kommunistov*, 1952, 106–7.

257. William Benbow, *Grand National Holiday and Congress of the Productive Classes*, L, 1832.

258. J. Kuypers, *Jacob Kats Agitator*, Brussels, 1930, 206–8; text in *The Constitutional*, Nov 12, 1836; discussion and references in Lehning, "Association," 189–91.

259. *Poor Man's Guardian*, 1833, Oct 19, 333–4, in Thompson, *The Making of the English Working Class*, 803, who attributes this passage to O'Brien. See also A. Plummer, "The Place of Bronterre O'Brien in the working class movement," *The Economic History Review*, 1929, Jan.

260. The substantial Irish role in Chartism provided not only an impetus towards extremism via O'Brien, but also a tendency (through Fergus O'Connor) to idealize the agrarian way of life and see in the worker an ex-peasant. See R. O'Higgins, "The Irish Influence in the Chartist Movement," *Past and Present*, 1965, Nov, 83–96.

261. B. Quarles, *Frederick Douglass*, NY, 1969, 81; K. Koszyk, *Deutsche Presse im 19. Jahrhundert*, 1966, II, 188.

262. Braunthal, *History*, 51.

263. Account in the section "Communist Intelligence" of Goodwyn Barmby's *Communist Chronicle*, I, no. 12, 133.

264. Ibid. The speaker was Barmby, who misspelled Babeuf in the text.

265. "Arrival of Weitling in England," *Communist Chronicle*, I, no. 12, 132–3.

266. Cited Schraepler, "Der Bund," 20.

267. According to Schapper in a letter to Marx of Jun 6, 1846, in Kandel', 112, the earlier membership figure is given without attribution in Kandel', 106. Schraepler ("Der Bund," 8), puts the number in 1847 at more than 1,000.

268. Schraepler, "Der Bund," 20, 24.

269. August Becker, *Was wollen die Kommunisten? Eine Rede, im Auszug vorgetragen, vor einer am 4ten August 1844, im Lokal des s.g. Kommunisten-Vereins zu Lausanne, von Mitgliedern verschiedener Arbeiter-Vereine abgehaltenen Versammlung*, Lausanne, 1844, 42–4, as cited in Bravo, "Il comunismo," *Annali*, VI, 545; and discussion 542–6.

270. K. Obermann, "Germano-Américains et presse ouvrière 1845–1854," in J. Godechot, ed., *La presse ouvrière 1819–1850*, 1966, 70 ff.; and, for more detail,

H. Schlüter, "Die Anfänge der deutschen Arbeiterbewegung in New York und ihre Presse," in *New Yorker Volkszeitung,* Feb 21, 1903.

271. Citation from the first issue of Jan 5, 1846, in Schlüter, 8.

272. Text in *Demokratisches Taschenbuch für 1848,* Leipzig, 1847, cited in Obermann, 72.

Chapter 7

1. Cited by T. Horton in *Gazette of the American Friends of Lafayette,* No. 15, 1952, Apr, 4.

2. Cited in ibid., 3.

3. Cited in Bardoux, *Les dernières Années,* 367. This remains the only major synthetic work on Lafayette's last years.

4. Ibid., 350.

5. Ibid., 424–5.

6. Jun 13, 1833, in ibid., 419.

7. Bardoux is not convincing with his sweeping generalization that the conspiracies of the era "began and ended with him" (284); but there is no other major study of the problem. The perceptive political memoir of Rémusat points to the difficulty of investigating a figure who early in life "acquired the habit of keeping secret not his opinions but his plans" and avoided lies "but not silence." *Mémoires de ma vie,* 1959, II, 246–7.

8. Rémusat, 57. In Rémusat's analysis, "the American revolution spoiled Lafayette . . . the creation of the fabulous government that came out of it, gave him illusions. He believed in the easiness of revolutions, and that he was born to make and lead them" (245). Then, when he found French youth agitating for revolution, "their enthusiasm recalled to him that of his own youthful years. Here again was his sacred battalion. . . . He believed that he owed them something, and saw them impatient to get on with it. He assigned to himself the duty of personally leading them—unable to endure the thought that anyone should risk more than he for liberty" (57).

9. Ibid., 57–8.

10. Bardoux, 422–3.

11. *Vie politique de . . . Lafayette,* published under the pseudonym of Gigault, 1833, 33 (Franklin collection, YU). He was ridiculed for avoiding revolutionary involvement by retreating to his estate at La Grange, then waking up "like a woodchuck after the winter" and expecting to be taken seriously.

12. Ibid., 1.

13. Cited in Harivel, 63.

14. *Vie politique,* 44.

15. Ibid., 46. England was denounced as insidiously cooptive ("the fortune of the aristocracy was fashioned out of insurrection") and maddeningly insular ("revolutions have been confined to its island without any continental result") 42.

16. Ibid., 34.

17. Even a neutral appraisal of Lafayette soon came to be regarded as "proof" of revolutionary insincerity or timidity. See Théodore Dézamy's denunciation of his onetime patron, Cabet, for overlooking Buonarroti's exposé and thus failing to denounce Lafayette with sufficient vigor, *Calomnies et politique de M. Cabet. Réfutation par des faits et par sa biographie,* 1842, 31–3.

18. Rémusat, II, 254.

19. Letter to Belgiosco of Aug 21, 1832, in A. Malvezzi, "Il generale La Fayette e la rivoluzione italiana del 1831," *PAN,* 1934, Jul 1, 366.

20. Letter of May 6, 1831, to Casimir Périer, commiserating with the Italians and acknowledging the "special obligations" of the French, ibid., 363–4. Lafayette was judged harshly by Pepe, however, as "one of those aristocrats who, by linking himself to ideas without understanding anything about them, renders a situation tragic that was not so." Falcionelli, *Sociétés,* 252; also 124, for Lafayette's promise of aid to him.

21. Bardoux, 406 ff; and the centennial work published in Paris: *La Fayette et la Pologne 1830–1834,* 1934.

22. Cited from a letter of Aug 31, 1836, in *Mémoires de Fazy,* 240.

23. Letter to Belgiosco of Aug 21, 1832, in Malvezzi, 366.

24. Cited by H. Voorhis, "Lafayette: Citizen and Freemason of Two Countries," *The American Lodge of Research, Transactions (Free and Accepted Masons),* 1936, II, no. 2, 337.

25. The standard life by his son, Henri Fazy, *James Fazy. Sa vie et son oeuvre,*

Geneva/Basel, 1887, 1–2, 4–5, should be supplemented by F. Ruchon, "Une Famille genevoise: Les Fazy d'Antoine Fazy, fabricant d'indiennes, à James Fazy, homme d'état et tribun," *Bulletin de l'institut national genevois*, LI, 1939, 3, 6, 8.

26. Vuilleumier, "Buonarroti . . . à Genève," 486–7; Henri Fazy, 3–16. See also the good discussion in F. Brokgauz and I. Efron, *Entsiklopedichesky slovar'*, XXXV, 235–6, and *Les Mémoires de James Fazy*, Geneva, 1947.

27. *De la Banque de France, considerée comme nuisible aux transactions commerciales*, 1819; the utopian allegory of popular sovereignty, *Voyage d'Ertelib*, Geneva, 1822; and the play *La mort de Lévrier*, Geneva, 1826.

28. *L'Homme aux portions ou conversations philosophiques et politiques*, 1821, 140, 211–3; see also the section "Observations sur la révolution française," 66–119, LC.

29. Ruchon, "Famille," 10–1.

30. Cited by H. Fazy, *James Fazy*, 17; see also *Mémoires de James Fazy*, 8.

31. Anonymous article in *Journal de Genève*, 1831, Sep, cited and discussed by W. Rappard, "Pennsylvania and Switzerland: The American Origins of the Swiss Constitution," in *University of Pennsylvania. Bicentennial Conference*, Philadelphia, 1941, 105.

32. Vuilleumier, 488; see also Ruchon, *Franc-Maçonnerie à Genève*, IV, 117–20, for the Fazys' links with Andryane and other associates of Buonarroti.

33. *Mémoires de Fazy*, 240 ff.

34. Report of the Hapsburg police agent C. von Engelshaufen, Mar 18, 1847, in Barnikol, *Geschichte*, 4.

35. Account of G. Kuhlmann based on information from A. Becker relayed through Engelshaufen: Barnikol, 20; see also discussion 19–23.

36. This account is based on W. Rappard, *L'Avènement de la démocratie moderne à Genève (1814–1847)*, Geneva, 1942, 253–63, 302–3; also Ruchon, "Famille," 12–5.

37. Ruchon, "Famille," 16–7, 20 ff.

38. Ibid., 18–9; also the highly critical biographical study by Th. de Saussure, *James Fazy, Sein Leben und Treiben*, Zürich, 1865.

39. Ruchon, 24.

40. *Gérontocratie*, 5–6.

41. Fazy, *Principes d'organisation industrielle pour le développement des richesses en France. Explication des malaises des classes productives et des moyens d'y porter remède*, 1830, title of section 271–82.

42. *Gérontocratie*, 6–7.

43. Ibid., 22.

44. Ibid., 5.

45. Ibid., 9.

46. Ibid., 22.

47. Herzen, *My Past*, II, 723.

48. Ibid.

49. *Mémoires*, 246.

50. Herzen, *My Past*, II, 726.

51. Ibid.

52. Cited in Rappard, *Avènement*, 366–7.

53. Ibid., 329–30.

54. Ibid., 329.

55. Fazy, in *Le Représentant du Peuple*, 1842, Mar 2, cited in Saitta, *Sinistra*, 399.

56. "Les Communistes allemands en Suisse," *Le Fédéral. Journal Genevois*, 1842, Mar 29, reproduced in Saitta, 402. The author is not identified, but the article is represented as, and seems to be, a continuation of Fazy's argument.

57. Ibid., 402.

58. Ibid., 403. August Becker, the leading German communist in Switzerland after Weitling's arrest in 1843, counter-attacked against Fazy's faith in the power of "political economy . . . to cure sufficiently the ills of society." *Les doctrinaires et les communistes dans la Suisse romande. Petit mémoire addressé aux hommes d'état et aux honnêtes gens de la Suisse et de l'Allemagne*, Lausanne, 1845, 2, cited in Saitta, 301.

After the revolutions of 1848, as he became preoccupied with writing *Capital*, Marx took a more positive view of Fazy. See A. Babel, "La Première Internationale, ses débuts et son activité à Genève de 1864 à 1870," in *Mélanges d'études économiques et sociales offerts à William E. Rappard*, Geneva, 1944, 244–5, 251.

59. Campanella, "Congress," 464 ff. esp. 476.

60. Henri Fazy, 315.

61. Ibid., 94, on the *Declaration des droits individuels*; and 313 ff. on *De l'intelli-*

gence collective des sociétés. Yet Fazy, in power in 1849, had to rein in the civil liberties of exiles in his realm in order to prevent external repression—much to the horror of Herzen, *My Past*, II, 727–34.

62. Onu, "Sotsiologicheskaia," 29–55, distinguishes this local revolution with universal aims from more widespread waves of revolution which have, however, more parochial objectives (as in 1848).

63. On the central role of Switzerland as a place of asylum and incubation for revolutionary movements, see G. Ferretti, *Esuli del Risorgimento in Svizzera*, Bologna, 1948, and A. Senn, *The Russian Revolution in Switzerland 1914–1917*, Wisconsin, 1971.

England played a multiform role: as a financier of revolution against Napoleon (J. Hirn, *Englische subsidien für Tirol und die Emigranten von 1809*, Innsbruck, 1912); as a base for later Italian revolutionaries (E. Morelli, *Mazzini in Inghilterra*, Florence, 1938; M. Wicks, *The Italian Exiles in London*, Manchester, 1937); and as a haven in the late nineteenth century for a wide variety of displaced revolutionaries (J. Hulse, *Revolutionists in London. A Study of Five Unorthodox Socialists*, Oxford, 1970).

64. "The 'Geneva idea' is the idea of virtue without Christ, my boy, the modern idea, or more correctly, the idea of all modern civilization." Dostoevsky, *A Raw Youth*, L, 1950, 208.

65. Title page of J. Eötvös, *Über die Gleichberechtigung der Nationalitäten in Oesterreich*, Vienna, 1851.

66. H. Butterfield, *The Whig Interpretation of History*, L, 1931.

67. K. Jürgensen, *Lamennais und die Gestaltung des belgischen Staates. Der liberale Katholizismus in der Verfassungsbewegung des 19 Jahrhunderts*, Wiesbaden, 1963. Lamennais tended to be influential in countries where revolution was frustrated: in Germany of the 1830s, as already discussed, and in Russia of the 1840s; see F. Nikitina, "Petrashevtsy i Lamenne," in *Dostoevsky. Materialy i issledovaniia*, III, 1978, 256–8, the first report on a long forthcoming study.

68. *Essai sur l'indifférence en matière de religion*, 4v, 1817–23.

69. The thesis of H. Commanger, *The Empire of Reason. How Europe Imagined and America Realized the Enlightenment*, NY, 1977, essentially echoed by P. Gay, "America the Paradoxical," The George Mason Lectures, Williamsburg, 1976.

Chapter 8

1. On the basic, recurring problem of satisfying a rapidly increasing educated population with expectations that run far ahead of vocational opportunities, see L. O'Boyle, "The Problem of an Excess of Educated Men in Western Europe 1800–1850," *Journal of Modern History*, 1970, Dec, 471–95. Some stimulating hypotheses about changing modes of discourse are mixed with turgid sociological prose in A. Gouldner, "Prologue to a Theory of Revolutionary Intellectuals," *Telos*, 1975–6, winter, 3–36. Marx's own complex views are described in S. Avineri, "Marx and the Intellectuals," *Journal of the History of Ideas*, 1967, Apr–Jun, 269–78. A. Gella provides the beginnings of a general sociological theory (though relatively little about the beginnings of the phenomenon in Poland itself) in "The Life and Death of the Old Polish Intelligentsia," *Slavic Review*, 1971, Mar, 1–27.

2. Definitions respectively of *Webster's Third International Dictionary*, repeated and discussed in E. Shils and H. Johnson, *International Encyclopedia of the Social Sciences*, VII, 66–85; and of W. Mullins, "On the Concept of Ideology in Political Science," *American Political Science Review*, 1972, Jun, 498–510. E. Lenberg suggests that ideologies are needed for survival in the modern world: *Ideologie und Gesellschaft*, Stuttgart, 1971. H. Schelsky sees the intellectuals committed to ideology as the priests of a new secular religion: *Die Arbeit tun die anderen: Klassenkampf und Priesterherrschaft der Intellektuellen*, Opladen, 1975.

3. See J. Dautry, "Sur un imprimé retrouvé du Comte de Saint-Simon," *Annales Historiques*, 1948, Oct–Dec, 289–321.

4. Republished in Saint-Simon, *Selected Writings* (ed. F. Markham), NY, 1952, 1–11. Of the many studies of Saint-Simon, special use is made here of F. Manuel, *The New World of Henri Saint-Simon*, Cambridge, Mass., 1956.

5. The name of his organization in Le Mans *cercle constitutionnel ambulant* suggests the Bonneville link. See J. Dautry, "Babuvistskaia traditsiia posle smerti Babefa i do revoliutsii 1830 g.," *Frantsuzsky ezhegodnik 1960*, 1961, 156–7, 165.

6. No copies have apparently survived of Bazin's confiscated *Esquisse d'un nouveau plan d'organisation sociale par un philanthrope*. See J. Dautry, "Saint-Simon et les anciens babouvistes de 1804 à 1809," in *Babeuf . . . deuxième centenaire*, 164.

Dautry doubts Mathiez's earlier hypothesis that Saint-Simon might have been influenced directly by Babeuf when both were in Picardy during 1790–3.

7. Saint-Simon's own *Esquisse d'un nouveau plan d'organisation sociale par un philanthrope* was written anonymously and remained unpublished until 1925. Discussion by Dautry is in Saint-Simon, *Textes choisis*, 1951, 20.

8. Cited from *Lettres philosophiques* in Dautry, "Saint-Simon et babouvistes," 165. His praise of Maréchal is in *Lettres*, 109–18 (BN). His Maréchal-like view of philosophy as the "point" of "the perfection of the human species" towards which all science converges is developed in *Lettres*, 203.

9. Cited in ibid., 166.

10. Interpretation suggested by Dautry (ibid., 169) and Tugan-Baranovsky, "Male," 179. Additional indication of Bazin's importance in the Philadelphians is in Vermale, *Didier*, 96–7.

11. Cited in "Saint-Simon et babouvistes," 170.

12. Ibid., 172 ff.

13. Saint-Simon did send Bazin a copy of his brochure of 1814, *On the Reorganization of European Society*; but Bazin disliked it ("Saint-Simon et babouvistes," 175). He returned to Le Mans after the fall of Napoleon, adopted a position that was more nationalistic than revolutionary, and was denied a Catholic burial in 1820 not because of his revolutionary past, but because he had died in a duel. See Dautry, "Traditsiia," 172–9, esp. n. 140.
A neglected early sketch of Bazin refers to "Bazinistes" as possessing a special kind of *sang froid* among revolutionaries: "une espèce de haine élégante et frondeuse, presqu'aussi aristocratique que la classe à laquelle elle s'adressait." *Biographie universelle ancienne et moderne*, 1843, III, 353.

14. See E. Kennedy, *A Philosophe in the Age of Revolution: Destutt de Tracy and the Origins of "Ideology,"* Philadelphia, 1978, 46–8. This is a full discussion with exhaustive references on usages of the term "ideology." See also his " 'Ideology' from Destutt de Tracy to Marx," *Journal of the History of Ideas*, 1979, Jul–Sep, 353–68.

15. *Eléments d'idéologie*, 1801, I, 1. See G. Lichtheim, *The Concept of Ideology and Other Essays*, NY, 1967, 3–46.

16. Cabanis, "Rapport du physique et du moral de l'homme," 123, cited in G. Boas, *French Philosophes of the Romantic Period*, Baltimore, 1925, 69.

17. The transfer of physiological into sociological categories is discussed in the works of G. Gurvitch on Saint-Simon, most succinctly in his introduction to *Comte Henri de Saint-Simon. La physiologie sociale*, 1965.

18. *Considérations sur les mesures à prendre pour terminer la révolution*, 1820.

19. The classic treatment of the group is F. Picavet, *Les idéologues*, 1891, though his concept of who were in fact *idéologues* is somewhat over-inclusive. See C. Van Duzer, *Contributions of the Ideologues to French Revolutionary Thought*, Baltimore, 1935. A comprehensive new account of the movement from prerevolutionary origins to its dissolution under Napoleon is S. Moravia, *Il Tramonto dell' illuminismo filosofia e politica nella società francese (1770–1810)*, Bari, 1968.

20. The title was *Projet d'elemens d'idéologie à l'usage des écoles centrales de la république française*. On the "revolutionary academy," see Kennedy, 78–9.

21. Napoleon was not their only critic. Moralistic philosophers like Mercier (who were also vying for Napoleon's favor) called them *idiologues*, *idiots* (Mormile, *Néologie*, 197; Mercier, *L'An* [ed. Trousson], 26). Napoleon's arch-critic among the intellectuals, Mme. de Staël, in turn called him an *idéophobe* (T. Jung, *Lucien Bonaparte et ses mémoires*, 1882, II, 233 ff., cited in Mme. de Staël, *Ten Years of Exile*, NY, 1973, 19).

22. His writings on this project are discussed and itemized in J. Walch, *Bibliographie du saint-simonisme*, 1967, 31. See also Gurvitch, ed., *Saint-Simon*, 17; and H. Gouhier, "Un 'projet d'encyclopédie' de Saint-Simon," *Revue Internationale de Philosophie*, XIV, no. 53–4, 1960, 387, 393.

23. *Mémoire sur la science de l'homme*, produced in several variants in 1813, though unpublished until 1858. Some sections translated in Markham, 21–7.

24. An isolated, parallel example of bizarre proposals from within France for a social revolutionary transformation of Napoleon's domain can be found in the works of two natives of Lorraine who met in Russia and moved to Paris, Pierre-Ignace Jaunez-Sponville and Nicolas Bugnet: *Catéchisme social ou exposition familière des principes posés par feu* (1808) and *La Philosophie du Ruvarebohni*, 2v (1809). The latter depicts the shipwrecked "icanarfs" (*français*) living on an island under a despotic "Ponélano" (Napoléon), and describes its transformation into "true happiness" (*vrai bonheur* being the anagram for *Ruvarebohni*) of a Christian communist "community of goods" that breaks down all vestiges of selfish acquisitiveness, including the family. See Ioannisian, "Iz utopicheskogo kommunizma vo

Frantsii v nachale xix stoletiia," *Novaia i Noveishaia Istoriia,* 1961, no. 3, 58–69; and E. Pariset, "L'Utopie de deux lorrains sous Napoléon I," in *Etudes,* 241–60.

25. In *L'Industrie* (1816–7) and *L'Organisateur* (1819), his *Du Système industriel* (1820–2) and his summary *Catéchisme des industriels* (1823–4). See Walch, 32.

26. *Le nouveau christianisme,* 1832, 116.

27. The importance of this work is stressed in F. Manuel, *The Eighteenth Century Confronts the Gods,* Cambridge, Mass., 1959.

28. According to one of their leaders, F. de Corcelle, *Documents,* 8; cited in Isambert, *De la Charbonnerie,* 118.

29. Corcelle, *Documents,* 68.

30. See R. Fakkar, *Sociologie, socialisme et internationalisme prémarxistes. Contribution à l'étude de l'influence internationale de Saint-Simon et de ses disciples,* Neuchâtel, 1968.

31. From his *Reorganization of the European Community* (1814), in Markham, 64.

32. Saint-Simon to the future Decembrist Lunin, cited in H. Auger, "Iz zapisok Ippolita Ozhe," *Russky Arkhiv,* 1877, kniga 2, 65.

33. *Framtidens religion, uppenbarad av Saint-Simon,* Stockholm, 1831; *Saint-Simons religionslāre,* Stockholm, 1833. Discussion and full bibliography by P. Cornell in *Svenskt biografiskt lexicon,* XVII, 1969, 685–8.

34. The work of J. de Puyjalon (*L'Influence des Saint-Simoniens sur la réalisation de l'isthme de Suez et des chemins de fer,* 1926) by no means exhausts the subject.

35. The link between the two men is discussed in H. Gouhier, *La Jeunesse d'Auguste Comte et la formation du positivisme,* 1963, 3v., which has added a rich bibliography on Saint-Simonianism in this second edition.
A new Soviet study discusses Saint-Simon's influence on Comte (270–302) and on other "bourgeois" thinkers more fully than his impact on revolutionaries: G. Kucherenko, *Sen-Simonizm v obshchestvennoi mysli xix v.,* 1975.

36. Fakkar, 95.

37. These appeals of Comte to accept his *Système de politique positive* discussed and referenced in Billington, "The Intelligentsia and the Religion of Humanity," *American Historical Review,* 1960, Jul, 807–8.

38. Itemized in G. Deville, "Origine des mots 'socialisme' et 'socialiste' et de certains autres," *La Révolution Française,* 1908, Jan–Jul, 395–9.

39. L. Reybaud, "Socialistes modernes. I. Les Saint-Simoniens," *Revue des Deux Mondes,* 1836, Jul 15, 341.

40. See J.-P. Callot, *Histoire de l'école polytechnique,* 1959, 65, 223–6; and for the integration of the school into the Napoleonic ethos, particularly after moving to its new location in 1805, see 33–54.

41. Phrases cited from the *Exposition* in Isambert, *De la charbonnerie,* 182–3. There is an English translation by G. Iggers: *The Doctrine of Saint-Simon: an exposition; first year, 1828–1829,* Boston, 1958. The proto-communist term "community of goods" was introduced and defended by Prati in the treatise: Fontana, chief, Prati, preacher, *Saint-Simonianism in London. On the Pretended Community of Goods or the Organization of Industry, on the Pretended Community of Women or Matrimony and Divorce,* L, 1834, 2d ed., esp. 7 (GL).

42. R. Parkhurst, *The Saint-Simonians Mill and Carlyle,* L, 1958.

43. These triadic emphases are stressed in the unpublished thesis of P. Mickey, "Le Livre Nouveau: The Vision of Monastic Saint-Simonism," Princeton, 1971, esp. 82–93. The thesis appends the first full reproduction of the unpublished *Livre Nouveau* from the manuscript in BA.

44. Mannheim, *Ideology and Utopia,* NY, 1936 (sections II–IV being the translation of the German original, Bonn, 1929); esp. "The Sociological Problem of the 'Intelligentsia,' " 153–64.

45. Fakkar, 204–5.

46. Fakkar, 159–60, 195.

47. *La République d'Andorre,* 1848; Fakkar, 181 n. 105.

48. Ibid., 235–6 n. 36.

49. Cited from *Jugement de la doctrine de Saint-Simon sur les derniers événements,* in Fakkar, 43 n. 43.

50. Salvemini flatly declares that "four-fifths of Mazzini's ideas were Saint-Simonian in origin," *Mazzini,* 161.

51. "El movimiento sansimoniano argentino señala el punto de divergencia definitiva entre la involución del espíritu hispano-colonial y el nacimiento de una mentalidad argentina." J. Ingenieros, "La filosofía social de Echeverría y la leyenda de la 'Asociación de Mayo,' " *Revista de Filosofía,* 1918, Mar, 236. Their leader Esteban

Echeverría had been in France 1826–30; and the journal planned by his circle in 1838 was to be a "periódico *puramente literario y socialista* nada político," with *Inteligencia* and several other such words emblazoned on the masthead, 240. See also Ingenieros, "Los Saintsimonianos Argentinos," *Revista de Filosofía*, 1915, Sep, 275–315.

52. On the *Zmartwychwstańcy*, neglected in all non-Polish histories, see Callier, *Jański*, and the official history of the order: *Historia zgromadzenia zmartwychwstania pańskiego*, Cracow, 1892–6, 4v. At the same time, the revolutionary émigré Polish Democratic Society officially defined its program in Saint-Simonian terms as working toward the "organic epoch" of social reconstruction. See Brock, "Program," 98.

53. J. S. Mill, *Correspondance inédite avec Gustave d'Eichtal*, 1898, 147.

54. A. Abdel-Malek, *Idéologie et renaissance nationale. L'Egypte moderne*, 1969, 197, lists the only earlier ones as Paris (1794), Berlin (1799), St. Petersburg (1809), Prague (1806), and Glasgow (1823). In the Near East as in Latin America, Saint-Simonian ideas tended to blend into Comtean posivitism and to strengthen statism rather than socialism (189–98).

55. Fakkar, 188–91.

56. *Système de la Méditerranée* in *The Globe*, Feb 5, 1832, and, separately, 1832; discussed in Fakkar, 198 ff.

57. Cited in Fakkar, 199.

58. Cited in Charléty, 224.

59. Cited in Fakkar, 223.

60. Chevalier, *Système*, in Fakkar, 199.

61. See the last verse of Félix Maynard's song of departure *À l'ouest*: ". . . Comme un riche divan de pourpre triomphale,/ Sera dans l'avenir, la couche nuptiale,/ Où deux mondes viendront s'épouser dans la paix." Vinçard aîné, *Chants*, 173.

62. Letter to Emile Barrault, head of the expedition, as printed in M. Emerit, *Les Saint-Simoniens en Algérie*, 1941, 53. The letter also promises that this is only the first canal to the East. "Plus tard nous percerons aussi l'autre à Panama." Emerit's study includes much new documentary material of wider interest than its title might suggest.

63. Discussion in Mickey, 125–6.

64. Puyjalon, *Influence*, 65.

65. For the sharing of this thought in Paris at the time, see references in J. Callot (pseud. Alem), *Enfantin*, Montreuil, 1963, 112 n. 1.

66. *Livre Nouveau*, second séance, text in Mickey, second pagination, 50.

67. Puyjalon, 63.

68. Published in 1861, when Enfantin was 65, 3 years before his death. Other late Saint-Simonian efforts to provide new religious statements are d'Eichtal, *Les Evangiles* (1863), and Barrault, *Le Christ* (1865).

69. Inherited from Freemasonry and from the neglected works of the mystic of Lyon, the politically reactionary Ballanche (*La Palingénésie sociale*). See references and discussions in Mickey, 131–45.

70. Urbain, *Notice autobiographique*, 1883, unpublished ms. 13737, BA, 6. This invaluable, unused testimony substantially supplements the only extant effort to provide a comprehensive account of Urbain's life by Emerit, *Saint-Simoniens*, esp. 67–83.

71. Urbain, *Notice*, 3–4 for discussion of *"ma triste origine."*

72. Ibid., 7–8; Emerit, *Saint-Simoniens*, 41–6; and Emerit, ed., *Révolution . . . en Algérie*, 88.

73. Fakkar, 207 n. 33.

74. Emerit, *Saint-Simoniens*, 70; *Notice*, 9–10; also Urbain's anonymously published "Une Conversion à l'Islamisme," *Revue de Paris*, 1852, Jul.

75. See Barrault's report to Urbain on Malabar in a letter of 1833: *Fonds Enfantins*, 7619, 17, BA.

76. Emerit, *Saint-Simoniens*, 73; Fakkar, 231–4.

77. Emerit, *Saint-Simoniens*, 74: "I am thirsty for your shade." Enfantin's thirst was equally intense, confessing to Urbain in a letter of Mar 11, 1835, that he misses "thy brown face," is fascinated by "black flesh," and regrets that "God has not yet given me communion with that flesh." *Fonds Enfantins*, 7619, 123–4, BA.

78. Booth, *Saint-Simon*, 215.

79. Fakkar, 207 n. 33; Emerit, *Saint-Simoniens*, 75.

80. *Notice*, 10. He also seemed something of a blend of the two literary characters that Enfantin considered symbols of East and West, respectively: Othello, representing absolutism and "constancy," and Don Juan, representing "ardent mobility" and anarchy. Fakkar, 198–9.

81. *Lettres sur la race noire et la race blanche*, 1839, 13 n. a, YU. Beyond the basic coupling of East with West, Eichtal fantasized natural intercourse between North and South America, Europe and Africa, Asia and Oceania—each linkage lubricated by a seminal sea: the Gulf of Mexico, the Mediterranean, and the South China Sea, respectively (61). Eichtal seems to hint even more than Enfantin at an element of homosexual attraction for Urbain: "When will you say to us, Ismayl, your name of *black* and of *fetishist*? When will we raise up together a chapel to the pine cones that we gathered together in the forest of Fontainebleau?" (30).

82. Ibid., 13, 20. Urbain anticipated and strikingly resembled the pan-Negro ideologist Edward Blyden (1832-1912), who also moved from the West Indies to Africa, learned Arabic, and became interested in Islam, and saw parallels between Jews and blacks. See H. Lynch, *Edward Wilmot Blyden*, Oxford, 1967.

83. *Lettres*, 26.

84. Ibid., 16. Eichtal waxed rhapsodic over the spectacle of black dancers at the Paris opera: "From the depths of my study, I transport myself with delight into the midst of black tribes. . . . I see them swaying on their haunches for hours on end" (29). Urbain points out in reply that African Muslims dance in the open air, not closed opera houses, both to pray and to celebrate (43-4, 48, in the only letter from Urbain in the volume).

85. Ibid., 52 ff.

86. Ibid., 58-9, 7.

87. G. d'Eichtal, *De l'état actuel et de l'avenir de l'islamisme dans l'Afrique centrale*, 1841. He had been the original apostle of Saint-Simonianism to the English. See Fakkar, 149 ff.; also B. Ratcliffe, "Saint-Simonism and Messianism: The Case of Gustave d'Eichtal," *French Historical Studies*, 1976, spring, 484-502, which, however, makes no mention of Urbain.

88. *L'Algérie: courrier d'Afrique, d'Orient et de la Méditerranée*.

89. *Notice*, 27.

90. Emerit, *Révolution . . . en Algérie*, 76-7; and more generally, 76-86 on this Carbonari-type group. One defendant anticipated Dostoevsky by calling another defendant Christ and his prosecutor the Inquisitor (81-2).

91. Ibid., 83.

92. *L'Algérie pour les algériens*, dated in *Notice*, 31. Not included in Fakkar is his *Correspondance du docteur A. Vital avec I. Urbain (1845-1874)*, with introduction and notes by A. Nouschi, *Collection de documents inédits et d'études sur l'histoire de l'Algérie*, second series, V, 1959.

93. Letter of Napoleon III to Pelissier, cited in Emerit, *Saint-Simoniens*, 270, including parallel text, showing Napoleon's borrowing from Urbain's *Indigènes et immigrants*, 1862. For details of the ultimately unsuccessful struggle of Urbain (together with Baron David, son of the revolutionary painter, and another former Saint-Simonian, Frederic Lacroix, a senator and sometime head of the Arab Bureau in Paris) to win over Napoleon III for a special *Royaume Arabe* inside Algeria, see Emerit, 233-87; also *1848 en Algérie*, 88 ff.

94. See the anonymous pamphlet of Lacroix commissioned by Napoleon III: *L'Algérie et la lettre de l'empereur*, 1863.

95. R. Labry, *Alexandre Ivanovič Herzen 1812-1870*, 1928, 236.

96. Fakkar, 38 n. 20.

97. A. Cieszkowski, *Prolegomena zur Historiosophie*, 1838; letter of Herzen to A. Vitberg, cited in A. Volodin, *Gegel' i russkaia sotsialisticheskaia mysl' XIX veka*, 1973, 139.

98. Cited in Labry, 237.

99. Fakkar, 101-3.

100. Ibid., 113, paraphrasing extended discussion by Gurvitch.

101. S. D'Irsay, *Histoire des universités françaises et étrangères*, 1935, II, 184-202.

102. An aphorism from his Jena period in *Dokumente zu Hegels Entwicklung*, Stuttgart, 1936, 360.

103. J. Ritter, *Hegel et la révolution française*, 1970, 19. Equally emphatic on this theme is A. Prior, *Revolution and Philosophy. The Significance of the French Revolution for Hegel and Marx*, Cape Town, 1972, who tends to suggest that the revolution was more directly and deeply inspirational for Hegel even than for Marx.

104. G. Lukács, *Der junge Hegel*, Zurich/Vienna, 1948, 20-6, 716-8.

105. L. Althuser, *Lenin and Philosophy and other essays*, L, 1971, 106 ff., esp. 118-9. More important than this link established by Althuser on the basis of Lenin's reading Hegel in 1914-5 might be Hegel's influence on one of his Russian translators, Lenin's older brother Alexander Ulyanov.

106. Letter of Oct 13, 1806, in the valuable introduction of Z. Pelczynski to *Hegel's Political Writings*, Oxford, 1964, 7.

107. See the penetrating essay on Hegel as the model modern intellect by K. Barth, *Protestant Thought from Rousseau to Ritschl*, L, 1959, 268–305. Among the many philosophical discussions of Hegel, this exposition owes most to F. Grégoire, *Etudes hégéliennes; les points capitaux du système*, Louvain, 1958. Some elements here included are implied rather than directly stated in Hegel (eg. thesis-antithesis-synthesis); but, since we are dealing with posthumous influence through secondary expositors, a composite picture is presented.

108. B. Baczko, "La gauche et la droite hégélienne en Pologne," *Annali*, 1963, VI, 137–63; and the anthology *Polskie spory o Hegla 1830–1860*, Warsaw, 1966.

109. A. Walicki, "Hegel, Feuerbach and the Russian 'philosophical left,'" in *Annali*, VI, 121–2.

110. Cited in Fakkar, 107.

111. Gurvitch, cited in Fakkar, 107.

112. E. Callier, *Bogdan Jański*, Poznań, 1876, 72. An earlier German use during the French Revolution (by Wieland, describing the Jacobins in *Neuer teutscher Merkur*, 1794, Feb, 141, cited in Seidler, 277) does not have the same suggestion of deep social changes: "Ihre Absicht sey, aus der französischen Revolution eine révolution sociale d.i., eine Umkehrung aller jetzt bestehenden Staaten zu machen."

113. See A. Walicki, "Two Polish Messianists: Adam Mickiewicz and Cieszkowski," *Oxford Slavonic Papers*, New Series, II, 1969, esp. 90–6. The concept of an "age of the Holy Spirit" dates back to Joachim of Flora and late medieval heresy. For Cieszkowski's influence on German and Russian revolutionary movements, see McLellan, *Hegelians*, 9–12; on Italians, Saitta, *Sinistra*, 125 ff.
Cieszkowski and other Slavs continued their interest in the cosmological aspects of Saint-Simonianism (the concept of palingenesis and of a coming "organic" era) even after moving on to Hegelianism. See his *Gott und Palingenesie*, 1842.

114. B. Trentowski, *Stosunek filozofii do cybernetyki*, Warsaw, 1974, 549 (original edition, Poznań, 1843).

115. *Inteligencja postępowa*, in *Rok*, XI, 1844, 3, cited in F. Pepłowski, *Sł ownictwo i frazeologia polskiej publicystyki okresu oświecenia i romantyzmu*, 1961, 167.

116. K. Libelt, *O miłości ojczyzny*, Poznań, 1844, as reprinted in Libelt's *Rozprawy*, Cracow, 1869, 111–2. The full title of Libelt's work is *Love of the Fatherland. The Year 1844 from the viewpoint of enlightenment, industry and current events*. See Z. Wójcik, *Rozwój pojęcia inteligencji*, Wrocław/Warsaw/Cracow, 1962, 21 n. 2; also I. Kosmowska, *Karol Libelt jako dzialacz polityczny i społeczny*, Poznań, 1918.
The word *intelligence* had, of course, been used earlier to suggest both a body of intellectual reformers as well as abstract intelligence in French rhetoric of the 1830s and among German reformers of the late 1840s. See, on the latter, R. Pipes, "'Intelligentsia' from the German," loc. cit., 615–8. Pipes's reference to the example that he incorrectly calls the first usage "in the modern sense" (616) is also inaccurate—the place of publication being Leipzig, the page reference 5251.

117. Cieszkowski, *De la pairie et de l'aristocratie moderne*, 1844. Though published in Paris, this work, like his others, had its main impact through Poznań, where he eventually became cofounder and president of the Poznań Association of the Friends of Learning. See Walicki, "Messianists," 104.

118. Pepłowski, 167. The usage of 1854 implies a distinction between the intelligentsia and the simple people; the usage of 1857 suggests that the intelligentsia is essentially snobbish.

119. Continuing Polish priority in origination of the terms is again indicated in the case of *inteligentny*, the adjectival form of *intelligentsia*. The Polish version is already listed in a Polish encyclopedia of 1863: ". . . in the broadest sense of the word we call *inteligentny* everyone who is a complete master of some branch of knowledge, for instance, a statesman, an architect, etc." *Encyklopedyja powszechna S. Orgelbranda*, XII, 1863, 617–8, as cited in Wójcik, 22 n. 6.

120. M. Malia, "Schiller and the Early Russian Left," in *Harvard Slavic Studies*, IV, 1957, 188.

121. *Polnoe sobranie sochinenii*, XI, 1956, 293–4.

122. Letter of Feb 4, 1837, in A. Kornilov, *Molodye gody Mikhaila Bakunina*, I, 1915, 376.

123. *Polnoe sobranie*, XII, 22.

124. A. Koyré, *Etudes sur l'histoire de la pensée philosophique en Russie*, 1950, 161. See also the informed bibliographical discussion of Hegel's influence in Russia.

125. The genesis of this "philosophy of action" among the Slavs is traced in Volodin, *Gegel'*, 138 ff.

126. Ogarev, cited from P. Sakulin, *Russkaia literatura i sotsializm*, 1924, 158–9, by Walicki, in *Annali*, VI, 1963, 122.

127. See A. Walicki, "Cieszkowski a Hercen," *Studia filozoficzne*, 1965, no. 2, 137–64; and *Polskie spory*, 153–242.

128. In a letter to C. von Bunsen, cited from Bunsen, *Aus seinen Briefen*, Leipzig, 1869, II, 133, in McLellan, *Marx*, 40–1.

129. Including the Danish theologian Søren Kierkegaard and the Russian novelist Ivan Turgenev. Subsequent lectures attracted an astonishing range of Russians, including the future reactionary leader Mikhail Katkov, the Slavophile philosopher Yury Samarin, and the theorist of conspiratorial revolution, Nicholas Ogarev. See Volodin, *Gegel'*, 280.

130. See the reprinted translation *Trubny glas strashnogo suda nad Gegelem*, 1933; also Volodin, 138.

131. Cited from *Deutsche Jahrbücher*, 1842, Oct, in M. Bakunin, *Sobranie sochinenii i pisem'*, 1935, III, 148; see also *Annali*, VI, 1963, 110.

132. It seems never to have been pointed out that this motto was very close to that held to be the "secret of masonry" revealed only to the final, 33d level of Scottish Masonry—at least in Italy in the nineteenth century: *Distruggere e rifabbricare*, Sòriga, *Albori*, 36. As in so many other revolutionary matters, Masonic derivation seems likely in the case of Proudhon, since he was active in the lodges of his native Besançon, where the Masonic and revolutionary traditions had early interconnections.

133. *God and the State*, Boston, 1883.

134. M. Stirner (pseud. of Johann K. Schmidt), *The Ego and His Own*, NY, 1918.

135. *Izbrannye proizvedeniia progressivnykh pol'skikh myslitelei v trekh tomakh*, 1958, II, 292. "Kilka myśli o eklektyzmie," *Rok*, 1843.

136. "Myśli o przyszłości filozofii," *Rok*, 1845; also *Polskie spory*, 277–368.

137. See discussion in Janion, *Gorgcka*, 456–8.

138. Description of J. Feldman in *The Cambridge History of Poland*, NY, 1971, II, 352–4. Still the best overall account of Dembowski is M. Stecka, "Edward Dembowski," *Przegląd Historyczny*, XII, 1910, nos. 1, 2.

139. The former published in 2v, Poznań, 1843, 1845; the latter, Brussels, 1844.

140. S. Edwards, *Selected Writings of Proudhon*, 16.

141. L. Namier, *1848: The Revolution of the Intellectuals*, NY, 1946. More recent scholarship is incorporated into P. Stearns, *1848: The Revolutionary Tide in Europe*, NY, 197. These events are set in the full European context in W. Langer, *Political and Social Upheaval 1832–1852*, NY, 1969, esp. 319–512.

142. Their importance is stressed in W. Langer, "The Pattern of Urban Revolution in 1848," in E. Acomb and M. Brown, *French Society and Culture Since the Old Regime*, NY, 1966, 90–108.

143. Langer, *Upheaval*, 89; J. Baughman, "The French Banquet Campaign of 1847–1848," *Journal of Modern History*, XXXI, 1959, Mar, 1–15.

144. R. Baldick, *The Life and Times of Frederick Lemaitre*, L, 1959, 79, also 80.

145. Ibid., 199.

146. P. Robertson, *Revolutions of 1848: A Social History*, Princeton, 1952, 54.

147. A. Zévaès, "Le mouvement social sous la restauration et sous la monarchie de juillet," *La Révolution de 1848*, 1936–37, Dec-Jan-Feb, 235.

148. Felix Pyat, cited in Baldick, 202; Zévaès, 235.
Théophile Gautier, who had been present at the tumultuous debut of *Hernani*, seemed to find the audience reaction of "fanaticism, frenzy" in 1848 even more extraordinary. See Zévaès, 236; also Baldick, 200. *Le Chiffonnier de Paris* was so popular that it gave birth to a parody, *Le chiffon-nié de par ici*.

149. Cited in Zévaès, 235.

150. Langer, *Upheaval*, 347–8; and articles by P. Amann, referenced n. 53.

151. "La chanson du banquet," of Feb 21, 1848, cited in A. Zévaès, "Pierre Dupont, chansonnier de 1848," *La Révolution de 1848*, 1931, Mar-Apr-May, 39.

152. "La Jeune République," in ibid., 40. See also Dupont's "La Marseillaise de l'atelier," 37–8.

153. Lamartine, "Manifesto to Europe," in Postgate, *Revolution*, 193.
For a major new study of the Hungarian Revolution, see I. Deak, *The Lawful Revolution: Louis Kossuth and the Hungarians 1848–1849*, NY, 1979; and, of the most important of the several Slavic national revolutions that eventually came into conflict with the Hungarian, see I. Leshchilovskaia, *Obshchestvenno-politicheskaia bor'ba v khorvatii 1848–1849*, 1977. See esp. 256–63, for the efforts of the Poles, who fought in leading roles for the Hungarians, simultaneously to aid the Croatians. For the conflict of a non-Slavic national minority with the Hungarian Revolution, see K. Hitchins, *Rumanian National Movement in Transylvania, 1780–1849*, Cambridge, Mass., 1969, 243–56.
The conflict between universalist advocates of constitutional liberty and nation-

alist advocates of fraternity had an echo in the new world in the general failure
of radical abolitionists to enlist Irish nationalists in the struggle against black
slavery. See G. Osofsky, "Abolitionists, Irish Immigrants and the Dilemmas of Romantic Nationalism," *American Historical Review*, 1975, Oct, esp. 911–2.

154. *Howitt's Journal*, 1848, Mar 25, 207.
155. Ibid., Apr 8, 235–6; Apr 22, 267–9.
156. Ibid., Apr 22, 269.
157. D. Mattheisen, "1848: Theory and Practice of the German *juste milieu*,"
The Review of Politics, 1973, Apr, 187–90.
158. H. Payne, *The Police State of Louis Napoleon Bonaparte 1851–1860*, Seattle,
1966.
159. J. Sloane, *Paul Marc Joseph Chenavard. Artist of 1848*, Chapel Hill, 1962;
Egbert, *Radicalism*, 183–6.
160. From the musically climactic statement of the revolutionary faith in the
third act of U. Giordano's opera about the Reign of Terror, *Andrea Chenier* (1896):
"Fare del mondo un Pantheon! Gli uomini in dei mutare e in un sol bacio e ab-
braccio tutte le genti amare!"
161. Sloane, 46–7, 112 ff. In addition to murals and mosaics, the four main pillars
were to be faced with statues symbolizing the four divisions of history and stages
of social development: the golden age of religion (Moses), the silver age of poetry
(Homer), the bronze age of philosophy (Aristotle), and the iron age of science
(Galileo). There were to be statues of Adam and Eve on either side of the main
entrance. Sloane relates this symbolism to the sexual theories of Enfantin (114–5),
without understanding the serious, androgynous ideal that underlies the whole
development of romantic thought from Ballanche through Enfantin to Chenavard.
162. Ibid., 109–10.
163. Text of letter of Sep 9, 1852, in *Przeglad Historyczny*, LVIII, 1967, 116–17;
discussion in S. Kieniewicz, *Les Insurrections polonaises du XIXe siècle et le
problème de l'aide de la France*, Warsaw, 1971, 4–5.

Chapter 9

1. Bertier de Sauvigny, "Liberalism," 147–66, analyzes three distinct (and usually successive) stages in the history of an important new political label: the *mor-
phological* creation of a new word, its *semantic* association with a new concept,
and its *lexical maturity*, when it comes into common usage. The birth of communism, which he does not discuss, provides a unique example of all three stages
occurring virtually simultaneously.
Even the previously discussed and altogether disconnected prehistory of this word
by Restif de la Bretonne in the eighteenth century was abrupt rather than evolutionary. Restif created the word to express a full-blown semantic meaning.
The only indication of any possible intervening printed use of the term between
Restif in the 1790s and 1840 is an undocumented attribution to Lamennais in
Dauzat, *Nouveau dictionnaire*, 182. I have found no usage by Lamennais in the
1830s, nor did Y. Le Hir in his study of terms: *Lamennais Ecrivain*, 1948.
Work in progress by J. Grandjonc of Aix, which I learned of too late for use in this
work, will apparently supplement, but not significantly modify, my account.
2. Sauvigny, 149.
3. Ibid., 157, also 155–60. During the French Revolution, the designation of
anything as an "ism" (*Jacobinisme, sans-culottisme*, etc.) was almost always a
form of insult if not denunciation. In exile after the Revolution of 1848, Metternich
argued that the ending *isme* invariably implied scorn (ibid., 150).
4. Ibid., 160.
5. The usage by Ferdinando Facchinei, *Note ed osservazioni sul libro intitolato
'Dei delitti e delle pene*,' directed against Beccaria, is discussed in F. Venturi,
" 'Socialista' e 'socialismo' nell'Italia del settecento," *Rivista Storica Italiana*, LXXV,
1963, 129–41. Earlier uses of the different term *socialista* among jurists of the natural law school following Grotius are discussed in H. Müller, *Ursprung und Geschichte des Wortes Sozialismus und seiner Verwandten*, Hanover, 1967, 30 ff.
6. By Giacomo Giuliani, *L'antisocialismo confutato—Opera filósofica*, Vicenza,
1903, 74, who also used the verb "to socialize oneself" (*socializzarsi*), 160, discussed
in Müller, 37.
7. G. Laurent, "Drouet sous le Directoire—A propos d'une lettre," *Annales Historiques*, X, 1925, 412–6. The full text of Drouet's letter has been lost, but he also
spoke in 1798 of the need to "watch over the intrigues of the *socialist* fanatics and
émigrés," 416. Sauvigny believes that the word was probably used in France before

Drouet ("Libéralisme," 162 n. 31). See also J. Godechot, "Pour un vocabulaire politique et social de la révolution française," *Actes du 89e Congrès des sociétés savantes*, I, 1964.

8. J. Gans, "L'Origine du mot 'socialiste' et ses emplois les plus anciens," *Revue d'Histoire Economique et Sociale*, XXX, 1957, 79–83, using the Owen correspondence in Manchester. Applegath (apparently also called Applegarth) had been an instructor at New Lanarck and belonged to a short-lived Education Society at New Harmony, Indiana. R. Leopold, *Robert Dale Owen. A Biography*, Harvard, 1940, 36–7.

9. 1827, Nov, 509; cited in Bestor, 277.

10. Adam Mickiewicz, cited in Walicki, "Messianists," 99.

11. First used in French publications apparently by a Swiss, Alexandre Vinet, "Catholicisme et Protestantisme," *Le Semeur*, 1831, Nov 23, cited in Müller, 97. Müller provides the most thorough discussion; and other references here are largely to materials either unused or underused by him.

12. Deville, "Origine," esp. 387–98, still provides the best basic references and discussion of these early usages. See also Bestor, 277 n. 95.

13. Charles Pellarin (the journalistic organizer of the conference, who had both Saint-Simonian and Fourierist links), cited in Müller, 102.

14. J. Kayser, *Les grandes batailles du radicalisme des origines aux portes du pouvoir 1820–1901*, 1962, 8; Müller, 54–5, for earlier British uses.

15. Metternich wrote that "*liberalism* has been replaced by *radicalism*" in a letter of Jun 10, 1832, to the Austrian ambassador in Berlin, Count von Trauttmansdorff, from text in V. Valentin, *Nationalfest*, 138–9.

16. See G. Alroy, "Les radicaux après la révolution de 1848," *Le Contrat Social*, 1966, Sep–Oct, 290–1.

17. M. Laffitte, quoted from *Siècle*, 1839, Mar 22, in *Procès de T. Thoré*, 1841, 19.

18. Cited from the first in a series of articles on communism in France in *Augsburger Allgemeine Zeitung*, 1840, Mar 11, in F. Klitzsch, *Sozialismus und soziale Bewegung im Spiegel der Augsburger "Allgemeinen Zeitung" 1840–1850*, Gütersloh, 1934, 32–3. The usage in this neglected journal (which also anticipated in its ABC des Kommunismus the title of the original Soviet indoctrination manual by Bukharin) thus antedates any of the usages documented in the best available discussion of the precise early uses of the word by Bestor, "Evolution," 278–81, or other works here referenced. The first Italian usage is traced from the French and dated 1840 without precise references in S. Battaglia, *Grande Dizionario della lingua italiana*, Turin, III, 448.

A. Bobkov indicates that shortly after Jan, 1837, an agent of Metternich reported that Schuster's League of Outlaws was conducting "now democratic, now communist, now republican agitation" ("K istorii raskola soiuza otverzhennykh v 1836–1837 godakh," *Novaia i Noveishaia Istoriia*, 1959, no. 5, 102). But the original article from which Bobkov took his reference makes it clear that this report dated in fact from 1843 (G. Wendel, "Vorläufer des Sozialismus," *Der Abend*, 1929. Nov 19).

19. The rapid spread of the new term can be traced in three early surveys: the generally sympathetic work of L. von Stein, *Der Socialismus und Communismus des heutigen Frankreichs*, Leipzig, 1842; the very alarmist L. de Carné, "De quelques publications démocratiques et communistes," *Revue des Deux Mondes*, 1841, Sep 1, 724–47; the antagonistic but relatively scholarly L. Reybaud, "Des idées et des sectes communistes," *Revue des Deux Mondes*, 1842, Jul 1, 5–47.

This latter work, which I discovered only after completing this section, has no precise documentation but suggests in general terms a direction close to that which I develop here—particularly stressing the roles of Buonarroti, Owen, and Cabet—and suggests (28) that communism as a conscious and organized movement began only after the failure of the Blanquist insurrection in May, 1839.

Numerous German newspaper usages of 1841 are documented in Schieder, *Anfänge*, 271 n. 1; also usage in the London *Times*, 1841, Nov 13, 5. For substance and controversy in early usage, see A. Cuvillier, "Action ouvrière et communisme en France vers 1840 et aujourd'hui," *La Grande Revue*, 1921, Dec, 25–35; and his "Les communistes allemands," in *Hommes et Idéologies de 1840*, 1956, 121–37.

20. From the Leipzig *Illustrierte Zeitung*, 1843, Sep 2, 9, as cited in K. Koszyk, "Das Jahr 1845 und der deutsche Sozialismus," *Annali*, 1963, VI, 516–7. The author goes on to speak of "Communism in the higher sense" as the provision of educational and other benefits for workers.

21. Schieder, *Anfänge*, 270–1; A. Zévaès, "L'Agitation communiste de 1840 à 1848," *La Révolution de 1848*, 1926, Oct, 974.

22. By Buffenoir, "Communisme à Lyon," 348, without any indication, however, that it was so designated by contemporaries.

23. M. McDougall, "After the Insurrections. The Workers' Movement in Lyon, 1834–1852," unpublished doctoral dissertation, Columbia, 1974, 201, and ff.

24. On the *Société des travailleurs*, and its Buonarrotian hierarchical structure under a secret directional committee that controlled special *agents révolutionnaires*, see Rémusat, *Mémoires de ma vie*, 1960, III, 390–1. There were 8 in a *métier* headed by "a worker," 3 *métiers* in an *atelier* headed by a foreman, and 3 *ateliers* in a *fabrique* headed by a shopman (*commis*).
The organization was said to number "less than 500 members" (ibid., 391). The best account of the emergence of the communists from the Babeuvist tradition (which does not mention this organization, however) is Zévaès, "Agitation," Oct, 971–81; Dec, 1035–44; 1927, Mar–Apr–May, 31–46.

25. McDougall, 223–4; J. Benoît, *Confessions d'un prolétaire*, 1968 (originally written in 1871), 61–2.

26. Benoît, *Confessions*, 37–40, 56–7. For details on his secret, hierarchical organization, which lasted until 1843, see McDougall, 223–5.

27. M. Mikhailov, *Istoriia soiuza kommunistov*, 1968, 54; Cabet, *Histoire du journal "Intelligence,"* 7 (undated fragment in BN, identified only as an extract from *Le Populaire*, no. 6). Cabet continues: "*L'Intelligence ne s'est jamais avoué communiste parce qu'elle ne jugeait pas qu'il fut opportun de le faire alors; mais les idées et les principes qu'elle développait menaient droit à la communauté.*"

28. On Lyon, Benoît, 59–60; McDougall, 222, 227. On Switzerland, Barnikol, *Geschichte*, 16; Pianzola, "Expulsion," 65.

29. *Intelligence*, 1838, Aug 7.

30. Report of the trial in *Intelligence*, 1838, Sep 3.

31. The slogan of Blanqui's journal of 1834, *Le Libérateur*. Dommanget (*Blanqui des origines*, 129) overlooks the significance of this substitution, but stresses (through 144) the importance of the journal in establishing the modern ideal of a class-based social revolution. Only one issue appeared (1834, Feb 2) with the revealing subtitle *Journal des opprimés voulant une réforme sociale par la République*. Blanqui prepared for the second issue his famous article "Who makes the soup should eat it," which Benoît Malon considered the first formulation of modern collectivist doctrine. Dommanget, 129–30.

32. J.-J. Pillot, Th. Dézamy, Dutelloz, Homberg, *Premier banquet communiste 1er juillet 1840*, 1840, 1. P. Angrand modifies to 1,000 the number of attendees from the 1,200 stated in the brochure: "Notes critiques sur la formation des idées communistes en France," *La Pensée*, 1948, Sep–Oct, 62.

33. *Banquet*, 1, 9.

34. Various toasts in ibid., 11–2.

35. Toast of the tailor Vellicus, 6–7.

36. Various toasts, 4, 3, 8. The first of these explicitly intended to insert "a new word" into "this motto."

37. This toast (by an otherwise unidentified Courmont, 12) concludes: "To the Government of Equals!"

38. Pillot, 14. The Saint-Simonian songwriter Vinçard had previously coined the slogan "Unite yourselves!" as the revolutionary answer to Louis Philippe's "Enrich yourselves!" and added "unity" to "liberty, equality, fraternity." See F. Isambert, "Une religion de la fraternité. A propos de quelques journaux ouvrièrs sous la monarchie de juillet," *Journal de Psychologie Normale et Pathologique*, 1957, Jul–Sep, 319.

39. This designation was first given the revolutionary intellectual fringe within the Parisian Society of Workers which arose in 1839 and, according to the unreferenced assertion of C. Johnson, "also called itself simply Les Communistes." *Utopian Communism in France. Cabet and the Icarians, 1839–1851*, Ithaca, 1974, 75.

40. Almost every point of view on the Left produced a supporting interpretation of the French Revolution during the period between the revolutions of 1830 and 1848. The basic text for egalitarian social revolutionaries remained Buonarroti's *History of the Conspiracy of Equals*; for revolutionary nationalists, Michelet's work; for liberal nationalists, Adolphe Thiers's *Histoire de la Révolution française* (1836 and numerous subsequent editions). Christian socialists leaned on Buchez's *Introduction à la science de l'histoire*, and his *Histoire parlementaire de la Révolution française* (written in collaboration with Roux-Lavargne between 1833 and 1838); idealistic secular socialists, on Louis Blanc's *Histoire de la Révolution française* (first two v, 1847); etc. *Annales Historiques de la Révolution Française*, 1966, Apr–Jun, is almost entirely devoted to analyzing the views on the French Revolution of early French socialists.

41. Text of his "Observations sur Maximilien Robespierre," reprinted (from its original anonymous publication as a supplement to the Brussels *Le Radical* in 1837,

and in *La Fraternité*, 1842, Sep, in *Revue Historique de la Révolution Française*, III, 1912, 479–87, esp. 481–2.

As early as Nov 24, 1832 (*Poor Man's Guardian*, lead story, 617–8), Buonarroti's translator, Bronterre O'Brien, had attempted to tell the "Real Character of Robespierre," quoting from Buonarroti and insisting that "Robespierre held nearly the same doctrines which the benevolent Robert Owen promulgates now—viz., a community of property, or rather an equitable distribution of the fruits of human labor among those who produce them. . . ." This anonymous article was followed by speeches and articles that climaxed in O'Brien's admiring *Life and Times of Maximilien Robespierre* in 1838.

42. See particularly his *Cours publique de l'histoire de France depuis 1789 jusqu'à 1830*; and his *Histoire de la révolution française*, 1838, 2v. The relevant passages are cited and his neglected ideas discussed in G. Santanastaso, *Il Socialismo francese*, Florence, 1954, 110–3.

43. *Oeuvres de Maximilien Robespierre*, 1840. See also his *Mémoires de Charlotte Robespierre sur ses deux frères*, 1835.

44. Laponneraye, "Babeuf et son système," *L'Intelligence*, 1840, Feb, 1–2.

45. Laponneraye, *Catéchisme démocratique*, n.d., 5.

46. Ibid., 3, 6.

47. Ibid., 12–3.

48. "Une révolution radicale dans les moeurs," *L'Intelligence*, 1838, Jul.

49. "Place au prolétariat," *L'Intelligence*, 1837, Sep, 4. This self-conscious rephrasing of Abbé Sieyès from the first issue of Laponneraye's journal was later repeated by Marx, whose borrowing of phrases and motifs from the original French communists has never been adequately recognized, let alone studied.

50. T. Dézamy, *Question proposée par l'Académie des Sciences Morales et Politiques. Les Nations avancent plus en connaissance en lumières qu'en morale pratique? Recherches la cause de cette différence dans leurs progrès, et indiques le remède*, 1839, 59. Revolutionary thought was powerfully stimulated by this essay contest, to which the young Dézamy wrote this neglected answer, dated in the text Dec 27, 1838.

51. Ibid., 59, 61.

52. Ibid., 63 n. 1.

53. *Code de la communauté*, 1842, 110; also 230–4.

54. *Patriotes français, lisez et rougissez de honte*, 1840. This antinationalist tone was also evident in Cabet's *Lettres sur la crise actuelle*, 1840.

55. Angrand, "Notes," 63 n. 1.

56. Leading some to assume incorrectly that Lamennais originated the word. See P. Gason, "Lamennais, a t'il lancé le mot 'communiste'?" *Le Monde*, 1954, Aug 18, 7; refuted by H. Desroche, "A propos de Lamennais et du mot 'communiste,'" *Actualité de l'histoire*, 1955, Mar, 28–32. For attacks by conservatives on Lamennais, see de Carné, "Publications," 728–31.

Lamennais left behind at his death a description of communism as "two doctrines within a single denomination . . . the one negative, the other positive, the one of destruction, the other of renovation." Desroche, "A propos," 31.

57. Cited and discussed in the only serious article ever written on this neglected figure: R. Garaudy, "Le Communisme matérialiste en France avant 1848: un précurseur Théodore Dézamy," *La Pensée*, 1848, May–Jun, 42. In 1841, when Lamennais began using the term himself (*Du passé et de l'avenir du peuple*, 1871, 91–5), he was denounced by a number of self-proclaimed communist correspondents from Lyon, Rouen, and elsewhere, who accused him of glorifying "the egoism of the family, which is in a small way what exclusive patriotism is in a large way, the egoism of the nation." A. Saitta, "Appunti e documenti per la storia del socialismo premarxista," *Movimento Operaio*, 1956, Sep–Oct, 772; also documents and references, 768–73.

58. *Calomnies et politique de M. Cabet*, 1842, 6. Cabet responded with *Toute la vérité au peuple ou réfutation d'un pamphlet calomniateur*, 1842. Garaudy (45) calls Dézamy the first to see "that philosophical intransigence was necessary to forge a Communist Party."

Once again, such was the dynamic of denunciation that Dézamy was denouncing Cabet for precisely the sin of religiosity of which Cabet had previously accused the "Constantinist" communist protégés of the Abbé Constant—Cabet's *Communist Credo* having been written in part to combat the influence of Constant's *Evangile de la liberté*, 1841, which was also translated into German. See Chacornac, *Levi*, 54 ff., and the Parisian police study of 1845: "Renseignements," *Actualité de l'histoire*, 1957, Oct, 26 n. 4. Only later in his *Le vrai Christianisme suivant Jésus-Christ*, 1846 (also 1847, 1850) did Cabet try to equate communism with "true Christianity," but never in such a way as to indicate that Christian teachings were for him (as they clearly were for many of the Germans like Schapper and Weitling) an independent source of some inspiration. See J. Prudhommeaux, *Icarie et son fondateur Etienne Cabet,* 1907, 162–3.

59. *Code,* 290.
60. Ibid., 291.
61. 268–9.
62. 157 n. 1.
63. 156–61.
64. *Le Jésuitisme vaincu et anéanti par le socialisme, ou les constitutions des Jésuites et leurs instructions secrètes en parallèle avec un projet d'organisation du travail,* 1845, 134.
65. *Calomnies,* 35–6, cited in Garaudy, 206–7. Dézamy is denouncing the new journalism of Emile de Girardin.
66. *Code,* 237.
67. *Question,* 14; also *Code,* 286–7.
68. *Question,* 58.
69. *Code,* 292.
70. Ibid., 261.
71. Ibid., 123.
72. Ibid.
73. Ibid., 285.
74. De la Hodde, 269.
75. On Dézamy's skillful self-defense in court as a "purely theoretical" writer, see G. Bourgin, "Le Communiste Dézamy," *Festschrift für Carl Grünberg,* Leipzig, 1932, 69–74, esp. 70.
See Ruge, "Dézamy und die Pressefreiheit," in *Zwei Jahre in Paris,* Leipzig, 1846, I, esp. 77, 92–3, on their close friendship. Hess began a German translation of his *Code* with the encouragement of Marx: *Gesetztbuch der Gemeinschaft nach Theodor Dézamy,* unpublished ms. dated about 1846 by E. Silberner, *The Works of Moses Hess,* Leiden, 1958, 77. See also Hess's letters to Marx (Hess, *Philosophische und sozialistische Schriften 1837–1850,* 1961, 482–4); Garaudy, *Sources,* 191; and the German translation of *Le Jésuitisme,* Leipzig, 1846, along with a shorter extract: *Organisations-Entwurf,* Leipzig, 1848. Dézamy's neglected impact on Marx is discussed in D. Riazanov, *Ocherki po istorii marksizma,* 1923, 76–7.
The mysterious figure of Nicholas Speshnev, who introduced the idea of revolutionary communism into Russia in the mid-forties, sided with Dézamy against Cabet. (See his letter to a Polish friend in V. Evgrafova, ed., *Filosofskie i obshchestvenno-politicheskie proizvedeniia petrashevtsev,* 1953, 488–502.) The early years of Speshnev, like the late ones of Dézamy, remain an enigma. Speshnev apparently fought in the Swiss civil war during the early 1840s and became the partial model for Stavrogin in Dostoevsky's *Possessed.* He never fulfilled his promise to explain fully the communist beliefs he propagated in Russia in the late forties (see *Literaturnoe nasledstvo,* LXIII, 1956, 171–2). His idea (later developed by Bakunin) that an inner communist group would supersede the Jesuits could have been inspired by Dézamy's *Le Jésuitisme* of 1845, though it dates back, as we have seen, to the Illuminists and Bonneville. Speshnev advocated that the central committee have three coequal subordinate bodies: Jesuitical, propagandistic, and revolutionary.
76. In addition to *Le Jésuitisme,* see his *Examen critique des huit discours sur le Catholicisme et la philosophie, prononcés à Notre-Dame, en décembre 1844 et en janvier 1845, etc. par M. Dézamy d'après les principes de la philosophie naturelle,* 1845; and his *Organisation de la liberté et du bien-être universel,* 1846, cited and discussed in Garaudy, *Sources,* 199–200. Garaudy, who was then a leading French communist intellectual, reproduces Dézamy's refutation of Lamennais (209–18) as a kind of model for answering objections to communism. Dézamy is also praised in the neglected brochure of Benoît Malon, *Le Parti ouvrièr en France,* 1882.
77. *Question,* 56.
78. Ibid., 65, also 64.
79. P. Schuller, "Karl Marx's Atheism," *Science and Society,* 1975, Fall, 331.
80. *Izbrannye sochineniia,* 1961, 118. Iconoclastic Russians of the 1950s also called themselves *nibonicho* (a contraction for "neither God nor the devil"). See Billington, *Icon,* 779–80 n. 26.
The use of the word "nihilist" as a political term also began with this idea. Cloots on Dec 27, 1793, said, "The Republic of the rights of man is properly speaking neither theist nor atheist but nihilist." Cited in A. Aulard, *Paris pendant la réaction thermidorienne et sous le directoire,* 1899, II, 285.
Pillot made a fetish of Babeuvist associations. His journal of 1839 was *Tribune of the People;* and his treatise of 1840 *History of the equals or ways of establishing*

equality among men, began with a "Manifesto of Contemporary Equals." See, in addition to the bibliographical sketch by I. Zil'berfarb in Pillot, *Sochineniia*, S. Bernstein, "Le Néo-Babouvisme·d'après la presse (1837–1848)," in *Babeuf et les problèmes*, 246–76; and V. Volgin, "Jean-Jacques Pillot, communiste utopique," *La Pensée*, 1959, Mar–Apr. Volgin also points out (*Frantsuzsky utopichesky kommunizm*, 1960, 25–6) that Pillot used a sophisticated if functional class analysis of the roles played in the reaction by different "castes."

81. After Cabet's *Voyage and Adventures of Lord William Carisdale in Icaria* was first published in a small London edition (the French original purportedly translated from English) in 1839, a Paris edition appeared in Jan 1840, closely followed by translations into German, Spanish, and English along with additional digested and paraphrased editions. (See F. Rudé, *Voyage en Icarie. Deux ouvriers viennois aux Etats-Unis en 1855*, 1952, esp. 5; and A. Lehning, "Discussions à Londres sur le communisme icarien," *Bulletin of the International Institute of Social History*, 1952, no. 2, 87 and ff.). The book was subtitled a "philosophical and social novel"—the exact term used as a subtitle by Flora Tristan's *Méphis ou le prolétaire* of 1838, one of the most influential of the artistically second-rate, but propagandistic "social novels" of the 1830s. See D. Evans, "Le roman social sous la monarchie du juillet, Romans démocratiques. L'apothéose du prolétaire," *French Quarterly*, 1931, Sep, esp. 104; also A. Zévaès, "Le Mouvement social sous la restauration et sous la monarchie de juillet," *La Révolution de 1848*, 1936–7, Dec–Jan–Feb, 232 ff.

The better prose fiction of the pre–1848 era, of course, also focused the attention of thinking people on the plight of the urban masses from the London of Dickens's *Oliver Twist* to the Paris of Hugo's *Les Misérables* and Sue's *Mystères de Paris*, to the St. Petersburg of Gogol and the early Dostoevsky. Thus, it might be said that the prosaic media (including Daumier's lithographed cartoons and the didactic pamphlets produced by the new high-speed printing as well as the programmatic novel) contributed to the rationalistic ideas of the social revolutionaries almost as much as the poetic media of romantic music and lyric poetry contributed to the rival and more emotional ideal of the national revolutionaries. If vernacular opera was in some ways, as we have suggested, the highest cultural expression of revolutionary nationalism, the ideological novel like *Icaria* may have played a similar role for social revolutionaries. Probably the most influential of all were the immensely popular novels of George Sand, which successfully fused propaganda and art into the quasi-religious communism of her *Le Meunier d'Angibault* (1845–6) and *Le péché de M. Antoine* (1847). See Evans, *Socialisme*, 124–31.

82. According to C. Tsuzuki, "Robert Owen and Revolutionary Politics," in S. Pollard and J. Salt, eds., *Robert Owen Prophet of the Poor*, Lewisburg, Pa., 1971, 34.

83. See H. Desroche, "Images and Echoes of Owenism in Nineteenth-Century France," in ibid., 246–7. See Saitta, *Buonarroti*, I, 64–9. Rey's exposition of Owen's ideas (reprinted from *Producteur*, 1826, Sep–Oct), *Lettres sur le système de la coopération mutuelle et de la communauté de tous les biens, d'après le plan de M. Owen*, 1828, called for "la communauté de jouissance des produits, basée sur l'égalité," 33. Rey then set up an Owenite Cooperative Society in Paris (J. Gans, "Robert Owen à Paris en 1837," *Le Mouvement Social*, 1962, Oct–Dec, 35).

Buonarroti himself hailed Owen as early as 1828 (*History of the Conspiracy*, cited in Pollard, *Owen*, 248) and grew to admire him even more in his late years. See the important article relating Owen much more intimately to the revolutionary tradition than is usual: A. Mathiez, "Babeuf et Robert Owen comparés et défendus par Buonarroti," *La Révolution de 1848*, 1910, 233–9.

Engels discovered Owen's teachings simultaneously with the English proletariat on his first visit to a factory in Manchester in 1843, contributing two important articles on continental socialism to Owen's *New Moral World*, 1843, Nov 4, 18 (Riazanov, *Ocherki*, 44–5, 100–1). There are some 300 extracts from Owen—by far the most from any earlier socialist thinker—in Marx's notebooks of 1845–7. See M. Rubel, "Les Cahiers de Lecture de Karl Marx," *International Review of Social History*, II, 1957, 401–2.

84. Berbrugger, cited in Sauvigny, "Liberalism," 163.

85. Owen was on his way to seeing Metternich—one of his periodic unsuccessful attempts to interest rulers in his communal ideas. See F. Podmore, *Robert Owen. A Biography*, L, 1906, II, 459–60. Desroche, 249–58.

86. Bestor, "Evolution," 278, corrects the otherwise valuable work of K. Grünberg, "Der Ursprung der Worte 'Sozialismus' und 'Sozialist,'" *Archiv für die Geschichte des Sozialismus und der Arbeiterbewegung*, II, 1912, 378, which has led many to assume that Owen used the term "communist" rather than these related words.

87. The last verse of a typical song from *Social Hymns* (Leeds, 1838, L, 1840)

in Podmore, II, 472. Owen also wrote a *Social Bible* (Manchester, 1835) and a *Catechism of the New Moral World* (Manchester, 1838; 2d ed. Leeds, 1838).

88. Gay tried unsuccessfully both to collaborate with Laponneraye's *Intelligence* in 1838–9 and to found his own journal *Communauté. Bulletin Mensuel de la Science Sociale* (Gans, 36–45). The latter effort probably inspired Dézamy's short-lived new journal of 1840, *Communautaire*. Gay and Dézamy collaborated in 1841 to publish *l'Humanitaire*, the first full-blown journal advocating revolutionary communism and "the most radical journal to see the light of day during the July Monarchy." (Johnson, *Communism*, 113. See also the confirming, contemporary judgment by a French student of Owen, A. Cochut, in *Revue des Deux Mondes*, 1841, Apr 1, 471.)

89. Desroche, in Pollard and Salt, *Owen*, 249. See also 262, 239–40. The substantial influence of both the ideas and example of Owen on Cabet is discussed in Prudhommeaux, *Cabet*, 133–9, but will almost certainly be stressed even more in the forthcoming study of Desroche, based on the unpublished work and personal archive of Prudhommeaux and other new materials.

90. Fourierist and Proudhonist attacks referenced in M. Rubel, "Robert Owen à Paris en 1848," *Actualité de l'Histoire*, 1960, Jan–Feb–Mar, 4–6.

91. Ibid., 10–2 for text of his *Proclamation au peuple français aux militaires et aux civils de toutes les classes, de tous les partis, de toutes les religions*, 1848, Jun; also 5–6 for Owen's other Parisian publications in 1848.

92. Cabet's interest in dictatorial revolutionary leadership was developed in England in the late 1830s and exemplified in his *Histoire populaire de la révolution française*, first ed. up to 1830, 1839–40, 4v; second ed., up to 1845, 1845, 6v; and especially in his *Rapport sur les mesures à prendre . . . le lendemain d'une insurrection victorieuse*, L, 1840, about which see Lehning, "Discussions," 91–3, 96. Cabet's *Voyage en Icarie*, 1845, 360, foresaw a "transient reign of 30–100 years." He may have derived these ideas from Teste, whom he knew in London, or even from Buonarroti, with whom he exchanged the first version of *Icaria* for a copy of his *History of the Babeuf Conspiracy* (see *Toute la vérité*, 85–6); but O'Brien, Buonarroti's translator (and follower in the cult of Robespierre), seems a more likely source for this emphasis, in view of his proximity and notoriety in London.

93. "Journal of a Social Mission to France," *The New Moral World*, I, 1840, Jul 11, no. 2, 21.

94. *New Moral World*, I, 1840, Jul 18, no. 3, 43.

95. Ibid., no. 2, 21.

96. Ibid.

97. Ibid., I, 1840, Aug 1, no. 5, 74.

98. Ibid.

99. Ibid.

100. Barmby says only that the prospectus was presented to an unidentifiable "M. Harve" (ibid). Since, however, Gay is prominently discussed on the same page along with a French bibliography of the works of Owen, which only Gay could have provided, it seems likely that Gay was in fact the "ardent friend" chosen to head the Association.

101. *New Moral World*, I, 1840, Aug 1, no. 5, 77, in a separate section labeled "French Correspondence" where Barmby speaks of a "Communitarian dinner." His earlier advance notice referred to "a social banquet of the adherents of the *Communist* or Communitarian school" (ibid., 75).

102. Barmby claimed that, while in Paris, "in the company of some disciples of Babeoeuf [sic], then called equalitarians, I first pronounced the name of Communist," in his lead article in *The Apostle, and Chronicle of the Communist Church*, I, 1848, Aug 1, no. 1, 2. The only known copy of this article (which provides his own detailed account of his early career) is in GL. This citation is inadequately referenced in the *Oxford English Dictionary*, II, 701; as is the article on Barmby in the *Dictionary of National Biography*, 1921, I, which says that Barmby claimed to have originated the word *communisme* in discussion with an unnamed "French celebrity" during the trip to Paris.

103. *New Moral World*, I, 1840, Aug 22, no. 8, 123.

104. Ibid., 122.

105. Explanation of the change in editorial in *The Promethean*, I, no. 1, 12.

106. Text in *The Promethean*, I, no. 1, 23.

107. Ibid., 38, for typical hymns by Owen Howell: "God is ALL IN ALL. . . . Nature, the material Christ, Teacheth that he doth exist. . . ."

108. Prospectus, ibid., 23.

109. Plan for "Administrative Gradations in Communization" by Barmby on the front page of *The Communist Chronicle*, I, no. 14.

110. *New Tracts for the Times: or, Warmth, Light, and Food for the Masses.*

Bible Proofs from Isaiah Against Jesus Christ's Being the Messiah, L (dated 1842 in BM catalogue), 14.

111. Ibid., 10–1.

112. Ibid., 10.

113. W. Armytage, *Heavens Below. Utopian Experiments in England 1560–1960,* L, 1961, 198–9.

114. Ibid., 208.

115. Thomas Frost, *Forty Years' Recollections: Literary and Political,* L, 1880, 58–62, 70–1; Armytage, 201–4.

116. Frost, 67–8; A. Morton, *The English Utopia,* L, 1952, 134.

117. Frost, 71.

118. According to Frost, 74, also 67. Barmby's *Chronicle* is in NP, invalidating Morton's indication (135) that no copies have survived.

119. *The truth on Baptism by Water, According to the Doctrine of the Communist Church,* published as no. 5 of *The Communist Miscellany,* n.p., n.d., 2–3, GL.

120. *Communist Chronicle,* I, no. 12, 133. The italics are Barmby's.

121. Concluding paragraph of Barmby's "The Truth Concerning the Devil," in Morton, 136. See the anticipation of this idea in the revolutionary song of the 1830s, "The Devil is Dead": J. Puech, "Chants d'il y a cent ans, autour des Saint-Simoniens," *La Révolution de 1848,* 1933, Mar–Apr–May, 26–9.

122. Barmby translated *Avenir des Ouvriers* as *The Workman's Future* in *New Moral World,* I, 1840, Sep 26, no. 13, 196.

123. *Polska Chrystusowa* (1842–6) was succeeded by a second journal also published in Paris, *Brotherhood* (*Zbratnienie,* 1847–8). Królikowski exercised considerable influence in France through his writings of the early forties in *Le Populaire* under the pseudonym of "Charles." After Cabet moved to America late in 1848, Królikowski became editor of *Le Populaire* and general "mandataire du citoyen Cabet." Brock, "Socialists," 160–1, and discussion following; also J. Turowski, *Utopia społeczna Ludwika Królikowskiego,* 1958.
See also Zenon Świętosławski's megalomaniacal "Statutes of the Universal Church," which proposed a world communist order with all property nationalized, a capital on the Isthmus of Suez, and Polish as the official language. Discussed in Brock, "Socialists," 157 ff.; text of statutes in *Lud Polski: Wybór,* 230–315; characterized as "revolutionary totalitarianism" by A. Walicki in his unpublished "The Problem of Revolution in Polish Thought of 1831–1848," 1976, 51.

124. Isambert, "Religion," 319.

125. Cited from edition of Apr 1844 in Isambert, 312.

126. Reproduced in Cuvillier, *Hommes,* opposite 78. For the central role of Buchez, the leader of Atelier, see ibid., 9–137; also Cuvillier, *Un Journal d'ouvriers. L'Atelier (1840–1850),* 1954.

127. Isambert, 320.

128. Ibid., 325.

129. Weitling, "Die Communion und die Kommunisten," *Der Hülferuf der deutschen Jugend,* 1841, Nov; as reprinted in W. Kowalski, *Vom Kleinbürgerlichen Demokratismus zum Kommunismus,* 1967, 149, 147.

130. See the example of radical hymnography in Schieder, 285 n. 23; and, on the already well established proliferation in Germany of revolutionary Ten Commandments, catechisms, and Lord's Prayers, 221–2. See also Barmby's "Exposition of the 'Lord's Prayer' According to the Doctrines of the Communist Church," *The Communist Miscellany,* I, no. 3, 49–50.

131. A. Scherzer, *Ermahnung zur Nächstenliebe, an die deutsche Jugend,* Paris, 1842, May, cited Schieder, 284.

132. A. Dietsch, *Gleichheit und Einigkeit, der Weg zur Freiheit und zum ewigen Frieden. Das tausendjährige Reich,* first published in the journal *Postthörnchen,* 1842, between Jul 22 and Aug 12, then separately in Aarau, 1843. These and many other examples are discussed in the section "Der religiöse Sozialismus der Weitlingianer," in Schieder, esp. 280–96. Dietsch soon shifted his millennial hopes to the New World (as Weitling was shortly to do). See his *Das tausendjährige Reich, nebst Plan und Statuten zur Gründung von New-Helvetia im Staate Missouri in Nordamerika,* Aarau, 1844.
This concept of a thousand-year kingdom also animated the radical prophecies of M. L. B. Müller (who called himself Ludwig Pröli) in Bavaria in the 1820s. After his arrest in 1830, he fled to the Millennarian Rappite communities of Pennsylvania. See F. Herrmann, "Maximilian Ludwig Proli, der Prophet von Offenbach," *Archiv für hessische Geschichte und Altertumskunde,* New Series, XIII, 1922, esp. 216–31.

133. Information from the official report of J. Bluntschli, *Die Kommunisten in der Schweiz nach den bei Weitling vorgefundenen Papieren,* Zürich, 1843; discussed

Wittke, 41. See also W. Seidel-Höppner, *Wilhelm Weitling, der erste deutsche Theoretiker und Agitator des Kommunismus*, 1961, 27–53; and G. Bravo, *Wilhelm Weitling e il comunismo tedesco prima del quarantotto*, Turin, 1963.

134. Cited in Wittke, 82.

135. Ibid., 98. Cabet also was interested in the revolutionary possibilities in Ireland. See his *Etat de la question sociale en Angleterre, en Ecosse, en Irlande et en France*, 1843.

136. Although Weitling backed down somewhat from his religiosity in *Garantien der Harmonie und Freiheit*, Vevey, 1842, which placed the word "God" in quotation marks, the religious strain reasserted itself in *Das Evangelium eines armen Sünders*, 1845.

August Becker (Weitling's leading associate, the son of a Lutheran pastor, and a former theology student) intensified the idea of a Christianized communism after Weitling's arrest in his oft-reprinted *Kommunisten-Vaterunser* and *Gebet des Armen* of 1843, as well as in his new journal at Lausanne in 1845: *Die frölische Botschaft von der religiösen und sozialen Bewegung*. See G. Bravo, "Il comunismo tedesco in Svizzera. August Becker 1843-1846," *Annali*, VI, 1963, bibliography 613, 616; article 521–608.

The Parisian police in 1845 distinguished materialistic, French communism from German communism, which was allegedly related to "the disfigured traditions of Christianity" that began with the Anabaptists and taught that "Jesus Christ was the head of a secret communist society founded in Galilee under the reign of Tiberius." "Renseignements," 14, 17.

137. See J. Droz, "Religious Aspects of the Revolutions of 1848 in Europe," in D. Acombe and M. Brown, Jr., eds., *French Society and Culture Since the Old Regime*, NY, 1966, 134–49; and his more specialized works referenced 149 n. 8.

138. Isambert (*De la Charbonnerie*, 187), speaking of Buchez's conversion from Saint-Simonianism to an explicitly Catholic socialism exemplified in the proletarian journal *Atelier*.

139. See the composite work, *L'Individualisme et le communisme par les citoyens Lefeul, Lamennais, Duval, Lamartine et Cabet*, 1848, 3–4, 33. Published in May in a third edition of 20,000, this may well have been the most widely read "communist" book of the revolutionary year in Paris.

140. See Barmby's ponderous reservations about communists who are "more politically social than religiously socially political," *Communist Chronicle*, I, no. 6, 86.

141. M. Nettlau, "Londoner deutsche kommunistische Discussionen 1845," *Archiv für die Geschichte des Sozialismus und der Arbeiterbewegung*, X, 1922, 382. Note also the effect of the translation of anticlerical pamphlets by French communists on Weitling's followers in Switzerland, discussed in Schieder, 296–300.

142. Andrea Mazzini, cited Saitta, *Sinistra*, 62.

143. Lehning, "Discussions," 94, 97. See also Zévaès, "Agitation," 37–9.

144. Lehning, "La réponse de Cabet à Schapper," *Bulletin of the International Institute of Social History*, VIII, 1953, 15, 7–8. See also the critique presumably written by Karl Schapper, "Nouveau journal allemand à Londres," *Populaire*, Oct 3 and 10, 1847; reprinted and discussed in Lehning, "Réponse," 9–15.

Cabet's projections were not entirely fanciful, since his revived *Populaire*, designed exclusively for workers, had soared in popularity, requiring a printing of 27,000 copies by its eighth issue. Garaudy, *Sources*, 166. For the complex development of Cabet's large following in France "from movement to sect" during the 1840s, see Johnson, *Communism*, esp. 207 ff.

145. In the new journal *Kommunistische Zeitschrift*, founded Sep, 1847. Lehning, "Réponse," 10; original German text in Lehning, "Discussions," 107–9.

146. Marx's "Circular against Kriege" (discussed in *Cahiers de l'Institut Maurice Thorez*, I, 1966, 56–8) denounced not only Kriege's *Volkstribun* in New York but the reformist and sentimental approach of the new organization "Young America." Marx nonetheless felt encouraged by the concern for community revealed beneath "their irrational religion." See H. Desroche, "Messianismes et utopies, note sur les origines du socialisme occidental," *Archives de Sociologie des Religions*, 1959, Jul-Dec, 42, also 32. Text of the article "Beschreibung der in neuerer Zeit entstandenen und noch bestehenden kommunistischen Ansiedlungen," *Deutsche Bürgerbuch*, 1845, in *Werke*, II, 521–35.

147. On Polish critiques of Kościuszko, Walicki, "Problem," 15; on Lafayette, Gigault, *Vie politique*, 1833. For discussion, Saitta, "L'idea de Europa," 420–1.

148. Also called the Irish Revolutionary Brotherhood, and, in America, the Fenian Brotherhood. See W. D'Arcy, *The Fenian Movement in the United States, 1858-1886*, Washington, D.C., 1947; T. Brown, *Irish American Nationalism, 1870-1890*, Philadelphia, 1966.

149. For use of the term "spirit of party" in the first large-scale history of the American Revolution in 1788 and of "party spirit" in a traveler's account of 1799, see H. Jones, *Revolution and Romanticism*, Cambridge, Mass., 1974, 208, 222.

150. Cited from Adams's first pamphlet on politics of 1774 (*Works*, IV, 193) in A. Ranney, "'The Divine Science': Political Engineering in American Culture," *The American Political Science Review*, 1976, Mar, 142.

151. Cabet argued that "the party of the movement 'must win or perish,'" *Révolution*, 382.

152. Cabet by 1839 included in his very definition of democracy "the material, intellectual and moral amelioration of the least fortunate classes . . . progressive, continual, incessant amelioration with no limit other than that of the possible." From the introduction to his *Histoire populaire*, cited in Angrand, "Notes," 40.

A. Ledru-Rollin, the dynamic leader of the new "radical" party within the French assembly, spoke in the name of "revolutionary democracy" in his *Manifesto to the Workers* of 1844 (discussed Kayser, "Batailles," 26 n. a).

153. Arguing that "the word democracy had not yet been corrupted" and retained "incomparable power," Considérant superseded his still-popular *Manifesto of the Societary School* of 1841 with his *Manifesto of Peaceful Democracy* in the first issue of his new journal on Aug 1, 1843. Originally entitled *Manifeste politique et sociale*, it was republished twice in 1847 as *Principes de socialisme. Manifeste de la démocratie au xixe siècle*, and thus posed an immediate model and challenge to Marx. See M. Dommanget, *Victor Considérant. Sa vie, son oeuvre*, 1929, 24, 22, and his description of Considérant as anti-revolutionary without being counter-revolutionary, 131–6.

154. B. Nikolaevsky, "Towards a History of 'the Communist League,' 1847–1852," *International Review of Social History*, I, part 2, 1956, 241–2. The report of the League's activities in London early in 1848 appended to this article reveals that the membership of the League in London was 84; of the Workers' Association within which it operated, 179, ibid., 241.

155. *L'Eclaireur de l'Indre*, Dec 6, 1844, cited in Evans, 129.

156. *Revue Encyclopédique*, 1832, Aug, cited in Evans, *Socialisme*, 78.

157. Subtitle of the new journal he founded and edited from 1845–50: *Revue Sociale, ou Solution Pacifique du Problème du Prolétariat*.

158. *La Vérité sur le parti démocratique*, 1840, 11. The work was dedicated "Aux prolétaires."

159. *Vérité*, 29.

160. His "Communism in France," in *Revue Indépendante*, is itemized with other articles in Prudhommeaux, xxi.

161. *Le Démocrate devenu Communiste malgré lui ou réfutation de la brochure de M. Thoré intitulée: "Du Communisme en France,"* 1847, originally published in *Populaire*, 1842, Sep. Hess translated the article from a Belgian version that appeared in 1842 into the unpublished manuscript *Der Communismus in Frankreich, von Thoré*; Silberner, *Works*, 90.

162. *Procès de Thoré*, 35.

163. Cited in Prudhommeaux, 19.

164. Conservative opponents of the anti-religious early writings of the Young Hegelians referred to them long before they did themselves as "this party" and "a new edition" of "the heroes of the French Revolution." H. Leo, *Die Hegelingen*, Halle, 1838; cited in McLellan, *Hegelians*, 13–4 and (without precise attribution) 24.

165. M. Hess, *Aufsätze*, 199–202, cited in McLellan, 148.

166. Dalin, "Historiographie," 75.

167. Suggested in Saint-Simon's *The Reorganization of the European Community*, 1814 (Markham, 63–8) and developed in the program of *The Globe*, which spoke of a triple alliance of German science, English industry, and French morality (Weill, *L'Ecole*, 68–9).

168. Hess likened Hegel to Saint-Simon and Fichte to Proudhon.

169. Later published in *21 Bogen aus der Schweiz*; reprinted in Hess, *Aufsätze*; and discussed in McLellan, 147 ff. In some ways, a "philosophy of action" (or "the deed") seems to have been advocated by Hegel himself in the brief period just after completing the *Phenomenology* when he served as editor of *Die Bamberger Zeitung*. See W. Beyer, *Zwischen Phänomenologie und Logik. Hegel als Redakteur der Bamberger Zeitung*, Frankfurt/Main, 1955, 86–108.

170. Belinsky, *Polnoe sobranie*, 1959, XII, 13, cited in Volodin, 139. Belinsky was comparing Heine to Schiller, the perpetual poet laureate of Slavic revolutionaries.

171. Herzen, *Polnoe sobranie*, II, 257.

172. Cited by Walicki, *Annali*, VI, 111.

173. Discussed by Walicki, *Annali*, VI, 121; see also the exhaustive compilation

of A. Zanardo, "Arnold Ruge giovane hegeliano 1824–1849," *Annali*, XII, 1970, 189–382; and A. Cornu, *Karl Marx et Friedrich Engels, leur vie et leur oeuvre. Tome premier. Les années d'enfance et de jeunesse. La gauche hégélienne, 1818/1820–1844*, 1955, esp. 172.

174. "Selbstkritik des Liberalismus," *Deutsche Jahrbücher*, 1843, Jan 2, cited in McLellan, 25; see also 28–32.

One of Ruge's erstwhile supporters complained in the same month that "the concept of a party has wandered from the church via belles lettres and scholarly philosophy into the state proper." *Über den Begriff der politischen Partei*, Königsberg, 1843, 13.

There was, once again, borrowing between extremes of Right and Left. The concept of a new, ideological party had been advanced earlier by the Right in much the form that was to be later adopted by the Left. Victor-Aimé Huber, who had fought with the Spanish revolutionary army in 1823, was converted from revolutionary militance to conservative pietism and published in 1841 an appeal for an ideologically-based conservative political party. See his *Über die Elemente, die Möglichkeit oder Notwendigkeit einer konservativen Partei in Deutschland*, Marburg, 1841; also J. Droz, "Victor-Aimé Huber: un conservateur social du milieu du XIXe siècle," *Archives de Sociologie des Religions*, 1960, Jul–Dec, 41–8.

175. Interpretation here leans heavily on S. Avineri, *The Social and Political Thought of Karl Marx*, Cambridge, 1968, 45–64. See also the discussion in Kolakowski, *Main Currents*, I, 81–181, which appeared too late for use in this section, but covers the subject in greater detail from the distinctive analytic perspective of a revisionist Marxist philosopher; also 9–80 for the prehistory of the concept of the dialectic.

176. *Zur Kritik der Hegelschen Rechtsphilosophie. Einleitung*, from *Deutsche-französische Jahrbücher*, 1844, in *Werke*, I, 391.

177. Characterization of McLellan, 22.

178. Ibid., 146, 152.

179. *Werke*, I, 494; McLellan, *Hegelians*, 147; L. Schwarzschild, *The Red Prussian. The Life and Legend of Karl Marx*, NY, 1947, 70–4; and G. Mayer, *Friedrich Engels in seiner Frühzeit, 1820 bis 1851*, 1920, 104–23, and materials referenced 410, 414–6.

180. Cited in Riazanov, *Ocherki*, 105–6. See also the entire article "Yunosheskie raboty Engel'sa," 99–106. M. Rubel traces to the origin of the modern idea of a Marxist party (then called a "Marx party") to Hess's writings on the Marx-Weitling controversy of 1846. "La charte de la première internationale," *Mouvement Social*, 1965, May–Jun, 4 n. 2.

181. *Kommunistisches Bekenntnis in Fragen und Antworten*, reprinted from a reprint of 1846 in *Philosophische und sozialistische Schriften, 1837–1850*, 1961, 359–68.

182. Riazanov, 105.

183. McLellan, 44.

184. MEGA, I, 65.

185. MEGA, VI, 191. See M. Rubel, "Remarques sur le concept du parti prolétarien chez Marx," *Revue Française de Sociologie*, 1961, II, no. 3, 166–76.

186. *Werke*, I, 108.

187. *Frühe Schriften*, I, 448.

188. Ruge, *Zwei Jahre*, I, 69 ff.

189. T. Oizerman, "Problema revoliutsii v trudakh Marksa i Engel'sa perioda formirovaniia Marksizma," *Moskovsky universitet. Uchenye zapiski (fil. fak.)*, CLXIX, 1954, 34.

190. *Frühe Schriften*, 593–4.

191. He suggested beans as a "manly," revolutionary substitute. See L. Feuerbach, *Sämtliche Werke*, X, 23, cited in R. Binkley, *Realism and Nationalism 1852–1871*, NY, 1935, 22–3.

192. McLellan, 106 ff.

193. Introduction to the first published version of 1888 in *Werke*, XXI, 264.

194. The 11th thesis, manuscript reprinted in McLellan, *Karl Marx. His Life and Thought*, NY, 1973, 141. The beginnings of the spread first of Feuerbachian and then of Marxist views in 1845 among German émigrés is documented for France and Belgium in Karl Grün, *Die soziale Bewegung in Frankreich und Belgien*, Darmstadt, 1845.

195. S. Avineri, "Hegel Revisited," *Journal of Contemporary History*, II, 1968, no. 3, 140.

196. The seriousness of religious interests and the priority of religious over social concerns among the Young Hegelians are stressed in W. Brazill, *The Young*

Hegelians, New Haven, 1970. Hostile critics in the late 1830s considered them pro-Jewish as well as anti-Christian (Avineri, 139–42).

197. Fakkar, esp. 98–103; G. Gurvitch, "Saint-Simon et Karl Marx," *Revue Internationale de Philosophie*, XIV, 1960, no. 53–4, 399 ff.

198. Belinsky's letter to Stankevich, Oct 2, 1839; in Belinsky, *Polnoe sobranie*, XI, 387.

199. Nettlau, "Londoner Discussionen," 368, 376, 379.

200. Ibid., 380. The phrase is that of H. Bauer, Schapper's principal supporter in the discussions; Kriege was Weitling's.

201. Ibid., 368. Simply to wait until the working class is ready is to "wait until cooked doves fly into our mouths."

202. Ibid., 382. Playing on the title of Weitling's *Guarantees of Harmony and Freedom*, Schapper finds "no guarantee of freedom" in a harmony that is too *soldatenmässig* (354).

203. Nettlau, "Discussionen," 384.

204. Marx may have adopted this distinction from the Young Hegelian Fröbel (McLellan, *Hegelians*, 34). Marx broke with Feuerbach's previous pairing of "egoism and communism" as being "inseparable as heart and head" (*Sämtliche Werke*, Stuttgart, 1959, II, 391). The only living, articulate survivor of the original Babeuf Conspiracy may, however, have suggested more than mere general affinity with his statement in 1845 that Buonarroti's *History* "has contributed to, better to say has founded, the Communist party" (Savary, in *La Fraternité*, cited in A. Lehning, "Buonarroti's Ideas on Communism and Dictatorship," *International Review of Social History*, 1957, no. 2, 282).

205. Account of the meeting in *The Northern Star*, 1845, Aug 23, mentions only the presence of Engels, but this is not surprising since he was far better known in England. For an account of this visit in which Engels formed close links with Harney, see I. Bakh, "Novye dannye o prebyvanii Marksa i Engel'sa v Londone v avguste 1845 goda," in *Iz istorii sotsial'no-politicheskikh idei*, 1955, 479–82.

206. *Werke*, II, 613, 624.

207. Ibid., 613. Earlier in the year Engels was speaking to Germans about "the party of community" (ibid., 535).

208. Schwarzschild, 132–4. Kuypers, "Marx en Belgique," 413 ff.

209. McLellan, *Marx*, 171.

210. Text of the letter in the handwriting of Schapper, first published in *Bund der Kommunisten*, 347.

211. Ibid., 348–9.

212. Ibid., 347.

213. B. Andréas, *Gründungsdokumente des Bundes der Kommunisten (Juni bis September 1847)*, Hamburg, 1969, 14. The invaluable discussion in the preface of these newly discovered documents unfortunately lacks precise references.

214. Ibid., 18.

215. Ibid.

216. *Misère*, 487–9.

217. Ibid., 492.

218. Answer to question 22 in text of *Entwurf des Kommunistischen Glaubensbekenntnisses*, in *Gründungsdokumente*, 58.

219. *Werke*, IV, 640, 237. For the text of Engels's *Grundsätze des Kommunismus*, ibid., 363–80. The "Kommunistisches Glaubensbekenntnis" of Schapper, Moll, and Bauer is apparently unpublished. The origin of this form probably lies in Moses Hess's *Kommunistisches Bekenntnis* of 1844. Among Andréas's newly discovered documents in Hamburg is the text of 22 questions and answers for a *Kommunistisches Glaubensbekenntnis* apparently drawn up for the June meeting of the League (*Gründungsdokumente*, 53–8). The body of the text is in the lithographed handwriting of Engels, but is signed by the president of the congress, Carl Schill, and by secretary Heide. See, in addition to Andréas, the discussion of Seleznev, "Novye dokumenty," 27–9.

220. *Gründungsdokumente*, 22. The reference is not given. For the text see *Werke*, IV, 596; for discussion, Lehning, "Association," 198; Andler, *Manifeste*, 39–42.

221. *Werke*, IV, 26.

222. Account of the meeting (at which Marx first met Harney) in *Northern Star*, 1847, Dec 4. For the interaction of the movements, see Engels, "The Revolutionary Movements of 1847," translated from Marx's *Deutsche Brüsseler Zeitung*, 1848, Jan 23, in Riazanov, *The Communist Manifesto*, L, 1930, 272–85. Early in 1847, Marx's correspondence committee formally joined the League of the Just, which in June changed its name to Communist League and (in the sole issue of its journal

in September) first invoked the device "Proletarians of all countries, unite!" See K. Grünberg, *Die Londoner Kommunistische Zeitschrift und andere Urkunden aus den Jahren 1847/1848*, Leipzig, 1921, 35; Lehning, "Association," 198–9.

223. *Werke*, IV, 603.

224. *Communist Manifesto*, section IV, in *Selected Works*, I, 241.

225. Citations from the article "Comunismo" in the Florentine *Tribuno della Plebe*, 1848, Dec 20, in *Presse ouvrière*, 234–5.

226. This confusion was particularly characteristic of widely circulated exposé literature such as Alfred Sudre, *Histoire du communisme ou réfutation des utopies socialistes*, 1849 (which by 1856 had undergone five editions and Italian and Spanish translations), and the explicitly "anti-communist" tract by an anonymous "friend of order": *L'antirouge, almanach antisocialiste, anticommuniste*, 1851. The first systematic discussion of the difference between the two concepts ("absolute equality" vs. rewards "according to works") was by Lamennais in 1841: his chapter 15 of *Du passé et de l'avenir du peuple*. See Saitta, *Sinistra*, 265. Saitta's discussion of the difference in usage of the two terms (250 ff.) is the richest available for France, Germany, and Italy.

227. *Gründungsdokumente*, 21–2.

228. See, for instance, G. Gaeta, "Première orientation sociale du journalisme," in *Presse ouvrière*, 234.

229. Lorenz von Stein saw "communism" as somehow more objectively real: "the condition of which socialism is merely a symptom." *The History of the Social Movement in France, 1789–1850* (ed. Mengelberg), Totowa, N.J., 1964, 286. This is translated from the third edition (1850) of a work first published in 1842. The section "Communism and Its Relationship to Socialism" (282–7) differentiates the two.

230. Johnson, *Communism*, 74–5.

231. Lamennais, *Du passé*, cited in Saitta, 265.

232. "La politique et le socialisme," in *Eclaireur de l'Indre*, 1844, Nov, cited in Saitta, 255.

233. Cabet, *Douze Lettres d'un communiste à un réformiste sur la communauté*, 1842. Conservatives like Saint-Marc Girardin saw communists as "the barbarian within" European civilization (*Souvenirs et reflections politiques d'un journaliste*, 1858, 143–4). See "les 'barbares de l'intérieur,' " in O. Hammen, "1848 et le 'Spectre du Communisme,' " *Contrat Social*, 1958, Jul, 191–200; also Gottfried Keller's outburst of Jul, 1843: Legge, *Rhyme*, 145.

234. C. Bouglé sees a commitment to egalitarianism as the root of differences between communists and socialists in the 1840s (*Le Sociologie de Proudhon*, 1911, 35–6).

235. *Gründungsdokumente*, 14. Dézamy defended "communists of all shades" from the charge that violence would be needed (*Presse ouvrière*, 137); and Marx and Engels mounted lengthy, diversionary counterattacks against "bloodthirsty" revolutionary republicans like Karl Heinzen (*Werke*, IV, 309–24, 331–59).

236. *Le Socialisme devant le vieux monde ou le vivant devant les morts*, 1848, 59–60.

237. *Polnoe sobranie*, III, 319. This definition of Mar 1844 is preceded by a more positive usage, describing Weitling and his Swiss followers in Nov 1843 (ibid., 140–1), the earliest use of the term I have found in Russian.

238. In his twelfth "Letter from France and Italy," *Polnoe sobranie*, VI, 116–7.

239. Cited from *Karmany slovar'*, II, reproduced in Evgrafova, *Filosofskie*, 294. The article on "Opposition," lists other terms on which subsequent articles are promised. Such an article never appeared in this incompleted, often "Aesopian" dictionary. The entry under "Owenism" (defined as "a system of mutual cooperation and community of goods") comes closest to an exposition of the communist ideal (ibid., 263–7).

240. K. Timkovsky to M. Petrashevsky in Evgrafova, *Filosofskie*, 378–9; also *Delo petrashevtsev*, I, 326, III, 272. This contrast was relatively commonplace in the 1840s. See, for instance, the essay "Fourieristen und Kommunisten," *Augsburger Allgemeine Zeitung*, May 7, 1841, discussed in Klitzsch, *Sozialismus*, 33; and Joseph Rey's discussion of "fouriéristes et communistes" as the two types of "socialistes complètes," *Appel au ralliement des socialistes*, 9.

241. Ivan-Ferdinand Yastrzhemsky, discussed in the unpublished doctoral thesis of F. Bartholomew, "The Petrashevshy Circle," Princeton, 1969.

242. Petrashevsky, cited in Evgrafova, 379.

243. Herzen, *Polnoe sobranie*, III, 319. Thoré provided confirming testimony already in 1840. See *Vérité*, 22–4; also Cuvillier, *Hommes*, 130.

244. The title of Pillot's most famous treatise *Ni châteaux ni chaumières*.

245. "Qui n'ont ni feu ni lieu," C. Louandre, "Statistique littéraire de la production intellectuelle en France depuis quinze ans," *Revue des Deux Mondes*, 1847, Oct 1, 284.

246. "Freed from all local and national limits": See *Die deutsche Ideologie*, 1953, 60, 32; and discussion in K. Papaisannou, "Marx et la politique internationale, Marx et l'unité du monde," *Contrat Social*, 1967, May–Jun, 157–60.

247. Papaisannou, "Marx et la politique internationale, est et ouest," *Contrat Social*, 1967, Sep–Oct, 304–7.

248. "Revolution in China and in Europe," from the *New York Daily Tribune*, 1853, Jun 14, in *The American Journalism of Marx and Engels* (H. Christmas, ed.), NY, 1966, 90.

249. Papaisannou, "Marx et la politique," 300–1.

250. Billington, *Mikhailovsky*, 195.

251. Even the best historians of working people still confuse these two. The varied material in E. M. Thompson's *Making of the British Working Class*, for instance, describes the imaginative, inventive, and almost uniformly nonrevolutionary ideas of working people in England during the early industrial era. Thompson nevertheless assumes (in his title, introduction, and conclusion) that his subject is a unitary, proto-revolutionary, self-conscious entity. There is almost no empirical evidence or extended argumentation for such an assumption. Thompson avoids the term "proletariat" but not the implication (recurrent among English intellectuals) that "the working class" in Britain might somehow have created a revolution if it had adopted the secular revolutionary consciousness of intellectuals rather than its own melange of religious, reformist, and rebellious impulses.

252. *Oxford English Dictionary*, VIII, 1447–8.

253. Michael Lepeletier, brother of the Babeuvist Felix Lepeletier, described his proposals for national communal education as "la révolution du citoyen-prolétaire." See Saitta, "Autour de la conjuration," *Annales Historiques*, 1960, Oct–Dec, 429.

254. Jean Reynaud, "De la nécessité d'une représentation speciale pour les prolétaires," *Revue Encyclopédique*, 1832, Apr.

255. Dommanget, *Idées*, 251, and discussion 232–51.
Laponneraye, echoed Blanqui in *Défense du citoyen Blanqui devant la cour d'assise*, 1832; *Lettre aux prolétaires*, Saint-Pélagie, 1833.

256. *Du passé*, cited Saitta, *Sinistra*, 264; also 391 for his phrase "the extinction of the proletariat."

257. Jules Leroux, *Le prolétaire et le bourgeois, dialogue sur la question des salaires*, 1840. See also Dézamy's discussion in *Almanach de la communauté*, 1843, 69–72; and the proclamation of the Lyon workers' journal *Le Travail* that "between the bourgeois and the proletarian it is manifest that there is no common interest," cited without precise reference in Cuvillier, *Hommes*, 122.

258. Savary, cited in J. Prudhommeaux, "Babeuf jugé par un communiste de 1840," *La Revue Française*, LV, 1908, 139.

259. *Svenskt biografiskt lexicon*, Stockholm, 1969, LXXXV, 685.

260. Anders Peter (Per) Götrek, *Om Proletariatet och dess befrielse genom den sanna kommunismen*, Stockholm, nd. There is no satisfactory discussion of Götrek or of the links of the Stockholm group (which reached a membership of some 1,500 in 1848–9 according to *Bund der Kommunisten*, 1072) with Lund. See, in addition to *Bund*, 1071–4; B. Andréas, *Le Manifeste Communiste de Marx et Engels*, Milan, 1963, 20 n. 2; Seleznev, "Dokumenty," 20–1; and the textual analysis of Götrek's pamphlet by E. Kandel' in *Novaia i Noveishaia Istoriia*, 1960, n. 2, 119–26.

261. Andréas, *Manifeste*, 15–6; *Catéchisme du prolétaire*, Liège, 1849; Kuypers, "Marx en Belgique," 416 ff.

262. From the extended citation in L. Bertrand, *Histoire de la démocratie et du socialisme en Belgique depuis 1830*, Brussels/Paris, 1906, I, 443. Andréas's echo theory (in *Manifeste*, 306) seems less convincing than that of Kuypers (in the work therein cited), who sees Tedesco influenced by Engels's earlier draft.

263. Bertrand, I, 441.

264. Tedesco's translation was begun in Mar 1848, but confiscated by the police and never published (Kuypers, "Marx en Belgique," 415). Götrek's translation changed "Proletarians of the world, unite!" into "The voice of the people is the voice of God"—apparently to avoid jail. See discussion of his *Kommunismens Rost* in K. Bäckström, *Arbetarrörelsen i Sverige*, Stockholm, 1971, I, 43.

265. J. Kuypers, "La Contribution de Victor Tedesco à l'élaboration du manifeste communiste de 1848," *Socialisme*, LXI, 1964, esp. 80 n. 1. See also Kuypers, "Wilhelm Wolff und der Deutsche Arbeiterverein (1847–1848) in Brüssel," *Archiv für Sozialgeschichte*, III, 1963, 103–7. While Tedesco was not a member of this organization, his *Catechism of the Proletariat* was almost immediately translated into

German by the poet and collaborator of Marx on *Neue Rheinische Zeitung,* Ferdinand Freiligrath, and disseminated in England and the United States. See Kuypers, "Marx en Belgique," 416.

266. The Buonarrotian influence was stronger in Belgium than France. In addition to works and figures referenced in Kuypers, Bertrand discusses (I, 174 ff.) the views set forth a decade before Tedesco by the Delhasse brothers: Félix Delhasse, *Le prolétariat veut être quelque chose;* and Alexandre Delhasse, *Catéchisme démocratique.*

267. Stein, *History,* 286; also 255 ff. The introduction by Kaethe Mengelberg (20–33) discusses Stein's influence on Marx, which has been described as a move from "dialectical idealism" to dialectical materialism. See J. Weiss, "Dialectical Idealism and the work of Lorenz von Stein," *International Review of Social History,* 1963, VIII, part I, 75–93. Stein's work played a decisive role in Bakunin's movement from German philosophy through French social thought to revolutionary activity. See V. Polonsky, *Materialy dlia biografii M. Bakunina,* 1923, I, 105–6.

268. Marx, *Selected Works,* I, 204.

269. Ibid., 216.

270. Ibid., 218.

271. Ibid., 219.

272. Engels, "Die Kommunisten und Karl Heinzen," *Deutsche Brüsseler Zeitung,* 1847, Oct 7, in *Werke,* IV, 321. This and the preceding article in the issue of Oct 3 contain a good discussion of the relation envisaged between the two putative bodies, the "Communist and Democratic Parties," ibid., 317.

273. Marx, *Selected Works,* 228.

274. Ibid., 237.

275. According to the League's report in Nikolaevsky, "Towards a History," 241, which discusses the paucity of material and the interpretive problems confronting any history of the League.

E. Kandel' provides a good bibliography of recent German books on revolutionary and workers' organization in Germany through the revolutionary crisis into the 1850s: "Protiv burzhuaznoi ideologii i revizionizma," *Voprosy Istorii KPSS,* 1976, no. 10, 66–78. The article shows, however, the survival of Stalinist scholarship within the USSR. Kandel' chides recent West German writings for failing to recognize the existence of a "proletarian wing" in these early organizations (69 ff.); but he is unable to establish precisely what this "proletarian" composition consisted of, and is unconvincing in arguing either that the Brussels Communist Correspondence Committee was a workers' organization or that Marx was personally of great importance during the revolution of 1848–50 (70–4).

276. See the thesis of W. Dohl, *Die deutsche Nationalversammlung von 1848 im Spiegel der 'Neuen Rheinischen Zeitung,'* Bonn, 1930; also A. Molok, *Karl Marx i iiun'skoe vosstanie 1848 goda v Parizhe,* M/Leningrad, 1934, 6 n. 6; 27 n. 1.

277. Cited from *Deutsche Zeitung,* 1848, Aug 18, in Noyes, 122.

278. From two members of the Cologne Workers' Union "in the name of many comrades," cited in Noyes, 286–7.

279. Noyes, 286–9, 366. Text in Marx, Engels, *Selected Works,* II, 154–68.

280. *Sochineniia,* VII, 573–4, n.

281. Ibid., 31.

282. Ibid.

283. Ibid., 31–2.

284. Ibid., 80; the documentation of the 1956 Soviet edition (579 n. 43) is careful to point out that this doctrine "was true for the period of pre-monopolistic capitalism," but has been invalid since Lenin's 1915 essay "On the Slogan of the United States of Europe."

285. Ibid., 80.

286. Ibid.

287. Ibid., 32.

288. Dommanget, *Drapeau,* 120. Already in an address to 300 political exiles on the last day of 1849, Harney predicted that "the red flag shall fly over the entire world and group all peoples behind it" (ibid., 119). The symbol appeared prominently in Harney's short-lived journal of 1850, in which the *Communist Manifesto* was printed for the first time in English (with a linguistic infelicity that begins with the opening "A frightful hobgoblin stalks throughout Europe"). *The Red Republican,* 1850, Nov 9, 161. The first volume of the two-volume facsimile reproduction (L, 1966) contains (i–xv) a synoptic account by J. Saville of Harney's career and of work on him since A. Schoyen, *The Chartist Challenge: A Portrait of George Julian Harney,* L, 1958. For Harney's long correspondence with Engels (1843–95), see P. Cadogan, "Harney and Engels," *International Review of Social History,* X, 1965, 66–104.

289. The way in which these revolutionaries became absorbed in the reformist politics of the New World is traced in H. Schlüter, *Der Anfang der deutschen Arbeiterbewegung in Amerika*, Stuttgart, 1907.

290. Mayer, *Engels*, I, 396; R. Stadelmann, *Social and Political History of the German 1848 Revolution*, Athens, Ohio, 1975, 177.

291. Text of the memorandum of association in *Unter dem Banner des Marxismus*, 1928, Mar, 144–5. See the contrast with the parallel passage in the memorandum of the Communist League, 141; also discussion of the original document of the association in Lehning, "Buonarroti," 285; "Association," 199.

292. Marx, Engels, *Sochineniia*, VIII, 651; Lehning, "Buonarroti," 282–5.

293. H. Draper, "Marx and the dictatorship of the proletariat," *Cahiers de l'Institut de Science Economique Apliquée*, 1962, Sep, 6 ff.

294. Ibid., 19–20.

295. Nettlau, "Discussionen," 380, and earlier usage by Weitling in Draper, 14.

296. "Die Krisis und die Konterrevolution," 1848, Sep 14, cited in Draper, 28.

297. Ibid., 27.

298. Letter of Jules Vidil (a former military man and leading Blanquist among the French émigrés in London) to Blanqui of 1850, Jul 19, cited in Dommanget, *Idées*, 383.

299. Kuypers, "Marx en Belgique," 415, also 412. Imbert played an important role in the German Workers' Association in Brussels. See Kuypers, "Wolff"; also Dommanget, *Idées*, 376.

300. Garaudy, *Sources*, 239–41.

301. In the first part of *Class War in France*, not published until Mar, 1850. See Draper, 31–2, 34.

302. *Sochineniia*, II, 239–41.

303. N. Plotkin, "Les Alliances des Blanquistes dans la Proscription," *Revue des Révolutions Contemporaines*, LXV, 1951, 120; *Werke*, VII, 615; McLellan, *Marx*, 235; Draper, 35–6.

304. *Sochineniia*, VII, 51.

305. Ibid., 91.

306. Ibid., 92–3.

307. Ibid., 91.

308. Draper, 15–8, 34 ff. Draper is not persuasive in suggesting (32) that Marx simply made up the slogan and attributed it retroactively to 1848. The possibilities of Blanquist influence on Marx cannot be ruled out and have never been systematically investigated. Marx was in touch with Blanquists during his visit to Paris in Jun 1849 (Dommanget, *Idées*, 377); and Marx's admiration for Blanqui was particularly strong in Feb 1850, just before the revival of the League (Mikhailov, *Istoriia*, 388–9).

Another possible French channel (not mentioned by Dommanget) is Jules Gay, whose journal *Le Communiste* appeared for one issue in Mar 1849 (*Babeuf et les problèmes*, 276). Marx had praised Gay along with Dézamy as "more scientific French Communists," who "are developing the doctrine of materialism in the sense of a doctrine of real humanism and as the logical base of Communism" (*Holy Family* cited in Garaudy, *Sources*, 191). The gap in the Marx-Engels correspondence from Aug 23, 1849, to Nov 19, 1850, deprives historians of direct testimony to influences on Marx during this critical period when Blanquist influence was at its height.

309. Noyes, 286–7, 366–7. The Germans had long nurtured a fascination, often based on fear, that revolution might become a permanent as well as global condition—from the complaint of 1814 about "der allgemeinen Weltrevolution unserer Zeit" (Malinkrodt, "Was tun bei Deutschlands und Europas Wiedergeburt?" cited in Seidler, 297) through the retrospective essay on the events of 1848–51, which spoke of "die grundsätzliche permanente Erhebung des Volkes über alle gegebene Obrigkeit" (F. Stahl, *Was ist Revolution?* 1852, in Seidler, 291 n. a).

As with so much else, this concept appears to have originally been derived from Illuminist usage. The Bavarian occultist Franz von Baader noted already in his diary for Aug 14, 1786, symptoms *einer uns allgemein bevorstehenden Revolution* (Grassl, "Zum Bedeutungswandel des Wortes 'Revolution,'" *Aufbruch*, 429–32), and appears to have returned to elaborate this idea in his 1834 essay *Revolutionismus* (Seidler, 291 n. a).

310. *Sochineniia*, VII, 267.

311. From the copy of the secret directive of the committee edited in London 1850, Mar, as captured by the Saxon police, sent to friendly German governments, and cited from the Wurtemberg Archives by Stadelmann, 164–5.

312. M. Kovalevsky, "Souvenirs sur Karl Marx," *Contrat Social*, 1967, Nov–Dec, 357–8.

313. B. Nikolaevsky, "Toward a History," 249. For other articles on the conflict of Marx with his "leftist" associates in 1850–1, see N. Belousova, *Iosif Moll', sbornik statei*, 1961; S. Na'aman, "Zur Geschichte des Bundes der Kommunisten in Deutschland in der zweiten Phase seines Bestehens," *Archiv für Sozialgeschichte*, V, 1965, 5–82; and L. Easton, "August Willich, Marx and Left Hegelian Socialism," *Etudes de Marxologie*, 1965.

314. The 22-year-old Johannes Miguel, later minister of finance in Prussia. See Draper, 41–2.

315. From the French text in M. Dommanget, *August Blanqui à Belle-Ile (1850– 1857)*, 1935, 65–6; also discussion, 63–87, and other materials referenced in Lehning, "Association," 204 n. 1. The Marx-Engels translation (*Sochineniia*, VII, 569– 70) had a German printing of 30,000 (ibid., 615) and was announced in an unpublished letter of Engels to the *Times* (text in ibid., 493–4).

316. In Marx's book defending the accused (*Enthüllungen über den Kommunistenprozess zu Köln*, Basel, 1853; tr. with intr. by R. Livingstone, *The Cologne Communist Trial*, L/NY, 1971), he attacked the Willich group for conspiratorial excesses and suggested that his own mission was to build "the opposition party of the future" on a new and different basis (*Werke*, VIII, 461; McLellan, 252). Marx attempted to start the germ of such a party by grouping 60 Germans into a Workers' Association that met twice a week late in 1851 before it disintegrated when its key members rejoined the larger Willich group in the late summer of 1852. See G. Becker, "Die neue Arbeiter-Verein in London 1852," *Zeitschrift für Geisteswissenschaft*, 1966.

317. The argument of Stadelmann, *History*.

318. Dommanget, *Belle-Ile*, 66; text in *Unter dem Banner des Marxismus*, 1928, Mar, 145.

319. The importance of this neglected uprising is stressed by C. Tilly (who points out that only 7,000 of 26,000 arrested were agrarian workers), "The Changing Place of Collective Violence," in M. Richter, ed., *Essays in Social and Political History*, Cambridge, Mass., 1970.

320. Draper, 46.

321. It appeared serially and is republished in *Selected Works*, 311–426.

322. Ibid., 323.

323. *Sochineniia*, VIII, 126.

324. Willich and Weydemeyer were former Prussian officers who later became military leaders of the Northern armies in the American Civil War: the former a major general who marched with Sherman through Georgia; the latter the military commandant of St. Louis. Both continued to hold Marx in the highest esteem despite earlier arguments. Weydemeyer arrived in the USA on Nov 7, 1851; published his article in the third issue of *Turn-Zeitung*, NY, 1852, Jan 1; and also included a reprint of the first installment of Engels's *Peasant War in Germany* (Draper, 44).

325. Marx, Engels, *Selected Correspondence*, Moscow, nd., 86.

326. In *Itogi i perspektivy*, written in prison early in 1906; published in *Nasha revoliutsiia*, St. Petersburg, 1906, 224–86; discussed E. Carr, *The Bolshevik Revolution*, L, 1950, I, 56–8, 61. Trotsky derived the idea from Alexander Helphand (Parvus) much as Marx took it from Blanqui. See Z. Zeman and W. Scharlau, *The Merchant of Revolution*, Oxford, 1965, 36, 110–1.

327. P. Foner, "Statuten des Kommunisten Klubs in New York," *Science and Society*, 1977, Fall, 334–7.

328. See his *Rom und Jerusalem, die letzte Nationalitätsfrage*, Leipzig, 1862.

329. Letter of Feb 29, 1860, to F. Freiligrath in Marx, *Sochineniia*, XXX, 400, 406; also Mikhailov, *Istoriia*, 14.

Chapter 10

1. P. Annenkov, *Reminiscences of Marx and Engels*, 270 ff., cited in McLellan, *Marx*, 156–7.

2. Moses Hess, *Briefwechsel*, 157, McLellan, 158.

3. *Werke*, IV, 10.

4. *Herr Vogt*, in *Werke*, XIV, 439, McLellan, 158–9.

5. A. Babel, "La première Internationale, ses débuts et son activité à Genève de 1864 à 1870," in *Mélanges d'études économiques et sociales offerts à William E. Rappard*, Geneva, 1944, 239.

6. Citations in P. Haubtmann, *Marx et Proudhon*, 1947, 31–2. There is still no comprehensive, scholarly treatment of this conflict. Perhaps the best survey of is-

sues is by E. Thier, "Marx und Proudhon," in I. Fetscher, ed., *Marxismusstudien*, Tübingen, 1957, 120–50.

J. Jackson, *Marx, Proudhon and European Socialism*, NY, 1962, is a useful introduction, lacking documentation or adequate bibliography. Among the better interpretive accounts are E. Dolléans, "La rencontre de Proudhon et de Marx," *Revue d'Histoire Moderne*, XI, 1936, 5–30; M. Bourguin, "Des rapports entre Proudhon et Karl Marx," *Le Contrat Social*, IX, 1965, 95–107; G. Gurvitch, "Proudhon et Marx," *Cahiers Internationaux de Sociologie*, 1966, Jan–Jun, 7–16; A. Cuvillier, "Marx et Proudhon," *Cercle de la Russie neuve, Paris. A la lumière de Marxisme*, 1937, II, 151–238; W. Pickles, "Marx and Proudhon," *Politica*, 1938, Sep, 236–60; E. Drumont, "Proudhon et Karl Marx," in *Les trétaux du succès; figures de bronze ou statues de neige*, 1902, 315–32; J. Dessaint, "Proudhon ou Karl Marx," *Nouvelle Revue*, XLIII, 1919, 97–106; G. Adler, *Die Grundlagen der Karl Marx'schen Kritik der bestehenden Volkswirtschaft*, Tübingen, 1887, 169–202; G. Pirou, "Proudhonisme et Marxisme," *Revue des Mois*, XX, 1919, 237–56; and V. Zastenker, "Proudhon et proudhonisme de 1846 à 1848," *Recherches soviétiques*, 1956, May–Jun, 151–94.

For a relatively favorable biography of Proudhon by a man on the way to becoming a Marxist, see M. Tugan-Baranovsky, *Prudon, ego zhizn' i obshchestvennaia deiatel'nost'*, St. Petersburg, 1891. Modern Marxism-Leninism follows the hostile pattern set by Yu. Steklov in his polemic attack just after the Soviet seizure of power: *Prudon otets anarkhii*, Petrograd, 1918. Marx's own views are summarized and developed more soberly in "Marx über Proudhon," *Die Neue Zeit*, XXXI, 1913, 821–30.

For more recent work on Proudhon, see the essays and discussion reprinted from a colloquium on the centenary of his death: *L'actualité de Proudhon*, Brussels, 1967; and A. Ritter, *The Political Thought of Pierre-Joseph Proudhon*, Princeton, 1969. Ritter's bibliographical discussion (3–25) counterbalances the more hostile earlier discussion in E. Carr, *Studies in Revolution*, L, 1950, 38–55.

7. A large section of Marx's *Holy Family*, written late in 1844, favorably contrasts Proudhon to the Germans. Citation and discussion in Dolléans, "Rencontre," 11.

8. Citation and discussion in Haubtmann, 33. Marx goes on to say, with a touch of envy, "Proudhon writes not simply in the interest of the proletariat, he is himself a proletarian, a worker" (34). Proudhon's promise to discover the correct future forms of society "by the observation of the causes and effects of property" represented a good statement of the mission that Marx himself adopted. It was also claimed as a new imperative and hailed as "a Communist work" by Barmby's *The Communist Chronicle*, I, no. 6, 36.

9. *Premier mémoire sur la propriété*, cited in Haubtmann, 35.

10. Argued in Haubtmann, 34–9.

11. Bourguin, 98 ff.

12. "On the Jewish Question" and "Contribution to the Critique of Hegel's *Philosophy of Right*," in Marx, *Early Writings*, L, 1963, 1–59.

13. Letter to Bergmann of Oct 24, 1844, in *Correspondance*, II, 166.

14. *Die soziale Bewegung in Frankreich und Belgien*, Darmstadt, 1845.

15. Cited in Bouglé, *Sociologie*, 89.

16. Haubtmann, 64 (which includes the full text of both letters).

17. Ibid.

18. Ibid., 68.

19. Ibid., 70–3.

20. The two volumes are republished together with an introduction and slight abridgement of Proudhon, 1964: Proudhon, *Système des contradictions économiques ou philosophie de la misère*, Marx, *Misère de la philosophie: Réponse à la philosophie de la misère de M. Proudhon*.

21. The only exception might be the later work of 1860, *Herr Vogt*, which is, however, more an extended pamphlet and a purely *ad hominem* attack.

22. *General Idea of the Revolution in the Nineteenth Century*, L, 1923, 74.

23. Discussion in Dolléans, "Rencontre," 13–4.

24. Letters of Aug 8 and 14 to Engels, discussed in Rubel, "Cahiers," 415. See also Rubel's *Marx devant le Bonapartisme*, The Hague/Paris, 1960; and R. Rosdolsky, *Zur Entstehungsgeschichte des Marxschen "Kapital,"* Frankfurt, 1968, 19–20.

25. Eventually published in *Arkhiv Marksa i Engel'sa*, 1948, X, 5–34. Engels had already written for Marx late in 1848 a savage attack on the way in which workers and revolutionaries in Paris seemed seduced by "Proudhon's pretentious monstrosity" and left "unprotected, exposed to the merciless claws of the wolf Proudhon" (Marx, Engels, *Collected Works*, M, 1977, VIII, 129, 131).

When Marx turned in 1857–8 to writing the seven notebooks that were the first sketch of his comprehensive analysis of modern political economy, Proudhon was still his principal target of criticism among the living. M. Nicolaus in his introduction to the first English publication of this work identifies Proudhon and Ricardo as Marx's "principal theoretical antagonists" (Marx, *Grundrisse*, NY, 1973, 10; and see Marx's text, esp. 424–6, 843–4).

26. This line of attack reached an intemperate climax in the indictment by the veteran French Stalinist G. Cogniot: *Proudhon et la démagogie bonapartiste: un "socialiste" en coquetterie avec le pouvoir personnel*, 1958.

27. Marx to Johann Schweitzer, Jan 24, 1865, cited in *The Poverty of Philosophy*, Moscow, 1956, 224; original usage in ibid., 141.

28. S. Stybe, *Frederik Dreier, hans liv, hans samtid og hans sociale taenkning*, Copenhagen, 1959, 41–3, 48, esp. 151 ff., and 297–8. His characteristically Proudhonist antinationalism is illustrated in *Folkenes Fremtid* and particularly *Fremtidens Folkeopdragelse*, both of 1848. See discussion in Stybe, 295–6; B. Malon, "Le Socialisme en Danemark," *La Revue Socialiste*, IX, 1889, 394 ff.

29. C. Jacker, *The Black Flag of Anarchy: Antistatism in the United States*, NY, 1968, 86–8. Proudhonist influence on other American radicals, such as Benjamin Tucker, is stressed in R. Rocker, *Pioneers of American Freedom*, Los Angeles, 1949.

30. Braunthal, 79–80.

31. Ibid., 88–91.

32. *Les Démocrates assermentés et les réfractaires*, 1863.

33. See the material added by the editor, M. Leroy, to the 1924 edition of *De la Capacité politique des classes ouvrières*.

34. Braunthal, 120–38 and ff., for the main facts; and, for a rich overall bibliography of the International by countries by J. Rougerie, see *Mouvement Social*, 1965, Apr–Jun, 127–38. The best Marxist account is still Yu. Steklov, *History of the First International*, L, 1929.

35. Cited in Braunthal, 125.

36. Cited in Rubel, "Charte," 20. De Paepe later described his own system of antidogmatic communism, which still bore traces of Proudhon's influence, as "Le Communisme relatif," *La Revue Socialiste*, XI, 1890, 547–53.

37. Characterization of the Franco-Swiss Proudhonist, Dr. Pierre Coullery, in Braunthal, 130.

38. Billington, *Mikhailovsky*, 22–3, 188; J. Skerlić, *Svetozar Marković*, Belgrade, 1922, 130–44. Likewise, those who wanted to turn Russian intellectuals away from populism to Marxism in the 1880s, began by seeking to translate Marx's *Poverty of Philosophy* into Russian. See the unpublished letter of Vera Zasulich to Engels in N. Naimark, "The Workers' Section and the Challenge of the 'Young' Narodnaia Volia, 1881–1884," *The Russian Review*, 1978, Jul, 296–7.

39. For differing interpretations of Proudhon's impact on Pi y Margal and the Spanish anarcho-federalist tradition, see A. Jutglar, *Federalismo y revolución*, Barcelona, 1966; and F. Urales, *La Evolución de la filosofía en España*, Barcelona, 1968, esp. 28 ff., 75 ff. For Proudhon's influence in Portugal after 1852, see the rich anthology: *Proudhon e la culturá portuguesa*, ed. García Petrus (Lisbon?), 1961–8, 5 v. For Mexico in the 1860s and 1870s, see G. García Cantú, *El socialismo en México, siglo xix*, Mexico, 1969, 11–2, 172–9.

40. Cited in Joll, 59.

41. Eduard Bernstein, cited in L. Febvre, "Une question d'influence. Proudhon et le syndicalisme contemporain," *Revue de Synthèse Historique*, 1909, Aug–Dec, 193. See also, for the influence of Proudhon during this period, E. Lagarde, *La Revanche de Proudhon ou l'avenir du socialisme mutuelliste*, 1905; J. Julliard, *Fernand Pelloutier et les origines du syndicalisme d'action directe*, 1971, 205 ff., 265 ff.; and, most incisively of all, A. Kriegel, *Le Pain et les roses. Jalons pour une histoire des socialismes*, 1973, 69–106.

42. J. Rougerie, "Sur l'Histoire de la Première Internationale," *Mouvement Social*, 1965, Apr–Jun, 28–34.

43. J. Clapham, *The Economic Development of France and Germany, 1815–1914*, Cambridge, 1963, 258–9.

44. Cited in Bouglé, *Sociologie*, 117.

45. Cited from *De la Justice* in H. de Lubac, *The Un-Marxian Socialist*, L, 1948, 149.

46. Cited in E. Dolléans, *Proudhon*, 1949, 338.

47. Marx, letter to P. Annenkov of Dec 28, 1846, in *Poverty*, 217. The Marxist tradition contends that this attitude arises logically from the class position of the *petit bourgeois*, who necessarily wavers between the bourgeoisie above him and the proletariat below.

For a differing explanation of the conflict in the understanding of contradictions by the two men, see Thier, 131–3.

48. See the section on Kant, Hegel, and Proudhon in Lubac, 140–65.

49. *Poverty*, 125. A fuller analysis of the ways in which Proudhon plays with a kind of dialectic is contained in Chen Kui-Si, *La Dialectique dans l'oeuvre de Proudhon*, 1936. Of Proudhon's basic moralism, D. Brogan has written "Proudhon was never asking '*Is this true?*', but always '*Is this right?*' " (*Proudhon*, L, 1934, 37).

50. *De la Justice dans la Révolution et dans l'Église*, 1858, I, 42; see the section "Adoration of Justice" in Lubac, 276–86.

51. "The will makes man a tyrant before wealth does; the proletarian's heart is the same as the rich man's, a sink of boiling sensuality, a center of lewdness and trickery." *Philosophie de la misère*, cited in Lubac, 61.

52. *Philosophie* as cited in Lubac, 296 n. 35.

53. *De la Justice*, cited in Lubac, 28.

54. D. Dillard noted Proudhonian anticipations of Keynesian ideas on money and interest: "Keynes and Proudhon," *Journal of Economic History*, 1942, May, 63–76. The quality of Proudhon's economic writings has perhaps been underestimated. *Manuel du spéculateur à la bourse* (1853), his most popular and heavily reprinted work, was a frequently penetrating guide to speculative investment by one with a purely intellectual interest in the process.

55. Interpretation suggested by the analysis of R. Tucker, *Philosophy and Myth in Karl Marx*, Cambridge, 1961, 108–54; and *The Marxian Revolutionary Idea*, NY, 1969, 51–3.

56. "I am anarchist in all the strength of the term." *Qu'est-ce que la propriété*, 1840, in *Oeuvres complètes*, 1866, I, 212. Sometimes he used the form *an-archique* (*Carnets de P. J. Proudhon*, 1960, I, 203).

57. F. Rudé, "Le mouvement ouvrier à Lyon," *Revue de Psychologie des Peuples*, XIII, 1958, 231–5. P. Ansart, *Naissance de l'anarchisme. Esquisse d'une explication sociologique du proudhonisme*, 1970, 165 ff.

58. Proudhon opposed Louis Blanc's state-organized social workshops as part of the "artificial centralization" (*Solution du problème social, Oeuvres*, VI, 13) that Parisians were forever imposing on the rest of France, and argued that the "working classes" (not, in his language, a unitary "proletariat") were best served not in "capturing, but in defeating both power and monopoly" (*Confessions*, 166, cited Allen, 5).

59. The unification of Italy and Germany in the 1860s is seen not just as the victory of modern nationalism, but also as the defeat of a prior predilection throughout Europe for ":federative experiments" in Binkley, *Realism*, 181 ff.

60. *De la Capacité*, 1924, 198 (see also 404); and *Idea of the Revolution*, 74. For the progression of Proudhon's views, see A. Bethod, "La théorie de l'état et du gouvernement dans l'oeuvre du Proudhon. De l'anarchie au fédéralisme," *Revue d'Histoire Economique et Sociale*, XI, 1923, 270–304; also Ansart, *Sociologie de Proudhon*, 1967, 131–42.

61. See his *Du Principe fédératif*, 1863; and L. Abensour, "P. J. Proudhon et la Pologne," *Grande Revue*, CIII, 1920, 3–15.

62. *La Fédération et l'unité de l'Italie*, 1862, 27–8. See discussion in Saitta, "L'idea di Europa," especially of Giuseppe Ferrari, the Italian sympathizer of Proudhon who feared that the advent of large states would destroy European dominance altogether in favor of America, Russia, and perhaps eventually China (Ferrari, *La Chine et l'Europe*, 1867, 598). Ferrari, though himself a professor, also shared Proudhon's fear of intellectuals in power. See his *Les philosophes salariés occupés à organiser une réaction occulte*, 1849. See Ferrari's study of Proudhon (1875) published in C. Sainte-Beuve, *P. J. Proudhon sa vie et correspondance 1838–1848*, Milan, 1947, 375–424; also C. Lovett, *Giuseppe Ferrari and the Italian Revolution*, Chapel Hill, 1979.

63. Jackson, *Marx, Proudhon*, 23. Yet Proudhon rejected decentralization that was purely political in nature, such as that urged by a German foe of Marx, Moritz Rittinghausen, who argued for a Swiss type of direct, local legislation. To Proudhon, this was even worse than electing representatives to a distant assembly, for direct legislation implicates people in transacting uniform and restrictive laws, while elected legislators might still retain flexibility and represent diversity. Rittinghausen, *Le Législation directe par le peuple ou la véritable démocratie*, 1850, is criticized in Proudhon, *Idea*, 143–53; defended by Rittinghausen in La *Législation directe par le peuple et ses adversaires*, Brussels, 1852 (English translation, intr. A. Harvey), *Direct Legislation by the People*, NY, 1897.

64. Marx, letter to Engels, Jun 20, 1866, cited in S. Bloom, *The World of Nations. A Study of the National Implications in the Work of Karl Marx*, NY, 1941, 28–9, a generally neglected study drawn on and further refined (on the basis of newly discovered manuscripts of Marx and Engels on the Polish question) in an unpublished

paper of A. Walicki, "Marx, Engels and Romantic Polish Nationalism," 1977, to which this analysis is indebted.

65. Bloom, 36.

66. Cited in K. Marx, F. Engels, *The Russian Menace to Europe*, Glencoe, 1952, 99–100.

67. Proudhon, *Idea*, 118.

68. A long, prophetic passage about the masses' inclination toward aesthetic criteria for politicians in an age when "le pouvoir s'était fait artiste" is cited from Proudhon by N. K. Mikhailovsky at the beginning of an article criticizing the modern state, which specially influenced the populist movement in Russia: "Count Bismarck," *Otechestvennye Zapiski*, 1871, Feb, in *Sochineniia*, St. Petersburg, 1897, VI, 71–2. See also V, 15.

69. *La Guerre et la paix*, 1861, III.

70. *La Guerre*, 451 and ff. through 456. The misinterpretations of Proudhon, which portray him as an advocate of war, take out of context his earlier section tracing the stubborn appeal of war and the dependence of much of history and art upon it. Proudhon has even been accused of proto-fascism. See J. Shapiro, "Pierre-Joseph Proudhon, Harbinger of Fascism," *American Historical Review*, 1945, Jul, 714–37.

71. Dolléans, *Proudhon*, 377–82.

72. This famous phrase, from Marx's "Contribution to the Critique of Hegel's Philosophy of Right," is cited with other similar passages in Lewy, *Religion and Revolution*, 542.

73. Jackson, *Marx, Proudhon*, 16–8.

74. Cited in Lubac, 81, 83.

75. The *raison d'église* of the Pharisees, "the Jesuits of Jerusalem," was the insidious forerunner of the *raison d'état* of the "new Jesuits," the political leaders of the modern, Jacobin state. In combating both church and state, Proudhon drew solace from the example of Christ ("I fight against the strong; I do not crush the weak"—cited in Lubac, 65) and from images of Christian apocalypse (looking forward in his "Revolutionary Manifesto" to the imminent time "when civilization will appear to us as a perpetual apocalypse . . . when by the reform of society Christianity will have found its second strength" [*Le Peuple*, 1848, Sep 2; in Dolléans, *Proudhon*, 149]). In his last work he characterized the French working classes as "this Paraclete for whose coming the apostles waited" (*De la Capacité*, 129–30). He left behind the manuscript for an uncompleted opus, *Caeserism and Christianity*, in part to answer Renan's portrayal of Christ as a dreamy mystic in his *Life of Jesus*.

76. E. Simmons, *Leo Tolstoy*, Boston, 1946, 649–50.

77. See particularly Proudhon's "Toast à la révolution," *Le Peuple*, 1848, Oct 17, in Dolléans, *Proudhon*, 150, 215; "il n'y a pas eu plusieurs révolutions, in n'y a eu qu'une révolution. La Révolution, il y a dix-huit siècles, s'appelait l'Evangile, la bonne nouvelle. . . . Ces chrétiens, ces révolutionnaires firent la première et la plus grande des révolutions . . . la Révolution est en permanence . . . il n'y a eu qu'une seule et même et perpétuelle révolution."

78. Tolstoy's debt to Proudhon has yet to be fully studied. A beginning has been made in S. Lafitte, "Tolstoi, Herzen et Proudhon," in *Studi in onore di Ettore Lo Gatto e Giovanni Maver*, Florence, 1962, 381–93. Proudhon not only influenced Tolstoy's opposition to war and to the state power that created it after meeting him in Brussels the year he published *La Guerre et la paix*; Proudhon also influenced the Russian émigré Baron F. Fircks (Schedo-Ferroti), who published in 1864 in Brussels *Le Program du congrès européen*. This was a Proudhonist project to deny capitalists the right to make armaments, and governments the right to declare war. See Dommanget, *Blanqui et l'opposition révolutionnaire à la fin du second empire*, 1960, 15 ff.

79. M. Buber, *Paths in Utopia*, L, 1949, 24–37, 86, 88, 146–9.
   J. Bancal has developed Buber's idea into a distinction between Proudhonian "topian socialism" (organically rooted somewhere, however minutely) and the "utopian socialism" of intellectuals (located only in the megalomanic mind). See *Proudhon pluralisme et autogestion*, 1970, II, 155. Bancal calls Proudhon a "prophet of the XXI century" (II, 232–4) with his advocacy of worker autonomy (*autogestion*), personalism (II, 219–20), and a radical pluralism compatible with the "functional pluralism of modern science" (I, 181).

80. G. Pirou, *Proudhonisme et le syndicalisme révolutionnaire*, 1910. The only important monograph documenting Proudhon's influence on any individual Russian is R. Labry, *Herzen et Proudhon*, 1928, which has now been substantially modified and supplemented by M. Mervand, "Herzen et Proudhon," *Cahiers du Monde Russe*

et Soviétique, 1971, Jan–Jun, 110–88. There is still no comprehensive survey of Proudhon's influence in either Russia or Eastern Europe.

81. Citations and discussion in Billington, *Mikhailovsky,* 27–41. Herzen, in a letter to Proudhon in Jul, 1855 (Mervand, 113), wrote: "You are the only *autonomous* thinker of the revolution."

82. The document "Dolzhny li my zaniat'sia izucheniem ideala budushchego?" was first published only in Russian (*Byloe,* 1921, no. 17); its influence is discussed in Venturi, 483 ff.

83. Bourguin, "Proudhon et Marx," 106.

84. *Idéomanie.* See Gurvitch, "Proudhon et Marx," 10.

85. See Saint-Beuve on Proudhon, discussed in Bourguin, 102.

86. Ansart, *Naissance,* 250–3, for the links with more recent youthful protest against the "externalization" of power; also 236, however, for the protest of the neo-romantics against Proudhon's antifeminism. Accused (or credited) with originating everything from fascism to deficit finance, Proudhon's views on women have now been read as indicating homosexuality. See D. Guérin, "Proudhon et l'amour 'unisexuel,'" *Arcadie,* 1965, Jan–Feb, 133–4.

87. A learned but rather pitiful Soviet scholar named N. Zastenker appears to have been condemned to spend his entire life denouncing Proudhon and anyone who has ever said a kind word about him. For samples, see his articles in *Istorichesky Zhurnal,* 1944, no. 10–1; *Literaturnoe Nasledstvo,* LXII, 1955; and *Frantsuzsky Ezhegodnik.* 1960. His "Ideinoe bankrotstvo sovremennogo neo-prudonizma," *Voprosy Istorii,* 1968, Sep, esp. 93–4; and "Marx et Proudhon aujourd'hui," *Cahiers du Communisme,* 1969, Feb–Mar, are particularly antagonistic to any suggestion of a future synthesis of Marxist and Proudhonist ideas—advanced by Gurvitch and in the summary to the centennial colloquium on Proudhon: *Actualité de Proudhon,* 251.

Chapter 11

1. Marrast, "La presse révolutionnaire," *Paris révolutionnaire,* 348.
2. Robertson, *1848,* 37.
3. Postgate, *Revolution,* 167; Robertson, *1848,* 28, 40–1; Weill, *Journal,* 225.
4. "The Placards of Paris," *Howitt's Journal,* 1848, Apr 15, 247–8.
5. Ibid., 248.
6. H. Innis, *The Bias of Communications,* Toronto, 1951, as paraphrased in G. Seldes, *The New Mass Media: Challenge to a Free Society,* Washington, D.C., 1968, 9.
7. According to Gans, "Origine," 81.
8. See G. Holyoake's article in *Dictionary of National Biography,* IX, 750–1; and his *Life of Henry Hetherington,* published in the year of Hetherington's death, L, 1849.
9. J. Harrison, *Utopianism and Education. Robert Owen and the Owenites,* NY, 1968, 9.
10. Morton, *Utopia,* 135.
11. Fahmy-Bey, *L'aventure,* 30.
12. "Renseignements," *Actualité de l'histoire,* 1957, Oct, 18–9.
13. Ibid., 20–2.
14. Ibid., 19–20.
15. A. Booth, *Saint-Simon and the Saint-Simonians,* L, 1871, 194.
16. Bertrand, *Histoire,* 436–9; also, for the role of foreign emigrants in the continuing revolutionary and journalistic ferment in Belgium, see Battistini, *Esuli italiani in Belgio,* 173–306.
17. Bertrand, 440.
18. H. Förder, *Marx und Engels am Vorabend der Revolution; die Ausarbeitung der politischen Richtlinien für die deutschen Kommunisten (1846–1848),* 1960, 75–95.
19. Cornu, *Marx et Engels,* I, 253 ff.
20. *Gründungsdokument,* 14–6; McLellan, *Marx,* 152–3.
21. The existing treatments of Marx's career as journalist by no means exhaust the subject: K. Bittel, *Karl Marx als Journalist,* 1953; A. Hutt, "Karl Marx as a Journalist," *Marxism Today,* 1960, May; and, with a fuller bibliography, K. Seleznev, *Rol' K. Marksa i F. Engel'sa v sozdanii rabochei pechati,* 1965.
22. G. Weill, *Le Journal. Origines, évolution et rôle de la presse périodique,* 1934, 195, and ff. for succinct account of the changes. See also L. Radiguer, *Maîtres im-*

primeurs et ouvriers typographes, 1903, 167 ff., for the technology and sociology of the changes.

23. W. Ong, *The Presence of the Word,* New Haven, 1967, uses these terms to designate the two stages that succeed and supplant an earlier oral culture. More generally, although less systematically, see M. McLuhan, *Understanding Media; the Extensions of Man,* NY, 1964; and the work of Innis, which largely inspired him. Useful bibliography on the typographical revolution is provided by E. Eisenstein, "Some Conjectures about the Impact of Printing on Western Society and Thought: A Preliminary Report," *Journal of Modern History,* 1968, Mar, 1–56.

24. J. Kirchner traces the origin of the term from the Arabic plural *mahâzin* to the Italian *magazino* (arsenal) on to England and thence to Germany in 1747 in *Die Grundlagen des deutschen Zeitschriftenwesens,* Leipzig, 1928, part I, 126–7. This German history (like Soviet histories) of journalism is rich in detail, but does not integrate its specialized subject into general historical context.

25. L. Faucher, "La Presse en Angleterre," *Revue des Deux Mondes,* 1826, Sep 15, 692. The date and the page reference to this useful article are incorrectly cited in L. O'Boyle, "The Image of the Journalist in France, Germany and England, 1815–1848," *Comparative Studies in Society and History,* 1968, Apr, 314.

26. Marrast in *Paris révolutionnaire,* 306.

27. Cited in C. Ledré, *Histoire de la presse,* 1958, 158.

28. Ibid.

29. E. Hamburger, "Episodes de la lutte entre Napoléon Ier et la presse anglaise," *Cahiers de la Presse,* 1938, Oct–Dec, 617–23. The author underscores the neglect of this subject by historians, but overlooks himself H. Klein, *Napoleon und die Presse. Napoleons Kampf gegen die Presse,* Bonn, 1918; also A. Periner, *Napoléon journaliste,* 1919.

30. Duchesse d'Abrantes, *Mémoires,* cited in Ledré, *Histoire,* 160.

31. G. Bourgin, "Note sur Robert Babeuf, fils de Gracchus et journaliste," *Cahiers de la Presse,* 1938, Apr–Jun, 223–9; Jul–Sep, 386–95.

32. Ibid., 394.

33. Etienne Arago, in *Paris révolutionnaire,* 405.

34. This is the only tradition of radical journalism whose lexicology and traditions have been subjected to careful study during the important formative period. See Pepłowski, *Słownictwo i frazeologie.* The impact of the Polish tradition on France and Europe is discussed by the works of L. Gocel, partly summarized in his "Les débuts de la presse de la grande émigration polonaise en France et son caractère clandestin (1832–1833)," *Revue d'Histoire Moderne et Contemporaine,* 1968, Apr–Jun, 304–20.

35. A. Saint-Prosper, *Du Monopole de l'imprimerie,* 1831, cited in Radiguer, 190.

36. C. Sainte-Foy, *Souvenirs,* 146, cited in Louis, *Histoire,* 438. Lamennais helped extend the revolutionary impulse beyond anticlerical intellectuals by insisting on the Christian qualities of the Polish and Belgian upheavals. See particularly C. de Coux, "Des Sociétés secrètes en Italie," *L'Avenir,* 1831, Apr 23.

37. Dubois, an early editor, cited in A. Lavi, " 'Le Globe' Sa fondation—sa redaction—son influence d'après des documents inédits," *Séances et Travaux de l'Académie des Sciences Morales et Politiques,* CLXI, 1904, 588–90.

38. Evans, *Socialisme,* 34. Beginning Jul 18, 1831, *The Globe* was formally subtitled "Journal of the Doctrine of Saint-Simon." See G. Weill, *L'Ecole Saint-Simonienne,* 1896, 65 and ff.

39. Cited from *The Globe,* Sep 9, 1831, in J. Vidalenc, "Les techniques de la propagande Saint-Simonienne à la fin de 1831," *Archives de Sociologie des Religions,* 1960, Jul–Dec, 8.

40. Vidalenc, 8, 14; also 12 for "the originality and amplitude of this propaganda."

41. Ibid., 13 ff. See 19 for a map of Saint-Simonian churches and correspondents throughout France.

42. Cited from his article "De l'individualisme et du socialisme," in Evans, *Socialisme,* 223–4. The article first appeared under a different title in *Revue Encyclopédique,* 1833, Oct, 94–117, but was formally published only in 1834.

43. See particularly his *De l'Humanité, de son principe, et de son avenir; où se trouve exposée la vraie définition de la religion, et où l'on explique le sens, la suite, et l'enchaînement du Mosaïsme et du Christianisme,* 1840, 2v; 2d ed. 1845. By investing this term with radical social content, he prepared for its use as the title of the first organ of the socialist Jean Jaurès, from whom it was taken as the name for the journal of the modern French Communist party.

44. This term had a varied subsequent usage, eventually even on the Right. See J. Hayward, "Solidarity: The Social History of an Idea in 19th Century France," *International Review of Social History,* IV, 1959, 261–84.

45. Cited in Evans, 39.

46. Originally entitled *Nouveau procédé typographique qui réunit les avantages de l'imprimerie mobile et du stéréotype,*" republished as "D'une nouvelle typographie," in *Revue Indépendante,* 1843, Jan. See Evans, *Socialisme,* 240.

47. Warren, *Manifesto,* Berkeley Heights, N.J., 1952 (originally 1841), 6.

48. Ibid., 1.

49. J. Leroux, *Aux ouvriers typographes. De la necessité de fonder une association ayant pour but de rendre les ouvriers propriétaires des instruments de travail,* 1833.

50. From the subtitle and epigraph respectively of his *Revue sociale ou solution pacifique du problème du prolétariat.* Leroux ended up after Napoleon III's coup retreating to the Isle of Jersey for agricultural experiments that might keep alive— even as they miniaturized—his ideal.

51. Cited in Ledré, *Histoire,* 201–2.

52. Ibid., 209.

53. They dramatized the threat of revolution in order to create the pressure for reform. See J. Hamburger, *James Mill and the Art of Revolution,* New Haven, 1963.

54. Cited in G. Perreux, *Au temps des sociétés secrètes,* 1931, 168.

55. Prospectus of *Le Siècle,* Jun 23, 1836, cited in V. Ainvelle, *La Presse en France. Genèse et évolution de ses fonctions psycho-sociales,* 1965, 205.

56. "Publicité des faits et non polémique des idées," ibid.

57. Hatin, *Histoire,* 149–52; also J.-P. Seguin, *Nouvelles à sensation. Canards du XIXe siècle,* 1959.

58. Ibid., 202.

59. Edouard Alletz, *De la Démocratie nouvelle,* 1838, II, 65–6.

60. Ibid., 64.

61. Characterization of Charles Philipon, founder of *La Caricature,* cited in O. Larkin, *Daumier: Man of His Time,* NY, 1966, 14. On the subsequent history and social significance of the political cartoon in the modern world, see the bibliography in L. Streicher, "David Low and the Sociology of Caricature," *Comparative Studies in Society and History,* VIII, 1965–6, no. 1, 1–2; and several other articles on the subject in subsequent editions of the same periodical, particularly W. Coupe, "The German Cartoon and the Revolution of 1848," IX, 1967, no. 2, 137–67.

62. Lamennais, *Correspondance,* II, 321, cited in Hatin, *Histoire,* 146; also 144 ff. and Ledré, *La Presse,* 142 ff.

63. Joseph Pennell, cited in Larkin, *Daumier,* 15. See also A. Blum, "La Caricature politique sous la monarchie de juillet," *Gazette des Beaux-Arts,* 1920, Mar–Apr, 257–77. Revolutionaries did not, of course, use lithography only for pictures. Louis Kossuth used it as a young delegate to the Hungarian diet in 1834 to publish the *procès-verbal* of that hitherto secret body. See Weill, *Journal,* 188–9. Caricature also flourished briefly in Prussia between the repeal of censorship on lithography in May 1842 and renewed police repression in Feb, 1843. See K. Koszyk, *Deutsche Presse im 19. Jahrhundert,* 1966, 88.

64. See *Progress of British Newspapers in the Nineteenth Century,* L, n.d., 45 (a compendium by the Swan Electric Engineering Company from the beginning of the century).

65. *Illustrated London News,* I (1842, May 14–Dec 31), iv.

66. A. Chesnier du Chesne, "L'Agence Havas," *Cahiers de la Presse,* 1938, Jan–Mar, 106.

67. Weill, *Journal,* 199.

68. Koszyk, *Deutsche Presse,* 212–3.

69. F. Mather, "The Railways, the Electric Telegraph and Public Order during the Chartist Period, 1837–48," *History,* 1953, Feb, esp. 48–51.

70. W. Schröder, "Politische Ansichten und Aktionen der 'Unbedingten' in der Burschenschaft," *Wissenschaftliche Zeitschrift der Universität Jena,* XV, 1966, no. 2, 236.

71. Ibid., 235.

72. *Freie Stimmen frischer Jugend,* 1819, discussed in Schröder, 237.

73. Cited in G. Bravo, "Il comunismo tedesco in Svizzera. August Becker 1843–1846," *Annali,* VI, 540 n. 63. See also other illustrations and materials referenced 538 ff., esp. Ludwig Seeger and August Becker's anonymously published *Politischsoziale Gedichte von Heinz und Kunz,* Bern, 1844; W. Schieder, "Wilhelm Weitling und die deutsche politische Handwerkerlyrik im Vormärz," *International Review of Social History* V, 1960, no. 2, 265–90. Cieszkowski's magnum opus "Our father," sought to derive an entire philosophy of social action from the prayer. See A. Chrzanowski, *Ojcze Nasz Augusta Cieszkowskiego,* Poznań, 1918.

74. Gabriel Pari, cited by R. Callas, "Le rôle considérable de notre presse dans la propagation des idées communistes," *Cahiers du Communisme,* 1958, Feb, 241.

75. Cited in J. Hamburger, *Intellectuals in Politics. J. S. Mill and the Philosophic Radicals*, New Haven, 1965, 127.

76. Cited in A. Schoyen, *The Chartist Challenge*, L, 1958, 6.

77. *Procès de T. Thoré*, 24.

78. "Address to our readers," *The Promethean or Communitarian Apostle*, 1842, Jan 12.

79. G. Barany, *Stephen Széchenyi and the Awakening of Hungary, 1791–1841*, Princeton, 1968, 382–3. Mazzini called his equally successful journalism "a sacerdotal act, the work of an apostolate." Ravenna, *Giornalismo*, 5.

80. Mikhailovsky's bust of Belinsky was a clear icon-substitute, and his writing desk on which the bust stood was described as "an altar on which he celebrated his holy rites," by V. Timofeeva: *Gleb Uspensky v Zhizni*, 1935, 115.
Soviet scholarship has now rescued Mikhailovsky from the total neglect of the Stalin era. But, because Mikhailovsky lived into the early twentieth century and incurred the polemic wrath of the young Lenin, he is still not incorporated into revolutionary hagiography. For his journalistic links and a summary of new Soviet literature since publication in 1958 of Billington, *Mikhailovsky*, see V. Tvardovskaia, "N.K. Mikhailovsky i 'Narodnaia Volia,' " *Istoricheskie Zapiski*, LXXXII, 1968, 163–203. See also Vilenskaia, *Mikhailovsky*, 1978.

81. Bittel, *Marx als Journalist*, 13–4.

82. *MEGA*, Erste Abteilung, I, Erster Halbband, 337. On Bastille Day, 1842, Marx called journalism the force for engaging "philosophy as such against the world." *Werke*, I, 97–8, as cited in O. Hamman, "The Young Marx, Reconsidered," *Journal of the History of Ideas*, 1970, Jan–Mar, 111. Engels's first signed journalistic piece was the translation of a poem "On the Invention of Printing." See Cornu, *Marx et Engels*, I, 227 n. 1. For both the Spanish and German texts with commentary by H. Koch, see "Die Ode auf die Erfindung der Buchdruckerkunst von José Manuel Quintana und Friedrich Engels," *Wissenschaftliche Zeitschrift der Universität Jena*, 1952/53, 1923.

83. Bittel, 30–1.

84. Ibid., 23.

85. Koszyk, 84. For more examples and details, see H. Keller, *Die politischen Verlagsanstalten und Druckereien in der Schweiz 1840–1848*, Bern, 1935.

86. An exception was the Irish Fenian movement, which sent back arms and pamphlets to several generations of Irish revolutionaries, and even launched a military attack on the English in Canada at the end of the American Civil War. Of the revolutionary nationalists, the Polish exile press within Europe continued to influence a wide spectrum of revolutionaries. See J. Borejsza, *W kręgu wielkich wygnańców 1848–1895*, Warsaw, 1963.

87. G. Becker, "Journaux de l'union ouvrière de Cologne," in *Presse ouvrière*, 264–83.

88. S. Na'aman, "In der Partei der *Neuen Rheinischen Zeitung*," in *Lassalle*, Hanover, 1970, 125–78, esp. 127.

89. F. Balser, "Une presse à rédaction ouvrière, 1848–1851," in *Presse ouvrière*, 238 ff.; and 286 ff., 309 ff.

90. The sixth étude of Corberon, *De la Justice*, discussed in M. Collinet, "Les débuts du machinisme devant les contemporains (1760–1840)," *Le Contrat Social*, 1965, May–Jun, esp. 195.

91. Noyes, *Organization*, esp. 131–43, and materials referenced therein.

92. Radiguer, *Maîtres Imprimeurs*, 252–3, 272.

93. One delegate from Lyon proclaimed: "That which exists among the typographers of Paris should exist among all typographers, not only of France, but of Europe, of the entire universe" (Radiguer, 254–5). Their professional journal *Typographia* of Mar 25, 1848, asserted that "L'ouvrier-imprimeur représente, pour parler franchement, l'état supérieur du prolétariat." Cited by J. Droz and P. Aycoberry, "Structures sociales et courants idéologiques dans l'Allemagne pré-révolutionnaire, 1835–1847," *Annali*, VI, 187.

94. Herzen, *My Past*, II, 806. The attribution to Duchêne is tentative.

95. Ibid. See also the entire chapter on Proudhon, 805–39.

96. On Herzen's aid to Proudhon, see E. Carr, "Some Unpublished Letters of Alexander Herzen," *Oxford Slavonic Papers*, III, 1952, 83 ff.; also 108 for a work Herzen tried to write against Girardin. For Proudhon as a journalist in this era, see A. Darimon, *A travers une Révolution (1847–1855)*, 1884.

97. *Presse ouvrière*, 176 and ff.

98. Cited in V. Kuleshov, "*Otechestvennye zapiski*" *i literatura 40-kh godov XIX veka*, 1959, 4.

99. Ibid., 357–9 n. 78.

100. Report of Bulgarin to the third section, cited without precise documentation

in ibid., 102. If, as it appears, the report dates from 1842, this would be the earliest usage of the term "communist" in Russia.

On the special importance of Sand's works in this journal (and on the formation of a literature with social content in Russia) see 105, and more fully K. Sanine, *Les Annales de la patrie et la diffusion de la pensée française en Russie (1868–1884)*, 1955, 60 ff.

101. Written in Nice and first published in abbreviated form in *L'Avènement du Peuple*, Paris, 1851, Nov 19, and in full as *Le Peuple russe et le socialisme. Lettre à Monsieur J. Michelet, Professeur au Collège de France*, 1852; and, in English, in *From the Other Shore*, L, 1956, 165–208.

102. *Poliarnaia Zvezda* like *Kolokol* has now been completely reproduced in facsimile, 1966. On the earlier *Polar Star* of the Decembrists, see V. Berezina, *Russkaia zhurnalistika pervoi chetverti XIX veka*, Leningrad, 1965, 74 ff.

103. A recent study has revealed this network to have been an important means of bringing together aristocratic and nonaristocratic elements (and to have included figures not previously known to have had revolutionary connections such as the ethnographer A. N. Afanas'ev). See N. Eidel'man, *Tainye korrespondenty 'poliarnoi zvezdy,'* 1966, and review thereof by A. Turkov, *Prometei*, 1967, no. 2, 314–5.

104. S. Svatikov, "Studenticheskaia pechat' s 1755 po 1915 g.," *Put' studenchestva*, 1916, 218, referenced in the unpublished doctoral dissertation of T. Hegarty, "Student Movements in Russian Universities, 1855–1861," Harvard, 1964. For another, later *Ekho* in Vilnius, see *Bol'shevistskaia pechat' v dooktiabr'sky period*, 1959, 11–2.

105. Cited in Venturi, *Roots*, 285.

106. Ibid., 286.

107. Venturi, 286; Yarmolinsky, 111.

108. From text in B. Bazilevsky (Bogucharsky), *Materialy dlia istorii revoliutsionnago dvizheniia v rossii v 60-kh gg.*, St. Petersburg, 1905, 43. The contemptuous term *liberalishki* was also used in Moscow circles. See N. Pirumova, "M. Bakunin ili S. Nechaev?" *Prometei*, V, 1968, 173.

109. See B. Koz'min, *Tkachev i revoliutsionnoe dvizhenie 1860kh godov*, The Hague, 1969 (reprinted from 1922); and P. G. *Zaichnevsky i "Molodaia Rossiia,"* 1932.

110. E. Vilenskaia, *Revoliutsionnoe podpol'e v Rossii (60-e gody XIX v.)*, 1965, 137. This work summarizes new scholarship on Land and Liberty and supplements Venturi, *Roots*.

111. On V. I. Bakst, see B. Koz'min, *Iz istorii revoliutsionnoi mysli v Rossii*, 1961, 506 ff.

112. N. Valentinov, *Encounters with Lenin*, L, 1968, esp. 63–8, stresses the importance of Chernyshevsky's example to Lenin. See also W. Woehrlin, *Chernyshevskii. The Man and the Journalist*, Cambridge, Mass., 1971.

113. On this journal, published between Jul 1862 and May 1863, by Kastus Kalinovsky, see E. Golomb and E. Fingerit, *Rasprostranenie pechati v dorevoliutsionnoi Rossii i v Sovetskom Soiuze*, 1959, 11–2.

Chapter 12

1. Milosz, *History*, 199, also 231. The best Polish work on Lévy is J. Borejsza, *Sekretarz Adama Mickiewicza*, 1969.

2. A. Lévy, *La Russie sur le Danube*, 1853, 175.

3. S. Märies, "Aspects des relations roumano-françaises: contribution d'Armand Lévy," *Revue Romaine d'Histoire*, 1973, no. 2, 375–94.

4. T. Huebner, *The Germans in America*, Philadelphia/NY, 1962, 99–101.

5. Cited in Huebner, 101. See also Theodore Poesche and Charles Goepp, *The New Rome*, NY, 1853. The militant, pro-union nationalism during the Civil War of Germans like Carl Schurz is well known. Some like Goepp went so far as to call for breaking up the state system in the South to insure strong national hegemony (*The National Club on the Reconstruction of the Union*, NY, 1864).

6. Lehning, "Association," 201–2.

7. Nearly 1,000 according to H. Payne and H. Grosshans, "The Revolutionaries and the French political police in the 1850's," *American Historical Review*, 1963, Jul, 954–5.

8. Ibid., 210, and n. 4.

9. These are the only two slogans appearing on the certificate issued to monetary contributors, reproduced in Lehning, "Association," opposite 210; see also the official *Manifesto* of Jun 24, 1858, 267.

10. For a reproduction of the *Bulletin of the International Association,* which published its key articles in all four languages—English, French, German, and Polish—see ibid., opposite 230.

11. Lehning's suggestion ("Association," 185) that it was "the first international organization of a proletarian and socialist character" is effectively challenged by Nikolaevsky ("Secret Societies and the First International," in *The Revolutionary Internationals,* 42–3), who points out that the words "workers" and "proletarian" never appear in its statutes. But Nikolaevsky underestimates their commitment to social revolution in labeling the association "a definite step backward from the international organizations that the English Chartists had tried to create in the 1840's" (42).

12. *Delo Petrashevtsev,* II, 95.

13. *Des socialistes français à M. Mazzini,* Brussels, 1852; and other works in this sustained feud are referenced in Lehning, "Association," 208–9 n. 8.

14. "Aux Républicains, Démocrates et Socialistes de l'Europe," in Lehning, "Association," 274. Lehning could find no copy of the English version published on 1858, Dec 7, and reproduces the French text from *Le Libertaire* of 1859, Feb 5 (233 n.1) of "the most important publication issued by the International and the International Committee" (233).

15. Ibid., 274–5.

16. Ibid., 276–7.

17. Ibid., 233. Lehning surprisingly does not connect the Polish defection with either the nationalist predilections or the aristocratic backgrounds of the Polish revolutionaries.

18. "Address of the International Association to the Democratic Party," in Lehning, 281–3.

19. Letter of Aug 28, 1858, from the London Central Committee of the International Association to the Icarian community of Nauvoo in Lehning, 272.

20. This journal, which considered itself both communistic and anarchistic, perpetuated the vigorous anti-Mazzinian criticism first sounded by Branciano (the Italian foe of nationalism, self-styled "friend of the red flag," and co-editor with Hugo of *L'Homme* on the Isle of Jersey). Déjacques's views are set forth in his *La Question révolutionnaire,* reprinted 1971.

21. Lehning, "Association," 236–8.

22. Cited in J. Saville, *Ernest Jones, Chartist,* L, 1952, 58–9. This was technically a public meeting (the first) of the International Committee out of which the International Association was formed (Braunthal, 77).

23. Cited in Lehning, 213–4.

24. M. St. John Packe, *Orsini, The Story of a Conspiracy,* Boston, 1957, 221. Although Orsini had by then broken with Mazzini, the extent of Mazzini's own encouragement of terrorist activities is stressed by Nikolaevsky in "Societies," 43–5, and A. Luzio, *Carlo Alberto e Giuseppe Mazzini,* Turin, 1923.

25. Nikolaevsky, "Societies," 44.

26. Ibid., 38 ff.

27. R. Grew, *A Sterner Plan for Italian Unity,* Princeton, 1963.

28. See the unpublished paper of Z. David on this friend of Bakunin and foe of the meliorative, pro-Hapsburg nationalism of Palacký: *Josef V. Frič and the Cause of Czech Independence (1859–1864),* esp. 5–6 and references 32–3; Marx, *Sochineniia,* VII, 208, 219.

29. Bakunin had also been in touch with an embryonic Finnish group when in Stockholm. See the newly discovered program set forth in Apr 25, 1863, to the Finnish nationalist poet Emile von Quanten: E. Rudnitskaia, "Neizvestnoe pis'mo M. Bakunina," *Prometei,* 1969, no. 7, 236–41. Freedom was projected (240) for Finland, Estonia, Latvia, Poland, Lithuania, the Ukraine, Little Russia, Bessarabia, Georgia, and all the Caucasus.

30. Text is in "Konwencja miedzy J. Garibaldim a J. Ordega 6 Juin 1864," *Kwartalnik Historyczny,* XXXVII, 1923, no. 2, 373; discussed in David, 27–8, 38.

31. A. Lehning, "Bakunin's Conceptions of Revolutionary Organisations and their Role: A Study of his 'Secret Societies,'" in C. Abramsky, ed., *Essays in Honour of E. H. Carr,* L, 1974, 61–5 and ff., contains new documentary materials. In addition, see M. Nettlau, *Ocherki po istorii anarkhicheskikh idei i stat'i po raznym sotsial'nym voprosam,* Detroit, 1951, 82–4 and ff; C. Marti, *Orígenes de anarquismo en Barcelona,* Barcelona, 1959, 70 n. 77.

In correctly stressing the transnational, social revolutionary nature of his projects during these last years, Lehning may go too far by contending that "after the failure of the Polish insurrection in 1863, Bakunin no longer believed in national liberation movements as a social and revolutionary force" (57).

32. The fundamental works on this period are by M. Nettlau, *Bakunin e l'Inter-*

nazionale in Italia dal 1864 al 1872, Geneva, 1928; and *Bakunin and the Interna-tional in Spain* (earlier German edition of the former in *Archiv für die Geschichte des Sozialismus und der Arbeiterbewegung*, II, 1911–2; earlier Spanish edition of the latter, Buenos Aires, 1925). On Switzerland and the Jura federation, see the annotated collection by Bakunin's principal Swiss follower, James Guillaume, *L'Internationale: documents et souvenirs (1864–1878)*, 1905–10, 4 v; and new material in A. Lehning's monumental *Archives Bakounine*, Leiden, 1961 et seq., 5 v. to date.

Discussions of other material and views are (for Switzerland) J. Freymond, ed., *Etudes et documents sur la première internationale en Suisse*, Geneva, 1964, and (for Italy) L. Valiani, *L'Historiographie de l'Italie contemporaine*, Geneva, 1968, 101–13.

33. For the rich subculture of conspiracy in Spain, see C. Lidi, *La Revolución de 1868*, NY, 1970; on Italy, see the classic study by N. Rosselli with new introduction by L. Valiani: *Mazzini e Bakunin*, Turin, 1967.

34. Citations in J. Joll, *The Anarchists*, L, 1964, 92, also 111–3.

35. Bakunin, *L'Empire knouto-germanique et la révolution sociale (1871)* in *Oeuvres*, II; and the uncompleted sequel (Nov–Dec, 1872) published in Lehning, ed., *Michel Bakounine et les conflits dans l'Internationale 1872. La question germaine-slave, le communisme d'état*, Leiden, 1965, 169–219.

36. Bakunin, *Ai miei amici d'Italia*, cited from Nettlau in Joll, *Anarchists*, 108.

37. Nikolaevsky, 41–2 and notes.

38. Paris, *Lion of Caprera*, 63.

39. Alexander Dumas, *On Board the Emma*, NY, 1929, 522.

40. There is a short description in B. King, *A History of Italian Unity*, NY 1967, II, 38–40; full information in L. Cassese, *La Spedizioni di sapri*, Bari, 1969; and N. Rosselli, *Carlo Pisacane nel risorgimento*, with a preface to the new edition (Milan, 1958) by W. Maturi, who adds more references and comment in his *Interpretazioni de risorgimento*, Turin, 1962, 465–71. Hales, *Mazzini*, 127, discusses an earlier Mazzinian plan to try something similar.

41. Cassese, 40 (esp. n. 15), discusses the "collective hallucination" involved in the multiplicity of inaccurate testimony that Pisacane used a red flag. A. Salomone, "The 'Great Fear' of 1860. Garibaldi and the Risorgimento," *Italian Quarterly*, 1971, Spring, 77–127, discusses the fear of social revolution that haunted Garibaldi even in victory.

42. T. Coogan, *The IRA*, L, 1970, 14.

43. He also issued a kind of manifesto calling for European confederation, his *Memorandum alle potenze dell'Europa* on Oct 22, 1860. See A. Tambora, "Garibaldi e l'Europa," *Atti del 39 congresso di storia del risorgimento italiano*, 1961, 515. On his links with Hungarians, see L. Lajos, *Garibaldi e l'emigrazione ungherese 1860–1862*, Modena, 1965.

44. K. Morawski, "Garibaldi e la Polonia," *Atti del 39 congresso*, 336.

45. Nikolaevsky seems to go beyond his evidence in suggesting ("Sociétés," 46) that in the 1860s "Mazzini, Garibaldi, and the Philadelphians formed a bloc that replaced the International Association of 1855–59."

46. The first public performance of the Boito text and Verdi melody was in London on May 24, 1962. The first international propagation came with the meeting of French and British workers in London on Aug 5 (which prepared for the First International). See P. Masini, "I Canti della Prima Internazionale in Italia," *Movimento Operaio e Socialista*, 1969, Jul–Sep, 229–43.

47. See particularly his "Die Polen, die Diplomatie und die Revolution," *Nordstern*, nos. 219–23, 1863, Jul. Nikolaevsky ("Sociétés," 329 n. 23) argues somewhat unconvincingly that Becker was also a Mason on the grounds that Mazzini addressed him as "Dear Brother."

48. On Coullery, a visionary Christian doctor who helped make the Jura a major center of organizing activity and anti-Marxist convictions within the First Inter-national, see J. Freymond and M. Molnár, "The Rise and Fall of the First Inter-national," in *The Revolutionary Internationals*, 14–6.

49. *The Return of the Swallow and Other Poems*, L, 1864, 40–1, also 21. For his more typical late writings, see *Aids to Devotion; or Religious Readings in the Order of the Natural and the Christian Years*, L, 1865.

50. Menu of the six-course dinner of Apr 17, amidst other material on Russo-Italian contacts, collected by V. Never, in *Atti del XLIII congresso di storia del risorgimento italiano*, 1968, 47.

51. *La France libre et Garibaldi*, L, 1864.

52. Dedijer, *The Road to Sarajevo*, L, 1966, 438–43, for the problematic but not entirely contrived question of the Masonic connections and forms of the revolu-tionaries. For evidence of a Masonic base to the Russian revolution of March 1917,

see G. Aronson, *Rossiia nakanune revoliutsii. Istoricheskie etiudy: monarkhisty, liberaly, masony, sotsialisti,* 1962.

53. Dedijer, *Road,* 178. Mazzini's revolutionary oath was reprinted in *Zora,* 1912 (479 notes).

54. Tambora, "Garibaldi," 462; and for Garibaldi's influence on Russians, 476 ff. For exhaustive bibliography on the Garibaldian impact see A. Campanella, *Giuseppe Garibaldi e la tradizione garibaldina,* Geneva, 1971, 2 v.

55. See discussion and references in Billington, *Mikhailovsky,* 191 n. 1. For the spread of nationalist insurrections from Bosnia and Herzegovina in the summer of 1875 to Romania and Bulgaria on the eve of the Russo-Turkish war of 1877–8, see V. Trajkov, "L'Insurrection d'avril 1876 en Bulgarie et les peuples balkaniques," *Etudes Balkaniques,* 1876, no. 1, 16–41.

56. This movement's *Mechanics' Free Press* of 1828 was "the first workers' journal edited by workers and for them," according to E. Pessen, "La première presse du travail. Origine, rôle, idéologie," *Presse ouvrière,* 43–4.

57. According to Obermann, "Germano-Américains," *Presse ouvrière,* 76.

58. Though the key new journal of 1845, *Der Volkstribun,* took its name from Babeuf, its reformist tone caused Marx's displeasure and switch to *Die Revolution,* a short-lived weekly of 1852 and the "first Marxist workers' journal in the United States." But Weydemeyer himself soon complained about the "embourgeoisation" of workers in America to Marx (ibid., 84) and switched to *Die Reform*—Cabet's isolated *Der Communist* being the only journal in the New World to keep a truly revolutionary name from the Old. See Obermann, *Joseph Weydemeyer. Ein Lebensbild 1818–1866,* 1968; and the unpublished doctoral thesis of D. Herreshoff, "American Disciples of Marx from the Age of Jackson to the Progressive Era," Wayne State, 1963.

59. D. Riazanov's careful analysis of this stage of Marx's career concludes that the English-language articles were largely written by Engels (*Ocherki,* 119–51), and discusses Marx's lesser known, more brief collaboration subsequently on the even more conservative *Die Presse* of Vienna (159–73).

60. See J. Wiener, *The War of the Unstamped: The Movement to Repeal the British Newspaper Tax, 1830–1836,* Cornell, 1969; *A Descriptive Finding List of Unstamped British Periodicals, 1830–1836,* L, 1970; and P. Hollis, *The Pauper Press: A Study in Working-Class Radicalism of the 1830's,* Oxford, 1970.

61. For the role of John Doherty in founding *The Voice of the People,* *Workmen's Expositor,* and others in Manchester, and of Bronterre O'Brien in imparting a more revolutionary flavor to *Poor Man's Guardian* before joining for a time Feargus O'Connor on his new *Northern Star,* founded in 1838, see M. Brooke, "Naissance de la presse ouvrière à Manchester," and D. Thompson "Créations d'O'Brien et d'O'Connor," in *Presse ouvrière,* 10 ff. and 21–33.

62. S. Gruner, "The Revolution of July 1830 and the expression 'Bourgeoisie,' " *Historical Journal,* XI, 1968, no. 3, 469; R. Gossez, "Presse parisienne à destination des ouvriers 1848–1851," *Presse ouvrière,* 130–1. See also G. Weill, "Les journaux ouvriers à Paris de 1830 à 1870," *Revue d'Histoire Moderne et Contemporaine,* 1907, Nov.

63. Cuvillier, *Hommes,* 91–3. Since, however, his itemization of earlier efforts (87–91) is incomplete, especially for Lyon, his implication that journals of this sort began only in 1839–40 is misleading.

64. Ibid., 99–154, and Cuvillier, *Un Journal d'ouvriers,* 1914, for the journal's substantial quarrels with other radical publications.

65. Cuvillier, *Hommes,* 124.

66. Ibid., 125.

67. According to Gossez, *Presse ouvrière,* 148. Proudhon's influential journals of this period built on links with the typographical society to help organize a Bank for the People offering cheap credit and mutual aid for workers (ibid., 176–82).

68. Barely one-quarter of the 171 new periodicals founded after the overthrow of Louis Philippe on Feb 25, 1848, survived for more than a brief period after Jun 17 (ibid., 183). The symbolic father figure of revolutionary journalism, "Père Duchène," reappeared briefly in Jun as an "author" in the official journal of the workers' delegates from the department of the Seine, *Journal des Travailleurs,* but was soon transformed (in the title of a new journal of July) into *Le Perdu Chêne de la Révolution* (the lost oak of the revolution) (ibid., 170).

69. The demise in 1858 of Ernest Jones's *People's Paper,* the last official journal of the Chartist movement, ended all British leadership for transnational working-class movements. The very title, *Bee-Hive,* of the most important new working-class newspaper of the 1860s (founded by the carpenter George Potter "in the interest of the working classes") suggests its mid-Victorian preoccupation with non-ideological day-to-day concerns. See S. Coltham, "The *Bee-Hive* Newspaper," in

A. Briggs and J. Saville, eds., *Essays in Labour History*, L, 1960, 174–204; and "George Potter, the Junta and the *Bee-Hive*," *International Review of Social History*, IX, 1964, 391–432; and X, 1965, 23–65.

70. The basic name of the First International was rich in Chartist association, their basic organization, the London Workingmen's Association of Jun 1836, having taken its name from a group founded in May to fight the "tax on knowledge," the Association of Working Men to Procure a Cheap and Honest Press. The Working-men's Association had begun the tradition of Chartist internationalism in Nov 1838 with a pioneering call for solidarity to Belgian workers appealing for Anglo-Belgian-Dutch-Rhineland worker collaboration. Text in *The Constitutional*, 1836, Nov 12; discussion in Lehning, "Association," 189–91, who also traces Anglo-continental collaboration through the late fifties, 191–284.

71. On this illustrated monthly *Russky rabochy*, see B. Esin, *Russkaia zhurnalistika 70–80 godov XIX veka*, 1963, 180 ff.

72. Citations in O. Anderson, *A Liberal State at War*, NY, 1967, 3, 85. For the support of the reformist press in provincial Sheffield, see A. Briggs, "John Arthur Roebuck and the Crimean War," *Victorian People*, L, 1954, 60–94.

73. For the richest documentation of this attitude including material not in subsequent Soviet editions, see D. Riazanov, *Anglo-russkiia otnosheniia v otsenke K. Marksa (Istoriko-kritichesky etiud)*, Petrograd (izdanie petrogradskago soveta rabochikh i krasnoarmeiskikh deputatov), 1918, LL.

74. Cited in Anderson, 3.

75. The poet laureate Alfred Tennyson sang of the 300 in the Heavy Brigade who had charged suicidally up a hill no less than the "noble six hundred" of the Light Brigade that charged "into the valley of death" (*The Poetic and Dramatic Works of Alfred, Lord Tennyson*, Boston, 1899, 640–1, 292). Elsewhere he directly chided reformers: "Better a rotten borough or so than a rotten fleet . . ." (*The Times*, 1859, May 9, cited in S. Maccoby, *English Radicalism 1853–1886*, L, 1938, 67).

76. Weill, *Journal*, 242.

77. Anderson, 71. Weill makes the differential less great.

78. *The Saturday Review*, cited in Weill, 240.

79. *Oxford English Dictionary*, V, second pagination, 585, for these, apparently the first, uses of "jingo" in this new sense. Ibid., II, 304, for *La Cocarde* of 1831 and the first use of "chauvinism" in 1870.

80. *Kolokol*, 1864, no. 44–45; cited in *Russkaia periodicheskaia pechat'* (1702–1894), 1959, 25.

81. Cited in M. Lemke, *Ocherki po istorii russkoi tsenzury i zhurnalistiki XIX stoletiia*, St. Petersburg, 1904, 279.

82. Ibid., 279; this figure was 4,000 more than its nearest competitor (ibid., 358).

83. Cited in Brokgauz-Efron, *Entsiklopedichesky slovar'*, XIV, 732. See also S. Nevedensky, *Katkov i ego vremia*, St. Petersburg, 1888.

84. Yarmolinsky, *Road*, 130.

85. Cited in Brokgauz-Efron, XIV, 732.

86. Ibid.

87. C. Moser, *Antinihilism in the Russian novel of the 1860's*, The Hague, 1964.

88. *Russkaia pechat'*, 342.

89. S. Pushkarev pointed this out to me convincingly in an extended discussion of my *Icon* (letter of Jul 30, 1966, 9–10) referring particularly to the characterization in A. Lobanov-Rostovsky, *Russia and Europe 1825–1878*, Ann Arbor, 1954, 259–63.

90. *Russkaia pechat'*, 436–7.

91. P. Pulzer, *The Rise of Political Anti-Semitism in Germany and Austria*, NY, 1964, 34 ff.

92. Brokgauz-Efron, LXII, 794; also *Russkaia pechat'*, 509–11.

93. Outside of France, the legend was both most intense and most revolutionary in Poland. H. Segel, "The Polish Napoleonic Cult from Mickiewicz to Żeromski," *Indiana Slavic Studies*, IV, 1963, 128–51.

94. In addition to his well-known contacts with the national revolutionaries, Napoleon also had 11 meetings in London with Cabet at precisely the time he was first popularizing the name and ideas of communism. See M. Prudhommeaux, "Louis Bonaparte et Etienne Cabet en 1839," *La Révolution de 1848*, 1909–10, Mar–Apr, 6–15.

95. S. Burchell, *Imperial Masquerade. The Paris of Napoleon III*, NY, 1971, 38 ff.

96. Ibid., 241.

97. Ibid., 44 ff.

98. The way in which the positivism of Saint-Simon's disciple Auguste Comte provided a kind of substitute ideology for both conservative Catholicism and revolutionary romanticism is fully traced in D. Charlton, *Positivist Thought in France*

during the Second Empire, 1852–1870, Oxford, 1959; and W. Simon, *European Positivism in the Nineteenth Century*, Ithaca, 1963, 73 ff.

99. Constantin Rossler, *System der Staatslehre*, Leipzig, 1857, xvii, cited in Ritter, *Hegel et la révolution*, 98.

100. Rémusat, *Mémoires*, II, 59.

101. Jules Faure, cited in D. Kulstein, *Napoleon III and the Working Class. A Study of Government Propaganda under the Second Empire*, Sacramento/Los Angeles, 1969, 41. This study (particularly 38–68) shows how elaborate was Napoleon's regulation of the press—involving reading 546 departmental newspapers in addition to the Paris press, and requiring four different types of financial subvention. See also L. Case, *French Opinion on War and Diplomacy during the Second Empire*, Philadelphia, 1954, and N. Isser, *The Second Empire and the Press. A Study of Government-Inspired Brochures on French Foreign Policy in their Propaganda Milieu*, The Hague, 1974.

102. Cited from Joly, *Dialogues aux enfers entre Machiavel et Montesquieu ou la politique de Machiavel au XIXe siècle*, Brussels, 1864, cited in Kulstein, 42–3. The famed anti-Jewish tract, *Protocols of the Elders of Zion*, was to a large extent a paraphrase of Joly's work.

103. Extracts from the various interpretations together with a bibliography (to be supplemented by Burchell, Kulstein, and other more recent works used here) are in B. Gooch, *Napoleon III—Man of Destiny. Enlightened Statesman or Proto-Fascist?*, 1963, and S. Osgood, *Napoleon III. Buffoon, Modern Dictator, or Sphinx?*, Boston, 1963. These infelicitously phrased alternatives do not exhaust the possibilities. More recent works often follow lines set out in Zeldin, *The Political System of Napoleon III*, 1958, and suggest that the image of first master manipulator of mass politics might be more appropriate. See, for instance, a work not included in Gooch or Osgood: T. Corley, *Democratic Despot. A Life of Napoleon III*, 1961.

104. R. Koebner, "The Emergence of the Concept of Imperialism," *Cambridge Journal*, V, 1952, 726–41; and, more fully, in his *Imperialism: the story and significance of a political word, 1840–1960*, Cambridge, 1964.

Koebner traces the term from English criticism of Napoleon III to English self-criticism in the 1870s; but there was a French usage of 1869 in the modern sense of contrasting "l'esprit impérialiste" with "nos institutions libérales" in J. Amigues, *La Politique d'un honnête homme*, 98, cited amidst many other uses from the period of the Franco-Prussian War in J. Dubois, *Le Vocabulaire politique et social en France de 1869 à 1872*, 1962, 319.

105. Inaugural article in the first issue of *La Marseillaise*, 1869, Dec 19, cited in A. Zévaès, *Henri Rochefort le pamphlétaire*, 1946, 77.

106. Unreferenced epigram, cited in ibid., 35.

107. Examples, which lose their mordant quality in translation, particularly for a modern reader not used to the *demi-mots* and *sous-entendus* that previously dominated nineteenth-century journalism in France, see ibid., 47–8.

108. I. Collins, *The Government and the Newspaper Press in France 1814–1881*, Oxford, 1959, 155–6.

109. *La Lanterne*, 1er série, no. 32, 10–1.

110. Paschal-Grousset in 1891 (Zévaès, *Rochefort*, 78); Eugene Varlin, in a letter of 1869 to James Guillaume (then secretary of the First International): ibid., 78.

111. Phrase of the Russian satirist Michael Saltykov, lamenting that the city under Napoleon had become preoccupied with "women's fashions and delicate condiments" (*Za Rubezhom* in *Izbrannye sochineniia*, 1940, 391).

112. Zévaès, *Rochefort*, 78.

113. According to Reclus, *Girardin*, 210, who also provides the circulation statistics and other information on Girardin. Already by the late 1860s, Girardin's anti-Prussian tone "surpassed anything that was permitted to the inarticulate tumult of deputies on the right." According to his contemporary Ollivier, cited in Koszyk, *Presse*, 214.

114. Weill, *Journal*, 285–91. For the role of the press on the continent in developing chauvinist sentiment after 1871, see H. Pross, *Literatur und Politik, Geschichte und Programme der politisch-literarischen Zeitschriften im deutschen Sprachgebiet seit 1870*, Otin/Freiburg, 1963; R. Manévy, *La Presse de la troisième république*, 1955; and material referenced in W. Haacke, "The Austrian and Viennese Press," *Gazette*, XIV, 1968, No. 3, 195–216.

115. Cited in F. Mott, *American Journalism. A History: 1690–1960*, NY, 3d ed., 1962, 529.

116. G. Grützner, *Die Pariser Kommune*, Cologne/Opladen, 1963, provides an

exhaustive history of the myth, particularly its intimidating effect on German Social Democrats.

117. Cheng Chih-Szu, "The Great Lessons of the Paris Commune," *Peking Review*, 1966, Apr 1, 23–6; Apr 8, 17–8, 25; Apr 15, 23–9.

118. G. Ionescu, "Lenin, the Commune and the State," *Government and Opposition*, 1970, Spring, 131–65. V. Eremina, "V. I. Lenin kak istorik parizhskoi kommuny," *Voprosy Istorii*, 1971, no. 2, 31–43.

119. M. Mashkin, "K istorii bor'by za Kommunu v Alzhire," *Voprosy Istorii*, 1949, no. 6, 85–99.

120. N. Goncharov, " 'Viselitsa'—revoliutsionnye listovki o parizhskoi kommune," *Literaturnoe Nasledstvo*, I, 1931, 161, 164, and material on 159.

121. R. Williams, *The French Revolution of 1870–1871*, NY, 1969, x.

122. S. Edwards, *The Communards of Paris, 1871*, L, 1973, 20, 53–4.

123. Williams, 152.

124. A. Decouflé, *La Commune de Paris (1871). Révolution populaire et pouvoir révolutionnaire*, 1969, 217–47.

125. Ibid., 248–9. The Parisian branch of the International took a strongly anti-nationalist tone, proclaiming in Apr that "country" is now an "empty word" and that "France is dead." See Jules Nostag, "Country—Humanity," *La Révolution politique et sociale*, no. 3, in Postgate, *Revolution*, 298.

126. Characterization of Sartre, cited in Decouflé, 18.

127. Jules Vallès in *Le Cri du Peuple*, Mar 30, cited in Edwards, *Communards*, 75.

128. Cited from an editorial in *Vengeur*, Mar 30, in Dubois, *Vocabulaire*, 50.

129. Villiers de l'Isle-Adam, "Paris as a Festival," reprinted in Edwards, 140.

130. M. Waldman, "The Revolutionary as Criminal in 19th Century France: A Study of the Communards and Deportees," *Science and Society*, 1973, Spring, 31–55; and 37–8, n. 26, for various estimates of deaths.

131. Borejsza, "Portrait," 153–4. So great was the European-wide revulsion at the Commune that Dąbrowski's two sons were driven to suicide and his brother to crime in exile. For the large Polish participation in the Commune, see K. Wyczańska, *Polacy w Komunie paryskiej*, 1971.

132. On this remarkable figure, see Borejsza, "Legend and Truth," *Poland*, 1973, Dec, 22–5.

133. His article "Communism" appeared without attribution in *Der Schweizerische Republikaner*, 1843, Jun 2, 6, 13, and is discussed in Yu. Steklov, *Mikhail Aleksandrovich Bakunin. Ego zhizn' i deiatel'nost'*, 1926, I, 148–58.

134. Cited in E. Pyziur, *The Doctrine of Anarchism of Michael A. Bakunin*, Chicago, 1968, 30 n. His reference to Steklov, III, 227, is inaccurate. Steklov notes one exception, when Bakunin referred to himself as a "communist" in Oct 1844 (I, 147 n. 1). Steklov further elaborates on Bakunin's opposition to communism in his retrospective apologia for Lenin's adoption of the label in 1918: *Kto zhe kommunisty? K voprosu o naimenovanii nashei partii*, NY, 1919.

135. Citations from A. Lehning, "Théorie et pratique du fédéralisme anti-étatique en 1870–1871," *International Review of Social History*, XVIII, 1972, 457. In addition, see Yu. Steklov, "Bakunin i franko-prusskaia voina 1870–1," *Golos Minuvshago*, 1915, no. 5, 5–43; and H. Temkin, "Marx and Bakunin: A Dispute on the Principle of Organization of the Labor Movement," unpublished paper of the Russian Research Center, Harvard, Jan 7, 1971. For his debt to Proudhon, see Lehning, "Conception," 71; and particularly "Letters to a Frenchman on the Present Crisis" (1870), in S. Dolgoff, ed., *Bakunin on Anarchy*, NY, 1972, 202.

136. Ibid., 213.

137. Ibid., 214.

138. Ibid., 197. Italics in the original.

139. Ibid., 202.

140. Ibid., 196; *Archives Bakounine*, IV, 235.

141. Lehning, "Théorie," 458–9; Dolgoff, 178–80.

142. Introduction by Lehning to Bakunin, *Selected Writings*, L, 1973, 23–4.

143. Letter of Aug 23, 1870, in Lehning, "Théorie," 460.

144. Letter of Sep 29, 1870, in Lehning, "Théorie," 465.

145. Letter of Oct 28, 1870, ibid., 465.

146. "The Paris Commune and the Idea of the State," written just after the fall of the Commune, in Bakunin, *Writings*, 199.

147. Ibid., 201; and "Réponse d'un international à Mazzini," in ibid., 214.

148. Bakunin, *Writings*, 203.

149. Johann Most, *Die Pariser Commune vor den Berliner Gerichten*, Braunschweig, 1875, esp. 14–5.

150. "Civil War in France," cited in Postgate, *Revolution*, 305, 311. Marx later qualified his support of the Commune, leading some scholars of Marxism, such as Bertram Wolfe and George Lichtheim, to suggest that Marx virtually repudiated the uprising. But it was this work that alone influenced the revolutionary tradition.

151. Ibid., 316.

152. Ibid., 310.

153. Ibid., 307–8.

154. Ibid., 335. Marx's voodoo rhetoric against the "French Sulla" was in part the special wrath of the gods against a fallen angel—Thiers having in his youth been for many the model of a radical man of ideas rising to power to change, rather than to be changed by, the system. See O'Boyle, 312.

155. Postgate, 319.

156. Ibid., 319, 336.

157. Ibid., 325. Marx even claimed that the counter-revolutionaries "knew that three months' free communication of Communal Paris with the provinces would bring about a general rising of the peasants."

158. Ibid., 322.

159. Text of *Instructions pour une prise d'armes* and discussion by G. Bourgin in *Archiv für die Geschichte des Sozialismus und der Arbeiterbewegung*, XV, 1930, 272–300.

160. Marxist historians downplay the extent of Marx's dependence on Blanquists even as they provide evidence of links with Marxism in the fight against Proudhonism/Bakuninism. S. Bernstein alleges that the rival Bakuninist Alliance was founded in the presence of Blanqui late in 1868 (*The Beginnings of Marxian Socialism in France*, NY, 1965, 2d ed., xiv), but also suggests that Marx persuaded Blanqui to send delegates to the Geneva Congress in 1867, only to have them rejected by Proudhonists then and in 1868.

M. Paz argues that "it is in their parallel and persistent animosity against Proudhon that Blanqui and Marx find each other" ("Auguste Blanqui, le révolutionnaire professionel," unpublished doctoral thesis, Aix-en-Provence, 1974, 132, BN; also 131–5 for Blanqui's conflict with Proudhon and his disciples, and 138–53 for his influence on Marx and Lenin). Another unpublished typescript of Paz ("Inventaire sommaire des papiers d'Auguste Blanqui," 1972, BN, 18–26) stresses parallels even more than links between Blanqui and Marx.

161. Cited in D. Stafford, *From Anarchism to Reformism*, Toronto, 1971, 10–1.

162. Cited in ibid., 15. See also Paul Brousse, *Le Marxisme dans l'internationale*, 1882; M. Rubel, "La Charte de la première internationale. Essai sur le "marxisme" dans l'association internationale des travailleurs," *Mouvement Social*, 1965, Apr–Jun, esp. 3–6; and M. Mande, "A propos du concept de 'marxisme,'" *Cahiers de l'Institut de Science Economique Appliqué*, VIII, 1974, 1397–1430.

163. Freymond, *Etudes*, 142.

164. The study of the origin and spread of this term by C. Weill ("A propos du terme 'bolchévisme,'" *Cahiers du Monde Russe et Soviétique*, 1975, Jul–Dec, 353–64) sees a parallel with Blanquism (355) but never considers Blanquist or any other precedents for the Leninist term.

165. In 1873, at the height of his struggle with Marx, Bakunin explained that he had changed the name of his Italian Alliance of Social Democracy of 1864 into the Alliance of Socialist Revolutionaries "as a result of the German state communists giving the term 'social democracy' a compromising, doctrinaire and state meaning" (*Istoricheskoe razvitie internatsionala*, Zurich, 1873, part I, cited in Lehning, "Conception," 62).

166. Lehning, "Conception," 73–4.

167. From the important work of Bakunin's principal Swiss follower, J. Guillaume, *Karl Marx pangermaniste et l'association internationale des travailleurs de 1864 à 1870*, 1915, I.

168. The militant federalists of the Jura after the Commune, cited in Stafford, *From Anarchism*, 76.

169. Bakunin, *Writings*, 263–4; and 232–70, for Bakunin's neglected side of this controversy, suggesting that Marx represents the future form of Bismarck's "worship of the state."

170. Cited in Lehning, "Théorie," 462. This predates the alleged origination of the term by Bakuninists in Spain in 1873 and/or in Malatesta's explanation in 1876 of the Bologna uprising of 1874 (Stafford, *From Anarchism*, 79).

171. Published in *Vpered*, 1905, Mar 23, discussed in B. Itenberg, *Rossiia i parizhskaia kommuna*, 1971, 179 ff.

172. "La Guerre des rues," from Cluseret, *Mémoires*, 1887, II, 273–89; reproduced in P. Kessel, ed., *1871. La Commune et la question militaire (Cluseret-Rossel)*, 1971, 337.

173. Ibid., 304.

174. 308–11.

175. 318.

176. Letter of Jun 21, 1868, cited in T. Marix-Spire, *Les Romantiques et la musique. Le cas George Sand 1804–1836*, 1954, 592 n. 8; also 591 n. 6, and the section "musique et philosophie," 419–57.

177. M. Reclus, *Emile de Girardin*, 1934, 215.

178. In some cases such as Spanish Cuba, revolutionary texts were skillfully coöpted for reactionary purposes, as when General Concha substituted the word "loyalty" for "liberty" in the second act duet of Bellini's *Puritani* (coolly jumping up to lead the applause when the baritone sang *Viva la libertà* anyhow) and defused the revolt scene of the *Mute Girl of Portici* by inserting a preceding tarantella that turned melodrama into *opera-bouffe* (Maretzek, *Revelations*, 29–30).

179. See the seminal critique by the Russian populist N. Mikhailovsky, "Darvinizm i operetki Offenbakha," *Otechestvennye Zapiski*, 1871, Oct; discussed in Billington, *Mikhailovsky*, 76–7.

180. Cited in N. Findeizen, "Vagner v Rossii," *Russkaia muzykal'naia gazeta*, 1903, no. 35, 767.

181. A. Orlova, *Trudy i Dni M. P. Musorgskogo*, 1963, 257, 234. The ideological implications of the Kromi scene discussed in Billington, *Icon*, 406 ff., can be supplemented by the only detailed musicological discussion by N. Briusova, "Stsena pod Kromami," in Yu. Keldysh and V. Yakovlev, *M. P. Musorgsky*, 1932, 90–105, which also contains a rich bibliography (241–90) and a full list of Mussorgsky's works and variant editions (291–310). A less substantial recent study is G. Khubov, *Musorgsky*, 1969, 486–92. Orlova's massive compilation traces derivations of elements of this scene from popular folklore (25–8, 234–6). Mussorgsky originally called it his "vagabondage" (*brodiazhnaia*), wrote it in white heat while preparing a second version of the opera in Sep 1871, and announced it to Stasov as "novelty and novelty, a novelty out of novelties" (ibid., 224).

The two basic variants of *Boris* are discussed in V. Belaiev, *Musorgsky's Boris Godunov and the new version*, Oxford, 1928. Letters and documents are in J. Leyda and S. Bertensson, eds., *The Mussorgsky Reader*, NY, 1947. There are English-language biographies by O. von Rieseman, NY, 1929; M. Calvocoressi, L, 1956; and V. Seroff, NY, 1968.

182. On the commission of 1886–7 launched by Boulanger as minister of war, see Chailley, "La Marseillaise," 14.

183. A. Zévaès, *Eugene Pottier et l'Internationale*, 1936, 46–53, for the material here contained.

184. On Pierre Degeyter and the Chorus "La Lyre des travailleurs," ibid., 35–7.

185. Ibid., 53.

186. M. Howard, *The Franco-Prussian War*, NY, 1962, 276, also 274.

Chapter 13

1. D. Showalter, *Railroads and Rifles, Soldiers, Technology and Unification of Germany*, Hamden, 1975.

2. J. Ellis, *The Social History of the Machine Gun*, NY, 1976.

3. C. Fall, *The Art of War: From the Age of Napoleon to the Present Day*, NY, 1961, 64; also H. Rogers, "The advent of rifled ordnance," *A History of Artillery*, Secaucus, 1975, 93–111.

4. G. Wilson, "The Evolution of Technology," in G. Metraux and F. Crouzet, eds., *The Nineteenth-Century World*, NY, 1963, 167.

5. See D. Billington, "Structures and Machines: The Two Sides of Technology," *Soundings*, 1974, Fall, 275–88.

6. Binkley, *Realism*, 9 ff.

7. D. Cardwell, *Turning Points in Western Technology*, NY, 1972, 129. The original work, *Réflexions sur la puissance motrice du feu et sur les machines propres à développer cette puissance*, 1824, is extensively discussed by Cardwell.

8. P. Nettl, "The German Social Democratic Party 1890–1914 as a Political Model," *Past and Present*, 1965, Apr, 67.

9. On the little-known prehistory of this term by Lenin's secretary, Vladimir Bonch-Bruevich in 1903, as well as Finnish, Yugoslav, and subsequent Eastern European usage in the mid–1940s as an alternative to the Stalinist model of "dictatorship of the proletariat" see Billington, *Icon*, 774 n. 40.

10. On the origin of this term during the Spanish Civil War in 1936 by Palmiro Togliatti and subsequent adoption by Mao during the Yenan Era and others as

an alternative to the Soviet model, see the unpublished doctoral dissertation, J. Urban, "Moscow and the Italian Communist Party: 1926–1945," Harvard, 1967; summarized in her "Contemporary Soviet Perspectives on Revolution in the West," *Orbis*, 1976, Winter, 1372–3.

11. W. Shinn, "The 'National Democratic State': A Communist Program for Less-Developed Areas," *World Politics*, 1963, Apr, 377–89. The phrase "national democratic state" was introduced publicly at the international conference of Communist parties in Moscow in Nov, 1960 (376), and apparently originated in the doctoral dissertation of the 1930s by the Soviet Africanist I. Potekhin (384 n. 10).

12. The many uses of this period are documented in Müller, "Die Wortfamilie Sozialdemokrat," in *Ursprung*, 156–9. The rival Proudhonists used the term "new democracy," which appeared in the subtitle of Proudhon's last book *De la Capacité politique des classes ouvrières*.

13. *Ursprung*, 161.

14. *Werke*, XXX, 259; cited in McLellan, *Marx*, 322.

15. Na'aman, 132.

16. Ibid., 132.

17. Ibid., 133, 154–5.

18. *Werke*, XXIX, 432.

19. G. Roth, *The Social Democrats in Imperial Germany*, Totowa, 1963, 42. See also R. Reichard, *Crippled from Birth, German Social Democracy, 1844–70*, Ames, Iowa, 1969; and E. Anderson, *The Social and Political Conflict in Prussia: 1858–1864*, Lincoln, 1954.

Lassalle's organizational activity during this period is covered in the documentary collection of S. Na'aman, *Die Konstituierung der deutschen Arbeiterbewegung 1862/63*, Assen, 1975; and B. Andréas, "Zur Agitation und Propaganda des Allgemeinen Deutschen Arbeitervereins 1863/64," *Archiv für Sozialgeschichte*, 1963, III, 297–332.

20. Cited in Roth, 43.

21. Ibid., 45.

22. Ibid., 46.

23. Ibid., 48 n. 3.

24. Roth, 49 ff. D. Groh, *Negative Integration und revolutionärer Attentismus. Die deutsche Sozialdemokratie am Vorabend des Ersten Weltkrieges*, Frankfurt/Main, 1972.

25. K. Kupisch, "Bismarck und Lassalle," in *Vom Pietismus zum Kommunismus*, 1953, esp. 132–3.

26. R. Hilferding, cited in Roth, 169.

27. Lassalle's boyhood statement of belief, cited in Reichard, 149.

28. Cited in ibid., 157.

29. Koszyk, 185, 189–90.

30. *Lucinde oder Kapital und Arbeit. Ein sozialpolitisches Zeitgemälde aus der Gegenwart*, which began to appear serially in Jun, 1863, is discussed Kupisch, 135.

31. *Werke*, XXXII, 620–1.

32. Koszyk, 191; see also R. Morgan, *The German Social Democrats and the First International 1864–1872*, Cambridge, Mass., 1965.

33. Roth, 49–55; see also the semi-official history of W. Schröder, *Geschichte der sozialdemokratischen Parteiorganisationen in Deutschland*, Dresden, 1912, 18 ff.

34. R. Tucker contends that this is the only time Marx ever used this phrase, and that the *Critique of the Gotha Program* shows that Marx's conception of communism was not based primarily on an ideal of distributive justice (*The Marxian Revolutionary Idea*, 46–50).

35. The more popular version of the work is the excerpt of key passages called *Socialism: Utopian and Scientific*, first published in French in 1880.

36. See the study based on the East German archives by D. Fricke, "Politseiskie presledovaniia sotsial-demokratov v Germanii v kontse xix veka," *Novaia i Noveishaia Istoriia*, 1959, no. 4, esp. 95.

37. M. Johnstone, "Marx and Engels and the Concept of the Party," *The Socialist Register*, 1967, 121–2. The author distinguishes four other types of party organization recognized by Marx as implementing his ideas: the small international cadre of the 1840s; parties that authentically represented labor but lacked organization in the 1850s and 1860s; the international federation of worker organizations (the First International); and broad national labor parties on the nonrevolutionary Chartist model which they saw appearing in England and America by the 1880s.

38. C. Schorske, *German Social Democracy, 1905–1917*, Cambridge, Mass., 1955, 3.

39. The painter Friedrich Zundel, husband of Clara Zetkin, cited by Rosa Luxemburg in a letter of Jan 25, 1902, in *Lettres à Léon Jogichès*, 1971, II, 80.

40. "Our task is not to organize the revolution, but to organize ourselves for the

revolution" (letter of Jul 11, 1900, cited in ibid., 52–3). According to G. Badia (*Rosa Luxemburg. journaliste, polémiste, révolutionnaire*, 1975, 147), this formulation first appeared in 1881. The way in which Kautskyism became a form of discipline as well as definition within German socialism is discussed not without some retrospective projection of later Soviet practices in E. Matthias, "Kautsky und der Kautskyanismus, Die Funktion der Ideologie in der deutschen Sozialdemokratie vor dem ersten Weltkrieg," in I. Tetscher, ed., *Marxismusstudien*, Tübingen, 1957, II, 151–97. The most thorough treatment of Kautsky's career is now M. Waldenberg, *Wzlot i upadek Karola Kautsky'ego*, Cracow, 1972 2 v; the most incisive is in Kolakowski, *Currents*, III, 31–57.

41. "Ein sozialdemokratischer Katechismus," *Die Neue Zeit*, 1893/1894, XII, i, 368.

42. Letter to Franz Mehring of Jul 8, 1893, discussed in Roth, 189.

43. He implicitly identified this technique with Marx in his "Zwischen Baden und Luxemburg" (*Die Neue Zeit*, 1909/1910, II, 667), where the juxtaposition of Marx's native city of Trier between these other cities to the right and left was said to be "a symbol of the camp of German Social Democracy." See also Nettl, *Luxemburg*, I, 429–35; Schorske, 186–7.

44. See S. Baron, *Plekhanov, the Father of Russian Marxism*, Stanford, 1963; and J. Braunthal, *Victor und Friedrich Adler. Zwei Generationen Arbeiterbewegung*, Vienna, 1965.

45. According to L. Derfler, *Socialism since Marx*, NY, 1973, 90.

46. Braunthal, 243–5.

47. Cited from the preamble to the resolution creating the bureau in L. Lorwin, *Labor and Internationalism*, NY, 1929, 85.

48. Joll, 105.

49. Joll, 133; Roth, 91.

50. A. Hall, "The War of Words: Anti-socialist Offensives and Counter-propaganda in Wilhelmine Germany 1890–1914," *Journal of Contemporary History*, 1976, Jul 13.

51. "It is necessary to fight populism everywhere—be it German, French, English or Russian," Engels wrote Vera Zasulich on Apr 3, 1890 (*Proletarskaia Revoliutsiia*, 1929, no. 2, 53).

52. Text in R. Tucker, ed., *Marx-Engels Reader*, 421. This preface was reprinted as *The Revolutionary Act*, NY, 1922.

53. Kolakowski (*Currents*, III, 51) develops the idea that Kautsky was, in effect, only extending the modifications that Engels had already made in Marx's philosophy (*Currents*, I, 376–408). This distinction (like the more fashionable one in the late 1960s) between the early Marx of the *Philosophical Manuscripts* and the later Marx of *Capital* is rejected for dogmatic reasons by the Marxist-Leninist hagiographical establishment. While too much can be made of these differences, the Engels introduction is clearly almost a direct, anticipatory rejection of the Leninism that was to come as well as of the Blanquism of the past in its insistence that the time "of revolutions carried through by small conscious minorities at the head of unconscious masses, is past" (*Reader*, 420).

54. Hall, 15.

55. A. Kriegel, "Le Parti Modèle: La Social-Democratie Allemande et la Ile Internationale," *Le Pain*, 254, 258, 253. She stresses the importance of the 74% worker representation in the Reichstag delegation (263). For another view of the secret of the international appeal of the German model, see G. Niemeyer, "The Second International: 1889–1914," in Drachkovich, *Internationals*, 106–7.

56. Nettl, "Party," 76–8.

57. See the key Reichstag speech of Hugo Haase (Joll, 175), who had previously helped the German Social Democrats oppose aiding Austria (159–64).

58. "Revisionism" originated in the call from South Germany for "practical reforming political action" aimed at "practical partial success" by Georg von Vollmar, *Über die Nächsten Aufgaben der deutschen Sozialdemokratie*, Munich, 1891, 19, cited in Joll, 91.

59. Text of Millerand's program in R. Ensor, *Modern Socialism*, L, 1904, 48–55; discussion in A. Kriegel and M. Perrot, *Le Socialisme français et le pouvoir*, 1966, 65–83.

60. Citations from Lafargue, *Le Socialisme et la conquête des pouvoirs publics*, Lille, 1899, in Kriegel and Perrot, 69–70.

61. For discussion of this neglected international movement, which functioned independently of the Second International, see Lorwin, 100–14.

62. Lorwin, 103.

63. The founding Fabian leader Herbert Bland, cited in A. McBriar, *Fabian Socialism and English Politics, 1884–1918*, Cambridge, 1962, 18.

64. Ibid., 66.

65. Cited from *Democratic Socialism*, in Braunthal, 264. An important group of new German books that recapture the complexity, richness, and genuine roots in Marxism of Bernstein's thought is conveniently itemized and discussed in D. Morgan, "The Father of Revisionism Revisited: Eduard Bernstein," *Journal of Modern History*, 1979, Sep, 525–32.

66. *Protokoll über die Verhandlungen des Parteitages*, Hanover, 1899, 149, cited in Braunthal, 271.

67. The importance of the spatial and structural elements in Masonic symbolism is stressed (without being related to revolutionary movements) by S. Baehr "The Masonic Component in Eighteenth Century Russian Literature," in A. Cross, ed., *Russian Literature in the Age of Catherine the Great*, Oxford, 1976, 121–39.

68. From the musically sumptuous evocation of the lost revolutionary dream at the end of the aria *Nemico della Patria* (U. Giordano, *Andrea Chenier*, Act III): "Fare del mondo un Pantheon! Gli uomini in dei mutare e in un sol bacio e abbracio tutte le genti amare!"

69. H. Marks, "The Sources of Reformism in the Social Democratic Party of Germany, 1890–1914," *Journal of Modern History*, XI, 1939, no. 3, 334; also Roth, 169 n. 18. For the complex forces that led to a parallel reformist bias within the German trade union movement at the same time, see D. Groh, "Intensification of Work and Industrial Conflict in Germany, 1896–1914," *Politics and Society*, VIII, 1978, no. 3–4, 349–97.

Chapter 14

1. For this reason, a bomb "resembles more a magical charm than a visible object manufactured in a factory," according to an Indian admirer of the Russian movement, the Congress party leader, Bal Gangadhar Tilak in 1908. See Z. Iviansky, "Individual Terror: Concept and Typology," *Journal of Contemporary History*, 1977, Jan, 61.

2. Billington, *Icon*, 40–2.

3. R. Sohlman, (*The Life of Alfred Nobel*, L, 1929, 127, 181; Iviansky, 60) suggests that Nobel had a deep sympathy for Russian radicals until the end of his life. The accomplishments of Ludwig Nobel (designer of the world's first tanker and Europe's first pipelines and tank cars) in creating the Russian oil industry is particularly stressed in R. Tolf, *The Russian Rockefellers: the Saga of the Nobel Family and the Russian oil industry*, Stanford, 1977.

4. According to their sister, Lenin's older brother, Alexander Ulyanov, was decisively influenced by Mendeleev even while still in secondary school. A. Ivansky, *Zhizn' kak fakel'*, 1966, 121; also 136 ff. for the impact of Mendeleev and other scientists on revolutionary students in St. Petersburg during the 1880s.

5. R. Kantor, "Dinamit 'Narodnoi Voli,'" *Katorga i Ssylka*, LVII–LVIII, 1929, 120. The leader of the People's Will in charge of explosives spoke of "leading propaganda to facts" (*vesti propagandu faktam*) as distinguished from the *propagande par le fait* of "Swiss anarchists." S. Shiriaev in his court deposition of Jul 21, 1880: "Avtobiograficheskaia zapiska Stepana Shiriaeva," *Krasny Arkhiv*, 1924, no. 7, 79.

6. Kantor, 120–8.

7. Michael Frolenko, a member of the executive committee of the People's Will "Nachalo narodnichestva," *Katorga i Ssylka*, XXIV, 1926, 22. I have modified the translation of this passage as presented (with inaccurate reference to the original) in Iviansky, 47.

8. P. Zavarzin, *Rabota tainoi politsii*, Paris, 1924, 94–7, on the *tekhnicheskoe biuro* of the Social Democrats in Rostov. Another provincial example of this phenomenon (even more marked within the rival Socialist Revolutionary party) was the student brotherhood formed under a chemistry student, the *boevaia druzhina* in Kazan, which prided itself on its own distinctive bomb, the *makedonka*, modeled on those of Macedonian revolutionaries. See S. Livshits, "Kazanskaia sotsial-demokraticheskaia organizatsiia v 1905 g.," *Proletarskaia Revoliutsiia*, 1923, no. 3, 104–5, diagram of the bomb opposite 104.

9. A Russian historian who later found favor with Stalin was one of the first to point to the key role of students in the 1848 revolution in the West: see E. Tarle, *Rol' studenchestva v revoliutsionnom dvizhenii v Evrope v 1848 g.*, St. Petersburg, 1906. For statistics on the student population under Alexander II (which had fallen from 65.3% aristocracy to 43.1% by 1875), see G. Shchetinina, "Universitety i obshchestvennoe dvizhenie v rossii v poreformenny period," *Istoricheskie Zapiski*, LXXXIV, 1969, 164–215, esp. 166.

A. Spitzer provides a comprehensive, skeptical survey of the vast recent literature on the concept of generational revolt in "The Historical Problem of Generations," *American Historical Review*, 1973, Dec, 1353–85.

10. On the complex question of whether the reactionary journalist Katkov originated the term slightly earlier or simply took it from reading Turgenev's manuscript prior to publication, see summary and references in Billington, "Intelligentsia," 810–1 n. 9. On the basis of a subsequent conversation with Professor Bialy of Leningrad, I now incline toward the latter conclusion.

Earlier, philosophical usages of the term are referenced in Benoît-Hepner, *Bakounine*, 193. Prior political usages during the French Revolution are completely overlooked in all studies referenced above. The first appears to have been by a Frenchman sent to Belgium to prepare for unification with France (*Antifédéraliste*, Oct 14, 1793, discussed in A. Mathiez, "Publica Chaussard, inventeur du nihiliste," *Annales Révolutionnaires*, X, 1918, 409–10). The first usage as a badge of pride is by Anacharsis Cloots on Dec 27, 1793; "The Republic of the Rights of Man is properly speaking neither theist nor atheist; it is nihilist" (M. Frey, *Les Transformations du vocabulaire français à l'époque de la révolution (1789–1800)*, 1925, 165). The first usage to designate a group was made in a negative usage similar to that of Chaussard in *Courier français*, 1795, Oct 1: "There was even under Robespierre a faction that was designated by the name *indifférentistes* or *nihilistes*" (A. Aulard, *Paris pendant la réaction thermidorienne et sous le directoire*, 1897, II, 285).

11. Their importance in raising student consciousness is stressed in A. Gleason, *Young Russia: The Genesis of Russian Radicalism in the 1860's*, NY, 1980. See also D. Brower, *Training the Nihilists, Education and Radicalism in Tsarist Russia*, Ithaca, 1975, 122 ff.; and Hegarty, "Movements."

12. K. Griewank, *Deutsche Studenten und Universitäten in der Revolution von 1848*, Weimar, 1949, esp. 55 ff. on the "free academic university" whose faculty included Kinkel; Droz, *Les Révolutions allemandes de 1848*, 1957, 618–20, on the Kinkel escape; 609, on the unique rallying of the army to revolution in Baden.

13. I follow here the modification by R. Brym ("A Note on the *Raznochintsy*," *Journal of Social History*, 1977, Mar, 354–9) of the downgrading by Brower (*Training*, esp. 114) of the importance of the social role of the "various ranks" (*raznochintsy*) in explaining the revolutionary turn of youth in the 1860s. On the term itself, see C. Becker, "Raznochintsy: The Development of the Word and of the Concept," *American Slavic and East European Review*, 1959, Feb, 63–74.

14. Brower, 144.

15. Ibid., 118.

16. From 476 to 1026; ibid., 121.

17. Ibid., 137.

18. Ibid., 137.

19. R. Zelnik, "The Sunday-School Movement in Russia, 1859–1862," *Journal of Modern History*, 1965, Jun, 151–70; and Ya. Abramov, *Nashi voskresnye shkoly. Ikh proshloe i nastoiashchee*, St. Petersburg, 1900.

20. W. Mathes, "Origins of Confrontation Politics in Russian Universities; Student Activism 1855–1861," *Canadian Slavic Studies*, 1968, Spring, 28–45; and Hegarty, for detail and statistics.

21. Cited as translated in Venturi, 249, 248.

22. Ibid., 249.

23. Characterization made by the religious philosopher Vladimir Solov'ev, *Sobranie sochinenii*, 1911, VI, 270.

24. Koz'min, *Iz istorii*, 261. Some suggested that landlords were burning St. Petersburg in retaliation for emancipation of the serfs—and even that the Tatars were attacking. See S. Chelishev, "Krestianskoe volnenie po povodu slukhov ozhigariakh," *Biblioteka dlia chteniia*, 1863, no. 1, 274, 280, 283.

25. *Young Russia*, as cited in Venturi, 295.

26. Ibid., 295–6.

27. Ibid., 290. Zaichnevsky identifies this program with Barbès, Blanqui's principal collaborator and associate of the 1830s.

28. Ibid., 285. Venturi's account must be supplemented by the posthumous account of B. Koz'min, *Iz istorii*, 127–345.

29. M. Lemke, *Politicheskie protsessy v Rossii 1860–kh gg.*, 1923, 19.

30. In addition to previous references on this subject, see B. Goldman (Gorev), "Rol' Prudona v istorii russkogo melkoburzhuaznogo sotsializma," *Krasnaia Nov'*, 1935, no. 1, 160–73, and other works itemized in Itenberg, *Dvizhenie*, 116, 137. See also, for Proudhon's influence on Chernyshevsky's collaborator, Dobroliubov, V. Bazanov, *Russkie revoliutsionnye demokraty i narodoznanie*, Leningrad, 1974, 134.

31. The core number of "about 20" given by Venturi (286) is scaled down by

Koz'min, *Iz istorii*, 134, who at the same time itemizes a larger number in some contact with the group, which might have attained, but could not have exceeded, 15–20 (146).

32. Koz'min, *Iz istorii*, 157–66.

33. Ibid., 181 ff.

34. Ibid., 185.

35. Peter Boborykin, *Za Polveka*, Moscow/Leningrad, 1926, 208.

36. Venturi, 292–3.

37. As was often to be the case with the new chauvinism, the call came not from the center of imperial power, but from the periphery: the treatise of an obscure Slovak, L'udovít Štúr, calling for unification of the Slavs under Russian leadership, with Moscow the capital, Russian the language, and Orthodoxy the religion. See the discussion of Štúr's *Slavdom and the World of the Future* by M. Petrovich in *Journal of Central European Affairs*, 1952, Apr, 1–19; and of the Moscow Congress in Petrovich's *The Emergence of Russian Panslavism, 1856–1870*, NY, 1956, 241–54.

38. Venturi's dating of 1865–6 is revised in the light of new material in R. Filippov, *Organizatsiia Ishutina*, 50 ff.

39. Chernyshevsky had broken with Herzen upon visiting him in London in 1859. For an example of the even more negative view of I. Khudiakov, who met Herzen as the emissary of Hell to Geneva in 1865 and denounced him for "living like a nobleman and not holding fast in his own life to those ideas about which he shouted so much," see Filippov, 126.

40. One leader of the group bracketed Chernyshevsky with Christ and St. Paul as one of the three great men of world history: "Delo Karakozova," *Krasny Arkhiv*, 1926, no. 4, 93. Khudiakov's tract of 1866 in Geneva was entitled "for true Christians" (*Dlia istinnykh khristian*).

41. Venturi, 349; also 336, 345–6.

42. For details of his grim youth, see P. Ekzempliarsky, "Selo Ivanovo v zhizni Sergeia Genad'evicha Nechaeva," *Trudy Ivanovo-Voznesenskogo gubernskogo nauchnogo obshchestva kraevedeniia*, vyp. 4, 1926, 7 ff.

43. P. Pomper, "Nechaev and Tsaricide: The Conspiracy within the Conspiracy," *The Russian Review*, 1973, Apr, 130.

44. Venturi, 359; and Ralli, "Sergei Genad'evich Nechaev," *Byloe*, 1906, VII, 137.

45. English translation of the text is in B. Dmytryshyn, *Imperial Russia: A Source Book, 1700–1917*, NY, 1967, 241–7. Discussion and analysis in Venturi, *Roots*, 359 ff., should be supplemented by the clearer differentiation of Nechaev from Bakunin in M. Confino, "Bakunun et Nečaev. Les débuts de la rupture. Introduction à deux lettres inédites de Michel Bakunin—2 et 9 Juin 1870," *Cahiers du Monde Russe et Soviétique*, 1966, Oct–Dec, 581–699. Various efforts to assign Bakunin a major role in authorizing the *Catechism* (and, to a lesser extent, Ogarev, Tkachev, and/or Enisherlov) are reviewed and refuted by A. Ivanov ("Kto avtor 'Katekhizisa revoliutsionera'?" *Novy Zhurnal*, CXXIII, 1976, 212–30). He concludes that the work "belongs in concept and in composition to Nechaev and no one else" (230). P. Pomper does not consider Ivanov's article, but insists (unconvincingly to me) on retaining a share of authorship for Bakunin: "Bakunin, Nechaev, and the 'Catechism of a Revolutionary': The Case for Joint Authorship," *Canadian-American Slavic Studies*, 1976, Winter, 535–46.

46. See the heavy-handed work by an unidentified P. H., *The Revolutionary Catechism in Four Languages* (English, French, Welsh, and Irish), Bath/L, 1849 (BO): "Q. What is the object of a Revolution? A. The destruction of things that are. Q. What is the pretence of a revolution? A. The substitution of things that never can be. . . ." The more radical, Southern section of the Decembrists used the catechism form in 1825 (Ivanov, 224). For the eighteenth-century German origins of the polemic use of catechisms, see J. Schmidt, *Der Kampf um den Katechismus in der Aufklärungsperiode Deutschlands*, Munich, 1935.

47. Venturi, 390.

48. Venturi, 395–6. Tkachev's initial reference in 1865 to a passage from *Critique of Political Economy* included the full-blown assertion that "this idea has now become common to all thinking and honest men, and no intelligent man can find any serious objection to it."

Philosophical materialism helped move Tkachev from a reformist to a revolutionary position (R. Theen, "The Political Thought of P. N. Tkachev in the 1860's: From Reform to Revolution," *Canadian Slavic Studies*, 1969, Summer, 200–23, esp. 220 n. 69), though Tkachev was hostile to Marxism (D. Hardy, "Tkachev and the Marxists," *Slavic Review*, 1970, Mar, 22–34).

The most thorough study of Tkachev is now Hardy, *Peter Tkachev, the Critic as Jacobin*, Seattle, 1977. Other works include A. Weeks, *The First Bolshevik, a Political Biography of Peter Tkachev*, NY, 1968; M. Charol, *The Unmentionable*

Nechaev, a Key to Bolshevism, NY, 1961; and R. Cannac, *Aux Sources de la Révolution Russe, Netchaiev du nihilisme au terrorisme*, 1961. The first two tend to overdraw direct links with Bolshevism; the latter lacks any documentation.

49. Nechaev introduced the revolutionary Marx to a Russian audience almost offhandedly: "Anyone who wants a detailed theoretical exposition of our viewpoint can find it in the Manifesto of the Communist Party published by us" (Venturi, 384). Venturi's attribution of the translation to Bakunin is almost certainly incorrect (B. Koz'min, "Kto byl pervym perevodchikom na russky iazyk 'Manifesta Kommunisticheskoi Partii'?" *Literaturnoe Nasledstvo*, LXIII, 1956, 700–1); but Confino's assumption of Nechaev's authorship (615) is also hypothetical.

50. From "liudi budushchego i geroi meshchanstva," *Delo*, 1868, nos. 4 and 5, as cited in Confino, "Bakunin," 617.

51. See the unpublished paper by P. Pomper, "Nechaev, Lenin, and Stalin: The Psychology of Leadership," 17, 18, 38 n. 34. Pomper inclines to the view that Nechaev was experimenting with explosives even before he went abroad.

52. Pomper, "Tsaricide," 126; G. Bakalov, "Khristo Botev i Sergei Nechaev," *Letopisi Marksizma*, 1929, IX–X; and discussion Venturi, 773–4 n. 29.

53. From text of the *Catechism* in Dmytryshyn, *Imperial Russia*, 241.

54. Ibid., 244–6; discussion (and translations of phraseology) from Venturi, 367.

55. Venturi, 367; Confino, 671 n. 1.

56. A hypothesis extrapolated from information in "Tsaricide," 133–4, and Venturi, 775 n. 44.

57. Venturi, 387.

58. Suggested by Pomper, "Nechaev, Lenin," 39 n. 44.

59. This earliest use as a collective noun by P. Lavrovsky of Kharkov is reproduced and discussed in the exhaustive study by O. Müller, *Intelligencija, Untersuchungen zur Geschichte eines politischen Schlagwortes*, Frankfurt, 1971, 27. His work overlooks, however, the richness and priority of Polish usages even in his one mention of Libelt (from Wójcik), 395.

60. Müller, *Intelligencija*, 105 ff. See especially Chaadaev's concept of 1835 about the advantages of backwardness for overtaking the West in national intelligence (109–10).

61. Ibid., 141 ff. See also A. Pollard, "The Russian Intelligentsia: The Mind of Russia," *California Slavic Studies*, III, 1964, 7 n. 19, 11–5.

62. A. Nikitenko, cited in Müller, 124–5; see also Aksakov's usage, 147.

63. Shelgunov, *Vospominaniii*, Moscow/Petersburg, 1923, 33. Shelgunov was the first to identify the term with rationalism and consciousness (Pollard, 15–6).

64. Müller, *Intelligencija*, 293 n. 126.

65. Pisarev, cited without precise attribution in *Bol'shaia Sovetskaia Entsiklopediia* (1st ed.), XXVIII, 609.

66. On Pisarev's seminal article of 1865, "Historical Ideas of Auguste Comte" (*Sochineniia*, St. Petersburg, 1897, IV, 313–464) and other materials introducing Comte to Russia in the late sixties and early 1870s, see Billington, "Intelligentsia," 812 ff.

67. P. Lavrov, *Istoricheskie Pis'ma*, St. Petersburg, 1906, 358.

68. A bewildering variety of philosophies of history was examined (and social Darwinism in particular rejected as a rationalization for perpetual conflict and reactionary chauvinism), see Billington, *Mikhailovsky*, 27–41.

69. See the article written in 1889 and chosen by Mikhailovsky for the introduction to his collected works (*Sochineniia N.K. Mikhailovskago*, St. Petersburg, 1896, I, v). He pays tribute to the "wonderful inner beauty" of the two meanings in *pravda* and defines his own mission as finding "a point of view in which *pravda-istina* and *pravda-spravedlivost'* . . . go hand in hand, one enriching the other."

Mikhailovsky also first used the term "Russian intelligentsia," popularizing it in his column "Letters on the Russian Intelligentsia." See Billington, "Intelligentsia," 812.

70. Pollard, 17.

71. Cited without precise reference in Pollard, 18. A similar phrase is in Tkachev, *Izbrannye Sochineniia*, 1932, I, 282.

72. Citation from Tkachev, not precisely referenced in Pollard, 19.

73. Tkachev, *Izbrannye*, I, 193, III, 91; originally published as *Offener Brief an Herrn F. Engels*, Zürich, 1874.

74. Tkachev died after a long illness five years after Blanqui. The emphasis on violence, elite discipline, and the execution of traitors in his principal journal, *Nabat* (1875–7), has been attributed to the influence of a wealthy Polish patron-collaborator, Gaspar-Mikhail Turski: D. Hardy, "The Lonely Emigré Petr Tkachev and the Russian Colony in Switzerland," *Russian Review*, 1976, Oct, 400–16.

75. *Partiinaia chestnost'*, cited from the confession of G. Enisherlov in Pirumova,

"Bakunin ili Nechaev," 178. Pirumova's suggestion that Enisherlov inspired Nechaev's *Catechism* seems doubtful to Pomper ("Tsaricide," 127–8), to B. Suvarin (letter to *Novy Zhurnal*, 1975, Dec, 281–3) and to Ivanov, "Kto," 68.

76. On the genealogy of this term, Billington, "Intelligentsia," 816–7.

77. From the summary by Isaiah Berlin of the London Conference of 1967, "To Define Populism," *Government and Opposition*, III, 1968, no. 2, 173. I have drawn particularly from Walicki and Berlin's contributions to this discussion, 137–79. See also the fuller published version edited by G. Ionescu and E. Gellner, *Populism: Its Meanings and National Characteristics*, 1969; and review by T. Di Tella, in *Government and Opposition*, IV, 1969, no. 4, 526–33.

78. On P. N. Rybnikov see M. Klevensky, "Vertepniki," *Katorga i Ssylka*, 1928, no. 10, 18–43.

79. Venturi, 375 ff. and references thereto.

80. N. Morozov, in *Revoliutsionnoe narodnichestvo*, 1964, I, 221; cited in Brower, 203.

81. See D. Hecht, *Russian Radicals Look to America*, Cambridge, Mass., 1947, 196–216.

82. Itenberg, *Dvizhenie*, 92–100, for the impact of this work by a slightly older governmental official influenced by his earlier contacts with the *Petrashevtsy*.

83. Testimony of a participant cited in M. Miller, "Ideological Conflicts in Russian Populism: The Revolutionary Manifestoes of the Chaikovsky Circle, 1869–1874," *Slavic Review*, 1970, Mar, 13; see also Itenberg, 186–93.

84. From the manifesto "Must We Concern Ourselves with an Examination of the Future Order," written by Kropotkin about Nov, 1873, and cited in Miller, 16.

85. Ibid., 17.

86. R. Zelnik, "Populists and Workers. The First Encounter between Populist Students and Industrial Workers in St. Petersburg, 1871–74," *Soviet Studies*, 1972, Oct, 258.

87. Itenberg, 338–9 and ff. for the remarkable case of the student who became a hauler, D. M. Rogachev. Others believed that the rebellious spirit of Razin and Pugachev could be conjured up anew from the Volga: V. Debagory-Mokrievich, *Ot Buntarstva k terrorizmu*, Moscow/Leningrad, 1930, I, 159; and V. Ginev, *Narodnicheskoe dvizhenie v srednem povolzh'e*, 1966, 21, 64 ff.

88. Details in M. Miller, *Kropotkin*, Chicago, 1976, 114–29.

89. The priest assumed that the "Nicholas" being honored was the grandson of the tsar, the future Nicholas II. See P. Kann, "Revoliutsionny forum Peterburga," *Voprosy Istorii*, 1976, no. 12, 198.

90. They were divided into 120 "Protestants" who refused to appear in Court and 73 (dubbed "Catholics") who did. See N. Troitsky, "Protsess '193–kh,' " in *Obshchestvennoe dvizhenie v poreformennoi Rossii* (a collection for B. Koz'min), 1965, 314–35.

91. Yarmolinsky, 197 and ff.

92. D. Field, *Rebels in the Name of the Tsar*, Boston, 1976, 113–207, provides documents and a narrative account.

93. Yarmolinsky, 219.

94. Characterizations of S. Kravchinsky (*Underground Russia*, NY, 1883, 100) whose admiring discussion of the two men remains a classic. For the little that is known of Lizogub, see E. Khir'iakova, "Vospominaniia i nekotorye svedeniia o Dmitrii Andreeviche Lizogube," *Zven'ia*, 1932, no. 1, 482–99: and the important and neglected biographical sketch included in the official publication of the People's Will, attesting to his central importance in validating the turn to terrorism: *Literatura sotsial'no-revoliutsionnoi partii narodnoi voli*, Paris, 1905, 363–74.

Lizogub provided the model for Svetlogub in Tolstoy's best treatment of terrorism (much neglected in comparison to those of Dostoevsky and Turgenev): *Bozheskoe i chelovecheskoe*. Completed just prior to the Revolution of 1905, Tolstoy's remarkable story traces both the "divine" and the "human" side of the terrorist's legacy by showing how a religious dissenter (of the kind Tolstoy admired) was inspired by the gospel that allegedly contained the essence of the terrorist's true faith, and how a subsequent revolutionary leader was driven to suicide by not realizing that this Christian-anarchist ideal was the true revolutionary message (*Sobranie sochinenii*, 1953, XIV, 205–38, 339).

95. S. Volk, *Narodnaia volia*, Moscow/Leningrad, 1966, 67–8. The basic source for this first appearance of organized terrorism in the south of Russia is Debagory-Mokrievich *Ot buntarstva*, I. The romanticized account in Kravchinsky (*Underground*, 70–81) can be countered by the antagonistic account of A. Ulam: *In the Name of the People*, NY, 1977, 269–96, which tends to avoid concrete, historical questions of origin in favor of editorial comment and general suggestions of deriva-

tion from Nechaev. See also J. Bachman, "Recent Soviet Historiography of Russian Revolutionary Populism," *Slavic Review*, 1970, Dec, 599–612.

96. Volk, 79.

97. Ibid., 69–70.

98. Alexander Solovev, cited in Venturi, 632.

99. Estimate in Volk, 277.

100. Ibid., 254–5, for careful tracing of the derivation of most of the statute of the People's Will from that of the second Land and Liberty.

101. Ibid., 259.

102. M. Katkov, cited in Ulam, 341.

103. Volk, 227, 255–9.

104. In the sketch of Lizogub from the last issue of the journal *Narodnaia Volia* to appear before the assassination of the tsar, in *Literatura "narodnoi voli,"* 371.

105. See the long chapter "The Ukrivateli" in Kravchinsky, *Underground*, 166–84.

106. See Kantor, "Dinamit," 118–28; Volk, 259.

107. Cited in Venturi, 680.

108. See the deposition of Ivan Emel'ianov in *Krasny Arkhiv*, XL, 1930, 184.

109. See the work of his distant relative, the later anarchist revolutionary Victor Serge, *Memoirs of a Revolutionist*, L, 1967 (corrected edition), 2.

110. Cited in Volk, 128.

111. Ibid., 81.

112. Cited in Volk, "Programmnye dokumenty," 423.

113. J. Waciorski, *Le Terrorisme politique*, 1939 (an excellent treatment of the history and vocabulary of terrorism by a Polish jurist which has been overlooked in recent studies) characterizes the Committee of Public Safety as believing that "terror is a legitimate means of defending the social order established by the revolution; terrorism is a criminal means" (30). The terms "terrorism," "terrorist," and "anti-terrorism" all came into general use only after the fall of Robespierre. See Brunot, IX, 871, 654; Frey, *Transformation*, 188–9.

For bibliographical guides to the vast recent literature on terrorism, see the works of two writers on guerrilla warfare: J. Bell, "Trends in Terror: The Analysis of Political Violence," *World Politics*, 1977, Apr, 476–88; and W. Laquer, "Interpretations of Terrorism: Fact, Fiction, and Political Science," *Journal of Contemporary History*, 1977, Jan, 1–42. The latter includes more historical material and surveys the rich fiction on the subject—as does W. May, "Terrorism as Strategy and Ecstasy," *Journal of the New School for Social Research*, 1974, Summer, 277–98. May's neglected theological study explores the peculiar appeal of living close to death, releasing "the violence latent in all things," and helping compensate for the "defective ritual life" of modern society. See also M. Hutchinson, "The Concept of Revolutionary Terrorism," *The Journal of Conflict Resolution*, 1972, Sep, 383–96; and the special issue on terrorism of *Stanford Journal of International Studies*, 1977, Spring.

The largely untouched subject of terrorist manipulation of the media for political effect is discussed in Y. Alexander, "Terrorism, the Media, and the Police," R. Kupperman and D. Trent, *Terrorism, Threat, Reality, Response*, Stanford, 1979, 331–48.

114. "Sieg der Kontrerevolution zu Wien," 1848, Nov, in *Werke*, V, 457. Italics added.

115. E. Walter, *Terror and Resistance. A Study of Political Violence*, NY/Oxford, 1969, 9. This valuable study develops general ideas from an examination of some primitive African political communities.

116. Nechaev, in his prison writings of the late seventies, called for a secret revolutionary tribunal to go into immediate action after an uprising and offer only two sentences: either acquittal or death. See Pomper, "Nechaev, Lenin," 19–21.

117. Morozov, *Terroristicheskaia Bor'ba*, L (but Geneva), 1880, 8 (BM).

118. Ibid., 11. The sharp opposition of social revolutionary goals to liberal ideals was already drawn in the pamphlet of the Petrashevsky circle of 1849, *What Is Socialism?* It defined socialism as "directly opposed to liberalism," which was in turn "destructive of social existence" (*Delo Petrashevtsev*, I, 92).

119. Morozov considered Zasulich's shot the *tochka pereloma* of the Russian struggle, after which people rose up to join it "as if from under the ground" (*Bor'ba*, 5).

In his attempt to prescribe terrorism as a kind of maturity test for radical youth (what he called *intelligentnaia russkaia molodezh'*), Morozov was in a sense generalizing from his own conversion from scientific scholarship to revolutionary activism. See his *V Nachale zhizni. Kak iz menia vyshel revoliutsioner vmesto uchenago*, 1907; also the collection edited by his wife, Ksenia Morozova, *Nikolai Aleksandrovich Morozov. K 90-letiiu so dnia rozhdeniia*, Moscow/Leningrad, 1944. Morozov apparently planned in the early 1880s to write a large-scale history of the Russian revolutionary movement (20–1, and, for bibliography, 38 ff.), materials for which have been assembled IA for forthcoming publication under the editorship of B. Sapir.

120. Suggested in S. Valk, "G.G. Romanenko," *Katorga i Ssylka*, 1928, no. 11, 47. No subsequent study seems ever to have been made of Romanenko; and the general question of the legacy of the People's Will has never been adequately dealt with. It is surprisingly neglected in the West, where one book after another (Ulam most recently and derivatively) ends with the assassination of Alexander II. Among Soviet scholars, V. Tvardovskaia substantially enriches the picture, insisting rather boldly (against Volk and conventional Soviet positions) that the final posture and legacy of the People's Will was essentially Blanquist, but that Blanqui himself was not a "Blanquist" in the caricatured way the term is used in Leninist polemics (*Sotsialisticheskaia mysl' Rossii na rubezhe 1870–1880kh godov*, 1969, 226–34). One of the few good Western treatments of the revolutionary activities of the neglected 1880s is V. Zilli, *La Rivoluzione russa del 1905. La formazione dei partiti politici (1881–1904)*, Naples, 1963, 57–79. For an excellent archival study of two small successor groups to the People's Will, see N. Naimark, "The Workers' Section and the Challenge of the 'Young': Narodnaia Volia, 1881–1884," *Russian Review*, 1978, Jul, 273–97. New material from the court records is in N. Troitsky, *"Narodnaia Volia" pered tsarskim sudom, 1880–1891*, Saratov, 1971.

121. Volk, "Programmnye dokumenty," 414; and ff. for unpublished material on this connection.

122. Valk, 39 ff.

123. Ibid., 38, 42, 48. *Terrorizm i rutina*, L (actually Geneva), 1880, was originally entitled "Terrorism and the Philistines," and was published under the pseudonym "V. Tarnovsky."

124. All of these ideas and terms are present in the proclamation by A. Prybyleva-Korba in their official journal in 1880, Dec: *Narodnaia Volia*, no. 4, cited Volk, 366. The word "party," implying "solidarity of thought" and totality of commitment, increasingly replaced the word "organization" as the basic term for the People's Will. See Volk, 259; Tvardovskaia, 227–8.

125. Tvardovskaia, 230–1. The letter "to the Ukrainian people," which Romanenko apparently drafted for the Executive Committee, cited the first anti-Jewish pogroms as evidence of rising popular resistance to the oppression of the Ukrainian peasantry (Valk, "Romanenko," 50–2); but this uncharacteristic note of anti-Semitism among the early revolutionaries was refuted in *Narodnaia Volia*, Oct, no. 6.

126. Valk, 53 ff. There is no record of the tsar's response; but the Right-Left vacillation evident in Romanenko's praise of pogroms foreshadowed his later turn to monarchism after exile in Central Asia (ibid., 59).

127. *Bor'ba*, 1882, Mar, cited in Volk, 346.

128. They called themselves "the preparatory group of practical organizers of the party of the People's Will" (Valk, 351). The university circle called itself a "party center" and its publication a "student party organ."

129. Billington, *Mikhailovsky*, 141–2.

130. L. Shternberg, *Politichesky terror v Rossii*, 1884, hectographed ed. in IA.

131. M. Krol', "Vospominaniia o Shternberge," *Katorga i Ssylka*, 1929, no. 8–9, esp. 226–8. Exiled for ten years to Sakhalin Island, Shternberg became a student of its culture and, after his return to St. Petersburg, a founding father of modern Russian anthropology and ethnography. See the memorial article in *Sbornik muzeia antropologii i etnografii*, Leningrad, VII, 1928, 1–70.

132. Naimark, 286 ff. The doctrine of *fabrichno-agrarny terror* resembles in some ways the parallel doctrine of "direct action" developed by Western revolutionary syndicalists.

133. New material of 1885 from Vladimir Burtsev, the future hagiographer of the revolutionary tradition, in Kazan, cited in Naimark, 294.

134. Ivansky, 159.

135. Ibid., 200.

136. Ibid., 143, 178–9, 186–9, and 249–73. His first illegal reading as a schoolboy had been from the most extreme of the scientistic nihilists of the 1860s, Pisarev (117–8), and nine days before the Dobroliubov demonstration, Ulyanov had been part of another delegation to visit the ailing satirist and former *Petrashevets*, Michael Saltykov-Shchedrin.

137. Account of I. Lukashevich, reprinted in Ivansky, 288–9. Ulyanov's party program, written in prison, was at variance with later Leninist doctrine in its insistence that the intelligentsia as an "independent social group" must lead the political struggle against a militarized government bureaucracy (also, in effect, "an

independent social force"). "Programma terroristicheskoi fraktsii partii 'Narodnaia Volia,' " reprinted in Ivansky, 297–8. The main weapon should be terror, which must be "systematic" and accompanied by "propagational" (*propagatorskaia*) activity that goes further than mere propaganda (ibid., 303, 300).

A recent Soviet study (I. Al'tman, "Programma gruppy A. I. Ulyanova," *Voprosy Istorii*, 1977, no. 4, 34–44) indicates that the program was first conceived in Dec 1886, formulated only in late Feb 1887, and was uncompleted at the time of Ulyanov's arrest. The article weakly attempts to sustain the view more congenial to Leninist hagiography that the group represented an ideologically progressive stage in the evolution from populism to Marxism. Al'tman finds some similarity of phraseology with Plekhanov, but relies mainly on the repeated attribution to Marxism of concepts equally shared by the Blanquist tradition.

138. Account of V. Dmitrieva in Ivansky, 193.

139. Ibid., 298 n. 1, and 300–2 for other comments by the tsar; for Ulyanov's explanation of the missile projectile on Feb 25, see Al'tman, 38.

140. The contrast between uniforms and masks in the exercise of political violence is developed with African illustrations but broader applications in Walter, *Terror*, 85–101.

141. This marginal group clearly deeply affected the former tsarist chief of the Kiev Okhrana and later personal secretary of the tsar: A. Spiridovich, *Histoire du terrorisme russe, 1886–1917*, 1930, 14–7.

142. Police report of Jan 2, 1887, in Ivansky, 275; also *Istorichesky Arkhiv*, 1960, no. 2, 204, on the almost certainly apolitical *kubantsy i dontsy*.

143. The basic account of this neglected group is "Istoricheskaia zapiska o tainom obshchestve 'zagovorshchikov,' " *Katorga i Ssylka*, 1928, no. 12, 49–58, esp. program 51–2. There were the familiar three layers of membership "amorphous" (*amorfny*), "preparatory," and "political circles," with the latter under the strict discipline of "constitutors" (*uchrediteli*), who also controlled the entire secret process of coöptation from lower to higher levels.

144. Cited from Kravchinsky's *Le Tsarisme et la révolution*, 1886, in Waciorski, *Terrorisme*, 37.

145. In his journal *Freiheit*, printed with a festive red border. See R. Hunter, *Violence and the Labour Movement*, L, 1916, 66–8; Iviansky, 48.

146. Cited in P. Hutton, "The Role of the Blanquist Party in Left-Wing Politics in France, 1879–90," *Journal of Modern History*, 1974, Jun, 293.

147. G. Haupt, "Role de l'exil dans la diffusion de l'image de l'intelligentsia révolutionnaire," *Cahiers du Monde Russe et Soviétique*, 1978, Jul–Sep, 236, 245, 247.

148. In addition to the general impact of the Russian women discussed in the final chapter of this work, G. Haupt has pointed to the marriage of key leaders of the European Left to Russian revolutionary women: Charles-Victor Jaclard in France, Fritz Adler in Austria, Karl Liebknecht in Germany, and Filippo Turati in Italy. Haupt particularly stresses the role played in Italy by Turati's wife, about whom see A. Schiavi, *Anna Kuliscioff*, Rome, 1955.

149. Miller, *Kropotkin*, 156–7. For an often prophetic contemporary work by a Ukrainian liberal predicting the impact of the Russian revolutionary tradition on the West, see Michael Dragomanov, *Le Tyrannicide en Russie et l'action de l'Europe occidentale*, Geneva, 1881.

150. Unlike most other key words in the modern revolutionary lexicon, anarchy and anarchical are terms with a relatively constant meaning, invoked by worried European rulers since at least the time of Philip the Fair. See the collection published by the Einaudi Foundation: *Anarchici e anarchia nel mondo contemporaneo*, Turin, 1971, 591.

151. *Pages choisis*, 265.

152. *Oeuvres complètes*, I, 212. Anarchism as an ideal *avant la lettre* has many antecedents, and is generally said to have first approached a systematic doctrine in William Godwin: Joll, *Anarchists*, 31–9; Woodcock, *Anarchism*, 60–93. A neglected early paean to the word is *The Anarchiad* of 1786, a semi-serious "epic poem from the banks of the Wabash" by Joel Barlow along with David Humphreys, John Trumbull, and Lemuel Hopkins, hailing the alleged "reign of anarchy" in primitive America as a "blessing." The rare published version, New Haven, 1861, is in the Beinecke Library, Yale University; see esp. 18, 20.

153. Intelligently discussed in M. Nomad, "The Anarchist Tradition," in Drachkovitch, *Internationals*, 69–79. The itemization of conferences in Miller, *Kropotkin*, 258–9, is fuller, listing the first four anarchist congresses (1873–7) under the First International (Bakuninist).

154. For comprehensive treatment, P. Masini, *Storia degli anarchici italiani de Bakunin a Malatesta (1862–1892)*, Milan, 1969.

155. Miller, "The Development of an Anarchist Ideology," *Kropotkin*, 138–47.

156. Tolstoy's dramatic rejection of the modern state, the industrial system, and all instruments of violence influenced the movement for nonviolent action through "the force of truth" (*satyagraha*) led by the most original revolutionary of the "third world" in the early twentieth century: Mahatma Gandhi. See M. Markovitch, *Tolstoi et Gandhi*, 1928; K. Nag, *Tolstoy and Gandhi*, Patna, 1950. For Tolstoy's more antagonistic relations with the revolutionary movement within Russia, see E. Oberländer, *Tolstoi und die revolutionäre Bewegung*, Munich/Salzburg, 1965.

Tolstoy and Gandhi will be presented by Martin Green as the authors of a radical religious alternative to both Marxism and liberalism in his *Tolstoy and Gandhi: An Essay in World History*, the last volume of a remarkable trilogy on imperialism. This work, to be pursued during 1980–81 at the Woodrow Wilson International Center for Scholars, returns to the key figures of the first volume of his trilogy, *The Challenge of the Mahatmas*, NY, 1978.

157. Cited in Joll, *Anarchists*, 127.
158. Cited from *La Révolte*, 1894, Mar 18–24, in Miller, 174.
159. Kropotkin's anticipations of Paul Goodman, Louis Mumford, and other social critics are itemized in Miller, 195–6.
160. Cited from "Le Gouvernement révolutionnaire," *Paroles d'un révolté*, 1885, in Miller, 192.
161. Estimate extrapolated from the magisterial study of J. Maitron, *Le Mouvement anarchiste en France*, 1976, I, by J. Joll, *Times Literary Supplement*, 1976, Sep 10, 1092.
162. See the challenge of Malatesta to the French syndicalist, Pierre Monatte, at the Amsterdam Congress of 1907: Woodcock, *Anarchism*, 267. See also Malatesta, *Anarchy*, L, 1949.
163. A delegate to the Geneva conference of 1882, cited in Woodcock, 260. Not until the International Workingmen's Association was founded in Berlin in Dec 1922, did anything like an Anarchist International exist. But this association, which gained some three million adherents, was more a syndicalist than a pure anarchist body. It led a dwindling, peripatetic existence after the Nazis took over power in 1932, still maintaining, however, a shadow existence in Sweden.
164. K. Porter, "The Never-ending Wrong," *Atlantic*, 1977, Jun, 39.
165. Ibid., 64.
166. O. Bayer, *Los Vengadores de la Patagonia Trágica*, Buenos Aires, 1972, 3 v; extensively reviewed by B. Chatwin, *Times Literary Supplement*, Dec 31, 1976, 1635–6. For the substantial anarchist influence in Brazil, see J. Dulles, *Anarchists and Communists in Brazil, 1900–1935*, Austin, 1973.
167. Avrich, *Anarchists*, 222, and more generally 204–33.
168. Kropotkin, cited in ibid., 226. See also Avrich, ed., *The Anarchists in the Russian Revolution*, Ithaca, 1973. All that remained were minute groups such as the Anarcho-Biocosmists, who professed total support for the Soviet state and agreed to press their social experiments "in interplanetary space but not upon Soviet territory" (G. Maximoff, *The Guillotine at Work: Twenty Years of Terror in Russia*, Chicago, 1940, 362; Avrich, 231). There was also, however, a much more substantial pacifistic movement of Tolstoyan anarchists within the Soviet Union than has ever been realized; its history is currently being written at the Woodrow Wilson Center by M. Popovsky on the basis of new materials from the USSR (*The Peasant Disciples of Tolstoy: 1918–1977*).

Chapter 15

1. G. Dangerfield, *The Strange Death of Liberal England, 1910–1914*, NY, 1961, itemizes the many forms of violence—some of them still without adequate study—that tore at England during this "peaceful" period; and the thesis suggested by his title could be extended to other "liberal" nations as well.
2. This subject was treated in "When Peace Was the Establishment," a presentation by R. Stromberg at the Woodrow Wilson International Center for Scholars on Aug 5, 1974. Published anticipations of his forthcoming major work on this subject are "The Intellectuals and the Coming of the War in 1914," *The Journal of European Studies*, III, 1973, 109–22; "Socialism and War in 1914," *Midwest Quarterly*, XVIII, 1977, Spring, 268–97; "1910: An Essay in Psychohistory," *Psychoanalytic Review*, LXIII, 1976, Summer, 235–48, and especially "Redemption by War: The Intellectuals and 1914," *Midwest Quarterly*, 1979, Spring, 211–27.
3. K. Deutsch and N. Wiener, "The Lonely Nationalism of Rudyard Kipling," *Yale Review*, 1963, Jun, 501. Deutsch and Wiener (502) characterize Kipling as the supreme spokesman for a widespread belief in "the all-or-nothing character of group

allegiance," which Kipling attributed to animals as well as to soldiers and school-boys.

4. William Booth, *In Darkest England and the Way Out*, L, 1890.

5. G. B. Shaw, *Major Barbara*, L, 1905.

6. C. Tilly, "The Changing Place of Collective Violence," in M. Richter, ed., *Essays in Theory and History*, Cambridge, Mass., 1970, 146, and 139–64; also Tilly, "Collective Violence in European Perspective," in H. Graham and T. Gurr, *The History of Violence in America*, NY, 1969, 4–44; and his further development of these ideas with L. and R. Tilly in *The Rebellious Century, 1830–1930*, Cambridge, Mass., 1975, which concludes that collective action, not violence as such, is what matters in history. The Tillys here distinguish (51–5 and elsewhere) among three different types of violence that tend to be successively dominant despite much overlapping: *competitive* (testing strength within a local system of power), *reactive* (fighting off a challenge to established rights), and *pro-active* (asserting new rights—as the "new unionists" and revolutionary syndicalists saw themselves doing).

7. Recent scholarship traces the rise of this more radical "new unionism" in Britain back to the 1870s. See A. Musson, *British Trade Unions, 1800–1875*, L, 1972, 65.

8. Maréchal, *Premières leçons du fils aîné d'un roi. Par un député présomptif aux futurs Etats-Généraux*, Leçon XXXIII, cited in M. Dommanget, "L'Idée de grève générale en France au XVIIIe siècle et pendant la Révolution," *Revue d'Histoire Economique et Sociale*, XLI, 1963, no. 1, 40. Dommanget is less convincing in tracing this idea to the even earlier work of the radical priest Jean Meslier, 35–8.

9. Cited in Dommanget, 51; also 48–53, and F. Braesch, ed., *Papiers de Chaumette*, 1908. In accord with revolutionary practice, particularly marked among militant anticlericals like Chaumette, he changed his Christian names to that of a classical hero: Anaxagoras, who was put to trial by political authorities in Athens for his scientific boldness and nonconformism.

10. Braunthal, 14; and brief history, 14–9. For their relationship to British radicalism of the day, see Bernstein, *Essays*, 48–56; and works referenced 204–5.

11. John Doherty, a spinner-turned-printer. See W. Crook, *The General Strike. A Study of Labor's Tragic Weapon in Theory and Practice*, Chapel Hill, 1931, 3–4.

12. William Benbow, *Grand National Holiday and Congress of the Productive Classes*, L, 1832. He called for a month of total withdrawal from the productive process during the summer by all "plundered fellow sufferers" during which a Congress of the Working Classes was to devise a social plan for the future. Elaborate preparations would assure that participation "be not partial but universal"; and delegations of workers would "speak daggers but use none" in persuading property holders to support this modern version of the Jewish sabbatical year and the year of Jubilee. Though there was no plan for annexing political power, Benbow's prescription for gradually escalating the size of delegations (from 20 to 100 to 1,000) to recalcitrant representatives of "the grasping and blood-sucking few" and his announcement in the pamphlet of his intention to found a "purely political" journal with the title taken from Babeuf—all point to a relatively full-blown conception of a revolutionary general strike. See citations from the reprinted text in E. Dolléans, "Le Naissance du chartisme (1830–1837)," *Revue d'Historie des Doctrines Economiques et Sociales*, 1909, II, 1–12, 412; also discussion in Crook, 9–10.

13. Richard Pilling, discussed in Crook, 17–27.

14. C. Jaurez, "Juillet 1855: La première grève générale en Espagne," *Cahiers Internationaux*, 1955, Jul–Aug, 69–74. R. Bezucha argues that the eight-day work stoppage of all 25,000 looms in Lyon in Feb, 1834, was in fact a general strike (*The Lyon Uprising of 1834*, Cambridge, Mass., 1974, 122–34).

A. Saulière points out that early discussions tended to envisage the "generalization of a strike rather than a general strike" (*La Grève générale de Robert Owen à la doctrine syndicaliste*, Bordeaux, 1913, 17).

15. Only in Spain was there a continuing anarcho-syndicalist tradition from the time of the First International, according to Rocker, *Anarcho-Syndicalism*, 131. For a sophisticated interpretive essay, see J. Romero-Maura, "The Spanish Case," *Government and Opposition*, 1970, Autumn, 456–79; for the anarchists in power during the Spanish Civil War, see the unpublished Oxford doctoral dissertation by J. Brademas, "Revolution and Social Revolution: A Contribution to the History of the Anarcho-Syndicalist Movement in Spain, 1930–1937," 1954.

The first academic study of strikes was made in nearby Portugal by Caetano d'Andrade Albuquerque, *Direitos dos operarios (estudos sobre as greves)*, an inaugural dissertation of 234 pages, Coimbra, 1870, a work not included in any of the studies referenced in this chapter.

16. Crook, 28–9; and more fully E. Georgi, *Theorie und Praxis des Generalstreiks in der modernen Arbeiterbewegung*, Breslau, 1908, 38–9. See also Proudhon's *De la*

Capacité politique des classes ouvrières, his last major work, in the edition of M. Leroy, 1924.

17. Report of Eugene Hins, cited in Rocker, *Anarcho-Syndicalism*, 72; also discussion, 70 ff.

18. Józef Hauke-Bosak, leader of the 1863 Polish rebellion, who dedicated his last pamphlet to the workers of Le Creusot, whom he called to armed combat (*Manuel d'organisation et du combat*). See Borejsza, 24.

19. Saulière, 15–33.

20. Rocker, 89, 83, 89.

21. D. Stafford, *From Anarchism to Reformism: A Study of the Political Activities of Paul Brousse within the First International and the French Socialist Movement 1870–90*, Toronto, 1971, especially 199 ff. on the activities of the Possibilists in France prior to their rival gathering (in Paris in 1889) to the founding congress of the Second International.

22. Selections from his *Collectivisme et révolution* (1879) and the 1880 *Programme du parti ouvrier* (worked out with Marx, Engels, and Guesde's close collaborator, Marx's Franco-Cuban son-in-law, Paul Lafargue) are in P. Louis, *Cent cinquante ans de pensée socialiste*, 1947, 208–11. See also 193–216.

23. Romero-Maura, 463.

24. C. Chambelland, 'La grève générale, thème de la pensée de F. Pelloutier et d'A. Briand," *Actualité de l'Histoire*, 1957, May, 22–3.

25. Crook, 36.

26. According to J. Julliard, *Fernand Pelloutier et les origines du syndicalisme d'action directe*, 1971, 171.

27. Text in Julliard, 279–303. Julliard argues (61 ff.) for Pelloutier's authorship and assigns a minor role to Briand.

28. Estimate in ibid., 257–8.

29. Crook, 154.

30. Cyrille van Overbegh, cited in ibid., 102.

31. Crook, 107; and 103–44 for a full account.

32. Romero-Maura, 466, 477, esp. materials n. 30. For a detailed history of French revolutionary syndicalism, defined as "the principles and practice of the C.G.T. in the years between 1902 and 1914," see F. Ridley, *Revolutionary Syndicalism in France the Direct Action of Its Time*, Cambridge, 1970.

33. V. Dalin, *Stachki i krizis sindikalizma v predvoennoi Frantsii*, Moscow/Leningrad, 1935, 7, for statistics. This neglected work is unsurpassed in detail and only lightly Leninist in interpretation.

34. Though an attempted general strike on May 1, 1906, did not altogether succeed, no major strike led by the C.G.T. altogether failed until the Paris builders' strike in Jul, 1911. See Dalin, 178; also J. Julliard, "Théorie syndicaliste révolutionnaire et pratique gréviste," *Mouvement Social*, 1968, Oct–Dec, 55–69.

35. E. Pouget, *Sabotage*, Chicago, 1913, indicates (37) that the C.G.T. was the first significant organization to endorse sabotage—at its Toulouse Congress in 1897.

36. Cited in C. de Goustine, *Pouget. Les Matins noirs du syndicalisme*, 1972, 174. On Pouget's "L'ABC de la révolution," see 20; Pouget's *Comment nous ferons la révolution* was co-authored with Emile Pataud and originally undated (1907), then published in 1909. He took the title of his journal *La Voix du Peuple* directly from Proudhon.

37. *Comment*, 226. See 158–70 on *le congrès fédéral*; 288–95 on *la libération de la femme*.

38. The number of strikers in the Paris region had been less than half that of the northern region in 1900–5 (about 91,000 to 196,000), but the number became more than twice as large during 1906–11 (about 382,000 to 169,000) (Dalin, 9).

Gustave Hervé (*La Guerre Sociale*, no. 37, 1913, cited in Dalin, 213–4) insisted that the C.G.T. had in fact become a political party capable of directly overthrowing capitalism. Dalin traces the passing of the leadership of the strike movement in France from textile workers to skilled metallurgical and transport workers at the beginning of the century (8), presumably permitting more sophisticated tactics. He attributes the decline in ardor in the immediate prewar period to the increasing dominance in Paris of that béte noire of Marxism, a "labor aristocracy" of building and light industrial unions (172). See also M. Reberroux, "Les Tendences hostiles à l'état dans la SFIO (1905–1914)," *Mouvement Social*, 1968, Oct–Dec, 21–37.

39. Sorel was influenced by the leader and strategist of the C.G.T., Victor Griffuelhes (see J. J. Stanley, ed., *From Georges Sorel*, NY, 1976, 297 n. 135; and Sorel's preface to Griffuelhes and L. Niel, *Les Objectifs de nos luttes de classe*, 1909). But even when Griffuelhes denied having read Sorel with his famous "I read Alexander Dumas" (Avrich, *Anarchists*, 99; Kriegel, *Pain*, 89), he illustrated some-

thing of the longing for romantic heroism and deliverance that was the essence of Sorel.

40. *Contribution à l'étude profane de la Bible; Le Procès de Socrate*, both 1889, discussed in J. Talmon, "The Legacy of Georges Sorel," *Encounter*, 1970, Feb, 48.

41. His long "Essai sur la philosophie de Proudhon," was written immediately upon his retirement and published in *Revue Philosophique*, XXXIII, XXXIV, 1892. The influence of Proudhon on Sorel is concisely traced in Stanley, 17–24.

42. I. Berlin, "Georges Sorel," *Times Literary Supplement*, 1971, Dec 31, 1617.

43. *Les Illusions du progrès*, 1908.

44. Sorel, preface to Pelloutier, *Histoire des bourses du travail*, 1902, 26; cited in the study of Sorel by I. Horowitz, *Radicalism and the Revolt against Reason*, NY, 1961, 28.

45. Phrases from Sorel's panegyric to the sublime pessimist (whom he distinguished from the "disheartened optimist" usually characterized as a pessimist) in *Reflections on Violence*, NY, 1961, 30–7. This English edition (hardcover, 1950, first French edition, 1908) includes supplementary materials from later editions and an introduction by E. Shils.

46. Phrase of Renan admired by Sorel, cited in Carr, "Sorel: Philosopher of Syndicalism," *Studies in Revolution*, 153–4.

47. Sorel distinguishes myths, which express "a determination to act," from "utopias," which are always concocted by cowardly intellectuals "to direct man's mind towards reforms which can be brought about by patching up the existing system" (*Reflections*, 50, and 41–53).

48. Talmon, "Legacy," 54.

49. *Reflections*, 177.

50. *Reflections* begins with a long section on "class war," seeking to recover the bellicosity of the original "Marxist vocabulary" (64 ff.).

51. See the successive sections, "The Proletarian Strike" and "The Political General Strike," *Reflections*, 119–79.

52. Ibid., 91, italicized in the original. Violence is contrasted with bourgeois "force," which is cunning, unacknowledged, and spiritually debasing—invariably camouflaged by "cleverness, social science or high-flown sentiments."

53. Ibid., 92, also 89. Violent revolutionary syndicalism reached a climax in Spain during the "tragic week" of upheaval centered on Barcelona in Jul, 1909 (J. Romero-Maura, "Terrorism in Barcelona and Its Impact on Spanish Politics 1904–1909," *Past and Present*, 1968, Dec, 130–83; J. Ullman, *Tragic Week: A Study of anticlericalism in Spain, 1875–1912*, Cambridge, Mass., 1968); and in England with the industrial strikes of 1911–2 led in large part by the Australian syndicalist Tom Mann and impelling unions to organize on the revolutionary syndicalist basis of nationwide industries capable of coordinating large-scale strikes. See G. Cole and R. Postgate, *The British Common People, 1746–1946*, L, 1947, 416.

54. J. Guillaume, ed., *L'Internationale. Documents et souvenirs 1864–1887*, IV, 1910, 114, cited in Iviansky, 45. For details, R. Hostetter, *The Italian Socialist Movement I: Origins (1860–1884)*, Princeton/Toronto/L, 1958, 321–81.

55. Crook, 185.

56. L. Lotti, *La Settimana rossa*, Florence, 1965.

57. Sorel became a regular contributor to the nationalist *L'Indépendance*, and a patron of the Cercle Proudhon, which (according to its leader, Edouard Berth) "came close to creating Fascism avant la lettre" (cited in Talmon, 58 n. 15). For Sorelian influence in Italy, see R. Paris, "Georges Sorel en Italie," *Mouvement Social*, 1965, Jan–Mar, 131–8; J. Roth, "The Roots of Italian Fascism: Sorel and Sorelismo," *Journal of Modern History*, 1967, Mar, 30–45. A leading student of comparative fascism, E. Nolte, tends, however, to stress the influence of Nietzsche more than of Sorel in providing the non-Marxist elements of Mussolini's critique of liberal democracy: "Marx und Nietzsche im Sozialismus des jungen Mussolini," *Historische Zeitschrift*, CXCI, 1960, 249–335. Stanley (2–5) strongly rejects bracketing Sorel with fascism.

For a more general discussion of the symbiosis between the extremes of Right and Left in common opposition to the liberal state in France, see Z. Sternhall, *La Droite révolutionnaire. Les origines françaises du fascisme, 1885–1914*, 1978.

58. P. Monelli, *Mussolini*, NY, 1950, 62–3; also R. De Felice, *Mussolini il rivoluzionario 1883–1920*, Turin, 1965, 136–76, esp. 182–3. De Felice's book is by far the richest study ever made of Mussolini's political formation. His basic conclusion that Mussolini was a product of the French revolutionary tradition and of the Left evoked stormy criticism in Italy to which De Felice responded vigorously in an interview with M. Ledeen, *Intervista sul fascismo*, Bari, 1975. D. Smith resumed the attack in a review of the fourth volume of De Felice's continuing biography of Mussolini

("A Monument for the Duce," *Times Literary Supplement*, 1975, Oct 31, 1278–90); Ledeen responded; and their conflicting appraisals have been published (1976) as *Un monumento al duce? Contributo al dibattito sul fascismo*. The controversy is discussed summarily in the introduction of C. Delzell to the English-language edition of an interpretive work first published in 1969: De Felice, *Interpretations of Fascism*, Cambridge, Mass., 1977. De Felice has also traced connections between revolutionary syndicalism and the even more romantic right-wing nationalist who contributed to the growth of fascism, *Gabriele D'Annunzio: Sindicalismo rivoluzionario e fiumanesimo nel carteggio De Ambris-D'Annunzio, 1919–1922*, Brescia, 1966. For an introduction to the vast recent literature on fascism written with special sympathy for the new social history, see C. Maier, "Some Recent Studies on Fascism," *The Journal of Modern History*, 1976, Sep, 506–21.

59. Cited from *Popolo d'Italia*, 1914, Dec 13, in H. Finer, *Mussolini's Italy*, NY, 1935, 103; see also 90–105. E. Saltarelli sees Mussolini skillfully pre-empting the enthusiasm that a new generation of Italian journalists (like Paolo Orana of *La Lupa*—"The She-wolf") had elicited during the Libyan campaign of 1911: "Le socialisme national en Italie: précédents et origines," *Mouvement Social*, 1965, Jan-Mar, 50 ff., esp. 59.

60. Six successive journals had perpetuated the name of Mazzini's original journal founded in May, 1848. See Ravinna, *Giornalismo*, 13–4.

61. C. Seton-Watson, *Italy from Liberalism to Fascism*, L, 1967, 518.

62. Horowitz, 182.

63. This aspect of monopolizing patriotic appeals and popularizing them as weapons against the Left is stressed in De Felice, *Il Fascismo e i partiti politici italiani: Testimonianze del 1921–1923*, Bologna, 1966. Use of fasci in a vaguely socialist sense began no later than 1871. See E. Wiskemann, *Fascism in Italy: Its Development and Influence*, NY, 1969, 9; also Tilly, *Century*, 120.

64. Tilly, *Century*, 169 ff.

65. P. Spriano, *L'Occupazione delle Fabriche*, Turin, 1964, follows the latter communist line in minimizing the syndicalist influence and maximizing the innovative aspects of the Togliatti-Gramsci group. For a more balanced account see M. Clark, *Antonio Gramsci and the Revolution that Failed*, New Haven/L, 1977.

66. The first title and the finally adopted title, respectively, of the socialist cultural periodical that provided the name (*Ordine Nuovo*) generally used to describe the Gramsci-Togliatti group, which eventually dominated the Italian Communist party.

67. Both the word and the concept of "hegemony" have generated an enormous literature verging on the mystical with the advent of the era of "Eurocommunism" and the effort of Italian Communists in particular to differentiate themselves from Soviet Communists. The concept is discussed (though not related adequately to the syndicalist heritage) in S. White, "Gramsci and the Italian Communist Party," *Government and Opposition*, 1972, Spring, esp. 191; G. Williams, "Gramsci's Concept of 'Egemonia,' " *Journal of the History of Ideas*, 1960, Oct–Dec, 586–99; and especially T. Bates, "Gramsci and the Theory of Hegemony," *Journal of the History of Ideas*, 1975, Apr–Jun, 351–66. The latter points out (352) that the concept was derived from the emphases on proletarian consent in Axelrod and Plekhanov. But Lenin and Leninists (particularly intellectuals) also used the term in the early Soviet period as a virtual synonym for dictatorship of the proletariat. V. Adoratsky ("Ideia gegemonii proletariata," in "Politicheskaia deiatel'nost' Lenina i ego lozungi," *Molodaia Gvardiia*, 1924, nos. 2–3, 488 ff.) places the term first among the "slogans" of Lenin. It has more recently been reassigned to Lenin as a rigid central concept used to refute almost all non-Soviet policies in the contemporary world, including those of Gramscian claimants to the concept (I. Aluf, "Leninskoe uchenie o gegemonii proletariata i sovremennost'," *Voprosy Istorii KPSS*, 1969, no. 1, 14–29).

68. Wiskemann, 22; Finer, 101; Tilly, 187–8. New evidence of Blanqui's direct, earlier influence on Clemenceau is provided in M. Paz, "Clemenceau, Blanqui's Heir," *The Historical Journal*, XVI, 1973, no. 3, 604–15.

69. "Neutralità attiva e operante," *Il Grido del Popolo*, 1914, Oct 31; discussed in Clark, 49, and more fully in R. Paris, "La première Expérience politique de Gramsci (1914–1915)," *Mouvement Social*, 1963, Jan–Mar, 31–57. A. del Noce has argued for a more permeating influence on Gramsci of the Fascist theorist Giovanni Gentile: *Il Suicidio della rivoluzione*, Milan, 1978.

70. On his journal of 1897 in Kaunas, see Golomb, 23.

71. K. Dziewanowski, *Joseph Pilsudski, A European Federalist, 1918–1922*, Stanford, 1969, 29–40, also Braunthal, 230–1.

72. P. Taft and P. Ross, "American Labor Violence: Its Causes, Character, and Outcome," in H. Graham and T. Gurr, *Violence in America: Historical and Com-*

parative Perspectives, NY, 1969, 281. A good recent account with bibliography is S. Lens, *The Labor Wars. From the Molly Maguires to the Sitdowns*, NY, 1974.

73. Only the isolated and idiosyncratic "Committees of Vigilance" in Louisiana specifically called itself a "revolutionary movement" (basing its illegal activity on the precedent of 1776). See R. Brown, "The American Vigilante Tradition," *Violence*, 181. Only the mysterious epidemic of assassinations in the New Mexico territory used political violence with revolutionary consistency against constituted authority. See Brown, "Historical Patterns of Violence in America," ibid., 58–60.

74. Taft and Ross, ibid., 283–4.

75. W. Broehl, Jr., *The Molly Maguires*, Cambridge, Mass., 1964, 73.

76. On the leader, "Peter Lalor," the "Tipperary Boys," and estimates that about half of the 863 participants were Irish, see *Historical Studies, Australia and New Zealand, Eureka Supplement*, Melbourne, 1954, 2d enlarged edition, 1965, 49, 79. See also 80 ff. for American participation in this event, which helped give birth to Australian nationalism and Australian trade unionism (according to a letter of Dec 20, 1971, from the Irish scholar and former ambassador to Australia, Eóin MacWhite).

77. Broehl, 25, and list of other societies, 26.

78. Ibid., 27–32, for varying legends about their origin and Molly Maguire's identity. This work, the first to use the Pinkerton papers, provides the basis for the account here.

79. W. D'Arcy, *The Fenian Movement in the United States: 1858–1886*, Washington, D.C., 1947, 243 ff. See also the collection edited by M. Harmon, *Fenians and Fenianism*, Seattle, 1970. For a transnational illustration of Left-Right interaction in the Irish movement, see the unpublished essay revealing that a pioneer of Russian radicalism in the 1830s, who became a Redemptorist monk in Ireland, ended up writing a special benediction for the Fenians: *De benedictione novi militis* (E. MacWhite, "The Mater's First Chaplain and the First Russian Political Emigré. Vladimir Pecherin, 1807–1885," 32–3).

See also new material in L. Ó Broin, *Revolutionary Underground: The Story of the Irish Republican Brotherhood, 1858–1924*, Totowa, 1976.

80. Their curious blend of violence with festivity is illustrated by the "Fenian Marseillaise" which was sung at the end of "Fenian picnics": "Away with speech, and brother, reach me down that rifle gun./ By her sweet voice, and hers alone, the rights of man are won." C. Wittke, *The Irish in America*, Baton Rouge, 1956, 154.

81. Z. Pease, *The Catalpa Expedition*, New Bedford, 1897.

82. D'Arcy, 404 ff.

83. T. Coogan, *The IRA*, L, 1970, 12, 14.

84. N. Mackenzie, *Secret Societies*, NY, 1967, 188 ff.

85. The AFL was the first body to promote the formal celebration of May 1 by laborers (see M. Dommanget, *Histoire du premier mai*, 1953, 35–7). But this campaign was linked to the cause of an eight-hour day, not to revolutionary solidarity as were later European "May Days." By 1894 American Labor settled on its own more recreational "Labor Day" on the first Monday in September.

86. Jacker, 138.

87. R. Drinnon, *Rebel in Paradise: A Biography of Emma Goldman*, Chicago, 1961, 69–77. See also the critical bibliography, 315–33.

88. Jacker, 128–41.

89. On the Russo-Jewish anarchists, see R. Rocker, *The London Years*, 1956; for their influence inside Russia, Avrich, 39–40. See also Rocker's transnational *Anarcho-Syndicalism*, L, 1938.

90. See the biographical preface by the translator R. Chase to Rocker, *Nationalism and Culture*, NY, 1937, xvi.

91. See Rocker's still valuable pamphlet, *The Tragedy of Spain*, NY, 1937.

92. See Rocker, *Pioneers of American Freedom*, Los Angeles, 1949, especially the examination of why American anarchism never found roots in European radicalism (145–54).

93. Goldman was brokenhearted in her last days over the crushing of anarchism in Catalonia during the Spanish Civil War: "It's as though you had wanted a child all your life, and at last, when you had almost given up hoping, it had been given to you—only to die soon after it was born" (E. Mannin, *Women and the Revolution*, NY, 1939, 137; Drinnon, 311). She followed the tradition of many American radicals of the period in asking that her body be returned to America to be buried near the martyrs of the Haymarket riot.

94. Drinnon, 3–27.

95. She was initially attracted to him by his gluttony in the restaurant, not by his ideas. See Goldman, *Living My Life*, NY, 1931, I, 5; Jacker, 129.

96. Jacker, 131.

97. "Forever is a long time," he told the court with characteristic bravado. "Who knows whether Austria will live that long." Goldman, "Johan Most," *American Mercury*, 1926, Jun, 162. See also Rocker, *Johann Most. Das Leben eines Rebellen*, 1924.

98. There were 28 delegates from 22 cities. See H. David, *The History of the Haymarket Affair*, NY, 1936, 99–101. "Communist Anarchism" was distinguished from the earlier indigenous pacifistic anarchism of men like Josiah Warren. See C. Machison, "Anarchism in the United States," *Journal of the History of Ideas*, 1945, Jan, 57 ff.

99. Most, *August Reinsdorf und die Propaganda der That*, NY, 1885, 28–30.

100. Copies of this rare work appear to have vanished from major American libraries during the revived interest in these matters in the late 1960s. Citations here are from the extended abstract entered as evidence into the Haymarket trials and reprinted in J. Lawson, ed., *American State Trials: A Collection of the Important and Interesting Criminal Trials which have taken place in the United States, from the beginning of our Government to the Present Day*, St. Louis, 1919, XII, 111–21. See also L. Adamic, *Dynamite. The Story of Class Violence in America*, NY, 1934, 41–8; Jacker, 94–6; Dedijer, *Sarajevo*, 167–8.

101. Lawson, 118.

102. Ibid., 116.

103. See the preceding deposition at the same trial in Lawson, 110.

104. Cited in Drinnon, 35.

105. C. Wittke, *Against the Current: The Life of Karl Heinzen*, Chicago, 1945.

106. Rocker, 403, 413; Goldman, 166.

107. Wittke, n. 8.

108. Heinzen, "Mord contra Mord," *Freiheit*, 1901, Sep 7, 2. Note how this article (which originally appeared in Johann Becker's *Die Evolution* of Jan–Feb, 1849) anticipated on the Left the later Bismarckian slogan of the Right: "blood and iron."

109. Estimate of P. Renshaw. *The Wobblies. The Story of Syndicalism in the United States*, NY, 1968, 8.

110. Renshaw, 160. See also J. Conlin, *Big Bill Haywood and the Radical Union Movement*, Syracuse, 1969.

111. By Haywood (Renshaw, 175; Kornbluh, *Rebel Voices*, 1), who saw his One Big Union "leading on to the great revolution which will emancipate the working class." See his speech, "The General Strike," NY, 1911, Mar 16, cited in Crook, 216.

A recent scholarly study is M. Dubofsky, *We Shall Be All: A History of the I.W.W.*, Chicago, 1969. Still the best account in many ways is P. Brissenden, *The IWW: A History of American Syndicalism*, NY, 1919 (reprinted 1957). For minutes of the first convention, attended by delegates from 34 states, see *The Founding Convention of the IWW*, NY, 1905 (reprinted 1969).

112. See, for instance, the picture "The Greatest Thing on Earth" (reproduced in Kornbluh, 33), of an endless stream of workers marching up out of a mire toward a sun containing a globe inscribed "IWW Universal."

113. Renshaw, 221–38, 4–5. There was also an independent and parallel syndicalist movement in Argentina that developed more directly from French and Spanish models and is exhaustively treated in the Hebrew doctoral thesis of Jacob Oved, Tel Aviv, 1975, scheduled for translation and publication as "El Anarquismo y el surgimiento del movimiento obrero en la Argentina," Mexico, 1977.

114. Renshaw, 36; Romero-Maura, "Case," 469. Estimate of numbers in Lens, 175.

115. From the text in Kornbluh, 45.

116. Williams, "Sabotage," *Solidarity*, 1911, Feb 25, in Kornbluh, 52. The term was first introduced in the IWW press in *Solidarity*, 1910, Jun 4 (Kornbluh, 37)—a journal started by Williams in Newcastle, Pa., during a 1909 steel strike (51). Other French influences are discussed in M. Lapitsky, *Uil'iam Kheivud*, 1974, 111.

Elizabeth Gurley Flynn (a later leader of the American Communist party), subsequently distinguished disciplined sabotage ("an internal industrial process") from crude violence. See *Sabotage*, 1915, cited in Kornbluh, 37.

117. Estimate of Gurley Flynn in Renshaw, 100–1.

118. Pouget, *Sabotage*, Chicago, 1913; A. Giovannitti, *Arrows in the Gale*, Riverside, Conn., 1914.

119. "The Revolutionary Strike," *The American Magazine*, 1912, May 25, cited in Kornbluh, 158; other comments cited in Renshaw, 106.

120. Kornbluh, 201.

121. Ibid., 202.

122. Cited in R. O'Connor and D. Walker, *The Lost Revolutionary: A Biography of John Reed*, NY, 1967, 33.

123. Cited in Kornbluh, 201.

124. *Ten Days That Shook the World*, NY, 1919, 16.

125. According to John Reed, cited in A. Peterson, *Daniel De Leon: Socialist Architect*, NY, 1941; Renshaw, 26.

126. Foster, cited in Lens, 231–2.

127. R. Friedheim, "Prologue to a General Strike: the Seattle Shipyard Strike of 1919," *Labor History*, VI, 1965, 121–42. For a more revolutionary reading of the strike, see H. O'Conner, *Revolution in Seattle*, NY, 1964.

128. Their main legacy to Soviet Communism may lie in the son that Dennis left behind in Moscow, Timur Timofeev, who now heads the Institute for the History of Workers' Movements, which supervises the scholarly side of Soviet revolutionary hagiography.

129. In 1919, Reed split from the American Communist party shortly after its founding in Chicago (Renshaw, 197–8) and, in 1921, died in Moscow largely disillusioned with Soviet Communism. See B. Wolfe, "The Harvard Man in the Kremlin Wall," *American Heritage*, 1960, Feb, 6–9, 94–103; also the new introduction to *Ten Days* by G. Hicks, revising some conclusions in his pioneering biography of 1938. New material on Reed's Russian period (though predictably little on his disillusionment) is in A. Startsev, *Russkie bloknoty Dzhona Rida*, 1968.

Most IWW activists went to the USSR as part of the 1,500 immigrants in the Kuzbas colony experiment (File 811.00B, Kuzbas, State Department, Washington, D.C.). Most returned disillusioned to America, and Heywood resigned as IWW head in 1923. The Soviet study of Heywood by Lapitsky creates the strong suspicion that Heywood's final views about the USSR were negative, by revealing (166) that Heywood had basically completed an autobiography in the USSR, and telling nothing about its contents.

130. D. Montgomery, "The 'New Unionism' and the Transformation of Workers' Consciousness in America, 1909–22," *Journal of Social History*, XVII, 1974, 517.

131. Renshaw, 146–7; also 143–60 for the vexed questions of the Hill legend, and supplementary material in Kornbluh, "Joe Hill: Wobbly Bard," *Voices*, 127–57; G. Smith, *Joe Hill: The Man and the Myth*, Utah, 1967; and *The IWW Songbook* and their *Little Red Songbook*. When the Congress of Industrial Organizations was formed in 1935—resuming industrial union organization after the depression—it took its official song directly from the IWW (sung to the tune of *John Brown's Body* and ending with the ringing affirmation that "the union makes us strong").

Chapter 16

1. Recent studies (as collated by M. Falkus, "Aspects of Foreign Investment in Tsarist Russia," *The Journal of European Economic History*, 1979, Spring, 5–36, esp. charts on 25, 31) suggest that total French investment in imperial Russia was about 12 billion French francs by 1914.

2. It began with votive reverence for *Das Kapital* without much understanding. Marx's anarchist foe, Bakunin, was the first to attempt to translate it into Russian in the late 1860s. Populist foes of Marxism, Mikhailovsky and Nicholas Danielson, became in the early seventies the first Russians respectively to praise him extravagantly in the legal press and to complete a translation. A liberal professor in Kiev, Nicholas Sieber, was one of the first ever to include Marx's work in a formal university course during the same 1870s. Marx himself as early as 1868 called it "the irony of fate that the Russians with whom I have fought for 25 years" should become "the first foreign nation to translate *Capital*" (*Letters to Dr. Kugelmann*, L, 1934, 77; also Billington, *Mikhailovsky*, 65–70; and A. Reuel, *'Kapitala' Karla Marksa v rossii 1870kh godov*, 1939, esp. 86–118).

3. Dan, 168; A. Ascher, *Pavel Axelrod and the Development of Menshevism*, Cambridge, Mass., 1972, 26. The primary source is Axelrod, "Pervye vstrechi s germanskoi sotsialdemokratiei," in *Perezhitoe i peredumannoe*, Berlin, 1923, 126–36.

4. Dan, 174, 178 n.; also E. Yaroslavsky, *Istoriia VKP (B)*, 1934, 2d ed., chast' I, 40. G. Zhuikov attempts, not altogether convincingly, to suggest greater influence of Plekhanov's group within St. Petersburg than has been generally thought (*Peterburgskie marksisty i gruppa "osvobozhdenie truda,"* Leningrad, 1975).

5. On these groups—led respectively by the Bulgarian, Dmitri Blagoev, and the Russian, Michael Brusnev—see Dan, 186–7.

6. For different aspects of this complex subject, see E. Mendelsohn, *Class Struggle in the Pale: The Formative Years of the Jewish Workers' Movement in Tsarist Russia*, Cambridge, 1970; N. Levin, *While Messiah Tarried, Jewish Socialist Movements, 1871–1917*, NY, 1977; the unpublished doctoral thesis of H. Shukman, "The Relations between the Jewish Bund and the RSDRP," Oxford, 1960; and H. Tobias, *The Jewish Bund in Russia from Its Origins to 1905*, Stanford, 1972.

7. An action organization, "The Union of Polish Workers," gained 6,000 members during the industrial unrest of 1889–91 (E. Yaroslavsky, *Istoriia velikoi kommunisticheskoi partii* [*bol'shevikov*], Moscow/Leningrad, 1926, Tom I, vyp. 1, 126): and Machajski was arrested in 1892 in an effort to bring a manifesto from the émigrés in Switzerland to the proletariat leading the large-scale uprising in Łodz in 1892. See Nomad, *Aspects*, 98–9.

8. Though his argument was directed at eastern Europe, Machajski framed it in terms of a challenge to Karl Kautsky's seemingly authoritative Marxist acceptance of the intellectuals as potential allies of a proletarian revolution: Kautsky, "Die Intelligenz und die Sozialdemokratie," *Die Neue Zeit*, 1894–5, no. 27, 10–6; no. 28, 43–9; no. 29, 74–80. Machajski argued that the intellectuals within the Social Democratic movement were "privileged employees of capitalism" pursuing a family quarrel on behalf of the "educated bourgeoisie" against the "bourgeois aristocracy," seeking to hold onto their special form of "property" (the education they had been given) and to use it as a weapon of control over the unwitting workers.

9. *The Intellectual Worker*, hectographed in 1898, was published in 1905 (*Umstvenny rabochy*, Geneva). See also his *Burzhuaznaia revoliutsiia i rabochee delo*, 1905. For discussions, see Nomad, *Aspects*, 96–117; Avrich, *Anarchists*, 102–6, and "Anarchism and Anti-intellectualism in Russia," *Journal of the History of Ideas*, 1966, Jul–Sep, 381–90; L. Feuer, "The Political Linguistics of 'Intellectual': 1898–1918," *Survey*, 1971, Winter, 156–83; and the unpublished Columbia dissertation of M. Schatz, "Anti-Intellectualism in the Russian Intelligentsia: Michael Bakunin, Peter Kropotkin, and Jan Wacław Machajski," 1963.

All of the above can be usefully supplemented by a discussion particularly rich in using Polish materials on and by Machajski: A. D'Agostino, "Machaevism: Intelligentsia Socialism and the Socialization of Intelligence," *Marxism and the Russian Anarchists*, San Francisco, 1977, 110–55.

The disproportionate political role of intellectuals in Communist Eastern Europe continues to prompt émigrés from that region to publish important studies of the subject. See particularly A. Gella, ed., *The Intelligentsia and the Intellectuals. Theory, Method and Case Study*, Oxford, 1976; and G. Konŕad and I. Szélenyi, *The Intellectuals on the Road to Class Power: A Sociological Study of the Role of the Intelligentsia in Socialism*, NY, 1979.

10. See the introduction of B. Volin to N. Fedoseev. *Stat'i i pis'ma*, 1958, 7 ff.; also the more informative earlier collection of articles, *Fedoseev Nikolai Evgrafovich. Odin iz pionerov revoliutsionnogo marksizma v Rossii*, Moscow/Petrograd, 1923, 104–10, 28 ff., 75.

11. *Fedoseev*, 74. He insisted that it be called "Social Democratic" rather than "Marxist" to avoid any suggestion of intellectual theorizing.

12. Ibid., *Stat'i*, 8, 23–7.

13. Cited in I. Getzler, *Martov*, Cambridge, 1967, 23. A. Kremer and Yu. Martov, *Ob agitatsii*, A. Gordon, *Pis'ma k intelligentam*, and S. Gozhansky, *Pis'ma k agitatoram* (which suggested "parallel activity" in both spheres and thus foreshadowed the later Soviet idea of an integrated *agitprop*), are discussed in Yaroslavsky, *Istoriia*, 1926, 128. See also Dan, 196–7; Getzler, 21–44.

14. Dan, 199.

15. See the important testimony by Klasson, "Vladimir Il'ich u R.E. Klassona," *Krasnaia Letopis'*, 1925, no. 2, 145. Klasson pointedly recalled in this deposition of 1925 that "then as now Marx was honored, but little read" (144).

16. Plekhanov's magisterial *In Defense of Materialism* of 1894 (L, 1947) reconciled the iconoclastic scientism with the moralistic idealism of the Russian revolutionary tradition, by urging the new generation to move from "mechanistic" to "historical" materialism: an "objective" and "monistic" worldview that would bridge "the seemingly bottomless abyss" between hard facts and high ideals (178, 220).

Kolakowski argues (*Currents*, II, 329, 340) that Plekhanov "wrote the first works which can be called manuals of Marxism" and was the first person to use the term "dialectical materialism" "to denote the whole of Marxist philosophy."

17. Plekhanov's close association with the German movement helped him become a leading figure in the Second International. He wrote its official tribute to Hegel in 1891 (reprinted in Plekhanov, *Les Questions fondamentales du Marxisme*, 1947, 107–35), was formally admitted as a Marxist to the Zürich Congress in 1893 (Joll, *International*, 72), collaborated in the German-led campaign to exclude the anarchists, and dramatically shook hands with a Japanese socialist at the opening of the Amsterdam Congress in 1904 when the Russo-Japanese war was raging (ibid., 106).

18. P. Struve, "My Contacts and Conflicts with Lenin," *The Slavonic Review*, 1934, Apr, 580. He brought back "a whole collection of contemporary Social-

Democratic literature in the German language" (578) which was unparalleled in St. Petersburg and widely used.

19. Ibid., 586. Struve, *Kriticheskie zametki k voprosu ob ekonomicheskom razvitii Rossii*, St. Petersburg, 1894.

20. Struve, "Contacts," 1934, Jul, 72–3; 204–5.

21. C. Weill, *Marxistes russes et social-démocratie allemande 1898–1904*, 1977, 185.

22. Dan, 208.

23. The scholarly, but necessarily Leninist study by the East German historian B. Brachman (*Russische Sozialdemokraten in Berlin, 1895–1914*, 1962) can now be supplemented by Weill's more interpretive account, which is focused on the pre–1905 period. For Lenin's own German associations, see K. Shterb, *Lenin v Germanii*, 1959.

24. Text in R. Tucker, ed., *Marx-Engels Reader*, 422–3.

25. Citations from Lenin attesting to his deep identification with his brother as a source of his own vocation are in L. Fischer, *The Life of Lenin*, NY, 1964, 17.

26. The decisive influence of Chernyshevsky on Lenin is attested in N. Valentinov, *Encounters with Lenin*, L, 1968, esp. 63–72; and stressed in A. Ulam, *The Bolsheviks*, NY, 1965, 19, 54–70.

27. Maria Yasneva (Golubeva), the wife of Zaichnevsky's closest associate, and a follower of Tkachev who later joined the Bolsheviks, cited in V. *I. Lenin v Samare 1889–1893. Sbornik vospominaniia*, 1933, 69. See also T. Szamuely, *The Russian Tradition*, NY, 1974, 318; Valentinov, *Encounters*, 73–5.
When Lenin first arrived in Geneva, he singled out the works of Tkachev as "closer to our viewpoint than any of the others" in addressing his future private secretary V. Bonch-Bruevich (see the latter's *Izbrannye Sochineniia*, 1962, II, 314–6). V. Adoratsky, a close friend of Lenin during that period and future editor of Lenin's works, also attested to the continuing importance of the elite and violent tradition of the People's Will for Lenin during the Samara period. See Fischer, *Lenin*, 19–20. Ulam dismisses Yasneva rather cavalierly as a "witch" (*Bolsheviks*, 106–7).

28. Lenin, *Sochineniia*, 1941, 4th ed., I, 380. For earlier Russian uses of *partiiny*, and later Leninist uses of *partiinost'* in the full sense of individual sacrifice for the sake of the party, see Billington, "Intelligentsia," 816, esp. n. 32. In the preface to a collection of party documents published in Geneva in 1904 (N. Shakhov, *Bor'ba za s'ezd*), Lenin insisted that all the material should "revolve around one central point, namely: the struggle of party spirit with circle spirit (*partiinosti s kruzhkovshchinoi*)"; cited in V. Morozova, "Izdatel'stvo sotsial-demokraticheskoi partiinoi literatury V. Bonch-Bruevicha i N. Lenina," *Voprosy Istorii KPSS*, 1962, no. 4, 101.

29. According to D. Kutsentov, V. *I. Lenin i mestnye partiinye organizatsii Rossii*, Perm, 1970, 95. The official Soviet view, which stretches every thread of authentic testimony to exaggerate the extent of both Lenin's leadership and his contacts with workers, is codified (and "bourgeois falsifications" duly rebuffed) in Ya. Volin, ed., *Istoriografiia peterburgskogo soiuza bor'by za osvobozhdenie rabochego klassa*, Perm, 1974.

30. D. Geyer seems to suggest that Lenin and the intellectuals superimposed a prior conspiracy on the workers (*Lenin in der russischen Sozialdemokratie*, Cologne/Graz, 1962). R. Pipes. *Social Democracy and the St. Petersburg Labor Movement, 1885–1897*, Cambridge, Mass., 1963, downplays Lenin's influence. A. Wildman, *The Making of a Workers' Revolution. Russian Social Democracy, 1891–1903*, Chicago, 1967, is a valuable social history.

31. For details, see Ya. Cherniavsky, *Bor'ba V. I. Lenina za organizatsionnye printsipy marksistskoi partii*, 1954, 9 ff.

32. Cited, from the first proclamation of the Union, by Dan (who was one of the members closest to Martov), 201.

33. According to the valuable fragment of Leonid Krasin's projected "revolutionary history of the Technological Institute," in M. Liadova and S. Pozner, eds., *Leonid Borisovich Krasin ("Nikitich"). Gody podpol'ia*, Moscow/Leningrad, 1928, 52. This project was never apparently completed, but there did appear in the following year an article by M. Rappeport, "Revoliutsionnaia istoriia tekhnologicheskogo instituta," in the centennial volume *Tekhnologichisky institut imeni leningradskogo soveta rabochikh, krestianskikh i krasnoarmeiskikh deputatov*, Leningrad, 1928, I, 271 ff. (LL). Key facts are taken from this rich, illustrated volume, esp. 97–9, 115, 273–7, 266, and picture of the special student building on 294. The enrollment was fixed at 500 in 1887 (105), but had increased to 630 by 1891 and to 841 by 1897 (113). D. Brower, "Student Political Attitudes and Social Origins: The Technological Institute of Saint Petersburg," *Journal of Social History*, VI, 1972–3, simply summarizes a questionnaire of 1909 showing that 56% of the students at

the institute considered themselves adherents of the radical Left (204), and points out that the radical component grew as the enrollment doubled from the late 1890s through 1908 (202).

34. N. Krupskaia, "O Krasine," in *Krasin*, 137. The otherwise unidentified Lelewel (usually omitted in subsequent Soviet accounts) is here assumed to be a Pole. See ibid., 52–7; Rappeport, 279; and (on Yakov Notkin's and Arkady Kremer's visit of 1885) Levin, *Messiah*, 232.

Krasin was attracted to the institute by an alumnus who was also a veteran of the People's Will and his chemistry teacher in Tiumen, Siberia (*Krasin*, 50). Valentinov, Krzhizhanovsky, and others were protected within the institute by another chemistry professor and his wife who were clandestine members of the Social Democratic movement (Valentinov, *Encounters*, 3–5).

35. The head of a circle invited Krasin to join with these words in Oct 1890; see Krasin, "Dela davno minuvshikh dnei, 1889–1892," *Proletarskaia revoliutsiia*, 1923, no. 3, 10; also 7–15.

36. *Krasin*, 67–71.

37. Fedor Afanas'evich and V. S. Golubev respectively: *Krasin*, 89, 394; also Rappeport, 281.

38. R. McNeal, *Bride of the Revolution: Krupskaya and Lenin*, Ann Arbor, 1972, 31–3.

39. See the important memoir of V. Karelina on this neglected group in Krasin, 86–92.

40. *Krasin*, 35–40.

41. Autobiographical testimony in *Gleb Maksimovich Krzhizhanovsky. Zhizn' i deiatel'nost'*, 1974, 186.

42. A. Mel'nikov, *Khranitel' partiinykh tain*, 1975, 13–4 (HU). The basic sources on Radchenko's life and activities remain the short memoirs by his brother, I. I. Radchenko (*Stary Bol'shevik*, 1933, Mar–Apr, 177–86) and his close associate, G. B. Krasin (ibid., 186–9). Modest increments of information, but no interpretation or insight, have been added in each of the only other accounts of any kind that I have found in an extensive search: D. Kutsentov, *Deiateli Peterburgskogo "Soiuza bor'by za osvobozhdenie rabochego klassa*," 1962, 115–22; A. Mel'nikov, "Leninets Stepan Radchenko," *Voprosy Istorii*, 1970, no. 4, 191–206; and E. S. Radchenko, "Odin iz pervykh soratnikov Il'icha," *Voprosy Istorii KPSS*, 1969, no. 7, 88–93. The latter memoir by his daughter, Evgeniia Stepanovna, is written in a purely scholarly form and gives no indication of this relationship.

43. For his role in arranging meetings, see M. Sil'vin, *Lenin v period zarozhdeniia partii*, Leningrad, 1958, 48–9, 103, 158–9. V. Akimov suggests that Radchenko in fact established a clandestine school in St. Petersburg during 1892–4 (*The Dilemmas of Russian Marxism 1895–1903*, Cambridge, 1969, 235).

44. Mel'nikov, "Radchenko," 196, *Khranitel'*, 98. "Engineer" seems to have been used internally within the empire by his Kievan contacts. See "Iz Vospominanii S.V. Parazich (S.V. Pomerants)," *Krasnaia Letopis'*, 1923, no. 7, 257.

45. Still another pseudonym used less often was Leibovich, a synthetic patronymic suggesting the russified form of both the German "lifeguard" (*leibgvardiia*) and the English "laborite" (*leiborist*). See *Perepiska V.I. Lenina i redaktsii gazety "Iskra" s sotsial-demokraticheskimi organizatsiiami v Rossii, 1900–1903*, 1970, III, 711. Though under police surveillance from 1891 (E. Radchenko, 89 ff.), Radchenko does not appear to have been effectively detected prior to the fall of 1894. See Mel'nikov, *Khranitel'*, 16.

46. Sil'vin, 104, 105.

47. N. Sergievsky, "Gruppa 'Osvobozhdeniia Truda' i marksistskie kruzhki," *Istoriko-revoliutsionny sbornik*, 1929, II, 152–3.

48. Sil'vin, 35. Other information from I. Radchenko, 177–8; G. Krasin, 186–7. More details on the Ukrainian activities and connections of Radchenko and his brothers are presumably contained in the Ukrainian-language study unavailable to me by E. Malenko, *Brat'ia Radchenki*, Kharkov, 1970.

49. Yu. Martov, *Zapiski sotsial-demokrata*, Berlin, 1922, 214, citing from the "sharp letter" he wrote to his comrades in St. Petersburg. Martov, like everyone else, is tantalizingly brief in his tributes to Radchenko.

50. For these aspects of Martov's legacy, see I. Getzler, *Martov*, 9 ff.; also A. Patkin, *The Origins of the Russian-Jewish Labour Movement*, Melbourne, 1947.

51. Martov claims that he was the first to use this term of denunciation (*Zapiski*, 214).

52. Stepan's father died when he was young, so that he was forced to take over the family business of supplying wood to the local railroad and immersed as a youth directly in a world of artisans, railroad workers, and so forth, generally unknown to most St. Petersburg intellectuals. See I. Radchenko, 177–8.

53. The remarkable memoir by Vera Karelina of this meeting (*Krasnaia Letopis'*, 1924, no. 1, 10–1) is generally overlooked in subsequent Soviet writings. The one author who cites it (Mel'nikov, "Radchenko," 195) presents the meeting as if it took place in 1893 and follows the usual practice of ritually exaggerating Lenin's influence even at this early date. It was apparently at a later meeting (at which Radchenko was also present) that Lenin was first introduced to broader revolutionary circles as "the brother of the well-known revolutionary A. I. Ulyanov," Kutsentov, *Deiateli*, 116–8.

54. G. Krasin, 187.

55. Kutsentov, 120; G. Krzhizhanovsky, in *O Vladimire Il'iche. Sbornik statei i vospominanii*, 1933, 39–40.

56. Kutsentov, 119; Sil'vin, 48–9, 103–5; E. Radchenko, 90.

57. Mel'nikov, "Radchenko," 201, on the basis of new archival material.

58. See the discussion of Radchenko's central role in Mel'nikov, *Khranitel'*, 102–10, which also suggests the possibility that Arkady Kremer, who quarreled with Radchenko over the word, may have been responsible for its insertion. The document was published at the press of the Bund; and the presence of these two at the meetings and their closeness to workers make either of them a more likely source of this addition than is Struve (to whom R. Pipes attributes the authorship without advancing any reasons or evidence: *Struve. Liberal on the Left 1870–1905*, Cambridge, Mass., 1970, 193). For detailed treatment of this neglected conference (which does not, however, clarify this question), see articles by I. Moshinsky and E. Gurvich in *Katorga i Ssylka*, 1928, no. 40. Russian Social Democratic Labor party remained the official name until after the Bolshevik Revolution.

The initial proletarian orientation of the Russian party (if not the introduction of the word "labor") almost certainly owes something to the Kiev Social Democrats and their remarkable leader, the locksmith Yuvenaly Mel'nikov. See B. Eidel'man, "K istorii vozniknoveniia rossiiskoi sotsial demokraticheskoi rabochei partii," *Proletarskaia Revoliutsiia*, 1921, no. 1, 20–65. The Kievans organized a conference of their own in Mar, 1897 (31–3), and their role at the Minsk gathering in 1898 would be better known had not many of their members been arrested in Mar, 1898. Mel'nikov died in 1899, and the Kievans' collective book *Rabochee delo v Rossii* disappeared without ever being published (49, 51). Mel'nikov, who may have been radicalized by his contact with technological students at the Kharkov colony of the St. Petersburg Technological Institute, summarized their worker-oriented economism anathema to later Leninizing historians: "Better to lift the masses an inch than one man to the second floor." (29).

59. Volin, *Istoriografiia*, 8–9.

60. *Za piatochok, za kipiatok*. This official party account of D. Kutsentov (in *Ocherki istorii Leningradskoi organizatsii KPSS. Ch.I, 1883–oktiabr' 1917*, Leningrad, 1962, 51) draws on archival material unavailable to ordinary Soviet (let alone foreign) scholars; but it is not precisely documented and is slanted to stress retroactively Lenin's leadership role and closeness to the working class.

The tantalizingly fragmentary use of an unpublished memoir by V. Solodilov (in Mel'nikov, *Khranitel'*, 90) depicts Radchenko arguing that the Russian movement should correct not just English trade unionism, but German Social Democracy as well, by fusing the class struggle of the proletariat with the political struggle against autocracy.

61. This distinction dates from Plekhanov in 1892 (Akimov, 17).

62. Getzler, 79. Martov also revived the Buonarrotian theme of vilifying Lafayette as the bourgeois who seeks "to contain the further development of the revolution." See his review (*Zhizn'*, 1900, Sep, 358–62) of Vasily Yakovlev, *Markiz Lafaiet (deiatel' trekh revoliutsii)*, 1889, cited in Getzler, 42–3.

63. Dan, 229.

64. Lenin, *What Is To Be Done?*, Oxford, 1963 (originally 1902), 182–3.

65. Cited in the intr. of S. Utechin to ibid., 109–10. Krupskaia cites Lenin as saying flatly that "*Iskra* created the Russian Social Democratic Workers' Party" (V. Stepanov, *Lenin i russkaia organizatsiia "Iskry" 1900–1903*, 1968, 397). Although the editorial offices were in Munich and the press in Stuttgart, she insisted that "its center of gravity is inside Russia" (ibid., 7).

66. Cited in A. Wildman, "Lenin's Battle with *Kustarnichestvo*: the *Iskra* Organization in Russia," *Slavic Review*, 1964, Sep, 486.

67. *What Is To Be Done?*, 187–8.

68. G. Deich, "Voprosy konspirativnoi tekhniki 'Iskry' v pis'makh V.I. Lenina 1900–1903 godov," *Voprosy Istorii*, 1969, no. 9, esp. 51 ff., 60–1.

69. Stepanov, *Lenin*, 7; Deich, "Voprosy," 63–6; and for details of his original proposals for *Iskra* and *Zaria* and of his key support organization near the border at Pskov, see B. Novikov, *V.I. Lenin i pskovskie iskrovtsy*, 1968; also *Bol'shevistskaia*

pechat'. Sbornik materialov, 1959–61. 4v; and the essays edited by A. Kostin on the seventieth anniversary of the founding of *Iskra: Leninskaia "Iskra,"* 1970.

70. Sil'vin, 238–40.

71. A conclusion that can be inferred from material in I. Radchenko, 183–4 (*Perepiska Lenina i redaktsii "Iskra",* III, 711); and from the testimony of E. Radchenko that Lenin visited the well-located yet effectively concealed Radchenko apartment in Pskov "almost every day" (91).

72. The correspondence to her from *Iskra* makes it clear she was in Kharkov as well as Poltava (*Perepiska,* I, 57–8, 70).

73. Wildman, 489; *Perepiska,* III, 711; and A. Mel'nikov, "Organizator sovetskoi torfianoi promyshlennosti. K 90-letiiu so dnia rozhdeniia I.I. Radchenko," *Torfianaia Promyshlennost',* 1964, no. 8, 25.

74. Mel'nikov, "Leninets," 205; E. Radchenko, 92.

75. That the name was initially unknown to Lenin and Krupskaia is evident from the latter's query of Sep 23 to a St. Petersburg correspondent: "Who is this you call General?" (*Perepiska,* I, 232, also 226, 245).

76. For details of this system, see V. Novikov, "Nepremenno vysylaite 'Iskru,'" *Voprosy Istorii,* 1977, no. 4, 118–26, esp. 119; *Leninsky sbornik,* VIII, 260; and S. Rozenoir, *Nelegal'ny transport,* 1932. The date of arrest (correcting I. Radchenko, 184, and others) is given in *Perepiska,* III, 711.

77. R. Obolenskaia, "Propaganda i agitatsiia v period staroi 'Iskry,'" *Stary Bol'shevik,* 1933, May–Jun, esp. 123–32.

78. "Doklad organizatsii 'Iskry' II s'ezdu RSDRP v 1903 g.," *Proletarskaia Revoliutsiia,* 1928, no. 1, 147–67, esp. 148, 154.

79. He called himself N. Lenin for the first time in an article written in his theoretical journal *Zaria:* "Gg. 'Kritiki' v agrarnom voprose," no. 2–3, in *Sobranie,* V, 1967, 99–156 (completed just as he was finishing *What Is To Be Done?*).

80. Lenin differentiated an "article" from the unfocused "thoughts and sketches" of bourgeois journalists. See P. Karasev, "Iz nabliudenii nad kompozitsiei leninskikh statei," *Problemy zhanrov v zhurnalistike,* Leningrad, 1968, 5–6. When asked later, Lenin formally listed his own occupation as "journalist" or "littérateur," the latter in its Russian form of *literator* being synonymous with "ideological journalism" since Belinsky. See V. Karpinski, "Lénine rédacteur," *Lénine tel qu'il fut. Souvenirs de contemporains,* Moscow, 1958, 382.

81. *What Is To Be Done?* 188.

82. Mel'nikov, "Leninets," 205–6; E. Radchenko, 92.

83. Krzhizhanovsky, 14–5; *What Is To Be Done?* 13.

84. Krzhizhanovsky, 16–7; Krasin, 261, 271–2, 195, 200, and (on the German phase) 233.

85. Krasin, 257.

86. Krzhizhanovsky became the founding head both of the Bolshevik Commission on Electrification (GOELRO) and of its successor organization, the State Planning Commission (GOSPLAN). Krasin became People's Commissar for Industry and Trade and then for Transportation. Ivan Radchenko, who had worked with Klasson to set up the first peat-burning electric power station at Noginsk in 1912, became head of the Directorate for Peat. See Mel'nikov, "Organizator," 25–6.

Though in prison or exile for most of the decade leading up to his death in 1911, Stepan Radchenko made use of a brief period of amnesty during the Revolution of 1905 to supply a revolver to his brother Leonty in Moscow and to bring another brother, Yury, to Vologda to learn revolutionary technique from fellow exiles there. After Stepan's death Yury was arrested when a lengthy Marxist study by Stepan was discovered in the secret compartment of a trunk that had been auctioned off to pay his debts. That piece of writing has not survived, and the first *apparatchik* thus left behind no written legacy of his own. See I. Radchenko, 183–6.

87. Strange as it may seem, there is still no comprehensive, scholarly biography of Lenin. The immense Soviet scholarship on the subject provides vast information, but is utterly hagiographical and devoid of interpretive—let alone critical—treatment. "Scholarship" on Lenin in the USSR is rather in the state of Christian scholarship about Jesus before modern Biblical criticism began to ask basic textual and interpretive questions. The "quest of the historical Lenin" is not yet acceptable to those who control access to the documents. A recent Western reviewer of the current Soviet chief hagiographer sees Lenin being treated not just as a historical actor but as a *figura,* validating the relationship between one event and another, and representing at all times "a goal imminent in the course of events" (A. Kimball, "I. I. Mints and the Representation of Reality in History," *Slavic Review,* 1976, Dec, 716).

Previously little-used material is incorporated in Fischer, *Lenin,* the best overall biography; but it should be supplemented (especially for the early period) by

Ulam, *Bolsheviks*, Shukman, *Lenin*, and D. Treadgold, *Lenin and His Rivals*, NY, 1955. See also R. Theen, *Lenin: Genesis and Development of a Revolutionary*, Philadelphia, 1973; B. Wolfe, *Three Who Made a Revolution*, NY, 1948; and *An Ideology in Power*, NY, 1969; L. Schapiro and P. Reddaway, eds., *Lenin: The Man, the Theorist, the Leader: A Reappraisal*, NY, 1967; and the bibliography of materials in Western languages by G. Heltai, *Books on Lenin*, np, 1969.

An ambitious new attempt to suggest that ideology was the essential feature of Leninism, the fulfillment of an inherently revolutionary "gnostic" tradition, is in A. Besançon, *Les Origines intellectuelles du léninisme*, 1977. "Lenin doesn't know that he believes. He believes that he knows" (15).

88. Cited in Utechin, *What Is To Be Done?* 20.
89. Ibid., 177.
90. "What does 'Freedom of Criticism' mean?," *What Is To Be Done?* 40–4, also 58–60.
91. Ibid., 100, 140, 191.
92. Lenin's two most important prescriptive writings, with broad programmatic significance for the international movement after coming into power, were *The Proletarian Revolution and the Renegade Kautsky* (written Autumn 1918, published L, 1920) and *"Left-Wing" Communism, an Infantile Disorder* (written and published Spring 1920, first disseminated at the all-important Second Congress of the Communist International in July, 1920).

A specially brilliant polemic accomplishment of his campaign in the pre-World War I period against both "right liquidators" (Mensheviks) and "left liquidators" (Bogdanov's Bolshevik faction, which was often dominant within Russia itself) was Lenin's success in ridiculing and bracketing together the genuinely Christian and conservative "God-seekers" with the anti-religious and ultra-revolutionary "God-builders." See J. Scherrer, " 'Ein gelber und ein blauer Teufel.' Zur Entstehung der Begriffe 'Bogostroitel'stvo' und 'Bogoiskatel'stvo,' " *Forschungen zur osteuropäischen Geschichte*, XXV, 1978, 319–29. A further act of polemic ingenuity was Lenin's bracketing together of the Left Bolsheviks' insistence on recalling Social Democratic deputies elected to the Duma ("recallism," *otzovizm*), with their insistence on building a new proletarian culture within the working class itself ("god-building," *bogotsroitel'stvo*) into the alleged sin of "god-recallism" (*bozhestvenny otzovizm*).

93. Isaiah Berlin has called this an "artificial dialectic" of planned alternation between relaxation and terror and identified it as Stalin's special contribution to politics in the twentieth century. See O. Utis, "Generalissimo Stalin and the Art of Government," *Foreign Affairs*, 1952, Jan, 197–214.
94. *What Is To Be Done?*, 145.
95. Letter of Jun 24, 1852, *What Is To Be Done?*, 37.
96. R. McNeal, ed., *Resolutions and Decisions of the Communist Party of the Soviet Union*, Toronto, 1974, I, 38.
97. A classic Menshevik account of the conflict is Dan's "Bolshevism and Menshivism," *Origins*, 236–407. The Leninist version codified for the USSR is "Vtoroi s'ezd partii. Vozniknovenie Bol'shevizma," in P. Pospelov et al., eds, *Istoriia kommunisticheskoi partii sovetskogo soiuze*, 1965, I, 446–531.

Lenin himself used the term "Bolshevism" as synonymous with "revolutionary social democracy," the implication being that others were less revolutionary. See V. Mochalov, "V.I. Lenin i vozniknovenie marksizma v Rossii," *Voprosy Istorii*, 1969, no. 4, 26 n. 21.

98. O. Znamensky and V. Shishkin, *Lenin, revoliutsionnoe dvizhenie i parlamentarizm*, Leningrad, 1977, 17 ff. Perhaps reflecting fear of "Eurocommunist" ideas, this book takes an antagonistic line to possible accommodation of Leninism to democratic forms.
99. Ibid., 22–5.
100. *What Is To Be Done?*, 100.
101. Ibid., 63.
102. "Zadachi revoliutsionnoi molodezhi," *Student*, 1903, Sep; *Polnoe sobranie*, VII, 355. See also P. Gusiatnikov, "Bor'ba V.I. Lenina, iskrovtsev za revoliutsionno-demokraticheskoe studenchestvo (1901–1903 gg.)," *Voprosy Istorii KPSS*, 1969, no. 1, 30–7.
103. "Sotsial Demokratiia i revoliutsionnoe dvizhenie krestianstva," *Polnoe sobranie*, IX, 409–10.
104. *Resolutions*, 63. Compare the specific Menshevik rejection of "the use of agrarian terror" (78).
105. *Two Tactics of Social Democracy in the Democratic Revolution*, NY, 1963, 65–73.
106. *Resolutions*, 94. The term was in fact originated by the Mensheviks (82–3).
107. O. Piatnitsky, *Memoirs of a Bolshevik*, Westport, Conn., 1973, 56.

108. Cited and discussed in B. Bociurkiw, "Lenin and Religion," in Schapiro and Reddaway, eds., *Lenin*, 113.

109. V. Bonch-Bruevich, from the text of his report to the congress in *Rassvet*, 1905, nos. 6–7, 173. This may be the first use of the term "people's democracy."

110. Resolution of the congress (notably less enthusiastic than Bonch-Bruevich's formulation), cited in Bociurkiw, 115.

Herzen's ambitious earlier attempt to enlist the Old Believers for revolutionary struggle in the early 1860s is made to appear not altogether unrealistic (despite its ultimate total failure) in the unpublished dissertation of R. Call, "The Revolutionary Activities of the Kolokol Group among the Raskolniks," Bloomington, 1964.

111. "Sotsializm i religiia," *Novaia Zhizn'*, 1905, Dec 3; B. Bociurkiw, 116.

112. For Lenin's struggle with the principal advocate of a proletarian culture and a kind of proletarian religion, see D. Grille, *Lenins Rivale: Bogdanov und seine Philosophie*, Cologne, 1966; and A. Yassour, "Bogdanov et son oeuvre," *Cahiers du Monde Russe et Soviétique*, 1969, Oct–Dec, for a massive bibliography. First materials on the major forthcoming study by J. Scherrer of the general struggle of Bogdanov's "left Bolsheviks" with Lenin (and with what they were the first to call "Leninism") is in "Gor'kij, Bogdanov, Lenin. Neue Quellen zur ideologischen Krise in der bolschewistischen Fraktion (1908–1910)," *Cahiers du Monde Russe et Soviétique*, 1978, Oct–Dec, 321–34.

113. M. Holdsworth, "Lenin and the Nationalities Question," in Schapiro and Reddaway, eds., *Lenin*, 270–2, points out that *avtonomiia* did not imply for Lenin the total independence it suggests to the modern reader in English.

114. "Goriuchy material' v mirovoi politike," *Proletarii*, 1908, Jul 23; *Polnoe Sobranie*, XVII, 174–83.

115. See his "Tasks of Revolutionary Social Democracy in the European War" and the manifestoes of the international conferences at Zimmerwald in 1915 and Kienthal in 1916 (H. Gruber, *International Communism in the Era of Lenin*, Ithaca, 1967, 53–80).

116. *Imperialism, the Highest Stage of Capitalism*, written in 1916, first published in Russian after his return in 1917. For a brief discussion, see M. Holdsworth, "Lenin's *Imperialism* in Retrospect," *Essays in Honour of E. H. Carr*, 341–51. For more detail, J. Freymond, *Lénine et l'impérialisme*, Lausanne, 1951.

117. Key metaphors used during the Revolution of 1905 by Lenin and discussed in Znamensky, 67–9.

118. *Gosudarstvo i revoliutsiia, Polnoe Sobranie*, XXXIII, 48.

119. Ibid., 91.

120. M. Perrie shows that the phrase and concept of a "permanent [*permanentnaia*] revolution" in *Revoliutsionnaia Rossiia*, 1905, Jul 1, was in fact used by the S.R. leader M. Gots even before Trotsky and Parvus: "The Socialist Revolutionaries on 'Permanent Revolution,'" *Soviet Studies*, 1973, Jan, 411–3.

121. Radek is the hero of the novel by Machajski's lifelong friend Stefan Zeromski, *Syzyfowe Prace*; see D'Agostino, *Marxism*, 114, and for a biography, W. Lerner, *Karl Radek. The Last Internationalist*, Stanford, 1970.

122. I. Deutscher, *The Prophet Armed*, NY/L, 1954, 254–62.

123. E. Bramstedt, *Dictatorship and Political Police. The Techniques of Control by Fear*, NY, 1945, 10 ff. stresses the founding importance of Joseph Fouché—as does P. Wilkinson, *Political Terrorism*, L, 1974, 51–3. The latter follows R. Cobb (*Terreur et subsistences, 1793–1795*, 1964, 207) in seeing the technique of preventive repression against categories suspected of potential opposition to the revolution as the major innovation of the revolutionary era—and in attributing it in good measure to Fouché.

The Prussian secret police, which later provided models for the Right, also first took shape as part of the Prussian reform movement on the Left—its pioneer, Justus Brunner, reacting symbiotically to Fouché. See W. Obenaus, *Die Entwicklung des preussischen Sicherheitspolizei bis zum Ende der Reaktionszeit*, 1940.

124. For the basic structure, see F. Zuckerman, "Vladimir Burtsev and the Tsarist Political Police in Conflict, 1907–14," *Journal of Contemporary History*, 1977, Jan, 215 n. 11. For history and much more detail, see the first two chapters of his unpublished doctoral dissertation—"The Russian Political Police at Home and Abroad (1880–1917): Its Structure, Functions and Methods and Its Struggle with the Organized Opposition," New York University, 1973, 1–92—using the invaluable archives of the foreign *agentura* from Paris, now at the Hoover Institution in Stanford. Another unpublished work identified by L. Gerson (*The Secret Police in Lenin's Russia*, Philadelphia, 1976, 325) as "Draft of a Ph. D. dissertation" at Columbia, 1957, is E. Hollis, "Police Systems of Imperial and Soviet Russia." For a published narrative account, see R. Hingley, *The Russian Secret Police; Muscovite, Imperial Russian and Soviet Political Security Operations 1565–1970*, 69–116. See also the

forthcoming doctoral thesis at Tel Aviv University by N. Schleifmann, "The Role and Influence of Agents Provocateurs in the Russian Revolutionary Movement: 1902–1917."

125. Zuckerman, *Police*, 5, 8, 19, 25, 39, 44–6; also "Burtsev," 215 n. 11.

126. H. Seton-Watson, *The Russian Empire 1801–1917*, Oxford, 1967, 464.

127. Bramstedt, "The Political Police under Napoleon III," in *Dictatorship*, 35–49.

128. Zuckerman, *Police*, 64. Collaboration with the German police appears to have been concentrated mainly on the handing over of suspects (discussed by the Social Democratic poet and critic Karl Frohme, *Politische Polizei und Justiz im monarchistischen Deutschland*, Hamburg, 1926), though it increased with the founding of a Berlin *agentura* in 1893.

129. See the account of Leonid Men'shchikov, leader of the Moscow Okhrana, who had previously been involved in the revolutionary movement and claimed after the Bolshevik Revolution to have always been secretly working for it: "Parizhskie 'Bombisty,'" *Okhrana i revoliutsiia*, 1925, ch. I, 89–93. Men'shchikov's papers are in the Nikolaevsky collection of the Hoover Institution, Stanford; and his notes and additions to a copy of V. Agafonov's history of the Okhrana's office in Paris (*Zagranichnaia okhranka*, Petrograd, 1918) is in the University of Wisconsin Library. See the note by A. Senn in *Cahiers du Monde Russe et Soviétique*, 1978, Oct–Dec, 444.

On the broader political context in which the revolutionary emigration operated in Paris during the 1880s and 1890s, see the unpublished doctoral dissertation of M. Millard, "Russian Revolutionary Emigration. Terrorism and the Political Struggle," Rochester, 1973.

130. Zuckerman, *Police*, 80 ff. for this and other code names which the revolutionaries often later adopted with satire and/or bravado. Among the flood of radical journals that appeared during the Revolution of 1905 was a *Skorpion*—as well as a *Vampir* (Vampire), *Pulemet* (Machine Gun), *Yad* (Poison), etc. All of these are in the Wisconsin Library (Senn, 447).

131. Degaev escaped to begin a new life as the amiable professor Alexander Pell at a series of American universities from South Dakota to Bryn Mawr; see Yarmolinsky, *Road*, 317–23.

132. R. Gaucher, *The Terrorists from Tsarist Russia to the O.A.S.*, L, 1968, 36, drawing from Victor Serge, *Les Coulisses d'une sûreté générale. Ce que toute révolutionnaire devait savoir sur la répression*, 1925, 49–50 (reissued 1970 under the subtitle).

133. Zuckerman, *Police*, 62–3, also 85 on the way the various lines, circles, and cards were collated on individual, synoptic cards.

134. Gaucher, 43, and the entire section "Okhrana vs. Terrorism," 28–56.

135. Men'shchikov, *Okhrana*, ch. III, 1932, 40: for different types of agent, 34 ff.; also 56. The *mamochki okhrankoi* were also called *babushki provokatsii*, 118 ff. The latter two volumes of Men'shchikov's invaluable work (NY) substantially enrich the picture in Zuckerman, who mistakenly says that nothing was published after part one of the work, which appeared in 1914 (*Police*, 69 n. 103).

136. Men'shchikov, *Okhrana*, ch. III, 58, on Gregory Kivo and the journals *Dal'ny Vostok* and *Vladivostok*. When seven innocent residents were executed because the local Okhrana leader, Lt. Col. Zavarnitsky, fabricated a revolutionary conspiracy, only a mild rebuke was made (ibid., 47).

137. Men'shchikov, "Okhranniki v Finliandii," *Okhrana*, ch. I, 219–26, esp. 221. Men'shchikov is less than candid in acknowledging his own leadership role.

138. Burtsev was the leading émigré chronicler of the revolutionary tradition up until 1905. Zuckerman (*Police*, 48–9) follows Bramstedt in suggesting that the first revolutionary police bureau protecting subversive groups was that of Raoul Rigault under Napoleon III ("Burtsev," 214 n. 1).

139. Men'shchikov, *Okhrana*, ch. I, 20–5. For two different aspects of Zubatov's remarkable movement, see D. Pospielovsky, *Russian Police Trade Unionism, Experiment or Provocation?* L, 1971; and J. Schneiderman, *Sergei Zubatov and Revolutionary Marxism. The Struggle for the Working Class in Tsarist Russia*, Ithaca/L, 1976.

140. Schneiderman, 105 ff.; Pospielovsky, 98 ff. About such a sensitive subject as Zubatov and "Police Socialism," one can even now learn only obliquely from Soviet scholarship. See V. Sviatlovsky, *Istoriia professional'nogo dvizheniia v Rossii*, Leningrad, 1925; V. Novikov, "Leninskaia 'Iskra' v bor'be s zubatovshchinoi," *Voprosy Istorii*, 1974, no. 8, 24–35; and I. Ionov, "Zubatovshchina i Moskovskie rabochie v 1905 g.," *Vestnik Moskovskogo Universiteta*, 1976, no. 3, 54–68. Zubatov's activities in the 1890s, neglected in these accounts, are described by his follower in the Moscow Okhrana, Men'shchikov, *Okhrana*, ch. I, 199–200, 339–48, 428 n. 8.

141. Novikov, 31–3.

142. W. Sablinsky, *The Road to Bloody Sunday: Father Gapon and the St. Peters-burg Massacre of 1905*, Princeton, 1976.

143. S. Harcave, *The Russian Revolution of 1905*, NY, 1970, 81, 69, text of petition, 285–92.

144. Hingley, 95, *Leninsky sbornik*, III, 123–6, V, 590. Rutenberg's oscillation between Left and Right was paralleled by that of Boris Savinkov, his original terrorist collaborator in the *Sotsialist* group of 1900 with which Lenin had instructed Stepan Radchenko to establish contact in 1900. Savinkov became a leading S.R. terrorist but then wrote two novels exposing terrorism (*The Pale Horse*, 1909, and *The Tale of What Was Not*, 1913) and joined the right-wing Kornilov rising against Kerensky's provisional government. Lenin's delegate for dealing with Gapon was Ivan Radchenko.

145. Estimate in Crook, 161; details in Harcave, 98–135.

146. M. Gordon, *Workers Before and After Lenin*, NY, 1941, 3. See also Harcave, 150–4; O. Anweiler, *The Soviets. The Russian Workers, Peasants and Soldiers Councils, 1905–1921*, NY, 1974; the account of an old Bolshevik F. Samoilov, *Pervy sovet rabochikh deputatov*, Leningrad, 1931; A. Shipulina and Yu. Yakobson, "Ivanovo-Voznesensky sovet rabochikh deputatov 1905 goda," *Voprosy Istorii*, 1977, Feb, 38–55; and W. Gard, "The Party and the Proletariat in Ivanovo-Voznesensk, 1905," *Russian History*, II, part 2, 1975, 101–23.

147. Shipulina, 48, 53–4; Gard, 110.

148. Hitherto unpublished material on M. Afanas'ev in Ionov, 60.

149. Novikov, 25–7.

150. Ionov, 64–6, in effect concedes as much and essentially validates the conclusion of S. Schwartz, *The Russian Revolution of 1905: The Workers' Movement and the Formation of Bolshevism and Menshevism*, Chicago, 1967 (elsewhere pilloried by Shipulina and other Soviet scholars), that purely economic demands dominated all mass worker organizations until Oct 1905.

151. Shipulina, 65 ff.

152. Cited from a pamphlet by a "group of the northern committee of the Russian Social Democratic Workers' Party" in Samoilov, 42, 93.

153. Deutscher, *Prophet*, 125 ff. Previously known as a "strike commission" or "workers' committee," the St. Petersburg group may have been the first formally to call itself a Soviet (see L. Petrova, "Peterburgsky sovet rabochikh deputatov," *Voprosy Istorii*, 1955, no. 11, 26). The insistence of Shipulina and other Soviet sources on the paternity of Ivanovo may reflect the fact of higher Bolshevik participation. Other works that imply St. Petersburg origins are L. Kleinbort, *Pervy sovet rabochikh deputatov*, Petrograd, 1917; and the 1925 work of L. Gorin, referenced and critiqued in Samoilov and Shipulina.

154. O. Anweiler, cited in R. McNeal, *Russia in Transition 1905–1914*, NY, 1970, 18.

155. Trotsky, *Stalin*, NY, 1946, 97; I. Deutscher, *Stalin: A Political Biography*, NY, 1949, 87, also 84–91. For Lenin's writings of this period on "partisan war" and the organization of *druzhiny* (Social Democratic fighting units of from 3 to 75 members with their own elected officers), see L. Senchakova, *Boevaia rat' revoliutsii. Ocherk o boevykh organizatsiiakh RSDRP i rabochikh druzhinakh 1905–1907 gg.*, 1975, esp. 34 and ff.
For the activities of the "forest brethren," who conducted partisan warfare in the Baltic region after the defeat of December, see N. Burenin, *Liudi bol'shevistskogo podpol'ia*, 1958, 60–2.

156. The evidence in E. Smith, *The Young Stalin*, NY, 1967, indicates the probability of such connections—at least from the time of his mysterious survival of Okhrana raids in Tbilisi in 1901—even if his particular hypotheses about the extent of these connections seem unduly conjectural. Isaac Don Levine, George Kennan, and others suggested earlier a Stalin-Okhrana link; and a prominent Soviet historian confirmed to me during the Khrushchev era that their findings were "right in essence though not in detail." Roy Medvedev, *Let History Judge: The Origins and Consequences of Stalinism*, NY, 1971, 315–24, provides a fascinating, if skeptical, discussion of these theories along with other rumors and theories within the USSR about Stalin's possible connections with the tsarist secret police. Much of his own material and his final comparison of Stalin with Azev raise doubts about his conclusion that "Stalin did not serve the tsarist secret police" (323); and he seems less certain in his more recent "New Pages from the Political Biography of Stalin," in R. Tucker, ed., *Stalinism*, NY, 1977, 199–201. Tucker shows that no connection has been proven and is skeptical about Smith's argument, though ultimately noncommittal (*Stalin As Revolutionary 1874–1929*, NY, 1973, 108–14).

157. Zuckerman, *Police*, 88.

158. Ibid., 614–5.
159. Fischer, *Lenin*, 81–4, itemizes the many unanswered questions about Lenin's links with Malinovsky. See also D. Anin, "Lenin and Malinovsky," *Survey*, 1975, Autumn, 145–56; and R. Elwood, *Roman Malinovsky: A Life without a Cause*, Newtonville, 1977.
160. As suggested, for instance, in the unconvincing and anti-Semitic article published under the pseudonym of Salluste, "Lénine Agent de l'Okhrana," *Revue de Paris*, 1927, Dec 15, 806–26.
161. Zuckerman, 654; S. Oppenheim, "The Making of a Right Communist—A.I. Rykov to 1917," *Slavic Review*, 1977, Sep, 438. Always a unifier, Rykov had begun his revolutionary career by forming a unique joint committee of S.R.'s and S.D.'s in Saratov in 1901 (ibid., 422).
162. H. Shukman, *Lenin and the Russian Revolution*, L, 1966, 138. *Pravda*, which Stalin founded in St. Petersburg in 1912, took its title from a prior journal published since 1905 in Vienna by Ukrainian Mensheviks, and given new life in 1908 when Trotsky became its editor. Deutscher, *Prophet*, 191–9. The police "unmasked" Chernomazov in Feb, 1914, in a move designed to deflect attention from Malinovsky.
163. Zuckerman, *Police*, 80.
164. Zilli, 445–64; and for Gershuni's early ideas, 298–303. See also Gershuni's "Terroristichesky element v nashei programme," *Revoliutsionnaia Rossiia*, 1902, Jun, 2–5; and for the early stage of S.R. development Spiridovich, 149–67.
165. A. Korov, V. Dalin, *Yunosheskoe dvizhenie v Rossii*, Moscow/Leningrad, 1925, 2d ed., 40, on the "South Russian League of Youth," and 44–5 on the Central Committee's proclamation to *Iskra*. For the more general leadership of South Russia in the coming together of student with more general discontent during 1900–2, see P. Gusiatnikov, *Revoliutsionnoe studencheskoe dvizhenie v Rossii, 1899–1907*, 1971, 41–2; for the spread of the student unrest to professional and secondary schools, see A. Ushakov, *Revoliutsionnoe dvizhenie demokraticheskoi intelligentsii v Rossii, 1895–1904*, 1976.
166. Of the 179 police entries for those accused of terrorist acts in which occupations are listed between 1902 and 1911, 90 (or 61%) were workers; 37, intellectuals; 23, students; and 20, peasants. M. Perrie, "The Social Composition and Structure of the Socialist-Revolutionary Party before 1917," *Soviet Studies*, 1972, Oct, 247–8. On student demands for *ideinoe ob'edinenie* and resistance to the moderate liberalism of *kul'turniki*, see Kirov and Dalin, 55 ff.
167. Zuckerman, *Police*, 88. Basic materials on Azev are in Gaucher, 57–70; Men'shchikov, *Okhrana*, ch. III, 5–33; and B. Nikolaevsky, *Aseff, the Spy—Russian Terrorist and Police Stool*, NY, 1934.
168. Nikolaevsky, *Aseff*, 29–30.
169. Avrich, *Anarchists*, 40–71, on this remarkable profusion of terror, bombings, and suicidal violence unleashed by the *beznachal'tsy* and *bezmotivniki*; and 105–6, on the *neprimirmye*.
170. Gaucher, *Terrorists*, 52.
171. Ibid., 52–3; Avrich, 64.
172. According to G. Tokmakoff, "Stolypin's Assassin," *Slavic Review*, 1965, Jun, 314; also Avrich, 55 n. 61. The purely individual nature of key political assassinations, such as that of President Garfield in 1881 (A. Robertson, "Murder Most Foul," *American Heritage*, 1964, Jul, 90–104) does not invalidate the imitative nature of the act (echoing the assassination of Alexander II earlier in the year).
173. See O. Radkey, *The Election to the Russian Constituent Assembly of 1917*, Cambridge, Mass., 1950, 16–7; also Radkey's history of the S.R. Party: *The Agrarian Foes of Bolshevism*, NY, 1958; and *The Sickle Under the Hammer*, NY, 1963.
174. Published in a good new English translation, Bloomington, 1978.
175. Morozov, *Otkrovenie v groze i bure; istoriia vozniknoveniia apokalipsisa*, St. Petersburg, 1907; summary translation by M. Kissell in *Popular Astronomy*, 1940, Dec; 1941, Jan; repr, as *The Revelation in Thunder and Storm*, Northfield, Minn., 1941. See also Morozov, *Proroki; istoriia vovniknoveniia bibleiskikh prorochestv*, 1914 (all in LC).
176. Merezhkovsky, *Józef Piłsudski*, L, 1921; also (with Hippius and others) *Das Reich des Antichrist: Russland und der Bolschewismus*, Munich, 1922.
177. *Taina trekh*, Prague, 1925; and discussion in B. Rosenthal, *D.S. Merezhkovsky and the Silver Age: The Development of a Revolutionary Mentality*, The Hague, 1975, 216–23, esp. 221; also "The Religious Revolution," 163–95, for the earlier apocalypticism that began with his *Approaching Beast* of 1906. See esp. 165 n. 9 for Hippius's scheme for concentric circles of threes.
178. Gerson, *Police*, 234–7, 311 n. 29; Hingley, 140–1.
179. Avrich, *Anarchists*, 64.

180. Dzerzhinsky, *Prison Diary and Letters*, Moscow, 1959, 20; Gerson, 13.
181. Cited by A. Khatskevich, *Soldat velikikh boev: Zhizn' i deiatel'nost'* F. E. *Dzerzhinskogo*, Minsk, 1961, 98; Gerson, 12.
182. Stalin, *Works*, Moscow, 1954, VIII, 203–4; Gerson, 266. When Stalin was deposed from the mausoleum next to Lenin in Oct 1961, he was appropriately interred in the Kremlin wall next to Dzerzhinsky. See G. Leggett, "Lenin, Terror and the Political Police." *Survey*, 1975, Autumn, 187.
183. Cited from an unpublished British intelligence report in Gerson, 35.
184. Questionnaire for the Tenth Party Congress in 1921, cited in N. Zubov, *F. E. Dzerzhinsky: Biografiia*, 1965, 2d ed. 272; Gerson, 267.
185. In addition to Alexander Solzhenitsyn, *Gulag Archipelago*, 1975, NY, see, for the origins of the concentration camp and forced labor systems: D. Dallin and B. Nikolaevsky, *Forced Labor in Soviet Russia*, New Haven, 1947; and S. Wolin and R. Slusser, eds., *The Soviet Secret Police*, NY, 1957.
186. Zuckerman, 88.
187. Fischer, *Lenin*, 121.

Chapter 17

1. L. Abensour, *La Femme et le féminisme avant la révolution*, 1923; also Abray, "Feminism."
2. W. Stephens, *Women of the French Revolution*, NY, 1922, 245, apparently citing Michelet, *Les Femmes de la révolution*, which created the first wide awareness of the special role of women in the revolution.
3. Among her biographies, see especially C. Tomelin, *The Life and Death of Mary Wollstonecraft*, L, 1974; also her *A Historical and Moral View of the Origins and Progress of the French Revolution, and the Effect It Has Produced in Europe*, L, 1794.
4. The only monograph on Palm (W. Koppius, *Etta Palm: Nederland's eerste Feministe*, Zeist, 1929) barely scratches the surface. See 30–41, 47, 67, for her role in the Social Circle. See 73–80 for her speech to its affiliated Confederation of the Friends of Truth.
5. Stephens, *Women*, 171.
6. Stephens, 274.
7. F. Picavet, *Les Idéologues*, 1891, 31 ff, 221 n. 2; A. Guillois, *Le Salon de Mme. Helvétius*, 1894; and P. Gautier, *Mme. de Staël et Napoléon*, 1903.
8. Prati in *Penny Satirist*, 1838, May 12, 1.
9. Ibid., 2.
10. Ibid., 1–2.
11. *Penny Satirist*, 1838, Sep 29, 4. He is referring to England later in the twenties.
12. J. West, *A History of the Chartist Movement*, Boston, 1920, 36–7.
13. The nonrevolutionary attitude was made explicit in the suffragette song of the early twentieth century: "For the safety of the nation/ To women give the vote./ For the hand that rocks the cradle/ Will never rock the boat." G. Lerner, "The Feminists: A Second Look," *Columbia Forum*, 1970, Fall, 19.
14. The classic account is still S. Charléty, *Histoire du saint-simonisme (1825–1884)*, 1931, 205–34. See also Fahmy-Bey (pseud. Johan d'Ivray), *L'Aventure saint-simonienne et les femmes*, 1928; and Ch. Patureau-Mirand, *De la Femme et son rôle dans la société, d'après les écrits saint-simoniens*, Limoges, 1910, for a more analytic study.
15. Charléty, 212–3.
16. Published in English as *Eternal Life*, Chicago, 1926.
17. Stephens, *Women*, 236 n. 1, traces the first use of the term to Fourier's *Le Théorie des quatre mouvements*, 1808—a usage that I have not found and is not included in the chronicle of Fourier's linguistic inventions in Bestor.
The interconnection between Fourier's often-ridiculed cosmology and his more seriously regarded social presumptions is stressed in N. Riasanovsky, *The Teaching of Charles Fourier*, Berkeley/Los Angeles, 1969.
18. Patureau-Mirand, 79–95.
19. Fahmy-Bey, 57–67; E. Sullerot, *La Presse féminine*, 1966, 19–20; also S. Voilquin, *Souvenirs d'une fille du peuple ou les saint-simoniennes en Egypte*, 1966. For bibliography, see Walch, 42.
20. Charléty, 212 n. 2; Parris, *Lion*, 5–12, 20–9, attaches great importance on the basis of new research to Garibaldi's voyage on the Clorinda with the Saint Simonians. He views their influence generally as, "the key to his whole life and conduct"

(22), but does not discuss the concept of a feminine messiah, which was then the main Saint-Simonian preoccupation.

21. Parris, 54 ff.

22. See "De la 'dame' à la 'femme,' " and illustration in Sullerot, *La Presse*, 15–7; also H. Haustein, "Transvestitismus und Staat am Ende des 18. und im 19. Jahrhundert," *Zeitschrift für Sexualwissenschaft*, XV, 1928–29.

For an attempt to derive the revolutionary image of women from their portrayal in propagandistic visual art largely prior to 1848, see E. Hobsbawn, "Man and Woman in Socialist Iconography," *History Workshop Journal*, 1978, Autumn, 121–38.

23. Gans, "Owen à Paris," 41–4.

24. Sullerot, 20. Delphine Gay, daughter of the writer Sophie Gay and wife of the editor Emile Girardin, was the most influential of the feminine social critics, and at the same time a final spokesman for the *idéologues'* belief in physiology as the all-liberating science. See her *Physiologie du ridicule*, 1833.

25. S. Kalembka, *Wielka Emigracja*, 1971, 284; Borejsza, "Portrait," 138.

26. See her *Union ouvrière*, Paris/Lyon, 1844 (reprinted 1967), esp. 47 ff.; also the neglected account by her German contemporary A. Ruge, "Flora Tristan und die Union ouvrière," *Sämtliche Werke*, 1848, V, 93–102.

J. Puech, *La Vie et l'oeuvre de Flora Tristan 1803–1844 (L'Union ouvrière)*, 1925, remains a basic study. See also C. Gattey, *Gauguin's Astonishing Grandmother: A Biography of Flora Tristan*, L, 1970; J. Baelen, *La Vie de Flora Tristan*, 1972; P. Leprohon, *Flora Tristan*, 1979; and the embellished account of D. Desanti, *Flora Tristan. La femme révoltée*, 1972.

27. For the best discussion see M. Thibert, "Féminisme et socialisme d'après Flora Tristan," *Revue d'Histoire Economique et Sociale*, IX, 1921, 115–36; also Puech, 337–56.

28. Title of second ed. 1842 of *Les Promenades dans Londres*, 1840. See Puech, 115 n. 3.

29. Puech, 100.

30. Ibid., 105–6. She referred to Bedlam henceforth as Bethlehem.

31. Ibid., 417 ff; also A. Zévaès, "Flora Tristan et l'Union Ouvrière", *La Révolution de 1848*, 1934, Dec, 1935, Jan–Feb, 213–22.

32. Puech, 402 ff. on *Méphis ou le Prolétaire*, 1838.

33. Thibert, 128–9.

34. Puech, 390–1, 2.

35. Abbé Alphonse-Louis Constant (later Eliphas Levy), *L'Assomption de la femme, ou le livre de l'amour*, 1841, n. 1, indicates an earlier intention to call the book "the gospel of love." She willed her head to the president of the Phrenological Society after death. J. Marillier, "Pierre Moreau, 'L'Union,' " *Actualité de l'Histoire*, 1953, no. 5, 13. Thibert discusses the feminism of Esquiros among others in her valuable *La Féminisme dans le socialisme français de 1830 à 1850*, 1926, 384.

36. For these and other details about the former sailor Louis de Tourreil his *doctrine fusionienne* and *religion fusionienne*, as well as Constant's development of these ideas, see Viatte, *Victor Hugo et les illuminés*, 82–97.

37. d'Eichtal and Urbain, *Lettres sur la race noire*, 18, 60–1. See also 62–3, where the new trinity of white, black, and mulatto is described as UNE NOUVELLE LOI DE FAMILLE; also 64–7 n. 2, for further attempts to derive prophetic social meaning from the doctrine of the Trinity. Eichtal, who was Jewish, was addressing Urbain, who was a Muslim convert.

38. *Nécessité de faire un bon accueil aux femmes étrangères*, 1835; and the posthumously published *L'Emancipation de la femme ou, le testament de la paria*, 1846.

39. Sullerot, "Journaux," 109–10.

40. *Presse ouvrière*, 132.

41. Cited in Thibert, 128.

42. Sarah Grimke, *Letters on the Equality of the Sexes and the Condition of Women*, Boston, 1838; other works discussed in W. O'Neill, *The Woman Movement: Feminism in the United States and England*, NY/L, 1969, 19–21.

43. W. Waterman, *Frances Wright*, NY, 1924, 64.

44. A. Perkins and T. Wolfson, *Frances Wright Free Enquirer: The Study of a Temperament*, NY/L, 1939, 64. See also 385–6 for a bibliography of her writings; but there is no scholarly life of Wright or complete listing of her work.

45. Waterman, 65.

46. Perkins, 54–84.

47. According to Perkins, 208. See also 127, 175–6, 193–4 for key elements of her utopian experiments; and Waterman, 94–7, on pamphlets of this period.

48. Perkins, 248–54.

49. See her lectures on "The Nature and History of Human Civilization," dis-

cussed Waterman, 246–54; and *England the Civilizer—Her History Developed in Its Principles*, L, 1848.

50. Perkins, 110, 372.

51. Perkins, 363; conference resolutions in O'Neill, 108–11. Elizabeth Cady Stanton, denied a seat at the former conference because of her sex, became a radical leader at the latter gathering. Its "Declaration of Sentiment" was modeled in part on the Declaration of Independence; and the journal she cofounded after the Civil War with Susan B. Anthony was called *Revolution*. See O'Neill, "Feminism as a Radical Ideology," in A. Young, ed., *Dissent: Explorations in the History of American Radicalism*, DeKalb, 1968, 279.

52. Women did play a crucial role in the social revolutionary ferment of early twentieth-century America. The key personalities ranged from Lucy Parsons, the widow of the only English-speaking Haymarket martyr, who appeared on the platform at the founding congress of the IWW, to the émigré anarchist editor, Emma Goldman. But the leading role was played by a remarkable series of Irish women as Irish radicals turned from national to social revolution in the New World. The line of leadership ran from the mythical "Molly Maguire," who lent her name to the conspiracy of the 1870s, through the miners' heroine Mary ("Mother") Jones, another founding figure of the IWW who lived to be one hundred, on to Elizabeth Gurley Flynn, the companion and correspondent of Joe Hill in his last days and the "rebel girl" of his ballads. See the latter's *I Speak My Own Piece*, NY, 1955.

A unique leadership role in the Irish revolutionary movement itself was played by Maude Gonne, who simultaneously inspired extremists of both Left and Right: working first with both French Boulangists and Irish republicans, later with both her revolutionary husband (John MacBride, who was a martyr of the Easter Rising in Dublin in 1916) and her lifelong reactionary admirer, the poet William Butler Yeats. Recent biographies by S. Levenson (NY, 1977) and N. Cardozo (NY, 1978) should be substantially supplemented for these aspects of her career by the projected study of L. O'Neill, *The Gyres of Gonne: The Influence of Maude Gonne MacBride on Modern History*.

More militant than Gonne's "daughters of Erin" of 1900 was the revolutionary rival to the Boy Scouts, the "Sons of Erin" founded by the even more professional revolutionary Constance Markiewicz in 1909. The daughter of Lord Gore-Booth, she married a Pole for revolutionary validation, once went directly to a revolutionary meeting in evening dress from Dublin castle, participated in the Easter rising of 1916, and became the first minister of labor in the first independent Irish government—and the first woman cabinet member in Western Europe. See J. van Voris, *Constance de Markievicz*, Old Westbury, 1972, 39 ff., 8. Eamon de Valera retrospectively noted that "women are at once the boldest and the most unmanageable revolutionaries." Ibid., 9.

53. Carlo Botta, *Storia della guerra del' independenza degli Stati Uniti d'America*, Paris, 1809, 4v.

Her frame of reference was generally European. On her first trip to America in 1818–9, she wrote a play glorifying a Swiss revolutionary, which she believed would begin an entirely new school of drama (*Altorf, a tragedy*, Philadelphia, 1819; discussed Perkins, 12–3). Its romantic, revolutionary message was, however, out of tune with the rising chauvinist temper of the new nation; and the play was, appropriately perhaps, replaced by *Pizzaro*, a melodrama of colonial conquest, on the occasion of General Andrew Jackson's triumphal visit to New York. Perkins, 36–41.

Again, it was a European event—the outbreak and spread of revolution in 1830—that inspired her to predict in an American journal (*Free Enquirer*, 1830, Nov 27) the imminent arrival of a new society that "no longer pitched nation against nation" by means of an altogether different form of war from "every other struggle in which the human race has been engaged . . . a *war of class* . . . that . . . is *universal*." Cited in Waterman, 228; also Perkins, 305.

54. P. Miller, ed., *Margaret Fuller, American Romantic*, NY, 1963, 286–300, includes her letters on her work (largely as director of a hospital in Rome during the siege of the revolutionary republic). Her manuscript on the history of the Italian Revolution, which she considered to be her most important work, was lost in the shipwreck that claimed her life off Fire Island, New York, on her way back to America.

55. Reproduction from the original of 1848, Jun, in Sullerot, *La Presse*, 27. See also her "Journaux," 88 ff. on the proliferation of these journals. For more details and another perspective, see L. Adler, *A l'Aube du féminisme: Les premières journalistes (1838–1852)*, 1979.

56. S. Rowbotham, *Women, Resistance and Revolution*, L, 1972, 123–4; Chacornac, *Levy*, 117; and E. Thomas, *Les Femmes de 1848*, 1948. The early parts of

Rowbotham's spirited volume are better for the English than the French side, where she never sorts out the players, confusing Desirée Gay with her sister-in-law Delphine Gay yet never identifying her with her own maiden name of Desirée Veret (117–21).

57. Sullerot, *La Presse*, 28.

58. Ibid., 26.

59. Cited from *Le Compagnon du Tour de France*, 1851, Oct 23, 9, in E. Thomas, *George Sand*, 1959, 59.

60. E. Dolléans, *Féminisme et mouvement ouvrier: George Sand*, 1951, 44. E. Thomas sees this attitude as providing a justification "before the fact of 'socialist realism,' which is neither realist nor socialist, but depicts the model man, the way one would like him to be." *Sand*, 59.

61. E. Thomas, *The Women Incendiaries*, L, 1967, xiv. Thomas recognizes that there is some presumptive truth to the allegations, 64–5 and elsewhere.

62. Thomas stresses the role of Elizabeth Dmitrieff, a friend and emissary of Marx and the leader of the union, which was the women's section of the French International; and of Anna Korvin-Krukovskaya, wife of the Blanquist leader Victor Jaclard, in the committee: 59–62 and 74–6.

The role of these two (and of a third key Russian woman E. Barteneva) is discussed more fully in I. Knizhnik-Vetrov, *Russkie deiatel'nitsy pervogo internatsionala i parizhskoi kommuny*, Moscow/Leningrad, 1964. See also W. McClellan, *Revolutionary Exiles: the Russians in the First International and the Paris Commune*, L, 1978.

63. E. Thomas, *Louise Michel ou la velléda de l'anarchie*, 1971, 10, 447, and the introductory epigraph from M. Barrès, *Mes Cahiers*, 1929, VI, 91.

64. Thomas, *Michel*, 432.

65. *À la Révolution tout entière:* S. Faure, cited in ibid., 444.

66. Ibid., 436.

67. Ibid., 433–4.

68. According to ibid., 447.

69. Ibid.

70. Ibid., 439. Her prophecy was almost unique in suggesting at this early time that in the coming Russian Revolution "the soldiers will be with the people," as they proved to be in 1917.

71. See Saltykov, *Za Rubezhom* in *Izbrannye sochineniia*, Moscow/Leningrad, 1940, 30; citations from Dostoevsky in Thomas, *Sand*, 126–7.

72. See materials referenced Billington, *Icon*, 739. She was the mother of the future theosophist leader Helena Blavatsky.

73. *Polski Słownik Biograficzny*, 1968, XIII/3, 478.

74. See A. Abdel-Malek, *Idéologie et renaissance nationale. L'Egypte moderne*, 1969, 306–14; also "La fin du rêve," in Fahmy-Bey, esp. 205–8.

75. Herzen's neglected *Who is Guilty?*, still untranslated into English, is related to "George Sandism" in Malia, *Herzen*, chapter XI, and to the developing Russian movement in R. McNeal, "Women in the Russian Radical Movement," *Journal of Social History*, 1971–2, Winter, 147.

76. One neglected early Western admirer believed that Chernyshevsky suggested a new doctrine of "sexualism" that might take humanity as far beyond socialism as the latter had progressed beyond "masculine individualism." See P. Bonnier, "Tchernychewski et l'évolution sexuelle," *Revue Socialiste*, 1885, II, 734, 837; and more generally 598–611, 731–8, 832–7; see also Sagnol, "L'Egalité des sexes," *Revue Socialiste*, 1889, IX, 685–97; 1889, X, 82–98.

77. Cited from an unidentified archimandrite in Irkutsk, in A. Shilov, intr., to M. Mikhailov, *Zapiski (1861–1862)*, Petrograd, 1922, 3.

78. *Zapiski*, 5–6. See also, more generally, R. Stites, "M.L. Mikhailov and the Emergence of the Woman Question in Russia," *Canadian Slavic Studies*, 1969, Summer, 178–99; and *The Women's Liberation Movement in Russia: Feminism, Nihilism, Bolshevism, 1860–1930*, Princeton, 1977; also V. Broido, *Apostles into Terrorists. Women and the Revolutionary Movement in the Russia of Alexander II*, NY, 1977.

For a definitive biography based on new material, see P. Fateev, *Mikhail Mikhailov—revoliutsioner, pisatel', publitsist*, 1969. For a good discussion of four other, less important recent books on this now much-covered subject, see R. Stites, "Wives, Sisters, Daughters and Workers: A Review Article," *Russian History*, 1976, III, 2, 237–44.

79. See Billington, *Mikhailovsky*, 17, materials referenced n. 3; and citations by E. Kolosov in Mikhailovsky, *Polnoe sobranie sochinenii*, St. Petersburg, 1913, X, lxi.

80. See A. Yanovsky, "Zhenskoe obrazovanie," in Brokgauz-Efron, *Entsiklopedi-*

chesky slovar, XXII, esp. 869–71. The thoroughness of articles on this subject in this late nineteenth-century Russian encyclopedia is in marked contrast to most Western encyclopedias then and since.

81. In May, 1873, J. Meijer, *Knowledge and Revolution: The Russian Colony in Zurich (1870–1873)*, Assen, 1955, 47. See also A. Amfiteatrov, *Zhenshchina v obshchestvennykh dvizheniiakh Rossii*, Geneva, 1905; and for the early twentieth century, *Zhenshchiny russkoi revoliutsii*, 1968.

82. Meijer, 69–72. See also A. Knight, "The Fritschi: A Study of Female Radicals in the Russian Populist Movement," *Canadian-American Slavic Studies*, 1975, spring, 1–17.

83. Cited without precise attribution in Yarmolinsky, *Road*, 238.

84. V. Figner, *Memoirs of a Revolutionist*, NY, 1927; also *Studencheskie gody (1872–6)*, 1924. She edited in the early Soviet period—along with A. Pribyleva-Korba another female veteran of the People's Will—a series of other memoirs of the movement. See the latter's *Narodnaia Volia, vospominaniia o 1870kh i 1880kh godov*, 1926. Less important, but better known in the West because of lectures and publications during exile, was C. Breshko-Breshkovskaya, *Hidden Springs of the Russian Revolution*, Stanford, 1931; and *The Little Grandmother of the Russian Revolution*, Boston, 1918.

85. The importance of Oshanina, née Olovennikova, the oldest of three revolutionary sisters, is only partly suggested in Venturi, *Roots*, 643–4; and is more fully developed in the materials referenced therein, 822–3, and by the late Boris Nikolaevsky in his course on the Russian revolutionary tradition given at Harvard in the spring of 1960.

86. P. Pomper, *Peter Lavrov and the Russian Revolutionary Movement*, Chicago, 1972, 176–9.

87. Kravchinsky (Stepniak), cited in Yarmolinsky, *Road*, 214.

88. Term cited from Panteleev in Vilenskaia, 145, who is apparently unaware of the sectarian associations of the term.

89. Tat'iana Lebedeva and Vera Zasulich (discussed in McNeal, "Women," 149); the figure of "Natasha" discussed in N. Burenin, *Liudi bol'shevistskogo podpol'ia*, 1958, 35–8. For the role of young women as ammunition carriers, see P. Gusiatnikov, *Revoliutsionnoe studencheskoe dvizhenie v Rossii*, 1971, 188.

90. McNeal, 153–4.

91. 21 of 43. This sentence was almost always imposed for terrorism. McNeal, 155.

92. A. Knight, "Female Terrorists in the Russian Socialist Revolutionary Party," *Russian Review*, 1979, Apr, 146, estimates that at least 25 of the about 78 total number of members were women. This important article is based on a chapter from her doctoral dissertation of 1977 at the London School of Economics: "The Participation of Women in the Revolutionary Movement in Russia: 1890–1914."

93. Phrase of A. Kelly ("Revolutionary Women," *New York Review of Books*, 1975, Jul 17, 22) used to characterize the distinctiveness while stressing the importance of the role of Russian women. Maria Spiridonova, whom Knight believes (150) "epitomized more than any other the Russian female terrorist," later defined the function of her Left S.R. party as being "to cleanse the moral atmosphere" (Knight, 159).

94. Zenzinov, cited in Knight, 147.

95. Knight, 152 ff.

96. I. Kakhovskaia, "Iz vospominanii o zhenskoi katorge," *Katorga i Ssylka*, 1926, no. 2, 178; cited Knight, 158.

97. See the cases of Dora Brilliant and Rahel Lurie, in Knight, 148–50.

98. Cases of Zinaida Konopliannikova and Maria Spiridonova, in ibid., 150–1.

99. P. Smirnov, "Znachenie zhenshchiny v istorii vozniknoveniia raskola," *Missionersky Sbornik*, 1891, Nov–Dec, 330–65.

100. McNeal, 158; Knight, 150. The most harrowing and moving of these immolations—and the one which had the greatest impact on society—was that of Maria Vetrova, a young student from Chernigov who had run an illegal press with several other women, had known Tolstoy, and burned herself with kerosene from her reading lamp. See N. Rostov, "Samoubiistvo M. F. Vetrovoi i studencheskie besporiadki 1897 g.," *Katorga i Ssylka*, 1926, n. 2, 50–66.

101. McNeal, 154; Knight, 154. Both of these secondary accounts misspell her name. The latter suggests that she did not detonate the dynamite for fear of hurting innocent bystanders; but there is no evidence for this in the only primary source, A. Friedberg, "E. Rogozinnikova (vospominaniia)," *Katorga i Ssylka*, 1929, no. 1, 154–77.

102. Description of Konopliannikova, cited in Knight, 150.

103. The speech had a powerful effect even on Russian-speaking anarchists in the United States when published there: *Rech' Matreny Prisiazhniuka v Kievskom voenno-okruzhnom sude 19-go iiulia 1908 goda*, NY, 1916; cited in Avrich, 66.

104. McNeal's analysis (150–1) of women revolutionaries listed in the most comprehensive Russian biographical codification of pre-1905 revolutionaries (*Deiateli revoliutsionnogo dvizheniia v Rossii: bio-bibliografichesky slovar'*, 1927–33, covering, however, only the letters a to g) finds that 60% of the 317 women involved from the 1860s through the 1880s came from the privileged estates (nobility and merchants). He suggests that this percentage is probably lower for men. Knight's analysis (144–5) of the biographies of female SR terrorists during the decade 1902–11, shows that the percentage of women from the privileged estates had declined only a little (and was demonstrably higher than among men), and that almost all of the women were highly educated—20 of the 27 women officially identified with terrorist acts by the party were designated as *intelligentki*.

105. See A. Meyer, "Marxism and the Women's Movement," in D. Atkinson, et al., eds., *Women in Russia*, Stanford, 1977, esp. 90–101; also C. Guettel, *Marxism and Feminism*, Toronto, 1974.

106. Cited without precise attribution in Gustav Scheidtmann, *Der Kommunismus und das Proletariat*, Leipzig, 1848, 53; cited without mention of Engels in Noyes, *Organization*, 46 n. 1.
Engels had scorned the nonrevolutionary efforts of Louise Otto-Peters to improve educational and professional opportunities for women; and subsequent Social Democrats often echoed this attitude in assessing her "Address of a Maiden" to the ministers of Saxony in May 1848, and her work as editor of the first German women's newspaper, *Frauen-Zeitung* from 1849–52. See Zetkin, *Zur Geschichte*, 25, 46–59, who was retroactively expressing her later insistence that Social Democratic women's organizations avoid all contact with bourgeois women's movements. (See Meyer, "Movement," 111).
Paralleling Peters's pioneering efforts (and even more neglected) was the woman's organization that coalesced in Brussels in response to the Fourierist Considérant's championing of female rights during the Revolution of 1848. Led by Desirée Veret Gay, widow of Robert Owen's original French disciple and outspoken foe of "authoritarian socialism" (See Dommanget, *Considérant*, 189; Zetkin, 32–3; and Jules Gay's unjustly forgotten major work, *Le Socialisme rationnel et le socialisme autoritaire*, Geneva, 1868), this group eventually formed links with the First International. An early champion of day-care centers for children, Gay and her husband saw equality of the sexes as a major deterrent to the paternal and authoritarian tendencies developing within the socialist movement. Humane treatment of children was to be the hallmark of a new morality, and they set up the first journal expressly for children. See Gans, "Owen à Paris," 45; and Desirée Gay, *Education rationelle de la première enfance: Manuel à l'usage des jeunes mères*, 1868.

107. Ten of the leading 16 members of the Baader-Meinhof terrorist group were women. See M. Getler, "Women Play Growing Role in Slayings by West German Terrorist Groups," *Washington Post*, 1977, Aug 6, A-15. Their resemblance to a medieval religious sect is suggested by M. Lasky, "Ulrike Meinhof and the Baader-Meinhof Gang," *Encounter*, 1975, no. 6, 9–23.

108. A textile union founded in 1869 in Saxony was "the first to treat women workers and wives of workers as equals" and to organize them "against the capitalist class enemy," according to Zetkin, *Zur Geschichte*, 7–8.

109. The extraordinary popularity of Bebel's work may be judged from the fact that the English translation made by the American Marxist Daniel de Leon was based on the 33d edition: *Woman under Socialism*, NY, 1904.

110. Koszyk, *Presse*, II, 208; Joll, *International*, 65; Zetkin, *Zur Geschichte*, 218–20; Meyer, "Movement," 111–2. Lively testimony to the resistance of the German working class to full rights for women and the often intimidating effect on Social Democratic women is provided by A. Popp, *Autobiography of a Working Woman*, L, 1912. For the rapid growth from a handful of women Social Democrats in 1890 to 175,000 in 1914, see the unpublished thesis of J. Strain, "Feminism and Political Radicalism in the German Social Democratic Movement 1890–1914," Berkeley, 1964.

111. Joll, *International*, 37. See also Zetkin, *Reminiscences of Lenin*, L, 1929.

112. L. Edmonson, "Russian Feminists and the First All-Russian Congress of Women," *Russian History*, 1976, III, 2, 123–49.

113. R. Stites, "Zhenotdel: Bolshevism and Russian Women, 1917–1930," *Russian History*, 1976, III, 2, esp. 175. The title was derived from the only important work of Russian revolutionary feminism written prior to the 1905 revolution, Krupskaia's *Zhenshchina-Rabotnitsa*, her first book, written in Siberia in 1899, first published illegally by *Iskra* in Switzerland in 1900 (dated 1901) and republished with an

explanatory introduction by the author, Moscow/Leningrad, 1926 (LC). See also
J. Fréville, *Inessa Armand: Une grande figure de la révolution russe*, 1957; B. Wolfe,
"Lenin and Inessa Armand," *American Slavic and East European Review*, 1963,
Mar, 96–114; and the early Comintern publication by Kollontai: *Rabotnitsa i
krest'ianka v Sovetskoi Rossii*, Petrograd, 1921.

114. L. Bryant, *Mirrors of Moscow*, NY, 1923, 121–2; cited in Stites, "Zhenotdel,"
180.

115. G. Massell, *The Surrogate Proletariat. Moslem Women and Revolutionary
Strategies in Soviet Central Asia: 1919–1929*, Princeton, 1974.

116. Useful for these early years is R. Evzerov and I. Yazhborovskaia, *Roza
Liuksemburg*, 1974, 20 ff.

117. For the key role of Anyuta Leibovich as the "soul" of the seminal Jewish
Youth Circle in Vilnius in 1885–7, and of Liuba Axelrod (no relation to Pavel) in
the new group of 1886, see Levin, *Messiah*, 228–9; and for the "legendary" role of
Jogiches as a link with the outside world, ibid., 233.

Important new research by L. Gerson for a biography of Dzerzhinsky indicates
that the first love of that Polish-Russian founder of the Soviet secret police was
Julia Goldman, the Jewish sister of a founder of the Bund. Jewish women continued
to play a disproportionately great role in those aspects of revolutionary activity that
required dedication and risk. Almost 30 percent of the women terrorists in the SR
Party were Jewish, though very few Jewish men were involved (Knight, 146).

On the broader question of the role and motivation of Jews in the revolutionary
tradition, see R. Wistrich, *Revolutionary Jews from Marx to Trotsky*, L, 1976, which
tends to stress self-hatred as the recurring motif in the variety of figures he
examines, and the more balanced treatment by L. Schapiro, "Jews in the Russian
Revolutionary Movement," *Slavonic and East European Review*, 1961, Dec, 148–67.

118. Evzerov, 34–6.

119. *Przegląd Socjaldemokratyczny*, modeled on Kautsky's *Neue Zeit*, was the
theoretical journal; *Czerwony Sztandar* (Red Flag) the daily party newspaper—
paralleling for Poland the same division of Party press that Lenin was to institute
in Russia. See J. Nettl, *Rosa Luxemburg*, L, 1966, I, 251–95, esp. 267–70. This
valuable basic study can be supplemented on some points by Badia, *Rosa
Luxemburg*.

120. "Sozial Reform oder Revolution," *Leipziger Volkszeitung*, 1899, Jul 6, translated as "Une question de tactique," *Le Mouvement Socialiste*, 1899, Aug, 132–7.

121. *Mass Strike, Party and Trade Unions*, completed in St. Petersburg, 1906,
Sep 15, modified translation in R. Howard, *Selected Political Writings of Rosa
Luxemburg*, NY/L, 1971, 237.

122. Luxemburg believed that the natural, proletarian-rooted nature of the mass
strike distinguished it from the anarchistic general strike so long caricatured by
Social Democrats ("the general strike is general nonsense"); and that its genesis in
relatively backward Russia ("In no country had one so little thought of 'propagating'
or even 'discussing' the mass strike.") prefigured even greater power for the mass
strike in more industrialized countries. See Howard, *Writings*, 230, paraphrasing
Luxemburg's own earlier article of 1905, Mar 3.

123. Nettl, *Luxemburg*, II, 504.

124. Her criticisms (related in Badia, 326 ff. and in Y. Bourdet, "Le Marxisme
anti-autoritaire de Rosa Luxemburg," *Autogestion*, 1977, Oct, 50) were in fact
preceded by Parvus's critique of Lenin's "ultracentralism" (Badia, 327 n. 306) on
Nov 30, 1903. Luxemburg's classic, "The Organizational Questions of Russian Social
Democracy" appeared in both *Iskra* and *Die Neue Zeit* in 1904, Jul, and is translated (with introduction by B. Wolfe) in R. Luxemburg, *"The Russian Revolution"
and "Leninism or Marxism?"*, Ann Arbor, 1961, 81–108.

The depth of her opposition to Leninist authoritarianism is played down by Badia,
but stressed by Bourdet and particularly by D. Guérin, *Rosa Luxemburg et la
spontanéité révolutionnaire*, 1966.

125. Badia, 354–5 n. 120.

126. Ibid., 303–4.

127. Zasulich accused Lenin in 1904 of substituting the hierarchical concept of
an "organization" for the mass concept of a "party" and condemned the Bolshevik
repudiation of democracy in 1918 just before her death. See J. Bergman, "The
Political Thought of Vera Zasulich," *Slavic Review*, 1979, Jun, 243–58.

128. Luxemburg taught at the German party school beginning in 1907 and was
asked by Bogdanov and Gorky to teach at the Russian party school at Capri, which
sought to produce from the proletariat "permanent cadres of the directors of the
party" (J. Scherrer, "Les Ecoles du parti de Capri et de Bologne: La formation de
l'intelligentsia du parti," *Cahiers du Monde Russe et Soviétique*, 1978, Jul–Sep,

261, 266). It seems likely that the Leninist tradition took over this concept of cadres within the party from Bogdanov (who saw them as bearers of a new collective consciousness and sense of "organizing skill" *organizovannost'*, *organizatsionnost'*: Scherrer, 266–7), who in turn derived it from the German Social Democrats.

As between Bogdanov's concept of a "worker's intelligentsia" stressing the class character and proletarian consciousness of those to be trained and Lenin's stress on a "party intelligentsia" more concerned with the Marxist orthodoxy of intellectuals and *their* consciousness of class struggle (the antipodes posed by Sherrer), Luxemburg was closer to the latter. In general, Badia suggests that the relationship between Lenin and Luxemburg was that of "privileged adversaries" rather than principled opponents: 325.

129. The first part of this brochure (first published Zürich, 1916 as *Die Krise der Sozialdemokratie*) is translated in *Writings of Luxemburg*, 322–35. A fuller and more representative set of extracts is translated by Badia in Luxemburg, *Textes*, 1969, 190–213.

130. Badia, *Luxemburg*, 344.

131. "Die kleinen Lafayette," *Spartacus*, 1918, Oct; itemization of articles and pseudonyms in Badia, 866.

132. Ibid., 374.

133. After participation in the Worker's Opposition, her subsequent career lay in diplomatic positions abroad, beginning with her ambassadorship to Norway in 1923 as the first woman to be accredited to a foreign country. On her early, erotic utopianism, see "The Path of Eros with Wings," in *Molodaia Gvardiia*, 1923, no. 3; other materials in Billington, *Icon*, 766 n. 100; B. Clements, *Bolshevik Feminist. The Life of Aleksandra Kollontai*, Bloomington, 1979; "Emancipation through Communism: The Ideology of A. M. Kollontai," *Slavic Review*, 1973, Jun, 323–38; and J. Stora-Sandor, *Alexandra Kollontai, Marxisme et l'évolution sexuelle*, 1973.

134. For a variety of views on this subject, see the Western symposium edited by D. Brown, *The Role and Status of Women in the Soviet Union*, NY, 1968; and the Eastern Bloc symposium summarized by M. Pavlova, in *Literaturnaia gazeta*, 1970, May 27. For a sympathetic discussion of the women's movement in China from the release from foot-binding during the 1911 revolution to the late years of Mao's rule, see H. Snow, *Women in Modern China*, The Hague, 1967.

135. Badia, 597–8; 148–9. The most spirited attempt to reclaim Luxemburg as a posthumous friend, if not advocate, of the Soviet system is Clara Zetkin's attack on Paul Levi: *Roza Liuksemburg i russkaia revoliutsiia*, Moscow/Petrograd, 1924.

136. Badia, 796–7.

137. Already in her last major article on the mass strike (in *Leipziger Volkszeitung*, 1913, Jun 26, 27, 28), Luxemburg noted that the German proletariat, despite its incomparable organization, was almost unique in never having produced—and not yet even being ripe for—a mass strike; and her invocation to struggle "whether ending in victory or defeat" clearly implies her belief in the latter result. See *Textes*, 160, 169.

138. "If one had to characterize the principal activity of Rosa Luxemburg in a word—not simply her profession but her vocation—one would have to say that she was first and above all else a journalist and more precisely a political journalist." Badia, 593, and the excellent analytical section, "La Journaliste," 593–643.

139. Luxemburg, *Briefe aus dem Gafängnes*, 1920, 17–8; and discussion of this passage from her posthumously published correspondence in Badia, esp. 712–3.

140. Luxemburg, *Briefe*, 18.

141. Cited from "Order reigns in Berlin" (*Die rote Fahne*, 1919, Jan 14) in Howard, 415. Her words conflate lines from two revolutionary poems by Marx's friend F. Freiligrath.

142. Bertolt Brecht had written a poem upon her death in 1919, but failed in his later, more favored days as court playwright of the East German Communist regime, to progress beyond the prologue to his proposed *Life and Death of Rosa Luxemburg*. See Badia, 798–800.

143. "What does the Spartacus League want?" from *Die rote Fahne*, 1918, Dec 14, cited in Bourdet, 55. See also Badia, *Le Spartakisme: Les dernières années de Karl Liebknecht et de Rosa Luxemburg 1914–1919*, 1967; and *Les Spartakistes 1918: L'Allemagne en révolution*, 1966.

144. Of all the *gauchiste* attempts to draw on Luxemburg to develop a practical political program to the Left of the bureaucratized Communist parties of the late sixties, the most serious was that of the head of the left-wing PSIUP in Italy, Lelio Basso. In addition to an important edition of her works (*Scritti politici*, 1967), see "Socialismo e rivoluzione in Rosa Luxemburg," *Problemi del Socialismo*, 1971, Jan–Feb, 40–63; and the proceedings of the conference he organized in Reggio

Emilia in Sep, 1973, on "The Contribution of Rosa Luxemburg to the development of Marxist thought."

Epilogue

1. Notably by the enthusiastic H. Brailsford: *Macedonia: Its Races and Their Future*, L, 1906.

2. Cited in Gaucher, 155. Discussion here is indebted to his account, 155–73, and to the more detailed account from the Greek point of view, which identifies IMRO with Bulgaria, by D. Dakin, *The Greek Struggle in Macedonia, 1897–1913*, Thessalonika, 1966, 92–106. Works from the Serbian and Bulgarian point of view are referenced in G. Zotiades, *The Macedonian Controversy*, Thessalonika, 1954, 5 n.

1. Russian ideological influences through Bulgaria on IMRO are stressed in V. Zuev, "Gotse Delchev—vydaiushchiisia deiatel' makedonskogo osvoboditel'nogo dvizheniia," *Institut slavianovedeniia: kratkie soobshcheniia*, 1954, No. 12.

3. Gaucher, 155.

4. P. Gusiatnokov, "Studencheskoe dvizhenie v 1905 godu," *Voprosy Istorii*, 1955, no. 10, 75.

5. This dramatic confrontation, which lasted several days and attracted great popular attention, is fully described in Rappeport, *Institut*, 284 ff. See also A. Mil'shtein, *Tekhnologichesky institut v 1905 godu*, Leningrad, 1955.

6. Krzhizhanovsky, *Sochineniia*, 1933, I, 61. He used as the epigraph to his basic brochure on the electrification of Russia: "The century of steam was the century of the bourgeoisie; the century of electricity is the century of socialism." *Krzhizhanovsky. Zhizn'*, 22.

7. Lenin first used the formulation at the 8th Congress of Soviets in the Bolshoi Theater in Moscow on Dec 22, 1920 (*Krzhizhanovsky. Zhizn'*, 33–4). The leading Socialist Revolutionary rival to Lenin and Trotsky in 1917 later complained of the "electric charges of will power" that those Bolshevik leaders imparted to the events of that year: V. Chernov, *The Great Russian Revolution*, New Haven, 1936, 445.

8. I. Spector, *The First Russian Revolution: Its Impact on Asia*, Englewood Cliffs, 1962, 40, 44, 50; discussion of Iran, 38–50; and for supplementary material, B. Aizin. "Mezhdunarodnoe znachenie revoliutsii 1905–1907 godov v Rossii," *Novaia i Noveishaia Istoriia*, 1975, no. 6, 21–41.

9. Spector, 80–3. Somewhat later, pioneering Japanese student revolutionaries also imitated the Russians, calling their journal *Narod*: H. Smith II, *Japan's First Student Radicals*, Cambridge, Mass., 1972, 55, also 63, 74–5.

10. Spector, 105–9; also new material in P. Sinha, *The Indian National Liberation Movement and Russia, 1905–1917*, New Delhi, 1975 (the revised version of a dissertation at Moscow University).

11. Ramsaur, *Young Turks*, 127; C. Buxton, *Turkey in Revolution*, NY/L, 1909, 43 ff.

12. A. Kriegel, "Aux Origines français du communisme chinois," *Preuves*, 1968, Aug–Sep, 24–41.

13. Cited from Ludwik Bystrzonowski in Halicz, *Warfare*, 144. His astonishing range of experiences in emigration (from active duty in the Algerian resistance movement to service as Turkish military attaché in Paris) is described in Halicz, 120–55. His unpublished "Mémoire sur Afghanistan," is in the Czartoryski Museum, Cracow, III, ms. 5555.

By the end of the century, Polish desperation for national regeneration led Polish revolutionaries to glorify distant and dispersed agitational movements (the Irish against the British) and non-revolutionary nationalisms (the Japanese against the Russians). "We were enamoured then with the Hindus, the inhabitants of the Caucasus, the Albanians, the Basques . . ." recalled Ignacy Daszyński, *Pamiętniki*, 1957, I, 23; Borejsza, "Portrait," 147.

14. F. Fanon, *The Wretched of the Earth*, Middlesex, England, 1970, 74–118; D. Caute, *Fanon*, L, 1970, 85. Caute stresses Sartre and Merleau-Ponty more than Sorel as the source of Fanon's ideas on violence: 92–4.

15. Fanon, *Wretched*, 19.

16. G. De Zendegni, "Martí in New York," *Américas*, 1973, Jan, 7–12. His journals were designed for other countries than Cuba, and *La Edad de Oro* was designed for children, who were not yet corrupted by social prejudice.

INDEX

This is an index to the text. Because of constraints of space, only major points of substance in the notes at the back of the book are included. Those historical figures, authors, and titles that are mentioned only in the notes are not included in the index, nor are subjects that are discussed in the notes in direct amplification of the text. Numbers in italics refer to the *Notes* (pp. 511–652); the first number represents the chapter, the number (or numbers) following the colon represents the note.

CPSIA information can be obtained at www.ICGtesting.com
Printed in the USA
BVOW03s2246210514

353817BV00001B/1/P